# SHEPARD'S
## ACTS AND CASES
## BY
## POPULAR NAMES

## FEDERAL AND STATE

A compilation of popular names by which federal and state acts and cases have been referred to or cited together with an identification of each act in terms of its constitutional or statutory references and each case in terms of the volume and page reference where the text of the decision may be found.

FIFTH EDITION - - - - - - - - - - - - - - - - - - - - - - - - - - - - - - - - - - - - 1999, PART 3

**SHEPARD'S**
555 Middle Creek Parkway
Colorado Springs, CO 80921-3622
1-800-899-6000

# EDITORIAL STAFF
## Shepard's Acts and Cases by Popular Names

---

*Team Leader:* LEE A. HENRY

*Editorial Staff Members:* CAROL SUE ANDERSEN, BRADLEY W. BAECKER, B.M. HANSON, THOMAS M. HENNEMAN, GLORIA S. LIKNESS, PETER J. PASQUALE, JEANNE SAMPLE-MCNEIL

*Editor:* CHERYL L. ROSS

*Editorial Quality Assurance Coordinator:* CHRISTOPHER J. WEST

*Publisher, Specialized Citations:* LISA M. PETERSON, J.D.

**To reach Shepard's call 1-800-899-6000 or visit our homepage at http://www.shepards.com.**



**0769833977**

## TABLE OF CONTENTS

PART 3

## PREFACE

Shepard's Acts and Cases by Popular Names is a reference tool that provides citation information for statutes and cases that are commonly referred to by popular name.

Federal and state acts are listed alphabetically and can be located by name (e.g., Pine Creek Scenic Rivers Act or Pilot Records Improvement Act of 1996). Shepard's Acts and Cases by Popular Names also provides a quick indexing system for locating a citation or list of citations from several states–including federal statutes–dealing with a specific topic (e.g., Lemon Law or Water Conservation). These indexes also include citations to Constitutional provisions (e.g., Equal Suffrage Amendment).

Where a particular case is known only by its popular name, the alphabetical indexes found in these volumes can be used to locate the needed citation to the case (e.g., Miranda).

## SUPPLEMENTATION

Shepard's Acts and Cases by Popular Names consists of the 1999 bound volume (Parts 1–3) and the current issue of the soft-covered cumulative supplement. Cumulative supplements are published bimonthly in February, April, June, August, October and December. Supplementation is cumulative, therefore, only the most recent supplement needs to be retained and used with the bound volume. From time to time, as the accumulation of citations necessitates, a cumulative supplement will be permanently bound. Each supplement-cover provides the necessary information as to "What Your Library Should Contain." Always consult these supplement covers before discarding any soft-covered supplements or bound volumes.

## ORGANIZATION

Shepard's Acts and Cases by Popular Names contains two divisions. Acts, i.e., federal and state statutory and constitutional materials, are listed alphabetically by popular name in the first division. Cases are listed alphabetically by popular name in the second division. Please consult the tables of abbreviations used in the division for Federal and State cases cited by Popular Names to identify the citing references that appear in these bound volumes.

Citations to federal statutes include the United States Code title and section numbers wherever this information is available. Sometimes a law is merely cited by the date on which it was enacted. The citation format contained in these volumes for federal statutes includes a citation to the date a law was enacted, the Public sequential number and Congressional Session that enacted the law, a Statutes at Large citation, and the citation to the U.S. Code where this information is available.

Parallel citations, cases that are published in more than one reporter, are included for the widely available reports (e.g., U.S., S. Ct., and L. Ed. citations for the United States Supreme Court decisions; official and regional reporter citations for state-court decisions in jurisdictions that publish a separate state official report).

## CITATIONS RESEARCH

After identifying a case or statute in Shepard's Acts and Cases by Popular Names, ascertain its status as authority and locate additional cases dealing with similar issues by consulting the pertinent Shepard's Citations.

SHEPARD'S

# ABBREVIATIONS—ACTS

Adm.–Administrative
AG–Agriculture
Ala.–Alabama
Am.–Amended
Amend.–Amendment
Ann.–Annotated
Appx.–Appendix
Ariz.–Arizona
Ark.–Arkansas
Art.–Article
Aug.–August
BO–Business Occupations and Professions
BR–Business Regulation
CA–Corporations and Associations
Cal.–California
Ch[s].–Chapter[s]
Civ.–Civil
CJ–Courts and Judicial Proceedings
CL–Commercial Law
Cl[s].–Clause[s]
Colo.–Colorado
Comp.–Compiled
Conn.–Connecticut
Consol.–Consolidated
Const.–Constitution
Crim.–Criminal
C.S.–Called Session
D.C.–District of Columbia
Dec.–December
Del.–Delaware
Div.–Division
ED–Education
EN–Environment
ET–Estates and Trusts
Ex.–Extra
Ex. Sess.–Extra Session
Feb.–February
Fla.–Florida
FI–Financial Institutions
FL–Family Law
Ga.–Georgia
G.A.–General Assembly
Gen.–General
H.B.–House Bill
Haw.–Hawaii
HE–Health-Environmental
HG–Health-General
HO–Health-Occupation
H.R.–House Reports
Ida.–Idaho
Ill.–Illinois
IN–Insurance Law
Ind.–Indiana
Init. Meas.–Initiative Measure
Jan.–January
Kan.–Kansas
Ky.–Kentucky
La.–Louisiana
L.B.–Legislative Bill
LE–Labor and Employment
Leg.–Legislature
Mass.–Massachusetts
Md.–Maryland
Me.–Maine
Mich.–Michigan
Minn.–Minnesota
Miss.–Mississippi
Mo.–Missouri
Mont.–Montana
N.C.–North Carolina
N.D.–North Dakota
Neb.–Nebraska
Nev.–Nevada
N.H.–New Hampshire
N.J.–New Jersey
N.M.–New Mexico
No.–Number
Nov.–November
NR–Natural Resources
nt[s].–note[s]
N.Y.–New York

Oct.–October
Okla.–Oklahoma
Ore.–Oregon
p[p].–page[s]
Pa.–Pennsylvania
Pamph. Laws–Pamphlet Laws
P.L.–Public Law
PP–State Personnel and Pension
prec.–preceding
Proc.–Procedure
P.R.–Puerto Rico
Rev.–Revised
R.I.–Rhode Island
RP–Real Property
§[§]–Section[s]
S.B.–Senate Bill
S.C.–South Carolina
S.D.–South Dakota
SF–State Finance & Procurement
SG–State Government
Sept.–September
Sess.–Session
Sp.–Special
Sp. Sess.–Special Session
S.R.–Senate Reports
Stat.–Statutes or United States Statutes at Large
Subd.–Subdivision
Subsec.–Subsection
Supp.–Supplement
Tenn.–Tennessee
Tex.–Texas
TG–Tax-General
TP–Tax Property
TR–Transportation
Unconsol.–Unconsolidated
U.S.–United States
Va.–Virginia
Vol[s].–Volume[s]
Vt.–Vermont
Wash.–Washington
Wis.–Wisconsin
W. Va.–West Virginia
Wyo.–Wyoming

# ABBREVIATIONS—CASES

The following abbreviations are used to identify the citing references that appear in this bound volume:

A.–Atlantic Reporter
A.2d–Atlantic Reporter, Second Series
Abb. N. Cas.–Abbott's New Cases, New York
Abb. Pr.–Abbott's Practice Reports, New York
Abb. Pr. (n.s.)–Abbott's Practice Reports, New Series, New York
Abs. (n.s.)–Abstracts, New Series (Treasury Decisions)
A.D.–Appellate Division Reports (New York Supreme Court)
A.D.2d–Appellate Division Reports, Second Series (New York Supreme Court)
Ala.–Alabama Reports
Ala. App.–Alabama Appellate Courts Reports
Alaska–Alaska Reports
Alaska Fed.–Alaska Federal Reports
Allen–Allen's Massachusetts Reports
Am. B.R. (n.s.)–American Bankruptcy Reports, New Series
A.M.C.–American Maritime Cases
App. D.C.–Appeal Cases, District of Columbia
Ariz.–Arizona Reports
Ariz. App.–Arizona Appeals Reports
Ark.–Arkansas Reports
Ark. App.–Arkansas Appellate Reports
Bailey–Bailey's South Carolina Law Reports
Barb.–Barbour's Supreme Court Reports, New York
Baxt.–Baxter's Tennessee Reports
B.C.R.–Baltimore City Reports
Bosw.–Bosworth's Superior Court Reports, New York
Boyce–Boyce's Reports, Delaware
B.R.–Bankruptcy Reporter
Bradf.–Bradford's Surrogate Reports, New York
Brewst.–Brewster's Reports, Pennsylvania
B.T.A.–Reports of the United States Board of Tax Appeals
Cal.–California Supreme Court Reports
Cal. 2d–California Supreme Court Reports, Second Series
Cal. 3d–California Supreme Court Reports, Third Series
Cal. 3d S.–California Supreme Court Reports, Third Series (Special Tribunal Supplement)
Cal. 4th–California Supreme Court Reports, Fourth Series
Cal. App.–California Appellate Reports
Cal. App. 2d–California Appellate Reports, Second Series
Cal. App. 3d–California Appellate Reports, Third Series
Cal. App. 3d S.–California Appellate Reports, Third Series Supplement
Cal. App. 4th–California Appellate Reports, Fourth Series
Cal. App. 4th S.–California Appellate Reports, Fourth Series Supplement
Cal. Comp. Cas.–California Compensation Cases
Cal. R. Com.–Opinions and Orders of the Railroad Commission of California
Cal. Rptr.–California Reporter
Cal. Rptr. 2d–California Reporter, Second Series
C.C.A.–Circuit Court of Appeals Reports
C.C.P.A.–United States Court of Customs and Patent Appeals Reports
C.D.–Decisions of the Commissioner of Patents
Civ. P. Rep.–Civil Procedure Reports, New York
Clark–Clark's Pennsylvania Law Journal Reports
Code Rep.–Code Reporter, New York
Colo.–Colorado Reports
Colo. App.–Colorado Court of Appeals Reports
Conn.–Connecticut Reports
Conn. App.–Connecticut Appellate Reports
Conn. Cir. Ct.–Connecticut Circuit Court Reports
Conn. Supp.–Connecticut Supplement
Cow.–Cowen's Common Law Reports, New York
Ct. Cl.–Court of Claims Reports, United States
Ct. Cust.–Court of Customs Appeals Reports, United States
Ct. Int'l Trade–United States Court of International Trade Reports
Cust. Ct.–Customs Court Reports, United States
Cush.–Cushing Massachusetts Reports
Dakota–Dakota Reports

Daly–Daly's Common Pleas Reports, New York
D.C.–District of Columbia Reports
D.C.H.–Reports of the United States District Court of Hawaii
Del.–Delaware Reports
Del. Ch.–Delaware Chancery Reports
Denio–Denio's Common Law Reports, New York
Dep't Rep.–State Department Reports, New York
Duer–Duer's Superior Court Reports, New York
E.D.R.–Education Department Reports, New York
Edm. Sel. Cas.–Edmond's Select Cases, New York
F.–Federal Reporter
F.2d–Federal Reporter, Second Series
F.3d–Federal Reporter, Third Series
F. Cas.–Federal Cases
F.C.C.–Federal Communications Commission Reports
F.C.C.2d–Federal Communications Commission Reports, Second Series
F. Supp.–Federal Supplement
F. Supp. 2d–Federal Supplement, Second Series
F.T.C.–Federal Trade Commission Decisions
Fla.–Florida Reports
Fla. Supp.–Florida Supplement
Fla. Supp. 2d–Florida Supplement, Second Series
F.P.C.–Federal Power Commission Reports
F.R.D.–Federal Rules Decisions
G. & J.–Gill and Johnson Reports, Maryland
Ga.–Georgia Reports
Ga. App.–Georgia Appeals Reports
Gen. Appraisers–United States General Appraisers
Gratt.–Grattan Virginia Reports
Gray–Gray Massachusetts Reports
Harr.–Harrington Delaware Reports
H.H.–Hayward and Hazleton's Reports, United States
Haw.–Hawaii Reports
Haw. App.–Hawaii Appellate Reports
Heisk.–Heiskell Tennessee Reports
Hill–Hill's Common Law Reports, New York
Hopk. Ch.–Hopkins' Chancery Reports
Houst.–Houston Reports, Delaware
How. Pr.–Howard's Practice Reports, New York
Hun–Hun's Supreme Court Reports, New York
I.C.–Interstate Commerce Reports
I.C.C.–Interstate Commerce Commission Reports
Idaho–Idaho Reports
Ill. Dec.–Illinois Decisions
Ill.–Illinois Reports
Ill. 2d–Illinois Reports, Second Series
Ill. App.–Illinois Appellate Court Reports
Ill. App. 2d–Illinois Appellate Court Reports, Second Series
Ill. App. 3d–Illinois Appellate Court Reports, Third Series
Ill. Cir. Ct.–Illinois Circuit Court Reports
Ill. Ct. Cl.–Illinois Court of Claims Reports
Ind.–Indiana Reports
Ind. App.–Indiana Court of Appeals Reports (Indiana Appellate Court Reports before 1972)
Interior Dec.–Decisions of the Department of the Interior
Iowa–Iowa Reports
Johns.–Johnson's Common Law Reports, New York
Johns. Ch.–Johnson's Chancery Reports, New York
Jones & S.–Jones and Spencer's Superior Court Reports, New York
Kan.–Kansas Reports
Kan. App.–Kansas Court of Appeals Reports
Kan. App. 2d–Kansas Court of Appeals Reports, Second Series
Keyes–Keyes' Reports, New York
Ky. Law Rep.–Kentucky Law Reporter
Ky.–Kentucky Reports
La.–Louisiana Reports
La. Ann.–Louisiana Annual Reports
La. App.–Louisiana Court of Appeals Reports
L. Ed.–Lawyer's Edition, United States Supreme Court Reports
L. Ed. 2d–Lawyer's Edition, United States Supreme Court Reports, Second Series
Leigh–Leigh Virginia Reports
Mart. (n.s.)–Martin Louisiana Reports, New Series (Louisiana Term Reports)
Mart. (o.s.)–Martin Louisiana Reports, Old Series (Louisiana Term Reports)
Marv.–Marvel Delaware Reports

Mass. App. Ct.–Massachusetts Appeals Court Reports
Mass. App. Div.–Appellate Division Reports Massachusetts
Mass.–Massachusetts Reports
McGrath–McGrath's Mandamus Cases, Michigan
M.C.C.–Interstate Commerce Commission Reports, Motor Carrier Cases
Md.–Maryland Reports
Md. App.–Maryland Appellate Reports
Me.–Maine Reports
Met.–Metcalf Massachusetts Reports
Mich.–Michigan Reports
Mich. App.–Michigan Appeals Reports
Mills–Mills' Surrogate's Court Reports, New York
Minn.–Minnesota Reports
Minor–Minor Alabama Reports
Misc.–New York Miscellaneous Reports
Misc. 2d–New York Miscellaneous Reports, Second Series
Miss.–Mississippi Reports
M.J.–Military Justice Reporter
Mo.–Missouri Reports
Mo. App.–Missouri Appeals Reports
Mont.–Montana Reports
N.C.–North Carolina Supreme Court Reports
N.C. App.–North Carolina Court of Appeals Reports
N.D.–North Dakota Reports
N.E.–North Eastern Reporter
N.E.2d–North Eastern Reporter, Second Series
Neb.–Nebraska Reports
Nev.–Nevada Reports
N.H.–New Hampshire Reports
N.J.–New Jersey Reports
N.J. Eq.–New Jersey Equity Reports
N.J.L.–New Jersey Law Reports
N.J. Misc.–New Jersey Miscellaneous Reports
N.J. Super.–New Jersey Superior Court Reports
N.L.R.B.–Decisions and Orders of the National Labor Relations Board
N.M.–New Mexico Reports
N.W.–North Western Reporter
N.W.2d–North Western Reporter, Second Series
N.Y.–New York Reports
N.Y.2d–New York Reports, Second Series
N.Y. Crim.–New York Criminal Reports
N.Y. St. Rep.–New York State Reporter
N.Y. Super. Ct.–New York Superior Court Reports
N.Y.S.–New York Supplement
N.Y.S.2d–New York Supplement, Second Series
Off. Gaz. Pat. Office–Official Gazette of the United States Patent Office
Ohio–Ohio Reports
Ohio Law Abs.–Ohio Law Abstract
Ohio App.–Ohio Appellate Reports
Ohio App. 2d–Ohio Appellate Reports, Second Series
Ohio App. 3d–Ohio Appellate Reports, Third Series
Ohio C.C. (n.s.)–Ohio Circuit Court Reports, New Series
Ohio Cir. Dec.–Ohio Circuit Decisions
Ohio Dec.–Ohio Decisions
Ohio Dec. Reprint–Ohio Decisions, Reprint
Ohio F. Des.–Ohio Federal Decisions
Ohio Law Rep.–Ohio Law Reporter
Ohio Misc.–Ohio Miscellaneous
Ohio Misc. 2d–Ohio Miscellaneous, Second Series
Ohio N.P. (n.s.)–Ohio Nisi Prius Reports, New Series
Ohio Op.–Ohio Opinions
Ohio Op. 2d–Ohio Opinions, Second Series
Ohio Op. 3d–Ohio Opinions, Third Series
Ohio St.–Ohio State Reports
Ohio St. 2d–Ohio State Reports, Second Series
Ohio St. 3d–Ohio State Reports, Third Series
Okla.–Oklahoma Reports
Okla. Crim.–Oklahoma Criminal Reports
Ore.–Oregon Reports
Ore. App.–Oregon Reports, Court of Appeals
P.–Pacific Reporter
P.2d–Pacific Reporter, Second Series
Pa.–Pennsylvania State Reports
Paige Ch.–Paige's Chancery Reports, New York
Park.–Parker's Criminal Reports, New York
Pa. Commw.–Pennsylvania Commonwealth Court Reports
Pa. D. & C.–Pennsylvania District and County Reports
Pa. D. & C.2d–Pennsylvania District and County Reports, Second Series
Pa. D. & C.3d–Pennsylvania District and County Reports, Third Series

Pa. D. & C.4th–Pennsylvania District and County Reports, Fourth Series
Pa. L.J. Rep.–Pennsylvania Law Journal Reports
Pa. Super.–Pennsylvania Superior Court Reports
Pelt.–Peltier's Decisions, Parish at Orleans, Louisiana
Penne.–Pennewill Delaware Reports
Phila.–Philadelphia Reports
Pick.–Pickering Massachusetts Reports
Pub. Lands Dec.–Public Lands Decisions
Quincy–Quincy's Massachusetts Reports
Reappr. Dec.–Reappraisement Decisions
Redf.–Redfield's Surrogates Reports, New York
R.I.–Rhode Island Reports
Sandf.–Sandford's Superior Court Reports, New York
Sandf. Ch.–Sandford's Chancery Reports, New York
S. Ct.–Supreme Court Reporter
S.C.–South Carolina Reports
S.C. Eq.–South Carolina Equity Reports
S.C.L.–South Carolina Law Reports
S.D.–South Dakota Reports
S.D.C. (n.s.)–Supreme Court, District of Columbia Reports, New Series
S.E.–South Eastern Reporter
S.E.2d–South Eastern Reporter, Second Series
S.E.C.–Securities and Exchange Commission Decisions and Reports
Serg. & Rawle–Sergeant and Rawle Pennsylvania State Reports
Silv.–Silvernail's Supreme Court Reports, New York
So.–Southern Reporter
So. 2d–Southern Reporter, Second Series
Stew.–Stewart Alabama Reports
S.W.–South Western Reporter
S.W.2d–South Western Reporter, Second Series
T.B. Mon.–Kentucky Reports, T.B. Monroe
T.C.–Tax Court Reports of the United States Tax Court
Tenn.–Tennessee Reports
Tenn. App.–Tennessee Appeals Reports
Tenn. Crim. App.–Tennessee Criminal Appeals Reports
Tex.–Texas Reports
Tex. Civ. App.–Texas Civil Appeals Reports
Tex. Crim.–Texas Criminal Reports
Thomp. & Cook's–Thompson and Cook's Supreme Court Reports, New York
Treas. Dec.–United States Treasury Decisions
U.S.–United States Reports
U.S. App. D.C.–United States Court of Appeals Reports
U.S.L.W.–United States Law Week
U.S.P.Q.–United States Patents Quarterly
Utah–Utah Reports
Utah 2d–Utah Reports, Second Series
Va.–Virginia Reports
Va. App.–Virginia Court of Appeals Reports
Va. Cir. Ct.–Virginia Circuit Court Opinions
Vt.–Vermont Reports
Wash.–Washington Reports
Wash. App.–Washing Appellate Reports
Wash. 2d–Washington Reports, Second Series
Wend.–Wendell's Common Law Reports, New York
Wheel. Crim. Cas.–Wheeler's Criminal Cases, New York
Wis.–Wisconsin Reports
Wis. 2d–Wisconsin Reports, Second Series
Wkly. L. Bull.–Weekly Law Bulletin, Ohio
W.L.J.–Western Law Journal, Ohio
W. Va.–West Virginia Reports
Wyo.–Wyoming Reports
Yates Sel. Cas.–Yates' Select Cases, New York

# FEDERAL AND STATE ACTS CITED BY POPULAR NAMES

## S – Z

## S

**S Corporation Income Tax Act**
Colo. Rev. Stat., 39-22-320 et seq.
Haw. Rev. Stat. Ann., § 235-121 et seq.
Miss. Code Ann. 1972, § 27-8-1 et seq.
N.C. Gen. Laws 1943, § 105-131 et seq.

**Sabbath Act**
Iowa Code 1954, 729.1
Ky. Rev. Stat. 1971, 436.160
Mass. Gen. Laws Ann., 136:5, 136:6 et seq.
Mich. Comp. Laws 1948, 435.1 et seq.
N.J. Stat. Ann., 2A:171-1 et seq.
N.Y. General Business Law (Consol. Laws Ch. 20) § 2 et seq.

**Sabbath Breaking Act**
Md. Ann. Code 1957, Art. 27, § 492 et seq.
Vt. Stat. Ann., Title 13, § 3301 et seq.

**Sabbath Day Act (World War II)**
Okla. Laws 1944, 1st Extraordinary Sess., p. 1, S.B. 6

**Sabbatical Leave Act**
La. Rev. Stat. Ann., 17:1171 et seq.
Pa. 1937 Pamph. Laws 2579, No. 481

**Sabbatino Amendment**
See Hickenlooper Amendment

**Sabine River Authority Act**
La. Rev. Stat. Ann., 38:2321 et seq.
Tex. Laws 51st Leg., 1949, p. 193, Ch. 110

**Sabine River Compact Act**
Tex. Water Code, § 44.001 et seq.

**Sabotage Act**
Wash. Rev. Code Ann., 9.05.060 et seq.

**Sabotage Act (Communist Control)**
Ala. Code 1958, Title 14, § 97(1) et seq.

**Sabotage Prevention Act**
Ark. Code Ann. 1987, 5-51-301 et seq.
Cal. Military and Veterans Code § 1630 et seq.
Colo. Rev. Stat. 1963, 40-22-1 et seq.
Fla. Stat. Ann., 876.37 et seq., 876.51
Ky. Rev. Stat. 1948, 39.100 et seq.
Md. Ann. Code 1957, Art. 27, § 535 et seq.
Me. Rev. Stat. Ann. 1964, Title 37-B, § 1001 et seq.
Mich. Comp. Laws 1948, 30.51 et seq.
N.H. Rev. Stat. 1955, 649:1 et seq.
N.M. Stat. Ann., 30-21-1 et seq.
Okla. Stat. Ann., Title 21, § 1265.1 et seq.
Pa. Purdon's Stat., Title 35, § 2101 et seq.
Tenn. Code Ann., 39-5-811 et seq.
Utah Code Ann. 1953, 76-8-801 et seq.
Vt. Stat. Ann., Title 13, § 3431 et seq.
Wis. Stat. Ann., 175.05, 946.02

**Saccharin Study and Labeling Act**
Nov. 23, 1977, P.L. 95-203, 21 U.S. Code §§ 301 nt., 343 et seq.; 42 U.S. Code § 3891-1 nt.
June 17, 1980, P.L. 96-273, 21 U.S. Code § 348 nt.
May 24, 1985, P.L. 99-46, 21 U.S. Code § 348 nt.
July 11, 1987, P.L. 100-71, 21 U.S. Code § 348 nt.
Oct. 28, 1991, P.L. 102-142, 21 U.S. Code § 348 nt.
Aug. 6, 1996, P.L. 104-180, 21 U.S. Code § 348 nt.

**Saccharin Study and Labeling Act Amendments of 1981**
Aug. 14, 1981, P.L. 97-42, 21 U.S. Code § 301 nt.

**Saco Watershed Compact Act**
N.H. Rev. Stat. 1955, 226-A:1 et seq.

**Sacramental Wine Act**
S.D. Codified Laws 1967, 35-1-8.1, 35-5-6

**Sacramento and San Joaquin Drainage District Act**
Cal. Water Code § 8500 et seq.

**Sacramento and San Joaquin Drainage District Refunding Act**
Cal. Water Code § 8935 et seq.

**Sacramento Area Flood Control Agency Act**
Cal. Statutes 1990, Ch. 510, p. 2421

**Sacramento County Court Services Consolidation Act**
Cal. Government Code § 26638.1

**Sacramento County Water Agency Act**
Cal. Water Code, Appendix, § 66-1 et seq.

**Sacramento Regional County Solid Waste Management District Act**
Cal. Public Resources Code § 60000 et seq.

**Sacramento Regional Transit District Act**
Cal. Public Utilities Code § 102000 et seq.

**Sacramento River West Side Levee District Act**
Cal. Statutes 1915, Ch. 361, p. 516

**Sacramento-San Joaquin Delta Protection Act**
Cal. Public Resources Code § 29700 et seq.

**Sacramento-San Joaquin Valley Wetlands Mitigation Bank Act**
Cal. Fish and Game Code 1957, § 1775 et seq.

**Sacramento State College (Desmond Act)**
Cal. Statutes 1949, Ch. 406, p. 748

**Saddleback Mountain-Arizona Settlement Act of 1996**
Feb. 6, 1996, P.L. 104-102, 110 Stat. 50

**Sadie Act**
Ga. Code Ann., 16-11-107

**Sadler Act (Deadly Weapons)**
Ill. Rev. Stat. 1991, Ch. 38, § 24-1 et seq.

**Safe and Clean Neighborhoods Act**
N.J. Stat. Ann., 52:27D-118.1 et seq.

**Safe and Secure Communities Act**
N.J. Stat. Ann., 52:17B-159 et seq.

**Safe and Unsafe Crossings Act (Railroad)**
Ga. Code Ann., 32-6-190 et seq.

**Safe Bicyclist Protection Act**
Cal. Vehicle Code §§ 2900, 21202, 21208, 21212, 21750, 39002, 39012

**Safe Boating Act**
Ida. Code 1947, 67-7001 et seq.

**Safe Cracking Act**
S.C. Code Ann. 1976, § 16-11-390
Tenn. Code Ann., 39-14-402

**Safe Cremation Act**
S.C. Code Ann. 1976, § 32-8-300 et seq.

**Safe Dams Act**
Ga. Code Ann., 12-5-370 et seq.
N.J. Stat. Ann., 58:4-8.1, 58:4-8.2
Tenn. Code Ann., 69-12-101 et seq.

**Safe Deposit Box Act**
Okla. Stat. Ann., Title 6, § 441 et seq.
Wash. Rev. Code Ann., 22.28.010 et seq.

**Safe Deposit Boxes Act (Credit Union)**
N.M. Stat. Ann., 58-11A-1 et seq.

**Safe Deposit Companies Act**
N.J. Stat. Ann., 17:14A-2 et seq.

**Safe Drinking Water Act**
Dec. 16, 1974, P.L. 93-523, 21 U.S. Code § 349; 42 U.S. Code §§ 201, 300f to 300j-9
Dec. 16, 1975, P.L. 93-523, 42 U.S. Code §§ 300f et seq.
Nov. 16, 1977, P.L. 95-190, 42 U.S. Code §§ 300f nt., 300j-1
June 19, 1986, P.L. 99-339, 42 U.S. Code §§ 300f, 300g-1 et seq., 300h et seq., 300i, 300i-1, 300j et seq.
Oct. 31, 1988, P.L. 100-572, 42 U.S. Code §§ 300j-4, prec. 300j- 21, 300j-21 to 300j-25
Oct. 20, 1994, P.L. 103-382, 42 U.S. Code § 300j-21
Ala. Code 1975, § 22-23-30 et seq.
Cal. Health and Safety Code § 4010 et seq.
Fla. Stat. Ann., 403.850 et seq.
Ga. Code Ann., 12-5-170 et seq.
Me. Rev. Stat. Ann. 1964, Title 22, § 2611 et seq.
Mich. Comp. Laws Ann., 325.1001 et seq.

Minn. Stat. Ann., 144.381 et seq.
Miss. Code Ann. 1972, § 41-26-1 et seq.
N.D. Cent. Code, 61-28.1-01 et seq.
Neb. Rev. Stat. 1943, 71-5301 et seq.
N.J. Stat. Ann., 58:12A-1 et seq.
Pa. Purdon's Stat., Title 35, § 721.1 et seq.
S.C. Code Ann. 1976, § 44-55-10 et seq.
Tenn. Code Ann., 68-221-101 et seq.
Utah Code Ann. 1953, 19-4-101 et seq., 26-12-1 et seq.
Wash. Rev. Code Ann., 70.119A.020 et seq.

**Safe Drinking Water Act (Calderon-Sher)**
Cal. Health and Safety Code §§ 116300, 116355, 116360, 116365, 116370, 116470

**Safe Drinking Water Act (Water Supply)**
Neb. Rev. Stat. 1943, 71-5301 et seq.

**Safe Drinking Water Act Amendments of 1986**
June 19, 1986, P.L. 99-339, 15 U.S. Code §§ 1261, 1263; 42 U.S. Code §§ 201 nts., 300f, 300g-1 et seq., 300h et seq., 300i, 300i-1, 300j et seq., 6939a, 6979a, 6779b
June 13, 1991, P.L. 102-54, 42 U.S. Code § 300g-6 nt.

**Safe Drinking Water Act Amendments of 1996**
Aug. 6, 1996, P.L. 104-182, 42 U.S. Code § 201 nt.

**Safe Drinking Water Amendments of 1977**
Nov. 16, 1977, P.L. 95-190, 42 U.S. Code §§ 201 nt., 300j-1 et seq.

**Safe Drinking Water and Drought Relief Act**
Cal. Water Code § 15125 et seq.

**Safe Drinking Water and Toxic Enforcement Act**
Cal. Health and Safety Code § 25249.5 et seq.

**Safe Drinking Water Bond Law**
Cal. Water Code §§ 13810 et seq., 13850 et seq., 13895 et seq., 14000 et seq., 23820 et seq.

**Safe Drinking Water State Revolving Fund Law**
Cal. Health and Safety Code § 116760 et seq.

**Safe Drinking Water Treatment Revolving Fund Act**
Mont. Code Ann., 75-6-201 et seq.

**Safe Driver Discount of Motor Vehicles Act**
S.C. Code Ann. 1976, § 38-73-760 et seq.

**Safe Driver Insurance Plan**
Mass. Gen. Laws Ann., 175:113P

**Safe Employment Act**
Ind. Code 1976, 35-2.1-1-1 et seq.
Ore. Rev. Stat., 654.001 et seq.

**Safe Homes for Women Act of 1994**
Sept. 13, 1994, P.L. 103-322, 42 U.S. Code § 13701 nt.

**Safe Medical Devices Act of 1990**
Nov. 28, 1990, P.L. 101-629, 21 U.S. Code § 301 nt.
June 16, 1992, P.L. 102-300, 21 U.S. Code §§ 360d, 360i nt.
Aug. 13, 1993, P.L. 103-80, 21 U.S. Code §§ 321, 360d, 360hh et seq., 371; 42 U.S. Code § 263b nt.

**Safe Neighborhood Act**
Fla. Stat. 1991, 163.501 et seq.

**Safe Packaging Act**
Pa. Purdon's Stat., Title 35, § 6024.101 et seq.

**Safe Place Act**
P.R. Laws Ann. 1954, Title 29, § 361

**Safe Place of Employment Act**
Wis. Stat. Ann., 101.11

**Safe Place to Work Act**
Conn. Gen. Stat. Ann., § 31-367
Ohio Rev. Code 1953, 4101.11 et seq.

**Safe Pursuit Police and Bystander Protection Act (Royce-Thompson)**
Cal. Statutes 1991, Ch. 1048

**Safe Rail Transportation Act**
Cal. Government Code § 8574.17
Cal. Public Resources Code § 765.5

**Safe Roads Act**
Mass. Gen. Laws Ann., 90:23, 90:24, 90:24D, 90:24G, 90:24K to 90:24O, 90C:2, 218:26, 258A:1
N.C. Laws 1990, Ch. 435

**Safe Schools Act**
Cal. Education Code 1976, § 17766 et seq.
Fla. Stat. Ann., 232.257
S.C. Code Ann. 1976, §§ 16-3-1040, 16-23-430, 20-7-430, 44-53-445, 59-5-65, 59-63-310 et seq.

**Safe Schools Act of 1994**
March 31, 1994, P.L. 103-227, 20 U.S. Code §§ 1221e-1, 5961 et seq.

**Safe Street Initiative**
Fla. Stat. Ann., 921.0001 et seq.

**Safe Streets Act**
Ala. Code 1975, § 32-5A-200 et seq.

**Safe Streets for Women Act of 1994**
Sept. 13, 1994, P.L. 103-322, 18 U.S. Code §§ 2247, 2248, 2259; 28 U.S. Code § 994 nt.; 42 U.S. Code § 13701 nt.

**Safe Toys Act**
Minn. Stat. Ann., 325F.08 et seq.

**Safe Transport Law (Keene-Hauser)**
Cal. Penal Code § 12026.2

**Safer Off-System Roads Act (Federal Aid For)**
Cal. Streets and Highways Code § 2520 et seq.

**Safer Streets and Neighborhoods Act of 1994**
Sept. 13, 1994, P.L. 103-322, 42 U.S. Code §§ 3711 nt., 3760, 3760 nt.

**Safety Act**
Colo. Rev. Stat., 42-4-101 et seq.
Mont. Code Ann., 50-71-101 et seq.
Tex. Transportation Code, § 723.001 et seq.

**Safety Act (Aerial Exhibitions)**
Ill. Rev. Stat. 1991, Ch. 38, § 50 et seq.

**Safety Act (Amusement Device)**
N.C. Gen. Stat. 1943, § 95-111.1 et seq.

**Safety Act (Amusement Rides and Amusement Attractions)**
W. Va. Code 1966 § 21-10-1 et seq.

**Safety Act (Boat)**
Ga. Code Ann., 52-7-1 et seq.

**Safety Act (Boiler and Pressure Vessel)**
See Boiler and Pressure Vessel Safety Act

**Safety Act (Carlucci Hunter)**
Fla. Stat. Ann., 372.5717

**Safety Act (Charter Boat)**
Wash. Rev. Code Ann., 88.04.005 et seq.

**Safety Act (Child Bicycle)**
Tenn. Code Ann., 55-52-101 et seq.

**Safety Act (Conditions of Employment)**
Pa. Purdon's Stat., Title 43, § 25-1 et seq.

**Safety Act (Construction)**
N.J. Stat. Ann., 34:5-1 et seq.

**Safety Act (Dam)**
Mich. Comp. Laws Ann., 281.1301 et seq.
Okla. Stat. Ann., Title 82, § 110.1 et seq.

**Safety Act (Driver)**
Cal. Vehicle Code 1959, § 23240 et seq.

**Safety Act (Elevator)**
See Elevator Safety Act

**Safety Act (Employees)**
Cal. Labor Code § 6400 et seq.

**Safety Act (Federal Highway)**
Ariz. Rev. Stat. Ann., § 28-611

**Safety Act (Fire in Public Buildings)**
Mass. Gen. Laws Ann., 143:3 et seq.

**Safety Act (Fire)**
Cal. Health and Safety Code § 13143.2
N.J. Stat. Ann., 52:27D-192 et seq.

**Safety Act (Food)**
Fla. Stat. Ann., 500.01 et seq.

**Safety Act (Heating Cable)**
Mich. Comp. Laws Ann., 125.2501 et seq.

**Safety Act (High-Rise)**
Okla. Stat. Ann., Title 19, § 863.44A et seq.

**Safety Act (High Voltage)**
Ga. Code Ann., 46-3-30 et seq.

**Safety Act (Highway)**
La. Rev. Stat. Ann., 48:1351 et seq.
N.J. Stat. Ann., 27:5F-1 et seq.

**Safety Act (Hoisting Operators)**
N.M. Stat. Ann., 60-15-1 et seq.

**Safety Act (Labor)**
Ore. Rev. Stat., 654.001 et seq.
Wash. Rev. Code Ann., 49.17.010 et seq.

**Safety Act (Liquefied Petroleum)**
See Liquefied Petroleum Safety Act

**Safety Act (Mining)**
N.M. Stat. Ann., 69-27-1

**Safety Act (Moonwalker)**
Utah Code Ann. 1953, 53-5-601 et seq.

**Safety Act (Motor Vehicle)**
Colo. Rev. Stat., 42-2-101 et seq.
S.C. Code Ann. 1976, § 56-5-4410 et seq.

**Safety Act (Natural Gas Pipelines)**
Neb. Rev. Stat. 1943, 81-542 et seq.

**Safety Act (Occupations)**
Md. Ann. Code 1974, Art. LE, § 5-101 et seq.

**Safety Act (Private Passenger Motor Vehicle)**
Cal. Vehicle Code 1959, § 27315

**Safety Act (Railroads)**
Ky. Rev. Stat. 1971, 277.310, 277.320
Me. Rev. Stat. Ann. 1964, Title 23, § 7081 et seq.

**Safety Act (Reservoirs)**
Colo. Rev. Stat., 37-87-105 et seq.

**Safety Act (Road Worker)**
Ill. Rev. Stat. 1991, Ch. 121, § 314.01 et seq.

**Safety Act (Roller Skating)**
Ga. Code Ann., 51-1-43

**Safety Act (Roller-Skating)**
Me. Rev. Stat. 1964, Title 8, § 603 et seq.

**Safety Act (School Bus)**
Alaska Stat. 1962, Replaced Titles, § 28.05.104

**Safety Act (School Zone)**
Utah Laws 1992, Ch. 91

**Safety Act (Seat Belt)**
Del. Code of 1974, Title 21, § 4801 et seq.

**Safety Act (Ski Lift)**
N.J. Stat. Ann., 34:4A-1 et seq.

**Safety Act (Skier)**
Nev. Rev. Stat. (1987 Reprint) 455A.010 et seq.

**Safety Act (Trench)**
Fla. Stat. 1962, 553.60 et seq.

**Safety Act (Workmen's Compensation)**
N.M. Stat. Ann., 52-1-10

**Safety Act (Workmen's)**
Cal. Labor Code § 6300 et seq.

**Safety Act (Workplace Violence)**
Cal. Code of Civil Procedure § 527.8

**Safety Act (Youth Camp)**
N.J. Stat. Ann., 26:12-1 et seq.

**Safety and Damage Prevention Act (Underground Utility)**
Del. Code of 1974, Title 26, § 801 et seq.

**Safety and Driver Education Act**
Tex. Rev. Civ. Stat., Art. 4413(29c)

**Safety and Financial Responsibility Act (Motor Vehicles)**
Iowa Code Ann., 321A.1 et seq.
N.C. Gen. Stat. 1943, § 20-279.1 et seq.
Wis. Stat. Ann., 344.01 et seq.

**Safety and Hazardous Materials Motor Carrier Act**
Okla. Stat. Ann., Title 47, §§ 230.1 to 230.14

**Safety and Health Act**
See also Occupational Safety and Health Act
Alaska Stat. 1962, § 18.05.010 et seq.
Colo. Rev. Stat. 8-11-100.1 et seq.
Ill. Rev. Stat. 1991, Ch. 48, § 137.1 et seq.
Minn. Stat. Ann., 182.65 et seq.

**Safety and Health Act (Industrial)**
Wash. Rev. Code Ann., 49.17.900

**Safety and Health Act (Mine)**
N.C. Gen. Stat. 1943, § 74-24.1 et seq.

**Safety and Health Act (Occupational)**
Alaska Stat. 1962, § 18.60.010 et seq.
Fla. Stat. Ann., 442.001 et seq.

**Safety and Liability Act (Amusement Rider)**
Pa. Purdon's Stat., Title 42, § 501 et seq.

**Safety and Licensing Act (Fireworks)**
N.M. Stat. Ann., 60-2C-1 et seq.

**Safety and Occupational Health Act (Farm)**
Pa. Purdon's Stat., Title 3, § 1901 et seq.

**Safety and Responsibility Act**
Tex. Transportation Code, § 601.001 et seq.

**Safety and Security Act (School)**
Kan. Stat. Ann., 72-89b01 et seq.

**Safety and Traffic Act**
Ark. Code Ann. 1987, 27-49-201 et seq.

**Safety Appliance Act**
Ill. Rev. Stat. 1985, Ch. 114, § 142 et seq.
Ind. Code 1971, 22-11-4-1 et seq.
Iowa Code Ann., 88.1 et seq.
Mich. Comp. Laws Ann., 469.211 et seq.
Minn. Stat. 1978, 219.58 et seq.
Ohio Rev. Code 1953, 4963.01 et seq.

**Safety Appliance Act (Railroads)**
Iowa Code 1971, 88.1 et seq.
Mo. Rev. Stat., 389.790 et seq.
Tex. Rev. Civ. Stat., Arts. 6382 to 6388
Va. Code 1950, § 40.1-42 et seq.
Wash. Rev. Code Ann., 81.44.031 et seq.

**Safety Appliance Acts (Interstate Commerce)**
Feb. 4, 1887, Ch. 104, 24 Stat. 379, 15 U.S. Code § 77c; generally distributed in 49 U.S. Code
March 2, 1893, Ch. 196, 27 Stat. 531, 45 U.S. Code §§ 1 to 7
March 2, 1903, Ch. 976, 32 Stat. 943, 45 U.S. Code §§ 8 to 10
April 14, 1910, Ch. 160, 36 Stat. 298, 45 U.S. Code §§ 11 to 16
Feb. 28, 1920, Ch. 91, 41 Stat. 499, 49 U.S. Code §§ 26, 27
Aug. 14, 1957, P.L. 85-135, 71 Stat. 352, 45 U.S. Code §§ 6, 13
April 11, 1958, P.L. 85-375, 72 Stat. 86, 45 U.S. Code § 9
July 9, 1976, P.L. 94-348, 90 Stat. 818, 45 U.S. Code § 6
Jan. 14, 1983, P.L. 97-468, 96 Stat. 2580, 45 U.S. Code § 13
June 22, 1988, P.L. 100-342, 45 U.S. Code §§ 1-14, 16
Sept. 3, 1992, P.L. 102-365, 45 U.S. Code §§ 6, 10, 13

**Safety Belt Use Act**
Ala. Code 1975, § 32-5B-1 et seq.
Fla. Stat. Ann., 316.614 et seq.
Kan. Stat. Ann., 8-2501 et seq.
N.M. Stat. Ann., 66-7-370 et seq.

**Safety Board Act (Pyrotechnic)**
S.C. Code Ann. 1976, § 23-8-10 et seq.

**Safety Code**
Ohio Rev. Code 1953, 4101.03 et seq., 4113.21, 4121.01 et seq.

**Safety Code (Construction)**
N.J. Stat. Ann., 34:5-1 et seq.

**Safety Code (Public)**
Utah Code Ann. 1953, 53-1-101 et seq.

**Safety Code (Scaffolding)**
Ky. Rev. Stat. 1971, Superseded Vol., 338.150 et seq.

**Safety Code for Amusement Rides**
S.C. Code Ann. 1976, § 41-18-10 et seq.

**Safety Commission Act**
Minn. Laws 1917, Ch. 261

**Safety Commission Act (Seismic)**
Cal. Government Code § 8870 et seq.
Mo. Laws 1993, S.B. No. 142

**Safety Commission Ordinance (Dalton)**
Ga. Laws 1992, p. 7205

**Safety Compact (Vehicle Equipment)**
Ind. Code Ann., 9-28-6-1 et seq.

**Safety Compliance Act (Bus)**
N.J. Stat. Ann., 48:4-2.1c et seq.

**Safety Council Act**
Alaska Stat. 1962, § 18.60.010 et seq.
Wash. Rev. Code 1951, 43.60.010 et seq.

**Safety Culture Act**
Mont. Code Ann., 39-71-1501 et seq.

**Safety Deposit Box Opening Act**
Ill. Rev. Stat. 1991, Ch. 17, §§ 1500, 1501

**Safety Deposit License Act**
Ill. Rev. Stat. 1991, Ch. 17, § 1450 et seq.

**Safety Fire Commissioner Act**
Ga. Code Ann., 25-2-1

**Safety for Dams and Reservoirs Act**
S.C. Code Ann. 1976, § 49-11-110 et seq.

**Safety Fund Act**
N.Y. Laws 1829, Ch. 94

**Safety Glass Act (Motor Vehicles)**
Ind. Code Ann., 9-8-6-40

**Safety Glazing Materials Act**
Ill. Rev. Stat. 1991, Ch. 111 1/2, § 3101 et seq.
Mich. Comp. Laws Ann., 125.1381

**Safety in Skiing Act**
N.Y. Labor Law (Consol. Laws Ch. 31) § 865 et seq.

**Safety Inspection Act**
Vt. Stat. Ann., Title 21, § 201 et seq.

**Safety Inspection and Education Act**
Ill. Rev. Stat. 1991, Ch. 48, § 59.01 et seq.

**Safety Inspection and Education in Commercial Establishments Act**
Ill. Rev. Stat. 1991, Ch. 48, § 59.1 et seq.

**Safety Inspection and Insurance Act (Amusement Rides)**
Tex. Insurance Code Art. 21.53

**Safety Instruction Law**
Cal. Education Code 1976, § 51202

**Safety Patrol Act**
Neb. Rev. Stat. 1943, 60-431 et seq.

**Safety Preparedness Act (Oil Refinery and Chemical Plant)**
Cal. Government Code § 51020 et seq.

**Safety Professional and Industrial Hygienist Title Protection Act**
Minn. Stat. 1986, 182A.01 et seq.

**Safety Program Act (Motorcycle)**
Md. Ann. Code 1974, Art. TR, § 16-606 et seq.

**Safety Radio Services Act (Public)**
Ga. Code Ann., 50-5-180 et seq.

**Safety Reform Act (Boating)**
Ala. Code 1975, § 33-5-50 et seq.

**Safety Regulation Act (Boating)**
Okla. Stat. Ann., Title 63, §§ 4200 to 4218

**Safety Regulations Act**
Neb. Rev. Stat. 1943, 48-401 et seq.

**Safety Responsibility Act (Motor Vehicles)**
Alaska Stat. 1962, § 28.20.010 et seq.
Ariz. Rev. Stat. Ann., § 28-1101 et seq.
Colo. Rev. Stat. 42-7-101 et seq.
D.C. Code Ann., § 40-401 et seq.
Del. Code of 1974, Title 21, § 2901 et seq.
Fla. Stat. Ann., 324.04 et seq.
Ga. Code Ann., 40-9-1 et seq.
Haw. Rev. Stat. § 287-1 et seq.
Ida. Code 1947, 49-1201 et seq.
Ill. Rev. Stat. 1991, Ch. 95 1/2, § 7-100 et seq.
Ind. Code Ann., 9-2.1-1 et seq.
Iowa Code Ann., 321A.1 et seq.
Kan. Laws 1957, Ch. 68
La. Rev. Stat. Ann., 32:851 et seq.
Md. Ann. Code 1974, Art. TR, § 17-104 et seq.
Minn. Stat. Ann., 65B.001 et seq.
Miss. Code Ann. 1972, § 63-15-1 et seq.
Mo. Rev. Stat., 303.010 et seq.
Mont. Code Ann., 61-6-101 et seq.
Neb. Rev. Stat. 1943, 60-501 et seq.
N.M. Stat. Ann. 1953, 64-24-5 et seq.
Okla. Stat. Ann., Title 47, § 7-101 et seq.
Pa. Cons. Stat., Title 75, § 701 et seq.
R.I. Gen. Laws 1956, 31-31-1 et seq.
S.D. Codified Laws 1967, 32-35-1 et seq.
Tex. Rev. Civil Stat., Art. 6701h
Va. Code 1950, § 46.1-388 et seq.
Wash. Rev. Code Ann., 46.29.010 et seq.
Wis. Stat. Ann., 344.12 et seq.
W. Va. Code 1966, § 17D-1-1 et seq.
Wyo. Stat. Ann., § 31-9-101 et seq.

**Safety Restraint for Children Act**
Wyo. Stat. Ann., § 31-5-1301 et seq.

**Safety Solicitation Act (Public)**
Mich. Comp. Laws Ann., 14.301 et seq.

**Safety Standards and Manufactured Housing Construction Law**
Va. Code 1950, § 36-85.2 et seq.
W. Va. Code 1966 § 21-9-1 et seq.

**Safety Training Act (Cycle Rider)**
Ill. Comp. Stat. 1992, Ch. 625, § 35/1 et seq.

**Sagebrush Rebellion Act**
N.M. Stat. Ann., 19-15-1 et seq.

**Saginaw Chippewa Indian Tribe of Michigan Distribution of Judgment Funds Act**
Nov. 5, 1987, P.L. 100-153, 101 Stat. 888

**Saguaro National Monument Expansion Act of 1991**
June 19, 1991, P.L. 102-61, 16 U.S. Code § 431 nt.

**Saguaro National Park Establishment Act of 1994**
Oct. 14, 1994, P.L. 103-364, 16 U.S. Code § 410zz nt.

**Sailing School Vessels Act of 1982**
Oct. 15, 1982, P.L. 97-322, 46 U.S. Code §§ 390, 390a to 390d, 446 to 446d, 446d nt., 672
Oct. 30, 1984, P.L. 98-577, 46 U.S. Code Appx. § 446b

**Sailors' and Soldiers' Children's Home Act**
Ind. Code Ann., 12-3-20-1 et seq.

**Sailors and Soldiers Relief Act**
Cal. Military and Veterans Code § 395.1
N.J. Stat. Ann., 38:23C-1 et seq.

**Saint Elizabeth's Hospital and District of Columbia Mental Health Services Act**
Oct. 31, 1991, P.L. 102-150, 24 U.S. Code §§ 225, 225 nt., 225b, 225f, 225h

**Saint Lawrence Seaway Act**
May 13, 1954, Ch. 201, 68 Stat. 92, 31 U.S. Code § 846; 33 U.S. Code §§ 981 to 990
July 17, 1957, P.L. 85-108, 71 Stat. 307, 33 U.S. Code §§ 984, 985, 989
Oct. 21, 1970, P.L. 91-469, 84 Stat. 1038, 33 U.S. Code §§ 985, 988
June 27, 1988, P.L. 100-352, 102 Stat. 664, 33 U.S. Code § 988

**Saint Lucie County Expressway Authority Act**
Fla. Stat. Ann., 348.9401 et seq.

**Saint Mary's Airport Authority Act**
Ga. Laws 1964, p. 2438

**Salamanca Hospital District Authority Act**
N.Y. Public Authorities Law (Consol. Laws Ch. 43A) § 1760 et seq.

**Salamanca Indian Lease Authority Act**
N.Y. Public Authorities Law (Consol. Laws Ch. 43A) 1790 et seq.

**Salaries and Fees Act**
Ill. Rev. Stat. 1991, Ch. 53

**Salaries and Fees Act (County Officers)**
Ind. Code Ann., 36-3-6-3 et seq.

**Salaries and Fees Act (State Officers)**
Ind. Code Ann., 4-2-1-1, 4-2-1-2

**Salaries of Public Officers (Gomez Clause)**
Fla. Stat. Ann., 111.045

**Salary Act**
Ariz. Laws 1952, Ch. 37

**Salary Act (Anti-Fee)**
Tenn. Code Ann., 8-22-101 et seq.

**Salary Act (Assigned Appellate Judges)**
Ill. Rev. Stat. 1991, Ch. 53, § 5.10 et seq.

**Salary Act (Counties)**
Mich. Comp. Laws Ann., 45.401 et seq.
Minn. Stat. 1982, 382.19 et seq.
N.D. Cent. Code, 11-10-10
N.M. Stat. Ann., 4-44-1 et seq.
Ohio Rev. Code 1953, 325.01 et seq.
Okla. Stat. Ann., Title 19, § 180.58 et seq.
Tex. Rev. Civ. Stat., Art. 3912e

**Salary Act (County Officers)**
Okla. Stat. Ann., Title 19, § 179.13 et seq.

**Salary Act (Garland County)**
Ark. Acts 1957, p. 976, No. 339

**Salary Act (Judicial)**
Ark. Code Ann. 1987, 8-8-202 et seq.

**Salary Act (Miller County)**
Ark. 1948 Initiated Act No. 2 of Miller County

**Salary Act (Public Officers and Employees)**
Ky. Rev. Stat. 1971, 64.480 et seq.

**Salary Act (Randolph County)**
Ark. 1948 Initiated Act No. 2 of Randolph County

**Salary Act (Sevier County)**
Ark. 1934 Initiated Act No. 1 of Sevier County

**Salary Act (State)**
Okla. Stat. Ann., Title 74, § 250.4 et seq.
Tex. Rev. Civ. Stat., Art. 6813 et seq.
Utah Code Ann. 1953, Miscellaneous Superseded Code Provisions, 67-8-11 et seq.

**Salary Act (Teachers, Supervisors)**
N.Y. Education Law 1947 (Consol. Laws Ch. 16) § 3101 et seq.

**Salary Act (Teachers)**
See Teachers' Salary Act

**Salary Act (Washington County)**
Ark. 1954 Initiated Acts of Washington County

**Salary Adjustment Act**
Ohio Laws Vol. 122, p. 576

**Salary Adjustment Act (Emergency)**
Wis. Stat. 1975, 66.195

**Salary Administration Act**
Okla. Stat. 1971, Title 74, § 701 et seq.

**Salary Alternative Policies Act (Teachers)**
Colo. Rev. Stat., 22-66-101 et seq.

**Salary and Classification Act (Cities)**
Ind. Code Ann., 36-3-6-2 et seq.

**Salary Board Act**
Pa. 1947 Pamph. Laws 1308, No. 524, § 23, Subsecs. 303 et seq.

**Salary Deduction Law**
Ky. Rev. Stat. 1971, 61.120 et seq.

**Salary Disclosure Act**
Mich. Comp. Laws Ann., 565.951

**Salary Freezing Law**
N.Y. Education Law 1947 (Consol. Laws Ch. 16) § 3112

**Salary Grab Act**
March 3, 1873, Ch. 226, 17 Stat. 485

**Salary Grant Act (Law Enforcement)**
Ill. Rev. Stat. 1991, Ch. 85, § 520 et seq.

**Salary Increase Act (State)**
Cal. Statutes 1945, Ch. 1364, p. 2554

**Salary Limitation Act**
Ind. Code Ann., 5-7-5-1

**Salary Payment Act (State Officer)**
Ill. Rev. Stat. 1991, Ch. 127, §§ 167w, 168

**Salary Procedures and Restrictions Act**
Ark. Act 1973, No. 284
N.M. Stat. Ann. 1953, 5-4-47 et seq.

**Salary Readjustment Act (State Employees)**
N.M. Stat. Ann. 1953, 5-4-47 et seq.

**Salary Reduction Act**
Iowa Laws 1933, (45th G. A.), Ch. 89
Ohio Laws Vol. 114, p. 70

**Salary Schedule Act**
Alaska Stat. 1962, § 39.27.011 et seq.

**Salary Supplement Act (Nonpublic School Teachers)**
R.I. Gen. Laws 1956, 16-51-1 et seq.

**Salary Withholding Act (Government)**
Ill. Rev. Stat. 1991, Ch. 85, § 470 et seq.

**Salary Withholding Act (State Employees)**
Ill. Rev. Stat. 1991, Ch. 127, § 351 et seq.

**Sale Act (Cigarettes)**
Fla. Stat. Ann., 210.01 et seq.

**Sale Below Cost Act (Milk)**
Tenn. Code Ann., 53-3-202

**Sale of Alcohol by Druggists Act**
S.C. Code Ann. 1976, § 61-11-10 et seq.

**Sale of Alcoholic Liquor by Individual Drink Act**
Ore. Rev. Stat., 472.010 et seq.

**Sale of Assets Act**
Del. Code of 1974, Title 8, § 271

**Sale of Business Opportunities Act**
Fla. Stat. Ann., 559.80 et seq.

**Sale of Checks Act**
Ala. Acts 1961, Sp. Sess., p. 2142
Ark. Code Ann. 1987, 23-41-102 et seq.
Del. Code of 1974, Title 5, § 2301 et seq.
Ga. Code Ann., 7-1-680 et seq.
Ky. Rev. Stat. 1971, 366.010 et seq.
La. Rev. Stat. Ann., 6:1031 et seq.
Mich. Comp. Laws Ann., 487.901 et seq.
Miss. Code Ann. 1972, § 75-15-1 et seq.
Mo. Rev. Stat., 361.700 et seq.
N.C. Gen. Stat. 1943, § 53-192 et seq.
N.D. Cent. Code, 51-17-01 et seq.
Neb. Rev. Stat. 1943, 8-1001 et seq.
Okla. Stat. Ann., Title 6, § 2101 et seq.
Ore. Rev. Stat., 717.010 et seq.
R.I. Gen. Laws 1956, 19-27-1 et seq.
Tex. Rev. Civ. Stat., Art. 489d

**Sale of Exchange Act**
Ill. Rev. Stat. 1991, Ch. 17, § 4701 et seq.

**Sale of Franchises Act (Public Utilities)**
Cal. Statutes 1905, p. 777

**Sale of Gold and Silver Act (Deceptive)**
Ill. Rev. Stat. 1991, Ch. 121 1/2, § 157.16 et seq.

**Sale of Goods**
See also Uniform Commercial Code-Sales
Ala. Code 1958, Title 57, § 1 et seq.
N.J. Rev. Stat. 12A:2-105 et seq.
N.Y. Uniform Commercial Code (Consol Laws, Ch, 38) § 2-101 et seq.

**Sale of Immoral Publications to Children Act**
Ill. Rev. Stat. 1991, Ch. 23, § 2362.9 et seq.

**Sale of Insurance by Banks Relative to the Consumer Protection Act**
Mass. Gen. Laws Ann., 167F.2A, 175.209 to 175.211, 178A.4, 183.68

**Sale of Insurance Securities Law**
N.M. Stat. Ann., 59A-35-1 et seq.

**Sale of Kosher Food Products Act of 1985**
Wash. Rev. Code Ann., 69.90.010 et seq.

**Sale of Land Act**
N.J. Stat. Ann., 2A:61-1 et seq.

**Sale of Maps Act**
Ill. Rev. Stat. 1991, Ch. 124, § 200 et seq.

**Sale of Meat, Slaughter, and Processing Animals Act**
Colo. Rev. Stat., 35-33-101 et seq.

**Sale of Money Orders Act**
Fla. Stat. Ann., 560.01 et seq.

**Sale of Residential Property Subject to Land Trust Act**
Ill. Rev. Stat. 1991, Ch. 29, § 8.30 et seq.

**Sale of Reversion or Remainder Interest Act**
Ky. Rev. Stat. 1971, Superseded Vols., 389.030

**Sale of Securities Act**
Cal. Statutes 1913, p. 715
Cal. Statutes 1917, p. 673
Fla. Stat. Ann., 517.011 et seq.
Haw. Rev. Stat. Ann., § 485-1 et seq.
La. Rev. Stat. Ann., 51:701 et seq.
Mass. Gen. Laws Ann., 110A:101 et seq.
S.C. Code Ann. 1976, § 35-1-10 et seq.
W. Va. Code 1966, § 32-1-101 et seq.

**Sale of Tobacco to Minors Act**
Ill. Rev. Stat. 1991, Ch. 23, § 2356.9 et seq.

**Sale of Unclaimed Property Act**
Ill. Rev. Stat. 1991, Ch. 141, § 0.01 et seq.

**Sale or Pledge of Goods by Minors Act**
Ill. Rev. Stat. 1991, Ch. 23, § 2365.9 et seq.

**Sale Price Ad Act**
Ill. Rev. Stat. 1991, Ch. 121 1/2, § 850 et seq.

**Salem Armory Act**
Ore. Laws 1991, Ch. 590

**Salem Civic Center Law**
Ill. Rev. Stat. 1991, Ch. 85, § 7101 et seq.

**Salem Police and Fire Alarm System Loan Act**
Mass. Acts 1952, Ch. 75

**Sales Act**
See Uniform Commercial Code—Sales

**Sales Act (Bulk)**
See Bulk Sales Act

**Sales Act (Cigarette)**
See Unfair Cigarette and Tobacco Products Sales Act

**Sales Act (Closing Out)**
See Closing Out Sales Act

**Sales Act (Conditional)**
See Conditional Sales Act

**Sales Act (Door-to-Door)**
Md. Ann. Code 1974, Art. CL, § 14-301 et seq.

**Sales Act (Franchise)**
N.Y. General Business Law (Consol. Laws Ch. 20) § 680 et seq.

**Sales Act (Home Solicitation)**
Ga. Code Ann., 10-1-1 et seq.

**Sales Act (Installment)**
Neb. Rev. Stat. 1943, 45-334 et seq.

**Sales Act (Motor Fuel)**
Ill. Rev. Stat. 1991, Ch. 121 1/2, § 1500 et seq.
Mass. Gen. Laws Ann., 94:295A et seq.

**Sales Act (Pyramid or Multilevel)**
N.M. Stat. Ann., 57-13-1 et seq.

**Sales Act (Retail Installments)**
See Retail Installment Sales Act

**Sales Act (Unfair)**
See Unfair Sales Act

**Sales and Leasing Act**
Tex. Rev. Civ. Stat., Art. 5421c

**Sales and Use Tax Act**
Cal. Revenue and Taxation Code § 6001 et seq.
Conn. Gen. Stat. Ann., § 12-406 et seq.
Fla. Stat. Ann., 212.01 et seq.
Ga. Code Ann., 48-8-1 et seq.
Ky. Rev. Stat. 1971, 139.010 et seq.
Me. Rev. Stat. Ann. 1964, Title 36, § 1751 et seq.
N.C. Gen. Stat. 1943, § 105-164.1 et seq.
N.D. Cent. Code, 57-39.2-01 et seq.
Nev. Rev. Stat. 1979 Reprint, 372.010 et seq.
N.J. Stat. Ann., 54:32B-1 et seq.
N.Y. Tax Law (Consol. Laws Ch. 60), § 1101 et seq.
Ore. Laws 1983, Sp. Sess., Ch. 3, §§ 2 to 117, 121 to 124, 128, 131 to 143
Ore. Laws 1985, Ch. 95, §§ 1 et seq., 134 et seq., 142, 145 et seq., 156 et seq.
Pa. Purdon's Stat., Title 72, § 7201 et seq.
R.I. Gen. Laws 1956, 44-18-1 et seq.
S.C. Code Ann. 1976, § 12-36-5 et seq.
Tex. Tax Code, § 151.001
Utah Code Ann. 1953, 59-12-101 et seq.

**Sales and Use Tax Act (Aircraft)**
Va. Code 1950, § 58.1-1500 et seq.

**Sales and Use Tax Act (Homestead Option)**
Ga. Code Ann., 48-8-100 to 48-8-109

**Sales and Use Tax Act (Local Government)**
Colo. Rev. Stat., 29-1-501 et seq.
N.C. Gen. Stat. 1943, § 105-463 et seq.

**Sales and Use Tax Act (Local Option)**
N.C. Gen. Stat. 1943, § 105-164.45 et seq.

**Sales and Use Tax Act (Motor Vehicle)**
Va. Code 1950, § 58.1-2400 et seq.

**Sales and Use Tax Act-Counties**
Tex. Tax Code, § 323.001 et seq.

**Sales and Use Tax Act-Municipalities**
Tex. Tax Code, § 321.001 et seq.
Utah Code Ann. 1953, 59-12-101 et seq.

**Sales and Use Tax Exemption Act**
Fla. Stat. Ann., 212.08

**Sales and Use Tax, Local Option Revenue Act**
Neb. Rev. Stat. 1943, 77-27, 142 et seq.

**Sales and Use Tax Refund Act**
Iowa Code Ann., 422.45

**Sales Below Cost Act**
Cal. Business and Professions Code § 17043
Conn. Gen. Stat. Ann., § 42-111 et seq.
Md. Ann. Code 1974, Art. CL, § 11-401 et seq.
Ore. Rev. Stat. 1953, 646.100
Utah Code Ann. 1953, 13-5-7

**Sales Discrimination Law**
Iowa Code Ann., 551.1 et seq.

**Sales Finance Act**
Del. Code of 1974, Title 5, § 2901 et seq.
Ga. Code Ann., 10-1-30 et seq.

Kan. Laws 1958, Ch. 9
Md. Ann. Code 1974, Art. FI, § 11-401 et seq.
Ohio Rev. Code 1953, 1317.01 et seq.

**Sales Finance Act (Automobiles)**
Cal. Civil Code § 2981 et seq.

**Sales Finance Act (Motor Vehicle Retail Installment)**
Vt. Stat. Ann., Title 9, § 2351 et seq.

**Sales Finance Act (Motor Vehicles)**
See Motor Vehicles Sales Finance Act

**Sales Finance Agency Act**
Ill. Rev. Stat. 1991, Ch. 17, § 5201 et seq.

**Sales Finance Companies Act**
Conn. Gen. Stat. Ann., § 36-254 et seq.
Md. Ann. Code 1974, Art. FI, § 11-401 et seq.
N.Y. Banking Law (Consol. Laws Ch. 2) § 491 et seq.

**Sales in Bulk Act**
See Bulk Sales Act

**Sales Limitation Act**
Tex. Penal Code 1925, Art. 1111m

**Sales of Checks Act**
Tex. Finance Code, § 152.001 et seq.

**Sales of Convict-Made Goods Regulatory Act**
Ind. Code Ann., 25-12-1-1 et seq.

**Sales Practices Act (Unfair Competition)**
Conn. Gen. Stat. Ann., § 42-115e et seq.

**Sales Price Ad Act**
Ill. Rev. Stat. 1991, Ch. 121 1/2, § 850 et seq.

**Sales Protection Act (Conditional)**
Ill. Rev. Stat. 1991, Ch. 121 1/2, §§ 157.40, 157.41

**Sales Protection Act (Door to Door)**
N.Y. Personal Property Law (Consol. Laws Ch. 41) § 425 et seq.

**Sales Representative Act**
Ill. Stat. 1991, Ch. 48, § 2250 et seq.

**Sales Representatives Recognition Act**
Okla. Stat. Ann., Title 15, § 675 et seq.

**Sales Ring Act (Livestock)**
Colo. Rev. Stat., 35-55-101 et seq.
N.M. Stat. Ann., 77-10-1 et seq.

**Sales Tax Act**
Ala. Code 1975, § 40-23-1 et seq.
Ariz. Rev. Stat. Ann., § 42-1301 et seq.
Colo. Rev. Stat., 39-26-101 et seq.
D.C. Code Ann., § 47-2001 et seq.
Ida. Code 1947, 63-3601 et seq.
Ill. Rev. Stat. 1991, Ch. 120, § 440 et seq.
Ind. Code Ann., 6-2.1-1-12 et seq.
Iowa Code Ann., 422.42 et seq.
Kan. Stat. Ann., 79-3601 et seq.
Ky. Acts 1930, Ch. 149
La. Rev. Stat. Ann., 47:301 et seq.
Mass. Gen. Laws Ann., 64H:1 et seq.
Mich. Comp. Laws Ann., 205.51 et seq.
Miss. Code Ann. 1972, § 27-65-1 et seq.
Mo. Rev. Stat., 144.010 et seq.
N.D. Cent. Code, 57-39.2-01 et seq.
N.J. Laws 1935, Chs. 268, 280
N.M. Stat. Ann. 1953, 72-16-1 et seq.
Ohio Rev. Code 1953, 5739.01 et seq.
Okla. Stat. Ann., Title 68, § 1350 et seq.
Ore. Laws 1935, Sp. Sess., Ch. 45
S.C. Code Ann. 1976, § 12-36-910 et seq.
S.D. Codified Laws 1967, 10-45-1 et seq.
Tenn. Code Ann., 67-6-101 et seq.
Tex. Tax Code, § 151.001 et seq.
Wash. Rev. Code Ann., 82.08.010 et seq.
Wis. Stat. Ann., 77.51 et seq.
Wyo. Stat. Ann., § 39-6-401 et seq.

**Sales Tax Act (Beer Consumers)**
Ark. Acts 1939, p. 758, No. 310

**Sales Tax Act (City Transportation)**
Miss. Code Ann. 1972, § 27-65-95 et seq.
Mo. Rev. Stat., 94.600 et seq.

**Sales Tax Act (Consumers)**
W. Va. Code 1966, § 11-15-1 et seq.

**Sales Tax Act (Counties)**
Ark. Code Ann. 1987, 26-74-307 et seq.
Mo. Rev. Stat., 67.500 et seq.
N.M. Stat. Ann., 7-21-1 et seq.

**Sales Tax Act (Emergency)**
Pa. Purdon's Stat., Title 72, § 3282
Wyo. Session Laws 1935, Ch. 74

**Sales Tax Act (New York City)**
N.Y. City Adm. Code '38, Ch. 46, § N46-1.0 et seq.

**Sales Tax Act (Occupational Privilege)**
Ga. Laws 1929, p. 103

**Sales Tax Act (Oleomargarine)**
Wyo. Session Laws 1931, Ch. 137

**Sales Tax Act (Retail Sales)**
See Retail Sales Tax Act

**Sales Tax Act (Retailers')**
Kan. Stat. Ann., 79-3601 et seq.

**Sales Tax Act (School)**
N.M. Stat. Ann. 1953, 72-16-1 et seq.

**Sales Tax Act (Temporary)**
Mass. Acts 1966, Ch. 14, § 1

**Sales Tax Emergency Revenue Act**
Miss. Code Ann. 1972, § 27-65-1 et seq.

**Sales Tax Exemption Act**
Ala. Code 1975, § 40-23-4 et seq.

**Sales Tax Law**
Mo. Rev. Stat., 144.010 et seq.

**Sales Tax Lien Act**
Iowa Code Ann., 422.56

**Sales Tax Relief Act**
Okla. Stat. 1981, Title 68, § 5010 et seq.

**Sales Taxation Act (Fairness in Retail)**
Fla. Stat. Ann., 212.215

**Salesmen's Tax Law**
Miss. Code Ann. 1972, § 27-67-501 et seq.

**Saline Act (Public Lands)**
Jan. 31, 1901, Ch. 186, 31 Stat. 745, 30 U.S. Code § 162

**Saline Water Conversion Act**
July 3, 1952, Ch. 568, 66 Stat. 328, 42 U.S. Code §§ 1951 to 1958
June 29, 1955, Ch. 227, 69 Stat. 198, 42 U.S. Code §§ 1952, 1953, 1958
Sept. 22, 1961, P.L. 87-295, 75 Stat. 628, 42 U.S. Code §§ 1951 to 1958
Aug. 11, 1965, P.L. 89-118, 79 Stat. 509, 42 U.S. Code §§ 1952, 1958
June 24, 1967, P.L. 90-30, 81 Stat. 78, 42 U.S. Code §§ 1951 nt., 1952, 1958
April 29, 1968, P.L. 90-297, 82 Stat. 110, 42 U.S. Code § 1958
Cal. Water Code § 12945 et seq.

**Saline Water Conversion Act of 1971**
July 29, 1971, P.L. 92-60, 85 Stat. 159, 42 U.S. Code § 1959 to 1959h
Aug. 2, 1977, P.L. 95-84, 42 U.S. Code §§ 1959h et seq.

**Saline Water Demonstration Act**
Sept. 2, 1958, P.L. 85-883, 72 Stat. 1706, 42 U.S. Code §§ 1958a to 1958g
Sept. 22, 1961, P.L. 87-295, 75 Stat. 630, 42 U.S. Code § 1958d

**Salinity Control Act (Irrigation District)**
Colo. Rev. Stat., 37-43-201 et seq.

**Salinity Control Barrier Act (Abshire-Kelly)**
Cal. Statutes 1953, Ch. 1104, p. 2601
Cal. Statutes 1957, Ch. 2092, p. 3717

**Salisbury Sewerage Loan Act**
Mass. Acts 1964, Ch. 81

**Salmon and Steelhead Conservation and Enhancement Act of 1980**
Dec. 22, 1980, P.L. 96-561, 16 U.S. Code § 3301 nt.

**Salmon Compact Act, Atlantic**
Conn. Gen. Stat. Ann., § 26-302

**Salmon Fisheries Act**
See Alaska Salmon Fisheries Act

**Salmon Fisheries Act (Alaska)**
Alaska Stat. 1962, § 16.10.010 et seq.

**Salmon Fishing Act**
Ore. Rev. Stat., 509.230

**Salmon Marketing and Development Act**
Cal. Food and Agricultural Code 1967, § 76501 et seq.

**Salmon Resources Conservation Law**
Wash. Rev. Code Ann., 75.48.005 et seq.

**Salmon, Steelhead Trout, and Anadromous Fisheries Program Act**
Cal. Fish and Game Code 1957, § 6900 et seq.

**Salt Lake City Watershed Improvement Act of 1990**
Nov. 28, 1990, P.L. 101-634, 104 Stat. 4580

**Salt River Bay National Historical Park and Ecological Preserve at St. Croix, Virgin Islands, Act of 1992**
Feb. 24, 1992, P.L. 102-247, 16 U.S. Code §§ 410tt et seq., 410tt nt.

**Salt River Pima-Maricopa Indian Community Water Rights Act**
Nov. 28, 1990, P.L. 101-628, 104 Stat. 4491

**Salt River Pima-Maricopa Indian Community Water Rights Settlement Act of 1988**
Oct. 20, 1988, P.L. 100-512, 102 Stat. 2549
Dec. 17, 1991, P.L. 102-238, 105 Stat. 1910

**Salt Severance Tax Act**
Miss. Code Ann. 1972, § 27-25-301 et seq.

**Salt Springs Law**
N.Y. Consol. Laws Ch. 52

**Salt Water Fishing Law (Hernando County)**
Fla. Special Laws 1969, Ch. 69-1097

**Salt Water Fishing Law (Pinellas County)**
Fla. Special Laws 1953, Ch. 29432

**Salt Water Haulers Act**
Tex. Water Code, § 29.001 et seq.

**Salten Sea Infrastructure Financing District**
Cal. Government Code § 53395.9

**Saltiel Law (Premarital Examination for Venereal Disease)**
Ill. Rev. Stat. 1991, Ch. 40, § 204

**Salton Sea Reclamation Act of 1998**
Nov. 12, 1998, P.L. 105-372, 112 Stat. 3377

**Saltonstall-Kennedy Act**
Aug. 11, 1939, Ch. 696, 53 Stat. 1412, 15 U.S. Code § 713c-3
July 1, 1954, Ch. 446, 68 Stat. 376
July 1, 1954, Ch. 447, 68 Stat. 376, 15 U.S. Code § 713c-3
Aug. 8, 1956, Ch. 1036, 70 Stat. 1124
Nov. 8, 1965, P.L. 89-348, 79 Stat. 1311
Dec. 22, 1980, P.L. 96-561, 94 Stat. 3287
Jan. 6, 1983, P.L. 97-424, 15 U.S. Code §§ 713c-3, 713c-3 nt.
Nov. 15, 1986, P.L. 99-659, 100 Stat. 3721
Nov. 28, 1990, P.L. 101-627, 15 U.S. Code § 713c-3
Oct. 29, 1992, P.L. 102-567, 15 U.S. Code § 713c-3

**Salvage Act**
Aug. 1, 1912, Ch. 268, 37 Stat. 242, 46 U.S. Code §§ 727 to 731
Mo. Rev. Stat. 1978, 420.010 et seq.
Neb. Rev. Stat. 1943, 78-101 et seq.
R.I. Gen. Laws 1956, 31-46-1 et seq.
Tex. Human Resources Code, § 432.001 et seq.

**Salvage and Surplus Act of 1957**
Tex. Rev. Civ. Stat., Art. 601b, § 9.01 et seq.

**Salvage Dealers Registration Act**
Ga. Code Ann., 43-48-1 et seq.

**Salvage Vehicles-Motor Vehicle Act**
Utah Code Ann. 1953, 41-1-36.1 et seq.

**Salvage Warehouse Store Act**
Ill. Rev. Stat. 1991, Ch. 114, § 400.1 et seq.

**Same Act Statute (Conviction of One as Bar)**
Va. Code 1950, § 19.2-294

**Sample-Everett Act (Optometry)**
Ky. Rev. Stat. 1971, 320.200 et seq.

**San Benito-Alameda-Santa Clara Water Authority Act**
Cal. Statutes 1955, Ch. 1289, p. 2349

**San Benito County Water Conservation and Flood Control District Act**
Cal. Statutes 1953, Ch. 1598, p. 3279
Cal. Water Code, Appendix, § 70-1 et seq.

**San Benito County Water Conservation and Flood Control District Merger Act**
Cal. Statutes 1961, Ch. 203

**San Bernadino County Transportation Sales Tax Act**
Cal. Public Utilities Code § 190000 et seq.

**San Bernardino County Flood Control Act**
Cal. Statutes 1939, Ch. 73, p. 1011
Cal. Water Code, Appendix, § 43-1 et seq.

**San Blas Marathon Act (Protection of Insignias and the Exclusive Rights for Commercial Advertisements in Radio and Television Transmissions of Marathon Activities on the Island)**
P.R. Laws Ann. 1954, Title 15, § 551a et seq.

**San Carlos Act**
June 7, 1924, Ch. 288, 43 Stat. 475
July 14, 1945, Ch. 301, 59 Stat. 469

**San Carlos Apache Tribe Water Rights Settlement Act of 1992**
Oct. 30, 1992, P.L. 102-575, 106 Stat. 4740
Nov. 2, 1994, P.L. 103-435, 25 U.S. Code § 390 nt.
Jan. 6, 1996, P.L. 104-91, 25 U.S. Code § 390 nt.
Oct. 9, 1996, P.L. 104-261, 25 U.S. Code § 390 nt.
June 12, 1997, P.L. 105-18, 25 U.S. Code § 390 nt.

**San Carlos Indian Irrigation Project Divestiture Act of 1991**
Dec. 12, 1991, P.L. 102-231, 105 Stat. 1722
Oct. 24, 1992, P.L. 102-497, 106 Stat. 3256

**San Carlos Mineral Strip Act of 1990**
Oct. 22, 1990, P.L. 101-447, 104 Stat. 1047

**San Diego Area Wastewater Management District Act**
Cal. Water Code, Appendix, § 133-101 et seq.

**San Diego County Flood Control District Act**
Cal. Statutes 1945, Ch. 1372, p. 2560
Cal. Water Code, Appendix, § 105-1.5 et seq.

**San Diego County Justice Facilities Financing Act**
Cal. Revenue and Taxation Code § 7286.30 et seq.

**San Diego County Justice Facility Financing Act**
Cal. Government Code § 26250 et seq.

**San Diego County Regional Transportation Commission Act**
Cal. Public Utilities Code § 132000 et seq.

**San Diego County Transit Act**
Cal. Public Utilities Code § 90000 et seq.

**San Diego County Transit District Act**
Cal. Public Utilities Code § 90000 et seq.

**San Diego Unified Port District Act**
Cal. Statutes 1962, 1st Ex. Sess., Ch. 67, p. 362

**San Domingo Resolution**
Jan. 12, 1871, No. 7, 16 Stat. 591

**San Francisco Bay Area Conservancy Program**
Cal. Public Resources Code § 31160 et seq.

**San Francisco Bay Area Metropolitan Rapid Transit District Act**
Cal. Statutes 1949, Ch. 1239, p. 2173

**San Francisco Bay Area Rapid Transit District Act**
Cal. Public Utilities Code, § 28500 et seq.

**San Francisco Bay Area Transportation Terminal Authority Act**
Cal. Government Code § 67500 et seq.

**San Francisco Bay Crossing Act**
Cal. Streets and Highways Code, § 30651 et seq.

**San Francisco Bay National Wildlife Refuge**
Oct. 28, 1988, P.L. 100-556, 102 Stat. 2780

**San Francisco Consolidation Act**
Cal. Statutes 1856, Ch. 125, p. 145

**San Francisco Court Act**
Cal. Statutes 1980, Ch. 578

**San Francisco Harbor Improvement Act**
Cal. Statutes 1929, Ch. 835, p. 1775

**San Francisco Harbor Revenue Bond Act**
Cal. Harbors and Navigation Code, § 3300 et seq.

**San Francisco Maritime National Historical Park Act of 1988**
June 27, 1988, P.L. 100-348, 102 Stat. 654, 16 U.S. Code §§ 410nn nt., 410nn to 410nn-4, 460bb-3
Nov. 2, 1994, P.L. 103-437, 16 U.S. Code §§ 410nn, 410nn-2

**San Francisco-Oakland Bay Bridge Act**
Cal. Streets and Highways Code § 30600 et seq.

**San Francisco Pilot Pension Plan Law**
Cal. Harbors and Navigation Code § 1160 et seq.

**San Francisco-San Mateo Consolidation Act**
Cal. Statutes 1929, Ch. 784, p. 1559

**San Gabriel Basin Water Quality Authority Act**
Cal. Water Code, Appendix, § 134-101 et seq.

**San Gorgonio Pass Water Agency Act**
Cal. Water Code, Appendix, § 101-1 et seq.

**San Joaquin County Flood Control and Water Conservation District Act**
Cal. Water Code, Appendix, § 79-1 et seq.

**San Joaquin Levee Water District Act (Lower)**
Cal. Water Code, Appendix, § 75-1 et seq.

**San Joaquin River Conservancy Act**
Cal. Public Resources Code § 32500 et seq.

**San Joaquin Valley Air Pollution Control District Law**
Cal. Health and Safety Code, § 24375 et seq.

**San Joaquin Valley Drainage Relief Act**
Cal. Water Code § 14900 et seq.

**San Juan Basin Wilderness Protection Act of 1984**
Oct. 30, 1984, P.L. 98-603, 98 Stat. 3155
Nov. 15, 1990, P.L. 101-556, 104 Stat. 2764
Nov. 12, 1996, P.L. 104-333, 16 U.S. Code § 1132 nt.; 43 U.S. Code § 178

**San Juan Island National Historical Park Act**
Sept. 9, 1966, P.L. 89-565, 80 Stat. 737, 16 U.S. Code §§ 282 to 282c

**San Juan New Center Corporation Act**
P.R. Laws Ann. 1954, Title 23, § 141 et seq.

**San Louis Obispo County Flood Control and Water Conservation District Act**
Cal. Water Code, Appendix, § 49-1 et seq.

**San Luis Obispo County Flood Control and Water Conservation District Act**
Cal. Statutes 1945, Ch. 1294, p. 2426

**San Luis Rey Indian Water Rights Settlement Act**
Nov. 17, 1988, P.L. 100-675, 102 Stat. 4000

**San Luis Rey Project Law (Water Authority)**
Cal. Water Code § 12000 et seq.

**San Mateo County Flood Control District Act**
Cal. Water Code, Appendix, § 87-1 et seq.

**San Mateo County Transit District Act**
Cal. Public Utilities Code, § 103000 et seq.

**Sanatorium Act (County)**
Mich. Comp. Laws Ann., 332.151 et seq.

**Sanatorium Act (State)**
Mich. Comp. Laws 1970, 332.51 et seq.

**Sanctions for Frivolous Civil Proceedings Act**
S.C. Code Ann. 1976, § 15-36-10 et seq.

**Sanctions for Medicaid Certified Nursing Home Act (Intermediate)**
S.C. Code Ann. 1976, § 44-6-400 et seq.

**Sanctuary Act (Coastal)**
Cal. Public Resources Code § 32500 et seq.

**Sanctuary Act (Manatee)**
Fla. Stat. Ann., 370.12

**Sand and Gravel Act**
Ore. Rev. Stat., 274.530 et seq.

**Sand and Gravel Removal Act**
Conn. Gen. Stat. Ann., § 22a-383

**Sand Creek Massacre National Historic Site Study Act of 1998**
Oct. 6, 1998, P.L. 105-243, 112 Stat. 1579

**Sand Dune Protection and Management Act**
Mich. Comp. Laws Ann., 281.651 et seq.

**Sanders-Reynolds Act (Taxation)**
Ky. Rev. Stat. 1971, 132.485

**Sanderson Act (Fair Trade)**
Ala. General Acts 1935, p. 746

**Sandy Hook Reservation Authority Act**
N.J. Stat. Ann., 13:15-1 et seq.

**Sandy Peters Memorial Act**
Cal. Penal Code § 12022.53

**Sanford Airport and Industrial Development Act**
Fla. Special Laws 1969, Ch. 69-1616

**Sanford Airport Authority Act**
Fla. Special Laws 1971, Ch. 71-924

**Sanford Downtown Development Corporation Act**
Fla. Special Laws 1976, Ch. 76-483

**Sangamon State University Act**
Ill. Rev. Stat. 1991, Ch. 144, § 320 et seq.

**Sanitarian Act (Registered)**
Utah Code Ann. 1953, 58-20-0.5 et seq.

**Sanitarian and Environmental Specialist Registration Act**
Okla. Stat. Ann., Title 59, § 1150.1 et seq.

**Sanitarians Act**
Conn. Gen. Stat. Ann., § 20-358 et seq.
Fla. Stat. Ann., 491.01 et seq.
Ky. Rev. Stat. 1971, 223.010 et seq.
Md. Ann. Code 1974, Art. HO, § 11-501 et seq.
Mich. Comp. Laws Ann., 338.2273 et seq.
N.M. Stat. Ann. 1953, 67-28-1 et seq.
Okla. Stat. Ann., Title 63, § 1-2201 et seq.
Wis. Stat. Ann., 140.45

**Sanitarium Act (Park Child Welfare)**
Ill. Rev. Stat. 1991, Ch. 105, §§ 327v9, 327w

**Sanitarium District Act (Tuberculosis)**
Ill. Rev. Stat. 1991, Ch. 23, § 1700 et seq.

**Sanitary Act (Barbers)**
Fla. Stat. 1983, 476.014 et seq.
Okla. Stat. Ann., Title 59, § 77

**Sanitary and Storm Sewer Districts Act (Metropolitan)**
Mont. Code Ann., 7-13-101 et seq.

**Sanitary Authorities Act**
Ore. Rev. Stat. 1953, 499.015 et seq.

**Sanitary Bakery Law**
Cal. Health and Safety Code § 28190 et seq.

**Sanitary Barber Law (Counties, 65,000 to 95,000)**
Ala. Code 1958, App., § 176(5n)

**Sanitary Code**
See also Sanitary Districts Act
N.J. Stat. Ann., 26:1-1 et seq.
Tex. Health and Safety Code, § 81.066

**Sanitary Commission Act (Barber)**
Fla. Stat. Ann., 476.01 et seq.

**Sanitary Control of Shellfish Pilot Program**
Cal. Health and Safety Code § 112290 et seq.

**Sanitary Disposal Projects Act**
Iowa Code 1971, 406.1 et seq.

**Sanitary District Act**
Md. Ann. Code 1974, Art. HE, § 9-601 et seq.

**Sanitary District Act (Chicago)**
Ill. Rev. Stat. 1985, Ch. 42, § 320 et seq.

**Sanitary District Act (Eastern Will)**
Ill. Comp. Stat. 1992, Ch. 70, § 3020/1 et seq.

**Sanitary District Act (Metro-East)**
Ill. Rev. Stat. 1991, Ch. 42, § 501-1 et seq.

**Sanitary District Act (New Castle County)**
Del. Code of 1974, Title 9, § 2301 et seq.

**Sanitary District Act (North Shore)**
Ill. Rev. Stat. 1991, Ch. 42, § 276.99 et seq.

**Sanitary District Act of 1907**
Ill. Rev. Stat. 1991, Ch. 42, § 246h et seq.

**Sanitary District and Municipality Mutual Expenditure Act**
Ill. Rev. Stat. 1991, Ch. 85, § 1620 et seq.

**Sanitary District Corporate Notes Act**
Ill. Rev. Stat. 1991, Ch. 42, § 319.30 et seq.

**Sanitary District Employees' and Trustees' Annuity and Benefit Fund Act**
Ill. Rev. Stat. 1991, Ch. 108 1/2, § 13-101 et seq.

**Sanitary District Enabling Act**
Me. Rev. Stat. Ann. 1964, Title 38, § 1061 et seq.

**Sanitary District Enlargement Act (Chicago-1st)**
Ill. Rev. Stat. 1989, Ch. 42, §§ 360.9, 361

**Sanitary District Enlargement Act (Chicago-2nd A)**
Ill. Rev. Stat. 1989, Ch. 42, § 361.01 et seq.

**Sanitary District Enlargement Act (Chicago-2nd B)**
Ill. Rev. Stat. 1989, Ch. 42, §§ 372m, 373

**Sanitary District Enlargement Act (Chicago-3rd)**
Ill. Rev. Stat. 1989, Ch. 42, §§ 374.9, 375

**Sanitary District Enlargement Act (Chicago-4th)**
Ill. Rev. Stat. 1989, Ch. 42, §§ 376.9, 377

**Sanitary District Enlargement Act (Chicago-5th)**
Ill. Rev. Stat. 1989, Ch. 42, §§ 378.9, 379

**Sanitary District Enlargement Act (Chicago-6th)**
Ill. Rev. Stat. 1989, Ch. 42, §§ 380.9, 380a

**Sanitary District Enlargement Act (Chicago-7th)**
Ill. Rev. Stat. 1989, Ch. 42, §§ 380b-9, 380c

**Sanitary District Enlargement Act (Chicago-8th)**
Ill. Rev. Stat. 1989, Ch. 42, §§ 380c.9, 380d

**Sanitary District Enlargement Act (Chicago-9th)**
Ill. Rev. Stat. 1989, Ch. 42, §§ 380e9, 380f

**Sanitary District Enlargement Act (Chicago-10th)**
Ill. Rev. Stat. 1989, Ch. 42, §§ 380f.9, 380g

**Sanitary District Enlargement Act (Chicago-11th)**
Ill. Rev. Stat. 1989, Ch. 42, §§ 380g.9, 380h

**Sanitary District Enlargement Act (Chicago-12th)**
Ill. Rev. Stat. 1989, Ch. 42, §§ 380h.9, 380i

**Sanitary District Enlargement Act (Chicago-13th)**
Ill. Rev. Stat. 1989, Ch. 42, §§ 380i.9, 380j

**Sanitary District Enlargement Act (Chicago-14th)**
Ill. Rev. Stat. 1989, Ch. 42, §§ 380j.9, 380k

**Sanitary District Enlargement Act (Chicago-15th)**
Ill. Rev. Stat. 1989, Ch. 42, §§ 380k.9, 380l

**Sanitary District Enlargement Act (Chicago-16th)**
Ill. Rev. Stat. 1989, Ch. 42, §§ 380l.9, 380m

**Sanitary District Enlargement Act (Chicago-17th)**
Ill. Rev. Stat. 1989, Ch. 42, §§ 380m.9, 380n

**Sanitary District Enlargement Act (Chicago-18th)**
Ill. Rev. Stat. 1989, Ch. 42, §§ 380n.9, 380o

**Sanitary District Enlargement Act (Chicago-19th)**
Ill. Rev. Stat. 1989, Ch. 42, §§ 380o.9, 380p

**Sanitary District Enlargement Act (Chicago-20th)**
Ill. Rev. Stat. 1989, Ch. 42, §§ 380p.9, 380q

**Sanitary District Enlargement Act (Chicago-21st)**
Ill. Rev. Stat. 1989, Ch. 42, §§ 380q.9, 380r

**Sanitary District Enlargement Act (Chicago-22nd)**
Ill. Rev. Stat. 1989, Ch. 42, §§ 380r.9, 380s

**Sanitary District Enlargement Act (Chicago-23rd)**
Ill. Rev. Stat. 1989, Ch. 42, §§ 380s.9, 380t

**Sanitary District Enlargement Act (Chicago-24th)**
Ill. Rev. Stat. 1989, Ch. 42, §§ 380t.9, 380u

**Sanitary District Enlargement Act (Chicago-25th)**
Ill. Rev. Stat. 1989, Ch. 42, §§ 380u.9, 380v

**Sanitary District Enlargement Act (Chicago-26th)**
Ill. Rev. Stat. 1989, Ch. 42, §§ 380v.9, 380w

**Sanitary District Enlargement Act (Chicago-27th)**
Ill. Rev. Stat. 1989, Ch. 42, §§ 380w.9, 380x

**Sanitary District Enlargement Act (Chicago-28th)**
Ill. Rev. Stat. 1989, Ch. 42, §§ 380x.9, 380y

**Sanitary District Enlargement Act (Chicago-29th)**
Ill. Rev. Stat. 1989, Ch. 42, §§ 380y.9, 380z

**Sanitary District Enlargement Act (Chicago-30th)**
Ill. Rev. Stat. 1989, Ch. 42, §§ 380z.9, 380z1

**Sanitary District Enlargement Act (Chicago-31st)**
Ill. Rev. Stat. 1989, Ch. 42, §§ 380z1.9, 380z2

**Sanitary District Enlargement Act (Chicago-32nd)**
Ill. Rev. Stat. 1989, Ch. 42, §§ 380z2.9, 380z3

**Sanitary District Enlargement Act (Chicago-33rd)**
Ill. Rev. Stat. 1989, Ch. 42, §§ 380z3.9, 380z4

**Sanitary District Enlargement Act (Chicago-34th)**
Ill. Rev. Stat. 1989, Ch. 42, §§ 380z4.9, 380z5

**Sanitary District Enlargement Act (Chicago-35th)**
Ill. Rev. Stat. 1989, Ch. 42, §§ 380z5.9, 380z6

**Sanitary District Enlargement Act (Chicago-36th)**
Ill. Rev. Stat. 1989, Ch. 42, §§ 380z6.9, 380z7

**Sanitary District Enlargement Act (Chicago-37th)**
Ill. Rev. Stat. 1989, Ch. 42, §§ 380z7.9, 380z8

**Sanitary District Enlargement Act (Chicago-38th)**
Ill. Rev. Stat. 1989, Ch. 42, §§ 380z8.9, 380z9

**Sanitary District Enlargement Act (Chicago-39th)**
Ill. Rev. Stat. 1989, Ch. 42, §§ 380z9.9, 380z10

**Sanitary District Enlargement Act (Chicago-40th)**
Ill. Rev. Stat. 1989, Ch. 42, §§ 380z10.9, 380z11

**Sanitary District Enlargement Act (Chicago-41st)**
Ill. Rev. Stat. 1989, Ch. 42, §§ 380z11.9, 380z12

**Sanitary District Enlargement Act (Chicago-42nd)**
Ill. Rev. Stat. 1989, Ch. 42, §§ 380z12.9, 380z13

**Sanitary District Enlargement Act (Chicago-43rd)**
Ill. Rev. Stat. 1989, Ch. 42, §§ 380z13.9, 380z14

**Sanitary District Enlargement Act (Chicago-44th)**
Ill. Rev. Stat. 1989, Ch. 42, §§ 380z14.9, 380z15

**Sanitary District Enlargement Act (Chicago-45th)**
Ill. Rev. Stat. 1989, Ch. 42, §§ 380z16.9, 380z17

**Sanitary District Enlargement Act (Chicago-46th)**
Ill. Rev. Stat. 1989, Ch. 42, §§ 380z17.9, 380z18

**Sanitary District Enlargement Act (Chicago-47th)**
Ill. Rev. Stat. 1989, Ch. 42, §§ 380z18.9, 380z19

**Sanitary District Enlargement Act (Chicago-48th)**
Ill. Rev. Stat. 1989, Ch. 42, §§ 380z19.9, 380z20

**Sanitary District Enlargement Act (Chicago-49th)**
Ill. Rev. Stat. 1989, Ch. 42, §§ 380z20.9, 380z21

**Sanitary District Enlargement Act (Chicago-50th)**
Ill. Rev. Stat. 1989, Ch. 42, §§ 380z21.9, 380z22

**Sanitary District Enlargement Act (Chicago-51st)**
Ill. Rev. Stat. 1989, Ch. 42, §§ 380z22.9, 380z23

**Sanitary District Enlargement Act (Chicago-52nd)**
Ill. Rev. Stat. 1989, Ch. 42, §§ 380z23.9, 380z24

**Sanitary District Enlargement Act (Chicago-53rd)**
Ill. Rev. Stat. 1989, Ch. 42, §§ 380z24.9, 380z25

**Sanitary District Enlargement Act (Chicago-54th)**
Ill. Rev. Stat. 1989, Ch. 42, §§ 380z25.9, 380z26

**Sanitary District Enlargement Act (Chicago-55th)**
Ill. Rev. Stat. 1989, Ch. 42, §§ 380z26.9, 380z27

**Sanitary District Enlargement Act (Chicago-56th)**
Ill. Rev. Stat. 1989, Ch. 42, §§ 380z27.9, 380z28

**Sanitary District Enlargement Act (Chicago-57th)**
Ill. Rev. Stat. 1989, Ch. 42, §§ 380z28.9, 380z29

**Sanitary District Enlargement Act (Chicago-58th)**
Ill. Rev. Stat. 1989, Ch. 42, §§ 380z29.9, 380z30

**Sanitary District Enlargement Act (Chicago-59th)**
Ill. Rev. Stat. 1989, Ch. 42, §§ 380z30.9, 380z31

**Sanitary District Enlargement Act (Chicago-60th)**
Ill. Rev. Stat. 1989, Ch. 42, §§ 380z31.9, 380z32

**Sanitary District Enlargement Act (Chicago-61st)**
Ill. Rev. Stat. 1989, Ch. 42, §§ 380z32.9, 380z33

**Sanitary District Enlargement Act (Chicago-62nd)**
Ill. Rev. Stat. 1989, Ch. 42, §§ 380z34.9, 380z35

**Sanitary District Enlargement Act (Chicago-63rd)**
Ill. Rev. Stat. 1989, Ch. 42, §§ 380z35.9, 380z36

**Sanitary District Enlargement Act (Chicago-64th)**
Ill. Rev. Stat. 1989, Ch. 42, §§ 380z36.9, 380z37

**Sanitary District Enlargement Act (Chicago-65th)**
Ill. Rev. Stat. 1989, Ch. 42, §§ 380z37.9, 380z38

**Sanitary District Enlargement Act (Chicago-66th)**
Ill. Rev. Stat. 1989, Ch. 42, §§ 380z38.9, 380z39

**Sanitary District Enlargement Act (Chicago-67th)**
Ill. Rev. Stat. 1989, Ch. 42, §§ 380z39.9, 380z40

**Sanitary District Enlargement Act (Chicago-68th)**
Ill. Rev. Stat. 1989, Ch. 42, §§ 380z40.9, 380z41

**Sanitary District Enlargement Act (Chicago-69th)**
Ill. Rev. Stat. 1989, Ch. 42, § 380z41.9 et seq.

**Sanitary District Enlargement Act (Chicago-70th)**
Ill. Rev. Stat. 1989, Ch. 42, §§ 380z44.9, 380z45

**Sanitary District Enlargement Act (Chicago-71st)**
Ill. Rev. Stat. 1989, Ch. 42, § 380z45.9, et seq.

**Sanitary District Enlargement Act (Chicago-72nd)**
Ill. Rev. Stat. 1989, Ch. 42, §§ 380z47.9, 380z48

**Sanitary District Enlargement Act (Chicago-73rd)**
Ill. Rev. Stat. 1989, Ch. 42, §§ 380z48.9, 380z49

**Sanitary District Enlargement Act (Chicago-74th)**
Ill. Rev. Stat. 1989, Ch. 42, § 380z49.9 et seq.

**Sanitary District Enlargement Act (Chicago-75th)**
Ill. Rev. Stat. 1989, Ch. 42, §§ 380z52.9, 380z53

**Sanitary District Enlargement Act (Chicago-76th)**
Ill. Rev. Stat. 1989, Ch. 42, §§ 380z53.9, 380z54

**Sanitary District Enlargement Act (Chicago-77th)**
Ill. Rev. Stat. 1989, Ch. 42, §§ 380z54.9, 380z55

**Sanitary District Enlargement Act (Chicago-78th)**
Ill. Rev. Stat. 1989, Ch. 42, §§ 380a55.9, 380z56

**Sanitary District Enlargement Act (Chicago-79th)**
Ill. Rev. Stat. 1989, Ch. 42, §§ 380z56.9 et seq.

**Sanitary District Enlargement Act (Chicago-80th)**
Ill. Rev. Stat. 1989, Ch. 42, §§ 380z58.9, 380z59

**Sanitary District Enlargement Act (Chicago-81st)**
Ill. Rev. Stat. 1989, Ch. 42, §§ 380z59.9, 380z60

**Sanitary District Enlargement Act (Chicago-82nd)**
Ill. Rev. Stat. 1989, Ch. 42, §§ 380z60.9, 380z61

**Sanitary District Enlargement Act (Chicago-84th)**
Ill. Rev. Stat. 1989, Ch. 42, §§ 380z62.9 et seq.

**Sanitary District Extension (1st) Act (North Shore)**
Ill. Rev. Stat. 1989, Ch. 42, §§ 297h, 298

**Sanitary District Extension (2nd) Act (North Shore)**
Ill. Rev. Stat. 1989, Ch. 42, §§ 298a, 298a1

**Sanitary District Navigable Streams Act (Chicago)**
Ill. Rev. Stat. 1989, Ch. 42, § 350m et seq.

**Sanitary District Obstruction Removal Act (Chicago)**
Ill. Rev. Stat. 1989, Ch. 42, § 372.9 et seq.

**Sanitary District Police Powers Act (Chicago)**
Ill. Rev. Stat. 1989, Ch. 42, §§ 359.9, 360

**Sanitary District, Purchasing Act (Chicago)**
Ill. Comp. Stat. 1992, Ch. 70, § 2605/11.1 et seq.

**Sanitary District Refunding Bond Act**
Ill. Rev. Stat. 1989, Ch. 42, § 298.01 et seq.

**Sanitary District Revenue Bond Act**
Ill. Rev. Stat. 1991, Ch. 42, § 319.1 et seq.

**Sanitary District Sewer Contract Act (Chicago)**
Ill. Rev. Stat. 1989, Ch. 42, §§ 380z99, 381

**Sanitary District Water Power Act (Chicago)**
Ill. Rev. Stat. 1989, Ch. 42, § 369.9 et seq.

**Sanitary Districts (1917 Act) Bond Act**
Ill. Rev. Stat. 1989, Ch. 42, § 319gl et seq.

**Sanitary Districts Act**
Cal. Health and Safety Code § 6400 et seq.
Ill. Rev. Stat. 1991, Ch. 42, § 246h et seq.
Ky. Rev. Stat. 1971, 220.010 et seq.
Md. Ann. Code 1974, Art. HE, § 9-601 et seq.
N.C. Gen. Stat. 1943, § 130A-47 et seq.
Ohio Rev. Code 1953, 6115.01 et seq.
Ore. Rev. Stat., 450.005 et seq.
Va. Code 1950, §§ 21-141 et seq., 21-224 et seq.

*Continued*

Wash. Rev. Code 1951, 55.04.010 et seq.

**Sanitary Districts and Sewage Disposal Act**
Ill. Rev. Stat. 1991, Ch. 42, § 411.99 et seq.

**Sanitary Drainage District Act**
Mo. Rev. Stat., 248.010 et seq.

**Sanitary Equipment Act (Hotels)**
Ill. Rev. Stat. 1991, Ch. 56 1/2, § 66.90 et seq.

**Sanitary Facilities Bond Act**
Md. Ann. Code 1974, Art. EN, § 9-801 et seq.

**Sanitary Food Act**
Neb. Rev. Stat. 1943, 81-216.01 et seq.

**Sanitary Food Preparation Act**
Ill. Rev. Stat. 1991, Ch. 56 1/2, § 66.90 et seq.

**Sanitary Food Transportation Act of 1990**
Nov. 3, 1990, P.L. 101-500, 49 U.S. Code Appx. §§ 2801 nt., 2801 to 2812
Oct. 31, 1994, P.L. 103-429, 49 U.S. Code Appx. §§ 2501 nt., 2801 nt.

**Sanitary Inspection Act**
Ill. Rev. Stat. 1991, Ch. 56 1/2, § 66.90 et seq.

**Sanitary Land Fill Areas Act**
Tenn. Code Ann., 68-213-101 et seq.

**Sanitary Landfill Facility Closure and Contingency Fund Act**
N.J. Stat. Ann., 13:1E-100 et seq.

**Sanitary Officers' Pension Act (Second Class Cities)**
Ind. Code Ann., 18-6-25-1 et seq.

**Sanitary Projects Act**
N.M. Stat. Ann., 3-29-1 et seq.

**Sanitary Requirements for Cold Storage Warehouses Act**
Ind. Code Ann., 16-1-21-1 et seq.

**Sanitary Requirements for Locker Plants Act**
Ind. Code Ann., 16-1-22-1 et seq.

**Sanitary Schoolhouse Act**
Ind. Code Ann., 16-1-24-1 et seq.

**Sanitary Sewer Act (Westchester County)**
N.Y. Laws 1926, Ch. 603
N.Y. Laws 1948, Ch. 852, § 161 et seq.

**Sanitary Sewer and Public Works Act (Onondaga County)**
N.Y. Laws 1933, Ch. 568

**Sanitary Sewer District Act (Hillsborough County)**
Fla. Special Laws 1927, Ch. 12868

**Sanitary Sewer Districts Act (Regional)**
Minn. Stat. Ann., 115.61 et seq.

**Sanitary Sewer Financing Act**
Fla. Stat. 1971, 184.01 et seq.

**Sanitary Sewer Financing Act (Counties)**
Fla. Stat. Ann., 153.01 et seq.

**Sanitary Sewer Financing Act (Miami)**
Fla. Special Laws 1945, Ch. 23407

**Sanitary Standards for Butterine and Ice Cream Factories Law**
Ill. Rev. Stat. 1971, Ch. 48, § 53 et seq.

**Sanitary Water Board Act**
Ill. Rev. Stat. 1991, Ch. 111 1/2, § 1049 et seq.
Pa. Purdon's Stat., Title 71, § 510-1

**Sanitation Act (Bakeries)**
Cal. Health and Safety Code § 28190 et seq.

**Sanitation Act (Dairy Establishment)**
N.M. Stat. Ann., 25-7B-1 et seq.

**Sanitation Act (Food)**
Ky. Rev. Stat. 1971, 217.280 et seq.

**Sanitation Act (Nassau County)**
N.Y. Laws 1936, Ch. 162

**Sanitation Agency Act (Tahoe-Truckee)**
Cal. Water Code, Appendix, § 114-1 et seq.

**Sanitation and Flood Control District Act (Vallejo)**
Cal. Statutes 1952, 1st Ex. Sess., Ch. 17, p. 351
Cal. Water Code, Appendix, § 67-1 et seq.

**Sanitation and Health Protection Act**
Tex. Health and Safety Code, § 341.001 et seq.

**Sanitation and Housing Act**
Pa. Purdon's Stat., Title 53, § 14891 et seq.

**Sanitation and Sewer Revenue Bond Act**
Cal. Statutes 1941, p. 2582

**Sanitation and Water Act**
Colo. Rev. Stat., 32-4-101 et seq.

**Sanitation and Water District Act**
N.M. Stat. Ann., 73-21-1 et seq.

**Sanitation Authority Act**
Cal. Water Code § 77000 et seq.

**Sanitation Commission Tri-State Compact**
Conn. Gen. Stat. Ann., § 22a-293 et seq.

**Sanitation District Act (County)**
Cal. Health and Safety Code § 4700 et seq.

**Sanitation of All Food-Producing and Sales Establishments Act**
Tenn. Code Ann., 53-8-101 et seq.

**Sanitation Registration Act**
Okla. Stat. Ann., Title 59, §§ 1150.1 to 1150.13

**Sanitation, Sewer and Water Revenue Bond Law**
Cal. Government Code, § 54300 et seq.

**Sanity Commission Act**
Mich. Comp. Laws 1948, 767.27

**Santa Barbara County Flood Control and Water Conservation District Act**
Cal. Water Code, Appendix, § 74-1 et seq.

**Santa Barbara County Special Health Care Authority Act**
Cal. Health and Safety Code § 1175 et seq.

**Santa Barbara County Water Agency Act**
Cal. Water Code, Appendix, § 51-1 et seq.

**Santa Barbara Metropolitan Transit District Act**
Cal. Public Utilities Code, § 95000 et seq.

**Santa Barbara Regional Health Authority Act**
Cal. Health and Safety Code § 1175 et seq.

**Santa Clara-Alameda-San Benito Water Authority Act**
Cal. Statutes 1955, Ch. 1289, p. 2349

**Santa Clara County Commuter Relief Act**
Cal. Public Utilities Code § 140000 et seq.

**Santa Clara County Flood Control and Water Conservation Act**
Cal. Statutes 1951, Ch. 1405, p. 3336

**Santa Clara County Open-Space Authority Act**
Cal. Public Resources Code § 35100 et seq.

**Santa Clara County Transit District Act**
Cal. Public Utilities Code § 100000 et seq.

**Santa Clara Valley Water District Act**
Cal. Water Code, Appendix, § 60-1 et seq.

**Santa Cruz County Flood Control and Water Conservation District Act**
Cal. Water Code, Appendix, § 77-1 et seq.

**Santa Cruz Metropolitan Transit District Act**
Cal. Public Utilities Code, § 98000 et seq.

**Santa Monica Bay Revitalization Act**
Cal. Fish and Game Code 1957, § 6580 et seq.

**Santa Monica Mountain Conservancy Act**
Cal. Public Resources Code, § 33000 et seq.

**Santa Monica Mountains Comprehensive Planning Act**
Cal. Government Code, § 67450 et seq.

**Santa Rosa Bay Bridge Authority Law**
Fla. Stat. Ann., 348.965 et seq.

**Sapelo Island Heritage Authority Act**
Ga. Code Ann., 12-3-440 et seq.

**SARA**
See Superfund Amendments and Reauthorization Act of 1986

**Sarasota Airport Authority Act**
Fla. Laws 1977, Ch. 77-651

**Sarasota Airport Traffic Control Act**
Fla. Laws 1967, Ch. 67-2053

**Sarasota County Antinuisance Act**
Fla. Special Laws 1953, Ch. 29527

**Sarasota County Lot Clearing Act**
Fla. Laws 1963, Ch. 63-1922

**Sarasota County Plumbing Control Act**
Fla. Special Laws 1953, Ch. 29526

**Sarasota County Public Hospital Board Act**
Fla. Laws 1949, Ex. Sess., Ch. 26468

**Sarasota County Utility Bond Act**
Fla. Special Laws 1967, Ch. 67-2048
Fla. Special Laws 1969, Ch. 69-1595

**Sarasota County Water and Navigation Control Authority Act**
Fla. Special Laws 1957, Ch. 57-1853

**Sarasota Erosion Control Act**
Fla. Special Laws 1969, Ch. 69-1571, § 3

**Sarasota Local Improvement Act**
Fla. Special Laws 1967, Ch. 67-2031, § 5

**Sarasota-Manatee Airport Authority Act**
Fla. Laws 1991, Ch. 358
Fla. Special Laws 1955, Ch. 31263
Fla. Special Laws 1977, Ch. 651

**Sarasota-Manatee Airport Traffic Control Act**
Fla. Special Laws 1967, Ch. 67-2053

**Sarasota Sewer Revenue Bond Act**
Fla. Special Laws 1945, Ch. 23528

**Sarasota Urban Renewal Act**
Fla. Laws 1963, Ch. 63-1888

**Sarasota Utility Bond Act**
Fla. Laws 1967, Ch. 67-2048

**Saratoga County Water Authority Act**
N.Y. Public Authorities Law (Consol. Laws Ch. 43A) § 1199aaa et seq.

**Saratoga Springs Authority Act**
N.Y. Public Authorities Law (Consol. Laws Ch. 43A) § 1600 et seq.

**Saratoga Springs City Center Authority Act**
N.Y. Public Authorities Law (Consol. Laws Ch. 43A), § 2490a et seq.

**Sardine Canning Inspection Act**
Me. Rev. Stat. Ann. 1964, Title 32, § 4151 et seq.

**Sardine Law**
Me. Rev. Stat. Ann. 1964, Title 32, § 4151 et seq.

**Sardine Tax Act**
Me. Rev. Stat. Ann. 1964, Title 36, § 4691 et seq.

**Sasser Amendment.**
Nov. 5, 1979, P.L. 96-103, 93 Stat. 787

**Satellite Home Viewer Act of 1988**
Nov. 16, 1988, P.L. 100-667, 17 U.S. Code § 101 nt.

**Satellite Home Viewer Act of 1994**
Oct. 18, 1994, P.L. 103-369, 17 U.S. Code § 101 nt.
Nov. 13, 1997, P.L. 105-80, 17 U.S. Code § 119

**Satisfaction and Accord Act**
Cal. Civil Code § 1521 et seq.

**Satisfaction of Judgments Act**
Wash. Rev. Code Ann., 4.56.100

**Saturday Half-Holiday Act**
D.C. Code 1968, § 28-2701

**Saturday Half-Holiday Acts (District of Columbia Code)**
March 3, 1901, Ch. 854, 31 Stat. 1405
June 30, 1902, Ch. 1329, 32 Stat. 543

**Saturday School Act**
Cal. Education Code 1976, § 42239.5

**Saulsbury Resolution (District of Columbia Rents)**
May 31, 1918, Ch. 90, 40 Stat. 593

**Sausage Act**
Mich. Comp. Laws Ann., 289.581 et seq.

**Sausage Act (Pure Food)**
Pa. Purdon's Stat., Title 31, § 1 et seq.

**Savannah-Chatham Authority for the Homeless Act**
Ga. Laws 1991, p. 4701

**Savannah-Chatham County Anti-Drug Commission Act**
Ga. Laws 1990, p. 4059

**Savannah-Chatham County Freedom of Choice School Assignment Law**
Ga. Laws 1971, Ex. Sess., p. 2198

**Savannah-Chatham Youth Futures Authority Act**
Ga. Laws 1988, p. 3743

**Savannah Civil Service Act**
Ga. Laws 1947, p. 938

**Savannah Development and Renewal Authority Act**
Ga. Laws 1992, p. 6764

**Savannah District Authority Act**
Ga. Laws 1951, p. 190

**Savannah Port Authority Act**
Ga. Laws 1925, p. 1451

**Savannah Transit Authority Act**
Ga. Laws 1960, p. 2620

**Save Harmless Act (Teachers)**
Conn. Gen. Stat. Ann., § 10-235
Mass. Gen. Laws 1932, Ch. 41, § 100C
N.J. Stat. Ann., 18A:16-6
N.Y. Education Law 1947 (Consol. Laws Ch. 16) § 2560
Wyo. Stat. Ann., § 21-3-128

**Save the Presidential Primary Act**
Cal. Elections Code 1961, §§ 2151, 13203, 13206, 13300 to 13302

**Save Your Vision Week Act**
Dec. 30, 1963, P.L. 88-242, 77 Stat. 629, 36 U.S. Code § 169a

**Saving Act**
Alaska Stat. 1962, § 01.10.100

**Saving Act (Procedure)**
Ark. Code Ann. 1987, 16-56-126
Ind. Code Ann., 34-1-2-8
Kan. Stat. Ann., 60-518
Wyo. Stat. Ann., § 1-3-118

**Saving Act (Prosecutions)**
Cal. Government Code § 9608
Ida. Code 1947, 67-513
Ill. Rev. Stat. 1991, Ch. 1, § 1103

**Saving Act (Statute of Limitations)**
Del. Code of 1974, Title 10, § 8116 et seq.
Ga. Code Ann., 9-2-61
Ky. Rev. Stat. 1971, 413.270
Mass. Gen. Laws Ann., 260:32
Mich. Comp. Laws Ann., 600.5856
Mo. Rev. Stat., 516.230
N.C. Gen. Stat. 1943, § 1-25
Ohio Rev. Code 1953, 2305.19
Ore. Rev. Stat., 12.220
Tenn. Code Ann., 28-1-105

*Continued*

Va. Code 1950, § 8.01-229
W. Va. Code 1966, § 55-2-18

**Saving Act (Statute Repeal)**
Colo. Rev. Stat. 1963, 135-1-7
Md. Ann. Code 1957, Art. 1, § 3
Minn. Stat. Ann., 645.35
Neb. Rev. Stat. 1943, 49-301
Ohio Rev. Code 1953, 1.58

**Saving Act (Venue)**
Tex. Rev. Civ. Stat., Art. 5539a

**Saving and Loan Holding Company Act**
Cal. Financial Code § 11500 et seq.

**Saving Clause Act**
Neb. Rev. Stat. 1943, 49-301

**Saving Quality Jobs Act**
Okla. Stat. Ann., Title 63, § 3701 et seq.

**Savings Account Act (First-Time Home Buyer)**
Mont. Code Ann., 15-63-101 et seq.

**Savings Account Act (Medical)**
Colo. Rev. Stat., 39-22-504.5 to 39-22-504.7
Ga. Code Ann., 33-20B-1 et seq.
Ida. Code 1947, 41-5301 et seq.
Ill. Comp. Stat. 1992, Ch. 820, § 152/1
Mich. Comp. Laws Ann., 550.981 et seq.
Miss. Code Ann. 1972, § 71-91-1 et seq.
Mont. Laws 1995, Ch. 295
N.M. Stat. Ann., 59A-23D-1 et seq.

**Savings Act (Baccalaureate)**
Ill. Comp. Stat. 1992, Ch. 110, § 920/1 et seq.

**Savings Act (Family Education)**
Mont. Code Ann., 15-62-101 et seq.

**Savings Act (Public Costs)**
Tenn. Code Ann., 68-11-1201 et seq.

**Savings Act (Retirement)**
Ill. Rev. Stat. 1991, Ch. 127, § 3751 et seq.

**Savings and Credit Unions Act**
P.R. Law Ann. 1954, Title 7, § 1101 et seq.

**Savings and Loan Acquisition Act (Regional Reciprocal)**
N.C. Gen. Stat. 1943, § 54B-48.1 et seq.

**Savings and Loan Act**
Ark. Code Ann. 1987, 23-37-801 et seq.
Ill. Rev. Stat. 1991, Ch. 17, § 3301-1 et seq.
Kan. Stat. Ann., 17-5101 et seq.
Md. Ann. Code 1974, Art. FI, § 9-102 et seq.
Mich. Comp. Laws 1948, 489.1 et seq.
Tex. Finance Code, § 61.001 et seq.

**Savings and Loan as Agent for Treasury Act**
Ill. Rev. Stat. 1991, Ch. 17, § 3610 et seq.

**Savings and Loan Association Act**
Ala. Code 1975, § 5-16-1 et seq.
Alaska Stat. 1962, § 06.30.005 et seq.
Ariz. Rev. Stat. Ann., § 6-401 et seq.
Ark. Code Ann. 1987, 23-37-101 et seq.
Cal. Financial Code, § 5000 et seq.
Colo. Rev. Stat., 11-40-101 et seq.
Ida. Code 1947, 26-1801 et seq.
Ill. Rev. Stat. 1991, Ch. 17, § 3301 et seq.
Iowa Code Ann., 534.1 et seq.
Kan. Stat. Ann., 17-5101 et seq.
Ky. Rev. Stat. 1971, 289.005 et seq.
La. Rev. Stat. Ann., 6:701 et seq.
Md. Ann. Code 1974, Art. FI, § 9.101 et seq.
Mich. Comp. Laws Ann., 491.102 et seq.
Miss. Code Ann. 1972, § 81-11-1 et seq.
Mo. Rev. Stat., 369.010 et seq.
N.C. Gen. Stat. 1943, § 54B-1 et seq.
N.J. Stat. Ann., 17:12B-46.1 et seq.
N.M. Stat. Ann., 58-10-1 et seq.
Okla. Stat. Ann., Title 18, § 381.1 et seq.
Ore. Rev. Stat., 722.002 et seq.
S.C. Code Ann. 1976, Superseded Vols., § 34-25-10 et seq.
S.D. Codified Laws 1967, 52-1-1 et seq.
Tenn. Code Ann., 45-3-101 et seq.
Tex. Rev. Civ. Stat., Art. 852a
Utah Code Ann. 1953, 7-7-1 et seq.
Va. Code 1950, § 6.1-195.1 et seq.
Vt. Stat. Ann., Title 8, § 1831 et seq.
Wash. Rev. Code Ann., 33.04.002 et seq.
Wis. Stat. Ann., 215.01 et seq.

**Savings and Loan Association Act (Guaranty Capital)**
Wyo. Stat. 1957, § 13-279.1

**Savings and Loan Association Act of 1964**
Mich. Comp. Laws Ann., 489.501 et seq.

**Savings and Loan Association and Interstate Banking Act**
Ariz. Rev. Stat. Ann., § 6-321 et seq.

**Savings and Loan Association Public Deposit Protection Act**
Colo. Rev. Stat., 11-47-101 et seq.

**Savings and Loan Emergency Closing Act**
N.J. Stat. Ann., 17:12B-46.1 et seq.

**Savings and Loan Guaranty Act**
Colo. Rev. Stat. 1973, 11-47.5-101 et seq.

**Savings and Loan Holding Company Amendments of 1967**
Feb. 14, 1968, P.L. 90-255, 82 Stat. 5, 12 U.S. Code § 1730a
Dec. 31, 1970, P.L. 91-609, 84 Stat. 1816, 12 U.S. Code § 1730a

**Savings and Loan Insurance Corporation Act**
La. Rev. Stat. Ann., 6:1121 et seq.

**Savings and Loan Interstate Branch Act**
N.C. Gen. Stat. 1943, § 54B-265 et seq.

**Savings and Loan Share and Account Act**
Ill. Rev. Stat. 1991, Ch. 17, § 3600 et seq.

**Savings and Loan Supplemental Fund Act**
Tex. Finance Code, § 273.001 et seq.
Tex. Rev. Civ. Stat., Art. 852b

**Savings and Loan Trust Powers Act**
Va. Code 1950, § 6.1-195.77 et seq.

**Savings are Vital to Everyone's Retirement Act of 1997**
Nov. 19, 1997, P.L. 105-92, 29 U.S. Code § 1001 nt.

**Savings Association Act**
Cal. Financial Code § 5000 et seq.
Fla. Stat. Ann., 665.011 et seq.
Minn. Stat. Ann., 51A.01 et seq.
Miss. Code Ann. 1972, § 81-12-1 et seq.
Ore. Rev. Stat., 722.002 et seq.
Pa. Purdon's Stat., Title 7, § 6020-1 et seq.
S.C. Code Ann. 1976, § 34-28-10 et seq.

**Savings Association Law**
Miss. Code Ann. 1972, § 81-12-1 et seq.

**Savings Associations Banking Act**
Ill. Rev. Stat. 1991, Ch. 17, § 3401 et seq.

**Savings Bank Acquisition Act**
Del. Code of 1974, Title 5, § 831 et seq.

**Savings Bank Act**
Fla. Stat. Ann., 667.001 et seq.
Ida. Code 1947, 26-1801 et seq.
Ill. Rev. Stat. 1991, Ch. 17, § 7301-1 et seq.
Ind. Code Ann., 28-6-1-1 et seq.
La. Rev. Stat. Ann., 6:1131 et seq.
Mich. Comp. Laws Ann., 487.3101 et seq.
Miss. Code Ann. 1972, § 81-14-1 et seq.
N.C. Gen. Stat. 1943, § 54C-1 et seq.
N.H. Rev. Stat. 1955, 386:1 et seq.
N.J. Stat. Ann., 17:9A-7 et seq.
P.R. Laws Ann. 1954, Title 7, § 1001 et seq.
Tex. Finance Code, § 91.001 et seq.
Va. Code 1950, § 6.1-194.109 et seq.

**Savings Bank Interstate Branch Act**
N.C. Gen. Stat. 1943, § 54C-199 et seq.

**Savings Bank Life Insurance Law**
N.Y. Insurance Law (Consol. Laws, Ch. 28) § 2201 et seq.

**Savings Bank Life Insurance Law (Officers and Employees)**
N.Y. Insurance Law 1984 (Consol. Laws Ch. 28) § 2201 et seq.

**Savings Bond Act**
Feb. 4, 1935, Ch. 5, 49 Stat. 20, 6 U.S. Code § 15; 31 U.S. Code §§ 752 to 754, 757b, 757c
Ky. Rev. Stat. 1971, 293.010 et seq.

*Continued*

**Savings Bond Act (College)**
Ark. Code Ann. 1987, 6-62-701 et seq.
Wash. Laws 1988, Ch. 125
Wash. Rev. Code Ann., 28B.106.005 et seq.

**Savings, Building and Loan Act**
Minn. Stat. 1967, 51.01 et seq.

**Savings Certificate Act**
N.M. Stat. Ann. 1953, 48-16-1 et seq.

**Savings in Construction Act of 1996**
Oct. 11, 1996, P.L. 104-289, 15 U.S. Code § 205a nt.

**Savings Institution Act (Regional Reciprocal)**
Tenn. Code Ann., 45-3-1401 et seq.

**Savings Institution Tax Act**
N.J. Stat. Ann., 54:10D-1 et seq.

**Savings Institutions Act**
Va. Code 1959, § 6.1-194.1 et seq.

**Sawed Off Shot Gun Act**
Va. Code 1950, § 18.2-299

**Sawtooth National Recreation Area Act**
Aug. 22, 1972, P.L. 92-400, 86 Stat. 612, 16 U.S. Code §§ 460aa to 460aa-14

**Sawyer Act (Annexation)**
Mo. Rev. Stat., 71.015

**Scabies Control Act**
Iowa Code Ann., 166A.1 et seq.

**Scabies Eradication Act (Livestock)**
Tex. Agriculture Code, § 164.001 et seq.

**Scaffold Act**
Cal. Labor Code § 7150 et seq.
Del. Code of 1974, Title 16, § 7701 et seq.
Ill. Rev. Stat. 1991, Ch. 48, § 55.90 et seq.
Mo. Rev. Stat., 292.090
Neb. Rev. Stat. 1943, 48-425
N.Y. Labor Law (Consol. Laws Ch. 31) § 240
Okla. Stat. 1981, Title 40, § 174 et seq.
Ore. Rev. Stat. 1953, 654.310
P.R. Laws Ann. 1954, Title 29, § 346 et seq.

**Scale Mechanics Act**
N.C. Gen. Stat. 1943, § 81A-70 et seq.

**Scalping Act (Railroad Tickets)**
Ore. Rev. Stat., 760.425

**Scavenger Act (Land Office)**
Mich. Comp. Laws 1948, 211.351 et seq.

**Scavenger Sales Act**
S.D. Laws 1901, Ch. 51

**Scavenger Tax Law**
Ill. Rev. Stat. 1991, Ch. 120, § 716a
Iowa Code Ann., 446.18
Neb. Rev. Stat. 1943, 77-1801 et seq.
S.D. Codified Laws 1967, 10-26-1 et seq.

**Scenic and Recreational Highway Act**
Wash. Rev. Code Ann., 47.39.010 et seq.

**Scenic and Wild River Act (Lower St. Croix)**
Minn. Stat. Ann., 103F.301 et seq.

**Scenic and Wild Rivers Act**
Ill. Rev. Stat. 1991, Ch. 105, § 491.90 et seq.
Minn. Stat. Ann., 103F.301 et seq.
N.J. Stat. Ann., 13:8-45 et seq.

**Scenic Areas Act**
Cal. Streets and Highways Code § 895 et seq.

**Scenic Highway Act**
Cal. Streets and Highways Code § 260 et seq.
Pa. Cons. Stat., Title 74, § 8301

**Scenic Highway Authority Act**
Ga. Laws 1947, p. 1480

**Scenic Highway System Act**
Tenn. Code Ann., 54-17-101 et seq.

**Scenic Highway Zoning Act**
N.M. Stat. Ann., 67-13-1 et seq.

**Scenic Railroad Act (Cumbres and Toltec)**
N.M. Stat. Ann., 16-5-1 et seq.

**Scenic Railroad Compact Act (Cumbres and Toltec)**
See Cumbres and Toltec Scenic Railroad Compact Act

**Scenic River Act (Le Tort Spring Run)**
Pa. Purdon's Stat., Title 32, § 820.101 et seq.

**Scenic River Act (Schuylkill)**
Pa. Purdon's Stat., Title 32, § 820.31 et seq.

**Scenic Rivers Act**
Ga. Code Ann., 12-5-350 et seq.
La. Rev. Stat. Ann., 56:1841 et seq.
Minn. Stat. 1988, 104.31 et seq.
N.C. Gen. Stat. 1943, § 113A-30 et seq.
N.Y. Labor Law (Consol. Laws Ch. 31) § 240
Okla. Stat. Ann., Title 82, § 1451 et seq.
Ore. Rev. Stat. 1953, 654.310
Pa. Purdon's Stat., Title 32, § 820.21 et seq.
P.R. Laws Ann. 1954, Title 29, § 346 et seq.
S.C. Code Ann. 1976, § 49-29-10 et seq.
Tenn. Code Ann., 11-13-101 et seq.
Va. Code 1950, § 10.1-400 et seq.

**Scenic Rivers Act (Brandywine)**
Pa. Purdon's Stat., Title 32, § 820.121 et seq.

**Scenic Rivers Act (French Creek)**
Pa. Purdon's Stat., Title 32, § 820.51 et seq.

**Scenic Rivers Act (LeTort Spring Run)**
Pa. Purdon's Stat., Title 32, § 820.101 et seq.

**Scenic Rivers Act (Octorara Creek)**
Pa. Purdon's Stat., Title 32, § 820.81 et seq.

**Scenic Rivers Act (Pine Creek)**
Pa. Purdon's Stat., Title 32, § 820.171 et seq.

**Scenic Rivers Act (Tucquan Creek and Bear Run)**
Pa. Purdon's Stat., Title 32, § 820.111 et seq.

**Scenic Rivers Act (Tulpehocken Creek and Yellow Breeches Creek)**
Pa. Purdon's Stat., Title 32, § 820.151 et seq.

**Scenic Rivers Act (Yellow Breeches Creek)**
Pa. Purdon's Stat., Title 32, § 820.141 et seq.

**Scenic Rivers System Act**
Ark. Code Ann. 1987, 15-23-301 et seq.

**Scenic Trails Act**
Ga. Code Ann., 12-3-110 et seq.

**Scenic Vistas Act**
Wash. Rev. Code Ann., 47.42.010 et seq.

**Schackno Act (Deficiency Judgments)**
N.Y. Real Property Actions and Proceedings Law (Consol. Laws Ch. 81) § 1371

**Schackno Act (Guaranteed Mortgages)**
N.Y. Laws 1933, Ch. 745

**Schackno Act (Mortgage Moratorium)**
N.Y. Civil Practice Act §§ 1077a to 1077g

**Schackno Act (State Recovery)**
N.Y. Laws 1933, 1st Ex. Sess., Ch. 781

**Schaumburg, DuPage County, Sterling, Elgin, Orland Park, and Centre East Civic Centers Act**
Ill. Rev. Stat. 1991, Ch. 85, § 3400 et seq.

**Scheben-Bach Act (Needy Blind)**
Ky. Rev. Stat. 1971, Superseded Vols., 207.010 et seq.

**Scheduling Act (Married Woman)**
Ark. Code Ann. 1987, 9-11-509 et seq.

**Schenectady City Court Practice Act**
N.Y. Laws 1927, Ch. 393

**Schenectady Metroplex Development Authority Act**
N.Y. Public Authorities Law (Consol. Laws Ch. 43A) § 2650 et seq.

**Schenectady Municipal Housing Authority Act**
N.Y. Public Housing Law (Consol. Laws 44A) § 405 et seq.

**Schenectady Parking Authority Act**
N.Y. Public Authorities Laws (Consol. Laws Ch. 43A) § 1599a et seq.

**Schiff-Bustamante Standards-Based Instructional Materials Program**
Cal. Education Code 1976, § 60450 et seq.

**Schley County Development Authority Act**
Ga. Laws 1967, p. 2795

**Schneider-Palmer Act (Breach of Promise)**
Mich. Comp. Laws Ann., 551.301 et seq.

**Schneider-Reid Act (Public Library Employees' Pensions)**
Mich. Comp. Laws Ann., 38.706

**Schoharie, Montgomery, Otsego Solid Waste Management Authority Act**
N.Y. Public Authorities Law (Consol. Laws Ch. 43A) § 2041 et seq.

**Scholars Act**
N.M. Stat. Ann., 21-21H-1 et seq.

**Scholars Program Act (Governor's)**
Ark. Code Ann. 1987, 6-82-301, 6-82-303

**Scholars-Tutors Program Act**
N.M. Stat. Ann., 22-2A-1 et seq.

**Scholarshare Trust Act (Golden State)**
Cal. Education Code 1976, § 69980 et seq.

**Scholarship Act (Competitive)**
N.J. Stat. Ann., 18A:62-1 et seq.

**Scholarship Act (Demonstration)**
Cal. Education Code 1976, § 58000 et seq.

**Scholarship Act (Edwin E. Aldrin)**
N.J. Laws 1969, Ch. 190

**Scholarship Act (Garden State)**
N.J. Stat. Ann., 18A:71-26.1 et seq.

**Scholarship Act (Legislative Endowment)**
N.M. Stat. Ann., 21-21J-1 et seq.

**Scholarship Act (Military School)**
Ill. Rev. Stat. 1991, Ch. 144, § 21a et seq.

**Scholarship Act (Nursing Education)**
Ill. Rev. Stat. 1991, Ch. 144, § 2751 et seq.

**Scholarship Act (Out-of-State)**
Md. Ann. Code 1974, Art. ED, § 18-307

**Scholarship Act (Rural Physician)**
Utah Code Ann. 1953, 26-9b-101 et seq.

**Scholarship Act (Surviving Child of Policeman or Fireman)**
Cal. Education Code 1976, §§ 68120, 68121

**Scholarship Act for the Daughters of the Confederacy**
Tenn. Public Acts 1919, Ch. 132

**Scholarship Agreement Act (Private Medical)**
Ill. Rev. Stat. 1991, Ch. 144, § 2700 et seq.

**Scholarship Assistance Act (College)**
Va. Code 1950, § 23-38.45 et seq.

**Scholarship Assistance Fund Act (Child Care Affordability)**
Mass. Gen. Laws Ann., 28A:5A

**Scholarship Consolidation Act**
P.R. Laws Ann. 1954, Title 18, § 861 et seq.

**Scholarship or Loan Act (Omnibus)**
Miss. Code Ann. 1972, § 37-143-1 et seq.

**Scholarship Program (Teacher)**
Kan. Stat. Ann., 74-32,100 et seq.

**Scholarship Program Act (National Guard)**
Ark. Code Ann. 1987, 6-82-801 et seq.

**Scholarships Act**
Ida. Code 1947, 33-4303 et seq.
Ill. Rev. Stat. 1991, Ch. 122, § 30-15 et seq.
Ind. Code Ann., 20-12-21-1 et seq.
Wis. Stat. Ann., 39.435

**Scholastic Achievement Act**
Colo. Rev. Stat., 22-2-201 et seq.

**School Accountability Funding for Excellence Program**
Md. Ann. Code 1974, Art. ED, § 5-206

**School Accreditation Act**
Neb. Rev. Stat. 1943, 79-1247.02

**School Act**
See Uniform School Act
Ala. Code 1975, § 16-1-1 et seq.
Alaska Stat. 1962, § 14.03.010 et seq.
Ark. Code Ann. 1987, 6-10-101 et seq.
Colo. Rev. Stat., 22-2-101 et seq.
Del. Code of 1974, Title 14, § 1001 et seq.
Fla. Stat. Ann., 228.001 et seq.
Ga. Code Ann., 20-2-1 et seq.
Ill. Rev. Stat. 1991, Ch. 122, § 1-1 et seq.
Iowa Code Ann., 257.1 et seq.
Ky. Rev. Stat. 1971, 156.010 et seq.
Md. Ann. Code 1974, Art. ED, § 1-101 et seq.
Mich. Comp. Laws Ann., 380.1 et seq.
Minn. Stat. Ann., 120.01 et seq.
Miss. Code Ann. 1972, § 37-1-1 et seq.
Mo. Rev. Stat., 160.011 et seq.
Mont. Code Ann., 20-1-101 et seq.
N.C. Gen. Stat. 1943, § 115C-1 et seq.
N.H. Rev. Stat. 1955, 21-N:2
N.J. Stat. Ann., 18A:1-1 et seq.
N.M. Stat. Ann., 22-1-1 et seq.
Okla. Stat. Ann., Title 70, § 1-101 et seq.
Ore. Rev. Stat., 326.011 et seq.
Pa. Purdon's Stat., Title 24, § 1-101 et seq.
P.R. Laws Ann. 1954, Title 18, § 1 et seq.
S.C. Code Ann. 1976, § 59-1-10 et seq.
S.D. Codified Laws 1967, 13-1-1 et seq.
Tenn. Code Ann., 49-1-101 et seq.
Tex. Education Code, §§ 31.01 et seq, 65.01 et seq.
Vt. Stat. Ann., Title 16
Wash. Rev. Code Ann., 28A.01.010 et seq.
Wis. Stat. Ann., 115.001 et seq.
W. Va. Code 1966, § 18-1-1 et seq.
Wyo. Stat. Ann., § 21-1-101 et seq.

**School Act (Cleveland County)**
N.C. Public-Local Laws 1935, Ch. 559

**School Act (Community)**
Fla. Stat. Ann., 228.071

**School Act (Compulsory Attendance)**
N.C. Gen. Stat. 1943, § 115C-378 et seq.

**School Act (County)**
Ore. Rev. Stat., 333.005 et seq.

**School Act (Developmental Research)**
Okla. Stat. Ann., Title 70, §§ 1210.571 to 1210.579

**School Act (Drug-free)**
Del. Code of 1974, Title 14, § 3801 et seq.

**School Act (Elmira)**
N.Y. Laws 1895, Ch. 370

**School Act (Indianapolis)**
Ind. Code Ann., 20-3-11-1 et seq.

**School Act (Industrial)**
Alaska Comp. Laws Ann. 1949, §§ 37-8-4, 37-8-5

**School Act (Proprietary)**
Colo. Rev. Stat., 12-59-101 et seq.
S.C. Code of 1976, § 40-60-70 et seq.

**School Act (Saturday)**
Cal. Education Code 1976, § 42239.5

**School Act (State Aid)**
S.C. Code Ann. 1976, § 59-21-10 et seq.

**School Act (Vocational)**
See Vocational School Act

**School Addition Loan Act (Charlemont)**
Mass. Acts 1948, Ch. 212

**School Addition Loan Act (Foxborough)**
Mass. Acts 1949, Ch. 16

**School Administration Act (Gilmer-Aikin)**
Tex. Education Code, § 11.01 et seq.

**School Age Act (Compulsory)**
Ohio Rev. Code 1953, 3321.01

**School-Age Child Care Program**
N.Y. Education Law 1947 (Consol. Laws Ch. 16) § 414, Subd. 1
N.Y. Social Services Law (Consol. Laws Ch. 55) § 410c, Subd. 5

**School Aid Act**
Mich. Comp. Laws Ann., 388.1601 et seq.,
Minn. Stat. Ann., 124.36 et seq.
N.J. Stat. Ann., 18A:7A-3, 18A:7A-7, 18A:7A-11, 18A:7A-17, 18A:7A-18, 18A:7A-28
Okla. Stat. Ann., Title 70, § 18-101 et seq.
Vt. Stat. Ann., Title 16, §§ 3469 nt., 3441 et seq.
Vt. Stat. Ann., Title 16, x

**School Aid Act for Asbestos**
N.J. 18A:58-68

**School Aid Acts**
Mich. Comp. Laws 1970, 388.671 et seq.

**School and College Registration Act**
Miss. Code Ann. 1972, § 75-60-1 et seq.

**School and Community Resource Grant Program**
Fla. Stat. Ann., 232.258

**School and Day Care Conference and Activities Leave Act**
La. Rev. Stat. Ann., 23:1015 et seq.

**School and Institutional Trust Lands Act**
Utah Code Ann. 1953, 53C-1-101 et seq.

**School and Municipal Tax Levy Validation Act**
Ill. Rev. Stat. 1991, Ch. 122, §§ 407.41h, 407.42

**School and State Sick Leave Act**
S.C. Code Ann. 1976, §§ 8-11-40 et seq., 59-1-400 et seq.

**School Antisegregation Act**
R.I. Gen. Laws 1956, 16-38-1

**School Architecture Act (Field)**
Cal. Education Code § 39140, 81130 et seq.

**School Asbestos Abatement Act**
La. Rev. Stat. Ann., 30:2341 et seq.

**School Asbestos Hazard Eliminations Act**
Miss. Code Ann. 1972, § 37-137-1 et seq.

**School Asbestos Safety Act**
N.Y. Education Law 1947 (Consol. Laws Ch. 16) § 430 et seq.

**School Assignment Act**
Fla. Stat. Ann., 230.232

**School Attendance Act**
Ala. Code 1975, § 16-28-1 et seq.
Ariz. Rev. Stat. Ann., § 15-802
Cal. Education Code 1976, § 48200 et seq.
Colo. Rev. Stat., 22-33-101 et seq.
Conn. Gen. Stat. Ann., § 10-184 et seq.
Fla. Stat. Ann., 232.01 et seq.
Ga. Code Ann., 20-2-690 et seq.
Haw. Rev. Stat. § 298-9
Ida. Code 1947, 33-201 et seq.
Ind. Code Ann., 20-8.1-3-1 et seq.
Ky. Rev. Stat. 1971, 159.010 et seq.
La. Rev. Stat. Ann., 17:221 et seq.
Mass. Gen. Laws Ann., 76:1 et seq.
Me. Rev. Stat. Ann. 1964, Title 20A, § 5001 et seq.
Miss. Code Ann. 1972, § 37-13-91
Mo. Rev. Stat., 167.031 et seq.
N.H. Rev. Stat. 1955, 193:1 et seq.
N.Y. Education Law 1947 (Consol. Laws Ch. 16) § 3204 et seq.
Okla. Stat. Ann., Title 70, § 18-107 et seq.
Ore. Rev. Stat., 339.010 et seq.
S.C. Code Ann. 1976, § 59-65-10 et seq.
Va. Code 1950, § 22-251 et seq.
Vt. Stat. Ann., Title 16, § 1121 et seq.
Wash. Rev. Code Ann., 28A.27.010 et seq.
Wis. Stat. Ann., 118.15
W. Va. Code 1966, § 18-8-1 et seq.

**School Attendance Act (Compulsory)**
Miss. Code Ann. 1972, § 37-13-91
N.Y. Education Law 1947 (Consol. Laws Ch. 16) § 3204 et seq.

**School Audit Law**
Okla. Stat. Ann., Title 70, § 22-101 et seq.

**School-Based Early Mental Health Intervention and Prevention Services for Children**
Cal. Welfare and Institutions Code § 4370 et seq.

**School-Based Early Mental Health Intervention and Prevention Services for Children Act**
Cal. Welfare and Institutions Code § 4370 et seq.

**School-Based Pupil Motivation and Maintenance Program and Dropout Recovery Act**
Cal. Education Code 1976, § 54720 et seq.

**School Board Member Recall Act**
N.M. Stat. Ann., 22-7-1 et seq.

**School Board Reapportionment and Reorganization Act**
La. Rev. Stat. Ann., 17:17.1 et seq.

**School Bond Act**
Mich. Comp. Laws Ann., 388.951 et seq.
Neb. Rev. Stat. 1943, 10-701 et seq.
N.J. Stat. Ann., 18A:24-1 et seq.
Ore. Rev. Stat., 328.205 et seq.
S.C. Code Ann. 1976, § 59-71-10 et seq.
Tenn. Code Ann., 49-3-1201 et seq.

**School Bond Act (Washington County)**
Md. Laws 1967, Ch. 352
Md. Laws 1971, Ch. 343

**School Bond Amendment**
W. Va. Const. 1872, Art. 10, § 8

**School Bond Guaranty Act**
Ore. Laws 1997, Ch. 614

**School Bond Reserve Act**
N.J. Stat. Ann., 18A:56-17 et seq.
Wyo. Stat. Ann., §§ 21-13-801, 21-13-802

**School Bond Sinking Fund Act**
N.C. Gen. Stat. 1943, Superseded Vol., § 115-226 et seq.

**School Bond Tax Act**
Iowa Code Ann., 298.1 et seq.

**School Bond Validation Law**
Cal. Statutes 1933, Ch. 19, p. 45
Cal. Statutes 1935, Ch. 13, p. 70; Ch. 21, p. 83; Ch. 114, p. 464

**School Book Bond Act**
N.C. Public Laws 1939, Ch. 67

**School Book Commission Act**
Mo. Rev. Stat. 1959, 170.010 et seq.

**School Budget Act**
Ark. Stat. 1947, 80-843 et seq.
Cal. Education Code 1976, § 42120 et seq.
Fla. Stat. Ann., 237.031 et seq.
Ill. Rev. Stat. 1991, Ch. 122, § 34-42 et seq.
N.J. Stat. Ann., 18A:22-7 et seq.
N.M. Stat. Ann., 22-8-1 et seq.

**School Budget Act (Charleston County)**
S.C. Code Ann. 1962, § 21-1662

**School Budget and Fiscal Control Act**
N.C. Gen. Stat. 1943, § 115C-422 et seq.

**School Building Accessibility Capital Improvement Grant Act**
Minn. Laws 1993, Ch. 373, §§ 20 to 22

**School Building Act**
Cal. Education Code 1976, § 39100 et seq.
Mich. Comp. Laws Ann., 388.851 et seq.
S.C. Code Ann. 1976, § 59-23-10 et seq.

**School Building Aid Act**
N.H. Rev. Stat. 1955, 198:15-a et seq.
N.J. Stat. Ann., 18A:58-20 et seq., 18A:58-33.6 et seq., 18A:58-33.22 et seq.

**School Building Aid and Earthquake Reconstruction and Replacement Bond Law**
Cal. Education Code 1976, §§ 17400 et seq., 17500 et seq.

**School Building Aid Bond Law of 1949-74**
Cal. Education Code 1976, §§ 15700 et seq., 15900 et seq., 16000 et seq., 16400 et seq., 16500 et seq., 16600 et seq., 16700 et seq., 16800 et seq., 17000 et seq., 17100 et seq., 17200 et seq., 17500 et seq., 17600 et seq.

**School Building Authority Act**
Ga. Code Ann., 20-2-550 et seq.
Ky. Rev. Stat. 1971, Superseded Vol., 157.800 et seq.
Me. Rev. Stat. Ann. 1964, Title 20-A, § 15701 et seq.
Pa. Purdon's Stat., Title 24, § 791.1 et seq.

**School Building Authority Act (Lake County)**
Fla. Special Laws 1951, Ch. 27668

**School Building Authority Act (Volusia County)**
Fla. Special Laws 1951, Ch. 27950

**School Building Authority for the Deaf and Blind Act**
Ga. Code 1933, 32-2801a et seq.

**School Building Construction Act**
Ind. Code Ann., 21-1-4-1 et seq.

**School Building Enlargement Loan Act (Manchester)**
Mass. Acts 1951, Ch. 348

**School Building Equalization Act**
Utah Code Ann. 1953, 53A-21-101 et seq.

**School Building Lease-Purchase Bond Law**
Cal. Education Code 1976, § 17600 et seq.

**School Building Lease-Purchase Law**
Cal. Education Code 1976, § 17700 et seq.

**School Building Loan Act (Belchertown)**
Mass. Acts 1951, Ch. 628

**School Building Loan Act (Brookfield)**
Mass. Acts 1950, Ch. 676

**School Building Loan Act (Greenfield)**
Mass. Acts 1959, Ch. 359

**School Building Loan Act (Lexington)**
Mass. Acts 1947, Ch. 186

**School Building Loan Act (Lunenberg)**
Mass. Acts 1949, Ch. 283

**School Building Loan Act (Lynnfield)**
Mass. Acts 1951, Ch. 723

**School Building Loan Act (New Braintree)**
Mass. Acts 1950, Ch. 675

**School Building Loan Act (North Brookfield)**
Mass. Acts 1950, Ch. 677

**School Building Loan Act (Oakham)**
Mass. Acts 1950, Ch. 701

**School Building Loan Act (Pittsfield)**
Mass. Acts 1949, Ch. 535

**School Building Loan Act (Shutesbury)**
Mass. Acts 1949, Ch. 15

**School Building Loan Act (Sturbridge)**
Mass. Acts 1949, Ch. 6

**School Building Loan Act (Swampscott)**
Mass. Acts 1952, Ch. 4

**School Building Loan Act (Wayland)**
Mass. Acts 1952, Ch. 49

**School Building Loan Act (Worcester)**
Mass. Acts 1950, Ch. 643
Mass. Acts 1952, Ch. 568

**School Building Program Act of 1951**
Del. Laws Vol. 48, p. 385, Ch. 148
Del. Laws Vol. 49, p. 697, Ch. 337
Del. Laws Vol. 50, p. 1230, Ch. 529
Del. Laws Vol. 52, p. 843, Ch. 345
Del. Laws Vol. 53, p. 842, Ch. 331

**School Bus Act**
Alaska Laws 1955, Ch. 39
Cal. Education Code 1976, §§ 39830 et seq., 82321
Ind. Code Ann., 20-9.1-1-1 et seq.
Iowa Code Ann., 321.372 et seq.
Mich. Comp. Laws Ann., 380.1321 et seq.
Mo. Rev. Stat., 304.050
N.M. Stat. Ann., 22-16-1 et seq.
Pa. Purdon's Stat., Title 24, § 13-1361 et seq.
S.C. Code Ann. 1976, § 59-64-410 et seq.
S.D. Codified Laws 1967, 13-29-1 et seq.
Wis. Stat. Ann., 121.51 et seq.

**School Bus Act (Catholic)**
N.Y. Education Law 1947 (Consol. Laws Ch. 16) §§ 1807, 1907, 2021, 3635

**School Bus Insurance Act**
Ga. Code Ann., 20-2-1090 et seq.
S.C. Code Ann. 1976, § 59-67-710 et seq.

**School Bus Operators' Tenure Act**
La. Rev. Stat. Ann., 17:491 et seq.

**School Bus Performance Bond Act**
Ill. Rev. Stat. 1991, Ch. 122, § 990 et seq.

**School Bus Registration Act**
Ind. Code Ann., 9-1-4-1 et seq., 20-9.1-4-8 et seq.

**School Bus Replacement Act**
Fla. Stat. Ann., 236.0835

**School Bus Safety Act**
Ala. Code 1975, § 16-27-1 et seq.
Alaska Stat. 1962, Replaced Titles, § 28.05.104

**School Bus Safety Act (Thomas Edward Lanni)**
Cal. Corporations Code § 39831.3
Cal. Vehicle Code 1959, § 22112

**School Bus Safety Interstate Compact Act**
Wash. Rev. Code Ann., 46.39.010, 46.39.020

**School Bus Transportation Act**
N.M. Stat. Ann., 22-16-1 et seq.

**School Buses Act (Insurance)**
S.C. Code Ann. 1976, § 59-67-710 et seq.

**School Capital Outlay Act (Public)**
N.M. Stat. Ann., 22-24-1 et seq.

**School Census Law**
Ark. Stat. 1947, 80-707 et seq.
Tenn. Code Ann., 49-6-3101 et seq.

**School Children's Vaccination Act**
Mont. Code Ann. 1991, 20-5-401 et seq.
N.H. Rev. Stat. 1955, 200:38
R.I. Gen. Laws 1956, 16-38-2

**School Closing Act**
Ala. Code 1958, Title 52, § 61(13) et seq.
Ark. Stat. 1947, 80-730 et seq.
Ga. Code Ann., 20-2-620 et seq.
La. Rev. Stat. Ann., 17:350.1 et seq.
Va. Code 1950, § 22-188.41 et seq.

**School Code (Greensboro)**
N.C. Laws 1949, Ch. 385

**School Code (Revised)**
Mich. Comp. Laws Ann., 380.1 et seq.

**School Codification Act**
Ind. Code Ann., 20-3-11-1 et seq.

**School Committee Act (County)**
Wis. Stat. Ann., 116.51 et seq.

**School Community Professional Development Act**
Fla. Stat. Ann., 231.600 et seq.

**School Compact Act (Interstate)**
Me. Rev. Stat. Ann. 1964, Title 20-A, § 3601 et seq.

**School Compact Act (Maine-New Hampshire)**
See Maine-New Hamsphire Interstate School Compact Act

**School Compact Act (New Hampshire-Vermont)**
See New Hampshire-Vermont Interstate School Compact Act

**School Compact Act (New York-Vermont)**
Vt. Stat. Ann., Title 16, § 791 et seq.

**School Consolidation Act**
Ind. Code Ann., 20-4-5-1 et seq.
Nev. Statutes 1947, Ch. 63, p. 91, § 54 et seq.

**School Consolidation Act (Voluntary)**
Okla. Stat. Ann., Title 70, § 7-201 et seq.

**School Consolidation and Annexation Act**
Okla. Stat. Ann., Title 70, § 7-201 et seq.

**School Construction Act**
Cal. Education Code 1976, §§ 15500 et seq., 39100 et seq.
Ill. Comp. Stat. 1992, Ch. 105, § 230/5-1 et seq.

**School Construction Aid Law (Urban)**
Cal. Education Code 1976, § 17300 et seq.

**School Construction Assistance Act**
N.M. Stat. Ann., 22-20-1 et seq.

**School Construction Authority Act (New York City)**
N.Y. Public Authorities Law (Consol. Laws Ch. 43A) § 1735 et seq.

**School Construction Bond Act**
Ill. Rev. Stat. 1991, Ch. 122, § 1201 et seq.
Wash. Rev. Code Ann., 28A.47.050 et seq.

**School Construction Loan Act (Leominster Northwest)**
Mass. Acts 1956, Ch. 673

**School Contracts Law (Public)**
N.J. Stat. Ann., 18A:18A-1 et seq.

**School Contracts Termination Act (Principals and Teachers)**
N.C. Gen. Stat. 1943, § 115-142

**School Corporation Financing Act**
Ind. Code Ann., 21-2-12-1 et seq.

**School Corporation Reorganization Act**
Ind. Code Ann., 20-4-1-1 et seq.

**School Crime Report Act**
S.C. Code Ann. 1976, § 59-63-310 et seq.

**School Crossing Guard Act (Ramon Turnquest)**
Fla. Laws 1992, Ch. 194

**School Depository Act**
Ohio Rev. Code 1953, 3313.51
Tex. Education Code, § 23.71 et seq.

**School Development Act (Exeter)**
R.I. Public Laws 1958, Ch. 160

**School Discipline Act**
Ark. Code Ann. 1987, 6-18-505
Fla. Stat. Ann., 228.041, 229.575, 230.23, 230.2313, 230.2315, 232.17, 232.19
Tenn. Code Ann., 49-6-4101 et seq.

**School Discrimination Law**
Mass. Gen. Laws Ann., 76:5, 151C:1 et seq.

**School Dismissal Act**
Ark. Code Ann. 1987, 6-18-506

**School District Act (Community Unit)**
Ill. Rev. Stat. 1991, Ch. 122, § 11A-1 et seq.

**School District Act (County)**
Mich. Comp. Laws 1948, 340.291 et seq.

**School District Act (Independent Districts)**
Ala. Code 1958, Title 52, § 197(1) et seq.

**School District Budget Act**
Colo. Rev. Stat., 22-44-101 et seq.
Mont. Rev. Code 1947, 75-6701 et seq.

**School District Building Authority Act (Houston County)**
Ga. Laws 1994, p. 3906

**School District Capital Construction Assistance Program**
Colo. Rev. Stat., 22-43.7-101 et seq.

**School District Consolidation Act**
Mo. Rev. Stat., 162.223 et seq.
N.M. Stat. Ann., 22-4-3 et seq.

**School District Educational Effectiveness and Fiscal Efficiency Act**
Ill. Rev. Stat. 1991, Ch. 122, § 870.1 et seq.

**School District Emergency Financial Assistance Law**
Ill. Rev. Stat. 1991, Ch. 122, § 1B-1 et seq.

**School District Eminent Domain Law**
Wash. Rev. Code Ann., 8.16.010 et seq.

**School District Equalization Act**
Kan. Stat. Ann., 72-7030 et seq.
Mich. Comp. Laws Ann., 388.1101 et seq.

**School District Finance and Quality Performance Act**
Kan. Stat. Ann., 72-6405 et seq.

**School District Indian Voter Qualification Act**
N.Y. Education Law 1947 (Consol. Laws Ch. 16) § 2012, Subd. 4

**School District Law (Rural)**
Ore. Rev. Stat., 334.005 et seq.

**School District Loan Act**
N.M. Stat. Ann., 22-18A-1 et seq.

**School District Local Option Single Member Representation Law**
Fla. Stat. 1981, 230.105

**School District Mercantile License Tax Act**
Pa. Purdon's Stat., Title 24, § 582.1 et seq.

**School District Organization Act**
Colo. Rev. Stat., 22-30-101 et seq.
Kan. Stat. Ann., 72-6734 et seq.
S.D. Codified Laws 1967, 13-5-1 et seq.
Wyo. Stat. Ann., § 21-5-101 et seq.

**School District Personal Property Tax Act**
Pa. Purdon's Stat., Title 24, § 581.1 et seq.

**School District Reorganization Act**
Ark. Code Ann. 1987, 6-13-501
Colo. Laws 1949, p. 636, Ch. 224
Del. Code of 1974, Title 14, §§ 1001 et seq., 1101 et seq.,
Ida. Code 1947, 33-301 et seq.
Mich. Comp. Laws Ann., 388.681 et seq.
Minn. Stat. Ann., 122.41 et seq.
Mo. Rev. Stat., 162.171 et seq.
N.D. Cent. Code, 15-53.1-08 et seq.
Okla. Stat. Ann., Title 70, § 7-101 et seq.
Ore. Rev. Stat., 330.505 et seq.
Pa. Purdon's Stat., Title 24, § 2-290 et seq.
S.D. Codified Laws 1967, 13-6-1 et seq.
Wyo. Stat. 1957, § 21-224 et seq.,

**School District Tax Act (First Class)**
Pa. Purdon's Stat., Title 24, § 584.1 et seq.

**School District Taxing Act (Philadelphia)**
Pa. Purdon's Stat., Title 24, §§ 584.1 et seq., 586.1 et seq.

**School District Taxing Act (Pittsburgh)**
Pa. Purdon's Stat., Title 24, §§ 584.1 et seq., 586.1 et seq.

**School District Validating Act**
Cal. Statutes 1957, Ch. 34, p. 589

**School District Validating Act (Second)**
Cal. Statutes 1957, Ch. 137, p. 731

**School District Validation Act**
Ill. Rev. Stat. 1991, Ch. 122, §§ 407.42h, 407.43, 407.43h et seq., 407.50, 407.51

**School Districts Act**
Iowa Code Ann., 274.1 et seq.
N.H. Rev. Stat. 1955, 194:1 et seq.
Ohio Rev. Code 1953, 3311.01 et seq.
Wash. Rev. Code Ann., 28A.57.010 et seq.

**School Districts Act (City)**
N.Y. Education Law 1947 (Consol. Laws Ch. 16) § 2501 et seq.

**School Districts Act (Interstate)**
Vt. Acts 1959, No. 230

**School Districts Aid Allocation Act (Collier)**
Cal. Education Code §§ 41200, 84200

**School Districts Local Partnership Act**
Minn. Stat. Ann., 124C.10 et seq.

**School Dropout Demonstration Assistance Act of 1988**
April 28, 1988, P.L. 100-297, 102 Stat. 265, 20 U.S. Code § 3241 et seq.
Aug. 23, 1988, P.L. 100-418, 102 Stat. 1491, 20 U.S. Code § 5051
Aug. 17, 1991, P.L. 102-103, 20 U.S. Code §§ 3243, 3244, 3245, 3246, 3248

**School Dropout Prevention Act**
Cal. Education Code 1976, § 54660 et seq.

**School Dropout Prevention and Basic Skills Improvement Act of 1990**
Nov. 16, 1990, P.L. 101-600, 20 U.S. Code § 2701 nt.

**School Dropout Prevention Program**
Pa. Purdon's Stat., Title 24, § 6601 et seq.

**School Education Assurance Act (Proprietary)**
Mich. Comp. Laws Ann., 395.251

**School Efficiency Program Act**
N.J. Stat. Ann., 18A:7E-6 et seq.

**School Election Act**
Kan. Stat. Ann., 25-2001 et seq., 72-7901 et seq., 72-8001 et seq., 72-8116 et seq.
N.M. Stat. Ann., 1-22-1 et seq.

**School Election Validation Act**
Ill. Rev. Stat. 1991, Ch. 122, §§ 407.36h, 407.37, 407.40h, 407.41

**School Employee Fair Hearing Act (Public)**
Ark. Acts 1991, No. 631

**School Employee Personnel Files Act**
La. Rev. Stat. Ann., 17:1231 et seq.

**School Employee's Minimum Sick Leave Law**
Ark. Code Ann. 1987, 6-17-1301 et seq.

**School Employees Retirement Act**
Neb. Rev. Stat. 1943, 79-1501 to 79-1566

**School Employees' Retirement Act**
Mich. Comp. Laws Ann., 38.201 et seq.
Mo. Rev. Stat. 1978, 169.010 et seq.
Ohio Rev. Code 1953, 3309.01 et seq.
Pa. Purdon's Stat., Title 24, § 8101 et seq.
Utah Code Ann. 1953, 49-2-101 et seq.

**School Employees Sick Leave Act**
S.C. Code Ann. 1976, §§ 8-11-40 et seq., 59-1-400 et seq.

**School Employment Procedures Act**
Miss. Code Ann. 1972, § 37-9-101 et seq.

**School Enrollment Act**
N.C. Gen. Stat. 1943, § 115C-364 et seq.

**School Equalizing Fund Law**
Ark. Stat. 1947, 80-821 et seq.

**School Ethics Act**
N.J. Laws 1991, Ch. 393

**School Facilities Act**
Cal. Statutes 1986, Ch. 886

**School Facilities Act (Leroy F. Green)**
Cal. Education Code 1976, § 17070.10 et seq.

**School Facilities Aid Act**
S.C. Code Ann. 1976, § 59-21-310 et seq.

**School Facilities Bond Act**
Cal. Education Code 1976,
Cal. Education Code 1976, §§ 17645 et seq., 17650 et seq.

**School Facilities Bond Act of 1988-1992**
Cal. Education Code 1976, §§ 17640 et seq., 17660 et seq., 17697 et seq.

**School Facilities Bond Act of 1992**
Cal. Education Code 1976, § 17645 et seq.

**School Facilities Construction Act**
Aug. 12, 1958, P.L. 85-620, 72 Stat. 548, 20 U.S. Code §§ 631 to 645
June 25, 1959, P.L. 86-70, 73 Stat. 144, 20 U.S. Code § 645
May 6, 1960, P.L. 86-449, 74 Stat. 89, 20 U.S. Code § 640
July 12, 1960, P.L. 86-623, 74 Stat. 414, 20 U.S. Code § 645
Oct. 3, 1961, P.L. 87-344, 75 Stat. 759, 20 U.S. Code §§ 633, 644 , 645
Dec. 18, 1963, P.L. 88-210, 77 Stat. 419, 20 U.S. Code §§ 633, 644, 645
Oct. 16, 1964, P.L. 88-665, 78 Stat. 1109, 20 U.S. Code §§ 633, 644, 645
July 21, 1965, P.L. 89-77, 79 Stat. 243, 20 U.S. Code § 640
April 13, 1970, P.L. 91-230, 84 Stat. 154, 20 U.S. Code §§ 241-1, 633, 635, 644 to 646
May 21, 1970, P.L. 91-260, 84 Stat. 254, 20 U.S. Code § 635

**School Facilities Finance Act**
N.C. Laws 1991, Ch. 622

**School Facilities Funding Act (Public)**
Tex. General and Special Laws 1991, p. 3726, Ch. 815
Tex. Rev. Civ. Stat., Art. 717t

**School Facility Health and Safety Bond Act**
N.Y. Laws 1997, Ch. 328

**School-Family Partnership Act**
La. Rev. Stat. Ann., 17:406 et seq.

**School Finance Act**
Ark. Code Ann. 1987, 6-20-301 et seq.
Colo. Rev. Stat., 22-53-101 et seq.
Kan. Stat. Ann., 72-7030 et seq.
Me. Rev. Stat. Ann. 1964, Title 20-A, §§ 15601 et seq., 15651 et seq.
N.M. Stat. Ann., 22-8-1 et seq.

**School Finance Act (Minimum)**
Utah Code Ann. 1953, 53A-17A-101 et seq.

**School Finance Act (Public)**
Colo. Rev. Stat., 22-54-101 et seq.

**School Finance Authority Act**
Cal. Education Code 1976, § 17870 et seq.
Ill. Rev. Stat. 1991, Ch. 122, § 34A-101 et seq.

**School Finance Authority Act (Elementary and Secondary)**
Neb. Rev. Stat. 1943, 79-1801 to 79-1852

**School Fire Alarm Law**
Cal. Education Code 1976, § 32000 et seq.

**School Food Service Financing Act**
N.Y. Laws 1980, Ch. 798

**School for the Performing and Visual Arts Act (South Florida)**
Fla. Stat. 1981, 240.535

**School Foundation Act**
Kan. Laws 1965, Ch. 402
Okla. Stat. Ann., Title 70, § 18-101 et seq.

**School Foundation and Equalization Act**
Neb. Rev. Stat. 1943, 79-1330 et seq.

**School Foundation Program Act**
See Foundation Program Act (Schools)

**School Foundation Program Fund Act**
Fla. Stat. 236.012 et seq.

**School Fraternities Act**
Okla. Stat. Ann., Title 70, § 24-105

**School Free Lunch Program Act**
Ill. Rev. Stat. 1991, Ch. 122, § 712.01 et seq.

**School Fund Apportionments Act**
Cal. Education Code 1976, §§ 41600 et seq., 45160 et seq, 84700 et seq., 88160 et seq.

**School Funds Act**
Ohio Rev. Code 1953, 3315.01 et seq.

**School Funds Depository Act**
Minn. Stat. 1953, 124.05

**School Funds Distribution Act**
Ind. Code Ann., 21-3-1.6-1 et seq.

**School Health Act**
Pa. 1945 Pamph. Laws 1222, No. 425

**School Health Services Act**
Fla. Stat. Ann., 402.32

**School House Holding Corporation Act**
Ind. Code 1971, 21-5-2-1 et seq.

**School Improvement Act**
Cal. Education Code 1976, § 54630 et seq.
Ida. Code 1947, 33-513, 33-1301 et seq.

**School Improvement and Accountability Act**
N.C. Laws 1991, Ch. 778

**School Improvement Incentives Act**
N.M. Stat. Ann., 22-13A-1 et seq.

**School Incentive Equalization Aid Law**
N.J. Stat. Ann., 18A:7A-3, 18A:7A-7, 18A:7A-11

**School Inspector Act**
Ind. Code 1971, 20-1-13-1 et seq.

**School Interstate Compact Act (Border State)**
Ill. Rev. Stat. 1991, Ch. 122, § 738.9 et seq.

**School Land Bank Act**
Cal. Public Resources Code § 8700 et seq.

**School Land Grant Act**
Alaska Comp. Laws Ann. 1949, § 47-2-21 et seq.

**School Land Sales Act**
Tex. Rev. Civ. Stat., Art. 5421c

**School Lands Act**
Tex. Natural Resources Code, § 51.001 et seq.

**School Lands Moratorium Act**
Cal. Statutes 1939, Ch. 609, p. 2030

**School Lease Rental Act**
Ind. Code Ann., 21-5-11-1 et seq.

**School Leasing Authority Act (Emergency)**
Miss. Code Ann. 1972, § 37-7-351

**School Leasing Law**
N.M. Stat. Ann. 1953, 77-17-1 et seq.

**School Libraries Act**
Cal. Education Code 1976, § 18100 et seq.
S.D. Codified Laws 1967, Superseded Vol., 14-5-1 et seq.
Wis. Stat. Ann., 43.17 et seq.

**School Library Act (County)**
Ore. Code 1930, § 35-4433 et seq.

**School License Act (Drivers' Training)**
Kan. Stat. Ann., 8-1212 et seq.

**School Loan Act**
Mass. Acts 1922, Ch. 571 (Cambridge)
Mass. Acts 1949, Ch. 9(Amherst)
Mass. Acts 1949, Ch. 523 (Danvers)
Mass. Acts 1950, Ch. 642 (Beverly)
Mass. Acts 1951, Ch. 356 (Lincoln)
Mass. Acts 1951, Ch. 358 (Lynn)
Mass. Acts 1951, Ch. 627 (Ware)
Mass. Acts 1952, Ch. 1 (Natick)
Mass. Acts 1952, Ch. 328 (Auburn)
Mass. Acts 1952, Ch. 528 (Chelsea)
Mass. Acts 1956, Ch. 57 (North Attleborough)
Mass. Acts 1956, Ch. 699 (Peabody)
Mass. Acts 1959, Ch. 420 (Lynn)

**School Location Act**
Me. Rev. Stat. Ann. 1964, Title 20, § 3561 et seq.; 20A, § 16101 et seq.

**School Lunch Act**
Mich. Comp. Laws Ann., 380.1272
N.D. Cent. Code, 15-54-01 et seq.
N.M. Stat. Ann., 22-13-13 et seq.
N.Y. Laws 1946, Ch. 632
N.Y. Laws 1947, Ch. 10
N.Y. Laws 1948, Ch. 511
S.D. Codified Laws 1967, 13-35-1 et seq.

**School Lunch and Child Nutrition Amendments of 1986**
Oct. 18, 1986, P.L. 99-500, 42 U.S. Code § 1751 nt.
Oct. 30, 1986, P.L. 99-591, 42 U.S. Code § 1751 nt.
Nov. 10, 1989, P.L. 101-147, 42 U.S. Code §§ 1758, 1760, 1761, 1761 nt., 1762a, 1762a nt., 1763, 1766 et seq., 1772, 1773, 1786

**School Lunch Employees' Retirement Act**
La. Rev. Stat. Ann., § 17:1231 et seq.

**School Machinery Act**
N.C. Gen. Stat. 1943, Superseded Vol., § 115-347 et seq.

**School Minimum Program Act**
See Minimum Foundation Program Act (Education)

**School Motor Vehicle Self-Insurance Act**
Ark. Acts 1991, No. 824

**School Nutrition Standards Act**
Tenn. Public Acts 1986, Ch. 904

**School of Mines and Agricultural College Act (Land Grant)**
Alaska Comp. Laws Ann. 1949, § 47-2-21 et seq.

**School of Technology Act (Thaddeus Stevens)**
Pa. Purdon's Stat., Title 24, § 19-1901-B

**School of the Arts Act**
Fla. Stat. Ann., 242.65

**School of Veterinary Medicine Act**
Tenn. Code Ann., 49-9-801

**School Officers Sabbatical Leave Act**
D.C. Code Ann., § 31-1014

**School Partnership Act (Family)**
La. Rev. Stat. Ann., 17:406 et seq.

**School Personnel Act (Certified)**
N.M. Stat. Ann., 22-10-1 et seq.

**School Placement Act**
Ala. Code 1958, Title 52, § 61(1) et seq.
La. Rev. Stat. Ann., 17:81.1

**School Plan Act (City)**
Wis. Stat. Ann., 120.40 et seq.

**School Powers Act**
Ind. Code Ann., 20-5-1-1 et seq.

**School Preference Law (Segregation)**
Tenn. Code Ann. 1955, Superseded Vol., 49-3704

**School Program Act (Charter)**
N.J. Stat. Ann., 18A:36A-1 et seq.

**School Program Act (Drug Offender)**
Tenn. Public Acts 1990, Ch. 992

**School Program Act (Minimum)**
Utah Code Ann. 1953, 53A-17a-101 et seq.

**School Qualified Bond Act**
N.J. Stat. Ann., 18A:24-85 et seq.

**School Redistricting Act**
Neb. Rev. Stat. 1943, 79-426.01 et seq.

**School Reform Act (Elementary and Secondary)**
N.C. Laws 1984, Ch. 1103

**School Reform and Student Protection Act (Maxine Waters)**
Cal. Education Code 1976, §§ 94316 et seq., 94840 et seq.

**School Reform for the Next Decade Act (Target 2000)**
S.C. Acts 1989, p. 1533, No. 194

**School Registration Act**
Miss. Code Ann. 1972, § 75-60-1 et seq.

**School Relief Fund Act**
Ind. Laws 1933, Ch. 167, p. 863

**School Remodeling Loan Act (Lexington)**
Mass. Acts 1958, Ch. 4

**School Reorganization Act**
See also Reorganization Act (Schools)
Ga. Code Ann., 20-2-61 et seq.
Iowa Code Ann., 275.1 et seq.
N.C. Laws 1965, Ch. 1051
Wis. Stat. Ann., 117.01 et seq.

**School Reorganization Curative Act**
Kan. Stat. Ann., 72-5629

**School Report Cards Act**
Ark. Code Ann. 1987, 6-15-801 et seq.

**School Reporting of Drug Violations Act**
Ill. Comp. Stat. 1992, Ch. 105, § 127/1 et seq.

**School Requirements Act**
Iowa Code Ann., 280.1 et seq.

**School Retirement Act**
Neb. Rev. Stat. 1943, 79-1501 et seq.

**School Revenue Bond Act**
N.M. Stat. Ann., 22-19-1 et seq.

**School Revolving Loan Fund Act**
Ark. Code Ann. 1987, 6-20-801 et seq.

**School Safety Act**
Cal. Health and Safety Code § 11353.5
Ga. Laws 1997, p. 1436
N.J. Stat. Ann., 18A:17-42 et seq.
S.C. Code Ann. 1976, §§ 16-3-612, 20-7-7210, 22-3-560, 59-63-370 to 59-63-390

**School Safety Act (Michelle Montoya)**
Cal. Education Code 1976, §§ 44237, 45125, 45125.1

**School Safety and Juvenile Justice Reform Act**
Ga. Laws 1994, p. 1012

**School Safety and Security Act**
Kan. Stat. Ann., 72-89b01 et seq.

**School Safety and Violence Protection Act**
Cal. Education Code 1976, § 32228 et seq.

**School Safety Supervision Act**
Tex. Education Code, § 21.301 et seq.

**School Security Act**
Tenn. Code Ann., 49-6-4201 et seq.

**School Security Corps Act**
P.R. Laws Ann. 1954, Title 18, § 141 et seq.

**School Segregation Act**
Ark. Code Ann. 1987, 6-13-620
Del. Code of 1953, Title 14, § 141
Ga. Code Ann., 20-2-670, 20-2-671
Ky. Rev. Stat. 1962, 158.020
Ohio Laws Vol. 5, p. 53
Okla. Stat. Ann., Title 70, § 1210.201 et seq.
S.C. Code Ann. 1976, Superseded Vols., § 59-63-10 et seq.

**School Site Act (Reversion)**
Iowa Code Ann., 297.15

**School Staff Institute Act**
R.I. Gen. Laws 1956, 16-66-1 et seq.

**School Student Records Act**
Ill. Rev. Stat. 1991, Ch. 122, § 50-1 et seq.

**School Students Immunization Act**
D.C. Code Ann., § 31-501 et seq.

**School Support Fund Act**
Ore. Rev. Stat., 327.006 et seq.

**School Support Tax Law (Local)**
Nev. Rev. Stat. 1979 Reprint, 374.010 et seq.

**School Survey and Reorganization Act**
Ill. Rev. Stat. 1963, Ch. 122, § 730 et seq.

**School System Act (Dougherty County)**
Ga. Laws 1951, p. 2233

**School Tax Act**
Miss. Code Ann. 1972, § 37-57-1 et seq.

**School Tax Act (Sales)**
N.M. Stat. Ann. 1953, 72-16-1 et seq.

**School Tax Act (Valdosta)**
Ga. Laws 1949, p. 1392

**School Tax Levies Limitations Act**
Ind. Code Ann., 6-1.1-19-1 et seq.

**School Tax Rate Validation Act of 1967-1969**
Ill. Rev. Stat. 1991, Ch. 122, §§ 407.37h, 407.38, 407.38h, 407.39, 407.39h, 407.40

**School Teachers (Nonpublic) Salary Supplement Act**
R.I. Gen. Laws 1956, 16-51-1 et seq.

**School Teachers Act**
Wash. Rev. Code Ann., 28A.67.010 et seq.

**School Teachers' Arbitration Act**
R.I. Gen. Laws 1956, 28-9.3-1 et seq.

**School Teachers' Certification Act**
See Teachers' Certification Act

**School Teachers' Minimum Salary Act**
See Teachers' Minimum Salary Act

**School Teachers' Retirement Act**
See Teachers' Retirement Act

**School Teachers' Tenure Act**
See Teachers' Tenure Act

**School Technology Revenue Bond Act (Archie-Hudson and Cunneen)**
Cal. Education Code 1976, § 17860 et seq.

**School Testing Act**
Cal. Education Code 1976, § 60600 et seq.

**School Testing Program Act**
Okla. Stat. 1981, Title 70, § 1210.505 et seq.

**School Textbook Act**
See Textbook Act (Schools)
N.M. Stat. Ann., 22-15-1 et seq.

**School Textbook Lending Law**
N.Y. Education Law 1947 (Consol. Laws Ch. 16) § 701

**School to Career Program (Certified)**
Iowa Code Ann., 15.361 to 15.367

**School-to-Work Opportunities Act of 1994**
May 4, 1994, P.L. 103-239, 20 U.S. Code §§ 6101 nt., 6101 et seq.
Oct. 20, 1994, P.L. 103-382, 20 U.S. Code §§ 6103, 6212
Aug. 22, 1996, P.L. 104-193, 20 U.S. Code § 6143
Oct. 7, 1998, P.L. 105-244, 20 U.S. Code § 6103

**School-to-Work Opportunity Act of 1994**
Nov. 10, 1998, P.L. 105-362, 20 U.S. Code § 6235

**School-to-Work Student Organization Act**
Minn. Stat. Ann., 121.615

**School Tort Liability Act**
Ill. Rev. Stat. 1981, Ch. 122, § 821 et seq.

**School Transfer Act**
Okla. Stat. Ann., Title 70, § 8-101 et seq.

**School Transit Subsidy Act**
D.C. Code Ann., § 44-216 et seq.

**School Transportation Act**
Cal. Education Code 1976, §§ 39800, 39830 et seq., 41850 et seq.
Ida. Code 1947, 33-1501 et seq.
Ind. Code Ann., 20-9.1-1-1 et seq.
N.D. Cent. Code, 15-34.2-01 et seq.
N.J. Stat. Ann., 18A:39-1 et seq.
Okla. Stat. Ann., Title 70, § 9-101 et seq.
Ore. Rev. Stat., 332.405 et seq.
S.C. Code Ann. 1976, § 59-67-410 et seq.
Vt. Stat. Ann., Title 16, § 1221 et seq.

**School Transportation Act (Blind or Deaf)**
Ill. Rev. Stat. 1991, Ch. 23, §§ 1209.9, 1210

**School Tuition Fund Act**
Ind. Burns' 1933, 28-912 to 28-920

**School Unification Act**
Kan. Stat. Ann., 72-6734 et seq., 72-6764 et seq.

**School Zone Act (Child Safe)**
Del. Code of 1974, Title 11, § 1112

**School Zone Act (Gun-Free)**
Cal. Penal Code § 626.9

**School Zone Safety Act**
Utah Laws 1992, Ch. 91

**Schools Act (Charter)**
Cal. Education Code 1976, § 47600 et seq.
Colo. Rev. Stat., 22-30.5-101 et seq.
Del. Code of 1974, Title 14, § 501 et seq.
N.M. Stat. Ann., 22-8A-1 et seq.

**Schools Act (Community)**
Ala. Code 1975, § 16-63-1 et seq.

**Schools Act (Twenty-First Century)**
N.Y. Education Law 1947 (Consol. Laws Ch. 16) § 309a et seq.

**Schools and School Districts Excellence in Education Act**
Mo. Rev. Stat. 1978, 160.251 et seq.

**Schools and School Districts Professional Teacher and Administration Act**
Mo. Rev. Stat. 1978, 168.400 et seq.

**Schools Charter Act**
Colo. Rev. Stat., 22-30.5-101 et seq.

**Schools for Arkansas' Future Act (Meeting the National Education Goals)**
Ark. Code Ann. 1987, 6-15-1001 et seq.

**Schools for Boys Act (Training)**
Ill. Rev. Stat. 1991, Ch. 122, § 660.9 et seq.

**Schools for Girls Act (Industrial)**
Ill. Rev. Stat. 1991, Ch. 122, § 645.9 et seq.

**Schools Professional Practices Act**
Ida. Code 1947, 33-1251 et seq.

**Schools Program Act**
N.J. Stat. Ann., 18A:6-33.7 et seq.

**Schools Program Act (Effective)**
N.J. Stat. Ann., 18A:6-33.7 et seq.

**Schools Racial Imbalance Act**
Mass. Gen. Laws Ann., 15:1I et seq., 71:37C, 71:37D

**Schools Toxic Art. Supplies Act**
Ill. Rev. Stat. 1991, Ch. 122, § 1601 et seq.

**Schrade-Belotti Reflectorized License Plates Act**
Cal. Vehicle Code 1959, § 4850

**Schumacher Act (Counterfeit Coins)**
Ohio Rev. Code 1953, 2911.35 et seq.

**Schuylkill County Act (Judicial Sales)**
Pa. 1871 Pamph. Laws 820, No. 752

**Schuylkill River Desilting Act**
Pa. Purdon's Stat., Title 32, § 751.1 et seq.

**Schuylkill Scenic River Act**
Pa. Purdon's Stat., Title 32, § 820.31 et seq.

**Science Act**
See Basic Science Act

**Science Advisory Council Act**
Ill. Rev. Stat. 1991, Ch. 127, § 420 et seq.

**Science and Engineering Equal Opportunities Act**
Dec. 12, 1980, P.L. 96-516., 42 U.S. Code §§ 1861 nt., 1885 et seq.
Nov. 22, 1985, P.L. 99-159, 42 U.S. Code §§ 1861 nt., 1885 et seq.
Oct. 31, 1988, P.L. 100-570, 42 U.S. Code § 1885c
July 29, 1998, P.L. 105-207, 42 U.S. Code §§ 1885b, 1885c

**Science and Mathematics Academy Law**
Ill. Rev. Stat. 1991, Ch. 122, § 1503 et seq.

**Science and Mathematics Teacher Tuition Assistance Act**
Neb. Rev. Stat. 1943, 79-12, 142 et seq.

**Science and Mathematics Teaching Student Assistance Act**
Neb. Rev. Stat. 1943, 79-12,122 et seq.

**Science and Natural History Museum Act**
N.M. Stat. Ann., 18-3A-1 et seq.

**Science and Technology Act**
Alaska Stat. 1962, § 37.17.010 et seq.

**Science and Technology Development Board Seed Capital Bond Act**
Mont. Code Ann. 1987, 90-3-401 et seq.

**Science and Technology Eminent Scholars and Research Equipment Act**
Okla. Stat. Ann., Title 74, §§ 2013 to 2016

**Science and Technology Equal Opportunities Act**
See Science and Engineering Equal Opportunities Act
Dec. 12, 1980, P.L. 96-516, 42 U.S. Code § 1861 nt.

**Science and Technology Financing Act**
Mont. Code Ann., 90-3-101 et seq.

**Science Center Authority**
Utah Code Ann. 1953, 9-3-401 et seq.

**Science in Motion Act**
Ala. Code 1975, § 16-61C-1 et seq.

**Science, Jobs and Technology Bond Act**
N.J. Laws 1984, Ch. 99

**Science, Mathematics, Technology Act (Magnet School)**
Colo. Rev. Stat., 22-84-101 et seq.

**Science Practice Act (Clinical Laboratory)**
R.I. Gen. Laws 1956, 23-16.3-1 et seq.

**Science, Technology, and Mathematics Improvement Act (K through 12)**
Colo. Rev. Stat., 22-81-101 et seq.

**Scientific and Advanced-Technology Act of 1992**
Oct. 23, 1992, P.L. 102-476, 42 U.S. Code §§ 1861 nt., 1862, 1862h, 1862i, 1862j
Oct. 7, 1998, P.L. 105-244, 42 U.S. Code § 1862i

**Scientific and Cultural Facilities District Act**
Colo. Rev. Stat., 32-13-101 et seq.

**Scientific and Natural Areas Preservation Act**
Kan. Stat. Ann., 74-6601 et seq.

**Scire Facias Act**
Pa. Purdon's Stat., Title 12, §§ 141, 291 et seq.

**Scituate Sewerage Loan Act**
Mass. Acts 1957, Ch. 636

**Scoliosis Screening Act**
Mich. Comp. Laws Ann., 333.9152

**Scott Act (Liquor Tax)**
Ohio Laws Vol. 80, p. 164

**Scott Miller Jr. Act (Horizonal Property)**
Ky. Rev. Stat. 1971, 381.805 et seq.

**Scott Water and Sewer Authority Act**
Ga. Laws 1972, p. 2831

**Scranton Extension Act (Pennsylvania Turnpike)**
Pa. 1949 Pamph. Laws 1050, No. 302

**Scrap Land Act**
Tex. Rev. Civ. Stat., Arts. 5323a, 5421c, § 6

**Scrap Metal Processing Facility (Junkyard Control) Act**
Okla. Stat. Ann., Title 69, § 1251 et seq.

**Scrap Tire Disposal Act**
N.C. Gen. Stat. 1943, § 130A-309.51 et seq.
N.M. Stat. Ann., 43-3-8

**Scrap Tire Regulatory Act**
Mich. Comp. Laws Ann., 299.561 et seq.

**Scrapping of Naval Vessels Act**
July 1, 1922, Ch. 263, 42 Stat. 814

**Screen Act (Coal)**
Kan. Stat. Ann., 49-301 et seq.

**Screen Law (Mining)**
Ark. Code Ann. 1987, 15-59-114

**Screen Law (Saloons)**
Del. Laws Vol. 18, p. 677, Ch. 555, § 4

**Screening Center Law (Commitment of Insane)**
Iowa Code Ann., 229.13

**Screening for Learning—Language Disabilities Act**
Wash. Rev. Code Ann., 28A.03.300 et seq.

**Screenings Act**
Minn. Stat. Ann., 21.71 et seq.

**Scribner Log Rule Act (Log Measurement)**
Pa. Purdon's Stat., Title 73, § 1872

**Scrip Act**
Kan. Laws 1897, Ch. 145

**Scriveners Act**
Ky. Rev. Stat. 1971, 382.335

**Sea and Shore Fisheries Act**
Me. Rev. Stat. Ann. 1964, Title 12, § 16001 et seq.

**Sea Food Act**
Miss. Code Ann. 1972, § 49-15-1 et seq.

**Sea Food Inspection Act**
Aug. 27, 1935, Ch. 739, 49 Stat. 871, 21 U.S. Code § 372a

**Sea Food Marketing Law (Cooperative)**
La. Rev. Stat. Ann., 12:441 et seq.

**Sea Grant Consortium Act**
S.C. Code Ann. 1976, § 48-45-10 et seq.

**Sea Grant Program Improvement Act of 1976**
Oct. 8, 1976, P.L. 94-461, 33 U.S. Code §§ 1121 et seq.
June 29, 1977, P.L. 95-58, 33 U.S. Code § 1124a
Nov. 8, 1984, P.L. 98-623, 33 U.S. Code § 1124a
Dec. 29, 1987, P.L. 100-220, 33 U.S. Code § 1124a
March 9, 1992, P.L. 102-251, 33 U.S. Code § 1124a
March 6, 1998, P.L. 105-160, 33 U.S. Code § 1124a

**Sea Island Cotton Law**
Fla. Stat. 1969, 579.01 et seq.

**Sea of Okhotsk Fisheries Enforcement Act of 1995**
Nov. 3, 1995, P.L. 104-43, Title V, 16 U.S. Code § 1823 nt.

**Sea Wall Loan Act (Duxbury)**
Mass. Acts 1952, Ch. 531

**Sea Wall Loan Act (Marshfield)**
Mass. Acts 1957, Ch. 340

**Seabury Investigation Act**
N.Y. Laws 1931, Ex. Sess., Ch. 773

**Seafood Marketing Law (Cooperatives)**
La. Rev. Stat. Ann., 12:441 et seq.

**Seafood Marketing, Research, and Development Act**
Cal. Food and Agricultural Code § 78401 et seq.

**Seal Act**
Ill. Rev. Stat. 1991, Ch. 1, § 2901-5

**Seal Farming Act**
Alaska Comp. Laws Ann. 1949, § 47-2-76 et seq.

**Seal Fisheries Act**
April 21, 1910, Ch. 183, 36 Stat. 326

**Seal of Quality Act**
Fla. Stat. Ann., 571.01 et seq.
Mich. Comp. Laws Ann., 289.631 et seq.

**Seals and Real Estate Contracts Act**
Ill. Rev. Stat. 1991, Ch. 29, § 0.01 et seq.

**Seamen Discharge Act**
March 24, 1937, Ch. 49, 50 Stat. 49, 46 U.S. Code § 643

**Seamen's Act**
March 4, 1915, Ch. 153, 38 Stat. 1164, 22 U.S. Code § 258; 33 U.S. Code §§ 365, 366; 46 U.S. Code §§ 222, 481, 569, 596, 597, 599, 601, 656, 660-1, 672, 673, 683, 688, 701, 703, 712, 713

**Seamen's Service Act**
Dec. 31, 1970, P.L. 91-603, 84 Stat. 1674, 10 U.S. Code § 2604; 46 U.S . Code §§ 1151, 1152, 1171, 1223

**Search and Rescue Act**
N.M. Stat. Ann., 24-15A-1 et seq.

**Search and Seizure Act**
Ala. Code 1975, § 15-5-1 et seq.
Del. Code of 1974, Title 11, § 2301 et seq.
Ga. Code Ann., 17-5-1 et seq.
Mich. Comp. Laws Ann., 780.651 et seq.
Mont. Code Ann., 46-5-101 et seq.
N.H. Rev. Stat. 1955, 595-A:1 et seq.
N.Y. Civil Rights Law (Consol. Laws Ch. 6) § 8
Ore. Rev. Stat., 133.525 et seq.
R.I. Gen. Laws 1956, 12-5-1 et seq.
Tex. Code of Criminal Procedure, Arts. 1.06, 18.01 et seq.
Vt. Stat. Ann., Title 13, § 4701 et seq.
Wash. Rev. Code Ann., 10.79.015 et seq.
W. Va. Code 1966, § 62-1-18

**Search and Seizure Act (Dram Shops)**
Ill. Rev. Stat. 1981, Ch. 43, § 190 et seq.

**Search and Seizure Act (Intoxicating Liquor)**
N.C. Gen. Stat. 1943, § 18B-502 et seq.

**Search Warrant Act**
June 15, 1917, Ch. 30, 40 Stat. 228, See 18 U.S. Code §§ 11, 957, 1621, 2231, 2234, 2235, 3105, 3109
Alaska Stat. 1962, § 12.35.010 et seq.
Ariz. Rev. Stat. Ann., § 13-3911 et seq.
Cal. Penal Code § 1523 et seq.
Ind. Code Ann., 35-33-5-7 et seq.
Md. Ann. Code 1957, Art. 27, § 551
Mich. Comp. Laws Ann., 780.651 et seq.
Mo. Rev. Stat., 542.010 et seq.
N.C. Gen. Stat. 1943, § 15A-241 et seq.

**Searches and Seizures Knock Not Act**
Neb. Rev. Stat. 1943, 29-411

**Seashore Act**
Cal. Public Resources Code §§ 5001.5, 5001.6

**Seasonal Farm Labor Act**
N.J. Stat. Ann.34:9A-1 et seq.
Pa. Purdon's Stat., Title 43, § 1301.101 et seq.

**Seasonal Labor Wages Law**
Cal. Labor Code § 250 et seq.

**Seastrand-Robbins Health Insurance Guaranty Association Act**
Cal. Insurance Code § 1066 et seq.

**Seat Belt Act**
Cal. Vehicle Code 1959, § 27300 et seq.
Ill. Rev. Stat. 1991, Ch. 95 1/2, § 12-603.1
Ind. Code Ann., 9-8-7-1 et seq.
N.J. Stat. Ann., 39:3-76.2e et seq.
N.M. Stat. Ann., 66-7-368 et seq.
N.Y. Vehicle and Traffic Law 1959 (Consol. Laws Ch. 71) § 1229c
Okla. Stat. Ann., Title 47, § 12-416 et seq.
Wis. Stat. Ann., 347.48

**Seat Belt Mandatory Use Law**
Miss. Code Ann. 1972, § 63-2-1 et seq.

**Seat Belt Safety Act**
Del. Code of 1974, Title 21, § 4801 et seq.

**Seat Belt Usage Act (Motor Vehicle)**
Utah Code Ann. 1953, 41-6-181

**Seat of Government Act**
Ill. Rev. Stat. 1991, Ch. 123, § 0.01 et seq.

**Seat of Government Act (Emergency)**
Ill. Rev. Stat. 1991, Ch. 123, § 6.9 et seq.

**Seat of State Government Act (Emergency)**
Neb. Rev. Stat. 1943, 72-701.D1

**Seatbelt Use Act**
Mont. Code Ann., 61-13-101 et seq.

**Seated Lands Act (Delinquent Taxes)**
Pa. Purdon's Stat., Title 72, § 5971a et seq.

**Seating and Improvement Bill**
Ky. Acts 1823-24, Ch. 709

**Seawall and Roads Act**
Ala. Local Acts 1931, p. 203

**Seawall Assessment Act (Cape Coral)**
Fla. Special Laws 1976, Ch. 76-342

**Sebring Airport Authority Act**
Fla. Special Laws 1967, Ch. 67-2070

**Second Amendment to the Building Code for the District of Columbia**
D.C. Law 1977 No. 2-18

**Second and First Class Cities and Villages Combined Improvements**
Neb. Rev. Stat. 1943, 19-2408 et seq.

**Second and First Class Cities and Villages Zoning Act**
Neb. Rev. Stat. 1973, 19-901 et seq.

**Second and First Class County Property Tax Relief Act**
Pa. Purdon's Stat., Title 72, § 4749.1 et seq.

**Second and Subsequent Offense Act**
Okla. Stat. Ann., Title 21, § 51 et seq.

**Second Avenue "El" Demolition Law**
N.Y. Laws 1942, Ch. 580

**Second Bond Issue Act**
Ill. Rev. Stat. 1957, Ch. 121, § 281a et seq.

**Second Budget Adjustment Act**
Vt. Acts 1979, No. 13
Vt. Acts 1981, No. 4

**Second Budget Adjustment Act for Fiscal Year 1985**
Vt. Acts 1985, No. 5

**Second Century Environmental Protection Act**
S.D. Laws 1992, Ch. 254

**Second Class A City Act**
Pa. Purdon's Stat., Title 53, § 30101 et seq.

**Second Class A City Permanent Registration Act**
Pa. Purdon's Stat., Title 25, § 951-1 et seq.

**Second Class A City Single Tax Collection Act**
Pa. Purdon's Stat., Title 53, § 30781 et seq.

**Second Class Cities Act**
Kan. Stat. Ann., 14-101 et seq.
N.Y. Consol. Laws Ch. 53
Pa. Purdon's Stat., Title 53, § 22101 et seq.
Wash. Rev. Code Ann., 35.23.010 et seq.

**Second Class Cities Sanitary Officers' Pension Act**
Ind. Code Ann., 18-6-25-1 et seq.

**Second Class City Building Code**
Pa. Purdon's Stat., Title 53, § 25081 et seq.

**Second Class City Civil Service Act**
Pa. Purdon's Stat., Title 53, § 23431 et seq.

**Second Class City Enabling Act**
Pa. Purdon's Stat., Title 53, § 25651 et seq.

**Second Class City Park Act**
Ind. Code Ann., 36-10-7-1 et seq.

**Second Class City Pension Fund Act**
Pa. Purdon's Stat., Title 53, § 23561 et seq.

**Second Class City Permanent Registration Act**
Pa. Purdon's Stat., Title 25, § 951-1 et seq.

**Second Class City Treasurer's Sale and Collection Act**
Pa. Purdon's Stat., Title 53, § 27101 et seq.

**Second Class City Zoning Act**
Pa. Purdon's Stat., Title 53, § 25651 et seq.

**Second Class Counties Magisterial Districts Act**
Pa. Purdon's Stat., Title 42, § 1401 et seq.

**Second Class County Authority Act**
Pa. Purdon's Stat., Title 16, § 12601 et seq.

**Second Class County Code**
Pa. Purdon's Stat., Title 16, § 3101 et seq.

**Second Class County Jury Selection Act**
Pa. Purdon's Stat., Title 17, § 1301 et seq.

**Second Class County Port Authority Act**
Pa. Purdon's Stat., Title 55, § 551 et seq.

**Second Class County Prison Board Act**
Pa. Purdon's Stat., Title 61, § 407.1 et seq.

**Second Class County Prothonotary Fee Act**
Pa. 1982 Pamph. Laws 303, No. 85

**Second Class County Tax Assessment Act**
Pa. Purdon's Stat., Title 72, § 5452.1 et seq.

**Second Class Township Code**
Pa. Purdon's Stat., Title 53, § 65101 et seq.

**Second Class Township Zoning Enabling Act**
Pa. Purdon's Stat., Title 53, § 10101 et seq.

**Second Conviction Statute (Intoxicating Liquors)**
Miss. Code Ann. 1972, § 97-31-27

**Second Decontrol Act of 1947**
July 15, 1947, Ch. 248, 61 Stat. 321, 50 U.S. Code Appx. § 645
June 4, 1948, Ch. 419, 62 Stat. 342, 50 U.S. Code Appx. § 645

**Second Defense Aid Supplemental Appropriation Act of 1942**
March 5, 1942, Ch. 141, 56 Stat. 130, 22 U.S. Code § 412 nt.

**Second Deficiency Appropriation Act**
Nov. 8, 1984, P.L. 98-620, 24 U.S. Code §§ 168, 176

**Second Deficiency Appropriation Act of 1938**
June 25, 1938, Ch. 681, 52 Stat. 1114, 42 U.S. Code § 1406a; 46 U.S. Code § 1111a

**Second Deficiency Appropriation Act of 1939**
May 2, 1939, Ch. 107, 53 Stat. 626, 21 U.S. Code § 376 nt.

**Second Deficiency Appropriation Act of 1940**
June 27, 1940, Ch. 437, 54 Stat. 628, 7 U.S. Code § 1504a; 21 U.S. Code § 46a
June 26, 1943, Ch. 145, 57 Stat. 180, See 3 U.S. Code § 107; 12 U.S. Code §§ 1439a, 1463 nt.; 29 U.S. Code § 48 to 48g nt.; 31 U.S. Code § 42 nt.; 36 U.S. Code § 121a; 49 U.S. Code § 305a

**Second Deficiency Appropriation Act of 1941**
July 3, 1941, Ch. 273, 55 Stat. 541

**Second Deficiency Appropriation Act of 1942**
July 2, 1942, Ch. 476, 56 Stat. 597, 7 U.S. Code §§ 174, 175

**Second Deficiency Appropriation Act of 1943**
July 12, 1943, Ch. 229, 57 Stat. 537, 42 U.S. Code § 1523 nt.

**Second Deficiency Appropriation Act of 1944**
June 28, 1944, Ch. 304, 58 Stat. 597, 31 U.S. Code § 18 nt.; 42 U.S. Code § 1523 nt.

**Second Deficiency Appropriation Act of 1945**
July 5, 1945, Ch. 271, 59 Stat. 412, 7 U.S. Code §§ 174, 176; 42 U.S. Code § 1523 nt.

**Second Deficiency Appropriation Act of 1946**
May 18, 1946, Ch. 263, 60 Stat. 185, 40 U.S. Code § 164a

**Second Deficiency Appropriation Act of 1947**
May 26, 1947, Ch. 82, 61 Stat. 106, 15 U.S. Code § 713a-4 nt.; 31 U.S. Code § 694

**Second Deficiency Appropriation Act of 1948**

June 25, 1948, Ch. 658, 62 Stat. 1027, 50 U.S. Code Appx. § 1193 nt.

**Second Deficiency Appropriation Act of 1949**

June 23, 1949, Ch. 236, 63 Stat. 231

**Second Degree Assault Act**

N.Y. Penal Law 1965 (Consol. Laws Ch. 40) § 120.05

**Second Hand Dealers Act**

Mich. Comp. Laws Ann., 445.401 et seq.

**Second-Hand Dealers and Secondary Metals Recyclers**

Fla. Stat. Ann., 538.03 et seq.

**Second-Hand Watch Act**

Ill. Rev. Stat. 1991, Ch. 121 1/2, § 191.1 et seq.

**Second Horizontal Property Regime Regulation Extension Act**

D.C. Laws 1975 No. 1-40

**Second Independent Offices Appropriation Act of 1954**

July 27, 1953, Ch. 241, 67 Stat. 195 (See 38 U.S. Code § 5011)

**Second Injury Fund Act**

S.C. Code Ann. 1976, § 42-7-310 et seq.

**Second Injury Fund Act (Workers' Compensation)**

Del. Code of 1974, Title 19, § 2327

Iowa Code Ann., 85.63 et seq.

Mich. Comp. Laws 1948, 412.8a

Mo. Rev. Stat., 287.220

N.C. Gen. Stat. 1943, § 97-35

N.Y. Worker's Compensation Law (Consol. Laws Ch. 67) § 15, Subd. 8

Tenn. Code Ann., 50-6-208

Tex. Rev. Civ. Stat., Art. 8308-2.14

Wash. Rev. Code Ann., 51.16.120

**Second Liberty Bond Act**

Sept. 24, 1917, Ch. 56, 40 Stat. 288, 31 U.S. Code §§ 745, 747, 752 to 754b, 757, 757b to 757e, 758, 760, 764 to 766, 769, 771, 773, 774, 801

June 17, 1930, Ch. 512, 46 Stat. 775, 31 U.S. Code § 754

May 26, 1938, Ch. 285, 52 Stat. 447, 31 U.S. Code §§ 752, 757b

March 28, 1942, Ch. 205, 56 Stat. 189, 31 U.S. Code §§ 754a, 754b, 757b

April 12, 1943, Ch. 52, 57 Stat. 63, 31 U.S. Code §§ 757b, 757c

June 9, 1944, Ch. 240, 58 Stat. 272, 31 U.S. Code § 757b

April 3, 1945, Ch. 51, 59 Stat. 47, 31 U.S. Code §§ 757b to 757e

June 26, 1946, Ch. 501, 60 Stat. 316, 31 U.S. Code § 757b, 757b nt.

Aug. 27, 1949, Ch. 517, 63 Stat. 668, 31 U.S. Code § 771

March 26, 1951, Ch. 19, 65 Stat. 26, 31 U.S. Code § 757c

Aug. 28, 1954, Ch. 1037, 68 Stat. 895, 31 U.S. Code § 757b

June 1, 1955, Ch. 119, 69 Stat. 82, 31 U.S. Code § 760

July 9, 1956, Ch. 536, 70 Stat. 519, 31 U.S. Code § 757b

April 20, 1957, P.L. 85-17, 71 Stat. 15, 31 U.S. Code § 757c

Sept. 2, 1958, P.L. 85-912, 72 Stat. 1758, 31 U.S. Code § 757b

June 30, 1959, P.L. 86-74, 73 Stat. 156, 31 U.S. Code § 757b

Sept. 22, 1959, P.L. 86-346, 73 Stat. 621, 31 U.S. Code §§ 747 nt., 753, 754, 757c, 757c-1

Nov. 13, 1966, P.L. 89-809, 80 Stat. 1590, 31 U.S. Code §§ 757f, 766

June 30, 1967, P.L. 90-39, 81 Stat. 99, 31 U.S. Code §§ 753, 757b , 757b-1, 757b-2

Jan. 2, 1968, P.L. 90-240, 81 Stat. 778, 31 U.S. Code § 757c-3

Oct. 17, 1968, P.L. 90-595, 82 Stat. 1155, 31 U.S. Code § 757c

April 7, 1969, P.L. 91-8, 83 Stat. 7, 31 U.S. Code § 757b

Dec. 1, 1969, P.L. 91-130, 83 Stat. 272, 31 U.S. Code § 757c

June 30, 1970, P.L. 91-301, 84 Stat. 368, 31 U.S. Code § 757b

Aug. 24, 1970, P.L. 91-388, 84 Stat. 830, 31 U.S. Code § 757c

July 1, 1973, P.L. 93-53, 87 Stat. 135, 31 U.S. Code §§ 752, 757c

Oct. 4, 1977, P.L. 95-120, 31 U.S. Code §§ 757b nt., 752

Aug. 3, 1978, P.L. 95-333, 31 U.S. Code §§ 752, 757b nt.

April 2, 1979, P.L. 96-5, 31 U.S. Code §§ 752, 757b nt., 757c nt.

Sept. 29, 1979, P.L. 96-78, 31 U.S. Code § 757b nt.

June 28, 1980, P.L. 96-286, 31 U.S. Code § 757b nt.

**Second Mortgage Loan Act**

Ohio Rev. Code 1953, 1321.51 et seq.

**Second Offender Act**

Conn. Gen. Stat. Ann., §§ 53a-40, 54-118a

Fla. Stat. Ann., 775.084

Ga. Code Ann., 17-10-7

Mich. Comp. Laws Ann., 769.10

Minn. Stat. 1978, 609.155

Mo. Rev. Stat., 558.019

N.Y. Penal Law 1965 (Consol. Laws, Ch. 40) § 70.10

Pa. Cons. Stat., Title 18, § 1103 et seq.

Tex. Penal Code, §§ 12.42, 12.43

**Second Omnibus Transportation Act**

Cal. Government Code § 14524.15

Cal. Statutes 1991, Ch. 928

**Second Railroad Settlement Act**

N.J. Stat. Ann.App. A:4-7.1 to App. A:4-7.11, App. A:4-7.14 to App. A:4-7.16

**Second Revenue Act of 1940**

Oct. 8, 1940, Ch. 757, 54 Stat. 947 (See 26 U.S. Code §§ 11, 312, 852, 855, 874, 882, 1551, 6401, 6402, 6404, 6407, 6501, 6502, 7423) 45 U.S. Code § 228c-1; 46 U.S. Code § 1155a

Feb. 11, 1942, Ch. 69, 56 Stat. 88 (See 38 U.S. Code §§ 701 to 721)

**Second Revisory Act (1989)1986-1989**

Ill. Laws 1986, P.A. 84-1438

Ill. Laws 1989, P.A. 86-820

Ill. Laws 1989, P.A. 87-828

**Second School District Validating Act**

Cal. Statutes 1957, Ch. 137, p. 731

**Second Skip Election Act**

Ind. Code 1982, 3-2-7-1 et seq.

**Second Supplemental Appropriation Act of 1948**

July 31, 1947, Ch. 414, 61 Stat. 695

**Second Supplemental Appropriation Act of 1950**

Oct. 28, 1949, Ch. 783, 63 Stat. 973, 2 U.S. Code §§ 60f, 60f nt.

**Second Supplemental Appropriation Act of 1951**

Jan. 6, 1951, Ch. 1213, 64 Stat. 1223, 2 U.S. Code § 36a

**Second Supplemental Appropriation Act of 1952**

Nov. 1, 1951, Ch. 665, 65 Stat. 760, U.S. Code Appx. § 1217a

**Second Supplemental Appropriation Act of 1953**

March 28, 1953, Ch. 12, 67 Stat. 9

**Second Supplemental Appropriation Act of 1955**

April 22, 1955, Ch. 26, 69 Stat. 28, 40 U.S. Code § 175 nt.

**Second Supplemental Appropriation Act of 1956**

May 19, 1956, Ch. 313, 70 Stat. 161, 2 U.S. Code §§ 60f, 61c nt.; 12 U.S. Code §§ 1701g-5, 1749d nt.; 15 U.S. Code § 713a-10; 16 U.S. Code § 669g-1 nt.; 46 U.S. Code § 1241b

**Second Supplemental Appropriation Act of 1957**

July 31, 1956, Ch. 805, 70 Stat. 763

**Second Supplemental Appropriation Act of 1958**

March 28, 1958, P.L. 85-352, 72 Stat. 50, 41 U.S. Code § 6b

**Second Supplemental Appropriation Act of 1959**

May 20, 1959, P.L. 86-30, 73 Stat. 33, 2 U.S. Code § 61i; 7 U.S. Code § 1704 nt.; 15 U.S. Code § 713a-10

**Second Supplemental Appropriation Act of 1960**

April 13, 1960, P.L. 86-424, 74 Stat. 42, 15 U.S. Code § 713a-10

**Second Supplemental Appropriation Act of 1961**

Sept. 8, 1960, P.L. 86-722, 74 Stat. 828, 25 U.S. Code § 70s

**Second Supplemental Appropriation Act of 1962**

July 25, 1962, P.L. 87-545, 76 Stat. 209, 2 U.S. Code § 60f nt.; 15 U.S. Code § 633 nt.; 40 U.S. Code 462 nt.

**Second Supplemental Appropriation Act of 1965**

April 30, 1965, P.L. 89-16, 79 Stat. 81, 15 U.S. Code § 63 nt.; 42 U.S . Code § 2881

**Second Supplemental Appropriation Act of 1966**

May 13, 1966, P.L. 89-426, 80 Stat. 141

**Second Supplemental Appropriation Act of 1967**

May 29, 1967, P.L. 90-21, 81 Stat. 30, 2 U.S. Code §§ 46a, 46d-3; 20 U.S. Code § 758; 40 U.S. Code § 756 nt.

**Second Supplemental Appropriation Act of 1968**

July 9, 1968, P.L. 90-392, 82 Stat. 307

**Second Supplemental Appropriation Act of 1969**

July 22, 1969, P.L. 91-47, 83 Stat. 49, 5 U.S. Code § 3101 nt.; 12 U.S . Code §§ 1715z nt., 1715z-1 nt., 1749 nt.

**Second Supplemental Appropriation Act of 1970**

July 6, 1970, P.L. 91-305, 84 Stat. 376

**Second Supplemental Appropriation Act to the General Appropriation Act of 1988**

Pa. 1991 Pamph. Laws, No. 3A

**Second Supplemental Appropriation Act, 1984**

Aug. 22, 1984, P.L. 98-396, 5 U.S. Code § 8340 nt.; 20 U.S. Code §§ 241ee, 645; 49 U.S. Code Appx. § 1604

**Second Supplemental Appropriation Acts, 1948-1984**

Pa. 1979 Pamph. Laws No. 595, No. 2-A

**Second Supplemental Appropriations Act of 1976**

June 1, 1976, P.L. 94-303, 2 U.S. Code § 61d-2

May 21, 1978, P.L. 95-283, 15 U.S. Code § 77c

Oct. 1, 1988, P.L. 100-458, 2 U.S. Code § 61f-1a

Nov. 5, 1990, P.L. 101-520, 2 U.S. Code §§ 61f-1a nt., 61f-1a

**Second Supplemental Appropriations Act, 1978**

Sept. 16, 1996, P.L. 104-197, 2 U.S. Code § 43d

**Second Supplemental General Appropriation Act**

Pa. 1984 Pamph. Laws 1311, No. 1A

Pa. 1985 Pamph. Laws 565, No. 4A

**Second Supplemental Housing Authorities Act**

Miss. Code Ann. 1972, § 43-33-61 et seq.

**Second Supplemental National Defense Appropriation Act of 1941**

Sept. 9, 1940, Ch. 717, 54 Stat. 884, 40 U.S. Code § 325a

Oct. 8, 1940, Ch. 756, 54 Stat. 968

Oct. 26, 1942, Ch. 629, 56 Stat. 1005, 31 U.S. Code § 665 nt.; 40 U.S. Code §§ 101 nt., 317

**Second Supplemental National Defense Appropriation Act of 1942**
Oct. 28, 1941, Ch. 460, 55 Stat. 745, 22 U.S. Code §§ 421, 422

**Second Supplemental National Defense Appropriation Act of 1943**
Oct. 26, 1942, Ch. 629, 56 Stat. 990, 7 U.S. Code § 171 nt.; 22 U.S. Code § 412 nts.; 31 U.S. Code § 665 nt.; 40 U.S. Code §§ 101 nt., 317
Oct. 26, 1949, Ch. 757, 63 Stat. 930, 40 U.S. Code § 317

**Second Supplemental Surplus Appropriation Rescission Act of 1946**
May 27, 1946, Ch. 271, 60 Stat. 221
Aug. 1, 1956, Ch. 473, 70 Stat. 884

**Second Unification Act**
Kan. Stat. Ann., 72-6764 et seq.

**Second Urgent Deficiency Appropriation Act of 1946**
March 28, 1946, Ch. 114, 60 Stat. 82

**Second Urgent Deficiency Appropriation Act of 1947**
June 27, 1947, Ch. 156, 61 Stat. 183
July 3, 1947, Ch. 206, 61 Stat. 243

**Second Urgent Deficiency Appropriation Act of 1955**
May 27, 1955, Ch. 107, 69 Stat. 68

**Second Urgent Deficiency Appropriation Act of 1957**
April 16, 1957, P.L. 85-15, 71 Stat. 11, 15 U.S. Code § 633 nt.

**Second Validating Act**
Cal. Statutes 1949, Ch. 782, p. 1511
Cal. Statutes 1950, 1st Ex. Sess., Ch. 72, p. 541
Cal. Statutes 1951, Ch. 1445, p. 3404
Cal. Statutes 1953, Ch. 1886, p. 3680
Cal. Statutes 1955, Ch. 1572, p. 2851
Cal. Statutes 1956, 1st Ex. Sess., Ch. 16, p. 307
Cal. Statutes 1957, Ch. 134, p. 724
Cal. Statutes 1958, 1st Ex. Sess., Ch. 20, p. 212
Cal. Statutes 1959, Ch. 31, p. 1980
Cal. Statutes 1960, 1st Ex. Sess., Ch. 10
Cal. Statutes 1961, Ch. 985
Cal. Statutes 1962, 1st Ex. Sess., Ch. 15, p. 168
Cal. Statutes 1963, Ch. 1029, p. 2307
Cal. Statutes 1964, 1st Ex Sess., Ch. 12, p. 119
Cal. Statutes 1965, Ch. 752, p. 2170
Cal. Statutes 1966, 1st Ex. Sess., Ch. 2
Cal. Statutes 1970, Ch. 365, p. 776
Cal. Statutes 1971, Ch. 564, p. 1079
Cal. Statutes 1972, Ch. 314, p. 583
Cal. Statutes 1974, Ch. 689
Cal. Statutes 1975, Ch. 680
Cal. Statutes 1976, Ch. 724
Cal. Statutes 1977, Ch. 613
Cal. Statutes 1978, Ch. 666
Cal. Statutes 1981, Ch. 568
Cal. Statutes 1983, Ch. 648
Cal. Statutes 1984, Ch. 691
Cal. Statutes 1985, Ch. 594
Cal. Statutes 1986, Ch. 580
Cal. Statutes 1988, Ch. 756
Cal. Statutes 1990, Ch. 810
Cal. Statutes 1991, Chs. 398, 441, 619

**Second Validating Act (General)**
Cal. Statutes 1946, 2nd Ex. Sess., Ch. 6, p. 336

**Second Validating Act (Public Bodies)**
Cal. Statutes 1947, Ch. 492, p. 1473

**Second Validating Act of 1992**
Cal. Statutes 1992, Ch. 568

**Second Validating Act of 1995**
Cal. Statutes 1995, Ch. 851

**Second Validating Act of 1996**
Cal. Statutes 1996, Ch. 479

**Second Validating Act of 1997**
Cal. Statutes 1997, Ch. 485

**Second War Powers Act of 1942**
March 27, 1942, Ch. 199, 56 Stat. 176, 12 U.S. Code § 355; 49 U.S. Code §§ 304, 310a, 911; 50 U.S. Code Appx. §§ 643 to 643c, 645 to 645b, 1152
June 30, 1942, Ch. 184, 61 Stat. 214, 50 U.S. Code Appx. § 645
Dec. 20, 1944, Ch. 614, 58 Stat. 827, 50 U.S. Code Appx. §§ 645, 1152
Dec. 28, 1945, Ch. 590, 59 Stat. 658, 50 U.S. Code Appx. § 645
June 29, 1946, Ch. 526, 60 Stat. 345, 50 U.S. Code Appx. §§ 645, 645b
Aug. 7, 1946, Ch. 770, 60 Stat. 868, 50 U.S. Code Appx. § 1152
March 31, 1947, Ch. 29, 61 Stat. 34, 50 U.S. Code Appx. § 645
July 15, 1947, Ch. 248, 61 Stat. 322, 50 U.S. Code Appx. § 645
Feb. 28, 1948, Ch. 85, 62 Stat. 58, 50 U.S. Code Appx. § 645
June 30, 1949, Ch. 289, 63 Stat. 404, 50 U.S. Code Appx. § 645
Oct. 15, 1970, P.L. 91-452, 84 Stat. 931, 50 U.S. Code Appx. § 643a

**Second Washington Airport Act**
Aug. 23, 1958, P.L. 85-726, 72 Stat. 807

**Second 1978, 1980 Combining Revisory Act**
Ill. Laws 1978, P.A. 80-1494
Ill. Laws 1980, P.A. 81-1550, Art. 1

**Second 1980 General Revisory Act**
Ill. Laws 1980, P.A. 81-1550, Art. 2

**Second 1982, 1984 Revisory Act**
Ill. Laws 1982, P.A. 82-1057
Ill. Laws 1984, P.A. 83-1528

**Secondary and Elementary Private Education Authorization Act**
Nev. Rev. Stat. 1979 Reprint, 394.201 et seq.

**Secondary and Elementary School Dropout Prevention Act**
Cal. Education Code 1976, § 54660 et seq.

**Secondary and Elementary School Reform Act**
N.C. Public Laws 1984, Ch. 1103

**Secondary and Elementary School Self Insurance Act**
Ark. Code Ann. 1987, 6-20-1501 et seq.

**Secondary and Feeder Roads Act**
Ill. Rev. Stat. 1951, Ch. 121, § 288h et seq.

**Secondary Boycott Act**
Cal. Labor Code § 1154.5
Ida. Code 1947, 44-801 et seq.
Minn. Stat. Ann., 179.41 et seq.
Ore. Laws 1953, Ch. 723, § 17

**Secondary Education Act (Nonpublic)**
N.J. Stat. Ann., 18A:58-59 et seq.
Pa. Purdon's Stat., Title 24, § 5601 et seq.

**Secondary Education Opportunity Program Act**
N.Y. Education Law 1947, (Consol. Laws Ch. 16) § 559 et seq.

**Secondary Evidence Rule**
Cal. Evidence Code § 1521

**Secondary Facilities Grant Act (Cooperative)**
Minn. Stat. Ann., 124.491 et seq.

**Secondary Highway Act**
Cal. Statutes 1951, Ch. 1321, p. 3207
Cal. Streets and Highways Code § 2200 et seq.

**Secondary Highway Routes Act**
Wash. Rev. Code 1951, 47.20.010 et seq.

**Secondary Injury Law**
N.Y. Workers' Compensation Law (Consol. Laws Ch. 67) § 15, Subd. 8

**Secondary Mortgage and Market Corporation Act**
Ga. Code Ann., 8-3-190 et seq.

**Secondary Mortgage Loan Act**
Md. Ann. Code 1974, Art. CL, § 12-401 et seq.
Md. Ann. Code 1974, Art. FI, § 12-301 et seq.
N.J. Stat. Ann., 17:11A-34 et seq.
Pa. Purdon's Stat., Title 7, § 6601 et seq.
R.I. Gen. Laws 1956, 19-25.2-1 et seq.

**Secondary Mortgage Loan Act-Credit Provisions**
Md. Ann. Code 1974, Art. CL, § 12-401 et seq.

**Secondary Mortgage Loan Act-Licensing Provisions**
Md. Ann. Code 1974, Art. FI, § 12-301 et seq.

**Secondary Mortgage Loans Act**
Mich. Comp. Laws Ann., 493.51 to 493.80
Tex. Rev. Civ. Stat., Art. 5069-5.01 et seq.

**Secondary Mortgage Market Enhancement Act of 1984**
Oct. 3, 1984, P.L. 98-440, 98 Stat. 1689, 12 U.S. Code §§ 24, 1423, 1423a, 1451, 1454, 1455, 1464, 1701 nt., 1717, 1723a, 1723c, 1757; 15 U.S. Code §§ 77r-1, 78c, 78g, 78h, 78k

**Secondary Mortgage Market Enhancement Act of 1994**
Sept. 23, 1994, P.L. 103-325, 15 U.S. Code § 77r-1

**Secondary Road Act**
Va. Code 1950, § 33.1-67 et seq.

**Secondary Road Assessment District Law**
Iowa Code Ann., 311.1 et seq.

**Secondary Road Bond Act**
N.C. Laws 1949, Ch. 1250

**Secondary School Pupils Act (Kansas Challenge to)**
Kan. Stat. Ann., 72-11a01 et seq.

**Secondary Schools Basic Skills Demonstration Act of 1988**
April 8, 1988, P.L. 100-297, 102 Stat. 270, 20 U.S. Code § 3261 et seq.
Aug. 23, 1988, P.L. 100-418, 102 Stat. 1496, 20 U.S. Code § 5061
Nov. 16, 1990, P.L. 101-600, 20 U.S. Code § 3263
Oct. 20, 1994, P.L. 103-382, 20 U.S. Code §§ 5061 to 5066

**Secondary Security Deed Act**
Ga. Code Ann., 7-4-30 et seq.

**Secondary Strikes and Boycotts Act**
Tex. Rev. Civ. Stat., Art. 5154f

**Secondhand Precious Metal Object Dealers and Pawnbrokers Act**
Md. Ann. Code 1974, Art. BR, § 12-601 et seq.

**Secondhand Watch Sales Act**
Cal. Business and Professions Code § 21500 et seq.

**Secrecy Act**
See Antisecrecy Act

**Secrecy Act (Local Legislative Meetings)**
Cal. Government Code, § 54950 et seq.

**Secrecy of Military Information Act**
Jan. 26, 1942, Ch. 19, 56 Stat. 19 (See 22 U.S. Code § 1934)

**Secret Ballot Act**
Also See Ga. Code Ann., 21-2-322, 21-2-350, 21-2-358
Ga. Code 1933, 34-1206, 34-1220, 34-1224
Ky. Rev. Stat. 1971, 118.025
R.I. Gen. Laws 1956, 17-19-1 et seq.

**Secret Marriage Act**
Mich. Comp. Laws Ann., 551.201 et seq.

**Secret Meeting Law**
Cal. Government Code § 54950 et seq.

**Secret Meeting Law (State Agencies)**
Cal. Government Code § 11120 et seq.

**Secret Primary Act**
Mich. Comp. Laws Ann., 168.576, 168.579

**Secret Primary Election Act**
Mich. Comp. Laws Ann., 168.531 et seq.

**Secret Societies Prohibition Act**
N.C. Gen. 1943, § 14-12.2 et seq.

**Secret Venire Act (Jefferson County)**
Ala. Code 1958, Title 62, § 196 et seq.

**Secretary of Education Act**
Del. Laws Vol. 71, Ch. 8

**Secretary of State Act**
Ill. Rev. Stat. 1991, Ch. 124, § 0.01 et seq.

**Secretary of State Buildings in Cook County Act**
Ill. Rev. Stat. 1991, Ch. 124, § 11.9 et seq.

**Secretary of State Merit Employment Code**
Ill. Rev. Stat. 1991, Ch. 124, § 101 et seq.

**Secretary of State Uniform Commercial Code Liability Act**
Ill. Rev. Stat. 1991, Ch. 124, §§ 13.9, 14

**Secrets Act**
See Uniform Trade Secrets Act

**Sector Development Act (Biotechnology)**
Ill. Comp. Stat. 1992, Ch. 20, § 230/1

**Secular Education Act (Nonpublic Schools)**
Conn. Gen. Stat. Ann., § 10-281a et seq.

**Secular Education Services Law**
La. Rev. Stat. Ann., 17:1321 et seq.

**Secure Residential Youth Care Facility Licensing Act**
Ill. Comp. Stat. 1992, Ch. 730, § 175/45-1

**Secured Creditors' Dividends in Liquidation Proceedings Act**
Ind. Code Ann., 30-2-7-1 et seq.
S.D. Codified Laws 1967, 54.10-1 et seq.
Wis. Stat. Ann., 128.25

**Secured Creditors Participation in Insolvent Estates Act**
N.Y. Debtor and Creditor Law (Consol. Laws Ch. 12) § 30 et seq.

**Secured Debt Tax Act**
Mich. Comp. Laws Ann., 205.131 et seq.
N.Y. Laws 1911, Ch. 802

**Secured Debts Act**
Kan. Stat. Ann., 79-3121 et seq.

**Secured Interest Act (Farm Products)**
N.M. Stat. Ann., 56-13-1 et seq.

**Securities Act**
See also Uniform Securities Act
Ariz. Rev. Stat. Ann., § 44-1801 et seq.
Cal. Corporations Code § 25000 et seq.
Fla. Stat. 1957, 517.011 et seq.
Ga. Code Ann., 10-5-1 et seq.
Ill. Rev. Stat. 1991, Ch. 121 1/2, § 137.1 et seq.
La. Rev. Stat. Ann., 51:701 et seq.
N.D. Cent. Code, 10-04-01 et seq.
Ohio Rev. Code 1953, 1707.01 et seq.
Okla. Stat. Ann., Title 71, § 1 et seq.
Pa. Purdon's Stat., Title 70, § 31 et seq.
S.D. Codified Laws 1967, 47-31-1 et seq.
Tenn. Code Ann., 48-2-101 et seq.
Tex. Rev. Civ. Stat., Art. 581-1 et seq.

**Securities Act (Mining)**
Wash. Laws 1937, Ch. 178

**Securities Act (Municipal)**
Tenn. Code Ann. 1955 Superseded Vols., 9-1401 et seq.

**Securities Act (Revised)**
Me. Rev. Stat. Ann. 1964, Title 32, § 10101 et seq.

**Securities Act (Sale of)**
Ark. Code Ann. 1987, 23-42-507 et seq.
Mass. Gen. Laws 1984, 110A:1 et seq.

**Securities Act Amendments of 1964**
Aug. 20, 1964, P.L. 88-467, 78 Stat. 565, 15 U.S. Code §§ 77d, 78c, 78l to 78o, 78o-3, 78p, 78t, 78w, 78ff

**Securities Act of Montana, 1961**
Mont. Code Ann., 30-10-101 et seq.

**Securities Act of 1933**
May 27, 1933, Ch. 38, 48 Stat. 74, 15 U.S. Code §§ 77a to 77aa
Aug. 22, 1940, Ch. 686, 54 Stat. 857, 15 U.S. Code § 77h
May 15, 1945, Ch. 122, 59 Stat. 167, 15 U.S. Code § 77c
Aug. 10, 1954, Ch. 677, 68 Stat. 683, 15 U.S. Code § 77b
Aug. 21, 1958, P.L. 85-699, 72 Stat. 694, 15 U.S. Code § 77c
Aug. 28, 1958, P.L. 85-791, 72 Stat. 945, 15 U.S. Code § 77i
June 25, 1959, P.L. 86-70, 73 Stat. 143, 15 U.S. Code § 77b
July 12, 1960, P.L. 86-624, 74 Stat. 412, 15 U.S. Code § 77b
Oct. 22, 1965, P.L. 89-289, 79 Stat. 1051, 15 U.S. Code § 77f
Aug. 10, 1970, P.L. 91-373, 84 Stat. 718, 15 U.S. Code § 77c
Oct. 15, 1970, P.L. 91-452, 84 Stat. 929, 15 U.S. Code § 77v
Dec. 14, 1970, P.L. 91-547, 84 Stat. 1433, 15 U.S. Code §§ 77b, 77c
Dec. 19, 1970, P.L. 91-565, 84 Stat. 1480, 15 U.S. Code § 77c
Dec. 22, 1970, P.L. 91-567, 84 Stat. 1498, 15 U.S. Code § 77c
June 4, 1975, P.L. 94-29, 89 Stat. 97, 15 U.S. Code §§ 78a to 78c
Nov. 6, 1978, P.L. 95-598, 15 U.S. Code § 77c
Sept. 20, 1982, P.L. 97-261, 15 U.S. Code § 77c
Oct. 15, 1990, P.L. 101-429, 15 U.S. Code §§ 77g, 77h-1, 77t
Sept. 23, 1994, P.L. 103-325, 15 U.S. Code § 77c
Dec. 8, 1995, P.L. 104-62, 15 U.S. Code § 77c
Dec. 22, 1995, P.L. 104-67, 15 U.S. Code §§ 77k, 77i, 77t, 77z-1, 77z-2
Oct. 11, 1996, P.L. 104-290, 15 U.S. Code §§ 77b, 77c, 77f, 77r, 77z-3
Nov. 3, 1998, P.L. 105-353, 15 U.S. Code §§ 77b, 77k, 77p, 77r, 77v, 77z-1 to 77z-3, 77aa

**Securities Acts Amendments of 1990**
Nov. 15, 1990, P.L. 101-550, 15 U.S. Code § 78a nt.

**Securities and Exchange Act**
Fla. Stat. Ann., 517.011 et seq.

**Securities and Exchange Commission Authorization Act of 1987**
Dec. 4, 1987, P.L. 100-181, 15 U.S. Code §§ 77b et seq., 77ccc, 78a nt., 78c, 78d to 78d-2, 78f, 78k-1, 78l, 78m, 78o, 78o-4, 78o-5, 78q, 78q-1, 78u, 78w, 78aa, 78bb, 78jj, 78kk, 78ll, 78lll, 79h, 79r, 79x, 79y, 79z-4, 80a-2 et seq., 80b-2 et seq.

**Securities and Exchange Commission Authorization Act of 1990**
Nov. 15, 1990, P.L. 101-550, 15 U.S. Code § 78a nt.

**Securities and Exchange Commission Authorization Act of 1996**
Oct. 11, 1996, P.L. 104-290, Title IV, 15 U.S. Code § 78a nt.

**Securities and Investor Protection Act**
Fla. Stat. Ann., 517.011 et seq.

**Securities Approval Act (Municipal)**
Me. Rev. Stat. Ann. 1964, Title 10, § 1061 et seq.

**Securities Broker Licensing Act**
Tex. Rev. Civ. Stat., Art. 581-12 et seq.

**Securities Commission Act**
N.D. Cent. Code, 10-04-01 et seq.

**Securities Depository Act**
Cal. Financial Code § 30000 et seq.

**Securities Enforcement Remedies and Penny Stock Reform Act of 1990**
Oct. 15, 1990, P.L. 101-429, 15 U.S. Code § 78a nt.

**Securities Exchange Act of 1933**

Sept. 23, 1994, P.L. 103-325, 15 U.S. Code §§ 77c, 78c, 78g, 78h , 78k

**Securities Exchange Act of 1934**

June 6, 1934, Ch. 404, 48 Stat. 881, 15 U.S. Code §§ 77b to 77e, 77j, 77k, 77m, 77o, 77s, 78a to 78o, 78o-3, 78p to 78hh

March 17, 1944, Ch. 101, 58 Stat. 117, 15 U.S. Code § 78ee

Aug. 10, 1954, Ch. 667, 68 Stat. 686, 15 U.S. Code §§ 78k, 78l

Aug. 28, 1958, P.L. 85-791, 72 Stat. 945, 15 U.S. Code § 78y

June 25, 1959, P.L. 86-70, 73 Stat. 143, 15 U.S. Code § 78c

July 12, 1960, P.L. 86-619, 74 Stat. 408, 15 U.S. Code § 78d

July 12, 1960, P.L. 86-624, 74 Stat. 412, 15 U.S. Code § 78c

Sept. 13, 1960, P.L. 86-771, 74 Stat. 913, 15 U.S. Code § 78d

Sept. 5, 1961, P.L. 87-196, 75 Stat. 465, 15 U.S. Code § 78s

July 27, 1962, P.L. 87-561, 76 Stat. 247, 15 U.S. Code § 78s

Aug. 14, 1964, P.L. 88-426, 78 Stat. 425, 15 U.S. Code § 78d

Aug. 20, 1964, P.L. 88-467, 78 Stat. 565, 15 U.S. Code §§ 78c, 78l, 78m to 78o, 78o-3, 78p, 78t, 78w, 78ff

July 29, 1968, P.L. 90-437, 82 Stat. 452, 15 U.S. Code § 78g

July 29, 1968, P.L. 90-438, 82 Stat. 453, 15 U.S. Code § 78s

July 29, 1968, P.L. 90-439, 82 Stat. 454, 15 U.S. Code §§ 78l to 78n

Oct. 20, 1969, P.L. 91-94, 83 Stat. 141, 15 U.S. Code § 78s

Aug. 10, 1970, P.L. 91-373, 84 Stat. 718, 15 U.S. Code § 78c

Sept. 25, 1970, P.L. 91-410, 84 Stat. 862, 15 U.S. Code § 78s

Oct. 15, 1970, P.L. 91-452, 84 Stat. 929, 15 U.S. Code § 78u

Oct. 26, 1970, P.L. 91-508, 84 Stat. 1124, 15 U.S. Code § 78g

Dec. 14, 1970, P.L. 91-547, 84 Stat. 1435, 15 U.S. Code §§ 78c, 78l

Dec. 22, 1970, P.L. 91-567, 84 Stat. 1497, 15 U.S. Code §§ 78c, 78m, 78n

Dec. 30, 1970, P.L. 91-598, 84 Stat. 1653, 15 U.S. Code § 78o

Apr 13, 1977, P.L. 95-20, 15 U.S. Code § 78kk

Dec. 19, 1977, P.L. 95-211, 15 U.S. Code § 78kk

Dec. 19, 1977, P.L. 95-213, 15 U.S. Code § 78m et seq.

May 21, 1978, P.L. 95-283, 15 U.S. Code §§ 78c, 78k

Oct. 13, 1982, P.L. 97-303, 15 U.S. Code §§ 78i, 78bb

Aug. 10, 1984, P.L. 98-376, 15 U.S. Code §§ 78c, 78o, 78t, 78u, 78ff

Oct. 3, 1984, P.L. 98-440, 98 Stat. 1689, 15 U.S. Code §§ 78c, 78g, 78h, 78k

Nov. 8, 1984, P.L. 98-620, 15 U.S. Code § 78k-1

Dec. 28, 1985, P.L. 99-222, 15 U.S. Code § 78n

Oct. 28, 1986, P.L. 99-571, 15 U.S. Code §§ 78o, 78o-3, 78o-5, 78q, 78w

Dec. 4, 1987, P.L. 100-181, 15 U.S. Code §§ 78b et seq., 78c et seq., 78kk, 78ll

Feb. 3, 1988, P.L. 100-241, 15 U.S. Code § 78m

Aug. 23, 1988, P.L. 100-418, 102 Stat. 1415, 15 U.S. Code §§ 78m, 78dd-1, 78ff

Nov. 19, 1988, P.L. 100-704, 15 U.S. Code §§ 78c, 78o, 78t-1, 78u 78ff, 78kk

Aug. 9, 1989, P.L. 101-73, 15 U.S. Code §§ 78c, 781, 78o-5

Oct. 15, 1990, P.L. 101-429, 15 U.S. Code §§ 78c, 78o, 78o nt., 78o-3, 78o-4, 78q-1, 78q-2, 78u, 78u-2, 78u-3, 78w, 78cc

Oct. 16, 1990, P.L. 101-432, 15 U.S. Code §§ 78i, 78l, 78m, 78o- 5, 78q, 78q-1, 78y

Nov. 15, 1990, P.L. 101-550, 15 U.S. Code §§ 78c, 78d, 78n, 78n nt., 78o, 78o-5, 78x, 78kk

Dec. 19, 1991, P.L. 102-242, 15 U.S. Code § 78aa-1

Aug. 11, 1993, P.L. 103-68, 15 U.S. Code § 78k

Dec. 17, 1993, P.L. 103-202, 15 U.S. Code §§ 78c, 78f, 78n, 78o, 78o-3, 78o-5, 78s, 78w

Oct. 22, 1994, P.L. 103-389, 15 U.S. Code § 781

Dec. 8, 1995, P.L. 104-62, 15 U.S. Code §§ 78c, 78l

Dec. 22, 1995, P.L. 104-67, 15 U.S. Code §§ 78j-1, 78i, 78t, 78u, 78u-4, 78u-5

Oct. 11, 1996, P.L. 104-290, 15 U.S. Code §§ 78c, 78d, 78g, 78h, 78o, 78q, 78bb, 78ee, 78kk, 78mm
Nov. 3, 1998, P.L. 105-353, 15 U.S. Code §§ 78c, 78d, 78g, 78n, 78o, 78o-4, 78o-5, 78q, 78s, 78t, 78u-4, 78z, 78bb, 78ee, 78kk, 78ll
Nov. 10, 1998, P.L. 105-366, 15 U.S. Code §§ 78dd-1, 78ff

**Securities in Fiduciary Accounts Act**
Ill. Rev. Stat. 1991, Ch. 17, § 2050 et seq.

**Securities Information Reporting Act (Public)**
Colo. Rev. Stat., 11-58-101 et seq.

**Securities, Insider Trading Statute Act**
S.C. Code Ann. 1976, § 38-23-10 et seq.

**Securities Investor Protection Act Amendments of 1978**
May 21, 1978, P.L. 95-283, 15 U.S. Code §§ 77c, 78c, 78k, 78k nt. , 78aaa nt., 78ccc et seq.

**Securities Investor Protection Act of 1970**
Dec. 30, 1970, P.L. 91-598, 84 Stat. 1636, 15 U.S. Code §§ 78o, 78aaa to 78lll
May 21, 1978, P.L. 95-283, 15 U.S. Code §§ 78aaa nt., 78ccc et seq.
Nov. 6, 1978, P.L. 95-598, 15 U.S. Code § 78eee et seq.
Oct. 13, 1982, P.L. 97-303, 15 U.S. Code § 78lll

**Securities Litigation Uniform Standards Act of 1998**
Nov. 3, 1998, P.L. 105-353, 112 Stat. 3227, 15 U.S. Code § 78a nt.

**Securities Ownership by Minors Act**
See Uniform Securities Ownership by Minors Act

**Securities Powers Act (Bank)**
Del. Code of 1974, Title 5, § 101 et seq.

**Securities Refunding Act (Public)**
Colo. Rev. Stat., 11-56-101 et seq.
S.D. Codified Laws 1967, 6-8A-1 et seq.

**Securities Safekeeping Act**
Ill. Rev. Stat. 1991, Ch. 130, §§ 50, 51

**Securities Sales Act**
See Sale of Securities Act

**Securities Transfer Act**
Ill. Rev. Stat. 1991, Ch. 32, § 439.49 et seq.

**Securities Validation Act (Public)**
N.M. Stat. Ann., 6-16-1 et seq.

**Security Act (Campus)**
Ill. Comp. Stat. 1992, Ch. 110, § 12/1
Okla. Stat. Ann., Title 74, § 360.16 et seq.

**Security Act (Convenience Business)**
Fla. Stat. Ann., 812.1701 et seq.

**Security Act (Convenience Store)**
Fla. Stat. Ann., 812.171 et seq.

**Security Act (Employment)**
Utah Code Ann. 1953, 35-4-101 et seq.

**Security Act (Library Materials)**
Miss. Code Ann. 1972, § 39-3-301 et seq.

**Security Act (Milk Producers)**
Pa. Purdon's Stat., Title 31, § 626.1 et seq.

**Security Act (Public Assistance)**
Wash. Rev. Code 1983, 74.04.005 et seq., 74.08.025 et seq.

**Security Agencies and Private Detective Act**
Ga. Code Ann., 43-38-1 et seq.

**Security and Defense Forces Act**
Mont. Rev. Code 1947, 77-1201 et seq.

**Security Assistance Act (Handicapped and Elderly)**
Fla. Stat. Ann., 426.001 et seq.

**Security Corps Act (School)**
P.R. Laws Ann. 1954, Title 18, § 141 et seq.

**Security Deposit Act (Child Support)**
R.I. Gen. Laws 1956, 15-19-1 et seq.

**Security Deposit Act (Landlord and Tenant)**
Colo. Rev. Stat., 38-12-101 et seq.
D.C. Code Ann., § 45-2527
Fla. Stat. 1983, 83.49
N.C. Gen. Stat. 1943, § 42-50 et seq.

**Security Deposit Interest Act**
Ill. Rev. Stat. 1991, Ch. 80, § 120 et seq.

**Security Deposit Return Act**
Ill. Rev. Stat. 1991, Ch. 80, § 100 et seq.

**Security Following Accident Act (Motor Vehicles)**
Cal. Vehicle Code 1959, § 16000 et seq.
N.J. Stat. 39:6A-1 et seq.

**Security for Costs Act**
Ill. Rev. Stat. 1991, Ch. 110, §§ 5-101 et seq,
Wis. Stat. Ann., 814.27 et seq.

**Security for Expenses Act (Corporations)**
Cal. Corporations Code § 800
Colo. Rev. Stat., 7-4-121
N.J. Stat. Ann., 14A:3-6
N.Y. Business Corporations Law (Consol. Laws, Ch. 4) §§ 721, 722, 726
Pa. Cons. Stat., Title 15, § 523 et seq.

**Security for Housing for the Elderly**
R.I. Gen. Laws 1956, 42-66.1-1 et seq.

**Security for Public Deposits Act**
Fla. Stat. 1983, 280.01 et seq.
Okla. Stat. Ann., Title 62, § 72.1 et seq.
Va. Code 1950, § 2:1-359 et seq.

**Security Fund Act (Workers Compensation)**
Pa. Purdon's Stat., Title 77, § 1051 et seq.

**Security Fund Act (Workmen's Compensation)**
N.C. Gen. Stat. 1943, § 97-105 et seq.
Pa. Purdon's Stat., Title 77, § 1051 et seq.

**Security Guard and Private Investigator Act**
Okla. Stat. Ann., Title 59, § 1750.1 et seq.

**Security Guards Act**
Md. Ann. Code 1974, Art. BO, § 19-101 et seq.
Me. Rev. Stat. Ann. 1964, Title 32, § 9401 et seq.
N.Y. General Business Law (Consol. Laws Ch. 20) § 89e et seq.

**Security Income Act (Supplemental)**
N.Y. Public Service Law (Consol. Laws Ch. 47) § 65b
N.Y. Social Services Law (Consol. Laws Ch. 55) §§ 207 et seq., 301 et seq.

**Security Information Act (College and University)**
Del. Code of 1974, Title 14, § 9001 et seq.
Pa. Purdon's Stat., Title 24, § 2502-1 et seq.
Tenn. Code Ann., 49-7-2201 et seq.

**Security Interest Act (Crop)**
Ill. Comp. Stat. 1992, Ch. 810, § 15/0.01 et seq.

**Security Law (Employment)**
Me. Rev. Stat. Ann. 1964, Title 26, § 1041 et seq.
S.C. Code Ann. 1976, § 41-27-10 et seq.

**Security Medical Facility Act**
Ida. Code 1947, 66-1301 et seq.

**Security of Communications Act**
Okla. Stat. Ann., Title 13, § 176.1 et seq.

**Security of Data and Information Technology Resources Act**
Fla. Stat. Ann., 282.318

**Security Officer Licensing Facilitation Act**
D.C. Laws 1977, No. 2-29

**Security Owners' Protection Law**
Cal. Corporations Code § 27000 et seq.

**Security Personnel for Housing for the Elderly Act**
R.I. Gen. Laws 1956, 42-66.1-1 et seq.

**Security Personnel Licensing and Regulation Act**
Utah Code Ann. 1953, 41-13a-1 et seq.

**Security, Privacy, and Dissemination of Criminal History Information Act**
Neb. Rev. Stat. 1943, 29-3501 et seq.

**Security Recording Act (Motor Vehicle)**
Miss. Code Ann. 1972, § 63-19-3, Subd. f

**Security Reform Act (Milk Control and Milk Producer)**
N.Y. Laws 1987, Ch. 540

**Security Registration Act (TOD)**
See Uniform TOD Security Registration Act

**Security Responsibility Law (Motor Vehicles)**
N.J. Rev. Stat. 1937, 39:6-23 et seq.

**Security Risk Act**
N.Y. Laws 1951, Ch. 233

**Security Systems Technicians Act**
Md. Ann. Code 1974, Art. BO, § 18-101 et seq.

**Security Takeover Disclosure Act**
N.H. Rev. Stat. 1955, 421-A:1 et seq.
N.Y. Business Corporation Law 1961 (Consol. Laws Ch. 4) §§ 1600 et seq., 1601 et seq.

**Security through Development of Correctional Facilities Bond Act**
N.Y. Laws 1981, Ch. 850

**Security Transfers Act (Fiduciary)**
Me. Rev. Stat. Ann. 1964, Title 13, § 641 et seq.

**Security Transfers Simplification Act (Fiduciaries)**
See Uniform Act for Simplification of Fiduciary Security Transfers

**Security Treatment Act**
Conn. Gen. Stat. Ann., § 17-238 et seq.

**Sedatives Sale Act**
Wash. Rev. Code 1951, 69.40.060, 69.40.070

**Sediment and Erosion Control Act**
Conn. Gen. Stat. Ann., 22a-325 et seq.
Del. Code of 1974, Title 7, § 4001 et seq.
Ga. Code Ann., 12-7-1 et seq.
Neb. Rev. Stat. 1943, 2-4601 et seq.
R.I. Gen. Laws 1956, 45-46-1 et seq.
S.C. Code Ann. 1976, § 48-18-10 et seq.
Va. Code 1950, § 21-89.1 et seq.

**Sediment and Erosion Reduction Act**
S.C. Code Ann. 1976, § 48-18-40 et seq.

**Sediment Control Act (Logging)**
W. Va. Code 1966 § 19-1B-1 et seq.

**Sediment Reduction and Stormwater Management Act**
S.C. Code Ann. 1976, § 48-14-10 et seq.

**Sedimentation Pollution Control Act**
N.C. Gen. Stat. 1943, § 113A-50 et seq.

**Sedition Act**
July 14, 1798, Ch. 73, 1 Stat. 596
May 16, 1918, Ch. 75, 40 Stat. 553
Alaska Stat. 1962, Replaced Titles, § 11.50.010 et seq.
Fla. Stat. Ann., 876.32 et seq.
Ga. Code Ann., 16-11-5 et seq.
Haw. Rev. Stat. 1968, § 124A-129 et seq.
Ill. Rev. Stat. 1991, Ch. 38, § 30-1 et seq.
Iowa Code Ann., 718.1
Ky. Rev. Stat. 1971, Superseded Vol., 432.030 et seq.
Mass. Gen. Laws Ann., 264:11
Md. Ann. Code 1957, Superseded Vol., Art. 85A
Mo. Rev. Stat. 1969, 559.310
Mont. Rev. Code 1947, 94-4401 et seq.
Neb. Laws 1918, Ex. Sess., Ch. 5
N.H. Rev. Stat. 1955, 648:1 et seq.
N.J. Stat. Ann., 2A:148-12 et seq.
Ohio Rev. Code 1953, 2921.21 et seq.
Pa. Purdon's Stat., Title 18, § 4207
R.I. Gen. Laws 1956, 11-43-11 et seq.
*Continued*

Vt. Stat. Ann., Title 13, § 3405

**Seduction Act**
Ala. Code 1975, § 13A-6-65
Mo. Rev. Stat. 1969, 559.310
Mont. Rev. Code 1947, 94-4108
R.I. Gen. Laws 1956, Superseded Vol., 11-37-4
Va. Code 1950, § 18.2-68
Wash. Rev. Code Ann., 4.24.020

**Seduction Act (Criminal)**
Wash. Rev. Code 1974, 9.79.070

**Seed Act**
Ala. Code 1975, § 2-26-1 et seq.
Ark. Code Ann. 1987, 2-18-101 et seq.
Cal. Food and Agricultural Code 1967, § 52251 et seq.
Colo. Rev. Stat., 35-27-101 et seq.
Del. Code of 1974, Title 3, § 1501 et seq.
Fla. Stat. Ann., 578.011 et seq.
Ga. Code Ann., 2-4-1 et seq., 2-11-20 et seq.
Ill. Rev. Stat. 1991, Ch. 5, § 401 et seq.
Ind. Code Ann., 15-4-1-1 et seq.
Iowa Code Ann., 199.1 et seq.
La. Rev. Stat. Ann., 3:1431 et seq.
Mass. Gen. Laws Ann., 128:84 et seq.
Md. Ann. Code 1974, Art. AG, § 9-201 et seq.
Me. Rev. Stat. Ann. 1964, Title 7, § 1041 et seq.
Mich. Comp. Laws Ann., 286.701 et seq.
Minn. Stat. Ann., 21.80 et seq.
Miss. Code Ann. 1972, § 69-3-1 et seq.
Mo. Rev. Stat., 266.011 et seq.
N.C. Gen. Stat. 1943, § 106-277 et seq.
N.D. Cent. Code, 4-09-01 et seq.
Neb. Rev. Stat. 1943, 81-2-147 et seq.
N.J. Stat. Ann.,4:8-17.13 et seq.
N.M. Stat. Ann., 76-10-11 et seq.
Ohio Rev. Code 1953, 907.01 et seq.
Okla. Stat. Ann., Title 2, § 8-21 et seq.
Pa. Purdon's Stat., Title 3, §§ 285-1 et seq., 291 et seq.
R.I. Gen. Laws 1956, 2-6-1 et seq.
S.C. Code Ann. 1976, § 46-21-10 et seq.
S.D. Codified Laws 1967, 38-12-1 et seq.
Tenn. Code Ann., 43-10-101 et seq.
Tex. Agriculture Code, § 61.001 et seq.
Utah Code Ann. 1953, 4-16-1 et seq.
Va. Code 1950, § 3.1-262 et seq.
Vt. Stat. Ann., Title 6, § 662 et seq.
Wash. Rev. Code Ann., 15.49.005 et seq.
Wis. Stat. Ann., 94.38 et seq.
W. Va. Code 1966, § 19-16-1 et seq.

**SEED Act**
See Support for East European Democracy (Seed) Act of 1989

**Seed and Feed Loan Act**
April 26, 1924, Ch. 132, 43 Stat. 110

**Seed and Grain Bonding Act**
N.D. Cent. Code, 11-29-01 et seq.

**Seed and Plant Certification Act**
Ida. Code 1947, 22-422 et seq., 22-1511 et seq.
Me. Rev. Stat. Ann. 1964, Title 7, § 2101 et seq.
N.H. Rev. Stat. 1955, 433:10 et seq.
Okla. Stat. Ann., Title 2, § 788.2 et seq.
Tex. Agriculture Code, § 62.001 et seq.

**Seed and Potatoes Act**
Minn. Stat. Ann., 30.01 et seq.

**Seed Capital Corporation Act**
Iowa Code 1995, 15E.81 et seq.

**Seed Capital Corporation and Partnership Act (Palmetto)**
S.C. Code Ann. 1976, § 41-44-10 et seq.

**Seed Free Forage Act (Noxious Weed)**
Mont. Code Ann., 80-7-901 et seq.

**Seed Grain Loan Act**
March 20, 1922, Ch. 109, 42 Stat. 467
Mont. Laws 1915, Ch. 13

**Seed Ground District Act**
N.J. Laws 1899, p. 160

**Seed Growers Registration Act**
Tex. Agriculture Code, § 62.001 et seq.

**Seed Industry Act (Alfalfa)**
Mont. Code Ann., 80-11-301 et seq.

**Seed Labeling Act**
Mont. Code Ann., 80-5-101 et seq.

**Seed Lien Act**
N.D. Cent. Code, 4-26-01 et seq.
Wash. Rev. Code Ann., 60.11.010 et seq.

**Seed Potato Act**
Ida. Code 1947, 22-505 et seq.
Minn. Stat. Ann., 30.01 et seq.
Mont. Laws 1989, Ch. 610
N.C. Gen. Stat. 1943, § 106-284.5 et seq.
N.D. Cent. Code, 4-26-01 et seq.
Va. Code 1950, § 3.1-285 et seq.

**Seed Testing Act**
Kan. Stat. Ann., 2-1415 et seq.
N.M. Stat. Ann., 76-10-11 et seq.

**Seed Warehousemen Act**
Mont. Code Ann., 80-5-201 et seq.

**Seeing Eye Dog Act**
Tex. Human Resources Code, § 121.001 et seq.

**Seeing-Eye Dogs on Railroads Act**
July 5, 1937, Ch. 432, 50 Stat. 475, 49 U.S. Code § 22

**Seeing Eye Law (Dogs Permitted on Omnibuses)**
N.Y. Transportation Law (Consol. Laws Ch. 61a) § 153

**Seeing Eye Law (Public Facilities)**
N.Y. Civil Rights Law (Consol. Laws Ch. 6) § 47 et seq.

**Seepage Act (Irrigation)**
Colo. Rev. Stat., 37-82-102

**Segregation Act**
La. Rev. Stat. Ann., 45:521 et seq.
Ohio Laws Vol. 5, p. 53
Tenn. Code Ann., Superseded Vol., 49-3701 et seq.

**Segregation Act (Buses)**
Ala. Code 1958, Title 48, § 301(31a) et seq.

**Segregation Act (Carriers)**
Ga. Code Ann., 46-9-133 et seq.
S.C. Code Ann. 1962, §§ 58-1491 et seq., 58-1491 et seq.

**Segregation Act (Cities)**
Tex. Rev. Civ. Stat., Art. 1015b

**Segregation Act (Coaches)**
Okla. Stat. Ann., Title 3, § 65.13

**Segregation Act (Public Assemblage)**
Va. Code 1950, §§ 18.1-356, 18.1-357

**Segregation Act (Schools)**
See School Segregation Act

**Segregation Act (Taxes)**
Va. Code 1950, §§ 58.1-100, 58.1-3000

**Segregation Act (Transportation)**
Tex. Penal Code 1925, Arts. 1659, 1660, 1661.1
Tex. Rev. Civ. Stat., Art. 6417

**Seining Law**
Ky. Rev. Stat. 1971, Superseded Vols., 150.590
Ky. Rev. Stat. 1971, 150.450

**Seismic Hazards Mapping Act**
Cal. Public Resources Code § 2690 et seq.

**Seismic Retrofit Earthquake Relief Bond Act**
Cal. Government Code § 8879 et seq.

**Seismic Safety Act (Essential Services Buildings)**
Cal. Health and Safety Code § 16000 et seq.

**Seismic Safety Commission Act**
Cal. Government Code § 8870 et seq.
Mo. Laws 1993, S.B. No. 142

**Seizure Act**
See Uniform Seizure Act

**Seizure Act (Public Utilities)**
See Public Utilities Seizure Act

**Seizure and Confiscation Act (Liquor)**
Tenn. Code Ann., 57-9-201 et seq.

**Seizure and Forfeiture Act (Asset)**
Kan. Stat. Ann., 60-4101 et seq.

**Seizure of Controlled Dangerous Substances Property Forfeiture Act**
La. Rev. Stat. Ann., 40:2601 et seq.

**Seizure of Firearm Act**
Ill. Rev. Stat. 1991, Ch. 38, § 161 et seq.

**Seizures Act**
Wash. Rev. Code Ann., 10.79.010 et seq.

**Selected Industrial Feasibility Act**
Miss. Code Ann. 1972, § 57-11-61 et seq.

**Selected Paroled Juvenile Offenders Pilot Program**
Ill. Comp. Stat. 1992, Ch. 730, § 5/3-16-5

**Selection and Service Act (Jury)**
Me. Rev. Stat. Ann. 1964, Title 14, § 1211 et seq.

**Selection of P.S.C. Act (Merit)**
S.C. Code Ann. 1976, § 58-3-21 et seq.

**Selective Draft Acts**
March 3, 1863, Ch. 75, 12 Stat. 731
Feb. 24, 1864, Ch. 13, 13 Stat. 6
July 4, 1864, Ch. 237, 13 Stat. 380
March 3, 1865, Ch. 79, 13 Stat. 490
May 18, 1917, Ch. 15, 40 Stat. 76
June 15, 1917, Ch. 29, 40 Stat. 217
Oct. 6, 1917, Ch. 92, 40 Stat. 393
Oct. 6, 1917, Ch. 105, 40 Stat. 410
April 20, 1918, Ch. 61, 40 Stat. 534
May 16, 1918, Ch. 76, 40 Stat. 554
May 20, 1918, Ch. 79, 40 Stat. 557
July 9, 1918, Ch. 143, 40 Stat. 885
Aug. 31, 1918, Ch. 166, 40 Stat. 955
Feb. 28, 1919, Ch. 79, 40 Stat. 1211
March 8, 1922, Ch. 101, 42 Stat. 421

**Selective Regulations Act (Coastal Wetlands)**
Mass. Gen. Laws Ann., 130:105

**Selective Sales and Use Tax Act**
Pa. Purdon's Stat., Title 72, § 7201 et seq.
Wis. Stat. Ann., 77.51 et seq.

**Selective Sales Tax Act**
Wyo. Stat. Ann., § 39-6-401 et seq.

**Selective Service Act of 1948**
See Military Selective Service Act of 1967
June 24, 1948, Ch. 625, 62 Stat. 604, 50 U.S. Code Appx. §§ 451 to 470, 1001 to 1017 nts.
June 30, 1950, Ch. 445, 64 Stat. 318, 50 U.S. Code Appx. §§ 460, 467, 471
Sept. 9, 1950, Ch. 939, 64 Stat. 826, 50 U.S. Code Appx. § 454
Sept. 27, 1950, Ch. 1059, 64 Stat. 1073, 50 U.S. Code Appx. §§ 454, 456, 459, 460, 464, 466, 470
June 19, 1951, Ch. 144, 65 Stat. 75, 50 U.S. Code Appx. §§ 451 to 454, 455, 456, 459, 460, 463, 466, 467, 471

**Selective Service Amendment Act of 1969**
Nov. 26, 1969, P.L. 91-124, 83 Stat. 220, 50 U.S. Code Appx. § 455

**Selective Service Extension Act of 1950**
June 30, 1950, Ch. 445, 64 Stat. 318, 50 U.S. Code Appx. §§ 460, 467, 471

**Selective Service Registration Act**
Cal. Education Code 1976, §§ 66500, 69400

**Selective Service Registration Awareness and Compliance Act**
Mo. Laws 1999, H.B. No. 415

**Selective Training and Service Act of 1940**
Sept. 16, 1940, Ch. 720, 54 Stat. 885
May 29, 1941, Ch. 155, 55 Stat. 211
Dec. 20, 1941, Ch. 602, 55 Stat. 844
March 28, 1942, Ch. 206, 56 Stat. 190
June 23, 1942, Ch. 443, 56 Stat. 386
July 28, 1942, Ch. 529, 56 Stat. 724
Nov. 13, 1942, Ch. 638, 56 Stat. 1018
Dec. 5, 1943, Ch. 342, 57 Stat. 596
July 1, 1944, Ch. 376, 58 Stat. 720

Dec. 8, 1944, Ch. 548, 58 Stat. 798
May 9, 1945, Ch. 112, 59 Stat. 166
May 14, 1946, Ch. 253, 60 Stat. 181
June 29, 1946, Ch. 522, 60 Stat. 341

**Self-Assessed Tax Lien Act**
Pa. Purdon's Stat., Title 53, § 7501 et seq.

**Self-Defense Act**
Neb. Rev. Stat. 1943, 28-1409
Okla. Stat. Ann., Title 21, § 643

**Self-Defense Act (Jack Hagler)**
Fla. Stat. Ann., 790.06 et seq.

**Self-Employed Individuals Tax Retirement Act of 1962**
Oct. 10, 1962, P.L. 87-792, 76 Stat. 809, 26 U.S. Code §§ 37, 62, 72, 101, 104, 105, 172, 401 to 405, 503, 805, 1361, 2039, 2517, 3306, 3401, 6047, 7207

**Self-Employment Assistance and Entrepreneurial Training Act**
N.J. Stat. Ann., 43:21-67 et seq.

**Self-Employment Contributions Act of 1954**
Aug. 16, 1954, Ch. 736, 68A Stat. 353, 26 U.S. Code §§ 1401 to 1403
Sept. 1, 1954, Ch. 1206, 68 Stat. 1087, 26 U.S. Code §§ 1401, 1402
Aug. 1, 1956, Ch. 836, 70 Stat. 840, 26 U.S. Code §§ 1401, 1402
Aug. 30, 1957, P.L. 85-239, 71 Stat. 521, 26 U.S. Code § 1402
July 30, 1965, P.L. 89-97, 79 Stat. 343, 26 U.S. Code § 1401

**Self-Funded Multiple Employer Welfare Arrangement Regulation Act**
Mont. Code Ann., 33-35-101 et seq.

**Self-Funded Research and Development Act (Trucking Industry)**
Okla. Stat. Ann., Title 47, § 1161 et seq.

**Self-Funding Benefits Act (Political Subdivisions)**
Neb. Rev. Stat. 1943, 13-1601 et seq.

**Self-Government and Governmental Reorganization Act**
D.C. Code Ann., § 1-201 et seq.

**Self-Help Clearing House Act**
Ill. Rev. Stat. 1991, Ch. 127, §§ 3350, 3351

**Self-Help Housing Authority Act**
R.I. Gen. Laws 1956, 42-53-1 et seq.

**Self-Improvement Act (Tree Fruit Industry)**
W. Va. Code 1966, § 19-2G-1 et seq.

**Self-Insurance Act (Local Government)**
La. Rev. Stat. Ann., 33:1341 et seq.

**Self-Insurance Act (Local)**
La. Rev. Stat. Ann., 33:1341 et seq.

**Self-Insurance Act (School Motor Vehicle)**
Ark. Acts 1991, No. 824

**Self-Insurance Fund Act (Commercial)**
Fla. Stat. Ann., 624.460 et seq.

**Self-Insurance Fund Guaranty Association Act**
Fla. Stat. Ann., 631.90 et seq.

**Self-Insurers Guaranty Fund Act**
Mont. Laws 1989, Ch. 244
N.M. Stat. Ann., 52-8-1 et seq.

**Self-Insurers' Security Act**
Cal. Labor Code § 3740 et seq.

**Self-Liquidating Bridge Act**
N.J. Stat. Ann., 27:19-26 to 27:19-39

**Self-Referral Act (Health Care Practitioner)**
Me. Rev. Stat. Ann. 1964, Title 22, § 2081 et seq.

**Self-Referral Act (Health Care Provider)**
S.C. Code Ann. 1976, § 44-113-30 et seq.

**Self-Referral Act (Patient)**
Fla. Laws 1992, Ch. 178
Ga. Code Ann., 43-1B-1 et seq.

**Self-Referral Act (Provider)**
S.C. Code Ann. 1976, § 44-113-10 et seq.

**Self-Service and Personal Property Storage Act (Liens)**
Minn. Stat. Ann., 514.970 et seq.

**Self-Service Storage Act**
Me. Rev. Stat. Ann. 1964, Title 10, § 1371 et seq.

**Self-Service Storage Facilities Act**
Mo. Rev. Stat. 1978, 415.400 et seq.

**Self-Service Storage Facility Act**
Ala. Code 1975, § 8-15-30 et seq.
Cal. Business and Professions Code, § 21700 et seq.
Del. Code of 1974, Title 25, § 4901 et seq.
Fla. Stat. Ann., 83.801 et seq.
Ga. Code Ann., 10-4-210 et seq.
Ill. Rev. Stat. 1991, Ch. 114, § 801 et seq.
Iowa Code Ann., 578A.1 et seq.
Kan. Stat. Ann., 58-813 et seq.
Ky. Rev. Stat. 1971, 359.200c et seq.
La. Rev. Stat. Ann., 9:4756 et seq.
Md. Ann. Code 1974, Art. CL, § 18-501 et seq.
Me. Rev. Stat. Ann. 1964, Title 10, § 1371 et seq.
Mich. Comp. Laws 1977, 570.521 et seq.
Mo. Rev. Stat. 1986, 415.400
N.J. Stat. Ann., 2A:44-187 et seq.
Pa. Purdon's Stat., Title 73, § 1901 et seq.
R.I. Gen. Laws 1956, 34-42-1 et seq.
S.C. Code Ann. 1976, § 39-20-10 et seq.
Tenn. Code Ann., 66-31-101 et seq.
Va. Code 1950, § 55-416 et seq.
Wash. Rev. Code Ann., 19.150.010 et seq.

**Self-Service Storage Facility Lien Act**
Iowa Code Ann., 578A.1 et seq.

**Self-Service Storage Lien Act**
N.M. Stat. Ann., 48-11-1 et seq.

**Self-Storage Facility Act**
Fla. Stat. Ann., 83.801 et seq.

**Self-Sufficiency and Employment Act**
Colo. Rev. Stat., 26-2-901 et seq.

**Self-Sufficiency and Rental Assistance Program Act**
Colo. Rev. Stat., 29-4-901 et seq.

**Self-Sufficiency and Welfare Reform Act**
Colo. Rev. Stat., 26-2-401 et seq.

**Self-Supported Municipal Improvement Districts Act**
Kan. Stat. Ann., 12-1794 et seq.

**Seller-Assisted Marketing Plan Act**
Neb. Rev. Stat. 1943, 59-1701 to 59-1761

**Seller Disclosure Act**
Mich. Comp. Laws Ann., 565.951 et seq.

**Seller of Checks Law**
Wis. Stat. Ann., 217.01 et seq.

**Sellers of Travel Act**
Fla. Stat. Ann., 559.926 et seq.

**Selma to Montgomery National Trail Study Act of 1989**
July 3, 1990. P.L. 101-321, 16 U.S. Code § 1241 nt.

**Semi-Centennial Commission Act**
Okla. Stat. 1951, Title 25, § 99.1 et seq.

**Semi-Monthly Pay Day Law**
Cal. Labor Code § 204

**Semi-Monthly Payment Law of Railroad Employees Act**
N.Y. Labor Law (Consol. Laws, Ch. 31), § 191

**Semiconductor Chip Protection Act of 1984**
Nov. 8, 1984, P.L. 98-620, 17 U.S. Code § 901 et seq.

**Semiconductor International Protection Extension Act of 1991**
June 28, 1991, P.L. 102-65, 8 U.S. Code § 1254a

**Semimonthly Pay Act**
Cal. Labor Code § 204
Ill. Rev. Stat. 1991, Ch. 48, § 39m-4
Ind. Code Ann., 22-2-5-1
Mich. Comp. Laws Ann., 408.472
Mo. Rev. Stat., 290.080, 290.090
Pa. Purdon's Stat., Title 43, § 251 et seq.
Wyo. Stat. Ann., § 27-4-101 et seq.

**Seminole County Air and Water Pollution Control Act**
Fla. Special Laws 1967, Ch. 67-2084

**Seminole County Comprehensive Planning Act**
Fla. Special Laws 1974, Ch. 74-612

**Seminole County Expressway Authority Law**
Fla. Stat. Ann., 348.95 et seq.

**Seminole County Water Conservation and Control Act**
Fla. Laws 1963, Ch. 63-1936

**Seminole Indian Land Claims Settlement Act of 1987**
Dec. 31, 1987, P.L. 100-228, 25 U.S. Code §§ 1772, 1772 nt.,

**Seminole Original Agreement.**
July 1, 1898, Ch. 542, 30 Stat. 567

**Seminole Supplemental Agreement.**
June 2, 1900, Ch. 610, 31 Stat. 250

**Senate Act**
Wash. Rev. Code 1951, 44.08.010 et seq.

**Senate and House of Representatives Apportionment Act**
Fla. Stat. Ann., 10.001 et seq.

**Senate Apportionment Act**
Okla. Stat. Ann., Title 14, § 80.10 et seq.
S.C. Code Ann. 1976, § 2-1-60

**Senate Reapportionment Act**
N.M. Stat. 1953, 2-9-1 et seq.
N.M. Stat. 1978, 2-8B-1 et seq.

**Senate Reapportionment Act (Temporary)**
N.J. Stat. Ann., 52:10B-1 et seq.

**Senate Redistricting Act**
N.M. Stat. Ann., 2-8C-1 et seq.
W. Va. Code 1966, § 1-2-1

**Senate Redistricting Act of 1991**
N.M. Laws 1991, 1st Sp. Sess., Ch. 3

**Senatorial Apportionment Act**
Kan. Stat. Ann., 4-4,101 et seq.
Okla. Laws 1961, p. 745
Pa. Purdon's Stat., Title 25, § 2201

**Senatorial Districts Act**
Ky. Rev. Stat. 1971, 6.011
N.M. Stat. Ann., 28-B-1 et seq.
W. Va. Code 1966, § 1-2-1

**Senatorial Reapportionment Act**
Ga. Code Ann., 28-1-1, 28-2-2
Pa. 1963 Ex. Pamph. Laws No. 2

**Senators' Election Act**
July 25, 1866, Ch. 245, 14 Stat. 243

**Seneca Nation Settlement Act of 1990**
Nov. 3, 1990, P.L. 101-503, 25 U.S. Code §§ 1774 to 1774h

**Seneca Regional Port District Act**
Ill. Rev. Stat. 1991, Ch. 19, § 351 et seq.

**Senior Care Act**
Kan. Stat. Ann., 75-5926 et seq.

**Senior Center Bond Act**
Cal. Welfare and Institutions Code § 9450 et seq.

**Senior Center Grant Program Act**
Pa. Purdon Stat., Title 35, § 7401 et seq.

**Senior Citizen and Disabled Resident Transportation Assistance Act**
N.J. Stat. Ann., 27:25-25 et seq.

**Senior Citizen Courses Act**
Ill. Rev. Stat. 1991, Ch. 144, § 1800 et seq.

**Senior Citizen Homeowner's Income Security Act**
N.J. Stat. Ann., 46:10B-16 et seq.

**Senior Citizen Property Tax Refund Act**
Ill. Rev. Stat. 1991, Ch. 24, §§ 1500, 1501

**Senior Citizens Advisory Committee Act**
Pa. 1998 Pamph. Laws, No. 152

**Senior Citizens Against Marketing Scams Act of 1994**
Sept. 13, 1994, P.L. 103-322, 18 U.S. Code §§ 2325 nt., 2325 et seq.

**Senior Citizens and Disabled Citizens Property Tax Postponement Law**
Cal. Revenue and Taxation Code § 20581 et seq.

**Senior Citizens and Disabled Persons Property Tax Relief and Pharmaceutical Assistance Act**
Ill. Rev. Stat. 1991, Ch. 67 1/2, § 401 et seq.

**Senior Citizens and Disabled Protected Tenancy Act**
N.J. Stat. Ann., 2A:18-61.22 et seq.

**Senior Citizens Centers and Services Companies Law**
N.Y. Private Housing Finance Law (Consol. Laws Ch. 44B) § 350 et seq.

**Senior Citizens Child Care Support Act**
Ill. Rev. Stat. 1991, Ch. 23, § 7001 et seq.

**Senior Citizens Day Act**
Ill. Rev. Stat. 1991, Ch. 1, § 3051-85

**Senior Citizens' Grants Act**
Wash. Rev. Code Ann., 74.08.025 et seq.

**Senior Citizens Higher Education Act**
Va. Code 1950, § 23-38.54 et seq.

**Senior Citizens Higher Education Assistance Act**
Ga. Code 1933, 32-175 et seq.

**Senior Citizens Homeowners and Renters Property Tax Assistance Law**
Cal. Revenue and Taxation Code § 20501 et seq.

**Senior Citizens Housing Act of 1962**
Sept. 28, 1962, P.L. 87-723, 76 Stat. 670, 12 U.S. Code §§ 84, 1701q, 1701r; 42 U.S. Code §§ 1471, 1472, 1474, 1476, 1481, 1485
May 25, 1967, P.L. 90-19, 81 Stat. 25, 12 U.S. Code § 1701r

**Senior Citizens Housing Assistance Act of 1986**
Cal. Health and Safety Code § 51450 et seq.

**Senior Citizens Mobile Home Property Tax Postponement Law**
Cal. Revenue and Taxation Code § 20639 et seq.

**Senior Citizens Nonprofit Rental Housing Tax Law**
N.J. Rev. Stat. 1937, 55:141-1 et seq.

**Senior Citizens on State Boards and Commissions Act**
Ill. Rev. Stat. 1991, Ch. 23, §§ 6150, 6151

**Senior Citizens Possessory Interest Holder Property Tax Postponement Law**
Cal. Revenue and Taxation Code § 20640 et seq.

**Senior Citizens Prescription Drug Payment Assistance Program**
Del. Code of 1974, Title 16, § 3001 et seq.

**Senior Citizens Property Tax Assistance Act**
Cal. Revenue and Taxation Code, § 20501 et seq.
Nev. Rev. Stat. 1979 Reprint, 361.800 et seq.
Pa. Purdon's Stat., Title 72, § 4751-1 et seq.

**Senior Citizens Property Tax Assistance and Postponement Law**
Cal. Revenue and Taxation Code § 20501 et seq.

**Senior Citizens Property Tax or Rent Rebate and Older Persons Inflation Needs Act**
Pa. Purdon's Stat., Title 72, § 4751-1 et seq.

**Senior Citizens Property Tax Postponement Act**
Cal. Revenue and Taxation Code, § 20581 et seq.

**Senior Citizens Real Estate Tax Deferral Act**
Ill. Rev. Stat. 1991, Ch. 67 1/2, § 401 et seq.

**Senior Citizens Rebate and Assistance Act**
Pa. Purdon's Stat., Title 72, § 4751-1 et seq.

**Senior Citizens Recreational Opportunities Act**
N.J. Stat. Ann., 52:27D-29.1 et seq.

**Senior Citizens Reduced Tuition Act**
N.M. Stat. Ann., 21-21D-1 et seq.

**Senior Citizens' Right to Work Act of 1996**
March 29, 1996, P.L. 104-121, Title I, 42 U.S. Code § 1305 nt.

**Senior Citizens Services Act**
Wash. Rev. Code Ann., 74.38.010 et seq.

**Senior Citizens Tax Deduction Act**
N.J. Stat. Ann., 54:4-8.40 et seq.

**Senior Citizens Tenant-Stockholder Property Tax Postponement Law**
Cal. Revenue and Taxation Code § 20625 et seq.

**Senior Companion Act**
Minn. Stat. Ann., 256.977

**Senior Executive Service Improvements Act**
Dec. 2, 1991, P.L. 102-175, 5 U.S. Code § 3301 nt.

**Senior Health Care Assessment Act**
Cal. Welfare and Institutions Code § 9760 et seq.
Ill. Rev. Stat. 1991, Ch. 24, §§ 1500, 1501

**Senior Judge Act**
Iowa Code Ann., 602.9201 et seq.

**Senior Judge Enabling Act**
Tenn. Code Ann., 17-2-301 et seq.

**Senior Services Act**
Ida. Code 1947, 67-5001 et seq.
W. Va. Code 1966, § 16-5P-1 et seq.

**Seniority Act for Rural Mail Carriers**
May 18, 1948, Ch. 298, 62 Stat. 236

**Seniority Rights Act (Post Office)**
Colo. Rev. Stat., 16-16-101 et seq.

**Sensible Transportation Policy Act**
Me. Rev. Stat. Ann. 1964, Title 23, § 73

**Sentence Act**
Pa. Cons. Stat., Title 42, § 9701 et seq.
Wash. Rev. Code Ann., 9.95.001 et seq., 9.95.150 et seq., 9.95.190

**Sentence and Commitment Act**
Ill. Rev. Stat. 1991, Ch. 38, § 1005-1-1 et seq.

**Sentence and Parole Act**
Ill. Rev. Stat. 1991, Ch. 38, § 1001-1-1 et seq.

**Sentence Suspension Act**
Miss. Code Ann. 1972, § 99-19-25 et seq.
Mont. Rev. Code 1947, 95-2206, Subsec. 1, Subd. b
N.C. Gen. Stat. 1943, § 15A-1341 et seq.

**Sentencing Act (Judge)**
Tenn. Code Ann., 40-35-101

**Sentencing Act of 1987**
Dec. 7, 1987, P.L. 100-182, 18 U.S. Code §§ 3006A nt., 3551 nt., 3553, 3561, 3563, 3583, 3663, 3742, 4106; 29 U.S. Code §§ 504, 1111; FRCrP 35
Sept. 13, 1994, P.L. 103-322, 28 U.S. Code § 994 nt.

**Sentencing and Policy Advisory Commission Act**
N.C. Laws 1990, Ch. 1076

**Sentencing Code**
Pa. Cons. Stat., Title 42, § 9701 et seq.

**Sentencing Commission Act**
Tenn. Public Acts 1985 Ex. Sess., Ch. 7

**Sentencing Guidelines Act**
Kan. Stat. Ann., 21-4701 et seq.
N.M. Stat. Ann., 31-18A-1 et seq.

**Sentencing Guidelines Act of 1986**
July 11, 1986, P.L. 99-363, 28 U.S. Code §§ 1 nt., 994

**Sentencing Improvements Act**
D.C. Code Ann., § 16-710 et seq.

**Sentencing Program for Young Adults (Delayed)**
Okla. Stat. Ann., Title 22, § 996 et seq.

**Sentencing Reform Act**
Ga. Laws 1994, p. 1959
N.Y. Laws 1995, Ch. 3
Wash. Rev. Code 1983, 9.94A.010 et seq.

**Sentencing Reform Act of 1984**
Oct. 12, 1984, P.L. 98-473, 18 U.S. Code § 3551 et seq.
Oct. 2, 1996, P.L. 104-232, 18 U.S. Code § 3551 nt.

**Sentencing Reform Amendments Act of 1985**
Dec. 26, 1985, P.L. 99-217, 18 U.S. Code § 3551 nt.; 28 U.S. Code § 994

**Sentry Dogs Act**
Cal. Health and Safety Code § 25970 et seq.

**SEPA (State Environmental Policy Act)**
Wash. Rev. Code Ann., 43.21C.900

**Separate Ballot Act**
Ill. Rev. Stat. 1991, Ch. 46, § 16-7

**Separate Coach Act**
Ark. Stat. 1947, 73-1218 et seq.
Ky. Rev. Stat. 1962, 276.440, 276.990
Okla. Stat. Ann., Title 13, § 181 et seq.
S.C. Code Ann. 1962, § 58-713 et seq.
Tex. Rev. Civ. Stat., Art. 6417

**Separate Compensation Funds Act**
Ohio Rev. Code 1953, 4131.01 et seq.

**Separate Juvenile Court Act**
Neb. Rev. Stat. 1943, 43-228 et seq.

**Separate Maintenance Act**
Ill. Rev. Stat. 1991, Ch. 40, § 402 et seq.
Kan. Stat. Ann., 60-1601
Mich. Comp. Laws Ann., 552.333
N.J. Stat. Ann., 2A:34-24
Ore. Rev. Stat. 1953, 107.105

**Separation Act**
La. Civil Code 1972, Art. 138 et seq.

**Separation Act (Contracts for Public Buildings)**
Pa. Purdon's Stat., Title 53, §§ 1003, 1618

**Separation Act (Drainage Districts)**
Ark. Code Ann. 1987, 14-121-603 et seq.

**Separation Act (Husband and Wife)**
Haw. Rev. Stat. Ann., § 580-71 et seq.
La. Civil Code, Art. 138
Md. Ann. Code 1974, Art. FL, § 1-203
N.H. Rev. Stat. 1955, 458:26 et seq.

**Separation Act (Maine)**
Mass. Acts 1819-20, January Session, Ch. 287
Mass. Acts 1819-20, May Session, Ch. 161

**Separation and Divorce Act**
R.I. Gen. Laws 1956, 15-5-1 et seq.

**Separation Districts Act (Grade)**
Cal. Streets and Highways Code § 8100 et seq.

**Separation of Grade District Act**
Cal. Streets and Highways Code, § 8100 et seq.

**Separation of Powers Act**
N.C. Gen. Stat. 1943, §§ 108A-33, 136-28.1, 140-5.15, 143B-426.11, 147-12
N.C. Laws 1982, Ch. 1191
N.C. Laws 1983, Ch. 717

N.C. Laws 1985, Ch. 955

**Separation of Powers Bond Act**
N.C. Laws 1983, Ch. 577
N.C. Laws 1985, Ch. 955

**Septage Waste Servicers Act**
Mich. Comp. Laws Ann., 325.311 et seq.

**September Housing Law**
N.Y. Laws 1920, Ex. Sess., Chs. 942 to 945, 947 to 952

**Septic System Maintenance Act**
R.I. Gen. Laws 1956, 45-24.5-1 et seq.

**SEQRA (State Environmental Quality Review Act)**
N.Y. Environmental Conservation Law 1972 (Consol. Laws Ch. 43B) § 8-0101 et seq.

**Sequestration of Witnesses Act**
Del. Code of 1974, Title 10, § 366
Ga. Code Ann., 24-9-61
N.J. Revised 1937, 2:29-88 to 2:29-109
Tex. Civ. Prac. and Rem. Code, § 62.001 et seq.
Tex. Rev. Civ. Stat., Art. 6840 et seq.
Tex. Rules of Civil Procedure as am. 1984, Rule 696 et seq.

**Sergeant-at-Arms Act**
N.J. Stat. Ann., 2A:11-19 et seq.

**Serial Numbers and Marks Act**
Ill. Rev. Stat. 1991, Ch. 121 1/2, §§ 157.13, 157.13a

**Series Partition and Subdivision Control Law**
Ore. Rev. Stat., 92.305 et seq.

**Serious and Habitual Juvenile Offender Act**
Okla. Stat. Ann., Title 10, § 1160.1 et seq.

**Serious Targeted Offenders Program Act**
Fla. Stat. Ann., 953.01 et seq.

**Serological Test Act (Syphilis)**
Okla. Stat. Ann., Title 43, § 31 et seq.; Title 63, § 1-515 et seq.

**Serve-America: The Community Service, Schools and Service-Learning Act of 1990**
Nov. 16, 1990, P.L. 101-610, 42 U.S. Code §§ 12501 nt., 12521 to 12527, 12531

**Serves Act**
Wash. Rev. Code Ann., 50.65.907

**Service Act (Civil)**
Neb. Rev. Stat. 1943, 19-801, et seq.

**Service Act (Foreign Corporations Substituted)**
Mass. Gen. Laws Ann., 181:4, 181:15

**Service Act (Long Arm)**
See Long Arm Service of Process Act (Civil Actions)

**Service Act (Motor Club)**
Wis. Stat. Ann., 616.71 et seq.

**Service Act (Nonresident Motorists)**
See Nonresident Motorist Substituted Service Act

**Service Act (Nonresident Property Owners)**
Pa. Cons. Stat., Title 42, § 5322 et seq.

**Service Act (Volunteer)**
Ala. Code 1975, § 6-5-336

**Service Administration Act (Municipal)**
P.R. Laws Ann. 1954, Title 21, § 1031 et seq.

**Service and Air Transportation Act**
Ala. Acts 1982, 3d Sp., p. 389

**Service and Repair Act (Motor Vehicles)**
Mich. Comp. Laws Ann., 257.1301 et seq.

**Service at Cost Act (Street Railways)**
Mass. Gen. Laws Ann., 161:115 et seq.

**Service Authority Act**
Colo. Rev. Stat., 32-7-101 et seq.

**Service by Mail Law**
S.C. Code Ann. 1976, § 15-9-930

**Service Compensation Records Transfer Act**
Ill. Rev. Stat. 1991, Ch. 126 1/2, §§ 62a, 62a.1

**Service Consent Act (Insurance Companies)**
Kan. Stat. Ann., 40-218

**Service Contract Act**
Ill. Comp. Stat. 1992, Ch. 215, § 152/1 et seq.

**Service Contract Act of 1965**
Oct. 22, 1965, P.L. 89-286, 79 Stat. 1034, 41 U.S. Code §§ 351 to 357
Oct. 9, 1972, P.L. 92-473, 86 Stat. 789, 41 U.S. Code §§ 351, 353 , 354, 358
July 6, 1973, P.L. 93-57, 87 Stat. 140, 41 U.S. Code § 357

**Service Contract Motor Vehicle Act**
Ida. Code 1947, 49-2801 et seq.

**Service Contract Reimbursement Insurance Act (Motor Vehicle)**
Neb. Rev. Stat. 1943, 44-3520 et seq.

**Service Corporation Law**
Wis. Stat. 1987, 180.99

**Service Corps Volunteers Act**
P.R. Laws Ann. 1954, Title 18, § 1411 et seq.

**Service Credit Act (Marks-Mello-Vasconcellos)**
Cal. Welfare and Institutions Code §§ 9500 to 9512

**Service Credit Act (Out-of-State)**
Cal. Education Code 1976, §§ 22820 to 22825

**Service District Budget Act (Emergency Medical)**
Okla. Stat. Ann., Title 19, § 1701 et seq.

**Service Extension Act of 1941**
Aug. 18, 1941, Ch. 362, 55 Stat. 626
Dec. 8, 1944, Ch. 548, 58 Stat. 799
Aug. 7, 1946, Ch. 770, 60 Stat. 871
Aug. 9, 1946, Ch. 936, 60 Stat. 971

**Service Flag and Button**
Oct. 17, 1942, Ch. 615, 56 Stat. 796, 36 U.S. Code §§ 179 to 182

**Service Letter Act (Employment Termination)**
Mo. Rev. Stat., 290.140
Okla. Stat. Ann., Title 40, § 171

**Service License Act (Liquors)**
Ore. Laws 1991, Ch. 271

**Service Lien Act (Stallion and Jack)**
Ill. Rev. Stat. 1991, Ch. 8, § 50.9 et seq.

**Service Mark Act**
Conn. Gen. Stat. Ann., § 35-11a et seq.
Va. Code 1950, § 59.1-77 et seq.

**Service Marks and Trademarks Act**
S.C. Code Ann. 1976, § 39-15-1105 et seq.
Va. Code 1950, §§ 59.1-92.1 to 59.1-92.20

**Service Members Occupational Conversion and Training Act of 1992**
Oct. 23, 1992, P.L. 102-484, 10 U.S. Code § 1143 nt.
Nov. 30, 1993, P.L. 103-160, 10 U.S. Code § 1143 nt.
Oct. 5, 1994, P.L. 103-337, 10 U.S. Code § 1143 nt.
Nov. 2, 1994, P.L. 103-446, 10 U.S. Code § 1143 nt.

**Service Network Act (Integrated)**
Minn. Stat. 1986, 62N.01 to 62N.24

**Service Occupation Tax Act**
Ill. Comp. Stat. 1992, Ch. 35, § 115/1 et seq.
Ill. Rev. Stat. 1991, Ch. 120, § 439.101 et seq.

**Service Occupation Tax Act (Counties)**
Ill. Rev. Stat. 1987, Ch. 34, § 409.2

**Service Occupation Tax Act (Municipal)**
Ill. Rev. Stat. 1991, Ch. 24, § 8-11-1.4

**Service Occupation Tax Act (Municipalities)**
Ill. Rev. Stat. 1991, Ch. 24, § 8-11-5

**Service of Process Act**
Fla. Stat. Ann., 48.011 et seq.
La. Rev. Stat. Ann., 13:3471 et seq.
Mich. Comp. Laws Ann., 600.1801 et seq.
Mo. Rev. Stat., 506.170 et seq.
Pa. Cons. Stat., Title 42, §§ 5322, 5323
Tenn. Code Ann., 20-2-101 et seq.
Vt. Stat. Ann., Title 12, § 654 et seq.
Wash. Rev. Code Ann., 4.28.080

**Service of Process Act (Corporations)**
Me. Rev. Stat. Ann. 1964, Title 13-A, § 1212

**Service of Process Act (Foreign Corporations)**
Ala. Code 1958, Title 7, § 199(1)
Conn. Gen. Stat. Ann., § 33-411
Me. Rev. Stat. Ann. 1964, Title 13A, § 1201 et seq.
Va. Code 1950, § 13.1-111

**Service of Process Act (Nonresident Motorists)**
See Nonresident Motorist Substituted Service Act

**Service of Process Act (Nonresident)**
Miss. Code Ann. 1972, §§ 11-11-11, 11-11-13, 13-3-57, 13-3-59, 13-3-61
N.M. Stat. Ann., 38-1-16 et seq.

**Service of Process Act (Unauthorized Insurers)**
Haw. Rev. Stat. Ann., § 431-342
N.Y. Insurance Law 1984 (Consol. Laws Ch. 28) § 1213
W. Va. Code 1966, § 33-4-13

**Service Organizations Preferred Provider Arrangement Act (Nonprofit)**
Me. Rev. Stat. Ann. 1964, Title 24, § 2333 et seq.; Title 24-A § 201 et seq.

**Service Patrol Act (Freeway)**
Cal. Streets and Highways Code § 2560 et seq.

**Service Pension Acts**
Feb. 6, 1907, Ch. 468, 34 Stat. 879
May 11, 1912, Ch. 123, 37 Stat. 112

**Service Quality Standards and Bill of Rights of Persons with Mental Retardation, Developmental Disabilities, Brain Injury, or Chronic Mental Illness**
Iowa Code Ann., 225C.25

**Service Recognition Board Termination Act**
Ill. Rev. Stat. 1991, Ch. 126 1/2, §§ 62m, 63

**Service Relief Act (Military)**
La. Rev. Stat. Ann., 29:401 et seq.

**Service Resource Bank Act**
P.R. Laws Ann. 1954, Title 10, § 2221 et seq.

**Service Sharing and Combination Incentives Law (Local Government)**
Minn. Stat. Ann., 465.80 et seq.

**Service Station Dealers Day in Court Act**
La. Rev. Stat. Ann., 51:1451 et seq.

**Service Tax Act**
Colo. Laws 1937, p. 1144, Ch. 240

**Service Technician and Service Agency Act**
Okla. Stat. Ann., Title 2, § 5-62.1 et seq.

**Service to the Visually Impaired Act**
S.D. Codified Laws 1967, 28-10-1 et seq.

**Service Trade Practices Act (Motor Vehicle)**
Iowa Code Ann., 537B.1 et seq.

**Service Use Tax Act**
Ill. Comp. Stat. 1992, Ch. 35, § 110/1 et seq.
Ill. Rev. Stat. 1991, Ch. 120, § 439.31 et seq.

**Service Warranty Associations Act**
Fla. Stat. Ann., 634.401 et seq.

**Service Warranty Insurance Act**
Okla. Stat. Ann., Title 36, § 6601 et seq.

**Servicemen's Absentee Voting Act**
Md. Ann. Code 1957, Art. 33, §§ 3-7, 27-1 et seq.
Wyo. Stat. 1957, § 22-242 et seq.

**Servicemen's Act (Divorce)**
Okla. Stat. Ann., Title 43, § 102

**Servicemen's and Veterans' Survivor Benefits Act**
Aug. 1, 1956, Ch. 837, 70 Stat. 857 (See 10 U.S. Code §§ 1441, 6148) 14 U.S. Code § prec. § 461; 26 U.S. Code §§ 121, 3121, 3122, 6051; 33 U.S. Code § 857 (See 38 U.S. Code §§ 410, 412, 422, 701 to 724, 781, 3101, 3107, 3501, 3502) 42 U.S. Code §§ 213, 402, 405 409, 410, 417; 45 U.S. Code §§ 228a, 228c-1
June 17, 1957, P.L. 85-56, 71 Stat. 160 (See 38 U.S. Code §§ 101, 106, 401 to 403, 410, 421, 3104)
Sept. 7, 1957, P.L. 85-311, 71 Stat. 632 (See 38 U.S. Code § 415)
Sept. 2, 1958, P.L. 85-857, 72 Stat. 1266
Sept. 2, 1958, P.L. 85-861, 72 Stat. 1557 (See 38 U.S. Code § 423)

**Servicemen's Bonus Act (World War I)**
Ore. Rev. Stat. 1953, 407.510 et seq.

**Servicemen's Bonus Act (World War II)**
Ore. Rev. Stat. 1953, 407.310

**Servicemen's Dependents Allowance Act of 1942**
June 23, 1942, Ch. 443, 56 Stat. 381
Aug. 20, 1942, Ch. 554, 56 Stat. 747
Oct. 26, 1943, Ch. 281, 57 Stat. 577
Oct. 6, 1945, Ch. 393, 59 Stat. 541

**Servicemen's Divorce Act**
Ala. Code 1975, § 6-7-20
N.M. Stat. Ann., 40-4-5
Okla. Stat. Ann., Title 12, § 1272
Tex. Family Code, § 3.23

**Servicemen's Employment Tenure Act**
Ill. Rev. Stat. 1991, Ch. 126 1/2, § 29 et seq.

**Servicemen's Indemnity Act of 1951**
April 25, 1951, Ch. 39, 65 Stat. 33
Aug. 24, 1954, Ch. 887, 68 Stat. 780
July 26, 1955, Ch. 380, 69 Stat. 374
July 29, 1955, Ch. 432, 69 Stat. 396
Aug. 1, 1956, Ch. 830, 70 Stat. 806

**Servicemen's Moratorium Act**
Ore. Rev. Stat., 408.440

**Servicemen's Readjustment Act**
Conn. Gen. Stat. Ann., § 36-152
La. Rev. Stat. Ann., 29:251 et seq.

**Servicemen's Readjustment Act of 1944**
June 22, 1944, Ch. 268, 58 Stat. 284 (See 38 U.S. Code § 1801 et seq.)
June 30, 1945, Ch. 204, 59 Stat. 267, 12 U.S. Code §§ 672, 712, 745, 751 to 753, 771, 781, 857, 861, 874, 880, 1016, 1020b, 1020d
July 6, 1945, Ch. 280, 59 Stat. 463
Oct. 6, 1945, Ch. 393, 50 Stat. 542
Dec. 28, 1945, Ch. 588, 59 Stat. 9
June 22, 1946, Ch. 447, 60 Stat. 299
Aug. 8, 1946, Ch. 882, 60 Stat. 932
March 31, 1947, Ch. 26, 61 Stat. 32
June 14, 1947, Ch. 106, 61 Stat. 133
April 3, 1948, Ch. 170, 62 Stat. 160
June 16, 1948, Ch. 487, 62 Stat. 472
July 1, 1948, Ch. 784, 62 Stat. 1209
Aug. 10, 1948, Ch. 832, 62 Stat. 70
July 26, 1949, Ch. 364, 63 Stat. 481
April 20, 1950, Ch. 94, 64 Stat. 74
Sept. 1, 1951, Ch. 378, 65 Stat. 316
Sept. 13, 1951, Ch. 381, 65 Stat. 320
April 18, 1952, Ch. 218, 66 Stat. 64
July 16, 1952, Ch. 875, 66 Stat. 682
July 1, 1953, Ch. 177, 67 Stat. 135
June 29, 1954, Ch. 410, 68 Stat. 320
Aug. 2, 1954, Ch. 649, 68 Stat. 643
Aug. 21, 1954, Ch. 780, 68 Stat. 756
June 16, 1955, Ch. 153, 69 Stat. 161
June 21, 1955, Ch. 171, 69 Stat. 167
Aug. 1, 1956, Ch. 854, 70 Stat. 913
Aug. 7, 1956, Ch. 1029, 70 Stat. 1115
June 17, 1957, P.L. 85-56, 71 Stat. 159
April 1, 1958, P.L. 85-364, 72 Stat. 74

**Servicemen's Readjustment Enabling Act**
D.C. Code Ann., §§ 45-2301, 45-2302

**Servicemen's Residence Act**
Ala. Code 1975, § 6-7-20

**Services Act**
Fla. Stat. Ann., 415.101 et seq.

**Services Act (Children's)**
Cal. Health and Safety Code § 248 et seq.

**Services Administration Act (Agricultural)**
P.R. Laws Ann. 1954, Title 5, § 31 et seq.

**Services and Goods Installment Sales Act**
Pa. Purdon's Stat., Title 69, § 1101 et seq.

**Services Code (Human)**
Colo. Rev. Stat., 26-1-101 et seq.

**Services Contract Act**
Ill. Comp. Stat. 1992, Ch. 215, § 152/1 et seq.

**Services Development and Health Facility Act**
Fla. Stat. Ann., 381.701 et seq., 408.031 et seq.

**Services for At-Risk Children and Youth Act (Coordinated)**
Utah Code Ann. 1953, 63-75-1 et seq.

**Services for Blind and Visually Impared Act**
R.I. Gen. Laws 1956, 40-9-1 et seq.

**Services for Children, Adolescents and Families Act (Interagency Provision)**
Kan. Laws 1992, Ch. 264

**Services for Emotionally Disturbed Children Law**
R.I. Gen. Laws 1956, 40.1-7-1 et seq.

**Services for Mentally Retarded Persons Act (Protective)**
Vt. Stat. Ann., Title 33, § 3601 et seq.

**Services for Older Oklahomans Act (Coordination of)**
Okla. Stat. Ann., Title 56, § 3001

**Services for Persons with Developmental Disabilities Act (Home and Community-based)**
Colo. Rev. Stat., 26-4-621 et seq.

**Services for Persons with Health Complexes Related to Acquired Immune Deficiency Syndrome Act (Home and Community-based)**
Colo. Rev. Stat., 26-4-641 et seq.

**Services for Persons with Major Mental Illnesses Act (Home and Community-Based)**
Colo. Rev. Stat., 26-4-671 et seq.

**Services for the Deaf Act (Telephone Communication)**
Fla. Stat. Ann., 427.501 et seq.

**Services Licensing Act (Delayed Deposit)**
Iowa Code Ann., 533D.1 et seq.

**Services Marks and Trademarks Act**
S.C. Code Ann. 1976, § 39-15-1105 et seq.

**Services of State Relevant to Establishment in Political Subdivisions Act**
Cal. Government Code §§ 13073, 13074

**Services Organization Act (Credit)**
Minn. Stat. Ann., 332.52 et seq.

**Services Program Act (Community)**
Kan. Stat. Ann., 79-32,194 et seq.

**Services Reorganization Act (Health and Rehabilitative)**
Fla. Laws 1992, Ch. 58

**Services Tax Act**
Tenn. Code Ann., 67-4-1801 et seq.

**Services to the Blind Act**
Mont. Code Ann. 1991, 53-7-301 et seq.

**Servitude Act (Conservation)**
La. Rev. Stat. Ann., 9:1271 et seq.

**Sesquicentennial Act**
Mich. Comp. Laws Ann., 399.21 et seq.

**Set-Aside Act (Emergency Petroleum)**
Vt. Stat. Ann., Title 9, § 4131 et seq.

**Set-Aside Act for Small Business, Female Business, and Minority Business**
N.J. Stat. Ann., 52:32-17 et seq.

**Set Back Act**
Tenn. Private Acts 1921, Ch. 163
Tenn. Private Acts 1923, Chs. 404, 415

**Setoff Act**
Mich. Comp. Laws 1948, 615.1 et seq., 600.2145 et seq.
N.H. Rev. Stat. 1955, 515:7 et seq.
R.I. Gen. Laws 1956, 9-6-16 et seq.
S.C. Code Ann. 1976, § 15-15-60
Vt. Stat. Ann. 1959, Superseeded Vol., Title 12, § 5461 et seq.
Wash. Rev. Code Ann., 4.32.120 et seq.
Wis. Stat. 1973, 895.07

**Setoff Act (Tax Refund)**
Neb. Rev. Stat. 1943, 77-27, 174 et seq.

**Setoff Debt Collection Act**
N.C. Gen. Stat. 1943, § 105A-1 et seq.
S.C. Code Ann. 1976, §§ 12-54-410 et seq., 12-56-10 et seq.
Va. Code 1950, § 58.1-520 et seq.
Vt. Stat. Ann., Title 32, § 5931 et seq.

**Settlement Act**
Conn. Gen. Stat. Ann., § 17-262 et seq.

**Settlement Act (Micmac)**
Me. Rev. Stat. Ann. 1964, Title 30, § 7201 et seq.

**Settlement Act (Viatical)**
N.Y. Civil Practice Laws and Rules (Consol. Laws Ch. 8) § 5205
N.Y. Insurance Law 1984 (Consol. Laws Ch. 28) §§ 3220, 7801 et seq.
N.Y. Public Health Law 1953 (Consol. Laws Ch. 45) § 20
N.Y. Social Services Law (Consol. Laws Ch. 55) § 366
N.Y. Tax Law (Consol. Laws Ch. 60) § 612

**Settlement and Homestead Act**
Haw. Rev. Laws 1955, § 99-1 et seq.

**Settlement Implementation Act (Indian Claims)**
Me. Rev. Stat. Ann. 1964, Title 30, § 6201 et seq.

**Settlement Law (Poor Relief)**
S.D. Codified Laws 1967, 28-13-1 et seq.

**Settlement of Claims Act**
D.C. Code Ann., § 1-1202 et seq.

**Settlement of Estates Act**
Wash. Rev. Code Ann., 11.76.010 et seq.

**Settlement of Mexican Claims Act Amendments of 1945**
April 3, 1945, Ch. 52, 59 Stat. 49

**Settlement of Mexican Claims Act of 1942**
Dec. 18, 1942, Ch. 766, 56 Stat. 1058
April 3, 1945, Ch. 52, 59 Stat. 49
March 28, 1947, Ch. 23, 61 Stat. 24

**Settlement of Persons Act**
N.H. Rev. Stat. 1955, 164-A:1 et seq.

**Settlement of Small Estates Act**
Ill. Rev. Stat. 1991, Ch. 110 1/2, §§ 25-1 et seq.

**Settlement of War Claims Act of 1928**
March 10, 1928, Ch. 167, 45 Stat. 254
March 10, 1930, Ch. 175, 46 Stat. 84
June 14, 1932, Ch. 259, 47 Stat. 318
March 3, 1933, Ch. 210, 47 Stat. 1488
June 12, 1933, Ch. 60, 48 Stat. 125
June 18, 1934, Ch. 608, 48 Stat. 1019
June 27, 1934, Ch. 851, 48 Stat. 1267
June 26, 1936, Ch. 852, 49 Stat. 1984
May 23, 1938, Ch. 263, 52 Stat. 437
Aug. 6, 1947, Ch. 506, 61 Stat. 789

**Settlement Practice Act (Unfair Claims)**
Ga. Code Ann., 33-6-30 et seq.
Okla. Stat. Ann., Title 36, §§ 1250.1 to 1250.16

**Settlers' Reclamation Act**
Wis. Laws 1935, Ch. 550, Subch. 96

**Seven Crimes Act**
March 3, 1885, Ch. 341, 23 Stat. 385

**Seven Million Dollar Bond Act**
N.J. Stat. Ann., Superseded Vol., 18:10-50, Subd. 1

**Seven-Months School Act**
Ga. Laws 1937, p. 882, § 2

**Seven Sister Act (Decedents' Estates)**
Pa. Cons. Stat., Title 20, § 8301 et seq.

**Seven Sisters Act (Corporations)**
N.J. Laws 1913, Ch. 18

**Seven Year Statute of Limitations (Adverse Possession)**
Ill. Rev. Stat. 1991, Ch. 110, § 13-107

**Seven Year Statute of Limitations (Real Property)**
Colo. Rev. Stat. 38-41-108

**Seventh Circuit Act**
Ark. Code Ann. 1987, 16-13-902 et seq.

**Seventh Supplemental National Defense Appropriation Act of 1942**
June 23, 1942, Ch. 444, 56 Stat. 389

**Seventy-five Million Dollar Bond Bill**
Ky. Acts 1924, Ch. 122

**Seventy-five Year Limitation Act (Real Property)**
Ill. Rev. Stat. 1985, Ch. 110, § 13-114

**Seventy Percent Law (Workers Compensation)**
Mich. Comp. Laws Ann., 418.862

**Seventy-Two Hour Act (Personal Injuries)**
Wis. Stat. Ann., 904.12

**Severability of Statutes Act**
Mo. Rev. Stat., 1.140

**Severance Act (Criminal)**
Tex. Code of Criminal Procedure, Art. 38.06

**Severance and Business Privilege Tax Act**
W. Va. Code 1966 § 11-13A-1 et seq.

**Severance Tax Act**
Ark. Code Ann. 1987, 26-58-101 et seq.
La. Rev. Stat. Ann., 47:631 et seq.
N.M. Stat. Ann., 7-26-1 et seq.
W. Va. Code 1966 § 11-13A-1 et seq.

**Severance Tax Act (Forest Products)**
Ala. Code 1975, § 9-13-80 et seq.

**Severance Tax Act (Minerals)**
Wyo. Stat. Ann., § 39-6-302 et seq.

**Severance Tax Act (Minimum)**
W. Va. Code 1966, § 11-12B-1 et seq.

**Severance Tax Act (Oil and Gas)**
Ind. Code Ann., 6-8-1-1 et seq.
Kan. Laws 1957, Ch. 516
Mich. Comp. Laws Ann., 205.301 et seq.

**Severance Tax Act (Oil)**
Cal. Revenue and Taxation Code § 42002 et seq.
Miss. Code Ann. 1972, § 27-25-501 et seq.

**Severance Tax Bonding Act**
N.M. Stat. Ann., 7-27-1 et seq.

**Severance Tax Income Bonding Act**
N.M. Stat. Ann., 7-27-28 et seq.

**Severe Chronic Disabilities Act (Community Trust for Persons with)**
N.C. Stat. 1943, § 36A-59.10 et seq.

**Severed Mineral Interest Act**
Ill. Rev. Stat. 1991, Ch. 96 1/2, § 9201 et seq.

**Severson Act (Prohibition Enforcement)**
Wis. Laws 1921, Ch. 441

**Sevier County Road Act**
Tenn. Private Acts 1933, Ch. 10

**Sewage and Waste Disposal Facilities Compact Act (New Hampshire-Vermont)**
See New Hampshire-Vermont Interstate Sewage and Waste Disposal Facilities Act

**Sewage and Waste Water Law (County)**
Nev. Rev. Stat. 1979 Reprint, Replaced pages, 244A.455 et seq.

**Sewage and Water Disposal Compact Act (New Hampshire-Vermont)**
N.H. Rev. Stat. 1955, 149-K:1

**Sewage and Water System Training Institute Act**
Ill. Rev. Stat. 1991, Ch. 144, § 690 et seq.

**Sewage Disposal Act**
Ill. Rev. Stat. 1991, Ch. 42, § 411.99 et seq.

**Sewage Disposal and Water Supply District Act**
Mich. Comp. Laws Ann., 323.151 et seq.

**Sewage Disposal and Waterworks Act**
Mich. Comp. Laws Ann., 325.201 et seq.

**Sewage Disposal District Act (Metropolitan Areas)**
Colo. Rev. Stat., 32-4-501 et seq.

**Sewage Disposal District Act (Regional)**
Cal. Health and Safety Code § 5900 et seq.

**Sewage Disposal Licensing Act (Private)**
Ill. Rev. Stat. 1991, Ch. 111 1/2, § 116.301 et seq.

**Sewage Disposal Planning Act**
N.C. Gen. Stat. 1943, § 162A-26 et seq.

**Sewage Disposal Plant Act**
Mich. Comp. Laws Ann., 123.201 et seq.

**Sewage Disposal System Act (Ground Absorption)**
N.C. Gen. Stat. 1943, § 130-166.22 et seq.

**Sewage Disposal Systems Act**
Ark. Code Ann. 1987, 14-236-101 et seq.

**Sewage Disposal Systems Act (Individual)**
Colo. Rev. Stat., 25-10-101 et seq.

**Sewage Disposal Systems Near Shorelines Act**
N.H. Rev. Stat. 1955, 485-A:1 et seq.

**Sewage Disposal through Public System Law**
Mich. Comp. Laws Ann., 123.281 et seq.

**Sewage District Act (Las Vegas)**
Nev. Statutes 1947, Ch. 164, p. 534

**Sewage Facilities Act**
Pa. Purdon's Stat., Title 35, § 750.1 et seq.

**Sewage Holding Tank Act**
Ga. Code Ann., 12-15-1 et seq.

**Sewage Infrastructure Improvement Act**
N.J. Stat. Ann., 58:25-23 et seq.

**Sewage Loan Act (Clinton)**
Mass. Acts 1954, Ch. 462

**Sewage Pollution Act**
Pa. Purdon's Stat., Title 35, § 691.1 et seq.

**Sewage Services Agency Law (Bay Area)**
Cal. Water Code § 16000 et seq.

**Sewage System Cleaner Control Act**
Pa. Purdon's Stat., Title 35, § 770.1 et seq.

**Sewage Treatment Act (State Aid)**
R.I. Public Laws 1967, Ch. 198

**Sewage Treatment Plant and Waterworks Operators' Certification Act**
Pa. Purdon's Stat., Title 63, § 1001 et seq.

**Sewage Treatment Plant Grant and Water Pollution Control Act**
Fla. Stat. Ann., 403.1821 et seq.

**Sewage Treatment Plant under Water Pollution Control Grant Act**
Fla. Stat. Ann., 403.1821 et seq.

**Sewer Act (Municipal Corporations)**
Ark. Code Ann. 1987, 14-235-201, 14-235-203, 14-235-205 et seq.

**Sewer and Small Water Public Utility Act**
Va. Code 1950, § 56-265.13:1 et seq.

**Sewer and Solid Waste Management Districts Act (Rural)**
Okla. Stat. Ann., Title 82, § 1324.1 et seq.

**Sewer and Water Authorities Act**
See Water and Sewer Authorities Act

**Sewer and Water Authority Act (Butts County, City of Flovilla, City of Jackson, City of Jenkinsburg)**
Ga. Laws 1986, p. 5457

**Sewer and Water Authority Act (Clayton-Rabun County)**
Ga. Laws 1992, p. 6403

**Sewer and Water Authority Act (Lamar County)**
Ga. Laws 1991, p. 3942

**Sewer and Water Authority Act (Peachtree City)**
Ga. Laws 1991, p. 5085

**Sewer and Water Districts Act**
Ida. Code 1947, 42-3201 et seq.
Wyo. Stat. Ann., § 41-10-101 et seq.

**Sewer and Water Districts Act (Regional)**
Ohio Rev. Code 1953, 6119.01 et seq.

**Sewer and Water Facilities Act**
Wash. Rev. Code Ann., 35.91.010 et seq.

**Sewer and Water Improvement Districts Act**
Utah Code Ann. 1953, 17A-2-301 et seq.

**Sewer and Water Revenue Act (Port Orange)**
Fla. Special Laws 1951, Ch. 27832

**Sewer and Water Revenue Bond Act**
Ida. Code 1947, 42-4101 et seq.
N.M. Stat. Ann., 3-31-1 et seq.

**Sewer and Water System Regulatory Act**
Fla. Stat. Ann., 367.011 et seq.

**Sewer and Water Utility Authority Act (Hart County)**
Ga. Laws 1992, p. 6828

**Sewer and Water Utility Authority Act (Walker County)**
Ga. Laws 1991, p. 3796

**Sewer Authorities Act**
Md. Ann. Code 1974, Art. EN, § 9-901 et seq.

**Sewer Authority Act (Bergen County)**
N.J. Stat. Ann., 40:14B-1 et seq.

**Sewer Authority Act (Buffalo)**
N.Y. Public Authorities Law (Consol. Laws Ch. 43A) § 1175 et seq.

**Sewer Authority Project Act (Alfred, Almond, Hornersville)**
N.Y. Public Authorities Law (Consol. Laws Ch. 43A) § 1147 et seq.

**Sewer Construction Assistance Act (Small Community)**
Fla. Stat. 403.1838

**Sewer Contract Act (Chicago Sanitary District)**
Ill. Rev. Stat. 1989, Ch. 42, §§ 380z99, 381

**Sewer District Act (Municipal)**
Cal. Statutes 1939, Ch. 24, p. 37

**Sewer District Act (Urban Counties)**
Fla. Laws 1957, Extra Session, Ch. 57-2028

**Sewer District Loan Act (Hillcrest)**
Mass. Acts 1954, Ch. 612

**Sewer District Loan Act (Monroe)**
Mass. Acts 1963, Ch. 559

**Sewer District Sewerage Loan Act (Lancaster)**
Mass. Acts 1952, Ch. 43

**Sewer Districts Act**
Vt. Stat. Ann., Title 24, § 3671 et seq.
Wash. Rev. Code Ann., 56.02.010 et seq.

**Sewer Districts Act (Metropolitan)**
Mont. Code Ann., 7-13-101 et seq.

**Sewer Districts Act of 1899, 1911**
Cal. Health and Safety Code §§ 4600 et seq., 4659 et seq.

**Sewer Districts in Unincorporated Territory Act**
Cal. Health and Safety Code, § 4659 et seq.

**Sewer Districts Revenue Bond Act**
Cal. Stat. 1939, Ch. 532, p. 1924

**Sewer Financing Act (Coral Gables)**
Fla. Special Laws 1949, Ch. 25743

**Sewer Financing Act (Counties)**
Fla. Stat. Ann., 153.01 et seq.

**Sewer Financing Act (Miami Shores Village)**
Fla. Special Laws 1947, Ch. 24715

**Sewer Financing Act (Miami)**
Fla. Special Laws 1945, Ch. 23407

**Sewer Loan Act (Ayer)**
Mass. Acts 1949, Ch. 300
Mass. Acts 1960, Ch. 167

**Sewer Loan Act (Falmouth)**
Mass. Acts 1928, Ch. 288, § 6

**Sewer Maintenance District Act**
Cal. Health and Safety Code, § 4860 et seq.

**Sewer Reconstruction Loan Act (Nantucket)**
Mass. Acts 1959, Ch. 275

**Sewer Rental Act**
N.Y. General Municipal Law (Consol. Laws Ch. 24), § 450 et seq.
Pa. Purdon's Stat., Title 53, § 2231 et seq.

**Sewer Revenue Act (Lake Wales)**
Fla. Special Laws 1947, Ch. 24648

**Sewer Revenue Bond Act**
Cal. Statutes 1933, Ch. 331, p. 909
Cal. Statutes 1939, Ch. 532, p. 1924
Cal. Statutes 1941, Ch. 322, p. 1506
Del. Laws Vol. 47, p. 546, Ch. 260

**Sewer Revenue Bond Act (Daytona Beach)**
Fla. Special Laws 1945, Ch. 23240

**Sewer Revenue Bond Act (Fort Myers)**
Fla. Special Laws 1945, Chs. 23284, 23293

**Sewer Revenue Bond Act (Sarasota)**
Fla. Special Laws 1945, Ch. 23528

**Sewer Revenue Bond Act (Tampa)**
Fla. Special Laws 1945, Ch. 23564

**Sewer Revenue Bond Act (Venice)**
Fla. Special Laws 1945, Ch. 23586

**Sewer Revenue Bond Act (Wilmington)**
Del. Laws Vol. 47, p. 581, Ch. 269

**Sewer Right of Way Law**
Cal. Government Code § 39000 et seq.

**Sewer, Sanitation and Water Revenue Bond Law**
Cal. Government Code, § 54300 et seq.

**Sewer Service Charge and Revenue Bond Act**
Ind. Code Ann., 19-2-5-1 et seq.

**Sewer System Act**
Ill. Rev. Stat. 1991, Ch. 24, § 11-141-1 et seq.
N.H. Rev. Stat. 1955, 149-I:1 et seq.
P.R. Laws Ann. 1954, Title 22, § 141 et seq.
S.D. Codified Laws 1967, 9-48-1 et seq.

**Sewer, Water, and Solid Waste Management Systems Finance Act**
Ark. Code Ann. 1987, 14-230-101 et seq.

**Sewerage Act (Municipal and County)**
N.J. Stat. Ann., 40A:26A-1 et seq.

**Sewerage and District Act**
Cal. Health and Safety Code § 5500 et seq.

**Sewerage and Water Authority Act (Bald Mountain)**
Ga. Laws 1983, p. 4466

**Sewerage and Water Authority Act (Barrow County)**
Ga. Laws 1991, p. 4444

**Sewerage and Water Authority Act (Bibb County)**
Ga. Laws 1966, p. 2737

**Sewerage and Water Authority Act (Douglasville-Douglas County)**
Ga. Laws 1985, p. 3584

**Sewerage and Water Authority Act (Ellijay-Gilmer County)**
Ga. Laws 1991, p. 5424

**Sewerage and Water Authority Act (Gilmer County)**
Ga. Laws 1984, p. 5215

**Sewerage and Water Authority Act (Hall County)**
Ga. Laws 1992, p. 6986

**Sewerage and Water Authority Act (Jackson County)**
Ga. Laws 1986, p. 5473

**Sewerage and Water Authority Act (Lumpkin County)**
Ga. Laws 1984, p. 4500

**Sewerage and Water Authority Act (Oak Ridge)**
Ga. Laws 1991, p. 4310

**Sewerage and Water Authority Act (Pike County)**
Ga. Laws 1991, p. 4180

**Sewerage and Water Authority Act (Stewart County)**
Ga. Laws 1988, p. 4498

**Sewerage and Water Authority Act (White County)**
Ga. Laws 1984, p. 4920

**Sewerage and Water District Act**
Cal. Health and Safety Code, § 5500 et seq.

**Sewerage and Water Facilities Act (Spalding County)**
Ga. Laws 1982, p. 4987

**Sewerage Authorities Act**
N.J. Stat. Ann., 40:14A-1 et seq.

**Sewerage Consolidation Law (Clark County)**
Nev. Statutes 1973, Ch. 447, p. 646

**Sewerage District Act (Metropolitan)**
See Metropolitan Sewerage District Act

**Sewerage Facilities Aid Program Act**
N.J. Stat. Ann., 58:25-1 et seq.

**Sewerage Facilities Bond Act**
Md. Ann. Code 1974, Art. EN, § 9-801 et seq.

**Sewerage Improvement District Act**
Wash. Rev. Code Ann., 85.08.010 et seq.

**Sewerage Improvement District Maintenance Act**
Wash. Rev. Code Ann., 85.16.010 et seq.

**Sewerage Loan Act (Brockton)**
Mass. Acts 1961, Ch. 453

**Sewerage Loan Act (Clarksburg)**
Mass. Acts 1951, Ch. 668

**Sewerage Loan Act (Cohasset)**
Mass. Acts 1962, Ch. 65

**Sewerage Loan Act (East Bridgewater)**
Mass. Acts 1964, Ch. 88

**Sewerage Loan Act (Holbrook)**
Mass. Acts 1964, Ch. 74

**Sewerage Loan Act (Ipswich)**
Mass. Acts 1946, Ch. 30

**Sewerage Loan Act (Lanesborough Garden Circle)**
Mass. Acts 1951, Ch. 133

**Sewerage Loan Act (Leominster)**
Mass. Acts 1961, Ch. 337

**Sewerage Loan Act (Longmeadow)**
Mass. Acts 1955, Ch. 178

**Sewerage Loan Act (Mansfield)**
Mass. Acts 1929, Ch. 348

**Sewerage Loan Act (Marlborough)**
Mass. Acts 1962, Ch. 355

**Sewerage Loan Act (Metropolitan North District)**
Mass. Acts 1951, Ch. 757
Mass. Acts 1954, Ch. 452
Mass. Acts 1955, Ch. 682

**Sewerage Loan Act (Metropolitan)**
Mass. Acts 1951, Ch. 645
Mass. Acts 1954, Ch. 580
Mass. Acts 1955, Ch. 551
Mass. Acts 1957, Ch. 710
Mass. Acts 1962, Ch. 658

**Sewerage Loan Act (Montague)**
Mass. Acts 1960, Ch. 440

**Sewerage Loan Act (Mount Pleasant)**
Mass. Acts 1955, Ch. 671

**Sewerage Loan Act (Newburyport)**
Mass. Acts 1963, Ch. 261

**Sewerage Loan Act (Randolph)**
Mass. Acts 1955, Ch. 273
Mass. Acts 1960, Ch. 278

**Sewerage Loan Act (Salisbury)**
Mass. Acts 1964, Ch. 81

**Sewerage Loan Act (Scituate)**
Mass. Acts 1957, Ch. 636

**Sewerage Loan Act (Shrewsbury)**
Mass. Acts 1954, Ch. 502

**Sewerage Loan Act (Weymouth)**
Mass. Acts 1960, Ch. 412

**Sewerage Loan Act (Whitman)**
Mass. Acts 1961, Ch. 460

**Sewerage Relief Loan Act (Metropolitan Districts)**
Mass. Acts 1962, Ch. 655

**Sewerage System Act (Cities and Towns)**
Wash. Rev. Code Ann., 35.67.010 et seq.

**Sewerage Treatment Loan Act (Northampton)**
Mass. Acts 1955, Ch. 462

**Sewers District Organization Act**
Mo. Rev. Stat., 249.010 et seq.
N.H. Rev. Stat. 1955, 149-I:1 et seq.
Pa. 1889 Pamph. Laws 220, No. 229
Pa. 1891 Pamph. Laws 75, No. 59
P.R. Laws Ann. 1954, Title 22, § 141 et seq.

**Sex and Child Offender Registration Act**
Ark. Code Ann. 1987, 12-12-901 et seq.

**Sex Crimes Act**
Cal. Penal Code § 288a
Ill. Rev. Stat. 1991, Ch. 38, § 11-6 et seq.
N.Y. Penal Law 1965 (Consol. Laws Ch. 40), § 130.00 et seq.
Pa. Cons. Stat., Title 18, § 3101 et seq.
Tenn. Code Ann., 39-2-601 et seq.
Wis. Stat. Ann., 975.01 et seq.

**Sex Crimes Against Children Prevention Act of 1995**
Dec. 23, 1995, P.L. 104-71, 28 U.S. Code § 994 nt.

**Sex Discrimination Act (Employment)**
Neb. Rev. Stat. 1943, 48-1219 et seq.
R.I. Gen. Laws 1956, 28-6-17 et seq.

**Sex Offender Community Notification Law (Child)**
Ill. Comp. Stat. 1992, Ch. 730, § 152/101 et seq.

**Sex Offender Management Board Act**
Ill. Comp. Stat. 1992, Ch. 20, § 4026/1 et seq.

**Sex Offender Registration Notification and Community Right-to-Know Act (Juvenile)**
Ida. Code 1947, 18-8401 et seq.

**Sex Offenders Act**
Colo. Rev. Stat., 16-13-201 et seq.
Kan. Stat. Ann., 62-1534 et seq.
Mass. Gen. Laws Ann., 123A:1 et seq.
Neb. Rev. Stat. 1943, 29-2911 et seq.
N.J. Stat. Ann., 2C:47-1 et seq.

**Sex Offenders Act (Lifetime Supervision of)**
Colo. Rev. Stat., 16-13-801 et seq.

**Sex Offenders Orchiectomy Law**
Tex. Government Code, §§ 501.061, 501.062

**Sex Offenders Registration Act**
Ark. Code Ann. 1987, No. 587
Cal. Penal Code § 290
Ida. Code 1947, 18-8301 et seq.
Ill. Rev. Stat. 1991, Ch. 38, § 221 et seq.
Kan. Stat. Ann., 22-3902 et seq.
Ky. Rev. Stat. 1971, 17.500 to 17.540
Me. Rev. Stat. Ann. 1964, Title 34-A, § 11001 et seq.
Mich. Comp. Laws Ann., 28.721 et seq.
Minn. Stat. Ann., 243.166
Mont. Laws 1991, Ch. 293
Neb. Rev. Stat. 1943, 29-4001 to 29-4013
N.M. Stat. Ann., 29-11A-1 et seq.
N.Y. Correction Law (Consol. Laws Ch. 43) § 168 et seq.
Okla. Stat. Ann., Title 57, § 581 et seq.
Tex. Code of Criminal Procedure, Art. 62.01 et seq.
W. Va. Code 1966 § 61-8F-1 et seq.

**Sex Offenders Registration Act (Habitual)**
Kan. Laws 1994, Ch. 253, §§ 17 to 26
Me. Rev. Stat. Ann. 1964, Title 34-A, § 11001

**Sex Offense Criminal History Record Information Act**
Miss. Code Ann. 1972, § 45-31-1 et seq.

**Sex Offense Victim Polygraph Act**
Ill. Rev. Stat. 1991, Ch. 38, §§ 1550, 1551

**Sex Psychopath Sentencing Act**
Pa. Cons. Stat., Title 18, § 3101 et seq.

**Sexual Abuse Act of 1986**
Nov. 10, 1986, P.L. 99-646, 18 U.S. Code § 2241 nt.
Nov. 14, 1986, P.L. 99-654, 18 U.S. Code § 2241 nt.

**Sexual Abuse Prevention Act (Child)**
Cal. Penal Code § 288
Ill. Comp. Stat. 1992, Ch. 325, § 15/0.01 et seq.

**Sexual Abuse Victim Protection Act (Children)**
Ala. Code 1975, § 15-25-30 et seq.

**Sexual and Physical Abuse Victim Protection Act**
Ala. Code 1975, § 15-25-30 et seq.

**Sexual and Violent Offenders Act (DNA Detection)**
Neb. Rev. Stat. 1943, 29-4101 to 29-4115
Pa. Purdon's Stat., Title 35, § 7651.101 et seq.

**Sexual Assault Act**
Ohio Rev. Code 1953, 2907.02
S.C. Code Ann. 1976, § 16-3-651 et seq.

**Sexual Assault Prevention Act**
Mo. Rev. Stat., 589.010 et seq.

**Sexual Assault Prevention and Crisis Services Act**
Tex. Health and Safety Code, §§ 44.001 et seq., 420.001 et seq.

**Sexual Assault Survivors Emergency Treatment Act**
Ill. Rev. Stat. 1991, Ch. 111 1/2, § 87-1 et seq.

**Sexual Assault Victims Act**
Wash. Rev. Code Ann., 70.125.010 et seq.

**Sexual Crimes Prosecution and Treatment Act**
N.M. Stat. 1978, 29-11-1 et seq.

**Sexual Deviant Act**
Ind. Code Ann., 35-42-4-2 et seq.
Wis. Stat. 1967, 959.15

**Sexual Deviation Research Act**
Cal. Welfare and Institutions Code, § 8050 et seq.

**Sexual Exploitation in Psychotherapy Act**
Ill. Rev. Stat. 1991, Ch. 70, § 800 et seq.

**Sexual Exploitation of Children Act**
N.M. Stat. Ann., 30-6A-1 et seq.

**Sexual or Violent Offender Registration Act**
Mont. Code Ann., 46-18-254, 46-18-255, 46-23-501 et seq.

**Sexual Predators Act**
Del. Laws 1995, Vol. 70, Ch. 600
Fla. Stat. Ann., 775.21 et seq.
Wash. Rev. Code Ann., 71.09.010

**Sexual Protection Act (Retarded Citizens)**
Ala. Code 1975, §§ 13A-6-62, 13A-6-64

**Sexual Psychopathic Act**
W. Va. Code 1966, § 27-6A-1 et seq.

**Sexual Psychopaths Act**
Ala. Code 1958, Title 15, § 434 et seq.
Cal. Welfare and Institutions Code, § 6300 et seq.
D.C. Code 1973, § 22-3501 et seq.
Fla. Stat. Ann., 916.10 et seq., 917.011 et seq.
Ill. Rev. Stat. 1991, Ch. 38, § 105-1.01 et seq.
Ind. Code 1971, 35-11-3-1 et seq.
Iowa Code 1977, 225A.1 et seq.
Mass. Gen. Laws Ann., 123A:1 et seq.
Mich. Comp. Laws 1948, 780.501 et seq.
Minn. Stat. Ann., 526.09 et seq.
Mo. Rev. Stat. 1978, 202.700 et seq.
Neb. Rev. Stat. 1943, 29-2911 et seq.
N.H. Rev. Stat. 1955, 173-A:1 et seq.
N.J. Stat. Ann., 2C:47-1 et seq.
Ohio Rev. Code 1953, 2947.24 et seq.
Ore. Rev. Stat., 137.111 et seq.
Wash. Rev. Code Ann., 71.06.010 et seq.
Wis. Stat. 1967, 959.15

**Sexual Sterilization Act**
Miss. Code Ann. 1972, § 41-45-1 et seq.
Va. Code 1950, § 37.1-156 et seq.

**Sexually Dangerous Persons Act**
Ill. Rev. Stat. 1991, Ch. 38, § 105 et seq.
Mass. Gen. Laws Ann., 123A:1 et seq.

**Sexually Dangerous Persons Act (Interstate Agreements)**
Ill. Rev. Stat. 1991, Ch. 38, §§ 205, 205-1

**Sexually Transmissable Disease Control Act**
Fla. Stat. Ann., 384.21 et seq.
Ill. Rev. Stat. 1991, Ch. 111 1/2, § 7401 et seq.

**Sexually Transmitted Disease Control Confidentiality Act**
Ky. Rev. Stat. 1971, 214.400 et seq.

**Sexually Violent Persons Commitment Act**
Ill. Comp. Stat. 1992, Ch. 725, § 207/1 et seq.

**Sexually Violent Predator Act**
Iowa Code 1995, 229A.1 to 229A.18
S.C. Code Ann. 1976, § 44-48-10 et seq.

**Seymour-Campbell Matriculation Act**
Cal. Education Code 1976, § 78210 et seq.

**Shackleford Act**
July 11, 1916, Ch. 241, 39 Stat. 355

**Shade Control Act**
Cal. Public Resources Code § 25980 et seq.

**Shade Tree Act**
Cal. Government Code § 25620 et seq.
Cal. Streets and Highways Code §§ 22000 et seq., 25620 et seq.
Mass. Gen. Laws Ann., 87:1 et seq.

**Shade Tree and Community Forestry Assistance Act**
N.J. Stat. Ann., 13:1L-17.1 et seq.

**Shaker Act**
N.Y. Religious Corporations Law (Consol. Laws Ch. 51), § 202

**Shanty Boat Law**
Ky. Rev. Stat. 1971, 182.140 et seq., 182.990

**Shapiro Act (Cooperative Marketing)**
Minn. Stat. Ann., 308.51 et seq.

**Share Act (Control)**
Miss. Code Ann. 1972, § 79-27-1 et seq.

**Share in Your Future Act**
W. Va. Code 1966 § 18-2F-1 et seq.

**Sharecroppers Act**
La. Code of Civil Procedure, Art. 4701 et seq.
P.R. Laws Ann. 1954, Title 5, § 201 et seq.

**Shared Appreciation Loan Law**
Cal. Civil Code § 1917 et seq.

**Shared Credit Rating Act**
Mich. Comp. Laws Ann., 141.1051 et seq.

**Shared Health Facilities Act (Medicaid Mills)**
N.Y. Public Health Law 1953 (Consol. Laws Ch. 45) § 4700 et seq.

**Shared Parental Responsibility Act**
Fla. Stat. Ann., 61.13

**Shareholder Communications Act of 1985**
Dec. 28, 1985, P.L. 99-222, 15 U.S. Code §§ 78a nt., 78 n, 78m nt.

**Shareholder Communications Improvement Act of 1990**
Nov. 15, 1990, P.L. 101-550, 15 U.S. Code § 78a nt.

**Shareholder Equity Act (Stacey, Bennett and Randall)**
Mich. Comp. Laws Ann., 450.1790 et seq.

**Shareholder Inspection Act**
Mo. Rev. Stat., 351.215

**Shareholder Protection Act**
Miss. Code Ann. 1972, § 79-25-1 et seq.
N.C. Gen. Stat. 1943, § 55-9-01 et seq.
Neb. Rev. Stat. 1943, 21-2431 et seq.
N.J. Stat. Ann., 14A:10A-1 et seq.
N.Y. Environmental Conservation Law 1972 (Consol. Laws Ch. 43B) §§ 70-0107, 70-0117

**Shareholders Appraisal Act**
Ala. Code 1975, § 10-2A-162
Colo. Rev. Stat., 7-7-108
Conn. Gen. Stat. Ann., § 33-373
Ga. Code 1933, 22-1202
Ill. Rev. Stat. 1991, Ch. 32, § 11.70
Ky. Rev. Stat. 1971, Superseded Vol., 271.415
Mass. Gen. Laws Ann., 156:46
Me. Rev. Stat. Ann. 1964, Title 13A, § 909
N.C. Gen. Stat. 1943, § 55-13-30, Subsec. e
Okla. Stat. Ann., Title 18, § 1091 et seq.
Tex. Business Corporation Act, Art. 5.12, Subds. B to D

**Shareholders' Liability Act**
Cal. Corporations Code § 410 et seq.

**Shares and Deposits Insurance Corporation for Cooperative Savings and Credit Unions Act**
P.R. Acts 1989, First Special Session, No. 5

**Shares and Deposits Insurance Fund for Savings and Credit Unions Act**
P.R. Laws Ann. 1954, Title 7, § 1151

**Sharing Act (Revenue)**
Fla. Stat. Ann., 218.20 et seq.

**Sharing Rides Act**
S.C. Code Ann. 1976, § 58-23-18 et seq.

**Sharkey-Brown-Isaacs Act (Discrimination)**
N.Y. City Adm. Code '38, Ch. 1, § D1-1.0 et seq.

**Shasta County Regional Library Facilities and Services Act**
Cal. Government Code § 26170 et seq.

**Shasta County Water Agency Act**
Cal. Water Code, Appendix, § 83-1 et seq.

**Shattuck-Gay Act (Intoxicating Liquor)**
La. Acts 1908, No. 176

**Shaver Act (Bar Association)**
Ala. Code 1975, § 34-3-17

**Shaw Act (Intoxicating Liquor)**
Ala. Code 1975, § 28-4-1 et seq.

**Shawano Municipal Court Act**
Wis. Laws 1957, Ch. 682

**Shawneetown Regional Port District Act**
Ill. Rev. Stat. 1991, Ch. 19, § 401 et seq.

**Shea Act (Aerial Photography)**
Mich. Comp. Laws Ann., 321.151 et seq.

**Shea Act (Military Service Overseas)**
Mass. Acts 1970, Ch. 174

**Shedding Act (Piers)**
N.Y. Laws 1875, Ch. 249

**Sheep Act**
Pa. 1878 Pamph. Laws 198, No. 231

**Sheep and Goat Act**
N.M. Stat. Ann., 77-8A-1 to 77-8A-11

**Sheep and Wool Authority Act**
Colo. Rev. Stat., 35-57.5-101 et seq.

**Sheep and Wool Producers Act**
Okla. Stat. Ann., Title 2, § 1501 et seq.

**Sheep and Wool Production Development and Marketing Act**
Ill. Rev. Stat. 1991, Ch. 5, § 1051 et seq.

**Sheep Commission Act**
Nev. Rev. Stat. 1979 Reprint, 562.010 et seq.

**Sheep Damage Act**
Pa. 1893 Pamph. Laws 136, No. 88

**Sheep, Lamb, and Wool Promotion, Research and Education Act**
Ida. Code 1947, 25-153 to 25-160

**Sheep License Limitation Act**
Cal. Business and Professions Code, § 16104

**Sheep Ownership Declaration Act**
Wyo. Stat. 1957, § 11-466 et seq.

**Sheep Producers' Indemnity Act**
Tenn. Code Ann., 44-14-101 et seq.

**Sheep Promotion, Research, and Information Act of 1994**
Oct. 22, 1994, P.L. 103-407, 7 U.S. Code §§ 7101 et seq., 7101 nt.

**Sheep Quarantine Act**
Ida. Code 1947, 25-126 et seq.

**Sheep Scabies Eradication Law**
Cal. Food and Agricultural Code 1967, § 9301 et seq.

**Shelby County, Alabama Civil Service Act**
Ala. Acts 1993, No. 664

**Shelby County Cemetery Act**
Tenn. Private Acts 1925, Ch. 405

**Shelby County Jury Commission Act**
Tenn. Acts 1905, Ch. 230

**Shelby County Water Agency Act**
Cal. Water Code, Appendix, § 83-1 et seq.

**Sheldon Civic Center Act**
Ill. Rev. Stat. 1991, Ch. 85, § 5201 et seq.

**Sheldon, Katherine Dunham, Oak Park, Aledo, Normal, Mason County, Jasper County, Brownstown Park District, Jo Daviess County, and Milford Civic Centers Act**
Ill. Rev. Stat. 1991, Ch. 85, § 4500 et seq.

**Shell-Cunningham Tidelands Act**
Cal. Statutes 1955, Ch. 1724, p. 3165

**Shelley-Maloney Apprentice Labor Standards Act**
Cal. Labor Code, § 3070 et seq.

**Shellfish Act**
Fla. Stat. Ann., 370.01 et seq.
Mass. Gen. Laws Ann., 130.37 et seq.
N.J. Stat. Ann., 50:1-5 et seq.
Va. Code 1950, § 28.1-1 et seq.

**Shellfish Pilot Program (Sanitary Control of)**
Cal. Health and Safety Code § 112290 et seq.

**Shellfish Protection Act**
Cal. Water Code § 14950 et seq.

**Shelter Assistance Trust Fund Act (Homeless)**
Neb. Laws 1992, L.B. 1192, §§ 1 to 8

**Shelter Belt Snow Fence Law**
Kan. Stat. Ann., 29-501 et seq.

**Shelter Care and Detention Home Act (County)**
Ill. Rev. Stat. 1991, Ch. 23, § 2681 et seq.

**Shelter House Act**
Mich. Comp. Laws Ann., 460.53

**Shelter Incentive Act**
Okla. Stat. Ann., Title 63, § 688.1 et seq.

**Shelter Rock Public Library Act**
N.Y. Laws 1962, Ch. 972

**Sheltered Care Licensing Act**
R.I. Gen. Laws 1956, 23-17.4-1 et seq.

**Sheltered Plan Act (Tax)**
S.C. Code Ann. 1976, § 8-23-10 et seq.

**Sheltered Workshop Act**
N.J. Stat. Ann., 34:16-39 et seq.

**Shelters Act (Domestic Violence)**
Ill. Rev. Stat. 1991, Ch. 40, § 2400 et seq.

**Shelters for Victims of Domestic Violence Act**
N.J. Stat. Ann., 30:14-1 et seq.

**Shenandoah National Park Act**
Va. Code 1950, § 7.1-19

**Shenandoah National Park Acts**
May 22, 1926, Ch. 363, 44 Stat. 616, 16 U.S. Code §§ 403, 403a to 403c
Feb. 16, 1928, Ch. 59, 45 Stat. 109, 16 U.S. Code §§ 403b, 403d
Feb. 4, 1932, Ch. 19, 47 Stat. 37, 16 U.S. Code §§ 403b, 403e
Aug. 19, 1937, Ch. 703, 50 Stat. 700, 16 U.S. Code §§ 403c-1, 403c-3, 403c-4. (See 18 U.S. Code §§ 3041, 3053, 3141) 18 U.S. Code Fed Rules Cr. Proc., Rules 4, 5(c), 9; 28 U.S. Code §§ 127, 604, 631 632, 634; 28 U.S. Code Fed Rules Civ. Proc. rule 4
June 13, 1939, Ch. 198, 53 Stat. 815, 16 U.S. Code § 403-1
June 5, 1942, Ch. 343, 56 Stat. 321, 16 U.S. Code § 403c-1
June 6, 1942, Ch. 380, 56 Stat. 327, 16 U.S. Code § 459s
June 30, 1961, P.L. 87-71, 75 Stat. 192, 16 U.S. Code § 403-3

**Shenandoah Valley Battlefields National Historic District and Commission Act of 1996**
Nov. 12, 1996, P.L. 104-333, § 606, 16 U.S. Code § 461 nt.

**Sheppard Air Corps Cadet Act**
See Army Aviation Cadet Act

**Sheppard Army Reserve Act**
See Army Reorganization Acts

**Sheppard Bone-Dry Law in District of Columbia**
March 3, 1917, Ch. 165, 39 Stat. 1123

**Sheppard-Towner Act (Maternity Hygiene)**
See Maternity Act

**Sheridan-McCollough Primary Reimbursement Act**
Mich. Comp. Laws Ann., 168.624f

**Sheriff Fee Act**
Pa. Cons. Stat., Title 42, § 21101 et seq.

**Sheriff Fees and Court Costs Transfer Act**
Ill. Rev. Stat. 1991, Ch. 33, § 28.9 et seq.

**Sheriff Offices Nomenclature Act**
Ga. Code Ann., 15-16-50 et seq.

**Sheriffs Act**
Ariz. Rev. Stat. Ann., § 11-441 et seq.
Ill. Rev. Stat. 1991, Ch. 125

**Sheriff's and Marshal's Bond Act (Attachments)**
Mo. Rev. Stat., 521.750 et seq.

**Sheriff's Civil Service Law (County)**
Tenn. Code Ann., 8-8-401 et seq.

**Sheriffs Fee Act**
Pa. Purdon's Stat., Title 42, § 21101 et seq.

**Sheriffs Fee Bill Act**
Pa. Purdon's Stat., Title 16, § 7861 et seq.

**Sheriffs Fees and Court Costs Transfer Act**
Ill. Comp. Stat. 1992, Ch. 55, § 40/0.01 et seq.

**Sheriffs Interpleader Act**
Pa. Purdon's Stat., Title 12, § 2358 et seq.

**Sheriffs Law Enforcement Training Act**
Neb. Rev. Stat. 1943, 81-1401 et seq.

**Sheriff's Merit System Act**
Ill. Rev. Stat. 1987, Ch. 125, § 151 et seq.

**Sheriffs Pension and Relief Fund Act**
La. Rev. Stat. Ann., 33:1451 et seq.

**Sheriffs' Retirement Act**
Mont. Code Ann., 19-7-105 et seq.

**Sheriffs' Retirement System Act**
Mo. Rev. Stat., 57.949 et seq.

**Sheriffs' Supplemental Pension Fund Act**
N.C. Gen. Stat. 1943, § 143-166.80 et seq.

**Sherley Amendment (Food and Drugs)**
Aug. 23, 1912, Ch. 352, 37 Stat. 416
March 3, 1913, Ch. 117, 37 Stat. 732

**Sherman Act (Purchase of Silver)**
July 14, 1890, Ch. 708, 26 Stat. 289

**Sherman Anti-Trust Act (Trusts)**
July 2, 1890, Ch. 647, 26 Stat. 209, 15 U.S. Code §§ 1 to 7
July 7, 1955, Ch. 281, 69 Stat. 282, 15 U.S. Code §§ 1 to 3
Oct. 8, 1982, P.L. 97-290, 15 U.S. Code § 6a
Nov. 16, 1990, P.L. 101-588, 15 U.S. Code §§ 1 to 3

**Sherman Food, Drug and Cosmetic Law**
Cal. Health and Safety Code, § 26000 et seq.

**Sherman Silver Act of 1890 (Repeal)**
Nov. 1, 1893, Ch. 8, 28 Stat. 4

**Shermantown Charter**
Nev. Statutes 1869, Ch. 102, p. 175

**Shern Act (City Employes)**
Pa. 1906 Ex. Pamph. Laws 19, No. 4

**Sherwood Act (Mexican, Civil War Pensions)**
May 11, 1912, Ch. 123, 37 Stat. 112
June 10, 1918, Ch. 96, 40 Stat. 603

**Shield Act**
Ore. Rev. Stat., 44.510 et seq.
Tenn. Code Ann., 24-1-208

**Shield Act (News Media)**
Mont. Code Ann., 26-1-901 et seq.
N.J. Rules of Evidence, Rule 27
N.Y. Civil Rights Law (Consol. Laws Ch. 6) § 79h
Pa. Cons. Stat., Title 42, § 5942

**Shield Law (Rape)**
N.M. Stat. Ann., 30-9-16
Wis. Stat. Ann., 972.11, 2

**Shields-Nickell Governmental Reorganization Act**
Ky. Rev. Stat. 1971, Superseded Vols., 12.025
Ky. Rev. Stat. 1971, 12.027

**Shields-Warriner-Webb Act (Married Woman's Property)**
Ky. Rev. Stat. 1971, 404.010

**Ship and Yacht Brokers' Act**
Cal. Harbors and Navigation Code § 76 et seq.
Fla. Stat. Ann., 236.001 et seq.

**Ship Brokers Act**
Cal. Harbors and Navigation Code § 700 et seq.

**Ship Canal Authority Act**
Fla. Stat. Ann., 374.011 et seq.

**Ship Lien Act**
Wash. Rev. Code Ann., 60.36.010 et seq.

**Ship Load Line Act**
July 3, 1941, Ch. 276, 55 Stat. 578, 46 U.S. Code § 88a

**Ship Mortgage Act**
La. Rev. Stat. Ann., 9:5521 et seq.

**Ship Mortgage Act of 1920**
June 5, 1920, Ch. 250, 41 Stat. 1000, 46 U.S. Code §§ 911, 921 to 927, 941, 951 to 954, 961, 971 to 975, 981 to 984
June 29, 1954, Ch. 419, 68 Stat. 323, 46 U.S. Code § 951
Sept. 26, 1961, P.L. 87-303, 75 Stat. 661, 46 U.S. Code § 922
Nov. 8, 1965, P.L. 89-346, 79 Stat. 1306, 46 U.S. Code § 961
Sept. 16, 1966, P.L. 89-582, 80 Stat. 795, 46 U.S. Code §§ 923, 927
Aug. 10, 1971, P.L. 92-79, 85 Stat. 285, 46 U.S. Code § 973

**Ship Mortgage Law**
La. Rev. Stat. Ann., 9:5521 et seq.

**Ship Operation Act (Watercraft)**
Mich. Comp. Laws 1948, 281.571 et seq.

**Ship Seizure Bill**
June 6, 1941, Ch. 174, 55 Stat. 242

**Ship Subsidies Act**
See Merchant Marine Act of 1936

**Shipbuilding Act**
May 10, 1892, Ch. 63, 27 Stat. 27

**Shipowner Service Act (Nonresident)**
Pa. Cons. Stat., Title 42, §§ 1722, 5322, 5323

**Shipping Act (Intoxicating Liquors)**
Ky. Rev. Stat. 1971, 242.260 et seq.

**Shipping Act Amendments of 1979**
June 19, 1979, P.L. 96-25, 46 U.S. Code §§ 815, 815 nt., 817, 820 to 822, 826, 828, 829, 831, 842 nt.

**Shipping Act of 1916**
Sept. 7, 1916, Ch. 451, 39 Stat. 728, 46 U.S. Code §§ 801 to 842
May 10, 1948, Ch. 269, 62 Stat. 212, 46 U.S. Code § 838
Aug. 12, 1958, P.L. 85-626, 72 Stat. 574, 46 U.S. Code § 812
Sept. 21, 1959, P.L. 86-327, 73 Stat. 597, 46 U.S. Code § 802
Sept. 19, 1961, P.L. 87-254, 75 Stat. 522, 46 U.S. Code §§ 801, 841b, 842
Oct. 3, 1961, P.L. 87-346, 75 Stat. 762, 46 U.S. Code §§ 813a, 814, 815, 817, 819, 841a
Aug. 22, 1963, P.L. 88-103, 77 Stat. 129, 46 U.S. Code § 817
Feb. 29, 1964, P.L. 88-275, 78 Stat. 148, 46 U.S. Code § 814
Oct. 30, 1965, P.L. 89-303, 79 Stat. 1124, 46 U.S. Code § 817
Nov. 8, 1965, P.L. 89-346, 79 Stat. 1305, 46 U.S. Code §§ 808, 835
Nov. 6, 1966, P.L. 89-778, 80 Stat. 1358, 46 U.S. Code § 833a
April 29, 1968, P.L. 90-298, 82 Stat. 111, 46 U.S. Code § 817
Oct. 15, 1970, P.L. 91-452, 84 Stat. 930, 46 U.S. Code § 827

*Continued*

Oct. 18, 1978, P.L. 95-483, 46 U.S. Code §§ 801, 817
June 19, 1979, P.L. 96-25, 46 U.S. Code §§ 815, 815 nt., 817, 820 to 822, 826, 828, 829, 831, 842 nt.
Aug. 8, 1980, P.L. 96-325, 46 U.S. Code §§ 801 et seq.
Mar 20, 1984, P.L. 98-237, 46 U.S. Code Appx. §§ 801, 812 to 817, 819 to 821, 824, 825, 828 to 831, 841c
Oct. 30, 1984, P.L. 98-595, 46 U.S. Code Appx. §§ 801, 815, 820, 1704, 1710
Nov. 23, 1988, P.L. 100-710, 46 U.S. Code Appx. §§ 808, 838, 840
Dec. 12, 1989, P.L. 101-225, 46 U.S. Code Appx. §§ 808, 836
Dec. 29, 1995, P.L. 104-88, 46 U.S. Code Appx. §§ 804, 812, 814 et seq., 826, 828 et seq., 833a, 841a, 841c
Oct. 8, 1996, P.L. 104-239, 46 U.S. Code Appx. § 808
Oct. 19, 1996, P.L. 104-324, 46 U.S. Code Appx. § 808

**Shipping Act of 1984**
March 20, 1984, P.L. 98-237, 46 U.S. Code Appx. §§ 1701, 1701 nt. , 1702 et seq.
Oct. 30, 1984, P.L. 98-595, 46 U.S. Code Appx. §§ 704, 1710, 1714
May 19, 1986, P.L. 99-307, 46 U.S. Code Appx. § 1702
Dec. 12, 1989, P.L. 101-225, 46 U.S. Code Appx. § 1720
Nov. 16, 1990, P.L. 101-595, 46 U.S. Code Appx. §§ 1709, 1709 nt., 1717, 1721, 1721 nt.
Aug. 17, 1991, P.L. 102-100, 46 U.S. Code Appx. § 1708
March 9, 1992, P.L. 102-251, 46 Appx. §§ 1709, 1721
Dec. 29, 1995, P.L. 104-88, 46 U.S. Code Appx. § 1704
Oct. 14, 1998, P.L. 105-258, 46 U.S. Code Appx. §§ 1701 to 1704, 1706 to 1710, 1712, 1714, 1715, 1717 to 1719, 1721
Nov. 13, 1998, P.L. 105-383, 46 U.S. Code Appx. §§ 1702, 1704, 1709

**Shipping Acts**
See also Merchant Marine Acts
June 26, 1884, Ch. 121, 23 Stat. 53, 22 U.S. Code § 1186; 46 U.S. Code §§ 8, 47, 101, 121, 189, 221, 541, 572, 573, 599, 658, 670, 679, 682 to 685, 703
June 19, 1886, Ch. 421, 24 Stat. 79, 46 U.S. Code §§ 45, 77, 121, 142, 188, 289, 319, 320, 329 to 331, 392, 393, 542a, 563, 599, 646, 671, 679
March 3, 1897, Ch. 389, 29 Stat. 687, 33 U.S. Code §§ 320, 323, 331, 341, 342, 350, 351, 364; 46 U.S. Code §§ 330, 366, 563, 564, 624, 625, 628, 660-1, 677
Dec. 6, 1967, P.L. 90-177, 81 Stat. 544, 46 U.S. Code § 826
Aug. 29, 1972, P.L. 92-416, 86 Stat. 653, 46 U.S. Code §§ 814, 815, 817, 822, 831

**Shipping Authority Act**
P.R. Laws Ann. 1954, Title 23, § 3051 et seq.

**Shipping Commissioners Acts**
June 7, 1872, Ch. 322, 17 Stat. 262
June 9, 1874, Ch. 260, 18 Stat. 64, 46 U.S. Code § 544
Aug. 19, 1890, Ch. 801, 26 Stat. 320, 46 U.S. Code § 563

**Ships Quarantine Law**
Wash. Rev. Code Ann., 70.16.010 et seq.

**Ships Regulation Act**
Wash. Rev. Code Ann., 88.04.010 et seq.

**Shipstead-Nolan Act**
July 10, 1930, Ch. 881, 46 Stat. 1020, 16 U.S. Code §§ 577 to 577b

**Shively-Spencer Act (Public Service Commission)**
Ind. Code Ann., 8-1-1-1 et seq.

**Shoalwater Bay Indian Tribe(Dexter-by-the-Sea Claim Settlement Act**
Sept. 28, 1984, P.L. 98-432, 98 Stat. 1671

**Shock Probation Statute**
Tex. Code of Criminal Procedure, Art. 42.12, § 3e

**Shoe-Fitting Devices Act**
Conn. Gen. Stat. Ann., § 53-212a

**Shoot-to-Kill Law**
N.Y. Penal Law 1965 (Consol. Laws Ch. 40) §§ 35.15, 35.30

**Shooting Preserve Act**
N.M. Stat. Ann., 17-3-35 et seq.

**Shooting Preserve Act (Private)**
S.D. Codified Laws 1967, 41-10-1 et seq.

**Shooting Range Fund Act**
N.M. Stat. Ann., 17-7-1 et seq.

**Shop Act (Dram)**
Mont. Code Ann., 27-1-710
Tenn. Code Ann., 57-10-101, 57-10-102
Vt. Stat. Ann., Title 7, § 501 et seq.

**Shop Book Act (Business Records)**
Ga. Code Ann., 24-3-14
Md. Ann. Code 1974, Art. CJ, § 10-101
Me. Rev. Stat. Ann. 1964, Title 16, § 356
Minn. Stat. Ann., 600.05
N.Y. Civil Practice Laws and Rules (Consol. Laws Ch. 8) Rule 4518
Pa. Cons. Stat., Title 42, § 6106

**Shop Rule Act (Office Records)**
Md. Ann. Code 1974, Art. CJ, § 10-101
Utah Code Ann. § 78-11-14

**Shoplifting Act**
Alaska Stat. 1962, § 11.46.220
Ariz. Rev. Stat. Ann., § 13-1805
Conn. Gen. Stat. Ann., § 53a-119a
Fla. Stat. 1977, 901.34
Ill. Rev. Stat. 1991, Ch. 38, § 16A-1 et seq.
Iowa Code Ann., 714.1 et seq.
La. Code of Crim. Proc. 1966, Art. 215
Md. Ann. Code 1957, Art. 27, § 551A
Miss. Code Ann. 1972, § 97-23-93 et seq.
Mo. Rev. Stat., 537.125
N.C. Gen. Stat. 1943, § 14-72.1
N.D. Cent. Code, 29-06-27
Nev. Rev. Stat. 1979 Reprint, 598.030
N.J. Stat. Ann., 2C:20-11
Ore. Rev. Stat., 131.655, 164.045, 164.055
Pa. Cons. Stat., Title 18, § 3929
S.C. Code Ann. 1976, § 16-13-105 et seq.
Tex. Penal Code, § 61-3A-1 et seq.
W. Va. Code 1966, § 61-3A-1 et seq.

**Shoplifting Act (Defense to Action for False Arrest)**
N.Y. General Business Law (Consol. Laws Ch. 20) § 217
Tex. Penal Code, § 31.03
Wash. Rev. Code Ann., 9A.16.080

**Shoplifting Act (False Arrest)**
N.Y. General Business Law (Consol. Laws Ch. 20) § 218

**Shoplifting Act of 1961**
Iowa Code 1977, 709.20 et seq.

**Shore and Beach Preservation Act**
Fla. Stat. Ann., 161.011 et seq.

**Shore Assistance Act**
Ga. Code Ann., 12-5-230 et seq.

**Shore Development Act**
R.I. Gen. Laws 1956, 46-3-1 et seq.

**Shore Fisheries Act**
Me. Rev. Stat. Ann. 1964, Title 12, § 6001 et seq.

**Shore Lands for Park Use Act**
Ill. Rev. Stat. 1991, Ch. 105, §§ 324.9, 324.10

**Shore Line Act (Lake Michigan)**
Ill. Rev. Stat. 1991, Ch. 19, § 1140 et seq.

**Shore Line Erosion Protection Act (Public Property)**
Oct. 27, 1965, P.L. 89-298, 79 Stat. 1095, 33 U.S. Code § 426g

**Shore Protection Act**
Ga. Code Ann., 12-5-230 et seq.

**Shore Protection Act of 1988**
Nov. 11, 1988, P.L. 100-688, 33 U.S. Code §§ 2601 nt., 2601 to 2609

**Shore Protection Bond Act**
N.J. Laws 1983, Ch. 356

**Shore Protection Loan Act (Barnstable County)**
Mass. Acts 1953, Ch. 98
Mass. Acts 1957, Ch. 518

**Shore Protection Loan Act (Plymouth County)**
Mass. Acts 1951, Ch. 396
Mass. Acts 1952, Ch. 531
Mass. Acts 1955, Ch. 381
Mass. Acts 1957, Ch. 239
Mass. Acts 1961, Ch. 366
Mass. Acts 1962, Ch. 464

**Shorelands Act**
Wash. Rev. Code Ann., 79.94.010 et seq.

**Shorelands Protection and Management Act**
Mich. Comp. Laws Ann., 281.631 et seq.

**Shoreline Erosion Control Demonstration Act of 1974**
March 7, 1974, P.L. 93-251, 88 Stat. 26, 42 U.S. Code § 1962d-5 nt.

**Shoreline Management Act**
Wash. Rev. Code Ann., 90.58.010 et seq.

**Shoreline Setback Act**
Haw. Rev. Stat. Ann., § 205-31 et seq.

**Shoreowner's Protection Act**
N.Y. Environmental Conservation Law, 1972 (Consol. Laws Ch. 43B) § 34-0101 et seq.

**Short Act (Montclair Created)**
N.J. Laws 1888, p. 483, Ch. 325

**Short and Long Haul Act**
Ky. Rev. Stat. 1971, 276.230
Minn. Stat. Ann., 218.021

**Short Cause Calendar Act**
Ill. Laws 1889, p. 222

**Short Check Act**
Colo. Rev. Stat. 18-5-205
Kan. Stat. Ann., 21-3707 et seq.

**Short-Doyle Act (Community Mental Health Services)**
Cal. Welfare and Institutions Code, § 5600 et seq.

**Short Firearms Act**
Wash. Rev. Code Ann., 9.41.010 et seq.

**Short Form Act**
Neb. Rev. Stat. 1943, 49-1501 et seq.

**Short Form Deeds Act**
Me. Rev. Stat. Ann. 1964 Title 33, § 761 et seq.

**Short Form Homicide Indictment Act**
Wyo. Stat. Ann., § 7-6-204

**Short Form Indictment Act**
Iowa Rules of Criminal Procedure, Rule 4
La. Code of Crim. Proc. 1966, Art. 465

**Short Form Manslaughter Indictment Act**
Wyo. Stat. Ann., § 7-6-204

**Short Form Mortgage Act**
Minn. Stat. Ann., 507.15

**Short Form of Deeds Act**
Mass. Gen. Laws Ann., 183:8 et seq.
Pa. Purdon's Stat., Title 21, § 2 et seq.

**Short Form Pleading Act (Criminal)**
Ohio Rev. Code 1953, 2941.05 et seq.

**Short Forms Conveyances Act**
N.M. Stat. Ann., 47-1-27 et seq.

**Short Homestead Exemption Act**
Ga. Code 1933, 51-1301 et seq.

**Short Jeopardy Act**
La. Code of Criminal Procedure, Art. 591 et seq.

**Short-Lanterman-Petris Act (Community Mental Health)**
Cal. Welfare and Institutions Code, § 5000 et seq.

**Short Merger Act (Corporations)**
Colo. Rev. Stat., 7-7-106
Del. Code of 1974, Title 8, § 253
Iowa Code 1989, 496A.72
Md. Ann. Code 1974, Art. CA, § 2-101 et seq.
Miss. Code Ann. 1972, § 79-3-149 et seq.
N.Y. Business Corporations Law (Consol. Laws, Ch. 4) § 901 et seq.
S.C. Code Ann. 1976, Superseded Vols., § 33-17-50
Utah Code Ann. 1953, 16-10-70
Wis. Stat. Ann., 180.685
W. Va. Acts 1953, Ch. 32

**Short Statute of Limitations (Administrative Review)**
N.Y. Civil Practice Law and rules (Consol. Laws, Ch. 8), § 217

**Short Statute of Limitations (Probate)**
Mass. Gen. Laws Ann., 197:9

**Short Statute of Limitations (Tax Sales-Land)**
Ala. Code 1975, § 40-10-82

**Short-Term Borrowing Act**
Ky. Rev. Stat. 1971, 65.7701 et seq.

**Short Term Borrowing Act**
Ill. Comp. Stat. 1992, Ch. 30, § 340/0.01

**Short-Term Cash Management Act**
N.M. Stat. Ann., 6-12A-1 to 6-12A-15

**Short-term Mortgage Redemption Act**
N.D. Cent. Code, 32-19.1-01 et seq.

**Short Term Public Securities Interest Rate Act**
N.M. Stat. Ann., 6-18-1 et seq.

**Short Weight Act**
Pa. Purdon's Stat., Title 73, § 1751

**Shorthand Reporters Act**
Cal. Business and Professions Code, § 8000 et seq.
Ida. Code 1947, 54-3101 et seq.
Nev. Rev. Stat. 1979 Reprint, 656.010 et seq.
Wash. Rev. Code Ann., 18.145.005 et seq.

**Shorthand Reporters Act (Certified)**
Ill. Comp. Stat. 1992, Ch. 225, § 415/1 et seq.

**Shot Firers Act**
Ill. Rev. Stat. 1951, Ch. 93, § 47 et seq.
Ind. Code Ann., 22-10-6-1 et seq.

**Shotgun and Rifle Registration Prohibition Act**
Cal. Statutes 1990, Ch. 177

**Shows and Exhibitions License Act**
R.I. Gen. Laws 1956, 5-22-1 et seq.

**Shreveport, Louisiana Redevelopment Agency Act**
La. Acts 1968, No. 179

**Shrewbury Sewerage Loan Act**
Mass. Acts 1954, Ch. 502

**Shrimp Act**
La. Rev. Stat. Ann., 56:491 et seq.

**Shrimp Conservation Act**
Tex. Parks and Wildlife Code, § 77.001 et seq.

**Shrimp Net Restriction Act (Bay County)**
Fla. Special Laws 1973, Ch. 73-404

**Shut-Off Protection Act (Low Income)**
Mich. Comp. Laws Ann., 400.1201 et seq.

**Shut-Off Protection Act (Public Assistance)**
Mich. Comp. Laws Ann., 400.1151 et seq.

**Shutesbury School Building Loan Act**
Mass. Acts 1949, Ch. 15

**Sick Doctor Statute**
Fla. Stat. 1975, 458.1201, Subsec. 1, Subd. n

**Sick Leave Act**
See Federal Sick Leave Act
Ohio Rev. Code 1953, 124.38

**Sick Leave Act (School Employee's)**
Ark. Code Ann. 1987, 6-17-1301 et seq.

**Sick Leave Act (Teachers')**
Ind. Code Ann., 20-6.1-6-3

**Sick Leave Act-State and School Employees**
S.C. Code Ann. 1976, §§ 8-11-40 et seq., 59-1-400 et seq.

**Sick Leave Bank Act (Special School Teachers)**
Tenn. Code Ann., 49-50-1101 et seq.

**Sickle Cell Anemia Information and Prevention Act**
Md. Ann. Code 1974, Art. HG, § 18-501

**Sickle Cell Disease Detection Act**
Ky. Rev. Stat. 1971, 402.310 et seq.

**Sickle Cell Trait and Anemia Act**
N.M. Stat. Ann., 24-3-1

**Sickness, Accident and Life Insurance Policy Readability Act**
Neb. Rev. Stat. 1943, 44-3401 et seq.

**Sickness and Accident and Medicare Supplement Insurance Minimum Standards Act**
Neb. Rev. Stat. 1943, 44-3601 et seq.

**Sickness and Accident Policy Provisions Act**
Cal. Insurance Code, § 10320 et seq.
Ind. Code. 1988, 27-8-5-2
Mo. Rev. Stat., 376.770 et seq.
Ohio Rev. Code 1953, 3923.01 et seq.

**Sickness and Life and Accident Insurance Policy Language Simplification Act**
W. Va. Code 1966, § 33-29-1 et seq.

**Sickness Compensation Act**
R.I. Gen. Laws 1956, 28-39-1 et seq.

**Sickness Insurance Act**
Mich. Comp. Laws Ann., 500.3400 et seq.

**Sickness Law (Disability Benefits)**
N.J. Stat. Ann., 43:21-25 et seq.

**Sickness, Life and Accident Insurance Guaranty Association Act**
Va. Code 1950, § 38.2-1700 et seq.

**Sidewalk Cafe Act**
D.C. Laws 1977, No. 2-7

**Sidewalk Construction Act**
Utah Code Ann. 1953, 27-14-1 et seq.

**Sidewalks Act**
Ill. Rev. Stat. 1991, Ch. 24, § 11-84-1 et seq.
N.H. Rev. Stat. 1955, 231:111 et seq.
R.I. Gen. Laws 1956, 24-7-1 et seq.
Utah Code Ann. 1953, 27-14-1 et seq.
Wash. Rev. Code Ann., 35.68.010 et seq.

**Sidney Martin Developmental Research School Act**
Fla. Stat. Ann., 228.053

**Sieroty-Dymally Children's Center Construction Law**
Cal. Election Code 1976, § 16260 et seq.

**Sierra County Flood Control and Water Conservation District Act**
Cal. Statutes 1959, Ch. 2123, p. 4979

**Sierra Valley Groundwater Basin Act**
Cal. Water Code, Appendix, § 119-101 et seq.

**Sign Act**
D.C. Code 1973, § 1-325 et seq.
W. Va. Code 1931, Miscellaneous Superseded Code Provisions, § 47-8-1

**Sign Act (Auction Sales)**
Ill. Comp. Stat. 1992, Ch. 720, § 225/0.01 et seq.
Ill. Rev. Stat. 1991, Ch. 121 1/2, § 219.01 et seq.

**Sign Act (Factors)**
Miss. Code Ann. 1972, § 15-3-7
Va. Code 1950, § 55-152

**Sign Control and Outdoor Advertising Act (Roadside)**
N.J. Stat. Ann., 43:10-46 et seq.

**Signage Act (Limited Winery)**
Pa. Purdon's Stat., Title 73, § 411 et seq.

**Signal at Railroad Crossing Law**
S.C. Code Ann. 1976, §§ 58-15-910, 58-17-1390, 58-17-3380

**Signal Inspection Act**
Sept. 3, 1992, P.L. 102-365, 49 U.S. Code Appx. § 26

**Signal Law (Railroad Crossing)**
S.C. Code Ann. 1976, §§ 58-15-910, 58-17-1390, 15-17-3380 et seq.

**Signatures and Records Act (Electronic)**
R.I. Gen. Laws 1956, 42-127-1 et seq.

**Sikes Act**
Dec. 31, 1982, P.L. 97-396, 16 U.S. Code §§ 670a, 670f to 670h, 670o
Oct. 27, 1986, P.L. 99-561, 16 U.S. Code §§ 670f, 670o
Nov. 14, 1988, P.L. 100-653, 16 U.S. Code § 670i
Nov. 29, 1989, P.L. 101-189, 16 U.S. Code §§ 670c-1, 670f
Nov. 18, 1997, P.L. 105-85, 16 U.S. Code §§ 670, 670 nt., 670a, 670b, 670c, 670c-1, 670e-1, 670e-2, 670f, 670o
Oct. 17, 1998, P.L. 105-261, 16 U.S. Code § 670c

**Sikes Act Improvement Act of 1997**
Nov. 18, 1997, P.L. 105-85, 16 U.S. Code § 670 nt.

**Silencer Act (Firearms)**
Cal. Penal Code § 12500 et seq.

**Silent Reflection Act**
Ill. Rev. Stat. 1991, Ch. 122, §§ 770, 771

**Siletz Indian Tribe Reorganization Act**
Nov. 18, 1977, P.L. 95-195, 25 U.S. Code §§ 711, 711 nt., 711a et seq.

**Silicosis Act**
Ky. Rev. Stat. 1971, 342.316
W. Va. Code 1966, § 23-4-8a et seq.

**Sills Act (Pensions, Spanish War, Philippine Insurrection, China Relief Expedition)**
June 5, 1920, Ch. 245, 41 Stat. 982

**Silver City Charter**
Nev. Statutes 1877, Ch. 83, p. 134

**Silver Coin Issue Resolution**
July 22, 1876, No. 17, 19 Stat. 215

**Silver Coin Proof Sets Act**
Nov. 15, 1990, P.L. 101-585, 31 U.S. Code §§ 5101 nt., 5132

**Silver Purchase Acts**
July 14, 1890, Ch. 708, 26 Stat. 289, 12 U.S. Code §§ 122, 145; 31 U.S. Code §§ 408, 410, 453
Nov. 1, 1893, Ch. 8, 28 Stat. 4, 31 U.S. Code § 311
June 19, 1934, Ch. 674, 48 Stat. 1178, 31 U.S. Code §§ 311a, 316a, 316b, 405a, 448 to 448e, 734a, 734b
June 25, 1959, P.L. 86-70, 73 Stat. 147, 31 U.S. Code § 448b

**Silverstein Law (Teachers' Salaries)**
N.Y. Laws 1913, Ch. 534

**Silvio O. Conte National Fish and Wildlife Refuge Act**
Dec. 11, 1991, P.L. 102-212, 16 U.S. Code § 668dd nt.

**Simmer Law (Municipal Utility)**
Iowa Code 1973, 397.9 et seq.

**Simmons Road Bill**
Ky. Acts 1922, p. 459 Appendix

**Simplification and Availability of Bank Credit Act**
Pa. 1994 Pamph. Laws, No. 167

**Simplification and Reduction of Paperwork Act**
Tenn. Code Ann., 4-25-101 et seq.

**Simplification for Credit Act**
S.C. Code Ann. 1976, § 29-3-40 et seq.

**Simplification of Fiduciary Security Transfers Act**
See also Uniform Act for Simplification of Fiduciary Security Transfers
Cal. Corporations Code § 30000 et seq.
Haw. Session Laws 1965, Act 44 39.49 et seq.

**Simplification of Land Titles Act**
Okla. Stat. Ann., Title 16, § 61 et seq.

**Simplified Estates Act**
Kan. Stat. Ann., 59-3201 et seq.

**Simpson-Brown Act (Teachers' Tenure)**
Ala. Code 1975, § 16-24-1 et seq.

**Simulcast Wagering of Horse and Dog Racing Act**
Mass. Gen. Laws Ann., 128C:1 et seq.

**Simulcasting Racing Act**
N.J. Stat. Ann., 5:5-110 et seq.

**Simultaneous Death Act**
See also Uniform Simultaneous Death Act
Mont. Code Ann., 72-2-205
Ohio Rev. Code 1953, 2105.21

**Simultaneous Tenure Act (Public Officer)**
Ill. Rev. Stat. 1991, Ch. 102, § 4.9 et seq.

**Sinclair Act (Schools)**
Me. Rev. Stat. Ann. 1964, Title 20A, § 1101 et seq.

**Sine Die Act, Mandatory**
S.C. Code Ann. 1976, § 2-1-180 et seq.

**Single Act Law (Foreign Corporations)**
Minn. Stat. Ann., 303.13
Mo. Rev. Stat., 351.633
N.C. Gen. MSCP, 55-145
N.H. Rev. Stat. 1955, 293-A:121
W. Va. Code 1966, § 31-1-56

**Single Act Law (Jurisdiction)**
Ida. Code 1947, 5-514 et seq.
Ill. Rev. Stat. 1991, Ch. 110, § 2-209
Iowa Code Ann., 617.3
Kan. Stat. Ann., 60-308
Me. Rev. Stat. Ann. 1964, Title 14, § 704A
Wis. Stat. Ann., 801.05

**Single Act Law (Nonresident Motorists)**
Minn. Stat. Ann., 170.55

**Single Act Law (Process)**
Miss. Code Ann. 1972, § 13-3-57
Vt. Stat. Ann., Title 12, § 855

**Single Audit Act**
Fla. Stat. Ann., 216.3491
Mass. Gen. Laws Ann., 44:40

**Single Audit Act Amendments of 1996**
July 5, 1996, P.L. 104-156, 31 U.S. Code § 7501 nt.

**Single Audit Act of 1984**
Oct. 19, 1984, P.L. 98-502, 31 U.S. Code § 7501 et seq.

**Single Business Tax Act**
Mich. Comp. Laws Ann., 208.1 et seq.

**Single Cooperative Interagency Merit System of Personnel Administration Established for Grant-Aided Agencies in the State**
S.C. Code Ann. 1976, § 8-19-10 et seq.

**Single County Ditch Act**
Ohio Rev. Code 1953, 6131.01 et seq.

**Single-Employer Pension Plan Amendments Act of 1986**
April 7, 1986, P.L. 99-272, 29 U.S. Code § 1001 nt.
Oct. 22, 1986, P.L. 99-514, 29 U.S. Code § 1002
Dec. 19, 1989, P.L. 101-239, 29 U.S. Code § 1367

**Single Filing Act (Mortgages)**
Ohio Rev. Code 1953, 1309.38

**Single Insurance Producer Licensing Act**
Colo. Rev. Stat., 10-2-101 et seq.

**Single Publication Act**
See Uniform Single Publication Act

**Single State Registration Act**
Tex. Transportation Code, § 645.001 et seq.

**Single Tax Collection Act (Second Class A Cities)**
Pa. Purdon's Stat., Title 53, § 30781 et seq.

**Single Transaction Act (Service on Nonresident)**
Fla. Stat. Ann., 48.181

**Single-Use Surgical Devices Act**
Ill. Comp. Stat. 1992, Ch. 410, § 620/16.5

**Sinking Fund Act**
Iowa Code 1985, 454.1 et seq.
N.J. Stat. Ann., 40:3-1 et seq.
R.I. Gen. Laws 1956, 35-8-3 et seq.

**Sinking Fund Act (General Fund Bonds)**
N.C. Gen. Stat. 1943, § 142-50 et seq.

**Sinking Fund Commission Act**
N.C. Gen. Stat. 1943, § 142-30 et seq.

**Sipsey Wild and Scenic River and Alabama Addition Act of 1988**
Oct. 28, 1988, P.L. 100-547, 16 U.S. Code § 1271 nt.

**Siskiyou County Flood Control and Water Conservation District Act**
Cal. Statutes 1959, Ch. 2121, p. 4946

**Sit-Down Strike Act**
Vt. Acts 1937, No. 210

**Sit-Down Strike Prohibition Act**
Md. Ann. Code 1957, Art. 27, § 552

**Site Development Act**
Pa. Purdon's Stat., Title 73, § 361 et seq.

**Site Identification Act**
N.M. Stat. Ann., 74-4A-15 et seq.

**Site Location of Development Law**
Me. Rev. Stat. Ann. 1964, Title 38, § 481 et seq.

**Site Value Tax Enabling Act**
Pa. Purdon's Stat., Title 53, § 25893 et seq.

**Siting Act (Energy Facility)**
Ore. Rev. Stat., 469.300 et seq.

**Siting Act (Hazardous Waste Facility)**
Ida. Code 1947, 39-5801 et seq.
Mass. Gen. Laws Ann., 21D:1 et seq.
Miss. Code Ann. 1972, § 17-18-1 et seq.

**Siting Act (Natural Gas Transmission Pipeline)**
Fla. Stat. Ann., 403.9401 et seq.

**Sitka National Cemetery Transfer Act of 1983**
July 30, 1983, P.L. 98-63, 97 Stat. 322

**Six Day Week Law**
Ill. Rev. Stat. 1991, Ch. 48, § 8a et seq.

**Six Foot Law**
Okla. Stat. Ann., Title 63, § 981

**Six-man Jury Statute**
Fla. Stat. Ann., 913.10

**Six Million Dollar Road Bonding Act**
Ore. Code 1991, §§ 44-501 to 44-513

**Six Month Claim Act (Probate)**
Fla. Stat. 1971, 733.16

**Six Months Statute of Limitations (Tax Lien Foreclosure)**
N.Y. Tax Law (Consol. Laws, Ch. 60), § 165h, Subd. 7

**Six O'Clock Act (Employment of Women)**
Mass. Gen. Laws 1932, Ch. 149, § 59

**Six Percent Act**
Mass. Gen. Laws Ann., 107:3

**Six Weeks Divorce Act**
Ida. Code 1947, 32-701
Nev. Rev. Stat. 1979 Reprint, 125.020
*Continued*

**Six Year Statute of Limitations**
Ala. Code 1975, 6-2-34
Alaska Stat. 1962, § 09.10.050
Ind. Code Ann., 34-1-2-1
Me. Rev. Stat. Ann. 1964, Title 14, § 752
Minn. Stat. Ann., 541.05
Miss. Code Ann. 1972, § 15-1-49
N.D. Cent. Code, 28-01-16
N.J. Stat. Ann., 2A:14-1
Wis. Stat. Ann., 893.19

**Six Year Statute of Limitations (Account and Replevin)**
R.I. Gen. Laws 1956, 9-1-16

**Six Year Statute of Limitations (Personal Actions)**
Colo. Rev. Stat. 13-80-103.5
N.Y. Civil Practice Laws and Rules (Consol. Laws, Ch. 8), § 213

**Sixteen Hour Law (Railroads)**
See Hours of Service Acts (Railraods)

**Sixth Supplemental National Defense Appropriation Act of 1942**
April 28, 1942, Ch. 247, 56 Stat. 226, 7 U.S. Code § 174; 22 U.S. Code § 412 nt.; 31 U.S. Code §§ 16, 82f; 42 U.S. Code § 1602; 50 U.S . Code Appx. § 1191
Oct. 26, 1942, Ch. 629, 56 Stat. 1005
July 1, 1943, Ch. 185, 57 Stat. 347, 31 U.S. Code §§ 493a, 649a, 650a; 50 U.S. Code Appx. § 1191
Feb. 25, 1944, Ch. 63, 58 Stat. 78, 50 U.S. Code Appx. §§ 1191, 1191 nt.
June 30, 1945, Ch. 210, 59 Stat. 294, 50 U.S. Code Appx. § 1191

**Sixty Day Act (Fire Insurance Contracts)**
N.Y. Insurance Law 1984 (Consol. Laws Ch. 28) § 3404, Subd. e

**Sixty Day Act (Oral Fire Insurance Contracts)**
N.Y. Insurance Law (Consol. Laws Ch. 28), § 168, Subd. 3

**Sixty-day Appeal Act**
Nev. Civil Practice Act 1911, § 387

**Sixty Day Waiting Law (Divorce)**
Ill. Rev. Stat. 1959, Ch. 40, § 7a et seq.

**Sixty Million Dollar Bond Issue Act**
Ill. Rev. Stat. 1957, Ch. 121, § 266 et seq.

**Sixty/Forty (60/40) Funding of Public Schools Act**
R.I. Gen. Laws 1956, 16-69-1 et seq.

**Size and Weight Act (Motor Vehicles)**
Ga. Code Ann., 32-6-20 et seq.

**Size, Weight and Load Regulations**
Miss. Code Ann. 1972, § 63-5-1

**Skarda Act**
Ill. Laws 1933, p. 873

**Skating Liability Immunity Act (Ice or Roller)**
S.C. Code Ann. 1976, § 52-19-10 et seq.

**Skeletal Remains Protection Act (Human)**
Ill. Rev. Stat. 1991, Ch. 127, § 2660 et seq.

**Skeleton Remains Protection and Unmarked Human Burial Sites Act**
Neb. Rev. Stat. 1943, 12-1201 et seq.

**Ski Area Safety Act**
Ga. Code Ann., 34-15-1 et seq.
Mich. Comp. Laws Ann., 408.321 et seq.

**Ski Area Safety and Liability Act**
Tenn. Code Ann., 68-114-101 et seq.

**Ski Lift Safety Act**
N.J. Stat. Ann., 34:4A-1 et seq.

**Ski Patrol Member Good Samaritan Law**
N.Y. Unconsol. Laws, § 7310

**Ski Safety Act**
Alaska Stat. 1962, § 05.45.210
Colo. Rev. Stat., 33-44-101 et seq.
N.M. Stat. Ann., 24-15-1 et seq.
N.Y. Labor Law (Consol. Laws Ch. 31) § 865 et seq.

**Skier Safety Act**
Nev. Rev. Stat. (1987 Reprint) 455A.010 et seq.

**Skiing Act (Cross-Country)**
Ida. Code 1947, 49-3101 et seq.

**Skiing Responsibility Act**
N.D. Cent. Code, 53-09-01 et seq.
Pa. 1980 Pamph. Laws 52, No. 19

**SKILL Act (State of Kansas Investments in Lifelong Learning)**
Kan. Stat. Ann., 74-50,102 et seq.

**Skip Election Act**
Ind. Code Ann., 3-1-16-1 et seq.

**Skip Mortgage Act**
La. Rev. Stat. Ann., 9:5521 et seq.

**Skippers Act (Family Desertion)**
Ala. Code 1975, § 30-4-80 et seq.
N.C. Gen. Stat. 1943, § 52A-1 et seq.

**Skullduggery Act**
Tenn. Code Ann., 2-5-101

**Skyjacking Act**
Miss. Code Ann. 1972, § 97-25-55

**Slander Act**
Cal. Civil Code § 44 et seq.
Cal. Code of Civil Procedure § 830 et seq.
Ga. Code Ann., 51-5-1 et seq.
Haw. Rev. Stat. 1968, § 751-1 et seq.
Ill. Rev. Stat. 1991, Ch. 126, §§ 0.01 et seq., 1 et seq.
Md. Ann. Code 1974, Art. CJ, § 3-501 et seq.
Mich. Comp. Laws Ann., 600.2911
Mont. Code Ann. 1991, 27-1-803
N.C. Gen. Stat. 1943, § 99-1 et seq.
Ohio Rev. Code 1953, 2739.01 et seq.
P.R. Laws Ann. 1954, Title 33, § 4101 et seq.
Tex. Civil Prac. and Rem. Code, § 73.001 et seq.
Wash. Rev. Code Ann., 9.58.110 et seq.

**Slander Act (Criminal)**
Ind. Code Ann., 35-13-6-1

**Slash Act (Forest Fire Hazards)**
Wash. Rev. Code Ann., 76.04.660

**Slash Disposal Law**
Mich. Comp. Laws Ann., 320.41 et seq.

**Slater-Marks Act (Monroe County Taxes)**
N.Y. Laws 1933, Ch. 833

**Slaughter Act (Livestock)**
Ill. Rev. Stat. 1991, Ch. 8, § 229.50 et seq.
N.H. Rev. Stat. 1955, 427:33 et seq.

**Slaughter Livestock Buyers Act**
Ill. Rev. Stat. 1991, Ch. 111, § 501 et seq.

**Slaughter, Processing, and Sale of Meat Animals Act**
Colo. Rev. Stat., 35-33-101 et seq.

**Slaughterhouse Act**
Cal. Food and Agricultural Code 1967, § 18651 et seq.
Me. Rev. Stat. Ann. 1964, Title 22, § 2541 et seq.
Minn. Stat. Ann., 31.51 et seq.
N.C. Gen. Stat. 1943, § 106-159 et seq.
Okla. Stat. Ann., Title 2, § 6-181 et seq.

**Slave Marriage Act**
S.C. Code Ann. 1976, §§ 20-1-30, 20-1-40

**Slave Trade Abolishment Act (District of Columbia)**
Sept. 20, 1850, Ch. 63, 9 Stat. 467

**Slave Trade Prohibition Act**
March 2, 1807, Ch. 22, 2 Stat. 426

**Slayers Act**
N.M. Stat. Ann., 45-2-803

**Slayers Act (Property Rights)**
D.C. Code Ann., § 19-320
Ida. Laws 1969, Ch. 242
N.C. Gen. Stat. 1943, § 31A-3 et seq.
Ohio Rev. Code 1953, 2105.19
Pa. Cons. Stat., Title 20, § 8801 et seq.
*Continued*

**Sleeping Drugs Sale Act**
Wash. Rev. Code 1951, 69.40.060, 69.40.070

**Slenker-Adams-Bates Act (Taxation-Public Utilities)**
Ind. Burns' 1933, 64-710 et seq.

**Slichter Act (Labor Relations)**
Mass. Gen. Laws Ann., 150A:1 et seq., 150B:1 et seq., 214:6A

**Sliding Scale Act (Taxation)**
Tenn. Public Acts 1919, Ch. 2

**Sloan Act (Fish and Game)**
Ky. Acts 1940, Ch. 86

**Slocum Primary Law**
S.D. Codified Laws 1967, 12-5-1

**Slogan Act**
Ill. Rev. Stat. 1991, Ch. 1, § 2901-30

**Slot Amusement Machine Tax Law**
Miss. Code Ann. 1972, § 27-27-1 et seq.

**Slot Machine Act**
Fla. Stat. Ann., 849.15 et seq.
Ill. Rev. Stat. 1991, Ch. 38, § 28-5
Ind. Code Ann., 35-45-5-3 et seq.
Minn. Stat. Ann., 349.30 et seq.
Mont. Code Ann., 23-5-112 et seq.
N.C. Gen. Stat. 1943, § 14-304 et seq.
N.Y. Penal Law 1965 (Consol. Laws Ch. 40), § 225.30, Subd. 1
Okla. Stat. Ann., Title 21, § 964 et seq.
Ore. Rev. Stat., 167.147 et seq.
Vt. Stat. Ann., Title 13, § 2135 et seq.
Wash. Rev. Code Ann., 9.46.230 et seq.

**Slot Machine License Tax Act**
Fla. Laws 1935, Ch. 17257

**Slot Machines Act (Prohibition)**
Tex. Penal Code, § 47.06

**Slow Speed Act**
Ill. Rev. Stat. 1991, Ch. 95 1/2, § 11-606
Minn. Stat. Ann., 169.15
Mo. Rev. Stat., 304.011
Mont. Code Ann., 61-8-311
Ore. Rev. Stat., 811.130

**Sludge Dumping Elimination Act (Ocean)**
N.J. Stat. Ann., 58:10A-44, 58:10A-45

**Slum Clearance Act**
Ill. Rev. Stat. 1991, Ch. 24, § 11-11-1
Ind. Code Ann., 18-7-8-1 et seq.
La. Rev. Stat. Ann., 40:561 et seq.
Mich. Comp. Laws Ann., 125.651 et seq.
Mo. Rev. Stat., 99.300 et seq.
Ohio Rev. Code 1953, 725.01 et seq.
Pa. Purdon's Stat., Title 35, § 1541 et seq.
P.R. Laws Ann. 1954, Title 17, § 131 et seq.
R.I. Gen. Laws 1956, 45-31-1 et seq.
Tenn. Code Ann., 13-20-201 et seq.

**Slum Clearance and Blight Elimination Act**
Wis. Stat. Ann., 66.431

**Slum Clearance and Low Rent Housing Law**
N.Y. Public Housing Law (Consol. Laws Ch. 44A), § 70 et seq.

**Slum Clearance and Redevelopment Authority Law**
Alaska Stat. 1962, § 18.55.480 et seq.
Del. Code of 1974, Title 31, § 4501 et seq.
Ky. Rev. Stat. 1971, 99.330 et seq.
Neb. Rev. Stat. 1943, 18-2101 et seq.
N.J. Stat. Ann.40:55-21.1 et seq.
W. Va. Code 1966, § 16-18-1 et seq.

**Slum Clearance and Redevelopment Authority Law (Portland)**
Me. Private and Special Laws 1951, Ch. 217

**Slum Clearance Corporation Act**
Ind. Code Ann., 18-7-10-1 et seq.

**Small Act (Lands across or under Streams)**
Tex. Rev. Civ. Stat., Art. 5414a

**Small and Minority Business Assistance Act**
Fla. Stat. Ann., 288.702 et seq.

**Small Board of Freeholders Act**
N.J. Stat. Ann.40:20-1 et seq.

**Small Brewery and Domestic Winery Act**
N.M. Stat. Ann., 60-6A-21 et seq.

**Small Business Access to Surety Bonding Survey Act of 1992**
Sept. 4, 1992, P.L. 102-366, 15 U.S. Code § 694b nt.

**Small Business Act**
July 30, 1953, Ch. 282, 67 Stat. 232
June 30, 1955, Ch. 251, 69 Stat. 225
Aug. 9, 1955, Ch. 628, 69 Stat. 547
Feb. 2, 1956, Ch. 29, 70 Stat. 10
Feb. 11, 1957, P.L. 85-4, 71 Stat. 4
Aug. 3, 1957, P.L. 85-120, 71 Stat. 341
Feb. 22, 1958, P.L. 85-332, 72 Stat. 27
July 18, 1958, P.L. 85-536, 72 Stat. 384, 12 U.S. Code § 371; 15 U.S. Code §§ 601 nt., 631 to 647
Aug. 21, 1958, P.L. 85-699, 72 Stat. 690, 15 U.S. Code § 633
Sept. 22, 1959, P.L. 86-367, 73 Stat. 647, 15 U.S. Code § 633, 636
June 30, 1961, P.L. 87-70, 75 Stat. 167, 15 U.S. Code §§ 631, 633 , 636
Sept. 5, 1961, P.L. 87-198, 75 Stat. 468, 15 U.S. Code § 633
Sept. 26, 1961, P.L. 87-305, 75 Stat. 666, 15 U.S. Code §§ 631, 633, 634, 636, 637, 639
Oct. 3, 1961, P.L. 87-341, 75 Stat. 757, 15 U.S. Code §§ 631 nt., 633
Oct. 4, 1961, P.L. 87-367, 75 Stat. 787, 15 U.S. Code § 634
July 25, 1962, P.L. 87-550, 76 Stat. 220, 15 U.S. Code §§ 633, 637a, 639a
Feb. 5, 1964, P.L. 88-264, 78 Stat. 7, 15 U.S. Code §§ 636, 645
Sept. 2, 1964, P.L. 88-560, 78 Stat. 786, 15 U.S. Code §§ 636, 637
June 30, 1965, P.L. 89-59, 79 Stat. 206, 15 U.S. Code §§ 633, 636
July 21, 1965, P.L. 89-78, 79 Stat. 243, 15 U.S. Code § 633
Aug. 10, 1965, P.L. 89-117, 79 Stat. 484, 15 U.S. Code § 633
Nov. 8, 1965, P.L. 89-334, 79 Stat. 1294, 15 U.S. Code § 633
May 2, 1966, P.L. 89-409, 80 Stat. 132, 15 U.S. Code §§ 633, 636
Nov. 3, 1966, P.L. 89-754, 80 Stat. 1295, 15 U.S. Code § 637
Nov. 6, 1966, P.L. 89-769, 80 Stat. 1319, 15 U.S. Code § 636
Nov. 6, 1966, P.L. 89-779, 80 Stat. 1364, 15 U.S. Code § 633
Oct. 11, 1967, P.L. 90-104, 81 Stat. 268, 15 U.S. Code §§ 633, 636, 637
Aug. 1, 1968, P.L. 90-448, 82 Stat. 567, 15 U.S. Code §§ 633, 636
Aug. 23, 1968, P.L. 90-495, 82 Stat. 835, 15 U.S. Code § 636
Dec. 30, 1969, P.L. 91-173, 83 Stat. 802, 15 U.S. Code §§ 633, 636
Aug. 12, 1970, P.L. 91-375, 84 Stat. 776, 15 U.S. Code § 637
Dec. 17, 1970, P.L. 91-558, 84 Stat. 1468, 15 U.S. Code § 633
Dec. 29, 1970, P.L. 91-596, 84 Stat. 1618, 15 U.S. Code §§ 633, 636
Dec. 29, 1970, P.L. 91-597, 84 Stat. 1633, 15 U.S. Code §§ 633, 636
May 18, 1971, P.L. 92-16, 85 Stat. 39, 15 U.S. Code § 633
June 6, 1972, P.L. 92-310, 86 Stat. 206, 15 U.S. Code § 634
June 27, 1972, P.L. 92-320, 86 Stat. 383, 15 U.S. Code § 633
Aug. 16, 1972, P.L. 92-385, 86 Stat. 554, 15 U.S. Code §§ 633, 636
Oct. 18, 1972, P.L. 92-500, 86 Stat. 898, 15 U.S. Code §§ 633, 636
Jan. 2, 1974, P.L. 93-237, 87 Stat. 1023, 15 U.S. Code §§ 633, 636, 639
Aug. 23, 1974, P.L. 93-386, 88 Stat. 742, 15 U.S. Code §§ 631, 633, 634, 636, 639, 647
March 24, 1977, P.L. 95-14, 15 U.S. Code § 633
Aug. 4, 1977, P.L. 95-89, 15 U.S. Code §§ 631 nt., 633 et seq.
July 4, 1978, P.L. 95-315, 15 U.S. Code §§ 633 et seq.
Oct. 24, 1978, P.L. 95-510, 15 U.S. Code §§ 634, 634 nt., 636, 637
July 25, 1979, P.L. 96-38, 15 U.S. Code §§ 636, 647
July 2, 1980, P.L. 96-302, 15 U.S. Code §§ 631 nt., 634 et seq.
April 18, 1984, P.L. 98-270, 15 U.S. Code §§ 631 to 633, 636, 636 nt., 647
July 10, 1984, P.L. 98-352, 15 U.S. Code §§ 633, 634, 639
July 16, 1984, P.L. 98-362, 15 U.S. Code §§ 632, 633, 637

*Continued*

July 18, 1984, P.L. 98-369, 98 Stat. 1116, 15 U.S. Code § 647
Aug. 21, 1984, P.L. 98-395, 15 U.S. Code §§ 631 nt., 636, 648
Oct. 12, 1984, P.L. 98-473, 15 U.S. Code § 650
Oct. 30, 1984, P.L. 98-577, 15 U.S. Code §§ 637, 644
Nov. 8, 1985, P.L. 99-145, 41 U.S. Code § 253
April 7, 1986, P.L. 99-272, 15 U.S. Code §§ 631, 631 nt., 632, 636, 644, 645, 647
Oct. 6, 1986, P.L. 99-443, 15 U.S. Code § 638
Oct. 18, 1986, P.L. 99-500, 15 U.S. Code §§ 632, 637, 644
Oct. 27, 1986, P.L. 99-567, 15 U.S. Code § 637
Oct. 30, 1986, P.L. 99-591, 15, U.S. Code §§ 644, 732, 737
Nov. 14, 1986, P.L. 99-661, 15 U.S. Code §§ 632, 632 nt., 637, 644
April 21, 1987, P.L. 100-26, 15 U.S. Code § 644
July 11, 1987, P.L. 100-72, 15 U.S. Code § 631 nt.
Dec. 4, 1987, P.L. 100-180, 15 U.S. Code §§ 644, 644 nt.
Aug. 23, 1988, P.L. 100-418, 102 Stat. 1553, 15 U.S. Code §§ 631, 631 nt., 636, 638 nt., 648, 649
Sept. 29, 1988, P.L. 100-456, 15 U.S. Code § 632
Oct. 17, 1988, P.L. 100-496, 15 U.S. Code § 644
Oct. 25, 1988, P.L. 100-533, 15 U.S. Code §§ 631, 631 nt., 631b, 636, 636 nt., 637
Nov. 3, 1988, P.L. 100-590, 15 U.S. Code §§ 631, 631 nt., 632 to 634, 636, 636 nt., 638, 644, 648
Nov. 15, 1988, P.L. 100-656, 15 U.S. Code §§ 631, 632, 632 nt., 633, 636, 637, 637 nt., 639, 644, 645
Nov. 23, 1988, P.L. 100-707, 15 U.S. Code § 636
June 15, 1989, P.L. 101-37, 15 U.S. Code §§ 631, 636, 636 nt., 637, 639, 644
Nov. 21, 1989, P.L. 101-162, 15 U.S. Code §§ 636, 637
Nov. 5, 1990, P.L. 101-510, 15 U.S. Code §§ 632, 637, 644
Nov. 5, 1990, P.L. 101-515, 15 U.S. Code §§ 633, 633 nt., 648, 648a, 651, 652
Nov. 15, 1990, P.L. 101-574, 15 U.S. Code §§ 631 nt., 633 et seq. generally
Oct. 28, 1991, P.L. 102-140, 15 U.S. Code §§ 633, 634, 636, 648a , 655
Dec. 5, 1991, P.L. 102-190, 15 U.S. Code §§ 637, 644
Dec. 5, 1991, P.L. 102-191, 15 U.S. Code §§ 636, 637, 656
Sept. 4, 1992, P.L. 102-366, 15 U.S. Code §§ 631 nt., 632, 636, 636 nt., 637, 644, 648
Oct. 23, 1992, P.L. 102-484, 15 U.S. Code §§ 638, 638 nt., 644
Oct. 28, 1992, P.L. 102-564, 15 U.S. Code §§ 634, 636, 638, 638 nt.
Oct. 29, 1992, P.L. 102-569, 15 U.S. Code § 644
Aug. 13, 1993, P.L. 103-81, 15 U.S. Code §§ 631 nt., 634, 636, 648, 652
Feb. 12, 1994, P.L. 103-211, 15 U.S. Code § 651
July 22, 1994, P.L. 103-282, 15 U.S. Code §§ 631 nt., 634
Aug. 26, 1994, P.L. 103-317, 15 U.S. Code § 651
Oct. 13, 1994, P.L. 103-355, 15 U.S. Code §§ 632, 637, 644, 645
Oct. 22, 1994, P.L. 103-403, 15 U.S. Code §§ 631 nt., 631, 632, 633, 634, 636, 637, 638, 644, 648, 652, 656
Oct. 12, 1995, P.L. 104-36, 15 U.S. Code §§ 634, 636
Dec. 21, 1995, P.L. 104-66, 15 U.S. Code §§ 639, 648
Feb. 10, 1996, P.L. 104-106, 15 U.S. Code §§ 637, 644
March 29, 1996, P.L. 104-121, 15 U.S. Code §§ 631 nt., 648, 657
Sept. 30, 1996, P.L. 104-208, 15 U.S. Code §§ 631 nt., 634
Nov. 18, 1997, P.L. 105-85, 15 U.S. Code §§ 637, 645
Dec. 2, 1997, P.L. 105-135, 15 U.S. Code §§ 631, 631 nt., 632, 636, 637, 638, 644, 645, 648, 656, 657a.
Oct. 21, 1998, P.L. 105-277, 15 U.S. Code §§ 636, 648, 654
April 2, 1999, P.L. 106-8, 15 U.S. Code § 636
April 5, 1999, P.L. 106-9, 15 U.S. Code § 631 nt.
April 6, 1999, P.L. 106-17, 15 U.S. Code § 656

April 27, 1999, P.L. 106-22, 15 U.S. Code § 636

April 27, 1999, P.L. 106-24, 15 U.S. Code §§ 631 nt., 636

Mont. Rev. Code 1947, 84-1501.1 et seq.

**Small Business Act (Comprehensive)**

Miss. Code Ann. 1972, § 57-10-151 et seq.

**Small Business Act (Development Finance Authority)**

Ark. Code Ann. 1987, 15-5-701 et seq.

**Small Business Act Amendments of 1961**

Sept. 26, 1961, P.L. 87-305, 75 Stat. 666, 15 U.S. Code §§ 633, 634, 636, 637, 639; 50 U.S. Code Appx. § 2158

**Small Business Act Amendments of 1967**

Oct. 11, 1967, P.L. 90-104, 81 Stat. 268, 15 U.S. Code §§ 633, 636, 637, 681 to 684, 686, 687, 692; 42 U.S. Code § 2902

**Small Business Act and Small Business Investment Act of 1958**

June 4, 1976, P.L. 94-305, 15 U.S. Code § 636 et seq.

March 24, 1977, P.L. 95-14, 15 U.S. Code § 694c

Aug. 4, 1977, P.L. 95-89, 15 U.S. Code § 682 et seq.

**Small Business Administration Reauthorization and Amendment Act of 1988**

Nov. 3, 1988, P.L. 100-590, 15 U.S. Code § 631 nt.

Nov. 5, 1990, P.L. 101-515, 15 U.S. Code § 697 nt.

Nov. 15, 1990, P.L. 101-574, 15 U.S. Code § 694b nt.

Oct. 22, 1994, P.L. 103-403, 15 U.S. Code §§ 694b, 697, 697 nt.

Oct. 12, 1995, P.L. 104-36, 15 U.S. Code § 694b nt.

Dec. 2, 1997, P.L. 105-135, 15 U.S. Code § 694b nt.

**Small Business Administration Reauthorization and Amendments Act of 1990**

Nov. 15, 1990, P.L. 101-574, 5 U.S. Code § 601 nt.; 15 U.S. Code §§ 631 nt., 637 nt., 648 nt., 648a nt., 652 nt.

Oct. 28, 1991, P.L. 102-140, 15 U.S. Code §§ 648a nt., 683 nt.

Oct. 28, 1992, P.L. 102-564, 15 U.S. Code § 648 nt.

**Small Business Administration Reauthorization and Amendments Act of 1994**

Oct. 22, 1994, P.L. 103-403, 15 U.S. Code § 631 nt.

**Small Business Advocate Act**

Pa. Purdon's Stat., Title 73, § 399.41 et seq.

**Small Business and Family Act**

Cal. Unemployment Insurance Code § 1118

**Small Business and Federal Procurement Competition Enhancement Act of 1984**

Oct. 30, 1984, P.L. 98-577, 41 U.S. Code §§ 251 nt., 403

Nov. 8, 1985, P.L. 99-145, 41 U.S. Code §§ 253c to 253g, 418a nt.

**Small Business and Household Pollution Prevention Program Act**

Pa. Purdon's Stat., Title 35, § 6029.201 et seq.

**Small Business Assistance Act**

Ala. Code 1975, § 25-10-1 et seq.

Cal. Corporations Code § 14150 et seq.

Fla. Stat. Ann., 288.701

Ga. Code Ann., 50-5-120 et seq.

Miss. Code Ann. 1972, § 57-10-501 et seq.

Tex. Gov. Code, § 481.101 et seq.

**Small Business Bonding Assistance Program**

La. Rev. Stat. Ann., 51:1121 et seq.

**Small Business Bridge Loan Program (Beverly-Murray)**

Cal. Statutes 1992, Ch. 61

**Small Business Budget Reconciliation and Loan Consolidation/Improvement Act of 1981**

Aug. 13, 1981, P.L. 97-35, 15 U.S. Code § 631 nt.

**Small Business Clean Air Assistance Act**

Mich. Comp. Laws Ann., 324.5701

**Small Business Competitiveness Demonstration Program Act of 1988**

Nov. 15, 1988, P.L. 100-656, 15 U.S. Code § 644 nt.

Nov. 15, 1990, P.L. 101-574, 15 U.S. Code § 644 nt.

Sept. 4, 1992, P.L. 102-366, 15 U.S. Code § 644 nt.

Oct. 23, 1992, P.L. 102-484, 15 U.S. Code § 644 nt.

Oct. 28, 1992, P.L. 102-564, 15 U.S. Code § 644 nt.

Nov. 30, 1993, P.L. 103-160, 15 U.S. Code § 632 nt.

Sept. 30, 1996, P.L. 104-208, 15 U.S. Code § 644 nt.

June 12, 1997, P.L. 105-18, 15 U.S. Code § 644 nt.

Dec. 2, 1997, P.L. 105-135, 15 U.S. Code §§ 637 nt., 644 nt., 697e nt.

**Small Business Computer Security and Education Act of 1984**

July 16, 1984, P.L. 98-362, 15 U.S. Code §§ 631 nt., 632, 633, 633 nt., 637, 637 nt.

Nov. 3, 1988, P.L. 100-590, 15 U.S. Code § 633 nt.

Nov. 5, 1990, P.L. 101-515, 15 U.S. Code § 633 nt.

Nov. 15, 1990, P.L. 101-574, 15 U.S. Code § 633

Oct. 28, 1991, P.L. 102-140, 15 U.S. Code § 633 nt.

Sept. 4, 1992, P.L. 102-366, 15 U.S. Code § 633 nt.

Oct. 22, 1994, P.L. 103-403, 15 U.S. Code § 633 nt.

**Small Business Corporation Law**

Cal. Corporations Code § 14000 et seq.

**Small Business Credit and Business Opportunity Enhancement Act of 1992**

Sept. 4, 1992, P.L. 102-366, 15 U.S. Code § 631 nt.

Aug. 13, 1993, P.L. 103-81, 15 U.S. Code § 648 nt.

**Small Business Credit Crunch Relief Act of 1992**

Sept. 4, 1992, P.L. 102-366, 15 U.S. Code § 631 nt.

**Small Business Development Act**

Ill. Rev. Stat. 1987, Ch. 127, § 2709-1 et seq.

La. Rev. Stat. Ann., 51:1120 et seq.

Ore. Rev. Stat., 285.500 et seq.

**Small Business Development Authority Act**

Neb. Rev. Stat. 1943, 58-301 et seq., 72-1701 et seq.

**Small Business Development Center Act of 1980**

July 2, 1980, P.L. 96-302, 15 U.S. Code §§ 631 nt., 648 et seq.

Aug. 21, 1984, P.L. 98-395, 15 U.S. Code § 648 nt.

Nov. 21, 1989, P.L. 101-162, 15 U.S. Code § 648 nt.

Nov. 5, 1990, P.L. 101-515, 15 U.S. Code § 648 nt.

Nov. 15, 1990, P.L. 101-574, 15 U.S. Code § 648 nt.

**Small Business Development Center Improvement Act of 1984**

Aug. 21, 1984, P.L. 98-395, 15 U.S. Code §§ 631 nt., 636, 648, 648 nt.

**Small Business Development Corporation Law**

Cal. Corporations Code § 14000 et seq.

**Small Business Development Credit Corporation Act**

Colo. Rev. Stat., 11-36-101 et seq.

**Small Business Development Financing Authority Act**

Md. Ann. Code 1974, Art. FI, § 13-202 et seq.

**Small Business Development Loan Act**

Mo. Rev. Stat., 348.005 et seq.

**Small Business Economic Policy Act of 1980**

July 2, 1980, P.L. 96-302, 15 U.S. Code §§ 631 nt., 631b et seq.

Nov. 15, 1990, P.L. 101-574, 15 U.S. Code § 631b

Dec. 2, 1997, P.L. 105-135, 15 U.S. Code § 631b

**Small Business Emergency Relief Act**

Dec. 31, 1975, P.L. 94-190, 89 Stat. 1095, 41 U.S. Code § 252 et seq.

**Small Business Employee Ownership Act of 1980**

July 2, 1980, P.L. 96-302, 15 U.S. Code §§ 631 nt., 636 nt.

**Small Business Energy Loan Act**

July 4, 1978, P.L. 95-315, 15 U.S. Code §§ 631 nt., 633 et seq.

**Small Business Equal Access to Justice Act**

Utah Code Ann. 1953, 78-27a-1 et seq.

**Small Business Equal Access to Justice Act (Carpenter-Katz)**

Cal. Code of Civil Procedure § 1028.5

**Small Business Equity Corporation Act**

La. Rev. Stat. Ann., 33:9081 et seq.

**Small Business Equity Enhancement Act of 1992**

Sept. 4, 1992, P.L. 102-366, 15 U.S. Code § 661 nt.

**Small Business Expansion Assistance Program**

W. Va. Code 1966, §§ 5B-6-1 to 5B-6-5

**Small Business Export Expansion Act of 1980**

Oct. 21, 1980, P.L. 96-481, 15 U.S. Code § 631 nt.

**Small Business, Female Business, and Minority Business Set-Aside Act**

N.J. Stat. Ann., 52:32-17 et seq.

**Small Business Financial Recovery Act**

Conn. Public Acts 1993, No. 382, §§ 39, 40, 42 to 49

**Small Business Financing Act**

Miss. Code Ann. 1972, § 57-10-201 et seq.

Va. Code 1950, § 9-197 et seq.

**Small Business Guaranteed Credit Enhancement Act of 1993**

Aug. 13, 1993, P.L. 103-81, 15 U.S. Code § 631 nt.

Sept. 30, 1996, P.L. 104-208, 15 U.S. Code § 634 nt.

**Small Business Health Access Corporation Act**

Fla. Stat. Ann., 409.701

**Small Business Health Insurance Initiative**

W. Va. Code 1966 § 5-16A-1 et seq.

**Small Business Incubator Act**

Ala. Code 1975, § 41-23-60 et seq.

**Small Business Incubators Act**

Cal. Statutes 1988, Ch. 634, § 1

Ill. Rev. Stat. 1991, Ch. 127, § 2711 et seq.

Mo. Rev. Stat., 620.495 et seq.

Neb. Rev. Stat. 1943, 72-1701 et seq.

Pa. Purdon's Stat., Title 73, § 395.1 et seq.

**Small Business Incubators Incentives Act**

Neb. Rev. Stat. 1943, 72-1701 et seq.

Okla. Stat. Ann., Title 74, § 5071 et seq.

**Small Business Innovation Development Act of 1982**

July 22, 1982, P.L. 97-219, 15 U.S. Code §§ 631 nt., 638, 638 nt.

Nov. 10, 1988, P.L. 100-647, 15 U.S. Code § 638 nt.

Oct. 23, 1992, P.L. 102-484, 15 U.S. Code § 638 nt.

Oct. 28, 1992, P.L. 102-564, 15 U.S. Code §§ 631 nt., 638, 638 nt.

**Small Business Innovation Research Program Reauthorization Act of 1992**

Oct. 28, 1992, P.L. 102-564, 15 U.S. Code § 631 nt.

**Small Business Innovation Research Promotion Act**

N.Y. Public Authorities Law (Consol. Laws Ch. 43A), § 3102b

**Small Business Insurers' Simplification Act of 1980**

Oct. 21, 1980, P.L. 96-477, 15 U.S. Code § 77a nt.

**Small Business International Trade and Competitiveness Act**

Aug. 23, 1988, P.L. 100-418, 102 Stat. 1553, 15 U.S. Code §§ 631, 631 nt., 636, 638 nt., 648, 649, 696

**Small Business Investment Act**

La. Rev. Stat. Ann., 33:9061 et seq.

**Small Business Investment Act Amendments of 1960**

June 11, 1960, P.L. 86-502, 74 Stat. 196, 15 U.S. Code §§ 662, 681, 682, 684

**Small Business Investment Act Amendments of 1961**

Oct. 3, 1961, P.L. 87-341, 75 Stat. 752, 15 U.S. Code §§ 631 nt., 633, 662, 681 to 687c, 696

**Small Business Investment Act Amendments of 1963**

Feb. 28, 1964, P.L. 88-273, 78 Stat. 146, 15 U.S. Code §§ 682, 683, 686, 687, 687d

**Small Business Investment Act Amendments of 1966**

Nov. 6, 1966, P.L. 89-779, 80 Stat. 1359, 5 U.S. Code §§ 5315, 5316; 15 U.S. Code §§ 633, 671, 687 to 687c, 687e to 687h

**Small Business Investment Act Amendments of 1972**

Oct. 27, 1972, P.L. 92-595, 15 § 662 nt.

**Small Business Investment Act of 1958**

Aug. 21, 1958, P.L. 85-699, 72 Stat. 689, 12 U.S. Code § 352a nts.; 15 U.S. Code §§ 77c, 77ddd, 80a-18, 633, 636, 661, 662, 671, 672, 681 to 688, 691, 695, 696; 18 U.S. Code §§ prec. 201, 217, 218, 221, 657, 1006, 1014

June 11, 1960, P.L. 86-502, 74 Stat. 196, 15 U.S. Code §§ 662, 681, 682, 684

May 1, 1961, P.L. 87-27, 75 Stat. 63, 15 U.S. Code § 696

Oct. 3, 1961, P.L. 87-341, 75 Stat. 752, 15 U.S. Code §§ 662, 681 to 687c, 696

Feb. 28, 1964, P.L. 88-273, 78 Stat. 146, 15 U.S. Code §§ 682, 683, 686, 687, 687d

Aug. 10, 1965, P.L. 89-117, 79 Stat. 482, 15 U.S. Code §§ 671, 692 to 694

Nov. 6, 1966, P.L. 89-779, 80 Stat. 1359, 15 U.S. Code §§ 671, 687 to 687c, 687e to 687h

Oct. 11, 1967, P.L. 90-104, 81 Stat. 269, 15 U.S. Code §§ 681 to 684, 686, 687

Dec. 31, 1970, P.L. 91-609, 84 Stat. 1812, 15 U.S. Code §§ 692, 693, 694 to 694b

Oct. 27, 1972, P.L. 92-595, 86 Stat. 1314, 15 U.S. Code §§ 633, 636, 662, 681, 683, 684, 686, 687i, 687j

Oct. 24, 1978, P.L. 95-507, 15 U.S. Code §§ 631 et seq., 681 et seq.

Nov. 5, 1979, P.L. 96-104, 15 U.S. Code § 687

Dec. 28, 1979, P.L. 96-161, 15 U.S. Code § 687

March 31, 1980, P.L. 96-221, 15 U.S. Code § 687

July 2, 1980, P.L. 96-302, 15 U.S. Code §§ 694c, 694c-2, 697 et seq.

Oct. 12, 1984, P.L. 98-473, 15 U.S. Code § 694-1

Nov. 8, 1984, P.L. 98-620, 15 U.S. Code § 687a

Dec. 28, 1985, P.L. 99-226, 15 U.S. Code § 687

April 7, 1986, P.L. 99-272, 15 U.S. Code §§ 687k, 687l, 694b, 697a

July 11, 1987, P.L. 100-72, 15 U.S. Code § 697a

Nov. 3, 1988, P.L. 100-590, 15 U.S. Code §§ 681, 687b, 687m, 694, 694b, 694c, 695 to 697, 697a to 697c

Nov. 21, 1989, P.L. 101-162, 15 U.S. Code §§ 683, 697l

Nov. 5, 1990, P.L. 101-515, 15 U.S. Code § 697

Nov. 15, 1990, P.L. 101-574, 15 U.S. Code §§ 683, 683 nt., 695, 696

Sept. 4, 1992, P.L. 102-366, 15 U.S. Code §§ 661, 662, 682, 683, 685, 686, 687, 687b, 687l

Oct. 22, 1994, P.L. 103-403, 15 U.S. Code §§ 683, 687, 697d, 697e, 697f

Oct. 12, 1995, P.L. 104-36, 15 U.S. Code § 697

Sept. 30, 1996, P.L. 104-208, 15 U.S. Code §§ 80a-18, 683, 687, 687b, 687d, 687i to 687m, 697f

Dec. 2, 1997, P.L. 105-135, 15 U.S. Code §§ 662, 681, 682, 683, 687b, 687m, 694b, 696, 697, 697e

April 5, 1999, P.L. 106-9, 15 U.S. Code §§ 661 nt., 662, 683, 687 , 687m

**Small Business Investment Corporations Act**

N.D. Cent. Code, 10-30-01 et seq.

**Small Business Investment Improvement Act of 1999**

April 5, 1999, P.L. 106-9, 113 Stat. 17, 15 U.S. Code § 661 nt.

**Small Business Investment Incentive Act of 1980**

Oct. 21, 1980, P.L. 96-477, 15 U.S. Code § 80a-51 nt.

Mont. Code Ann., 15-33-101 et seq.

**Small Business Job Protection Act of 1996**

Aug. 20, 1996, P.L. 104-188, 26 U.S. Code § 1 nt.

Aug. 5, 1997, P.L. 105-34, 26 U.S. Code §§ 529 nt., 6501 nt., 7701 nt.

July 22, 1998, P.L. 105-206, 26 U.S. Code §§ 167 nt., 219, 414, 679, 4091 nt., prec. 6041

**Small Business Lending Enhancement Act of 1995**

Oct. 12, 1995, P.L. 104-36, 15 U.S. Code § 631 nt.

**Small Business Licensing Coordination Act**

Mont. Code Ann., 30-16-101 et seq.

**Small Business Linked Deposit Act**

Okla. Stat. Ann., Title 62, § 88.1 et seq.

**Small Business Loan Act**

Me. Rev. Stat. Ann. 1964, Title 5, § 15001 et seq.

N.J. Stat. Ann., 17:9A-59.25 et seq.

**Small Business Loan Act (Veterans)**

Me. Rev. Stat. Ann. 1964, Title 37-B, § 551 et seq.

**Small Business Loan Securitization and Secondary Market Enhancement Act of 1994**

Sept. 23, 1994, P.L. 103-325, 15 U.S. Code § 78a nt.

**Small Business Mobilization Law**

June 11, 1942, Ch. 404, 56 Stat. 351

Dec. 8, 1944, Ch. 549, 58 Stat. 799

Minn. Stat. 1982, 16.081 et seq.

**Small Business New Jobs Training Act**

Iowa Code Ann., 280C.1 et seq.

**Small Business Prepayment Penalty Relief Act of 1994**

Oct. 22, 1994, P.L. 103-403, 15 U.S. Code § 661 nt.

**Small Business Procurement Act**

Kan. Stat. Ann., 75-6001 et seq.

La. Rev. Stat. Ann., 39:1731 et seq.

Minn. Stat. Ann., 16B.19 et seq.

**Small Business Procurement Act (Female and Minority)**

Iowa Laws 1985 (71st G.A.), H.F. 225

**Small Business Procurement and Contract Act**

Cal. Government Code, § 14835 et seq.

**Small Business Product Development Act**

Cal. Corporations Code §§ 14000, 14029.9 et seq.

**Small Business Programs Improvement Act of 1996**

Sept. 30, 1996, P.L. 104-208, Division D, 15 U.S. Code § 631 nt.

**Small Business Protection Act of 1967**

Oct. 11, 1967, P.L. 90-104, 81 Stat. 272, 15 U.S. Code § 634 nt.

**Small Business Purchasing Act**

Ill. Rev. Stat. 1991, Ch. 127, § 132.21

Mont. Code Ann., 18-5-301 et seq.

**Small Business Reauthorization Act of 1997**
Dec. 2, 1997, P.L. 105-135, 15 U.S. Code § 631 nt.

**Small Business Recovery Act**
Conn. Gen. Stat. Ann., §§ 32-347 to 32-349

**Small Business Regulatory Enforcement Fairness Act of 1996**
March 29, 1996, P.L. 104-121, Title II, 5 U.S. Code § 601 nt.

**Small Business Research and Development Enhancement Act of 1992**
Oct. 28, 1992, P.L. 102-564, 15 U.S. Code § 631 nt.

**Small Business Secondary Market Improvements Act of 1984**
July 10, 1984, P.L. 98-352, 15 U.S. Code §§ 631 nt., 633, 634, 634 nt., 639

**Small Business Set-Aside Act**
N.J. Stat. Ann., 52:32-17

**Small Business Surety Bond Guaranty Program Act**
Okla. Stat. Ann., Title 74, § 85.47 et seq.

**Small Business Tax Policy Act**
Ill. Rev. Stat. 1991, Ch. 127, §§ 3881, 3882

**Small Business Tax Revision Act of 1958**
Sept. 2, 1958, P.L. 85-866, 72 Stat. 1676, 26 U.S. Code §§ 165, 172, 179, 535, 1244, 1551, 6161, prec. 6166, 6166, 6503, 6601

**Small Business Technology Growth Program**
Fla. Stat. Ann., 288.95155

**Small Business Technology Transfer Act of 1992**
Oct. 28, 1992, P.L. 102-564, 15 U.S. Code § 631 nt.

**Small Business Training Assistance Act**
Ore. Rev. Stat., 285.540 et seq.

**Small Business Utility Advocate Act**
Ill. Rev. Stat. 1991, Ch. 111 2/3, § 1201 et seq.

**Small Business Utility Deposit Relief Act**
Ill. Rev. Stat. 1991, Ch. 111 2/3, § 1001 et seq.

**Small Business Year 2000 Readiness Act**
April 2, 1999, P.L. 106-8, 113 Stat. 13, 15 U.S. Code § 631 nt.

**Small Businessman's Loan Assistance Act**
Miss. Code Ann. 1972, § 57-10-101 et seq.

**Small Cause Court Acts**
N.J. Stat. Revised 1937, 2:8-46, 2:9-1 to 2:9-26, 2:33-1 to 2:33-180

**Small Cities Assistance Act**
N.M. Stat. Ann., 3-37A-1 et seq.

**Small Cities Community Development Block Grant Program Act**
Fla. Stat. Ann., 290.0401 et seq.

**Small Claims Act**
Cal. Code of Civil Procedure § 116.110 et seq.
Ky. Rev. Stat. 1971, 24A.200 et seq.
Me. Rev. Stat. Ann. 1964, Title 14, § 7481 et seq.
N.C. Gen. Stat. 1943, §§ 1-539.3 et seq., 7A-210 et seq.
N.H. Rev. Stat. 1955, 503:1 et seq.
N.J. Rev. Stat. 1937, 2A:18-65 et seq.
R.I. Gen. Laws 1956, 10-16-1 et seq.
S.D. Codified Laws 1967, 15-39-45 et seq.
S.D. Supreme Court Rule, 81-4
Wash. Rev. Code Ann., 12.40.010 et seq.

**Small Claims Arbitration Act**
Pa. Cons. Stat., Title 42, §§ 7361, 7362

**Small Claims Court Act**
Cal. Code of Civil Procedure § 117 et seq.
Mont. Code Ann., 3-12-101 et seq.
N.M. Stat. Ann. 1953, 16-5-1 et seq.
N.Y. City Civil Court Act § 1801 et seq.
Utah Code Ann. 1953, 78-6-1 et seq.
Wis. Stat. Ann., 779.01 et seq.

**Small Claims Procedure Act**
Ark. Code Ann. 1987, 16-17-601 et seq.
Kan. Stat. Ann., 61-2701 et seq.

Okla. Stat. Ann., Title 12, § 1751 et seq.

**Small Claims Settlement Act**
La. Rev. Stat. Ann., 13:5141 et seq.

**Small Community Environmental Flexibility Act**
Colo. Rev. Stat., 25-19-101 et seq.

**Small Community Sewer Construction Assistance Act**
Fla. Stat. Ann., 403.1838

**Small Construction Business Act**
Ill. Rev. Stat. 1981, Ch. 127, § 132.41 et seq.

**Small Counties Assistance Act**
N.M. Stat. Ann., 4-61-1 et seq.

**Small Craft Harbor District Act**
Cal. Harbors and Navigation Code, § 7000 et seq.

**Small Craft Harbors Act**
Cal. Harbors and Navigation Code § 5008 et seq.

**Small Employer Group Health Coverage Reform Act**
N.C. Gen. Stat. 1943, § 58-50-100 et seq.
Tenn. Public Acts 1992, Ch. 808

**Small Employer Health Benefit Act**
Minn. Stat. 1986, 62L.01 et seq.

**Small Employer Health Coverage Incentive Act**
Cal. Revenue and Taxation Code §§ 17053.20, 23615

**Small Employer Health Insurance Act**
Neb. Rev. Stat. 1943, 44-5201 et seq.
Utah Code Ann. 1953, 31A-30-101 et seq.

**Small Employer Health Insurance Availability Act**
Colo. Rev. Stat., 10-8-601 et seq.
Ida. Code 1947, 41-4701 et seq.
Mont. Code Ann., 33-22-1801 to 33-22-1814
Neb. Rev. Stat. 1943, 44-5223 et seq.
R.I. Gen. Laws 1956, 27-50-1 et seq.
Tex. Insurance Code, § 26.01 et seq.
Wyo. Stat. 1977, § 26-19-301 et seq.

**Small Employer Health Insurance Reform Act**
Okla. Stat. Ann., Title 36, § 6511 et seq.

**Small Employer Rating, Renewability and Portability Health Insurance Act**
Ill. Comp. Stat. 1992, Ch. 215, § 95/1-1 et seq.

**Small Enterprise Development Finance Act**
Miss. Code Ann. 1972, § 57-71-1 et seq.

**Small Estates Act**
Ala. Code 1975, § 43-2-690 et seq.
Colo. Rev. Stat. 15-12-1201
Fla. Stat. Ann., 735.201 et seq.
Ida. Code 1947, 15-3-1201 et seq.
Ill. Rev. Stat. 1991, Ch. 110 1/2, § 25-1 et seq.
Kan. Stat. Ann., 59-2287 et seq.
Md. Ann. Code 1974, Art. ET, § 5-601 et seq.
Mich. Comp. Laws Ann., 700.101 et seq.
Mo. Rev. Stat., 473.090 et seq.
Neb. Rev. Stat. 1943, 30-24-127; 30-24-128
N.Y. Surrogate's Court Procedure Act (Consol. Laws Ch. 59A) § 1301 et seq.
S.D. Codified Laws 1967, 30-11A-1 et seq.
Tenn. Code Ann., 30-4-101 et seq.
Va. Code 1950, § 64.1-132.1 et seq.

**Small Facility Loan Guarantee for Developmental Disability Programs**
Cal. Health and Safety Code § 436.40 et seq.

**Small Games of Chance Act (Local Option)**
Pa. Purdon's Stat., Title 10, § 311 et seq.

**Small Group Rate and Renewability Act**
N.M. Stat. Ann., 59A-23C-3

**Small Group Rating Law (Model)**
Iowa Code Ann., 513B.1

**Small Groups Rate and Renewability Act**
N.M. Stat. Ann., 59a-23c-1 et seq.

**Small Insurance Policy Law**
Tenn. Code Ann., 56-7-702

**Small Investor-Owned Telephone Utility Act**
Va. Code 1950, § 56-531 et seq.

**Small Lakes Program Act (Multipurpose)**
Kan. Stat. Ann., 82a.1601 et seq.

**Small Loan Act**
Ala. Code 1975, § 5-18-1 et seq.
Alaska Stat. 1962, § 06.20.010 et seq.
Ariz. Rev. Stat. Ann., § 6-601 et seq.
Ark. Stat. 1947, 67-1301 et seq.
Cal. Financial Code § 24000 et seq.
Colo. Rev. Stat., 5-3-101 et seq.
Conn. Gen. Stat. Ann., § 36-225 et seq.
D.C. Code Ann., § 26-701 et seq.
Del. Code of 1974, Title 5, § 2101 et seq.
Fla. Stat. Ann., 516.001 et seq.
Ga. Code Ann., 7-3-1 et seq.
Haw. Rev. Stat. Ann., § 409-1 et seq.
Ida. Code 1947, 26-2027 et seq.
Ill. Rev. Stat. 1991, Ch. 17, § 6400 et seq.
Iowa Code Ann., 536.1 et seq.
Ky. Rev. Stat. 1971, 288.410 et seq.
La. Rev. Stat. Ann., 9:3577.1 et seq.
Mass. Gen. Laws Ann., 140:96 et seq.
Md. Ann. Code 1974, Art. CL, § 12-201 et seq.
Me. Rev. Stat. Ann. 1964, Title 9A, § 1-201 et seq.
Mich. Comp. Laws Ann., 493.1 et seq.
Minn. Stat. Ann., 56.01 et seq.
Miss. Code Ann. 1972, § 75-67-1 et seq.
Mo. Rev. Stat., 367.100 et seq.
N.C. Gen. Stat. 1943, § 53-164 et seq.
N.D. Cent. Code, 13-03-01 et seq.
Neb. Rev. Stat. 1943, 45-114 et seq.
Nev. Rev. Stat. 1979 Reprint, 675.010 et seq.
N.H. Rev. Stat. 1955, 399-A:1 et seq.
N.J. Stat. Ann.17:10-1 et seq.
N.M. Stat. Ann., 58-15-1 et seq.
N.Y. Banking Law (Consol. Laws Ch. 2), § 340 et seq.
Ohio Rev. Code 1953, 1321.01 et seq.
Okla. Stat. 1961, Title 36, § 4501 et seq.
Ore. Rev. Stat., 725.010 et seq.
Pa. Purdon's Stat., Title 7, § 6151 et seq.
R.I. Gen. Laws 1956, 19-25-1 et seq.
S.C. Code Ann. 1962, § 8-701 et seq.
Tenn. Code Ann., 47-9-201
Tex. Rev. Civ. Stat., Art. 5069-1.01 et seq.
Utah Laws 1945, Miscellaneous Superseded Code Provisions, Ch. 15A
Va. Code 1950, § 6.1-244 et seq.
Vt. Stat. Ann., Title 8, § 2201 et seq.
Wash. Rev. Code Ann., 31.08.010 et seq.
Wis. Stat. 1973, 214.01 et seq.
Wyo. Stat. 1957, § 13-489 et seq.

**Small Loan Act—Credit Provisions**
Md. Ann. Code 1974, Art. CL, § 12-201 et seq.

**Small Loan Act—Licensing Provisions**
Md. Ann. Code 1974, Art. FI, § 11-201 et seq.

**Small Loan and Consumer Finance Act**
S.D. Codified Laws 1967, 54-4-1 et seq., 54-6-1 et seq.

**Small Loan Companies Act**
Ind. Code 1971, 28-7-4-1 et seq.

**Small Loan License Act**
Ohio Rev. Code 1953, 1321.02

**Small Loan Privilege Tax Act**
Miss. Code Ann. 1972, § 75-67-201 et seq.

**Small Loan Regulatory Act**
Miss. Code Ann. 1972, § 75-67-101 et seq.

**Small Lottery and Raffle Act**
Neb. Rev. Stat. 1943, 9-501 et seq.

**Small Offense Law**
Tenn. Code Ann., Superseded Vol., 40-407 et seq.

**Small or Small Minority Business Purchasing Act**
Ky. Rev. Stat. 1971, 45.470 et seq.

**Small Personal Loan Act**
P.R. Laws Ann. 1954, Title 10, § 941 et seq.

**Small Power Production Act**
Me. Rev. Stat. Ann. 1964, Title 35-A, § 3301 et seq.

**Small Reclamation Projects Act of 1956**
Aug. 6, 1956, Ch. 972, 70 Stat. 1047, 43 U.S. Code § 422k
June 5, 1957, P.L. 85-47, 71 Stat. 48, 43 U.S. Code §§ 422d, 422e
Sept. 2, 1966, P.L. 89-553, 80 Stat. 376, 43 U.S. Code §§ 422b, 422d, 422e, 422h, 422j
Dec. 27, 1975, P.L. 94-181, 89 Stat. 1049, 43 U.S. Code §§ 422b, 422d, 422e, 422j
Sept. 4, 1980, P.L. 96-336, 43 U.S. Code §§ 422e, 422j, 422j nt.
Oct. 27, 1986, P.L. 99-546, 43 U.S. Code §§ 422a to 422d
Nov. 2, 1994, P.L. 103-437, 43 U.S. Code § 422d

**Small Stock Act**
Tenn. Acts 1903, Ch. 177

**Small Town Development Act**
Miss. Code Ann. 1972, § 57-79-1 et seq.

**Small Tract Act of 1938**
June 1, 1938, Ch. 317, 52 Stat. 609, 43 U.S. Code § 682a
July 14, 1945, Ch. 298, 59 Stat. 467, 43 U.S. Code § 682a

**Small Tract Financing Act**
Mont. Code Ann., 71-1-301 et seq.

**Small Tract Optional Tax Act (Western Oregon)**
Ore. Rev. Stat., 321.705 et seq.

**Small Tracts Act**
Jan. 12, 1983, P.L. 97-465, 16 U.S. Code § 521c et seq.

**Small Value Cases Transfer Act**
Mass. Gen. Laws Ann., 231:102C

**Small Water and Sewer Public Utility Act**
Va. Code 1950, § 56-265.13:1 et seq.

**Small Water Systems Assistance Act**
Pa. Purdon's Stat., Title 35, § 724.1 et seq.

**Smaller War Plants Corporation**
April 27, 1945, Ch. 98, 59 Stat. 95

**Smallpox Immunization Act**
N.C. Gen. Stat. 1943, § 130A-152 et seq.

**SMART Schools Act (Soundly Made, Accountable, Reasonable and Thrifty)**
Fla. Stat. Ann., 235.175 et seq.

**Smith Act**
Ala. Code 1975, § 16-13-52.1

**Smith Act (Coal Research)**
Ky. Rev. Stat. 1971, 152A.210

**Smith Act (Cold Storage)**
Ohio Rev. Code 1953, 915.01 et seq.

**Smith Act (Eggs)**
Ky. Rev. Stat. 1971, 260.600 et seq.

**Smith Act (Reclamation and Irrigation)**
Aug. 11, 1916, Ch. 319, 39 Stat. 506, 43 U.S. Code §§ 621 to 630

**Smith Act (Tax Assessments)**
Ga. Code 1933, 92-6701 et seq.

**Smith Act of 1940**
June 28, 1940, Ch. 439, 54 Stat. 670 (See 18 U.S. Code § 2385)

**Smith-Connally Anti-Strike Act**
See War Labor Disputes Act

**Smith-Hughes Act (State Board of Education)**
Ohio Laws Vol. 107, p. 579

**Smith-Hughes Act (Vocational Education)**
See Vocational Education Acts

**Smith-Hughes Vocational Education Act**
Aug. 5, 1997, P.L. 105-33, 20 U.S. Code § 11 et seq.

**Smith-Lever Act**
Nov. 28, 1990, P.L. 101-624, 7 U.S. Code § 344
April 4, 1996, P.L. 104-127, 7 U.S. Code § 343
June 23, 1998, P.L. 105-185, 7 U.S. Code §§ 341 nt., 343, 344, 346
Oct. 21, 1998, P.L. 105-277, 7 U.S. Code § 343
*Continued*

**Smith-Lever Act (Agricultural Extension Work)**
See Agricultural Extension Work Acts

**Smith Martin-Hittle-Burke-Rowell Act (Occupational Disease)**
Mich. Comp. Laws 1948, 417.1 et seq.

**Smith-McNitt-Holbeck Act (Township Highways)**
Mich. Comp. Laws 1948, 247.1 et seq.

**Smith One Per Cent Act**
Ohio Rev. Code 1953, 5705.02 et seq

**Smith River Management Act**
Mont. Laws 1989, Ch. 512

**Smith River National Recreation Area Act**
Nov. 16, 1990, P.L. 101-612, 16 U.S. Code §§ 431 nt., 460bbb et seq.

**Smith-Sears Act (Vocational Rehabilitation)**
June 27, 1918, Ch. 107, 40 Stat. 617

**Smithfield Pinball Arcade and Pinball Machine Ordinance**
R.I. Public Laws 1982, Ch. 119

**Smithsonian Institution Sesquicentennial Commemorative Coin Act of 1995**
Jan. 10, 1996, P.L. 104-96, 31 U.S. Code § 5112 nt.

**Smoke Abatement Act**
Mont. Code Ann., 7-31-101 et seq.
R.I. Gen. Laws 1956, 23-23-1 et seq.

**Smoke Control Act**
N.Y. City Adm. Code '38, Ch. 26, § D26-1.0 et seq.

**Smoke Detector Act**
D.C. Code Ann., § 5-529 et seq.
Ill. Rev. Stat. 1991, Ch. 127 1/2, § 801 et seq.

**Smoke Detectors Act (Facilities Requirements)**
Ill. Rev. Stat. 1991, Ch. 127 1/2, § 820 et seq.

**Smoke Detectors Act (Facilities Requiring)**
Ill. Comp. Stat. 1992, Ch. 425, § 10/0.01 et seq.

**Smoke Nuisance Abatement Act**
Mo. Rev. Stat., 71.760 et seq.
Mont. Code Ann., 7-31-101 et seq.
R.I. Gen. Laws 1956, Superseded Vol., 23-23-1 et seq.

**Smoke Nuisance Act**
Mass. Gen. Laws 1932, Ch. 140, § 132 et seq.

**Smoke Prevention Act**
D.C. Code 1973, § 6-811 et seq.

**Smokeless Tobacco Limitation Act**
Ill. Rev. Stat. 1991, Ch. 23, § 2358-21 et seq.

**Smokeless Tobacco Outdoor Advertising Act**
Ill. Rev. Stat. 1991, Ch. 23, § 2358-30 et seq.

**Smokeless Tobacco Products Act**
N.M. Stat. Ann., 30-48-1 et seq.

**Smoking Herbs and Tobacco Accessories Control Act**
Ill. Rev. Stat. 1991, Ch. 23, § 2358-1 et seq.

**Smoking in Public Places Act**
Okla. Stat. Ann., Title 63, § 1-5216 et seq.

**Smoking in Workplace Act**
Haw. Rev. Stat. Ann., § 328K-11 et seq.
Me. Rev. Stat. Ann. 1964, Title 22, § 1580-A
N.M. Stat. Ann., 24-16-1 et seq.
R.I. Gen. Laws 1956, 23-20.7-1 et seq.

**Smoking Restriction Act**
D.C. Code Ann., § 6-911 et seq.

**Smoking Restrictions in Schools Act**
R.I. Gen. Laws 1956, 23-20.9-1 et seq.

**Smoot-Burton Act (British War Debt)**
Feb. 28, 1923, Ch. 146, 42 Stat. 1325

**Smyer-Bentley Act (War Emergency Council)**
Ala. General Acts 1943, p. 169, No. 185

**Smyrna Development Authority Act (Downtown)**
Ga. Laws 1991, p. 4382

**Snake River Compact Act**
Ida. Code 1947, 42-3313 et seq.
Wyo. Stat. Ann., §§ 41-12-501, 41-12-502

**Sniffer Law (Paint)**
Mont. Code Ann., 45-9-121

**Sno-Park Permit Program**
Cal. Health and Safety Code § 5091.01 et seq.

**Snob Zoning Law**
Mass. Gen. Laws Ann., 40B:20

**Snow Act**
D.C. Code 1973, § 7-901 et seq.

**Snow and Ice Act (Compulsory Removal)**
D.C. Code Ann., § 7-901 et seq.
Ill. Rev. Stat. 1991, Ch. 70, § 200 et seq.
Ind. Code 1971, 18-1-4-1, Subd. 31
Wis. Stat. Ann., 66.615, Subsec. 5

**Snow and Ice Act (Notice of Claim)**
Ind. Code 1971, 18-2-2-1

**Snowmobile Act**
Ill. Rev. Stat. 1991, Ch. 95 1/2 § 601-1 et seq.
Mich. Comp. Laws Ann., 257.1501 et seq.
Mont. Code Ann., 23-2-601 et seq.
N.D. Cent. Code, 39-24-01 et seq.
N.M. Stat. Ann., 66-9-1 et seq.
S.D. Codified Laws 1967, 32-20A-1 et seq.
Wash. Rev. Code Ann., 46.10.010 et seq.

**Snowmobile and All-Terrain Vehicle Law**
Pa. Cons. Stat., Title 75, § 7701 et seq.

**Snowmobile Numbering Act**
Ida. Code 1947, 67-7102 et seq.

**Snuff and Cigarette Tax Act**
N.D. Cent. Code, 57-36-01 et seq.

**Snyder Act (Indian Affairs Bureau)**
Nov. 2, 1921, Ch. 115, 42 Stat. 208, 25 U.S. Code § 13
Oct. 12, 1976, P.L. 94-482, 90 Stat. 2233
Oct. 7, 1998, P.L. 105-244, 25 U.S. Code § 13

**Snyder-Armstrong Act (Liquor Control)**
Pa. 1923 Pamph. Laws 34, No. 25

**Social and Biomedical Research Act**
Fla. Stat. Ann., 402.105

**Social Psychotherapist Regulation Act**
Tex. Rev. Civ. Stat., Art. 4512f

**Social Security Act**
Aug. 14, 1935, Ch. 531, 49 Stat. 620
March 24, 1943, Ch. 26, 57 Stat. 46, 42 U.S. Code § 409
Feb. 25, 1944, Ch. 63, 58 Stat. 93, 42 U.S. Code § 401
April 4, 1944, Ch. 161, 58 Stat. 188, 42 U.S. Code § 409
Oct. 3, 1944, Ch. 480, 58 Stat. 789, 42 U.S. Code §§ 1104, 1321
Oct. 23, 1945, Ch. 433, 59 Stat. 548, 42 U.S. Code § 409
Dec. 29, 1945, Ch. 652, 59 Stat. 671, 42 U.S. Code § 409 and nt.
Aug. 10, 1946, Ch. 951, 60 Stat. 979, 42 U.S. Code §§ 303, 402, 403, 409, 410, 503, 603, 701, 702, 711, 712, 721, 731, 1203, 1301
Aug. 6, 1947, Ch. 510, 61 Stat. 794, 42 U.S. Code §§ 1104, 1321
April 20, 1948, Ch. 222, 62 Stat. 195, 42 U.S. Code § 409
June 14, 1948, Ch. 468, 62 Stat. 438, 42 U.S. Code §§ 303, 603, 1203, 1301
July 16, 1949, Ch. 342, 63 Stat. 445
Aug. 28, 1950, Ch. 809, 64 Stat. 482, 42 U.S. Code §§ 301, 302, 303, 304, 306, 401, 402, 403, 404, 405 and others
Sept. 23, 1950, Ch. 994, 64 Stat. 947, 42 U.S. Code § 411
July 12, 1951, Ch. 233, 65 Stat. 120, 42 U.S. Code § 410
June 28, 1952, Ch. 483, 66 Stat. 285, 42 U.S. Code § 418

*Continued*

July 18, 1952, Ch. 945, 66 Stat. 767, 42 U.S. Code §§ 303, 403, 405, 413 to 417, 420, 421, 603, 1203, 1309, 1353
Aug. 14, 1953, Ch. 483, 67 Stat. 580, 42 U.S. Code § 417
Aug. 15, 1953, Ch. 504, 67 Stat. 587, 42 U.S. Code § 418, 418 nt.
Aug. 5, 1954, Ch. 657, 68 Stat. 668, 42 U.S. Code §§ 503, 1101 to 1104, 1321 to 1323
Sept. 1, 1954, Ch. 1206, 68 Stat. 1052, 42 U.S. Code §§ 228e, 402 to 405, 408 to 411, 413 to 418, 420 to 422
Aug. 9, 1955, Ch. 685, 69 Stat. 621, 42 U.S. Code §§ 402, 417
Aug. 1, 1956, Ch. 836, 70 Stat. 807, 42 U.S. Code §§ 301, 302, 303, 401 to 403, 405, 409, 410, 411, 413 to 416, 418, 421 to 425, 601 to 603, 606, 721, 906, 1201 to 1203, 1301, 1308, 1310, 1351 to 1353
July 17, 1957, P.L. 85-109, 71 Stat. 308, 42 U.S. Code §§ 416, 424
Aug. 30, 1957, P.L. 85-226, 71 Stat. 511, 42 U.S. Code § 418
Aug. 30, 1957, P.L. 85-238, 71 Stat. 518, 42 U.S. Code §§ 402, 416
Aug. 30, 1957, P.L. 85-239, 71 Stat. 523, 42 U.S. Code § 411
Aug. 27, 1958, P.L. 85-786, 72 Stat. 938, 42 U.S. Code § 409
Aug. 27, 1958, P.L. 85-787, 72 Stat. 939, 42 U.S. Code § 418
Aug. 28, 1958, P.L. 85-798, 72 Stat. 964, 42 U.S. Code §§ 402, 418
Aug. 28, 1958, P.L. 85-840, 72 Stat. 1013, 42 U.S. Code §§ 302, 303, 401 to 403, 406, 408 to 411, 413 to 418, 422, 423, 425, 603, 701, 702, 711, 712, 721 to 725, 1202a nt., 1203, 1301, 1306, 1308, 1311, 1353
Aug. 28, 1958, P.L. 85-848, 72 Stat. 1087, 42 U.S. Code §§ 1361, 1367, 1371
Sept. 2, 1958, P.L. 85-857, 72 Stat. 1265, 42 U.S. Code §§ 402, 417, 1371
Sept. 6, 1958, P.L. 85-927, 72 Stat. 1782, 42 U.S. Code §§ 402, 1104
June 25, 1959, P.L. 86-70, 73 Stat. 149, 42 U.S. Code §§ 402, 410 , 724, 1301
Aug. 18, 1959, P.L. 86-168, 73 Stat. 389, 42 U.S. Code § 410
Sept. 22, 1959, P.L. 86-346, 73 Stat. 622, 42 U.S. Code §§ 401, 1404
April 8, 1960, P.L. 86-415, 74 Stat. 35, 42 U.S. Code § 415
April 22, 1960, P.L. 86-442, 74 Stat. 81, 42 U.S. Code §§ 413, 1365 nt., 1371
June 11, 1960, P.L. 86-507, 74 Stat. 202, 42 U.S. Code § 405
July 12, 1960, P.L. 86-624, 74 Stat. 419, 42 U.S. Code §§ 402, 410, 418, 724, 1301, 1361
Sept. 13, 1960, P.L. 86-778, 74 Stat. 928, 42 U.S. Code §§ 301 to 304, 306, 401 to 403, 405, 408 to 411, 413 to 418, 422 and others
March 24, 1961, P.L. 87-6, 75 Stat. 14, 42 U.S. Code § 1105
May 8, 1961, P.L. 87-31, 75 Stat. 75, 42 U.S. Code §§ 303, 604, 607, 608, 906, 1101, 1308
June 30, 1961, P.L. 87-64, 75 Stat. 131, 42 U.S. Code §§ 303, 402 , 403, 409, 413 to 416, 418, 423, 1203, 1308, 1313, 1353
Sept. 21, 1961, P.L. 87-256, 75 Stat. 537, 42 U.S. Code § 410
Sept. 22, 1961, P.L. 87-293, 75 Stat. 626, 42 U.S. Code §§ 405, 409, 410
July 25, 1962, P.L. 87-543, 76 Stat. 173, 42 U.S. Code §§ 301 to 303, 306, 601 to 609, 721 to 723, 726 to 728, 906, 1201, 1202, 1203, 1206, 1301 and others
Oct. 24, 1962, P.L. 87-878, 76 Stat. 1202, 42 U.S. Code § 418
May 29, 1963, P.L. 88-31, 77 Stat. 51, 42 U.S. Code §§ 1101, 1103 , 1105
Oct. 24, 1963, P.L. 88-156, 77 Stat. 273, 42 U.S. Code §§ 701, 702, 711, 712, 729, 729a, 1391 to 1394
Feb. 26, 1964, P.L. 88-272, 78 Stat. 63, 42 U.S. Code §§ 409, 411
June 30, 1964, P.L. 88-347, 78 Stat. 236, 42 U.S. Code § 1313
July 2, 1964, P.L. 88-350, 78 Stat. 240, 42 U.S. Code § 418
July 23, 1964, P.L. 88-382, 78 Stat. 335, 42 U.S. Code § 418
Oct. 13, 1964, P.L. 88-641, 78 Stat. 1042, 42 U.S. Code §§ 606, 607
Oct. 13, 1964, P.L. 88-650, 78 Stat. 1075, 42 U.S. Code §§ 409, 416, 1202, 1382
July 30, 1965, P.L. 89-97, 79 Stat. 290, 42 U.S. Code §§ 302, 303 , 306, 401, 402 to 406, 409, 410, 411, 413, 415 to 418, 422, 423, 424a and others
March 15, 1966, P.L. 89-368, 80 Stat. 67, 42 U.S. Code § 428
April 8, 1966, P.L. 89-384, 80 Stat. 105, 42 U.S. Code §§ 1395p, 1395s, 1395v

Nov. 2, 1966, P.L. 89-713, 80 Stat. 1111, 42 U.S. Code § 1395x
June 29, 1967, P.L. 90-36, 81 Stat. 94, 42 U.S. Code §§ 607, 1313 , 1315
Jan. 2, 1968, P.L. 90-248, 81 Stat. 821, 42 U.S. Code §§ 302 to 304, 401 to 404, 409 to 411, 413, 415 to 418, 421 to 423, 425 to 429, 601 to 604, 606 to 608, 609 nt., 610, 620 to 626, 630 to 644, 701 to 715, 729, 907, 908, 1202 to 1204, 1306, 1308 to 1311, 1313 to 1320a, 1352 to 1354, 1361, 1382, 1383, 1395b-1, 1395d to 1395f, 1395j nt., 1395k, 1395l, 1395n, 1395p to 1395s, 1395u to 1395y, 1395aa, 1395cc, 1395dd, 1395gg, 1395ll, 1396a, 1396b, 1396d to 1396g
June 28, 1968, P.L. 90-364, 82 Stat. 273, 42 U.S. Code §§ 603, 607, 1396b
July 26, 1968, P.L. 90-430, 82 Stat. 447, 42 U.S. Code § 1103
Aug. 13, 1968, P.L. 90-486, 82 Stat. 759, 42 U.S. Code § 418
July 9, 1969, P.L. 91-41, 83 Stat. 45, 42 U.S. Code §§ 603, 1313
Aug. 7, 1969, P.L. 91-53, 83 Stat. 93, 42 U.S. Code § 1101
Aug. 9, 1969, P.L. 91-56, 83 Stat. 99, 42 U.S. Code §§ 1396a, 1396b
Dec. 30, 1969, P.L. 91-172, 83 Stat. 737, 42 U.S. Code §§ 401 to 403, 415, 427, 428
Aug. 10, 1970, P.L. 91-373, 84 Stat. 703, 42 U.S. Code §§ 504, 1101 to 1103, 1105 to 1108, 1323
Oct. 15, 1970, P.L. 91-452, 84 Stat. 930, 42 U.S. Code § 405
Jan. 12, 1971, P.L. 91-690, 84 Stat. 2074, 42 U.S. Code § 1395x
March 17, 1971, P.L. 92-5, 85 Stat. 6, 42 U.S. Code §§ 403, 409, 411, 413, 415, 427, 428
July 1, 1971, P.L. 92-40, 85 Stat. 96, 42 U.S. Code § 1313
Dec. 28, 1971, P.L. 92-223, 85 Stat. 802, 42 U.S. Code §§ 402, 602, 603, 607, 630 to 636, 638, 639, 641 to 644, 1396a, 1396d
Dec. 29, 1971, P.L. 92-224, 85 Stat. 810, 42 U.S. Code § 1103
June 30, 1972, P.L. 92-329, 86 Stat. 398, 42 U.S. Code §§ 1103, 1105
July 1, 1972, P.L. 92-336, 86 Stat. 411, 42 U.S. Code §§ 403, 409 , 411, 413, 415, 427, 428, 430
July 10, 1972, P.L. 92-345, 86 Stat. 456, 42 U.S. Code §§ 702, 705, 708, 709, 710
Oct. 20, 1972, P.L. 92-512, 86 Stat. 945, 42 U.S. Code §§ 303, 603, 1203, 1320b, 1353, 1383
Oct. 30, 1972, P.L. 92-603, 86 Stat. 1333, 42 U.S. Code §§ 402, 403, 405, 408, 409, 410, 411, 414 to 416, 418
July 1, 1973, P.L. 93-53, 87 Stat. 135, 42 U.S. Code §§ 702, 705, 708 to 710, 716
July 6, 1973, P.L. 93-58, 87 Stat. 142, 42 U.S. Code § 426
July 9, 1973, P.L. 93-66, 87 Stat. 152, 42 U.S. Code §§ 402, 403, 409, 411, 413, 415, 1320b, 1382, 1383b, 1396a nt., 1396b
Dec. 31, 1973, P.L. 93-233, 87 Stat. 947, 42 U.S. Code §§ 401 to 403, 409, 411, 413, 415, 426 to 428, 430, 1301, 1315, 1316, 1320a-1, 1320b, 1382, 1382c, 1382e, 1383, 1395f, 1395v, 1395y, 1395mm, 1396a, 1396b, 1396d, 1396g
Aug. 7, 1974, P.L. 93-368, 88 Stat. 420, 42 U.S. Code §§ 411, 1103, 1382, 1382f, 1383, 1396a
June 28, 1975, P.L. 94-44, 89 Stat. 235, 42 U.S. Code § 1313
July 1, 1975, P.L. 94-48, 89 Stat. 247, 42 U.S. Code § 1396a
Aug. 9, 1975, P.L. 94-88, 89 Stat. 433, 19 U.S. Code § 1202; 42 U.S. Code §§ 602, 603, 654, 655
Oct. 21, 1975, P.L. 94-120, 89 Stat. 609, 42 U.S. Code §§ 1397a, 1397b
Dec. 31, 1975, P.L. 94-182, 89 Stat. 1051, 42 U.S. Code §§ 1320c-1, 1320c-17, 1395g, 1395r, 1395u, 1395x, 1395y, 1396a, 1396b
Jan. 2, 1976, P.L. 94-202, 89 Stat. 1135, 42 U.S. Code §§ 401, 403, 405, 405a, 418, 424a, 430, 432, 1382a, 1383
May 23, 1977, P.L. 95-30, 42 U.S. Code § 652 et seq.
June 30, 1977, P.L. 95-59, 42 U.S. Code §§ 655, 1397a
Aug. 1, 1977, P.L. 95-83, 42 U.S. Code § 701 et seq.
Oct. 25, 1977, P.L. 95-142, 42 U.S. Code §§ 1395u, 1395g et seq.
Nov. 12, 1977, P.L. 95-171, 42 U.S. Code §§ 603 et seq., 1397a nt.,
Dec. 13, 1977, P.L. 95-210, 42 U.S. Code § 1395 et seq.
Dec. 20, 1977, P.L. 95-216, 42 U.S. Code § 401 et seq.

*Continued*

June 13, 1978, P.L. 95-292, 42 U.S. Code §§ 426, 426-1, 1395 et seq.
Nov. 1, 1978, P.L. 95-559, 42 U.S. Code §§ 1320a-1, 1396a, 1396a nt., 1396b
Nov. 6, 1978, P.L. 95-600, 42 U.S. Code §§ 402, 405, 410, 411, 1308, 1318
Nov. 10, 1978, P.L. 95-626, 42 U.S. Code § 1396b
Oct. 4, 1979, P.L. 96-79, 42 U.S. Code § 1396b
Jan. 2, 1980, P.L. 96-178, 42 U.S. Code §§ 655, 655 nt., 1397a, 1397f
April 1, 1980, P.L. 96-222, 42 U.S. Code §§ 602, 1382a, 1383
May 26, 1980, P.L. 96-249, 42 U.S. Code §§ 503, 504
Oct. 13, 1982, P.L. 97-300, 42 U.S. Code §§ 602, 632, 633
Dec. 21, 1982, P.L. 97-375, 42 U.S. Code § 1320
Dec. 21, 1982, P.L. 97-377, 42 U.S. Code §§ 603 nt., 1382g, 1383 nt.
Dec. 31, 1982, P.L. 97-404, 42 U.S. Code § 603 nt.
Jan. 6, 1983, P.L. 97-424, 42 U.S. Code §§ 602, 602 nt., 1382
Jan. 12, 1983, P.L. 97-455, 42 U.S. Code §§ 402, 402 nt., 405, 421, 433
Oct. 24, 1983, P.L. 98-135, 42 U.S. Code §§ 1323, 1397
July 18, 1984, P.L. 98-369, 98 Stat. 622, 42 U.S. Code §§ 1063 et seq., 1122 et seq.
Aug. 16, 1984, P.L. 98-378, 42 U.S. Code §§ 602, 602 nt., 603, 606, 651 et seq., 665, 666, 667, 671, 1315, 1396a
Aug. 22, 1984, P.L. 98-396, 20 U.S. Code § 645
Oct. 9, 1984, P.L. 98-460, 98 Stat. 1794, 42 U.S. Code §§ 405, 408, 416, 421 to 423, 1382c, 1382d, 1382h, 1383 to 1383b
Nov. 8, 1984, P.L. 98-617, 42 U.S. Code §§ 402 nt., 672, 674, 1395, 1395f
Nov. 8, 1984, P.L. 98-620, 42 U.S. Code § 504
Nov. 8, 1985, P.L. 99-145, 10 U.S. Code § 1451
Dec. 12, 1985, P.L. 99-177, 42 U.S. Code § 911
Dec. 23, 1985, P.L. 99-198, 42 U.S. Code § 503
Dec. 26, 1985, P.L. 99-221, 26 U.S. Code § 3121; 42 U.S. Code §§ 410, 410 nt.
April 7, 1986, P.L. 99-272, 42 U.S. Code §§ 401 to 404, 409, 410, 415, 418, 424a, 503, 602, 673, 674, 677, 701, 907, 909, 910, 1301, 1310, 1315, 1320a-2, 1320c-2, 1320c-3, 1320c-13, 1382g, 1383, 1383c, 1395e, 1395f, 1395i, 1395i-2, 1395l, 1395p, 1395q, 1395r, 1395t, 1395u, 1395w-1, 1395x, 1395y, 1395cc, 1395mm, 1395ww, 1395yy, 1396a, 1396b, 1396d, 1396k, 1396n, 1396o, 1396r, 1396s
June 6, 1986, P.L. 99-335, 42 U.S. Code § 410
July 2, 1986, P.L. 99-349, 42 U.S. Code § 1395
Oct. 18, 1986, P.L. 99-500, 42 U.S. Code § 645
Oct. 21, 1986, P.L. 99-509, 42 U.S. Code §§ 415, 418, 666, 679, 701, 1320a-7a, 1320b-5, 1320b-7, 1320c-2, 1320c-3, 1395b-8, 1395e, 1395k, 1395g, 1395h, 1395l, 1395u, 1395u nt., 1395w-1, 1395x, 1395y, 1395cc, 1395dd, 1395ff, 1395ff nt., 1395hh, 1395ll, 1395mm, 1395nn, 1395pp, 1395rr, 1395ww, 1396a, 1396b, 1396d, 1396n, 1396s
Oct. 22, 1986, P.L. 99-514, 42 U.S. Code §§ 301, 402, 409 to 411, 415, 418, 421, 423, 602, 602 nt., 657, 657 nt., 658, 664, 670, 670 nt., 671, 673 to 675, 678, 1320b-6, 1320c-13, 1382a, 1383, 1395p, 1395u, 1395u nt., 1395y nt., 1395cc, 1395dd, 1395mm, 1395mm nt., 1395ww, 1395ww nt., 1395yy, 1396a, 1396b, 1396d, 1396s, 1397b, 1397f
Oct. 27, 1986, P.L. 99-570, 42 U.S. Code § 1383
Oct. 28, 1986, P.L. 99-576, 42 U.S. Code § 1395cc
Oct. 30, 1986, P.L. 99-591, 42 U.S. Code § 645
Nov. 6, 1986, P.L. 99-603, 42 U.S. Code §§ 303, 502, 602, 603, 672, 673, 1203, 1320b-7, 1353, 1383 nt., 1396b
Nov. 10, 1986, P.L. 99-643, 42 U.S. Code §§ 1382, 1382c, 1382h, 1383, 1383c, 1396, 1396a
Dec. 22, 1987, P.L. 100-203, 42 U.S. Code §§ 300bb-6 and nt., 402 , 409 to 411, 418, 423, 426, 429, 602, 603, 616, 621, 626, 674, 675, 912, 1301, 1302, 1308, 1320a-7a, 1320a-7b, 1320a-8, 1320b-5, 1320b-9, 1320c-2 and nt., 1320c-3 and nt., 1320c-5, 1382 nt., 1382b, 1383, 1383c nt. generally 1395 et seq., 1396a and nt., 1396b to 1396d, 1396j, 1396l, 1396n to 1396p, 1396r, 1396r-3, 1396s, 1397b

April 29, 1988, P.L. 100-300, 102 Stat. 441, 42 U.S. Code § 663

Oct. 13, 1988, P.L. 100-485, generally 42 U.S. Code §§ 401 et seq., 503, 504, 602 et seq., prec. 681, 681 to 687, 1301 et seq., 1320a-7a, 1320b- 10, 1395 et seq., 1396 et seq., 1397e

Nov. 7, 1988, P.L. 100-628, 42 U.S. Code §§ 503, 504

Nov. 10, 1988, P.L. 100-647, 42 U.S. Code §§ 401 et seq., 617, 669, 677, 1320b-9, 1320b-11, 1382a, 1382b, 1383, generally §§ 1395 et seq., generally §§ 1396 et seq.

Nov. 18, 1988, P.L. 100-690, 42 U.S. Code § 408

Nov. 23, 1988, P.L. 100-707, 42 U.S. Code § 1382a

Dec. 13, 1989, P.L. 101-234, 42 U.S. Code §§ 1395m, 1395u, 1395cc , 1395ll, 1395ww, 1396d

Dec. 19, 1989, P.L. 101-239, generally 42 U.S. Code § 301 et seq.

Aug. 20, 1990, P.L. 101-382, 42 U.S. Code § 1313

Oct. 1, 1990, P.L. 101-403, 42 U.S. Code § 1395ww

Nov. 5, 1990, P.L. 101-508, 42 U.S. Code §§ 401 et seq. generally, 601 et seq. generally, 705, 1103, 1313, 1320a-3a, 1320a-6, 1320a-7b, 1320b-9, 1320b-13, 1320c-3, 1320c-5, 1320c-6, 1320c-9, 1381 et seq. generally, 1395 et seq. generally, 1396 et seq. generally

Nov. 16, 1990, P.L. 101-597, 42 U.S. Code §§ 1320c-5, 1395l, 1395u, 1395x

Nov. 28, 1990, P.L. 101-624, 42 U.S. Code § 405

Nov. 29, 1990, P.L. 101-649, 42 U.S. Code §§ 402, 1382c

June 13, 1991, P.L. 102-54, 42 U.S. Code §§ 402, 417, 428, 662, 1320a-7, 1320b-3, 1395f, 1395cc, 1396s

Aug. 17, 1991, P.L. 102-107, 26 U.S. Code § 3304 nt.; 42 U.S. Code § 1108

Oct. 7, 1991, P.L. 102-119, 42 U.S. Code §§ 1396b, 1396n

Nov. 20, 1991, P.L. 102-164, 42 U.S. Code § 1108

Dec. 12, 1991, P.L. 102-234, 42 U.S. Code §§ 1396a, 1396b, 1396r -4

July 3, 1992, P.L. 102-318, 42 U.S. Code §§ 502, 503, 1101, 1102 , 1104, 1105, 1110

Sept. 30, 1992, P.L. 102-375, 42 U.S. Code §§ 1395i-3, 1396r

Nov. 4, 1992, P.L. 102-585, 42 U.S. Code § 1396r-8

April 12, 1993, P.L. 103-18, 42 U.S. Code § 1396r-8

Aug. 10, 1993, P.L. 103-66, 42 U.S. Code §§ 303, 602, 620, 622, 629 to 629e, 652, 666, 1203, 1308, 1382 et seq., 1395b-1 et seq., 1396a et seq., 1397f

Nov. 24, 1993, P.L. 103-152, 42 U.S. Code §§ 503, 504, 1105, 1108, 1382j

Dec. 3, 1993, P.L. 103-178, 42 U.S. Code § 410

May 18, 1994, P.L. 103-252, 42 U.S. Code § 1396r-5

Aug. 15, 1994, P.L. 103-296, 42 U.S. Code §§ 401 et seq., 901 et seq., 1301, 1306, 1307, 1310, 1320a-6, 1320a-7, 1320a-8, 1320b-1, 1320b-10, 1320b-11, 1320c-4, 1382 et seq., 1383 et seq., 1395i, 1395s, 1395t, 1395cc, 1395ff, 1395ii, 1395rr, 1395mm, 1396a, 1396i, 1396q,

Oct. 20, 1994, P.L. 103-382, 42 U.S. Code §§ 602, 622, 1320a-2

Oct. 22, 1994, P.L. 103-387, 42 U.S. Code §§ 401, 402, 404, 409, 410, 1383

Oct. 31, 1994, P.L. 103-432, 42 U.S. Code §§ 602, 608, 622, 623, 624, 627, 628a, 652, 663, 666, 672, 673, 674, 675, 679, 682, 687, 701, 1320a- 1a, 1320a-3a, 1320a-7b, 1320a-9, 1320a-10, 1320b-5, 1320b-7, 1320b-8, 1320c-9, 1320c-13, 1382a, 1382c, 1383, 1395d, 1395e, 1395f, 1395h, 1395i-3, 1395i-4, 1395l, 1395m, 1395p, 1395q, 1395r, 1395u, 1395x, 1395y, 1395w-1, 1395w-4, 1395aa, 1395cc, 1395nn, 1395pp, 1395ss, 1395ww, 1395yy, 1395zz

Nov. 2, 1994, P.L. 103-448, 42 U.S. Code § 1396a

Dec. 8, 1994, P.L. 103-465, 42 U.S. Code § 503

July 27, 1995, P.L. 104-19, 42 U.S. Code § 603

Oct. 12, 1995, P.L. 104-35, 42 U.S. Code §§ 652, 654

March 29, 1996, P.L. 104-121, 42 U.S. Code §§ 401, 402, 403, 405 , 422, 423, 425, 902, 903, 1320b-15, 1382, 1382c, 1383, 1383c, 1383e

April 26, 1996, P.L. 104-134, 42 U.S. Code §§ 404, 664, 1395aa, 1395bb, 1395bbb

Aug. 20, 1996, P.L. 104-188, 42 U.S. Code §§ 409, 410, 671, 674

*Continued*

Aug. 22, 1996, P.L. 104-193, 42 U.S. Code §§ 611a, 618, 628b, 671, 672, 710, 1320a-2a, 1383, 1396a, 1396g, 1397a, 1397b

Sept. 30, 1996, P.L. 104-208, 42 U.S. Code § 1320b-7

Oct. 2, 1996, P.L. 104-224, 42 U.S. Code §§ 1320b-14, 1395y

Oct. 9, 1996, P.L. 104-248, 42 U.S. Code §§ 1396a, 1396b

Oct. 11, 1996, P.L. 104-299, 42 U.S. Code §§ 1395x, 1396d

Oct. 19, 1996, P.L. 104-315, 42 U.S. Code § 1396r

Oct. 19, 1996, P.L. 104-316, 42 U.S. Code § 404

Oct. 19, 1996, P.L. 104-327, 42 U.S. Code § 603

April 30, 1997, P.L. 105-12, 42 U.S. Code §§ 701, 1395y, 1395cc, 1396a, 1396b, 1397d

May 15, 1997, P.L. 105-15, 42 U.S. Code §§ 1395i-3, 1396r

Aug. 5, 1997, P.L. 105-33, 42 U.S. Code §§ 503, 602 to 604, 607 to 609, 611 to 613, 652, 653, 653a, 654, 654b, 655, 657 to 659, 663, 664, 666, 672, 673, 903, 909 nt., 911, 1101 to 1103, 1301, 1308, 1310, 1315, 1320a-1, 1320a-3, 1320a-3a, 1320a-7, 1320a-7a, 1320a-7b, 1320a-7d, 1320a-7e, 1320b-4, 1320c-11, 1322, 1382, 1382c, 1382d, 1382e, 1383, 1395a, 1395b-2, 1395b-6, 1395b-7, 1320b- 8, 1395b-16, 1395d to 1395h, 1395i-2, 1395i-5, 1395k to 1395n, 1395p to 1395r, 1395u, 1395v, 1395w-1, 1395w-3, 1395w-4, 1395w-21 to 1395w-28, 1395x, 1395y, 1395aa, 1395cc, 1395dd, 1395ff, 1395mm, 1395nn, 1395pp, 1395ss, 1395tt, 1395ww, 1395yy, 1395bbb, 1395eee, 1395fff, 1395ggg, 1396a, 1396b, 1396d, 1396g-1, 1396n, 1396o, 1396r, 1396r-1a, 1396r-4 to 1396r-8, 1396u-2, 1396u-3, 1396u-4, 1397aa to 1397jj

Aug. 5, 1997, P.L. 105-34, 42 U.S. Code §§ 405, 411, 1320b-14

Oct. 10, 1997, P.L. 105-61, 42 U.S. Code § 410

Oct. 27, 1997, P.L. 105-65, 42 U.S. Code § 503

Nov. 13, 1997, P.L. 105-78, 42 U.S. Code §§ 603, 1320b-13, 1382 nt., 1382e, 629, 629a, 629b, 653, 671, 672, 673, 673b, 674, 675, 677, 678, 679b, 1320a-9

June 9, 1998, P.L. 105-178, 42 U.S. Code §§ 604, 1397b

July 16, 1998, P.L. 105-200, 42 U.S. Code §§ 603, 604, 609, 613, 622, 629b, 652, 653, 655, 658, 658a, 666, 669, 669a, 671, 673b, 674

Oct. 21, 1998, P.L. 105-277, 42 U.S. Code §§ 407, 603, 1320a-7a, 1320a-7d, 1395b-6, 1395r, 1395x, 1395fff, 1397b, 1397dd

Oct. 28, 1998, P.L. 105-306, 42 U.S. Code §§ 404, 603, 655, 1320b -17, 1382a, 1382b, 1383

Nov. 10, 1998, P.L. 105-362, 42 U.S. Code § 1395ss

March 25, 1999, P.L. 106-4, 42 U.S. Code § 1396r

May 21, 1999, P.L. 106-31, 42 U.S. Code § 1396b

**Social Security Act (Acceptance)**

Ind. Code Ann., 12-1-2-12

**Social Security Act (Public Employees)**

N.Y. Retirement and Social Security Law (Consol. Laws Ch. 51A) § 130 et seq.

Wash. Rev. Code Ann., 41.48.010 et seq.

**Social Security Act (State)**

Cal. Statutes 1935, p. 1226

Ky. Rev. Stat. 1971, 205.010 et seq.

Miss. Code Ann. 1972, § 25-11-1 et seq.

Mo. Rev. Stat., 207.010 et seq., 208.010 et seq.

N.J. Stat. Ann., 43:21-1 et seq.

N.Y. Retirement and Social Security Law (Consol. Laws Ch. 51A) § 130 et seq.

Okla. Stat. Ann., Title 56, § 161 et seq.

S.D. Codified Laws 1967, 28-1-1 et seq.

Tenn. Code Ann., 11-1-101 et seq.

Wis. Stat. Ann., 49.20 et seq.

**Social Security Act Amendments of 1939**

Aug. 10, 1939, Ch. 666, 53 Stat. 1360, 7 U.S. Code § 642; 12 U.S. Code § 1464; 29 U.S. Code § 45b; 42 U.S. Code §§ 302, 303, 306, 401 to 409, 502, 503, 602, 603, 606, 701 to 703, 711 to 714, 721, 1011, 1102 nt., 1107 nt., 1202, 1203, 1206, 1301, 1306, 1307; 45 U.S. Code § 363 nt.

March 24, 1943, Ch. 26, 57 Stat. 47

**Social Security Act Amendments of 1946**

Aug. 10, 1946, Ch. 951, 60 Stat. 978, 42 U.S. Code §§ 303, 402, 403, 409, 409 nts., 410, 503, 603, 701, 702, 711, 712, 721, 731, 1203, 1301

Aug. 6, 1947, Ch. 510, 61 Stat. 794, 42 U.S. Code § 303 nt.

**Social Security Act Amendments of 1947**

Aug. 6, 1947, Ch. 510, 61 Stat. 793, 42 U.S. Code §§ 303 nt., 1104, 1321

**Social Security Act Amendments of 1950**

Aug. 28, 1950, Ch. 809, 64 Stat. 477, 42 U.S. Code §§ 301, 304, 306, 401 to 406, 408, 409, 410, 411 to 419, 503, 602, 603, 604, 606, 701 to 705, 711 to 715, 721, 731, 901 to 904, 1104, 1201, 1202, 1202a, 1203, 1204, 1206, 1301, 1302, 1306 to 1308, 1321, 1351 to 1355

July 18, 1952, Ch. 945, 66 Stat. 775, 42 U.S. Code § 402 nt.

Sept. 1, 1954, Ch. 1206, 68 Stat. 1097, 42 U.S. Code § 1202a nt.

April 25, 1957, P.L. 85-26, 71 Stat. 27, 42 U.S. Code § 1202a nt.

Sept. 13, 1960, P.L. 86-778, 74 Stat. 936, 42 U.S. Code §§ 402 nt., 1202a nt.

**Social Security Act Amendments of 1952**

July 18, 1952, Ch. 945, 66 Stat. 767, 42 U.S. Code §§ 303, 402 nts., 403, 405, 413 to 417, 420, 421, 603, 1203, 1309, 1353; 45 U.S. Code §§ 228a, 228e

Sept. 1, 1954, Ch. 1206, 68 Stat. 1097, 42 U.S. Code § 303 nt.

Sept. 13, 1960, P.L. 86-778, 74 Stat. 936, 42 U.S. Code §§ 402 nt., 417 nt.

**Social Security Act Amendments of 1972**

Oct. 30, 1972, P.L. 92-603, 86 Stat. 1329, 5 U.S. Code §§ 5315, 5316; 7 U.S. Code §§ 1431, 2012, 2019, 2023; 26 U.S. Code §§ 639, 911, 3101, 3111, 6051, 6413; 42 U.S. Code §§ 302, 306, 306a, 401 to 403, 405, 409 to 411, 414 to 416, 418, 422 to 430, 705 to 709, 801 to 805, 1202, 1352, 1382, 1395 et seq., 1396 et seq., 1401, 1402

Aug. 1, 1977, P.L. 95-83, 42 U.S. Code § 1396b nt.

**Social Security Act Amendments of 1994**

July 16, 1998, P.L. 105-200, 42 U.S. Code § 1314a

**Social Security Amendments of 1954**

Sept. 1, 1954, Ch. 1206, 68 Stat. 1052, 26 U.S. Code §§ 176, 1401, 1402, 1426, 3101, 3102, 3111, 3121, 3122, 6413; 42 U.S. Code §§ 303, 402 to 408, 411, 413 to 418, 420 to 422, 1202a nt.; 45 U.S. Code §§ 228a, 228b, 228e

Aug. 1, 1956, Ch. 836, 70 Stat. 855, 26 U.S. Code § 3121 nt.

Sept. 13, 1960, P.L. 86-778, 74 Stat. 948, 42 U.S. Code § 415 nt.

July 30, 1965, P.L. 89-97, 79 Stat. 366, 42 U.S. Code § 415 nt.

**Social Security Amendments of 1956**

Aug. 1, 1956, Ch. 836, 70 Stat. 807, 26 U.S. Code §§ 1401, 1402, 3101, 3102, 3111, 3113, 3121; 42 U.S. Code §§ 301, 302, 303, prec. § 401, 401, 401a, 402, 403, 405, 409 to 411, 413 to 416, 418, 421 to 425, 601 to 603, 606, 721, 906, 1201 to 1203, 1301, 1308, 1310, 1351 to 1353; 45 U.S. Code §§ 228a, 228e

July 17, 1957, P.L. 85-110, 71 Stat. 308, 42 U.S. Code § 303 nt.

Sept. 13, 1960, P.L. 86-778, 74 Stat. 994, 42 U.S. Code § 401a

July 30, 1965, P.L. 89-97, 79 Stat. 340, 42 U.S. Code § 401a nt.

**Social Security Amendments of 1958**

Aug. 28, 1958, P.L. 85-840, 72 Stat. 1013, 26 U.S. Code [I.R.C. 1954], §§ 1401, 1402, 3101, 3111, 3121, 3122, 6334, 6413; 42 U.S. Code §§ 302, 303, 401 to 403, 406, 408 to 411, 413 to 418, 422, 423, 425, 603, 701, 702, 711, 712, 721 to 725, 1202a nt., 1203, 1301, 1306, 1308, 1311, 1353; 45 U.S. Code § 228a

Sept. 13, 1960, P.L. 86-778, 74 Stat. 935, 42 U.S. Code § 418 nt.

July 2, 1964, P.L. 88-350, 78 Stat. 240, 42 U.S. Code § 418 nt.

July 30, 1965, P.L. 89-97, 79 Stat. 409, 42 U.S. Code § 418 nt.

**Social Security Amendments of 1960**

Sept. 13, 1960, P.L. 86-778, 74 Stat. 924, 26 U.S. Code §§ 1402, 1403, 3121, 3125, 3126, 3301, 3302, 3304 nt., 3305, 3306, 3308, 3309, 6205, 6413, 7213, 7701; 26 U.S. Code [I.R.C. 1939] § 1426 nt.; 29 U.S. Code § 49d; 42 U.S. Code §§ 301 to 304, 306, 401 to 403, 405, 408 to 411, 413 to 418, 422, 423, 501, 701, 702, 704, 711, 712, 714, 721, 722, 726, 1101 to 1104, 1202, 1301, 1308, 1312, 1321 to 1324, 1361 to 1364, 1367, 1371, 1400c; 45 U.S. Code §§ 228a, 228c, 228e; 48 U.S. Code § 1421h

June 30, 1961, P.L. 87-64, 75 Stat. 138, 42 U.S. Code §§ 402, 415 nt.

July 30, 1965, P.L. 89-97, 79 Stat. 366, 26 U.S. Code § 3121 nt.; 42 U.S. Code §§ 415 nt., 418 nt.

**Social Security Amendments of 1961**

June 30, 1961, P.L. 87-64, 75 Stat. 131, 26 U.S. Code §§ 1401, 1402, 3101, 3111; 42 U.S. Code §§ 303, 402, 403, 409, 413 to 416, 418, 423, 1203, 1308, 1313, 1353; 45 U.S. Code § 228a

July 25, 1962, P.L. 87-543, 76 Stat. 196, 42 U.S. Code §§ 303 nt. , 1308

**Social Security Amendments of 1965**

July 30, 1965, P.L. 89-97, 79 Stat. 286, 26 U.S. Code §§ 72, 79, 213, 401, 405, 451, 1401, 1402, 3101, 3102, 3111, 3121, 3122, 3125, 3201, 3211, 3221, 3401, 3402, 6051, 6053, 6205, 6413, 6652, 6674; 42 U.S. Code §§ 242b nt., 302, 303, 306, 401 to 406, 409, 410, 411, 413, 415 to 418, 422, 423, 424a, 425 to 427, 602, 603, 606, 701, 703, 704, 711, 713, 714, 716, 721 to 723, 729a, 729-1, 907, 1202, 1203, 1206, 1301, 1306, 1308, 1309, 1312, 1315 to 1318, 1352, 1353, 1355, 1382, 1383, 1385, 1391, 1392, 1395 to 1396d, 2981 nt.; 45 U.S. Code §§ 228a, 228e, 228s-2

April 8, 1966, P.L. 89-384, 80 Stat. 105, 42 U.S. Code § 1395p nt.

Jan. 2, 1968, P.L. 90-248, 81 Stat. 854, 42 U.S. Code § 426a

**Social Security Amendments of 1967**

Jan. 2, 1968, P.L. 90-248, 81 Stat. 821, 26 U.S. Code §§ 1401, 1402, 3101, 3111, 3121, 3306, 6051, 6413; 42 U.S. Code §§ 242b nt., 302 to 304, 401 to 404, 409 to 411, 413, 415 to 418, 421 to 423, 424a to 429 and others; 45 U.S . Code §§ 228e, 228s-2

July 18, 1984, P.L. 98-369, 98 Stat. 1088, 42 U.S. Code § 1395b-1

Nov. 5, 1990, P.L. 101-508, 42 U.S. Code § 413 nt.

Aug. 22, 1996, P.L. 104-193, 42 U.S. Code § 602 nt.

**Social Security Amendments of 1969**

Dec. 30, 1969, P.L. 91-172, 83 Stat. 737, 42 U.S. Code §§ 401, 402, 403, 415, 427, 428

July 6, 1970, P.L. 91-306, 84 Stat. 407, 42 U.S. Code § 415 nts.

Jan. 11, 1971, P.L. 91-669, 84 Stat. 2038, 42 U.S. Code § 415 nt.

**Social Security Amendments of 1977**

Dec. 20, 1977, P.L. 95-216, 26 U.S. Code §§ 3101 et seq., 42 U.S. Code §§ 401 et seq., 1305 nt.

July 18, 1984, P.L. 98-369, 98 Stat. 1097, 42 U.S. Code § 907a

**Social Security Amendments of 1983**

April 20, 1983, P.L. 98-21, 97 Stat. 65, 42 U.S. Code § 1305 nt.

July 18, 1984, P.L. 98-369, 42 U.S. Code §§ 1080 et seq., 1159 et seq.

April 7, 1986, P.L. 99-272, 42 U.S. Code § 1394y nt.

Oct. 21, 1986, P.L. 99-509, 42 U.S. Code § 1395ww

Nov. 5, 1990, P.L. 101-508, 42 U.S. Code § 411

Aug. 10, 1993, P.L. 103-66, 42 U.S. Code § 401 nt.

Dec. 21, 1995, P.L. 104-66, 42 U.S. Code § 1395ww nt.

**Social Security and Retirement Act**

S.C. Code Ann. 1976, § 9-5-10 et seq.

**Social Security Benefits Act**

Vt. Stat. Ann., Title 3, § 571 et seq.

**Social Security Coverage Act (Public Employees)**
Mich. Comp. Laws Ann., 38.851 et seq.

**Social Security Disability Amendments of 1980**
June 9, 1980, P.L. 96-265, 42 U.S. Code § 1305 nt.
June 9, 1980, P.L. 97-265, 42 U.S. Code § 1305 nt.
Oct. 9, 1984, P.L. 98-460, 98 Stat. 1808, 42 U.S. Code § 1382h nt.
April 7, 1986, P.L. 99-272, 42 U.S. Code § 1310 nt.
Nov. 10, 1986, P.L. 99-643, 42 U.S. Code § 1382h nt.
Dec. 19, 1989, P.L. 101-239, 42 U.S. Code § 1310 nt.
Nov. 5, 1990, P.L. 101-508, 42 U.S. Code § 1310 nt.
Aug. 15, 1994, P.L. 103-296, 42 U.S. Code § 1310 nt.

**Social Security Disability Benefits Reform Act of 1984**
Oct. 9, 1984, P.L. 98-460, 42 U.S. Code §§ 405, 408, 416, 421 to 423, 907 nt., 1303 nt., 1305 nt., 1382c, 1382d, 1382h, 1383 to 1383b
April 7, 1986, P.L. 99-272, 42 U.S. Code § 907 nt.

**Social Security Domestic Employment Reform Act of 1994**
Oct. 22, 1994, P.L. 103-387, 26 U.S. Code § 1 nt.

**Social Security Domestic Reform Act of 1994**
April 26, 1996, P.L. 104-134, 31 U.S. Code § 3701 nt.

**Social Security Enabling Act**
Ill. Rev. Stat. 1991, Ch. 108 1/2, § 21-101 et seq.
Iowa Code 1983, 97C.1 et seq.

**Social Security Enabling Act (Old Age and Survivors Insurance)**
Ind. Code Ann., 5-10-2-1 et seq.
Iowa Code Ann., 97C.1 et seq.
Mo. Rev. Stat., 105.300 et seq.
Pa. Purdon's Stat., Title 65, § 201 et seq.

**Social Security Independence and Program Improvements Act of 1994**
Aug. 15, 1994, P.L. 103-296, 42 U.S. Code § 1305 nt.
March 29, 1996, P.L. 104-121, 42 U.S. Code § 425 nt.
Aug. 22, 1996, P.L. 104-193, 42 U.S. Code §§ 405, 1382 nt.
Aug. 5, 1997, P.L. 105-33, 42 U.S. Code §§ 425, 1382

**Social Security Integration Act (Public Employees)**
N.J. Rev. Stat. 1937, 43:15A-1 et seq.

**Social Security Integration Act (Teachers' Pensions)**
N.J. Rev. Stat. 1937, 18A:66-1 et seq.

**Social Security Integration and Supplemental Retirement Benefits Act (Public Employees)**
Ind. Code Ann., 5-10-3-1 et seq.

**Social Security Pass-On Act**
Cal. Welfare and Institutions Code § 11008.1

**Social Service Community Centers Act**
Okla. Stat. Ann., Title 63, § 2051 et seq.

**Social Service Transportation Improvement Act**
Cal. Government Code, § 15950 et seq.

**Social Services Act**
Alaska Stat. 1962, § 47.05.010 et seq.
Colo. Rev. Stat. 26-1-101 et seq.
Fla. Stat. Ann., 409.016 et seq.
N.Y. Consol. Laws, Ch. 55
Utah Code Ann. 1953, 62A-1-101 et seq.

**Social Services Act (Community)**
Minn. Stat. Ann., 256E.01 et seq.

**Social Services Act of 1973 (Priority)**
Me. Rev. Stat. Ann. 1964, Title 22, § 6101 et seq.

**Social Services Block Grant Act**
Aug. 13, 1981, P.L. 97-35, 42 U.S. Code § 1305 nt.

**Social Services Department Organic Act**
P.R. Laws Ann. 1954, Title 3, § 211 et seq.

**Social Services Planning Act**
Cal. Welfare and Institutions Code, § 10100 et seq.

**Social Services Transportation Improvement Act**
Cal. Government Code § 15950 et seq.

**Social Welfare Act**
Cal. Welfare and Institutions Code, § 10550 et seq.
Fla. Stat. Ann., 409.016 et seq.
Iowa Code Ann., 217.1 et seq.
Kan. Stat. Ann., 39-701 et seq.
Mich. Comp. Laws Ann., 400.1 et seq.
Vt. Stat. Ann., Title 33, § 2501 et seq.

**Social Welfare Facilities Act**
P.R. Laws Ann. 1954, Title 24, § 331 et seq.

**Social Work Act (Professional)**
Tex. Human Resources Code, § 50.001 et seq.

**Social Work Licensing Act**
Utah Code Ann. 1953, 58-35-1 et seq.

**Social Work Practice Act**
Ala. Code 1975, § 34-30-1 et seq.
Ark. Code Ann. 1987, 17-39-101 et seq.
Cal. Business and Professions Code, § 9000 et seq.
Colo. Rev. Stat., 12-63.5-101 et seq.
Ga. Code Ann., 43-7A-1 et seq.
Ida. Code 1947, 54-3201 et seq.
La. Rev. Stat. Ann., 37:2701 et seq.
Mass. Gen. Laws Ann., 112:130 et seq.
Md. Ann. Code 1974, Art. HO, § 19-101 et seq.
N.C. Gen. Stat. 1943, § 90B-1 et seq.
N.J. Stat. Ann., 2A:162-11 et seq.
N.M. Stat. Ann., 61-31-1 et seq.
Okla. Stat. Ann., Title 59, § 1250 et seq.
Pa. Purdon's Stat., Title 63, § 1901 et seq.

**Social Work Practice Act (Clinical)**
Ill. Comp. Stat. 1992, Ch. 225, § 20/1 et seq.

**Social Workers Act**
Md. Ann. Code 1974, Art. HO, § 19-101 et seq.

**Social Workers Licensing Act**
Mass. Gen. Laws Ann., 112:130 et seq.
Okla. Stat. Ann., Title 59, § 1250 et seq.
R.I. Gen. Laws 1956, 5-39.1-1 et seq.
Utah Code Ann. 1953, 58-60-201 et seq.

**Sockeye Salmon or Pink Salmon Fishing Act of 1947**
July 29, 1947, Ch. 345, 61 Stat. 511, 16 U.S. Code §§ 776, 776 nts., 776a to 776f
July 11, 1957, P.L. 85-102, 71 Stat. 293, 16 U.S. Code §§ 776 to 776e
Oct. 18, 1972, P.L. 92-504, 86 Stat. 907, 16 U.S. Code § 776f
March 15, 1985, P.L. 99-5, 16 U.S. Code §§ 776, 776a to 776f, 776 nt.

**Sod Act**
Va. Code 1950, § 3.1-296.1 et seq.

**Sodbuster Law**
Dec. 23, 1985, P.L. 99-198, 16 U.S. Code §§ 3801, 3811 to 3813, 3821 to 3823, 3831 to 3836, 3841 to 3845
July 2, 1986, P.L. 99-349, 16 U.S. Code § 3801
Oct. 18, 1986, P.L. 99-500
Oct. 30, 1986, P.L. 99-591, 16 U.S. Code § 3831
Nov. 10, 1986, P.L. 99-641, 16 U.S. Code § 3831
April 24, 1987, P.L. 100-28, 16 U.S. Code § 3812

**Sodomy Act**
Ga. Code Ann., 16-6-2
N.Y. Penal Law 1965 (Consol. Laws Ch. 40), § 130.20 et seq.
Ohio Rev. Code 1953, 2907.12
Wash. Rev. Code Ann., 9A.44.010 et seq.
Wis. Stat. Ann., 944.17

**Soft Drink Interbrand Competition Act**
July 9, 1980, P.L. 96-308, 15 U.S. Code §§ 3501 et seq., 3501 nt.

**Soft Drinks Act**
Mich. Comp. Laws 1948, 289.401 et seq.
Mo. Rev. Stat., 196.365 et seq.
Neb. Laws 1921, Ch. 8
Pa. 1925 Pamph. Laws 730, No. 399

**Soft Drinks Tax Act**
La. Rev. Stat. Ann., 47:881 et seq
N.C. Gen. Stat. 1943, § 105.113.41 et seq.
Pa. 1947 Pamph. Laws 249, No. 102
S.C. Code Ann. 1976, § 12-21-1710 et seq.
Va. Code 1950, § 58.1-1700 et seq.

**Soft Tree Fruits Act**
Wash. Rev. Code Ann., 15.28.010 et seq.

**Software License Enforcement Act**
Ill. Rev. Stat. 1985, Ch. 29, § 801 et seq.
La. Rev. Stat. Ann., 51:1961 et seq.

**Soil Additives Act**
N.C. Gen. Stat. 1943, § 106-50.28 et seq.

**Soil Amendment Act**
Ark. Code Ann. 1987, 2-19-401 et seq.
Ga. Code Ann., 2-12-70 et seq.
Ill. Rev. Stat. 1991, Ch. 5, § 2801-1 et seq.
Kan. Stat. Ann., 2-2801 et seq.
Me. Rev. Stat. Ann. 1964, Title 7, § 775 et seq.
Okla. Stat. Ann., Title 2, § 1701 et seq.
R.I. Gen. Laws 1956, 2-22-1 et seq.

**Soil and Plant Amendment Act**
Ida. Code 1947, 22-2201 et seq.
Miss. Code Ann. 1972, § 69-24-1 et seq.

**Soil and Plant Analysis Laboratory Act**
Neb. Rev. Stat. 1943, 2-3101 et seq.

**Soil and Water Conservation District Law**
Minn. Stat. 1986, 103C.005 et seq.

**Soil and Water Conservation Districts Act**
Ala. Code 1975, § 9-8-20 et seq.
Alaska Stat. 1962, § 41.10.010 et seq.
Ariz. Rev. Stat. Ann., § 37-1001 et seq.
Ark. Code Ann. 1987, 14-125-101 et seq.
Cal. Public Resources Code § 9074 et seq.
Conn. Gen. Stat. 1983, § 22a-314 et seq.
D.C. Code Ann., § 1-2801 et seq.
Del. Code of 1974, Title 7, § 3901 et seq.
Fla. Stat. Ann., 582.01 et seq.
Ga. Code Ann., 2-6-20 et seq.
Ida. Code 1947, 22-2715 et seq.
Ill. Rev. Stat. 1991, Ch. 5, § 106 et seq.
Ind. Code Ann., 13-3-1-1 et seq.
Iowa Code Ann., 467A.1 et seq.
Kan. Stat. Ann., 2-1901 et seq.
Ky. Rev. Stat. 1971, 262.010 et seq.
La. Rev. Stat. Ann., 3:1201 et seq.
Md. Ann. Code 1974, Art. AG, § 8-101 et seq.
Me. Rev. Stat. Ann. 1964, Title 12, § 1 et seq.
Mich. Comp. Laws Ann., 282.1 et seq.
Minn. Stat. Ann., 103C.001 et seq.
Miss. Code Ann. 1972, § 69-27-1 et seq.
Mo. Rev. Stat., 278.060 et seq.
Mont. Rev. Code 1991, 76-15-101 et seq.
N.C. Gen. Stat. 1943, § 139-1 et seq.
N.D. Cent. Code, 4-22-01 et seq.
Neb. Rev. Stat. 1943, 2-1575 et seq.
Nev. Rev. Stat. Ann., 548.010 et seq.
N.J. Stat. Ann., 4:24-1 et seq.
N.M. Stat. Ann., 73-20-25 et seq.
N.Y. Consol. Laws Ch. 9B
Ohio Rev. Code 1953, 1515.01 et seq.
Okla. Stat. 1961, Title 45, § 745.5 et seq.
Ore. Rev. Stat., 568.210 et seq.
Pa. 1937 Pamph. Laws 2704, No. 557
P.R. Laws Ann. 1954, Title 5 § 241 et seq.
S.C. Code Ann. 1976, § 48-9-10 et seq.
S.D. Codified Laws 1967, 38-8-1 et seq.
Tenn. Code Ann., 43-14-201 et seq.
Utah Code Ann. 1953, 4-18-1 et seq.
Va. Code 1950, § 21-1 et seq.
Wash. Rev. Code Ann., 89.08.005 et seq.
Wis. Stat. 1983, 92.01 et seq.
W. Va. Code 1966, § 19-21A-1 et seq.
Wyo. Stat. Ann., § 11-16-101 et seq.

**Soil and Water Resources Conservation Act of 1977**

Nov. 18, 1977, P.L. 95-192, 16 U.S. Code §§ 2001, 2001 nt.

Dec. 23, 1985, P.L. 99-198, 16 U.S. Code §§ 2004 to 2006, 2009

Oct. 13, 1994, P.L. 103-354, 16 U.S. Code §§ 2001, 2002, 2005

**Soil Bank Act**

May 28, 1956, Ch. 327, 70 Stat. 188, 7 U.S. Code §§ 1801 to 1814, 1821 to 1824, 1831 to 1837

Aug. 28, 1957, P.L. 85-203, 71 Stat. 478, 7 U.S. Code § 1802

May 16, 1958, P.L. 85-413, 72 Stat. 118, 7 U.S. Code § 1815

June 25, 1959, P.L. 86-70, 73 Stat. 142, 7 U.S. Code § 1837

Sept. 14, 1959, P.L. 86-265, 73 Stat. 552, 7 U.S. Code § 1816

April 9, 1960, P.L. 86-423, 74 Stat. 42, 7 U.S. Code § 1813

June 11, 1960, P.L. 86-507, 74 Stat. 200, 7 U.S. Code § 1831

July 12, 1960, P.L. 86-624, 74 Stat. 411, 7 U.S. Code § 1837

Sept. 14, 1960, P.L. 86-793, 74 Stat. 1030, 7 U.S. Code § 1836

June 29, 1961, P.L. 87-62, 75 Stat. 129, 7 U.S. Code § 1831

July 3, 1962, P.L. 87-521, 76 Stat. 135, 7 U.S. Code § 1831

**Soil Conditioner Act**

Colo. Rev. Stat., 35-12-101 et seq.

Del. Code of 1974, Title 3, § 2101 et seq.

Ida. Code 1947, 22-4001 et seq.

Neb. Rev. Stat. 1943, 81-2.162.01 et seq.

N.J. Stat. Ann., 4:9-15.1 et seq.

**Soil Conditioners and Fertilizers Act**

N.D. Cent. Code, 19-20.1-01 et seq.

Neb. Rev. Stat. 1943, 81-2.162.01 et seq.

**Soil Conservation Act**

Colo. Rev. Stat., 35-70-101 et seq.

Mass. Gen. Laws Ann., 128B:1 et seq.

N.H. Rev. Stat. 1955, 432:8 et seq.

Pa. Purdon's Stat., Title 3, § 849 et seq.

R.I. Gen. Laws 1956, 2-4-1 et seq.

Tex. Agriculture Code, § 201.001 et seq.

Vt. Stat. Ann., Title 10, § 701 et seq.

**Soil Conservation and Domestic Allotment Act**

April 27, 1935, Ch. 85, 49 Stat. 163, 16 U.S. Code §§ 590a to 590i, 590j to 590q

Feb. 29, 1936, Ch. 104, 49 Stat. 1151, 7 U.S. Code §§ 612c, 624; 16 U.S. Code §§ 590g to 590i, 590j to 590q

June 28, 1937, Ch. 395, 50 Stat. 329, 16 U.S. Code §§ 590g to 590i

Feb. 16, 1938, Ch. 30, 52 Stat. 31, 16 U.S. Code §§ 590h, 590o

May 14, 1940, Ch. 200, 54 Stat. 216, 16 U.S. Code § 590h

July 2, 1940, Ch. 521, 54 Stat. 727, 7 U.S. Code §§ 608-1, 1301, 1372, 1385, 1391; 16 U.S. Code §§ 590h, 590l

Dec. 26, 1941, Ch. 626, 55 Stat. 860, 7 U.S. Code §§ 1330, 1340; 16 U.S. Code § 590h

Feb. 6, 1942, Ch. 44, 56 Stat. 53, 16 U.S. Code § 590h

Sept. 29, 1942, Ch. 568, 56 Stat. 761, 16 U.S. Code § 590h

Sept. 21, 1944, Ch. 412, 58 Stat. 737, 16 U.S. Code §§ 590f, 590h

July 25, 1946, Ch. 642, 60 Stat. 663, 16 U.S. Code § 590h

July 26, 1947, Ch. 339, 61 Stat. 494, 16 U.S. Code § 590q

July 3, 1948, Ch. 827, 62 Stat. 1250, 16 U.S. Code § 590h

Sept. 23, 1950, Ch. 997, 64 Stat. 978, 16 U.S. Code § 590h

May 26, 1952, Ch. 335, 66 Stat. 95, 16 U.S. Code § 590h

Aug. 28, 1954, Ch. 1041, 68 Stat. 907, 16 U.S. Code §§ 590h, 590o

Aug. 9, 1955, Ch. 624, 69 Stat. 545, 16 U.S. Code § 590h

April 6, 1956, Ch. 186, 70 Stat. 105, 16 U.S. Code § 590h

July 24, 1956, Ch. 668, 70 Stat. 597, 16 U.S. Code § 590h

Aug. 3, 1956, Ch. 950, 70 Stat. 1033, 16 U.S. Code §§ 590k, 590n

Aug. 7, 1956, Ch. 1030, 70 Stat. 1115, 16 U.S. Code § 590p

July 25, 1958, P.L. 85-553, 72 Stat. 414, 16 U.S. Code § 590h

June 25, 1959, P.L. 86-70, 73 Stat. 143, 16 U.S. Code §§ 590h, 590q
July 12, 1960, P.L. 86-624, 74 Stat. 412, 16 U.S. Code §§ 590h, 590q
Sept. 14, 1960, P.L. 86-793, 74 Stat. 1030, 16 U.S. Code § 590p
March 22, 1961, P.L. 87-5, 75 Stat. 6, 16 U.S. Code § 590p
Aug. 8, 1961, P.L. 87-128, 75 Stat. 302, 16 U.S. Code § 590p
March 30, 1962, P.L. 87-425, 76 Stat. 50, 16 U.S. Code § 590p
May 15, 1962, P.L. 87-451, 76 Stat. 70, 16 U.S. Code § 590p
Sept. 27, 1962, P.L. 87-703, 76 Stat. 605, 16 U.S. Code §§ 590g, 590h, 590p
Oct. 2, 1962, P.L. 87-732, 76 Stat. 696, 16 U.S. Code § 590p-1
May 20, 1963, P.L. 88-26, 77 Stat. 45, 16 U.S. Code § 590p
Aug. 31, 1964, P.L. 88-534, 78 Stat. 743, 16 U.S. Code § 590h
Nov. 3, 1965, P.L. 89-321, 79 Stat. 1190, 16 U.S. Code § 590p
Nov. 2, 1966, P.L. 89-742, 80 Stat. 1167, 16 U.S. Code § 590h
Oct. 11, 1968, P.L. 90-559, 82 Stat. 996, 16 U.S. Code § 590p
Nov. 18, 1969, P.L. 91-118, 83 Stat. 194, 16 U.S. Code § 590p
Nov. 30, 1970, P.L. 91-524, 84 Stat. 1379, 16 U.S. Code § 590p
Aug. 30, 1972, P.L. 92-419, 86 Stat. 676, 16 U.S. Code §§ 590g, 590h, 590o
Sept. 29, 1977, P.L. 95-113, 16 U.S. Code §§ 590h, 590o
June 6, 1980, P.L. 96-263, 16 U.S. Code § 590p
June 30, 1980, P.L. 96-294, 16 U.S. Code § 590h
Dec. 21, 1982, P.L. 97-374, 16 U.S. Code § 590i
Dec. 23, 1985, P.L. 99-198, 16 U.S. Code §§ 590g, 590h, 590h nt.
Feb. 24, 1986, P.L. 99-253, 16 U.S. Code § 590h
Oct. 18, 1986, P.L. 99-500, 16 U.S. Code § 590h
Oct. 30, 1986, P.L. 99-591, 16 U.S. Code § 590h
Nov. 10, 1986, P.L. 99-641, 16 U.S. Code § 590h
Nov. 28, 1990, P.L. 101-624, 16 U.S. Code §§ 590h, 590p
Dec. 13, 1991, P.L. 102-237, 16 U.S. Code § 590h
Oct. 13, 1994, P.L. 103-354, 16 U.S. Code §§ 590e, 590h
Nov. 2, 1994, P.L. 103-437, 16 U.S. Code § 590p
April 4, 1996, P.L. 104-127, 16 U.S. Code §§ 590h, 590k, 590n to 590p
Ore. Rev. Stat., 568.010 et seq.

**Soil Conservation Commission Act**
Utah Code Ann. 1953, 4-18-1

**Soil Conservation Districts Law**
Md. Ann. Code 1974, Art. AG, § 8-101 et seq.

**Soil Conservation Domestic Allotment Act**
Ill. Rev. Stat. 1991, Ch. 5, § 138.99 et seq. .

**Soil Erosion Act**
See Soil Conservation and Domestic Allotment Act

**Soil Erosion and Dust Blowing Act**
Colo. Rev. Stat., 35-72-101 et seq.

**Soil Erosion and Sedimentation Control Act**
Conn. Gen. Stat. Ann., 22a-325 et seq.
D.C. Code Ann., § 45-508
D.C. Laws 1976, No. 1-55
Mich. Comp. Laws 1948, 282.101 et seq.
N.J. Stat. Ann., 4:24-39 et seq.
R.I. Gen. Laws 1956, 45-46-1 et seq.

**Soil Survey Act**
Mich. Comp. Laws Ann., 321.41 et seq.
Mont. Code Ann. 1991, 76-11-201 et seq.

**Soils Conditioners and Liming Materials Act**
Ga. Code Ann., 2-12-40 et seq.

**Solano County Flood Control and Water Conservation District Act**
Cal. Statutes 1951, Ch. 1656, p. 3748

**Solano County Integrated Health and Human Services Pilot Program**
Cal. Welfare and Institutions Code §§ 18986.80 to 18986.82

**Solano County Water Agency Act**
Cal. Statutes 1991, Ch. 573

**Solar Access Act**
Tenn. Code Ann., 66-9-201 et seq.

**Solar and Energy Conservation Mortgage Corporation Act**
Cal. Health and Safety Code, § 53000 et seq.

**Solar Collector Standards Act**
N.M. Stat. Ann., 71-6-4 et seq.

**Solar Easement Act**
Fla. Stat. Ann., 704.07
Ga. Code Ann., 44-9-20 et seq.
N.J. Stat. Ann., 46:3-24 to 46:3-26
Va. Code 1950, § 55-352 et seq.

**Solar Energy Act (Comprehensive)**
Ill. Comp. Stat. 1992, Ch. 30, § 725/1 et seq.

**Solar Energy and Energy Conservation Act of 1980**
June 30, 1980, P.L. 96-294, 12 U.S. Code §§ 3601 nt., 8601 et seq.

**Solar Energy and Energy Conservation Bank Act**
June 30, 1980, P.L. 96-294, 12 U.S. Code §§ 3601 et seq., 3601 nt.
Nov. 30, 1983, P.L. 98-181, 12 U.S. Code §§ 3602, 3606, 3609, 3612, 3615, 3618
Oct. 17, 1984, P.L. 98-479, 12 U.S. Code §§ 3612, 3618
Sept. 30, 1987, P.L. 100-122, 12 U.S. Code § 3603
February 5, 1988, P.L. 100-242, 12 U.S. Code §§ 3604, 3607, 3613

**Solar Energy Development Act**
N.M. Stat. Ann., 71-6-1 et seq.

**Solar Energy Products Warranty Act**
N.Y. Energy Law (Consol. Laws Ch. 17A), § 12-101 et seq.

**Solar Energy Research and Development Act**
Colo. Rev. Stat., 24-82-501 et seq.

**Solar Energy Research, Development, and Demonstration Act of 1974**
Oct. 26, 1974, P.L. 93-473, 42 U.S. Code § 5551 et seq.

**Solar Energy Standards Act**
Fla. Stat. Ann., 377.705

**Solar Energy Tax Credit Act**
Ga. Code Ann., 48-7-29.2

**Solar Heating and Cooling Demonstration Act of 1974**
Sept. 3, 1974, P.L. 93-409, 42 U.S. Code § 5501 et seq.

**Solar Photovoltaic Energy Research, Development, and Demonstration Act of 1978**
Nov. 4, 1978, P.L. 95-590, 42 U.S. Code §§ 5501 nt., 5581, 5581 nt., 5582 et seq.
Sept. 21, 1993, P.L. 103-82, 42 U.S. Code § 5590

**Solar Power Loan Act**
N.M. Stat. Ann., 71-1-1 et seq.

**Solar Recordation Act**
N.M. Stat. Ann., 47-3-6 et seq.

**Solar Rights Act**
Cal. Civil Code § 714
Cal. Statutes 1978, Ch. 1154
N.M. Stat. Ann., 47-3-1 et seq.
Wyo. Stat. Ann., § 34-22-101 et seq.

**Solar Shade Control Act**
Cal. Public Resources Code § 25980 et seq.

**Solar Tax Credit Act**
Ariz. Rev. Stat. Ann., §§ 42-123.01, 43-1031, 43-1053, 43-1074, 43-1075

**Solar, Wind, Waste, and Geothermal Power Production Incentives Act of 1990**
Nov. 15, 1990, P.L. 101-575, 16 U.S. Code §§ 791a nt., 796 nt.

**Soldiers' Adjusted Compensation Act**
Kan. Gen. Stat. 1949, 73-101 et seq.

**Soldiers' and Sailors' Absentee Ballot Act (World War II)**
Okla. Laws 1944, 1st Extraordinary Session, p. 3, S. B. 1

**Soldiers' and Sailors' Children's Home Act**
Ind. Code Ann., 12-3-20-1 et seq.

**Soldiers' and Sailors' Civil Relief Act**
La. Rev. Stat. Ann., 29:251 et seq.
N.J. Stat. Ann., 38:23C-1 et seq.
N.Y. Military Law (Consol. Laws Ch. 36) § 300 et seq.
Wis. Stat. Ann., 45.53

**Soldiers' and Sailors' Civil Relief Act Amendments of 1942**
Oct. 6, 1942, Ch. 581, 56 Stat. 769, 50 U.S. Code Appx. §§ 501 nt., 513 to 518, 525, 526, heading prec. 530, 530 to 536, 540 to 548, 560, 569, 572, 574, 590

**Soldiers' and Sailors' Civil Relief Act Amendments of 1991**
March 18, 1991, P.L. 102-12, 50 U.S. Code Appx. § 501 nt.

**Soldiers' and Sailors' Civil Relief Act of 1918**
March 8, 1918, Ch. 20, 40 Stat. 440
Sept. 3, 1919, Ch. 55, 41 Stat. 282
March 4, 1923, Ch. 284, 42 Stat. 1510

**Soldiers' and Sailors' Civil Relief Act of 1940**
Oct. 17, 1940, Ch. 888, 54 Stat. 1178, 50 U.S. Code Appx. §§ 501, 510 to 517, 520 to 525, 530 to 533, 535 to 537, 540 to 554, 560 to 574, 580 to 585, 590
Oct. 6, 1942, Ch. 581, 56 Stat. 769, 50 U.S. Code Appx. §§ 501 nt., 513 to 518, 525, 526 heading prec. § 530, 530 to 536, 540 to 548, 560, 569, 572, 574, 590
July 3, 1944, Ch. 397, 58 Stat. 722, 50 U.S. Code Appx. § 574 and nt.
April 3, 1948, Ch. 170, 62 Stat. 160, 50 U.S. Code Appx. § 546
June 23, 1952, Ch. 450, 66 Stat. 151, 50 U.S. Code Appx. § 532
July 11, 1956, Ch. 570, 70 Stat. 528, 50 U.S. Code Appx. § 540
Sept. 2, 1958, P.L. 85-857, 72 Stat. 1272, 50 U.S. Code Appx. § 547
Sept. 8, 1960, P.L. 86-721, 74 Stat. 820, 50 U.S. Code Appx. § 520
Oct. 9, 1962, P.L. 87-771, 76 Stat. 768, 50 U.S. Code Appx. § 574
March 3, 1966, P.L. 89-358, 80 Stat. 28, 50 U.S. Code Appx. §§ 530, 511, 591
March 18, 1991, P.L. 102-12, 50 U.S. Code Appx. §§ 511 to 513, 515, 516, 518, 525, 526, 530 to 532, 534, 535, 540 to 545, 547, 548, 564 to 567, 570, 574, 580, 581, 584, 591, 592, 593
Feb. 10, 1996, P.L. 104-106, 50 U.S. Code Appx. § 592

**Soldiers' and Sailors' Homestead Acts**
April 4, 1872, Ch. 85, 17 Stat. 49
June 8, 1872, Ch. 338, 17 Stat. 333
March 3, 1873, Ch. 274, 17 Stat. 605

**Soldiers and Sailors Memorial Bridge Act**
Pa. 1919 Pamph. Laws 1049, No. 420

**Soldiers' and Sailors' Relief Act**
Cal. Military and Veterans Code, § 395.1
Mich. Comp. Laws Ann., 35.21 et seq.

**Soldiers' and Sailors' Vote Act**
Ohio Rev. Code 1953, 3511.01 et seq.

**Soldiers' Bonus Act**
See World War Adjusted Compensation Act
Nov. 8, 1984, P. O. 98-616, 42 U.S. Code §§ 6916, 6931, 6933, 6948
June 19, 1986, P.L. 99-339, 42 U.S. Code §§ 6939a, 6979a, 6979b
Oct. 17, 1986, P.L. 99-499, 42 U.S. Code §§ 6926, 6928, 2991 to 2991d, 2991g
Nov. 1, 1988, P.L. 100-582, 42 U.S. Code §§ 6903, prec. 6992 6992, 6992a to 6992k
Ill. Rev. Stat. 1939, Ch. 126 1/2, § 1 et seq.
Iowa Code 1977, 35A.1 et seq.
Kan. Laws 1921, Ch. 255
Minn. Laws 1919, Extra Session, Ch. 49
Mo. Laws 1921, 2d., Extra Session, p. 6
N.D. Laws 1919, Ch. 206
N.D. Laws 1921, Ch. 103
N.Y. Laws 1920, Ch. 872
*Continued*

N.Y. Laws 1921, Ch. 315, 344
Ore. Rev. Stat., 407.085 et seq.
Wis. Laws 1919, Ch. 667

**Soldiers' Bonus Fund Act**
Mass. Gen. Laws 1924, Ch. 480

**Soldiers' Burial Act**
Ohio Rev. Code 1953, 5901.16 et seq.

**Soldiers' Compensation Act**
Ill. Rev. Stat. 1939, Ch. 126 1/2, § 1 et seq.
Kan. Gen. Stat. 1949, 73-101 et seq.
S.D. Laws 1921, Ch. 363

**Soldiers' Exemption Act**
Wyo. Stat. Ann., § 39-1-202

**Soldiers' Families Freedom Resolution**
March 3, 1865, No. 30, 13 Stat. 571

**Soldiers' Home Act**
Ind. Code Ann., 10-6-1-1 et seq.

**Soldiers' Land Settlement Act**
Ore. Laws 1991, Ch. 303

**Soldiers Memorial Hall Act**
Ill. Rev. Stat. 1991, Ch. 23, § 3050 et seq.

**Soldiers' Preference Act**
Iowa Code Ann., 70.1 et seq., 400.10
Kan. Stat. Ann., 73-201 et seq.
Minn. Stat. Ann., 197.455 et seq.
S.D. Codified Laws 1967, 3-3-1 et seq.

**Soldiers' Relief Act**
Iowa Code Ann., 250.3 et seq.
Ohio Rev. Code 1953, 5901.01 et seq.

**Soldiers, Sailors and Marines Act**
N.J. Stat. Ann., 38:16-1 et seq.

**Soldiers', Sailors' and Marines' Educational Aid Act (World War I)**
Ore. Laws 1991, Ch. 428

**Soldiers' Settlement Act**
Mo. Laws 1919, p. 704
Tenn. Public Acts 1919, Ch. 140

**Soldiers' Tax Exemption Act**
Iowa Code Ann., 427.3
N.M. Stat. Ann., 7-37-5 et seq.

**Soldier's Tax Relief Act**
Tenn. Public Acts 1991, Ch. 397

**Soldier's Vote Act**
Sept. 16, 1942, Ch. 561, 56 Stat. 753
April 1, 1944, Ch. 150, 58 Stat. 136

**Soldiers' Voting Act**
Conn. Gen. Stat. Ann., § 9-134 et seq.
Del. Laws Vol. 21, p. 134, Ch. 39
N.J. Rev. Stat. 19:57-1 et seq.
N.Y. Election Law 1976 (Consol. Laws Ch. 17), § 10-102 et seq.
R.I. Gen. Laws 1956, 17-21.1-1 et seq.
Wyo. Stat. 1957, § 22-242 et seq.

**Sole Traders Law (Married Women)**
Cal. Code of Civil Procedure § 1811 et seq.
Fla. Stat. 1969, 62.021
Nev. Rev. Stat. 1979 Reprint, Replaced Pages, 124.010 et seq.
Pa. Purdon's Stat., Title 48, § 41 et seq.
Tex. Family Code, § 4.04

**Solicitation Act (Legal Business)**
Ill. Rev. Stat. 1991, Ch. 13, § 14.9 et seq.

**Solicitation Act (Prostitution)**
Haw. Rev. Stat. 1968, § 712-1200 et seq.
Mich. Comp. Laws Ann., 750.448 et seq.

**Solicitation and Charitable Organization Act**
Kan. Stat. Ann., 17-1759 et seq.

**Solicitation of Charitable Funds Act**
Colo. Rev. Stat., 6-16-101 et seq.
Conn. Gen. Stat. Ann., §§ 17-21a et seq., 21a-175 et seq.
D.C. Code Ann., § 2-701 et seq.
Fla. Stat. 1983, 492.401 et seq.
Ga. Code Ann., 43-17-1 et seq.
Ill. Rev. Stat. 1991, Ch. 23, § 5100 et seq.
Iowa Code Ann., 122.1 et seq.
Kan. Stat. Ann., 17-1759 et seq.
Ky. Rev. Stat. 1971, 367.650 et seq.

Mass. Gen. Laws Ann., 68:16 et seq.
Me. Rev. Stat. Ann. 1964, Title 9, § 5001 et seq.
N.C. Gen. Stat. 1943, §§ 108-75.1 et seq., 131C-1 et seq.
N.M. Stat. Ann., 57-22-1 et seq.
Ohio Rev. Code 1953, 1716.01 et seq.
Okla. Stat. Ann., Title 18, § 552.1 et seq.
Ore. Laws 1985, Ch. 729, §§ 1 to 20, 23, 24
Pa. Purdon's Stat., Title 10, § 162.1 et seq.
S.C. Code Ann. 1976, § 33-55-10 et seq.
Tenn. Code Ann., 48-3-501 et seq.
W. Va. Code 1966, § 29-19-1 et seq.

**Solicitation of Employees Law**
Cal. Labor Code §§ 973, 974

**Solicitation of Funds Act**
Fla. Stat. Ann., 496.001 et seq.

**Solicitation of Funds Act (Law Enforcement and Emergency Service)**
Fla. Stat. Ann., 496.401 et seq.

**Solicitation Reform Act (Charitable)**
Tenn. Code Ann., 48-3-501, 48-3-503 to 48-3-507, 48-3-509, 48-3-511 to 48-3-514, 48-3-518, 48-3-520

**Solicitor General Retirement Fund Act**
Ga. Code Ann., 47-10-1 et seq.

**Solicitorial Retirement Act**
N.C. Gen. Stat. 1943, §§ 135-77, 135-78

**Solicitors' Act**
Ala. Code 1975, § 12-17-180 et seq.

**Solicitors, Agents and Brokers**
Ill. Rev. Stat. 1991, Ch. 73, § 1065.37-1 et seq.

**Solid and Hazardous Waste Act**
Utah Code Ann. 1953, 19-6-101 et seq., 26-14-1 et seq.

**Solid and Hazardous Waste Recycling and Treatment Act**
Ill. Rev. Stat. 1991, Ch. 127, § 2703-1 et seq.

**Solid Fuel Act**
Md. Ann. Code 1974, Art. AG, § 11-501 et seq.
N.Y. City Adm. Code '38, Ch. 36, § B36-22.0 et seq.
Pa. Purdon's Stat., Title 73, § 1831 et seq.

**Solid Waste Act (Palm Beach County)**
Fla. Special Laws 1974, Ch. 74-564
Fla. Special Laws 1975, Ch. 75-473

**Solid Waste and Energy Producing Disposal Service Act (Metro East)**
Ill. Rev. Stat. 1991, Ch. 111 1/2, § 7101 et seq.

**Solid Waste Authority Act**
N.M. Stat. Ann., 74-10-1 et seq.
Tenn. Code Ann., 68-211-901 et seq.

**Solid Waste Authority Act (Stewart County)**
Ga. Laws 1992, p. 6867

**Solid Waste Authority Act (Western Finger Lakes)**
N.Y. Public Authorities Law (Consol. Laws Ch. 43A) § 2725 et seq.

**Solid Waste Collection and Disposal Assistance Act (Local Government)**
Miss. Laws 1994, Ch. 624

**Solid Waste Collection Regulatory Reform Act**
N.J. Stat. Ann., 40:37-153 et seq.

**Solid Waste Combustion Institute Act**
N.Y. Laws 1987, Ch. 615, § 21 et seq.

**Solid Waste Compact Act (Interstate)**
N.H. Rev. Stat. 1955, 53-D:1

**Solid Waste Compact Act (New Hampshire-Vermont)**
Vt. Stat. Ann., Title 10, § 1222 et seq.

**Solid Waste Control Act**
Cal. Government Code § 66795 et seq.
D.C. Code Ann., § 6-502 et seq.

**Solid Waste Control Act (County)**
Tex. Health and Safety Code, § 364.001 et seq.

**Solid Waste Disposal Act**
Oct. 20, 1965, P.L. 89-272, 79 Stat. 997, 42 U.S. Code §§ 3251 to 3259
Oct. 15, 1968, P.L. 90-574, 82 Stat. 1013, 42 U.S. Code § 3259
Oct. 26, 1970, P.L. 91-512, 84 Stat. 1227, 42 U.S. Code §§ 3251 to 3254f, 3256 to 3259
April 9, 1973, P.L. 93-14, 87 Stat. 11, 42 U.S. Code § 3259
Oct. 21, 1976, P.L. 94-580, 42 U.S. Code § 6901 et seq.
Nov. 8, 1978, P.L. 95-609, 42 U.S. Code § 6901 et seq.
Oct. 21, 1980, P.L. 96-482, 42 U.S. Code § 6901 nt.
Dec. 21, 1982, P.L. 97-375, 42 U.S. Code § 6962
Nov. 8, 1984, P.L. 98-616, 42 U.S. Code §§ 6916, 6931, 6933, 6948
June 19, 1986, P.L. 99-339, 42 U.S. Code §§ 6939a, 6979a, 6979b
Oct. 17, 1986, P.L. 99-499, 42 U.S. Code §§ 6926, 6928, 6991 to 6991d, 6991g
Nov. 1, 1988, P.L. 100-582, 42 U.S. Code §§ 6903, prec. 6992, 6992a to 6992k
Oct. 6, 1992, P.L. 102-386, 42 U.S. Code §§ 6903, 6924, 6927, 6939c to 6939e, 6961
Oct. 24, 1992, P.L. 102-508, 42 U.S. Code § 6991
Oct. 13, 1994, P.L. 103-355, 42 U.S. Code § 6962
Oct. 31, 1994, P.L. 103-429, 42 U.S. Code § 6991
Nov. 2, 1994, P.L. 103-437, 42 U.S. Code § 6907
March 26, 1996, P.L. 104-119, 42 U.S. Code §§ 6921, 6924, 6925, 6947, 6949a
Aug. 20, 1996, P.L. 104-186, 42 U.S. Code § 6964
Sept. 30, 1996, P.L. 104-208, 42 U.S. Code § 6991b
Nov. 10, 1998, P.L. 105-362, 7 U.S. Code § 6977; 42 U.S. Code §§ 6992g to 6992k
Ala. Code 1975, § 22-27-1 et seq.
Haw. Rev. Stat. § 340A-1 et seq.
Kan. Stat. Ann., 65-3401 et seq.
Mass. Gen. Laws Ann., 16:18 et seq.
Miss. Code Ann. 1972, § 17-17-1 et seq.
N.M. Stat. Ann., 74-9-1 et seq.
S.D. Codified Laws 1967, 34A-6-1 et seq.
Tenn. Code Ann., 68-211-101 et seq.
Tex. Health and Safety Code, § 361.001 et seq.

**Solid Waste Disposal Act (Brevard County)**
Fla. Special Laws 1967, Ch. 67-1146

**Solid Waste Disposal Act (Evangeline Parish)**
La. Rev. Stat. Ann., 33:8001

**Solid Waste Disposal Act (Joint County and Municipal)**
Ark. Code Ann. 1987, 14-233-101 et seq.

**Solid Waste Disposal Act (Local)**
Ill. Rev. Stat. 1991, Ch. 85, § 5901

**Solid Waste Disposal Act (St. Landry Parish)**
La. Acts 1980, No. 289

**Solid Waste Disposal Act Amendments of 1980**
Nov. 10, 1998, P.L. 105-362, 42 U.S. Code § 6981 nt.

**Solid Waste Disposal and Codisposal Site Cleanup Program Law**
Cal. Public Resources Code § 48020 et seq.

**Solid Waste Disposal and Resource Act (Hillsborough Count)**
Fla. Laws 1981, Ch. 81-387

**Solid Waste Disposal and Resource Recovery Act**
Fla. Laws 1983, Ch. 83-370

**Solid Waste Disposal and Resource Recovery Act (Bay County)**
N.J. Stat. Ann., 13:1E-136 et seq.

**Solid Waste Disposal and Resource Recovery Act (Pinellas County)**
Fla. Special Laws 1975, Ch. 75-487

**Solid Waste Disposal and Resource Recovery Authority Act**
W. Va. Code 1966, § 16-26-1 et seq.

**Solid Waste Disposal and Resource Recovery Facility Bond Act**
N.J. Laws 1985, Ch. 330

**Solid Waste Disposal Authority Act (Onondago County)**
N.Y. Public Authorities Law (Consol. Laws Ch. 43A), § 2015 et seq.

**Solid Waste Disposal Authority Act (St. Lawrence County)**
N.Y. Public Authorities Law (Consol. Laws, Ch. 43A), § 2048a et seq.

**Solid Waste Disposal District Act**
Ill. Rev. Stat. 1991, Ch. 85, § 1651 et seq.

**Solid Waste Disposal Facilities Act**
Ind. Code Ann., 36-9-31-1 et seq.

**Solid Waste Disposal Financing Law (Counties)**
N.J. Stat. Ann., 40:66A-31.1 et seq.

**Solid Waste Disposal Regulatory Reform Act**
Cal. Public Resources Code § 43100 et seq.

**Solid Waste Disposal Resource Recovery Facilities Act**
S.C. Code Ann. 1976, § 6-16-10 et seq.

**Solid Waste Disposal Site Cleanup and Maintenance Bill of Rights**
Cal. Revenue and Taxation Code § 45856 et seq.

**Solid Waste Disposal Site Hazard Reduction Act**
Cal. Public Resources Code § 46000 et seq.

**Solid Waste Dumping Elimination Act (Ocean)**
Del. Code of 1974, Title 7, § 6070 et seq.

**Solid Waste Facilities Act**
Ida. Code 1947, 39-7401 et seq.

**Solid Waste Management Act**
See also Waste Disposal Act
Ark. Code Ann. 1987, 8-6-201 et seq.
Cal. Government Code § 68000 et seq.
Conn. Gen. Stat. Ann., §§ 20-7a, 22a-207 et seq.
Ga. Code Ann., 12-8-20 et seq.
Me. Rev. Stat. Ann. 1964, Title 38, § 1301 et seq.
Mich. Comp. Laws Ann., 324,11501 et seq.
Minn. Stat. Ann., 400.01 et seq.
Mont. Code Ann. 1991, 75-10-201 et seq.
N.J. Stat. Ann., 13:1E-1 et seq., 40:66A-32 et seq.
N.Y. County Act 1950 (Consol. Laws Ch. 11) § 626
N.Y. Environmental Conservation Law 1972 (Consol. Laws Ch. 43B) §§ 3-0301, 19-0306, 27-0103, 27-0106, 27-0107, 27-0109, 27-0305, 27-0401, 27-0702, 27-0703, 27-0707, 27-0715, 27-0717
N.Y. General Municipal Law (Consol. Laws Ch. 24) §§ 104a, 120aa
N.Y. Local Laws 1973, County of Monroe, p. 1099
N.Y. Public Authorities Law (Consol. Laws Ch. 43A) §§ 1285i, 2878a, 2878b
N.Y. Public Authorities Law (Consol. Laws Ch. 43A), § 2041 et seq.
N.Y. State Finance Law 1940 (Consol. Laws Ch. 56) §§ 161a, 177
N.Y. Town Law (Consol. Laws Ch. 62) § 122a
N.Y. Village Law 1972 (Consol. Laws Ch. 64) § 5-525
Okla. Stat. Ann., Title 27A, § 2-10-101 et seq.; Title 63, § 1-2300 et seq.
Pa. Purdon's Stat., Title 35, § 6018.101 et seq.
P.R. Laws Ann. 1954, Title 12, § 1301 et seq.
S.D. Codified Laws 1967, 7-33-1 et seq.
Tenn. Code Ann., 68-211-801 et seq.
Utah Code Ann. 1953, 19-6-501 et seq., 26-32-1 et seq.
Vt. Stat. Ann., Title 10, § 6601 et seq.
W. Va. Code 1966 § 20-5F-1 et seq.

**Solid Waste Management Act (County Department)**
Mich. Comp. Laws Ann., 45.581 et seq.

**Solid Waste Management Act (Hazardous)**
N.C. Gen. Stat. 1943, § 130A-290 et seq.

**Solid Waste Management Act (Integrated)**
Neb. Laws 1992, L.B. 1257, §§ 1 to 43

**Solid Waste Management and Hazardous Waste Septage Act**
Me. Rev. Stat. Ann. 1964, Title 38, § 1301 et seq.

**Solid Waste Management and Land Protection Act**
N.D. Cent. Code, 23-29-01 et seq.

**Solid Waste Management and Recycling Fund Act**
Ark. Code Ann. 1987, 8-6-601 et seq.

**Solid Waste Management and Resource Recovery Act**
Cal. Government Code, § 66700 et seq.
La. Rev. Stat. Ann., 30:1121 et seq.

**Solid Waste Management Authorities Act (Regional)**
Ga. Code Ann., 12-8-50 et seq.

**Solid Waste Management Authority Act (Eastern Rensselaer County)**
N.Y. Public Authorities Law (Consol. Laws Ch. 43A) § 2050aa et seq.

**Solid Waste Management Authority Act (Essex-Franklin)**
N.Y. Public Authorities Law (Consol. Laws Ch. 43A) §§ 2051a to 2051x

**Solid Waste Management Authority Act (Greater Troy Area)**
N.Y. Public Authorities Law (Consol. Laws Ch. 43A) § 2052a et seq.

**Solid Waste Management Authority Act (Multi-town)**
N.Y. Public Authorities Law (Consol. Laws Ch. 43A), § 2040a et seq.

**Solid Waste Management Authority Act (North Hempstead)**
N.Y. Public Authorities Law (Consol. Laws, Ch. 43A), § 2049a et seq.

**Solid Waste Management Authority Act (Oneida-Herkimer)**
N.Y. Public Authorities Law (Consol. Laws Ch. 43A) §§ 2049aa to 2049yy

**Solid Waste Management Authority Act (Regional)**
Miss. Code Ann. 1972, § 17-17-301 et seq.

**Solid Waste Management Board Act**
W. Va. Code 1966 §§ 16-26-1 et seq., 22C-3-1 et seq.

**Solid Waste Management Corporation Act**
R.I. Gen. Laws 1956, 23-19-1 et seq.

**Solid Waste Management Districts Act (Rural)**
Okla. Stat. Ann., Title 82, § 1324.1 et seq.

**Solid Waste Management Grant Program**
Wis. Stat. Ann., 144.60 et seq.

**Solid Waste Management Loan Program**
N.C. Gen. Stat. 1943, § 159I-1 et seq.

**Solid Waste Management, Resource Recovery and Conservation Act (Municipal)**
Tex. Health and Safety Code, § 363.001 et seq.

**Solid Waste Planning Act (Nonhazardous)**
Miss. Code Ann. 1972, § 17-17-1 et seq.

**Solid Waste Planning and Recovery Act**
Tenn. Code Ann., 68-211-601 et seq.

**Solid Waste Policy and Management Act**
S.C. Code Ann. 1976, § 44-96-10 et seq.

**Solid Waste Recycling Act**
Ariz. Rev. Stat. Ann., § 49-831 et seq.
La. Rev. Stat. Ann., 30:2411 et seq.
Wis. Stat. 1987, 144.794 et seq.

**Solid Waste Resource Recovery Development Act**
Pa. Purdon's Stat., Title 35, § 755.1 et seq.

**Solid Waste-Resource Recovery Development Act**
Pa. Purdon's Stat., Title 35, § 755.1 et seq.

**Solid Waste Resource Recovery Financing Act**
Tex. Health and Safety Code, § 362.001 et seq.

**Solid Waste Reuse and Recycling Access Act**
Cal. Public Resources Code § 42900 et seq.

**Solid Waste Site Operator Certification Law**
Ill. Rev. Stat. 1991, Ch. 111, § 7851 et seq.

**Solid Waste Utility Control Act**
N.J. Stat. Ann., 48:13A-1 et seq.

**Solid Waste, Water, and Sewer Management Systems Finance Act**
Ark. Code Ann. 1987, 14-230-101 et seq.

**Solomon Act (Public Employees-Labor Unions)**
Ala. Code 1958, Title 55, § 317(1) et seq.

**Solution, Oil and Gas Mining Law**
N.Y. Environmental Conservation Law 1972 (Consolidated Laws Ch. 43B) § 23-0101 et seq.

**Solvang Municipal Improvement District Act**
Cal. Statutes 1951, Ch. 1635, p. 3676

**Somerset Hospital Conversion Security and Quehanna Boot Camp Project Itemization Act**
Pa. 1995 Pamph. Laws, Special Session, Nos. 1, 34

**Somerset Water Loan Act**
Mass. Acts 1957, Ch. 622

**Somerville Court House Loan Act**
Mass. Acts 1963, Ch. 519

**Sommerville Act (Foreign Corporations)**
Minn. Stat. Ann., 303.01 et seq.

**Son of Sam Act**
Colo. Rev. Stat. 24-4.1-201 et seq.
Ky. Rev. Stat. 1971, 346.165
Minn. Stat. Ann., 611A.68
Neb. Rev. Stat. 1943, 81-1836
N.J. Stat. Ann., 52:4B-28 et seq.
N.M. Stat. Ann., 31-22-1 et seq.
N.Y. Executive Law 1951 (Consol. Laws Ch. 18) § 632a
S.C. Code Ann. 1976, §§ 15-59-40 et seq., 44-53-520
Tenn. Code Ann., 29-13-201
Tex. Rev. Civ. Stat., Art. 8309-1, §§ 16 to 18

**Son of Sam Law**
Mich. Comp. Laws Ann., 600.4701 et seq.

**Song Act (State)**
Ill. Rev. Stat. 1991, Ch. 1, § 2901-35

**Song-Beverly Consumer Warranty Act**
Cal. Civil Code § 1790 et seq.

**Song-Beverly Credit Card Act**
Cal. Civil Code § 1747 et seq.

**Song-Brown Family Physician Training Act**
Cal. Education Code 1976, § 69270 et seq.

**Song-Cobey Evidence Act**
Cal. Statutes 1965, Ch. 299, p. 1297

**Sonny Bono Copyright Term Extension Act**
Oct. 27, 1998, P.L. 105-298, Title I, 112 Stat. 2827, 17 U.S. Code § 101 nt.

**Sonoma County Flood Control and Water Conservation District Act**
Cal. Water Code, Appendix, § 53-1 et seq.

**Sordoni Act (Bank Moratorium)**
Pa. 1933 Pamph. Laws 9, No. 6

**Sour Gas Act**
Tex. Natural Resources Code, § 87.001 et seq.

**Sour Gas Pipeline Facilities Act**
Tex. Rev. Civ. Stat., Art. 6053-4

**South African Democratic Transition Support Act of 1993**
Nov. 23, 1993, P.L. 103-149, 22 U.S. Code § 5001 nt.

**South Brevard Airport District Act**
Fla. Special Laws 1969, Ch. 69-880

**South Carolina Family Week Act**
S.C. Code Ann. 1976, § 53-3-10 et seq.

**South Carolina National Heritage Corridor Act of 1996**
Nov. 12, 1996, P.L. 104-333, Division II, Title VI, 16 U.S. Code § 461 nt.

**South Central Interstate Forest Fire Protection Compact Act**
Okla. Stat. Ann., Title 2, § 1301-215
Tex. Education Code, § 88.116 et seq.

**South Cobb Development Authority Act**
Ga. Laws 1982, p.3772

**South Dakota Domestic Public Corporation Takeover**
S.D. Codified Laws 1967 Miscellaneous Superseded, § 47-32-1 et seq.

**South Dakota-Nebraska Boundary Compact**
Nov. 28, 1989, P.L. 101-183, 103 Stat. 1328

**South Delta Water Agency Act**
Cal. Water Code, Appx., § 116-1.1

**South Florida School for the Performing and Visual Arts Act**
Fla. Stat. Ann., 240.535

**South Hadley Water Loan Act (Fire District No. 2)**
Mass. Acts 1954, Ch. 412

**South Jersey Food Distribution Authority Law**
N.J. Stat. Ann., 4:26-1 et seq.

**South Jersey Port Corporation Act**
N.J. Stat. Ann., 12:11A-1 et seq.

**South Jersey Transportation Authority Act**
N.J. Stat. Ann., 27:25A-1 et seq.

**South Newton Special Utility District Act**
Tex. General and Special Laws 1997, Ch. 597

**South Pacific Tuna Act**
June 7, 1988, P.L. 100-329, 102 Stat. 588, 16 U.S. Code §§ 973 nt., 973 et seq.
June 27, 1988, P.L. 100-350, 102 Stat. 660, 16 U.S. Code §§ 973f, 973i
Oct. 26, 1992, P.L. 102-523, 16 U.S. Code § 973r
Nov. 3, 1995, P.L. 104-43, 16 U.S. Code § 973g

**South Platte River Compact**
March 8, 1926, Ch. 46, 44 Stat. 195

**South Seminole and North Orange County Wastewater Transmission Authority Act**
Fla. Special Laws 1978, Ch. 78-617

**South Shore Estuary Reserve Act (Long Island)**
N.Y. Executive Law 1951 (Consol. Laws Ch. 18) § 960 et seq.

**Southeast Interstate Low-Level Radioactive Waste Compact Act**
Ala. Code 1975, § 22-32-1 et seq.
Fla. Stat. Ann., 404.30
Tenn. Code Ann., 68-202-101 et seq.

**Southeast Interstate Low-Level Radioactive Waste Compact Amendments Consent Act of 1989**
Nov. 22, 1989, P.L. 101-171, 42 U.S. Code § 2021d nt.

**Southeast Interstate Low-Level Radioactive Waste Management Compact**
Jan. 15, 1986, P.L. 99-240, 99 Stat. 1871

**Southeast Interstate Low-Level Radioactive Waste Management Compact Act**
Ga. Code Ann., 12-8-120 et seq.
Miss. Code Ann. 1972, § 57-47-1 et seq.

N.C. Gen. Stat. 1943, § 104F-1 et seq.
S.C. Code Ann. 1976, § 48-47-10 et seq.
Va. Code 1950, § 32.1-238.6:1 et seq.

**Southeastern Interstate Forest Fire Protection Compact Act**
Ga. Code Ann., 12-10-60 et seq.
Ky. Rev. Stat. 1971, 149.310
N.C. Gen. Stat. 1943, § 113-60.11 et seq.
S.C. Code Ann. 1976, § 48-37-10 et seq.
Tenn. Code Ann., 11-4-301 et seq.

**Southeastern Nassau County Water Authority Act**
N.Y. Public Authorities Law (Consol. Laws Ch. 43A) § 1174a et seq.

**Southern Arizona Water Rights Settlement Act of 1982**
Oct. 24, 1992, P.L. 102-497, 106 Stat. 3256

**Southern Arizona Water Rights Settlement Technical Amendments Act of 1992**
Oct. 24, 1992, P.L. 102-497, 106 Stat. 3256

**Southern Bay Crossing Act**
Cal. Streets and Highways Code § 30651 et seq.

**Southern California Rapid Transit District Law**
Cal. Public Utilities Code § 30000 et seq.

**Southern California Transportation Study Commission Act**
Cal. Government Code § 67410 et seq.

**Southern California World Trade Center Authority Law**
Cal. Government Code § 8420 et seq.

**Southern Dairy Compact**
Ala. Acts 1998, No. 305
Ga. Code Ann., 2-18-1 et seq.
La. Rev. Stat. Ann., 3:4021 to 3:4025

**Southern Growth Policies Agreement Act**
Ala. Code 1975, § 41-18-1 et seq.
Ark. Code Ann. 1987, 15-2-101
Fla. Stat. Ann., 23.140
Ga. Code Ann., 12-10-20 et seq.
Ky. Rev. Stat. 1971, 147.580
La. Rev. Stat. Ann., 49:61
N.C. Gen. Stat. 1943, § 143-490 et seq.
Okla. Stat. Ann., Title 74, §§ 3501, 3502
S.C. Code Ann. 1976, § 13-13-10
Tenn. Code Ann., 13-2-101 et seq.
Va. Code 1950, § 2.1-339.1 et seq.

**Southern Illinois University Management Act**
Ill. Rev. Stat. 1991, Ch. 144, § 650 et seq.

**Southern Illinois University Name Change Act**
Ill. Rev. Stat. 1991, Ch. 144, §§ 599, 600

**Southern Illinois University Objects Act**
Ill. Rev. Stat. 1991, Ch. 144, § 601.9 et seq.

**Southern Illinois University Revenue-Producing Buildings and Structures Act**
Ill. Rev. Stat. 1991, Ch. 144, § 641 et seq.

**Southern Indiana Tuberculosis Hospital Act**
Ind. Code 1971, 16-11-12-1 et seq.

**Southern Interstate Nuclear Compact Act**
Ala. Acts 1961, Sp. Sess., p. 1909
Del. Code of 1953, Title 6, § 7201 et seq.
Fla. Stat. Ann., 377.71 et seq.
Ga. Code Ann., 12-10-1 et seq.
Ky. Rev. Stat. 1971, 152.210
Md. Ann. Code 1957, Art. 41, § 16-101 et seq.
Miss. Code Ann. 1972, § 57-25-1 et seq.
Mo. Rev. Stat., 18.060 et seq.
N.C. Gen. Stat. 1943, § 104D-1 et seq.
Okla. Stat. Ann., Title 74, § 1051 et seq.
P.R. Laws Ann. 1954, Title 1, § 201 et seq.
S.C. Code Ann. 1976, § 13-7-420 et seq.
Tex. Rev. Civ. Stat. 1974, Art. 4413C-1
Va. Code 1950, § 2.1-336 et seq.

**Southern Nevada Project Act**
Oct. 22, 1965, P.L. 89-292, 79 Stat. 1068, 43 U.S. Code §§ 616ggg to 616mmm
July 19, 1966, P.L. 89-510, 80 Stat. 312, 43 U.S. Code § 616lll

**Southern Nevada Public Land Management Act of 1998**
Oct. 19, 1998, P.L. 105-263, 112 Stat. 2343, 31 U.S. Code § 6901 nt.

**Southern New Jersey Children's Hospital Act**
N.J. Stat. Ann., 26:2H-1 et seq.

**Southern Products Mart Authority Act**
Ala. Code 1975, § 41-10-50 et seq.

**Southern Regional Education Compact Act**
Ky. Acts 1950, Ch. 252
Md. Ann. Code 1974, Art. ED, § 25-201 et seq.
Tenn. Code Ann., 49-12-101 et seq.

**Southern Regional Emergency Management Compact**
Ga. Code Ann., 38-3-80, 28-3-81
Miss. Code Ann. 1972, §§ 45-18-1, 45-18-3
S.C. Code Ann. 1976, §§ 25-9-410, 25-9-420

**Southern Sandoval County Arroyo Flood Control Act**
N.M. Stat. Ann., 72-19-1 et seq.

**Southern State Police Compact Act**
La. Rev. Stat. Ann., 40:1312.1 et seq.

**Southern States Energy Compact Act**
Ala. Code 1975, § 9-18A-1 et seq.
Ark. Code Ann. 1987, 15-10-401 et seq.
Ga. Code Ann., 12-10-1 et seq.
Ky. Rev. Stat. 1971, 152.200 et seq.
Md. Ann. Code 1957, Art. 41, § 16-101 et seq.
Miss. Code Ann. 1972, § 57-25-1
N.C. Gen. Stat. 1943, § 104D-1 et seq.
Okla. Stat. Ann., Title 74, § 1051 et seq.
S.C. Code Ann. 1976, § 13-7-420 et seq.
Va. Code 1950, § 2.1-336 et seq.

**Southern States Nuclear Compact Act**
Tenn. Code Ann., 68-202-101 et seq.

**Southold Housing Code**
N.Y. Local Laws 1967, Town of Southold, p. 1941

**Southold Town Code**
N.Y. Local Laws 1973, Town of Southold, p. 2976

**Southside Regional Airport Authority at Blackstone Act**
Va. Acts 1992, Ch. 371

**Southwest Regional Port District Act**
Ill. Rev. Stat. 1991, Ch. 19, § 451 et seq.

**Southwestern Extension Act (Pennsylvania Turnpike)**
Pa. Purdon's Stat., Title 36, § 669.1 et seq.

**Southwestern Illinois Development Authority Act**
Ill. Rev. Stat. 1991, Ch. 85, § 6151 et seq.

**Southwestern Illinois Metropolitan and Regional Planning Act**
Ill. Rev. Stat. 1991, Ch. 85, § 1151 et seq.

**Southwestern Low-Level Radioactive Waste Disposal Compact Consent Act**
Nov. 23, 1988, P.L. 100-712, 42 U.S. Code § 2021d nt.

**Southwestern Pennsylvania Regional Renaissance Initiative Act**
Pa. Purdon's Stat., Title 16, § 3011 et seq.

**Southworth-Symons Act (Banks)**
Ind. Laws 1919, Ch. 50, p. 112

**Sovereign Immunity Act**
S.C. Code Ann. 1976, § 15-3-530 et seq.

**Soviet-Eastern European Research and Training Act of 1983**
See Research and Training for Eastern Europe and the Independent States of the Former Soviet Union Act of 1983
Nov. 22, 1983, P.L. 98-164, 22 U.S. Code §§ 4501, 4501 nt., 4509

**Soviet Nuclear Threat Reduction Act of 1991**
Dec. 12, 1991, P.L. 102-228, 22 U.S. Code § 2551 nt.
Oct. 23, 1992, P.L. 102-484, 22 U.S. Code § 2551 nt.
Oct. 24, 1992, P.L. 102-511, 22 U.S. Code § 5856

**Soviet Scientists Immigration Act of 1992**
Oct. 24, 1992, P.L. 102-509, 8 U.S. Code § 1153 nt.

**Soybean Act**
Okla. Stat. Ann., Title 2, § 1801 et seq.

**Soybean Ink Act**
Ill. Comp. Stat. 1992, Ch. 50, § 20/1 et seq.

**Soybean Marketing Act**
Fla. Stat. Ann., 573.830 et seq.
Ill. Rev. Stat. 1991, Ch. 5, § 551 et seq.

**Soybean Promotion Act**
Tenn. Code Ann., 43-20-201 et seq.

**Soybean Promotion, Research, and Consumer Information Act**
Nov. 28, 1990, P.L. 101-624, 7 U.S. Code §§ 6301 to 6311

**Soybean Resources Act**
Neb. Rev. Stat. 1943, 2-3301 et seq.

**Spa Act (Health)**
Tex. Rev. Civ. Stat., Art. 52211

**Space Authority Act**
La. Rev. Stat. Ann., 51:1351 et seq.

**Space Basis Act (Carriage of Mail by Railroads)**
July 28, 1916, Ch. 261, 39 Stat. 425

**Space Center Act**
N.M. Stat. Ann., 18-7-1 et seq.

**Space Heating Safety Act**
Ill. Rev. Stat. 1991, Ch. 127 1/2, § 701 et seq.

**Space Management Act (State)**
Ga. Code Ann., 50-5-30 et seq.

**Space Needs Law (Leyden Township)**
Ill. Rev. Stat. 1991, Ch. 85, § 7701-1 et seq.

**Space Port Committee Act**
Utah Laws 1971, Ch. 159

**Space Preservation Bond Act (Open)**
N.J. Laws 1991, Ch. 183

**Space Tax Law (Farm and Open)**
Me. Rev. Stat. Ann. 1964, Title 36, § 1102 et seq.

**Spaceport Development Act**
N.M. Stat. Ann., 9-15-42 et seq.

**Spaceport Florida Authority Act**
Fla. Stat. Ann., 331.301 et seq.

**Spacing Act (Oil Wells)**
Okla. Stat. Ann., Title 52, § 87.1

**Spafford Local Law for Retention of Elected Assessors**
N.Y. Local Laws 1971, Town of Spafford, p. 3491

**Spalding County Water and Sewerage Facilities Authority Act**
Ga. Laws 1982, p.4987

**Spalding-Griffin County Charter Commission Act**
Ga. Laws 1991, p. 3802

**Spalding-Griffin County Personal Care Health Board Act**
Ga. Laws 1991, p. 4609

**Spanish-American Peace Treaty Proclamation**
Dec. 10, 1898, 30 Stat. 1754

**Spanish Colonization Commemorative Act of 1988**
Oct. 28, 1988, P.L. 100-559, 102 Stat. 2798

**Spanish Friendship Treaty (1863)**
Haw. Session Laws 1870, p. 85, Sept. 2, 1870

**Spanish War Claims Act**
March 2, 1901, Ch. 800, 31 Stat. 877

**Spanish War Tax Act (Reduction)**
March 2, 1901, Ch. 806, 31 Stat. 938

**Spanish War Veterans' Relief Act**
Minn. Laws 1931, Ch. 405

**Spanking Act**
Nev. Rev. Stat. 1979 Reprint, 392.465

**Spark Arrester Act (Steam Engines)**
Tex. Penal Code 1925, Art. 1329

**Spark M. Matsunaga Hydrogen Research, Development, and Demonstration Act of 1990**
Nov. 15, 1990, P.L. 101-566, 42 U.S. Code §§ 12401 to 12408

**Sparks Charter**
Nev. Statutes 1905, Ch. 83, p. 158
Nev. Statutes 1949, Ch. 180, p. 372
Nev. Statutes 1971, Ch. 545, p. 1142
Nev. Statutes 1975, Ch. 470, p. 724

**SPARS Act**
Nov. 23, 1942, Ch. 639, 56 Stat. 1020 (See 14 U.S. Code §§ 751, 752, 756, 759, 826)

**Sparta-Hancock Public Facilities Authority Act**
Ga. Laws 1991, p. 4394

**Spartanburg Civil Service Act**
S.C. Code Ann. 1962, § 47-800.51

**Spartanburg County Supervising Auditor Act**
S.C. Acts 1923, p. 842, No. 497

**Spas and Health Resorts Act**
Ind. Code 1971, 23-9-9-1 et seq.

**Spaulding County-Griffin Anti-Drug Commission Act**
Ga. Laws 1988, p. 4053

**Spears Bill (Firemen's and Policemen's Hours)**
Tex. Rev. Civ. Stat., Art. 911b, § 5a

**Special Ad Hoc Municipal Police and Firefighter Postretirement Adjustment Act**
Pa. Purdon's Stat., Title 53, § 896.101 et seq.

**Special Adult Offender Act**
Ga. Code 1933, 77-365 et seq.

**Special Airport Districts Act**
N.C. Gen. Stat. 1943, § 63-78 et seq.

**Special Alternative Incarceration Act**
Mich. Comp. Laws Ann., 798.11 et seq.

**Special Appellate Compensation Act**
Ohio Rev. Code 1953, 4123.519

**Special Appropriation Act**
N.M. Laws 1977, Ch. 363

**Special Assault Act**
Ohio Rev. Code 1953, 2903.11 et seq.

**Special Assessment Act**
Ill. Rev. Stat. 1991, Ch. 24, § 9-2-1 et seq.

**Special Assessment and Bond Refunding Act**
Cal. Government Code § 59100 et seq.

**Special Assessment Apportionment Act**
Ill. Rev. Stat. 1991, Ch. 120, §§ 370.9, 371

**Special Assessment Apportionment Law**
Ill. Comp. Stat. 1992, Ch. 35, § 230/1 et seq.

**Special Assessment Benefiting State Property Act**
Ill. Rev. Stat. 1991, Ch. 120, § 1350 et seq.

**Special Assessment Benefiting State Property Law**
Ill. Comp. Stat. 1992, Ch. 35, § 240/1 et seq.

**Special Assessment Investigation, Limitation and Majority Protest**
Cal. Streets and Highways Code § 2800 et seq. Act

**Special Assessment Relief Act**
Cal. Streets and Highways Code § 1900 et seq.

**Special Assessment Supplemental Bond and Procedures Act**
Ill. Comp. Stat. 1992, Ch. 50, § 460/1 et seq.

**Special Care Disclosure Act (Alzheimer's)**
Neb. Rev. Stat. 1943, 71-516.01 et seq.
S.C. Code Ann. 1976, §§ 44-36-510, 44-36-520

**Special Care Facility Licensing Act**
Tex. Health and Safety Code, § 248.001 et seq.

**Special Central American Assistance Act of 1979**
May 31, 1980, P.L. 96-257, 22 U.S. Code § 2346e

**Special Charter Not for Profit Corporations Act**
Ill. Rev. Stat. 1991, Ch. 32, § 197.9 et seq.

**Special Child Support Act**
P.R. Laws Ann. 1954, Title 8, § 501 et seq.

**Special Commodity Carrier Act**
Tex. Rev. Civ. Stat., Art. 911b, § 5a

**Special County Hospital Gasoline Tax Act**
N.M. Stat. Ann., 7-24B-1 et seq.

**Special County Hospital Gross Receipts Tax Act**
N.M. Stat. Ann., 7-20-19 et seq.

**Special Days Act**
S.C. Code Ann. 1976, § 53-3-10 et seq.

**Special Development District Enabling Act**
R.I. Gen. Laws 1956, 45-24.4-1 et seq.

**Special Disability Fund Act (Workmen's Compensation)**
Fla. Stat. Ann., 440.49

**Special Disabled Veterans Employment Act**
Okla. Stat. Ann., Title 72, § 401 et seq.

**Special District Accountability Act**
See also Uniform Special District Accountability Act
Fla. Stat. Ann., 189.401 et seq.

**Special District Act**
Colo. Rev. Stat. 32-1-101 et seq.

**Special District Consolidation Assistance Act**
Cal. Government Code § 60350 et seq.

**Special District Control Law**
Colo. Rev. Stat., 32-1-201 et seq.
Nev. Rev. Stat. 1979 Reprint, 308.010 et seq.

**Special District Dissolution Act**
Ida. Code 1947, 63-4101 et seq.

**Special District Elections Act**
Wyo. Stat. 1977, § 22-29-101 et seq.

**Special District Procedures Act**
N.M. Stat. Ann., 4-53-1 et seq.

**Special Districts Disclosure Act**
Fla. Stat. Ann., 189.416 et seq.

**Special Districts Fiscal Procedures Act**
Utah Code Ann. 1953, 17A-1-401 et seq.

**Special Drawing Rights Act**
June 19, 1968, P.L. 90-349, 82 Stat. 188, 12 U.S. Code §§ 412, 415, 417, 467; 22 U.S. Code §§ 286n to 286r
Dec. 30, 1970, P.L. 91-599, 84 Stat. 1657, 22 U.S. Code § 286q
Nov. 30, 1983, P.L. 98-181, 22 U.S. Code § 286q

**Special Drug Prosecutor Act**
Ga. Laws 1998, S.B. 523

**Special Education Act**
Neb. Rev. Stat. 1943, 79-3301 et seq.

**Special Education Act (Preschool)**
Ala. Code 1975, § 16-39A-1 et seq.

**Special Education for Exceptional Children Act**
Kan. Stat. Ann., 72-961 et seq.

**Special Education Program Act**
P.R. Laws Ann. 1954, Title 18, § 1331 et seq.

**Special Education Reform Act (Poochigian and Davis)**
Cal. Statutes 1997, Ch. 854

**Special Education Services Act**
Cal. Education Code 1976, § 56030 et seq.

**Special Equipment Registration and License Fee Exemption Act**
Cal. Vehicle Code 1959, § 4010

**Special Farm Drainage Act**
Ill. Rev. Stat. 1953, Ch. 42, § 134 et seq.

**Special Foreign Assistance Act of 1971**
Jan. 5, 1971, P.L. 91-652, 84 Stat. 1942, 22 U.S. Code §§ 2242, 2261, 2302 nt., 2411
Feb. 7, 1972, P.L. 92-226, 86 Stat. 35, 22 U.S. Code § 2411 nt.

**Special Foreign Assistance Act of 1986**
Oct. 24, 1986, P.L. 99-529, 22 U.S. Code § 2151 nt.

**Special Franchise Tax Act**
N.Y. Real Property Tax Law (Consol. Laws Ch. 50A) § 102, Subd. 17
N.Y. Tax Law (Consol. Laws, Ch. 60), §§ 2 Subd. 6, 44 et seq.

**Special Fuel and Gasoline Excise Tax Act**
W. Va. Code 1966, § 11-14-1 et seq.

**Special Fuel and Motor Fuel Tax Act**
Va. Code 1950, § 58.1-2100 et seq.

**Special Fuel and Motor Fuel Tax Law**
Iowa Code Ann., 452A.1 et seq.

**Special Fuel and Motor Fuel Use Tax Act**
Fla. Stat. Ann., 207.001 et seq.

**Special Fuel and Motor Tax Act**
Utah Code Ann. 1953, 59-13-101 et seq.

**Special Fuel Excise Act**
Mass. Gen. Laws Ann., 64E:1 et seq.

**Special Fuel Tax Act**
Fla. Stat. Ann., 206.85 et seq.
Ida. Code 1947, 49-1228 et seq.
Ind. Code Ann., 6-6-2.1-101 et seq.
Iowa Code Ann., 324.31 et seq.
Kan. Stat. Ann., 79-3474 et seq.
Ky. Rev. Stat. 1971, 138.210 et seq.
La. Rev. Stat. Ann., 47:801 et seq.
Mass. Gen. Laws Ann., 64E:1 et seq.
Me. Rev. Stat. Ann. 1964, Title 36, § 3201 et seq.
Mont. Code Ann. 1991, 15-70-301 et seq.
N.C. Gen. Stat. 1943, § 105-449.1 et seq.
N.D. Cent. Code, 57-43.2-01
Neb. Rev. Stat. 1943, 66-601 et seq.
Nev. Rev. Stat. 1979 Reprint, 366.010 et seq.
N.M. Stat. Ann., 7-16-1 et seq.
Okla. Stat. Ann., Title 68, § 701 et seq.
Tex. Taxation-General 1959, Art. 10.01 et seq.
Va. Code 1950, § 58.1-2100 et seq.
Wash. Rev. Code Ann., 82.38.010 et seq.

**Special Fuels Supplier Tax Act**
N.M. Stat. Ann., 7-16A-1 et seq.

**Special Fund Abolition Law**
Cal. Government Code § 16350

**Special Fund Act (Workmen's Compensation)**
Minn. Stat. Ann., 176.131

**Special Guardian Act (Minors)**
N.J. Stat. Ann., 3B:12-19 et seq.

**Special Hospital District Act**
N.M. Stat. Ann., 4-48A-1 et seq.

**Special Identification-Registration-Parking Regulations for Physically Disabled Persons Act**
Ark. Stat. 1947, 75-266.19 et seq.

**Special Improvement District Act**
Utah Code Ann. 1953, 17A-2-301 et seq.

**Special Improvement Districts Act**
Colo. Rev. Stat., 31-25-501 et seq.

**Special Incinerator Ash Disposal Act**
Wash. Rev. Code Ann., 70.138.010 et seq.

**Special Indemnity Fund Act (Workmen's Compensation)**
Okla. Stat. Ann., Title 85, § 171 et seq.

**Special Inquiry Judge Act**
Wash. Rev. Code Ann., 10.29.010 et seq.

**Special International Security Assistance Act of 1979**
July 20, 1979, P.L. 96-35, 22 U.S. Code §§ 2349 to 2349b, 3401, 3401 nt., 3402 et seq.

**Special Investigations Bureau of the Department of Justice Act**
P.R. Laws Ann. 1954, Title 3, § 138 et seq.

**Special Issue Act**
Tex. Rules of Civil Procedure as am. 1984, Rules 277, 279

**Special Judges Act**
Ky. Rev. Stat. 1971, 26A.020

**Special Jury Act**
N.Y. Judiciary Law (Consol. Laws Ch. 30) § 749aa

**Special Law Enforcement Officer Act**
Ky. Rev. Stat. 1971, 61.900 et seq.
N.J. Stat. Ann., 40A:14-146.8 et seq.

**Special Laws Act**
Conn. Gen. Stat. Ann., §§ 2-14, 2-58

**Special Laws Prohibition Act (Territories)**
July 30, 1886, Ch. 818, 24 Stat. 170, 48 U.S. Code §§ 1471 to 1473, 1475, 1478, 1479

**Special Legal Proceedings Act**
P.R. Laws Ann. 1954, Title 32, § 2241 et seq.

**Special Local Finance and Budget Act of the City of Yonkers**
N.Y. Laws 1976, Ch. 488

**Special Master Act (Condemnation)**
Ga. Code Ann., 22-2-100 et seq.

**Special Medical Needs Act**
N.M. Stat. Ann., 27-4-1 et seq.

**Special Method Referendum Act**
Ala. Code 1975, § 28-2-20 et seq.

**Special Military Wills and Powers of Attorney Act**
P.R. Laws Ann. 1954, Title 25, § 2901 et seq.

**Special Motor Fuels Use Tax Law**
Ark. Code Ann. 1987, 26-56-101 et seq.
Mo. Rev. Stat., 142.362 et seq.

**Special Municipal Aid Act**
N.J. Stat. Ann., 52:27D-118.24 et seq.
N.Y. Laws 1981, Ch. 1019
N.Y. Laws 1982, Ch. 431

**Special Municipal Gross Receipts Tax Act**
N.M. Stat. Ann., 7-19A-1 et seq.

**Special Needs Adoption Tax Credit Act**
Mo. Rev. Stat. 135.325 et seq.

**Special Needs Housing Act**
N.Y. Laws 1988, Ch. 261

**Special Needs Housing Municipal Assistance Act**
N.Y. Laws 1982, Ch. 338

**Special Needs Prison Program**
Miss. Laws 1994, Ch. 450

**Special Obligation Bonds for Refunding Act**
S.C. Code Ann. 1976, § 11-15-600 et seq.

**Special Peace Officers Act**
Alaska Comp. Laws Ann. 1949, § 45-1-2

**Special Police Act (Westchester County)**
N.Y. Village Law 1909 Consol. Laws Ch. 64) § 199j et seq.

**Special Practice Act (District Courts)**
Tex. Rev. Civ. Stat., Art. 2092
Tex. Rules of Civil Procedure as Am. 1984, Rule 330

**Special Primary Election Law**
N.M. Laws 1982, Third Special Session, Ch. 3

**Special Projects District Act**
N.C. Laws 1990, Ch. 999

**Special Provisions for Village Police Departments Law**
N.Y. Laws 1972, Ch. 891, § 2
N.Y. Unconsolidated Laws, § 5711 et seq.

**Special Road and Bridge District No. 5 of Palm Beach County Act**
Fla. Special Laws 1935, Ch. 17640

**Special Road District Act**
Mo. Rev. Stat., 233.010 et seq.

**Special Road Maintenance District Act**
Cal. Streets and Highways Code § 1550.1 et seq.

**Special School Taxes Act (Limitations)**
Ind. Burns' 1933, 28-1101 et seq.

**Special School Teachers' Sick Leave Bank Act**
Tenn. Code Ann., 49-50-1101 et seq.

**Special Senses and Communication Disorders Act**
Tex. Health and Safety Code, § 36.001 et seq.

**Special Service Area Tax Act**
Ill. Comp. Stat. 1992, Ch. 35, § 235/1 et seq.
Ill. Rev. Stat. 1991, Ch. 120, § 1300 et seq.

**Special Service Districts Act**
N.D. Cent. Code, 11-28.1-01 et seq.
Utah Code Ann. 1953, 11-23-1 et seq.

**Special Service Force Memorial Monument Permanent Trust Act (First)**
Mont. Code Ann., 35-21-901 to 35-21-903

**Special Service Paroles Law**
Cal. Penal Code § 3100 et seq.

**Special Services Tax Districts Act (De Kalb County)**
Ga. Laws 1982, p. 4396

**Special Session Bond Act**
N.C. Public Laws 1938, Extra Session, Ch. 1

**Special Session Corrections and Secure Facilities Capital Budget Project Itemization Act of 1995**
Pa. 1995 Pamph. Laws, Special Session, Nos. 1, 19

**Special Session Somerset Hospital Conversion and Quehanna Boot Camp Project Itemization Act of 1995**
Pa. 1995 Pamph. Laws, Special Session, Nos. 1, 34

**Special Sessions Act**
Ill. Rev. Stat. 1991, Ch. 63, § 190 et seq.

**Special Studies Zones Act**
Cal. Public Resources Code § 2621 et seq.

**Special Tax on Petroleum Products Law**
Tenn. Code Ann., 67-3-901 et seq.

**Special Verdict Act**
Ohio Civ. Rule, 48 et seq.
Wis. Stat. Ann., 805.12

**Special Voting Rights Act**
S.D. Codified Laws 1967, Superseded Vol., 12-19A-1 et seq.

**Special Zoning District Act**
N.M. Stat. Ann., 3-21-15 et seq.

**Specialist Licensing Act (Hearing Instrument)**
Utah Code Ann. 1953, 58-46a-102 et seq.

**Specialized Living Centers Act**
Ill. Rev. Stat. 1991, Ch. 91 1/2, § 601 et seq.

**Specialized Manufacturing Production Property Valuation Act**
W. Va. Code 1966, § 11-6E-1 et seq.

**Specialized Motor Carrier Act**
Tex. Rev. Civ. Stat., Art. 911b, § 5a

**Specie Payment Resumption Act**
Jan. 14, 1875, Ch. 15, 18 Stat. 296, 31 U.S. Code §§ 332, 402, 417

**Species Act (Endangered)**
S.C. Code Ann. 1976, § 50-15-10 et seq.

**Species Management Act (Nongame)**
N.H. Rev. Stat. 1955, 212-B:1 et seq.

**Specific Contract Act (Payment in Money)**
Cal. Code of Civil Procedure § 667

**Specific Performance Act**
Mont. Code Ann., 27-1-411 et seq.

**Specific Skills Training Grant Program (Additional Employer)**
N.Y. Education Law 1947 (Consol. Laws Ch. 16) § 3032

**Specified Disease and Medicare Supplement Act**
Md. Ann. Code 1957, Art. 48A, §§ 468B to 468H

**Specified Disease Insurance Act**
Wash. Rev. Code Ann., 48.70.010 et seq.

**Specious Cash Sales Act**
N.Y. General Business Law (Consol. Laws Ch. 20) § 252 et seq.

**Spectator Safety Act (Baseball)**
Colo. Rev. Stat., 13-21-120

**Speculative Securities Act**
Kan. Stat. Ann., 17-1252 et seq.

**Speech-Language Pathologists, Audiologists, and Hearing Aid Dealers Act**
Md. Ann. Code 1974, Art. HO, § 2-101 et seq.

**Speech Language Pathology, Audiology and Hearing Aid Dispensing Practices Act**
N.M. Stat. Ann., 61-14B-1 to 61-14B-25

**Speech Pathologists and Audiologists Licensure Act**
Ark. Code Ann. 1987, 17-97-101 et seq.
Cal. Business and Professions Code § 2530 et seq.
Fla. Stat. Ann., 468.1105 et seq.
Ga. Code Ann., 43-44-1 et seq.
Ill. Rev. Stat. 1991, Ch. 111, § 7901 et seq.
Md. Ann. Code 1974, Art. HO, § 20-101 et seq., NO, § 19-101 et seq.
Me. Rev. Stat. Ann. 1964, Title 32, § 6001 et seq.
Mo. Rev. Stat., 345.010 et seq.
N.M. Stat. Ann., 61-14B-1 et seq.
Okla. Stat. Ann., Title 59, § 1601 et seq.
Pa. Purdon's Stat., Title 63, § 1701
P.R. Laws Ann. 1954, Title 20, § 3101 et seq.
S.C. Code Ann. 1976, § 40-67-10 et seq.
Tenn. Code Ann., 63-17-101 et seq.
Utah Code Ann. 1953, 58-41-1 et seq.
Wyo. Stat. Ann., § 33-33-101 et seq.

**Speed Act (Motor Vehicle)**
Ga. Offical Code Ann., 40-6-180 et seq.
Iowa Code Ann., 321-285 et seq.

**Speed Act (Railroad)**
Miss. Code Ann. 1972, § 77-9-237

**Speed and Minimum Tire Width Law**
Ky. Rev. Stat. 1971, Superseded Vol., 84.160

**Speed Exemption Act (Emergency Vehicles)**
N.C. Gen. Stat. 1943, § 20-145

**Speed Limit Act**
Ala. Code 1975, § 32-5A-171
Ariz. Rev. Stat. Ann., § 28-701 et seq.
Cal. Vehicle Code 1959, §§ 22348 et seq., 22350 et seq.
Ga. Code Ann., 40-6-180 et seq.
Ind. Code Ann., 9-4-1-57 et seq.
Iowa Code Ann., 321.285 et seq.
La. Rev. Stat. Ann., 32:61 et seq.
Me. Rev. Stat. Ann. 1964, Title 29, § 1251 et seq.
Mich. Comp. Laws Ann., 257.627 et seq.
Miss. Code Ann. 1972, §§ 63-3-501 et seq., 63-7-75
Mo. Rev. Stat., 304.010 et seq.
Mont. Code Ann. 1991, 61-8-303 et seq.
N.C. Gen. Stat. 1943, § 20-141
Neb. Rev. Stat. 1943, 39-662 et seq.
N.H. Rev. Stat. 1955, 265:60
N.J. Stat. Ann., 39:4-95 et seq.
N.Y. Vehicle and Traffic Law 1959 (Consol. Laws Ch. 71) § 1180
Ohio Rev. Code 1953, 4511.21 et seq.
*Continued*

Okla. Stat. Ann., Title 47, § 11-801 et seq.
R.I. Gen. Laws 1956, 31-14-1 et seq.
S.C. Code Ann. 1976, § 56-5-1510 et seq.
Tex. Rev. Civ. Stat., Art. §§ 166 to 172, 6701d-8
Vt. Stat. Ann., Title 23, § 1081 et seq.
Wash. Rev. Code Ann., 46.61.400 et seq.

**Speed Trap Act (Motor Vehicles)**
Cal. Vehicle Code 1959, §§ 40801 to 40805
Ore. Rev. Stat. 1953, 483.112
Wash. Rev. Code Ann., 46.61.470

**Speeder Patrol Act**
Wash. Rev. Code 1951, 76.04.260

**Speeding Act (Motor Vehicle)**
Miss. Code Ann. 1972, §§ 63-3-501 et seq., 63-7-75

**Speedway Law**
N.Y. Laws 1893, Ch. 102

**Speedy Trial Act**
Cal. Government Code § 68600 et seq.
Ga. Code Ann., 17-7-170
Ill. Rev. Stat. 1991, Ch. 38, § 103-5
Mass. Gen. Laws Ann., 231:59A et seq.
Me. Rev. Stat. Ann. 1964, Title 15, § 1201
Mich. Comp. Laws Ann., 767.38, 768.1
N.C. Gen. Stat. 1943, § 15-10
S.C. Code Ann. 1976, § 17-23-90

**Speedy Trial Act Amendments Act of 1979**
Aug. 2, 1979, P.L. 96-43, 18 U.S. Code §§ 3161, 3161 nt., 3164 to 3168, 3170, 3174

**Speedy Trial Act of 1974**
Jan. 3, 1975, P.L. 93-619, 18 U.S. Code §§ 3152 to 3156, 3161 to 3174; 28 U.S. Code § 604

**Speedy Trial Victim's Rights Act**
Ga. Code Ann., 17-7-173

**Speicher Act**
Fla. Stat. Ann., 295.0195

**Spence Act (Savings and Loan Holding Companies)**
Sept. 23, 1959, P.L. 86-374, 73 Stat. 691, 12 U.S. Code § 1730a
Sept. 13, 1960, P.L. 86-746, 74 Stat. 883, 12 U.S. Code § 1730a
Oct. 16, 1966, P.L. 89-695, 80 Stat. 1046, 12 U.S. Code § 1730a
Feb. 14, 1968, P.L. 90-255, 82 Stat. 5, 12 U.S. Code § 1730a

**Spencer Stream Improvements Loan Act**
Mass. Acts 1957, Ch. 440

**Spending Limitation Act**
N.Y. State Finance Law 1940 (Consol. Laws Ch. 56) § 30 et seq.
S.C. Code Ann. 1976, § 11-11-410 et seq.
S.C. Constitution Article 10, §§ 7, 13 et seq.

**Spending Limitation Act (Westchester County)**
N.Y. Tax Law (Consol. Laws Ch. 60) § 1262b nt.

**Spending Philosphy Act (State Employees Compensation)**
Fla. Stat. 1967, 282.051, Subsec. 6

**Spending Reduction Act of 1984**
July 18, 1984, P.L. 98-369, 98 Stat. 1057

**Spendthrift Act (Guardian and Ward)**
Haw. Rev. Stat. Ann., § 551-30 et seq.
Ore. Rev. Stat. 1953, 126.006 et seq.

**Spendthrift Trust Act**
Del. Code of 1974, Title 12, § 3536
N.C. Gen. Stat. 1943, § 36A-115
Nev. Rev. Stat. 1979 Reprint, 166.010 et seq.
Okla. Stat. Ann., Title 60, § 175.25
Pa. Cons. Stat., Title 23 § 4301 et seq.

**Speno-Brennan Act (Public Moneys; Transportation)**
N.Y. Education Law 1947 (Consol. Laws Ch. 16) § 3635

**Spent Nuclear Fuel Act**
Ill. Rev. Stat. 1991, Ch. 111 1/2, § 230.20 et seq.

**Spiegel Act (Rent Relief)**
N.Y. Social Services Law (Consol. Laws Ch. 55) § 143b

**Spill Compensation and Control Act**
N.J. Stat. Ann., 58:10-23.11 et seq.

**Spill Containment and Abatement Act (Hazardous Substances, Highway)**
Cal. Vehicle Code 1959, § 2450 et seq.

**Spill Prevention and Response Act (Oil)**
La. Rev. Stat. Ann., 30:2451 et seq.
Tex. Natural Resources Code, § 40.001 et seq.

**Spinal Cord and Head Injury Act**
Ill. Rev. Stat. 1991, Ch. 111 1/2, § 7850 et seq.

**Spinners' Lien Act**
Mass. Gen. Laws Ann., 255:31A

**Spiritous and Vinous Liquor Tax Law**
Pa. Purdon's Stat., Title 47, § 745 et seq.

**Spirits and Alcoholic Beverages Act**
P.R. Laws Ann. 1954, Title 13, § 6001 et seq.

**Spirituous and Vinous Liquor Tax Law**
Pa. Purdon's Stat., Title 47, § 745 et seq.

**Spirituous Liquor Act**
See Alcoholic Beverages Act

**Spite Fence Act**
Cal. Civil Code § 841.4
Mass. Gen. Laws Ann., 49:21 et seq.
N.H. Rev. Stat. 1955, 476:1 et seq.
R.I. Gen. Laws 1956, 34-10-20
Vt. Stat. Ann., Title 24, § 3817

**Splash Guard Act**
Ill. Rev. Stat. 1991, Ch. 95 1/2, § 12-710

**Split-Listing Act (Real Estate Assessment)**
Ohio Rev. Code 1953, 5713.04

**Split Sentence Act**
Ala. Code 1975, § 14-3-38

**Split Tax Bills Act**
Ohio Rev. Code 1953, 319.20

**Split Verdict Act**
Pa. Cons. Stat., Title 18, § 1102, 2502

**Spoils of War Act of 1994**
April 30, 1994, P.L. 103-236, 50 U.S. Code §§ 2201 nt., 2201 et seq.

**Sponge Act**
Aug. 15, 1914, Ch. 253, 38 Stat. 692, 16 U.S. Code §§ 781 to 785

**Spooner Act (Isthmian Canal)**
June 28, 1902, Ch. 1302, 32 Stat. 481, 31 U.S. Code § 744

**Sportfishing and Boating Safety Act of 1998**
June 9, 1998, P.L. 105-178, Title VII, Subtitle D, 16 U.S. Code § 777 nt.

**Sports Agents Act**
Md. Ann. Code 1974, Art. BR, § 4-426 et seq.

**Sports Agents Regulation Act**
Va. Code 1950, § 18.2-501.1 et seq.

**Sports and Community Venue Districts Act**
Tex. Local Government Code, § 335.001 et seq.

**Sports and Community Venues Act**
Tex. Local Government Code, § 334.001 et seq.

**Sports and Exposition Authority Act**
N.J. Stat. Ann., 5:10-1 et seq.

**Sports and Exposition Authority Refunding Bond Guaranty Act**
N.J. Laws 1978, Ch. 48
P.R. Laws Ann. 1954, Title 3, § 442 et seq.

**Sports Authorities Act**
Tenn. Code Ann., 7-67-101 et seq.

**Sports Authorities Funding Act**
Tenn. Code Ann., 67-6-103, 67-6-601, 67-6-712

**Sports Authority Act**
N.Y. Public Authorities Law (Consol. Laws Ch. 43A) § 2460 et seq
Utah Code Ann. 1953, Miscellaneous Superseded Code Provisions, 62-1-1 et seq.
Utah Code Ann. 1953, 9-1-301 et seq.

**Sports Authority Act (New York City)**
N.Y. Public Authorities Law (Consol. Laws Ch. 43A) § 2500 et seq.

**Sports Bribery Act**
Wash. Rev. Code Ann., 67.24.010 et seq.

**Sports Bribery Points Shaving Act**
N.Y. Penal Law 1965 (Consol. Laws Ch. 40) § 180.35 et seq.

**Sports Center Authority Act (Broome County)**
N.Y. Public Authorities Law (Consol. Laws, Ch. 43A) § 2050 et seq.

**Sports Complex Authority Act**
Md. Ann. Code 1957, Art. 41, § 141 et seq.

**Sports Facilities Authority Act**
Ill. Rev. Stat. 1991, Ch. 85, § 6001 et seq.

**Sports Facility Authority Act (Oneida County)**
N.Y. Public Authorities Law (Consol. Laws Ch. 43A) § 2052a et seq.

**Sports Facility, Convention, Meeting and Tourism Act (State and Local Government)**
Mo. Rev. Stat. 1978, 70.840 et seq.

**Sports Fishing Act**
Mich. Comp. Laws Ann., 301.1 et seq.

**Sports Fraud Act**
Wash. Rev. Code Ann., 67.24.010

**Sports Hall of Fame Act**
Ga. Code Ann., 50-12-60 et seq.

**Sports Hall of Fame Authority Act**
Ga. Code Ann., 12-3-561 et seq.

**Sports Law (Sunday Amateur)**
Me. Rev. Stat. Ann. 1964, Title 17, § 3205

**Sports Stadium Act**
Ill. Rev. Stat. 1991, Ch. 85, § 6031 et seq.

**Sports Volunteer Immunity Act**
Ill. Rev. Stat. 1991, Ch. 70, §§ 700, 701

**Sportsmen Fishing Act**
Mich. Comp. Laws Ann., 301.1 et seq.

**Spot Pond Drainage and Flood Control Act**
Mass. Acts 1955, Ch. 574

**Spotter Reports Law**
Cal. Public Utilities Code § 8251, 8252

**Spousal Pension Rights Act**
Neb. Rev. Stat. 1943, 42-1101 to 42-1113

**Spouse or Child Abandonment Act**
Ga. Code Ann., 19-10-1, 19-10-2

**Spouse's Right of Election Act (Testamentary)**
N.Y. Estates, Powers, and Trusts Law (Consol. Laws Ch. 17B) § 5-1.1

**Sprayer's and Duster's Lien Law**
Wash. Rev. Code Ann., 60.14.010 et seq.

**Spring and Seepage Act**
Colo. Rev. Stat., 37-82-102

**Spring Hill Adequate Facilities Tax Act**
Tenn. Private Acts 1988, Ch. 173

**Spring Hill Construction Impact Fee Act**
Tenn. Private Act 1988, Ch. 176

**Spring Mountains National Recreation Area Act**
Aug. 4, 1993, P.L. 103-63, 16 U.S. Code §§ 460hhh nt., 460hhh et seq.

**Spring Run Scenic River Act (Le Tort)**
Pa. Purdon's Stat., Title 32, § 820.101 et seq.

**Spring Valley Parking Authority Act**
N.Y. Public Authorities Law (Consol. Laws Ch. 43A) § 1599aa et seq.

**Springbrook Golf Course Commission Act**
Ga. Laws 1999, H.B. 1021

**Springer Act**
July 30, 1886, Ch. 818, 24 Stat. 170, 48 U.S. Code §§ 1471 to 1473, 1475, 1478, 1479

**Sprinkler Systems for Fire Protection Act**
S.C. Code Ann. 1976, § 23-45-10 et seq.

**Sproul Act (State Highways)**
Pa. 1911 Pamph. Laws 468

**Spruce Budworm Management Act**
Me. Rev. Stat. 1964, Title 12, § 8401 et seq.

**Spruce Knob-Seneca Rocks National Recreation Area Act**
Sept. 28, 1965, P.L. 89-207, 79 Stat. 843, 16 U.S. Code §§ 460p to 460p-5

**Spruce Pond Brook of Franklin Drainage Loan Act**
Mass. Acts 1958, Ch. 387

**St. Clair County Bingo Act**
Ala. Acts 1991, p. 1378, No. 710

**St. Clair Flats Leasing Act**
Mich. Comp. Laws Ann., 322.401 et seq.

**St. Clair Land Cession Act**
Ill. Rev. Stat. 1991, Ch. 1, §§ 3800, 3801

**St. Cloud Metropolitan Transit Commission Act**
Minn. Stat. Ann., 458A.01 et seq.

**St. Elizabeth's Hospital Mental Patient Voluntary Admissions Act**
D.C. Code 1961, § 32-412 et seq.

**St. Landry Parish Industrial District Act**
La. Acts 1986, No. 693

**St. Landry Parish Solid Waste Disposal Act**
La. Acts 1980, No. 289

**St. Laudry Parish Industrial District Act of 1986**
La. Rev. Stat. Ann., 33:130.31

**St. Lawrence County Solid Waste Disposal Authority Act**
N.Y. Public Authorities Law (Consol. Laws Ch. 43A), § 2048a et seq.

**St. Louis County Act (Annexation)**
Mo. Rev. Stat., 71.860 et seq.

**St. Louis Metropolitan Area Airport Authority Act**
Ill. Rev. Stat. 1983, Ch. 15 1/2, § 301 et seq.

**St. Louis Metropolitan Police Act**
Mo. Rev. Stat., 84.010 et seq.

**St. Louis-Missouri Metropolitan Airport Authority Act**
Mo. Rev. Stat. 1978, 305.500 et seq.

**St. Louis Police Retirement or Pension System Act**
Mo. Rev. Stat., 86.010 et seq.

**St. Louis Public School Retirement System Act**
Mo. Rev. Stat., 169.410 et seq.

**St. Lucie County and Municipality Tax Collection Act**
Fla. Laws 1963, Ch. 63-1858

**St. Lucie County Beach Preservation Act**
Fla. Special Laws 1961, Ch. 61-2755

**St. Lucie County Environmental Control Act**
Fla. Special Laws 1983, Ch. 83-511

**St. Lucie County Erosion District Act**
Fla. Special Laws 1967, Ch. 67-2001

**St. Lucie County Expressway Authority Act**
Fla. Stat. Ann., 348.9401 et seq.

**St. Lucie County Water District Act**
Fla. Special Laws 1984, Ch. 84-522

**St. Mary Parish Mass Transit Authority Act**
La. Rev. Stat. Ann., 48:1631 et seq.

**St. Mary's City Commission Act (Historic)**
Md. Ann. Code 1974, Art. ED, § 24-501 et seq.

**St. Mary's County Open Meetings Law**
Md. Ann. Code 1957, Art. 24, § 4-201 et seq.

**St. Paul Municipal Court Act**
Minn. Stat. Ann., 488A.18 et seq.

**St. Paul People Mover Act**
Minn. Stat. 1980, 458B.01 et seq.

**St. Petersburg Civil Service Act**
Fla. Special Laws 1937, Ch. 18890

**St. Petersburg Downtown Improvement Authority Act**
Fla. Special Laws 1974, Ch. 74-603

**St. Petersburg Expressway Authority Law**
Fla. Stat. 1965, 348.011 et seq.

**St. Petersburg Urban Renewal Law**
Fla. Special Laws 1961, Ch. 61-2781
Fla. Special Laws 1965, Ch. 65-2207

**Stabilization Act (Banks)**
See Bank Stabilization Act

**Stabilization Act (Citrus)**
Fla. Stat. Ann., 601.154

**Stabilization Act (Dairy Farm)**
Me. Rev. Stat. Ann. 1964, Title 36, § 4541 et seq.

**Stabilization Act of 1942**
Oct. 2, 1942, Ch. 578, 56 Stat. 765, 16 U.S. Code §§ 713a-8, 713a-8 nt.
June 30, 1944, Ch. 325, 58 Stat. 642
Oct. 3, 1944, Ch. 479, 58 Stat. 784
June 30, 1945, Ch. 214, 59 Stat. 306
July 25, 1946, Ch. 671, 60 Stat. 664, 677

**Stabilization and Reintegration Act**
N.J. Stat. Ann., 52:17B-181 et seq.

**Stabilization Extension Act of 1944**
June 30, 1944, Ch. 325, 58 Stat. 632

**Stabilization Fund-Dollar Devaluation Act**
See Gold Reserve Act of 1934

**Stabilization of Commercial Rents Law**
N.Y. Laws 1945, Ch. 3

**Stabilization of Fluid Milk and Cream Act**
Cal. Food and Agricultural Code 1967, §§ 61801 et seq., 62730 et seq.

**Stabilization Reserve Corporation Act (New York City)**
N.Y. Public Authorities Law (Consol. Laws Ch. 43A) § 2530 et seq.

**Stable and Reliable Source of Revenues for WMATA Act**
D.C. Code Ann., §§ 1-2466, 1-2467

**Stacey, Bennett, and Randall Shareholder Equity Act**
Mich. Comp. Laws Ann., 450.1790 et seq.

**Stadium Act**
Ark. Code Ann. 1987, 22-3-1001 et seq.
D.C. Code Ann., § 2-321 et seq.
Ill. Rev. Stat. 1991, Ch. 85, § 6031 et seq.
N.C. Gen. Stat. 1943, § 143-236.2 et seq.

**Stadium Authority Act**
Md. Ann. Code 1974, Art. FI, § 13-701 et seq.

**Stadium Authority Act (Cobb County)**
Ga. Laws 1984, p. 4727

**Stadium Revenue Bond Act**
N.C. Laws 1963, Ch. 686

**Staff Assistants Act (General Assembly)**
Ill. Rev. Stat. 1991, Ch. 63, § 131.01 et seq.

**Staff Attorney and Judicial Law Clerk Recruitment Act**
Tex. Government Code, §§ 72.041, 72.042

**Staff Development Buy-Out Program**
Cal. Education Code 1976, § 44579 et seq.

**Staff Performance Incentive Act (Certificated)**
Cal. Education Code 1976, § 44650 et seq.

**Stage Coach Corporations Law**
N.Y. Transportation Corporation Law Consol. Laws Ch. 63) § 60 et seq.

**Stagecoach Reservoir Project Act of 1994**
Oct. 31, 1994, P.L. 103-434, 108 Stat. 4547

**Staggering Act**
N.J. Laws 1935, Ch. 13
N.J. Laws 1936, Ch. 218

**Staggers Rail Act of 1980**
Oct. 14, 1980, P.L. 96-448, 49 U.S. Code § 10101
Dec. 21, 1982, P.L. 97-375, 49 U.S. Code § 1654a

**STAKE Act (Stop Tobacco Access to Kids Enforcement Act)**
Cal. Business and Professions Code § 22950 et seq.

**Stale Check Act**
Vt. Acts 1923, No. 50

**Stale Uses and Reversions Act**
Iowa Code Ann., 614.24

**Stalking Act**
Mass. Gen. Laws Ann., 265:43
Pa. Cons. Stat., Title 18, § 2709
Wash. Rev. Code Ann., 9A.46.110

**Stalking and Harassment Act**
N.M. Stat. Ann., 30-3A-1 et seq.

**Stallion and Jack Pedigree Act**
Ill. Rev. Stat. 1991, Ch. 8, §§ 32.9, 33
Kan. Stat. Ann., 47-107 et seq.

**Stallion and Jack Service Lien Act**
Ill. Rev. Stat. 1991, Ch. 8, § 50.9 et seq.

**Stallion Registration Act**
Ill. Rev. Stat. 1977, Ch. 8, § 39 et seq.
Ind. Code Ann., 35-1-88-1
Ore. Code 1991, §§ 20-1401 to 20-1422

**Stamp Act (Documentary)**
Neb. Rev. Stat. 1943, 76-901 et seq.

**Stamp Act (Mineral Documentary)**
Miss. Code Ann. 1972, § 27-31-71 et seq.

**Stamp Act (Trading)**
See Trading Stamp Act

**Stamp Act (Waterfowl)**
N.J. Stat. Ann., 23:3-75 et seq.

**Stamp Note Act**
Iowa Laws 1933 (45th G. A.), Ch. 103

**Stamp Out Breast Cancer Act**
Aug. 13, 1997, P.L. 105-41, 39 U.S. Code § 101 nt.

**Stamp Payments Act**
July 17, 1862, Ch. 196, 12 Stat. 592

**Stamp Tax Act (Cigarettes)**
Okla. Stat. Ann., Title 68, § 301 et seq.
Tex. Tax Code, § 154.001 et seq.

**Stamp Tax Act (Documents)**
Fla. Stat. Ann., 201.01 et seq.
Haw. Session Laws 1876, Ch. 55
Mass. Gen. Laws Ann., 64D:1 et seq.
Mich. Comp. Laws Ann., 207.501 et seq.
Pa. 1935 Pamph. Laws 203, No. 90
S.C. Code Ann. 1976, § 12-21-310 et seq.

**Stamp Tax Act (Illegal Drug)**
Ida. Code 1947, 63-4201 et seq.

**Stamp Tax Act (Intangibles)**
Ind. Code Ann., 6-5-1-1 et seq.

**Stamp Tax Act (Tobacco)**
Okla. Stat. Ann., Title 68, § 401 et seq.

**Stancel Act (Highways)**
Miss. Code Ann. 1972, § 65-1-3 et seq.

**Standard Apple Act**
Cal. Food and Agricultural Code 1967, §§ 43801 et seq., 75501
Kan. Laws 1933, Ch. 1

**Standard Appropriation Act**
Ida. Code 1947, 67-3531

**Standard Appropriations Act**
Ida. Code 1947, 67-3601 et seq.

**Standard Auto Accident Reparations Act**
Colo. Rev. Stat., 10-4-701 et seq.

**Standard Barrel Act (Apple Barrels)**
Aug. 3, 1912, Ch. 273, 37 Stat. 250, 15 U.S. Code §§ 231 to 233; 21 U.S. Code §§ 20 to 23

**Standard Barrel Act (Fruits, Vegetables, etc.)**
March 4, 1915, Ch. 158, 38 Stat. 1186, 15 U.S. Code §§ 234 to 236

**Standard Barrel Act (Lime Barrels)**
Aug. 23, 1916, Ch. 396, 39 Stat. 530, 15 U.S. Code §§ 237 to 242

**Standard-Based Mathematics Staff Development Act**
Cal. Education Code 1976, § 44695 et seq.

**Standard Baskets Act**
Aug. 31, 1916, Ch. 426, 39 Stat. 673, 15 U.S. Code §§ 251 to 256

**Standard Building Code**
N.J. Stat. Ann., 34:5-166

**Standard Clearance Act (Railroads)**
Minn. Stat. Ann., 219.45 et seq.

**Standard Code for Manufactured Homes and Recreational Vehicles**
See also Uniform Standard Code for Manufactured Homes and Recreational Vehicles
Neb. Rev. Stat. 1943, 71-4601 et seq.
Okla. Stat. Ann., Title 63, § 2451 et seq.

**Standard Code for Mobile Home Parks**
Ala. Code 1975, 24-5-1 et seq.
Neb. Rev. Stat. 1943, 71-4621 et seq.

**Standard Fire Insurance Policy Act**
Cal. Insurance Code § 2070 et seq.
La. Rev. Stat. Ann., 22:691
Mich. Comp. Laws Ann., 500.2832
Minn. Stat. Ann., 65A.01

**Standard Gas Measurement Law**
Ark. Code Ann. 1987, 15-74-301 et seq.
La. Rev. Stat. Ann., 55:151 et seq.
Okla. Stat. Ann., Title 52, § 471 et seq.
Tex. Natural Resources Code, § 91.051 et seq.

**Standard Loaf Act**
Cal. Business and Professions Code § 19800 et seq.

**Standard Measurements Act**
Colo. Rev. Stat. 35-14-101 et seq.

**Standard Milk Bottle Act**
Mich. Comp. Laws 1948, 288.351 et seq.

**Standard Nonforfeiture Act (Insurance)**
Ala. Code 1975, § 27-15-28
Ariz. Rev. Stat. Ann., §§ 20-1231, 20-1231.01
Cal. Insurance Code § 10159.1 et seq.
Conn. Gen. Stat. Ann., § 38a-438 et seq.
D.C. Code Ann., § 35-507
Del. Code of 1974, Title 18, § 2929
Fla. Stat. Ann., 627.476
Haw. Rev. Stat. Ann., § 431-561
Ida. Code 1947, 41-1927
Ky. Rev. Stat. 1971, 304.15-300 et seq.
La. Rev. Stat. Ann., 22:168
Md. Ann. Code 1957, Art. 48A, § 414
Me. Rev. Stat. Ann. 1964, Title 24-A, § 2528 et seq.
Mich. Comp. Laws Ann., 500.4060
Minn. Stat. Ann., 61A.24
Miss. Code Ann. 1972, § 83-7-25
Mo. Rev. Stat., 376.670
Mont. Rev. Code 1947, 40-3831
N.C. Gen. Stat. 1943, § 58-55

Neb. Rev. Stat. 1943, 44-407 et seq.
Nev. Rev. Stat. 1979 Reprint, 688A.290 et seq.
N.H. Rev. Stat. 1955, 409:1 et seq.
N.J. Stat. Ann., 17B:25-19
N.M. Stat. Ann., 59A-20-31
N.Y. Insurance Law (Consol. Laws Ch. 28) § 4221
Ohio Rev. Code 1953, 3915.07
Ore. Rev. Stat., 743.204 et seq.
Pa. Purdon's Stat., Title 40, § 510.1
S.C. Code Ann. 1976, § 38-7-10 et seq.
S.D. Codified Laws 1967, 58-15-31 et seq.
Tenn. Code Ann., 56-7-401
Tex. Insurance Code, Art. 3.44a
Utah Code Ann. 1953, 31A-22-407
Va. Code 1950, § 38.2-3200 et seq.
Vt. Stat. Ann., Title 8, § 3741 et seq.
Wash. Rev. Code Ann., 48.76.010 et seq.
W. Va. Code 1966, § 33-13-30
Wyo. Stat. Ann., § 26-16-201 et seq.

**Standard Nonforfeiture and Valuation Act**

Colo. Rev. Stat. 1973, 10-7-301 et seq.
Conn. Gen. Stat. Ann., § 4b-11 et seq.

**Standard Nonforfeiture Law for Individual Deferred Annuities**

Ala. Code 1975, § 27-15-28.1
Ark. Code Ann. 1987, 23-81-201 et seq.
Colo. Rev. Stat., 10-7-501 et seq.
Ga. Code Ann., 33-28-3
Haw. Rev. Stat. Ann., § 431-564
Ida. Code 1947, 41-1927A
Iowa Code Ann., 508.38
Ky. Rev. Stat. 1971, 304.15-315
La. Rev. Stat. Ann., 22:173.1
Md. Ann. Code 1957, Art. 48A, § 408B
Me. Rev. Stat. Ann. 1964, Title 24-A, § 2541 et seq.
Mich. Comp. Laws Ann., 500.4072
Minn. Stat. Ann., 61A.245
Mont. Code Ann., 33-20-501 et seq.
N.C. Gen. Stat. 1943, § 58-58-60
Neb. Rev. Stat. 1943, 44-407.10 et seq.
N.H. Rev. Stat. 1955, 409-A:1 et seq.
N.J. Stat. Ann., 17B:25-20
Ohio Rev. Code 1953, 3915.071
Ore. Rev. Stat., 743.275 et seq.
Pa. Purdon's Stat., Title 40, § 510b
S.C. Code Ann. 1976, § 38-69-210 et seq.
S.C. Code Ann. 1976, Superseded Vols., § 38-8-10 et seq.
Tenn. Code Ann., 56-36-101 et seq.
Utah Code Ann. 1953, 31A-22-409
Vt. Stat. Ann., Title 8, § 3750
Wash. Rev. Code Ann., 48.23.410 et seq.
W. Va. Code 1966, § 33-13-30a et seq.
Wyo. Stat. Ann., § 26-16-401 et seq.

**Standard Nonforfeiture Law for Individual Deferred Annuities Act**

Md. Ann. Code 1974, Art. IN, § 16-501 et seq.
R.I. Gen. Laws 1956, 27-4.4-1 et seq.

**Standard Nonforfeiture Law for Life Insurance**

Ala. Code 1975, § 27-15-28
Alaska Stat. 1962, § 21-45-300
Ark. Code Ann. 1987, 23-81-201 et seq.
Fla. Stat. Ann., 627.476
Ill. Rev. Stat. 1991, Ch. 73, § 841.2
Iowa Code Ann., 508.37
Ky. Rev. Stat. 1971, 304.15-300 et seq.
Md. Ann. Code 1957, Art. 48A, § 414
Md. Ann. Code 1974, Art. IN, § 16-301 et seq.
Me. Rev. Stat. Ann. 1964, Title 24-A, § 2528 et seq.
Mich. Comp. Laws Ann., 500.4060
Minn. Stat. Ann., 61A.24
Mont. Code Ann., 33-20-201 et seq.
Neb. Rev. Stat. 1943, 44-407 to 44-407.09
N.H. Rev. Stat. 1955, 409:1 et seq.
Pa. Purdon's Stat., Title 40, § 510.1
R.I. Gen. Laws 1956, 27-4.3-1 et seq.
S.C. Code Ann. 1976, § 38-63-510 et seq.
Tex. Insurance Code, Art. 3.44a
Utah Code Ann. 1953, 31A-22-408
Vt. Stat. Ann., Title 8, § 3741 et seq.
Wash. Rev. Code Ann., 48.76.010 et seq.
Wyo. Stat. Ann., § 26-16-201 et seq.

**Standard Policy Act (Insurance)**

Ore. Rev. Stat., 742.001
Va. Code 1950, § 38-177 et seq.

**Standard Provisions Act (Life Insurance Policies)**
Cal. Insurance Code § 10330 et seq.
Ill. Rev. Stat. 1991, Ch. 73, § 836

**Standard Reference Data Act**
July 11, 1968, P.L. 90-396, 82 Stat. 339, 15 U.S. Code §§ 290 to 290f

**Standard State Zoning and Enabling Act**
Del. Code of 1974, Title 22, § 301 et seq.
Mont. Code Ann., 76-2-301 et seq.
N.D. Cent. Code, 40-47-01 et seq.
Tex. Rev. Civ. Stat., Arts. 1011a to 1011j

**Standard Time Act**
Minn. Stat. Ann., 645.071
Tenn. Code Ann., 4-1-401

**Standard Time Acts**
March 19, 1918, Ch. 24, 40 Stat. 450, 15 U.S. Code §§ 261 to 263
Aug. 20, 1919, Ch. 51, 41 Stat. 280
March 4, 1921, Ch. 173, 41 Stat. 1446, 15 U.S. Code § 265
March 3, 1923, Ch. 216, 42 Stat. 1434, 15 U.S. Code § 264
April 13, 1966, P.L. 89-387, 80 Stat. 107, 15 U.S. Code §§ 261 to 263

**Standard Travel Pay and Allowance Act**
Ida. Code 1947, 67-2007, 67-2008

**Standard Valuation Act (Insurance)**
Ala. Code 1975, § 27-36-7
Ariz. Rev. Stat. Ann., § 20-510
Ark. Code Ann. 1987, 23-84-101 et seq.
Cal. Insurance Code § 10489.1 et seq.
Conn. Gen. Stat. Ann., § 38a-77 et seq.
Fla. Stat. Ann., 625.121
Haw. Rev. Stat. Ann., § 431-269
Ida. Code 1947, 41-612
Iowa Code Ann., 508.36
Ky. Rev. Stat. 1971, 304.6-120 et seq.
La. Rev. Stat. Ann., 22:163
Me. Rev. Stat. Ann. 1964, Title 24-A, § 951 et seq.
Minn. Stat. Ann., 61A.25
Miss. Code Ann. 1972, § 83-7-23
Mo. Rev. Stat., 376.380
N.C. Gen. Stat. 1943, § 58-50
N.D. Cent. Code, 26.1-35-01 et seq.
N.H. Rev. Stat. 1955, 410:1 et seq.
N.J. Stat. Ann., 17B:19-8
N.M. Stat. Ann., 59A-8-5
N.Y. Insurance Law (Consol. Laws Ch. 28) § 4217
Ore. Laws 1991, Ch. 401, §§ 17 to 28
Ore. Rev. Stat. 1989, 733.110, 733.120, 733.127, 733.129, 733.130, 733.132, 733.134, 733.136
S.C. Code Ann. 1976, § 38-9-180
S.D. Codified Laws 1967, 58-26-13 et seq.
Tex. Insurance Code, Art. 3.28
Utah Code Ann. 1953, 31A-17-403
Vt. Stat. Ann., Title 8, § 3781 et seq.
Wash. Rev. Code Ann., 48.74.010 et seq.
Wyo. Stat. Ann., § 26-6-201 et seq.

**Standard Valuation and Nonforfeiture Amendments Act**
D.C. Code Ann., §§ 35-501, 35-503, 35-505, 35-507, 35-508, 35-526

**Standard Valuation Law**
Ariz. Rev. Stat. Ann., § 20-510
Miss. Code Ann. 1972, § 83-7-23
R.I. Gen. Laws 1956, 27-4.5-1 et seq.
Utah Code Ann. 1953, 31A-17-501 et seq.

**Standard Valuation of Reserve Liabilities Law-Life Insurance**
Mont. Code Ann., 33-2-521 et seq.

**Standard Water District Enabling Act**
July 18, 1997, P.L. 105-28, 111 Stat. 245
Me. Rev. Stat. Ann. 1964, Title 35-A, § 6401 et seq.

**Standard Weight Bread Law**
Neb. Laws 1931, Ch. 162
Wash. Rev. Code Ann., 19.92.100

**Standard Weights and Measures Act**
D.C. Code Ann., § 10-101 et seq.
Md. Ann. Code 1974, Art. AG, § 11-101 et seq.
N.C. Gen. Stat. 1943, § 81A-37 et seq.

**Standardization and Inspection Act (Fruits and Vegetables)**
Fla. Stat. Ann., 603.11 et seq.

**Standardized Health Claim Form Act**
Neb. Rev. Stat. 1943, 44-524 et seq.

**Standardized State Position and Salary Act**
Ill. Rev. Stat. 1955, Ch. 127, § 168-1 et seq.

**Standardized Testing Act (Aptitude Tests)**
N.Y. Education Law 1947 (Consol. Laws Ch. 16) § 340 et seq.

**Standardized Testing and Reporting Program (STAR)**
Cal. Education Code 1976, § 60640 et seq.

**Standardized Treatment Program for Sex Offenders Act**
Tenn. Code Ann., 39-13-701 et seq.

**Standards-Based Instructional Materials Program**
Cal. Education Code 1976, § 60450 et seq.

**Standards Code for Manufactured Housing Act and Recreational Vehicles Act**
See also Uniform Standards Code for Manufactured Housing Act
Ga. Code Ann., 8-2-130 et seq.
La. Rev. Stat. Ann., 51:911.21 et seq.
Miss. Code Ann. 1972, § 75-49-1 et seq.
Neb. Rev. Stat. 1943, 71-1555 et seq.
S.C. Code Ann. 1976, Superseded Vols., § 31-17-10 et seq.
Tenn. Code Ann., 68-126-101 et seq.

**Standards Code for Mobile Homes**
See Uniform Standards Code for Mobile Homes

**Standards for Crime Victims' Act (Fair Treatment)**
Also known as the Crime Victims' Bill of Rights
N.Y. Executive Law 1951 (Consol. Laws Ch. 18) § 640 et seq.

**Standards for Rental or Unoccupied Premises Law**
N.Y. Local Laws 1967, Town of Evans, p. 1532
N.Y. Local Laws 1973, Village of Angola, p. 3135

**Standards for Workplace Drug and Alcohol Testing Act**
Okla. Stat. Ann., Title 40, § 551 et seq.

**Standards HUD Construction and Safety Standards for Mobile Homes Act**
Ark. Code Ann. 1987, 20-25-101 et seq.

**Standards of Assistance for Public Assistance Applicants and Recipients**
D.C. Laws 1976, No. 1-74

**Standards of Assistance Relating to Persons Residing in Community Residence Facilities Act**
D.C. Code Ann. § 3-205,49

**Standby Charge Procedures Act**
See Uniform Standby Charge Procedures Act

**Standby Guardianship Act**
Ga. Code Ann., 29-4-50 et seq.
N.J. Stat. Ann., 3B:12-67 et seq.

**Standing Up Service Act**
D.C. Code Ann. § 25-111

**Stanford Assessors Act**
N.Y. Local Laws 1971, Town of Stanford, p. 3506

**Stanford Disposal Act**
N.Y. Local Laws 1969, Town of Stanford, p. 2102

**Stanford Junk Car Act**
N.Y. Local Laws 1967, Town of Stanford, p. 1963

**Stanford Trailer Act**
N.Y. Local Laws 1967, Town of Stanford, p. 1965

**Stanislaus County Court Services Consolidation Act**
Cal. Statutes 1992, Ch. 181

**Stanislaus County Flood Control Enabling Act**
Cal. Statutes 1981, Ch. 421

**Stanly County Emergency Reserve Fund Act**
N.C. Laws 1963, Ch. 691

**Stansel Act (Highways)**
Miss. Code Ann. 1972, § 65-1-1 et seq.

**STAR Markets Act (State Assistance for Recycling)**
Cal. Public Contract Code § 12150 et seq.

**Star Schools Assistance Act**
March 31, 1994, P.L. 103-227, 20 U.S. Code § 4085

**Star Schools Program Assistance Act**
Oct. 27, 1986, P.L. 99-570, 42 U.S. Code § 3711 nt.
April 28, 1988, P.L. 100-297, 102 Stat. 320, 20 U.S. Code § 4081 et seq.
July 25, 1991, P.L. 102-73, 20 U.S. Code § 4086
Aug. 17, 1991, P.L. 102-103, 20 U.S. Code §§ 4081 to 4084, 4085a to 4085d, 4086
Oct. 20, 1994, P.L. 103-382, 20 U.S. Code §§ 4081, 4081 nt., 4802 to 4085d, 4086

**State Accident Fund Act**
Md. Ann. Code 1974, Art. LE, § 9-301 et seq.

**State Accounting Act (State Funds)**
Ky. Rev. Stat. 1971, 46.010 et seq.

**State Accounting and Fiscal Responsibility Account Act**
Mich. Comp. Laws Ann., 21.421 et seq.

**State Acid Deposition Control Act**
N.Y. Environmental Conservation Law, 1972 (Consol. Laws Ch. 43B) § 19-0901 et seq.
N.Y. Tax Law (Consol. Laws Ch. 60) §§ 208 Subd. 9, Pg, 612 Subd. h, P1

**State Act**
N.Y. Consol. Laws, Ch. 57

**State ADA Flat Grant Act**
Ind. Code Ann., 21-3-4.5-1 et seq.

**State Administrative Board Act**
Mich. Comp. Laws Ann., 17.1 et seq.

**State Administrative Procedure Act**
Colo. Rev. Stat., 24-4-101 et seq.
Mont. Code Ann., 2-4-101 et seq.
N.Y. Consol. Laws, Ch. 82
S.C. Code Ann. 1976, § 1-23-10 et seq.

**State Administrative Rules Act (Registration)**
N.C. Gen. Stat. 1943, § 150B-18 et seq.

**State Adverse Interest Act**
Pa. Purdon's Stat., Title 71, § 776.1 et seq.

**State Aeronautical Regulatory Act**
Mont. Rev. Code 1947, 1-101 et seq.

**State Aeronautics Act**
See also Aeronautics Act
Iowa Code Ann., 328.1 et seq.
N.J. Stat. Ann., 6:2-1 to 6:2-12
Ore. Rev. Stat., 491.002 et seq.
Vt. Stat. Ann., Title 5, § 201 et seq.

**State Aeronautics Commission Act**
Wash. Rev. Code Ann., 47.68.010 et seq.
W. Va. Code 1966, § 29-2A-1 et seq.

**State Aeronautics Department Act**
Del. Code of 1974, Title 2, § 101 et seq.
Minn. Stat. Ann., 360.011 et seq.
Neb. Rev. Stat. 1943, 3-101 et seq.
Vt. Stat. Ann., Title 5, § 1 et seq.

**State Agencies Audit Act**
N.M. Stat. Ann., 12-6-1 et seq.

**State Agency Act**
Cal. Government Code § 11120 et seq.
Ky. Rev. Stat. 1971, 13A.010 et seq.

**State Agency Employees Child Care Services Act**
Ill. Rev. Stat. 1991, Ch. 127, § 3001 et seq.

**State Agency Entity Creation Act**
Ill. Rev. Stat. 1991, Ch. 127, § 4201 et seq.

**State Agency Historic Resources Preservation Act**
Ill. Rev. Stat. 1991, Ch. 127, § 133c21 et seq.

**State Agency Leasing Act**
La. Rev. Stat. Ann., 30:151 et seq.

**State Agency Regulations Filing Act**
Ky. Rev. Stat. 1971, Superseded Vols., 13.085

**State Agency Reorganization Act**
S.C. Code Ann. 1976, § 1-19-10 et seq.

**State Agency Transfer Act**
N.J. Stat. Ann., 52:14D-1 et seq.

**State Agricultural and Forestry Residue Utilization Act**
Cal. Public Resources Code § 25630 et seq., § 25675

**State Aid Act (County Roads)**
Ky. Rev. Stat. 1971, 179.400 et seq.

**State Aid Act (Roads and Bridges)**
Ill. Rev. Stat. 1957, Ch. 121, §§ 9 et seq.

**State Aid Act (Schools)**
Okla. Stat. Ann., Title 70, § 18-101 et seq.
S.C. Code Ann. 1976, § 59-21-10 et seq.

**State Aid Act (Student)**
N.Y. Education Law 1947 (Consol. Laws Ch. 16) § 601 et seq.

**State Aid for Nonstate Agencies Act**
N.C. Laws 1991, Ch. 830

**State Aid for Sewage Treatment Facilities Act**
R.I. Public Laws 1967, Ch. 198

**State Aid for Urban Renewal Projects Act**
N.J. Stat. Ann., 52.27D-44 et seq.

**State Aid Highway Act**
Wash. Rev. Code Ann., 36.75.010 et seq., 36.77.010 et seq., 36.87.010 et seq., 47.08.080 et seq., 47.24.010 et seq.

**State Aid Intercept Act**
N.M. Stat. Ann., 6-21-1 et seq.

**State Aid Road Act**
Ga. Code 1933, 95-1701 et seq.
Minn. Stat. Ann., 162.01 et seq.
N.J. Stat. Ann., 27:13A-1 et seq.

**State Aid to Densely Populated Municipalities Act**
N.J. Stat. Ann., 52:27D-384 et seq.

**State Aid to Education Act**
Mich. Comp. Laws Ann., 388.671 et seq.

**State Aid to Public Libraries Act**
Mich. Comp. Laws Ann., 397.551 et seq.

**State Aid to Redevelopment Agencies Act**
R.I. Public Acts 1966, Ch. 49

**State Aid to Subdivisions Act**
S.C. Code Ann. 1976, § 6-27-10 et seq.

**State Aircraft Act**
N.M. Stat. Ann., 15-9-1 et seq.

**State Aircraft Motor Vehicle Registration Law**
Fla. Stat. Ann., 329.01 et seq.

**State Aircraft Pooling Act**
Tex. Government Code, § 2205.001 et seq.
Tex. Rev. Civ. Stat. 1974, Art. 4413(34b)

**State Airline Authority Act**
Neb. Rev. Stat. 1943, 3-801 et seq.

**State Airport Licensing Law**
Fla. Stat. Ann., 330.27 et seq.

**State Airports Act**
Nev. Rev. Stat. 1979 Reprint, 494.010 et seq.

**State and City Civil Service Act**
La. Const. 1974, Art. 10

**State and County College Tenure Act**
N.J. Stat. Ann., 18A:60-6 et seq.

**State and Education Employees Group Insurance Act**
Okla. Stat. Ann., Title 74, § 1301 et seq.

**State and Federal Employment Cooperation Act**
Ill. Rev. Stat. 1991, Ch. 48, § 172a et seq.

**State and Federal Land Jurisdiction Act**
Ill. Rev. Stat. 1991, Ch. 1, § 7151 et seq.

**State and Local Coastal Resources Management Act**
La. Rev. Stat. Ann., 49.213.1 et seq.

**State and Local Fiscal Assistance Act Amendments of 1980**
Dec. 28, 1980, P.L. 96-604, 31 U.S. Code § 1221 nt.

**State and Local Fiscal Assistance Act of 1972**
Oct. 20, 1972, P.L. 92-512, 31 U.S. Code § 1221 nt.

**State and Local Government Convention, Sports Facility, Meeting and Tourism Act**
Mo. Laws 1991, S.B. No. 295, 312, §§ 21 to 31
Mo. Rev. Stat. 1978, 70.840 et seq.

**State and Local Government Cost Estimate Act of 1981**
Dec. 23, 1981, P.L. 97-108, 31 U.S. Code § 1301 nt.

**State and Local Government Partnership Act**
S.C. Code Ann. 1976, §§ 28-5-47 to 28-5-54

**State and Local Government Revenue Bond Act**
N.C. Gen. Stat. 1943, § 159-80 et seq.

**State and Local Government Volunteers Act**
Ark. Code Ann. 1987, 21-13-101 et seq.

**State and Local Law Enforcement Assistance Act of 1986**
Oct. 27, 1986, P.L. 99-570, Title I, Subtitle K, 100 Stat. 3207-41, 42 U.S . Code §§ 3711 nt., 3741, 3782, 3783, 3789, 3793, 3796h to 3796s, 3797

**State and Local Records Law**
Mo. Rev. Stat., 109.200 et seq.

**State and Municipal Court Compact**
R.I. Gen. Laws 1956, 8-18-1 et seq.

**State and Municipal Traffic Bail Bond Procedure Act**
Okla. Stat. Ann., Title 22, § 1115 et seq.

**State and Regional Planning Act**
Fla. Stat. Ann., 186.001 et seq.

**State and Regional Planning and Community Development Act**
Mo. Rev. Stat., 251.150 et seq.

**State and School Sick Leave Act**
S.C. Code Ann. 1976, §§ 8-11-40 et seq., 59-1-400 et seq.

**State and Veterans Nursing Homes Act**
Colo. Rev. Stat., 26-12-101 et seq.

**State Animal Act**
Ill. Rev. Stat. 1991, Ch. 1, § 2901-45

**State Antiparamilitary Training Act**
Fla. Stat. Ann., 790.29

**State Appellate Defender Act**
Ill. Rev. Stat. 1985, Ch. 38, § 208-1 et seq.

**State Appellate Public Defenders Act**
Ida. Code 1947, 19-867 to 19-872

**State Appraiser Licensing and Certifying Act**
Ariz. Rev. Stat. Ann., § 32-3601 et seq.

**State Appraisers' Act (Canal Lands)**
N.Y. Laws 1908, Ch. 195

**State Appropriation Act (Power Authority)**
N.Y. Public Authorities Law (Consol. Laws Ch. 43A) § 1007

**State Appropriations and Tax Limitation Act**
Utah Code Ann. 1953, 59-17A-101 et seq.

**State Appropriations Limitation Act**
N.J. Stat. Ann., 52:9H-24 et seq.

**State Architectural Act**
Okla. Stat. Ann., Title 59, § 46.1 et seq.

**State Archives Act**
Cal. Government Code § 12220 et seq.
Minn. Stat. 1969, 138.13 et seq.
Utah Code Ann. 1953, 63-2-901 et seq.

**State Archives Act (Lost)**
Ill. Rev. Stat. 1991, Ch. 124, §§ 10.9, 11

**State Archives and Historical Records Act**
R.I. Gen. Laws 1956, 42-8.1-1 et seq.

**State Archives Partnership Trust Act**
N.Y. Laws 1992, Ch. 758

**State Armory Board Act**
N.M. Stat. Ann., 20-7-1 et seq.
Utah Code Ann. 1953, 39-2-1 et seq.

**State Army Reserve Officers' Training Corps Law**
Ill. Rev. Stat. 1991, Ch. 122, § 30-16.1 et seq.

**State Assistance for Fire Equipment Act**
Cal. Government Code § 8589.8 et seq.

**State Assistance for Recycling (STAR) Markets Act**
Cal. Public Contract Code § 12150 et seq.

**State Assistance Fund for Energy Act**
Cal. Financial Code § 32000 et seq.

**State Assistance Fund for Recreational Marinas Act**
Cal. Financial Code § 35000 et seq.

**State Athletic Commission Act**
N.D. Cent. Code, 53-01-01 et seq.
N.Y. Unconsolidated Law, § 8901 et seq.
Pa. Purdon's Stat., Title 4, § 31.101 et seq.

**State Atomic Energy Law**
See Atomic Energy Law

**State Audit Act**
Ill. Rev. Stat. 1991, Ch. 15, § 301-1 et seq.
Iowa Code Ann., 11.24 et seq.

**State Authorities Eminent Domain Act**
S.C. Code Ann. 1976, § 28-3-10 et seq.

**State Authority Act**
Pa. Purdon's Stat., Title 71, § 1707.1 et seq.

**State Aviation Commission Act**
See Aviation Commission Act

**State Avifaunal Emblem Law**
Cal. Government Code § 423

**State Ballot Law Commission Act**
Mass. Gen. Laws Ann., 55B:1 et seq.

**State Bank Aid Act**
March 24, 1933, Ch. 8, 48 Stat. 20

**State Bank Holding Company Act**
S.C. Code Ann. 1976, § 34-23-10 et seq.

**State Bank Parity Act**
Cal. Financial Code §§ 753, 857, 1757, 1935, 3359, 3371, 3372, 3372.5, 3373
N.J. Stat. Ann., 17:13B-1, 17:13B-2

**State Banking Act**
See also Banking Act
Ark. Code Ann. 1987, 23-31-201 et seq.
W. Va. Code 1966, § 31A-1-1 et seq.

**State Bar Act**
Ala. Code 1975, § 34-3-40 et seq.
Ariz. Rev. Stat. Ann., § 32-201 et seq.
Cal. Business and Professions Code § 6000 et seq.

*Continued*

Ga. Code Ann., 15-19-30 et seq.
Ida. Code 1947, 3-401 et seq.
Ky. Supreme Court Rules, Rule 3.010 et seq.
Mich. Comp. Laws 1948, 691.51 et seq.
Miss. Code Ann. 1972, § 73-3-101 et seq.
Nev. Rev. Stat. 1979 Reprint, 7.275, 7.285
N.M. Stat. Ann., 36-2-1 et seq.
Okla. Laws 1929, Special Session, p. 376
Ore. Rev. Stat., 9.005 et seq.
S.D. Codified Laws 1967, 16-17-1 et seq.
Tex. Government Code, 81.001 et seq.
Utah Code Ann. 1953, 78-51-1 et seq.
Va. Code 1950, § 54.1-3909
Wash. Rev. Code Ann., 2.48.010 et seq.
Wis. Stat. 1981, 758.25

**State Bar Board Act**
N.D. Cent. Code, 27-11-06 et seq.

**State Bar Dues Act**
Ky. Supreme Court Rules, Rule 3.010 et seq.

**State Beach Development Act**
R.I. Public Laws 1958, Ch. 177

**State Beach, Park, Recreational, and Historical Facilities Bond Act**
Cal. Public Resources Code § 5096.71 et seq.

**State Beauticians Act**
Del. Rev. Code 1935, § 6287 et seq.

**State Beauty Culture Act**
Pa. Purdon's Stat., Title 63, § 507 et seq.

**State Beef Commission Act**
Wash. Rev. Code Ann., 16.67.010

**State Beneficiary Public Trusts-Publicly Owned Treatment Works Act**
Okla. Stat. Ann., Title 27A, §§ 1011 to 1017

**State Bingo Control Law**
N.Y. Executive Law 1951 (Consol. Laws, Ch. 18), § 430 et seq.

**State Bird Act**
Ill. Rev. Stat. 1991, Ch. 1, § 2901-10

**State Blind or Deaf School Transportation Act**
Ill. Rev. Stat. 1991, Ch. 23, §§ 1209.9, 1210

**State Blind Pension Law**
See Blind Pension Act

**State Blue Book Act**
Cal. Government Code §§ 14885, 14886

**State Board of Accounts Retirement Act**
Ind. Code Ann., 5-1-15-1 et seq.

**State Board of Adjustment Act**
Ala. Code 1975, § 41-9-60 et seq.

**State Board of Administration Act**
Fla. Stat. Ann., 215.44 et seq.

**State Board of Agriculture Act**
Tenn. Code Ann., 43-2-101

**State Board of Control Act**
Tex. Rev. Civ. Stat., Art. 601b et seq.

**State Board of Control for State Homes for the Aged Act**
Colo. Rev. Stat. 1963, 133-1-1 et seq.

**State Board of Education Act**
Kan. Stat. Ann., 72-7501 et seq.

**State Board of Education Bond Act**
Del. Laws Vol. 53, p. 864, Ch. 334

**State Board of Equalization Act (Taxation)**
Mich. Comp. Laws Ann., 209.1 et seq.

**State Board of Financial Institutions Act**
S.C. Code Ann. 1976, § 33-1-10 et seq.

**State Board of Higher Education Act**
See Board of Higher Education Act

**State Board of Housing Law**
Pa. 1937 Pamph. Laws 1705, No. 359
Pa. 1945 Pamph. Laws 984, No. 384

**State Board of Registration for Foresters Act**
Ark. Code Ann. 1987, 17-28-101 et seq.

**State Board of Tourism Commissioners Act**
N.Y. Laws 1977, Ch. 357, § 2

**State Boards and Commissions Law**
N.Y. Consol. Laws, Ch. 54

**State Boards Rule Making Act**
Ind. Code Ann., 4-22-2-1 et seq.

**State Boat Act**
Ky. Rev. Stat. 1971, 235.010 et seq.
Md. Ann. Code 1974, Art. NR, § 8-701 et seq.
Neb. Rev. Stat. 1943, 37-1201 et seq.
Tenn. Public Acts 1959, Ch. 212

**State Bond Act**
Alaska Stat. 1962, § 37.15.010 et seq.
Fla. Stat. Ann., 215.57 et seq.
S.D. Codified Laws 1967, Miscellaneous Superseded Code, 4-12-1 et seq.
Va. Code 1950, § 33.1-267 et seq.

**State Bondholders Committee Act**
Mich. Comp. Laws 1948, 451.351 et seq.

**State Bonding Fund Act**
N.D. Cent. Code, 26.1-21-01 et seq.
Neb. Laws 1935, Ch. 23

**State Boundary Commission Act**
Mich. Comp. Laws Ann., 123.1001 et seq.

**State Boxing Commission Act**
Ind. Code Ann., 25-9-1-1 et seq.

**State Boxing Law**
N.Y. Laws 1920, Ch. 912
N.Y. Laws 1921, Ch. 714

**State Brand Act (Animals)**
Okla. Stat. Ann., Title 2, § 4-1 et seq.

**State Bridge Authority Act**
N.Y. Public Authorities Law (Consol. Laws Ch. 43A) § 525 et seq.

**State Bridge Commission Act**
Mich. Comp. Laws Ann., 254.151 et seq.

**State Budget Commission Act**
Ida. Code 1947, 67-3501 et seq.
Ind. Code Ann., 4-12-1-1 et seq.
Ky. Rev. Stat. 1971, 42.010 et seq.
Mich. Comp. Laws Ann., 21.1 et seq.
Miss. Code Ann. 1972, § 27-103-1 et seq.
N.D. Cent. Code, 54-44.1-01 et seq.
Nev. Rev. Stat. 1979 Reprint, 353.150 et seq.
N.H. Rev. Stat. 1955, 9:1 et seq.
N.J. Stat. Ann., 52:27B-10 et seq.
R.I. Gen. Laws 1956, 35-3-1 et seq.
S.D. Codified Laws 1967, 4-7-1 et seq.
Wyo. Stat. 1957, § 9-504 et seq.

**State Building Act (Contracts)**
Cal. Government Code § 14250 et seq.

**State Building Authority Act**
Alaska Stat. 1962, § 18.55.010 et seq.
Ga. Code 1933, 91-501a et seq.
Ida. Laws 1974, Ch. 111
Ill. Rev. Stat. 1991, Ch. 127, § 213.1-1 et seq.
N.J. Stat. Ann., 52:18A-50 et seq.

**State Building Code**
Iowa Code Ann., 103A.1 et seq.
Mont. Code Ann., 50-60-203
N.D. Cent. Code, 54-21.3-01 et seq.
N.Y. Executive Law 1951, (Consol. Laws Ch. 18) § 370 et seq.
Wash. Rev. Code Ann., 19.27.010 et seq.

**State Building Commission Act**
W. Va. Code 1966, § 5-6-1 et seq.

**State Building Construction Act**
Cal. Government Code § 15800 et seq.

**State Building Construction Administration Act**
Tex. Rev. Civ. Stat., Art. 601b, § 5.01 et seq.

**State Building Energy Conservation Act**
Mont. Code Ann., 90-4-601 et seq.

**State Building Financing Authority Act**
Wash. Rev. Code 1951, 43.76.010 et seq.

**State Building Ownership Act**
Utah Code Ann. 1953, 63-9a-1 et seq.

**State Building Services Act**
Ark. Code Ann. 1987, 22-2-101 et seq.

**State Building Standards Act**
Cal. Health and Safety Code § 18901 et seq.

**State Bureau of Identification Act**
N.J. Stat. Ann., 53:1-12 et seq.

**State Canvassers Act (Elections)**
Mich. Comp. Laws Ann., 168.841 et seq., 200.301 et seq.

**State Capital Improvement Act**
N.C. Laws 1959, Ch. 1039

**State Capital Improvement Bond Act**
N.C. Laws 1957, Ch. 935
N.C. Laws 1961, Ch. 951

**State Capital Improvement Legislative Bond Act**
N.C. Laws 1963, Ch. 838
N.C. Laws 1965, Ch. 915

**State Capital Improvement Voted Bond Act**
N.C. Laws 1961, Ch. 1037

**State Capital Preservation Act**
Pa. Purdon's Stat., Title 71, § 1047.21 et seq.

**State Capitol Environs Act**
Neb. Rev. Stat. 1943, 90-301 et seq.

**State Capitol Environs Protection and Improvement Act**
Neb. Rev. Stat. 1943, 90-301 et seq.

**State Capitol Expansion Act**
N.M. Stat. Ann. 1953, 6-2-14 et seq.

**State Capitol Joint Management Commission Act**
N.J. Stat. Ann., 52:31-34 et seq.

**State Carbon Dioxide Act**
N.M. Stat. Ann., 19-10A-1 et seq.

**State Case Registry Act**
Ill. Comp. Stat. 1992, Ch. 305, § 5/10-27

**State Caustic Alkali or Acid Law**
Wis. Stat. Ann., 100.37

**State Certification of Need and Health Facility Licensure Act**
S.C. Code Ann. 1976, § 44-7-320 et seq.

**State Charities Act**
N.Y. Consol. Laws, Ch. 55

**State Charity Hospital Act**
Miss. Code Ann. 1972, § 4-11-1 et seq.

**State Chemical Dependency Plan**
Mont. Code Ann., 53-24-204

**State Chemical Laboratory Authorization Act**
Miss. Code Ann. 1972, § 57-21-1 et seq.

**State Civil Defense Act**
Mont. Code Ann., 10-3-101 to 10-3-208

**State Civil Emergency Preparedness Act**
N.M. Stat. Ann., 12-10-1 et seq.

**State Civil Service Act**
Cal. Government Code § 18500 et seq.
Colo. Rev. Stat. 1963, 26-5-1 et seq.
Mich. Public Acts 1937, No. 346
Minn. Stat. Ann., 43A.01 et seq.
Ore. Rev. Stat., 240.005 et seq.
R.I. Gen. Laws 1956, 36-3-1 et seq.
Wash. Rev. Code Ann., 41.06.010 et seq.

**State Claims Act (Uncollected)**
Ill. Rev. Stat. 1991, Ch. 15, § 100 et seq.

**State Clean Water Assistance Act**
Mich. Comp. Laws Ann., 323.451 et seq.

**State Coastal Conservancy Act**
Cal. Public Resources Code § 31000 et seq.

**State Collection Act**
Ill. Rev. Stat. 1991, Ch. 15, § 151 et seq.

**State College and University Employees Uniform Insurance Benefits Act**
Tex. Insurance Code, Art. 3.50-3

**State College Building Program Amendment**
Tex. Const. 1876, Art. 7, § 17, 18

**State College Contract Act**
Cal. Education Code 1976, § 90100 et seq.
N.J. Stat. Ann., 18A:64-52 et seq.

**State College Revenue Bond Act**
Cal. Education Code 1976, § 90010 et seq.

**State Colleges Act**
N.C. Gen. Stat. 1943, § 116-45 et seq.

**State Colleges and Universities Gasohol Use Act**
Ill. Rev. Stat. 1991, Ch. 144, § 2851 et seq.

**State Colleges and Universities Revenue Bond Act**
Ill. Rev. Stat. 1991, Ch. 144, § 1201 et seq.

**State Colleges and Universities Revenue Bond Act (Board of Governors of)**
Ill. Comp. Stat. 1992, Ch. 110, § 610/1 et seq.

**State Commerce Act**
Conn. Gen. Stat. Ann., §§ 4-5, 4-24a, 4-60a, 10-321, Subsec. a, 32-1a et seq., 36-322, Subsec. a, Subd. 9

**State Commission for Higher Education Facilities Act**
Me. Rev. Stat. Ann. 1964, Title 20-A, § 10501 et seq.

**State Commission of Investigation Act (Temporary)**
N.Y. Unconsolidated Law, § 7507 et seq.

**State Commissions and Councils Code**
Utah Code Ann. 1953, 63C-1-101 et seq.

**State Commodity Code**
N.M. Stat. Ann., 58-13a-1 et seq.

**State Commodity Code (Model)**
Iowa Code Ann., 502A.1 et seq.

**State Communications Act**
Cal. Statutes 1947, Ch. 1071, p. 2472

**State Competitive Scholarship Act**
N.J. Stat. Ann., 18A:71-1 et seq.

**State Comprehensive Health Association Act**
Fla. Stat. Ann., 627.648 et seq.

**State Comprehensive Health Planning Act**
S.C. Code Ann. 1976, § 44-5-10 et seq.

**State Comprehensive Mental Health Service Plan Act of 1986**
Nov. 14, 1986, P.L. 99-660, 42 U.S. Code § 201 nt.

**State Comprehensive Plan Appeals Board**
R.I. Gen. Laws 1956, 45-22.3-1 et seq.

**State Comprehensive Planning Act**
Fla. Stat. Ann., 186.001 et seq.

**State Comptroller Act**
Ill. Rev. Stat. 1991, Ch. 15, § 201 et seq.

**State Compulsory Meat Inspection Act**
Ore. Rev. Stat., 619.010 et seq.

**State Conciliation Act**
Ore. Rev. Stat., 662.405 et seq.

**State Conservation and Planning Act**
Cal. Statutes 1947, Ch. 807, p. 1909

**State Conservation Districts Law**
Mont. Rev. Code 1947, 76-101 et seq.

**State Constitutions Act (Virginia, Texas, Mississippi)**
April 10, 1869, Ch. 17, 16 Stat. 40

**State Construction Code**
See also Uniform State Construction Code
Mich. Comp. Laws Ann., 125.1501 et seq.

**State Construction Program Bond Act**
Cal. Statutes 1955, Ch. 1709, p. 3142
Cal. Statutes 1958, 1st Ex. Sess., Ch. 88, p. 320

*Continued*

Cal. Statutes 1962, 1st Ex. Sess., Ch. 23, p. 193
Cal. Statutes 1962, 3rd Ex. Sess., Ch. 2, p. 564
Cal. Statutes 1964, 1st Ex. Sess., Ch. 143, p. 513

**State Construction Projects Liability Act**
Tenn. Code Ann., 12-4-501 et seq.

**State Contract Act**
Cal. Public Contract Code § 10100 et seq.

**State Contracts Act**
Cal. Government Code § 14404 et seq.
Ill. Rev. Stat. 1965, Ch. 127, § 64 et seq.

**State Contracts Prevailing Wage Act**
Ind. Code Ann., 5-16-7-1 et seq.

**State Convention Facility Development Act**
Mich. Comp. Laws Ann., 207.621 et seq.

**State Correctional Facility Reimbursement Act**
Mich. Comp. Laws Ann., 800.401 et seq.

**State Council for the Preservation of Natural Areas Act**
Ga. Laws 1966, p. 330

**State Council of Civil Defense Act**
Pa. Purdon's Stat., Title 35, § 7110.101 et seq.

**State Council of Defense Act**
Del. Laws Vol. 43, p. 1173, Ch. 285
Ill. Rev. Stat. 1949, Ch. 127, § 63j et seq.
Kan. Laws 1941, Ch. 347
Mo. Laws 1941. p. 669 §§ 1-3
S.C. Code Ann. 1976, § 25-9-10 et seq.
Utah Code Ann. 1953, 63-5-1 et seq.

**State Council on Developmental Disabilities Act**
Ida. Code 1947, 67-6701 et seq.

**State Council on Maternal Infant, and Child Health Act**
S.C. Code Ann. 1976, § 20-7-5410 et seq.

**State Council on the Deaf and Hard of Hearing Act**
Ida. Code 1947, 67-7301 et seq.

**State Credit Card Crime Act**
Ark. Code Ann. 1987, 5-37-101 et seq.
Tenn. Code Ann., 39-14-101 et seq.

**State Credit Union Act**
Wash. Rev. Code Ann., 31.12.005 et seq.

**State Crime Laboratory Commission Act**
R.I. Gen. Laws 1956, 12-1.1-1 et seq.

**State Dairy and Food Act**
Ore. Rev. Stat., 662.405 et seq.

**State Dairy Law**
Tenn. Code Ann., 53-3-101 et seq.

**State Debit Card Crime Act**
Tenn. Code Ann., 39-14-101 et seq.

**State Debt Impact Note Act**
Ill. Rev. Stat. 1981, Ch. 63, § 42.71 et seq.

**State Debt Policy Law and Procedure Act**
La. Rev. Stat. Ann., 39:1361 et seq.

**State Defense Act**
Ind. Laws 1949, Ch. 275, p. 1016

**State Defense Council Act**
Ky. Rev. Stat. 1948, 39.010 et seq.

**State Defense Emergency Act (New York)**
N.Y. Unconsolidated Laws, § 9101 et seq.

**State Defense Force Act**
Colo. Rev. Stat., 28-4-101 et seq.
Haw. Rev. Stat. Ann., § 122A-1 et seq.
Utah Code Ann. 1953, 39-4-1 et seq.
Wis. Stat. Ann., 21.025

**State Dental Act**
Okla. Stat. Ann., Title 59, § 328.1 et seq.

**State Department Authorities Act of 1956**
April 26, 1996, P.L. 104-134, 22 U.S. Code § 2708
Oct. 21, 1998, P.L. 105-277, 22 U.S. Code §§ 2695, 2697, 2698, 2704

**State Department Basic Authorities Act of 1956**

Aug. 1, 1956, Ch. 841, 22 U.S. Code §§ 2662, 2669 to 2679, 2679a, 2680, 2680a, 2684, 2687 to 2689s, 2695 to 2704
July 12, 1960, P.L. 86-624, 22 U.S. Code § 2669
Sept. 6, 1960, P.L. 86-707, 22 U.S. Code § 2669
Sept. 8, 1960, P.L. 86-723, 22 U.S. Code § 2678
Aug. 1, 1962, P.L. 87-565, 22 U.S. Code § 2669
Feb. 2, 1972, P.L. 92-226, 22 U.S. Code § 2680
July 13, 1972, P.L. 92-352, 22 U.S. Code § 2680
Oct. 26, 1974, P.L. 93-475, 22 U.S. Code §§ 2679a, 2680, 2680a
Nov. 29, 1975, P.L. 94-141, 22 U.S. Code §§ 2679a, 2687, 2688
July 12, 1976, P.L. 94-350, 22 U.S. Code §§ 2689, 2690
June 15, 1977, P.L. 95-45, 22 U.S. Code § 2760
Aug. 17, 1977, P.L. 95-105, 22 U.S. Code §§ 2691, 2693
Oct. 7, 1978, P.L. 95-426, 22 U.S. Code §§ 2680a, 2680, 2691, 2695
Aug. 15, 1979, P.L. 96-60, 22 U.S. Code § 2696
Oct. 17, 1980, P.L. 96-465, 22 U.S. Code § 2651 nt.
Aug. 24, 1982, P.L. 97-241, 22 U.S. Code §§ 2651 nt., 2679a, 2680a, 2684, 2696, 2705, 4301 et seq.
Nov. 22, 1983, P.L. 98-164, 22 U.S. Code §§ 2671, 2675, 2706, 2707, 4303, 4304a
Oct. 19, 1984, P.L. 98-533, 22 U.S. Code § 2651 nt., 2708
Nov. 8, 1984, P.L. 98-618, 22 U.S. Code § 4303, 4303 nt.
Aug. 16, 1985, P.L. 99-93, 22 U.S. Code §§ 2651 nt., 2669, 2704, 2709, 2710, 4301, 4302, 4305, 4309a, 4314
July 2, 1986, P.L. 99-349, 100 Stat. 716
Aug. 27, 1986, P.L. 99-399, 22 U.S. Code §§ 2651 nt., 2708
Oct. 27, 1986, P.L. 99-550, 22 U.S. Code § 2678
Oct. 27, 1986, P.L. 99-569, 22 U.S. Code § 4302
Dec. 22, 1987, P.L. 100-204, 22 U.S. Code §§ 2652 nt., 2670, 2697 , 2702, 2702 nt., 2706, 2713, 4302, 4303, 4305, 4315, 4315 nt., 4316, prec. 4341, 4341 nt., 4341 to 4343
Nov. 18, 1988, P.L. 100-690, 22 U.S. Code §§ 2651 nt., 2708, 2714
Dec. 13, 1989, P.L. 101-231, 22 U.S. Code § 2708
Feb. 16, 1990, P.L. 101-246, 22 U.S. Code §§ 2651 nt., 2669, 2678 , 2684, 2696, 2698, 2703, 2708, 2709, 2715 to 2719, 4303, 4304
Nov. 29, 1990, P.L. 101-649, 22 U.S. Code § 2691
March 27, 1991, P.L. 102-20, 22 U.S. Code § 2669
Oct. 28, 1991, P.L. 102-138, 22 U.S. Code §§ 2651 nt., 2669, 2670, 2695, 2696, 2703, 2706, 2717, 2718, 2720 to 2723, 4351 to 4357
April 30, 1994, P.L. 103-236, 22 U.S. Code §§ 2651a, 2662, 2669, 2670, 2671, 2696, 2703 et seq., 2724, 4302 et seq., 4309a, 4314, 4316
Oct. 25, 1994, P.L. 103-415, 22 U.S. Code § 2651a
Oct. 19, 1996, P.L. 104-316, 22 U.S. Code § 2671
Oct. 17, 1998, P.L. 105-261, 22 U.S. Code § 2717
Oct. 21, 1998, P.L. 105-277, 22 U.S. Code §§ 2651a, 2695, 2697, 2698, 2701, 2704 to 2706, 2708, 2710, 2717, 2724 to 2728
Oct. 30, 1998, P.L. 105-323, 22 U.S. Code § 2708
Nov. 12, 1998, P.L. 105-375, 22 U.S. Code § 4304b

**State Department Financial Responsibility and Accountability Act**

Colo. Rev. Stat., 24-17-101 et seq.

**State Department of Agriculture Act**

Colo. Rev. Stat., 35-1-101 et seq.

**State Department of Air Transportation Act**

Ga. Code Ann., 50-19-20 et seq.

**State Department of Defense Act**

N.J. Stat. Ann., 38A:3-1 et seq.

**State Department of Education Act**
Colo. Rev. Stat., 22-2-101 et seq.

**State Department of Health Act**
N.J. Stat. Ann.26:1A-2 et seq.

**State Department of Health Building Expansion Act**
Ark. Acts 1977, p. 1641, No. 686

**State Department of Health Services Cooperative Agreement Act**
Cal. Health and Safety Code § 38070

**State Department of Parole Reorganization Act**
Colo. Rev. Stat., 17-2-101 et seq.

**State Department of Public Health Reorganization Act**
Colo. Rev. Stat., 25-1-101 et seq.

**State Department—USIA Authorization Act, Fiscal Year 1975**
Aug. 24, 1982, P.L. 97-241, 22 U.S. Code § 2151 nt.

**State Departments Act**
N.Y. Consol. Laws Ch. 78

**State Dependent Care Development Grants Act**
Sept. 30, 1986, P.L. 99-425, 42 U.S. Code § 9801 nt.
Nov. 3, 1990, P.L. 101-501, 42 U.S. Code §§ 9871, 9874, 9875, 9877
May 18, 1994, P.L. 103-252, 42 U.S. Code § 9871
Oct. 20, 1994, P.L. 103-382, 42 U.S. Code § 9877

**State Depository Act of 1919**
Ida. Code 1947, 67-2725 et seq.
Ill. Rev. Stat. 1991, Ch. 130, § 20 et seq.
Mo. Rev. Stat., 110.070 et seq.
Ore. Rev. Stat., 295.005 et seq.
Tenn. Code Ann., 9-5-101 et seq.
Tex. Rev. Civ. Stat., Art. 2525 et seq.
Utah Laws 1933, Ch. 47

**State Designer Selection Board Act**
Minn. Stat. Ann., 16B.33

**State Detention Homes Act**
Ga. Code Ann., 42-4-30 et seq.

**State Development Department Act**
Del. Code of 1974, Title 29, § 8631 et seq.

**State Directory of New Hires Act**
N.M. Stat. Ann., 50-13-1 to 50-13-4

**State Disaster Preparedness Act**
Fla. Stat. Ann., 252.31 et seq.

**State Disaster Relief Fund Act**
Tenn. Code Ann., 58-2-501 et seq.

**State Disbursements to Counties Act**
Ill. Rev. Stat. 1987, Ch. 34, §§ 6651, 6652

**State Documents Act**
Md. Ann. Code 1974, Art. SG, § 7-201 et seq.

**State Drug Abuse Control Act**
Haw. Rev. Stat. § 328-81 et seq.

**State Drugs and Substances Control Act**
S.D. Codified Laws 1967, 34-20B-1 et seq.

**State Economic Development Act**
Okla. Stat. Ann., Title 74, § 671 et seq.

**State Economic Development Assistance Act**
N.J. Rev. Stat. 1937, 13:16-1 et seq.

**State Education Assistance Act**
S.C. Code Ann. 1976, § 59-115-10 et seq.

**State Education Building Expansion Act**
Ark. Acts 1977, p. 1447, No. 554

**State Education Tax Act**
Mich. Comp. Laws Ann., 211.901 et seq.

**State Educational Institution Improvement Bond Act**
N.M. Laws 1975, 1st Sp. Sess., Ch. 4

**State Egg Act**
Ind. Code Ann., 16-6-1-1 et seq.

**State Election Campaign Fund Act**
Cal. Revenue and Taxation Code § 18701 et seq.

**State Electric Corporation Law**
S.D. Code 1939, 55.3101 et seq.

**State Electrical Act**
Neb. Rev. Stat. 1943, 81-571 et seq., 81-2101 et seq.

**State Emergency Defense Act**
R.I. Public Laws 1950, July Session, Ch. 2641

**State Emergency Management Act**
Fla. Stat. Ann., 252.31 et seq.

**State Emergency Management and Civil Defense Act**
Md. Ann. Code 1957, Art. 41, § 17-101 et seq.

**State Emergency Rent Control Act**
Minn. Laws, 1947, Ch. 632

**State Emergency War Powers Act**
Mont. Laws 1943, Ch. 155
Vt. Acts 1943, No. 6

**State Employee and Retiree Direct Deposit Act**
Fla. Stat. Ann., 17.076

**State Employee Bill of Rights**
Okla. Stat. Ann., Title 74, § 841.6 et seq.

**State Employee Bonding Act**
Tex. Government Code, § 653.001 et seq.

**State Employee Charitable Contribution Act**
Okla. Stat. Ann., Title 74, § 7001 et seq.

**State Employee Combined Charitable Campaign Act**
Ala. Code 1975, § 36-1A-1 et seq.

**State Employee Grievance Procedure Act**
S.C. Code Ann. 1976, § 8-17-310 et seq.

**State Employee Health Insurance Plan Act**
Ga. Code Ann., 45-18-1 et seq.

**State Employee Incentive Plan Act**
Tenn. Public Acts 1992, Ch. 908

**State Employee Indemnification Act**
Ill. Rev. Stat. 1991, Ch. 127, § 1300 et seq.

**State Employee Industrial Commission Awards Act**
Ill. Rev. Stat. 1991, Ch. 127, § 179.9 et seq.

**State Employee Job Sharing Act**
Ill. Rev. Stat. 1991, Ch. 127, §§ 1350, 1351

**State Employee Prevailing Wage Act**
Ill. Rev. Stat. 1991, Ch. 127, §§ 390.9, 391

**State Employee Protection Act**
Ala. Code 1975, § 36-26A-1 et seq.
Mont. Code Ann., 2-18-1201 et seq.

**State Employee Salary Readjustment Act**
N.M. Stat. Ann. 1953, 5-4-47 et seq.

**State Employee Vacation Time Act**
Ill. Rev. Stat. 1991, Ch. 127, §§ 63b120.01, 63b121

**State Employees' Alternative Work Schedule Act**
R.I. Gen. Laws 1956, 36-3.1-1 et seq.

**State Employees and Officials Group Health Insurance Act**
Wyo. Stat. Ann., § 9-3-202 et seq.

**State Employees and Officials Group Insurance Act**
Colo. Rev. Stat., 10-8-201 et seq.
Ill. Rev. Stat. 1991, Ch. 247 § 521 et seq.
N.H. Rev. Stat. 1955, 21-I:26 et seq.

**State Employees' and Teachers' Retirement Act**
Wyo. Stat. Ann., § 9-3-401 et seq.

**State Employees Benefits Act**
Okla. Stat. Ann., Title 74, § 1362 et seq.

**State Employees Collective Bargaining Act**
Neb. Rev. Stat. 1943, 81-1369 et seq.

**State Employees Compensation Act (Workmen's Compensation)**
Ill. Rev. Stat. 1991, Ch. 48, § 138.1 et seq.

**State Employees Cost of Living Salary Increase Act**
W. Va. Code 1966, § 5-5-1 et seq.

**State Employees' Dental Care Act**
Cal. Government Code § 22950 et seq.

**State Employees Direct Deposit Act**
Okla. Stat. Ann., Title 74, § 294.10 et seq.

**State Employees Disability Program Act**
Okla. Stat. Ann., Title 74, § 1331 et seq.

**State Employees Flexible Benefits Act**
Okla. Stat. Ann., Title 74, § 1341 et seq.

**State Employees Group Benefits Act**
Colo. Rev. Stat., 24-50-601 et seq.

**State Employees Group Health, Dental and Life Insurance Act**
Mass. Gen. Laws Ann., 32A:1 et seq.
Okla. Stat. Ann., Title 74, § 1301 et seq.

**State Employees Group Life Insurance Law**
Pa. Purdon's Stat., Title 71, § 780.1 et seq.

**State Employees Health Fitness and Education Act**
Tex. Government Code, § 664.001 et seq.

**State Employees Labor Relations Act**
Vt. Stat. Ann., Title 3, § 901 et seq.
Wis. Stat. Ann., 111.80 et seq.

**State Employees Leave Act**
Alaska Stat. 1962, § 39.20.200 et seq.

**State Employees' Medical and Hospital Care Act**
Cal. Government Code § 22751 et seq.

**State Employees Minimum Wage Act**
S.C. Code Ann. 1976, § 8-11-140 et seq.

**State Employees' Oath Act**
Cal. Government Code § 18150 et seq.

**State Employees, Officers and Officials' Code of Conduct**
Del. Code of 1974, Title 29, § 5801 et seq.

**State Employees' Pension Act**
Del. Code of 1974, Title 29, § 5501 et seq.

**State Employees' Personnel Act**
Iowa Code Ann., 19A.1 et seq.
N.H. Rev. Stat. 1955, 21-I:48 et seq.

**State Employees Political Activity Act**
Ill. Rev. Stat. 1991, Ch. 24 1/2, § 38r.9 et seq.

**State Employees Pretax Benefits Program Act**
Fla. Stat. Ann., 110.161

**State Employees Protection Act**
Ala. Code 1975, § 36-26A-1 et seq.

**State Employees' Retirement System Act**
Ala. Code 1975, § 36-27-1 et seq.
Ariz. Rev. Stat. Ann., § 38-741 et seq.
Ark. Code Ann. 1987, 24-4-101 et seq.
Cal. Government Code § 20000 et seq.
Colo. Rev. Stat., 24-51-101 et seq.
Conn. Gen. Stat. Ann., § 5-152 et seq.
Fla. Stat. Ann., 112.05 et seq., 122.01 et seq.
Ga. Code Ann., 47-2-1 et seq.
Haw. Rev. Stat. Ann., § 88-21 et seq.
Ill. Rev. Stat. 1991, Ch. 108 1/2, § 14-101 et seq.
Ky. Rev. Stat. 1971, 61-510 et seq.
La. Rev. Stat. Ann., 42:541 et seq.
Md. Ann. Code 1957, Art. 73B, § 1 et seq.
Me. Rev. Stat. Ann. 1964, Title 5, § 1001 et seq.
Mich. Comp. Laws Ann., 38.1 et seq.
Mo. Rev. Stat., 104.310 et seq.
N.C. Gen. Stat. 1943, § 135-1 et seq.
Neb. Rev. Stat. 1943, 84-1301 et seq.
N.H. Rev. Stat. 1955, 100-A:1 et seq.
N.J. Stat. Ann., 43:15A-6 et seq.

N.Y. Retirement and Social Security Law (Consol. Laws Ch. 51A), § 2 et seq.
Ohio Rev. Code 1953, 145.01 et seq.
Pa. Cons. Stat., Title 71, § 5101 et seq.
R.I. Gen. Laws 1956, 36-8-1 et seq.
S.C. Code Ann. 1976, § 9-1-10 et seq.
Tenn. Code Ann. 1955, 8-3501 et seq.
Tex. Rev. Civ. Stat., 6228a-5 et seq.
Utah Code Ann. 1953, 49-2-101 et seq.
Vt. Stat. Ann., Title 3, §§ 371 et seq., 455 et seq.
Wash. Rev. Code Ann., 41.40.005 et seq.
Wis. Stat. Ann., 40.20 et seq.
Wyo. Session Laws 1949, Ch. 42

**State Employees' Salary Readjustment Act**
N.M. Stat. Ann. 1953, 5-4-47 et seq.

**State Employees Telecommuting Act**
Fla. Stat. Ann., 110.171 et seq.

**State Employees' Training Act**
Tex. Rev. Civ. Stat., Art. 6252-11a

**State Employees Training Act**
Tex. Government Code, § 656.041 et seq.

**State Employees Uniform Nepotism Policy Act**
Tenn. Code Ann., 8-31-101 et seq.

**State Employer-Employee Relations Act**
Cal. Government Code § 3512 to 3524

**State Employers' Liability Act**
Ky. Rev. Stat. 1971, 277.310, 277.320

**State Employment and Training Act**
Fla. Stat. 1981, 450.50 et seq.

**State Employment Labor Relations Act**
Wis. Stat. Ann., 111.80 et seq.

**State Energy Act**
Ore. Rev. Stat., 672.002 et seq.

**State Energy Assistance and Information Program Act**
Md. Ann. Code 1957, Art. 41, § 6-401 et seq.

**State Energy Conservation Construction Code Act**
N.Y. Energy Law (Consol. Laws Ch. 17A) § 11-101 et seq.

**State Energy Crisis Management Act**
R.I. Gen. Laws 1956, 42-60-1 et seq.

**State Energy Efficiency Programs Improvement Act of 1990**
Oct. 18, 1990, P.L. 101-440, 42 U.S. Code § 6201 nt.

**State Energy Resources Act**
Me. Rev. Stat. Ann. 1964, Title 5, § 5001 et seq.

**State Enforcement of Foreign Judgments Act**
Fla. Stat. Ann., 55.501 et seq.

**State Engineering Act**
Ore. Rev. Stat., 672.002 et seq.

**State Entomologist Act**
Colo. Rev. Stat., 35-4-101 et seq.

**State Environmental Laboratory Certification Program Act**
Ark. Code Ann. 1987, 8-2-201 et seq.

**State Environmental Policy Act**
Wash. Rev. Code Ann., 43.21C.010 et seq.

**State Environmental Quality Review Act**
N.Y. Environmental Conservation Law 1972 (Consol. Laws, Ch. 43B), § 8-0101 et seq.

**State Equal Access to Justice Act**
N.Y. Civil Practice Laws and Rules (Consol. Laws Ch. 8) § 8600 et seq.

**State Equalization Aid Act (Schools)**
Ark. Stat. 1947, 80-821 et seq.
N.D. Cent. Code, 15-40.1-01 et seq.
Tex. General & Special Laws 50th Leg., 1947, p. 401, Ch. 228

**State Executive Succession Act**
La. Rev. Stat. Ann., 49:851 et seq.

**State Expenditures Limitation Act**
N.J. Stat. Ann., 52:9H et seq.

**State Export Promotion Coordinating Act**
Ill. Comp. Stat. 1992, Ch. 20, § 225/1 et seq.

**State Exposition and Fair Law**
Cal. Food and Agricultural Code 1967, § 3551 et seq.

**State Facilities Education Act**
N.J. Stat. Ann., 18A:7B-1 et seq.

**State Fair Act**
Ill. Rev. Stat. 1991, Ch. 127, § 1701 et seq.
Ky. Rev. Stat. 1971, 247.090 et seq.

**State Fair Board Act**
Ill. Rev. Stat. 1991, Ch. 127, § 1151 et seq.

**State Fair Board Reorganization Act**
Ind. Code Ann., 15-1-1-1 et seq.

**State Fair Employment Practices Act**
R.I. Gen. Laws 1956, 28-5-1 et seq.

**State Fair Housing Act**
N.C. Gen. Stat. 1943, § 41A-1 et seq.

**State Fair Trade Act (Intoxicating Liquors)**
Minn. Stat. Ann., 340A.301 et seq.

**State Family Farm Development Authority Act**
S.C. Code Ann. 1976, § 46-47-10 et seq.

**State Farm Act**
Ill. Rev. Stat. 1971, Ch. 118, § 14 et seq.
Ind. Code Ann., 11-2-5-1 et seq.

**State Finacing Act (Aircraft Maintenance and Engine Repair Facilities)**
Minn. Stat. Ann., 116R.01 et seq.

**State Finance Act**
Ill. Rev. Stat. 1991, Ch. 127, § 137 et seq.
N.Y. Consol. Laws, Ch. 56
Utah Code Ann. 1953, 63-1-12 et seq.

**State Financing and Investment Commission Act**
Ga. Code Ann., 50-17-20 et seq.

**State Fire and Tornado Insurance Act**
N.D. Cent. Code, 26.1-22-01 et seq.

**State Fire Code**
Mont. Code Ann. 1987, 2-5-2011

**State Fire Commissioner Act**
Pa. Purdon's Stat., Title 71, § 1199.21 et seq.

**State Fire Marshal Act**
Ill. Rev. Stat. 1991, Ch. 127 1/2, § 0.01 et seq.

**State Fire Prevention Law**
Utah Code Ann. 1953, 63-29-1 et seq.

**State Fireworks Law**
Cal. Health and Safety Code § 12500 et seq.
Wash. Rev. Code Ann., 70.77.120 et seq.

**State Fiscal Year 1990 Project Priority List**
N.J. Laws 1991, Chs. 189, § 2, 190, § 3

**State Fish Act**
Ill. Rev. Stat. 1991, Ch. 1, § 2901-50

**State Flood Control Facilities Act**
N.J. Stat. Ann., 58:16A-1 et seq.

**State Flower Law**
Cal. Government Code § 421

**State Folk Dance Act**
Ill. Rev. Stat. 1991, Ch. 1, § 2901-65

**State Food, Drug and Cosmetic Law**
See Food, Drug and Cosmetic Act

**State Food Purchase Program Act**
Pa. 1992 Pamph. Laws, No. 129

**State Food Stamp Distribution Act**
Mich. Comp. Laws Ann., 400.751

**State Forest Aid Act**
Aug. 29, 1935, Ch. 808, 49 Stat. 963, 16 U.S. Code §§ 567a, 567c

**State Forest Research and Experimental Tax Act**
Ore. Rev. Stat., 321.005 et seq.

**State Forestry Act**
Cal. Public Resources Code § 4376 et seq.
Del. Code of 1974, Title 7, § 2901 et seq.
Ill. Rev. Stat. 1991, Ch. 96 1/2, § 5900 et seq.
Mo. Rev. Stat., 254.010 et seq.

**State Forests Lands Prospecting Act**
Pa. Purdon's Stat., Title 32, § 141 et seq.

**State Forfeiture Act**
Wis. Stat. Ann., 778.01 et seq.

**State Funded Homestead Tax Relief Act**
Mont. Laws 1977, Ch. 457

**State-Funded Local Projects Construction Bidding Act**
Colo. Rev. Stat., 29-1-701 et seq.

**State Funds Accounting Act**
Mich. Comp. Laws Ann., 21.101 et seq.

**State Funds Investment Act**
Neb. Rev. Stat. 1943, 72-1237 et seq.

**State Funds Law**
Cal. Government Code § 16300 et seq.

**State Funds Reform Act**
Tex. Government Code, § 404.091 et seq.

**State Gambling Law**
Ore. Rev. Stat., 167.117 et seq.

**State Games Commission Act**
Ga. Code Ann., 50-12-40 et seq.

**State Gasoline Tax Law**
See Gasoline Tax Act

**State General Fund Bond Sinking Fund Act**
N.C. Gen. Stat. 1943, § 142.50 et seq.

**State General Obligation Bond Law**
Cal. Government Code § 16720 et seq.
Conn. Gen. Stat. Ann., § 3-20

**State Gift Ban Act**
Ill. Comp. Stat. 1992, Ch. 5, § 425/1 et seq.

**State Government Act**
Pa. Purdon's Stat., Title 71, § 1781 et seq.

**State Government Act (Emergency Seat of)**
Neb. Rev. Stat. 1943, 72-701.D1
S.D. Codified Laws 1967, 4-5-12 et seq.

**State Government Council Act**
Ariz. Laws 1967, Ch. 109

**State Government Effectiveness Act**
Neb. Rev. Stat. 1943, 81-2701 et seq.

**State Government Evaluation and Justification Act**
Me. Rev. Stat. Ann. 1964, Title 3, §§ 921 et seq., 951 et seq.

**State Government Quality Improvement Act**
Tenn. Public Acts 1992, Ch. 774

**State Government Recylcing Management Act**
Neb. Rev. Stat. 1943, 81-1642 et seq.

**State Government Reorganization Act**
Haw. Rev. Stat. Ann., § 26-1 et seq.

**State Government Reorganization Revisory Act**
Ill. Laws 1980, P.A. 81-1509, Art. 4

**State Government Strategic Planning and Performance and Review Act**
Cal. Government Code § 11810 et seq.

**State Government Volunteers Act**
Cal. Government Code § 3110 et seq.
Va. Code 1950, § 2.1-554 et seq.

**State Government Wellness and Physical Fitness Act**
Cal. Government Code § 12040 et seq.

**State Government Workers Act (Volunteer)**
Utah Code Ann. 1953, 67-20-1 et seq.

**State Governmental Ethics Act**
Kan. Stat. Ann., 46-215 et seq.

**State Grading Act (Uniform)**
N.D. Laws 1917, Ch. 56

**State Grading and Inspection Act (Grain)**
N.D. Laws 1919, Ch. 138
N.D. Laws 1923, p. 549

**State Grand Jury Act**
Miss. Code Ann. 1972, § 13-7-1 et seq.
N.J. Stat. Ann., 2A:73A-1 et seq.
S.C. Code Ann. 1976, § 14-7-1600 et seq.

**State Grant Act (Housing Development)**
Ill. Rev. Stat. 1991, Ch. 67 1/2, § 53 et seq.

**State Gross Retail Tax Act (Income)**
Ind. Code Ann., 6-2.1-1-1 et seq.

**State Group Insurance Program Law**
Fla. Stat. Ann., 110.123

**State Growth Policy Act**
Ga. Code Ann., 50-12-130 et seq.

**State Guard Act**
Ala. Code 1958, Title 35, § 203 et seq.
Cal. Military and Veterans Code, § 120 et seq.
Colo. Rev. Stat., 28-4-101 et seq.
Del. Code of 1974, Title 20, § 301 et seq.
Haw. Rev. Stat. Ann., § 122A-1 et seq.
Ill. Rev. Stat. 1991, Ch. 129, §§ 228h et seq., 229 et seq.
Kan. Stat. Ann., 48-501 et seq.
Ky. Rev. Stat. 1971, 36.010 et seq.
Md. Ann. Code 1957, Art. 65, § 1 et seq.
Neb. Rev. Stat. 1943, 55-201 et seq.
N.H. Rev. Stat. 1955, 111:1 et seq.
N.M. Stat. Ann., 20-10-1 et seq.
Okla. Stat. Ann., Title 44, § 241 et seq.
Ore. Rev. Stat. 1953, 397.005 et seq.
P.R. Laws Ann. 1954, Title 25, § 2201 et seq.
S.C. Code Ann. 1976, § 25-3-10 et seq.
S.D. Codified Laws 1967, 33-14-1 et seq.
Tenn. Code Ann., 58-1-401 et seq.
Tex. Rev. Civ. Stat., Art. 5768
Utah Code Ann. 1953, 39-4-1 et seq.
Vt. Stat. Ann., Title 20, § 1151 et seq.
Wis. Stat. Ann., 21.025
W. Va. Code 1966, § 15-4-1 et seq.

**State Guard Reserve Act**
Ind. Code Ann., 10-2-8-1 et seq.

**State Guard Reserve Corps Act**
Tex. Rev. Civ. Stat., Art. 5891c

**State Hail Insurance Act**
See Hail Insurance Act

**State Hazardous Aerosol Act**
La. Rev. Stat. Ann., 40:1057 et seq.

**State Hazardous Waste Incineration Siting Act**
Colo. Rev. Stat., 25-15-501 et seq.

**State Hazardous Waste Siting Act**
Colo. Rev. Stat., 25-15-200.1 et seq.

**State Health Aid Act**
N.J. Stat. Ann., 26:2F-1 et seq.

**State Health Benefits Program Act**
N.J. Stat. Ann., 52:14-17.25 et seq.

**State Health Care Information System Act**
Okla. Stat. Ann., Title 63, § 1-115 et seq.

**State Health Care Policy and Financing Act**
Colo. Rev. Stat., 25.5-1-102 et seq.

**State Health Department Capital Improvement Fund**
Miss. General Laws 1996, Ch. 469

**State Health Facilities Authority Law**
Fla. Stat. 1983, 154.401 et seq.

**State Health Insurance Coverage Access Act**
Wash. Rev. Code Ann., 48.41.010 et seq.

**State Health Plan**
Mont. Code Ann., 50-5-402 et seq.

**State Health Planning and Development Act**
Ala. Code 1975, § 22-4-1 et seq.
Ga. Code Ann., 31-6-1 et seq.

S.C. Code Ann. 1976, 44-5-10 et seq.
Wash. Rev. Code Ann., 70.38.015 et seq.

**State Higher Education Administrative Procedure Act**
Wash. Rev. Code Ann., 28B.19.010 et seq.

**State Higher Education And Urban School Construction Program Bond Act of 1968**
Cal. Education Code 1959, § 17300 et seq.

**State Higher Education Construction Program Bond Act**
Cal. Statutes 1966, 1st Ex Sess., Ch. 156

**State Higher Education Personnel Law**
Wash. Rev. Code Ann., 28B.16.010 et seq.

**State Highway Access Management Act**
N.J. Stat. Ann., 27:7-89 et seq.

**State Highway Act**
Cal. Streets and Highways Code § 230 et seq.
Del. Code of 1974, Title 17, § 101 et seq.
Kan. Stat. Ann., 25-1901 et seq., 68-401 et seq.
Ky. Rev. Stat. 1971, 176.010 et seq.
Mo. Rev. Stat., 227.010 et seq.
N.J. Rev. Stat. 1937, 27:6-1 et seq.
Ohio Rev. Code 1953, 5501.01 et seq.
Pa. Purdon's Stat., Title 36, § 670-101 et seq.
Vt. Stat. Ann., Title 19, § 1 et seq.
Wash. Rev. Code Ann., 47.17.005 et seq.

**State Highway Act (Condemnation)**
Mich. Comp. Laws Ann., 213.171 et seq.

**State Highway Act (Districts)**
S.C. Acts 1929, p. 670, No. 297

**State Highway and Bridge Authority Act**
Pa. Purdon's Stat., Title 36, § 3601 et seq.

**State Highway Bonds Act**
Colo. Rev. Stat., 43-4-101 et seq.
N.C. Laws 1927, Ch. 95
N.C. Laws 1943, Ch. 322
N.C. Laws 1965, Ch. 46
N.C. Laws 1977, Ch. 643

**State Highway Classification Act**
Cal. Streets and Highways Code § 230 et seq.

**State Highway Commission Act**
S.D. Codified Laws 1967, 31-2-2 et seq.

**State Highway Construction Bonds Act**
Ark. Acts 1949, p. 11, No. 5
Ark. Acts 1959, No. 485
Ark. Acts 1961, No. 68
Ark. Acts 1965, No. 23

**State Highway Department Act**
Mo. Rev. Stat. 1986, 226.010 et seq.
N.J. Stat. Ann., 27:1A-1 et seq.

**State Highway Department Organization Act**
Mich. Comp. Laws Ann., 247.801 et seq.

**State Highway Employees Retirement Act**
Ark. Code Ann. 1987, 24-5-101 et seq.

**State Highway Patrol, Game and Fish Warden and Criminal Investigator Retirement Act**
Wyo. Stat. Ann., § 9-3-601 et seq.

**State Highway Patrol Pension Act**
Ohio Rev. Code 1953, 5505.01 et seq.

**State Highway Pedestrians Act**
Mich. Comp. Laws Ann., 257.655

**State Highway Permit Law**
Cal. Streets and Highways Code § 670 et seq.

**State Highway Police Act**
Ill. Rev. Stat. 1991, Ch. 121, § 307.1

**State Highway Refunding Bonds Act**
Colo. Stat. Ann. 1935, Ch. 153, § 135 et seq.

**State Highway Regulatory Act**
La. Rev. Stat. Ann., 32:1 et seq.

**State Highway System Access Management Act**
Fla. Stat. Ann., 335.18 et seq.

**State Highway Toll Bridge Act**
Ky. Rev. Stat. 1971, 180.010 et seq.

**State Highway Treasury Anticipation Debenture Act of 1938-1945**
Mont. Laws 1939, p. 743
Mont. Laws 1943, Ch. 217
Mont. Laws 1945, Ch. 39

**State Highway Treasury Anticipation Note Act**
Ida. Laws 1939, Ch. 252
Ida. Laws 1946, First Extra Session, Ch. 36

**State Highway Warrants Act**
Colo. Rev. Stat., 43-4-301 et seq.

**State Highways Act of 1921**
Ill. Rev. Stat. 1957, Ch. 121, § 291 et seq.

**State Historic Preservation Act**
Mo. Rev. Stat., 253.408

**State Historical Building Code**
Cal. Health and Safety Code, § 18950 et seq.

**State Historical Library Act**
Ill. Rev. Stat. 1991, Ch. 128, §§ 12.99, 13

**State Historical Museum Act**
Cal. Public Resources Code § 5013

**State Homes for Boys and Girls Act**
N.J. Stat. Ann., 30:4-156 et seq.

**State Hospital Act**
Tenn. Code Ann., 68-11-101 et seq.

**State Hospital Act (Mental Diseases)**
Ohio Rev. Code 1953, 5123.03 et seq.

**State Hospital and Medical Facilities Survey and Construction Act**
Haw. Rev. Stat. 1968, § 323D-11 et seq.
Wyo. Stat. Ann., § 35-2-301 et seq.

**State Hospital Authority Act**
Ga. Code Ann., 31-7-20 et seq.

**State Hospital Commission Act**
Mich. Comp. Laws 1970, 330.11 et seq.

**State Hospital Construction and Franchising Act**
S.C. Code Ann. 1976, § 44-7-110 et seq.

**State Hospital Survey and Construction Act**
See Hospital Survey and Construction Act

**State Hostel Facilities Act**
Cal. Public Resources Code § 5050 et seq.

**State House Fellows Program Act**
Utah Code Ann. 1953, 63-39-1 et seq.

**State House of Representatives Apportionment Act**
Okla. Stat. Ann., Title 14, § 116 et seq.

**State House of Representatives Redistricting Act**
Okla. Stat. Ann., Title 14, § 121 et seq.

**State Housing Act**
Ark. Code Ann. 1987, 14-169-201 et seq.
Cal. Health and Safety Code, § 17910 et seq.
Del. Code of 1974, Title 31, § 4101 et seq.
Fla. Stat. Ann., 424.001 et seq.
Ill. Rev. Stat. 1977, Ch. 67 1/2, § 151 et seq.
Kan. Laws 1933, Ch. 225
N.C. Public Laws 1933, Ch. 384
N.J. Stat. Ann., 55:14H-1 et seq.
N.Y. Public Housing Law (Consol. Laws Ch. 44A)
Ohio Rev. Code 1953, 3735.01 et seq.
S.C. Code Ann. 1976, § 31-1-10 et seq.
Tex. Rev. Civ. Stat., Art. 1528a

**State Housing Development Authority Act**
Mich. Comp. Laws Ann., 125.1401 et seq.

**State Housing Incentive Partnership Act**
Fla. Stat. Ann., 420.0001 et seq.

**State Housing Initiatives Partnership Act**
Fla. Stat. Ann., 420.907 et seq.

**State Housing Strategy Act**
Fla. Stat. Ann., 420.0001 et seq.

**State Housing Trust Fund for the Homeless Act**
Ga. Code Ann., 8-3-300 et seq.

**State Immunity Act**
Ill. Rev. Stat. 1991, Ch. 127, § 801

**State Improvement Commission Law**
Fla. Stat. 1953, 420.01 et seq.

**State Income Tax Act**
Colo. Rev. Stat., 39-22-101 et seq.

**State Industrial Recovery Act**
Cal. Statutes 1933, Ch. 1037, p. 2632
Ill. Rev. Stat. 1935, Ch. 38, § 246a et seq.
S.C. Acts 1934, p. 2281, No. 1213
W. Va. Acts 1933, 2nd. Ex. Sess., Ch. 86
Wyo. Session Laws 1935, Ch. 123

**State Inland Ports Act**
Miss. Code Ann. 1972, § 59-17-1 et seq.

**State Inmate Escapees' Medical Fees Act**
Ill. Rev. Stat. 1991, Ch. 37, §§ 439.25, 439.26

**State Insect Act**
Ill. Rev. Stat. 1991, Ch. 1, § 2901-15

**State Inservice Education Opportunities Act**
Kan. Stat. Ann., 72-9601 et seq.

**State Inspection Act (Deceased Animals)**
N.Y. Agricultural and Markets Law (Consol. Laws Ch. 69) § 72 et seq.

**State Institutional Buildings Bond Act**
Ark. Stat. 1947, 13-1010 et seq.

**State Institutions Label Law**
Cal. Penal Code § 2895 et seq.

**State Institutions of Higher Education Capital Improvement Voted Bond Act**
N.C. Laws 1975, Ch. 854

**State Insurance Act**
Mich. Comp. Laws Ann., 550.701 et seq.

**State Insurance Plan and Tort Claims Act (Comprehensive)**
Mont. Code Ann., 2-9-101 to 2-9-318

**State Judicial Unification Act**
N.J. Stat. Ann., 2B:10-1 et seq.

**State Justice Institute Act of 1984**
Nov. 18, 1988, P.L. 100-690, 42 U.S. Code §§ 10702, 10704, 10705, 10713
Nov. 19, 1988, P.L. 100-702, 42 U.S. Code §§ 10704 to 10706, 10708, 10713
Nov. 21, 1989, P.L. 101-162, 42 U.S. Code § 10713
Oct. 27, 1992, P.L. 102-528, 42 U.S. Code §§ 10701, 10702, 10705
Oct. 29, 1992, P.L. 102-572, 42 U.S. Code §§ 10703, 10705, 10713

**State Kosher Law**
N.Y. General Business Law (Consol. Laws, Ch. 20)

**State Labor Relations Act**
Mass. Gen. Laws Ann., 150A:1 et seq.
N.Y. Labor Law (Consol. Laws Ch. 31) § 700 et seq.
Tex. Rev. Civ. Stat., Art. 5154a
Vt. Stat. Ann. 1959, Title 21, § 1501 et seq.

**State Land Forfeiture Law**
Cal. Public Resources Code § 7771 et seq.

**State Land Transfer Act**
Ill. Laws 1994, P.A. 88-661

**State Land Use Planning Act**
Wyo. Stat. Ann., § 9-8-101 et seq.

**State Lands Act**
Cal. Public Resources Code § 6001 et seq.

**State Lands Act (Sale to Veterans)**
Colo. Rev. Stat., 36-5-101 et seq.

**State Lands Leasing Law**
Cal. Public Resources Code § 6501 et seq.

**State Law Enforcement Division Act (SLED)**
S.C. Code Ann. 1976, § 23-3-10 et seq.

**State Law Enforcement Officers' Death Benefit Act**
N.C. Gen. Stat. 1943, § 143-166.1 et seq.

**State Law for Aeronautics**
Ind. Code Ann., 8-21-4-1 et seq.
Mont. Code Ann., 67-1-20 et seq.
S.C. Code Ann. 1976, § 55-3-10 et seq.

**State Laws Commission Act**
See Uniform State Laws Commission Act

**State Lawsuit Immunity Act**
Ill. Rev. Stat. 1991, Ch. 127, §§ 800, 801

**State Lease Purchase Act**
La. Rev. Stat. Ann., 39:1780 et seq.

**State Legislatures Act (National Conference)**
Ill. Rev. Stat. 1991, Ch. 63, §§ 122.9, 123

**State Librarian Act**
Ga. Code Ann., 50-11-1 et seq.

**State Library Act**
Ill. Rev. Stat. 1991, Ch. 128, § 101 et seq.
Me. Rev. Stat. Ann. 1964, Title 27, § 1 et seq.
Mo. Rev. Stat., 181.021 et seq., 182.010 et seq.
Wyo. Stat. Ann., §§ 9-2-404, 9-2-417

**State Library Aid Act**
N.J. Stat. Ann., 18A:74-1 et seq.

**State Library Building Act**
Ark. Acts 1969, p. 1011, No. 341

**State License Fee Act**
Mich. Comp. Laws Ann., 338.2201 et seq.

**State Licensing and Certified Real Estate Appraisers Law**
Tenn. Code Ann., 62-39-101 et seq.

**State Lighting Efficiency Standards for Existing Public Buildings Act**
N.Y. Energy Law (Consol. Laws Ch. 17A) § 8-101 et seq.

**State Limitation Law (Retail Liquor Licenses)**
N.J. Rev. Stat. 1937, 33:1-12.14

**State Liquor Control Act**
See Liquor Control Act

**State-Local Financial Coordination Act**
Cal. Government Code § 65591 et seq.

**State Lottery Act**
Ariz. Rev. Stat. Ann., § 5-501 et seq.
Cal. Government Code § 8880 et seq.
Mass. Gen. Laws Ann., 10:22 et seq.
Md. Ann. Code 1974, Art. SG, § 9-101 et seq.
Mo. Rev. Stat., 313.200 et seq.
Mont. Laws 1985, Ch. 669
N.J. Stat. Ann., 5:9-1 et seq.
N.Y. Tax Law (Consol. Laws, Ch. 60), § 1600 et seq.
Ore. Laws 1985, Ch. 2
Ore. Rev. Stat., 461.010
Pa. Purdon's Stat., Title 72, § 3761-101 et seq.
Tex. Government Code, § 466.001 et seq.
Vt. Stat. Ann., Title 31, § 651 et seq.
W. Va. Code 1966 § 29-22-1 et seq.

**State Lottery Control Act**
N.Y. Executive Law 1951 (Consol. Laws Ch. 18) § 430 et seq.

**State Mandates Act**
Ill. Rev. Stat. 1991, Ch. 85, § 2201 et seq.
Iowa Code Ann., 25B.1 et seq.

**State Map Act**
Cal. Public Resources Code § 8002 et seq.

**State Market Road Act**
Ore. Rev. Stat., 369.020 et seq.

**State Markets Act**
Cal. Food and Agricultural Code 1967, § 58001 et seq.

**State Meat Inspection Act**
Ore. Rev. Stat., 619.010 et seq.

**State Medical Act**
N.J. Stat. Ann., 45:9-1 et seq.

**State Medical Examiner Act**
N.J. Stat. Ann., 52:17B-78 et seq.

**State Medical Facility Plan**
Mont. Code Ann., 50-5-402 et seq.

**State Medical Library Law**
Cal. Business and Professions Code, § 525 et seq.

**State Memorial Act (Dickson Mounds)**
Ill. Rev. Stat. 1991, Ch. 105, §§ 4681.9, 468m

**State Mental Health Act**
Wis. Stat. Ann., 51.001 et seq.

**State Mental Hospital Act**
Pa. Purdon's Stat., Title 50, § 1051
Tenn. Code Ann., 33-2-101 et seq.

**State Mental Institution Act (Acquisition)**
Cal. Statutes 1950, 1st Ex. Sess., Ch. 29, p. 471

**State Mental Institutions Bond Act**
N.C. Laws 1953, Ch. 1148

**State Merit System Act**
Ala. Code 1975, § 36-26-1 et seq.
Conn. Gen. Stat. Ann., § 5-193 et seq.
Mo. Rev. Stat., 36.010 et seq.
Ore. Rev. Stat., 240.005 et seq.
R.I. Gen. Laws 1956, 36-3-1 et seq.

**State Military Reserve Act**
Cal. Military and Veterans Code § 550 et seq.

**State Milk Control Act**
N.J. Stat. Ann., App. A:8-1 to App. A:8-49

**State Milk Marketing Act**
Wash. Rev. Code Ann., 15.42.010 et seq.

**State Mineral Act**
Ill. Rev. Stat. 1991, Ch. 1, § 2901-25

**State Mineral Leasing Act**
Cal. Public Resources Code § 6890 et seq.

**State Mineral Water Act**
Cal. Public Resources Code § 6961 et seq.

**State Money Management Act**
Utah Code Ann. 1953, 51-7-1 et seq.

**State Moneys Act**
Ill. Rev. Stat. 1991, Ch. 127, § 170 et seq.

**State Moneys Deposit Act**
Ill. Rev. Stat. 1991, Ch. 130, § 19m et seq.

**State Moneys Disposal Law**
Cal. Government Code § 16301

**State Moratorium Act (Military Service)**
N.D. Laws 1918 Spec. Sess., Ch. 10

**State Moratorium Act (Mortgages)**
N.D. Laws 1935, Ch. 242
N.D. Laws 1937, Ch. 161
N.D. Laws 1939, Ch. 165
S.D. Laws 1935, Ch. 178
S.D. Laws 1937, Ch. 207

**State Moratorium Act (War Service)**
S.D. Laws 1918, Spec. Sess., Ch. 55

**State Museum Construction Act**
Ill. Rev. Stat. 1991, Ch. 127, §§ 59.01, 59.1

**State Narcotic Drug Act**
S.D. Codified Laws 1967, Miscellaneous Superseded Code 39-16-1 et seq.

**State Nature and Historic Preserve Dedication Act**
N.C. Gen. Stat. 1943, § 143-260.6 et seq.

**State Nature and Historical Preserve Act**
N.Y. Environmental Conservation Law 1972 (Consol. Laws Ch. 43B), § 45-0101 et seq.

**State Normal School Act**
Ky. Rev. Stat. 1971, 164.290 et seq.

**State Norris-La Guardia Act (Labor Injunctions)**
See Little Norris-La Guardia Act (Labor Injunctions)

**State Nursery Act**
Cal. Public Resources Code § 4681 et seq.
Ore. Rev. Stat., 571.005 et seq.

**State Nursing Training Facilities Construction Act**
Va. Code 1950, § 32-391 et seq.

**State Nutrition Act**
Mich. Comp. Laws Ann., 325.871 et seq.

**State Nutrition Assistance Program (SNAP)**
Ga. Code Ann., 2-17-1 et seq.

**State Occupational Diseases Act**
Ill. Rev. Stat. 1991, Ch. 48, § 172.36 et seq.

**State Occupational Therapy Act**
Ala. Code 1975, § 34-39-1
Ga. Code Ann., 42-28-1 et seq.

**State Occupational Therapy Practice Act**
Ala. Code 1975, § 34-39-1 et seq.

**State of Entry Act (Insurance)**
Ga. Code Ann., 33-3A-1 et seq.

**State of Kansas Investments in Lifelong Learning Act (SKILL)**
Kan. Stat. Ann., 74-50,102 et seq.

**State Off Street Parking in Rockford Act**
Ill. Rev. Stat. 1991, Ch. 127, §§ 3470, 3471

**State Office Building Authority Act**
Ga. Code Ann., 50-9-1 et seq.
Ind. Code Ann., 4-13-11-1 et seq.
Kan. Laws 1945, Ch. 314
N.J. Stat. Ann., 52:18A-50 et seq.

**State Office of Rehabilitation Act**
Utah Code Ann. 1953, 53A-24-101 et seq.

**State Officer Salary Payment Act**
Ill. Rev. Stat. 1991, Ch. 127, §§ 167w, 168

**State Officers Act**
Wash. Rev. Code Ann., 43.01.010 et seq.

**State Officers and Employees Employment Labor Relations Act**
Wis. Stat. Ann., 111.80 et seq.

**State Officers and Employees Group Insurance Program Law**
Fla. Stat. 1977, 112.075

**State Officers and Employees Money Disposition Act**
Ill. Rev. Stat. 1991, Ch. 127, § 170 et seq.

**State Officers' Fees and Salaries Act**
Ind. Code Ann., 4-2-1-1, 4-2-1-2

**State Officers Pay Act**
Ga. Code 1933, 89-707 et seq.

**State Offices Appointment Act (Vacancies)**
Ohio Rev. Code 1953, 3.03

**State Officials' Compensation Commission Act**
Colo. Rev. Stat., 2-3-801 et seq.

**State Ombudsman Program for the Protection of Children Act**
Ga. Code Ann., 15-11-120 et seq.

**State or Local Employee Grievance Procedure Act**
S.C. Code Ann. 1976, § 8-17-110 et seq.

**State Organization Act**
Alaska Stat. 1962, § 44.17.005 et seq.

**State-Owned Coastal Wetlands Coastal Management Plan**
Tex. Parks and Wildlife Code, § 14.001

**State Owned Lands Protection Act**
Mich. Comp. Laws Ann., 322.141 et seq.

**State Paper Purchasing Act**
Ill. Rev. Stat. 1991, Ch. 127, § 132.100 et seq.

**State Parental Grant Act (Nonpublic Schools)**
Ill. Rev. Stat. 1973, Ch. 122, § 1021 et seq.

**State Parental Grant Plan for Children of Low Income Families Act (Nonpublic Schools)**
Ill. Rev. Stat. 1973, Ch. 122, § 1001 et seq.

**State Park Act (Rio Grande Valley)**
N.M. Stat. Ann., 16-4-9 et seq.

**State Park and Forestry Resources Act**
N.J. Stat. Ann., 13:1L-1 et seq.

**State Park and Recreation Bond Act**
N.M. Laws 1965, Ch. 280
N.M. Stat. Ann., 16-2-20

**State Park and Recreation Bond Act (Cameron-Unruh)**
Cal. Public Resources Code, § 5096.1 et seq.

**State Park Audit Act**
Ill. Rev. Stat. 1991, Ch. 105, §§ 489.9, 490

**State Park Authority Act**
Ga. Code Ann., 12-3-1 et seq.

**State Park Bonds Act**
Cal. Statutes 1927, Ch. 765, p. 1480

**State Park Commission Law**
Cal. Public Resources Code § 5001 et seq.

**State Park Development Revenue Bond Act**
Va. Code 1950, § 10.1-300 et seq.

**State Parks Act**
Ill. Rev. Stat. 1991, Ch. 105, § 464h et seq.
N.C. Gen. Stat. 1943, § 113-44.7 et seq.

**State Parks Designation Act**
Ill. Rev. Stat. 1991, Ch. 105, § 468f.9 et seq.

**State Parks Development Act**
Ala. Code 1975, §§ 40-25-2, 40-25-23

**State Parks Foundation Act**
Mich. Comp. Laws Ann., 318.331 et seq.

**State Parks Revenue Bond Act**
Ill. Rev. Stat. 1991, Ch. 105, § 490.01 et seq.

**State Patrol Act**
Ga. Code Ann., 35-2-30 et seq.
Neb. Rev. Stat. 1943, 81-2001 et seq.
Wash. Rev. Code Ann., 43.43.010 et seq.

**State Patrol Retirement Act**
Wash. Rev. Code Ann., 43.43.120 et seq.

**State Peace Officers and Firefighters Retirement Act**
Cal. Government Code § 21252.02

**State Penal and Rehabilitation Authority Act**
Ga. Code Ann., 42-3-1 et seq.

**State Penitentiary Act**
Ill. Rev. Stat. 1991, Ch. 38, § 1001-1-1 et seq.

**State Penitentiary Work Release Act**
Wyo. Stat. Ann., § 7-13-717 et seq.

**State Permanent Improvement Bond Act**
N.C. Laws 1953, Ch. 1149

**State Personal Property Tax Act**
Pa. Purdon's Stat., Title 72, § 3242 et seq.

**State Personnel Act**
See Personnel Act (State)
Conn. Gen. Stat. 1983, § 5-193 et seq.

**State Personnel Management Act**
Utah Code Ann. 1953, 67-19-1 et seq.

**State Personnel Office Act**
Neb. Rev. Stat. 1943, 81-1301 et seq.

**State Personnel Practices Act**
La. Rev. Stat. Ann., 39:85 et seq.

**State Personnel Relations Law**
Ore. Rev. Stat., 240.005 et seq.

**State Personnel System Act**
Colo. Rev. Stat., 24-50-101 et seq.

**State Personnel System Salary Act**
Colo. Rev. Stat. 24-50-101 et seq.

**State Pesticide Control Act**
Ore. Rev. Stat., 634.006 et seq.

**State Pharmacy Law**
See Pharmacy Act

**State Planning Act**
Cal. Statutes 1929, p. 1805
Colo. Rev. Stat., 24-32-201 et seq.
Del. Code of 1974, Title 29, § 9101 et seq.
Haw. Rev. Stat. Ann., § 226-1 et seq.
Me. Rev. Stat. Ann. 1964, Title 5, § 3301 et seq.
N.J. Stat. Ann., 52:18A-197 et seq.
N.M. Stat. Ann., 9-14-1 et seq.
Pa. Purdon's Stat., Title 71, § 1049.1 et seq.
S.D. Codified Laws 1967, 11-1-1 et seq.

**State Planning Board Law**
Pa. Purdon's Stat., Title 71, § 1050.9 et seq.

**State Plumbing License Act**
N.J. Stat. Ann., 45:14C-1 et seq.

**State Police Act**
Ill. Rev. Stat. 1991, Ch. 121, § 307.1 et seq.
Ind. Code Ann., 10-1-1-1 et seq.
La. Rev. Stat. Ann., 40:1371 et seq.
Md. Ann. Code 1957, Art. 88B, § 1 et seq.
Mich. Comp. Laws Ann., 38.1 et seq.
N.H. Rev. Stat. 1955, 106-B:1 et seq.
Ore. Rev. Stat., 181.010 et seq.
R.I. Gen. Laws 1956, 42-28-1 et seq.
Tenn. Code 1932, § 11450 et seq.

**State Police and Motor Vehicle Inspectors' Retirement Act**
Vt. Stat. Ann., Title 3, § 501 et seq.

**State Police Arbitration Act**
R.I. Gen. Laws 1956, 28-9.5-1 et seq.

**State Police Communications Equipment Leasing Act**
Ark. Code Ann. 1987, 12-8-301 et seq.

**State Police Compact Act**
Conn. Gen. Stat. Ann., § 29-162 et seq.
Me. Rev. Stat. 1964, Title 25, § 1665 et seq.
N.H. Rev. Stat. 1955, 106-D:1 et seq.
Vt. Stat. Ann., Title 20, § 1951 et seq.

**State Police Compact Act (Mid-Atlantic)**
See Mid-Atlantic State Police Compact Act

**State Police Compact Act (New England)**
See New England State Police Act

**State Police Compact Act (Southern)**
La. Rev. Stat. Ann., 40:1312.1 et seq.

**State Police Headquarters Facility and Wireless Data Equipment Financing Act (Department of Arkansas)**
Ark. Acts 1997, No. 1057

**State Police Minimum Salary Act**
Del. Code of 1974, Title 11, § 8303

**State Police Pension Act**
Del. Code of 1974, Title 11, § 8321 et seq.
Ind. Code Ann., 10-1-2-1 et seq.

**State Police Radio Act**
Ill. Rev. Stat. 1991, Ch. 121, § 307.20 et seq.

**State Police Retirement Act**
Mich. Comp. Laws Ann., 38.1601 et seq.

**State Police Retirement System Act**
Ky. Rev. Stat. 1971, 16.505 et seq.
Md. Ann. Code 1957, Art. 88B, § 49 et seq.
Me. Rev. Stat. Ann. 1964, Title 25, § 1592 et seq.
N.J. Rev. Stat. 1937, 53:5A-1 et seq.
W. Va. Code 1966, § 15-2A-1 et seq.

**State Port Authority Act**
Ga. Code Ann., 52-2-1 et seq.
N.H. Rev. Stat. 1955, 271-A:1 et seq.

**State Ports and Harbors Act**
Miss. Code Ann. 1972, § 59-5-1 et seq.

**State Ports Bond Act**
N.C. Laws 1949, Ch. 820

**State Postwar Construction Act**
Cal. Statutes 1947, Ch. 1342, p. 2895

**State Power Act**
Ore. Laws 1933, Ch. 357

**State Power Authority Act**
La. Rev. Stat. Ann., 33:4545.1 et seq.

**State Power Authority Act (Electricity)**
La. Rev. Stat. Ann., 33:4545.1 et seq.

**State Prairie Grass Act**
Ill. Rev. Stat. 1991, Ch. 1, § 2901-55

**State Preserves Act**
Iowa Code Ann., 111B.1 et seq.

**State Primary Election Law**
See Primary Election Act
Ky. Rev. Stat. 1971, Superseded Vols., 119.010 et seq.

**State Printing Act**
Ark. Stat. 1947, 14-301 et seq.
Ind. Code Ann., 4-13-4.1-1 et seq.
Mich. Comp. Laws 1948, 19.151 et seq.
Mo. Rev. Stat., 34.170 et seq.
S.C. Code Ann. 1976, § 11-25-10 et seq.

**State Printing and Public Documents Law**
N.Y. Consol. Laws, Ch. 58

**State Printing Contracts Act**
Ill. Rev. Stat. 1991, Ch. 127, § 132.201 et seq.

**State Printing Control Act**
Mont. Code Ann. 1991, 18-7-301 et seq.

**State Prison Act**
N.J. Stat. Ann., 30:4-136 et seq.

**State Prison and Youth Services Facilities Bond Act**
N.C. Laws 1990, Ch. 935

**State Prison Inmate Care and Custody Reimbursement Act**
Ark. Code Ann. 1987, 12-29-501 et seq.
Colo. Rev. Stat., 17-10-101 et seq.

**State Private Correctional Facility Siting Act**
Ida. Code 1947, 20-801 et seq.

**State Procurement Act**
Del. Laws 1995, Vol. 70, Ch. 601

**State Procurement Code**
Alaska Stat. 1962, § 36.30.005 et seq.
La. Rev. Stat. Ann., 39:1551 et seq.

**State Products Mart and Coliseum Authority Act**
Ala. Code 1975, § 41-10-80 et seq.

**State Prohibition Act (Liquor)**
Ala. Code 1975, § 28-4-1 et seq.
Ark. Acts 1915, p. 98, No. 30
N.D. Laws 1890, Ch. 110
N.D. Laws 1921, Ch. 97
N.Y. Laws 1921, Chs. 155, 156

**State Project Area School Construction Law**
Cal. Education Code 1976, § 15500 et seq.

**State Project Finance Agency Act**
N.Y. Laws 1975, Ch. 7

**State Projects Water Conservation in Landscaping Act**
Colo. Rev. Stat., 37-96-101 et seq.

**State Prompt Payment Act**
Ill. Rev. Stat. 1991, Ch. 127, § 132.400 et seq.

**State Proof Act**
Mich. Comp. Laws Ann., 600.2113 et seq.

**State Properties Acquisition Law**
Ga. Code Ann., 22-1-1 et seq.

**State Properties Code**
Ga. Code Ann., 50-16-30 et seq.

**State Properties Insurance Reserve Fund Act**
Utah Code Ann. 1953, Miscellaneous Superseded Code Provisions, 63-9-23 et seq.

**State Property and Buildings Commission Act**
Ky. Rev. Stat. 1971, 56.440 et seq.

**State Property Control Act**
Ill. Rev. Stat. 1991, Ch. 127, § 133b1 et seq.

**State Property Insurance Law**
Cal. Government Code § 11007

**State Property Special Assessment Benefiting Law**
Ill. Comp. Stat. 1992, Ch. 35, § 230/1 et seq.

**State Public Assistance Programs Act**
Md. Ann. Code 1974, Department of Human Resources, § 63

**State Public Assistance Reserve Fund Act**
R.I. Gen. Laws 1956, Superseded Vol., 40-10-1 et seq.

**State Public Health Statistics Act**
Haw. Rev. Stat. Ann., § 338-1 et seq.

**State Public Sanitary Sewerage Facilities Assistance Act**
N.J. Rev. Stat. 1937, 58:24-1 et seq.

**State Public School Building Authority Act**
Pa. Purdon's Stat., Title 24, § 791.1 et seq.

**State Puformatory Act**
Neb. Rev. Stat. 1943, 83-465

**State Purchasing Act**
Ark. Stat. 1947, 14-201 et seq.
Cal. Government Code § 13370 et seq.
Ga. Code Ann., 50-5-50 et seq.
Mo. Rev. Stat., 34.010 et seq.

**State Purchasing Agent Act**
See Purchasing Agent Act (State)
Mich. Comp. Laws Ann., 17.21 et seq.
N.M. Stat. Ann., 13-1-21 et seq.

**State Purchasing and General Services Act**
Tex. Government Code, § 2151.001 et seq.
Tex. Rev. Civ. Stat. 1974, Art. 601b

**State Purchasing Bid Act**
Alaska Stat. 1962, § 37.05.220 et seq.

**State Rail Authority Act**
W. Va. Code 1966, § 29-18-1 et seq.

**State Rail Preservation Act**
Mo. Rev. Stat. 1978, 680.130 et seq.

**State Railroad Police Act**
Me. Rev. Stat. Ann. 1964, Title 23, § 6071 et seq.; Title 35, § 1301 et seq.

**State Railroad Preservation Act**
Ala. Code 1975, § 37-10-1 et seq.
Mo. Rev. Stat., 620.994 et seq.
R.I. Gen. Laws 1956, 39-6.1-1 et seq.

**State Railroad Preservation and Assistance Act**
Me. Rev. Stat. Ann. 1964, Title 23, § 7101 et seq.

**State Real Property Leasing Act**
Ill. Comp. Stat. 1992, Ch. 30, § 562/1

**State Real Property Tax Act**
N.Y. Laws 1976, Ch. 349, § 3

**State Reclamation Act**
Wash. Rev. Code Ann., 89.16.005 et seq.

**State Reconstruction and Reemployment Law**
Cal. Government Code, § 15530 et seq.

**State Records Act**
Ill. Rev. Stat. 1991, Ch. 116, § 43.4 et seq.

**State Records Management Act**
Cal. Government Code § 14740 et seq.

**State Recovery Act**
N.Y. Laws 1933, 1st Ex. Sess., Ch. 781

**State Recycling and Recycled Materials Procurement Act**
Okla. Stat. Ann., Title 74, § 85.50 et seq.

**State Redistricting Act**
Wash. Rev. Code Ann., 44.05.010 et seq.

**State Reformatory Act**
See Reformatory Act

**State Reformatory for Women Act**
Ill. Rev. Stat. 1977, Ch. 23, § 2801 et seq.

**State Refunding Bond Act**
N.C. Gen. Stat. 1943, § 142-29.1 et seq.
W. Va. Code 1966 § 13-2G-1 et seq.

**State Regents' Academic Scholars Act**
Okla. Stat. Ann., Title 70, §§ 2401 to 2407

**State Regional Centers of Artistic Excellence Act**
N.J. Stat. Ann., 52:16A-1 et seq.

**State Regional Centers of Artistic Excellent Act**
N.J. Stat. Ann., 52:16A-26.1 et seq.

**State Register Act**
N.M. Laws 1947, Ch. 19
S.C. Code Ann. 1976, § 1-23-10 et seq.
Wash. Rev. Code Ann., 34.08.010 et seq.

**State Register of Critical Areas Act**
Me. Rev. Stat. Ann. 1964, Title 5, § 3310 et seq.

**State Register of Historic Places Act**
Okla. Stat. Ann., Title 53, § 351 et seq.

**State Register of Natural Heritage Areas Act**
Okla. Stat. Ann., Title 74, § 1840 et seq.

**State Regulated Farmers Warehouse Act**
La. Rev. Stat. Ann., 54:241 et seq.

**State Regulatory Act (Aircraft)**
Va. Code 1950, § 5.1-1 et seq.

**State Relief Commission Act**
Ohio Laws Vol. 116, pp. 133, 240
Ohio Laws Vol. 117, p. 13

**State Rent Control Act**
N.J. Stat. Ann., 2A:42-11, 2A:42-14 et seq.

**State Reorganization Act**
Mo. Rev. Stat., Appendix B
Tenn. Code Ann., 4-3-101 et seq.

**State Reorganization Bill (Administrative Departments)**
Tenn. Code Ann. 1955, 4-301 et seq.

**State Resort Facility Act**
Haw. Rev. Stat. Ann., § 184-11 et seq.

**State Resource Recovery Policy Act**
N.Y. Environmental Conservation Law 1972 (Consol. Laws, Ch. 43B), § 27-0101 et seq.

**State Retail Liquor License Act**
W. Va. Code 1966 § 60-3A-1 et seq.

**State Retirement Act**
Ark. Code Ann. 1987, 24-4-101 et seq.
Utah Code Ann. 1953, 49-1-101 et seq.
Vt. Stat. Ann., Title 3, § 455 et seq.

**State Retirement and Social Security Act**
S.C. Code Ann. 1976, § 9-5-10 et seq.

**State Retirement System Act**
Me. Rev. Stat. Ann. 1964, Title 5, § 17001 et seq.

**State Revenue Bond Act**
N.M. Stat. Ann. 1953, Superseded Vol., 11-10-1 et seq.

**State Revenue Officers Registration Act**
D.C. Code Ann., §§ 4-1001, 4-1002

**State Revenue Sharing Act**
Mich. Comp. Laws Ann., 141.901 et seq.
N.J. Stat. Ann., 54A:10-1 et seq.

**State Revolving Fund Law (Safe Drinking Water)**
Cal. Health and Safety Code § 116760 et seq.
Neb. Rev. Stat. 1943, 71-5314 to 71-5327
N.M. Stat. Ann., 6-21A-1 to 6-21A-9 et seq.

**State Road Act**
Ky. Rev. Stat. 1971, 176.010 et seq.
Md. Ann. Code 1974, Art. TR, § 8-210 et seq.

*Continued*

**State Road and Highway Bonding Act**
Ore. Code 1991, §§ 44-501 to 44-513, 44-601 to 44-617, 44-701 to 44-709

**State Road Commission Act**
Utah Laws 1909, Ch. 119

**State Rules Act**
N.M. Stat. Ann., 14-4-1 et seq.

**State Rural Electrification Authority Act**
Ala. General Acts 1935, p. 110
Miss. Code Ann. 1972, § 77-5-1 et seq.
N.M. Stat. Ann. 1953, 45-3-1 et seq.
S.C. Code Ann. 1976, § 58-29-10 et seq.
Tenn. Code Ann., 65-23-101 et seq.

**State Rural Rehabilitation Law**
N.C. Public Laws 1935, Ch. 459

**State Safe Drinking Water Act**
Wash. Rev. Code Ann., 70.119A.020 et seq.

**State Salaries Act**
Utah Code Ann. 1953, Miscellaneous Superseded Code Provisions 67-8-11 et seq.
Wash. Rev. Code Ann., 43.03.010 et seq.

**State Salary Administration Act**
Okla. Stat. 1971, Title 74, § 701 et seq.

**State Salary and Annuity Withholding Act**
Ill. Rev. Stat. 1991, Ch. 127, § 351 et seq.

**State Salary Standardization Act**
Ill. Rev. Stat. 1991, Ch. 127, § 168-1 et seq.

**State Sales Tax Act**
See Sales Tax Act

**State Sanitary Code**
N.J. Stat. Ann., 26:1-1 et seq.

**State Sanitorium Act**
Mich. Comp. Laws 1970, 332.51 et seq.

**State Savings and Loan Insurance Corporation Act**
La. Rev. Stat. Ann., 6:1121 et seq.

**State Savings Bank Act**
S.C. Code Ann. 1976, § 34-30-10 et seq.

**State Scholarship Award Program Act**
Neb. Rev. Stat. 1943, 85-980 et seq.

**State Scholarships Law**
Ill. Rev. Stat. 1991, Ch. 122, § 30-15 et seq.

**State School Aid Act**
Mich. Comp. Laws Ann., 388.1401 et seq., 388.1601 et seq.
Mich. Comp. Laws 1970, 388.671 et seq.
N.J. Stat. Ann., 18A:7A-3, 18A:7A-7, 18A:7A-8, 18A:7A-11, 18A:7A-17, 18A:7A-18, 18A:7A-28

**State School Aid Act for Asbestos**
N.J. Stat. Ann., 18A:58-68 et seq.

**State School Bond Sinking Fund Act**
N.C. Gen. Stat. 1943, Superseded Vol., § 115-226 et seq.

**State School Building Aid Act**
N.J. Stat. Ann., 18A:58-33.6 et seq., 18A:58-33.22 et seq.

**State School Building Aid and Earthquake Reconstruction and Replacement Bond Law**
Cal. Education Code 1976, §§ 17400 et seq., 17500 et seq.

**State School Building Aid Bond Law of 1949-1978**
Cal. Education Code 1976, §§ 15900 et seq., 16400 et seq., 16500 et seq., 16600 et seq., 16700 et seq., 16800 et seq., 17000 et seq., 17100 et seq., 17200 et seq., 17600 et seq.

**State School Building Aid Law 1949, 1952**
Cal. Education Code 1976, §§ 15700 et seq., 16000 et seq.

**State School Building Authority Act**
Ga. Code Ann., 20-5-550 et seq.

**State School Building Authority for the Deaf and Blind Act**
Ga. Code 1933, 32-2801a et seq.

**State School Building Lease-Purchase Bond Law**
Cal. Education Code 1976, § 17600 et seq.

**State School Building Lease-Purchase Bond Law of 1976-1984**
Cal. Education Code 1976, §§ 17680 et seq., 17695 et seq., 17700 et seq.

**State School Fund Apportionment Act**
Cal. Statutes 1951, Ch. 1259, p. 3127
Cal. Statutes 1952, 1st Ex. Sess., Ch. 12, p. 414

**State School Incentive Equalization Aid Law**
N.J. Rev. Stat. 18A:7A-3, 18A:7A-7, 18A:7A-11, 18A:7A-17, 18A:7A-18, 18A:7A-28

**State Seal Act**
Ill. Rev. Stat. 1991, Ch. 1, § 2901-5

**State Securities Act**
Nev. Rev. Stat. 1979 Reprint, 349.150 et seq.

**State Selection Acts (Public Lands)**
Sept. 4, 1841, Ch. 16, 5 Stat. 453
Aug. 18, 1894, Ch. 301, 28 Stat. 394, 15 U.S. Code § 203; 20 U.S. Code § 83; 43 U.S. Code §§ 276, 641, 863

**State Senate Apportionment Act**
Okla. Stat. Ann., Title 14, § 80.10 et seq.

**State Sickness Law (Disability Benefits)**
N.J. Stat. Ann., 43:21-25 et seq.

**State Sinking Fund Act**
R.I. Gen. Laws 1956, 35-8-3 et seq.

**State Slogan Act**
Ill. Rev. Stat. 1991, Ch. 1, § 2901-30

**State Soil Conservation Law**
Tex. Agriculture Code, § 201.011 et seq.

**State Soil Survey Act**
Mich. Comp. Laws Ann., 321.41 et seq.

**State Song Act**
Ill. Rev. Stat. 1991, Ch. 1, § 2901-35

**State Sovereignty Commission Act**
Ark. Stat. 1947, 6-801 et seq.

**State Space Management Act**
Ga. Code Ann., 50-5-30 et seq.

**State Special School Teachers' Sick Leave Bank Act**
Tenn. Code Ann., 49-50-1101 et seq.

**State Speech Pathologist and Audiologist Licensing Act**
Ga. Code Ann., 43-44-1 et seq.

**State Spending Lid Act**
Kan. Stat. Ann., 75-6701 et seq.

**State Subsidy of Special Education of Private Institutions Act**
Ill. Rev. Stat. 1991, Ch. 122, § 14-7.02

**State Superfund Act (Hazardous Waste Remedial Fund)**
N.Y. Environmental Conservation Law 1972 (Consol. Laws Ch. 43B) §§ 27-0923, 27-1301 et seq.
N.Y. State Finance Law 1940 (Consol. Laws Ch. 56) § 97b

**State Supplies Purchasing Act**
W. Va. Code 1966, § 5A-3-1 et seq.

**State Supported Salary Schedule for Teachers Act**
Del. Code of 1974, Title 14, § 1301 et seq.

**State Surplus Funds Investment Law**
Cal. Government Code § 16470 et seq., § 16420 et seq.

**State Surplus Personal Property Act**
Tenn. Code Ann., 12-2-401 et seq.

**State Surplus Property Act**
Kan. Stat. Ann., 75-6601 et seq.

**State Survey and Remonumentation Act**
Mich. Comp. Laws Ann., 54.261 et seq.

**State Tax Commission Act**
Md. Ann. Code 1957, Art. 81, § 224 et seq.
Mo. Rev. Stat., 138.190 et seq.
*Continued*

**State Tax Lien Registration Act**
Mich. Comp. Laws Ann., 211.681 to 211.687

**State Tax Lien Registration and Enforcement Act**
Neb. Rev. Stat. 1943, 77-3901 et seq.

**State Tax Uniform Procedure Act**
N.J. Stat. Ann., 54:48-1 et seq.
Okla. Stat. Ann., Title 68, § 201 et seq.

**State Taxation of Depositories Act**
Aug. 16, 1973, P.L. 93-100, 87 Stat. 347, 12 U.S. Code § 548 nt.
Feb. 27, 1976, P.L. 94-222, 15 U.S. Code § 1666f et seq.

**State Teachers College Board Act**
Ill. Rev. Stat. 1991, Ch. 144, § 1001 et seq.

**State Teachers' Retirement Act**
Cal. Education Code 1976, § 22000 et seq.
Wis. Stat. Ann., 40.20 et seq.

**State Teachers Retirement Lands Act**
Cal. Public Resources Code § 6475 et seq.

**State Teachers' Retirement System Home Loan Program Act (Dave Elder)**
Cal. Education Code 1976, § 22360

**State Technical Services Act of 1965**
Sept. 14, 1965, P.L. 89-182, 79 Stat. 679, 15 U.S. Code §§ 1351 to 1368
Nov. 6, 1966, P.L. 89-771, 80 Stat. 1322, 15 U.S. Code § 1352
July 24, 1968, P.L. 90-422, 82 Stat. 423, 15 U.S. Code § 1360

**State Technical-Vocational Education Act**
Tex. Education Code, § 31.01 et seq.

**State Telecommunications Consolidation Act**
Tex. Rev. Civ. Stat., Art. 601b, § 10.01 et seq.

**State Tenement House Act**
N.J. Stat. Ann., 55:1-1 et seq.

**State Textbook Act**
Ky. Rev. Stat. 1971, 157.100 et seq.
Miss. Code Ann. 1972, § 37-43-1 et seq.

**State Tollway Authority Act**
Ga. Code Ann., 32-10-60 et seq.

**State Tort Claims Act**
Neb. Rev. Stat. 1943, 81-8,209 et seq.

**State Tort Liability Act**
Haw. Rev. Stat. Ann., § 662-1 et seq.

**State Trademark Act**
N.H. Rev. Stat. 1955, 350-A:1 et seq.

**State Trails System Act**
N.M. Stat. Ann., 16-3-1 et seq.

**State Transfer of Development Rights Bank Act**
N.J. Stat. Ann., 4:1C-49 et seq.

**State Transitional Bilingual-Bicultural Education Act**
R.I. Gen. Laws 1956, 16-54-1 et seq.

**State Transportation Act**
Conn. Gen. Stat. Ann., § 13b-1 et seq.

**State Transportation Preservation Act**
Mich. Comp. Laws Ann., 474.51 et seq.

**State Travel Reimbursement Act**
Okla. Stat. Ann., Title 74, § 500.1 et seq.

**State Treasurer Act**
Ill. Rev. Stat. 1991, Ch. 130, § 0.01 et seq.

**State Treasurer Employment Code**
Ill. Rev. Stat. 1991, Ch. 130, § 101 et seq.

**State Treasurer's Bank Compensation Pilot Program Act**
Ill. Rev. Stat. 1991, Ch. 130, § 201 et seq.

**State Treasury Management Act**
Ark. Code Ann. 1987, 19-3-201 et seq., 19-3-501 et seq.

**State Treasury Money Management Act**
Ark. Code Ann. 1987, 11-9-301, 19-3-601 et seq.

**State Tree and State Flower Act**
Ill. Rev. Stat. 1991, Ch. 1, § 2901-40

**State Tree Law**
Cal. Government Code § 422

**State-Tribal Cooperative Agreements Act**
Mont. Code Ann., 18-11-101 et seq.
Neb. Rev. Stat. 1943, 13-1501 et seq.

**State Trust for Outdoor Recreation Enhancement (STORE) Act**
Ida. Code 1947, 67-4245 et seq.

**State Tuberculosis Control Act**
Ky. Rev. Stat. 1971, 215.520 et seq.

**State Tuition Law**
N.Y. Education Law 1956 (Consol. Laws Ch. 16) § 2045

**State Underground Petroleum Environmental Response Act**
Fla. Stat. 1983, 206.485 et seq.

**State Underground Petroleum Environmental Response Bank Act**
S.C. Code Ann. 1976, § 44-2-10 et seq.

**State Unemployment Compensation Law**
Ore. Rev. Stat., 657.005 et seq.

**State Uniform Construction Code Act**
La. Rev. Stat. Ann., 40:1725 et seq.
N.J. State Ann., 52:27D-119 et seq.

**State Uniform Laws Commission Act**
Ariz. Rev. Stat. Ann., §§ 41-1306, 41-1307

**State Universities Civil Service Act**
Ill. Rev. Stat. 1955, Ch. 24 1/2, § 380.01 et seq.

**State University Act**
Ill. Rev. Stat. 1991, Ch. 144, §§ 500, 502a, 502b

**State University Act (Chicago)**
Ill. Rev. Stat. 1991, Ch. 144, § 1100 et seq.

**State University Act (Governor's)**
Ill. Rev. Stat. 1991, Ch. 144, § 1110 et seq.

**State University Act (Rutgers)**
N.J. Stat. Ann., 18A:65-1 et seq.

**State University Act (Sangamon)**
Ill. Rev. Stat. 1991, Ch. 144, § 320 et seq.

**State University and Colleges Contract Law**
Cal. Education Code 1976, § 90100 et seq.

**State University and Colleges Educational Opportunity Act**
Cal. Education Code 1976, § 69620 et seq.

**State University Housing Loan Fund Act**
Fla. Stat. Ann., 240.296

**State University of New York and the City University of New York Retirement Incentive Act**
N.Y. Laws 1992, Ch. 494, §§ 1 to 14

**State University Revenue Bond Act**
Cal. Education Code 1976, § 90010 et seq.

**State, Urban and Coastal Park Bond Act**
Cal. Public Resources Code, § 5096.111 et seq.

**State Urban Development Corporation Act**
N.Y. Laws 1998, Ch. 58

**State Use Act**
N.J. Stat. Ann., 30:4-92 et seq.
N.Y. Correction Law (Consol. Laws Ch. 43) § 184

**State Use System of Industries in the Public Welfare Institutions Act**
R.I. Gen. Laws 1956, 13-7-1 et seq.

**State Vehicle Identification Act**
Ill. Rev. Stat. 1991, Ch. 127, § 133e et seq.

**State Vehicle Mileage Act**
Ill. Rev. Stat. 1991, Ch. 127, § 132.500 et seq.

**State Veterans' Home Assistance Improvement Act of 1977**
July 5, 1977, P.L. 95-62, 38 U.S. Code §§ 101 nt., 5031 et seq.

**State Vital Statistics Law**
See Vital Statistics Act

**State Voluntary Poultry Inspection Act**
Ore. Rev. Stat., 619.410 et seq.

**State War Powers Act (Emergency)**
Cal. Military and Veterans Code, § 1500 et seq.

**State Warehouse Act**
Ga. Code Ann., 10-4-1 et seq.

**State Warrants Escheat Act**
Ill. Rev. Stat. 1991, Ch. 15, § 210-14 et seq.

**State Water Commission Act**
N.Y. Laws 1905, Ch. 723

**State Water Conservation Act**
N.D. Cent. Code, 61-02-01 et seq.

**State Water Control Act**
Va. Code 1950, § 62.1-44.2 et seq.

**State Water Plan**
Mont. Code Ann., 85-1-203 et seq.

**State Water Plan Act**
Kan. Stat. Ann., 82a-901 et seq.

**State Water Plan Storage Act**
Kan. Stat. Ann., 82a-1301 et seq.

**State Water Pollution Act**
See Water Pollution Act

**State Water Quality Control Act**
Ariz. Rev. Stat. Ann., § 36-1851 et seq.

**State Water Quality Laboratory Certification Act**
Md. Ann. Code 1974, Art. EN, § 9-1001

**State Water Resources Board Act**
Ore. Rev. Stat., 536.210 et seq.

**State Water Resources Law**
Cal. Water Code § 12570 et seq.
Va. Code 1950, § 62.1-44.45 et seq.

**State Water Resources Planning Act**
Kan. Stat. Ann., 82a-901 et seq.

**State Welfare Act**
Nev. Rev. Stat. 1979 Reprint, 422.005 et seq.

**State Welfare Home Act**
Del. Code of 1953, Title 31, § 701 et seq.

**State Wilderness System Act**
Fla. Stat. Ann., 259.01 et seq.

**State Wildlife and Recreation Lands Management Act**
Wash. Rev. Code Ann., 43.98A.010 et seq.

**State Witness Immunity Act**
Ill. Rev. Stat. 1991, Ch. 38, § 106.1 et seq.
Ohio Rev. Code 1953, 101.44, 2945.44,

**State Workers Act (Volunteer)**
Utah Code Ann. 1953, 67-30-1 et seq.

**State Zoning Enabling Act**
Mont. Code Ann., 76-2-301 et seq.

**Statehood Act**
Haw. Rev. Laws 1955, § 360-1 et seq.

**Statehood Acts (Arizona and New Mexico)**
June 20, 1910, Ch. 310, 36 Stat. 557

**Statehood Commission Act**
Haw. Rev. Laws 1955, § 360-1 et seq.

**Statehood Convention Procedural Amendments Act**
D.C. Code Ann., §§ 1-113, 1-119

**Statement Publication Act (Public Funds)**
Ill. Rev. Stat. 1991, Ch. 102, § 4.90 et seq.

**State's Attorney Act**
Ill. Rev. Stat. 1987, Ch. 14

**State's Attorney Appellate Service Commission Act**
Ill. Rev. Stat. 1991, Ch. 14, § 201 et seq.

**State's Attorney Salary Act**
Ill. Rev. Stat. 1991, Ch. 53, § 7 et seq.

**Statewide Accounting Project Act**
See also Uniform Statewide Accounting Project Act
Tex. Rev. Civ. Stat., Art. 4348f

**Statewide Alzheimer's Disease and Related Disorders Registry Act**
S.C. Code Ann. 1976, §§ 44-36-10 to 44-36-30

**Statewide Building and Housing Codes**
Md. Ann. Code 1957, Art. 83B, § 6-101 et seq.

**Statewide Cancer Registry Act**
Ala. Code 1975, § 22-13-30 et seq.

**Statewide Certified Master Teacher Law**
Cal. Education Code 1976, § 44490 et seq.

**Statewide City Employees' Retirement System Law**
Wash. Rev. Code Ann., 41.44.010 et seq.

**Statewide Classification and Pay Plan**
Mont. Code Ann., 2-18-201 to 2-18-305

**Statewide Economic Development and Planning Act**
Miss. General Laws 1991, Ch. 484, p. 499

**Statewide Economic Development and Planning Act of 1987**
Miss. Code Ann. 1972, § 57-63-1 et seq.

**Statewide Emergency Medical Services and Trauma Care System Act**
Wash. Rev. Code Ann., 70.168.010 et seq.

**Statewide Emergency Services Retirement Act**
Tex. Rev. Civ. Stat., Art. 6243e.3 et seq.

**Statewide Emergency Telecommunications Board Act**
Mass. Gen. Laws 1991, 6A:18B et seq.

**Statewide-Family Investment Program**
Minn. Stat. 1986, 256J.01 et seq., 256K.01 et seq.

**Statewide Fire Prevention Code Act**
Va. Code 1950, § 27-94 et seq.

**Statewide Grand Jury Act**
Fla. Stat. Ann., 905.31 et seq.
Ill. Rev. Stat. 1991, Ch. 38, § 1701 et seq.

**Statewide Health Care Act**
N.M. Stat. Ann., 27-10-1 et seq.

**Statewide Library Development System Act**
Miss. Code Ann. 1972, § 39-3-351 et seq.

**Statewide Mandatory Source Separation and Recycling Act**
N.J. Stat. Ann., 13:1E-99.11 et seq.

**Statewide Multipurpose Hazardous Waste Facility Siting Act**
Fla. Stat. Ann., 403.78 et seq.

**Statewide Personnel System Law**
Miss. Code Ann. 1972, § 25-9-101 et seq.

**Statewide Primary Act**
N.C. Gen. Stat. 1943, § 163-104 et seq.

**Statewide Privilege Tax Law**
Miss. Code Ann. 1972, § 27-15-1 et seq.

**Statewide Probation Act**
Ga. Code Ann., 42-8-20 et seq.

**Statewide Public Defender System Act**
Miss. Code Ann. 1972, §§ 25-32-31 to 25-32-65

**Statewide Registration Act**
Ky. Rev. Stat. 1971, Superseded Vol., 117.600 et seq.

**Statewide Rural Health Care System Act**
Tex. Insurance Code, Art. 20C.01 et seq.

**Statewide Special Inquiry Judge Act**
Wash. Rev. Code Ann., 10.29.010 et seq.

**Statewide Stock Law**
Miss. Code Ann. 1972, § 69-13-1 et seq.

**Statewide Testing Program Act**
Miss. Code Ann. 1972, § 37-16-1 et seq.

**Statewide Trauma System Act**
Neb. Rev. Stat. 1943, 71-8201 to 71-8253

**Statewide Volunteer Firefighters Retirement Act**
Tex. Rev. Civ. Stat., Art. 6243e.3

**Stationery Act (University Use)**
Ill. Rev. Stat. 1991, Ch. 38, § 70 et seq.

**Statistic Law (Agricultural Lands)**
Ore. Laws 1991, Ch. 124

**Statistics Act (Agricultural)**
Ill. Comp. Stat. 1992, Ch. 505, § 15/0.01 et seq.

**Statistics Act (Court)**
Ill. Rev. Stat. 1991, Ch. 25, §§ 29.9, 30

**Statistics Act (Vital)**
Fla. Stat. Ann., 382.001 et seq.

**Statistics Commission Act (Veterans)**
Wash. Laws 1945, Ch. 258

**Statue of Liberty-Ellis Island Commemorative Coin Act**
July 9, 1985, P.L. 99-61, 31 U.S. Code §§ 5112, 5116, 5132

**Status of Convicted Persons Act**
Haw. Rev. Stat. Ann., § 831-1 et seq.
Mont. Code Ann., 46-18-801
N.H. Rev. Stat. 1955, 607-A:1 et seq.

**Status of Women Act**
Haw. Rev. Stat. Ann., § 367-1 et seq.

**Status of Women Commission Act**
Ga. Code Ann., 50-12-80 et seq.

**Status Quo Act**
Ind. Burns' 1933, 60-1101 et seq.

**Statute Against Accumulations**
Pa. 1853 Pamph. Laws 503, No. 304

**Statute and Rule Construction Act**
See Uniform Statute and Rule Construction Act

**Statute Computerization Act**
Ill. Rev. Stat. 1991, Ch. 63, § 150 et seq.

**Statute of Accumulations**
Ill. Rev. Stat. 1991, Ch. 30, §§ 152.9, 153

**Statute of Advancements**
Ill. Rev. Stat. 1939, Ch. 39, § 4 et seq.

**Statute of Ann (Trusts)**
S.C. Code Ann. 1976, § 15-71-310 et seq.

**Statute of Charitable Uses**
Conn. Gen. Stat. Ann., § 47-2
Ill. Rev. Stat. 1991, Ch. 14, § 51 et seq.

**Statute of Conveyances**
Ky. Rev. Stat. 1971, 382.010 et seq.
Tex. Property Code, § 5.001 et seq.

**Statute of Deeds**
W. Va. Code 1966, § 36-3-1 et seq.

**Statute of Descent**
See also Descent Act
Ark. Stat. 1947, 61-101 et seq.
Ga. Code Ann., 53-4-1 et seq.
Haw. Rev. Stat., § 532-1 et seq.
Ind. Code Ann., 29-1-2-1 et seq.
Kan. Stat. Ann., 59-501 et seq.
Md. Ann. Code 1974, Art. ET, § 3-101 et seq.
Minn. Stat. Ann., 525.13 et seq.
N.J. Stat. Ann., 3B:5-2 et seq.

**Statute of Descent and Distribution**
See Descent and Distribution Act

**Statute of Distribution**
See also Distribution Act
Ala. Code 1975, 43-8-40 et seq.

**Statute of Distributions (Probate)**
Conn. Gen. Stat. Ann., § 45a-425 et seq.

**Statute of Entails**
Ill. Rev. Stat. 1991, Ch. 30, § 5
Ohio Rev. Code 1953, 2131.08

**Statute of Escheat**
Ill. Rev. Stat. 1939, Ch. 39, §§ 1, 2

**Statute of Frauds**
Ala. Code 1975, § 8-9-1 et seq.
Alaska Stat. 1962, § 09.25.010
Ariz. Rev. Stat. Ann., § 44-101
Ark. Code Ann. 1987, 4-59-101 et seq.
Cal. Civil Code §§ 852, 1091, 1624, 1624a
Cal. Commercial Code, §§ 1206, 2201, 8319
Colo. Rev. Stat., 38-10-101 et seq.
Conn. Gen. Stat. Ann., § 52-550 et seq.
D.C. Code 1973, § 28-3501 et seq.
Del. Code of 1974, Title 6, § 2711 et seq.
Fla. Stat. 1983, 689.01 et seq., 725.01 et seq.
Ga. Code Ann., 13-5-30
Haw. Rev. Stat. Ann., § 656-1 et seq.
Ida. Code 1947, 9-505
Ind. Code Ann., 32-2-1-1 et seq.
Iowa Code 1977, 557.10, 622.32 et seq.
Kan. Stat. Ann., 33-101 et seq.
Ky. Rev. Stat. 1971, 371.010
La. Civil Code, Art. 2278
Mass. Gen Laws 1984, 259:1 et seq.
Md. Ann. Code 1957, Art. 39C, § 1
Me. Rev. Stat. Ann. 1964, Title 33, § 51 et seq.
Mich. Comp. Laws Ann., 566.106, 566.108, 566.132
Minn. Stat. Ann., 513.01 et seq.
Miss. Code Ann. 1972, § 15-3-1
Mo. Rev. Stat., 432.010 et seq.
Mont. Code Ann., 28-2-903
N.C. Gen. Stat. 1943, § 22-1 et seq.
N.D. Cent. Code, 9-06-04
Neb. Rev. Stat. 1943, 36-101 et seq.
Nev. Rev. Stat. 1979 Reprint, 111.205 et seq.
N.H. Rev. Stat. 1955, 506:1 et seq.
N.J. Stat. Ann., 25:1-1 et seq.
N.Y. General Obligations Law (Consol. Laws Ch. 24A) § 5-701
N.Y. Uniform Commercial Code (Consol. Laws Ch. 38) §§ 1-206, 2-201, 8-319
Ohio Rev. Code 1953, 1335.01 et seq.
Okla. Stat. Ann., Title 15, § 136
Ore. Rev. Stat., 112.015 et seq.
R.I. Gen. Laws 1956, 9-1-4
S.C. Code Ann. 1976, §§ 27-23-50, 32-3-10, 32-3-20
S.D. Codified Laws 1967, 53-8-2
Tenn. Code Ann., 29-2-101 et seq.
Tex. Business and Commerce Code, § 26.01 et seq.
Utah Code Ann. 1953, 25-5-1 et seq.
Vt. Stat. Ann., Title 12, § 181
Wash. Rev. Code Ann., 19.36.010, 62A.2-201
Wis. Stat. Ann., 241.02
Wyo. Stat. Ann., § 1-23-105

**Statute of Frauds (Commissions)**
Wis. Stat. Ann., 240.10

**Statute of Frauds (Contracts)**
Va. Code 1950, §§ 11-1, 11-2

**Statute of Frauds (General)**
W. Va. Code 1966, § 55-1-1

**Statute of Frauds (Public Pay Roll)**
La. Rev. Stat. Ann., 14:138, 14:139

**Statute of Frauds (Real Property)**
N.Y. General Obligations Law (Consol. Laws Ch. 24A) § 5-703
Va. Code 1950, §§ 55-2, 55-3
Wash. Rev. Code Ann., 64.04.010
Wis. Stat. 1985, 240.06 et seq.
W. Va. Code 1966, § 36-1-3

**Statute of Frauds (Sales)**
Ida. Code 1947, 28-2-201
Ill. Rev. Stat. 1991, Ch. 26, §§ 1-206, 2-201, 8-319
Md. Ann. Code 1974, Art. CL, § 2-201

*Continued*

N.C. Gen. Stat. 1943, § 25-1-206
N.D. Cent. Code, 41-02-08
N.Y. Uniform Commercial Code (Consol. Laws Ch. 38) § 2-201
Pa. Cons. Stat., Title 13, § 2201

**Statute of Frauds (Securities)**
N.Y. Uniform Commercial Code (Consol. Laws Ch. 38) § 8-319
Pa. Cons. Stat., Title 13, § 8319

**Statute of Frauds (Uniform Commercial Code Sales)**
Alaska Stat. 1962, § 45.05.050

**Statute of Frauds and Perjuries**
Ill. Rev. Stat. 1991, Ch. 59

**Statute of Frauds-Personal Property**
D.C. Code 1973, § 28:1-206

**Statute of Jeofails**
Fla. Stat. 1953, 54.26
Ky. Civil Code of Practice 1932, § 134
Md. Ann. Code 1957, Superseded Vol., Art. 5, § 16
Miss. Code Ann. 1972, § 11-7-167
Mo. Rev. Stat., 546.080
N.Y. Civil Practice Law and Rules (Consol. Laws Ch. 8) § 2001 et seq.
Tenn. Code Ann., Superseded Vol., 20-1505
Va. Code 1950, § 8.01-678

**Statute of Jeofails (Criminal)**
W. Va. Code 1966, § 62-2-11

**Statute of Limitations**
Conn. Gen. Stat. 1983, § 52-575 et seq.
Del. Code of 1974, Title 10, § 7901 et seq.
Md. Ann. Code 1974, Art. CJ, § 5-101 et seq.
Neb. Rev. Stat. 1943, 25-201 et seq.
Okla. Stat. Ann., Title 12, § 91 et seq.

**Statute of Limitations (1 Year)**
Ariz. Rev. Stat. Ann., §§ 12-522, 12-541, 12-542
Kan. Stat. Ann., 60-514
La. Civil Code, Art. 3534 et seq.
Me. Rev. Stat. Ann. 1964, Title 14, § 753
Miss. Code Ann. 1972, § 91-7-235
Mo. Rev. Stat., 516.140
Pa. Cons. Stat., Title 42 §§ 5524, 5536
Wash. Rev. Code Ann., 4.16.130

**Statute of Limitations (2 Years-Misdemeanors)**
Ga. Offical Code Ann., 17-13-1

**Statute of Limitations (2 Years)**
Ariz. Rev. Stat. Ann., §§ 15-522, 12-543
Kan. Stat. Ann., 60-513
Wash. Rev. Code Ann., 4:16.130

**Statute of Limitations (3 Years)**
Ariz. Rev. Stat. Ann., §§ 12-523, 12-543
Fla. Stat. 1973, 95.11
Kan. Stat. Ann., 60-512
Me. Rev. Stat. Ann. 1964, Title 14 § 868
Mo. Rev. Stat., 516.130
Wash. Rev. Code Ann., 4.16.080
Wis. Stat. Ann., 893.20

**Statute of Limitations (4 Years)**
Ariz. Rev. Stat. Ann., § 12-544 et seq.
Ga. Code Ann., 9-3-25, 9-3-30 et seq.
Miss. Code Ann. 1972, § 15-1-25

**Statute of Limitations (5 Years)**
Mo. Rev. Stat., 516.120

**Statute of Limitations (5 Years—Written Instruments)**
Ark. Code Ann. 1987, 16-56-111

**Statute of Limitations (6 Months)**
Pa. Cons. Stat., Title 42 § 5522

**Statute of Limitations (6 Years)**
Ala. Code 1975, 6-2-34
Ariz. Rev. Stat. Ann., § 12-548
Ind. Code Ann., 34-1-2-1
Me. Rev. Stat. Ann. 1964, Title 14, § 752
Miss. Code Ann. 1972, § 15-1-49
N.J. Stat. Ann., 2A:14-10
Wis. Stat. Ann., 893-19

**Statute of Limitations (10 Years)**
Ga. Code Ann., 9-3-27
Mo. Rev. Stat., 516.110

**Statute of Limitations (15 Years-Color of Title)**
Ark. Code Ann. 1987, 18-11-103

**Statute of Limitations (20 Years-Judgments)**
N.Y. Civil Practice Law and Rules (Consol. Laws, Ch. 8), § 211 Subd. b

**Statute of Limitations (20 Years)**
Ind. Code Ann., 34-1-2-2, Subd. 6

**Statute of Limitations (21 Year Act)**
Pa. Cons. Stat., Title 42, § 5530

**Statute of Limitations (30 Days-Validity of Proceedings)**
Cal. Streets and Hignways Code § 3012

**Statute of Limitations (40 Years)**
Ill. Rev. Stat. 1991, Ch. 110, § 13-118 et seq.

**Statute of Limitations (Account and Replevin)**
R.I. Gen. Laws 1956, 9-1-16

**Statute of Limitations (Actions against Public Authorities)**
N.Y. Public Authorites Law (Consol. Laws Ch. 43A) § 1212

**Statute of Limitations (Actions by State)**
Mo. Rev. Stat., 516.360

**Statute of Limitations (Administrative Review)**
N.Y. Civil Practice Law and Rules (Consol. Laws Ch. 8), § 217

**Statute of Limitations (Adoption)**
Colo. Rev. Stat. 1963, § 4-1-16
Tex. Family Code, § 16.01 et seq.

**Statute of Limitations (Adverse Possession)**
Ill. Rev. Stat. 1991, Ch. 110, § 13-107

**Statute of Limitations (Assessment, Validity of Proceedings)**
Cal. Streets and Highways Code § 3012

**Statute of Limitations (Catch All Act)**
Ohio Rev. Code 1953, 2305.09, Subd. D

**Statute of Limitations (Civil)**
Ala. Code 1975, § 6-2-30 et seq.
Alaska Stat. 1962, § 09.10.010 et seq.
Ariz. Rev. Stat. Ann., § 12-501 et seq.
Ark. Code Ann. 1987, 18-61-101 et seq.
Cal. Code of Civil Prodedure, § 312 et seq.
Conn. Gen. Stat. Ann., § 52-573 et seq.
D.C. Code 1973, § 12-301 et seq.
Del. Code of 1974, Title 10, § 8101 et seq.
Fla. Stat. Ann., 95.011 et seq.
Ga. Code Ann., 9-3-20 et seq.
Haw. Rev. Stat. Ann., § 657-1 et seq.
Ida. Code 1947, 5-201 et seq.
Ind. Code Ann., 34-1-2-1 et seq.
Iowa Code 1977, 614.1 et seq.
Kan. Stat. Ann., 60-501 et seq.
Ky. Rev. Stat. 1971, 413.010 et seq.
La. Civil Code, Art. 3457 et seq.
Mass. Gen. Laws Ann., 260:1 et seq.
Md. Ann. Code 1974, Art. CJ, § 5-101 et seq.
Me. Rev. Stat. Ann. 1964, Title 14, § 751 et seq.
Mich. Comp. Laws 1979, 600.5801 et seq.
Minn. Stat. Ann., 541.01 et seq.
Miss. Code Ann. 1972, § 15-1-1 et seq.
Mo. Rev. Stat., 516.010 et seq.
Mont. Code Ann., 70-19-301 et seq.
N.C. Gen. Stat. 1943, § 1-15 et seq.
N.D. Cent. Code, 28-01-01 et seq.
Neb. Rev. Stat. 1943, 25-201 et seq.
Nev. Rev. Stat. 1979 Reprint, 11.010 et seq.
N.H. Rev. Stat. 1955, 508:1 et seq.
N.J. Stat. Ann., 2A:14-1 et seq.
N.M. Stat. Ann., 37-1-1 et seq.
N.Y. Civil Practice Law and Rules (Consol. Laws Ch. 8), § 201 et seq.
Ohio Rev. Code 1953, 2305.03 et seq.
Okla. Stat. Ann., Title 12, § 91 et seq.
Ore. Rev. Stat., 12.010 et seq.
Pa. Cons. Stat., Title 42, § 5523 et seq.
R.I. Gen. Laws 1956, 9-1-13 et seq.
S.C. Code Ann. 1976, § 15-3-10 et seq.
S.D. Codified Laws 1967, 15-2-1 et seq.
Tenn. Code Ann., 28-3-101 et seq.
Utah Code Ann. 1953, 78-12-1 et seq.
Va. Code 1950, § 8.01-236
Vt. Stat. Ann., Title 12, § 461 et seq.
*Continued*

Wash. Rev. Code Ann., 4.16.005 et seq.
Wis. Stat. Ann., 893.01 et seq.
W. Va. Code 1966, §§ 55-2-1 et seq., 55-7-8
Wyo. Stat. Ann., § 1-3-101 et seq.

**Statute of Limitations (Claims against City)**
N.Y. Court of Claims Act, § 10, Subd. 3

**Statute of Limitations (Claims against Estates)**
Ohio Rev. Code 1953, 2117.06

**Statute of Limitations (Claims against Government)**
Cal. Government Code, § 715

**Statute of Limitations (Contract)**
N.Y. Civil Practice Laws and Rules (Consol. Laws Ch. 8) § 213

**Statute of Limitations (Contractor's Bond)**
Cal. Civil Code, §§ 3249, 4206

**Statute of Limitations (Contracts of Sale)**
D.C. Code 1973, § 28:2-725
Ill. Rev. Stat. 1991, Ch. 26, § 2-725
Iowa Code Ann., 554.2725
Pa. Cons. Stat., Title 13, § 2725
Tenn. Code Ann., 47-2-725

**Statute of Limitations (Contracts)**
Ga. Code Ann., 9-3-20 et seq.
N.Y. Civil Practice Law and Rules (Consol. Laws Ch. 8), § 213, Subd. 2

**Statute of Limitations (Contribution among Joint Tortfeasors)**
R.I. Gen. Laws 1956, 10-6-4

**Statute of Limitations (Court of Claims)**
Mich. Comp. Laws Ann., 600.6452

**Statute of Limitations (Criminal)**
Ala. Code 1975, § 15-3-1 et seq.
Ariz. Rev. Stat. Ann., § 13-106
Ark. Stat. 1947, 43-1601 et seq.
Cal. Penal Code § 799 et seq.
Colo. Rev. Stat., 13-80-102
Colo. Rev. Stat. 1963, 39-1-3
Conn. Gen. Stat. Ann., § 54-193
D.C. Code Ann., § 23-113
Del. Code of 1974, Title 11, § 205
Fla. Stat. Ann., 775.15
Ga. Code Ann., 17-3-1 et seq.
Haw. Rev. Stat. Ann., § 701-108
Ida. Code 1947, 19-401 et seq.
Iowa Code Ann., 802.1 et seq.
Kan. Stat. Ann., 21-3106
La. Code of Crim. Proc. 1966, Art. 571 et seq.
Mass. Gen. Laws Ann., 277:63
Mich. Comp. Laws Ann., 767.24
Mont. Code Ann., 45-1-205, 45-1-206
N.C. Gen. Stat. 1943, § 15-1
Neb. Rev. Stat. 1943, 29-110
N.H. Rev. Stat. 1955, 625:8
N.J. Stat. Ann., 2C:64-8
N.M. Stat. Ann., 30-1-8, 30-1-9
Okla. Stat. Ann., Title 22, § 151 et seq.
Pa. Cons. Stat., Title 42, § 5551 et seq.
R.I. Gen. Laws 1956, 12-21-2
Tenn. Code Ann., 40-2-101 et seq.
Tex. Code of Criminal Procedure, Art. 12.01 et seq.
Vt. Stat. Ann., Title 13, § 4501 et seq.
Wash. Rev. Code Ann., 9A.04.080
W. Va. Code 1966, § 61-11-9

**Statute of Limitations (Death Actions)**
Pa. Cons. Stat., Title 42, §§ 5524, 8301
Va. Code 1950, § 8.01-229

**Statute of Limitations (Debt and Covenant)**
R.I. Gen Laws 1956, 9-1-17

**Statute of Limitations (Debts in Writing)**
Ill. Rev. Stat. 1991, Ch. 110, § 13-206

**Statute of Limitations (Decedent's Estates)**
Fla. Stat. Ann., 733.705

**Statute of Limitations (Disciplinary Action, Ship Brokers)**
Cal. Harbors and Navigation Code, § 78.1

**Statute of Limitations (Dissent from Will)**
N.C. Gen. Stat. 1943, § 30-2

**Statute of Limitations (District and Special Improvements)**
N.Y. Town Law (Consol. Laws Ch. 62) § 195, Subd. 2

**Statute of Limitations (Dower)**
N.Y. Real Property Actions and Proceedings Law (Consol. Laws Ch. 81) § 1001 et seq.

**Statute of Limitations (Eminent Domain)**
Tenn. Code Ann., 29-16-124 et seq.

**Statute of Limitations (Estate Tax Liens)**
N.Y. Tax Law (Consol. Laws Ch. 60), § 24911

**Statute of Limitations (Fire Insurance Contracts)**
N.Y. Insurance Law 1984 (Consol. Laws Ch. 28) § 3404, Subd. e

**Statute of Limitations (Foreign Claims)**
Okla. Stat. Ann., Title 12, § 104 et seq.
Pa. Cons. Stat., Title 42, § 5521 et seq.
W. Va. Code 1966, § 55-2A-1 et seq.

**Statute of Limitations (Foreign Judgments)**
Tex. Civ. Prac. and Rem. Code, § 36.001 et seq.

**Statute of Limitations (Foreign Laws)**
Okla. Stat. Ann., Title 12, § 104 et seq.

**Statute of Limitations (Injuries)**
Ohio Rev. Code 1953, 2305.10

**Statute of Limitations (Justices of Peace)**
Pa. Cons. Stat., Title 42, § 5522

**Statute of Limitations (Land Patents)**
La. Rev. Stat. Ann., 9:5661

**Statute of Limitations (Malicious Prosecutions)**
Pa. 1935 Pamph. Laws 503, No. 196

**Statute of Limitations (Malpractice)**
N.Y. Civil Practice Law and Rules (Consol. Laws, Ch. 8), § 214 Subd. 6, 214a
Ohio Rev. Code 1953, 2305.11

**Statute of Limitations (Matrimonial Actions)**
Wis. Stat. Ann., 767.03, Subsec, 2

**Statute of Limitations (Misdemeanors)**
N.C. Gen. Stat. 1943, § 15-1
Tenn. Code Ann., 40-2-102

**Statute of Limitations (Motor Vehicle Indemnification Corporation)**
N.Y. Insurance Law (Consol. Laws Ch. 28) § 608, Subd. c

**Statute of Limitations (Negligence Actions against State)**
N.Y. Court of Claims Act, § 10

**Statute of Limitations (Negligence)**
N.Y. Civil Practice Law and Rules (Consol. Laws, Ch. 8), § 214, Subd. 5

**Statute of Limitations (Nonsuit or Dismissal)**
Ga. Code Ann., 9-2-61

**Statute of Limitations (Occupational Diseases)**
Ind. Code Ann., 22-3-7-32, Subd. c
Pa. Purdon's Stat., Title 77, § 1415
Tenn. Code Ann., 50-6-306

**Statute of Limitations (One Year, Personal Actions)**
N.Y. Civil Practice Laws and Rules (Consol. Laws Ch. 8) § 215

**Statute of Limitations (Paternity)**
Ala. Code 1975, § 26-12-7
N.Y. Family Court Act § 517

**Statute of Limitations (Personal Actions)**
Ariz. Rev. Stat. Ann., 1956, § 12-541 et seq.
Ark. Code Ann. 1987, 16-56-104 et seq.
Cal. Code of Civil Procedure § 337 et seq.
Colo. Rev. Stat., 13-80-101 et seq.
Del. Code of 1974, Title 10, § 8101 et seq.
Fla. Stat. Ann., 95.11
Ga. Code Ann., 9-3-33
Ill. Rev. Stat. 1981, Ch. 110, § 13-118 et seq.
Ky. Rev. Stat. 1971, 413.080 et seq.
Mich. Comp. Laws Ann., 600.5805 et seq.
Mont. Rev. Code 1947, 93-2601 et seq.
Pa. Cons. Stat., Title 42, § 5523 et seq.

*Continued*

Tenn. Code Ann., 28-3-101 et seq.
Tex. Rev. Civ. Stat., Art. 5524 et seq.
Utah Code Ann. 1953, 78-12-22 et seq.

**Statute of Limitations (Personal Injury)**
N.J. Stat. Ann., 2A:14-2
Pa. Cons. Stat., Title 42, § 5524
R.I. Gen. Laws 1956, 9-1-14

**Statute of Limitations (Port Authority of New York and New Jersey Actions)**
N.Y. Unconsolidated Law, § 7107

**Statute of Limitations (Port of New York Authority)**
N.Y. Laws 1950, Ch. 301, § 7

**Statute of Limitations (Probate)**
Ark. Code Ann. 1987, 28-40-103
Cal. Probate Code § 714
Mass. Gen. Laws Ann., 197:9

**Statute of Limitations (Property Injury)**
Mont. Code Ann., 27-2-207

**Statute of Limitations (Public Works Contractor's Bond)**
Fla. Stat. Ann., 255.05

**Statute of Limitations (Realty Color of Title)**
N.D. Cent. Code, 47-06-03

**Statute of Limitations (Realty)**
Ark. Code Ann. 1987, 18-61-101 et seq.
Cal. Code of Civil Procedure § 315 et seq.
Colo. Rev. Stat., 38-41-101 et seq.
Del. Code of 1974, Title 10, § 7901 et seq.
Fla. Stat. 1983, 95.12 et seq.
Ill. Rev. Stat. 1981, Ch. 110, § 13-101 et seq.
Ky. Rev. Stat. 1971, 413.010 et seq.
Mich. Comp. Laws Ann., 600.5801 et seq.
N.C. Gen. Stat. 1943, § 1-35 et seq.
Pa. Cons. Stat., Title 42, § 5530
Tenn. Code Ann., 28-2-101 et seq.
Tex. Rev. Civ. Stat., Art. 5507 et seq.
Va. Code 1950, § 8.01-236

**Statute of Limitations (Recovery of Land)**
Ill. Rev. Stat. 1991, Ch. 110, § 13-101

**Statute of Limitations (Rejected Probate Claims)**
Cal. Probate Code, § 714

**Statute of Limitations (Sales)**
Ida. Code 1947, 28-2-725

**Statute of Limitations (Savings)**
See Saving Act (Statute of Limitations)

**Statute of Limitations (Schools)**
Ill. Rev. Stat. 1985, Ch. 122, § 822

**Statute of Limitations (Seizin)**
Cal. Code of Civil Procedure, § 318

**Statute of Limitations (Slander)**
R.I. Gen. Laws 1956, 9-1-14

**Statute of Limitations (Street Improvements)**
Okla. Stat. Ann., Title 11, § 36-323

**Statute of Limitations (Survival of Actions)**
Miss. Code Ann. 1972, § 91-7-235
Pa. Cons. Stat., Title 42, § 5524

**Statute of Limitations (Tax Collectors)**
Me. Rev. Stat. Ann. 1964, Title 36, § 761

**Statute of Limitations (Tax Deeds)**
Cal. Revenue and Taxation Code, § 175

**Statute of Limitations (Tax Lien Foreclosure)**
N.Y. Real Property Tax Law (Consol. Laws Ch. 50A), §§ 1110 et seq., 1136, Subd. 7
N.Y. Tax Law (Consol. Laws, Ch. 60) § 165h., Subd. 7

**Statute of Limitations (Tax Purchasers)**
Mo. Rev. Stat., 140.590

**Statute of Limitations (Tax Sale Redemption)**
Colo. Rev. Stat., 39-10-101

**Statute of Limitations (Tax Sales-Land)**
Ala. Code 1975, § 40-10-82

**Statute of Limitations (Taxation)**
Fla. Stat. 1967, 192.21
Tenn. Code Ann., 67-1-1501

**Statute of Limitations (Torts)**
Ga. Code Ann., 9-3-30
La. Civil Code, Art. 2315

**Statute of Limitations (Toxic Torts)**
N.Y. Civil Practice Laws and Rules (Consol. Laws Ch. 8) § 214c

**Statute of Limitations (Trespass)**
R.I. Gen. Laws 1956, 9-1-15

**Statute of Limitations (Uninsured Motorists, Actions against) (MVAIC)**
N.Y. Insurance Law 1984 (Consol. Laws Ch. 28) § 5208

**Statute of Limitations (Usury)**
Ky. Rev. Stat. 1971, 413.140

**Statute of Limitations (Utilities Rates)**
Cal. Public Utilities Code, § 735

**Statute of Limitations (Wills)**
Cal. Probate Code § 20 et seq.

**Statute of Limitations (Workers' Compensation)**
Ala. Code 1975, § 25-5-80
Ark. Code Ann. 1987, 11-9-702
Fla. Stat. Ann., 440.19
Ga. Code Ann., 34-9-82
Ill. Rev. Stat. 1991, Ch. 48, § 138.6
Iowa Code Ann., 85.26
La. Rev. Stat. Ann., 23:1209
Mo. Rev. Stat. 1978, 287.430
Neb. Rev. Stat. 1943, 48-137
N.Y. Workmen's Compensation Law (Consol. Laws Ch. 67), § 40
Okla. Stat. Ann., Title 85, § 43
Pa. Purdon's Stat., Title 77, § 602
R.I. Gen. Laws 1956, 28-35-57, 28-35-57.1
S.C. Code Ann. 1976, § 42-15-40
Tenn. Code Ann., 50-6-203
Wis. Stat. Ann., 102.17, Subsec. 4

**Statute of Limitations (Wrongful Death)**
Ala. Code 1975, § 6-5-410
Del. Code of 1974, Title 10, § 8107
Ind. Code Ann., 34-1-1-2
Mo. Rev. Stat., 537.100

**Statute of Limitations on Foreign Claims Act**
Pa. Cons. Stat., Title 42, § 5521 et seq.

**Statute of Local Governments**
N.Y. Statute of Local Governments (Consol. Laws Ch. 58A)

**Statute of Mortmain**
Ohio Rev. Code 1953, 2107.06

**Statute of Nonclaim**
Ark. Code Ann. 1987, 28-50-101
Okla. Stat. Ann., Title 58, § 333

**Statute of Nonclaim (Decedents' Estates)**
See Nonclaim Act (Estates)

**Statute of Perpetuities**
Ala. Code 1975, 35-4-4
Conn. Gen. Stat. Ann., § 45a-503 et seq.
N.Y. Estates Powers and Trusts Law (Consol. Laws, Ch. 17B), § 9-1.1

**Statute of Proof Act**
See Proof of Statutes Act

**Statute of Religious Freedom**
Va. Code 1950, §§ 57-1, 57-2

**Statute of Repose**
Tex. Civil Practice and Remedies Code, §§ 16.008, 16.009

**Statute of Uses**
Ala. Code 1975, § 35-4-250
Fla. Stat. Ann., 689.05 et seq.
Ga. Code Ann., 53-12-1 et seq.
Ill. Rev. Stat. 1991, Ch. 30, § 3
Md. Ann. Code 1974, Art. RP, § 6-105
Mo. Rev. Stat., 456.020
N.C. Gen. Stat. 1943, § 41-7
S.C. Code Ann. 1976, § 62-7-107 et seq.
W. Va. Code 1966, § 36-1-17

*Continued*

**Statute of Usury**
See Usury Act

**Statute of Wills**
See Wills Act

**Statute on Statutes**
Ill. Rev. Stat. 1991, Ch. 1, § 1000 et seq.

**Statute Proof Act**
Ind. Code Ann., 34-3-1-1 et seq.
Md. Ann. Code 1974, Art. CJ, § 10-202 et seq.
Mich. Comp. Laws Ann., 600.2113 et seq.

**Statutes Annotated Act**
Vt. Stat. Ann., Title 3, § 51 et seq.

**Statutes of Amendments**
Haw. Rev. Stat. 1968, § 634-20

**Statutes of Decents and Distributions**
Mo. Rev. Stat., 474.010 et seq.

**Statutes of Frauds**
Pa. Purdon's Stat., Title 33, § 1 et seq.

**Statutes of Limitations (Bond for Wages)**
Tex. Rev. Civ. Stat., Art. 5160

**Statutes of Limitations (Generally)**
N.Y. Civil Practice Laws and Rules (Consol. Laws Ch. 8) § 201 et seq.

**Statutes of Limitations (Prosecutions)**
Ind. Code Ann., 35-41-4-2 et seq.
Pa. Cons. Stat., Title 42, § 5551 et seq.

**Statutes of Limitations Act**
Aug. 24, 1942, Ch. 555, 56 Stat. 747 (See 18 U.S. Code § 3287)

**Statutes Savings Act (1874)**
Ill. Rev. Stat. 1991, Ch. 1, §§ 1650, 1651

**Statutory Close Corporation Supplement**
Ill. Rev. Stat. 1991, Ch. 144, § 1100 et seq.
S.C. Code Ann. 1976, § 33-18-101 et seq.
Wyo. Stat. Ann., § 17-17-101 et seq.

**Statutory Construction Act**
See also Uniform Statutory Construction Act
Ill. Rev. Stat. 1991, Ch. 1, § 1001 et seq.
Kan. Stat. Ann., 77-201
Minn. Stat. Ann., 645.01 et seq.
N.Y. General Construction Law (Consol. Laws Ch. 22)
Pa. Cons. Stat., Title 1, § 1501 et seq.

**Statutory Employer Act**
Conn. Public Acts 1991, p. 1735, Ch. 138
Kan. Stat. Ann., 44-503
Mich. Comp. Laws Ann., 418.171
Mont. Code Ann., 39-71-118
Va. Code 1950, § 65.1-29

**Statutory Employer Act (Workmen's Compensation)**
Ga. Code Ann., 34-9-8

**Statutory Form Power of Attorney Act**
See also Uniform Statutory Form Power of Attorney Act
See Uniform Statutory Form Power of Attorney Act
La. Rev. Stat. Ann., 9:3861 et seq.

**Statutory Interpretation Act**
Pa. Cons. Stat., Title 1, § 1501 et seq.

**Statutory Joint Account Act**
Mich. Comp. Laws Ann., 487.711 et seq.

**Statutory Lien Act (Personalty)**
Mo. Rev. Stat., 430.010 et seq.

**Statutory Precautions Act (Railroads)**
Tenn. Code Ann., 65-12-108 et seq.

**Statutory Rape Act**
See Rape Act

**Statutory Recount Act (Elections)**
Wash. Rev. Code Ann., 29.64.010 et seq.

**Statutory Rule Against Perpetuities**
See also Uniform Statutory Rule Against Perpetuities
Cal. Probate Code § 21200 et seq.
Colo. Rev. Stat. 15-11-1101 et seq.
Conn. Public Acts 1991, No. 44

Fla. Stat. Ann., 689.225
Ga. Code Ann., 44-6-200 et seq.
Mich. Comp. Laws Ann., 554.71 et seq.
Minn. Stat. Ann., 501A.01 et seq.
Mont. Laws 1989, Ch. 250
Neb. Rev. Stat. 1943, 76-2001 et seq.
N.J. Stat. Ann., 46:2F-1 et seq.
Ore. Rev. Stat., 105.950 et seq.

**Statutory Rule against Perpetuities**
See also Uniform Statutory Rule against Perpetuities
Mass. Gen. Laws Ann., 184A:1 et seq.
Me. Rev. Stat. Ann. 1964 Title 33, § 101 et seq.
N.Y. Estates, Powers and Trusts Law (Consol. Laws Ch. 17B) § 9-1.1 et seq.

**Statutory Salary Act (State Agencies)**
Okla. Stat. Ann., Title 74, § 250.4 et seq.

**Statutory Short Form Power of Attorney Act**
Conn. Gen. Stat. Ann., § 1-42 et seq.

**Statutory Short Form Power of Attorney for Property Law**
Ill. Rev. Stat. 1991, Ch. 110 1/2, § 803-1 et seq.

**Statutory Short Forms of Acknowledgment Act**
Fla. Stat. Ann., 695.25

**Statutory Suit Act (Master and Servant)**
Ala. Code 1958, Title 7, § 176(1) et seq.

**Statutory Tenement Law**
Ky. Rev. Stat. 1953, 101.010 et seq.

**Statutory Trust Act**
Wyo. Stat. 1977, § 17-23-101 et seq.

**Statutory Unitization Act**
N.M. Stat. Ann., 70-7-1 et seq.

**Statutory Will Act**
N.M. Stat. Ann., 45-2A-1 et seq.

**Stavisky-Goodmens Law (New York City Funding)**
N.Y. Education Law 1947 (Consol. Laws Ch. 16) § 2576, Subd. 5

**Stay Act (Death Action Limitation)**
Va. Code 1950, § 8.01-229

**Stay Act (Land Foreclosures)**
Tex. General & Special Laws 43rd Leg., 1934, 2nd C. S., p. 2, Ch. 2
Tex. General & Special Laws 43rd Leg., 1934, 2nd C. S., p. 42, Ch. 16
Tex. General Laws 43rd Leg., 1933, p. 225, Ch. 102

**Stay of Execution Act (Civil)**
Mo. Rev. Stat., 513.365, 513.370
Pa. 1861 Pamph. Laws 770, No. 696

**Stay of Judgement Act**
Mo. Rev. Stat., 511.785 et seq.

**Steagall Commodity Credit Act**
July 1, 1941, Ch. 270, 55 Stat. 498, 15 U.S. Code §§ 713a-1, 713a-4, 713a-8

**Steagall National Housing Act of 1938**
See National Housing Act

**Steagall National Housing Act of 1939**
June 3, 1939, Ch. 175, 53 Stat. 804, 12 U.S. Code §§ 1703, 1708 to 1711, 1713, 1715c, 1716

**Steagall R. F. C. Relief Obligations Act**
Feb. 24, 1938, Ch. 32, 52 Stat. 79, 15 U.S. Code §§ 603, 611a, 611b

**Steagall Stock Liability Act**
See Federal Reserve Act

**Steagall-Wagner National Housing Act of 1938**
See National Housing Act Amendments of 1938

**Stealing by Deceit Act**
Mo. Rev. Stat., 570.030

**Steam Boiler Inspection Act**
Cal. Labor Code § 7680 et seq.
Okla. Stat. Ann., Title 40, § 184 et seq.
Tex. Rev. Civ. Stat., Art. 5221c

**Steam Fitters Act**
Ga. Laws 1937, p. 748

**Steam Signal Act**
Va. Code 1950, § 56-414 et seq.

**Steamboat Companies Act**
Wash. Rev. Code Ann., 81.84.010 et seq.

**Steamboat Inspection Act**
May 27, 1936, Ch. 463, 49 Stat. 1380 (See 28 U.S. Code § 411) 31 U.S. Code § 72; 33 U.S. Code §§ 152, 157; 46 U.S. Code §§ 2 to 4, 12, 18, 28, 39, 40, 43, 44, 49, 51, 52, 55, 56, 63, 77, 79, 222, 225, 234, 239, 260, 265, 275, 369, 372, 375, 382b, 408, 416

**Steamship Authority Funding Loan Act (New Bedford)**
Mass. Acts 1961, Ch. 470

**Steamship Tonnage Tax Act**
Mich. Comp. Laws 1970, 207.51 et seq.

**Steamtown National Historic Site Act of 1986**
Oct. 18, 1986, P.L. 99-500, 100 Stat. 3590
Oct. 30, 1986, P.L. 100 Stat. 3590

**Steel and Aluminum Energy Conservation and Technology Competitiveness Act of 1988**
Nov. 17, 1988, P.L. 100-680, 15 U.S. Code § 5101 nt.
Oct. 24, 1992, P.L. 102-486, 15 U.S. Code §§ 5103, 5107, 5108, 5110

**Steel Import Stabilization Act**
Oct. 30, 1984, P.L. 98-573, 19 U.S. Code § 2253 nt.
Dec. 12, 1989, P.L. 101-221, 19 U.S. Code § 2253 nt.

**Steel Industry American Heritage Area Act of 1996**
Nov. 12, 1996, P.L. 104-333, Division II, Title IV, 16 U.S. Code § 461 nt.

**Steel Industry Compliance Extension Act of 1981**
July 17, 1981, P.L. 97-23, 42 U.S. Code § 7401 nt.

**Steel Products Procurement Act**
Ill. Rev. Stat. 1991, Ch. 48, § 1801 et seq.
Pa. Purdon's Stat., Title 73, § 1881 et seq.
R.I. Gen. Laws 1956, 37-2.1-1 et seq.

**Steel Trade Liberalization Program Implementation Act**
Dec. 12, 1989, P.L. 101-221, 19 U.S. Code § 2101 nt.
Aug. 20, 1990, P.L. 101-382, 19 U.S. Code § 2703 nt.

**Steele-Baldwin Act (Workmen's Death Benefits)**
Mich. Comp. Laws 1948, 412.8

**Steinberg Law (Increase after Budget Approval)**
N.Y. General City Law (Consol. Laws Ch. 21), § 25

**Steingut Act (State Papers)**
N.Y. State Departments Law (Consol. Laws Ch. 78), § 183

**Stenographers Act (Court)**
Tex. Gov. Code, 22.009, 52.041

**Step-Parent Adoption Facilitation Act**
D.C. Code 1973, § 16-308

**Stephens Act (Commercial Rent)**
N.Y. Laws 1945, Ch. 3

**Stephens County-Toccoa Airport Authority Act**
Ga. Laws 1961, p. 2423

**Stephenson Budget Act**
Ky. Acts 1926, Chs. 170, 172

**Stepmother Act**
Fla. Stat. 1973, 731.34

**Sterilization Act**
Ariz. Laws 1929, Ch. 44
Cal. Welfare and Institutions Code §§ 7254, 6624
Conn. Gen. Stat. Ann., § 19-569g
Del. Code of 1974, Title 16, § 5701 et seq.
Ga. Code Ann., 31-20-1 et seq.
Ida. Code 1947, 39-3901 et seq.
Ind. Code 1971, 16-13-13-1 et seq.
Iowa Code 1977, 145.1 et seq.
Kan. Laws 1917, Ch. 299
Mich. Comp. Laws 1970, 720.301 et seq.
Minn. Stat. Ann., 256.08 et seq.
Miss. Code Ann. 1972, § 41-45-1 et seq.
Mont. Code Ann. 1979, 53-23-101 et seq.
N.C. Gen. Stat. 1943, § 35-36 et seq.
N.D. Cent. Code, 25-04.1-01 et seq.
N.H. Rev. Stat. 1955, Superseded Vol., 174:1 et seq.
N.Y. Laws 1912, Ch. 445
Okla. Stat. Ann., Title 43A, § 341 et seq.
Ore. Rev. Stat., 436.010 et seq.
S.C. Code Ann. 1976, § 44-47-10 et seq.
S.D. Codified Laws 1967, Superseded Vol., 27-11-1 et seq., 27-17-1 et seq.
Tenn. Code Ann., 68-34-101
Utah Code Ann. 1953, 64-10-1 et seq.
Va. Code 1950, § 37.1-156 et seq.
Vt. Stat. Ann., Title 18, § 8701 et seq.
Wis. Stat. 1975, 46.12
W. Va. Code 1966, § 16-11-1 et seq.

**Sterilization Act (Dog and Cat)**
Okla. Stat. Ann., Title 4, § 499 et seq.

**Sterilization Act (Habitual Criminals)**
Okla. Laws 1935, p. 94

**Sterilization Act (Mentally Ill)**
N.C. Gen. Stat. 1943, § 35-36

**Sterilization Act (Pet)**
N.M. Stat. Ann., 77-1-18 et seq.

**Sterilization Act (Voluntary)**
See Voluntary Sterilization Act

**Sterilization Due Process Act**
Me. Rev. Stat. Ann. 1964, Title 34-B, § 7001 et seq.

**Sterilization of Bedding Act**
Colo. Rev. Stat., 25-5-301 et seq.

**Sterling Act (Civil Service Retirement)**
See Civil Service Retirement Acts

**Sterling Act (Employers' Liability)**
April 22, 1908, Ch. 149, 35 Stat. 65, 45 U.S. Code §§ 51 to 60, 71

**Sterling Act (Local Taxes)**
Pa. Purdon's Stat., Title 53, § 15971 et seq.

**Sterling Civic Center Act**
Ill. Rev. Stat. 1991, Ch. 85, § 3501 et seq.

**Sterling, Elgin, Orland Park, Centre East, Schaumburg, and DuPage County Civic Centers Act**
Ill. Rev. Stat. 1991, Ch. 85, § 3400 et seq.

**Sterling-Lehlbach Act (Classification, Federal Employees)**
See Classification Act of 1923

**Steroid Control Act**
Ill. Rev. Stat. 1989, Ch. 56 1/2, § 2301 et seq.

**Steroids Act (Anabolic)**
S.C. Code Ann. 1976, § 44-53-10 et seq.

**Steroids Control Act (Anabolic)**
S.C. Code Ann. 1976, § 44-53-10 et seq.

**Stetson-Eshleman Act (Railroad Commission)**
Cal. Statutes 1911, p. 13

**Stevedoring Industry Act (Labor Disputes)**
Haw. Rev. Stat. Ann., § 382-1 et seq.

**Stevenson-Wydler Technology Innovation Act of 1980**

Oct. 21, 1980, P.L. 96-480, 15 U.S. Code § 3701 nt.

Aug. 14, 1986, P.L. 99-382, 15 U.S. Code § 3704

Oct. 20, 1986, P.L. 99-502, 15 U.S. Code §§ 3701 to 3714

Aug. 20, 1987, P.L. 100-107, 15 U.S. Code §§ 3708, 3711a to 3714

Aug. 23, 1988, P.L. 100-418, 102 Stat. 1433, 15 U.S. Code §§ 3706 , 3710, 3713

Oct. 24, 1988, P.L. 100-519, 15 U.S. Code §§ 3703, 3704, 3710, 3710a, 3710b, 3710c

Nov. 29, 1989, P.L. 101-189, 15 U.S. Code §§ 3710, 3710a, 3710c

Nov. 5, 1990, P.L. 101-510, 15 U.S. Code §§ 3705 nt., 3715

April 6, 1991, P.L. 102-25, 15 U.S. Code § 3710a

Dec. 5, 1991, P.L. 102-190, 15 U.S. Code § 3715

Dec. 18, 1991, P.L. 102-240, 15 U.S. Code §§ 3708, 3711b, 3711c, 3712 to 3715

Feb. 14, 1992, P.L. 102-245, 15 U.S. Code §§ 3703, 3704, 3710, 3710a, 3711a

Oct. 23, 1992, P.L. 102-484, 15 U.S. Code § 3710a

Oct. 30, 1992, P.L. 102-575, 43 U.S. Code § 390h-3

Nov. 30, 1993, P.L. 103-160, 15 U.S. Code § 3710a

Dec. 21, 1995, P.L. 104-66, 15 U.S. Code § 3710

March 7, 1996, P.L. 104-113, 15 U.S. Code §§ 3710, 3710a, 3710c, 3710d

Oct. 30, 1998, P.L. 105-309, 15 U.S. Code §§ 3704, 3711a

Nov. 13, 1998, P.L. 105-394, 15 U.S. Code § 3710

**Stewart B. McKinney Homeless Assistance Act**

July 22, 1987, P.L. 100-77, 7 U.S. Code §§ 612c nt., 2012, 2014, 2020, 2025; 20 U.S. Code §§ 1205, 1207a; 29 U.S. Code §§ 1503 , 1551, 1721 nt., 40 U.S. Code § 484; 42 U.S. Code §§ 254e, 256, 256a, 290aa-3 nt., 290bb-1a, 290bb-2, 290cc-21 et seq., 11301 et seq., 11301 nt., 11401 et seq.

Feb. 5, 1988, P.L. 100-242, 42 U.S. Code §§ 11382, 11391

April 28, 1988, P.L. 100-297, 102 Stat. 423, 42 U.S. Code §§ 11421et seq.

Nov. 4, 1988, P.L. 100-607, 42 U.S. Code § 290aa-3 nt.

Nov. 7, 1988, P.L. 100-628, 42 U.S. Code generally §§ 11301 et seq., generally §§ 11421 et seq.

Aug. 16, 1989, P.L. 101-93, 42 U.S. Code §§ 256, 290aa-3 nt., 290bb-2, 290cc-21, 290cc-28, 290cc-29, 290cc-35, 290cc-36, 290dd, 290ee, 290ee-1

Nov. 21, 1989, P.L. 101-165, 42 U.S. Code § 11499

Dec. 12, 1989, P.L. 101-220, 7 U.S. Code § 2014 nt.

Oct. 1, 1990, P.L. 101-402, 42 U.S. Code § 11319

Nov. 28, 1990, P.L. 101-625, 42 U.S. Code §§ 11302, 11361 et seq. generally

Nov. 29, 1990, P.L. 101-645, 42 U.S. Code §§ 290aa-3 nt., 302, 11312 et seq. generally, 11411 et seq. generally, 11481 to 11489

Oct. 23, 1992, P.L. 102-484, 42 U.S. Code § 11411

Oct. 28, 1992, P.L. 102-550, 42 U.S. Code §§ 11318, 11319, 11346 , 11352, 11374, 11375, 11377, prec. 11381, 11381, 11382 to 11389, prec. 11391, 11391 to 11399, 11401, 11403 et seq., prec. 11404, 11404, 11404a, 11404b, 11405 to 11405c, 11406 to 11406c, prec. 11407, 11407, 11407a, 11407b, prec. 11408, 11408, 11408a

Nov. 4, 1992, P.L. 102-590, 42 U.S. Code §§ 11448 to 11450

May 4, 1994, P.L. 103-239, 42 U.S. Code §§ 11449, 11550

May 18, 1994, P.L. 103-252, 42 U.S. Code § 11464

Oct. 20, 1994, P.L. 103-382, 42 U.S. Code §§ 11421, 11431 et seq.

Oct. 25, 1994, P.L. 103-421, 42 U.S. Code § 11411
Feb. 13, 1996, P.L. 104-110, 42 U.S. Code §§ 11448, 11450
Oct. 3, 1996, P.L. 104-235, 42 U.S. Code §§ 11481 to 11489
Oct. 9, 1996, P.L. 104-275, 42 U.S. Code § 11448
Oct. 19, 1996, P.L. 104-316, 42 U.S. Code § 11304
Oct. 26, 1996, P.L. 104-330, 42 U.S. Code §§ 11371, 11372, 11373, 11374, 11375, 11376, 11382, 11401, 11403, 11408
Nov. 21, 1997, P.L. 105-114, 42 U.S. Code §§ 11448, 11450
Aug. 7, 1998, P.L. 105-220, 42 U.S. Code §§ 11421, 11441 to 11447, 11449, 11450, 11461 to 11466, 11471, 11472
Oct. 21, 1998, P.L. 105-276, 42 U.S. Code § 3544
Oct. 21, 1998, P.L. 105-277, 42 U.S. Code § 11302
Cal. Health and Safety Code § 50805.5

**Stewart B. McKinney Homeless Assistance Amendments Act of 1988**
Nov. 7, 1988, P.L. 100-628, 42 U.S. Code § 11301 nt.
Nov. 29, 1990, P.L. 101-645, 104 Stat. 4760
April 21, 1992, P.L. 102-273, 42 U.S. Code § 1437f nt.
Oct. 9, 1992, P.L. 102-405, 106 Stat. 1978
Oct. 28, 1992, P.L. 102-550, 42 U.S. Code §§ 1437f nt., 3544
Nov. 4, 1992, P.L. 102-590, 102 Stat. 5139
Aug. 10, 1993, P.L. 103-66, 42 U.S. Code § 3544
Sept. 21, 1993, P.L. 103-82, 42 U.S. Code § 11312
Aug. 22, 1996, P.L. 104-193, 42 U.S. Code § 11381 nt.

**Stewart B. McKinney Homeless Assistance Amendments Act of 1990**
Nov. 29, 1990, P.L. 101-645, 42 U.S. Code §§ 5118 nt., 11301 nt., 11332

**Stewart B. McKinney Homeless Housing Assistance Amendments Act of 1992**
Oct. 28, 1992, P.L. 102-550, 42 U.S. Code § 11301 nt.

**Stewart B. McKinney National Wildlife Refuge Designation Act of 1987**
May 13, 1987, P.L. 100-38, 16 U.S. Code § 668dd nt.

**Stewart B. McKinny National Wildlife Refuge Designation Act**
Ga. Laws 1988, p. 4498

**Stewart County Road Act**
Tenn. Private Acts 1951, Ch. 171

**Stewart County Solid Waste Authority Act**
Ga. Laws 1992, p. 6867

**Stewart County Water and Sewerage Authority Act**
Ga. Laws 1988, p. 4498

**Still Act**
Colo. Laws 1925, p. 220, Ch. 80

**Stillwater Trailer Law**
N.Y. Local Laws 1968, Town of Stillwater, p. 3036

**Stilwell Act (Imprisonment for Debt—Abolishment)**
N.Y. Laws 1831, Ch. 300

**Stimulant and Barbituric Acid Control Act**
Miss. Code Ann. 1972, § 41-29-117 et seq.

**Stimulant and Depressant Drug Control Act**
N.Y. Penal Law 1965 (Consol. Laws Ch. 40) § 220.00 et seq.
N.Y. Public Health Law 1953 (Consol. Laws Ch. 45) § 3370 et seq.

**Stimulating Small Business Growth for Creation of Jobs Act**
Ark. Code Ann. 1987, 15-4-401 et seq.

**Stink Bomb Act**
Ala. Code 1975, §§ 13A-7-27, 13A-7-28
Iowa Code 1977, 732.10 et seq.

**Stipulated Premium Plan Act (Insurance)**
Mo. Rev. Stat., 377.200 et seq.

**Stirling-Areias Contractors State License Board Enforcement Act**
Cal. Business and Professions Code §§ 7019, 7020, 7065.3, 7091

**Stirling-Davis Common Interest Development Act**
Cal. Civil Code § 1350 et seq.
Cal. Statutes 1985, Ch. 874, Title 6

**Stobb Act (National Prohibition)**
Jan. 15, 1931, Ch. 29, 46 Stat. 1036

**Stock Act (Injuries to Livestock)**
Kan. Stat. Ann., 66-295 et seq.

**Stock Act (Livestock)**
Ark. Code Ann. 1987, 14-387-301 et seq.
Colo. Rev. Stat., 35-41-100.3 et seq.
Ga. Code 1933, 62-501 et seq.
Ky. Rev. Stat. 1971, 259.110 et seq.
La. Rev. Stat. Ann., 3:2801 et seq.
Miss. Code Ann. 1972, § 69-13-1 et seq.
Mo. Rev. Stat., 270.010
S.C. Code Ann. 1976, § 47-7-110 et seq.
Tex. Agricultural Code, § 143.021 et seq.
W. Va. Code 1966, § 19-18-1 et seq.

**Stock Act (Local Option)**
Ala. Code 1975, § 3-5-1 et seq.
W. Va. Code 1931, Ch. 19, Art. 19, § 1 et seq.

**Stock Act (Pasco County)**
Fla. Special Laws 1927, Ch. 13250

**Stock and Bond Act (Railroads)**
Tex. Rev. Civ. Stat., Art. 6520 et seq.

**Stock and Fence Law**
N.C. Gen. Stat. 1943, § 68-1 et seq.

**Stock and Poultry Act (Preparations)**
S.C. Code Ann. 1976, § 46-27-820 et seq.

**Stock Appraisal Act**
Del. Code of 1974, Title 8, § 262

**Stock Appraisal Act (Dissenting Shareholders)**
Ohio Rev. Code 1953, 1701.85

**Stock at Large Act**
Ga. Code Ann., 14-3-1 et seq.

**Stock Attachment Law**
Del. Code of 1974, Title 8, § 324

**Stock Branding Law**
Colo. Rev. Stat., 35-43-101 et seq.

**Stock, Commodity, or Options Transaction Tax Exemption Act**
Ill. Comp. Stat. 1992, Ch. 35, §§ 820/1, 820/2
Ill. Rev. Stat. 1991, Ch. 121 1/2, § 1000 et seq.

**Stock Company Act**
Haw. Session Laws 1890, Ch. 43

**Stock Company Act (Insurance)**
Ind. Code Ann., 27-1-6-1 et seq.

**Stock Corporation Act**
Conn. Gen. Stat. Ann., § 33-282 et seq.
Md. Ann. Code 1974, Art. CA, § 1-101 et seq.
N.Y. Consol. Laws, Ch. 59
Va. Code 1950, § 13.1-601 et seq.

**Stock District Act**
Ark. Code Ann. 1987, 14-387-201 et seq.

**Stock Fence Act (Railroads)**
Tex. Rev. Civ. Stat., Art. 6402

**Stock Fencing Act**
Colo. Rev. Stat., 35-46-101 et seq.

**Stock Grazing Act**
Colo. Rev. Stat., 35-45-101 et seq.
Nev. Rev. Stat. 1979 Reprint, 568.010 et seq.

**Stock Guard Law (Railroads)**
Ark. Code Ann. 1987, 23-12-412

**Stock Installment Sales Law**
Iowa Code 1979, 501.1 et seq.

**Stock Jobbing Act**
N.Y. Laws 1801 (Reprint, Vol. 5), Ch. 116, § 17

**Stock Killing Law**
Colo. Rev. Stat., 40-27-101 et seq.

**Stock Law (Benton County)**
Tenn. Private Acts 1925, Ch. 496

**Stock Law (County)**
Ark. Pope's Digest 1937, § 335 et seq.

**Stock Law (Statewide)**
Miss. Code Ann. 1972, § 69-13-1 et seq.

**Stock Option Act (Corporations)**
Del. Code of 1974, Title 8, § 157

**Stock Option Plan Act (Bank Officers and Employees)**
N.J. Rev. Stat. 1937, 17:9A-27.50 et seq.

**Stock Ownership Plan Act (Employees)**
N.J. Stat. Ann., 52:27H-90 et seq.

**Stock Raising Homestead Act**
April 16, 1993, P.L. 103-23, 43 U.S. Code § 299, 299 nt.

**Stock-Raising Homestead Act**
See Enlarged Homestead Acts

**Stock Reservoir Act**
Jan. 13, 1897, Ch. 11, 29 Stat. 484, 43 U.S. Code §§ 952 to 955

**Stock Restricted Area Act**
Wash. Rev. Code Ann., 16.24.010 et seq.

**Stock Transfer Act**
See also Uniform Stock Transfer Act
Ariz. Rev. Stat. Ann., § 47-8101 et seq.
N.Y. Uniform Commercial Code (Consol. Laws Ch. 38) § 8-301 et seq.

**Stock Transfer Tax Act**
N.Y. Tax Law (Consol. Laws Ch. 60), § 270 et seq.

**Stock Transfer Tax Act (Corporations)**
Ga. Code Ann., 14-2-117
Tex. Rev. Civ. Stat., Art. 1358-1 et seq.

**Stock Watering Act**
Nev. Rev. Stat. 1979 Reprint, 533.485 et seq.

**Stocker and Feeder Act**
Mo. Rev. Stat., 267.010 et seq.

**Stockfish-Wood Act (Costs and Fees)**
Mich. Comp. Laws 1948, 649.2

**Stockholder Wage Liability Act**
Mass. Gen. Laws Ann., 156:35
Pa. 1933 Pamph. Laws 364, No. 106, § 514

**Stockholders Double Liability Act (Banks)**
Okla. Stat. Ann., Title 6, § 701

**Stockholders' Liability Act**
See Federal Reserve Act

**Stockholder's Liability Act (Banks)**
Vt. Stat. Ann. 1959, Superseded Vol., Title 8, § 663

**Stockholder's Voting Act (Corporations)**
Ga. Code Ann., 14-2-720 et seq.

**Stockholm Snowmobile Local Law**
N.Y. Local Laws 1972, Town of Stockholm, p. 2879

**Stockman Act (Intangibles Tax)**
Mich. Comp. Laws Ann., 205.131 et seq.

**Stocks and Bonds Act (Utilities)**
Neb. Rev. Stat. 1943, Superseded Vols. 75-701 et seq.

**Stockton Metropolitan Transit District Act**
Cal. Public Utilities Code § 50000 et seq.

**Stockyards Act**
Neb. Rev. Stat. 1943, 54-503 et seq.

**Stockyards and Packers Act**
Minn. Stat. Ann., 31B.01 et seq.

**Stokes Act (Reservoirs)**
N.Y. Environmental Conservation Law (Consol. Laws, Ch. 43B) § 15-1307

**Stolen and Altered Property Act (Motor Vehicle Chop Shop)**
Ga. Code Ann., 16-8-80 et seq.
Okla. Stat. Ann., Title 47, § 1501 et seq.

**Stolen, Chop Shop and Altered Property Motor Vehicle Act**
S.C. Code of Law 1976, § 56-29-10 et seq.

**Stolen Motor Vehicle Chop Shop and Altered Property Act**
R.I. Gen. Laws 1956, 31-48-1 et seq.

**Stolen Property Act**
Mich. Comp. Laws Ann., 750.535 et seq.

**Stolen Property Possession Act**
Ill. Rev. Stat. 1991, Ch. 38, § 16-1

**Stone Act**
Aug. 4, 1892, Ch. 375, 27 Stat. 348, 30 U.S. Code § 161

**Stone and Pome Fruit Pest Control District Law**
Cal. Food and Agricultural Code 1967, § 8760 et seq.

**Stone-McDonald Act (Recreational Corporations)**
Ala. Code 1975, § 11-60-1 et seq.

**Stone Mountain Memorial Association Act**
Ga. Code Ann., 12-3-190 et seq.

**Stoneham Brook Clearance Loan Act**
Mass. Acts 1959, Ch. 404
Mass. Acts 1960, Ch. 105

**Stones River National Battlefield Act**
March 3, 1927, Ch. 374, 44 Stat. 1399, 16 U.S. Code §§ 426 to 426j
April 22, 1960, P.L. 86-443, 74 Stat. 82, 16 U.S. Code §§ 426k to 426m

**Stonier-Brunner Act (Local Taxes)**
Pa. 1947 Pamph. Laws 1145, No. 481

**Stony Creek Wild and Scenic River Act**
Pa. Purdon's Stat., Title 32, § 820.41 et seq.

**Stop Act (Motor Vehicles)**
N.C. Gen. Stat. 1943, § 20-158

**Stop Act (Railroad Crossings)**
Ind. Code Ann., 9-4-1-106 et seq.
La. Rev. Stat. Ann., 32:169 et seq.
Tex. Rev. Civ. Stat., Art. 6701d, § 86

**Stop and Finish Law**
Ore. Rev. Stat., 131.605 et seq.

**Stop and Frisk Act**
Ala. Code 1975, §§ 15-5-30, 15-5-31
Fla. Stat. 1977, 901.151
Ind. Code Ann., 35-3-1-1 et seq.
Kan. Stat. Ann., 22-2402
La. Code of Criminal Procedure, Art. 215.1
Mass. Gen. Laws Ann., 41:98
Neb. Rev. Stat. 1943, 29-829
N.Y. Criminal Procedure Law (Consol. Laws Ch. 11A), § 140.50
Wis. Stat. Ann., 968.24, 968.25

**Stop and Render Aid Act**
Ga. Code Ann., 40-6-270, 40-6-271
S.C. Code Ann. 1976, § 56-5-1210 et seq.

**Stop, Look and Listen Act**
Ark. Stat. 1947, 75-640 et seq.
Ky. Rev. Stat. 1971, 189.560

**Stop Notice Act**
N.M. Stat. Ann., 48-2A-1 et seq.

**Stop Notice Act (Mechanics' Liens)**
Cal. Civil Code §§ 3083, 3103, 3158 et seq., 3181, 3183 et seq., 3196 et seq.

**Stop Sign Act (Motor Vehicles)**
Del. Code of 1974, Title 17, § 147

**Stop Tobacco Access to Kids Enforcement Act (STAKE Act)**
Cal. Business and Professions Code § 22950

**Stop Turning Out Prisoners Act**
Fla. Laws 1995, Ch. 294

**Stopping and Standing Act (Vehicles)**
Okla. Stat. Ann., Title 47, § 11-1003

**Stopping, Standing and Parking Act**
S.C. Code Ann. 1976, § 56-5-2510 et seq.

**Storage Act (Controlled Atmosphere)**
N.J. Stat. Ann., 4:10-26 et seq.

**Storage Act (Gas)**
See Gas Storage Act
Ill. Rev. Stat. 1991, Ch. 96 1/2, § 5500 et seq.

**Storage Act (Intoxicating Liquors)**
Tenn. Code Ann., 39-6-921, 39-17-713

**Storage Act (Liens on Personal Property and Self-Service)**
Minn. Stat. Ann., 514.970 et seq.

**Storage Act (Marina and Boatyard)**
Me. Rev. Stat. Ann. 1964, Title 10, § 1381 et seq.

**Storage Act (Personal Property)**
Ill. Rev. Stat. 1991, Ch. 111 1/2, § 118.9 et seq.

**Storage Act (Underground)**
Pa. Purdon's Stat., Title 58, § 451 et seq.

**Storage and Grain Act**
Kan. Stat. Ann., 34-101 et seq.

**Storage and Labor Lien Act**
Ill. Rev. Stat. 1991, Ch. 82, § 39.9 et seq.

**Storage and Labor Lien Act (Small Amount)**
Ill. Rev. Stat. 1991, Ch. 82, § 47.9 et seq.

**Storage and Towing Act**
La. Rev. Stat. Ann., 32:1711 et seq.

**Storage and Use Tax Act**
Pa. 1953 Pamph. Laws 377, No. 85

**Storage Facility Act (Self-Service)**
La. Rev. Stat. Ann., 9:4756 et seq.
Mo. Rev. Stat. 1978, 415.400 et seq.
S.C. Code Ann. 1976, § 39-20-10 et seq.
Wash. Rev. Code Ann., 19.150.010 et seq.

**Storage Lien Act (Self-Service)**
N.M. Stat. Ann., 48-11-1 et seq.

**Storage of Gas Law (Underground)**
See Underground Gas Storage Act

**Storage Tank Act**
Kan. Stat. Ann., 65-34,101 et seq.

**Storage Tank Act (Underground)**
Ga. Code Ann., 12-13-1 et seq.
Miss. Code Ann. 1972, § 49-17-401 et seq.
Utah Code Ann. 1953, 19-6-401 et seq.

**Storage Tank and Spill Prevention Act**
Pa. Purdon's Stat., Title 35, § 6021.101

**Storage Tank Cleanup Fund Act (Underground)**
Mass. Gen. Laws Ann., 215:1 et seq.

**Storage Tank Cleanup Trust Fund Act (Underground)**
Cal. Health and Safety Code § 25299.10

**Storage Tank Finance Act (Underground)**
N.J. Stat. Ann., 58:10A-37.1 et seq.

**Storage Tank Petroleum Trust Fund Act**
Ark. Code Ann. 1987, No. 173

**Storage Tank Regulatory Act (Underground)**
Mich. Comp. Laws Ann., 299.701a et seq.
Okla. Stat. Ann., Title 17, § 301 et seq.

**Storage Tank Release Indemnity Program (Petroleum)**
Okla. Stat. Ann., Title 17, § 350 et seq.

**Storage Tank Trust Fund Act (Underground and Aboveground)**
Ala. Code 1975, § 22-35-1 et seq.

**Storage Warehouse Act**
Wash. Rev. Code 1979, 81.92.010 et seq.

**STORE Act (State Trust for Outdoor Recreation Enhancement)**
Ida. Code 1947, 67-4245 et seq.

**Store and Theatre Tax Act**
Pa. Purdon's Stat., Title 72, § 3420-1 et seq.

**Store License Act**
Ind. Burns' 1933, 42-301 et seq.
Tex. Taxation-General 1959, Art. 17.01 et seq.
W. Va. Code 1966, § 11-13A-1 et seq.

**Store License Tax Act**
Mont. Code Ann. 1989, 15-57-101 et seq.

**Store Order Act (Wages)**
Pa. 1881 Pamph. Laws 147, No. 173

**Storm Damage Loan Act (Emergency)**
Mass. Acts 1939, Ch. 63

**Storm Drain Maintenance District Act**
Cal. Water Code, Appendix, § 42-1 et seq.

**Storm Drainage Act (Contra Costa County)**
Cal. Water Code, Appendix, § 69-1 et seq.

**Storm Drainage District Act (ContraCosta County)**
Cal. Statutes 1953, Cj. 1532, p. 3191

**Storm Emergency Fund Act**
Neb. Laws 1949, Ch. 306

**Storm Water District Act**
Cal. Statutes 1909, Ch. 222, p. 339

**Storm Water Management Act**
Pa. Purdon's Stat., Title 32, § 680.1 et seq.

**Storm Water Management and Combined Sewer Overflow Abatement Bond Act**
N.J. Laws 1991, Ch. 181

**Storm Water Management and Sediment Reduction Act**
S.C. Code Ann. 1976, § 48-14-10 et seq.

**Stout Act (Alcoholic Beverages)**
Ind. Code 1971, 7-1-1-1 et seq.

**Stout Act (Delinquent Taxes)**
N.J. Stat. Ann., App. 54:4-123

**Stout-DeLano-Brake Act (Unemployment Compensation)**
Mich. Comp. Laws 1970, 421.1 et seq.

**Stranded Gas Development Act**
Alaska Stat. 1962, § 43.82.010 et seq.

**Strange-Bartlett Act (Parks)**
Ky. Rev. Stat. 1962, 148.110 et seq.

**Strange-McBrayer Act**
Ky. Acts 1930, Ch. 152

**Stranger Picketing Act**
S.D. Codified Laws 1967, 60-10-9 et seq.
Wis. Stat. Ann., 103.535

**Strategic and Critical Materials Stock Piling Revision Act of 1979**
July 30, 1979, P.L. 96-41, 7 U.S. Code §§ 1743, 1745; 15 U.S. Code §§ 714b; 40 U.S. Code § 485; 50 U.S. Code §§ 98, 98 nt., 98a to 98h-3; 50 U.S. Code Appx. § 2039

**Strategic and Critical Materials Stockpiling Act**
July 23, 1946, Ch. 590, 60 Stat. 596, 50 U.S. Code §§ 98, 98 nt., 98a to 98h
July 30, 1979, P.L. 96-41, 50 U.S. Code §§ 98, 98 nt., 98a to 98h-3
Nov. 14, 1986, P.L. 99-661, 50 U.S. Code §§ 98c to 98e, 98e-1, 98e-1 nt., 98h, 98h-2
Dec. 4, 1987, P.L. 100-180, 50 U.S. Code §§ 98 nt., 98a, 98b, 98d , 98e-1, 98h-2, 98h-4, 98h-5
Aug. 23, 1988, P.L. 100-418, 102 Stat. 1159, 50 U.S. Code § 98h-4
Sept. 29, 1988, P.L. 100-456, 50 U.S. Code §§ 98b, 98h-2
Nov. 29, 1989, P.L. 101-189, 50 U.S. Code §§ 98e, 98e-1, 98g, 98h-2, 98h-6, 98h-7
Nov. 5, 1990, P.L. 101-510, 50 U.S. Code §§ 98e, 98h
Dec. 5, 1991, P.L. 102-190, 50 U.S. Code §§ 98e, 98h, 98h-2, 98h-5, 98h-7
Oct. 23, 1992, P.L. 102-484, 50 U.S. Code §§ 98b, 98d, 98h, 98h-1
May 31, 1993, P.L. 103-35, 50 U.S. Code § 98h-2
Nov. 30, 1993, P.L. 103-160, 50 U.S. Code §§ 98a, 98d, 98h, 98h-5

Oct. 5, 1994, P.L. 103-337, 50 U.S. Code § 98e
Feb. 10, 1996, P.L. 104-106, 50 U.S. Code §§ 98c, 98e, 98f
Sept. 23, 1996, P.L. 104-201, 50 U.S. Code §§ 98a, 98b, 98e, 98h-4, 98h-5
Nov. 18, 1997, P.L. 105-85, 50 U.S. Code § 98e
Oct. 17, 1998, P.L. 105-261, 50 U.S. Code § 98h

**Strategic and Critical Minerals Act of 1990**
Nov. 2, 1990, P.L. 101-498, 30 U.S. Code § 1201 nt.

**Strategic Fund Act**
Mich. Comp. Laws Ann., 125.2001 et seq.

**Strategic Investment Fund Program**
Iowa Code Ann., 15:311 et seq.

**Strategic Lawsuits against Public Participation Law (Anti-SLAPP)**
Mass. Gen. Laws Ann., 231:59H

**Strategic Material Loan Act**
See Reconstruction Finance Corporation Act

**Strategic Petroleum Reserve Amendments Act of 1981**
Aug. 13, 1981, P.L. 97-35, 42 U.S. Code § 6201 nt.

**Strategic Planning Act for Educational Excellence**
Utah Code Ann. 1953, 53A-1a-101 et seq.

**Strategic Planning and Performance and Review Act (State Government)**
Cal. Government Code § 11810 et seq.

**Strategic Planning and Performance Budget Act**
Miss. Laws 1994, Ch. 602

**Strategic Planning Assistance Act (Community)**
Kan. Stat. Ann., 74-5092 et seq.

**Strategic Planning for Public Education Act**
N.M. Laws 1996, Ch. 86

**Strategic Training for Accelerated Reemployment Program (STAR)**
Me. Rev. Stat. Ann. 1964, Title 26, § 2015-A

**Strategic War Materials Act**
June 7, 1939, Ch. 190, 53 Stat. 811, 50 U.S. Code §§ 98, 98 nt., 98a, 98b, 98c, 98d, 98e, 98f, 98g, 98h
May 28, 1941, Ch. 135, 55 Stat. 206, 50 U.S. Code § 98e
Aug. 5, 1955, Ch. 580, 69 Stat. 539, 50 U.S. Code §§ 591, 591 nt.
Aug. 1, 1956, Ch. 849, 70 Stat. 899, 22 U.S. Code §§ 611, 618 (See 50 U.S. Code §§ 851, 852)
Aug. 28, 1958, P.L. 85-791, 72 Stat. 950, 50 U.S. Code §§ 793, 820, 821
May 31, 1962, P.L. 87-474, 76 Stat. 91, 50 U.S. Code §§ 782, 784
March 26, 1964, P.L. 88-290, 78 Stat. 168, 50 U.S. Code §§ 402 nt., 831 to 835
Jan. 2, 1968, P.L. 90-237, 81 Stat. 765, 50 U.S. Code §§ 781 to 784, 788 to 794
Oct. 15, 1970, P.L. 91-452, 84 Stat. 931, 50 U.S. Code § 792

**Strawberry Assessment Act**
N.C. Gen. Stat. 1943, § 106-781 et seq.

**Strawberry Marketing Act**
La. Rev. Stat. Ann., 3:471 et seq.

**Strawberry Marketing and Labeling Act**
Ky. Rev. Stat. 1971, 260.130 et seq.

**Stray Act**
N.C. Gen. Stat. 1943, § 68-15 et seq.

**Stray Animal Act**
Mo. Rev. Stat., 271.010 et seq.
Mont. Code Ann., 23-2-301 et seq.
N.C. Gen. Stat. 1943, § 79-1 et seq.

**Stream and Lake Mineral Extraction Law**
Cal. Public Resources Code, § 6961 et seq.

**Stream and Water Pollution Act**
Miss. Code Ann. 1972, § 40-64-01 et seq.
Miss. Code 1942, § 5929-01 et seq.

**Stream Control Act (Rockland County)**
N.Y. Laws 1975, Ch. 846

**Stream Control Commission Act**
La. Rev. Stat. Ann., 24:253 et seq.
Mich. Comp. Laws Ann., 323.1 et seq.

**Stream Control Law (Westchester County)**
N.Y. Laws 1948, Ch. 852, § 191 et seq.
N.Y. Laws 1956, Ch. 853

**Stream Improvements Loan Act (Spencer)**
Mass. Acts 1957, Ch. 440
Tenn. Code Ann., 69-3-101 et seq.

**Stream Partners Program Act**
W. Va. Code 1966, § 20-13-1 et seq.

**Stream Pollution Control Board Act**
Ind. Code Ann., 13-1-3-1 et seq.

**Stream Sanitation Act**
Cal. Statutes 1909, Ch. 93, p. 140
N.C. Gen. Stat. 1943, § 143-211 et seq.

**Streambank Erosion Control Evaluation and Demonstration Act of 1974**
March 7, 1974, P.L. 93-251, 88 Stat. 21, 42 U.S. Code § 1962d-5
Mont. Code Ann., 75-7-101 et seq.

**Streambed and Land Preservation Act**
Mont. Code Ann., 75-7-101 et seq.

**Streams Preservation Act (Natural)**
W. Va. Code 1966, § 22-13-1 et seq.

**Streams, Rivers and Lakes Act**
Ill. Rev. Stat. 1991, Ch. 19, § 51.9 et seq.

**Street, Alley and Other Improvement Act**
D.C. Laws 1978, No. 2-65
Ind. Code Ann., 36-1-3.5-2 et seq.

**Street and Alley Closing and Acquisition Procedures Act**
D.C. Code Ann., § 7-411 et seq.

**Street and Bridge Tax Act (Cities)**
Ill. Rev. Stat. 1991, Ch. 24, §§ 11-81-1, 11-81-2

**Street and Parking Revenue Bond Act**
Ark. Code Ann. 1987, 14-302-101 et seq.

**Street and Sewer Department Act (Wilmington)**
Del. Laws Vol. 18, p. 352, Ch. 188

**Street Car Law (Jim Crow)**
Tenn. Code Ann., Superseded Vol., 65-1704 et seq.

**Street Closing Act**
N.Y. Laws 1895, Ch. 1006

**Street Control Act (Park Commissioners-1879-1917)**
Ill. Rev. Stat. 1991, Ch. 105, §§ 119.9. et seq., 124.9 et seq., 142.9 et seq., 153.9 et seq., 158.9 et seq.

**Street-Core Act (Congressional Districts)**
Ind. Laws 1931, Ch. 113, p. 447

**Street Crimes Act**
Cal. Penal Code §§ 12025, 12031

**Street Improvement Act**
N.C. Private Laws 1927, Ch. 156
Okla. Stat. Ann., Title 11, § 36-201 et seq.
Tex. Rev. Civ. Stat., Art. 1086 et seq.

**Street Improvement Act (Baxley)**
Ga. Laws 1927, p. 902

**Street Improvement Act (Dalton)**
Ga. Laws 1923, p. 593

**Street Improvement Act (Municipalities)**
Ariz. Rev. Stat. Ann., § 48-571 et seq.

**Street Improvement Act (Waycross)**
Ga. Laws 1925, p. 1557

**Street Improvement Act of 1911, 1913**
Cal. Streets and Highways Code §§ 5000 et seq., 7000 et seq.

**Street Improvement Bond Act**
Cal. Streets and Highways Code § 8500 et seq.

**Street Improvement Loan Act (Worcester)**
Mass. Acts 1951, Ch. 385

**Street Improvement Ordinance (Dalton)**
Ga. Laws 1991, p. 5309

**Street Improvement Petition Act**
N.M. Stat. Ann., 3-33-14 et seq.

**Street Improvement Provisional Order Act**
N.M. Stat. Ann., 3-33-13 et seq.

**Street Light District Act**
Ill. Rev. Stat. 1991, Ch. 121, § 354.9 et seq.

**Street Lighting Act of 1919, 1931**
Cal. Streets and Highways Code, §§ 18000 et seq., 18300 et seq.

**Street Occupations Law**
Ky. Rev. Stat. 1971, 339.230, 339.240, 339.990

**Street Opening Act**
N.Y. Local Laws 1971, Town of Philipstown, p. 3100
N.Y. Local Laws 1971, Village of Cold Spring, p. 4007

**Street Opening Act of 1889, 1903**
Cal. Streets and Highways Code §§ 3200 et seq., 4000 et seq.

**Street Opening Bond Act of 1911, 1921**
Cal. Streets and Highways Code §§ 3400 et seq., 4500 et seq.

**Street or Highway Law of the Town of Hunter**
N.Y. Local Laws 1966, Town of Hunter, p. 1113

**Street Paving Act**
La. Rev. Stat. Ann., 33:3381 et seq.

**Street Railroad Bridge Act**
Ill. Rev. Stat. 1991, Ch. 131 1/4, §§ 4.9, 5

**Street Railroad Right of Way Act**
Ill. Rev. Stat. 1991, Ch. 131 1/4, § 0.01 et seq.

**Street Railroad Vestibule Act**
Ill. Rev. Stat. 1991, Ch. 131 1/4, § 5.9 et seq.

**Street Railway Act**
Cal. Public Utilities Code § 7801 et seq.
D.C. Code 1973, § 44-201 et seq.
Ill. Rev. Stat. 1991, Ch. 131 1/4, § 1 et seq.
Mich. Comp. Laws Ann., 472.1 et seq.
Minn. Stat., 1961, 220.01 et seq.
N.J. Stat. Ann.48:15-1 et seq.
Pa. Purdon's Stat., Title 15, § 3601 et seq.
Wash. Rev. Code Ann., 81.64.010 et seq.

**Street Railway Bonds Act (Municipal)**
Wash. Rev. Code Ann., 35.93.010 et seq.

**Street Railway Merger Act**
Jan. 14, 1933, Ch. 10, 47 Stat. 752
D.C. Code Ann., § 43-801 et seq.

**Street Railways Services at Cost Act**
Mass. Gen. Laws Ann., 161:115 et seq.

**Street Readjustment Act**
D.C. Code Ann., § 7-401 et seq.

**Street, Road and Highway Classification Act**
Mich. Comp. Laws 1970, 247.651 et seq.

**Street Special Assessment Relief Act**
Cal. Streets and Highways Code § 1900 et seq.

**Street Surface Railroad Law**
N.Y. Railroad Law (Consol. Laws Ch. 49), § 170 et seq.

**Street Terrorism Enforcement and Prevention Act**
Cal. Penal Code § 186.20 et seq.
Fla. Stat. Ann., 874.01 et seq.
La. Rev. Stat. Ann., 15:1401 et seq.
Mont. Code Ann., 45-8-401, et seq.
R.I. Gen. Laws 1956, 11-61-1 et seq.

**Street Traders Act (Minors)**
La. Rev. Stat. Ann., 23:271 et seq.

**Street Trades Act**
Ill. Rev. Stat. 1991, Ch. 48, § 31.51 et seq.
Wis. Stat. Ann., 103.21 et seq.

**Street Vacation Act**
Cal. Streets and Highways Code § 8300 et seq.
Wash. Rev. Code Ann., 35.79.010 et seq.

**Street Work Revolving Fund Law**
Cal. Government Code § 43420 et seq.

**Street Work Validation Law**
Cal. Statutes 1929, Ch. 360, p. 684

**Streetgang Act**
Miss. Code Ann. 1972, § 97-44-1 et seq.

**Streetgang Terrorism and Prevention Act**
Ga. Code Ann., 16-15-1 et seq.

**Streets and Highways Code**
Cal. Statutes 1935, Ch. 29, p. 248

**Streets and Neighborhoods Act (Safer)**

**Streets and Parks Act**
Minn. Stat. Ann., 430.01 et seq.

**Streets and Roads Authority Act (Harris County)**
Ga. Laws 1995, p. 3752

**Streit Act (Trust Indentures)**
N.Y. Real Property Law (Consol. Laws Ch. 50), § 124 et seq.

**Stress Debriefing Act (Critical Incident)**
Neb. Rev. Stat. 1943, 71-7101 et seq.

**Strict Foreclosure Act**
S.D. Codified Laws 1967, 21-50-1 et seq.

**Strike Act (Public Employees)**
See Public Employees' Antistrike Act

**Strike Act (Sit-Down Prohibition)**
Md. Ann. Code 1957, Art. 27, § 552

**Strike Control Act**
Mich. Comp. Laws Ann., 423.9 et seq.

**Strike Regulation Act**
Ala. Code 1975, § 25-7-1 et seq.
Ga. Code Ann., 34-6-1 et seq.

**Strike Suit Act (Stockholders' Derivative Action)**
Fla. Stat. Ann., 607.0304, 607.0622, 607.07401

**Strike Vote Act**
Fla. Stat. Ann., 447.301 et seq.
Kan. Stat. Ann., 44-809

**Strike Workers Act (Advertisement for)**
Ill. Comp. Stat. 1992, Ch. 820, § 25/0.01 et seq.

**Strike Workers' Advertisement Act**
Ill. Rev. Stat. 1991, Ch. 48, § 21b.9 et seq.

**Strikebreaker Act**
June 24, 1936, Ch. 746, 49 Stat. 1899 (See 18 U.S. Code § 1231)
Ill. Rev. Stat. 1991, Ch. 48, § 2d.9 et seq.
Minn. Stat. Ann., 179.12, 179A.13
Okla. Stat. Ann., Title 11, § 51-102 et seq.

**Strikes by Public Employees Act**
See Public Employees' Antistrike Act

**Strip and Underground Mine Reclamation Act**
Mont. Code Ann. 1983, 82-4-201 et seq.

**Strip and Underground Mine Siting Act**
Mont. Code Ann., 82-4-101 et seq.

**Strip Mined Coal Conservation Act**
Mont. Code Ann. 1979, 82-3-101 et seq.

**Strip Mined Land Reclamation Act**
N.D. Cent. Code, 38-14.1-01 et seq.

**Strip Mining Act**
Ill. Rev. Stat. 1991, Ch. 96 1/2, § 4501 et seq.
Ind. Code Ann., 13-4-6-1 et seq.
Ky. Rev. Stat. 1971, 350.010 et seq.
Md. Ann. Code 1974, Art. NR, § 7-501 et seq.

Mo. Rev. Stat., 444.500 et seq.
Tenn. Code Ann., 59-8-101 et seq.
W. Va. Code 1966, §§ 20-6-1 et seq., 22A-3-1 et seq.

**Strip Mining Act (Anthracite)**
Pa. Purdon's Stat., Title 52, § 681.1 et seq.

**Strip Mining and Reclamation Act**
Ky. Rev. Stat. 1971, 350.010 et seq.

**Strip Mining Reclamation Act**
Ohio Rev. Code 1953, 1513.01 et seq.

**Strip Search Act**
Iowa Code Ann., 804.30

**Striped Bass Act**
N.J. Stat. Ann., 23:5-43 et seq.

**Striped Bass Act of 1991**
Oct. 17, 1991, P.L. 102-130, 16 U.S. Code § 757a nt.

**Strom Thurmond National Defense Authorization Act for Fiscal Year 1999**
Oct. 17, 1998, P.L. 105-261, 112 Stat. 1920
Oct. 21, 1998, P.L. 105-277, 22 U.S. Code § 2778 nt.

**Strong Act (Boards of Freeholders)**
N.J. Laws 1902, p. 65, Ch. 34

**Strong-Biddle Act**
Ala. Code 1975, § 36-21-2

**Strong Mayor Form of Municipal Government Act**
Ill. Rev. Stat. 1991, Ch. 24, § 6-1-1 et seq.

**Stroud-McKool Primary Financing Law**
Tex. Election Code, §§ 173.001 et seq., 13.08c-1 et seq.

**Struck Jury Act**
N.J. Stat. 1937, 2A:75-1 et seq.

**Structural Engineering Act**
Ill. Rev. Stat. 1991, Ch. 111, § 6501 et seq.

**Structural Engineering Licensing Act**
Ill. Rev. Stat. 1987, Ch. 111, § 6601 et seq.

**Structural Pest Control Act**
Cal. Business and Professions Code § 8500 et seq.
Colo. Rev. Stat., 35-11-101 et seq.
Fla. Stat. Ann., 482.011 et seq.
Ga. Code Ann., 43-45-1 et seq.
Ill. Rev. Stat. 1991, Ch. 111 1/2, § 2201 et seq.
La. Rev. Stat. Ann., 3:3361 et seq.
N.C. Gen. Stat. 1943, § 106-65.22 et seq.
Okla. Stat. Ann., Title 2, § 3-171 et seq.
Tex. Rev. Civ. Stat., Art. 135b-6

**Structural Pest Control Act (Montoya)**
Cal. Business and Professions Code § 8516

**Structural Work Act**
Ill. Rev. Stat. 1991, Ch. 48, § 59.90 et seq.

**Stub Ballot Act**
Tex. Election Code, § 64.008

**Stud License Tax Law**
Ky. Stat. 1936, §§ 4223d-1 to 4223d-5

**Student Academic Partnership Program**
Cal. Education Code 1976, § 99300 et seq.

**Student Aid Act (Scholarships)**
N.Y. Education Law 1947 (Consol. Laws Ch. 16), § 601 et seq.

**Student Aid Commission Act (College)**
Iowa Code Ann., 261.1 et seq.

**Student Assistance Act (Mathematics and Science Teaching)**
Neb. Rev. Stat. 1943, 79-12,122 et seq.

**Student Assistance Award Restoration Act**
Tenn. Code Ann., 49-4-801 et seq.

**Student Borrower Right to Know Law (Sale of Student Loans)**
N.Y. Banking Law (Consol. Laws Ch. 2) § 9i
N.Y. Education Law 1947 (Consol. Laws Ch. 16) § 683a

**Student Capacity to Borrow Act (Minors)**
See also Uniform Minor Student Capacity to Borrow Act
Okla. Stat. Ann., Title 15, § 31 et seq.

**Student Choice Act**
N.M. Stat. Ann., 21-21C-1 et seq.

**Student Discipline Act**
Neb. Rev. Stat. 1943, 79-4,170 to 79-4,205

**Student Educational Enhancement Deposit Act**
Me. Rev. Stat. Ann. 1964, Title 20-A, § 12601 et seq.

**Student Exchange Act**
Neb. Rev. Stat. 1943, 79-3601 et seq.

**Student Finance Authority Act**
Ga. Code Ann., 20-3-310 et seq.

**Student Finance Commission Act**
Ga. Code Ann., 20-3-230 et seq.

**Student Financial Assistance Act**
Tex. Education Code, § 56.001 et seq.

**Student Financial Assistance Amendments of 1985**
April 7, 1986, P.L. 99-272, 20 U.S. Code § 1001 nt.

**Student Financial Assistance Program Act (Residential)**
Mont. Code Ann. 1991, 20-26-101 et seq.

**Student Financial Assistance Technical Amendments Act of 1982**
Oct. 13, 1982, P.L. 97-301, 20 U.S. Code §§ 1001 nt., 1070a nt., 1070a, 1070b-3 nt., 1078 nt., 1083a, 1087bb nt., 1087cc, 1087-2, 1089 nt., 1221e-1, 2752
Oct. 19, 1984, P.L. 98-511, 20 U.S. Code §§ 1070a, 1078 nt., 2701 nt., 3804 nt.
Nov. 22, 1985, P.L. 99-159, 20 U.S. Code § 1087bb nt.
April 7, 1986, P.L. 99-272, 20 U.S. Code § 1078 nt.

**Student Financial Assistance Technical Corrections Act of 1986**
May 23, 1986, P.L. 99-320, 20 U.S. Code § 1001 nt.

**Student Grant Program Act**
Ala. Code 1975, § 16-33A-1 et seq.

**Student Interne Act**
Pa. Purdon's Stat., Title 35, §§ 435, 436

**Student Learning Environment and Discipline Act (Improved)**
Ga. Laws 1999, H.B. 605

**Student Loan Act**
Ark. Stat. 1947, 80-4032 et seq.
N.M. Stat. Ann., 21-21-1 et seq.

**Student Loan Act (Medical)**
Kan. Stat. Ann., 76-380 et seq.
N.M. Stat. Ann., 21-22-1 et seq.

**Student Loan Act (Nursing)**
N.M. Stat. Ann., 21-22B-1 et seq.

**Student Loan Act of 1969**
Okla. Stat. Ann., Title 70, § 695.1 et seq.

**Student Loan and Finance Authority Act**
Cal. Education Code 1976, § 69905 et seq.

**Student Loan Authority Act**
Cal. Education Code 1976, § 69905 et seq.
Mass. Gen. Laws Ann., 15C:1 et seq.
R.I. Gen. Laws 1956, 16-62-1 et seq.

**Student Loan Authority Act (College)**
Mass. Gen. Laws Ann., 15C:1 et seq.

**Student Loan Debt Income Tax Setoff Act**
Miss. Code Ann. 1972, § 27-7-701 et seq.

**Student Loan Default Prevention Initiative Act of 1990**
Nov. 5, 1990, P.L. 101-508, 11 U.S. Code §§ 362, 541, 1328; 20 U.S. Code § 1001 nt.

**Student Loan for Service Act (Allied Health)**
N.M. Stat. Ann., 21-22C-1 et seq.

**Student Loan Foundation Act**
Conn. Gen. Stat. Ann., § 10a-201 et seq.

**Student Loan Funds Act**
Va. Code 1950, § 23-38.10:2 et seq.

**Student Loan Guarantee Act**
N.M. Stat. Ann., 21-21-14 et seq.
W. Va. Acts 1968, Ch. 54
W. Va. Code 1966, § 18-220-1 et seq.

**Student Loan Marketing Association Reorganization Act of 1996**
Sept. 30, 1996, P.L. 104-208, 20 U.S. Code § 1001 nt.

**Student Loan Purchase Program Law**
Ill. Rev. Stat. 1991, Ch. 122, § 30-15.14a et seq.

**Student Loan Reconciliation Amendments of 1989**
Dec. 19, 1989, P.L. 101-239, 20 U.S. Code § 1001 nt.

**Student Loan Reform Act of 1993**
Aug. 10, 1993, P.L. 103-66, 20 U.S. Code § 1001 nt.

**Student Loans to Minors Act**
Ill. Rev. Stat. 1991, Ch. 17, §§ 6300, 6301

**Student Organization Act (School-to-Work)**
Minn. Stat. Ann., 121.615

**Student Organization Responsibility for Drug Abuse Act**
Ga. Code Ann., 20-3-90 et seq.

**Student Protection and School Reform Act (Maxine Waters)**
Cal. Education Code 1976, § 94316 et seq.

**Student Publications Act**
Kan. Laws 1992, Ch. 5

**Student Records Act**
Ill. Rev. Stat. 1991, Ch. 122, § 50-1 et seq.

**Student Right-To-Know Act**
Nov. 8, 1990, P.L. 101-542, 20 U.S. Code §§ 1001 nt., 1092 nt.

**Student Right-To-Know and Campus Security Act**
Nov. 8, 1990, P.L. 101-542, 20 U.S. Code § 1001 nt.
April 9, 1991, P.L. 102-26, 20 U.S. Code § 1092 nt.

**Student Scholarship Program Act (Nursing)**
Kan. Stat. Ann., 74-3291 et seq.

**Student Services Act**
Fla. Stat. Ann., 203.2313

**Student Services Act (Public School)**
Ark. Acts 1991, No. 908

**Student State Aid Act**
N.Y. Education Law 1947 (Consol. Laws Ch. 16) § 601 et seq.

**Student-to-Student Grant Act**
Ill. Rev. Stat. 1991, Ch. 144, § 270 et seq.

**Student Transfer Program Act**
Colo. Rev. Stat. 23-1-501, 23-1-502

**Student Travel Act**
P.R. Laws Ann. 1954, Title 18, § 921 et seq.

**Students FIRST Act**
Ariz. Rev. Stat. Ann., §§ 15-901 et seq., 15-2001 et seq.

**Studies Act**
N.C. Laws 1990, Ch. 1078
N.C. Laws 1991, Ch. 754
N.C. Laws 1991, Ch. 802

**Study Commissions and Committees Act**
N.C. Gen. Stat. 1943, § 120-180 et seq.
N.C. Laws 1991, Ch. 873

**Study Commissions and Committees Act (Independent)**
N.C. Laws 1985, Ch. 792

**Study Commissions and Committees Act of 1987**
N.C. Gen. Stat. 1943, § 120-180 et seq.

**Stuffed Toy Act**
Me. Rev. Stat. Ann. 1964, Title 26, § 121 et seq.

**Stull Act (Certificated Employees)**
Cal. Education Code 1976, § 44660 et seq.

**Stull-Burton Vietnam Veterans Employment Act**
Cal. Government Code, § 7280 et seq.

**Sturbridge School Building Loan Act**
Mass. Acts 1949, Ch. 6

**Stuyvesant Mobile Home and Travel Trailer Law**
N.Y. Local Laws 1968, Town of Stuyvesant, p. 3049

**Subchapter S Corporations**
Mont. Code Ann., 15-31-201 et seq.

**Subchapter S Revision Act Of 1982**
Oct. 19, 1982, P.L. 97-354, 26 U.S. Code § 1 nt.
July 18, 1984, P.L. 98-369, 98 Stat. 966

**Subcontractor and Contractor Payment Act**
Pa. Purdon's Stat., Title 73, § 501 et seq.

**Subcontractors Fair Practices Act**
N.M. Stat. Ann., 13-4-31 et seq.

**Subcontractors' Gratuities and Kick-Backs Act (Public Contracts)**
March 8, 1946, Ch. 80, 60 Stat. 37, 41 U.S. Code §§ 51 to 54
Sept. 2, 1960, P.L. 86-695, 74 Stat. 740, 41 U.S. Code §§ 51 to 54

**Subcontractors' Lien Act**
Ohio Rev. Code 1953, 1311.04 et seq.

**Subdivided Land Sales Act**
Ida. Code 1947, 55-1801 et seq.
Minn. Stat. Ann., 83.20 et seq.
N.D. Cent. Code, 43-23.1-01 et seq.
Okla. Stat. Ann., Title 71, § 601 et seq.
Va. Code 1950, § 55-336 et seq.

**Subdivision Act**
Cal. Business and Professions Code, § 11000 et seq.
N.M. Stat. Ann., 47-5-1 et seq., 47-6-1 et seq.

**Subdivision and Land Development Review Enabling Act**
R.I. Gen. Laws 1956, 45-23-25 et seq.

**Subdivision and Platting Act**
Mont. Code Ann., 76-3-101 et seq.

**Subdivision and Series Partition Control Law**
Ore. Rev. Stat., 92.305 et seq.

**Subdivision Control Act**
Conn. Gen. Stat. Ann., § 8-25 et seq.
Ill. Rev. Stat. 1991, Ch. 109, § 1 et seq.
Mass. Gen. Laws Ann., 41:81K et seq.
Mich. Comp. Laws Ann., 560.101 et seq.
Ore. Rev. Stat., 92.305 et seq.
Va. Code 1950, § 15.1-465 et seq.
Wash. Rev. Code Ann., 58.17.010 et seq.
Wis. Stat. Ann., 236.01 et seq.

**Subdivision Control Act (Municipal)**
N.C. Gen. Stat. 1943, § 160A-371 et seq.

**Subdivision Land Exclusion Law**
Cal. Government Code § 66499.21 et seq.

**Subdivision Map Act**
Cal. Government Code § 66410 et seq.

**Subdivision Regulation Act**
S.C. Code Ann. 1976, § 6-7-1010 et seq.

**Subdivision Road and Bridge Act (Alachua County)**
Fla. Special Laws 1953, Ch. 28872

**Subletting and Subcontracting Fair Practices Act**
Cal. Public Contract Code § 4100 et seq.

**Submarine Cable Act**
Feb. 29, 1888, Ch. 17, 25 Stat. 41, 47 U.S. Code §§ 21 to 33

**Submerged Land Act (Parks)**
Ill. Rev. Stat. 1991, Ch. 105, § 79 et seq.

**Submerged Lands Act**
May 22, 1953, Ch. 65, 67 Stat. 29 (See 10 U.S. Code §§ 7421 to 7426, 7428 to 7438) 43 U.S. Code §§ 1301 to 1303, 1311 to 1315
April 7, 1986, P.L. 99-272, 43 U.S. Code § 1301
Fla. Stat. Ann., 253.67 et seq.
Ill. Rev. Stat. 1991, Ch. 19, § 149.9 et seq.

**Submerged Lands Act (Chicago)**
Ill. Comp. Stat. 1992, Ch. 70, §§ 1550/0.01, 1550/1, 1555/1, 1555/1.1

**Submerged Lands Act (Great Lakes)**
Mich. Comp. Laws Ann., 322.701 et seq.

**Submerged Lands Act (Lincoln Park)**
Ill. Rev. Stat. 1991, Ch. 105, § 437.9 et seq.

**Submerged Lands and Ocean Leasing Act**
Haw. Rev. Stat. § 190D-1 et seq.

**Submission Act (Arbitration)**
See Arbitration Act

**Subrogation Act (Attaching Creditor)**
Conn. Gen. Stat. Ann., § 52-340

**Subrogation Act (Insurance)**
Conn. Gen. Stat. Ann., § 38a-321

**Subrogation Act (Joint Tortfeasor)**
Ill. Rev. Stat. 1991, Ch. 70, § 302

**Subrogation Act (Mechanic's Lien)**
Conn. Gen. Stat. Ann., § 49-33

**Subrogation Act (Public Welfare)**
La. Rev. Stat. Ann., 46:8 et seq.

**Subrogation Act (Remainderman)**
Conn. Gen. Stat. Ann., § 12-48

**Subrogation Act (Workmen's Compensation)**
Colo. Rev. Stat., 8-52-107, 8-52-108
Ida. Code 1947, 72-223
Ind. Code Ann., 22-3-2-13
La. Rev. Stat. Ann., 23:1162
Me. Rev. Stat. Ann. 1964, Title 39, § 68
Mo. Rev. Stat., 287.150
S.C. Code Ann. 1976, § 42-9-360 et seq.
Vt. Sat. Ann., Title 21, § 624
Wash. Rev. Code Ann., 51.24.030 et seq.
Wyo. Stat. 1957, § 27-154

**Subscription Television Act**
Cal. Revenue and Taxation Code § 35001 et seq.

**Subsequent Injury Act (Workmen's Compensation)**
Cal. Labor Code, § 4750 et seq.
Ky. Rev. Stat. 1971, 342.120 et seq.
Minn. Stat. Ann., 176.131
N.M. Stat. Ann., 52-2-1 et seq.

**Subsequent Injury Fund Act**
Md. Ann. Code 1957, Art. 101, § 66

**Subsequent Marriage Act (Illegitimate Children)**
Ind. Code Ann., 31-6-6.1-1 et seq.

**Subsequent Offender Act**
N.Y. Penal Law 1965 (Consol. Laws Ch. 40), § 70.10

**Subsidence Act (Mines)**
Pa. Purdon's Stat., Title 52, § 1406.1 et seq.

**Subsidence Assistance Act (Abandoned Mine)**
Pa. Purdon's Stat., Title 52, § 3351 et seq.

**Subsidiary Trust Company Act**
Mont. Code Ann. 1991, 32-1-801 et seq.

**Subsidiary Trust Company Formation Act (Bank Holding Company)**
Ark. Code Ann. 1987, 23-32-1901 et seq.

**Subsidized Adoption Act**
Ala. Code 1975, § 26-10-20 et seq.
Ark. Code Ann. 1987, 9-9-401 et seq.
Me. Rev. Stat. Ann. 1964, Title 19, § 541 et seq.
Mont. Code Ann. 1991, 52-2-501 et seq.
Okla. Stat. Ann., Title 10, § 60.25 et seq.

**Subsistence Act**
Kan. Stat. Ann., 75-3206 et seq.

**Subsistence Expense Act of 1926**
June 3, 1926, Ch. 457, 44 Stat. 688
April 30, 1940, Ch. 172, 54 Stat. 174

**Substance Abuse Administrative Act (Comprehensive)**
R.I. Gen. Laws 1956, 39-25-1 et seq.

**Substance Abuse and Alcoholism Act**
Ill. Rev. Stat. 1987, Ch. 111 1/2, § 6301 et seq.
N.Y. Mental Hygiene Law 1977 (Consol. Laws Ch. 27) § 19.01 et seq.

**Substance Abuse and Alcoholism Services Consolidation Act**
N.Y. Laws 1992, Ch. 223

**Substance Abuse Assistance Act**
Mich. Comp. Laws Ann., 325.751 et seq.

**Substance Abuse Community Correctional Treatment Act**
Cal. Penal Code § 6240 et seq.

**Substance Abuse Counselor Certification Act**
La. Rev. Stat. Ann., 37:3371 et seq.

**Substance Abuse Intervention and Prevention Act (Teens)**
Utah Code Ann. 1953, 62A-8-201 et seq.

**Substance Abuse, Mental Health and Act**
N.C. Gen. Stat. 1943, § 122C-1 et seq.

**Substance Abuse Prevention Act**
R.I. Gen. Laws 1956, 16-21.2-1 et seq.

**Substance Abuse Prevention Act (Juvenile)**
Fla. Stat. Ann., 396.1816, 397.215

**Substance Abuse Prevention Act (Omnibus)**
R.I. Gen. Laws 1956, 42-109-1 et seq.

**Substance Abuse Prevention and Comprehensive Health Education Act**
Fla. Stat. Ann., 233.067

**Substance Abuse Prevention and Treatment Act**
Me. Rev. Stat. Ann. 1964, Title 5, § 20001 et seq.

**Substance Abuse Services Act**
Mich. Comp. Laws Ann., 325.711 et seq.

**Substance Abuse Treatment and Prevention Act**
Ill. Rev. Stat. 1991, Ch. 91 1/2, § 1001

**Substance Abuse Treatment Program**
Ill. Rev. Stat. 1991, Ch. 38, § 1531 et seq.

**Substance and Alcohol Abuse Services Oversight Act**
Tex. Health and Safety Code, § 468.001 et seq.

**Substance Mitigation Act (Hazardous)**
Utah Code Ann. 1953, 19-6-301 et seq.

**Substances Act (Controlled)**
Neb. Rev. Stat. 1943, 28-401 et seq.
P.R. Laws Ann. 1954, Title 24, § 2101

**Substances Act (Precursor)**
Okla. Stat. Ann., Title 63, § 2-321

**Substances Act (Regulation of Percursors to Controlled)**
Haw. Rev. Stat. Ann., § 329-81 et seq.

**Substances Act (Regulation of Precursors to Controlled)**
Haw. Rev. Stat. Ann., §§ 329-81 to 329-91

**Substances Act (Toxic)**
Mass. Gen. Laws Ann., 111F:1 et seq.

**Substances Labeling Act (Hazardous)**
Me. Rev. Stat. Ann. 1964, Title 7, § 501 et seq.
Wis. Stat. Ann., 100.37

**Substances Spill Prevention and Control Act (Hazardous)**
Tex. Water Code, § 26.261 et seq.

**Substantive Act (Workmen's Compensation)**
N.J. Stat. Ann., 34:15-1 to 34:15-69

**Substituted Service Act**
Ala. Code 1958, Title 7, § 199(1)
Fla. Stat. Ann., 49.011 et seq.
Kan. Stat. Ann., 60-307
La. Rev. Stat. Ann., 13:3471 et seq.
N.J. Stat. Ann., 39:7-2
Wis. Stat. Ann., 801.11, Subsec. 5

**Substituted Service Act (Foreign Corporations)**
Mass. Gen. Laws Ann., 181:15
Me. Rev. Stat. Ann. 1964, Title 13A, § 1201 et seq.
Minn. Stat. Ann., 303.13
Ohio Rev. Code 1953, 1703.19
S.C. Code Ann. 1976, § 15-9-240
Tenn. Code Ann., 20-2-201 et seq.
Va. Code 1950, § 13.1-111

**Substituted Service Act (Insurance)**
Mo. Rev. Stat., 375.256 et seq.

**Substituted Service Act (Motor Vehicles)**
Ohio Rev. Code 1953, 2703.20
S.C. Code Ann. 1976, § 15-9-350

**Substituted Service Act (Nonresident Motorists)**
See Nonresident Motorists Act and Nonresident Motorist Substituted Service

**Substituted Service Act (Nonresidents)**
Fla. Stat. Ann., 48.161 et seq.
Mich. Comp. Laws Ann., 257.403

**Substituted Service of Process Statute**
Tenn. Code Ann., 20-2-201 et seq.

**Suburban Communities Code**
Del. Code of 1974, Title 9, § 501 et seq.

**Suburban Development Act**
Neb. Rev. Stat. 1943, 16-901 et seq.

**Suburban Fire District Act**
Neb. Rev. Stat. 1943, 35-501 et seq.

**Suburban Improvement District Act**
Ark. Code Ann. 1987, 14-92-201, 14-92-204

**Suburban Town Law**
N.Y. Town Law (Consol. Laws Ch. 62) § 50 et seq.

**Subversive Activities Act**
Fla. Stat. Ann., 876.22 et seq.
Ga. Code Ann., 16-11-5 et seq.
Haw. Rev. Stat. Ann., § 131-1 et seq.
Kan. Stat. Ann., 21-3803 et seq.
Md. Ann. Code 1957, Art. 85A
Mich. Comp. Laws Ann., 752.311 et seq.
Miss. Code Ann. 1972, § 45-19-51 et seq.
N.C. Gen. Stat. 1943, § 14-11 et seq.
N.H. Rev. Stat. 1955, 648:1 et seq.
Ohio Rev. Code 1953, 2921.21 et seq.
P.R. Laws Ann. 1954, Title 33, § 1471
Wash. Rev. Code Ann., 9.81.010 et seq.

**Subversive Activities and Communist Control Act**
La. Rev. Stat. Ann., 14:358 et seq.

**Subversive Activities Control Act**
Haw. Rev. Stat. Ann., § 131-1 et seq.
Mass. Gen. Laws Ann., 264:16 et seq.

**Subversive Activities Control Act of 1950**
Sept. 23, 1950, Ch. 1024, 64 Stat. 987 (See 8 U.S. Code §§ 1102, 1182, 1225, 1251 to 1254, 1301, 1327, 1423, 1424, 1427, 1429, 1446 to 1448, 1451) 18 U.S. Code §§ 792 nt., 793, prec. § 1501, § 1507; 22 U.S. Code §§ 611, 618; 50 U.S. Code §§ 781 to 826
June 18, 1952, Ch. 442, 66 Stat. 138, 8 U.S. Code § 156
July 12, 1952, Ch. 697, 66 Stat. 590, 50 U.S. Code § 791
July 29, 1954, Ch. 646, 68 Stat. 586, 50 U.S. Code § 786
Aug. 24, 1954, Ch. 886, 68 Stat. 777, 50 U.S. Code §§ 782, 784, 785, 789 to 793
July 26, 1955, Ch. 381, 69 Stat. 375, 50 U.S. Code § 792a
Nov. 8, 1984, P.L. 98-620, 50 U.S. Code § 792a
Dec. 17, 1993, P.L. 103-199, 50 U.S. Code §§ 781 et seq.
*Continued*

**Subversive Activities Control Board Tenure Act**
Aug. 5, 1955, Ch. 580, 69 Stat. 539, 50 U.S. Code § 791, 791 nt.

**Subversive Activities Investigation Act**
Mich. Comp. Laws 1970, 28.51 et seq.

**Subversive Activities Law (Public Employees)**
N.Y. Civil Services Law (Consol. Laws Ch. 7) § 105

**Subversive Activities Registration Act**
S.C. Code Ann. 1976, § 23-29-10 et seq.

**Subversive Conduct Law (Public Employees)**
N.Y. Laws 1951, Ch. 233

**Subversive Control Act**
Alaska Stat. 1962, § 11.56.810 et seq.
Ind. Code 1976, 35-26-2-1 et seq.

**Subversive Groups Act**
Mich. Comp. Laws 1970, 752.321 et seq.

**Subversive Organization Registration Law**
Cal. Corporations Code § 35000 et seq.
Mont. Rev. Code 1947, 94-4411 et seq.

**Subway Act**
Ill. Rev. Stat. 1991, Ch. 24, § 11-121-1 et seq.

**Subway Act (County)**
Ohio Rev. Code 1953, 307.701

**Subway Act (Electrical Conductors)**
N.Y. Laws 1884, Ch. 534
N.Y. Laws 1885, Ch. 499

**Subway Loitering Act**
N.Y. Penal Law 1965 (Consol. Laws Ch. 40), § 240.35, Subds. 7, 8

**Succession Act**
Mont. Code Ann., 72-11-101 et seq.
N.C. Gen. Stat. 1943, § 29-1 et seq.
P.R. LAws Ann. 1954, Title 25, § 161 et seq.

**Succession Act (Civil Defense)**
Vt. Stat. Ann., Title 20, § 181 et seq.

**Succession Act (Emergency Interim)**
See Emergency Interim Succession Act

**Succession Act (Estates)**
Okla. Stat. Ann., Title 84, § 211 et seq.

**Succession Act (Executive and Judicial)**
See Emergency Interim Executive and Judicial Succession Act

**Succession Act (Intestacy)**
See Intestacy Act

**Succession Act (Judicial)**
S.C. Code Ann. 1976, § 1-9-10 et seq.

**Succession Act (Legislative)**
Okla. Stat. Ann., Title 63, § 686.1 et seq.

**Succession and Distribution Act (Estates)**
See Intestacy Act

**Succession and Inheritance Tax Law**
Colo. Rev. Stat., 39-23-101 et seq.

**Succession and Legacy Tax Act**
N.H. Rev. Stat. 1955, 86:1 et seq.

**Succession and Procedures Act (Legislative Emergency)**
Neb. Rev. Stat. 1943, 50-501 et seq.

**Succession and Transfer Tax Act**
Conn. Gen. Stat. Ann., § 12-340 et seq.

**Succession Law**
Cal. Probate Code § 200 et seq.

**Succession Law (Estates)**
Okla. Stat. Ann., Title 84, § 211 et seq.

**Succession of Property Ilfeld Act**
N.M. Laws 1927, Ch. 163

**Succession Tax Act**
Haw. Rev. Stat. Ann., § 236A-1 et seq.
Mass. Gen. Laws Ann., 65:1 et seq.
Md. Ann. Code 1957, Art. 81, § 149 et seq.
Minn. Stat. Ann., 291.005 et seq.

N.D. Cent. Code, 57-37.1-01 et seq.
N.M. Stat. Ann., 7-7-1 et seq.
Ohio Rev. Code 1953, 5731.01 et seq.
Tex. Taxation-General 1959, Art. 14.01 et seq.

**Successive Verdict Act**
Miss. Code Ann. 1972, § 11-7-213, § 99-17-47

**Successor Employer Act (Collective Bargaining)**
Ill. Comp. Stat. 1992, Ch. 820, § 10/0.01 et seq.

**Successor Trustee Act (Land Trust)**
Ill. Rev. Stat. 1991, Ch. 148, § 60 et seq.

**Sudbury, Assabet, and Concord Wild and Scenic River Act**
April 9, 1999, P.L. 106-20, 113 Stat. 30, 16 U.S. Code § 1271 nt.

**Sudbury, Assabet, and Concord Wild and Scenic River Study Act**
Nov. 28, 1990, P.L. 101-628, 16 U.S. Code § 1271 nt.

**Sudden Infant Death Syndrome Act**
Ark. Code Ann. 1987, 20-15-501 et seq.

**Sudden Infant Death Syndrome Act of 1974**
April 22, 1974, P.L. 93-270, 88 Stat. 90, 42 U.S. Code §§ 289d, 289g, 300c-11

**Sudden Infant Death Syndrome Amendments of 1979**
Dec. 12, 1979, P.L. 96-142, 42 U.S. Code §§ 201 nt., 300c-11, 300c-12

**Sudden Infant Death Syndrome Assistance Act**
N.J. Stat. Ann., 26:50-1 et seq.

**Sudden Infant Death Syndrome Study Commission Act**
Ill. Rev. Stat. 1985, Ch. 111 1/2, § 5801 et seq.

**Suffolk and Nassau Counties Improvement Act**
N.Y. Laws 1939, Ch. 276

**Suffolk County Consumer Protection Act**
N.Y. Local Laws 1973, County of Suffolk, p. 1260

**Suffolk County Court House Act**
Mass. Acts 1935, Ch. 474

**Suffolk County District Court Act**
N.Y. Laws 1962, Ch. 811

**Suffolk County Highway Improvement Act**
N.Y. Laws 1927, Ch. 190

**Suffolk County Tax Act**
N.Y. Laws 1920, Ch. 311

**Suffolk County Water Authority Act**
N.Y. Public Authorities Law (Consol. Laws Ch. 43A), § 1074 et seq.

**Suffrage Act**
Tex. Election Code, § 11.001 et seq.

**Suffrage Amendment.**
Aug. 26, 1920, 41 Stat. 1823

**Sugar Act**
P.R. Laws Ann. 1954, Title 5, § 371 et seq.

**Sugar Act Amendments of 1962**
July 13, 1962, P.L. 87-535, 76 Stat. 156, 7 U.S. Code §§ 1101 nts., 1111, 1112, 1114 to 1119, 1121 to 1123, 1131, 1132, 1154, 1158; 26 U.S. Code §§ 4501, 6412

**Sugar Act Amendments of 1965**
Nov. 8, 1965, P.L. 89-331, 79 Stat. 1271, 7 U.S. Code §§ 1101 nt. , 1111, 1112, 1114 to 1117, 1119, 1122, 1132, 1152, 1158; 26 U.S. Code §§ 4501, 6418, 6511

**Sugar Act Amendments of 1971**
Oct. 14, 1971, P.L. 92-138, 85 Stat. 379, 7 U.S. Code § 1101 nt.

**Sugar Act of 1937**
Sept. 1, 1937, Ch. 898, 50 Stat. 903, 7 U.S. Code §§ 1100, 1101, 1111 to 1115, 1117 to 1122, 1131 to 1137
Feb. 4, 1938, Ch. 14, 52 Stat. 26
June 25, 1940, Ch. 423, 54 Stat. 571, 7 U.S. Code § 1131

*Continued*

Oct. 15, 1940, Ch. 887, 54 Stat. 1178, 7 U.S. Code § 1117
Dec. 26, 1941, Ch. 638, 55 Stat. 872, 7 U.S. Code §§ 1131(a), 1134(a), 1134(c), 1137 and nt.
June 20, 1944, Ch. 266, 58 Stat. 283
July 27, 1946, Ch. 685, 60 Stat. 706

**Sugar Act of 1948**
Aug. 8, 1947, Ch. 519, 61 Stat. 922, 7 U.S. Code §§ 1100, 1101, 1111 to 1122, 1131 to 1137, 1151 to 1160
Sept. 1, 1951, Ch. 379, 65 Stat. 318, 7 U.S. Code §§ 1101 nt., 1112, 1114, 1117, 1118
May 29, 1956, Ch. 342, 70 Stat. 217, 7 U.S. Code §§ 1101, 1111, 1112, 1114, 1115, 1117, 1131, 1132, 1155, 1157, 1161
Aug. 28, 1958, P.L. 85-791, 72 Stat. 950, 7 U.S. Code § 1115
June 25, 1959, P.L. 86-70, 73 Stat. 141, 7 U.S. Code § 1101
July 6, 1960, P.L. 86-592, 74 Stat. 330, 7 U.S. Code §§ 1101, 1113, 1115, 1119, 1137, 1158; 26 U.S. Code §§ 4501, 6412
March 31, 1961, P.L. 87-15, 75 Stat. 40, 7 U.S. Code §§ 1101 nt., 1158
July 13, 1962, P.L. 87-535, 76 Stat. 156, 7 U.S. Code §§ 1101 nts., 1111, 1112, 1114 to 1119, 1121 to 1123, 1131, 1132, 1154, 1158
July 19, 1962, P.L. 87-539, 76 Stat. 169, 7 U.S. Code §§ 1112, 1114, 1117, 1123
Nov. 8, 1965, P.L. 89-331, 79 Stat. 1271, 7 U.S. Code §§ 1101 nt. , 1111, 1112, 1114 to 1117, 1119, 1122, 1132, 1152, 1158

**Sugar Beet Weighing and Testing Act**
Neb. Rev. Stat. 1943, 89-201 et seq.

**Sugar Control Act**
May 9, 1934, Ch. 263, 48 Stat. 670, 7 U.S. Code §§ 608 to 611, 613, 615 to 618, 620

**Sugar Control Extension Act of 1947**
March 31, 1947, Ch. 30, 61 Stat. 35

**Suggestion System Act**
Ga. Code Ann., 50-31-1 to 50-31-7

**Suicide Act**
Colo. Rev. Stat., 10-7-109
Wash. Rev. Code Ann., 9.80.060 et seq.

**Suicide Act (Insurance)**
Mo. Rev. Stat., 376.620

**Suisun-Fairfield Sewer District Act**
Cal. Statutes 1951, Ch. 303, p. 553

**Suisun Marsh Preservation Act**
Cal. Public Resources Code § 29000 et seq.

**Suit Tax Act**
Wis. Stat. Ann., 814.22

**Suitable Home Law**
Ky. Rev. Stat. 1971, Superseded Vol., 205.410 et seq.

**Suits Against the Commonwealth Act**
P.R. Laws Ann. 1954, Title 32, § 3077 et seq.

**Suits in Admiralty Act**
March 9, 1920, Ch. 95, 41 Stat. 525, 46 U.S. Code §§ 741 to 752
Dec. 13, 1950, Ch. 1136, 64 Stat. 1112, 46 U.S. Code § 745
Aug. 30, 1954, Ch. 1076, 68 Stat. 968, 46 U.S. Code § 752
Sept. 13, 1960, P.L. 86-770, 74 Stat. 912, 46 U.S. Code § 742
Oct. 29, 1972, P.L. 92-417, 86 Stat. 656, 46 U.S. Code § 749

**Sulfa Drugs Sale Act**
Wash. Rev. Code 1951, 69.40.060, 69.40.070

**Sullivan Act**
Ky. Acts 1908, Ch. 56

**Sullivan Act (Dangerous Weapons)**
N.Y. Penal Law 1965 (Consol. Laws Ch. 40) § 265.05

**Sullivan Act (Gasoline Tax)**
Ohio Laws Vol. 112, p. 508

**Sullivan Act (Plain Language Law)**
N.Y. General Obligations Law (Consol. Laws Ch. 24A) § 5-702

**Sullivan and Madison Resolution (World Government)**
Ala. General Acts 1943, p. 117, No. 117

**Sulloway Act (Pensions)**
See Widows' Pension Act

**Sulphur Tax Act**
Tex. Tax Code, § 203.001 et seq.

**Summary Abatement of Life-or-Health Threatening Conditions Act**
D.C. Code of 1981, §§ 5-513, 5-604, 5-605, 45-1311

**Summary Administration of Small Estates Act**
Ida. Code 1947, 15-3-1201 et seq.

**Summary Conviction Appeal Act**
Pa. Cons. Stat., Title 42, § 5105

**Summary Courts-Martial Act**
June 18, 1898, Ch. 469, 30 Stat. 483

**Summary Eviction Act**
D.C. Code Ann., § 45-1410
Ga. Code Ann., 44-7-50 et seq.

**Summary Investigation Act**
N.J. Stat. Ann., 40A:5-22 et seq.

**Summary Judgment Act**
Ark. Code Ann. 1987, 16-65-201 et seq.
Cal. Code of Civil Procedure § 437c
Ga. Code Ann., 9-11-56
Ill. Rev. Stat. 1991, Ch. 110, § 2-1005
Ill. Rev. Stat. 1991, Ch. 110A, §§ 191, 192
Kan. Stat. Ann., 60-256
La. Code of Civil Procedure, Art. 966 et seq.
Mich. Comp. Laws 1948, 618.9 et seq.
Neb. Rev. Stat. 1943, 25-1330 et seq.
N.H. Rev. Stat. 1955, 491:8a
Ohio Civ. Rule 56
R.I. Rules Civil Procedure, Rule 56
Tex. Rules of Civil Procedure as am. 1984, Rule 166-A
Wis. Stat. Ann., 802.08

**Summary Jurisdiction Act (Elections)**
N.Y. Election Law 1976 (Consol. Laws Ch. 17) § 16-100 et seq.

**Summary Proceedings Act**
Mich. Comp. Laws Ann., 600.5701 et seq.

**Summary Proceedings Act (Disorderly House)**
N.Y. Multiple Dwelling Law 1946 (Consol. Laws Ch. 61A) § 352

**Summary Process Act**
Conn. Gen. Stat. Ann., § 47a-23 et seq.
Mass. Gen. Laws Ann., 239:1 et seq.

**Summer Resort Owners Corporation Act**
Mich. Comp. Laws Ann., 455.201 et seq.

**Summer School for the Arts Act**
Ill. Rev. Stat. 1991, Ch. 122, § 1751 et seq.

**Summer Vocational and Technical Education Act**
Cal. Education Code 1976, § 52380 et seq.

**Summons Law**
Ore. Rules Civil Procedure, Rule 7

**Sumner County Purchasing Law**
Tenn. Private Acts 1975, Ch. 6

**Sumners-Amherst Act**
Oct. 14, 1940, Ch. 872, 18 U.S. Code § 1761

**Sumners Courts Act**
June 29, 1940, Ch. 445, 54 Stat. 688 (See 18 U.S. Code §§ 3141, 3144, 3287, 3289, 3771)

**Sumners-McCarran Act**
March 1, 1937, Ch. 21, 50 Stat. 24 (See 28 U.S. Code §§ 294, 371)

**Sumter County Financing Community Improvement Districts Act**
Ga. Laws 1991, p. 3592

**Sumter County Industrial Development Authority Act**
Ga. Laws 1992, p. 5062

**Sunday Act**
Ark. Stat. 1947, 41-3805 et seq.
Conn. Gen. Stat. Ann., § 53-300a et seq.
Fla. Stat. 1967, 855.01 et seq.
Ga. Code Ann., 10-1-570 et seq.
Haw. Session Laws 1886, Ch. 43, § 1
Ill. Rev. Stat. 1991, Ch. 43, § 129
Ind. Code Ann., 35-1-86-1
Mass. Gen. Laws Ann., 136:1 et seq.
Md. Ann. Code 1957, Art. 27, § 492 et seq.
Mich. Comp. Laws 1948, 435.1 et seq.
Minn. Stat. Ann., 624.01 et seq.
Miss. Code Ann. 1972, § 97-23-63 et seq.
Mo. Rev. Stat., 578.100 et seq.
N.D. Cent. Code, 12.1-30-01 et seq.
Nev. Rev. Stat. 1957, 201.260
N.H. Rev. Stat. 1955, 332-D:1 et seq.
Ohio Rev. Code 1953, 3773.23 et seq.
Okla. Stat. Ann., Title 21, § 907 et seq.
Pa. Apr. 22, 1794, 3 Sm. L. 177, Ch. 1746
Pa. 1705, 1 Sm. L. 25, Ch. 119
Pa. 1939 Pamph. Laws 872, No. 375, § 699.4
Pa. 1959 Pamph. Laws 585, No. 192
Pa. 1959 Pamph. Laws 660, No. 212
Pa. 1959 Pamph. Laws 777, No. 278
Pa. 1959 Pamph. Laws 1530, No. 540
Pa. 1959 Pamph. Laws 1874, No. 684
R.I. Gen. Laws 1956, 11-40-1 et seq.
S.C. Code Ann. 1976, § 53-1-5 et seq.
S.D. Codified Laws 1967, 22-26-1 et seq.
Tenn. Code Ann., Superseded Vols., 39-4001, 39-4002
Vt. Stat. Ann. 1959, Title 13, § 3301 et seq.
Wash. Rev. Code Ann., 9.76.010 et seq.
Wis. Laws 1915, Ch.296
W. Va. Code 1966, § 61-10-25 et seq.

**Sunday Act (Amusements)**
Tex. Penal Code 1925, Art. 286

**Sunday Act (Contracts)**
Ala. Code 1958, Title 9, § 21

**Sunday Act (Dram Shop)**
Ill. Rev. Stat. 1991, Ch. 43, § 129

**Sunday Act (Hunting)**
N.C. Gen. Stat. 1943, § 103-2

**Sunday Act (Sale of Goods)**
Tex. Penal Code 1925, Art. 286 et seq.

**Sunday Amateur Sports Law**
Me. Rev. Stat. Ann. 1964, Title 17, § 3205 et seq.

**Sunday Barbering Act**
N.Y. General Business Law (Consol. Laws Ch. 20) § 16

**Sunday Baseball Law**
N.Y. General Business Law (Consol. Laws Ch. 20) § 7

**Sunday Blue Laws**
Conn. Gen. Stat. Ann., § 53-302a et seq.
Iowa Code 1954, 729.1
Ky. Rev. Stat. 1971, 436.160
Md. Ann. Code 1957, Art. 2B, § 90 et seq.
Md. Ann. Code 1957, Art. 27, § 492 et seq.
Md. Ann. Code 1974, Art. BR, § 18-101 et seq.
N.M. Stat. Ann. 1953, 40-44-1 et seq.
Ohio Rev. Code 1953, 3773.23 et seq.
Tenn. Code Ann., Superseded Vol., 39-4001 et seq.
Vt. Stat. Ann., Title 13, § 3351 et seq.

**Sunday Business Activities Act**
Ga. Code 1933, 96-801 et seq.

**Sunday Closing Act**
Ala. Code 1975, § 13A-12-1 et seq.
Ill. Rev. Stat. 1937, Ch. 38, § 547
Kan. Stat. Ann., 21-967 et seq.
La. Rev. Stat. Ann., 51:191 et seq.
Md. Ann. Code 1957, Art. 2B, § 90 et seq.
Md. Ann. Code 1957, Art. 27, §§ 521, 522
Mont. Rev. Code 1947, 94-35-216
N.C. Gen. Stat. 1943, § 14-346.2
N.J. Stat. Ann.2A:171-1.1 et seq.
P.R. Laws Ann. 1954, Title 33, § 2201
Utah Code Ann. 1953, 76-55-1 et seq.
Va. Code 1950, § 18.2-341 et seq.
Wyo. Stat. 1957, § 15-160, Subsec. 12

**Sunday Closing Act (Liquor)**
Ky. Rev. Stat. 1971, 244.290

**Sunday Closing Act (Motor Vehicle Dealers)**
Colo. Rev. Stat., 12-6-301 et seq.

**Sunday Closing Act (Sales)**
Neb. Rev. Stat. 1943, Superseded Vol., 69-901 et seq.

**Sunday Labor Act**
Kan. Gen. Stat. 1949, 21-952, 21-953
Tex. Penal Code 1925, Arts. 283, 284

**Sunday License Act**
R.I. Gen. Laws 1956, 5-23-1 et seq.

**Sunday Liquor Act**
Ohio Rev. Code 1953, 4301.22, Subd. D
Tex. Alcoholic Beverage Code, § 105.01 et seq.
Wyo. Stat. Ann., § 12-5-101

**Sunday Movie Referendum Act**
Pa. Purdon's Stat., Title 4, § 61 et seq.

**Sunday Observance Act**
Me. Rev. Stat. Ann. 1964, Title 17, § 3201 et seq.

**Sunday Observance Act (Horse Racing)**
Del. Code of 1953, Title 28, § 906
Ida. Code 1947, 18-6202 et seq.
Ky. Rev. Stat. 1971, 436.160
Neb. Rev. Stat. 1943, 14-102, 24, 15-258, 16-226, 17-128
N.Y. General Business Law (Consol. Laws Ch. 20) § 2 et seq.
S.C. Code Ann. 1976, § 53-1-10 et seq.
Wyo. Stat. 1957, § 15-160, Subsecs. 11, 12

**Sunday or Holiday Burial Act**
Ill. Rev. Stat. 1991, Ch. 21, § 100 et seq.

**Sunday Retail Sales Act**
Conn. Gen. Stat. Ann., § 53-302a
Pa. Cons. Stat., Title 18, § 7363

**Sunday Sales Act**
Kan. Stat. Ann., 21-964 et seq.

**Sunday Work Act**
Va. Code 1950, § 18.1-358

**Sundown Act**
Fla. Stat. Ann., 11.611

**Sundry Claims Act**
Ohio Rev. Code 1953, 127.11

**Sunflower Industry Promotion Act**
N.D. Cent. Code, 4-10.2-01 et seq.

**Sunny Day Fund Act**
Pa. Purdon's Stat., Title 72, § 3741.101 et seq.

**Sunrise Act**
Fla. Stat. Ann., 11.62
N.M. Stat. Ann., 12-9A-1 et seq.
Wash. Rev. Code Ann., 43.133.010 et seq.

**Sunset Act**
Me. Rev. Stat. Ann. 1964, Title 3, § 921 et seq.
Wash. Rev. Code Ann., 43.131.010 et seq.

**Sunset Law**
Ala. Code 1975, § 41-20-1 et seq.
Ariz. Rev. Stat. Ann., § 41-2351 et seq.
Ark. Stat. 1947, 5-1201 et seq.
Colo. Laws 1976, Ch. 115
Conn. Gen. Stat. Ann., § 2c-1 et seq.
Fla. Stat. Ann., 119.14
Ga. Code Ann., 43-2-1 et seq.
Haw. Rev. Stat. Ann., § 26H-1 et seq.
Ill. Rev. Stat. 1991, Ch. 127, § 1901 et seq.
Kan. Stat. Ann., 74-7245 et seq.
La. Rev. Stat. Ann., 49:190 et seq.
Md. Ann. Code 1974, Art. SG, § 10-701 et seq.
Me. Rev. Stat. Ann. 1964, Title 3, § 921
Miss. Code Ann. 1972, § 5-9-1 et seq.
Mont. Code Ann., 2-8-101 et seq.
N.C. Gen. Stat. 1943, § 143-34.15 et seq.
N.H. Rev. Stat. 1955, 17-G:1 et seq.
N.M. Stat. Ann., 12-9-1 et seq.
Okla. Stat. Ann., Title 74, § 3901 et seq.
Ore. Rev. Stat., 182.605 et seq.
Pa. Purdon's Stat., Title 71, § 1795.1 et seq.
*Continued*

S.C. Code Ann. 1976, § 1-20-10 et seq.
S.D. Laws 1978, Ch. 4
Tenn. Code Ann., 4-29-101 et seq.
Tex. Government Code, § 325.001 et seq.
Utah Code Ann. 1953, 63-55-1 et seq.
Va. Code 1950, § 30-65 et seq.
Vt. Stat. Ann., Title 26, § 3101 et seq.
W. Va. Code 1966, § 4-10-1 et seq.
Wyo. Stat. Ann., § 28-10-101 et seq.

**Sunset Law (Independent Agency)**
Fla. Special Laws 1977, Ch. 77-584

**Sunset Review Act (Open Government)**
Fla. Stat. Ann., 119.15

**Sunshine Act**
Sept. 13, 1976, P.L. 94-409, 5 U.S. Code §§ 552b et seq.
Ark. Code Ann. 1987, 25-19-106
Cal. Government Code § 9027 et seq.
Colo. Rev. Stat., 24-6-101 et seq.
Fla. Stat. Ann., 286.011
Ga. Code Ann., 50-14-1 et seq.
Haw. Rev. Stat. Ann., § 92-1 et seq.
Ill. Rev. Stat. 1991, Ch. 102, § 41 et seq.
Iowa Code Ann., 21.1 et seq., 22.1 et seq.
La. Rev. Stat. Ann., 42:5 et seq.
Mich. Comp. Laws Ann., 15.261 et seq.
Minn. Stat. Ann., 471.705
Mont. Rev. Code 1947, 82-3401 et seq.
N.C. Gen. Stat. 1943, § 143-318.9 et seq.
N.J. Stat. Ann., 46:3-24
N.M. Rev. Stat. Ann. 1978, 10-15-1.1
N.Y. Public Officers Law (Consol. Laws Ch. 47), § 95 et seq.
Ohio Rev. Code 1953, 121.22
Okla. Stat. Ann., Title 25, § 301 et seq.
Pa. Purdon's Stat., Title 65, § 271 et seq.
R.I. Gen. Laws 1956, 42-46-1 et seq.
S.C. Code Ann. 1976, § 30-4-70 et seq.
Tenn. Code Ann., 8-44-101 et seq.
Tex. Rev. Civ. Stat., Art. 6252-17
Utah Code Ann. 1953, 52-4-1 et seq.
Vt. Stat. Ann., Title 1, § 315 et seq.
Wash. Rev. Code Ann., 42.30.010 et seq.
Wis. Stat. Ann., 19.81 et seq.
W. Va. Code 1966, § 6-9A-1 et seq.

**Sunshine Act (Department of Revenue)**
Ill. Rev. Stat. 1991, Ch. 127, § 2001 et seq.

**Sunshine Act, Open Public Meetings**
Neb. Rev. Stat. 1943, 84-1408 et seq.

**Sunshine in Litigation Act**
Fla. Stat. Ann., 69.081

**Sunshine Law (Access to Public Records)**
Vt. Stat. Ann., Title 1, § 315 et seq.

**Sunshine Law (Freedom of Information)**
N.Y. Public Officers Law (Consol. Laws Ch. 47) § 84 et seq.

**Sunshine Law (Open Meetings Law)**
N.Y. Public Officers Law (Consol. Laws Ch. 47) § 100

**Sunshine Law (Public Meetings)**
Ind. Code Ann., 5-14-1.5-1 et seq.

**Super Collider Bond Act**
Cal. Government Code § 8790.50 et seq.

**Super Speed Ground Transportation Act (California-Nevada)**
Cal. Government Code § 93000 to 93002
Cal. Statutes 1988, Ch. 149
Cal. Statutes 1992, Ch. 27

**Superconducting Super Collider Act**
Ill. Rev. Stat. 1991, Ch. 127, § 2751
Mich. Comp. Laws Ann., 3.811 et seq.
Miss. Code Ann. 1972, § 57-61-1 et seq.

**Superfund Act**
Mass. Gen. Laws Ann., 21E:1 et seq.
Minn. Stat. Ann., 115B.01 et seq.

**Superfund Amendments and Reauthorization Act of 1986**
Oct. 17, 1986, P.L. 99-499, 42 U.S. Code § 9601 nt.
Oct. 27, 1986, P.L. 99-563, 42 U.S. Code §§ 9671 to 9675
Dec. 22, 1987, P.L. 100-202, 29 U.S. Code § 655
Nov. 9, 1989, P.L. 101-144, 42 U.S. Code § 9611

Nov. 10, 1998, P.L. 105-362, 42 U.S. Code § 7401 nt.

**Superfund Revenue Act of 1986**
Oct. 17, 1986, P.L. 99-499, 26 U.S. Code § 1 nt.
Nov. 10, 1988, P.L. 100-647, 26 U.S. Code § 9506
Nov. 5, 1990, P.L. 101-508, 26 U.S. Code § 9507 nt.

**Superhighway Act**
Ill. Rev. Stat. 1951, Ch. 121, § 314a et seq.
Ky. Rev. Stat. 1971, 177.390 et seq.
Mich. Comp. Laws Ann., 252.1 et seq.
Miss. Code Ann. 1972, § 65-3-29 et seq.

**Superhighway Act (Electronic)**
Conn. Public Acts 1994, May Special Session No. 2, § 193

**Superior Court Act**
Colo. Rev. Stat., 13-7-101 et
Okla. Stat. Ann., Title 20, § 91.1 et seq.
Pa. Cons. Stat., Title 42, § 541 et seq.
Wash. Rev. Code Ann., 2.08.010 et seq.

**Superior Court Building Elevator Loan Act (Hampden County)**
Mass. Acts 1953, Ch. 403
N.C. Gen. Stat. 1943, § 2-26 et seq.

**Superior Court Clerks' Retirement Act**
Ga. Code Ann., 47-14-1 et seq.
N.C. Gen. Stat. 1943, §§ 135-84, 135-85

**Superior Court Emeritus Act (Judges)**
Ga. Code Ann., 15-6-1

**Superior Court Judges Retirement System Act**
Ga. Code Ann., 47-9-1 et seq.

**Supernumerary Judge Act**
Ala. Code 1958, Title 13, § 31 et seq.

**Supersedeas Act**
Neb. Rev. Stat. 1943, 25-1916

**Supersession Act (Prosecutors)**
Pa. Purdon's Stat., Title 71, § 297

**Supervising and Conservation Commission Act**
Ore. Rev. Stat., 294.605 et seq.

**Supervising Auditor Act (Spartanburg County)**
S.C. Acts 1923, p. 842, No. 497

**Supervision Act (Municipal Bond)**
Colo. Rev. Stat., 11-59-101 et seq.

**Supervision and Regulation Law (Building and Loan Associations)**
Okla. Stat. Ann., Title 18, § 381.5, 381.6 et seq.

**Supervision Model Act (Administrative Insurance)**
Minn. Stat. Ann., 60G.01 et seq.

**Supervision of Charitable Trusts and Trustees Act**
Minn. Stat. Ann., 501B.33 et seq.

**Supervision of Children Act (Improper)**
Ill. Rev. Stat. 1991, Ch. 23, § 2368.9 et seq.

**Supervision of Insurers Act (Administrative)**
S.C. Code Ann. 1976, § 38-26-10 et seq.

**Supervision of International Student Exchange Visitor Placement Organizations Act**
See Uniform Supervision of International Student Visitor Placement Organizations Act

**Supervision of Juvenile in Need Act**
Ark. Code Ann. 1987, 9-28-301 et seq.

**Supervision of Probationers and Parolees Act (Interstate)**
Mass. Gen. Laws Ann., 127:151A et seq.

**Supervision of Trustees for Charitable Purposes Act**
See also Uniform Supervision of Trustees for Charitable Purposes Act
Iowa Code 1962, 682.48 et seq.
Mich. Comp. Laws Ann., 14.251 et seq.

**Supervision, Rehabilitation and Liquidation Act (Insurers)**
Mo. Rev. Stat., 375.1150 et seq.
S.C. Code Ann. 1976, § 38-27-10 et seq.

**Supervision, Rehabilitation, and Liquidation Model Act**
Mont. Code Ann., 33-2-1301 et seq.

**Supervisors Salary Act**
N.Y. Education Law 1947 (Consol. Laws Ch. 16) § 3101 et seq.

**Supplement Medicare Act**
Cal. Statutes 1992, Ch. 287
N.M. Stat. Ann., 59A-24A-1 et seq.

**Supplement to Second Liberty Bond Act**
Sept. 24, 1918, Ch. 176, 40 Stat. 965

**Supplement to the California Industrial Recovery Act**
Cal. Statutes 1933, Ch. 1037, p. 2632

**Supplemental (Emergency) Revenue Act of 1935**
W. Va. Acts 1935, Ch. 84

**Supplemental Aid Act**
Minn. Stat. Ann., 256D.33 et seq.

**Supplemental Appropriation Act of 1948**
July 30, 1947, Ch. 361, 61 Stat. 610, 2 U.S. Code § 72a

**Supplemental Appropriation Act of 1949**
Aug. 13, 1948, Ch. 835, 62 Stat. 1291

**Supplemental Appropriation Act of 1950**
Oct. 14, 1949, Ch. 694, 63 Stat. 869

**Supplemental Appropriation Act of 1951**
Sept. 27, 1950, Ch. 1052, 64 Stat. 1044, 2 U.S. Code § 46a nt.; 31 U.S. Code § 695; 41 U.S. Code § 219 nt.
May 27, 1958, P.L. 85-426, 72 Stat. 143, 31 U.S. Code § 695

**Supplemental Appropriation Act of 1952**
Nov. 1, 1951, Ch. 664, 65 Stat. 736, 31 U.S. Code § 871
June 5, 1952, Ch. 369, 66 Stat. 122
Aug. 6, 1965, P.L. 89-144, 79 Stat. 448

**Supplemental Appropriation Act of 1953**
July 15, 1952, Ch. 758, 66 Stat. 637, 2 U.S. Code §§ 46a nt., 46b nt.; 31 U.S. Code §§ 699a, 724, 871; 50 U.S. Code Appx. § 1894

**Supplemental Appropriation Act of 1954**
Aug. 7, 1953, Ch. 340, 67 Stat. 418, 31 U.S. Code § 655 nt.; 40 U.S. Code § 33a
Oct. 9, 1962, P.L. 87-777, 76 Stat. 777

**Supplemental Appropriation Act of 1955**
Aug. 26, 1954, Ch. 935, 68 Stat. 813, 12 U.S. Code § 1749d nts.; 15 U.S . Code § 603 nt.; 25 U.S. Code § 372-1; 31 U.S. Code § 200; 33 U.S. Code § 984a; 40 U.S. Code § 33a (See 44 U.S. Code § 2910)
July 8, 1959, P.L. 86-79, 73 Stat. 167, 31 U.S. Code § 200

**Supplemental Appropriation Act of 1956**
Aug. 4, 1955, Ch. 541, 69 Stat. 450, 15 U.S. Code § 714h
Oct. 4, 1961, P.L. 87-367, 75 Stat. 788, 15 U.S. Code § 714h nt.

**Supplemental Appropriation Act of 1957**
July 27, 1956, Ch. 748, 70 Stat. 678, 31 U.S. Code § 724a
Aug. 30, 1961, P.L. 87-187, 75 Stat. 416, 31 U.S. Code § 724a
July 23, 1970, P.L. 91-350, 84 Stat. 449, 31 U.S. Code § 724a
March 7, 1978, P.L. 95-240, 31 U.S. Code § 724a

**Supplemental Appropriation Act of 1958**
Aug. 28, 1957, P.L. 85-170, 71 Stat. 426, 15 U.S. Code §§ 633 nts.; 31 U.S. Code § 665

**Supplemental Appropriation Act of 1959**
Aug. 27, 1958, P.L. 85-766, 72 Stat. 864, 15 U.S. Code § 633 nt.; 22 U.S. Code § 1754; 42 U.S. Code § 2459 nt.; 50 U.S. Code § 407

**Supplemental Appropriation Act of 1961**
July 14, 1960, P.L. 86-651, 74 Stat. 509

**Supplemental Appropriation Act of 1962**
Sept. 30, 1961, P.L. 87-332, 75 Stat. 733, 15 U.S. Code § 633 nt.

**Supplemental Appropriation Act of 1963**
May 17, 1963, P.L. 88-25, 77 Stat. 20, 2 U.S. Code § 60f nt.

**Supplemental Appropriation Act of 1965**
Oct. 7, 1964, P.L. 88-635, 78 Stat. 1023, 15 U.S. Code § 633 nt.

**Supplemental Appropriation Act of 1966**
Oct. 31, 1965, P.L. 89-309, 79 Stat. 1133, 15 U.S. Code § 633 nt.; 40 U.S. Code § 166f-3
Jan. 2, 1968, P.L. 90-239, 81 Stat. 775, 40 U.S. Code § 166b-3

**Supplemental Appropriation Act of 1967**
Oct. 27, 1966, P.L. 89-697, 80 Stat. 1057, 2 U.S. Code § 60f nt.

**Supplemental Appropriation Act of 1968**
Jan. 2, 1968, P.L. 90-239, 81 Stat. 773, 2 U.S. Code §§ 60f nt., 126-1; 40 U.S. Code § 166b-3

**Supplemental Appropriation Act of 1969**
Oct. 21, 1968, P.L. 90-608, 82 Stat. 1190, 2 U.S. Code § 61b-2; 12 U.S. Code §§ 1715 nt., 1715z-1 nt., 1730a, 1749 nt.; 18 U.S. Code § 3056; 50 U.S. Code Appx. § 2271 nt.

**Supplemental Appropriation Act of 1970**
Dec. 26, 1969, P.L. 91-166, 83 Stat. 447

**Supplemental Appropriation Act, 1971**
Jan. 8, 1971, P.L. 91-665, 84 Stat. 1981
Dec. 28, 1985, P.L. 99-225, 2 U.S. Code § 31b-1

**Supplemental Appropriation Act, 1975**
Aug. 15, 1985, P.L. 99-88, 2 U.S. Code § 59
July 22, 1994, P.L. 103-283, 40 U.S. Code § 166b-2

**Supplemental Appropriations Act**
Haw. Session Laws 1992, Act 300
Haw. Session Laws 1996, Act 176
Haw. Session Laws 1996, Act 287
Haw. Session Laws 1997, Act 328
Haw. Session Laws 1998, Act 116

**Supplemental Appropriations Act (Federal)**
Pa. 1978 Pamph. Laws No. 62-A

**Supplemental Appropriations Act (Judiciary)**
Haw. Session Laws 1986, Act 348

**Supplemental Appropriations Act of 1993**
July 2, 1993, P.L. 103-50, 107 Stat. 241
Feb. 12, 1994, P.L. 103-211, 2 U.S. Code §§ 1207a, 1207a nt.
Jan. 23, 1995, P.L.104-1, 2 U.S. Code § 1207a

**Supplemental Appropriations Act of 1996**
April 26, 1996, P.L. 104-134, Title II, 110 Stat. 1321-335

**Supplemental Appropriations Act, 1959-1991**
Haw. Session Law 1974, Act 218
Haw. Session Laws 1972, Act 202
Haw. Session Laws 1976, Act 226
Haw. Session Laws 1978, Act 243
Haw. Session Laws 1980, Act 300
Haw. Session Laws 1982, Act 264
Haw. Session Laws 1984, Act 285
Haw. Session Laws 1986, Act 345
Haw. Session Laws 1988, Act 390
Haw. Session Laws 1990, Act 299
Pa. 1976 Pamph. Laws 1464, No. 55-A
Pa. 1978 Pamph. Laws 1664, No. 62-A
Pa. 1979 Pamph. Laws 587, No. 1-A
Pa. 1979 Pamph. Laws 595, No. 2-A
Pa. 1982 Pamph. Laws 1638, No. 51-A
Pa. 1983 Pamph. Laws 411, No. 1-A
Pa. 1983 Pamph. Laws 603, No. 7-A
Wash. Laws 1959, Extra Session, Ch. 11

**Supplemental Appropriations Act, 1972**
July 17, 1984, P.L. 98-367, 2 U.S. Code § 64b

**Supplemental Appropriations Act, 1973**
Aug. 5, 1977, P.L. 95-94, 2 U.S. Code § 58
March 7, 1978, P.L. 95-240, 2 U.S. Code § 58
July 8, 1980, P.L. 96-304, 2 U.S. Code § 58
Sept. 10, 1982, P.L. 97-257, 2 U.S. Code §§ 58, 58 nt. Oct. 2, 1982, P.L. 97-276, 2 U.S. Code §§ 43b, 43b nt., 46a, 46a nt., 46a-1, 46a-1 nt., 46a-3, 46d-4 nt., 46e nt., 52 nt., 53 nt., 58, 58 nt.

*Continued*

Nov. 30, 1983, P.L. 98-191, 2 U.S. Code § 58
July 12, 1985, P.L. 99-65, 2 U.S. Code § 58
Oct. 21, 1987, P.L. 100-137, 2 U.S. Code § 58
Oct. 1, 1988, P.L. 100-458, 2 U.S. Code §§ 58, 58 nt.
Nov. 21, 1989, P.L. 101-163, 2 U.S. Code § 58
Nov. 5, 1990, P.L. 101-520, 2 U.S. Code §§ 58, 58 nt., 58c-1
Aug. 14, 1991, P.L. 102-90, 2 U.S. Code § 58
Oct. 7, 1997, P.L. 105-55, 2 U.S. Code § 58
Oct. 21, 1998, P.L. 105-275, 2 U.S. Code § 58

**Supplemental Appropriations Act, 1976**
Dec. 18, 1975, P.L. 94-157, 2 U.S. Code § 61-1 et seq.

**Supplemental Appropriations Act, 1977**
May 4, 1977, P.L. 95-26, 2 U.S. Code § 31a-1 et seq.
Aug. 5, 1977, P.L. 95-94, 2 U.S. Code § 61h-6
Oct. 1, 1988, P.L. 100-458, 2 U.S. Code §§ 58 nt., 61h-6
May 25, 1990, P.L. 101-302, 2 U.S. Code § 61h-6
Aug. 14, 1991, P.L. 102-90, 2 U.S. Code § 61h-6
Oct. 21, 1998, P.L. 105-275, 2 U.S. Code § 61h-6

**Supplemental Appropriations Act, 1979**
Aug. 15, 1985, P.L. 99-88, 2 U.S. Code § 69a
Dec. 22, 1987, P.L. 100-202, 2 U.S. Code § 69a nt.

**Supplemental Appropriations Act, 1983**
July 30, 1983, P.L. 98-63, 2 U.S. Code §§ 31-1, 61-1, 65c, 65e, 88b-6, 11b, 136a-2; 5 U.S. Code § 5901 nt.; 12 U.S. Code § 1709; 18 U.S . Code § 1114; 25 U.S. Code § 292b; 31 U.S. Code §§ 6901, 6903 , 6907; 33 U.S. Code §§ 569b, 569c, 610; 40 U.S. Code §§ 166, 761; 49 U.S. Code Appx. §§ 1324 nt., 1603 nt.
Aug. 22, 1984, P.L. 98-396, 98 Stat. 1387
Oct. 12, 1984, P.L. 98-473, 98 Stat. 1964
Dec. 19, 1985, P.L. 99-190, 2 U.S. Code §§ 31-1, 31-1 nt.
Nov. 30, 1989, P.L. 101-194, 2 U.S. Code § 31-1
May 4, 1990, P.L. 101-280, 2 U.S. Code § 31-1
Aug. 14, 1991, P.L. 102-90, 2 U.S. Code §§ 31-1, 31 nt., 358 nt.
Nov. 19, 1995, P.L. 104-53, 2 U.S. Code § 88b-6
Aug. 20, 1996, P.L. 104-186, 2 U.S. Code § 88b-6

**Supplemental Appropriations Act, 1984**
Nov. 30, 1983, P.L. 98-181
July 12, 1985, P.L. 99-65, 2 U.S. Code § 58a
Oct. 2, 1986, P.L. 99-439, 100 Stat. 1085
Nov. 17, 1988, P.L. 100-676, 102 Stat. 4040
Dec. 19, 1989, P.L. 101-240, 22 U.S. Code § 276c-3

**Supplemental Appropriations Act, 1985**
July 2, 1986, P.L. 99-349, 100 Stat. 747
Dec. 22, 1987, P.L. 100-202, 2 U.S. Code § 68-5
Oct. 28, 1991, P.L. 102-138, 105 Stat. 665
Sept. 16, 1996, P.L. 104-197, 2 U.S. Code § 61g-7

**Supplemental Appropriations Act, 1987**
July 11, 1987, P.L. 100-71, 2 U.S. Code § 31a-2a, 65f, 84b, 117e, 166f , 184b to 184f; 4 U.S. Code § 7301 nt., 7 U.S. Code §§ 1308, 1989 nt., 5001, 5002; 8 U.S. Code § 1356; 12 U.S. Code § 2001 nt., 15 U.S. Code § 633 nt., 16 U.S. Code § 1406l-10a nt., 19 U.S. Code §§ 1613a, 1613b; 22 U.S. Code § 2764; 30 U.S. Code § 1235k; 36 U.S. Code § 1405; 42 U.S. Code §§ 1760, 1784, 1786; 44 U.S. Code § 1719

**Supplemental Appropriations and Rescission Act of 1981**
Oct. 21, 1987, P.L. 100-137, 2 U.S. Code § 58b

**Supplemental Appropriations and Rescission Act, 1980**
Nov. 5, 1990, P.L. 101-520, 2 U.S. Code §§ 123b-1 nt., 123b-1

**Supplemental Appropriations for the New Independent States of the Former Soviet Union Act, 1993**
Sept. 30, 1993, P.L. 103-87, 107 Stat. 974

**Supplemental Armed Forces Appropriation Act of 1966**
March 15, 1966, P.L. 89-367, 80 Stat. 36

**Supplemental Armed Forces Appropriation Act of 1967**
June 5, 1967, P.L. 90-22, 81 Stat. 52, 10 U.S. Code §§ 3034, 5081 , 5201, 8034

**Supplemental Benefits Act (Adoption)**
Miss. Code Ann. 1972, § 93-17-51 et seq.
S.C. Code Ann. 1976, § 20-7-1900 et seq.

**Supplemental Budget Act**
Wash. Laws 1959, Extra Session, Ch. 11

**Supplemental Defense Appropriation Act of 1958**
Feb. 11, 1958, P.L. 85-322, 72 Stat. 8, 10 U.S. Code § 1581 nt.
Oct. 4, 1961, P.L. 87-367, 75 Stat. 788, 10 U.S. Code § 1581 nt.

**Supplemental Defense Appropriation Act of 1966**
March 25, 1966, P.L. 89-374, 80 Stat. 79

**Supplemental Defense Appropriation Act of 1967**
April 4, 1967, P.L. 90-8, 81 Stat. 8

**Supplemental Emergency Services District Act**
Okla. Stat. Ann., Title 63, § 330.84 et seq.

**Supplemental Federal Augmentation Appropriation Act**
Pa. 1981 Pamph. Laws 776, No. 56A

**Supplemental Federal Security Agency Appropriation Act of 1949**
June 16, 1948, Ch. 472, 62 Stat. 443, 42 U.S. Code §§ 703a nt., 704a nt., 1901 nt., 1905, 1905 nt., 1913, 1915 to 1918

**Supplemental Fund Act (Savings and Loan)**
Tex. Finance Code, § 273.001 et seq.

**Supplemental General Appropriation Act**
N.M. Laws 1990, Special Session, Ch. 7
Pa. 1984 Pamph. Laws 1311, No. 1-A

**Supplemental Government Corporations Appropriation Act of 1948**
July 29, 1947, Ch. 346, 61 Stat. 514

**Supplemental Housing Authorities Act**
Ala. Code 1975, § 24-1-100 et seq.
Miss. Code Ann. 1972, § 43-33-101 et seq., § 43-33-61 et seq.

**Supplemental Housing Authorization Act of 1977**
April 30, 1977, P.L. 95-24, 12 U.S. Code § 1701 nt., 1706 et seq.

**Supplemental Income Act of 1974 (Blind, Disabled, and Eldery Persons)**
Me. Rev. Stat. Ann. 1964, Title 22, § 3200 et seq.

**Supplemental Independent Offices Appropriation Act of 1949**
June 30, 1948, Ch. 775, 62 Stat. 1196, 46 U.S. Code § 864a
Feb. 21, 1949, Ch. 7, 63 Stat. 6

**Supplemental Labor Department Appropriation Act of 1960**
June 29, 1960, P.L. 86-535, 74 Stat. 250

**Supplemental Local Government Sales and Use Tax Act**
N.C. Gen. Stat. 1943, § 105-480 et seq.

**Supplemental Military Appropriation Act**
July 1, 1939, Ch. 258, 53 Stat. 992

**Supplemental Municipal Gross Receipts Tax Act**
N.M. Stat. Ann., 7-19-10 et seq.

**Supplemental Municipal Property Tax Relief Act**
N.J. Stat. Ann., 52:27D-118.32 et seq.

**Supplemental National Defense Appropriation Act of 1948**
May 21, 1948, Ch. 333, 62 Stat. 259, 50 U.S. Code Appx. § 1193

**Supplemental Naval Appropriation Act of 1943**
March 31, 1943, Ch. 30, 57 Stat. 52

**Supplemental Nutrition Assistance Contingency Fund Act**
N.J. Stat. Ann., 26:1A-36.1 et seq.

**Supplemental Pension Act**
N.Y. Laws 1952, Ch. 319
N.Y. Laws 1955, Ch. 687, § 160 et seq.

**Supplemental Pension Fund Act (Register of Deeds)**
N.C. Gen. Stat. 1943, § 161-50 et seq.

**Supplemental Pension Fund Act (Sheriffs')**
N.C. Gen. Stat. 1943, § 143-166.80 et seq.

**Supplemental Post Office Department Appropriation Act of 1949**
June 19, 1948, Ch. 558, 62 Stat. 564

**Supplemental Proceedings Act**
N.C. Gen. Stat. 1943, § 1-352 et seq.

**Supplemental Proceedings Act (Executions)**
Wash. Rev. Code Ann., 6.32.010 et seq.

**Supplemental Public Securities Act**
N.M. Stat. Ann., 6-14-8 et seq.

**Supplemental Retirement Act**
Fla. Stat. Ann., 112.361
Va. Code 1950, § 51-111.9 et seq.

**Supplemental Retirement Act for Retired Members of State Retirement Systems**
Fla. Stat. Ann., 112.351 et seq.

**Supplemental Retirement Allowance Act**
N.Y. Retirement and Social Security Law (Consol. Laws Ch. 51A) § 190 et seq.

**Supplemental Retirement Benefit Act (Commissioned Law Enforcement and Custodial Officer)**
Tex. Rev. Civ. Stat. 1974, Art. 6228f-1

**Supplemental Retirement Benefits Act (Public Employees)**
Ind. Code Ann., 5-10-3-1 et seq.

**Supplemental Retirement Income Act of 1984**
N.C. Gen. Stat. 1943, § 135-90 et seq.

**Supplemental School Corporation Financing Act**
Ind. Code Ann., 21-2-12-1 et seq.

**Supplemental Security Income Act**
Colo. Rev. Stat., 26-2-201 et seq.

**Supplemental Transit Aid Program Act**
Minn. Laws, 1974, Ch. 534

**Supplemental Treasury and Post Office Departments Appropriation Act of 1949**
June 19, 1948, Ch. 558, 62 Stat. 560

**Supplemental Treasury Department Appropriation Act of 1949**
June 19, 1948, Ch. 588, 62 Stat. 561

**Supplemental Veterans Administration Appropriation Act of 1962**
Feb. 13, 1962, P.L. 87-404, 76 Stat. 8

**Supplemental World War II Veterans Compensation Bond Act**
Pa. Cons. Stat., Title 51, § 20072 et seq.

**Supplementary Appropriation Act**
Del. Laws Vol. 55, p. 451, Ch. 134
Del. Laws Vol. 57, 1733, Ch. 586
Del. Laws Vol. 57, 1778, Ch. 599
Del. Laws Vol. 57, 1806, Ch. 619
Del. Laws Vol. 57, 1841, Ch. 642
Del. Laws Vol. 58, p. 135, Ch. 55
Del. Laws Vol. 58, p. 161, Ch. 73
Del. Laws Vol. 58, p. 162, Ch. 74
Del. Laws Vol. 58, p. 183, Ch. 89
Del. Laws Vol. 58, p. 290, Ch. 136

**Supplementary Assistance Act to Certain Persons**
Iowa Code Ann., 249.1 et seq.

**Supplementary Benefits Act**
P.R. Laws Ann. 1954, Title 29, § 725 et seq.

**Supplementary Neighborhood Commissions Act**
D.C. Code Ann., § 1-251 et seq.

**Supplementary Program for the Aged, Blind and Disabled**
Cal. Welfare and Institutions Code § 12000 et seq.

**Supplementary School District Reorganization Act**
Ark. Acts 1965, 2nd Ex. Sess., No. 21

**Supplementary School Tax Assistance Act**
Ind. Code Ann., 21-2-13-1 et seq.

**Supplier-Wholesale Distributor Equity Agreement Act**
Wash. Rev. Code Ann., 19.126.010 et seq.

**Supply Act (Cherokee County)**
S.C. Acts 1945, p. 745, No. 274

**Supply Act (Water)**
Ga. Code Ann., 12-5-470 et seq.

**Supply Designations Act (Laundry)**
Cal. Business and Professions Code § 14480 et seq.

**Supply Lien Act**
Va. Code 1950, § 43-1 et seq.

**Support Act**
D.C. Code 1973, § 30-301 et seq.
Mich. Comp. Laws Ann., 400.231 et seq.
N.Y. Domestic Relations Law (Consol. Laws Ch. 14) § 30 et seq.
Pa. Purdon's Stat., Title 62, § 1971 et seq.
Tex. Family Code, § 21.01 et seq.

**Support Act (Business Expansion)**
Ga. Code Ann., 48-7-40.1 et seq.

**Support Act (Children)**
R.I. Gen. Laws 1956, 15-9-1 et seq.

**Support Act (Civil Liability)**
See Civil Liability for Support Act

**Support Act (Civil Procedural)**
Pa. Cons. Stat., Title 23, § 4502 et seq.

**Support Act (Dependents)**
Conn. Gen. Stat. Ann., § 46b-215
Md. Ann. Code 1974, Art. FL, § 10-301 et seq.
Me. Rev. Stat. Ann. 1964, Title 19, § 331 et seq.
Mo. Rev. Stat., 454.010 et seq.
N.J. Stat. Ann., 2A:4-30.24 et seq.
Ore. Rev. Stat., 416.010 et seq.

**Support Act (Family Desertion)**
Wash. Rev. Code Ann., 26.20.030 et seq.

**Support Act (Family)**
See also Uniform Interstate Family Support Act
N.J. Stat. Ann., 30:6D-33 et seq.
N.Y. Domestic Relations Law (Consol. Laws, Ch. 14) § 30 et seq.
N.Y. Family Court Act § 411 et seq.

**Support Act (Indigents)**
Pa. Purdon's Stat., Title 62, § 1971 et seq.

**Support Act (Office of Child)**
Mich. Comp. Laws Ann., 400.231 et seq.

**Support Act (Parents)**
R.I. Gen. Laws 1956, 15-10-1 et seq.

**Support Act (Reciprocal Enforcement)**
See also Uniform Reciprocal Enforcement of Support Act
Ala. Code 1975, 30-4-80 et seq.
Alaska Stat. 1962, § 25.25.010 et seq.
Ariz. Rev. Stat. Ann., § 12-1651 et seq.
Conn. Gen. Stat. Ann., § 46b-180 et seq.
Ga. Code Ann., 19-11-40 et seq.
Ky. Rev. Stat. 1971, 407.010 et seq.
Mass. Gen. Laws Ann., 273A:1 et seq.
Minn. Stat. Ann., 518C.01 et seq.
Mont. Rev. Code 1947, 93-2601-1 et seq.
N.C. Gen. Stat. 1943, § 52A-1 et seq.
N.H. Rev. Stat. 1955, 546:1 et seq.

*Continued*

Ore. Rev. Stat., 110.005 et seq.
R.I. Gen. Laws 1956, 15-11-1 et seq.
Utah Code Ann. 1953, 77-31-1 et seq.

**Support Act (Working Parents)**
N.H. Laws 1993, Ch. 269

**Support and Maintenance Act (Child)**
Miss. Code Ann. 1972, § 9-11-101 et seq.

**Support and Parenting Time Enforcement Act**
Mich. Comp. Laws Ann., 552.601 et seq.

**Support and Treatment Act (Alcholism and Drug Addiction)**
Wash. Rev. Code Ann., 74.50.010 et seq.

**Support and Visitation Enforcement Act**
Mich. Comp. Laws Ann., 552.601 et seq.

**Support Dog Act**
Miss. Code Ann. 1972, § 43-6-151 et seq.

**Support Enforcement Act**
Ida. Code 1947, 7-1048 et seq.
Mass. Gen. Laws Ann., 273A:1 et seq.
Mich. Comp. Laws Ann., 780.151 et seq.
N.D. Cent. Code, 14-12.1-01 et seq.
N.J. Stat. Ann., 2A:17-56.7 et seq.
N.M. Stat. Ann., 40-4A-1 et seq.
N.Y. Civil Practice Law and Rules (Consol. Laws Ch. 8) § 5421
N.Y. Laws 1986, Ch. 892
N.Y. Laws 1987, Ch. 815
P.R. Laws Ann. 1954, Title 32, § 3311 et seq.

**Support Enforcement Act (Child)**
Mont. Code Ann., 40-5-401 et seq.

**Support Enforcement Act (New York State)**
N.Y. Civil Practice Laws and Rules (Consol. Laws Ch. 8) §§ 211, 5242, 5252
N.Y. Domestic Relations Law (Consol. Laws Ch. 14) §§ 34, 35, 37, 37a, 236, 237, 240, 241, 244, 245
N.Y. Executive Law 1951 (Consol. Laws Ch. 18) § 256
N.Y. Family Court Act §§ 117, 171a, 421, 424, 424a, 425, 426, 433 to 435, 438 to 440, 448, 451, 454, 460, 471, 475, 513, 516a, 517, 522, 536, 545, 571
N.Y. Social Services Law (Consol. Laws Ch. 55) §§ 111b, 111c, 111f to 111h, 111k, 111m, 111n
N.Y. Tax Law (Consol. Laws Ch. 60) § 171c
N.Y. Worker's Compensation Law (Consol. Laws Ch. 67) §§ 33, 218

**Support for East European Democracy (SEED) Act of 1989**
Nov. 28, 1989, P.L. 101-179, 22 U.S. Code § 5401 nt.
Oct. 24, 1992, P.L. 102-511, 22 U.S. Code § 5402
Nov. 26, 1997, P.L. 105-118, 22 U.S. Code § 5421
July 22, 1998, P.L. 105-206, 22 U.S. Code § 5401

**Support for the Aged Act**
P.R. Laws Ann. 1954, Title 3, § 211 1-5 et seq.

**Support Income Deduction Act (Child)**
Mont. Code Ann., 40-5-301 et seq.

**Support of Dependents Act**
See also Uniform Support of Dependents Act
Iowa Code Ann., 252A.1 et seq.
Ohio Rev. Code 1953, 3115.01 et seq.
S.C. Code Ann. 1976, § 20-7-110 et seq.

**Support of Dependents Law**
Okla. Stat. Ann., Title 10, § 1601 et seq.

**Support of Minor Children Act**
Ga. Code Ann., 19-6-17

**Support Personnel Policies Act (Family)**
Fla. Stat. Ann., 110.1521 et seq.

**Support Program Act (Primary Care)**
W. Va. Code 1966 § 16-2H-1 et seq.

**Support Reform Act (Medical)**
Mont. Code Ann., 40-5-801 et seq.

**Support Registry Act (Centralized)**
Okla. Stat. Ann., Title 43, § 410 et seq.

**Support Services Law for Mentally Disabled Adults (Home-Based)**
Ill. Rev. Stat. 1991, Ch. 91 1/2, § 1802-1 et seq.

**Support Systems for Mentally Deficient and Mentally Ill Persons Act**
Sept. 23, 1994, P.L. 103-325, 108 Stat. 2243, Title 4
Ill. Comp. Stat. 1992, Ch. 405, § 35/1 et seq.

**Supported Employees Act**
Ill. Rev. Stat. 1991, Ch. 127, § 3901 et seq.

**Supportive Residences Licensing Act**
Ill. Rev. Stat. 1989, Ch. 111 1/2, § 9001 et seq.

**Suppression Act (Communism)**
Tex. Rev. Civ. Stat., Art. 6889-3A

**Suppression Eradication Act (Boll Weevil)**
Ark. Acts 1991, No. 710

**Suppression of Illegitimate Traffic in Narcotic Drug Act**
Mich. Comp. Laws 1970, 335.151 et seq.

**Supreme Court Act**
Ill. Rev. Stat. 1991, Ch. 37, § 8.9 et seq.
Wash. Rev. Code Ann., 2.04.010 et seq.

**Supreme Court Building Act**
Ill. Rev. Stat. 1991, Ch. 37, §§ 24a1, 24, 24a

**Supreme Court Jurisdiction Act**
Tex. Government Code, § 22.001

**Supreme Court Relief Act**
Tex. Government Code, § 22.007

**Supreme Court Terms Act**
Ill. Rev. Stat. 1991, Ch. 37, § 5.9, 6

**Surcharge Law (Energy Resources)**
Cal. Revenue and Taxation Code § 40001 et seq.

**Sureties Relief Act**
Ind. Code Ann., 5-4-4-1 et seq.

**Surety Act**
Ill. Rev. Stat. 1991, Ch. 132, § 0.01 et seq.
Mont. Code Ann., 28-11-401 et seq.

**Surety and Casualty Rate Regulation Act**
Mo. Rev. Stat., 379.420 et seq.
Pa. Purdon's Stat., Title 40, § 1181 et seq.

**Surety Bond Act**
N.M. Stat. Ann., 10-2-13 et seq.

**Surety Bond Exemption Act**
Ark. Code Ann. 1987, 23-32-1401 et seq.

**Surety Bond Guaranty Program Act (Small Business)**
Okla. Stat. Ann., Title 74, § 85.47 et seq.

**Surety Bond Law (Public Works Contractors')**
Me. Rev. Stat. Ann. 1964, Title 14, § 871 et seq.

**Surety Bonds**
June 6, 1972, P.L. 92-310, 86 Stat. 202, 6 U.S. Code § 6

**Surety Bonds Act**
Alaska Stat. 1962, § 09.65.030 et seq.
Ida. Code 1947, 59-801 et seq.

**Surety Companies Act**
See Corporate Surety Act

**Surety Company Act**
Ill. Rev. Stat. 1935, Ch. 32, § 272 et seq.
Mich. Comp. Laws Ann., 550.101 et seq.

**Surety Insurance Fund Act**
Ala. Code 1958, Title 28, § 329 et seq. seq.

**Surety Lien Act**
Kan. Stat. Ann., 60-1111

**Surety Market Assistance Association Act**
Okla. Stat. Ann., Title 36, § 6423 et seq.

**Surety of Peace Act**
Pa. Purdon's Stat., Title 19, § 23

**Surety Release Act (Fiduciary)**
Ill. Rev. Stat. 1991, Ch. 103, § 17.9 et seq.

**Surety Release Act (Trustee)**
Ill. Rev. Stat. 1991, Ch. 103, §§ 20.9, 21

**Surety Statute (Release)**
Ky. Rev. Stat. 1971, 62.090 et seq.

**Suretyship Act**
Wash. Rev. Code Ann., 19.72.001 et seq.

**Surface and Air Transportation Commission Act (Middle Georgia)**
Ga. Laws 1990, p. 5170

**Surface and Air Transportation Commission Act (Northeast Georgia)**
Ga. Laws 1991, p. 4596

**Surface and Ground Water Drainage Act**
Md. Laws 1971, Ch. 344

**Surface and Underground Mine Reclamation Act**
Mich. Comp. Laws Ann., 425.1101 et seq.

**Surface Coal Mining Act**
Mo. Rev. Stat., 444.800 et seq.

**Surface Coal Mining and Reclamation Act**
Tex. Natural Resources Code, § 134.001 et seq.
W. Va. Code 1966, § 22-3-1 et seq.

**Surface Coal Mining Fee Act**
Ill. Rev. Stat. 1991, Ch. 96 1/2, § 7500 et seq.

**Surface Coal Mining Land Conservation and Reclamation Act**
Ark. Code Ann. 1987, 15-58-101 et seq.
Colo. Rev. Stat. 34-33-101 et seq.
Miss. Code Ann. 1972, § 53-9-1 et seq.
Tex. Rev. Civ. Stat. 1974, Art. 5920-11
W. Va. Code 1966 § 22A-3-1 et seq.

**Surface Damages Act**
Okla. Stat. Ann., Title 52, § 318.2 et seq.

**Surface Freight Forwarder Deregulation Act of 1986**
Oct. 22, 1986, P.L. 99-521, 49 U.S. Code § 10101 nt.

**Surface Land Conservation and Reclamation Act (Coal Mining)**
Ill. Comp. Stat. 1992, Ch. 225, § 720/1.o1 et seq.

**Surface Mining Act**
Ala. Code 1975, § 9-16-1 et seq.
Ga. Code Ann., 12-4-70 et seq.
Ida. Code 1947, 47-1501 et seq.
Ind. Code Ann., 13-4-6-1 et seq.
Ky. Rev. Stat. 1971, 350.010 et seq.
Md. Ann. Code 1974, Art. NR, § 7-6A-01 et seq.
N.M. Stat. Ann., 69-25A-1 et seq.
Tenn. Code Ann., 59-8-201 et seq.

**Surface Mining and Reclamation Act**
Ala. Code 1975, § 9-16-107 et seq.
Cal. Public Resources Code § 2710 et seq.
Ill. Rev. Stat. 1991, Ch. 96 1/2, § 4501 et seq.
La. Rev. Stat. Ann., 30:901 et seq.
Miss. Code Ann. 1972, § 53-7-1 et seq.
N.D. Cent. Code, 38-14.1-01 et seq.
Pa. Purdon's Stat., Title 52, § 1396.1 et seq.
S.D. Codified Laws 1967, 45-6B-81 et seq.
Tex. Natural Resources Code, § 131.001 et seq.

**Surface Mining Control and Reclamation Act**
Ala. Code 1975, § 9-16-70 et seq.
Va. Code 1950, § 45.1-226 et seq.

**Surface Mining Control and Reclamation Act of 1977**
Aug. 3, 1977, P.L. 95-87, 18 U.S. Code § 1114; 30 U.S. Code §§ 1201 et seq.
March 7, 1978, P.L. 95-240, 30 U.S. Code § 1211
Aug. 11, 1978, P.L. 95-343, 30 U.S. Code § 1302
Dec. 21, 1982, P.L. 97-377, 30 U.S. Code § 1235 nt.
Oct. 12, 1984, P.L. 98-473, 30 U.S. Code § 1231

Oct. 18, 1986, P.L. 99-500, 30 U.S. Code § 1265

Oct. 30, 1986, P.L. 99-591, 30 U.S. Code § 1265

May 7, 1987, P.L. 100-34, 30 U.S. Code §§ 1232, 1278, 1278 nt.

July 11, 1987, P.L. 100-71, 30 U.S. Code § 1235

Nov. 5, 1990, P.L. 101-508, 30 U.S. Code §§ 1231 to 1237, 1239, 1240a, 1241 to 1243, 1257, 1302

Oct. 24, 1992, P.L. 102-486, 30 U.S. Code §§ 1231 to 1234, 1257, 1260, 1265, 1291, 1300, 1309a, 1309b

Oct. 7, 1998, P.L. 105-244, 30 U.S. Code § 1291

**Surface-Mining Land Conservation and Reclamation Act**

Kan. Stat. Ann., 49-601 et seq.

Pa. Purdon's Stat., Title 52, § 1396.1 et seq.

**Surface Mining Law (Noncoal)**

La. Rev. Stat. Ann., 30:961 et seq.

**Surface Transportation and Uniform Reallocation Assistance Act of 1987**

April 2, 1987, P.L. 100-17, 101 Stat. 132

Oct. 1, 1988, P.L. 100-462, 102 Stat. 2269

**Surface Transportation and Uniform Relocation Assistance Act of 1987**

April 2, 1987, P.L. 100-17, 23 U.S. Code § 101 nt.

Dec. 22, 1987, P.L. 100-202, 23 U.S. Code §§ 202 nt., 401 nt.

Nov. 21, 1989, P.L. 101-164, 103 Stat. 1096

Dec. 18, 1991, P.L. 102-240, 23 U.S. Code § 104 nt.; 49 U.S. Code Appx. . § 1608 nt.

Nov. 28, 1995, P.L. 104-59, 109 Stat. 607

**Surface Transportation Assistance Act of 1978**

Nov. 6, 1978, P.L. 95-599, 15 U.S. Code § 1418; 16 U.S. Code § 460l-11; 23 U.S. Code §§ 101 to 105, 109, 111, 116 et seq., 215, 217, 219c, 303, 307 nt., 320, 401 nt., 402, 403 nt., 406; 26 U.S. Code §§ 39, 4041, 4061, 4071, 4081, 4481, 4482, 6156, 6412, 6421, 6427, 7210, 7603 to 7605, 7609, 7610; 40 U.S. Code Appx. §§ 201, 201 nt.; 42 U.S. Code § 5904 nt.; 46 U.S. Code § 883 nt.; 49 U.S. Code §§ 303, 1601 nt., 1602 et seq.

Nov. 9, 1979, P.L. 96-106, 42 U.S. Code § 5904

Oct. 15, 1982, P.L. 97-327, 23 U.S. Code § 101 nt.

Oct. 31, 1994, P.L. 103-429, 49 U.S. Code Appx. § 1602-1

June 9, 1998, P.L. 105-178, 40 U.S. Code Appx. § 201 nt.

**Surface Transportation Assistance Act of 1982**

Jan. 6, 1983, P.L. 97-424, 23 U.S. Code § 101 nt., 49 U.S. Code § 1602 nt.

March 9, 1984, P.L. 98-229, 23 U.S. Code § 101 nt.

July 17, 1984, P.L. 98-363, 98 Stat. 435

July 18, 1984, P.L. 98-369, 98 Stat. 1145, 42 U.S. Code §§ 602, 602 nt., 1382a

Oct. 30, 1984, P.L. 98-554, 49 U.S. Code Appx. §§ 2311, 2316

Nov. 8, 1984, P.L. 98-620, 49 U.S. Code 2305

Oct. 27, 1986, P.L. 99-570, 49 U.S. Code Appx. § 2304

April 2, 1987, P.L. 100-17, 23 U.S. Code §§ 101 nt., 104 nt., 127 , 146 nt., 217, 49 U.S. Code Appx. §§ 1607a, 1607a-1, 2311, 2314

Nov. 5, 1990, P.L. 101-516, 49 U.S. Code Appx. § 2311

Dec. 18, 1991, P.L. 102-240, 23 U.S. Code §§ 101 nt., 146 nt.; 49 U.S. Code Appx. §§ 2302 to 2304, 2306, 2307, 2311, 2312

Oct. 31, 1994, P.L. 103-429, 49 U.S. Code Appx. § 2315 nt.

**Surface Transportation Efficiency Act (Intermodal)**
Fla. Stat. Ann., 334.03 et seq.

**Surface Transportation Extension Act of 1997**
Dec. 1, 1997, P.L. 105-130, 23 U.S. Code § 101 nt.

**Surface Transportation Revenue Act of 1991**
Dec. 18, 1991, P.L. 102-240, 26 U.S. Code § 1 nt.
Aug. 20, 1996, P.L. 104-188, 26 U.S. Code § 4481

**Surface Transportation Revenue Act of 1998**
June 9, 1998, P.L. 105-178, Title IX, 26 U.S. Code § 1 nt.

**Surface Water Act**
Tex. Water Code, § 11.086

**Surface Water Drainage Utility Act**
Wyo. Stat. 1977, §§ 16-10-101 to 16-10-110

**Surface Water Improvement and Management Act**
Fla. Stat. Ann., 373.451 et seq., 689.225

**Surface Water Protection District Act**
Ill. Rev. Stat. 1991, Ch. 42, § 447.99 et seq.

**Surgeons and Physicians Act**
N.H. Rev. Stat. 1955, 329:1 et seq.
R.I. Gen. Laws 1956, 5-37-1 et seq.
Vt. Stat. Ann., Title 26, § 1311 et seq.
W. Va. Code 1966, § 30-3-1 et seq.

**Surgeons and Physicians College Act**
P.R. Laws Ann. 1954, Title 20, § 72 et seq.

**Surgeons' and Physicians' Registration Act**
N.M. Stat. Ann., 61-6-22 et seq.

**Surgery and Medicine Act**
Ky. Rev. Stat. 1971, 311.250 et seq.

**Surgery Practice Act**
Wash. Rev. Code Ann., 18.71.005 et seq.

**Surgical and Medical Plan Act**
S.D. Codified Laws 1967, 58-38-1 et seq.

**Surgical Facility Licensure Act (Ambulatory)**
N.C. Gen. Stat. 1943, § 131E-145 et seq.

**Surgical Institute for Children Act**
Ill. Rev. Stat. 1991, Ch. 23, § 2200 et seq.

**Surgical Treatment Center Act (Ambulatory)**
Ill. Comp. Stat. 1992, Ch. 210, § 5/1 et seq.

**Surplus Agricultural Commodities Disposal Act of 1982**
Oct. 21, 1982, P.L. 97-358, 7 U.S. Code §§ 1421 nt., 1433b

**Surplus Commodities Corporation Act**
June 27, 1942, Ch. 454, 56 Stat. 461, 15 U.S. Code § 713c and nt.

**Surplus Federal Property Acquisition Act**
Cal. Statutes 1945, Ch. 796, p. 1488

**Surplus Federal Property for Schools Act**
Ill. Rev. Stat. 1991, Ch. 122, §§ 737.9, 738

**Surplus Food Commodities Distribution Program Act**
Haw. Rev. Laws 1955, § 12-14 et seq.

**Surplus Food Distribution Act (Commodities)**
Mich. Comp. Laws Ann., 400.181 et seq.

**Surplus Fund-Certified Claims Act of 1949**
July 6, 1949, Ch. 299, 63 Stat. 407, 31 U.S. Code §§ 712a, 712a nts.

**Surplus Funds Investment Law (Municipal)**
Cal. Statutes 1913, Ch. 73, p. 76

**Surplus Funds Investment Law (State)**
Cal. Government Code § 16470 et seq.

**Surplus Funds Investment Pool Act**
Mich. Comp. Laws Ann., 129.111 et seq.

**Surplus Funds of Local Government Investment Act**
Fla. Stat. Ann., 218.40 et seq.

**Surplus Housing Facilities Act**
Cal. Statutes 1947, Ch. 27, p. 509

**Surplus Line Insurance Act**
Ala. Code 1975, 27-10-20 et seq.
Alaska Stat. 1962, § 21.34.010 et seq.
Ark. Code Ann. 1987, 23-65-301 et seq.
Colo. Rev. Stat., 10-5-101 et seq.
Del. Code of 1974, Title 18, § 1901 et seq.
Fla. Stat. Ann., 626.913 et seq.
Ga. Code Ann., 33-5-20 et seq.
Ida. Code 1947, 41-1211 et seq.
Ill. Rev. Stat. 1991, Ch. 73, § 1057 et seq.
Ky. Rev. Stat. 1971, 304.10-010 et seq.
Md. Ann. Code 1957, Art. 48A, § 183 et seq.
Md. Ann. Code 1974, Art. IN, § 3-301 et seq.
Me. Rev. Stat. Ann. 1964, Title 24-A, § 2001 et seq.
Mich. Comp. Laws Ann., 500.1901 et seq.
Minn. Stat. Ann., 60A.195 et seq.
Mo. Rev. Stat., 384.011 et seq.
Mont. Code Ann. 1991, 33-2-301 et seq.
N.C. Gen. Stat. 1943, § 58-21-1 et seq.
Neb. Laws 1992, L.B. 1006, §§ 1 to 14
Nev. Rev. Stat. 1979 Reprint, 685A.010 et seq.
N.J. Stat. Ann.17:22-6.40 et seq.
Ohio Rev. Code 1953, 3905.30 et seq.
Ore. Rev. Stat., 735.400 et seq.
Ore. Rev. Stat., 750.003 et seq.
Pa. Purdon's Stat., Title 40, § 1006.1 et seq.
S.D. Codified Laws 1967, 58-32-1 et seq.
Tenn. Code Ann., 56-14-101 et seq.
Wis. Stat. Ann., 618.41
Wyo. Stat. Ann., § 26-11-101 et seq.

**Surplus Lines Insurance Guaranty Fund Act**
N.J. Stat. Ann., 17:22-6.70 et seq.

**Surplus Personal Property Act**
Tenn. Code Ann., 12-2-401 et seq.

**Surplus Property Act**
Ill. Rev. Stat. 1991, Ch. 127, § 176d et seq.
Okla. Stat. Ann., Title 80, § 34.2 et seq.

**Surplus Property Act (State)**
Kan. Stat. Ann., 75-6601 et seq.

**Surplus Property Act of 1944**
Oct. 3, 1944, Ch. 479, 58 Stat. 765, 50 U.S. Code Appx. §§ 1622, 1641
Oct. 22, 1945, Ch. 432, 59 Stat. 546
May 3, 1946, Ch. 248, 60 Stat. 168, 50 U.S. Code Appx. § 1622
July 23, 1946, Ch. 590, 60 Stat. 599
Aug. 1, 1946, Ch. 723, 60 Stat. 754, 50 U.S. Code Appx. § 1641
Aug. 7, 1946, Ch. 790, 60 Stat. 886
July 30, 1947, Ch. 404, 61 Stat. 678, 50 U.S. Code Appx. § 1622
June 10, 1948, Ch. 433, 62 Stat. 350, 50 U.S. Code Appx. § 1622
June 29, 1948, Ch. 727, 62 Stat. 1103, 50 U.S. Code Appx. § 1622
Oct. 1, 1949, Ch. 589, 63 Stat. 700, 50 U.S. Code Appx. § 1622
June 20, 1952, Ch. 449, 66 Stat. 151, 50 U.S. Code Appx. § 1641
July 18, 1956, Ch. 627, 70 Stat. 563, 50 U.S. Code Appx. § 1641
July 20, 1961, P.L. 87-90, 75 Stat. 211, 50 U.S. Code Appx. § 1622
Aug. 17, 1961, P.L. 87-153, 75 Stat. 390, 50 U.S. Code Appx. § 1641
May 21, 1970, P.L. 91-258, 84 Stat. 235, 50 U.S. Code Appx. § 1622
Oct. 22, 1970, P.L. 91-485, 84 Stat. 1085, 50 U.S. Code Appx. § 1622
Aug. 4, 1972, P.L. 92-362, 86 Stat. 504, 50 U.S. Code Appx. § 1622
July 2, 1986, P.L. 99-349, 100 Stat. 749

**Surplus Property and Public Airport Authority Act**
Kan. Stat. Ann., 27-315 et seq.

**Surplus Property Purchase Act**
Wash. Rev. Code Ann., 39.32.010 et seq.

**Surplus Return Act (Corporate)**
Me. Rev. Stat. Ann. 1964, Title 36, § 6501 et seq.

**Surplus Return Act (Individual)**
Me. Rev. Stat. Ann. 1964, Title 36, § 6401 et seq.

**Surplus Soldiers' Bonus Fund Act**
Mass. Acts 1924, Ch. 480

**Surplus Statute (Sales)**
Mich. Comp. Laws Ann., 600.3252

**Surplus Town Funds Transfer Act**
Ill. Rev. Stat. 1991, Ch. 139, § 163.9 et seq.

**Surplus Water Act**
Mich. Comp. Laws Ann., 281.301 et seq.

**Surprise Valley Groundwater Basin Act**
Cal. Statutes 1995, Ch. 698

**Surrender Act (Children)**
Kan. Stat. Ann., 38-112 et seq.

**Surrender and Cost Act**
Iowa Code Ann., 811.6

**Surrender or Merger of Reversion Act**
Ill. Rev. Stat. 1991, Ch. 30, §§ 38.9, 39

**Surrogacy Act**
Me. Rev. Stat. Ann. 1964, Title 19-A, § 1521 et seq.

**Surrogate Act (Health Care)**
Fla. Stat. Ann., 765.201 et seq.
W. Va. Code 1966 § 16-30B-1 et seq.

**Surrogate Parenting Act**
Mich. Comp. Laws Ann., 722.851 et seq.

**Surrogates' Court Procedure Act**
N.Y. Consol. Laws, Ch. 59A

**Surveillance Act (Electronic)**
La. Rev. Stat. Ann., 15:1301 et seq.

**Surveillance Control Act (Wiretapping and Electronics)**
Pa. Cons. Stat., Title 18, § 5701 et seq.

**Survey Act**
Ill. Rev. Stat. 1991, Ch. 133, § 10.9 et seq.
Tenn. Code Ann., 62-18-101 et seq.

**Survey Act (Coast and Geodetic)**
Ill. Comp. Stat. 1992, Ch. 765, § 230/0.01 et seq.

**Survey and Construction Act (Hospitals)**
Wis. Stat. Ann., 50.20 et seq.

**Survey and Construction Act (Medical Facilities)**
Kan. Stat. Ann., 65-411 et seq.

**Survey and Construction Act (State Hospital)**
Neb. Rev. Stat. 1943, 71-2001 et seq.

**Survey and Construction of Hospital and Medical Facilities Act**
See Hospital and Medical Facilities Survey and Construction Act

**Survey and Corner Recordation Act**
N.D. Cent. Code, 47-20.1-01 et seq.

**Survey and Remonumentation Act (State)**
Mich. Comp. Laws Ann., 54.261 et seq.

**Survey Manual Legalization Act (Public Lands)**
Oct. 1, 1890, Ch. 1262, 26 Stat. 650
Aug. 15, 1894, Ch. 288, 28 Stat. 285
April 26, 1902, Ch. 592, 32 Stat. 120

**Survey of Public Lands Restoration and Perpetuation Act**
Fla. Stat. Ann., 177.501 et seq.

**Survey Recording Act**
Wash. Rev. Code Ann., 58.09.010 et seq.

**Survey Restoration and Perpetuation of Public Land Act**
Fla. Stat. Ann., 177.501 et seq.

**Surveying and Engineering Practice Act**
N.M. Stat. Ann., 61-23-1 et seq.

**Surveyors Act (County)**
Ill. Rev. Stat. 1991, Ch. 133, §§ 4.9, 5

**Surveyors Act (Land)**
Ark. Code Ann. 1987, 17-41-103, 17-41-201 et seq.
Cal. Business and Professions Code § 8700 et seq.
Mich. Comp. Laws Ann., 338.551 et seq.
Nev. Rev. Stat. 1979 Reprint, 625.250 et seq.
Ore. Rev. Stat., 672.002 et seq.

**Surveyors' and Engineers' Registration Act**
Ind. Code Ann., 25-31-1-1 et seq.

**Surveyors, Architects and Engineers Examining Board Act**
P.R. Laws Ann. 1954, Title 20, § 711 et seq.

**Surveyors' License Act**
Cal. Business and Professions Code § 8725 et seq.
Pa. 1921 Pamph. Laws 1131, No. 422

**Survival Act**
Ill. Rev. Stat. 1991, Ch. 110 1/2, § 27-6
La. Civil Code 1972, Art. 2315
Okla. Stat. Ann., Title 12, § 1051

**Survival Act (Corporations)**
Md. Ann. Code 1974, Art. CA, § 3-408, Subd. b.

**Survival Act (Injuries)**
N.Y. Estates, Powers and Trusts Law (Consol. Laws Ch. 17B) § 11-3.2b
Tex. Rev. Civ. Stat., Arts. 4671 to 4678

**Survival Act (Rights of Action)**
Wis. Stat. Ann., 895.01

**Survival Act (Torts)**
Cal. Civil Code § 956
Cal. Code of Civil Procedure § 385
Cal. Probate Code §§ 573, 574
La. Civil Code, Art. 2315.1
Mo. Rev. Stat., 537.010 et seq.

**Survival Act (Wrongful Death)**
Ky. Rev. Stat. 1971, 411.130
N.H. Rev. Stat. 1955, 556:12 et seq.
Ore. Rev. Stat., 30.080

**Survival Law (Actions)**
Ala. Code 1975, § 6-5-460 et seq.
Ariz. Rev. Stat. Ann., § 14-3110
Ark. Code Ann. 1987, 16-62-101 et seq.
Cal. Code of Civil Procedure § 385
Colo. Rev. Stat. 13-20-101 et seq.
Conn. Gen. Stat. Ann., § 52-599 et seq.
D.C. Code 1973, § 12-101 et seq.
Del. Code of 1974, Title 10, § 3701 et seq.
Fla. Stat. Ann., 46.021
Ga. Code Ann., 9-2-40 et seq.
Haw. Rev. Stat. Ann., § 663-4 et seq.
Ida. Code 1947, 5-327
Ind. Code Ann., 34-1-1-1
Iowa Code Ann., 611.20
Kan. Stat. Ann., 60-1801
Mass. Gen. Laws Ann., 228:1
Md. Ann. Code 1974, Art. ET, § 7-401
Me. Rev. Stat. Ann. 1964, Title 18A, § 3-817
Mich. Comp. Laws Ann., 600.2921
Minn. Stat. Ann., 573.01
Miss. Code Ann. 1972, § 91-7-233
Mont. Code Ann., 27-1-501
N.C. Gen. Stat. 1943, § 28A-18-1
N.J. Rev. Stat. 1937, 2A:15-3, 2A:15-4
N.M. Stat. Ann., 37-2-1
Ohio Rev. Code 1953, 2125.01 et seq., 2305.21
Okla. Stat. Ann., Title 12, § 1051
Pa. Cons. Stat., Title 20, § 3371 et seq.
R.I. Gen. Laws 1956, 9-1-6 et seq.
S.C. Code Ann. 1976, § 15-5-90
S.D. Codified Laws 1967, 15-4-1
Tenn. Code Ann., 20-5-101 et seq.
Tex. Rev. Civ. Stat., Art. 5525
Utah Code Ann. 1953, 78-11-12, 78-11-13
Va. Code 1950, § 8.01-25
Vt. Stat. Ann., Title 14, § 1451 et seq.
Wash. Rev. Code Ann., 4.20.005 et seq.
Wyo. Stat. Ann., § 1-4-101

**Surviving Partners Act (Closing-up Business)**
Ind. Code Ann., 23-4-3-1 et seq.

**Survivor and Old Age Insurance Act**
N.D. Cent. Code, 52-09-01 et seq.

**Survivor Benefit Plan Amendments of 1985**
Nov. 8, 1985, P.L. 99-145, 10 U.S. Code §§ 1447, 1447 nt., 1448, 1450 to 1452, 1455
Nov. 4, 1986, P.L. 99-661, 10 U.S. Code § 1448 nt.

**Survivors and Old Age Insurance Act (State and Municipal Employees)**
Ind. Code Ann., 5-10-2-1 et seq.

**Survivors Compensation Act (Veterans)**
Ill. Rev. Stat. 1991, Ch. 126 1/2, § 57.80 et seq.

**Survivors Scholarship Act (Peace Officer and Fire Fighter)**
N.M. Stat. Ann., 21-21F-5 et seq.

**Survivors Supplemental Benefits Act (Police Officers')**
N.M. Stat. Ann., 29-4A-1 et seq.

**Survivorship Act (Real Property)**
Mont. Code Ann., 70-20-310

**Survivorship Act (Wrongful Death)**
Minn. Stat. Ann., 573.02
Miss. Code Ann. 1972, § 11-7-13

**Susan B. Anthony Dollar Coin Act of 1978**
Oct. 10, 1978, P.L. 95-447, 31 U.S. Code § 5112

**Suspended Sentence Act**
Miss. Code Ann. 1972, § 99-19-25 et seq.
Mont. Code Ann., 46-18-201
N.C. Gen. Stat. 1943, § 15-197 et seq.
P.R. Laws Ann. 1954, Title 34, § 1026 et seq.
Tenn. Code Ann., 40-21-101 et seq.
Wash. Rev. Code Ann., 9.92.060

**Suspended Sentence and Probation Law**
La. Code of Crim. Proc. 1966, Art. 893 et seq.

**Suspension Act (Executions)**
Ky. Acts 1820, Ch. 150

**Suspension Act (Limitations)**
Mo. Rev. Stat., 537.100

**Suspension Act (Rights)**
Ariz. Rev. Stat. Ann., § 13-904

**Suspension of Sentance Act**
N.C. Gen. Stat. 1943, § 15A-1341

**Susquehanna River Basin Compact Act**
Md. Ann. Code 1974, Art. NR, § 8-301
N.Y. Environmental Conservation Law 1972 (Consol. Laws Ch. 43B) § 21-1301 et seq.
Pa. Purdon's Stat., Title 32, § 820.1 et seq.

**Sussex County Employees Retirement Act**
Del. Code of 1974, Title 9, § 7008 et seq.

**Sustainable Agriculture Act**
Ill. Rev. Stat. 1991, Ch. 5, § 2651 et seq.
Pa. Purdon's Stat., Title 3, § 2101 et seq.

**Sustainable Agriculture Research and Education Act**
Mont. Laws 1989, Ch. 659

**Sustainable Fisheries Act**
Oct. 11, 1996, P.L. 104-297, 16 U.S. Code § 1801 nt.

**Sustained Yield Act (Forests)**
Wash. Rev. Code Ann., 79.60.010 et seq.

**Sutter County Flood Control and Water Conservation District Act**
Cal. Water Code, Appx. § 125-1 et seq.
Tex. Code of Criminal Procedure, Arts. 776 to 781
Wash. Rev. Code Ann., 9.92.060

**Sutter County Water Agency Act**
Cal. Water Code, Appendix, § 86-1 et seq.

**Swamp and Overflow Land Act**
Ark. Code Ann. 1987, 22-6-401 et seq.

**Swamp Fever Act**
S.C. Code Ann. 1976, § 47-13-1310 et seq.

**Swamp Land Act**
Sept. 28, 1850, Ch. 84, 9 Stat. 519 (See 43 U.S. Code §§ 982 to 984)
March 12, 1860, Ch. 5, 12 Stat. 3
La. Rev. Stat. Ann., 41:421 et seq.

**Swampscott School Building Loan Act**
Mass. Acts 1952, Ch. 4

**Swampy or Barren Land Reclamation Act**
P.R. Laws Ann. 1954, Title 28, § 71 et seq.

**Sweating Act**
Ky. Rev. Stat. 1971, 422.110

**Sweden Commemorative Act**
N.J. Laws 1986, C128

**Swedish and Norwegian Friendship Treaty (1852)**
Haw. Session Laws 1855, p. 64, April 5, 1855

**Sweepstakes Act**
N.H. Rev. Stat. 1955, 284:21-a et seq.

**Sweepstakes Races Act**
Colo. Rev. Stat., 12-60.1-101 et seq.

**Sweet Act (War Risk Insurance Amendment)**
Dec. 24, 1919, Ch. 16, 41 Stat. 371
March 4, 1923, Ch. 291, 42 Stat. 1521

**Sweet Corn and Celery Marketing Act**
Fla. Stat. Ann., 573.01 et seq.

**Sweet Potato Industry Promotion and Assessment Act**
N.J. Rev. Stat. 1937, 54:47E-1 et seq.

**Sweet Potato Inspection and Classification Act**
Tex. Agriculture Code, § 91.141 et seq.

**Sweet Potato Seed and Plant Law**
Okla. Stat. Ann., Title 2, § 3-181 et seq.

**Swift Rail Development Act of 1994**
Nov. 2, 1994, P.L. 103-440, 49 U.S. Code § 20101 nt.

**Swimming Facilities Loan Act (Milford)**
Mass. Acts 1953, Ch. 360

**Swimming Pool Act (Public)**
Mich. Comp. Laws Ann., 333.12521 et seq.

**Swimming Pool and Bathing Beach Act**
Ill. Rev. Stat. 1991, Ch. 111 1/2, § 1201 et seq.

**Swimming Pool District Law**
Nev. Rev. Stat. 1957, 316.010 et seq.

**Swimming Pool Loan Act (Chicopee)**
Mass. Acts 1962, Ch. 428

**Swimming Pool Safety Act**
Ill. Rev. Stat. 1991, Ch. 111 1/2, § 1250 et seq.

**Swimming Pool Safety Law (Yasmin Paleso'o)**
Cal. Health and Safety Code § 116049.1

**Swimming Pool Sanitation Law**
Cal. Health and Safety Code § 24100 et seq.

**Swindling Act**
Iowa Code Ann., 713.1 et seq.
Minn. Stat. Ann., 609.52
Tex. Penal Code, § 31.01 et seq.
Wash. Rev. Code Ann., 9.45.020 et seq.

**Swine Brucellosis Act**
Neb. Rev. Stat. 1943, 54-1348 et seq.

**Swine Brucellosis and Pseudorabies Control and Eradication Act**
Mich. Comp. Laws Ann., 287.801 et seq.

**Swine Brucellosis Eradication Act**
Ill. Rev. Stat. 1991, Ch. 8, § 148f et seq.

**Swine Dealers Act**
S.D. Codified Laws 1967, Miscellaneous Superseded Code, § 40-16-1 et seq.

**Swine Disease Control and Eradication Act**
Ill. Rev. Stat. 1991, Ch. 8, § 501 et seq.

**Swine Garbage Feeding Act**
Ind. Code Ann., 15-2-1-18-20

**Swine Health Protection Act**
Oct. 17, 1980, P.L. 96-468, 7 U.S. Code § 3801 nt.
April 4, 1996, P.L. 104-127, 7 U.S. Code §§ 3809 to 3813

*Continued*

**Swine Mycobacteriosis Indemnification Act**
Ga. Code Ann., 4-4-140 et seq.

**Swiss Cheese Grading Act**
Wis. Laws 1933, Ch. 405

**Switchblade Knives Act**
Mont. Code Ann., 45-8-331
Pa. Cons. Stat., Title 18, §§ 907, 908

**Swope Act (Junior Municipal Colleges)**
Ky. Rev. Stat. 1971, 165.010 et seq.

**Swope, Blake, Moore and Howard Act (Elections)**
Ky. Acts 1944, Ch. 5

**Swope-Conley Act (Atomic Energy)**
Ky. Rev. Stat. 1971, Superseded Vol., 152.510 et seq.

**Swope-Hunt Act (State Theatre)**
Ky. Rev. Stat. 1971, 153.110 et seq.

**Sylacauga Civil Service Act**
Ala. Acts 1951, p. 763

**Symms National Recreational Trails Act of 1991**
Dec. 18, 1991, P.L. 102-240, 16 U.S. Code §§ 1261, 1261 nt., 1262

**Symons-Otterbacher Renal Disease Act**
Mich. Comp. Laws Ann., 333.5401 et seq.

**Symons-Southworth Act (Banks)**
Ind. Laws 1919, Ch. 50, p. 112

**Syndicalism Act**
Cal. Penal Code § 11400 et seq.
Haw. Rev. Stat. 1968, § 721-1 et seq.
Ida. Code 1947, 18-2001 et seq.
Ind. Code 1976, 35-26-1-1 et seq.
Kan. Stat. Ann., 21-3803 et seq.
Ky. Rev. Stat. 1971, Superseded Vol., 432.020 et seq.
Mich. Comp. Laws 1970, 750.46 et seq.
Minn. Stat. Ann., 185.06
Mont. Code Ann., 45-8-105
Neb. Laws 1919, Ch. 261
N.Y. Penal Law 1965 (Consol. Laws Ch. 40) § 240.15
Ohio Rev. Code 1953, 2923.12 et seq.
Okla. Stat. Ann., Title 21, § 1261 et seq.
Ore. Code 1991, §§ 14-3,110 to 14-3,113

**Syndicalism and Sabotage Act**
Cal. Penal Code § 11400 et seq.

**Synthetic Fuels Corporation Act of 1985**
April 7, 1986, P.L. 99-272, 42 U.S. Code prec. § 8791 nt.

**Synthetic Liquid Fuels Act**
April 5, 1944, Ch. 172, 58 Stat. 189, 30 U.S. Code §§ 321, 321 nt.
March 15, 1948, Ch. 117, 62 Stat. 79, 30 U.S. Code § 321
Sept. 22, 1950, Ch. 988, 64 Stat. 905, 30 U.S. Code § 321 nt.

**Syphilis Act (Prenatal)**
Ill. Rev. Stat. 1991, Ch. 111 1/2, § 4800 et seq.

**Syracuse City Court Act**
N.Y. Laws 1962, Ch. 513

**Syracuse Department of Finance Act**
N.Y. Laws 1905, Ch. 681

**Syracuse Grade Crossing Elimination Act**
N.Y. Laws 1926, Ch. 439

**Syracuse Municipal Court Code**
N.Y. Laws 1937, Ch. 742

**Syracuse Parking Authority Act**
N.Y. Public Authorities Law (Consol. Laws Ch. 43A) § 1475 et seq.

**Syracuse Public Works Act**
N.Y. Laws 1905, Ch. 684

**Syracuse Tax Assessment Act**
N.Y. Laws 1906, Ch. 75

**Syrup Act**
Wis. Laws 1905, Ch. 152

**System Act (Metric)**
S.C. Code Ann. 1976, § 39-9-230 et seq.

**System Development Act (Trauma Care)**
Iowa Code 1995, 147A.20 et seq.

**System Development Permitting Act (Geothermal and Cable)**
Haw. Rev. Stat. Ann., § 196D-1 et seq.

**System Labor Relations Act (University of Maine)**
Me. Rev. Stat. Ann. 1964, Title 26, § 1021 et seq.

**System of Accounting Act**
Ala. Code 1958, Title 41, § 3 Insurance

**System Regulatory Law (Insurance Company)**
La. Rev. Stat. Ann., 22:1001 et seq.

**System Support Act (Emergency Medical Services)**
Minn. Stat. Ann., 144.8093

**Systems Act (Drainage Utility)**
Tex. Government Code., § 402.041 et seq.

**Systems Act (Water Supply)**
Okla. Stat. Ann., Title 27A, § 2-6-301 et seq.

## T

**T. B. Hospital Loan Act (Bristol County)**
Mass. Acts 1953, Ch. 131

**T. V. A. Amendment Act**
July 26, 1939, Ch. 366, 53 Stat. 1083, 16 U.S. Code §§ 831n-2, 831n-3

**T. V. A. National Defense Act**
July 31, 1940, Ch. 648, 54 Stat. 781

**Table and Kitchen Wine Act (County Option)**
Ida. Code 1947, 23-1301 et seq.

**Table Wine Act**
Ala. Code 1975, § 28-7-1 et seq.

**Tabor Amendment**
Also known as Colorado Taxpayer's Bill of Rights
Colo. Const. Art. 10, § 20

**Tackett-Carter Act (Jailers)**
Ky. Acts 1936, 4th Sp. Sess., Ch. 14

**Taconite Environmental Protection Fund Act**
Minn. Stat. Ann., 298.222 et seq.

**Tactical Incident Assistance Act**
Mont. Laws 1989, Ch. 455

**Taft-Hartley Act**
See Labor Management Relations Act of 1947

**Taft-Porter Act (County Library Districts)**
Ohio Rev. Code 1953, 3375.19 et seq.

**Tag Act (Vehicles)**
Mass. Gen. Laws Ann., 90:20C

**Tag Permit Act (Motor Vehicle Dealers)**
Miss. Code Ann. 1972, § 27-19-301 et seq.

**Tagging Law (Game and Fish)**
Ore. Rev. Stat., 496.175, 496.180

**Tagging Law (Game Animals)**
Ore. Rev. Stat., 497.510 et seq.

**Tahoe Regional Planning Compact Act**
Cal. Government Code § 66800 et seq.
Nev. Rev. Stat. 1979 Reprint, 277.200

**Tahoe-Truckee Sanitation Agency Act**
Cal. Statutes 1971, Ch. 1566, p. 3084
Cal. Water Code, Appx., § 114-1 et seq.

**Taiwan Relations Act**
April 10, 1979, P.L. 96-8, 22 U.S. Code §§ 3301, 3301 nt., 3302 et seq.
Nov. 22, 1983, P.L. 98-164, 22 U.S. Code § 3311

**Take-Over Act (Corporate)**
S.C. Code Ann. 1976, § 33-1-101 et seq.
Wis. Stat. Ann., 552.01 et seq.

**Take-Over Act (Investor Protection)**
Ark. Code Ann. 1987, 23-43-101 et seq.

**Take-Over Disclosure Act**
Okla. Stat. Ann., Title 71, § 451 et seq.

**Take-Over Offer Disclosure Act**
Utah Code Ann. 1953, Miscellaneous Superseded Code Provisions, 61-4-1 et seq.

**Take Pride In America Act**
Nov. 28, 1990, P.L. 101-628, 16 U.S. Code § 4601 et seq.

**Takeover Act (Domestic Public Corporation)**
S.D. Codified Laws 1967 Miscellaneous Superseded, 47-32-1 et seq.

**Takeover Bid Act**
Ky. Rev. Stat. 1971, Superseded Vols., 292.560 et seq.

**Takeover Bid Disclosure Act**
Me. Rev. Stat. Ann. 1964, Title 13, § 801 et seq.
Mo. Rev. Stat., 409.500 et seq.
N.J. Stat. Ann. 49:5-1 et seq.
S.C. Code Ann. 1976, § 35-2-10 et seq.
Va. Code 1950, § 13.1-528 et seq.

**Takeover Disclosure Act**
Alaska Stat. 1962, § 45.57.010 et seq.
Okla. Stat. Ann., Title 71, § 451 et seq.
Pa. Purdon's Stat., Title 70, § 71 et seq.
Va. Code 1950, § 13.1-528 et seq.

**Takeover Law (Corporations)**
N.Y. Business Corporations Law 1961 (Consol. Laws Ch. 4) §§ 513, Subd. e, 912, 1600 et seq.

**Takeover Offers Act (Business)**
Ind. Code. Ann., 23-2-3.1-1 et seq.

**Takings Act (Regulatory)**
Wyo. Stat. Ann. 1977, §§ 9-5-301 to 9-5-305

**Talbert Act (Telegraph and Telephone Companies)**
Tenn. Code Ann., 65-21-101, 65-21-103, 65-21-107, 65-21-108

**Talbot Act (Unemployment Relief)**
Pa. 1931 Pamph. Laws 1503, No. 7E
Pa. 1932 Ex. Pamph. Laws 90, No. 52

**Talent Agencies Act**
Cal. Labor Code § 1700 et seq.

**Talented and Gifted Education Act**
Ore. Laws 1991, Ch. 337

**Tall Structure Act (Airport Zoning)**
Mich. Comp. Laws Ann., 259.481 et seq.
Minn. Stat. Ann., 360.061 et seq.

**Tallahassee and Leon County Consolidated Government Charter**
Fla. Special Laws 1971, Ch. 71-747
Fla. Special Laws 1973, Ch. 73-628
Fla. Special Laws 1976, Ch. 76-492

**Tallahassee Downtown Improvement Authority Act**
Fla. Special Laws 1971, Ch. 71-935

**Tallentire Act (Brokerage)**
Ohio Rev. Code 1953, 2911.04 et seq.

**Tallentire Act (Budget)**
Ohio Laws Vol. 111, p. 422

**Tallgrass Prairie National Preserve Act of 1996**
Nov. 12, 1996, P.L. 104-333, Subtitle A, 16 U.S. Code § 698u nt.

**Tally Act (Medical Practice Penalties)**
Ohio Rev. Code 1953, 4731.41

**Talmadge-Aiken Act**
Sept. 28, 1962, P.L. 87-718, 7 U.S. Code § 450

**Tampa Bay Commuter Rail Authority Act**
Fla. Stat. Ann., 343.71 et seq.

**Tampa-Hillsborough County Charter**
Fla. Special Laws 1970, Ch. 70-724

**Tampa-Hillsborough County Expressway Authority Law**
Fla. Stat. Ann., 348.50 et seq.

**Tampa Local Improvement Act**
Fla. Special Laws 1925, Ch. 11232

**Tampa Police and Firemen Pension Act**
Fla. Special Laws 1941, Ch. 21590

**Tampa Recreational Facilities Revenue Bond Act**
Fla. Special Laws 1949, Ch. 26255

**Tampa Sewer Revenue Bond Act**
Fla. Special Laws 1945, Ch. 23564

**Tampa Urban Renewal Act**
Fla. Special Laws 1957, Ch. 57-1904

**Tampering Act (Telephone Coin Box)**
Ill. Rev. Stat. 1991, Ch. 134, § 16.01 et seq.

**Tampering with Electric Meters Act**
S.C. Code Ann. 1976, § 16-13-385

**Tampering with Food or Drugs Act**
S.C. Code Ann. 1976, §§ 16-1-10, 16-3-75 et seq.

**Tandem Truck Safety Act of 1984**
Oct. 30, 1984, P.L. 98-554, 49 U.S. Code Appx. §§ 2301, nt., 2301 et seq.

**Tangelo Act**
Fla. Stat. 1969, 601.231, 601.232

**Tangerine Advertising Act**
Fla. Stat. Ann., 601.15

**Tank Act (Storage)**
Kan. Stat. Ann., 65-34,101 et seq.

**Tank Maintenance Fee Law (Underground Storage)**
Cal. Revenue and Taxation Code § 50101 et seq.

**Tank Regulation Act (Aboveground)**
Okla. Stat. Ann., Title 17, § 401 et seq.

**Tank Regulation Act (Underground Storage)**
Okla. Stat. Ann., Title 17, § 301 et seq.

**Tank Release Cleanup Act (Petroleum)**
Minn. Stat. Ann., 115C.01 et seq.

**Tank Trust Fund Act (Underground and Aboveground Storage)**
Ala. Acts 1993, No. 628

**Tank Vessel Act**
July 10, 1972, P.L. 92-340, 86 Stat. 427, 46 U.S. Code § 391a

**Tank Vessel Safety Act**
R.I. Gen. Laws 1956, 46-12.6-1 et seq.

**Tank Vessel Traffic Regulation Act**
Alaska Stat. 1962, Replaced Titles, § 30.20.010 et seq.

**Tanner Consumer Protection Act**
Cal. Civil Code § 1793.22

**Tanning Device Operation Act (Artificial)**
Colo. Rev. Stat., 25-5-1001 et seq.

**Tanning Facility Control Act**
Tenn. Code Ann., 68-117-101 et seq.

**Tanning Facility Regulation Act**
Iowa Code Ann., 136D.1 et seq.
La. Rev. Stat. Ann., 40:2701 et seq.
Tex. Health and Safety Code, § 145.001 et seq.

**Tape Piracy Act**
Ida. Code 1947, 18-7601 et seq.

**Tapp-Rives Bill**
Ky. Rev. Stat. 1971, 131.030, 131.130, 140.010 et seq.

**Tar River Port Commission Act**
N.C. Laws 1951, Ch. 593

**Target Area Contract Preference Act**
Cal. Government Code § 4530 et seq.

**Target Shooting Act**
P.R. Laws Ann. 1954, Title 15, § 371 et seq.

**Target 2000-School Reform for the Next Decade Act**
S.C. Acts 1989, p. 1533, No. 194

**Targeted Outreach for Pregnant Women Act**
Fla. Stat. Ann., 381.0045

**Tariff Act (Railroads)**
Minn. Stat. Ann., 218.011 et seq.

**Tariff Act of 1930**
June 17, 1930, Ch. 497, 46 Stat. 590, 6 U.S. Code § 1; 19 U.S. Code §§ 6, 11, 31, 32, 43, 44, 257, 258, 528, 1001 to 1654; 22 U.S. Code § 401; 31 U.S. Code §§ 541, 549; 46 U.S. Code §§ 28, 58, 274, 321, 333
March 1, 1937, Ch. 22, 50 Stat. 24, 19 U.S. Code § 1352(c)
Aug. 14, 1937, Ch. 620, 50 Stat. 638, 19 U.S. Code § 1441 and nt.
April 12, 1940, Ch. 96, 54 Stat. 107, 19 U.S. Code § 1352
May 14, 1942, Ch. 313, 56 Stat. 283
June 7, 1943, Ch. 118, 57 Stat. 125, 19 U.S. Code §§ 1351, 1352
June 3, 1944, Ch. 233, 58 Stat. 269, 19 U.S. Code §§ 1451 and nt., 1451a
July 1, 1944, Ch. 377, 58 Stat. 721, 19 U.S. Code § 1584

July 5, 1945, Ch. 269, 59 Stat. 410, 19 U.S. Code §§ 1351, 1352, 1354
Dec. 28, 1945, Ch. 605, 59 Stat. 667, 19 U.S. Code § 1551
March 8, 1946, Ch. 81, 60 Stat. 39, 19 U.S. Code § 1584
Aug. 1, 1947, Ch. 435, 61 Stat. 716
Feb. 25, 1948, Ch. 67, 62 Stat. 34
April 5, 1948, Ch. 173, 62 Stat. 161
April 20, 1948, Ch. 218, 62 Stat. 176
May 3, 1948, Ch. 247, 62 Stat. 207
May 19, 1948, Ch. 313, 62 Stat. 242
June 8, 1948, Ch. 425, 62 Stat. 344
June 12, 1948, Ch. 454, 62 Stat. 383
June 24, 1948, Ch. 614, 62 Stat. 583
May 17, 1949, Ch. 123, 63 Stat. 67
Sept. 26, 1949, Ch. 585, 63 Stat. 698, 19 U.S. Code §§ 1351, 1354
Oct. 25, 1949, Ch. 720, 63 Stat. 896
Feb. 8, 1950, Ch. 4, 64 Stat. 4
June 17, 1950, Ch. 296, 64 Stat. 247
Aug. 3, 1950, Ch. 535, 64 Stat. 406
Sept. 7, 1950, Ch. 911, 64 Stat. 785
Sept. 8, 1950, Ch. 924, 64 Stat. 798
Sept. 27, 1950, Ch. 1061, 64 Stat. 1075
June 16, 1951, Ch. 141, 65 Stat. 73, 19 U.S. Code §§ 1352, 1354
Oct. 25, 1951, Ch. 587, 65 Stat. 655
March 29, 1952, Ch. 123, 66 Stat. 27
June 12, 1952, Ch. 421, 66 Stat. 137
July 17, 1952, Ch. 928, 66 Stat. 755
Aug. 7, 1953, Ch. 348, 67 Stat. 472, 19 U.S. Code § 1352
July 1, 1954, Ch. 445, 68 Stat. 360, 19 U.S. Code §§ 1352, 1352a, 1366 nt.
July 8, 1954, Ch. 466, 68 Stat. 454
Aug. 16, 1954, Ch. 740, 68 Stat. 731
Aug. 28, 1954, Ch. 1040, 68 Stat. 896
Aug. 28, 1954, Ch. 1044, 68 Stat. 913
Aug. 28, 1954, Ch. 1045, 68 Stat. 914
Sept. 1, 1954, Ch. 1213, 68 Stat. 1137, 19 U.S. Code 1301a, 1441, 1451, 1581, 1595a, 1605, 1607, 1610, 1612
June 21, 1955, Ch. 169, 69 Stat. 162, 19 U.S. Code §§ 1351, 1352, 1352a
June 30, 1955, Ch. 258, 69 Stat. 242, 19 U.S. Code §§ 1401, 1557, 1562
April 2, 1956, Ch. 157, 70 Stat. 85
July 16, 1956, Ch. 624, 70 Stat. 554
Aug. 2, 1956, Ch. 887, 70 Stat. 943, 19 U.S. Code §§ 1336, 1401a, 1402, 1500, 1583; 31 U.S. Code § 372
Aug. 6, 1956, Ch. 989, 70 Stat. 1066
Aug. 6, 1956, Ch. 1021, 70 Stat. 1076, 19 U.S. Code § 1313
Aug. 30, 1957, P.L. 85-235, 71 Stat. 516
Sept. 4, 1957, P.L. 85-284, 71 Stat. 609
April 16, 1958, P.L. 85-378, 72 Stat. 87
April 16, 1958, P.L. 85-379, 72 Stat. 88, 19 U.S. Code § 1308
May 16, 1958, P.L. 85-408, 72 Stat. 115
May 16, 1958, P.L. 85-410, 72 Stat. 117
May 16, 1958, P.L. 85-414, 72 Stat. 118, 19 U.S. Code § 1308
May 16, 1958, P.L. 85-417, 72 Stat. 120
May 19, 1958, P.L. 85-418, 72 Stat. 120
June 11, 1958, P.L. 85-454, 72 Stat. 185
June 13, 1958, P.L. 85-458, 72 Stat. 187
Aug. 14, 1958, P.L. 85-645, 72 Stat. 602
Aug. 18, 1958, P.L. 85-673, 72 Stat. 624, 19 U.S. Code § 1313
Aug. 20, 1958, P.L. 85-686, 72 Stat. 673, 19 U.S. Code §§ 1333, 1335, 1336, 1337, 1351
Aug. 20, 1958, P.L. 85-696, 72 Stat. 687
Aug. 28, 1958, P.L. 85-791, 72 Stat. 945, 19 U.S. Code § 1641
Aug. 28, 1958, P.L. 85-808, 72 Stat. 976
Sept. 2, 1958, P.L. 85-867, 72 Stat. 1685, 19 U.S. Code § 1;
Sept. 14, 1959, P.L. 86-262, 73 Stat. 549
Sept. 16, 1959, P.L. 86-288, 73 Stat. 568
Sept. 21, 1959, P.L. 86-325, 73 Stat. 596
April 4, 1960, P.L. 86-402, 74 Stat. 13
June 30, 1960, P.L. 86-557, 74 Stat. 263
July 7, 1960, P.L. 86-606, 74 Stat. 361, 19 U.S. Code § 1309
Sept. 15, 1960, P.L. 86-795, 74 Stat. 1051
Sept. 16, 1960, P.L. 86-800, 74 Stat. 1054
June 27, 1961, P.L. 87-59, 75 Stat. 121
July 20, 1961, P.L. 87-95, 75 Stat. 214
July 26, 1961, P.L. 87-110, 75 Stat. 224
Aug. 10, 1961, P.L. 87-132, 75 Stat. 335
Sept. 21, 1961, P.L. 87-261, 75 Stat. 541, 19 U.S. Code § 1321
May 21, 1962, P.L. 87-455, 76 Stat. 72
May 24, 1962, P.L. 87-456, 76 Stat. 72, 19 U.S. Code § 1312
Aug. 24, 1962, P.L. 87-598, 76 Stat. 400, 19 U.S. Code § 1551

*Continued*

Aug. 24, 1962, P.L. 87-604, 76 Stat. 403
Aug. 24, 1962, P.L. 87-606, 76 Stat. 404
Oct. 9, 1962, P.L. 87-770, 76 Stat. 768
Oct. 10, 1962, P.L. 87-790, 76 Stat. 808
Oct. 11, 1962, P.L. 87-794, 76 Stat. 881, 19 U.S. Code §§ 1323, 1351
Oct. 23, 1962, P.L. 87-854, 76 Stat. 1130, 19 U.S. Code § 1551
Oct. 24, 1962, P.L. 87-878, 76 Stat. 1202
June 29, 1963, P.L. 88-53, 77 Stat. 73
Aug. 5, 1963, P.L. 88-86, 77 Stat. 118
June 25, 1964, P.L. 88-323, 78 Stat. 222, 19 U.S. Code § 1202
June 29, 1964, P.L. 88-324, 78 Stat. 222, 19 U.S. Code § 1202
June 29, 1964, P.L. 88-329, 78 Stat. 225, 19 U.S. Code § 1202
June 30, 1964, P.L. 88-331, 78 Stat. 226, 19 U.S. Code § 1202
June 30, 1964, P.L. 88-334, 78 Stat. 231, 19 U.S. Code § 1202
June 30, 1964, P.L. 88-336, 78 Stat. 231, 19 U.S. Code § 1202
June 30, 1964, P.L. 88-337, 78 Stat. 232, 19 U.S. Code § 1202
June 30, 1964, P.L. 88-338, 78 Stat. 232, 19 U.S. Code § 1202
June 30, 1964, P.L. 88-342, 78 Stat. 234, 19 U.S. Code § 1202
July 7, 1964, P.L. 88-362, 78 Stat. 298, 19 U.S. Code § 1202
Aug. 22, 1964, P.L. 88-482, 78 Stat. 594, 19 U.S. Code § 1202
June 30, 1965, P.L. 89-61, 79 Stat. 207, 19 U.S. Code § 1202
June 30, 1965, P.L. 89-62, 79 Stat. 208, 19 U.S. Code §§ 1202, 1321
Sept. 27, 1965, P.L. 89-204, 79 Stat. 839, 19 U.S. Code § 1202
Oct. 1, 1965, P.L. 89-229, 79 Stat. 901, 19 U.S. Code § 1202
Oct. 7, 1965, P.L. 89-241, 79 Stat. 934, 19 U.S. Code § 1202
Oct. 21, 1965, P.L. 89-283, 79 Stat. 1022, 19 U.S. Code § 1202
March 15, 1966, P.L. 89-368, 80 Stat. 71, 19 U.S. Code § 1202
April 13, 1966, P.L. 89-388, 80 Stat. 109, 19 U.S. Code § 1202
April 14, 1966, P.L. 89-392, 80 Stat. 118, 19 U.S. Code § 1202
April 19, 1966, P.L. 89-405, 80 Stat. 130, 19 U.S. Code § 1202
May 31, 1966, P.L. 89-432, 80 Stat. 169, 19 U.S. Code § 1202
May 31, 1966, P.L. 89-433, 80 Stat. 169, 19 U.S. Code § 1202
May 31, 1966, P.L. 89-434, 80 Stat. 169, 19 U.S. Code § 1202
May 31, 1966, P.L. 89-436, 80 Stat. 189, 19 U.S. Code § 1202
May 31, 1966, P.L. 89-437, 80 Stat. 190, 19 U.S. Code § 1202
May 31, 1966, P.L. 89-439, 80 Stat. 191, 19 U.S. Code § 1202
May 31, 1966, P.L. 89-440, 80 Stat. 192, 19 U.S. Code § 1202
May 31, 1966, P.L. 89-468, 80 Stat. 218, 19 U.S. Code § 1202
Sept. 13, 1966, P.L. 89-573, 80 Stat. 765, 19 U.S. Code § 1202 nt.
Sept. 13, 1966, P.L. 89-575, 80 Stat. 771, 19 U.S. Code § 1202
Oct. 8, 1966, P.L. 89-634, 80 Stat. 879, 19 U.S. Code § 1202
July 3, 1967, P.L. 90-45, 81 Stat. 111, 19 U.S. Code § 1202
July 7, 1967, P.L. 90-48, 81 Stat. 119, 19 U.S. Code § 1202
July 7, 1967, P.L. 90-49, 81 Stat. 119, 19 U.S. Code § 1202
Dec. 15, 1967, P.L. 90-201, 81 Stat. 600, 19 U.S. Code § 1;
Dec. 30, 1967, P.L. 90-234, 81 Stat. 752, 19 U.S. Code § 1202
Jan. 2, 1968, P.L. 90-240, 81 Stat. 776, 19 U.S. Code §§ 1202, 1551
Oct. 12, 1968, P.L. 90-564, 82 Stat. 1001, 19 U.S. Code § 1202
Oct. 12, 1968, P.L. 90-571, 82 Stat. 1004, 19 U.S. Code § 1202
Oct. 21, 1968, P.L. 90-615, 82 Stat. 1210, 19 U.S. Code § 1202
Oct. 22, 1968, P.L. 90-630, 82 Stat. 1328, 19 U.S. Code § 1313
Oct. 24, 1968, P.L. 90-635, 82 Stat. 1351, 19 U.S. Code § 1202
Oct. 24, 1968, P.L. 90-638, 82 Stat. 1359, 19 U.S. Code §§ 1202, 1981 nt.
June 13, 1969, P.L. 91-25, 83 Stat. 35, 19 U.S. Code § 1202
June 13, 1969, P.L. 91-26, 83 Stat. 36, 19 U.S. Code § 1202

June 13, 1969, P.L. 91-28, 83 Stat. 36, 19 U.S. Code § 1202
June 30, 1969, P.L. 91-36, 83 Stat. 42, 19 U.S. Code § 1202
July 9, 1969, P.L. 91-41, 83 Stat. 44, 19 U.S. Code § 1202
Aug. 9, 1969, P.L. 91-56, 83 Stat. 99, 19 U.S. Code § 1202
Aug. 25, 1969, P.L. 91-65, 83 Stat. 105, 19 U.S. Code § 1202
Dec. 30, 1969, P.L. 91-180, 83 Stat. 837, 19 U.S. Code § 1202
June 2, 1970, P.L. 91-271, 84 Stat. 283, 19 U.S. Code §§ 1305, 1311, 1315, 1401, 1402, 1432, 1434, 1438, 1441, 1443 to 1455, 1457, 1467, 1482, 1484, 1485, 1490 to 1493, 1496, 1499, 1501 to 1503, 1505, 1506, 1509 to 1516, 1520, 1521, 1523, 1555, 1557, 1560, 1562, 1564, 1565, 1584, 1586, 1595, 1602 to 1607, 1609, 1610, 1612 to 1614, 1617, 1618, 1623, 1641, 1648
June 30, 1970, P.L. 91-298, 84 Stat. 367, 19 U.S. Code § 1202
July 6, 1970, P.L. 91-;, 84 Stat. 407, 19 U.S. Code § 1202
July 7, 1970, P.L. 91-309, 84 Stat. 411, 19 U.S. Code § 1202
Oct. 15, 1970, P.L. 91-452, 84 Stat. 930, 19 U.S. Code § 1333
Oct. 27, 1970, P.L. 91-513, 84 Stat. 1293, 19 U.S. Code § 1584
Dec. 23, 1970, P.L. 91-570, 84 Stat. 1503, 19 U.S. Code § 1202
Dec. 31, 1970, P.L. 91-613, 84 Stat. 1835, 19 U.S. Code § 1202
Dec. 31, 1970, P.L. 91-615, 84 Stat. 1847, 19 U.S. Code § 1202
Dec. 31, 1970, P.L. 91-635, 84 Stat. 1877, 19 U.S. Code § 1202
Jan. 5, 1971, P.L. 91-654, 84 Stat. 1944, 19 U.S. Code § 1466
Jan. 5, 1971, P.L. 91-655, 84 Stat. 1945, 19 U.S. Code § 1202
Jan. 8, 1971, P.L. 91-662, 84 Stat. 1973, 19 U.S. Code § 1305
Jan. 12, 1971, P.L. 91-674, 84 Stat. 2058, 19 U.S. Code § 1202
Jan. 12, 1971, P.L. 91-685, 84 Stat. 2069, 19 U.S. Code § 1557
Jan. 12, 1971, P.L. 91-689, 84 Stat. 2073, 19 U.S. Code § 1202
Jan. 12, 1971, P.L. 91-692, 84 Stat. 2075, 19 U.S. Code §§ 1202, 1313
July 2, 1971, P.L. 92-44, 85 Stat. 100, 19 U.S. Code § 1202
Oct. 25, 1972, P.L. 92-549, 86 Stat. 1162, 19 U.S. Code § 1322
Oct. 27, 1972, P.L. 92-587, 86 Stat. 1296, 19 U.S. Code § 1202
July 30, 1973, P.L. 93-77, 87 Stat. 176, 19 U.S. Code § 1202
July 30, 1973, P.L. 93-78, 87 Stat. 177, 19 U.S. Code § 1202
July 30, 1973, P.L. 93-79, 87 Stat. 177, 19 U.S. Code § 1202
Aug. 16, 1973, P.L. 93-99, 87 Stat. 341, 19 U.S. Code § 1202
Aug. 16, 1973, P.L. 93-101, 87 Stat. 348, 19 U.S. Code § 1202
Aug. 17, 1977, P.L. 95-106, 19 U.S. Code § 1330 et seq.
Nov. 6, 1978, P.L. 95-598, 19 U.S. Code § 1485
April 3, 1979, P.L. 96-6, 19 U.S. Code § 1303
July 26, 1979, P.L. 96-39, 19 U.S. Code §§ 1303, 1311, 1311 nt., 1332, 1336, 1337, 1351, 1401a, 1402, 1466, 1500, 1514 to 1516a, 1671 et seq.
Jan. 12, 1983, P.L. 97-446, 19 U.S. Code §§ 1311, 1321, 1321 nt., 1483 to 1485, 1487, 1494, 1505, 1557
Jan. 12, 1983, P.L. 97-456, 19 U.S. Code §§ 1330, 1331
Nov. 30, 1983, P.L. 98-181, 19 U.S. Code §§ 1671a, 1671b, 1671g
Oct. 12, 1984, P.L. 98-473, 19 U.S. Code §§ 1607 to 1616
Oct. 25, 1984, P.L. 98-547, 19 U.S. Code § 1627
Oct. 30, 1984, P.L. 98-573, 19 U.S. Code §§ 1313, 1322, 1330, 1339, 1504, 1505, 1520, 1555, 1602, 1605 to 1607, 1609 et seq., 2463
Nov. 8, 1984, P.L. 98-620, 19 U.S. Code § 1337
April 7, 1986, P.L. 99-272, 19 U.S. Code § 1330
Oct. 2, 1986, P.L. 99-514, 19 U.S. Code §§ 1304, 1313, 1339, 1514 , 1516, 1613a, 1641, 1671, 1671a to 1671c, 1671e, 1671g, 1673b, 1673e, 1675, 1677, 1677-1, 1677b, 1677d, 1677f, 2703 nt.

*Continued*

Oct. 27, 1986, P.L. 99-570, 19 U.S. Code §§ 1401, 1433, 1436, 1459, 1497, 1509, 1584 to 1586, 1590, 1594, 1595, 1595a, 1608, 1613, 1613a, 1613b, 1616a, 1619, 1622, 1628, 1629

Dec. 22, 1987, P.L. 100-202, 19 U.S. Code § 1613b

Dec. 22, 1987, P.L. 100-203, 19 U.S. Code § 1330

Aug. 23, 1988, P.L. 100-418, generally 19 U.S. Code §§ 1304 et seq.

Nov. 10, 1988, P.L. 100-647, 19 U.S. Code §§ 1330, 1332, 1337, 1507, 1671, 1677, 1677-2

Nov. 18, 1988, P.L. 100-690, 19 U.S. Code §§ 1305, 1431, 1497, 1589, 1594, 1603, 1608 to 1610, 1612, 1613b, 1616a, 1627

Dec. 7, 1989, P.L. 101-207, 19 U.S. Code §§ 1330, 1616a, 1333, 1466, 1516a, 1553, 1555, 1607, 1613b, 1673h, 1677, 1677f, 2703 nt.

Nov. 5, 1990, P.L. 101-508, 19 U.S. Code § 1613b

Dec. 4, 1991, P.L. 102-185, 19 U.S. Code § 1330

Oct. 25, 1992, P.L. 102-519, 19 U.S. Code §§ 1646b, 1646c

Oct. 28, 1992, P.L. 102-563, 19 U.S. Code § 1337

Aug. 10, 1993, P.L. 103-66, 19 U.S. Code § 1450

Dec. 8, 1993, P.L. 103-182, 19 U.S. Code § 1304 et seq.

Nov. 2, 1994, P.L. 103-447, 19 U.S. Code § 1616a

Dec. 8, 1994, P.L. 103-465, 19 U.S. Code §§ 1303, 1;, 1313, 1315, 1337, 1466, 1504, 1516a, 1592a, 1671 et seq., 1673 et seq., 1676a, 1677 et seq.

April 24, 1996, P.L. 104-132, 19 U.S. Code § 1595a

July 2, 1996, P.L. 104-153, 19 U.S. Code §§ 1431; 1484; 1526

Oct. 3, 1996, P.L. 104-237, 19 U.S. Code § 1607

Oct. 11, 1996, P.L. 104-295, 19 U.S. Code §§ 1304, 1313, 1321, 1337, 1401, 1413, 1431, 1436, 1441, 1484, 1490, 1491, 1504, 1505, 1508, 1509, 1514, 1515, 1516a, 1555, 1592, 1592a, 1625, 1631, 1641, 1671a, 1671d, 1673a, 1673f, 1675, 1677, 1677n, 1673a

Oct. 19, 1996, P.L. 104-316, 19 U.S. Code § 1613b

Oct. 14, 1998, P.L. 105-258, 19 U.S. Code § 1641

June 25, 1999, P.L. 106-36, 19 U.S. Code §§ 1304, 1313, 1411, 1441, 1484b, 1505, 1514, 1515, 1520, 1555, 1557, 1558, 1584, 1675

**Tariff Acts**

March 2, 1861, Ch. 68, 12 Stat. 178

March 3, 1883, Ch. 121, 22 Stat. 488, 12 U.S. Code §§ 541, 544, 545

Oct. 1, 1890, Ch. 1244, 26 Stat. 567

Aug. 27, 1894, Ch. 349, 28 Stat. 509, 15 U.S. Code §§ 8 to 11

July 24, 1897, Ch. 11, 30 Stat. 151

Aug. 5, 1909, Ch. 6, 36 Stat. 11, 31 U.S. Code §§ 745, 756; 46 U.S . Code §§ 104, 121

Oct. 3, 1913, Ch. 16, 38 Stat. 114, 19 U.S. Code §§ 124, 128, 130, 131; 46 U.S. Code § 146

Sept. 21, 1922, Ch. 356, 42 Stat. 858, 19 U.S. Code §§ 5, 257, 258, 261, 1333; 31 U.S. Code §§ 372, 521, 549; 46 U.S. Code §§ 11, 58, 321, 333

Oct. 21, 1975, P.L. 94-120, 89 Stat. 609, 19 Appx. U.S. Code § 1202

**Tariff and Trade Act of 1984**

Aug. 23, 1988, P.L. 100-418, 102 Stat. 1240, 19 U.S. Code § 2112 nt.

**Tariff Board Act**

Aug. 5, 1909, Ch. 6, 36 Stat. 83

**Tariff Classification Act of 1962**

May 24, 1962, P.L. 87-456, 76 Stat. 72, 7 U.S. Code § 1856; 19 U.S. Code prec. § 1202, §§ 1312, 1861, nt.; 21 U.S. Code § 41; 26 U.S . Code §§ 4501, 6412, 6418; 40 U.S. Code § 470; 42 U.S. Code § 2201

Oct. 11, 1962, P.L. 87-794, 76 Stat. 882, 19 U.S. Code prec. § 1202

Aug. 23, 1988, P.L. 100-418, 102 Stat. 1155, 19 U.S. Code prec. § 1202 nt.

**Tariff Commission of 1882**

May 15, 1882, Ch. 146, 22 Stat. 64

**Tariff Schedules of the United States**
June 17, 1930, Ch. 497, 46 Stat. 590, 19 U.S. Code § 1202
Oct. 7, 1965, P.L. 89-241, 79 Stat. 934, 19 U.S. Code § 1202
April 13, 1966, P.L. 89-388, 80 Stat. 109, 19 U.S. Code § 1202
April 14, 1966, P.L. 89-392, 80 Stat. 118, 19 U.S. Code § 1202
April 19, 1966, P.L. 89-405, 80 Stat. 130, 19 U.S. Code § 1202
May 26, 1966, P.L. 89-431, 80 Stat. 168, 19 U.S. Code § 1202
May 31, 1966, P.L. 89-432, 80 Stat. 169, 19 U.S. Code § 1202
May 31, 1966, P.L. 89-433, 80 Stat. 169, 19 U.S. Code § 1202
May 31, 1966, P.L. 89-434, 80 Stat. 169, 19 U.S. Code § 1202
May 31, 1966, P.L. 89-436, 80 Stat. 189, 19 U.S. Code § 1202
May 31, 1966, P.L. 89-437, 80 Stat. 190, 19 U.S. Code § 1202
May 31, 1966, P.L. 89-439, 80 Stat. 191, 19 U.S. Code § 1202
May 31, 1966, P.L. 89-440, 80 Stat. 192, 19 U.S. Code § 1202
May 31, 1966, P.L. 89-468, 80 Stat. 218, 19 U.S. Code § 1202
Sept. 13, 1966, P.L. 89-573, 80 Stat. 765, 19 U.S. Code § 1202 nt.
Sept. 13, 1966, P.L. 89-575, 80 Stat. 771, 19 U.S. Code § 1202
Oct. 8, 1966, P.L. 89-634, 80 Stat. 879, 19 U.S. Code § 1202
July 3, 1967, P.L. 90-45, 81 Stat. 111, 19 U.S. Code § 1202
July 7, 1967, P.L. 90-48, 81 Stat. 119, 19 U.S. Code § 1202
July 7, 1967, P.L. 90-49, 81 Stat. 119, 19 U.S. Code § 1202
Dec. 30, 1967, P.L. 90-234, 81 Stat. 752, 19 U.S. Code § 1202
Jan. 2, 1968, P.L. 90-240, 81 Stat. 776, 19 U.S. Code § 1202
Oct. 12, 1968, P.L. 90-564, 82 Stat. 1001, 19 U.S. Code § 1202
Oct. 12, 1968, P.L. 90-571, 82 Stat. 1004, 19 U.S. Code § 1202
Oct. 21, 1968, P.L. 90-615, 82 Stat. 1210, 19 U.S. Code § 1202
Oct. 22, 1968, P.L. 90-630, 82 Stat. 1329, 19 U.S. Code § 1202
Oct. 24, 1968, P.L. 90-635, 82 Stat. 1351, 19 U.S. Code § 1202
Oct. 24, 1968, P.L. 90-638, 82 Stat. 1359, 19 U.S. Code §§ 1202, 1981 nt.
June 13, 1969, P.L. 91-25, 83 Stat. 35, 19 U.S. Code § 1202
June 13, 1969, P.L. 91-26, 83 Stat. 36, 19 U.S. Code § 1202
June 13, 1969, P.L. 91-28, 83 Stat. 36, 19 U.S. Code § 1202
June 30, 1969, P.L. 91-36, 83 Stat. 42, 19 U.S. Code § 1202
July 9, 1969, P.L. 91-41, 83 Stat. 44, 19 U.S. Code § 1202
Aug. 9, 1969, P.L. 91-56, 83 Stat. 99, 19 U.S. Code § 1202
Aug. 25, 1969, P.L. 91-65, 83 Stat. 105, 19 U.S. Code § 1202
Dec. 30, 1969, P.L. 91-180, 83 Stat. 837, 19 U.S. Code § 1202
June 30, 1970, P.L. 91-298, 84 Stat. 367, 19 U.S. Code § 1202
July 6, 1970, P.L. 91-;, 84 Stat. 407, 19 U.S. Code § 1202
July 7, 1970, P.L. 91-309, 84 Stat. 411, 19 U.S. Code § 1202
Aug. 24, 1970, P.L. 91-388, 84 Stat. 830, 19 U.S. Code § 1202
Dec. 23, 1970, P.L. 91-570, 84 Stat. 1503, 19 U.S. Code § 1202
Dec. 31, 1970, P.L. 91-613, 84 Stat. 1835, 19 U.S. Code § 1202
Dec. 31, 1970, P.L. 91-615, 84 Stat. 1847, 19 U.S. Code § 1202
Dec. 31, 1970, P.L. 91-635, 84 Stat. 1877, 19 U.S. Code § 1202
Jan. 5, 1971, P.L. 91-655, 84 Stat. 1945, 19 U.S. Code § 1202
Jan. 12, 1971, P.L. 91-674, 84 Stat. 2058, 19 U.S. Code § 1202
Jan. 12, 1971, P.L. 91-689, 84 Stat. 2073, 19 U.S. Code § 1202
Jan. 12, 1971, P.L. 91-692, 84 Stat. 2075, 19 U.S. Code § 1202
July 2, 1971, P.L. 92-44, 85 Stat. 100, 19 U.S. Code § 1202
Oct. 27, 1972, P.L. 92-587, 86 Stat. 1296, 19 U.S. Code § 1202
July 30, 1973, P.L. 93-77, 87 Stat. 176, 19 U.S. Code § 1202

*Continued*

July 30, 1973, P.L. 93-78, 87 Stat. 177, 19 U.S. Code § 1202
July 30, 1973, P.L. 93-79, 87 Stat. 177, 19 U.S. Code § 1202
Aug. 16, 1973, P.L. 93-99, 87 Stat. 341, 19 U.S. Code § 1202
Aug. 16, 1973, P.L. 93-101, 87 Stat. 348, 19 U.S. Code § 1202
June 8, 1974, P.L. 93-310, 88 Stat. 235, 19 U.S. Code § 1202
June 30, 1975, P.L. 94-46, 89 Stat. 245, 19 U.S. Code § 1202
Aug. 8, 1975, P.L. 94-75, 89 Stat. 408, 19 U.S. Code § 1202
Aug. 8, 1975, P.L. 94-76, 89 Stat. 409, 19 U.S. Code § 1202
Aug. 9, 1975, P.L. 94-88, 89 Stat. 433, 19 U.S. Code § 1202
Aug. 9, 1975, P.L. 94-89, 89 Stat. 438, 19 U.S. Code § 1202
Oct. 21, 1975, P.L. 94-120, 89 Stat. 609, 19 U.S. Code § 1202 Appx.
Nov. 8, 1977, P.L. 95-159, 19 U.S. Code § 1202
Nov. 8, 1977, P.L. 95-160, 19 U.S. Code § 1202
Nov. 8, 1977, P.L. 95-161, 19 U.S. Code § 1202
Nov. 8, 1977, P.L. 95-162, 19 U.S. Code § 1202

**Tariff Schedules Technical Amendments Act of 1965**
Oct. 7, 1965, P.L. 89-241, 79 Stat. 933, 19 U.S. Code prec. § 1202 nt., §§ 1202, 1981. nt.
June 29, 1967, P.L. 90-36, 81 Stat. 94, 19 U.S. Code prec. § 1202 nt.

**Tarrytown Parking Authority Act**
N.Y. Public Authorities Law (Consol. Laws Ch. 43A) § 1600a et seq.

**Tarsney Act (Erection of Public Buildings)**
Feb. 20, 1893, Ch. 146, 27 Stat. 468

**Task Force Act (First Aid)**
Ill. Comp. Stat. 1992, Ch. 20, § 3937/1 et seq.

**Task Force on Child Abuse and Neglect Act**
N.J. Stat. Ann., 9:6-8.74 et seq.

**Tattooing, Body Piercing and Permanent Cosmetics Act**
Cal. Health and Safety Code § 119300 et seq.

**Taunton Electric Loan Act**
Mass. Acts 1955, Ch. 201

**Taunton Water Loan Act**
Mass. Acts 1953, Ch. 540

**Tavern Liability Act**
Ill. Rev. Stat. 1991, Ch. 43, § 135

**Tavern, Restaurant, and Bar Wage Protection Act**
Mont. Code Ann., 39-3-601 et seq.

**Tax Abatement Act**
N.D. Cent. Code 57-23-01 et seq.
Pa. Purdon's Stat., Title 72, § 5567.1 et seq.

**Tax Abatement Act (Gasohol Fuels)**
Ill. Comp. Stat. 1992, Ch. 35, §§ 125/1 to 125/10
Ill. Rev. Stat. 1991, Ch. 5, § 1751 et seq.

**Tax Abatement and Property Redevelopment Act**
Tex. Tax Code, § 312.001 et seq.

**Tax Act**
Conn. Gen. Stat. Ann., § 12-1 et seq.
Ga. Code Ann., 48-1-1 et seq.
Ind. Code. Ann., 6-1.1-1-1 et seq.
Kan. Stat. Ann., 79-101 et seq.
Ky. Rev. Stat. 1971, 131.010 et seq.
Md. Ann. Code 1957, Art. 81, § 1 et seq.
Mont. Code Ann. 1991, 15-1-101 et seq.
N.D. Cent. Code, 57-01-01 et seq.
N.J. Laws 1903, Ch. 208
N.Y. Consol. Laws, Ch. 60
Ore. Rev. 1953, 305.005 et seq.
Tex. Tax Code, 1.01 et seq.
W. Va. Code 1966, § 11-1-1 et seq.

**Tax Act (Accommodations)**
S.C. Code Ann. 1976, §§ 12-35-30 et seq., 12-35-710 et seq.

**Tax Act (Ad Valorem)**
Miss. Code Ann. 1972, § 27-51-1 et seq.

**Tax Act (Alternative Fuel)**
Neb. Rev. Stat. 1943, 66-684 et seq.

**Tax Act (Asparagus Industry)**
N.J. Stat. Ann., 54:47C-1 et seq.

**Tax Act (Beer)**
Ga. Code Ann., 3-5-60, 3-5-61

**Tax Act (Beneficial Use)**
Tenn. Code Ann., 67-4-1501 et seq.

**Tax Act (Central Railroad)**
Ill. Comp. Stat. 1992, Ch. 35, §§ 605/18, 605/22

**Tax Act (Cigarette)**
Ill. Comp. Stat. 1992, Ch. 35, § 130/1 et seq.

**Tax Act (Cigarettes)**
Fla. Stat. Ann., 210.01 et seq.
Ida. Code 1947, 63-2501 et seq.
Ind. Code. Ann., 6-7-1-1 et seq.
Okla. Stat. Ann., Title 68, § 301 et seq.
W. Va. Code 1966, § 11-17-1 et seq.

**Tax Act (City Utility Users)**
Miss. Code Ann. 1972, § 21-33-201 et seq.

**Tax Act (Compensating)**
Miss. Code Ann. 1972, § 27-67-1 et seq.

**Tax Act (Controlled Substance)**
N.M. Stat. Ann., 7-18A-1 et seq.

**Tax Act (Controlled Substances)**
Mass. Gen. Laws Ann., 64K:1 to 64K:4

**Tax Act (Corporate Franchise)**
Miss. Code Ann. 1972, § 27-31-1 et seq.

**Tax Act (Corporation)**
N.Y. Tax Law (Consol. Laws Ch. 60) § 180 et seq.

**Tax Act (County Automobile Renting Occupation)**
Ill. Rev. Stat. 1989, Ch. 34, §§ 5-1032, 5-1033

**Tax Act (Diesel Fuel)**
Neb. Rev. Stat. 1943, 66-650 et seq.

**Tax Act (Documentary Stamp)**
Fla. Stat. Ann., 201.01 et seq.

**Tax Act (Estate)**
Mich. Comp. Laws Ann., 205.231 et seq.

**Tax Act (Estates)**
Fla. Stat. Ann., 198.01 et seq.
Ga. Code Ann., 48-12-1 et seq.
Iowa Code Ann., 451.1 et seq.
Neb. Rev. Stat. 1943, 77-2101.01 et seq.
S.C. Code Ann. 1976, § 12-16-10 et seq.

**Tax Act (Franchise)**
Ga. Code Ann., 48-5-420 et seq.
Ga. Code 1933, 92-2401 et seq.

**Tax Act (Gas Revenue)**
Ill. Comp. Stat. 1992, Ch. 35, § 615/1 et seq.

**Tax Act (Gasoline)**
Fla. Stat. 1969, 208.01 et seq.
Ind. Code. Ann., 6-6-1.1-101 et seq.
S.C. Code Ann. 1976, § 12-27-10 et seq.

**Tax Act (General Assistance)**
Ill. Rev. Stat. 1991, Ch. 107, §§ 36.9, 36a

**Tax Act (Home Rule County Use)**
Ill. Rev. Stat. 1989, Ch. 34, § 5-1008

**Tax Act (Home Rule Municipal)**
Ill. Rev. Stat. 1989, Ch. 24, § 8-11-5

**Tax Act (Hot Dog)**
N.Y. Tax Law (Consol. Laws Ch. 60) § 1105

**Tax Act (Income)**
Ariz. Rev. Stat. Ann., § 43-101 et seq.
Ga. Code Ann., 48-7-1 et seq.
Ill. Comp. Stat. 1992, Ch. 35, § 5/101 et seq.
Iowa Code Ann., 422.1 et seq.

**Tax Act (Inheritance)**
Ga. Code 1933, 92-2401 et seq.
Ind. Code. Ann.,6-4.1-1-1 et seq.
Me. Rev. Stat. Ann. 1964, Title 36, §§ 3401 et seq., 3461 et seq.

**Tax Act (Insurers)**
N.J. Stat. Ann., 54:18A-1 et seq.

**Tax Act (Intangible Personal Property)**
Fla. Stat. Ann., 199.012 et seq.

**Tax Act (Intangible Property)**
Ga. Code Ann., 48-6-20 et seq.

**Tax Act (Intangibles)**
Fla. Stat. Ann., 199.012 et seq.
Ind. Code. Ann., 6-5.1-1-1 et seq.

**Tax Act (Interstate Telecommunications Gross Receipts)**
N.M. Stat. Ann., 7-9C-1 et seq.

**Tax Act (Local Government Sales and Use)**
Colo. Rev. Stat., 29-1-501 et seq.

**Tax Act (Local Occupational License)**
Fla. Stat. Ann., 205.013 et seq.

**Tax Act (Mechanical Amusement Device)**
Neb. Rev. Stat. 1943, 77-3001 et seq.

**Tax Act (Messages)**
Ill. Comp. Stat. 1992, Ch. 35, § 610/1 et seq.

**Tax Act (Motor Fuel)**
Ga. Code Ann. 48-9-1 et seq.
Iowa Code Ann., 452A.1 et seq.

**Tax Act (Multistate)**
Haw. Rev. Stat. § 255-1 et seq.

**Tax Act (Municipal Automobile Renting Occupation)**
Ill. Rev. Stat. 1989, Ch. 24, § 8-11-8

**Tax Act (Municipal Service Corporation)**
Ill. Rev. Stat. 1989, Ch. 24, § 8-11-5

**Tax Act (Non-Home Rule Municipal Service Occupation)**
Ill. Rev. Stat. 1989, Ch. 24, § 8-11-5

**Tax Act (Property)**
Ill. Comp. Stat. 1992, Ch. 35, § 205/1-1 et seq.
Mich. Comp. Laws Ann., 211.1

**Tax Act (Public Utilities)**
Wis. Stat. Ann., 76.01 et seq.

**Tax Act (Realty Interest Transfer)**
Miss. General Laws 1958, Ch. 589, p. 1111

**Tax Act (Refund)**
Okla. Stat. Ann., Title 68, § 227 et seq.

**Tax Act (S Corporation Income)**
Haw. Rev. Stat. Ann., § 235-121 et seq.

**Tax Act (S Corporation)**
Colo. Rev. Stat., 39-22-320 et seq.
Haw. Rev. Stat. Ann., §§ 235-121 to 235-130

**Tax Act (Sales)**
Iowa Code Ann., 422.42 et seq.

**Tax Act (Single Business)**
Mich. Comp. Laws Ann., 208.1 et seq.

**Tax Act (Special Fuel Use)**
Okla. Stat. Ann., Title 68, § 701 et seq.

**Tax Act (Special Fuel)**
Mass. Gen. Laws Ann., 64E:1 et seq.
Neb. Rev. Stat. 1943, 66-601 et seq.

**Tax Act (Special Service Area)**
Ill. Comp. Stat. 1992, Ch. 35, § 235/1 et seq.
Ill. Rev. Stat. 1991, Ch. 120, § 1300 et seq.

**Tax Act (State Education)**
Mich. Comp. Laws Ann., 211.901 et seq.

**Tax Act (State Income)**
Ill. Rev. Stat. 1989, Ch. 120, § 1-101 et seq.

**Tax Act (State Real Estate Transfer)**
Mich. Comp. Laws Ann., 207.521 et seq.

**Tax Act (Tobacco Products)**
Ill. Comp. Stat. 1992, Ch. 35, § 142/1-1 et seq.
Mich. Comp. Laws Ann., 205.421 et seq.
Ore. Rev. Stat., 323.645

**Tax Act (Tobacco)**
Ga. Code Ann., 48-11-1 et seq.

**Tax Act (Tourism and Convention Facility Promotion)**
Mich. Comp. Laws Ann., 436.141 et seq.

**Tax Act (Uncollectable)**
Ill. Comp. Stat. 1992, Ch. 35, § 710/1 et seq.
Ill. Rev. Stat. 1991, Ch. 120, § 890 et seq.

**Tax Act (Use)**
Fla. Stat. Ann., 212.01 et seq.
Ga. Code Ann., 48-8-1 et seq.
Ill. Comp. Stat. 1992, Ch. 35, § 105/1 et seq.
Iowa Code Ann., 423.1 et seq.
Miss. Code Ann. 1972, § 27-67-1 et seq.

**Tax Act (Village Library and Gymnasium)**
Ill. Rev. Stat. 1991, Ch. 81, § 73.9 et seq.

**Tax Act (Withholding)**
Ga. Code Ann., 48-7-100 et seq.

**Tax Act of 1963 for Education**
Pa. Purdon's Stat., Title 72, § 7201

**Tax Adjustment Act**
July 31, 1945, Ch. 340, 59 Stat. 517

**Tax Adjustment Act of 1966**
March 15, 1966, P.L. 89-368, 80 Stat. 38, 19 U.S. Code § 1202; 26 U.S. Code §§ 276, 1402, 1403, 3402, 4061, 4251, 4253, 6015, 6154, 6211, 6412, 6654, 6682, 7205, 7701; 42 U.S. Code § 428

**Tax Adjustment Law**
Okla. Stat. Ann., Title 68, § 2479

**Tax Administration Act**
N.M. Stat. Ann., 7-1-1 et seq.

**Tax Administration Act (Chain Store)**
Fla. Stat. Ann., 214.01 et seq.

**Tax Administration Act of 1971**
Fla. Stat. Ann., 214.09 et seq.

**Tax Allocation Act**
Mich. Comp. Laws Ann., 211.211

**Tax Allocation Act (County Economic Development Project Area Project)**
Ill. Rev. Stat. 1989, Ch. 34, § 7001 et seq.

**Tax Amnesty Act**
Iowa Code Ann., 98.13
Ky. Rev. Stat. 1971, 131.400 et seq.
La. Rev. Stat. Ann. Acts 1991, No. 894
R.I. Gen. Laws 1956, 44-6.1-1 et seq.

**Tax Amnesty Program (Unemployment)**
Ga. Official Code Ann., 34-8-270 et seq.

**Tax and Bond Act (Municipal Federal Grant)**
Ill. Rev. Stat. 1991, Ch. 24, § 808.01 et seq.

**Tax and Budget Act**
Ohio Rev. Code 1953, 5705.01 et seq.

**Tax and Financing Policy Commission Act**
Ind. Code. Ann., 2-5-3-1 et seq.

**Tax and Municipal Lien Act**
Pa. Purdon's Stat., Title 53, § 7101 et seq.

**Tax and Public Account Lien Act**
Pa. Purdon's Stat., Title 72, § 4061 et seq.

**Tax and Rent Refund Act (Elderly Householders)**
Me. Rev. Stat. Ann. 1964, Title 36, § 6201 et seq.

**Tax and Trade Relief Extension Act of 1998**
Oct. 21, 1998, P.L. 105-277, Division J, 112 Stat. 2681, 26 U.S. Code § 1 nt.

**Tax Anticipation Note Act**
Colo. Rev. Stat., 29-15-101 et seq.
Ill. Rev. Stat. 1991, Ch. 85, § 820 et seq.

**Tax Anything Act**
Pa. 1947 Pamph. Laws 1145, No. 481

**Tax Apportionment Act**
Neb. Rev. Stat. 1943, 77-2108

**Tax Apportionment Act (Estate)**
See also Uniform Estate Tax Apportionment Act
Miss. Code Ann. 1972, § 27-10-1 et seq.

**Tax Apportionment Act (Federal Estate)**
Nev. Rev. Stat. 1979 Reprint, 150.290 et seq.

**Tax Apportionment Act (Income)**
Utah Code Ann. 1953, 59-7-302 et seq.

**Tax Appraisal Board Act**
Neb. Rev. Stat. 1943, Superseded Vols., 77-1325 et seq.

**Tax Assessment Act**
Mass. Gen. Laws Ann., 59:11 et seq.
Md. Ann. Code 1957, Art. 81, § 13 et seq.
N.J. Stat. Ann., 54:1-1 et seq.
Tenn. Code Ann., 9-2-101 et seq.
Wash. Rev. Code Ann., 84.12.200 et seq., 84.16.010 et seq., 84.24.010 et seq., 84.40.020 et seq., 84.48.010 et seq.

**Tax Assessment Act (Second Class Counties)**
Pa. Purdon's Stat., Title 72, § 5452.1 et seq.

**Tax Assessment Act (Syracuse)**
N.Y. Laws 1906, Ch. 75

**Tax Assessment and Tax Collection Act (Alachua County and Muncipility)**
Fla. Special Laws 1967, Ch. 67-1075

**Tax Assessment Arbitration Act**
Fla. Stat. 1969, 194.033

**Tax Assessment Freeze Act**
N.J. Stat. Ann., 54:3-26, 54:51A-8

**Tax Assessments (Cotty Act)**
Mo. Rev. Stat., 1375.035 et seq.

**Tax Assessments Act (Special, Streets, and Relief)**
Cal. Streets and Highways Code § 1900 et seq.

**Tax Assessments Equalization Act**
Ga. Code Ann., 48-5-290 et seq.
Wash. Rev. Code Ann., 84.48.010 et seq.

**Tax Assessors Registration and Professional Certification Act**
Tex. Rev. Civ. Stat., Art. 8885

**Tax Assistance Act (Local Economic Revitalization)**
Pa. 1977 Pamph. Laws No. 237, No. 76

**Tax Assistance Act (Property)**
Cal. Revenue and Taxation Code § 20501 et seq.

**Tax Authorization Act**
N.J. Stat. Ann., 40:48C-1 et seq.

**Tax Authorization Act (Relief)**
Ill. Rev. Stat. 1991, Ch. 107, § 46.9, 47

**Tax Bill Act (Local Improvements)**
Kan. Laws 1927, Ch. 133

**Tax Budget Act**
Wis. Stat. Ann., 20.005

**Tax Certificate Issuance and Return Duplicating User Charges Act**
D.C. Code Ann., §§ 47-405, 47-406, 47-1805.4, 47-2018

**Tax Certificates of Delinquency Act**
Wash. Rev. Code Ann., 84.64.010 et seq.

**Tax Claims Act (Municipal)**
Pa. 1901 Pamph. Laws 364, No. 228
Pa. 1921 Pamph. Laws 1089, No. 403
Pa. 1923 Pamph. Laws 207, No. 153

**Tax Classification Act**
Mont. Code Ann., 15-6-101 et seq.

**Tax Classification Act (Intangibles)**
Ga. Code Ann., 48-6-20

**Tax Code**
Okla. Stat. Ann., Title 68, § 101 et seq.
Va. Code 1950, § 58.1 et seq.
Wash. Rev. Code Ann., 82.01.050 et seq.

**Tax Code (Ad Valorem)**
Okla. Stat. Ann., Title 68, § 2801 et seq.

**Tax Collection Act**
R.I. Gen. Laws 1956, 44-7-1 et seq.
Wash. Rev. Code Ann., 84.56.010 et seq.

**Tax Collection Act (Brevard County)**
Fla. Special Laws 1961, Ch. 61-1917

**Tax Collection Act (Indian River County and Municipality)**
Fla. Special Laws 1967, Ch. 67-1517

**Tax Collection Act (Local Government)**
Ill. Comp. Stat. 1992, Ch. 35, § 715/1 et seq.

**Tax Collection Act (Local)**
Ill. Comp. Stat. 1992, Ch. 35, § 720/1
Ill. Rev. Stat. 1991, Ch. 120, §§ 1801 et seq., 1900, 1901
Pa. Purdon's Stat., Title 72, § 5511.1 et seq.

**Tax Collection Suit Act**
Ill. Comp. Stat. 1992, Ch. 35, §§ 705/1 to 705/3
Ill. Rev. Stat. 1991, Ch. 120, § 880 et seq.

**Tax Commission Act**
Ill. Rev. Stat. 1991, Ch. 120, § 611 et seq.
Md. Ann. Code 1957, Art. 81, § 231A et seq.
Mo. Rev. Stat., 138.190 et seq.
Nev. Rev. Stat. 1979 Reprint, 360.010 et seq.
N.H. Rev. Stat. 1955, 71:1 et seq.
Okla. Stat. Ann., Title 68, § 101 et seq.
Ore. Rev. Stat., 305.005 et seq.
Wash. Rev. Code Ann., 82.01.050 et seq.

**Tax Commissioner Act (Berrien County)**
Ga. Laws 1931, p. 390

**Tax Compact Act**
Mont. Code Ann., 15-1-601 et seq.
Neb. Rev. Stat. 1943, 77-2901

**Tax Compact Act (Multistate)**
See Multistate Tax Compact Act

**Tax Compliance Act (Municipal)**
Ill. Rev. Stat. 1991, Ch. 24, 1551 et seq.

**Tax Compromise Act**
Pa. Purdon's Stat., Title 72, §§ 5876 et seq., 5878a et seq.

**Tax Conformity Act (Klehs-Alquist)**
Cal. Statutes 1991, Ch. 117

**Tax Control Act (Local Option)**
Neb. Rev. Stat. 1943, 77-3401 et seq.

**Tax Court Act**
Md. Ann. Code 1957, Art. 81, § 224 et seq.
Ore. Rev. Stat., 305.405 et seq.

**Tax Court Appeals Act**
Md. Ann. Code 1957, Art. 81, § 248 et seq.

**Tax Credit Act (Agricultural Lands)**
Iowa Code Ann., 426.1 et seq.

**Tax Credit Act (Business Investment and Jobs Expansion)**
W. Va. Code 1966 § 11-13C-1 et seq.

**Tax Credit Act (Education Assistance and Development)**
R.I. Gen. Laws 1956, 44-42-1 et seq.

**Tax Credit Act (Homesteads)**
Iowa Code Ann., 425.1 et seq.

**Tax Credit Act (Military Service)**
Iowa Code Ann., 426A.1 et seq.

**Tax Credit Act (Special Needs Adoption)**
Mo. Rev. Stat. 1978, 135.325 et seq.

**Tax Credit Information Act (Earned Income)**
Del. Laws, Vol. 69, Ch. 443
Ill. Comp. Stat. 1992, Ch. 820, § 170/1 et seq.

**Tax Credit Law**
Wash. Rev. Code Ann., 82.04.440 et seq.

**Tax Credit Law (Job Creation)**
Pa. Purdon's Stat., Title 72, § 8801 et seq.

**Tax Credit Law (Research and Development)**
Pa. Purdon's Stat., Title 72, § 8701-B et seq.

**Tax Crimes and Penalties Act**
W. Va. Code 1966 § 11-9-1 et seq.

**Tax Deed Prescription Act**
Ga. Code 1933, 92-8315

**Tax Deeds Statute of Limitations**
Cal. Revenue and Taxation Code § 175

**Tax Deferral Act (Homestead Property)**
Fla. Stat. Ann., 197.242 et seq.

**Tax Deferral for Elderly Act (Decatur)**
Ga. Laws 1991, p. 3985

**Tax Deferral for the Elderly Act**
Ga. Code Ann., 48-5-70 et seq.

**Tax-Deferred Tuition Savings Program Act**
Ark. Code Ann. 1987, 6-83-101 et seq.

**Tax Delinquency Amnesty Act**
Ill. Laws 1984, P.A. 83-1428
La. Rev. Stat. Ann. Acts 1985, No. 301

**Tax Department Act**
Ohio Rev. Code 1953, 5703.01 et seq.

**Tax Discount Act (Dillon County)**
S.C. Code Ann. 1962, § 65-1989

**Tax Districts Act (Boyle)**
Tenn. Acts 1905, Ch. 345

**Tax Election Act (Unlimited)**
Mich. Comp. Laws Ann., 141.161 et seq.

**Tax Enabling Act**
Pa. Purdon's Stat., Title 53, § 6901 et seq.

**Tax Enabling Act (Local)**
Pa. Purdon's Stat., Title 53, § 6901 et seq.

**Tax Enforcement Act (Liquid Fuels and Fuel Use)**
Pa. Cons. Stat., Title 75, § 9401 et seq.

**Tax Enforcement Act (Reciprocal)**
Tex. Tax Code, 151.615

**Tax Enforcement and Compliance Act**
Ala. Acts 1983, 4th Sp., p. 128

**Tax Enforcement Procedures Act**
Tenn. Code Ann., 67-1-1401 et seq.

**Tax Equalization and Review Commission Act**
Neb. Rev. Stat. 1943, 77-5001 to 77-5021

**Tax Equity Act**
Colo. Rev. Stat., 39-22-101 et seq.

**Tax Equity and Educational Opportunities Support Act**
Neb. Rev. Stat. 1943, 79-801 et seq.

**Tax Equity and Enforcement Act**
N.Y. Laws 1985, Ch. 65

**Tax Equity and Fiscal Responsibility Act of 1982**
Sept. 3, 1982, P.L. 97-248, 26 U.S. Code § 1 nt.
Jan. 6, 1983, P.L. 97-424, 26 U.S. Code § 3304 nt.
July 18, 1984, P.L. 98-369, 98 Stat. 942, 1048
Oct. 30, 1984, P.L. 98-601, 26 U.S. Code §§ 3301 nt., 3302, 3302 nt.
Sept. 30, 1985, P.L. 99-107, 26 U.S. Code § 5701 nt.
Nov. 14, 1985, P.L. 99-155, 26 U.S. Code § 5701 nt.
Dec. 13, 1985, P.L. 99-181, 26 U.S. Code § 5701 nt.
Dec. 18, 1985, P.L. 99-189, 26 U.S. Code § 5701 nt.
Dec. 23, 1985, P.L. 99-201, 26 U.S. Code § 5701 nt.
April 7, 1986 P.L. 99-272, 26 U.S. Code § 5701 nt., 42 U.S. Code §§ 1395c nt., 1395h nt.
Oct. 21, 1986, P.L. 99-509, 42 U.S. Code § 1395mm

Aug. 22, 1996, P.L. 104-193, 42 U.S. Code § 602 nt.

**Tax Equivalent Property Act**
Utah Code Ann. 1953, 59-3-101 et seq.

**Tax Escrow Act (Mortgage)**
Ill. Rev. Stat. 1991, Ch. 17, §§ 5000, 5001

**Tax-Exempt Bond Allocation Act**
Pa. Purdon's Stat., Title 73, § 397.1 et seq.

**Tax Exempt Bond Allocation Act**
Pa. Purdon's Stat., Title 73, § 397.1 et seq.

**Tax Exemption Act**
Ala. Code 1975, § 40-9-1 et seq.
Cal. Revenue and Taxation Code § 201 et seq.
Ga. Code Ann., 48-5-40 et seq.
Iowa Code Ann., 427.1 et seq.
Mass. Gen. Laws Ann., 59:5
Md. Ann. Code 1957, Art. 81, § 9
Me. Rev. Stat. Ann. 1964, Title 36, § 651 et seq.
N.D. Cent. Code, 57-02-08, 57-02-09
Neb. Rev. Stat. 1943, 77-202
N.H. Rev. Stat. 1955, 72:22 et seq.
N.J. Stat. Ann., 54:4-3.3 et seq.
Ohio Rev. Code 1953, 5709.01 et seq.
Ore. Rev. Stat., 307.010 et seq.
S.C. Code Ann. 1976, § 12-37-220 et seq.
S.D. Codified Laws 1967, 10-4-7 et seq.
Tenn. Code Ann., 67-5-201 et seq.
Tex. Tax Code, § 11.11 et seq.
Wash. Rev. Code Ann., 84.36.005 et seq.
Wyo. Stat. Ann., §§ 39-1-101, 39-1-201

**Tax Exemption Act (Farm Woodlots)**
Wis. Laws 1989, 70.113, Subsec. 2

**Tax Exemption Act (Forest Lands)**
N.Y. Real Property Tax Law (Consol. Laws Ch. 50A) § 480

**Tax Exemption Act (Glenview Naval Air Station)**
Ill. Rev. Stat. 1991, Ch. 1, §§ 3400, 3401

**Tax Exemption Act (Great Lakes Naval Station)**
Ill. Rev. Stat. 1991, Ch. 1, §§ 3450, 3451

**Tax Exemption Act (Homestead)**
Haw. Rev. Stat. Ann., § 246-27 et seq.

**Tax Exemption Act (New Industries)**
N.D. Cent. Code, 40-57.1-01 et seq.

**Tax Exemption Act (Personal Property)**
Mich. Comp. Laws Ann., 211.9

**Tax Exemption Act (Property)**
Ida. Code 1947, 63-105
Mont. Code Ann., 15-6-201 et seq.

**Tax Exemption Act (Real Estate)**
Mich. Comp. Laws Ann., 211.7

**Tax Exemption Act (Stock, Commodity, or Options Transactions)**
Ill. Rev. Stat. 1991, Ch. 121 1/2, § 1000 et seq.

**Tax Exemption Act (Veterans' Homesteads)**
Mich. Comp. Laws Ann., 211.7b

**Tax Exemption Act (Veterans)**
Iowa Code Ann., 427.3
N.H. Rev. Stat. 1955, 72:28 et seq.
Wyo. Stat. Ann., § 39-1-202

**Tax Exemption for Air Pollution Control Facilities Act**
Mich. Comp. Laws Ann., 336.1 et seq.

**Tax Exemption Law (Long Term)**
N.J. Stat. Ann., 40A:20-1 et seq.

**Tax-Exemption on Property Act**
S.C. Code Ann. 1976, § 12-37-220

**Tax Expenditure Annual Report Act**
Miss. Code Ann. 1972, §§ 57-13-45, 57-13-47

**Tax Expenditure Reporting Act**
Neb. Rev. Stat. 1943, 77-379 et seq.

**Tax Extension Act**
Ill. Rev. Stat. 1991, Ch. 120, § 643a

**Tax Extension Act of 1991**
Dec. 11, 1991, P.L. 102-227, 26 U.S. Code § 1 nt.

**Tax Fairness Act**
N.C. Laws 1991, Ch. 728

**Tax Fairness, Simplification, and Conformity Act**
Cal. Statutes 1992, Ch. 698

**Tax Fairness, Simplification and Conformity Act (Bank and Corporation)**
Cal. Business and Professions Code § 23438
Cal. Revenue and Taxation Code § 17087.5 et seq.

**Tax Ferret Law**
Iowa Code 1981, 443.20

**Tax Foreclosure Act**
Fla. Stat. 1977, 197.012 et seq.
Kan. Stat Ann. 79-2801 et seq.
Ore. Rev. Stat., 312.005 et seq.
Wash. Rev. Code Ann., 84.64.030 et seq.

**Tax Foreclosure Act (In rem)**
N.J. Stat. Ann., 54:5-104.29 et seq.

**Tax Foreclosure Act (Monroe County)**
N.Y. Laws 1938, Ch. 440
N.Y. Laws 1962, Ch. 905

**Tax Foreclosure Act (Unknown or Nonresident)**
Tex. Rules of Civil Procedure, Rule 117a

**Tax Fund Bond Act (Motor Fuel)**
Ill. Rev. Stat. 1991, Ch. 121, § 101-90 et seq.

**Tax Incentive and Administration Act (Alcohol)**
Mont. Code Ann., 15-70-501 et seq.

**Tax Incentive Reform Act**
Ala. Code 1975, §§ 40-7-35, 40-9B-1 et seq.

**Tax Incentive Time Extension Act**
D.C. Code 1973, § 47-651, Subd. a

**Tax Incentives Act**
P.R. Laws Ann. 1954, Title 13, § 256 et seq.

**Tax Incentives Act (Energy)**
Ark. Stat. 1947, 87-2093 et seq.

**Tax Increases Act (Advertisement of Proposed Ad Valorem)**
Miss. General Laws 1994, Ch. 414, p. 238

**Tax Increment Allocation Act (County Economic Development Project Area)**
Ill. Rev. Stat. 1991, Ch. 34, § 8001 et seq.

**Tax Increment Allocation Economic Development Area Act**
Ill. Rev. Stat. 1991, Ch. 67 1/2, § 1001 et seq.

**Tax Increment Development Act**
La. Rev. Stat. Ann., 47:8001 et seq.

**Tax Increment Finance Authority Act**
Mich. Comp. Laws Ann., 125.1801 et seq.

**Tax Increment Financing Act**
Haw. Rev. Stat. Ann., § 46-101 et seq.
Md. Ann. Code 1957, Art. 41, § 14-201 et seq.
Minn. Stat. 1986, 273.71 et seq.
N.J. Stat. Ann., 52:27D-250 et seq.
Pa. Purdon's Stat., Title 53, § 6930.1 et seq.
R.I. Gen. Laws 1956, 45-33.2-1 et seq.
S.C. Code Ann. 1976, § 31-6-10 et seq.
Tex. Tax Code, § 311.001 et seq.
W. Va. Code 1966, § 7-11B-1 et seq.

**Tax Increment Financing Industrial Development Act**
Mont. Laws 1989, Ch. 712, §§ 1 to 3

**Tax Increment Law**
N.M. Stat. Ann., 3-60A-19 et seq.
Wis. Stat. Ann., 66.46

**Tax Inquisitor Act**
Ohio Laws Vol. 82, p. 152
Ohio Laws Vol. 85, p. 170

**Tax Law (Farm and Open Space)**
Me. Rev. Stat. Ann. 1964, Title 36, § 1101 et seq.

**Tax Law (Motor Fuel First Importation)**
N.Y. Law 1985, Ch. 44

**Tax Law (Motor Fuel)**
Ill. Comp. Stat. 1992, Ch. 505/1 et seq.

**Tax Law (Pistols or Other Firearms Local)**
Mich. Comp. Laws Ann., 123.1101 et seq.

**Tax Law (Real Estate Transfer)**
Ill. Comp. Stat. 1992, Ch. 35, § 305/1 et seq.

**Tax Law Conformance Act (Charitable Trust)**
Ill. Comp. Stat. 1992, Ch. 760, § 60/0.01 et seq.
Ill. Rev. Stat. 1991, Ch. 148, § 50 et seq.

**Tax Laws Administration Act**
Ga. Code Ann., 48-2-1 et seq.

**Tax Levy Act**
Ohio Rev. Code 1953, 5705.01 et seq.
Wash. Rev. Code Ann., 84.52.010 et seq.

**Tax Levy Limitation Act**
Wash. Rev. Code Ann., 84.52.050

**Tax Levy Validation Act (Municipal and School)**
Ill. Rev. Stat. 1991, Ch. 122, §§ 407.41h, 407.42

**Tax Lid Law**
Kan. Stat. Ann., 79-5001 et seq.

**Tax Lien Act**
Iowa Code Ann., 422.26
Ky. Rev. Stat. 1971, 134.420
Me. Rev. Stat. Ann. 1964, Title 36, § 941 et seq.
Pa. Purdon's Stat., Title 72, § 5971a et seq.
S.D. Codified Laws 1967, 10-19-1 et seq.
Wash. Rev. Code Ann., 84.60.010 et seq.

**Tax Lien Act (Municipal)**
Conn. Gen. Stat. Ann., § 12-171 et seq.
Pa. Purdon's Stat. Title 53, § 7101 et seq.

**Tax Lien Act (Occupation)**
Neb. Rev. Stat. 1943, 21-312, 21-323

**Tax Lien Foreclosure Act**
N.C. Gen. Stat. 1943, § 105-349 et seq.
N.D. Cent. Code, 32-31-01 et seq.

**Tax Lien Foreclosure Act (New York City)**
N.Y. City Adm. Code '38, Ch. 17, § D17-1.0 et seq.

**Tax Lien Registration Act**
Cal. Government Code § 27330 et seq.
Colo. Rev. Stat. 38-25-101 et seq.
Ida. Code 1947, 45-201 et seq.
N.H. Rev. Stat. 1955, 454-B:1 et seq.
S.C. Code Ann. 1976, § 12-57-10 et seq.

**Tax Lien Registration Act (Federal Revised)**
See Revised Uniform Federal Tax Lien Regristration Act

**Tax Lien Registration Act (Federal)**
See Revised Uniform Federal Tax Lien Registration Act
See Uniform Federal Tax Lien Registration Act;

**Tax Lien Registration Act (State)**
Mich. Comp. Laws Ann., 211.687 et seq.

**Tax Lien Registration and Enforcement Act**
See Uniform Tax Lien Registration And Enforcement Act

**Tax Limitation Act**
Ind. Code. Ann., 6-1.1-18-1 et seq.
Kan. Stat. Ann., 79-1945 et seq.

**Tax Limitation Act (Property)**
Mich. Comp. Laws Ann., 211.201 et seq.

**Tax Limitation Act (Schools)**
Ind. Burns' 1933, 28-1106, 28-1107

**Tax Limitation and Appropriations Act**
Utah Code 1953, 59-17A-101 et seq.

**Tax Loophole Act of 1937**
Aug. 26, 1937, Ch. 815, 50 Stat. 813

**Tax Machinery Act**
N.C. Gen. Stat. 1943, § 105-271 et seq.

**Tax Moratorium Act**
Kan. Stat. Ann., 79-2415 et seq.
Mich. Comp. Laws Ann., 211.301 et seq.
N.M. Laws 1935, Ch. 133
Okla. Laws 1941, p. 338, H. B. 68
Tenn. Public Acts 1935, Ch. 38
Tenn. Public Acts 1937, Ch. 101
Tenn. Public Acts 1939, Ch. 50

**Tax Moratorium Act (Railroads)**
N.Y. Real Property Tax Law (Consol. Laws Ch. 50A) § 489a et seq.

**Tax on Capital Gains and Other Unearned Income Act**
N.J. Stat. Ann., 54A:9-24

**Tax on Investments Law**
N.Y. Laws 1917, Ch. 700

**Tax on Wills and Administrations Act**
Va. Code 1950, § 58.1-1711 et seq.

**Tax Payment Loan Act**
Ore. Rev. Stat., 82.140

**Tax Penalty Amnesty Act**
Ark. Acts 1997, No. 1001
Ark. Code Ann. 1987, 26-18-201 et seq.

**Tax Policy Act**
Colo. Laws 1988, Ch. 273

**Tax Policy Act (Small Business)**
Ill. Rev. Stat. 1991, Ch. 127, §§ 3881, 3882

**Tax Policy Commission Act**
Ind. Code. Ann., 2-5-3-1 et seq.

**Tax Preparers Act**
Cal. Business and Professions Code § 9891 et seq.

**Tax Prepayment Act**
Ida. Code 1947, 63-1601 et seq.

**Tax Procedure Act**
See Uniform Tax Procedure Act

**Tax Procedure Act (State)**
Ark. Code Ann. 1987, 26-18-101 et seq.
N.J. Stat. Ann., 54:48-1 et seq.

**Tax Procedure and Administration Act**
W. Va. Code 1966, § 11-10-1 et seq.

**Tax Procedures Act (Local)**
Ala. Acts 1998, No. 191

**Tax Procedures and Practices Act**
Iowa Code 1995, 421.60

**Tax Proceedings Act (Curative Act of 1943)**
Cal. Statutes 1943, Ch. 458, p. 1993

**Tax Proceedings Act (Curative Act of 1945)**
Cal. Statutes 1945, Ch. 1134, p. 2176

**Tax Proration Act (Estate Taxes)**
Pa. Cons. Stat., Title 20, § 3701 et seq.

**Tax Quality Act**
Colo. Rev. Stat., 39-22-101 et seq.

**Tax Rate Extension Act of 1955**
March 30, 1955, Ch. 18, 69 Stat. 14, 26 U.S. Code §§ 11, 821, 4041, 4041 nt., 4061, 4081, 5001, 5022, 5041, 5051, 5063, 5134, 5701, 5701 nt., 5757, 6412

**Tax Rate Extension Act of 1956**
March 29, 1956, Ch. 115, 70 Stat. 66, 26 U.S. Code §§ 11, 821, 4041, 4061, 4081, 5001, 5022, 5041, 5051, 5063, 5134, 5701, 5707, 6412

**Tax Rate Extension Act of 1957**
March 29, 1957, P.L. 85-12, 71 Stat. 9, 26 U.S. Code §§ 11, 821, 4061, 5001, 5022, 5041, 5051, 5063, 5134, 5701, 5707, 6412

**Tax Rate Extension Act of 1958**
June 30, 1958, P.L. 85-475, 72 Stat. 259, 26 U.S. Code §§ 11, 821 , 4061, 4292, 5001, 5022, 5041, 5051, 5063, 5134, 5701, 5707, 6412, 6415, 6416, 7012, 7272

**Tax Rate Extension Act of 1959**
June 30, 1959, P.L. 86-75, 73 Stat. 157, 26 U.S. Code §§ 11, 821, 4061, 4251, 4261, 5001, 5022, 5041, 5051, 5063, 5701, 5707, 6412

**Tax Rate Extension Act of 1961**
June 30, 1961, P.L. 87-72, 75 Stat. 193, 26 U.S. Code §§ 11, 821, 4061, 4251, 4261, 5001, 5022, 5041, 5051, 5063, 5701, 5707, 6412

**Tax Rate Extension Act of 1962**
June 28, 1962, P.L. 87-508, 76 Stat. 114, 26 U.S. Code §§ 11, 821 , 4061, 4251 to 4253, 4261 to 4264, 5001, 5022, 5041, 5051, 5063, 5701, 5707, 6412, 6416, 6421
June 30, 1964, P.L. 88-348, 78 Stat. 237, 26 U.S. Code § 4261 nt.

**Tax Rate Extension Act of 1963**
June 29, 1963, P.L. 88-52, 77 Stat. 72, 26 U.S. Code §§ 11, 821, 4061, 4251, 4261, 5001, 5022, 5041, 5051, 5063, 5701, 5707, 6412

**Tax Reassessment Act**
Wash. Rev. Code Ann., 84.24.010 et seq.

**Tax Rebate Act**
Cal. Revenue and Taxation Code § 17070 et seq.

**Tax Receivership Act**
N.J. Stat. Ann., 54:5-53.1
Tenn. Code Ann., 67-5-2201 et seq.

**Tax Reciprocity Act**
Ark. Code Ann. 1987, 26-17-402 et seq.
Me. Rev. Stat. Ann. 1964, Title 36, § 174
Minn. Stat. Ann., 290.081
Miss. Code Ann. 1972, § 27-75-1 et seq.
Tenn. Code Ann., 20-13-109

**Tax Recordation Act**
Va. Code 1950, § 58.1-800 et seq.

**Tax Records Act (Lost or Destroyed)**
Cal. Revenue and Taxation Code § 4838

**Tax Redemption Act**
Iowa Code Ann., 447.1 et seq.
La. Rev. Stat. Ann., 47:2221 et seq.
Md. Ann. Code 1974, Art. TP, § 14-827

**Tax Reduction Act**
N.C. Laws 1985, Ch. 656
Tenn. Public Acts 1985, Ch. 395

**Tax Reduction Act of 1975**
March 29, 1975, P.L. 94-12, 89 Stat. 26, 26 U.S. Code § 1 nt.
Dec. 23, 1975, P.L. 94-164, 89 Stat. 970, 26 U.S. Code §§ 42 nt., 43 nt.
Nov. 6, 1978, P.L. 95-600, 26 U.S. Code §§ 43 nt., 48 nt.

**Tax Reduction and Simplification Act of 1977**
May 23, 1977, P.L. 95-30, 5 U.S. Code § 5520 et seq.
Nov. 6, 1978, P.L. 95-600, 26 U.S. Code § 42 nt.

**Tax Reform Act**
Cal. Revenue and Taxation Code § 16720 et seq.
Cal. Statutes 1977, Ch. 1079

**Tax Reform Act (Estate and Transfer)**
Ida. Code 1947, 14-401 et seq.

**Tax Reform Act (Foreign Franchise)**
Ala. Code 1975, § 40-14-41

**Tax Reform Act (Insurance Premium)**
Ala. Code 1975, § 27-4A-1 et seq.

**Tax Reform Act (Local)**
Pa. Purdon's Stat., Title 72, § 4750.101 et seq.

**Tax Reform Act of 1969**

Dec. 30, 1969, P.L. 91-172, 83 Stat. 487, 26 U.S. Code §§ 1 to 5, 11, 12, 21, 46 to 49, 51, 56 to 58, 62, 72, 82, 83, 101, 103, 123, 124, 141, 143, 151, 152 and others; 42 U.S. Code §§ 401, 402, 403, 415, 427, 428

Dec. 31, 1970, P.L. 91-642, 84 Stat. 1880, 26 U.S. Code § 217

Jan. 12, 1971, P.L. 91-675, 84 Stat. 2059, 26 U.S. Code § 311 nts.

Nov. 6, 1978, P.L. 95-600, 26 U.S. Code § 4940 nt.

July 18, 1984, P.L. 98-369, 98 Stat. 787, 26 U.S. Code § 4940 nt.

**Tax Reform Act of 1976**

Oct. 4, 1976, P.L. 94-455, 26 U.S. Code § 1 nt., 170 nt., 447 nt., 911 nt.

Nov. 12, 1977, P.L. 95-171, 42 U.S. Code § 167 nt.

Nov. 6, 1978, P.L. 95-600, 26 U.S. Code §§ 42 nt., 46, 120 nt., 382 nt., 904 nt., 907 nt., 995 nt., 2011 nt., 4041, 6504

Nov. 8, 1978, P.L. 95-615, 26 U.S. Code § 382 nt.

Jan. 2, 1980, P.L. 96-178, 26 U.S. Code § 162 nt.

April 2, 1980, P.L. 96-223, 26 U.S. Code § 1001 et seq.

July 18, 1984, P.L. 98-369, 98 Stat. 1047, 26 U.S. Code § 190 nt.

**Tax Reform Act of 1984**

July 18, 1984, P.L. 98-369, 98 Stat. 494, 26 U.S. Code § 1 nt.

Oct. 31, 1984, P.L. 98-612, 26 U.S. Code § 1271 nt.

May 24, 1985, P.L. 99-44, 26 U.S. Code §§ 3402, 6653, 6695

Oct. 11, 1985, P.L. 99-121,

April 7, 1986, P.L. 99-272, 26 U.S. Code § 132 nt.

Oct. 22, 1986, P.L. 99-514, 26 U.S. Code §§ 1 nt., 51 nt., 57, 57 nt., 72 nt., 79 nt., 83 nt., 103 nt., 103A nt., 125 nt., 141 nt., 168 nt., 172 nt., 208B nt., 267 nt., 291 nt., 311 nt., 321 nt., 382 nt., 402 nt., 414 nt., 419 nt., 422A nt., 425 nt., 461 nt., 513 nt., 643 nt., 801 nt., 806 nt., 807 nt., 881, 904 nt., 921 nt., 959 nt., 991 nt., 999, 1059 nt., 1092, 1092 nt., 1212, 1256 nt., 1271 nt., 1278, 1362 nt., 1504 nt., 2039 nt., 5001 nt., 5101 nt., 6050H nt., 6501 nt., 6611 nt., 6655 nt., 7702 nt., 7871; 100 Stat. pp. 2512, 2871, 2892, 2903

Nov. 10, 1988, P.L. 100-647, 26 U.S. Code §§ 801 nt., 921 nt., 959 nt., 963 nt., 6013 nt.

**Tax Reform Act of 1986**

Oct. 17, 1986, P.L. 99-499, 26 U.S. Code §§ 4221, 6427

Oct. 21, 1986, P.L. 99-509, 42 U.S. Code § 1395ww

Oct. 22, 1986, P.L. 99-514, 26 U.S. Code § 1 nt.

Dec. 22, 1987, P.L. 100-203, 19 U.S. Code § 58c nt.

Aug. 23, 1988, P.L. 100-418, 102 Stat. 1319, 19 U.S. Code § 2703 nt.

Nov. 10, 1988, P.L. 100-647, generally 26 U.S. Code §§ 1 et seq.

Aug. 9, 1989, P.L. 101-73, 26 U.S. Code §§ 368, 368 nt., 597, 597 nt.

Nov. 8, 1989, P.L. 101-140, 26 U.S. Code §§ 79, 79 nt., 89, 89 nt., 105, 119, 120, 125, 127, 129, 132, 162, 401, 414, 505, 6652

Nov. 28, 1989, P.L. 101-179, 26 U.S. Code § 7872 nt.

Dec. 12, 1989, P.L. 101-221, 42 U.S. Code § 2703 nt.

Dec. 19, 1989, P.L. 101-239, generally 26 U.S. Code §§ 1 et seq.; 29 U.S. Code §§ 1052 to 1055

Nov. 5, 1990, P.L. 101-508, 26 U.S. Code §§ 56 nt., 832 nt., 860A nt.

Aug. 20, 1996, P.L. 104-188, 26 U.S. Code § 414 nt.

Aug. 21, 1996, P.L. 104-191, 26 U.S. Code § 864 nt.

Aug. 5, 1997, P.L. 105-34, 26 U.S. Code § 453C nt.

June 9, 1998, P.L. 105-178, 26 U.S. Code §§ 172 nt., 4041 nt.

July 22, 1998, P.L. 105-206, 26 U.S. Code §§ 1 nt., prec. 21, 39, 59, 101 nt., 121 nt., 172 nt., 219, 351 nt., 401 nt., 404, 408A, 453c nt., 475 , 512 nt., 1045, 1397D, 1397F, 2001 nt., 4973, 6011 nt., 6038B, 6050S, 6103, 6213 nt., 6724, 7232

Oct. 21, 1998, P.L. 105-277, 26 U.S. Code §§ 1301 nt., 7508A nt.

**Tax Reform and Rate Reduction Act (Business)**

N.Y. Laws 1987, Ch. 817

**Tax Reform and Reduction Act**
N.Y. General City Law (Consol. Laws Ch. 21) § 25m
N.Y. Laws 1987, Ch. 28
N.Y. Tax Law (Consol. Laws Ch. 60) §§ 601 to 603, 605 to 607, 611, 612, 614 to 616, 618, 620A, 622, 624, 631 to 635, 637, 638, 651, 659, 671, 681, 683, 685, 687, 689, 699, 1303

**Tax Reform and Relief Act**
Minn. Laws 1967, Extra Session, Ch. 32

**Tax Reform Code**
Pa. Purdon's Stat., Title 72, § 7101 et seq.

**Tax Reform Technical Corrections and Tax Reduction Act (New York City)**
N.Y. Laws 1987, Ch. 333

**Tax Refund Act**
Ala. Code 1975, §§ 40-1-11, 40-1-12
Ga. Code 1933, 92-1403, Subd. I
Ind. Code. Ann., 6-1.1-26-1 et seq.
Okla. Stat. Ann., Title 68, § 227 et seq.
Pa. Purdon's Stat., Title 72, §§ 5566b, 5566c
Wash. Rev. Code Ann., 84.69.010 et seq.

**Tax Refund Act (Air and Water Pollution Control)**
Neb. Rev. Stat. 1943, 77-27, 149 et seq.

**Tax Refund Act (Federal Excise)**
Ill. Rev. Stat. 1991, Ch. 127, § 39d-1, 39d-1.1

**Tax Refund Act (Gasoline License)**
Mont. Code Ann., 15-70-225 et seq.

**Tax Refund Act (Use and Occupation)**
Ill. Comp. Stat. 1992, Ch. 35, § 150/1
Ill. Rev. Stat. 1991, Ch. 120, §§ 1500, 1501

**Tax Refund Intercept Program Act**
N.M. Stat. Ann., 7-2C-1 et seq.

**Tax Refund Limitations Act**
Pa. Purdon's Stat., Title 72, § 503

**Tax Refund Setoff Act**
Neb. Rev. Stat. 1943, 77-21, 174 et seq.

**Tax Registration Act (Gross Receipts)**
N.M. Stat. Ann., 7-10-1 et seq.

**Tax Reimbursement Act (Local)**
Ill. Comp. Stat. 1992, Ch. 35, § 740/1 et seq.
Ill. Rev. Stat. 1991, Ch. 85, § 751-1 et seq.

**Tax-Related Job Creation and Economic Development Act**
Del. Code of 1974, Title 30, § 1102

**Tax Release Act**
Ga. Code 1933, 92-5712

**Tax Relief Act (Homeowner's Property)**
Wash. Rev. Code Ann., 84.09.080, 84.33.040, 84.33.077, 84.33.078, 84.36.473, 84.36.475, 84.36.477, 84.40.405, 84.52.015, 84.55.005, 84.55.090

**Tax Relief Act (Property)**
Neb. Rev. Stat. 1943, 77-4201 et seq.

**Tax Relief Act (Residential Property)**
D.C. Code Ann., § 47-849 et seq.

**Tax Relief Act (Resident's)**
Fla. Laws 1998, Ch. 341, §§ 1 to 4

**Tax Relief Act (Sales)**
Okla. Stat. Ann., Title 68, § 5010 et seq.

**Tax Relief Act (Senior Citizens and Disabled Persons)**
Ill. Rev. Stat. 1991, Ch. 67 1/2, § 401 et seq.

**Tax Relief Act (Soldier's)**
Tenn. Public Acts 1991, Ch. 397

**Tax Relief for Flood Victims Act**
Ky. Rev. Stat. 1971, 141.011

**Tax Remission Act (Port Lavaca)**
Tex. Laws 47th Leg., 1941, p. 780, Ch. 485

**Tax Repeal Act (Gender)**
Cal. Civil Code § 51.6

**Tax Return Filing Act (Electronic)**
Ala. Code 1975, § 40-18-240 et seq.

**Tax Return Preparer Act**
Tenn. Code Ann., 62-29-101 et seq.

**Tax Revenue Act**
Haw. Rev. Stat. Ann., § 231-1 et seq.

**Tax Revision Committee Act**
Utah Code Ann. 1953, 36-4-18 et seq.

**Tax Revision Law**
Tenn. Public Acts 1991, Ch. 428

**Tax Rollback Law**
S.D. Laws 1957, Ch. 482

**Tax Sale Act (Baltimore City)**
Md. Laws 1941, Ch. 540

**Tax Sale Act (Real Property)**
Okla. Stat. Ann., Title 68, § 3104 et seq.

**Tax Sales Act**
Ala. Code 1975, 40-10-1 et seq.
D.C. Code Ann., § 47-1301 et seq.
Md. Ann. Code 1957, Art. 81, § 70 et seq.
Me. Rev. Stat. Ann. 1964, Title 36, § 891 et seq.
Mont. Code Ann., 15-17-101 et seq.
N.J. Stat. Ann., 54:5-1 et seq.
Pa. Purdon's Stat., Title 72, § 5860.101 et seq.
R.I. Gen. Laws 1956, 44-9-1 et seq.
S.C. Code Ann. 1976, § 12-49-410 et seq.
Wash. Rev. Code Ann., 84.64.070 et seq.

**Tax Sales Law (Delinquent Taxes)**
Neb. Rev. Stat. 1943, 77-1801 et seq.

**Tax Settlements Act**
N.J. Stat. Ann., A:4:7-1 et seq.

**Tax Sheltered Plan Act**
S.C. Code Ann. 1976, § 8-23-10 et seq.

**Tax Simplification Act**
See Individual Income Tax Act of 1944

**Tax Simplification Act (Fee in Lieu of)**
S.C. Code Ann. 1976, § 12-44-10 et seq.

**Tax Simplification Act (Local)**
Ala. Acts 1998, No. 192

**Tax Simplification and Equalization Act**
N.D. Cent. Code, 57-02-04 et seq.

**Tax Stability and Trust Fund Act**
Utah Code Ann. 1953, 17-4-12 et seq.

**Tax Stabilization Act (Pinelands Municipal Property)**
N.J. Stat. Ann., 54:1-68 et seq.

**Tax Stabilization Act (Preserved Farmland)**
Pa. Purdon's Stat., Title 72, § 5491.1 et seq.

**Tax Stabilization Reserve Fund Act**
Pa. Purdon's Stat., Title 72, § 3741.201 et seq.

**Tax Stamp Act (Cigarettes)**
Kan. Stat. Ann., 79-3301 et seq.

**Tax Stamp Act (Secured Debts)**
Kan. Laws 1927, Ch. 327

**Tax Supervising and Conservation Commission Act**
Ore. Rev. Stat., 294.605 et seq.

**Tax Technical Corrections Act of 1998**
July 22, 1998, P.L. 105-206, Title VI, 26 U.S. Code § 1 nt.

**Tax Termination Act**
Cal. Revenue and Taxation Code § 3511.3 et seq.

**Tax Title Act**
Mass. Gen. Laws Ann., 60:64 et seq.

**Tax Title Reconveyance Act**
Ill. Rev. Stat. 1991, Ch. 120, § 736 et seq.

**Tax Titles (Confirmation Act)**
Ark. Code Ann. 1987, 18-60-601 et seq.

**Tax Treatment Extension Act of 1977**
Nov. 8, 1978, P.L. 95-615, 26 U.S. Code §§ 1 nt., 43, 61 nt., 62, 117 nt., 119, 167, 217, 382 nt., 401 nt., 911, 913, 1302, 1304, 6011, 6012, 6091

**Tax Tribunal Act**
Mich. Comp. Laws Ann., 205.701 et seq.

**Tax Uniform Procedure Law (State)**
N.J. Stat. Ann., 54:48-1 to 54:52-3

**Tax Validation Act**
Cal. Statutes 1943, Ch. 458, p. 1993
Cal. Statutes 1945, Ch. 1134, p. 2176
Cal. Statutes 1947, Ch. 605, p. 1615
Cal. Statutes 1949, Ch. 465, p. 811
Cal. Statutes 1951, Ch. 494, p. 1647
Cal. Statutes 1953, Ch. 978, p. 2465

**Taxable Bond Act**
Ark. Code Ann. 1987, 19-9-701 et seq.
Fla. Stat. Ann., 159.821 et seq.

**Taxable Transfer Act**
N.Y. Tax Law (Consol. Laws Ch. 60) § 220 et seq.

**Taxation Act (Exemption)**
Iowa Code Ann., 427.1 et seq.

**Taxation Act (Fairness in Retail Sales)**
Fla. Stat. Ann., 212.215

**Taxation Act (Foreign Dividends)**
Ala. Code 1975, § 40-18-35

**Taxation Act (General)**
Tex. Tax. Code, § 101.001 et seq.

**Taxation Act (Inheritance)**
Iowa Code Ann., 450.1 et seq.

**Taxation Act (Jacobson-Turner)**
Ark. 1911, Ex. Sess., p. 495, No. 1

**Taxation Act (Truth in)**
Ill. Comp. Stat. 1992, Ch. 35, §§ 215/1 to 215/9.2
Tenn. Code Ann., 67-5-1701

**Taxation and Revenue Department Act**
N.M. Stat. Ann., 9-11-1 et seq.

**Taxation Law**
S.C. Const. Article 10, § 1-15 et seq.

**Taxation of Costs Act**
N.J. Stat. Ann., 2A:15-59 et seq.

**Taxation of Motor Fuels Consumed by Interstate Buses Act**
Me. Rev. Stat. Ann. 1964, Title 36, § 3091 et seq.

**Taxation of Motor Fuels Consumed by Interstate Buses Compact**
N.H. Rev. Stat. 1955, 260:66 et seq.

**Taxation Professional Certification Act (Property)**
Tex. Rev. Civ. Stat., Art. 8885

**Taxation Proration Agreement (Bus)**
Vt. Stat. Ann., Title 23, § 561 et seq.

**Taxation Proration and Reciprocity Agreement (Bus)**
Me. Rev. Stat. Ann. 1964, Title 29, § 431 et seq.
Me. Rev. Stat. Ann. 1964, Title 36, § 1492 et seq.

**Taxation Sliding Scale Act**
Tenn. Public Acts 1919, Ch. 2

**Taxes Act (Estate and Gift)**
Vt. Stat. Ann., Title 32, § 7401 et seq.

**Taxi Bonding Law**
N.Y. Vehicle and Traffic Law 1959 (Consol. Laws Ch. 71) § 370

**Taxicab Act**
N.C. Gen. Stat. 1943, §§ 20-37, 160A-304
R.I. Gen. Laws 1956, 39-14-1 et seq.

**Taxicab Insurance Act**
D.C. Code 1973, § 44-301 et seq.

**Taxicab Insurance Rate Approval Act**
D.C. Laws 1977, No. 1-127

**Taxicab Regulation Act**
N.Y. Local Laws 1973, Town of New Windsor, p. 2644
Wash. Rev. Code Ann., 46.72.010 et seq.

**Taxicab Tax Law (New York City)**
N.Y. City Adm. Code '38, Ch. 46, § K46-1.0 et seq.

**Taxing Agency Validation Act**
Cal. Statutes 1955, Ch. 382, p. 841

**Taxing and Licensing Act (Merchants)**
Tenn. Code Ann., Superseded Vol., 67-4701 et seq.

**Taxing District Relief Act**
Wash. Rev. Code Ann., 39.64.005 et seq.

**Taxing District Reserve Fund Act**
Ill. Comp. Stat. 1992, Ch. 35, §§ 725/1 to 725/4
Ill. Rev. Stat. 1991, Ch. 120, § 2101 et seq.

**Taxpayer Bill of Rights 2**
July 30, 1996, P.L. 104-168, 26 U.S. Code § 1 nt.

**Taxpayer Bill of Rights 3**
July 22, 1998, P.L. 105-206, Title III, 26 U.S. Code § 1 nt.

**Taxpayer Browsing Protection Act**
Aug. 5, 1997, P.L. 105-35, 26 U.S. Code § 1 nt.
Aug. 5, 1997, P.L. 105-35, 111 Stat. 1104
Cal. Revenue and Taxation Code §§ 7056.5, 19542.1
Cal. Unemployment Insurance Code § 13018

**Taxpayer Convenience Act**
Ala. Code 1975, § 40-7-2.1

**Taxpayer Protection Act**
Wash. Rev. Code. Ann., 43.135.902

**Taxpayer Protection and Technical Corrections Act**
Ala. Code 1975, §§ 40-2A-5, 40-2A-7, 40-2A-9 to 40-2A-11

**Taxpayer Relief Act of 1997**
Aug. 5, 1997, P.L. 105-34, 26 U.S. Code § 1 nt.

**Taxpayers' Bill of Rights**
Ariz. Rev. Stat. Ann., § 42-139 et seq.
Ark. Code Ann. 1987, 26-18-801 et seq.
Cal. Revenue and Taxation Code § 21001 et seq.
Colo. Const. Art. 10, § 20
Fla. Stat. Ann., 213.015
Ga. Official Code Ann., 48-1-8
Kan. Stat. Ann., 79-3268
Minn. Stat. Ann., 270.0602 et seq.
Mont. Code Ann., 15-1-221 to 15-1-223
Mont. Laws 1991, Ch. 619
N.Y. Tax Law (Consol. Laws Ch. 60) § 3000 et seq.
Ore. Rev. Stat., 305.860 to 305.900
Pa. Purdon's Stat., Title 35, § 3310-101 et seq.
S.C. Code Ann. 1976, §§ 12-54-710 et seq., 12-58-10 et seq.
Tenn. Public Acts 1992, Ch. 857
Va. Code 1950, § 58.1-1845

**Taxpayer's Bill of Rights (Employment)**
Cal. Unemployment Insurance Code §§ 650, 1206, 1222, 1231 et seq., 13004.1

**Taxpayers Bill of Rights (Local)**
Pa. Cons. Stat., Title 53, § 8421 et seq.

**Taxpayers Bill of Rights (Morgan Property)**
Cal. Revenue and Taxation Code § 5900 et seq.

**Taxpayers' Bill of Rights and Uniform Revenue Procedures Act**
See Uniform Revenue Procedures and Taxpayers' Bill of Rights Act

**Taxpayers Information Act**
Mont. Code Ann., 15-10-201 et seq.

**Taxpayers' Rights and Responsibilities Act**
Wash. Rev. Code Ann., 82.32A.002 et seq.

**Taxpreparer Disclosure of Information Act**
Ill. Rev. Stat. 1991, Ch. 38, § 65-10 et seq.
Ill. Rev. Stat. 1991, Ch. 120, § 2301 et seq.

Ore. Rev. Stat., 305.865 et seq.
S.C. Code Ann. 1976, § 12-54-710 et seq.

**Taylor Act (Grazing)**
Nev. Rev. Stat. 1979 Reprint, 568.010 et seq.

**Taylor Act (Public Employees' Fair Employment)**
N.Y. Civil Service Law 1958 (Consol. Laws Ch. 7) § 200 et seq.

**Taylor Act (Streets)**
Ohio Laws Vol. 83, p. 140

**Taylor County Water and Sewerage Authority Act**
Ga. Laws 1995, p. 3589

**Taylor Grazing Act**
June 28, 1934, Ch. 865, 48 Stat. 1269, 43 U.S. Code §§ 315 to 315n, 315o-1, 485, 1171
Aug. 6, 1947, Ch. 507, 61 Stat. 790, 43 U.S. Code §§ 315b, 315i, 315j
June 19, 1948, Ch. 548, 62 Stat. 533, 43 U.S. Code §§ 315g, 315h
May 28, 1954, Ch. 243, 68 Stat. 151, 43 U.S. Code §§ 315, 315m

**Taylor-Lybrand-Timmons Insurance Code**
Ala. Code 1975, § 27-1-1 et seq.

**Taylor T. V. A. Act**
July 16, 1941, Ch. 303, 55 Stat. 597

**Tea Importation Act**
March 2, 1897, Ch. 358, 29 Stat. 604, 21 U.S. Code §§ 41 to 50
July 12, 1943, Ch. 221, 57 Stat. 498
Aug. 10, 1993, P.L. 103-66, 21 U.S. Code § 46a
April 9, 1996, P.L. 104-128, 21 U.S. Code § 41 et seq.

**TEA 21 Restoration Act**
July 22, 1998, P.L. 105-206, 23 U.S. Code § 101 nt.

**Teacher Affidavit Act**
Ark. Stat. 1947, 80-1229 et seq.

**Teacher and Supervisor Grant Program (Child Development)**
Cal. Education Code 1976, § 69620 et seq.

**Teacher Bargaining Act**
Ind. Code. Ann., 20-7.5-1-1 et seq.

**Teacher Credentialing Law (Bergeson Act)**
Cal. Education Code 1976, § 44200 et seq.

**Teacher Credentials Interstate Transfer Act**
N.J. Stat. Ann., 18A:26-11 et seq.

**Teacher Due Process Act**
Okla. Stat. Ann., Title 70, § 6-101.20 et seq.

**Teacher Education Act (Cooperative)**
Colo. Rev. Stat., 22-62-101 et seq.

**Teacher Education Center Act**
Fla. Stat. Ann., 231.600 et seq.

**Teacher Education Internship Act**
Cal. Education Code 1976, § 44450 et seq.

**Teacher Employment Act**
Wyo. Stat. Ann., § 21-7-101 et seq.

**Teacher Employment, Compensation, and Dismissal Act**
Colo. Rev. Stat., 22-63-101 et seq.

**Teacher Exchange and Recruitment Law (Foreign Language)**
Cal. Education Code 1976, § 44610 et seq.

**Teacher Fair Dismissal Act**
Ark. Code Ann. 1987, 6-17-1501 et seq.

**Teacher Incentive Program**
Cal. Education Code 1976, § 44760 et seq.

**Teacher Loan Forgiveness Act (Rural and Urban)**
Pa. Purdon's Stat., Title 24, § 5191 et seq.

**Teacher Negotiation (Employment Relations)**
Conn. Gen. Stat. Ann., § 10-153a et seq.

**Teacher Preparation Act (Award for Excellence)**
Wash. Rev. Code Ann., 28A.625.350 et seq.

**Teacher Preparation and Licensing Law**
Cal. Education Code 1976, § 44200 et seq.

**Teacher Preparation and Training Act (Bilingual-Crosscultural)**
Cal. Education Code 1976, § 10100 et seq.

**Teacher Program Act (Mentor)**
Cal. Education Code 1976, § 4490 et seq.

**Teacher Quality Employment Act**
N.J. Stat. Ann., 18A:29-5.1 et seq.

**Teacher Recognition Act**
N.J. Stat. Ann., 18A:29A-1 et seq.

**Teacher Recognition Act (Governors Annual)**
N.J. Stat. Ann. 18A:29A-1 et seq.

**Teacher Scholarship Act (Child Development)**
Ill. Comp. Stat. 1992, Ch. 110, § 922/1 et seq.

**Teacher Scholarship Program**
Kan. Stat. Ann., 74-32,100 et seq.

**Teacher Shortage Act (Critical)**
Miss. Code Ann. 1972, § 37-159-1 et seq.

**Teacher Shortage Scholarship Program (David A. DeBolt)**
Ill. Comp. Stat. 1992, Ch. 110, § 947/52

**Teacher Termination Act**
Iowa Code Ann., 279.13 et seq.

**Teacher Testing Act**
Ark. Stat. 1947, 80-1267 et seq.

**Teacher Training Act (Educational Technology)**
N.J. Stat. Ann., 18A:6-103 et seq.

**Teachers Act**
Wash. Rev. Code Ann., 28A.67.010 et seq.

**Teachers Alternative Salary Policies Act**
Colo. Rev. Stat., 22-66-101 et seq.

**Teachers' and Principals' Contracts Termination Act**
N.C. Gen. Stat. 1943, § 115-142

**Teachers' and Public Employees' Reciprocal Service Credit Act**
W. Va. Code 1966, § 5-13-1 et seq.

**Teachers' and School Employees' Retirement System Act**
Mo. Rev. Stat., 169.010 et seq.

**Teachers' and State Employees' Retirement Act**
Ala. Code 1975, § 36-27-1 et seq.
N.C. Gen. Stat. 1943, § 135-1 et seq.
Wis. Stat. Ann., 40.20 et seq.
Wyo. Stat. Ann., § 9-3-401 et seq.

**Teachers' Appointment and Tenure Law (Richland County)**
S.C. Acts 1941, p. 125, No. 97

**Teachers as Advisors Act**
Fla. Stat. Ann., 230.2314

**Teachers' Certification Act**
Colo. Rev. Stat., 22-60-101 et seq.
N.D. Cent. Code, 15-36-01 et seq.
Tex. Education Code, § 13.031 et seq.
Wash. Rev. Code Ann., 28A:70.005 et seq.

**Teachers College Board Act**
Ill. Rev. Stat. 1991, Ch. 144, § 1001 et seq.

**Teachers College Board Revenue Bond Act**
Ill. Rev. Stat. 1991, Ch. 144, § 1011 et seq.

**Teachers' Compensation Act**
Tenn. Public Acts 1951, Ch. 132

**Teachers' Compulsory Retirement Act**
Ill. Rev. Stat. 1991, Ch. 122, § 34-87

**Teachers' Continuing Contract Act**
S.D. Laws 1951, Ch. 87
Tenn. Code Ann., 49-5-409

**Teachers' Continuing Service Act**
Ala. Code 1975, § 16-24-1 et seq.

**Teachers Continuous Contract Act**
Wis. Stat. Ann., 118.22 et seq.

**Teachers' Corps Act**
Mass. Acts 1966, Ch. 517

**Teachers' Disclosure of Association Act**
Ark. Stat. 1947, 80-1229 et seq.

**Teachers Education Act (Cooperative)**
Wyo. Stat. Ann., § 21-21-101 et seq.

**Teachers' Employment Act (Tenure)**
Ala. Code 1975, § 16-24-1 et seq.

**Teachers' Equal Pay Act**
Mass. Gen. Laws Ann., 71:40

**Teachers' Exam Act (National)**
S.C. Code of 1976, § 59-26-10 et seq.

**Teachers' Institute Act**
Mo. Rev. Stat., 168.011 et seq.

**Teachers' Insurance and Retirement Fund Act**
N.D. Cent. Code, 15-39.1-01 et seq.

**Teachers' Leave Act**
D.C. Code Ann., § 31-1020 et seq.

**Teachers' Loyalty Bill**
N.Y. Laws 1921, Ch. 666

**Teachers Loyalty Oath Act**
Cal. Education Code 1976, § 44244
Mass. Gen. Laws Ann., 71:30A
Mich. Comp. Laws Ann., 388.401 et seq.
N.H. Rev. Stat. 1955, 191:1 et seq.
N.J. Stat. Ann., 18A:6-7
N.Y. Education Law 1947 (Consol. Laws Ch. 16) § 3002
Ore. Rev. Stat. 1953, 342.615 et seq.
Wash. Rev. Code 1989, 28A.67.020

**Teachers' Minimum Salary Act**
Ark. Code Ann. 1987, 6-17-1001 et seq.
Ida. Code 1947, 33-1219
Ind. Code. Ann., 20-6.1-5-1 et seq.
Iowa Code 1962, 294.6
Me. Rev. Stat. Ann. 1964, Title 20-A, § 13402
Tex. Education Code, § 16.157
Wash. Superseded Code 1951, 28.67.090

**Teachers' Minimum Sick Leave Law**
Ark. Code Ann. 1987, 6-17-1201 et seq.

**Teachers' Organizational Affidavit Act**
Ark. Stat. 1947, 80-1229

**Teachers' Pension Act**
Iowa Code Ann., 294.15
Mich. Comp. Laws Ann., 38.201 et seq.
N.J. Stat. Ann., 18:13-24 et seq.
N.J. Stat. Ann., 18A:66-1 et seq.
R.I. Gen. Laws 1956, 16-15-1 et seq.
Wyo. Session Laws 1943, Ch. 59

**Teachers' Pension Act (Fulton County)**
Ga. Laws 1945, p. 528

**Teachers' Pension and Annuity Fund Act**
N.J. Stat. Ann., 18A:66-1 et seq.

**Teachers' Pension and Retirement Act (Fulton County)**
Ga. Laws 1937, p. 892

**Teachers' Pension and Retirement Fund Act**
N.M. Stat. Ann., 22-11-1 et seq.

**Teachers' Pension and Retirement Fund Act (Over 500,000)**
Ill. Rev. Stat. 1991, Ch. 108 1/2, § 17-101 et seq.

**Teachers' Professional Negotiations Act**
Fla. Laws 1969, Ch. 69-665
Mont. Rev. Code 1947, 75-6115 et seq.
Neb. Rev. Stat. 1943, 79-1287 et seq.

**Teachers' Professional Negotiations Act (Hillsborough County)**
Fla. Special Laws 1971, Ch. 71-686

**Teachers' Professional Negotiations Act (Pinellas County)**
Fla. Special Laws 1971, Ch. 71-875

**Teachers' Professional Practices Act**
Tex. Education Code, § 13.201 et seq.

**Teachers' Retirement Act**
Ala. Code 1975, § 16-25-1 et seq.
Alaska Stat. 1962, § 14.25.010 et seq.
Ariz. Rev. Stat. Ann., § 15-1401 et seq.
Ark. Stat. 1947, 80-1412 et seq.
Cal. Education Code 1976, § 22000 et seq.
Conn. Gen. Stat. Ann., § 10-183b et seq.
D.C. Code Ann., § 31-1201 et seq.
Fla. Stat. Ann., 238.01 et seq.
Ga. Code Ann., 47-3-1 et seq.
Ida. Code 1947, 33-1301 et seq.
Kan. Stat. Ann., 72-1726 et seq., 72-1758 et seq., 72-1788 et seq., 72-5501 et seq.
La. Rev. Stat. Ann., 17:571 et seq.
Md. Ann. Code 1957, Art. 73B, § 81 et seq.
Me. Rev. Stat. Ann. 1964, Title 5, § 17001 et seq.
Mich. Comp. Laws Ann., 38.201 et seq.
Minn. Stat. Ann., 354.045 et seq.
Miss. Code Ann. 1972, § 25-11-201 et seq.
Mont. Code Ann., 19-4-101 et seq.
N.D. Cent. Code, 15-39.1-01 et seq.
Nev. Rev. Stat. 1979 Reprint, 391.360
N.H. Rev. Stat. 1955, 100-A:1 et seq.
N.Y. City Adm. Code '85, § 13-501 et seq.
Ohio Rev. Code 1953, 3307.01 et seq.
Okla. Stat. Ann., Title 70, § 17-101 et seq.
Ore. Rev. Stat., 239.002 et seq.
P.R. Laws Ann. 1954, Title 18, § 321 et seq.
R.I. Gen. Laws 1956, 16-16-1 et seq.
Tenn. Code Ann., 8-34-101 et seq.
Tex. Government Code 821.001 et seq.
Utah Code Ann. 1953, 49-2-101 et seq.
Vt. Stat. Ann., Title 16, § 1931 et seq.
Wash. Rev. Code Ann., 41.32.005 et seq.
Wis. Stat. Ann., 40.20 et seq.
W. Va. Code 1966, § 18-7A-1 et seq.
Wyo. Session Laws 1943, Ch. 59
Wyo. Session Laws 1951, Ch. 159

**Teachers' Retirement Act (Milwaukee)**
Wis. Stat. Ann., 40.20 et seq.

**Teachers' Retirement Act (Under 500,000)**
Ill. Rev. Stat. 1991, Ch. 108 1/2, § 16-101 et seq.

**Teachers' Retirement and Tenure Act**
Ky. Rev. Stat. 1971, 161.220 et seq.

**Teachers' Retirement Fund Act**
Ind. Code. Ann., 21-6.1-1-1 et seq.

**Teachers' Retirement Lands Act**
Cal. Public Resources Code § 6475 et seq.

**Teachers' Retirement Law (District of Columbia)**
Jan. 15, 1920, Ch. 39, 41 Stat. 387

**Teacher's Retirement Reform Act**
W. Va. Code 1966, § 18-7B-1 et seq.

**Teachers' Retirement System Act**
Ark. Code Ann. 1987, 24-7-201 et seq.
S.D. Codified Laws 1967, 3-12-1 et seq.

**Teachers' Salary Act**
Ark. Code Ann. 1987, 6-17-901 et seq.
D.C. Code Ann., § 31-1101 et seq.
Me. Rev. Stat. Ann. 1964, Title 20-A, § 13401 et seq.
N.Y. Education Law 1947 (Consol. Laws Ch. 16) §§ 3015, 3101 et seq.
Vt. Stat. Ann., Title 16, § 1792 et seq.

**Teachers' Salary Act Amendments (District of Columbia)**
D.C. Code Ann., § 31-1101, 31-1111, 31-1135, 31-1141

**Teachers' Salary Policy Planning Grants Act**
Colo. Rev. Stat., 22-67-101

**Teachers' Sick Leave Act**
Ind. Code. Ann., 20-6.1-6-3

**Teachers' Sick Leave Bank Act**
Tenn. Code Ann., 49-5-801 et seq.

**Teachers' Sick Leave Bank Act (Special School)**
Tenn. Code Ann., 49-50-1101 et seq.

**Teachers' Temporary Contract Act**
Ind. Code. Ann., 20-6.1-4-7

**Teachers' Tenure Act**
Ala. Code 1975, § 16-24-1 et seq.
Alaska Stat. 1962, § 14.20.130 et seq.
Ariz. Rev. Stat. Ann., § 15-531 et seq.
Cal. Education Code 1976, §§ 44000 et seq., 87000 et seq.
Colo. Rev. Stat. 22-63-101 et seq.
Conn. Gen. Stat. Ann., § 10-151 et seq.
Del. Code of 1974, Title 14, § 1401 et seq.
Ga. Laws 1937, p. 879
Ill. Rev. Stat. 1991, Ch. 122, § 24-11 et seq.
Ind. Code. Ann., 20-6.1-4-9 et seq.
Ky. Rev. Stat. 1971, 161.720 et seq.
La. Rev. Stat. Ann., 17:441 et seq.
Mich. Comp. Laws Ann., 38.71 et seq.
Minn. Stat. Ann., 125.17 et seq.
Mo. Rev. Stat., 168.102 et seq.
Mont. Code Ann., 20-4-203
Neb. Rev. Stat. 1943, 79-1255 et seq.
N.J. Stat. Ann., 18A:28-1 et seq.
N.M. Stat. Ann., 22-10-1
N.Y. Education Law 1947 (Consol. Laws Ch. 16) §§ 2573, 3011, 3012, 6202
Ohio Rev. Code 1953, 3319.07 et seq.
Ore. Rev. Stat., 342.805 et seq.
Pa. Purdon's Stat., Title 24, § 11-1121 et seq.
P.R. Laws Ann. 1954, Title 18, § 214 et seq.
R.I. Gen. Laws 1956, 16-13-1 et seq.
Tenn. Code Ann., 49-5-501 et seq.
W. Va. Code 1966, § 18A-2-2

**Teachers' Tenure Act (Atlanta)**
Ga. Laws 1968, p. 3697

**Teachers' Tenure Act (Duval County)**
Fla. Special Laws 1941, Ch. 21197

**Teachers' Tenure Act (Knox County)**
Tenn. Private Acts 1937, 3rd Ex. Sess., Ch. 18

**Teachers' Tenure Act (Milwaukee)**
Wis. Stat. Ann., 119.42

**Teachers' Tenure Act (Orange County)**
Fla. Special Laws 1937, Ch. 18743

**Teachers Tenure of Service Act**
Colo. Stat. Ann. 1935, Ch. 146 § 288 et seq.

**Teachers' Week Act (Retired)**
Ill. Rev. Stat. 1991, Ch. 1, § 3051-80 et seq.

**Teaching Act (Prescriptive)**
Okla. Stat. Ann., Title 70, § 1210.271 et seq.

**Teaching Practice Program of the Department of Education Act**
Apr. 9, 1996, P.L. 104-128, 110 Stat. 1198
P.R. Acts 1989, No. 79

**Teaching Practices Act**
Iowa Code 1989, 272A.1 et seq.
La. Rev. Stat. Ann., 17:1331 et seq.

**Tear Gas Weapons Act**
Cal. Penal Code §§ 12400, 12401 et seq.

**Tech-Prep Education Act**
Sept. 25, 1990, P.L. 101-392, 20 U.S. Code § 2394 nt.
Aug. 17, 1991, P.L. 102-103, 20 U.S. Code § 2394a
May 4, 1994, P.L. 103-239, 2 U.S. Code §§ 2394b, 2394c

**Technical Amendments Act of 1958**
Sept. 2, 1958, P.L. 85-866, 72 Stat. 1606, 26 U.S. Code §§ 35, 75 , 101, 120 nt., 152, 162, 164 to 168, 170 to 172, 178, 213, 243, 246, 337, 341, 358, 372, 381, 391, 403, 404, 421, 453, 455, 481, 503, 534, 535, 545, 556, 558, 582, 611, 613, 614, 813, 851, 852, 871, 904, 905, 911, 1015, 1016, 1031, 1033, 1034, 1053, 1071, 1231 to 1235, 1237, 1239, 1242, 1243, 1;, 1307, 1312, 1314, 1341, 1347, 1361 nt., 1371 to 1377, 1441, 1482, 1504, 2011, 2014, 2015, 2039, 2053, 2055, 2106, 2208, 2501, 2517, 2522, 3121, 3122, 3504, 6012, 6013, 6015, 6033, 6037, 6038, 6104, 6163, 6164, 6212, 6325, 6338, 6339, 6501, 6504, 6511, 6532, 6601, 6611, 6652, 6653, 6851, 6871, 7213, 7324, 7325, 7422, 7455, 7502, 7513, 7514
June 8, 1960, P.L. 86-496, 74 Stat. 164, 26 U.S. Code § 162 nt.
*Continued*

Oct. 17, 1963, P.L. 88-153, 77 Stat. 272, 26 U.S. Code § 162 nt.

Aug. 31, 1964, P.L. 88-554, 78 Stat. 761, 26 U.S. Code § 162 nt.

Oct. 15, 1966, P.L. 89-692, 80 Stat. 1025, 26 U.S. Code § 162 nt.

**Technical Amendments to the Federal Courts Improvement Act of 1982**

Nov. 8, 1984, P.L. 98-620, 28 U.S. Code § 1 nt.

**Technical Amendments to Various Indian Laws Act of 1991**

Dec. 17, 1991, P.L. 102-238, 25 U.S. Code § 2201 nt.

**Technical and Community College Act**

Wash. Rev. Code Ann., 28B.50.010 et seq.

**Technical and Miscellaneous Civil Service Amendments Act of 1991**

Oct. 2, 1992, P.L. 102-378, 5 U.S. Code § 1101 nt.

**Technical and Miscellaneous Revenue Act of 1988**

Nov. 10, 1988, P.L. 100-647, 26 U.S. Code § 1 nt.

Aug. 9, 1989, P.L. 101-73, 26 U.S. Code § 597 nt. Nov. 8, 1989, P.L. 101-140, 26 U.S. Code §§ 89, nts., 117, 120, 127, 129, 129 nts., 132, 414 nt., 505, 515 nt., 3101 nt., 3121, 3121 nt., 3231, 3;, 3401, 4976; 42 U.S. Code § 409

Dec. 19, 1989, P.L. 101-239, generally 26 U.S. Code §§ 1 et seq., 29 U.S. Code §§ 1167

Nov. 6, 1990, P.L. 101-508, 26 U.S. Code §§ 858, 892, 2051, 2642 , 4091

July 22, 1998, P.L. 105-206, 26 U.S. Code § 7803 nt.

**Technical and Vocational Education Act**

Cal. Education Code 1976, § 52380 et seq.

**Technical and Vocational Institute Act**

N.M. Stat. Ann., 21-16-1 et seq.

**Technical Changes Act of 1953**

Aug. 15, 1953, Ch. 512, 67 Stat. 615, 15 U.S. Code § 376, 376 nt.

Feb. 20, 1956, Ch. 63, 70 Stat. 23

**Technical Correction Act to Assembly Bill No. 1 of the 1971 First Extraordinary Session**

Cal. Statutes 1971, 1st Ex. Sess., Ch. 2, p. 5134

**Technical Corrections Act of 1979**

April 1, 1980, P.L. 96-222, 26 U.S. Code §§ 1 et seq., 1 nt.; 42 U.S. Code § 1382 et seq.

**Technical Corrections Revisory Act**

Ill. Laws 1978, P.A. 80-1495

Ill. Laws 1979, P.A. 81-759

Ill. Laws 1980, P.A. 81-1509, Art. 2

Ill. Laws 1986, P.A. 84-1308, § 3, Art. III

**Technical Corrections Tax Act of 1981**

Ark. Code Ann. 1987, 26-18-;, 26-18-208, 26-51-404, 26-51-432

**Technical Corrections Tax Act of 1983**

Ark. Acts 1983, p. 593, No. 379

**Technical Excellence in Engineering Research**

Utah Code Ann. 1953, 63-62-2 et seq.

**Technical Institute Act**

Kan. Stat. Ann., 72-4331 et seq.

Miss. Code Ann. 1972, § 37-133-1 et seq.

**Technical Registration Act**

Ariz. Rev. Stat. Ann., § 32-101 et seq.

**Technical Revenue Act (Income Tax)**

Ark. Acts 1989, No. 826

**Technical School Registration Act**

Ind. Code. Ann., 20-12-62-1 et seq.

**Technical Training for Minorities and Women Act**

N.J. Stat. Ann., 18A:54D-1 et seq.

**Technical-Vocational Education Act**

Tex. Education Code, § 31.01 et seq.

**Technician Act (Pharmacy)**

Wyo. Stat. Ann. 1977, § 33-24-301 et seq.

**Technician Certification Act (Alternative Fuels)**
Okla. Stat. Ann., Title 74, § 130.11 et seq.

**Technician Certification Act (Underground Storage Tank)**
Ida. Code 1947, 41-276 et seq.

**Technician Training Act (Hemodialysis)**
Cal. Business and Professions Code §§ 1247 to 1247.9

**Technologist and Practical Technician Licensing Act (Radiology)**
Utah Code Ann. 1953, 58-54-1 et seq.

**Technologist Certification Act (Radiologic)**
Fla. Stat. Ann., 468.3001 et seq.
Tex. Rev. Civ. Stat., Art. 4512m, § 2.01 et seq.
Wash. Rev. Code Ann., 18.84.010 et seq.

**Technology Act (Education)**
Minn. Stat. Ann., 124C.21 et seq.

**Technology Act (Fusion/Energy)**
Utah Code Ann. 1953, 9-2-801 et seq.

**Technology Act (Institute of)**
N.J. Stat. Ann., 18A:64E-12 et seq.

**Technology Administration Act of 1998**
Oct. 30, 1998, P.L. 105-309, 112 Stat. 2935, 15 U.S. Code § 271 nt.

**Technology Administration Authorization Act of 1991**
Feb. 14, 1992, P.L. 102-245, 15 U.S. Code § 3701 nt.

**Technology Advancement and Development Act**
Ill. Rev. Stat. 1991, Ch. 127, § 3701 et seq.

**Technology and Defense Conversion Act**
N.M. Stat. Ann., 9-15-37 et seq.

**Technology and Innovation Act**
Utah Code Ann. 1953, 63-60-1 et seq.

**Technology and Science Financing Act**
Mont. Code Ann., 90-3-101 et seq.

**Technology Assessment Act of 1972**
Oct. 13, 1972, P.L. 92-484, 86 Stat. 797, 2 U.S. Code §§ 471 to 481; 42 U.S. Code § 1862
Jan. 2, 1986, P.L. 99-234, 2 U.S. Code § 476

**Technology Competitiveness Act**
Aug. 23, 1988, P.L. 100-418, 102 Stat. 1426, 15 U.S. Code § 271 nt.

**Technology Deployment Act**
Conn. Public Acts 1993, No. 382, §§ 30 to 38

**Technology Development Corporation Act**
Mass. Gen. Laws Ann., 40G:1 et seq.

**Technology Enterprise Corporation Act**
Kan. Stat. Ann., 74-5050, 748101 et seq.

**Technology Equipment Act (Education)**
N.M. Stat. Ann., 6-15A-1 to 6-15A-16

**Technology Evaluation and Training Centers Act (Assistive)**
Ill. Comp. Stat. 1992, Ch. 20, § 1320/1 et seq.

**Technology Finance Corporation Act**
Utah Code Ann. 1953, 9-2-701 et seq.

**Technology for Education Act**
N.M. Stat. Ann., 22-15A-1 et seq.

**Technology for Education Act of 1994**
Sept. 30, 1996, P.L. 104-208, 20 U.S. Code §§ 6813, 7001 to 7005

**Technology Information Commission Act**
Utah Code Ann. 1953, 63C-2-101 et seq.

**Technology Infrastructure Fund Act (Higher Education)**
N.J. Stat. Ann., 18A:72A-59 et seq.

**Technology Initiative Act (Advanced)**
Miss. Code Ann. 1972, § 57-54-1 et seq.

**Technology Investment Act (Telecommunications)**
Del. Laws, Vol. 69, Ch. 99

**Technology, Jobs and Science Bond Act**
N.J. Laws 1984, Ch. 99

**Technology, Mathematics, and Science Improvement Act (K through 12)**
Colo. Rev. Stat., 22-81-101 et seq.

**Technology, Mathematics, Science Act (Magnet School)**
Colo. Rev. Stat., 22-84-101 et seq.

**Technology Park Development Act**
Mich. Comp. Laws Ann., 207.701 et seq.

**Technology Policy Act (Information)**
Ga. Official Code Ann., 50-29-1 et seq.

**Technology Regulation Act (Assistive)**
Neb. Rev. Stat. 1943, 69-2601 to 69-2619

**Technology Related Assistance for Individuals with Disabilities Act**
Ga. Official Code Ann., 30-9-1 et seq.

**Technology-Related Assistance for Individuals with Disabilities Act Amendments of 1994**
March 9, 1994, P.L. 103-218, 29 U.S. Code § 2201 nt.

**Technology-Related Assistance for Individuals With Disabilities Act of 1988**
Aug. 19, 1988, P.L. 100-407, 102 Stat. 1044, generally 29 U.S. Code §§ 2201 nt., 2201 et seq.
Oct. 30, 1990, P.L. 101-476, 20 U.S. Code § 1400 nt.
Oct. 29, 1992, P.L. 102-569, 29 U.S. Code §§ 2251, 2252, 2261
March 9, 1994, P.L. 103-218, 29 U.S. Code § 2201 et seq.
Oct. 20, 1994, P.L. 103-382, 29 U.S. Code § 2271
Aug. 7, 1998, P.L. 105-220, 29 U.S. Code §§ 2211, 2212
Oct. 7, 1998, P.L. 105-244, 29 U.S. Code § 2202
Nov. 13, 1998, P.L. 105-394, 29 U.S. Code § 2201, 2201 nt., 2202, 2211 to 2216, 2231, 2241 to 2246, 2251, 2281 to 2288

**Technology Resources Act (Security Data and Information)**
Fla. Stat. Ann., 282.318

**Technology Task Force Act (Year 2000)**
Ill. Comp. Stat. 1992, Ch. 20, § 4035/1 et seq.

**Technology Warranty Act (Assistive)**
Haw. Rev. Stat. Ann., § 481K-1 et seq.
Ida. Code 1947, 48-1401 et seq.

**Technology 2000 Partnership Act**
Mass. Gen. Laws Ann., 23F:1 to 23F:9

**Ted Weiss Child Support Enforcement Act of 1992**
Oct. 27, 1992, P.L. 103-537, 15 U.S. Code § 1601 nt.

**Teen Age Draft Act**
Nov. 13, 1942, Ch. 638, 56 Stat. 1018

**Teen Court Pilot Program Act**
Miss. Code Ann. 1972, § 43-21-751 et seq.

**Teen Driver Safety Act (Brady-Jared)**
Cal. Vehicle Code 1959, § 12814.6

**Teen Drug/Alcohol Intervention and Prevention Act**
Utah Code Ann. 1953, 62A-8-203 et seq.

**Teen Smoking Act**
Ga. Official Code Ann., 16-12-171, 40-5-57.3

**Teenage and Adult Driver Responsibility Act**
Ga. Laws 1997, H.B. 681

**Teenage Protection Act (Automobile)**
Ga. Official Code Ann., 40-5-63, 40-6-255

**Teenage Services Act**
N.Y. Social Services Law (Consol. Laws Ch. 55) § 409i et seq.

**Teenager Pregnancy Prevention Act**
Cal. Penal Code § 261.5

**Teeter Plan Bond Law**
Cal. Government Code § 54773

**Tehama County Flood Control and Water Conservation District Act**
Cal. Water Code, Appx., § 82-1 et seq.

**Tehran American School Claim Act of 1985**
May 29, 1986, P.L. 99-330, 100 Stat. 509

**Telecommunication Device Distribution and Dual Party Relay Service Program Act**
Pa. Purdon's Stat., Title 35, § 6701 et seq.

**Telecommunication Devices for the Deaf Act**
Ill. Rev. Stat. 1991, Ch. 111 1/2, § 4200 et seq.

**Telecommunication Line Tapping Act**
Ill. Rev. Stat. 1991, Ch. 134, §§ 15m, 16

**Telecommunications Access Act**
N.M. Stat. Ann., 63-9F-1 et seq.

**Telecommunications Access System Act**
Fla. Stat. Ann., 427.701 et seq.

**Telecommunications Accessibility Enhancement Act of 1988**
Oct. 28, 1988, P.L. 100-542, 40 U.S. Code § 762 nt.

**Telecommunications Act**
Ida. Code 1947, 62-601 et seq.
Mich. Comp. Laws Ann., 484.2101 et seq.
Mont. Code Ann., 69-3-801 et seq.
N.M. Stat. Ann., 63-9A-1 et seq.
Va. Code 1950, § 22-344.4 et seq.
Wyo. Stat. Ann. 1977, § 37-14-101 et seq.

**Telecommunications Act of 1934**
Oct. 7, 1998, P.L. 105-244, 47 U.S. Code § 223

**Telecommunications Act of 1996**
Feb. 8, 1996, P.L. 104-104, 47 U.S. Code § 609 nt.

**Telecommunications and Competition Development Act**
Ga. Official Code Ann., 46-5-160 to 46-5-174

**Telecommunications Authorization Act of 1992**
Oct. 27, 1992, P.L. 102-538, 106 Stat. 3533
Oct. 25, 1994, P.L. 103-414, 47 U.S. Code § 318

**Telecommunications Board Act (Statewide Emergency)**
Mass. Gen. Laws Ann., 6A:18B et seq.

**Telecommunications Consolidation Act**
Ga. Code Ann., 50-5-160 et seq.
Tex. Rev. Civ. Stat., Art. 601b, § 10.01 et seq.

**Telecommunications Consumer Choice Act (Long Distance)**
Cal. Public Utilities Code § 709.2

**Telecommunications Consumer Protection Act**
Fla. Stat. Ann., 364.601 to 364.604

**Telecommunications Crimes Act**
Tex. Code of Criminal Procedure, Arts. 13.25, 13.26, 59.01, Subd. 2
Tex. Penal Code, § 33A.01 et seq.

**Telecommunications Customer Service Act**
Cal. Public Utilities Code § 2895 et seq.

**Telecommunications Excise Tax Act**
Ill. Comp. Stat. 1992, Ch. 35, § 630/1 et seq.
Ill. Rev. Stat. 1991, Ch. 120, § 2001 et seq.

**Telecommunications Facility Fire and Emergency Act**
Ill. Rev. Stat. 1991, Ch. 111 2/3, § 1550 et seq.

**Telecommunications for the Disabled Act of 1982**
Jan. 3, 1983, P.L. 97-410, 47 U.S. Code §§ 609 nt., 610, 610 nt.

**Telecommunications for the Hearing-Impaired Act**
Okla. Stat. Ann., Title 63, § 2416 et seq.

**Telecommunications Gross Receipts Tax Act (Interstate)**
N.M. Stat. Ann., 7-9C-1 et seq.

**Telecommunications in Evidence Act**
Fla. Stat. 1983, 120.52, 120.53

**Telecommunications Infrastructure Development Act**
Cal. Government Code § 50030

**Telecommunications Marketing Act**
Ga. Official Code Ann., 46-5-180 et seq.

**Telecommunications Municipal Infrastructure Maintenance Fee Act**
Ill. Comp. Stat. 1992, Ch. 35, § 635/1 et seq.

**Telecommunications Regulatory Authorization Act**
Del. Code of 1974, Title 26, § 701 et seq.

**Telecommunications Regulatory Reform Act**
Ark. Acts 1997, No. 77

**Telecommunications Relay System Act**
Neb. Laws 1993, L.B. 305, §§ 23 to 29

**Telecommunications Research Facilities of the United States Protection Act**
Colo. Rev. Stat., 30-11-601 et seq.

**Telecommunications Research Facilities Protection Act**
Colo. Rev. Stat., 30-11-601 et seq.

**Telecommunications Service Theft Act**
N.M. Stat. Ann., 30-33A-1 to 30-33A-5

**Telecommunications Services Regulation Act**
Pa. Cons. Stat., Title 66, § 3001 et seq.

**Telecommunications System Act**
Neb. Rev. Stat. 1943, 81-1120.01 et seq.

**Telecommunications Tax Act**
W. Va. Code 1966, § 11-13B-1 et seq.

**Telecommunications Technology Investment Act**
Del. Laws, Vol. 69, Ch. 99

**Telecommunications Trade Act of 1988**
Aug. 23, 1988, P.L. 100-418, 102 Stat. 1216, 19 U.S. Code § 3101 nt.

**Telecommunications Universal Service Fund Act**
Neb. Rev. Stat. 1943, 86-1401 to 86-1411

**Telecommuting Act (State Employee)**
Fla. Stat. Ann., 110.171 et seq.

**Telefacsimile Advertising Act (Unsolicited)**
Tenn. Code Ann., 47-18-1601 et seq.

**Telegraph Act**
Ill. Rev. Stat. 1991, Ch. 134, § 0.01 et seq.
N.Y. Transportation Corporations Law (Consol. Laws Ch. 63) § 25 et seq

**Telegraph and Telephone Companies Act**
Md. Ann. Code 1957, Art. 23, § 317 et seq.

**Telegraph and Telephone Tax Acts**
Oct. 3, 1917, Ch. 63, § 500, 40 Stat. 314
Feb. 24, 1919, Ch. 18, 40 Stat. 1102
Nov. 23, 1921, Ch. 136, 42 Stat. 284

**Telegraph Companies Act**
Mich. Comp. Laws Ann., 484.151 et seq.

**Telegraph Companies-Liability for Causing Mental Anguish Act**
S.C. Code Ann. 1976, § 58-9-1860

**Telegraph Companies Regulation Act**
Wash. Rev. Code Ann., 80.36.010 et seq.

**Telegraph Company Merger Act**
See Communications Act OF 1934

**Telegraph Rates Regulation Act**
Wash. Rev. Code Ann., 80.36.010 et seq.

**Telemarketer Registration Act**
Pa. Purdon's Stat., Title 73, § 2241 et seq.

**Telemarketing Act**
Ala. Code 1975, § 8-19A-1 et seq.
Fla. Stat. Ann., 501.601 et seq.

**Telemarketing Act (Fraudulent)**
Aug. 15, 1994, P.L. 103-297, 108 Stat. 1545
N.M. Stat. Ann., 30-50-1 et seq.

**Telemarketing and Consumer Fraud and Abuse Prevention Act**
Aug. 16, 1994, P.L. 103-297, 15 U.S. Code §§ 6101 et seq., 6101 nt.

**Telemarketing Fraud Act**
Del. Code of 1974, Title 6, § 2501A et seq.

**Telemarketing Fraud Prevention Act of 1998**
June 23, 1998, P.L. 105-184, 18 U.S. Code § 1 nt.

**Telemarketing Protection Act (Consumer)**
La. Rev. Stat. Ann., 45:810 et seq.

**Telemedicine Act**
Tex. Insurance Code, Art. 21.53F

**Telemedicine and Distance Learning Act**
Ga. Official Code Ann., 50-5-190 et seq.

**Telephone Access Act (Emergency)**
Colo. Rev. Stat., 40-3.4-101 et seq.

**Telephone Act**
Kan. Stat. Ann., 17-1901 et seq.

**Telephone Act (Emergency Public Safety)**
Pa. Purdon's Stat., Title 35, § 7011 et seq.

**Telephone Act (Public Safety)**
N.C. Gen Stat. 1943, § 62A-1 et seq.

**Telephone and Electric Cooperative Act**
Alaska Stat. 1962, § 15.05.010 et seq.

**Telephone and Mail Consumer Product Promotion Fair Practices Act**
Ark. Acts 1991, No. 680

**Telephone and Telegraph Company Certification Act**
N.M. Stat. Ann., 63-9-1 et seq.

**Telephone Authority Act**
P.R. Laws Ann. 1954, Title 27, § 401 et seq.

**Telephone Authority Act (Perry)**
Ga. Laws 1973, p. 3776

**Telephone Buyers' Protection Act**
Wash. Rev. Code Ann., 19.130.010 et seq.

**Telephone Call Act (Malicious)**
N.Y. Penal Law 1965 (Consol. Laws Ch. 40) § 240.31

**Telephone Call Act (Right of Accused)**
Cal. Penal Code § 851.5

**Telephone Charge Fraud Act**
Ill. Rev. Stat. 1991, Ch. 134, §§ 15b.9, 15c

**Telephone Coin Box Tampering Act**
Ill. Rev. Stat. 1991, Ch. 134, § 16.01 et seq.

**Telephone Communication Services for the Deaf Act**
Fla. Stat. Ann., 427.501 et seq.

**Telephone Companies Act**
Md. Ann. Code 1957, Art. 23, § 317 et seq.
Mich. Comp. Laws Ann., 484.1 et seq.

**Telephone Companies' Exchange Law**
Ky. Rev. Stat. 1971, 278.520, 278.530, 278.990

**Telephone Companies Regulation Act**
Mich. Comp. Laws Ann., 484.101 et seq.
Wash. Rev. Code Ann., 80.36.010 et seq.

**Telephone Company Act**
Ill. Rev. Stat. 1991, Ch. 134, § 16.90 et seq.

**Telephone Consumer Protection Act of 1991**
Dec. 20, 1991, P.L. 102-243, 47 U.S. Code § 609 nt.
Oct. 28, 1992, P.L. 102-556, 47 U.S. Code § 227 nt.

**Telephone Cooperative Act**
S.C. Code Ann. 1976, § 33-46-10 et seq.
Tenn. Code Ann., 65-29-101 et seq.
Tex. Rev. Civ. Stat., Art. 1528c
Tex. Utilities Code, § 162.001 et seq.
Va. Code 1950, § 56-485 et seq.

**Telephone Cooperative Act (Rural)**
Ga. Code Ann., 46-5-60 et seq.
Mont. Code Ann., 35-18-101 et seq.
Okla. Stat. Ann., Title 18, § 438.1 et seq.

**Telephone Cooperative Corporation Act**
Ky. Rev. Stat. 1971, 279.310 et seq.

**Telephone Cooperative Corporations Act**
Okla. Stat. Ann., Title 18, § 438.1 et seq.

**Telephone Dialers Act (Automatic)**
Ill. Comp. Stat. 1992, Ch. 815, § 305/1 et seq.

**Telephone Disclosure and Dispute Resolution Act**
Oct. 28, 1992, P.L. 102-556, 15 U.S. Code § 5701 et seq.
Feb. 8, 1996, P.L. 104-104, 15 U.S. Code § 5714

**Telephone Emergency Notification or Information Act**
La. Rev. Stat. Ann., 45:840 to 45:844

**Telephone Fraud Prevention Act**
Utah Code Ann. 1953, 13-26-1 et seq.

**Telephone Line Interference Act**
Ill. Rev. Stat. 1991, Ch. 134, § 15a, 15a.1

**Telephone Line Right of Way Act**
Ill. Rev. Stat. 1991, Ch. 134, § 11.9 et seq.

**Telephone Number Act (Emergency)**
Tex. Health and Safety Code, § 772.301 et seq.

**Telephone Number '911' Emergency Service Act**
Ga. Code Ann., 46-5-120 et seq.

**Telephone Operator Consumer Services Improvement Act of 1990**
Oct. 17, 1990, P.L. 101-435, 47 U.S. Code §§ 226, 226 nt., 609 nt.

**Telephone Privacy Act**
Cal. Penal Code § 653m

**Telephone Rates Regulation Act**
Wash. Rev. Code Ann., 80.36.010 et seq.

**Telephone Sales Protection Act**
N.Y. Personal Property Law (Consol. Laws Ch. 41) § 440 et seq.

**Telephone Service Act (Emergency)**
Wyo. Stat. Ann., § 16-9-101 et seq.

**Telephone Service Act (Universal)**
Ark. Code Ann. 1987, 23-17-301 et seq.
Cal. Public Utilities Code § 871 et seq.
Cal. Revenue and Taxation Code § 44000 et seq.

**Telephone Service Assistance Act (Low Income)**
N.M. Stat. Ann., 63-9C-1 et seq.

**Telephone Service Enabling Act (Emergency)**
Mich. Comp. Laws Ann., 484.1101 et seq.
N.M. Stat. Ann., 63-9B-1 et seq.

**Telephone Service Law (Emergency)**
Utah Code Ann. 1953, 69-2-1 et seq.

**Telephone Services Act (Cellular)**
Mich. Comp. Laws Ann., 484.1101 et seq.
N.M. Stat. Ann., 63-9B-1 et seq.

**Telephone Solicitation Act**
Ida. Code 1947, 48-1001 et seq.

**Telephone Users Surcharge Act**
Cal. Revenue and Taxation Code § 41001 et seq.

**Telephone Utility Act (Investor-Owned)**
Va. Code 1950, § 56-531 et seq.

**Televised University Athletics Act**
Ill. Rev. Stat. 1991, Ch. 144, §§ 254, 255

**Television Act (Cable)**
S.C. Code Ann. 1976, § 58-12-10 et seq.

**Television Act (Western Illinois University)**
Ill. Rev. Stat. 1991, Ch. 144, § 919 et seq.

**Television and Film Investment Act**
Fla. Stat. Ann., 288.015 et seq.

**Television and Film Production Law**
Tenn. Code Ann., 4-3-5001 et seq.

**Television and Motion Picture Development Act**
N.J. Stat. Ann. 34:1B-22 et seq.

**Television and Radio Defamation Act**
Neb. Rev. Stat. 1943, 86-601 et seq.

**Television and Radio Licensing Act**
Ind. Code. Ann., 25-36-1-1 et seq.

**Television and Radio Technician Act**
P.R. Laws Ann. 1954, Title 20, § 2401 et seq.

**Television Authority Act (Educational)**
Okla. Stat. Ann., Title 70, § 23-101 et seq.

**Television Broadcasting to Cuba Act**
Feb. 16, 1990, P.L. 101-246, 22 U.S. Code §§ 1465aa nt., 1465aa to 1465ff
Oct. 28, 1991, P.L. 102-138, 22 U.S. Code § 1465ee
March 12, 1996, P.L. 104-114, 22 U.S. Code § 1465 et seq.
Oct. 21, 1998, P.L. 105-277, 22 U.S. Code §§ 1465c nt., 1465bb, 1465cc, 1465dd

**Television Decoder Circuitry Act of 1990**
Oct. 15, 1990, P.L. 101-431, 47 U.S. Code §§ 303, 303 nt., 609 nt.

**Television, Motion Picture, and Commercial Industries Act**
Cal. Government Code § 14998 et seq.

**Television Program Improvement Act of 1990**
Dec. 1, 1990, P.L. 101-650, 47 U.S. Code § 303c

**Television Systems Act (Cable)**
W. Va. Code § 5-18-1 et seq.

**Television Translator Districts Act**
Ida. Code 1947, 31-4101 et seq.

**Telfair-Wheeler Airport Authority Act**
Ga. Laws 1998, H.B. 1908

**Teller Act (Omnibus Statehood Act)**
Feb. 22, 1889, Ch. 180, 25 Stat. 676

**Teller Resolution (Cuba)**
April 20, 1898, No. 24, 30 Stat. 738

**Temperance Act**
Ill. Rev. Stat. 1991, Ch. 43, § 135
Tenn. Code Ann., 39-17-701 et seq.

**Temperance Commissioner Law**
N.D. Laws 1907, Ch. 187

**Temple Act (Topographical Survey)**
Feb. 27, 1925, Ch. 360, 43 Stat. 1011

**Temple University—Commonwealth Act**
Pa. Purdon's Stat., Title 24, § 2510-1 et seq.

**Temporary Appointment Act**
N.J. Stat. Ann., 52:10B-1 et seq.

**Temporary Appointment Acts**
July 24, 1941, Ch. 320, 55 Stat. 603
Sept. 22, 1941, Ch. 414, 55 Stat. 728
Nov. 30, 1942, Ch. 643, 56 Stat. 1023

**Temporary Assessment Act (Medicaid Hospital Provider)**
Utah Code Ann. 1953, 26-36-101 et seq.

**Temporary Assistance Program**
Alaska Stat. 1962, § 47.27.900

**Temporary Child Care for Children With Disabilities and Crisis Nurseries Act Amendments of 1992**

May 28, 1992, P.L. 102-295, 42 U.S. Code § 5117 nt.

**Temporary Child Care for Children With Disabilities and Crisis Nurseries Act of 1986**

Aug. 19, 1986, P.L. 100-403, 102 Stat. 1013, 42 U.S. Code § 5117

Aug. 27, 1986, P.L. 99-401, 42 U.S. Code §§ 5117 nt., 5117a to 5117d

Oct. 25, 1989, P.L. 101-127, 42 U.S. Code §§ 5117 nt., 5117a, 5117a nt., 5117c, 5117d

Oct. 30, 1990, P.L. 101-476, 42 U.S. Code § 5117c

May 28, 1992, P.L. 102-295, 42 U.S. Code §§ 5117c, 5117d

Oct. 3, 1996, P.L. 104-235, 42 U.S. Code §§ 5117, 5117 nt., 5117a to 5117d

**Temporary Child Care for Handicapped Children and Crisis Nurseries Act of 1986**

See Temporary Child Care for Children with Disabilities and Crisis Nurseries Act of 1986

**Temporary Clerk Hire Bill**

Ala. Code 1958, Title 55, § 175

**Temporary Contract Act (Teachers)**

Ind. Code. Ann., 20-6.1-4-7

**Temporary Disability Benefit Act**

N.J. Rev. Stat. 1937, 43:21-25 et seq.

**Temporary Disability Insurance Act**

Haw. Rev. Stat. Ann., § 392-1 et seq.

R.I. Gen. Laws 1956, 28-39-1 et seq.

**Temporary Dispenser's Act**

N.M. Stat. Ann., 60-6A-1 et seq., 60-6B-1 et seq.

**Temporary Election Act**

Ohio Laws Vol. 120, p. 711

**Temporary Emergency Food Assistance Act of 1983**

Aug. 15, 1985, P.L. 99-88, 7 U.S. Code § 612c nt.

Dec. 23, 1985, P.L. 99-198, 7 U.S. Code § 612c nt.

July 2, 1986, P.L. 99-349, 100 Stat. 712

July 22, 1987, P.L. 100-77, 7 U.S. Code § 612c nt.

Sept. 19, 1988, P.L. 100-435, 7 U.S. Code § 612c nt.

Nov. 28, 1990, P.L. 101-624, 7 U.S. Code § 612c nt.

**Temporary Emergency Relief Administration Act**

N.Y. Laws 1931, Ch. 798

**Temporary Emergency Unemployment Benefit Law**

N.Y. Laws 1959, Ch. 229

**Temporary Emergency Wildfire Suppression Act**

Sept. 9, 1988, P.L. 100-428, 42 U.S. Code § 1856a nt.

April 7, 1989, P.L. 101-11, 42 U.S. Code § 1856p

**Temporary Employment Services Act**

Tex. Labor Code, §§ 93.001 to 93.003

**Temporary Extended Railroad Unemployment Insurance Benefits Act of 1961**

March 24, 1961, P.L. 87-7, 75 Stat. 16, 45 U.S. Code §§ 401 to 404

Oct. 5, 1963, P.L. 88-133, 77 Stat. 222, 45 U.S. Code § 403

**Temporary Extended Unemployment Compensation Act of 1961**

March 24, 1961, P.L. 87-6, 75 Stat. 8, 26 U.S. Code §§ 3301, 3302 ; 42 U.S. Code §§ 1101 nt., 1105, 1400l to 1400v

**Temporary Health Care Placement Decision Maker for an Adult Act**

Ga. Official Code Ann., 31-36A-1 et seq.

**Temporary Housing Act**
Miss. Code Ann. 1972, § 43-41-301 et seq.

**Temporary Housing Act (Veterans of World War II)**
Conn. Public Acts 1991, May Special Session, p. 7, No. 3

**Temporary Insanity Act (Crimes)**
Tex. Penal Code, § 8.04

**Temporary Joint Underwriting Association Act (Malpractice)**
Minn. Stat. Ann., 62F.01 et seq.

**Temporary Larceny Act (Vehicles)**
N.C. Gen. Stat. 1943, § 14-72.2

**Temporary Milk Control Act**
N.J. Stat. Ann., App. A:8-1 to App. A:8-49

**Temporary State Commission of Investigation Act**
N.Y. Unconsolidated Law, § 7507 et seq.

**Temporary Unemployment Compensation Act of 1958**
June 4, 1958, P.L. 85-441, 72 Stat. 171, 42 U.S. Code §§ 1400 to 1400k
March 31, 1959, P.L. 86-7, 73 Stat. 14, 42 U.S. Code § 1400
Sept. 13, 1960, P.L. 86-778, 74 Stat. 982, 42 U.S. Code § 1400c
Nov. 7, 1963, P.L. 88-173, 77 Stat.;, 42 U.S. Code § 1400c
N.Y. Labor Law (Consol. Laws Ch. 31) § 536, Subd. 2

**Ten Day Statute of Limitations (Motor Vehicle Idemnification Corporation)**
N.Y. Insurance Law 1939 (Consol. Laws, Ch. 28), § 608, Subd. c

**Ten Hour Act (Females)**
Ky. Rev. Stat. 1971 Superseded Vols., 337.370, 337.380
Ore. Rev. Stat., 653.255

**Ten Hour Act (Labor)**
Ga. Code Ann., § 34-3-1

**Ten Hour Act (Street Cars)**
R.I. Gen. Laws 1956, 28-11-2 et seq.

**Ten Hour Act (Women and Minors)**
N.H. Rev. Stat. 1955, 275:15

**Ten Hour Day Act**
Ohio Laws Vol. 89, p. 311

**Ten Mile Zone Law (Intoxicating Liquors)**
Tex. General Laws 35th Leg., 1918, 4th C. S., p. 18, Ch. 12

**Ten Million Dollar Road Bonding Act**
Ore. Code 1930, § 44-601 et seq.

**Ten O'Clock Closing Act (Employment of Women)**
Mass. Gen. Laws Ann., 149:59

**Ten Year Color of Title Act**
N.D. Cent. Code, 47-06-03

**Ten Year Lien Law**
Del. Code of 1974, Title 10, § 4711 et seq.

**Ten Year Life Act (Parole)**
Mich. Comp. Laws Ann., 791.234

**Ten Year Limitations Act (Written Contracts)**
Ill. Rev. Stat. 1991, Ch. 110, § 13-206

**Ten Year Statute of Limitations (Color of Title)**
N.D. Cent. Code, 47-06-03

**Ten Year Statute of Limitations (Matrimonial Actions)**
Wis. Stat. Ann., 767.03, Subsec. 4

**Ten Year Statute of Limitations (Personal Actions)**
N.Y. Civil Practice Law and Rules (Consol. Laws, Ch. 8), § 212

**Ten Year Statute of Limitations Act**
Ala. Code 1975, § 6-2-33
Alaska Stat. 1962, § 09.10.030
Ga. Code Ann., 9-3-27
N.D. Cent. Code, 28-01-15

**Tenancy Act**
Wash. Rev. Code Ann., 59.04.010 et seq.

**Tenancy Act (Manufactured Home Park)**
S.C. Code Ann. 1976, § 27-47-10 et seq.

**Tenancy Law (Emergency)**
N.Y. Laws 1945, Chs. 3, 314, 315
N.Y. Laws 1946, Ch. 274
N.Y. Laws 1949, Chs. 534, 535, 591

**Tenant Act**
Ga. Code Ann., 44-7-1 et seq.
N.C. Gen. Stat. 1943, § 42-1 et seq.

**Tenant and Landlord Act**
Md. Ann. Code 1974, Art. RP, § 8-101
N.H. Rev. Stat. 1955, 540:1 et seq.
N.M. Stat. Ann., 47-8-1 et seq.
S.C. Code Ann. 1976, § 27-33-10 et seq.
Wash. Rev. Code Ann., 59.18.010 et seq.
W. Va. Code 1966, § 37-6-1 et seq.

**Tenant and Landlord Act (Mobile Homes)**
Ida. Code 1947, 55-2001 et seq.
Iowa Code Ann., 562B.1 et seq.
Neb. Laws 1984, L.B. 916, §§ 1 to 62

**Tenant and Landlord Act (Residential)**
See Residential Landlord and Tenant Act
Miss. General Laws 1991, Ch. 478, p. 505

**Tenant and Landlord Security Deposit Act**
Fla. Stat. Ann., 83.49

**Tenant and Residential Landlord Act**
S.C. Code Ann. 1976, § 27-40-10 et seq.

**Tenant Dispossession Act**
N.J. Stat. Ann., 2A:18-53 et seq.

**Tenant Manager Training Act (Public Housing)**
Ill. Rev. Stat. 1991, Ch. 67 1/2, § 1201 et seq.

**Tenant Protection Act**
N.Y. Laws 1974, Ch. 576, § 4

**Tenant Protection Act (Emergency)**
N.Y. Unconsolidated Law, § 8621 et seq.

**Tenant Security Deposit Act**
N.C. Gen. Stat. 1943, § 42-50 et seq.

**Tenant-Stockholder Property Tax Postponement Law (Senior Citizens)**
Cal. Revenue and Taxation Code § 20625 et seq.

**Tenants' and Remaindermen Principal and Income Law**
Cal. Civil Code § 730 et seq.

**Tenants Property Tax Rebate Act**
N.J. Stat. Ann., 54:4-6.2 et seq.

**Tenants Rights Act (Utility Service)**
Pa. Purdon's Stat. Title 68, § 399.1 et seq.

**Tenants' Rights to Cable Television Services Act**
Pa. Purdon's Stat., Title 68, § 250.501-B et seq.
W. Va. Code 1966 § 5-18A-1 et seq.

**Tender Act**
Ill. Rev. Stat. 1991, Ch. 135, § 0.01 et seq.

**Tender Offer Disclosure Act**
Conn. Gen. Stat. Ann., § 36-456
N.C. Gen. Stat. 1943, § 78B-1 et seq.
S.C. Code Ann. 1976, § 35-2-10 et seq.

**Tenement House Act**
Cal. Health and Safety Code § 17910 et seq.
Conn. Gen. Stat. Ann., § 19a-356 et seq.
Ind. Laws 1913, Ch. 149, p. 377
Ky. Rev. Stat. 1953, 101.010 et seq.
Mass. Gen. Laws Ann., 144:1 et seq., 145:1 et seq.
Mich. Comp. Laws Ann., 125.401 et seq.
N.J. Stat. Ann., 55:1-1 to 55:13-4
N.Y. (Consol. Laws, Ch. 61)
Pa. 1895 Pamph. Laws 135, No. 105
Pa. 1895 Pamph. Laws 350, No. 258
Wis. Laws 1909, Ch. 394

**Tennessee Boundary Confirmatory Act**
N.C. Laws 1821, Ch. 41

**Tennessee Restoration Resolution**
July 24, 1866, No. 73, 14 Stat. 364

**Tennessee River Basin Water Pollution Control Compact**
Ky. Rev. Stat. 1971, 224.18-780
Tenn. Code Ann. 1955, 70-1901 et seq.

**Tennessee River Four-County Port Authority Act**
Tenn. Code Ann., 64-4-101 et seq.

**Tennessee Teaching Scholars Act**
Tenn. Code Ann., 49-4-212

**Tennessee-Tombigbee Waterway Development Compact**
Ky. Rev. Stat. 1971, 182.300 et seq.
Tenn. Code Ann., 69-9-101 et seq.

**Tennessee Valley Authority Act**
June 6, 1972, P.L. 92-310, 86 Stat. 206, 16 U.S. Code §§ 831b, 831c
July 25, 1974, P.L. 93-356, 88 Stat. 390, 16 U.S. Code § 831h
Nov. 28, 1975, P.L. 94-139, 89 Stat. 750, 16 U.S. Code § 831n-4
Ky. Rev. Stat. 1971, 96.550 et seq.

**Tennessee Valley Authority Act of 1933**
May 18, 1933, Ch. 32, 48 Stat. 58, 16 U.S. Code §§ 831 to 831dd
July 18, 1941, Ch. 309, 55 Stat. 599, 16 U.S. Code § 831c
Nov. 21, 1941, Ch. 485, 55 Stat. 775, 16 U.S. Code § 831h
Oct. 15, 1949, Ch. 695, 63 Stat. 880, 16 U.S. Code § 831a
July 12, 1952, Ch. 700, 66 Stat. 591, 16 U.S. Code § 831x
Aug. 30, 1954, Ch. 1076, 68 Stat. 968, 16 U.S. Code § 831h
Aug. 6, 1959, P.L. 86-137, 73 Stat. 280, 16 U.S. Code §§ 831d, 831n-4
Aug. 14, 1959, P.L. 86-157, 73 Stat. 338, 16 U.S. Code § 831n-4
Aug. 12, 1966, P.L. 89-537, 80 Stat. 346, 16 U.S. Code § 831n-4
Sept. 28, 1968, P.L. 90-536, 82 Stat. 885, 16 U.S. Code § 831x
Oct. 14, 1970, P.L. 91-446, 84 Stat. 915, 16 U.S. Code § 831n-4
Oct. 31, 1979, P.L. 96-97, 16 U.S. Code § 831n-4
Nov. 1, 1985, P.L. 99-141
July 2, 1986, P.L. 99-349, 100 Stat. 749
Sept. 13, 1994, P.L. 103-322, 16 U.S. Code § 831c-3

**Tennessee Valley Authority Act of 1983**
Dec. 1, 1983, P.L. 98-191, 16 U.S. Code § 831h

**Tennessee Valley Authority Bond Limitation Act**
Aug. 12, 1966, P.L. 89-537, 80 Stat. 346, 16 U.S. Code § 831n-4

**Tennessee Valley Authority Bridge Act**
Nov. 21, 1941, Ch. 480, 55 Stat. 773, 16 U.S. Code § 831c-1
Sept. 26, 1968, P.L. 90-524, 82 Stat. 876, 16 U.S. Code § 831c-1

**Tennessee Valley Authority Payment Act**
Ill. Rev. Stat. 1991, Ch. 120, §§ 1600, 1601

**Tennessee Wilderness Act of 1984**
Oct. 30, 1984, P.L. 98-578, 16 U.S. Code § 1132 nt.

**Tennessee Wilderness Act of 1986**
Oct. 16, 1986, P.L. 99-490, 100 Stat. 1235

**Tenure Act (Augusta Employees and Officers)**
Ga. Laws 1937-38 Ex. Sess., p. 938

**Tenure Act (Firemen and Policemen)**
Ind. Code. Ann., 36-8-3.5-1 et seq.
Ky. Rev. Stat. 1971, 95.440

**Tenure Act (Policemen)**
Pa. Purdon's Stat., Title 53, § 811 et seq.

**Tenure Act (Richmond County)**
Ga. Laws 1937-38 Ex. Sess., p. 938

**Tenure Act (School Teachers)**
Mont. Code Ann., 20-4-203

**Tenure Act (State, County and Municipal Employees)**
N.J. Rev. Stat. 11:9-2.1 to 11:28-3

**Tenure Act (Teachers)**
See Teachers' Tenure Act

**Tenure Act (Town Treasurer)**
N.J. Stat. Ann., 40:132-11

**Tenure Act (Veterans')**
Mass. Gen. Laws 1991, 31:21 et seq.

**Tenure Employees Hearing Act**
N.J. Stat. Ann., 18A:6-10 et seq.

**Tenure of Instructors Act**
Kan. Stat. Ann., 72-5410 et seq.

**Tenure of Office Act (Exempt Firemen)**
N.J. Stat. Ann., 40:47-60 et seq.

**Tenure of Office Act (Teachers)**
Ore. Rev. Stat. 1953, 342.205 et seq.

**Tenure of Office Act (Veterans)**
N.J. Stat. Ann., 38:16-1 et seq.

**Tenure of Office Acts**
May 15, 1820, Ch. 102, 3 Stat. 582
March 2, 1867, Ch. 154, 14 Stat. 430
April 5, 1869, Ch. 10, 16 Stat. 6

**TERA (Temporary Emergency Relief Administration)**
N.Y. Laws 1931, Ch. 798

**Term Contract Nonrenewal Act**
Tex. Education Code, § 21.201 et seq.

**Term Extender Act (County Recorders)**
Ohio Laws Vol. 115, p. 191, § 3

**Term Limitations Act**
Cal. Elections Code 1961, § 25003
Utah Code Ann. 1953, 20A-10-101 et seq.
Wash. Rev. Code. Ann., 44.04.010, Wash. Init. Meas. No. 670, § 8 preceding

**Term Limitations Act (Congressional)**
Me. Rev. Stat. Ann. 1964, Title 21-A, § 421 et seq.

**Terminable Permit Act**
Ill. Rev. Stat. 1991, Ch. 131 1/4, § 17 et seq.

**Terminal Act**
N.J. Stat. Ann., 32:1-146.6 et seq.

**Terminal Authority Act**
Tenn. Private Acts 1947, Ch. 875

**Terminal Commission Act (Buffalo)**
N.Y. Laws 1911, Ch. 842

**Terminal Company Act**
Mass. Acts 1896, Ch. 516

**Terminal Facilities Loan Act (East Boston)**
Mass. Acts 1952, Ch. 505

**Terminal Warehouse Act**
Wash. Rev. Code Ann., 22.09.011 et seq.

**Terminal Weighing Law**
Cal. Business and Professions Code § 12801 et seq.

**Terminally Ill Act (Rights of the)**
Me. Rev. Stat. Ann. 1964, Title 18-A, § 5-701

**Terminally Ill Act (Rights)**
R.I. Gen. Laws 1956, 23-4.11-1 et seq.

**Terminally Ill or Permanently Unconscious Rights Act**
Ark. Code Ann. 1987, No. 713

**Terminally Ill Rights Act**
See also Uniform Rights of the Terminally Ill Act
Mont. Code Ann. 1991, 50-9-101 et seq.

**Termination and Re-Creation of Statutory Entities, Sunset Act**
La. Rev. Stat. Ann., 49:190 et seq.

**Termination from Employment and Governmental Reorganization Act**
Ga. Official Code Ann., 45-24-1 et seq.

**Termination of Parental Rights Act**
Mo. Rev. Stat., 211.442 et seq.
Utah Code Ann. 1953, 78-3a-101 et seq.

**Termination of Powers Act**
Ill. Rev. Stat. 1991, Ch. 30, § 176.90 et seq.

**Termination of Rights of Unfit Parents Law**
Miss. Code Ann. 1972, § 93-15-101 et seq.

**Terrebonne Parish Artificial Reef Act**
La. Rev. Stat. Ann., 56:2021 et seq.

**Terrebonne Parish Mass Transit Authority Act**
La. Rev. Stat. Ann., 48:1501 et seq.

**Terrell Election Law**
Tex. Election Code, Art. 1.01 et seq.
Tex. Penal Code, § 36.02

**Territorial Electric Service Act**
Ga. Code Ann., 46-3-1 et seq.

**Territorial Enabling Act of 1950**
July 18, 1950, Ch. 466, 64 Stat. 344, 48 U.S. Code §§ 910 to 910b, 1408 to 1408e
Aug. 11, 1956, Ch. 783, 70 Stat. 637, 48 U.S. Code §§ 910, 910a, 1408 nt., 1408b, 1408c
May 25, 1967, P.L. 90-19, 81 Stat. 22, 48 U.S. Code § 1408c

**Territorial Home Guard Act**
See Army Reorganization Acts

**Territorial Hospital and Medical Facilities Survey and Construction Act**
Haw. Rev. Laws 1955, § 48A-1 et seq.

**Territorial Integrity Act**
Mont. Code Ann., 69-5-101 et seq.

**Territorial Practice Act**
April 7, 1874, Ch. 80, 18 Stat. 27, 48 U.S. Code § 1464

**Territorial Waters Act**
Fla. Stat. Ann., 370.21
Tex. Parks and Wildlife Code, § 66.301 et seq.

**Territory Act (Uninhabited)**
Cal. Government Code § 35300 et seq.

**Terrorism and Prevention Act (Street Gangs)**
Ga. Official Code Ann., 16-15-1 et seq.

**Terrorism Enforcement and Prevention Act (Street)**
Fla. Stat. Ann., 874.01 et seq.
Mont. Code Ann., 45-8-401 et seq.

**Terry Beirn Community Based AIDS Research Initiative Act of 1991**
Aug. 14, 1991, P.L. 102-96, 42 U.S. Code § 201 nt.

**Tertiary Care and Medical Education Act**
Fla. Stat. Ann., 395.60 et seq.
Fla. Stat. Ann., 395.801 et seq.

**Test Animals Fund Act**
Neb. Laws 1952, Ex. Sess., Ch. 4

**Testamentary Additions to Trusts Act**
See Uniform Testamentary Additions to Trusts Act

**Testers' and Creamery License Act**
Ind. Code. Ann., 15-6-1-1 et seq.

**Testimonial Dinner Act**
Mass. Gen. Laws Ann., 268:9A

**Testimony Perpetuation Act**
Neb. Rev. Stat. 1943, 25-1267.08 et seq.
Okla. Stat. Ann., Title 12, § 538.1 et seq.

**Testing Act (Admission)**
N.Y. Education Law 1947 (Consol. Laws Ch. 16) § 340 et seq.

**Testing Act (Cattle)**
Minn. Stat. Ann., 30.245

**Testing for Employment (Drug)**
Mont. Code Ann., 39-2-304

**Testing Programs Act (Statewide)**
Miss. Code Ann. 1972, § 37-16-1 et seq.

**Texans Work Program Act**
Tex. Labor Code, § 308.001 et seq.

**Texas Annexation Resolution**
March 1, 1845, No. 7, 5 Stat. 797

**Texas Band of Kickapoo Act**
Jan. 8, 1983, P.L. 97-429, 25 U.S. Code §§ 1300b-11 et seq., 1300b-11 nt.

**Texas Cattle Act**
Kan. Stat. Ann., 47-607, 47-637 et seq.

**Texas Low-Level Radioactive Waste Disposal Compact Consent Act**
Sept. 20, 1998, P.L. 105-236, 42 U.S. Code § 2021d nt.

**Texas-New Mexico State Line School District Compact Act**
N.M. Laws 1933, Ch. 110

**Texas Volunteer Pensions Act**
May 30, 1908, Ch. 230, 35 Stat. 553

**Texas Wilderness Act Amendments of 1986**
Oct. 29, 1986, P.L. 99-584, 100 Stat. 3322

**Texas Wilderness Act of 1984**
Oct. 30, 1984, P.L. 98-574

**Texshare Library Consortium Act**
Tex. Government Code, § 441.201 et seq.

**Textbook Act (Schools)**
Ala. Code 1975, § 16-36-1 et seq.
Ark. Code Ann. 1987, 6-21-401 et seq.
Ga. Code Ann., 20-2-1010 et seq.
Ill. Rev. Stat. 1991, Ch. 122, § 28-1 et seq.
Kan. Stat. Ann., 72-4107 et seq.
Ky. Rev. Stat. 1971, 156.405, 156.447, 156.474, 157.100 et seq.
Miss. Code Ann. 1972, § 37-43-1 et seq.
N.D. Cent. Code, 15-43-01 et seq.
N.M. Stat. Ann., 22-15-1 et seq.
Okla. Stat. Ann., Title 70, § 16-101 et seq.
Ore. Rev. Stat., 337.011 et seq.
S.D. Codified Laws 1967, 13-34-1 et seq.
Tenn. Code Ann., 49-6-2201 et seq.
Tex. Education Code, § 12.01 et seq.

**Textbook Aid Act**
R.I. Gen. Laws 1956, 16-23-2

**Textbook and Instructional Materials in Center Program Act (Pupil)**
Cal. Education Code 1976, § 60117

**Textbook Lending Act**
N.Y. Education Law 1947 (Consol. Laws Ch. 16) § 701

**Textbook Purchase, Distribution and Sale Act**
Ind. Code. Ann., 20-10.1-11-1 et seq.

**Textile Fiber Products Identification Act**
Sept. 2, 1958, P.L. 85-897, 72 Stat. 1717, 15 U.S. Code §§ 70 to 70k
June 5, 1965, P.L. 89-35, 79 Stat. 124, 15 U.S. Code § 70b
Sept. 24, 1984, P.L. 98-417, 98 Stat. 1603, 15 U.S. Code § 70b

**Textile Products Labeling Act**
P.R. Laws Ann. 1954, Title 10 § 2151

**Thaddeus Stevens State School of Technology Act**
Pa. Purdon's. Stat., Title 24, § 19-1901-B

**Thames River Valley Flood Control Compact Act**
Conn. Gen. Stat. Ann., § 25-101 et seq.

**Thanatopractice Act**
N.M. Stat. Ann., 61-32-1 et seq.

**Thanatopractice License Law**
N.M. Stat. Ann., 61-29A-1 et seq.

**Thanksgiving Day Act**
Dec. 26, 1941, Ch. 631, 55 Stat. 862 (See 5 U.S. Code § 6103)

**Thayer Act (Bronx River Parkway Extension)**
N.Y. Laws 1925, Ch. 197

**THC Therapeutic Research Act**
Minn. Stat. Ann., 152.21

**The Life Insurance Company Guaranty Corporation of New York Act**
N.Y. Insurance Law 1984 (Consol. Laws, Ch. 28), § 7701 et seq.

**Theater Bank Night Act**
N.M. Stat. Ann., 30-19-1 et seq.

**Theater Competition Act (Motion Picture)**
Wash. Rev. Code Ann., 19.58.010 et seq.

**Theatre and Store Tax Act**
Pa. Purdon's Stat., Title 72, § 3420-1 et seq.

**Theatrical Employment Agencies Law**
Colo. Rev. Stat., 12-24-201 et seq.

**Theatrical Performer's Act**
P.R. Laws Ann. 1954, Title 20, § 3301 et seq.

**Theatrical Syndication Financing Act**
N.Y. General Business Law (Consol. Laws Ch. 20) § 399b et seq.

**Theft Act**
Ariz. Rev. Stat. Ann., § 13-1801 et seq.
Colo. Rev. Stat., 18-4-401
Ill. Rev. Stat. 1991, Ch. 38, § 16-1 et seq.
Wis. Stat. Ann., 943.20

**Theft Act (Motor Vehicles)**
Cal. Statutes 1991, Ch. 930
Colo. Rev. Stat., 42-5-101 et seq.
Okla. Stat. Ann., Title 47, § 4-101 et seq.

**Theft and Arson Reporting Immunity Act**
Okla. Stat. Ann., Title 36, § 6301 et seq.

**Theft and Insurance Fraud Reporting Act (Motor Vehicle)**
Cal. Insurance Code § 1874 et seq.

**Theft and Insurance Fraud Reporting Immunity Act (Motor Vehicle)**
N.J. Stat. Ann. 17:23-8 et seq.
S.C. Code Ann. 1976, § 38-77-1110 et seq.

**Theft and White Collar Crimes Act**
D.C. Code Ann., §§ 22-711 et seq., 22-2511 et seq., 22-3801 et seq.

**Theft from Vehicles Act**
D.C. Code 1973, § 22-2204a

**Theft Liability Act**
Tex. Civil Practice and Remedies Code, § 134.001 et seq.

**Theft of Cable Television Service Act**
S.C. Code Ann. 1976, § 16-11-810 et seq.

**Theft of Motor Vehicle, Aircraft, Boat or Boat Motor Act**
Fla. Stat. 1973, 814.01 et seq.

**Theft of Public Transportation Services Act**
Colo. Rev. Stat., 18-4-801 et seq.

**Theft Prevention Act (Automobile)**
Pa. Purdon's Stat., Title 40, § 3601 et seq.

**Theft Prevention Act (Motor Vehicle)**
Ill. Rev. Stat. 1991, Ch. 95 1/2, § 1301 et seq.

**Theft Prevention Act (Wireless Services)**
Ark. Acts 1997, No. 1310
Ill. Comp. Stat. 1992, Ch. 720, § 5/16F-1 et seq.

**Theft Reporting Act (Motor Vehicle)**
Ill. Comp. Stat. 1992, Ch. 625, § 10/1

**Thelluson Act (Accumulations)**
Ill. Rev. Stat. 1991, Ch. 30, §§ 152.9, 153
Pa. 1853 Pamph. Laws 503, No. 304

**Theodore R. Montoya Memorial Hemophilia Program Act**
N.M. Stat. Ann., 24-2A-1 et seq.

**Therapeutic Abortion Act**
Cal. Health and Safety Code § 25950 et seq.

**Therapeutic Recreation Personnel Certification Act**
N.C. Gen. Stat. 1943, § 90C-1 et seq.

**Therapeutic Research Act (Controlled Substances)**
Ga. Code Ann., 43-34-120 et seq.
Mass. Gen. Laws Ann., 94D:1 et seq.
N.Y. Public Health Law 1953 (Consol. Laws Ch. 45) §§ 3397a to 3399g

*Continued*

N.Y. Public Health Law 1953 (Consol. Laws Ch. 45) § 3397a et seq.

**Therapeutic Research Act (THC)**
Minn. Stat. Ann., 152.21

**Therapeutic Use Act (Marijuana)**
S.C. Code Ann. 1976, § 44-53-610 et seq.

**Therapist Act (Licensed Marriage and Family)**
Tex. Rev. Civ. Stat., Art. 4512c-1

**Therapist Grant and Scholarship Program (Mental Health)**
Utah Code Ann. 1953, 62A-13-101 et seq.

**Therapist Licensing Act (Marriage and Family)**
Utah Code Ann. 1953, 58-60-301 et seq.

**Therapist Licensure Act (Marital and Family)**
Okla. Stat. Ann., Title 59, § 1925.1 et seq.

**Therapist Sexual Misconduct Victims Compensation Act**
Tenn. Code Ann., 29-26-201 et seq.

**Therapists Registration Act (Marriage and Family)**
Kan. Stat. Ann., 65-6401 et seq.

**Therapy Act (Physical)**
See Physical Therapy Act

**Therapy Licensing Act (Marriage and Family)**
Ill. Rev. Stat. 1989, Ch. 111, § 8351-1 et seq.

**Therapy Licensing Act (Occupational)**
N.J. Stat. Ann., 45:9-37.51 et seq.

**Therapy Practice Act (Massage)**
N.M. Stat. Ann., 61-12C-1 et seq.

**Therapy Practice Act (Occupational)**
Ala. Code 1975, § 34-39-1 et seq.
Kan. Stat. Ann., 65-5401 et seq.
Pa. Purdon's Stat., Title 63, § 1501 et seq.
Tex. Rev. Civ. Stat., Art. 851 et seq.
Utah Code Ann. 1953, 58-42a-101 et seq.

**Therapy Practice Act (Respiratory)**
Kan. Stat. Ann., 65-5501 et seq.

**Therapy Practice and Counseling Act**
N.M. Stat. Ann., 61-9A-1 et seq.

**Therapy Technology Act**
Ark. Code Ann. 1987, 17-98-101 et seq.

**Thermal Efficiency Code**
Fla. Stat. Ann., 553.900 et seq.

**Thermal Power Plant Siting Act**
Wash. Rev. Code Ann., 80.50.010 et seq.

**Thibodaux, Louisiana Redevelopment Agency Act**
La. Acts 1968, No. 439

**Thieves Act**
Md. Ann. Code 1957, Art. 27, § 558
Pa. Purdon's Stat., Title 18, § 4821

**Third Amendment to the Revenue Act for Fiscal Year 1978 and Other Purposes**
D.C. Code Ann., §§ 47-1509, 25-103, 25-111, 25,124

**Third Amendment to the Revenue Act of 1975 Act**
D.C. Code Ann., § 47-2001

**Third Class Cities Act**
Kan. Stat. Ann., 15-101 et seq.
Pa. Purdon's Stat., Title 53, § 35101 et seq.
Wash. Rev. Code Ann., 35.24.010 et seq.

**Third Class City Civil Service Act**
Pa. Purdon's Stat., Title 53, § 35901 et seq.

**Third Class City Code**
Pa. Purdon's Stat., Title 53, § 35101 et seq.

**Third Class City Employees' Retirement Law**
Pa. Purdon's Stat., Title 53, § 39371 et seq.

**Third Class City Pension Fund Act**
Pa. Purdon's Stat., Title 53, § 39340 et seq.

**Third Class City Port Authority Act**
Pa. Purdon's Stat., Title 55, § 571 et seq.

**Third Class City Registration Act**
Pa. Purdon's Stat., Title 25, § 951-1 et seq.

**Third Class City Zoning Enabling Act**
Pa. Purdon's Stat., Title 53, § 10601 et seq.

**Third Class County Assessment Act**
Pa. Purdon's Stat., Title 72, § 5342 et seq.

**Third Class County Convention Center Authority Act**
Pa. Purdon's Stat., Title 16, § 13101 et seq.

**Third Class County Employees' Retirement Act**
Pa. Purdon's Stat., Title 16, § 11501 et seq.

**Third Conviction for Felonies Act**
Tex. Penal Code, § 12.42

**Third Deficiency Appropriation Act of 1939**
Aug. 9, 1939, Ch. 633, 53 Stat. 1301, 42 U.S. Code § 704a nt.

**Third Deficiency Appropriation Act of 1946**
June 28, 1946, Ch. 161, 61 Stat. 190
July 23, 1946, Ch. 591, 60 Stat. 600, 2 U.S. Code §§ 46a nt., 46b nt.; 22 U.S. Code § 295a nt.; 31 U.S. Code § 487a
Aug. 8, 1946, Ch. 870, 60 Stat. 911
Feb. 26, 1947, Ch. 6, 61 Stat. 6

**Third Deficiency Appropriation Act of 1949**
Oct. 10, 1949, Ch. 662, 63 Stat. 738, 2 U.S. Code §§ 46a, 46b nts.
Oct. 10, 1949, Ch. 662, 63 Stat. 744

**Third Degree Act**
Mont. Rev. Code 1947, 94-3918

**Third Felony Act**
Ind. Code. Ann., 35-50-2-8

**Third Liberty Bond Act**
April 4, 1918, Ch. 44, 40 Stat. 502, 31 U.S. Code §§ 752, 752a, 754, 765, 766, 771, 774

**Third-Party Administrator Act**
Neb. Laws 1992, L.B. 1006, §§ 76 to 91

**Third Party Administrator Act**
Mich. Comp. Laws Ann., 550.901 et seq.
Okla. Stat. Ann., Title 36, § 1441 et seq.

**Third Party Beneficiary Act**
Mich. Comp. Laws Ann., 600.1405

**Third Party Beneficiary Contract Act**
Ill. Rev. Stat. 1991, Ch. 110 1/2, § 400 et seq.

**Third Party Liability Act (Medicaid)**
Fla. Stat. Ann., 409.910

**Third Party Liability Act (Workmens Compensation)**
Mich. Comp. Laws Ann., 418.827

**Third Party Practice Act (Joinder)**
Ark. Code Ann. 1987, 16-61-207
La. Code of Civil Procedure Art. 1111 et seq.
Mo. Rev. Stat., 507.080
Neb. Rev. Stat. 1943, 25-331
N.Y. Civil Practice Law and Rules (Consol. Laws Ch. 8) § 1007
Tenn. Public Acts 1955, Ch. 145
Tex. Rules of Civil Procedure as am. 1984, Rule 38

**Third Party Prescription Program Act**
Ala. Code 1975, § 34-23-110 et seq.
Ga. Code Ann., 26-4-140 et seq.
Ill. Rev. Stat. 1991, Ch. 73, § 1065.59-1 et seq.
Me. Rev. Stat. Ann. 1964, Title 32, § 13771 et seq.
Okla. Stat. Ann., Title 15, § 781 et seq.
Tenn. Code Ann., 63-10-301 et seq.

**Third Party Proceedings Act**
P.R. Laws Ann. 1954, Title 32, § 1171 et seq.

**Third Supplemental Appropriation Act of 1948**
Dec. 23, 1947, Ch. 524, 61 Stat. 941

**Third Supplemental Appropriation Act of 1951**
June 2, 1951, Ch. 121, 65 Stat. 52, 31 U.S. Code § 696; 46 U.S. Code § 1241a; 50 U.S. Code Appx. §§ 2094, 2264

**Third Supplemental Appropriation Act of 1952**
June 5, 1952, Ch. 369, 66 Stat. 101, 50 U.S. Code Appx. § 460 nt.
Aug. 20, 1996, P.L. 104-186, 2 U.S. Code §§ 38b, 102a, 125a

**Third Supplemental Appropriation Act of 1954**
May 11, 1954, Ch. 200, 68 Stat. 87, 20 U.S. Code § 275 nt.

**Third Supplemental Appropriation Act of 1957**
June 21, 1957, P.L. 85-58, 71 Stat. 176, 2 U.S. Code §§ 46a-1, 102a; 42 U.S. Code § 267
Aug. 20, 1996, P.L. 104-186, 2 U.S. Code § 102a

**Third Supplemental Appropriation Act of 1961**
March 31, 1961, P.L. 87-14, 75 Stat. 20, 2 U.S. Code § 127

**Third Supplemental National Defense Appropriation Act of 1941**
Oct. 8, 1940, Ch. 756, 54 Stat. 968

**Third Supplemental National Defense Appropriation Act of 1942**
Dec. 17, 1941, Ch. 591, 55 Stat. 810, 22 U.S. Code § 412 nt.; 24 U.S. Code § 41 nt.; 31 U.S. Code § 529h; 42 U.S. Code § 1523 nt.

**Third Supplemental Surplus Appropriation Rescission Act of 1946**
July 23, 1946, Ch. 591, 60 Stat. 624

**Third Unification Act**
Kan. Stat. Ann., 72-6793 et seq.

**Third Validating Act**
Cal. Statutes 1947, Ch. 1335, p. 2889
Cal. Statutes 1955, Ch. 1565, p. 2844
Cal. Statutes 1965, Ch. 855, p. 2453
Cal. Statutes 1967, Ch. 938, p. 2429
Cal. Statutes 1970, Ch. 1149, p. 2029
Cal. Statutes 1971, Ch. 712, p. 1379
Cal. Statutes 1972, Ch. 337, p. 632
Cal. Statutes 1974, Ch. 911
Cal. Statutes 1975, Ch. 681
Cal. Statutes 1976, Ch. 725
Cal. Statutes 1978, Ch. 667
Cal. Statutes 1981, Ch. 586
Cal. Statutes 1982, Ch. 458
Cal. Statutes 1983, Ch. 638
Cal. Statutes 1984, Ch. 692
Cal. Statutes 1985, Ch. 590
Cal. Statutes 1986, Ch. 581
Cal. Statutes 1988, Ch. 757
Cal. Statutes 1990, Ch. 811
Cal. Statutes 1991, Chs. 399, 442, 777
Cal. Statutes 1992, Ch. 569
Cal. Statutes 1995, Ch. 688
Cal. Statutes 1996, Ch. 172
Cal. Statutes 1997, Ch. 486

**Third 1984 Revisory Act**
Ill. Laws 1984, P.A. 83-1539

**Thirty Day Statute (Judgments)**
Ala. Code 1958, Title 13, § 119

**Thirty Day Statute of Limitations (District and Special Improvements)**
N.Y. Town Law (Consol. Laws, Ch. 62), § 195, Subd. 2

**Thirty-Five Million Dollar Highway Note Act**
Okla. Laws 1937, p. 367

**Thirty Foot Act (Navigable Streams)**
Tex. Natural Resources Code, § 21.001 et seq.

**Thistle Act**
Mo. Rev. Stat., 263.190 et seq.

**Thomas Alva Edison Commemorative Coin Act**
Oct. 31, 1998, P.L. 105-331, 112 Stat. 3073, 31 U.S. Code § 5112 nt.

**Thomas Amendment.**
May 12, 1933, Ch. 25, 48 Stat. 51, 12 U.S. Code § 462b; 31 U.S. Code §§ 314, 316, 462, 771, 821 to 823

**Thomas County Higher Education Authority Act**
Ga. Laws 1979, p. 3288

**Thomas County Hospital Assets Act**
Kan. Stat. Ann., 19-18,133, 19-18,134

**Thomas Edward Lanni Schoolbus Safety Act**
Cal. Education Code 1976, § 39831.3
Cal. Vehicle Code 1959, § 22112

**Thomas J. Anderson, Gordon Rockwell Environmental Protection Act**
Mich. Comp. Laws Ann., 691.1201 et seq.

**Thomas Jefferson Commemoration Commission Act**
Aug. 17, 1992, P.L. 102-343, 36 U.S. Code § 149 nt.
Dec. 14, 1993, P.L. 103-191, 36 U.S. Code § 149 nt.

**Thomas Jefferson Commemorative Coin Act of 1993**
Dec. 14, 1993, P.L. 103-186, 31 U.S. Code § 5112 nt.

**Thomas-McCurdy Act**
Ala. Acts 1990, No. 339

**Thomas Zoul Act (Taxation)**
Ohio Laws Vol. 117, p. 32

**Thomaston-Upson County Airport Authority Act**
Ga. Laws 1988, p. 4225

**Thomasville Convention and Visitors Bureau Authority Act**
Ga. Laws 1991 Ex. Sess., p. 434

**Thomasville Payroll Development Authority Act**
Ga. Laws 1960, p. 2567

**Thompson Act (Discrimination by Hospitals)**
Mont. Rev. Code 1947, 94-3557, 94-3558

**Thompson-Hunter Patient Protection Act**
Cal. Statutes 1991, Ch. 1180

**Thompson-Killea Limited Partner Protection Act**
Cal. Corporations Code § 25014.5 et seq.

**Thompson-King Act (Labor Relations)**
Mo. Rev. Stat., 295.010 et seq.

**Thompson-Maddy-Ducheny-Ashburn Welfare-to-Work Act**
Cal. Education Code 1976, § 8208 et seq.

**Thompson-Richter Underground Storage Tank Reform Act**
Cal. Health and Safety Code § 25289 et seq.

**Thompson-Royce Police and Bystander Protection and Safe Pursuit Act**
Cal. Statutes 1991, Ch. 1048

**Thompson's Law (Vacation of Default Judgments)**
N.Y. Civil Practice Laws and Rules (Consol. Laws Ch. 8) § 5015

**Thomson Anti-Gambling Act**
Wis. Stat. Ann., 945.041

**Thomson Budget Act**
Wis. Stat. Ann., 65.90

**Thomson-McDuffie County Industrial Development Authority Act**
Ga. Laws 1962, p. 2120

**Thorn Liquor Act (Local Option)**
Ark. Code Ann. 1987, 3-8-301 et seq., 3-3-310

**Thoroughbred Racing Capital Investment Fund Act**
N.Y. Racing, Pari-Mutual Wagering and Breeding Law (Consol. Laws Ch. 47A) § 251 et seq.

**Thoroughfare Authority Act (Metropolitan)**
Ind. Code 1976, 19-5-4-1 et seq.

**Thorp Act (Marketing of Milk)**
Cal. Food and Agricultural Code 1967, §§ 35751, 61301 et seq.

**Thousand Islands Bridge Authority Act**
N.Y. Public Authorities Law (Consol. Laws Ch. 43A) § 575 et seq.

**Threatened and Endangered Species Act**
Fla. Stat. Ann., 372.072

**Threatened, Endangered, or Nongame Species Conservation Act**
Colo. Rev. Stat., 33-2-101 et seq.

**Threatened Species Act**
Haw. Rev. Stat. Ann., § 195D-1 et seq.

**Threatening Communication Act**
May 15, 1939, Ch. 133, 53 Stat. 742 (See 18 U.S. Code §§ 875 to 877, 3239)

**Three Affiliated Tribes and Standing Rock Sioux Tribe Equitable Compensation Act**
Oct. 30, 1992, P.L. 102-575, 106 Stat. 4731

**Three and Two Month Statutes of Limitations (Probate Claims)**
Cal. Probate Code § 714

**Three Assessor Act (Eminent Domain)**
Ga. Code Ann., 22-1-40 et seq.

**Three Brakemen Act (Railroads Full Crew)**
Ark. Stat. 1947, 73-720 et seq.

**Three-Day Marriage Act**
Mass. Gen. Laws Ann., 207:19 et seq.

**Three Factor Apportionment Act (Corporate Income)**
Ga. Code Ann., 48-7-31

**Three Felony Offender Act**
Tex. Penal Code, § 12.42

**Three-Fourths Jury Act**
Ohio Civ. Rule 48 et seq.

**Three-Hundred-Ten (310) Law**
Mont. Code Ann. 1987, 75-7-101 et seq.

**Three Judge Act (Labor Disputes)**
Mass. Gen. Laws Ann., 212:30

**Three Lakes Water and Sanitation District Act**
Colo. Rev. Stat., 32-10-101 et seq.

**Three Mile Local Option Law**
Ark. Acts 1881, p. 140, No. 74

**Three Mile Road Act**
Ind. Code. Ann., 8-20-1-61

**Three Million Dollar Act**
March 3, 1847, Ch. 50, 9 Stat. 174

**Three Months Divorce Law**
Ark. Code Ann. 1987, 9-12-307

**Three Per Cent. Act (Immigration)**
May 19, 1921, Ch. 8, 42 Stat. 5

**Three Point Tax Law**
Iowa Code Ann., 422.1 et seq.

**Three Rivers Local Flood Protection Project Loan Act**
Mass. Acts 1962, Ch. 692

**Three Strikes and You're Out Law**
Cal. Penal Code § 1170.12
Wash. Rev. Code. Ann., 9.94A.392

**Three Term Act (Criminal Trials)**
Ind. Code 1976, 35-1-27-1
Ohio Rev. Code 1953, 2945.72

**Three Year Separation Act**
Ark. Code Ann. 1987, 9-12-301

**Three Year Statute of Limitation (Personal Injury)**
R.I. Gen. Laws 1956, 9-1-14 et seq.

**Three Year Statute of Limitations (Criminal Actions)**
Cal. Penal Code § 800

**Three Year Statute of Limitations Act**
Ala. Code 1975, § 6-2-37
Alaska Stat. 1962, § 09.10.060
Cal. Code of Civil Procedure § 338
Fla. Stat. 1973, 95.11, Subsec. 5
Kan. Stat. Ann., 60-512
Me. Rev. Stat. Ann. 1964, Title 14, § 868
N.Y. Civil Practice Law and Rules (Consol. Laws, Ch. 8), § 214
Wash. Rev. Code Ann., 4.16.080
Wis. Stat. Ann., 893.20

**Threshers Lien Act**
Ind. Code. Ann., 32-8-33-1 et seq.
Iowa Code Ann., 571.1 et seq.
Minn. Stat. Ann., 514.65, 514.66
Okla. Stat. Ann., Title 42, § 111 et seq.

**Thrift and Loan Law**
Cal. Financial Code § 18000 et seq.

**Thrift Companies Act**
Nev. Rev. Stat. 1979 Reprint, 677.010 et seq.

**Thrift Industry Recovery Act**
Aug. 10, 1987, P.L. 100-86, 12 U.S. Code §§ 226 nt., 1436 nt., 1441 nt., 1442a, 1464, 1467 nt., 1467 to 1467a nt., 1729 to 1730a, 1730h, 1730i

**Thrift Institutions Restructuring Act**
Oct. 15, 1981, P.L. 97-320, Title III, 12 U.S. Code § 1641 nt.
Nov. 30, 1983, P.L. 98-181, 12 U.S. Code § 1701j-3

**Thrift Savings Fund Investment Act of 1987**
May 22, 1987, P.L. 100-43, 5 U.S. Code §§ 8401 nt., 8438

**Thrift Savings Investment Funds Act of 1996**
Sept. 30, 1996, P.L. 104-208, 5 U.S. Code § 8401 nt.

**Thrift Savings Plan Act of 1996**
Sept. 30, 1996, P.L. 104-208, Title II, 5 U.S. Code § 8401 nt.

**Thrift Savings Plan Technical Amendments Act of 1990**
July 17, 1990, P.L. 101-335, 5 U.S. Code §§ 3392, 3392 nt., 8351, 8351 nt. prec. 8401, 8401, 8401 nt., 8432a, 8433, 8433 nt., 8434, 8434 nt., 8435, 8438, 8438 nt., 8440a, 8440b, 8477, 8477 nt.
Oct. 2, 1992, P.L. 102-378, 5 U.S. Code § 3392 nt.

**Throughway Act**
Ore. Rev. Stat., 374.005 et seq.

**Thruway Authority Act**
N.Y. Public Authorities Law (Consol. Laws Ch. 43A) § 350 et seq.

**Thurman Act (Flu Vaccine for Elderly)**
Cal. Welfare and Institutions Code § 9310

**Thurman Act (Pacific Railroads)**
May 7, 1878, Ch. 96, 20 Stat. 56

**Thurman Agricultural Policy Act**
Cal. Food and Agricultural Code § 801 et seq.

**Tice Road Act**
Ill. Rev. Stat. 1957, Ch. 121, § 47

**Tick Eradication Act**
Ark. Code Ann. 1987, 2-40-904 et seq.
Fla. Stat. Ann., 585.01 et seq.
Ga. Code Ann., 4-4-60 et seq.
Tex. Agricultural Code, § 167.001 et seq.

**Ticket Act (Traffic)**
S.C. Code Ann. 1976, § 56-7-10 et seq.

**Ticket Brokers' License Act**
Tex. Rev. Civ. Stat., Art. 9008

**Ticket Scalping Act**
Ill. Rev. Stat. 1991, Ch. 121 1/2, § 157.30 et seq.
Mich. Comp. Laws Ann., 750.465
S.C. Code Ann. 1976, § 16-17-710 et seq.

**Tidal Waters Act (Boat Regulation)**
N.J. Stat. Ann. 12:7-44 et seq.

**Tidal Wetlands Acquisition Act**
Conn. Gen. Stat. Ann., § 26-17a

**Tidal Wetlands Act**
N.Y. Environmental Conservation Law 1972 (Consol. Laws Ch. 43B) § 25-0101 et seq.

**Tide Gate Loan Act (Marshfield)**
Mass. Acts 1962, Ch. 464

**Tidelands**
See Submerged Lands Act

**Tidelands Act**
Ga. Code Ann., 44-8-6 et seq.
Ore. Rev. Stat., 274.040 et seq.
S.C. Code Ann. 1976, § 48-39-10 et seq.
Wash. Rev. Code Ann., 79.93.010 et seq., 79.94.340 et seq.

**Tidelands Act (Cunningham-Shell)**
Cal. Statutes 1955, Ch. 1724, p. 3165

**Tidewater Fisheries Act**
Md. Ann. Code 1974, Art. NR, § 4-701 et seq.

**Tidewater Recreation and Stadium Authority Act**
Va. Acts 1968, Ch. 288

**Tidwell Act (Motor Carriers)**
Ala. Code 1975, § 37-3-1 et seq.

**Tied House Act (Liquor)**
Wis. Stat. Ann., 125.33

**Tied House Evil Act**
Fla. Stat. Ann., 561.42

**Tift County Trade Center Authority Act**
Ga. Laws 1980, p. 4520

**Tift County Water and Sewerage Authority Act**
Ga. Laws 1972, p. 2808

**Tifton-Tift County Charter Commission Act**
Ga. Laws 1983, p. 3590

**Tilden Act (Trusts)**
N.Y. Estates, Powers and Trusts Law (Consol. Laws. Ch. 17B) § 8-1.1

**Tillman-Gillespie Resolution (Transportation of Coal and Oil)**
March 7, 1906, Ch. 8, 34 Stat. 823

**Timber Act**
Alaska Comp. Laws Ann. 1949, § 47-2-111 et seq.
Minn. Stat. Ann., 90.01 et seq.

**Timber and Stone Act**
June 3, 1878, Ch. 151, 20 Stat. 89, 43 U.S. Code §§ 311 to 313

**Timber Buyers Licensing Act**
Ill. Rev. Stat. 1991, Ch. 111, § 701 et seq.

**Timber Culture Acts**
March 3, 1873, Ch. 277, 17 Stat. 605
March 13, 1874, Ch. 55, 18 Stat. 21

**Timber Culture Repeal Act**
See Forest Reserve Acts (General)

**Timber Cutter's Act (Injunction)**
Ga. Code 1933, 55-204

**Timber Cutting Damages Act**
Va. Code 1950, § 55-331 et seq.

**Timber Inspection Act**
Ark. Code Ann. 1987, 15-32-201 et seq.

**Timber Lien Law**
Wash. Rev. Code Ann., 60.24.020 et seq.

**Timber Supply Stabilization Act**
Ida. Code 1947, 58-1001 et seq.

**Timber Tax Act**
Ida. Code 1947, 63-324 et seq.
N.H. Rev. Stat. 1955, 79:1 et seq.
Wash. Rev. Code 1983, 84.33.010 et seq.

**Timber Theft Equipment Condemnation Act**
Ala. Acts 1987, p. 1256

**Timber Trespass Act**
Del. Code of 1974, Title 25, § 1401 et seq.

**Timber Yield Tax Law**
Cal. Revenue and Taxation Code § 38101 et seq.

**Timberland Productivity Act**
Cal. Government Code § 51100 et seq.

**Timberlands Control Act (Mississippi River)**
Miss. Code Ann. 1972, § 49-20-1 et seq.

**Time Act**
Ind. Laws 1957, Ch. 172, p. 356
Md. Ann. Code 1957, Art. 94

**Time Act (Voting)**
Neb. Rev. Stat. 1943, 32-1046

**Time Off for Official Meetings Act**
Ill. Rev. Stat. 1991, Ch. 102, §§ 250, 251

**Time Off to Vote Act**
Colo. Rev. Stat., 1-7-102
Ill. Rev. Stat. 1991, Ch. 46, § 17-15
W. Va. Code 1966, § 3-1-42

**Time Sales Act (Motor Vehicles)**
Mo. Rev. Stat., 365.010 et seq.

**Time-Share Act**
Ark. Code Ann. 1987, 18-14-101 et seq.
Ga. Code Ann., 44-3-160 et seq.
Iowa Code Ann., 557A.1 et seq.
La. Rev. Stat. Ann., 9:1131.1 et seq.
Mass. Gen. Laws Ann., 183B:1 et seq.
Md. Ann. Code 1974, Art. RP, § 11A-101 et seq.
Mont. Code Ann., 37-53-101 et seq.
N.C. Gen. Stat. 1943, § 93A-39 et seq.
Neb. Rev. Stat. 1943, 76-1701 et seq.
N.M. Stat. Ann., 41-11-1 et seq.
Tenn. Code Ann., 66-32-101 et seq.
Tex. Property Code, § 221.001 et seq.
Wash. Rev. Code Ann., 64.36.010 et seq.
W. Va. Code 1966 § 36-9-1 et seq.

**Time-Share Act (Real Estate)**
Fla. Stat. Ann., 721.01 et seq.
Ill. Rev. Stat. 1991, Ch. 30, § 701 et seq.

**Time-Share Resale Broker Act**
Tenn. Code Ann., 66-32-102 et seq.

**Time Sharing and Vacation Plan Act**
Fla. Stat. Ann., 721.01 et seq.

**Time Sharing Plans Act (Vacation)**
S.C. Code Ann. 1976, § 27-32-10 et seq.

**Time Standardization Act**
Ill. Rev. Stat. 1991, Ch. 1, § 3200 et seq.

**Timeshare and Camp Resort Act**
Utah Code Ann. 1953, 57-19-1 et seq.

**Timeshare and Land Sales Practices Act**
Utah Code Ann. 1953, 57-11-1 et seq.

**Timeshare Lien Foreclosure Act**
Fla. Stat. Ann., 721.80 to 721.86

**Timmons-Taylor-Lybrand Insurance Code**
Ala. Code 1975, § 27-1-1 et seq.

**Tin Parachute Law**
Mass. Gen. Laws Ann., 149:183

**Tin Protection Act**
Feb. 15, 1936, Ch. 74, 49 Stat. 1140

**Tincher-Capper Act (Grain Futures)**
See Grain Futures Act

**Tip Credit Act**
Alaska Stat. 1962, § 23.10.065

**Tipping Act**
Ark. Acts 1913 p. 364, No. 98
Cal. Labor Code § 350 et seq.
Ill. Rev. Stat. 1961, Ch. 38, § 551 et seq.

**Tipplers Act**
Ark. Code Ann. 1987, Ch. 148

**Tippling House Act**
Ill. Rev. Stat. 1937, Ch. 38, § 547

**Tipton County Road Act**
Tenn. Private Acts 1943, Ch. 120

**Tire Recycling Act**
Cal. Government Code §§ 66799.100 et seq., 66799.110 et seq., 66799.120 et seq., 66799.130 et seq., 66799.140 et seq., 66799.150, 66799.151
Cal. Public Resources Code § 42860 et seq.
Cal. Statutes 1990, Ch. 33 § 1
N.M. Stat. Ann., 74-11-1 et seq.

**Tire Recycling Act (Waste)**
Pa. Purdon's Stat., Title 35, § 6029.101 et seq.

**Tire Regulatory Act (Scrap)**
Mich. Comp. Laws Ann., 299.561 et seq.

**Tissue Bank Act**
D.C. Code Ann., § 2-1602 et seq.

**Tithing Act (State Finances)**
Ore. Rev. Stat., 293.145 et seq.
S.D. Laws 1943, Ch. 277

**Title Act (Automobiles)**
Neb. Rev. Stat. 1943, 60-101 et seq.

**Title Act (Certificate of)**
Neb. Rev. Stat. 1943, 60-101 et seq.
N.Y. Vehicle and Traffic Law 1959 (Consol. Laws Ch. 71) § 2101 et seq.

**Title Act (Marketable)**
N.Y. Real Property Law (Consol. Laws Ch. 50) § 345

**Title Act (Motor Vehicles)**
See Motor Vehicle Title Act

**Title Act (Quiet)**
Mass. Gen. Laws Ann., 240:1 et seq.

**Title Act (Tax)**
Mass. Gen. Laws Ann., 60:64 et seq.

**Title Certificate Act (Motor Vehicles)**
See Motor Vehicle Certificate of Title Act

**Title Certificate Law**
S.C. Code Ann. 1976, § 56-19-210 et seq.

**Title Defects Act**
Mass. Gen. Laws Ann., 184:24

**Title Examination Act (Real Property)**
Neb. Rev. Stat. 1943, 76-601 et seq.

**Title Guaranty Act**
Ill. Rev. Stat. 1991, Ch. 73, § 478 et seq.

**Title I of the Elementary and Secondary Education Act of 1965**
Nov. 3, 1966, P.L. 89-750, 80 Stat. 1191, 20 U.S. Code §§ 241a nt., 241b, 241c, 241e to 241h, 241j to 241m, 244, 331a, 332a, 332b, 821 to 823, 841 to 844, 861 to 864, 867, 871 to 886; 42 U.S. Code § 2000d-5

**Title Insurance Act**
Ala. Code 1958, Title 10, § 169 et seq.
Cal. Insurance Code § 12340 et seq.
Conn. Gen. Stat. Ann., § 38a-400 et seq.
Ill. Rev. Stat. 1991, Ch. 73, § 1401 et seq.
Mo. Rev. Stat., 381.011 et seq.
Mont. Code Ann., 33-25-104 et seq.
Neb. Rev. Stat. 1943, 44-1901 et seq.
N.H. Rev. Stat. 1955, 416-A:1 et seq.
N.J. Stat. Ann., 17:46B-1 et seq.
N.M. Stat. Ann., 59A-30-1 et seq.
Okla. Stat. Ann., Title 36, § 5001 et seq.
Tenn. Code Ann., 56-35-101 et seq.
Tex. Insurance Code, Art. 9.01 et seq.
Utah Code Ann. 1953, 31A-23-403 et seq.
Wash. Rev. Code Ann., 48.29.010 et seq.
Wyo. Stat. Ann., § 26-23-301 et seq.

**Title Insurance Agent Act**
Neb. Laws 1997, L.B. 53

**Title Insurance and Abstract Law**
Ind. Code. Ann., 27-7-3-1 et seq.

**Title Insurance Code of Colorado**
Colo. Rev. Stat., 10-11-101 et seq.

**Title Insurance Guaranty Act**
Tex. Insurance Code, Art. 9.48

**Title Insurance Rate Regulatory Act**
Pa. 1953 Pamph. Laws 1312, No. 372

**Title Insurers Act**
Neb. Rev. Stat. 1943, 44-1978 to 44-19,105

**Title Page Act**
Ill. Rev. Stat. 1991, Ch. 121 1/2, §§ 157.14, 157.14a

**Title Pledge Act**
Miss. Code Ann. 1972, § 75-67-401 et seq.
Tenn. Code Ann., 45-15-101 et seq.

**Title Protection Act (Certified Industrial Hygienist)**
Neb. Rev. Stat. 1943, 71-8001 to 71-8008

**Title Registration Act**
Iowa Code Ann., 321.17 et seq.

**Title Registration Act (Automobiles)**
Ark. Code Ann. 1987, 27-14-201 et seq.
La. Rev. Stat. Ann., 32:701 et seq.

**Title Registration Act (Motor Vehicles)**
See Motor Vehicle Title and Regristration Act

**Title Registration Act (Real Property)**
Ill. Rev. Stat. 1991, Ch. 30, § 44n et seq.
Minn. Stat. Ann., 508.01 et seq.
N.Y. Real Property Law (Consol. Laws Ch. 50) § 370 et seq.

**Title Simplification Act**
Okla. Stat. Ann., Title 16, § 61 et seq.

**Title to Movable Property Act**
July 29, 1954, Ch. 616, 68 Stat. 580, 43 U.S. Code § 499a
Aug. 2, 1956, Ch. 884, 70 Stat. 940, 43 U.S. Code § 499a
June 24, 1965, P.L. 89-48, 79 Stat. 172, 43 U.S. Code § 499a

**Title Transfer Act (Motor Vehicles)**
Mich. Comp. Laws Ann., 257.233 et seq.

**Title XX, Restrictions Act**
S.C. Code Ann. 1976, § 43-1-230 et seq.

**Titles to Manufactured Homes Act**
Colo. Rev. Stat., 38-29-101 et seq.

**Titling Act (Watercraft)**
N.C. Gen. Stat. 1943, § 75A-32 et seq.

**Titusville-Cocoa Airport District Act**
Fla. Special Laws 1963, Ch. 63-1143

**Titusville Urban Renewal Law**
Fla. Special Laws 1967, Ch. 67-2137

**Tiwa Indians Act**
Aug. 18, 1987, P.L. 100-89, 25 U.S. Code § 1300g-5

**Tlingit and Haida Status Clarification Act**
Nov. 2, 1994, P.L. 103-454, 25 U.S. Code §§ 1212 nt., 1212 et seq.
Feb. 12, 1996, P.L. 104-109, 25 U.S. Code § 1215

**Tobacco Accessories and Smoking Herbs Control Act**
Ill. Rev. Stat. 1991, Ch. 23, § 2358-1 et seq.

**Tobacco Act (Minors)**
Ore. Rev. Stat. 1953, 167.250

**Tobacco Act (Prevention of Youth Access to)**
Miss. Code Ann. 1972, §§ 45-37-1 et seq., 97-2-25, 97-5-43 to 97-5-47, 97-27-35

**Tobacco Act (Youth)**
Mich. Comp. Laws Ann., 722.645

**Tobacco Adjustment Act of 1983**
Nov. 29, 1983, P.L. 98-180, Title II, 7 U.S. Code § 1421 nt.
Aug. 23, 1988, P.L. 100-418, 102 Stat. 1156, 7 U.S. Code § 511r
Nov. 28, 1990, P.L. 101-624, 7 U.S. Code §§ 509, 511r
Dec. 13, 1991, P.L. 102-237, 7 U.S. Code § 509
Aug. 10, 1993, P.L. 103-66, 7 U.S. Code § 511r
April 4, 1996, P.L. 104-127, 7 U.S. Code § 509

*Continued*

**Tobacco Control Act**
June 28, 1934, Ch. 866, 48 Stat. 1275
April 25, 1936, Ch. 249, 49 Stat. 1239, 7 U.S. Code §§ 515 to 515k
Va. Code 1950, § 61.1-38 et seq.

**Tobacco Control Act (Gilbert-Wells)**
Ky. Rev. Stat. 1971, 248.010, 248.280 et seq.

**Tobacco Excise Tax Law**
Ore. Laws 1925, Ch. 342

**Tobacco Identification Act**
Ga. Code Ann., 10-4-100 et seq.

**Tobacco Inspection Act**
Aug. 23, 1935, Ch. 623, 49 Stat. 731, 7 U.S. Code §§ 511 to 511q
April 7, 1986, P.L. 99-272, 7 U.S. Code § 511d
Ky. Acts 1820, Ch. 96
Md. Ann. Code 1974, Art. AG, § 7-301 et seq.

**Tobacco License Act**
Neb. Rev. Stat. 1943, 28-1418 et seq.
Utah Code Ann. 1953, 59-14-1 et seq.

**Tobacco Marketing Act**
Ga. Official Code Ann., 10-4-106

**Tobacco Marketing Act (Flue-Cured)**
Fla. Stat. Ann., 573.857 et seq.

**Tobacco Master Settlement Agreement Act**
Ida. Code 1947, 39-7801 et seq.

**Tobacco or Cigarette Products License Act**
Vt. Stat. Ann., Title 32, § 7731 et seq.

**Tobacco Products Act**
N.M. Stat. Ann., 30-49-1 et seq.

**Tobacco Products Act (Prevention of Access by Children)**
Fla. Laws 1992, Ch. 285

**Tobacco Products Act (Smokeless)**
N.M. Stat. Ann., 30-48-1 et seq.

**Tobacco Products Tax Act**
Ark. Stat. 1947, 84-4212 et seq.
Ida. Code 1947, 63-2551 et seq.
Ill. Comp. Stat. 1992, Ch. 35, § 142/1-1 et seq.
Ill. Rev. Stat. 1977, Ch. 120, § 453.81 et seq.
Mich. Comp. Laws Ann., 205.421 et seq.
N.C. Gen. Stat. 1943, § 105-113.2 et seq.
N.D. Cent. Code, 57-36-01 et seq.
Neb. Rev. Stat. 1943, 77-4001 et seq.
N.M. Stat. Ann., 7-12A-1 et seq.
Okla. Stat. Ann., Title 68, § 401 et seq.
Ore. Rev. Stat., 323.500 et seq.
Tex. Tax Code, § 155.021 et seq.
Vt. Stat. Ann., Title 32, § 7811 et seq.

**Tobacco Products Tax Act of 1977**
Ark. Code Ann. 1987, 26-57-201 et seq.

**Tobacco Sale to Minors Act**
Ill. Rev. Stat. 1991, Ch. 23, § 2356.9 et seq.

**Tobacco Sales to Minors Act**
Colo. Rev. Stat., 24-35-501 et seq.

**Tobacco Stamp Tax Act**
Okla. Stat. Ann., Title 68, § 401 et seq.

**Tobacco Statistics Act**
April 30, 1912, Ch. 102, 37 Stat. 106

**Tobacco Tax Act**
Ala. Code 1975, § 40-25-1 et seq.
Alaska Stat. 1962, § 43.50.010 et seq.
Ga. Code Ann., 48-11-1 et seq.
Haw. Rev. Stat. Ann., § 245-1 et seq.
La. Rev. Stat. Ann., 47:841 et seq.
Md. Ann. Code 1974, Art. TP, § 9-212
Miss. Code Ann. 1972, § 27-69-1 et seq.
N.H. Rev. Stat. 1955, 78:1 et seq.
N.M. Stat. Ann. 1953, 7-12-1 et seq.
Tenn. Code Ann., 67-4-1001 et seq.

**Tobacco Use by Minors Act**
Tex. Health and Safety Code, § 161.251 et seq.

**Tobacco-Use Prevention Act (Adolescent)**
N.Y. Public Health Law 1953 (Consol. Laws Ch. 45) § 1399aa nt.

**Tobacco Warehouse Law**
Ky. Rev. Stat. 1971, 248.280 et seq.

**Toccoa-Stephens County Airport Authority Act**
Ga. Laws 1961, p. 2423

**TOD Security Registration Act**
See Uniform TOD Security Registration Act

**Todd Act (Franklin County Road and Bridge Repair)**
Ala. General Acts 1951, p. 378, No. 143

**Todd Act (Nurses' Registration)**
N.Y. Education Law 1947 (Consol. Laws Ch. 16) § 6901 et seq.

**Todd Act (Penalties)**
N.Y. Alcoholic Beverage Control Law (Consol. Laws Ch. 3B) § 130

**Todd-Desmond Act (Marriage Licenses)**
N.Y. Domestic Relations Law (Consol. Laws Ch. 14) § 13 et seq.

**Toddler and Infant Early Intervention Act**
Miss. Code Ann. 1972, § 41-87-1 et seq.

**Toddlers and Infants with Disabilities Act**
S.C. Code Ann. 1976, § 44-7-2510 et seq.

**Toddlers and Infants with Handicapping Conditions Act**
S.C. Code Ann. 1976, § 44-7-2510 et seq.

**Tohono O'Oodham Tat Momolikot Dam Settlement Act**
Oct. 14, 1986, P.L. 99-469, 100 Stat. 1195

**Tokyo Exposition Act**
May 22, 1908, Ch. 185, 35 Stat. 183

**Tolerance Law (Zero)**
Ore. Rev. Stat., 813.300 et seq.

**Toleration Act (Religious Societies)**
N.H. Laws 1819, Ch. 76, § 3

**Toll Act (Westchester County)**
N.Y. Public Authorities Law (Consol. Laws Ch. 43A) § 404, Subd. 9

**Toll Bridge Acquisition Act**
Ida. Laws 1939, Ch. 223

**Toll Bridge Act**
Ill. Rev. Stat. 1991, Ch. 137, § 0.01 et seq.
Ind. Code. Ann., 8-16-2-1 et seq.
Ky. Rev. Stat. 1971, 180.010 et seq.
Wash. Rev. Code Ann., 47.56.010 et seq.
W. Va. Code 1966, § 17-17-1 et seq.

**Toll Bridge Authority Act**
Cal. Streets and Highways Code § 30000 et seq.
Mont. Rev. Code 1947, 32-1901 et seq.
Wash. Rev. Code Ann., 47.56.010 et seq.

**Toll Bridge Corporations Act**
Okla. Stat. Ann., Title 18, § 191 et seq.

**Toll Highway Act**
Ill. Rev. Stat. 1991, Ch. 121, § 100-1 et seq.
N.J. Stat. Ann., 27:12B-14

**Toll Highway Commission Act**
Ill. Rev. Stat. 1987, Ch. 121, § 314a.26 et seq.

**Toll Logging Roads Law**
Wash. Rev. Code Ann., 76.24.010 et seq.

**Toll Mills Law**
Neb. Rev. Stat. 1943, 56-201 et seq.

**Toll Road Act**
Colo. Rev. Stat., 43-3-301 et seq.
Ky. Rev. Stat. 1971, 177.390 et seq.
Mo. Rev. Stat. 1959, 225.010 et seq.
Wash. Laws 1955, Ch. 268

**Toll Road and Turnpike Organization, Extension, and Conversion Act**
Pa. Purdon's Stat., Title 36, § 651.1 et seq.

**Toll Road, Bridge and Tunnel Authority Act**
Ala. Code 1975, § 23-2-140 et seq.

**Toll Road Commission Act**
Ind. Code. Ann., 8-15-2-1 et seq.

**Toll Roads and Turnpikes Act**
Kan. Stat. Ann., 68-2001 et seq.

**Tolling Act (Statute of Limitations)**
Cal. Code of Civil Procedure § 351
Fla. Stat. Ann., 95.051
Kan. Stat. Ann., 60-517
Mass. Gen. Laws Ann., 260:12
Mich. Comp. Laws Ann., 600.5856
N.C. Gen. Stat. 1943, § 1-21
Okla. Stat. Ann., Title 12, § 98
Ore. Rev. Stat., 12.150
W. Va. Code 1966, § 55-2-17

**Tolling Act (Wrongful Death)**
Mo. Rev. Stat., 537.100

**Tollway Authority Act**
Ark. Code Ann. 1987, 14-303-101 et seq.
Ga. Code Ann., 32-10-60 et seq.
Tenn. Code Ann., 54-15-101 et seq.

**Tollway Authority Act (Regional)**
Tex. Transportation Code, § 366.001 et seq.

**Toltec and Cumbres Scenic Railroad Act**
N.M. Stat. Ann., 16-5-1 et seq.

**Toltec and Cumbres Scenic Railroad Compact Act**
Colo. Rev. Stat., 24-60-1701, 24-60-1702

**Tom Bane Civil Rights Act**
Cal. Civil Code § 51
Cal. Statutes 1991, Ch. 1277

**Tom Beville Act (Obstructing Justice)**
Ala. Code 1975, §§ 13A-10-2, 13A-10-123, 13A-10-127e
Cal. Labor Code § 7950 et seq.

**Tom Carrell Memorial Tunnel and Mine Safety Act**
Cal. Labor Code § 7950 et seq.

**Tomato Standardization and Inspection Act**
Tex. Agriculture Code, § 92.001 et seq.

**Tombigbee Valley Development Authority Act**
Ala. Code 1975, § 33-17-1 et seq.

**Tomlin-Van Eenenaam-Watson Act (State Bridge Commission)**
Mich. Comp. Laws Ann., 254.151 et seq.

**Ton Mile Tax Act**
Colo. Rev. Stat., 42-3-123
Wis. Laws 1989, 341.25 et seq.

**Tonapah Charter**
Nev. Statutes 1903, Ch. 89, p. 163

**Tonawanda City Court Act**
N.Y. Laws 1942, Ch. 906

**Tongass Timber Reform Act**
Nov. 28, 1990, P.L. 101-626, 16 U.S. Code §§ 539d nt., 539e nt.

**Tonnage Measurement Simplification Act**
Dec. 24, 1980, P.L. 96-594, 46 U.S. Code § 71 nt.

**Tontine Company Act**
Mich. Comp. Laws 1948, 494.1 et seq.

**Tool Act (Burglary Tools)**
N.C. Gen. Stat. 1943, § 14-55

**Tool and Die Lien Act**
Ill. Rev. Stat. 1991, Ch. 82, § 350 et seq.

**Tool Equipment Act (Railroad Cars)**
Mich. Comp. Laws Ann., 469.141 et seq.

**Topographic Mapping Act**
Cal. Public Resources Code § 8831 et seq.

**Torrens Act (Instruments Creating Liens)**
Ill. Rev. Stat. 1991, Ch. 30, § 103 et seq.

**Torrens Act (Land Title Registration)**
Cal. Statutes 1915, p. 1932
Colo. Rev. Stat., 38-36-101 et seq.
Ga. Code Ann., 44-2-40 et seq.
Haw. Rev. Stat. Ann., § 501-1 et seq.

Ill. Rev. Stat. 1991, Ch. 30, § 44h et seq.
Mass. Gen. Laws Ann., 185:1 et seq.
Minn. Stat. Ann., 508.01 et seq.
N.C. Gen. Stat. 1943, § 43-1 et seq.
Neb. Laws 1915, Ch. 225
N.Y. Real Property Law (Consol. Laws Ch. 50) § 370 et seq.
Ohio Rev. Code 1953, 5309.01 et seq.
Ore. Rev. Stat. 1953, 94.005 et seq.
Tenn. Public Acts 1917, Ch. 63
Utah Laws 1917, Ch. 28
Va. Code 1950, § 55-112
Wash. Rev. Code 1976, 65.12.005 et seq.

**Torrens Act (Mechanics' Lien-Notice of Claim)**
Ill. Rev. Stat. 1991, Ch. 82, § 24

**Torrens Act (Registered Titles)**
Ill. Rev. Stat. 1991, Ch. 30, § 44h et seq.

**Torrens Repeal Law**
Ill. Rev. Stat. 1991, Ch. 30, § 1201 et seq.

**Torres-Felando Long Term Care Reform Act**
Cal. Statutes 1982, Ch. 1453

**Tort Actions General Survival Act**
D.C. Code Ann., § 12-101

**Tort Claims Act**
Alaska Stat. 1962, § 09.50.250 et seq.
Cal. Government Code § 900 et seq.
Del. Code of 1974, Title 10, § 4001 et seq.
Ga. Official Code Ann., 50-21-20 et seq.
Ida. Code 1947, 6-901 et seq.
Ind. Code. Ann., 34-4-16.5-1 et seq.
Iowa Code Ann., 25A.1 et seq.
Kan. Stat. Ann., 75-6101 et seq.
Md. Ann. Code 1974, Art. SG, § 12-101 et seq.
Md. Code 1974, CJ, § 5-401 et seq.
Me. Rev. Stat. Ann. 1964, Title 14, § 8101 et seq.
Mont. Code Ann., 2-9-301 et seq.
N.J. Stat. Ann., 59:1-1 et seq.
N.M. Stat. Ann., 41-4-1 et seq.
N.Y. Laws 1939, Ch. 860, § 8 et seq.
Okla. Stat. Ann. Title 51, § 151 et seq.
Ore. Rev. Stat., 30.260 et seq.
S.C. Code Ann. 1976, § 15-78-10 et seq.
Tex. Civil Practice and Remedies Code, 101.001 et seq.
Va. Code 1950, § 8.01-195.1 et seq.

**Tort Claims Act (Municipal)**
Iowa Code Ann., 613A.1 et seq.

**Tort Claims Act (Political Subdivisions)**
See Political Subdivision Tort Claims Act

**Tort Claims Act (State)**
N.C. Gen. Stat. 1943, § 143-291 et seq.
Neb. Rev. Stat. 1943, 81-8209 et seq.

**Tort Claims and Comprehensive State Insurance Plan Act**
Mont. Rev. Code Ann. 1947, 82-4301 et seq.

**Tort Counterclaim Act**
Miss. Code Ann. 1972, § 11-7-69

**Tort-Feasors Act (Joint)**
Md. Ann. Code 1957, Art. 50, § 16 et seq.

**Tort Immunity Act (Local Governmental and Governmental Employees)**
Ill. Rev. Stat. 1991, Ch. 85, § 1-101 et seq.

**Tort Liability Act (Government)**
Okla. Stat. Ann., Title 51, § 151 et seq.
Ore. Rev. Stat., 30.260 et seq.
Tenn. Code Ann., 29-20-101 et seq.

**Tort Liability Act (Municipalities)**
Minn. Stat. Ann., 466.01 et seq.

**Tort Liability Act (Parents)**
Mont. Code Ann., 40-6-237, 40-6-238
R.I. Gen. Laws 1956, 9-1-3, 9-1-3.1

**Tort Liability Act (Public Agencies)**
Cal. Government Code § 800 et seq.

**Tort Liability Act (Schools)**
Ill. Rev. Stat. 1991, Ch. 122, § 821 et seq.

**Tort Liability Act (State)**
Haw. Rev. Stat. Ann., § 662-1 et seq.

**Tort Liability of Schools Act**
Ill. Rev. Stat. 1991, Ch. 122, § 820 et seq.

**Tort Reform Act**
Ga. Code Ann., 51-1-20, 51-12-1, 51-12-5 to 51-12-6, 51-12-12, 51-12-31 to 51-12-33
Minn. Stat. Ann., 60A.06 et seq.
Mo. Rev. Stat., 408.040, 490.715, 509.050, 510.263, 537.067, 537.068, 537.117, 537.760 et seq., 538.300
Wash. Rev. Code Ann., 4.16.160, 4.16.300, 4.16.310, 4.24.005, 4.24.264, 4.24.420, 4.56.250, 4.56.260, 5.40.050, 5.40.060, 5.60.060, 7.70.090, 48.19.450, 48.22.050, 51.24.060

**Tort Reform and Insurance Act**
Fla. Laws 1977, Ch. 468
Fla. Stat. Ann., 57.105, 458.320, 459.0085, 624.460 et seq., 768.13

**Tortfeasor Contribution Act (Joint)**
Ariz. Rev. Stat. Ann., § 12-2501 et seq.
Ark. Code Ann. 1987, 16-61-201 et seq.
Ill. Rev. Stat. 1991, Ch. 70, § 300 et seq.
R.I. Gen. Laws 1956, 10-6-1 et seq.

**Tortfeasors Act (Uniform Contribution)**
Del. Code of 1974, Title 10, § 6301 et seq.

**Tortfeasors Contribution Act**
See also Uniform Contribution Among Tortfeasors Act
Alaska Stat. 1962, § 09.16.010 et seq.
Ark. Code Ann. 1987, 16-61-201 et seq.
Cal. Code of Civil Procedure §§ 588 et seq., 875
Colo. Rev. Stat. 13-50.5-101 et seq.
Ga. Code Ann., 51-12-32
Haw. Rev. Stat. § 663-11 et seq.
Ky. Rev. Stat. 1971, 412.030
Mich. Comp. Laws Ann., 600.2925a et seq.
Miss. Code Ann. 1972, § 85-5-5
Mo. Rev. Stat., 537.060
N.C. Gen. Stat. 1943, § 1B-1 et seq.
N.D. Cent. Code, 32-38-01
Nev. Rev. Stat. 1979 Reprint, 17.225 et seq.
N.J. Stat. Ann., 2A:53A-1 et seq.
N.M. Stat. Ann., 41-3-8
Pa. Cons. Stat. Title 42, § 8321 et seq.
R.I. Gen. Laws 1956, 10-6-1 et seq.
Tenn. Code Ann., 29-11-101
Tex. Civil Practice and Remedies Code, § 32.001 et seq.
Wyo. Stat. Ann., § 1-1-110 et seq.

**Torts Act**
La. Civil Code, Art. 2315 et seq.
Mo. Rev. Stat., 537.010 et seq.

**Torture Victim Protection Act of 1991**
March 12, 1992, P.L. 102-256, 28 U.S. Code § 1350 nt.

**Torture Victims Relief Act of 1998**
Oct. 30, 1998, P.L. 105-320, 112 Stat. 3016, 22 U.S. Code § 2152 nt.

**Total Compensation Act (Public Employees Retirement System)**
Cal. Statutes 1974, Ch. 374

**Total Quality Government Act (Legislative Commission)**
Ala. Code 1975, § 41-9-940 et seq.

**Totten Trusts Act**
N.Y. Estates, Powers and Trusts Law (Consol. Laws Ch. 17B) § 7-5.1 et seq.

**Tourism and Convention Facility Promotion Tax Act**
Mich. Comp. Laws Ann., 436.141 et seq.

**Tourism and Convention Marketing Act**
Mich. Comp. Laws Ann., 141.881 et seq.
Okla. Stat. Ann., Title 74, § 1801 et seq.

**Tourism and Recreation Act**
Okla. Stat. Ann., Title 74, § 1801 et seq.

**Tourism Authority Act**
Va. Code 1950, § 2.1-548.53 et seq.

**Tourism, Conventions and Other Special Events Promotion Act**
Ill. Rev. Stat. 1991, Ch. 24, § 8-3-13

**Tourism Department Act**
N.M. Stat. Ann., 9-15A-1 et seq.

**Tourism Department and Economic Development Act**
N.M. Stat. Ann., 9-15-1 et seq.

**Tourism Development Act**
Ark. Code Ann. 1987, 15-11-501 et seq.

**Tourism Improvement and Development District Act**
N.J. Stat. Ann., 40:540-1 et seq.

**Tourism Infrastructure Admissions Tax Act**
S.C. Code Ann. 1976, §§ 12-21-6510 to 12-21-6580

**Tourism Marketing Act (Regional)**
Mich. Comp. Laws Ann., 141.891 et seq.

**Tourism, Melting, Sports Facility and Convention Act (State and Local Government)**
Mo. Rev. Stat. 1978, 70.840 et seq.

**Tourism or Convention Marketing Act (Community)**
Mich. Comp. Laws Ann., 141.871 et seq.

**Tourism Policy Act**
Cal. Government Code § 15364.50 et seq.
Mich. Comp. Laws Ann., 2.101

**Tourism Policy and Export Promotion Act of 1992**
Sept. 30, 1992, P.L. 102-372, 22 U.S. Code §§ 2121 nt., 2122 nt., 2124 nt., 2124c
Oct. 11, 1996, P.L. 104-288, 22 U.S. Code § 2124c

**Tourism Promotion Act**
Okla. Stat. Ann., Title 68, § 50010 et seq.

**Tourism Promotion District Act**
La. Rev. Stat. Ann., 51:1281 et seq.

**Tourism, Sports and Entertainment Special District Act (Multi-Jurisdictional)**
Fla. Laws 1994, Ch. 338

**Tourist Camps Act**
Colo. Rev. Stat., 43-5-201 et seq.
Ind. Burns' 1933, 35-2801 et seq.
Minn. Stat. Ann., 450.19

**Tourist Court Act**
Ga. Code Ann., 31-28-1 et seq.

**Tourist Development Company Act**
P.R. Laws Ann. 1954, Title 23, § 671 et seq.

**Tourist Development Local Option Act**
Fla. Stat. Ann., 125.0104

**Tourist Incentives Act**
P.R. Laws Ann. 1954, Title 23 § 693 et seq.

**Tourist Information Act**
Vt. Stat. Ann., Title 10, § 481 et seq.

**Tourist Meeting and Entertainment Facilities Assistance Act**
Ark. Code Ann. 1987, 14-171-201 et seq.

**Tourist Promotion Act**
N.Y. Laws 1974, Ch. 457
Pa. Purdon's Stat., Title 73, § 401 et seq.

**Tourist Service Training Act**
N.M. Stat. Ann., 21-20-1 et seq.

**Tow Truck Act (Professional)**
Mont. Code Ann., 61-8-901 et seq.

**Tow Truck and Impound Regulation Act**
Utah Code Ann. 1953, 41-6-187 et seq.

**Towing Act**
Mass. Gen. Laws Ann., 40:22D

**Towing and Storage Act**
La. Rev. Stat. Ann., 32:1711 et seq.

**Towline Brooks Drainage and Flood Control Act**
Mass. Acts 1955, Ch. 574

**Town Act**
N.J. Stat. Ann., 40:123-1 et seq.
N.Y. Consol. Laws, Ch. 62
Wash. Rev. Code Ann., 35.27.010 et seq.

**Town Act (Suburbs)**
N.Y. Town Law (Consol. Laws Ch. 62) § 50 et seq.

**Town and City Development Act**
Conn. Gen. Stat. Ann., § 7-480 et seq.

**Town and City Street Alley and Other Public Improvements Act**
Ind. Code 1976, 19-8-16-1 et seq.

**Town and Country Planning Act**
Mass. Gen. Laws Ann., 41:81D

**Town and Village Free Library Act**
Cal. Education Code 1976, § 19600 et seq.

**Town-Boylan Act (Drugs)**
N.Y. Laws 1914, Ch. 363

**Town Claims Act**
Wash. Rev. Code Ann., 35.31.040 et seq.

**Town Depositaries Act**
Wash. Rev. Code Ann., 35.38.010 et seq.

**Town Funds Transfer Act (Surplus)**
Ill. Rev. Stat. 1991, Ch. 139, § 163.9 et seq.

**Town Government Act**
Ind. Code 1976, 18-3-1-1 et seq.

**Town Government Law (Unincorporated)**
Nev. Rev. Stat. 1979 Reprint, 269.500 et seq.

**Town Hall Act**
Ill. Rev. Stat. 1991, Ch. 139, § 149.9 et seq.

**Town Hall Building Loan Act (Conway)**
Mass. Acts 1950, Ch. 722

**Town Hall Purchase Act**
Ill. Rev. Stat. 1991, Ch. 139, § 143.990 et seq.

**Town Health Board Act**
Wash. Rev. Code Ann., 70.05.005 et seq.

**Town Hospital Act**
Ill. Rev. Stat. 1991, Ch. 139, § 160.5h et seq.

**Town Incorporation Act**
Wyo. Stat. Ann. § 15-1-201 et seq.

**Town Incorporation Validation Act**
Ill. Rev. Stat. 1991, Ch. 24, § 808d.12h et seq.

**Town Libraries Act**
N.H. Rev. Stat. 1955, 202-A:1 et seq.

**Town Local Improvements Act**
Wash. Rev. Code Ann., 35.43.010 et seq.

**Town Manager Act**
Vt. Stat. Ann., Title 24, § 1231 et seq.

**Town Meeting Act**
Mass. Gen. Laws Ann., 43A:1 et seq.
Okla. Stat. Ann., Title 11, § 16-301 et seq.

**Town Meeting Act (Falmouth)**
Mass. Acts 1935, Ch. 349

**Town Mutual Act**
Wis. Stat. Ann., 612.01 et seq.

**Town of Brookhaven Resource Recovery Agency Act**
N.Y. Public Authorities Law (Consol. Laws Ch. 43A) § 2051e et seq.

**Town of Clifton Park Water Authority Act**
N.Y. Public Authorities Law (Consol. Laws Ch. 43A) § 1120 et seq.

**Town of Gordonsville Charter**
Va. Acts 1975, Ch. 346

**Town of North Hempstead Solid Waste Management Authority Act**
N.Y. Laws 1984, Ch. 638
N.Y. Public Authorities Law (Consol. Laws Ch. 43A) § 2049a et seq.

**Town of Tyrone Public Facilities Authority Act**
Ga. Laws 1979, p. 3938

**Town of Wilton Water and Sewer Authority Act**
N.Y. Public Authorities Law (Consol. Laws Ch. 43A) § 1121 et seq.

**Town Offices Project Loan Act (Abington)**
Mass. Acts 1957, Ch. 237

**Town Planning Commission Act**
Wash. Rev. Code Ann., 35.63.010 et seq.

**Town Plat Act**
Mo. Rev. Stat., 445.010 et seq.

**Town Roads Act**
Minn. Stat. Ann., 164.01 et seq.

**Town Sewerage System Act**
Wash. Rev. Code Ann., 35.67.010 et seq.

**Town Sidewalks Law**
Wash. Rev. Code Ann., 35.68.010 et seq.

**Town Site Act**
Alaska Comp. Laws Ann. 1949, § 47-2-31 et seq.
Colo. Rev. Stat. Replaced Vols., 31-1-501- et seq.

**Town Unit School Law**
N.Y. Laws 1917, Ch. 328

**Town Zoning Act**
N.Y. Town Law (Consol. Laws Ch. 62) § 261 et seq.

**Towner-Sheppard Act (Maternity Hygiene)**
See Maternity Act

**Townhouse Ownership Act**
Kan. Stat. Ann., 58-3701 et seq.

**Towns and Cities Act**
Colo. Rev. Stat., 31-1-101 et seq.
Ind. Code. Ann., 36-3-1-1 et seq.
Wash. Rev. Code Ann., 35.01.010 et seq.

**Towns and Cities Incorporation Act**
Ind. Code 1976, 18-1-1-1 et seq.

**Towns County Mountain Fair Authority Act**
Ga. Laws 1980, p. 3134

**Towns County Water and Sewerage Authority Act**
Ga. Laws 1972, p. 3407

**Townscape Preservation Act**
Vt. Stat. Ann. Title 24, § 4407

**Townsend Curative Act (Recorded Instruments)**
Tex. Rules of Criminal Evidence, Rules 201, 901

**Townsend-Wedworth Paramedic Act**
Cal. Health and Safety Code § 1480 et seq.

**Township Act**
Ill. Rev. Stat. 1991, Ch. 139, § 0.1 et seq.
Mich. Comp. Laws Ann., 41.1 et seq.
N.J. Rev. Stat. 40A:61-1, 40A:62-1, 40A:63-1 et seq.
Ohio Rev. Code 1953, 501.01 et seq.
Pa. Purdon's. Stat., Title 53, § 54101 et seq.
Wash. Rev. Code Ann., 45.04.010 et seq.

**Township Act (First Class)**
Pa. Purdon's Stat., Title 53, § 55101 et seq.

**Township Act (Second Class)**
Pa. Purdon's Stat., Title 53, § 65101 et seq.

**Township Advisory Board Act**
Ind. Code. Ann., 17-4-28-1 et seq.

**Township and Village Public Improvements Act**
Mich. Comp. Laws Ann., 41.411 et seq.

**Township Annexation Act**
Ill. Rev. Stat. 1991, Ch. 139, § 126.90 et seq.

**Township Artesian Well Law**
S.D. Code 1939, 61.0701 et seq.

**Township Bond Money Refund Act**
Ill. Rev. Stat. 1991, Ch. 139, § 160.90 et seq.

**Township Building Code**
Mich. Comp. Laws Ann., 125.351 et seq.

**Township Charter Act**
Mich. Comp. Laws Ann., 42.1 et seq.

**Township Claims Act**
Wash. Rev. Code Ann., 45.52.010 et seq.

**Township Code**
Ill. Comp. Stat. 1992, Ch. 60, § 1/1-1 et seq.

**Township Code (First Class)**
Pa. Purdon's Stat., Title 53, § 55101 et seq.

**Township Code (Second Class)**
Pa. Purdon's Stat., Title 53, § 65101 et seq.

**Township Comfort Station Act**
Ill. Rev. Stat. 1991, Ch. 139, § 160d.9 et seq.

**Township Community Building Act**
Ill. Rev. Stat. 1991, Ch. 139, § 151.9 et seq.

**Township Consolidation Act**
Ill. Rev. Stat. 1991, Ch. 139, § 140m et seq.

**Township Emergency Equipment Act**
Ill. Rev. Stat. 1991, Ch. 139, § 350 et seq.

**Township Fire Protection Act**
Mich. Comp. Laws Ann., 41.801 et seq.

**Township Funds for Guidance Centers Act**
Ill. Rev. Stat. 1991, Ch. 139, § 167.20 et seq.

**Township Funds for Historical Societies Act**
Ill. Rev. Stat. 1991, Ch. 139, § 167.30 et seq.

**Township Funds for Schools Act**
Ill. Rev. Stat. 1991, Ch. 139, § 167.3m et seq.

**Township High School Act**
Ill. Rev. Stat. 1949, Ch. 122, § 10-1 et seq.

**Township Highway Act**
Mich. Comp. Laws Ann., 247.651 et seq.

**Township Hospital Leasing Act**
Ill. Rev. Stat. 1991, Ch. 139, § 160.28 et seq.

**Township Improvement Act**
Mich. Comp. Laws Ann., 41.411 et seq.

**Township Library Bond Act**
Ill. Rev. Stat. 1991, Ch. 81, § 45.9 et seq.

**Township Library Bond Validation Act (1963)**
Ill. Rev. Stat. 1991, Ch. 81, §§ 16.1h, 16.2

**Township Library Bond Validation Act (1969)**
Ill. Rev. Stat. 1991, Ch. 81, §§ 16.2h, 16.3

**Township License Law (Amusements)**
Iowa Code 1954, 361.1 et seq.

**Township Monument Act**
Ill. Rev. Stat. 1991, Ch. 139, §§ 150.9, 151

**Township Non-Sectarian Hospital Act**
Ill. Rev. Stat. 1991, Ch. 139, § 160.01 et seq.

**Township Official Bond Approval Act**
Ill. Rev. Stat. 1991, Ch. 103, §§ 16.9, 17

**Township Open Space Act**
Ill. Rev. Stat. 1991, Ch. 139, § 321 et seq.

**Township Organization Act**
Ill. Rev. Stat. 1991, Ch. 139, § 0.1 et seq.
Mo. Rev. Stat., 65.010 et seq.
Neb. Rev. Stat. 1943, 23-201 et seq.

**Township Park Bond Act**
Ill. Rev. Stat. 1991, Ch. 105, § 224.9 et seq.

**Township Park Land Acquisition Act**
Ill. Rev. Stat. 1991, Ch. 105, § 318.90 et seq.

**Township Planning Act**
Mich. Comp. Laws Ann., 125.321 et seq.

**Township Planning and Zoning Act**
Ind. Code. Ann., 36-7-1-1 et seq.

**Township Purchasing Act**
Ill. Rev. Stat. 1991, Ch. 139, § 190 et seq.

**Township Reform Act**
Ind. Code. Ann., 36-6-6-1 et seq.

**Township Refunding Bond Act**
Ill. Rev. Stat. 1991, Ch. 139, § 173.9 et seq.

**Township Refuse Collection and Disposal Act**
Ill. Rev. Stat. 1991, Ch. 139, § 331 et seq.

**Township Road Fund Transfer Act**
Ill. Rev. Stat. 1991, Ch. 139, § 167.01 et seq.

**Township Rural Zoning Act**
Mich. Comp. Laws Ann., 125.271 et seq.

**Township-Service Areas Act**
N.J. Stat. Ann., 40:156A-1 et seq.

**Township Trustees Salary Act**
Ind. Code 1976, 17-4-1-1 et seq.

**Township Trustees: Authority to Perform Nortarial Acts**
Ind. Code. Ann., 33-16-8-1 et seq.

**Township Water System Act**
Mich. Comp. Laws Ann., 486.501 et seq.

**Township Waterworks Act**
Ill. Rev. Stat. 1991, Ch. 139, § 160.30h et seq.

**Township Zoning Act**
Ill. Rev. Stat. 1991, Ch. 139, § 301 et seq.

**Township Zoning Enabling Act**
Ohio Rev. Code 1953, 519.01 et seq.

**Townships within Cities Act**
Ill. Rev. Stat. 1991, Ch. 139, § 133m et seq.

**Townsite Act**
Utah Code Ann. 1953, 57-7-1 et seq.

**Townsite Acts**
May 23, 1844, Ch. 17, 5 Stat. 657
March 3, 1863, Ch. 80, 12 Stat. 754
July 1, 1864, Ch. 205, 13 Stat. 343
March 3, 1865, Ch. 107, 13 Stat. 529
March 2, 1867, Ch. 177, 14 Stat. 541
June 8, 1868, Ch. 55, 15 Stat. 67
July 1, 1870, Ch. 193, 16 Stat. 183

**Toxic "Hot Spots" Information and Assessment Act of 1991 (Air)**
Cal. Health and Safety Code §§ 44300 to 44304, 44; to 44309, 44320 et seq., 44340 et seq., 44360 et seq., 44380 et seq.
Tex. Health and Safety Code, § 370.001 et seq.

**Toxic and Hazardous Materials Emergency Notification Act**
Ark. Acts 1991, No. 917

**Toxic Art. Supplies in Schools Act**
Ill. Rev. Stat. 1991, Ch. 122, § 1601 et seq.

**Toxic Art. Supplies Labeling Act**
Tenn. Code Ann., 68-131-301 et seq.

**Toxic Catastrophe Prevention Act**
N.J. Stat. Ann., 131K-19 et seq.

**Toxic Chemical Release Reporting Act**
Tex. Health and Safety Code, § 370.001 et seq.

**Toxic Household Cleaners Act**
N.C. Gen. Stat. 1943, § 66-85 et seq.

**Toxic Injection Well Control Act**
Cal. Health and Safety Code § 25159.10 et seq.

**Toxic Packaging Reduction Act**
R.I. Gen. Laws 1956, 23-18.13-1 et seq.

**Toxic Pits Cleanup Act**
Cal. Health and Safety Code § 25208 et seq.

**Toxic Pollution Prevention Act**
Ill. Rev. Stat. 1991, Ch. 111 1/2, § 7951 et seq.
Minn. Stat. Ann., 115D.01 et seq.

**Toxic Substance Control Commission Act**
Mich. Comp. Laws Ann., 286.181 et seq.

**Toxic Substances Act**
Mass. Gen. Laws Ann., 111F:1 et seq.
N.Y. Labor Law (Consol. Laws Ch. 31) § 875 et seq.

**Toxic Substances Control Act**
Oct. 11, 1976, P.L. 94-469, 15 U.S. Code § 2601 et seq.
Nov. 8, 1984, P.L. 98-260, 15 U.S. Code § 2622 Oct. 22, 1986, P.L. 99-519, 15 U.S. Code §§ prec. 2601, 2601 to 2629, 2641 to 2654
July 18, 1988, P.L. 100-368, 15 U.S. Code §§ 2645, 2646, 2647, 2655
*Continued*

Aug. 23, 1988, P.L. 100-418, 15 U.S. Code §§ 2602, 2612 Oct. 28, 1988, P.L. 100-551, 15 U.S. Code §§ prec. 2661, 2661 et seq.
Nov. 5, 1990, P.L. 101-508, 15 U.S. Code § 2665
Nov. 28, 1990, P.L. 101-637, 15 U.S. Code §§ 2643, 2646, 2646 nt., 2647, 2656, 2656 nt.
Oct. 28, 1992, P.L. 102-550, 15 U.S. Code §§ 2606, 2610, 2612, 2615, 2616, 2618, 2619, prec. §§ 2681, 2681 to 2692
Oct. 20, 1994, P.L. 103-382, 15 U.S. Code §§ 2642, 2662
Dec. 21, 1995, P.L. 104-66, 15 U.S. Code §§ 2626, 2665

**Toxic Substances Disclosure Act**
Ill. Rev. Stat. 1985, Ch. 48, § 2501 et seq.

**Toxic Substances Disclosure to Employees Act**
Ill. Rev. Stat. 1991, Ch. 48, § 1401 et seq.

**Toxic Substances Information Act**
Va. Code 1950, § 32.1-239 et seq.

**Toxic Torts Act (Limitations)**
N.Y. Civil Practice Laws and Rules (Consol. Laws Ch. 8) § 214c

**Toxic Vapors Act**
N.C. Gen. Stat. 1943, § 90-113.8A et seq.

**Toxicological Laboratory Service Act**
Ill. Rev. Stat. 1991, Ch. 111 1/2, §§ 200.9, 201

**Toxics Enforcement and Training Act (Local)**
Cal. Penal Code § 14300 et seq.

**Toxics Use Reduction Act**
Mass. Gen. Laws Ann., 21I:1 et seq.

**Toxics Use Reduction and Hazardous Waste Reduction Act**
Ore. Rev. Stat., 465.003 et seq.

**Toy Safety Act of 1984**
Oct. 17, 1984, P.L. 98-491, 14 U.S. Code § 1261

**Track Buyers Act**
Ida. Code 1947, 22-1401 et seq.

**Tracking and Permitting Act (Radioactive Waste)**
Ill. Comp. Stat. 1992, Ch. 420, § 37/1

**Traction Act (Street Railways)**
N.J. Stat. Ann., 48:15-1 et seq.

**Tractor Act**
Neb. Rev. Stat. 1943, 2-2701 et seq.

**Tractor Code**
Pa. 1929 Pamph. Laws 1005, No. 404

**Tractor Gas Act**
Ala. Code 1975, § 40-17-100 et seq.

**Tractor, Lawn and Garden, and Light Industrial Equipment Franchise Act**
Ala. Code 1975, § 8-21A-1 et seq.

**Tractor Warranty Act (Farm)**
Ga. Code Ann., 10-1-810 et seq.

**Tracy-Copps Act (Vocational Rehabilitation)**
Ohio Laws Vol. 109, p. 310

**Trade Act (Monopoly or Restraint of)**
N.Y. General Business Law (Consol. Laws Ch. 20) § 340 et seq.

**Trade Act of 1974**
Jan. 3, 1975, P.L. 93-618, 19 U.S. Code §§ 160, 162 to 164, 170a, 1303 et seq., 1484, 1515n, 1516, 1862, 1863, 1872, 1981, 2101 et seq., 2211 et seq., 2311 et seq., 2411 et seq., 2631, 2632; 26 U.S. Code § 3302; 31 U.S. Code § 665
July 26, 1979, P.L. 96-39, 19 U.S. Code §§ 1315, 2101 nt., 2112, 2119, 2131, 2155, 2192, 2194, 2253, 2411 to 2416, 2432, 2434, 2435, 2462 to 2464, 2481, 2482
Jan. 12, 1983, P.L. 97-456, 19 U.S. Code § 2171
July 18, 1984, P.L. 98-369, 98 Stat. 1172, 19 U.S. Code §§ 2293, 2297, 2298, 2355
Oct. 30, 1984, P.L. 98-573, 19 U.S. Code §§ 2112, 2192, 2253, 2251, 2415, 2461, 2642, 2464, 2465, 2466

June 11, 1985, P.L. 99-47, 19 U.S. Code §§ 2112, 2462, 2463, 2464
Sept. 30, 1985, P.L. 99-107, 19 U.S. Code prec. § 2271, nt.
Nov. 14, 1985, P.L. 99-155, 19 U.S. Code prec. § 2271 nt.
Dec. 13, 1985, P.L. 99-181, 19 U.S. Code prec. § 2271 nt.
Dec. 18, 1985, P.L. 99-189, 19 U.S. Code prec. § 2271 nt.
April 7, 1986, P.L. 99-272, 19 U.S. Code §§ 2171 nt., prec. 2271, 2271, 2272, 2291 to 2293, 2296, 2297, 2311, 2341 to 2344
Oct. 22, 1986, P.L. 99-514, 19 U.S. Code §§ 2112, 2138, 2155, 2171, 2462, 2464
Oct. 27, 1986, P.L. 99-570, 19 U.S. Code §§ 2462, 2491 et seq. Dec. 22, 1987, P.L. 100-204, 19 U.S. Code §§ prec. 2491, 2492
Dec. 22, 1987, P.L. 100-203, 19 U.S. Code § 2171
Aug. 23, 1988, P.L. 100-418, 19 U.S. Code § 2131 et seq.
Nov. 10, 1988, P.L. 100-647, 19 U.S. Code §§ 2131, 2212, 2253, 2254, 2296, 2397 nt.
Nov. 18, 1988, P.L. 100-690, 19 U.S. Code § 2492
Nov. 28, 1989, P.L. 101-179, 19 U.S. Code § 2462
Dec. 7, 1989, P.L. 101-207, 19 U.S. Code § 2171
Aug. 20, 1990, P.L. 101-382, 19 U.S. Code §§ 2075, 2171, 2191- 2194, 2318, 2432, 2435, 2437, 2462, 2463
April 1, 1992, P.L. 102-266, 19 U.S. Code § 2787
July 3, 1992, P.L. 102-318, 19 U.S. Code § 2291
Aug. 10, 1993, P.L. 103-66, 19 U.S. Code §§ prec. 2271 nt., 2296, 2317, 2346, 2462, 2465
Nov. 23, 1993, P.L. 103-149, 19 U.S. Code § 2462
Dec. 8, 1993, P.L. 103-182, 19 U.S. Code §§ 2242, 2252, 2271 et seq., 2317, 2331, 2322, 2395
Dec. 8, 1994, P.L. 103-465, 19 U.S. Code §§ 1303, 2155, 2171, 2191, 2192, 2194, 2242, 2252, 2253, 2254, 2411, 2414, 2416, 2420, 2463, 2465
Dec. 19, 1995, P.L. 104-65, 19 U.S. Code § 2171
Aug. 20, 1996, P.L. 104-188, 19 U.S. Code §§ prec. 2461, 2461- 2467
Oct. 11, 1996, P.L. 104-295, 19 U.S. Code §§ 2171, 2252, 2411, 2414, 2440, 2462
Aug. 5, 1997, P.L. 105-34, 19 U.S. Code § 2465
July 22, 1998, P.L. 105-206, 19 U.S. Code §§ 2432, 2481
Aug. 7, 1998, P.L. 105-220, 19 U.S. Code § 2311
Oct. 21, 1998, P.L. 105-277, 19 U.S. Code §§ 2241, prec. 2271 nt. , 2296, 2311,2317, 2331, 2346, 2465
Nov. 10, 1998, P.L. 105-362, 19 U.S. Code §§ 2136, 2441
June 25, 1999, P.L. 106-36, 19 U.S. Code §§ 2171, 2194, 2293, 2436, 2441, 2463, 2492, 2494, 2495

**Trade Adjustment Assistance Reform and Extension Act of 1986**
April 7, 1986, P.L. 99-272, 19 U.S. Code § 2101 nt.

**Trade Agreements Act**
June 12, 1934, Ch. 474, 48 Stat. 943, 19 U.S. Code §§ 1001, 1201, 1351 to 1354

**Trade Agreements Act of 1979**
July 26, 1979, P.L. 96-39, 5 U.S. Code § 5315, 13 U.S. Code §§ 301, 301 nt., 19 U.S. Code §§ 160 et seq.; 26 U.S. Code §§ 1 nt., 993 et seq.; 28 U.S. Code § 1541 et seq.
June 11, 1985, P.L. 99-47, 19 U.S. Code § 2518
Aug. 23, 1988, P.L. 100-418, 19 U.S. Code §§ 2511, 2515, 2581
Dec. 8, 1993, P.L. 103-182, 19 U.S. Code §§ 2511, 2512, 2518, 2575 et seq.
Dec. 8, 1994, P.L. 103-465, 19 U.S. Code §§ 2512 et seq., 2531, 2532, 2544, 2571, 2573
Oct. 11, 1996, P.L. 104-295, 19 U.S. Code §§ 2514, 2515, 2518, 2532, 2544, 2571, 2578a

**Trade Agreements Extension Act of 1948**
June 26, 1948, Ch. 678, 62 Stat. 1053, 19 U.S. Code § 1351 nt., 1354, 1357, 1357 nt., 1358, 1359

**Trade Agreements Extension Act of 1949**
Sept. 26, 1949, Ch. 585, 63 Stat. 697, 19 U.S. Code §§ 1351, 1351 nt., 1352, 1354

**Trade Agreements Extension Act of 1951**

June 16, 1951, Ch. 141, 65 Stat. 72, 7 U.S. Code § 624; 19 U.S. Code §§ 1352, 1354, 1360, 1360 nt., 1361 to 1367, 1516 nt.

Aug. 7, 1953, Ch. 348, 67 Stat. 472, 19 U.S. Code §§ 1364, 1364 nt..

June 21, 1955, Ch. 169, 69 Stat. 165, 19 U.S. Code §§ 1352a, 1363, 1364

Aug. 20, 1958, P.L. 85-686, 72 Stat. 675, 19 U.S. Code §§ 1360, 1364

**Trade Agreements Extension Act of 1953**

Aug. 7, 1953, Ch. 348, 67 Stat. 472, 7 U.S. Code § 624; 19 U.S. Code §§ 1330, 1351 nt., 1352, 1364, 1366 nt.

**Trade Agreements Extension Act of 1955**

June 21, 1955, Ch. 169, 69 Stat. 162, 19 U.S. Code §§ 1351, 1352, 1352a, 1363, 1364

**Trade Agreements Extension Act of 1958**

Aug. 20, 1958, P.L. 85-686, 72 Stat. 673, 19 U.S. Code §§ 1333, 1335 to 1337, 1351, 1352 nt., 1352a, 1360, 1364

**Trade and Development Enhancement Act of 1983**

Aug. 23, 1988, P.L. 100-418, 12 U.S. Code §§ 635q, 635s

**Trade and Industrial Competitiveness Act (International)**

N.Y. Agriculture and Markets (Consol. Laws. Ch. 69) § 16

N.Y. Laws 1990, Ch. 291

N.Y. Public Authorities Law (Consol. Laws Ch. 43A) §§ 3102, 3102a, 3102d

**Trade and Manufacturing Site Act**

Alaska Comp. Laws Ann. 1949, § 47-2-71

**Trade and Tariff Act of 1984**

Oct. 30, 1984, P.L. 98-573, 19 U.S. Code §§ 1564 nt., 1654 et seq..

June 11, 1985, P.L. 99-47, 19 U.S. Code § 2112 nt.

Dec. 19, 1985, P.L. 99-190, 19 U.S. Code § 58b

April 7, 1986, P.L. 99-272, 19 U.S. Code § 58b

Oct. 22, 1986, P.L. 99-514, 19 U.S. Code §§ 1520, 1564, 1671 nt., 1677f, 2112 nt., 2114, 2463

Aug. 23, 1988, P.L. 100-418, 102 Stat. 1160, 19 U.S. Code §§ 58b, 2112 nt., 2253 nt.

Dec. 7, 1989, P.L. 101-207, 19 U.S. Code §§ 58b, 58c

Oct. 28, 1992, P.L. 102-549, 12 U.S. Code §§ 635q, 635r, 635s

Oct. 21, 1998, P.L. 105-277, 19 U.S. Code § 2114b

**Trade Center Act**

Wash. Rev. Code Ann., 53.29.010 et seq.

**Trade Center Act (Port Districts)**

Wash. Rev. Code. Ann., 53.29.900

**Trade Center Authority Act (International and Marine)**

Ga. Laws 1995, p. 4499

**Trade Center Authority Act (Tift County)**

Ga. Laws 1980, 9. 4520

**Trade Commission Act**

See Federal Trade Commission Act

Mont. Rev. Code 1947, 70-201 et seq.

**Trade Deficit Review Commission Act**

Oct. 21, 1998, P.L. 105-277, sect127, 112 Stat. 2681, 19 U.S. Code § 2213 nt.

**Trade Development Act (Export)**

Miss. Code Ann. 1972, § 57-57-1 et seq.

**Trade Development Act (International)**

Okla. Stat. Ann., Title 2, § 3001 et seq.

**Trade Development Act (World)**

Okla. Stat. Ann., Title 74, § 2050 et seq.

**Trade Dollar Retirement Act**

March 3, 1887, Ch. 396, 24 Stat. 634

**Trade Enhancement Act (International)**

Ore. Rev. Stat., 285.069 et seq.

**Trade Expansion Act of 1962**

Oct. 11, 1962, P.L. 87-794, 76 Stat. 872, 19 U.S. Code prec. § 1202, §§ 1323, 1351, 1352, 1352a nt., 1362 nt., 1364 nt., 1801 to 1806, 1821, 1822, 1831 to 1833, 1841 to 1846, 1861, 1862, 1871 to 1873, 1881 to 1888, 1901, 1902, 1911 to 1920, 1931, 1941 to 1944, 1951, 1952, 1961 to 1963, 1971 to 1978, 1981, 1982, 1991; 26 U.S. Code §§ 172, 6501, 6511

Dec. 16, 1963, P.L. 88-205, 77 Stat. 390, 19 U.S. Code § 1861

July 26, 1979, P.L. 96-39, 19 U.S. Code § 1982

April 2, 1980, P.L. 96-223, 19 U.S. Code § 1862

July 12, 1985, P.L. 99-64, 19 U.S. Code § 1864

Aug. 23, 1988, P.L. 100-418, 102 Stat. 1257, 19 U.S. Code §§ 1862 , 1872, 1964

July 22, 1998, P.L. 105-206, 19 U.S. Code § 1881

**Trade Fair Act of 1959**

April 22, 1959, P.L. 86-14, 73 Stat. 18, 19 U.S. Code §§ 1751 to 1756

**Trade-Mark Act of 1946**

July 5, 1946, Ch. 540, 60 Stat. 427, 15 U.S. Code §§ 1051, 1051 nt., 1052 to 1072, 1091 to 1096, 1111 to 1121, 1123 to 1127. (See 28 U.S. Code § 1254)

Aug. 17, 1950, Ch. 773, 64 Stat. 459, 15 U.S. Code § 1057

July 19, 1952, Ch. 950, 66 Stat. 814, 15 U.S. Code § 1071

Aug. 8, 1958, P.L. 85-609, 72 Stat. 540, 15 U.S. Code §§ 1067, 1070, 1071, 1092, 1113

Oct. 3, 1961, P.L. 87-333, 75 Stat. 748, 15 U.S. Code § 1126

Oct. 9, 1962, P.L. 87-772, 76 Stat. 769, 15 U.S. Code §§ 1051, 1052, 1056, 1057, 1059, 1060, 1062 to 1066, 1071, 1091, 1092, 1111, 1112, 1114, 1115, 1117, 1126, 1127

July 24, 1965, P.L. 89-83, 79 Stat. 260, 15 U.S. Code § 1113

Aug. 8, 1982, P.L. 97-247, 15 U.S. Code §§ 1058, 1061, 1063 to 1066, 1113

Oct. 12, 1982, P.L. 97-296, 15 U.S. Code § 1121a

Nov. 16, 1988, P.L. 100-667, 15 U.S. Code § 1058 nt.

Dec. 10, 1991, P.L. 102-204, 15 U.S. Code § 1113

Oct. 27, 1992, P.L. 102-542, 15 U.S. Code §§ 1114, 1122, 1125, 1127

Dec. 8, 1993, P.L. 103-182, 15 U.S. Code §§ 1091, 1052

Dec. 8, 1994, P.L. 103-465, 15 U.S. Code § 1052

Jan. 16, 1996, P.L. 104-98, 15 U.S. Code §§ 1125, 1127

Oct. 30, 1998, P.L. 105-330, 15 U.S. Code §§ 1051, 1051 nt., 1052 , 1057, 1058, 1059, 1060, 1062, 1064, 1091, 1094, 1113, 1114, 1115, 1121, 1124, 1126

**Trade-Mark Acts**

March 3, 1881, Ch. 138, 21 Stat. 502

Aug. 5, 1882, Ch. 393, 22 Stat. 300

Feb. 20, 1905, Ch. 592, 33 Stat. 724

Feb. 18, 1911, Ch. 113, 36 Stat. 918

Jan. 8, 1913, Ch. 7, 37 Stat. 649

June 10, 1938, Ch. 332, §§ 1, 2, 3, 5, 52 Stat. 638

**Trade Marks Registration Act**

Neb. Rev. Stat. 1943, 87-111 et seq.

**Trade Name Certification Act**

Iowa Code Ann., 547.1 et seq.

La. Rev. Stat. Ann., 51:211 et seq.

W. Va. Code 1966, § 47-8-2 et seq.

**Trade Name Registration Act**

Ga. Code Ann., 10-1-490 et seq.

Neb. Rev. Stat. 1943, 87-208 et seq.

Wash. Rev. Code Ann., 19.80.001 et seq.

Wyo. Stat. Ann., § 40-2-101 et seq.

**Trade Names Act**

Cal. Business and Professions Code § 14400 et seq.

Colo. Rev. Stat., 7-71-101, 7-71-102

Iowa Code Ann., 547.1 et seq.

La. Rev. Stat. Ann., 51:1431 et seq.

N.H. Rev. Stat. 1955, 349:1 et seq.

N.Y. General Business Law (Consol. Laws Ch. 20) § 130

**Trade Practices Act**

Fla. Stat. Ann., 626.951 et seq.

**Trade Practices Act (Deceptive)**
Fla. Stat. Ann., 501.201 et seq.

**Trade Practices Act (Insurance)**
Ark. Code Ann. 1987, 23-66-201 et seq.
Md. Ann. Code 1957, Art. 48A, § 212 et seq.
Mich. Comp. Laws Ann., 500.2001 et seq.
Vt. Stat. Ann., Title 8, § 4721 et seq.

**Trade Practices Act (Intoxicating Liquor)**
N.M. Stat. Ann., 60-8A-1 et seq.

**Trade Practices Act (Petroleum)**
Tenn. Code Ann., 47-25-601 et seq.

**Trade Practices Act (Unfair Insurance)**
Fla. Stat. Ann., 626.951 et seq.

**Trade Practices Act (Unfair)**
Me. Rev. Stat. Ann. 1964, Title 5, § 206 et seq.

**Trade Practices Act (Unlawful)**
Ore. Rev. Stat., 646.608 et seq.

**Trade Promotions Act**
N.M. Stat. Ann., 9-15-8.1 et seq.

**Trade School Act (Private)**
Mich. Comp. Laws Ann., 395.101 et seq.
Pa. Purdon's Stat., Title 24, § 1725.1 et seq.

**Trade School Act (Regional)**
Ala. Code 1975, § 16-60-190 et seq.

**Trade School and College Authority Act**
Ala. Acts 1963, p. 259

**Trade School and Junior College Act**
Ala. Code 1975, § 16-60-1 et seq.

**Trade School Registration Act**
Ind. Code. Ann., 20-12-62-1 et seq.

**Trade School Regulation Law**
Cal. Labor Code § 1649

**Trade Secret Theft Act**
Ind. Code. Ann., 35-17-3-1 et seq.

**Trade Secrets Act**
See also Uniform Trade Secrets Act
Conn. Gen. Stat. Ann., § 35-50 et seq.
Ga. Code Ann., 10-1-760 et seq.
W. Va. Code 1966, § 47-22-1 et seq.

**Trade Show Promotion Act**
Kan. Stat. Ann., 74-5075 et seq., 74-50,141 et seq.

**Trade Suspension Adjustment Act (Agricultural)**
Va. Code 1950, § 59.1-336 et seq.
W. Va. Code 1966, § 47-22-1 et seq.

**Trade Union Label Act**
Ark. Code Ann. 1987, 70-539 et seq.
Conn. Gen. Stat. Ann., § 35-18a et seq.

**Trade Zones Act (Foreign)**
Ill. Rev. Stat. 1991, Ch. 24, § 1360 et seq.

**Trademark Act**
Ala. Code 1975, § 8-12-6 et seq
Alaska Stat. 1962, §§ 45.50.010 to 45.50.205
Cal. Business and Professions Code § 14200 et seq.
Conn. Gen. Stat. Ann., § 35-11a et seq.
Del. Code of 1974, Title 6, § 3301 et seq.
Ill. Rev. Stat. 1991, Ch. 140, § 7.9 et seq.
Ind. Code. Ann., 24-2-1-1 et seq.
Iowa Code Ann., 548.1 et seq.
Mass. Gen. Laws Ann., 110:1 et seq.
Mich. Comp. Laws, 1979, 429.31 et seq.
Minn. Stat. Ann., 333.18 et seq.
Mo. Rev. Stat., 417.005 et seq.
Mont. Code Ann. 1979, 30-13-301 et seq.
N.D. Cent. Code, 47-22-01 et seq.
N.H. Rev. Stat. 1955, 350-A:1 et seq.
N.J. Stat. Ann., 56:3-13.1 et seq.
N.M. Stat. Ann., 57-3B-1 to 57-3B-17
N.Y. General Business Law (Consol. Laws Ch. 20) § 360 et seq.
Ohio Rev. Code 1953, 1329.01 et seq.
Ore. Rev. Stat., 647.005 et seq.
Pa. Cons. Stat., Title 54, § 1101 et seq.
P.R. Laws Ann. 1954, Title 10, § 191 et seq.
R.I. Gen. Laws 1956, 6-2-1 et seq.
S.C. Code Ann. 1976, § 39-15-110 et seq.

S.D. Codified Laws 1967, 37-6-1 et seq.
Tenn. Code Ann., 47-25-501 et seq.
Tex. Business and Commerce Code, § 16.01 et seq.
Wash. Rev. Code Ann., 19.77.010 et seq.
W. Va. Code 1966, § 47-2-1 et seq.
Wyo. Stat. Ann., § 40-1-101 et seq.

**Trademark Act (Counterfeit)**
Ill. Rev. Stat. 1991, Ch. 140, § 22.9 et seq.

**Trademark Act (Registered Container)**
Ill. Rev. Stat. 1991, Ch. 140, § 121 et seq.

**Trademark and Brand Act**
N.Y. Agriculture and Markets Law (Consol. Laws Ch. 69) §§ 156h, 156i

**Trademark and Service Mark Act**
Va. Code 1950, § 59.1-77 et seq.

**Trademark and Service Marks Act**
S.C. Code Ann. 1976, § 39-15-1105 et seq.
Va. Code 1950, §§ 59.1-92.1 to 59.1-92.20

**Trademark Counterfeiting Act**
N.J. Stat. Ann., 2C:21-32

**Trademark Counterfeiting Act of 1984**
Oct. 12, 1984, P.L. 98-473, 18 U.S. Code §§ 2311, 2320

**Trademark Dilution Act**
Mass. Gen. Laws Ann., 110B:12
N.Y. General Business Law (Consol.Laws Ch. 20) § 368d

**Trademark Law Revision Act of 1988**
Nov. 16, 1988, P.L. 100-667, 15 U.S. Code § 1051 nt.

**Trademark Law Treaty Implementation Act**
Oct. 30, 1998, P.L. 105-330, Title I, 112 Stat.;4, 15 U.S. Code § 1051 nt.

**Trademark Registration Act**
Colo. Rev. Stat., 7-70-101 et seq.
Fla. Stat. Ann., 495.011 et seq.
Ga. Code Ann., 10-1-440 et seq.
Ill. Rev. Stat. 1991, Ch. 140, § 7.9 et seq.
Kan. Stat. Ann., 81-111 et seq.
La. Rev. Stat. Ann., 51:211 et seq.
Md. Ann. Code 1974, Art. BR, § 1-404
Miss. Code Ann. 1972, § 75-25-1 et seq.
N.C. Gen. Stat. 1943, § 80-1 et seq.
Okla. Stat. Ann., Title 78, § 21 et seq.
S.D. Codified Laws 1967, 37-6-4 et seq.
Utah Code Ann. 1953, 70-3-1 et seq.
Vt. Stat. Ann., Title 9, § 2521 et seq.
Wash. Rev. Code Ann., 19.77.010 et seq.

**Trademark Registration and Protection Act**
Ill. Comp. Stat. 1992, Ch. 765, § 1036/1 et seq.

**Trademark Remedy Clarification Act**
Oct. 27, 1992, P.L. 102-542, 15 U.S. Code § 1051 nt.

**Trademarks, Trade Names and Labels Act**
Pa. Cons. Stat., Title 54, § 1101 et seq.

**Tradeport Development Authority Act (International)**
Mich. Comp. Laws Ann., 125.2521 et seq.

**Traders Act**
Miss. Code Ann. 1972, § 15-3-7
Va. Code 1950, § 55-152
W. Va. Code 1931, Ch. 47, Art. 8, § 1

**Trader's License Act**
Md. Ann. Code 1974, Art. BR, § 17-1804

**Trades Act (Street)**
Wis. Stat. Ann., 103.21 et seq.

**Trades Unions Act**
June 29, 1886, Ch. 567, 24 Stat. 86

**Trading Bonus Statute**
Colo. Rev. Stat. 1963, 40-16-15

**Trading Company Act (Export)**
Okla. Stat. Ann., Title 74, § 2101 et seq.

**Trading Stamp Act**
Haw. Rev. Stat. 1968, § 770-1
Kan. Stat. Ann., 21-2801 et seq.
Mass. Gen. Laws Ann., 93:14L et seq.
N.D. Cent. Code, 51-06-01 et seq.
Neb. Laws 1905, Ch. 204
N.H. Rev. Stat. 1955, 357-A:1 et seq.

*Continued*

N.J. Stat. Ann., 45:23-1 et seq.
S.D. Codified Laws 1967, 37-19-1 et seq.
Tenn. Code Ann., Superseded Vol., 67-4203
Utah Code Ann. 1953, 13-6-1 et seq.
Vt. Stat. Ann., Title 9, § 4021 et seq.
Wash. Rev. Code Ann., 19.84.010 et seq.
Wis. Stat. Ann., 100.15
Wyo. Stat. Ann., § 40-16-101 et seq.

**Trading Stamp Companies Act**
Cal. Business and Professions Code § 17750 et seq.

**Trading With the Enemy Acts**
Oct. 6, 1917, Ch. 106, 40 Stat. 411, 12 U.S. Code § 95a; 50 U.S. Code Appx. §§ 1 to 6, 7 to 39
March 28, 1918, Ch. 28, 40 Stat. 460, 50 U.S. Code § 176; 50 U.S. Code Appx. § 12
Sept. 24, 1918, Ch. 176, 40 Stat. 966, 12 U.S. Code § 95a; 50 U.S. Code Appx. § 5
Nov. 4, 1918, Ch. 201, 40 Stat. 1020, 31 U.S. Code §§ 484, 762, 763; 40 U.S. Code § 485; 50 U.S. Code Appx. § 7
July 11, 1919, Ch. 6, 41 Stat. 35, 50 U.S. Code Appx. § 9
June 5, 1920, Ch. 241, 41 Stat. 977, 50 U.S. Code Appx. § 9
Feb. 27, 1921, Ch. 76, 40 Stat. 1147, 50 U.S. Code Appx. § 9
Dec. 21, 1921, Ch. 13, 42 Stat. 351, 50 U.S. Code Appx. § 9
Dec. 27, 1922, Ch. 13, 42 Stat. 1065, 50 U.S. Code Appx. § 9
March 4, 1923, Ch. 285, 42 Stat. 1511, 50 U.S. Code Appx. §§ 9, 20- -24
May 7, 1926, Ch. 252, 44 Stat. 406, 50 U.S. Code Appx. § 9
March 10, 1928, Ch. 167, 45 Stat. 267, 50 U.S. Code Appx. §§ 9, 10, 20, 22 to 31
Feb. 21, 1929, Ch. 291, 45 Stat. 1255, 50 U.S. Code Appx. § 25
June 11, 1929, Ch. 14, 46 Stat. 6, 50 U.S. Code Appx. § 26
March 10, 1930, Ch. 75, 46 Stat. 84, 50 U.S. Code Appx. § 25
March 9, 1933, Ch. 1, 48 Stat. 1, 12 U.S. Code § 95a; 50 U.S. Code Appx. § 5
March 28, 1934, Ch. 102, 48 Stat. 510, 3 U.S. Code § 46; 5 U.S. Code § 636; 50 U.S. Code Appx. § 24
June 18, 1934, Ch. 567, 48 Stat. 977, 50 U.S. Code Appx. § 24
Aug. 24, 1937, Ch. 745, 50 Stat. 748, 50 U.S. Code Appx. § 9
May 7, 1940, Ch. 185, 54 Stat. 179, 12 U.S. Code § 95a; 50 U.S. Code Appx. § 5
Dec. 18, 1941, Ch. 593, 55 Stat. 839, 12 U.S. Code § 95a; 50 U.S. Code Appx. § 5
March 8, 1946, Ch. 83, 60 Stat. 50, 50 U.S. Code Appx. §§ 20, 32, 619
May 16, 1946, Ch. 260, 60 Stat. 182, 50 U.S. Code Appx. § 38
Aug. 8, 1946, Ch. 878, 69 Stat. 925, 50 U.S. Code Appx. §§ 32 to 38
Aug. 5, 1947, Ch. 499, 61 Stat. 784, 50 U.S. Code Appx. §§ 32, 33
July 1, 1948, Ch. 794, 62 Stat. 1218, 50 U.S. Code Appx. § 33
July 3, 1948, Ch. 826, 62 Stat. 1246, 50 U.S. Code Appx. § 39
Sept. 29, 1950, Ch. 1108, 64 Stat. 1080, 50 U.S. Code Appx. § 32
Aug. 7, 1953, Ch. 344, 67 Stat. 461, 50 U.S. Code Appx. § 39
Feb. 9, 1954, Ch. 4, 68 Stat. 7, 50 U.S. Code Appx. § 33
Aug. 23, 1954, Ch. 830, 68 Stat. 767, 50 U.S. Code Appx. §§ 32, 33
June 25, 1956, Ch. 436, 70 Stat. 331, 50 U.S. Code Appx. § 20
Aug. 6, 1956, Ch. 1016, 70 Stat. 1073, 50 U.S. Code Appx. § 9
Oct. 22, 1962, P.L. 87-846, 76 Stat. 1113, 50 U.S. Code Appx. §§ 9, 32, 33, 39, 41, 42
Oct. 23, 1962, P.L. 87-861, 76 Stat. 1139, 50 U.S. Code Appx. §§ 39, 43, 44
Aug. 26, 1964, P.L. 88-490, 78 Stat. 607, 50 U.S. Code Appx. § 42
Oct. 4, 1966, P.L. 89-619, 80 Stat. 871, 50 U.S. Code Appx. § 39
June 6, 1972, P.L. 92-310, 86 Stat. 214, 50 U.S. Code Appx. § 6
Dec. 28, 1977, P.L. 95-223, 50 U.S. Code Appx. §§ 3, 3 nt., 16
Aug. 16, 1985, P.L. 99-93, 50 U.S. Code Appx. § 39
Aug. 23, 1988, P.L. 100-418, 102 Stat. 1370, 50 U.S. Code Appx. §§ 5, 6, 39
Oct. 6, 1992, P.L. 102-393, 50 U.S. Code Appx. § 16
Oct. 23, 1992, P.L. 102-484, 50 U.S. Code Appx. § 16

March 12, 1996, P.L. 104-114, 50 U.S. Code Appx. § 16

**Traditional Housing Participant Misconduct Act**
Cal. Health and Safety Code § 50580 et seq.

**Traffic Act**
Ill. Rev. Stat. 1991, Ch. 95 1/2, § 11-100 et seq.
Md. Ann. Code 1974, Art. TR, § 21-103 et seq.
P.R. Laws Ann. 1954, Title 9 § 301 et seq.

**Traffic Act (Bicycles)**
Mont. Code Ann., 61-8-601 et seq.

**Traffic Act (Boulevard Stop)**
Md. Ann. Code 1974, Art. TR, §§ 21-403, 21-707, 25-109

**Traffic Act (Highways)**
Ala. Code 1975, § 32-1-1 et seq.
Alaska Stat. 1962, § 28.05.010 et seq.
Ariz. Rev. Stat. Ann., § 28-601 et seq.
Ark. Code Ann. 1987, 27-49-201 et seq.
Cal. Vehicle Code 1959, § 21000 et seq.
Conn. Gen. Stat. Ann., § 14-212 et seq.
D.C. Code Ann., § 40-701 et seq.
Del. Code of 1974, Title 21, § 4101 et seq.
Fla. Stat. Ann., 316.001 et seq.
Iowa Code Ann., 321.1 et seq.
Kan. Stat. Ann., 8-1401 et seq.
Ky. Rev. Stat. 1971, 189.010 et seq.
Md. Ann. Code 1974, Art. TR, § 21-101 et seq.
Mich. Comp. Laws Ann., 257.601 et seq.
Minn. Stat. Ann., 169.01 et seq.
N.C. Gen. Stat. 1943, § 20-138 et seq.
N.D. Cent. Code, 39-07-01 et seq.
Neb. Rev. Stat. 1943, 39-601 et seq.
Nev. Rev. Stat. 1979 Reprint, 484.011 et seq.
N.H. Rev. Stat. 1955, 265:1 et seq.
N.J. Stat. Ann., 39:4-1 et seq.
N.M. Stat. Ann. 1953, 64-1-1 et seq.
Ohio Rev. Code 1953, 4511.01 et seq.
Okla. Stat. Ann., Title 47, §§ 1-101, 121.1 et seq.
Ore. Rev. Stat., 810.010 et seq.
Pa. Purdon's Stat., Title 75, § 3301 et seq.
P.R. Laws Ann. 1954, Title 9, § 841 et seq.
R.I. Gen. Laws 1956, 31-12-1 et seq.
S.C. Code Ann. 1976, § 56-5-10 et seq.
Tex. Rev. Civ. Stat., Art. 6701d
Wash. Rev. Code Ann., 46.61.005 et seq.
Wis. Stat. Ann., 346.01 et seq.
W. Va. Code 1966, § 17C-1-1 et seq.
Wyo. Stat. Ann., § 31-5-101 et seq.

**Traffic Act (Municipalities)**
Fla. Stat. 1969, 186.01 et seq.

**Traffic Adjudication Act**
D.C. Code Ann., § 40-601 et seq.
N.J. Stat. Ann., 39:1-1 et seq.

**Traffic and Motor Vehicle Laws**
N.J. Stat. Ann., 39:1-1 to 39:11-11

**Traffic Bail Bond Procedure Act**
Okla. Stat. Ann., Title 22, §§ 1115 to 1115.5

**Traffic Checkpoint Act (Administrative)**
Utah Code Ann. 1953, 77-23-101 et seq.

**Traffic Congestion and Air Pollution Control Act**
N.J. Stat. Ann., 27:26A-1 et seq.

**Traffic Control Act**
See Uniform Traffic Control Act

**Traffic Control Signals Act**
Okla. Stat. Ann., Title 47, § 11-201 et seq.

**Traffic Court Act (Albany)**
N.Y. Laws 1937, Ch. 135

**Traffic Court Act (Philadelphia)**
Pa. Cons. Stat., Title 42, § 1302 et seq.

**Traffic Engineering Act (Municipalities)**
Ind. Code 1976, 18-4-19-1 et seq.

**Traffic Infractions Act**
Ida. Code 1947, 49-1401 et seq.

**Traffic Infractions Disposition Act**
Fla. Stat. Ann., 318.11 et seq.

**Traffic Law (Highway)**
N.C. Gen. Stat. 1943, § 20-138.1 et seq.

**Traffic Laws Act**
Alaska Stat. 1962, §§ 28.01.010, 28.01.020

**Traffic Mitigation Act (Travelink)**
Del. Code of 1974, Title 30, § 2030 et seq.

**Traffic Offenders Act (Habitual)**
Wash. Rev. Code Ann., 46.65.010 et seq.

**Traffic on Highways Act**
S.C. Code Ann. 1976, § 56-5-10 et seq.

**Traffic Records and Criminal Information System Act**
Iowa Code Ann., 692.1 et seq.

**Traffic Regulation Act**
Ga. Code Ann., 40-1-1 et seq.
Ida. Code 1947, 49-501 et seq.
Ind. Code. Ann., 9-4-1-1 et seq.
Iowa Code Ann., 321.228 et seq.
La. Rev. Stat. Ann., 32:221 et seq.
Minn. Stat. Ann., 169.01 et seq.
Miss. Code Ann. 1972, § 63-3-1 et seq.
Mont. Code Ann., 61-8-101 et seq.
S.D. Codified Laws 1967, 32-14-1 et seq.
Utah Code Ann. 1953, 41-6-1 et seq.

**Traffic Regulation Law (Highway)**
Miss. Code Ann. 1972, § 63-3-1 et seq.

**Traffic Rules and Regulations, Nonresident Violator Compact**
N.J. Stat. Ann., 39:5F-1 et seq.

**Traffic Safety Act**
Ind. Code. Ann., 9-6-2-1 et seq.
Mont. Code Ann., 61-2-101 et seq.
N.M. Stat. Ann., 66-7-501 et seq.
Tenn. Code Ann., 55-8-101 et seq.
Tex. Rev. Civ. Stat., Art. 6701j-1

**Traffic Safety Act (Omnibus)**
Cal. Statutes 1990, Ch. 33, § 1
Cal. Vehicle Code 1959, § 27315 et seq.

**Traffic Safety and Driver Education Act**
Tex. Rev. Civ. Stat., Art. 4413(29c)

**Traffic Safety Program**
Cal. Vehicle Code 1959, § 2900 et seq.

**Traffic Stops Statistics Act**
R.I. Gen. Laws 1956, 31-21.1-1 et seq.

**Traffic Stops Statistics Study Act**
Ala. Acts 1999, H.B. 63

**Traffic Ticket Act**
See Uniform Traffic Ticket Act

**Traffic Violations Bureau Act**
Ga. Code Ann., 40-13-50 et seq.

**Traffic Violations Compact Act**
La. Rev. Stat. Ann., 32:1441 et seq.

**Traffic Violator Compact Act (Nonresident)**
Miss. Code Ann. 1972, § 63-10-1 et seq.
S.C. Code Ann. 1976, § 56-25-10 et seq.

**Traffic Violator Compacts Act (Nonresident)**
S.C. Code Ann. 1976, § 56-25-10 et seq.

**Trafficking Control Act (Food Stamp)**
Del. Code of 1974, Title 31, § 610 et seq.

**Trafficking Enterprise Act (Drug)**
Ala. Code 1975, § 13A-12-233

**Trafficking in Children Act**
Okla. Stat. Ann., Title 21, § 865 et seq.

**Trafficking in Illegal Drugs Act**
Okla. Stat. Ann., Title 63, § 2-414 et seq.

**Trafficway Act**
Kan. Laws 1929, Ch. 132

**Trail Act (Alaska)**
See Alaska Road and Trail Act

**Trail System Act**
Okla. Stat. Ann., Title 74, § 1853 et seq.

**Trailer Act (Home-made)**
Tenn. Code Ann., 55-4-101

**Trailer Act (Mobile Homes)**
Iowa Code Ann., 135D.1 et seq.

**Trailer Camp Act**
Mich. Comp. Laws Ann., 125.1101 et seq.

**Trailer Camp and Coach Act**
Cal. Health and Safety Code §§ 18000 et seq., 18200 et seq.

**Trailer Coach Park Act**
Ill. Rev. Stat. 1991, Ch. 111 1/2, § 711 et seq.
Mich. Comp. Laws Ann., 125.1101 et seq.

**Trailer Home Park Act**
Mich. Comp. Laws Ann., 125.1035 et seq.

**Trailer Park and Auto Court Act**
Cal. Health and Safety Code §§ 18000 et seq., 18200 et seq.

**Trailer Parks Licensing Act**
Minn. Stat. Ann., 327.14 et seq.

**Trailer Registration Act**
Wis. Stat. 1985, 341.25, Subsec. 1, Subds. f to m

**Trails of Illinois Act (Recreational)**
Ill. Comp. Stat. 1992, Ch. 20, § 862/1 et seq.

**Trails System Act**
Ark. Code Ann. 1987, 22-4-401 et seq.
Colo. Rev. Stat., 33-42-101 et seq.
Ky. Rev. Stat. 1971, 148.610 et seq.
N.C. Gen. Stat. 1943, § 113A-83 et seq.
N.J. Stat. Ann., 13:8-30 et seq.
N.M. Stat. Ann., 16-3-1 et seq.
Okla. Stat. Ann., Title 74, § 3451 et seq.
Tenn. Code Ann., 11-11-101 et seq.

**Trailways Act**
Mich. Comp. Laws Ann., 299.131 et seq.

**Train Crew Act**
Ark. Code Ann. 1987, 73-720 et seq.

**Train Employees' Hours Law**
Cal. Labor Code § 600 et seq.

**Train Length Act**
Ariz. Laws 1912, Ch. 43

**Train Manning Law**
Cal. Labor Code § 6901 et seq.

**Train Medicine Kit Law**
Cal. Public Utilities Code § 7608

**Train Order Law**
Cal. Public Utilities Code § 7677

**Trained Attendant Law (Psychiatry)**
Cal. Business and Professions Code § 4500 et seq.

**Trained Nurse Act**
Ky. Rev. Stat. 1971, 314.011 et seq.

**Trainers Licensure Act (Athletic)**
Ala. Acts 1993, No. 617

**Trainers Practice Act (Athletic)**
Ill. Comp. Stat. 1992, Ch. 225, § 5/1 et seq.

**Training Academy Act**
Miss. Code Ann. 1972, § 45-5-1 et seq.

**Training Act (Customized)**
Colo. Rev. Stat., 23-60-;

**Training Act (Education Management)**
Fla. Stat. Ann., 231.087

**Training Act (Existing Industry)**
Colo. Rev. Stat., 23-60-307

**Training Act (Law Enforcement)**
Neb. Rev. Stat. 1943, 81-1401 et seq.

**Training Act (Municipal Clerk)**
Ill. Rev. Stat. 1991, Ch. 144, § 61.50 et seq.

**Training Act (Rural Leadership)**
Pa. Purdon's Stat., Title 53, § 897.1 et seq.

**Training Act (Sheriffs Law Enforcement)**
Neb. Rev. Stat. 1943, 81-1401 et seq.

**Training Act (State Employees)**
Tex. Government Code, § 656.041 et seq.

**Training and Apprentice Act (Public Works)**
N.M. Stat. Ann., 13-4D-1 et seq.

**Training and Apprenticeship Act**
Pa. Purdon's Stat., Title 43, § 90.1 et seq.

**Training and Education Act (High Technology)**
Wash. Rev. Code Ann., 28B.65.010 et seq.

**Training and Employment Act**
Fla. Stat. 1981, 450.50 et seq.
N.C. Gen. Stat. 1943, § 143B-438.1 et seq.
N.C. Laws 1985, Ch. 543

**Training and Employment Council Act**
Mo. Rev. Stat. 1978, 620.521

**Training and Employment Programs for Older Californians Act**
Cal. Unemployment Insurance Code § 16000 et seq.

**Training and Jobs Law**
Minn. Stat. Ann., 268.001 et seq.

**Training and Standards Act (911 Training and Standards Act)**
Mo. Rev. Stat., 650.340

**Training Assistance Act (Dislocated Worker)**
Pa. Purdon's Stat., Title 43, § 690a-1 et seq.

**Training Evaluation Act (Job)**
Ill. Comp. Stat. 1992, Ch. 20, § 2220/5-1 et seq.

**Training Information Program Act**
Kan. Stat. Ann., 72-4450 et seq.

**Training Partnership Act (Job)**
Me. Rev. Stat. Ann. 1964, Title 26, § 2001 et seq.

**Training Reform Act (Prison Inmate)**
La. Rev. Stat. Ann., 15:731 to 15:733

**Training School Act**
D.C. Code Ann., § 32-801 et seq.
Wyo. Stat. Ann., § 25-5-101 et seq.

**Training Schools for Boys Act**
Ill. Rev. Stat. 1991, Ch. 122, § 660.9 et seq.

**Training Technology Transfer Act of 1988**
Aug. 23, 1988, P.L. 100-418, 102 Stat. 1500, 20 U.S. Code § 5091
Nov. 16, 1990, P.L. 101-600, 20 U.S. Code § 5092
March 31, 1994, P.L. 103-227, 20 U.S. Code § 5093
Oct. 20, 1994, P.L. 103-382, 20 U.S. Code § 5124

**Trammell Corrupt Practices Act**
Fla. Laws 1913, Ch. 6470

**Tramp Act**
Neb. Laws 1879, p. 64
N.Y. Penal Law 1909 (Consol Laws Ch. 40) §§ 2370 to 2372
Ohio Rev. Code 1953, 2923.28

**Tramroad Act**
Jan. 21, 1895, Ch. 37, 28 Stat. 635, 43 U.S. Code § 956

**Tramway Safety Act (Passenger)**
N.H. Rev. Stat. 1955, 225-A:1 et seq.

**Tranportation Sales Tax (City and County)**
Mo. Rev. Stat., 94.600 et seq.

**Trans-Alaska Pipeline Authorization Act**
Nov. 16, 1973, P.L. 93-153, 87 Stat. 584, 43 U.S. Code §§ 1651 to 1655
Nov. 8, 1984, P.L. 98-630, 43 U.S. Code § 1652
June 27, 1988, P.L. 100-352, 43 U.S. Code § 1652
Aug. 18, 1990, P.L. 101-380, 43 U.S. Code §§ 1653, 1656

**Trans-Alaska Pipeline System Reform Act of 1990**
Aug. 18, 1990, P.L. 101-380, 43 U.S. Code § 1651 nt.

**Transacted Business with a Producer Controlled Property or Casualty Insurer Act**
Ky. Rev. Stat. 1971, 304.3-400c et seq.

**Transacting Business Act (Jurisdiction)**
La. Rev. Stat. Ann., 13:3201

**Transaction Card Crime Act (Financial)**
S.C. Code Ann. 1976, § 16-14-10 et seq.

**Transaction Privilege Tax Act**
Ariz. Rev. Stat. Ann., § 42-1301 et seq.

**Transaction Tax Exemption Act (Stock, Commodity, or Options)**
Ill. Comp. Stat. 1992, Ch. 35, §§ 820/1, 820/2

**Transactional Rule**
Mont. Code Ann., 26-1-103

**Transactions Act (Brokerage Relationships in Real Estate)**
Ga. Official Code Ann., 10-6A-1 et seq.

**Transactions Act (Disclosure of Material)**
Iowa Code 1995, 521D.1 et seq.

**Transactions and Use Tax Law**
Cal. Revenue and Taxation Code § 7251 et seq.

**Transboundary Pollution Reciprocal Access Act**
See Uniform Transboundary Pollution Reciprocal Access Act

**Transcript Act (Court Reporter)**
Ill. Rev. Stat. 1991, Ch. 37, § 660.9 et seq.

**Transcript Act (Debate)**
Ill. Rev. Stat. 1991, Ch. 63, § 200 et seq.

**Transcript and Certificate Act**
N.Y. Judiciary Law (Consol. Laws Ch. 30) § 255c

**Transfer Act (Equitable Claims)**
Ala. Code 1958, Title 13, § 153

**Transfer Act (Fraudulent)**
See Uniform Fraudulent Transfer Act

**Transfer Act (Motor Vehicles)**
Mich. Comp. Laws Ann., 257.233 et seq.

**Transfer Act (Pupils)**
Ind. Code. Ann., 20-8.1-6.1-1 et seq.

**Transfer Act (Small Value Cases)**
Mass. Gen. Laws Ann., 231:102C

**Transfer Act (Stock)**
See Uniform Stock Transfer Act

**Transfer Agency Act (Securities)**
Utah Code Ann. 1953, Miscellaneous Superseded Code Provisions, 61-3-1 et seq.

**Transfer and Estate Tax Reform Act**
Haw. Rev. Stat. § 236D-1 et seq.
Ida. Code 1947, 14-401 et seq.
Wash. Rev. Code Ann., 83.100.010 et seq.

**Transfer and Inheritance Tax Act**
Ida. Code 1947, 14-401 et seq.
Ill. Rev. Stat. 1991, Ch. 120, § 405A-1 et seq.
N.J. Rev. Stat. 1937, 54:33-1 et seq.
Pa. Purdon's Stat., Title 72, § 2301 et seq.

**Transfer Inheritance Tax Act (Joint Property)**
Pa. Purdon's Stat., Title 72, § 2301

**Transfer Law (Nonprobate)**
Mo. Rev. Stat., 461.003 et seq.

**Transfer Liability Act**
Ore. Rev. Stat., 314.310

**Transfer of Accounts Receivable Act**
Pa. 1941 Pamph. Laws 606, No. 255

**Transfer of Actions Act (Law and Equity)**
Mich. Comp. Laws 1948, 611.2

**Transfer of Causes Law**
N.J. Stat. Revised 1937

**Transfer of Court Costs and Sheriff Fees Act**
Ill. Rev. Stat. 1991, Ch. 33, § 28.9 et seq.

**Transfer of Custody Act**
Okla. Stat. Ann., Title 10, § 25 et seq.

**Transfer of Dependents Act**
See also Uniform Transfer of Dependents Act
Conn. Gen. Stat. 1983, § 17-293

**Transfer of Development Rights Demonstration Act (Burlington County)**
N.J. Stat. Ann., 40:55D-113 et seq.

**Transfer of Funds Act (Fair and Exposition)**
Ill. Comp. Stat. 1992, Ch. 135, §§ 135/0.01, 135/1
Ill. Rev. Stat. 1991, Ch. 127, §§ 167f1.9, 167f2

**Transfer of Funds Act (Health and Finance)**
Ill. Rev. Stat. 1991, Ch. 127, §§ 167f2.9, 167f3

**Transfer of Funds Act (Public Welfare)**
Ill. Rev. Stat. 1991, Ch. 127, §§ 167b.9, 167c

**Transfer of Funds Act (University Building)**
Ill. Rev. Stat. 1991, Ch. 127, §§ 167c.9, 167d

**Transfer of Local Government Property Act**
Ill. Rev. Stat. 1991, Ch. 127, § 155h et seq.

**Transfer of Property Act (Lifetime)**
Ill. Rev. Stat. 1991, Ch. 110 1/2, § 600 et seq.

**Transfer of Securities Act**
Ill. Rev. Stat. 1991, Ch. 32, § 439.49 et seq.

**Transfer of Shares Act**
Pa. Purdon's Stat., Title 72, § 2041 et seq.

**Transfer of Teacher Credentials Act**
N.J. Stat. Ann. 18A:26-11 et seq.

**Transfer of Venue Act**
Fla. Stat. Ann., 47.091 et seq.
Ind. Code. Ann., 34-1-13-1 et seq.
Kan. Stat. Ann., 60-609 et seq.
Mass. Gen. Laws Ann., 223:15
N.C. Gen. Stat. 1943, § 1-83
N.D. Cent. Code, 28-04-07
Nev. Rev. Stat. 1979 Reprint, 13.050
Ore. Rev. Stat., 14.110
S.C. Code Ann. 1976, § 15-7-100
S.D. Codified Laws 1967, 15-5-11 et seq.
Va. Code 1950, § 8.01-265
Wash. Rev. Code Ann., 4.12.030
Wis. Stat. Ann., 801.53
W. Va. Code 1966, § 56-9-1
Wyo. Stat. 1957, § 1-53 et seq.

**Transfer-on-Death of Interest in Real Property and Nonregistered Personal Property Act**
Miss. Laws 1999, H.B. 321

**Transfer-on-Death Security Registration Act**
See Uniform Transfer-on-Death Security Registration Act

**Transfer Simplification Act (Fiduciary Security)**
See Uniform Act for Simplification of Fiduciary Security Transfers

**Transfer Tax Act**
Haw. Rev. Laws 1955 § 122-11
Mich. Comp. Laws Ann., 205.201 et seq.
Minn. Stat. Ann., 291.01 et seq.
R.I. Gen. Laws 1956, 44-22-1 et seq.
Wyo. Stat. Ann., § 39-6-801

**Transfer Tax Act (Estate and Generation-Skipping)**
Ill. Comp. Stat. 1992, Ch. 35, § 405/1 et seq.

**Transfer Tax Act (Estate)**
Ill. Rev. Stat. 1991, Ch. 120, § 405A-1 et seq.
N.J. Stat. Ann., 54:33-1 et seq.
N.Y. Tax Law (Consol. Laws Ch. 60) § 220 et seq.
W. Va. Code 1966, § 11-11-1 et seq.

**Transfer Tax Act (Generation Skipping)**
Cal. Revenue and Taxation Code § 16700 et seq.
Tenn. Code Ann., 67-8-601 et seq.

**Transfer Tax Act (Intestate Succession)**
Mont. Code Ann., 72-16-301 et seq.

**Transfer Tax Act (Real Estate)**
Cal. Revenue and Taxation Code § 11901 et seq.
Pa. Purdon's Stat., Title 72, § 8101-C et seq.

**Transfer Tax Act (Reciprocal)**
See Reciprocal Transfer Tax Act

**Transfer Tax Act (State Real Estate)**
Mich. Comp. Laws Ann., 207.521 et seq.

**Transfer Tax and Land Trust Recordation Act**
Ill. Rev. Stat. 1987, Ch. 115, § 9.2a

**Transfer Tax Law (Nonresidents)**
N.Y. Tax Law (Consol. Laws Ch. 60) § 248 et seq.

**Transfer Tax Law (Real Estate)**
Ill. Comp. Stat. 1992, Ch. 35, § 305/1 et seq.

**Transfer Tax Law (Residents)**
N.Y. Tax Law (Consol. Laws Ch. 60) § 220 et seq.

**Transferee Liability Act**
Ore. Rev. Stat., 314.310

**Transference of the Rice Corporation, Inc. and the Vegetable Corporation, Inc. to the Land Authority of Puerto Rico Act**
P.R. Acts 1985, No. 10

**Transfers Act (Fraudulent)**
Ariz. Rev. Stat. Ann., § 44-1001 et seq.
W. Va. Code 1966, § 40-1A-1 et seq.

**Transfers Act (Stock)**
See also Uniform Stock Transfers Act
N.Y. Uniform Commercial Code (Consol. Laws Ch. 38) § 8-301 et seq.

**Transfers of Funds Abroad Act**
P.R. Laws Ann. 1954, Title 7, § 1401 et seq.

**Transfers to Minors Act**
See also Uniform Transfers to Minors Act
Ala. Code 1975, § 35-5A-1 et seq.
Fla. Stat. Ann., 944.701 et seq.

**Transient Farmer Tax Act**
S.D. Codified Laws 1967, 10-42-1 et seq.

**Transient Merchant Act**
Ill. Rev. Stat. 1991, Ch. 121 1/2, § 1651 et seq.

**Transient Merchant Licensing Act**
Ark. Code Ann. 1987, 17-42-101 et seq.
Kan. Stat. Ann., 1-2231 et seq.
Okla. Stat. Ann., Title 19, § 1601 et seq.
W. Va. Code 1966 § 47-11E-1 et seq., § 11-12-20 et seq.

**Transient Merchant Tax Statute**
Tenn. Code Ann., Superseded Vol., 67-4801 et seq.

**Transient Merchants Act**
Ga. Code Ann., 43-46-1 et seq.
Ill. Rev. Stat. 1985, Ch. 121 1/2, § 158 et seq.
Ind. Code. Ann., 25-37-1-1 et seq.
Iowa Code 1981, 332.45 et seq.
Ky. Stat. 1936, § 4217b-1 et seq.
Mich. Comp. Laws Ann., 445.371 et seq.
N.D. Cent. Code, 51-04-01 et seq.
S.D. Codified Laws 1967, 37-12-1 et seq.

**Transient Minors Act**
Cal. Military and Veterans Code § 1509.5

**Transient Pauper Relief Act**
Wis. Stat. Ann., 49.02, Subsec. 2m

**Transient Property Act**
Okla. Territory Laws 1895, p. 229, Art. 5

**Transient Retail Merchants' License Act**
Mont. Code Ann., 7-21-2401 et seq.

**Transient Vendors Act**
Mass. Gen. Laws Ann., 101:1 et seq.

**Transit Act**
N.J. Laws 1869, p. 226, Ch. 104
N.Y. Rapid Transit Law (Consol. Laws, Ch. 48A) § 2 et seq.

**Transit Authority Act**
Ga. Code Ann., 32-9-9
Mass. Acts 1947, Ch. 544
N.Y. Public Authorities Law (Consol. Laws Ch. 43A) § 1200 et seq.

**Transit Authority Act (Central Pinellas)**
Fla. Special Laws 1970, Ch. 70-907

**Transit Authority Act (Chatham)**
Ga. Laws 1986, p. 5082

**Transit Authority Act (Chattanooga)**
Tenn. Private Acts 1967, Ch. 460

**Transit Authority Act (Duluth)**
Minn. Laws 1969, Ch. 720

**Transit Authority Act (Macon-Bibb County)**
Ga. Laws 1980, p. 4313, §§ 1.1 to 5.1

**Transit Authority Act (Macon)**
Ga. Laws 1973, p. 2914

**Transit Authority Act (Metropolitan)**
Ill. Rev. Stat. 1991, Ch. 111 2/3, § 301 et seq.
Neb. Rev. Stat. 1943, 14-1801 et seq.

**Transit Authority Act (New York City)**
N.Y. Public Authorities Law (Consol. Laws Ch. 43A) § 1200 et seq.

**Transit Authority Act (Savannah)**
Ga. Laws 1960, p. 2620

**Transit Authority Law**
Neb. Rev. Stat. 1943, 14-1801 et seq.
Neb. Rev. Stat. 1943, 14-1801 to 14-1826

**Transit Authority of River Parishes Act**
La. Rev. Stat. Ann., 48:1601 et seq.

**Transit Commission Act**
Ill. Rev. Stat. 1991, Ch. 121, §§ 5-701.8, 7-202.14

**Transit Construction Fund Act**
N.Y. Public Authorities Law (Consol. Laws Ch. 43A) § 1225a et seq.

**Transit Development Act**
Cal. Public Utilities Code § 120000 et seq.

**Transit Development Board Act (North San Diego County)**
Cal. Public Utilities Code § 125000 et seq.

**Transit District Act**
Cal. Public Utilities Code § 24501 et seq.

**Transit District Act (San Mateo County)**
Cal. Public Utilities Code § 103000 et seq.

**Transit District Act (Santa Clara County)**
Cal. Public Utilities Code § 100000 et seq.
Cal. Statutes 1969, Ch. 180, p. 431

**Transit Districts Act (Coordinated)**
Kan. Stat. Ann., 75-5051 et seq.

**Transit Fare Payment Act**
D.C. Code Ann., § 44-223 et seq.

**Transit Fare Referendum Act**
N.Y. Rapid Transit Law (Consol. Laws Ch. 48A) § 36 et seq.

**Transit Law (Municipalities)**
N.M. Stat. Ann., 3-52-1 et seq.

**Transit Safety Act (Bi-State)**
Ill. Comp. Stat. 1992, Ch. 45, § 111/1 et seq.

**Transit Village Development Planning Act**
Cal. Government Code § 65460 et seq.

**Transition Act**
Tenn. Code Ann., 8-1-201 et seq.

**Transition Act (Cities and Towns)**
Va. Code 1950, § 15.1-1003

**Transition Act (Gubernatorial)**
Md. Ann. Code 1974, Art. SG, § 3-201 et seq.

**Transition Act (State Administration)**
Tenn. Code Ann., 8-1-201 et seq.

**Transition Assistance Program Act**
Fla. Stat. Ann., 944.701 et seq.

**Transitional Assistance Department Act**
Mass. Gen. Laws Ann., 18:1 et seq.

**Transitional Bilingual Education Act**
Ill. Rev. Stat. 1991, Ch. 122, § 14C-1 et seq.
R.I. Gen. Laws 1956, 16-54-1 et seq.

**Transitional Billingual Instruction Act**
Wash. Rev. Code Ann., 28A.58.800 et seq.

**Transitional Finance Authority Act (New York City)**
N.Y. Public Authorities Law (Consol. Laws Ch. 43A) § 2799aa et seq.

**Transitional Housing Participant Misconduct Act**
Cal. Health and Safety Code § 50580 et seq.

**Transmission Act (Electricity)**
Mich. Comp. Laws Ann., 460.551 et seq.

**Transmission Line Prescriptive Right Prohibition Act**
Ill. Rev. Stat. 1991, Ch. 134, §§ 14.9, 15

**Transmission Line Siting Act**
Fla. Stat. Ann., 403.52 et seq.

**Transmission of Money Act**
D.C. Code Ann., § 47-3101 et seq.

**Transmission Pipeline Intrastate Regulatory Act (Natural Gas)**
Fla. Laws 1992, Ch. 284, § 2 et seq.

**Transmission Pipeline Siting Act (Natural Gas)**
Fla. Stat. Ann., 403.9401 et seq.

**Transmission Siting and Regulatory Act (Electric)**
R.I. Gen. Laws 1956, 39-25-1 et seq.

**Transmitters Act (Money)**
N.C. Gen. Stat. 1943, § 53-192 et seq.

**Transmitters Code (Money)**
Fla. Stat. Ann., 560.101 et seq.

**Transmitters of Money Act**
Ill. Comp. Stat. 1992, Ch. 205, § 657/1

**Transmitting Utility Act**
Ark. Code Ann. 1987, 4-19-101 et seq.
Wyo. Stat. Ann., § 37-4-101 et seq.

**Transplant Amendments Act of 1990**
Nov. 16, 1990, P.L. 101-616, 42 U.S. Code §§ 201 nt., 273 nt.

**Transportation Act**
Conn. Gen. Stat. Ann., § 13b-1 et seq.
Fla. Stat. Ann., 23.041 et seq.
Me. Rev. Stat. Ann. 1964, Title 23, § 4202 et seq.
Neb. Rev. Stat. 1943, 19-3901 et seq.
N.J. Stat. Ann., 27:1A-1 et seq.
N.Y. Consol. Laws, Ch. 61a
Tenn. Code Ann., 54-13-31
Tenn. Public Acts 1972, Ch. 829
Wash. Rev. Code Ann., 81.04.010 et seq.

**Transportation Act (Augusta-Richmond)**
Ga. Laws 1970, p. 3208

**Transportation Act (Auto Truck)**
Cal. Statutes 1917, Ch. 213, p. 330

**Transportation Act (Bicycle)**
Cal. Streets and Highways Code § 890 et seq.

**Transportation Act (Child Safety)**
N.Y. Education Law 1947 (Consol. Laws Ch. 16) §§ 3635, 3635b
N.Y. Transportation Law (Consol. Laws Ch. 61A) § 14

**Transportation Act (Emergency)**
N.M. Stat. Ann., 22-17-1 et seq.

**Transportation Act (Food Safety)**
Ill. Rev. Stat. 1991, Ch. 56 1/2, § 2401 et seq.

**Transportation Act (Hazardous Materials)**
Pa. Cons. Stat., Title 75, § 8301 et seq.

**Transportation Act (High-Speed Rail)**
Fla. Stat. Ann., 341.3201 et seq.

**Transportation Act (Katz-Robbins)**
Cal. Statutes 1990, Ch. 95

**Transportation Act (Limousine)**
Mich. Comp. Laws Ann., 257.1901 et seq.

**Transportation Act (Liquors)**
Ala. Code 1975, § 28-4-120 et seq.
Tex. General Laws 35th Leg., 1918, 4th C. S., p. 55, Ch. 31

**Transportation Act (Local)**
Wash. Rev. Code Ann., 39.92.010 et seq.

**Transportation Act (Motor Vehicles)**
Fla. Stat. 1983, 323.01 et seq.
Minn. Stat. Ann., 221.011 et seq.
S.C. Code Ann. 1976, § 58-23-10 et seq.
Utah Code Ann. 1953, 54-6-1 et seq.
Wis. Stat. Ann., 194.01 et seq.

**Transportation Act (Nuclear Materials)**
Colo. Rev. Stat., 40-2.2-101 et seq.

**Transportation Act (Omnibus)**
Cal. Statutes 1991, Ch. 13
Cal. Statutes 1993, Ch. 272
Cal. Statutes 1996, Ch. 10

**Transportation Act (Public)**
Neb. Rev. Stat. 1943, 13-1201 to 13-1212
Pa. Cons. Stat., Title 74, § 1101 et seq.

**Transportation Act (Pupil)**
Mich. Comp. Laws Ann., 257.1801 et seq.

**Transportation Act (Safe Rail)**
Cal. Government Code § 8574.17
Cal. Public Resources Code § 765.5
Cal. Statutes 1991, Ch. 763

**Transportation Act (School Bus)**
See School Bus Act

**Transportation Act (Schools)**
See School Transportation Act

**Transportation Act (War Emergency)**
Wash. Laws 1943, Ch. 243

**Transportation Act (West Palm Beach)**
Fla. Special Laws 1947, Ch. 24979

**Transportation Act of 1940**
Sept. 18, 1940, Ch. 722, 54 Stat. 898, 49 U.S. Code Ch. 1, prec. § 1, §§ 1, 3 to 5, 6, 12, 13, 15, 15a, 16 to 17, 20, 22, 25, 65, 66, 67, 153, Ch. 8 prec. § 301, §§ 301 to 305,;, 309 to 312, 314, 316 to 318, 320 to 322, 324a, 325 nt., Ch. 12 prec. § 901, §§ 901 to 923
Dec. 12, 1945, Ch. 573, 59 Stat. 606, 49 U.S. Code § 65
Aug. 26, 1958, P.L. 85-762, 72 Stat. 860, 49 U.S. Code § 66

**Transportation Act of 1958**
Aug. 12, 1958, P.L. 85-625, 72 Stat. 568, 49 U.S. Code §§ 1, 13, 13a, 15a, 303, 1231 to 1240

**Transportation Act of 1977 (Hazardous Materials)**
Ark. Code Ann. 1987, 27-2-101 et seq.

**Transportation Acts**
Feb. 28, 1920, Ch. 91, 41 Stat. 456, 49 U.S. Code §§ 1 to 6, 10 to 18, 19a, 20, 20a, 26, 27, 71 to 74, 76 to 80, 137, 141, 142, 316, 1361 nt.
May 8, 1920, Ch. 172, 41 Stat. 590, 49 U.S. Code § 75
Aug. 13, 1940, Ch. 666, 54 Stat. 788, 40 U.S. Code § 316
Jan. 7, 1941, Ch. 938, 54 Stat. 1226, 49 U.S. Code § 73
Oct. 25, 1972, P.L. 92-550, 86 Stat. 1163, 49 U.S. Code § 66
Nov. 6, 1978, P.L. 95-598, 40 U.S. Code § 316

**Transportation Agencies Procurement of Architectural and Engineering Services Act**
Md. Ann. Code 1974, Art. TR, § 2-301 et seq.

**Transportation Agents Act (Motor Carriers)**
Wash. Rev. Code Ann., 81.76.010 et seq.

**Transportation and Energy Planning Act**
Miss. Code Ann. 1972, § 57-39-1 et seq.

**Transportation and Highway Act**
Ark. Code Ann. 1987, 27-1-101 et seq.

**Transportation and Planning Act (Regional)**
Ind. Burns' 1933, 53-1301 et seq.
Ind. Laws 1965, Ch. 349, p. 1034

**Transportation and Production Act**
Okla. Stat. Ann., Title 52, § 21 et seq.

**Transportation and Related Agencies Appropriations Act, 1995**
Oct. 11, 1996, P.L. 104-287, 49 U.S. Code § 5302

**Transportation and Resource Development Act**
N.M. Stat. Ann., 73-23-1 et seq.

**Transportation Assistance Act (Elderly and Handicapped Coordinated Public)**
Kan. Stat. Ann., 75-5032 et seq.

**Transportation Assistance Act (Local Government)**
Fla. Stat. Ann., 335.20

**Transportation Assistance Act (Senior Citizen and Disabled Resident)**
N.J. Stat. Ann., 27:25-25 et seq.

**Transportation Assistance Authority Act**
Pa. Purdon's Stat., Title 66, § 1901 et seq.

**Transportation Assistance Capital Budget Act**
Pa. 1984 Pamph. Laws No. 1199, No. 228

**Transportation Authorities Act**
Mich. Comp. Laws Ann., 124.401 et seq.

**Transportation Authority Act (Central Florida Regional)**
Fla. Stat. Ann., 343.61 et seq.

**Transportation Authority Act (North Lake Tahoe)**
Cal. Government Code § 67960 et seq.

**Transportation Authority Act (Regional)**
See Regional Transportation Authority Act

**Transportation Authority and Improvement Act (Local)**
Cal. Public Utilities Code § 18000 et seq.

**Transportation Authority Law (Broward County)**
Fla. Special Laws 1971, Ch. 561

**Transportation Authority Law (Jacksonville)**
Fla. Stat. Ann., 349.01 et seq.

**Transportation Authority Law (Pinellas County)**
Fla. Stat. 1975, 348.012 et seq.

**Transportation Authority Law (Regional)**
S.C. Code Ann. 1976, § 58-25-10 et seq.

**Transportation Authority Reform Act (Los Angeles County Metropolitan)**
Cal. Statutes 1992, Ch. 60

**Transportation Benefits Tax Act**
N.J. Stat. Ann., 54:8A-58 et seq.

**Transportation Blueprint for Twenty-First Century (Katz-Kopp-Baker-Campbell)**
Cal. Statutes 1991, Ch. 106

**Transportation Blueprint for Twenty-First Century (Katz-Kopp-Baker)**
Cal. Statutes 1991, Ch. 105

**Transportation Bond Act**
Ill. Rev. Stat. 1991, Ch. 127, § 701 et seq.
N.J. Laws 1968, Ch. 126
N.J. Laws 1972, Ch. 46
N.J. Laws 1975, Ch. 209

**Transportation Brokers Act (Aircraft)**
Cal. Public Utilities Code § 24001 et seq.

**Transportation Brokers Act (Buses)**
Tex. Rev. Civ. Stat., Art. 911d

**Transportation Capital Facilities Bond Act**
N.Y. Laws 1967, Ch. 715

**Transportation Capital Facilities Development Act**
N.Y. Laws 1967, Ch. 717, § 1 et seq.

**Transportation Code**
Fla. Stat. Ann., 334.01 et seq., 341.11 et seq.

**Transportation Commission Act (County)**
Cal. Public Utilities Code § 130000 et seq.

**Transportation Commission Act (Metropolitan)**
Cal. Government Code § 66500 et seq.

**Transportation Commission Revenue Bond Act (Los Angeles County)**
Cal. Public Utilities Code § 130500 et seq.

**Transportation Companies Fee Act**
Wash. Rev. Code Ann., 81.24.010 et seq.

**Transportation Contract Bond Act**
Va. Acts 1988, Chs. 653, 676
Va. Acts 1990, Ch. 710
Va. Code 1950, §§ 33.1-268, 33.1-269, 33.1-277

**Transportation Contract Bond Act (1991-A)**
Va. Acts 1991, Chs. 619, 639

**Transportation Cooperation Act**
Ill. Rev. Stat. 1991, Ch. 111 2/3 § 601 et seq.

**Transportation Coordinating Committee Act**
Ill. Rev. Stat. 1991, Ch. 23, § 6751 et seq.

**Transportation Corporation Act**
Fla. Stat. Ann., 339.401 et seq.
Mo. Rev. Stat. 1978, 238.300
Tex. Rev. Civ. Stat., Art. 15281
Tex. Transportation Code, § 431.001 et seq.

**Transportation Corporations Law**
N.Y. Consol. Laws, Ch. 63

**Transportation Department Act**
N.M. Stat. Ann., 9-11-4, 67-3-6
Utah Code Ann. 1953, 63-49-1 et seq.

**Transportation Development District Act**
Mo. Rev. Stat. 1978, 238.200
N.J. Stat. Ann., 27:1C-1 et seq.

**Transportation District Act**
Cal. Statutes 1939, p. 3042
Colo. Rev. Stat., 32-9-101 et seq.
Va. Code 1950, § 15.1-1342 et seq.

**Transportation District Act (Urban)**
Ill. Rev. Stat. 1983, Ch. 111 2/3, § 501 et seq.

**Transportation Efficiency Act**
Fla. Laws 1992, Ch. 152

**Transportation Efficiency Act (Intermodal Surface)**
Cal. Streets and Highways Code §§ 163, 2600
Fla. Stat. Ann., 334.03 et seq.

**Transportation Equity Act for the 21st Century**
June 9, 1998, P.L. 105-178, 23 U.S. Code § 101 nt.
July 22, 1998, P.L. 105-206, 2 U.S. Code §§ 900, 901 nt., 902 nt.; 16 U.S. Code §§ 668dd nt., 777c, 777g, 777g-1; 23 U.S. Code §§ prec. 101, 101 nt., 104, 104 nt., 105, 109 nt., 110, 115, 118, 119, 120, 124, 126, 129, 134, 143, 144, 144 nt., 149 nt., 150, 154, 164, 188, 202, 322, 402 nt., 502 nt.; 26 U.S. Code §§ 9503, 9504; 38 U.S. Code §§ prec. 1101, 1103, 1103 nt., 1110, 1110 nt., 3532, 3532 nt., 3534, 3542, 3687; 49 U.S. Code § 111 nt., 5505, 30105, 31136 nt., 31314
Oct. 21, 1998, P.L. 105-277, 23 U.S. Code § 502 nt.; 49 U.S. Code § 5307 nt.
May 21, 1999, P.L. 106-31, 49 U.S. Code § 5307 nt.

**Transportation Facilities Bond Act**
Va. Acts 1973, Ch. 230
Va. Acts 1979, Ch. 221
Va. Acts 1984, Ch. 89
Va. Acts 1991, Chs. 615, 620

**Transportation Finance and Administration Act**
Ill. Laws 1979, Second Special Session, P.A. 81-3

**Transportation Funding Act (High-Cost)**
Ark. Code Ann. 1987, 6-20-1701 et seq.

**Transportation Improvement Act (Costa Rail)**
Cal. Streets and Highways Code §§ 2701 to 2701.02, 2701.02 to 2701.05, 2701.10 to 2701.23, 2702 to 2702.02, 2702.02 to 2702.05, 2702.10 to 2702.22, 2703 to 2703.02, 2703.05 to 2703.08, 2703.10 et seq.

**Transportation Improvement Act (Fresno County)**
Cal. Public Utilities Code § 142000 et seq.

**Transportation Improvement Act (Social Service)**
Cal. Government Code § 15950 et seq.

**Transportation Improvement and Reform Act (Deddeh)**
Cal. Government Code § 14524.15
Cal. Streets and Highway Code § 2700
Cal. Streets and Highways Code §§ 163, 2600

**Transportation Improvement District in Individual Counties Act**
Va. Code 1950, § 15.1-1372.21 et seq.

**Transportation Improvement District in Individual Localities Act (Primary Highway)**
Va. Code 1950, § 15.1-1372.21 et seq.

**Transportation Improvement District in Multi-County Areas Act**
Va. Code 1950, § 15.1-1372.1 et seq.

**Transportation Infrastructure Bank Act**
S.C. Code Ann. 1976, § 11-43-110 et seq.

**Transportation Infrastructure Finance and Innovation Act of 1998**
June 9, 1998, P.L. 105-178, Subtitle E, Chapter 1, 23 U.S. Code § 101 nt.

**Transportation Infrastructure Renewal Bond Act**
N.Y. Transportation Law (Consol. Laws, Ch. 63), § 420 et seq.

**Transportation Law (Commercial)**
Ill. Comp. Stat. 1992, Ch. 625, § 5/18a-1101 et seq.

**Transportation License Tax Law (Motor Vehicles)**
Cal. Revenue and Taxation Code § 9601 et seq.

**Transportation of Foreign Mail by Aircraft Act**
Aug. 23, 1958, P.L. 85-726, 72 Stat. 809, 49, §§ 485a, 485b
Colo. Rev. Stat., 4-2.1-101 et seq.
Ga. Code Ann., 32-6-220 et seq.

**Transportation of Handicapped Children Act**
Tenn. Code Ann., 49-6-2114

**Transportation of Hazardous Materials Act**
Colo. Rev. Stat. 40-2.1-101 et seq.
Ga. Code Ann., 32-6-220 et seq.

**Transportation of Money and Valuables Act**
Del. Code of 1974, Title 5, § 3201 et seq.

**Transportation of Poor and Indigent Persons Act**
Conn. Gen. Stat. Ann., § 17-293

**Transportation Partnership Act**
Pa. Purdon's Stat., Title 53, § 1621 et seq.

**Transportation Passenger Rights Act (Public)**
S.C. Code Ann. 1976, § 58-23-1810 et seq.

**Transportation Payment Act of 1972**
Oct. 25, 1972, P.L. 92-550, 49 U.S. Code § 66 nt.

**Transportation Policy Act (Sensible)**
Me. Rev. Stat. Ann. 1964, Title 23, § 73

**Transportation Preservation Act**
Mich. Comp. Laws Ann., 474.51 et seq.

**Transportation Rate Fund Act**
Cal. Public Utilities Code § 5001 et seq.

**Transportation Reform, Accountability and Cooperation Act**
Fla. Laws 1985, Ch. 180

**Transportation Rehabilitation and Improvement Bond Act**
N.J. Laws 1979, Ch. 165

**Transportation Replacement Housing and Relocation Act**
N.J. Stat. Ann., 27:7-72 et seq.

**Transportation Research Act**
Tex. Education Code, Art. 150.001 to 150.003

**Transportation Revisory Act**
Ill. Laws 1979, P.A. 81-840

**Transportation Security Act**
Ala. Code 1975, § 13A-7-1

**Transportation Service District Act**
Va. Code 1950, § 15.1-791.1 et seq.

**Transportation Services Act**
N.M. Stat. Ann., 15-8-1 et seq.

**Transportation Services Bureau Act**
Neb. Rev. Stat. 1943, 81-1008 et seq.

**Transportation Study Commission Act (Bay Area)**
Cal. Government Code § 66500 et seq.

**Transportation System Assistance and Financing Act**
N.Y. Highway Law (Consol. Laws Ch. 25) §§ 10a, 10c
N.Y. Public Authorities Law (Consol, Laws Ch. 43A) §§ 376, 552, 553, 553e, 1203a, 1205, 1207m, 1209, 1219a, 1266, 1266c, 1269a to 1269c, 1277
N.Y. State Finance Law (Consol. Laws Ch. 56) §§ 88 et seq.

**Transportation Tax Acts**
Oct. 3, 1917, Ch. 63, 40 Stat. 314
Feb. 24, 1919, 40 Stat. 1101
Nov. 23, 1921, Ch. 136, 42 Stat. 320

**Transportation Terminal Authority Act (San Francisco Bay Area)**
Cal. Government Code § 67500 et seq.

**Transportation Ticket Fraud Act**
Ill. Rev. Stat. 1989, Ch. 114, § 104.9 et seq.

**Transportation Trust Fund Act**
Del. Code of 1974, Title 2, § 1401 et seq.

**Transportation Trust Fund Authority Act**
N.J. Stat. Ann., 27:1B-1 et seq.

**Trap Act (Corporate Officers)**
N.J. Stat. Ann., Superseded Vol., 14:8-16

**Trapping Act**
Va. Code 1950, § 29-51 et seq.

**Trauma Act (Roy E. Campbell)**
Fla. Stat. Ann., 395.0146, 395.031, 395.033 to 395.0345, 395.037

**Trauma Care Act**
Fla. Stat. Ann., 395.031 et seq.

**Trauma Care System Act**
Colo. Rev. Stat., 25-3.5-701 et seq.

**Trauma Care System and Statewide Emergency Medical Services Act**
Wash. Rev. Code Ann., 70.108.010 et seq.

**Trauma Care Systems Development Act**
Iowa Code 1995, 147A.20 et seq.
Neb. Rev. Stat. 1943, 71-5166 et seq.

**Trauma Care Systems Planning and Development Act of 1990**
Nov. 16, 1990, P.L. 101-590, 42 U.S. Code § 201 nt.

**Trauma Reduction Act (Child Witness)**
Ill. Rev. Stat. 1991, Ch. 37, §§ 800, 801

**Trauma Scene Waste Management Act**
Cal. Health and Safety Code § 118321 et seq.

**Trauma System Act (Statewide)**
Neb. Rev. Stat. 1943, 71-8201 to 71-8253

**Trautman Act (Wills)**
Tenn. Code Ann., 32-3-107

**Travel Act**
Sept. 13, 1961, P.L. 87-228, 75 Stat. 498, 18 U.S. Code § 1952
July 7, 1965, P.L. 89-68, 79 Stat. 212, 18 U.S. Code § 1952

**Travel Act (Hospitality and Visitor)**
La. Rev. Stat. Ann., 51:1251 et seq.

**Travel Act (Mental Health Patient)**
Ill. Rev. Stat. 1991, Ch. 91 1/2, §§ 1450, 1451

**Travel Act (Student)**
P.R. Laws Ann. 1954, Title 18, § 921 et seq.

**Travel and Transportation Reform Act of 1998**
Oct. 19, 1998, P.L. 105-264, 112 Stat. 2350, 5 U.S. Code § 5701 nt.

**Travel Expense Act (Circuit Court Judges)**
Ill. Rev. Stat. 1991, Ch. 53, § 5.01, 5.1

**Travel Expense Act of 1949**
June 9, 1949, Ch. 185, 63 Stat. 166 (U.S. Code 5 U.S. Code §§ 102, 105, 2105, 2106, 5701, 5702, 5704 to 5708)
April 26, 1950, Ch. 108, 64 Stat. 89 (U.S. Code 5 U.S. Code §§ 2105, 5701, 5702, 5707)
July 28, 1955, Ch. 424, 69 Stat. 393 (U.S. Code 5 U.S. Code §§ 105,5701, 5702, 5704, 5707)
Aug. 14, 1961, P.L. 87-139, 75 Stat. 339 (U.S. Code 5 U.S. Code §§ 2105, 5701, 5702, 5704, 5707)

**Travel Expense Amendments Act of 1975**
May 19, 1975, P.L. 94-22, 89 Stat. 84, 2 U.S. Code § 68b; 5 U.S. Code § 5701 et seq.

**Travel Pay and Allowance Act**
Ida. Code 1947, 67-2007, 67-2008

**Travel Promotion Consumer Protection Act**
Ill. Rev. Stat. 1991, Ch. 121 1/2, § 1851 et seq.

**Travel Regulation Act**
Alaska Stat. 1962, § 39.20.110 et seq.

**Travel Regulations Act**
Tex. Government Code, § 660.001 et seq.

**Travel Reimbursement Act**
Okla. Stat. Ann., Title 74, § 500.1 et seq.

**Travel Service Training Act**
N.M. Stat. Ann., 21-20-1 et seq.

**Traveler Information Logo Signing Act**
Okla. Stat. Ann., Title 69, § 4021 et seq.

**Travelers Check and Money Order Licensees Act**
Conn. Gen. Stat. Ann., § 36-530 et seq.

**Travelers Check Licensees Act**
Conn. Gen. Stat. Ann., § 36-530 et seq.

**Travelers Checks Act**
Cal. Financial Code § 1851 et seq.

**Traveling Library Act**
Wash. Laws 1907, Ch. 164

**Travelink Traffic Mitigation Act**
Del. Code of 1974, Title 30, § 2030 to 2035

**Travis, May, Overbey and Davidson Act (State Colleges)**
Ky. Rev. Stat. 1971, 164.290, 164.310

**Traxler-McCauley-Law-Bowman Bingo Act**
Mich. Comp. Laws Ann., 432.102 et seq.

**Traxler-McCauley-Law-Bowman-McNeely Lottery Act**
Mich. Comp. Laws Ann., 432.1 et seq.

**Traylor-Neill Act (Highways)**
Ga. Code Ann., 32-4-1

**Treason Act**
Mich. Comp. Laws Ann., 750.544 et seq.
N.H. Rev. Stat. 1955, 648:1 et seq.
R.I. Gen. Laws 1956, 11-43-1 et seq.
Wash. Rev. Code Ann., 9.82.010 et seq.

**Treasure Island Conversion Act**
Cal. Health and Safety Code § 33492.5
Cal. Statutes 1968, Ch. 1333, § 2.1

**Treasurer Act**
Ill. Rev. Stat. 1991, Ch. 130, § 0.01 et seq.

**Treasurer as Custodian of Funds Act**
Ill. Rev. Stat. 1991, Ch. 130, § 19.9, et seq.

**Treasurer's Sales Act (Second Class Cities)**
Pa. Purdon's Stat., Title 53, § 27101 et seq.

**Treasury and General Government Appropriations Act, 1998**
Oct. 10, 1997, P.L. 105-61, 111 Stat. 1272
Oct. 27, 1997, P.L. 105-66, 5 U.S. Code § 8331 nt.

**Treasury and General Government Appropriations Act, 1999**
Oct. 21, 1998, P.L. 105-277, 112 Stat. 2681

**Treasury and Post Office Departments Appropriation Acts**
March 25, 1940, Ch. 71, 54 Stat. 55
May 31, 1941, Ch. 156, Stat. 212, 7 U.S. Code §§ 610, 641
Feb. 21, 1942, Ch. 108, 56 Stat. 109
March 10, 1942, Ch. 178, 56 Stat. 152, 7 U.S. Code § 610 nt., prec. 641 nt.
June 30, 1943, Ch. 179, 57 Stat. 250, 7 U.S. Code §§ 610, prec. 641; 19 U.S. Code § 5 nt.
April 22, 1944, Ch. 175, 58 Stat. 195, 7 U.S. Code §§ 610, nts. prec. 641
April 24, 1945, Ch. 92, 59 Stat. 56, 7 U.S. Code §§ 610, prec. 641; 31 U.S. Code § 760 nt.
July 20, 1946, Ch. 588, 60 Stat. 568, 7 U.S. Code §§ 610, prec. 641; 31 U.S. Code § 760 nt.
July 1, 1947, Ch. 186, 61 Stat. 216, 31 U.S. Code § 760 nt.
June 14, 1948, Ch. 466, 62 Stat. 408, 31 U.S. Code § 760 nt.
June 30, 1949, Ch. 286, 63 Stat. 356, 12 U.S. Code § 362; 15 U.S. Code §§ 603b, 603c; 19 U.S. Code §§ 6e 2074; 31 U.S. Code § 760 nt.
Aug. 11, 1951, Ch. 301, 65 Stat. 182, 3 U.S. Code § 203 nt.; 12 U.S. Code § 362; 31 U.S. Code §§ 418a, 760 nt.
June 30, 1952, Ch. 523, 66 Stat. 289, 3 U.S. Code § 203 nt.; 12 U.S. Code § 362; 31 U.S. Code § 760 nt.
June 18, 1953, Ch. 132, 67 Stat. 67, 12 U.S. Code § 362; 20 U.S. Code § 241 nt.; 31 U.S. Code § 760 nt.

**Treasury Department Appropriation Acts**
March 25, 1940, Ch. 71, 54 Stat. 55
May 31, 1941, Ch. 156, 55 Stat. 212, 7 U.S. Code §§ 610, 641
March 10, 1942, Ch. 178, 56 Stat. 152, 7 U.S. Code § 610, nts. prec. § 641
June 30, 1943, Ch. 179, 57 Stat. 250, 7 U.S. Code §§ 610, prec. 641; 19 U.S. Code § 5 nt.
April 22, 1944, Ch. 175, 58 Stat. 195, 7 U.S. Code §§ 610, nts. prec. 641
April 24, 1945, Ch. 92, 59 Stat. 56, 7 U.S. Code §§ 610, prec. 641; 31 U.S. Code § 760 nt.
July 20, 1946, Ch. 588, 60 Stat. 568, 7 U.S. Code §§ 610, prec. 641; 31 U.S. Code § 760 nt.
July 1, 1947, Ch. 186, 61 Stat. 216, 31 U.S. Code § 760 nt.
June 14, 1948, Ch. 466, 62 Stat. 408, 31 U.S. Code § 760 nt.
June 30, 1949, Ch. 286, 63 Stat. 356, 12 U.S. Code § 362; 19 U.S. Code §§ 6e, 2074; 31 U.S. Code § 760 nt.
Sept. 6, 1950, Ch. 896, 64 Stat. 634, 12 U.S. Code § 362; 31 U.S. Code § 760 nt.
Aug. 11, 1951, Ch. 301, 65 Stat. 182, 3 U.S. Code § 203 nt.; 12 U.S. Code § 362; 31 U.S. Code §§ 418a, 760 nt.
June 30, 1952, Ch. 523, 66 Stat. 289, 3 U.S. Code § 203 nt.; 12 U.S. Code § 362; 31 U.S. Code § 760 nt.
June 18, 1953, Ch. 132, 67 Stat. 67, 12 U.S. Code § 362; 20 U.S. Code § 241 nt.; 31 U.S. Code § 760 nt.
May 28, 1954, Ch. 242, 68 Stat. 144, 12 U.S. Code §§ 362, 363; 20 U.S. Code § 241 nt.; 31 U.S. Code § 760 nt.

June 11, 1959, P.L. 86-39, 73 Stat. 67, 20 U.S. Code § 241 nt.
June 30, 1960, P.L. 86-561, 74 Stat. 283, 20 U.S. Code § 241 nt.
Aug. 21, 1961, P.L. 87-159, 75 Stat. 393, 20 U.S. Code § 241 nt.
Aug. 6, 1962, P.L. 87-575, 76 Stat. 310, 20 U.S. Code § 241 nt.
June 13, 1963, P.L. 88-39, 77 Stat. 58, 20 U.S. Code § 241 nt.
Aug. 1, 1964, P.L. 88-392, 78 Stat. 367, 20 U.S. Code § 241 nt.
June 30, 1965, P.L. 89-57, 79 Stat. 196, 20 U.S. Code § 241 nt.
June 29, 1966, P.L. 89-474, 80 Stat. 222, 14 U.S. Code § 92 nt.; 20 U.S. Code § 241 nt.
July 7, 1967, P.L. 90-47, 81 Stat. 113
June 19, 1968, P.L. 90-350, 82 Stat. 190
Sept. 29, 1969, P.L. 91-74, 83 Stat. 118, 31 U.S. Code § 1032
Sept. 26, 1970, P.L. 91-422, 84 Stat. 872
July 9, 1971, P.L. 92-49, 85 Stat. 108
Aug. 9, 1975, P.L. 94-91, 89 Stat. 441, 26 U.S. Code § 7443 nt.; 31 U.S. Code §§ 638c nt., 699b; 33 U.S. Code § 776; 40 U.S. Code § 490
Oct. 18, 1986, P.L. 99-500, 100 Stat. 3656
Oct. 30, 1986, P.L. 99-591, 100 Stat. 3656
Dec. 22, 1987, P.L. 100-202, 101 Stat. 1329
Sept. 22, 1988, P.L. 100-440, 39 U.S. Code § 403 nt.
Nov. 3, 1989, P.L. 101-136, 103 Stat. 783

**Treasury Department Appropriations Act, 1991**
Nov. 5, 1990, P.L. 101-509, 42 U.S. Code § 3771 nt.

**Treasury Department Appropriations Act, 1992**
Oct. 28, 1991, P.L. 102-141, 105 Stat. 834

**Treasury Department Appropriations Act, 1993**
Oct. 6, 1992, P.L. 102-393, 26 U.S. Code § 7803 nt.; 31 U.S. Code sect; nt.; 42 U.S. Code § 3771 nt.

**Treasury Department Appropriations Act, 1994**
Oct. 28, 1993, P.L. 103-123, 107 Stat. 1226

**Treasury Department Appropriations Act, 1995**
Sept. 30, 1994, P.L. 103-329, 108 Stat. 2382

**Treasury Department Appropriations Act, 1996**
Nov. 19, 1995, P.L. 104-52, Title I, 109 Stat. 468

**Treasury Department Appropriations Act, 1997**
Sept. 30, 1996, P.L. 104-208, Title I, 110 Stat. 3009

**Treasury Department Appropriations Act, 1998**
Oct. 10, 1997, P.L. 105-61, Title I, 111 Stat. 1272

**Treasury Department Appropriations Act, 1999**
Oct. 21, 1998, P.L. 105-277, 101(h), Title I, 112 Stat. 2681

**Treasury Forfeiture Fund Act of 1992**
Oct. 6, 1992 P.L. 102-393, 31 U.S. Code § 9701 nt.

**Treasury Fund Structure Act**
Mont. Code Ann., 17-2-101 et seq.

**Treasury Investment Act**
Ohio Rev. Code 1953, 731.56 et seq.

**Treasury Management Act (State)**
Ark. Code Ann. 1987, 19-3-201

**Treasury, Post Office, and Executive Office Appropriation Acts**
June 13, 1963, P.L. 88-39, 77 Stat. 58, 12 U.S. Code § 364; 20 U.S. Code § 241 nt.
Aug. 1, 1964, P.L. 88-392, 78 Stat. 367, 12 U.S. Code § 364; 20 U.S. Code § 241 nt.
June 30, 1965, P.L. 89-57, 79 Stat. 196, 12 U.S. Code § 364; 20 U.S Code § 241 nt.
June 29, 1966, P.L. 89-474, 80 Stat. 222, 3 U.S. Code § 102 nt.; 12 U.S. Code § 364; 14 U.S. Code § 92 nt.; 20 U.S. Code § 241 nt.; 26 U.S. Code § 7443 nt.
June 19, 1968, P.L. 90-350, 82 Stat. 190, 3 U.S. Code § 102 nt.; 12 U.S. Code § 364; 18 U.S. Code § 1461 nt.; 26 U.S. Code § 7443 nt.
*Continued*

July 7, 1968, P.L. 90-47, 81 Stat. 113, 3 U.S. Code § 102 nt.; 12 U.S. Code § 364; 26 U.S. Code § 7443

Sept. 29, 1969, P.L. 91-74, 83 Stat. 116, 3 U.S. Code § 102 nt.; U.S. Code § 364; 18 U.S. Code § 1461 nt.; 26 U.S. Code § 7443 nt.; 31 U.S. Code § 1032

Sept. 26, 1970, P.L. 91-422, 84 Stat. 879

**Treasury-Post Office Appropriation Acts**

May 6, 1939, Ch. 115, 53 Stat. 654, 31 U.S. Code § 529b

June 1, 1955, Ch. 113, 69 Stat. 72, 12 U.S. Code §§ 362, 363; 20 U.S. Code § 241 nt.; 31 U.S. Code §§ 760 nt., 1031

April 2, 1956, Ch. 161, 70 Stat. 92, 20 U.S. Code § 241 nt.

May 27, 1957, P.L. 85-37, 71 Stat. 35, 20 U.S. Code § 241 nt.

March 28, 1958, P.L. 85-354, 72 Stat. 61, 12 U.S. Code § 364; 20 U.S. Code § 241 nt.

June 11, 1959, P.L. 86-39, 73 Stat. 65, 12 U.S. Code § 364; 20 U.S. Code § 241 nt.

June 30, 1960, P.L. 86-561, 74 Stat. 283, 12 U.S. Code § 364; 20 U.S. Code § 241 nt.

Aug. 21, 1961, P.L. 87-159, 75 Stat. 393, 12 U.S. Code § 364; 20 U.S. Code § 241 nt.

**Treasury-Post Office Departments and Executive Office Appropriation Act, 1963**

Aug. 6, 1962, P.L. 87-575, 76 Stat. 310, 12 U.S. Code § 364; 20 U.S. Code § 241 nt.

**Treasury-Post Office Departments Appropriation Act, 1951**

Sept. 6, 1950, Ch. 896, 64 Stat. 634, 12 U.S. Code § 362; 31 U.S. Code § 760 nt.

**Treasury-Post Office Supply Act**

March 28, 1938, Ch. 55, 52 Stat. 120, 31 U.S. Code § 529b

**Treasury, Postal Service, and General Government Appropriation Act, 1970**

July 9, 1971, P.L. 92-49, 85 Stat. 108, 3 U.S. Code § 102 nt.; 26 U.S. Code § 7443 nt.; 31 U.S. Code § 638c

**Treasury, Postal Service, and General Government Appropriations Act, 1976**

Aug. 9, 1975, P.L. 94-91, 89 Stat. 441, 26 U.S. Code § 7443 nt.; 31 U.S. Code §§ 638c nt., 699b; 33 U.S. Code § 776; 40 U.S. Code § 490

**Treasury, Postal Service and General Government Appropriations Act, 1988**

Dec. 22, 1987, P.L. 100-202, 101 Stat. 1329

**Treasury, Postal Service and General Government Appropriations Act, 1989**

Sept. 22, 1988, P.L. 100-446, 3 U.S. Code § 102 nt.,; 5 U.S. Code §§ 3101 nt., 3341 nt., 5305 nt., 5343 nt., 5724, 6302 nt.; 22 U.S. Code § 211a; 26 U.S. Code § 7443 nt.; 31 U.S. Code §§ 343 nt., 5114 nt.; 33 U.S. Code § 776; 39 U.S. Code § 403 nt.; 40 U.S. Code §§ 490a, 490c, 490d; 50 U.S. Code § 98h

Nov. 3, 1989, P.L. 101-136, 103 Stat. 815

**Treasury, Postal Service and General Government Appropriations Act, 1990**

Nov. 3, 1989, P.L. 101-136, 103 Stat. 783

**Treasury, Postal Service and General Government Appropriations Act, 1991**

Nov. 5, 1990, P.L. 101-509, 5 U.S. Code §§ 1701 nt., 3101 nt., 5303 nt., 5304a, 5343 nt., 6307 nt., 18 U.S. Code § 3056 nt., 28 U.S. Code § 509 nt., 31 U.S. Code 1343 nt., 39 U.S. Code §§ 3401, 3401 nt., 40 U.S. Code § 490c, 41 U.S. Code § 261

**Treasury, Postal Service and General Government Appropriations Act, 1992**

Oct. 28, 1991, P.L. 102-141, 105 Stat. 834

Sept. 23, 1992, P.L. 102-368, 106 Stat. 1131

Sept. 30, 1994, P.L. 103-329, 5 U.S. Code § 5941 nt.

Nov. 19, 1995, P.L. 104-52, 5 U.S. Code § 5941 nt.

Oct. 10, 1997, P.L. 105-61, 5 U.S. Code § 5941 nt.

**Treasury, Postal Service, and General Government Appropriations Act, 1993**
Oct. 6, 1992, P.L. 102-393, 3 U.S. Code § 102 nt.; 5 U.S. Code §§ 1101 nt., 3101 nt., prec. 3341 nt., 5343 nt., 8902, 8902 nt.; 16 U.S. Code § 403 nt.; 18 U.S. Code §§ 981, 982, 1761, 1762; 19 U.S. Code § 2071 nt., 21 U.S. Code § 1509; 26 U.S. Code § 7443 nt., 7803 nt., 9003, 9003 nt.; 28 U.S. Code § 524; 31 U.S. Code § sect; 306 nt., 1343 nt., prec. 9701, 9701 nt., 9703; 33 U.S. Code § 776; 39 U.S. Code §§ 403 nt., 2003, prec. 3001, 3015, 3015 nt.; 40 U.S. Code §§ 490b, 490c, 490f, 490g; 41 U.S. Code § 261; 42 U.S. Code §§ 415 nt., 3771 nt., 6962; 50 U.S. Code § 1705; 50 U.S. Code App. § 16
Dec. 21, 1995, P.L. 104-66, 5 U.S. Code prec. § 3341 nt.

**Treasury, Postal Service, and General Government Appropriations Act, 1994**
Oct. 28, 1993, P.L. 103-123, 107 Stat. 1226

**Treasury, Postal Service and General Government Appropriations Act, 1995**
Sept. 30, 1994, P.L. 103-329, 108 Stat. 2382
Nov. 19, 1995, P.L. 104-52, 109 Stat. 468

**Treasury, Postal Service, and General Government Appropriations Act, 1996**
Nov. 19, 1995, P.L. 104-52, 109 Stat. 468
April 26, 1996, P.L. 104-134, 26 U.S. Code § 7801 nt.
Sept. 30, 1996, P.L. 104-208, 5 U.S. Code § 5343 nt.; 26 U.S. Code § 7801 nt.

**Treasury, Postal Service, and General Government Appropriations Act, 1997**
Sept. 30, 1996, P.L. 104-208, 110 Stat. 3009

**Treasury Warrant Act**
Ky. Rev. Stat. 1971, 41.120 et seq.

**Treated Fence Post Act**
Fla. Stat. Ann., 501.90

**Treated Timber Products Act**
Ga. Code Ann., 2-14-100 et seq.
Mo. Rev. Stat., 280.005 et seq. Rev. Stat. 1973, 27-10.5-101 et seq.

**Treatment Act (Insect Sting Emergency)**
Fla. Stat. Ann., 402.60

**Treatment Act (Mandatory)**
Ala. Acts 1990, No. 390

**Treatment Act for Drug Abusers**
Kan. Stat. Ann., 65-5201 et seq.

**Treatment and Care of the Developmentally Disabled Act**
Colo. Rev. Stat., 27-10.5-101 et seq.

**Treatment and Corrections Act**
Neb. Rev. Stat. 1943, 83-170 et seq.

**Treatment and Corrections Act (Prisons and Prisoners)**
Neb. Rev. Stat. 1943, 83-170 et seq.

**Treatment and Prevention Act (Substance Abuse)**
Me. Rev. Stat. Ann. 1964, Title 5, § 20001 et seq.
N.M. Stat. Ann., 43-3-8

**Treatment and Support Act (Alcoholism and Drug Addiction)**
Wash. Rev. Code Ann., 74.50.010 et seq.

**Treatment Facilities Marketing Practices Act**
Tex. Health and Safety Code, § 164.001 et seq.

**Treatment of Dependent Neglected and Delinquent Children Act**
Ill. Rev. Stat. 1991, Ch. 37, § 801-1 et seq.

**Treatment of Minors Act (Psychiatric Inpatient)**
Va. Code 1950, § 16.1-335 et seq.

**Treatment of Wastewater Act (Revolving Fund)**
Mont. Laws 1989, Ch. 678

**Treatment Plant and Water Pollution Control Grant Act (Sewage)**
Fla. Stat. Ann., 403.1821 et seq.

**Treatment Works Penalty Law (Publicly Owned)**
Pa. 1992 Pamph. Laws, No. 9

**Treaty of Annexation (1897)**
Haw. Fundamental Law of 1904, p. 243

**Treaty of Friendship (Austro-Hungary 1875)**
Haw. Session Laws 1876, p. 166, June 2, 1876

**Treaty of Friendship (Bremen 1851)**
Haw. Session Laws 1855, p. 61, March 27, 1854

**Treaty of Friendship (Denmark 1846)**
Haw. Statute Laws Vol. 2, p. 103, Oct. 19, 1846

**Treaty of Friendship (France 1846)**
Haw. Statute Laws Vol. 2, p. 101, March 26, 1846

**Treaty of Friendship (France 1857)**
Haw. Session Laws 1858-59, p. 489, Sept. 8, 1858

**Treaty of Friendship (Great Britain 1846)**
Haw. Statute Laws Vol. 2, p. 100, March 26, 1846

**Treaty of Friendship (Great Britain 1951)**
Haw. Session Laws 1858-59, p. 467, May 6, 1852

**Treaty of Friendship (Hamburg 1848)**
Haw. Statute Laws Supplement, p. 59, Jan. 8, 1848

**Treaty of Friendship (Italy 1863)**
Haw. Session Laws 1870, p. 73, Feb. 27, 1869

**Treaty of Friendship (Japan 1871)**
Haw. Session Laws 1872, p. 44, Sept. 27, 1871

**Treaty of Friendship (Russia 1869)**
Haw. Session Laws 1870, p. 83, June 19, 1869

**Treaty of Friendship (Spain 1863)**
Haw. Session Laws 1870, p. 85, Sept. 2, 1870

**Treaty of Friendship (Sweden and Norway 1852)**
Haw. Session Laws 1855, p. 64, April 5, 1855

**Treaty of Friendship (United States 1849)**
Haw. Session Laws 1850, p. 208, Dec. 20, 1849

**Treaty of Reciprocity (United States Export-Import)**
Haw. Session Laws 1876, p. 161, Jan. 30, 1875

**Treble Damage Act (Contracts)**
Tenn. Code Ann. 1955, 47-50-109

**Treble Damage Act (Timber)**
Cal. Civil Code § 3346
Wash. Rev. Code Ann., 64.12.030

**Treble Damage Law (Contracts)**
Tenn. Code Ann., 47-50-109

**Tree and Flower Act**
Ill. Rev. Stat. 1991, Ch. 1, § 2901-40

**Tree Cutting Act (Wrongful)**
Ill. Rev. Stat. 1991, Ch. 96 1/2, § 9400 et seq.

**Tree Expert Act**
N.J. Stat. Ann., 45:15C-1 et seq.

**Tree Fruit Industry Self-Improvement Act**
W. Va. Code 1966 § 19-2G-1 et seq.

**Tree Fruit Research Act**
Wash. Rev. Code Ann., 15.26.010 et seq.

**Tree Growth Tax Act**
Me. Rev. Stat. Ann. 1964, Title 36, § 571 et seq.
Minn. Stat. Ann., 270.31 et seq.

**Tree Planting Act**
Cal. Streets and Highways Code § 22000 et seq.

**Tree Seedling Act**
Pa. Purdon's Stat., Title 32, § 453 et seq.

**Tree Trimming Act (Railroad)**
Wis. Stat. Ann., 195.29, Subsec. 6

**Trees and Shrubs Act**
Mich. Comp. Laws Ann., 286.201 et seq.

**Trench Safety Act**
Fla. Stat. Ann., 553.60 et seq.

**Trespass Act**
Ala. Code 1975, § 13A-7-2 et seq.
Cal. Penal Code § 602
Fla. Stat. Ann., 810.08 et seq.
Ga. Code Ann., 16-7-21
La. Rev. Stat. Ann., 14:63 et seq.
Md. Ann. Code 1957, Art. 27, § 577
Mich. Comp. Laws Ann., 600.2918, 600.2919
N.C. Gen. Stat. 1943, § 14-134
Pa. 1905 Pamph. Laws 169, No. 124
S.C. Code Ann. 1976, § 16-11-510 et seq.
Wash. Rev. Code Ann., 9A.52.010 et seq.

**Trespass Act (Civil)**
Mich. Comp. Laws Ann., 600.2918, 600.2919

**Trespass Act (Criminal)**
Ind. Code. Ann., 35-43-2-2
Mich. Comp. Laws Ann., 750.546 et seq.
Ohio Rev. Code 1953, 2911.21

**Trespass Act (Industrial Property)**
Cal. Penal Code § 552 et seq.

**Trespass Act (Timber)**
Del. Code of 1974, Title 25, § 1401 et seq.

**Trespass by Animals Act**
S.D. Codified Laws 1967, 40-28-1 et seq.

**Trespass to Try Title Act**
Tex. Property Code, § 22.001 et seq.

**Trespassing Law (Animal)**
Iowa Code Ann., 169B.1 et seq.

**Tri-City Regional Port District Act**
Ill. Rev. Stat. 1991, Ch. 19, § 284 et seq.

**Tri-County Authority Act (Santa Clara-Alameda-San Benito)**
Cal. Statutes 1955, Ch. 1289, p. 2349

**Tri-County Commuter Rail Authority Act**
Fla. Stat. Ann., 343.51 et seq.

**Tri-County River Valley Development Authority Law**
Ill. Rev. Stat. 1991, Ch. 85, § 7501 et seq.

**Tri-County Water Authority Act**
Ga. Laws 1986, p. 5318

**Tri-State Compact (Sanitation Commission)**
Conn. Gen. Stat. Ann., § 22a-293 et seq.

**Tri-State Compact Act (Interstate Sanitation)**
Conn. Gen. Stat. Ann., § 22a-293 et seq.
N.J. Stat. Ann., 32:18-1 et seq.

**Tri-State Delta Economic Compact**
La. Rev. Stat. Ann., 51:1021 to 51:1024

**Tri-State High Speed Rail Line Compact Act**
Ill. Rev. Stat. 1991, Ch. 114, §§ 650, 651

**Tri-State Lotto Compact Act**
Me. Rev. Stat. Ann. 1964, Title 8, § 401 et seq.
Me. Rev. Stat. Ann. 1964, Title 8, § 401 et seq.
N.H. Rev. Stat. 1955, 287-F:1 et seq.
Vt. Stat. Ann., Title 31, § 671 et seq.

**Tri-State Regional Planning Compact**
Conn. Gen. Stat. Ann., § 16-339
N.J. Stat. Ann., 32:22B-1 et seq.
N.Y. Unconsolidated Laws § 8301 et seq.

**Tri-State Transportation Compact Act**
N.J. Stat. Ann., 32:22B-1 et seq.
N.Y. Laws 1963, Ch. 617
N.Y. Laws 1964, Ch. 316
N.Y. Laws 1965, Ch. 413

**Trial Commissioner Act (County Courts)**
Ky. Rev. Stat. 1971, Superseded Vol., 25.280

**Trial Consolidation Act**
Ala. Code 1958, Title 7, § 221

**Trial Court Delay Reduction Act**
Cal. Government Code § 68600 et seq.

**Trial Court Funding Act**
Cal. Government Code § 77000 et seq.

**Trial Court Funding Act (Lockyer-Isenberg)**
Cal. Statutes 1997, Ch. 850

**Trial Court Realignment and Efficiency Act**
Cal. Government Code § 12419.10
Cal. Statutes 1991, Ch. 90

**Trial Judges and Solicitors Retirement Fund Act**
Ga. Code Ann., 47-10-1 et seq.

**Trial Jury Selection and Management Act**
Cal. Code of Civil Procedure § 190 et seq.

**Trial Justices Act**
Conn. Gen. Stat. Ann., § 51-111 et seq.
Va. Code 1950, § 16-41 et seq.

**Trial Law (Misdemeanor)**
N.Y. Criminal Procedure Law (Consol. Laws Ch. 11A) §§ 340.40, Subd. 2, 400.22
N.Y. Penal Law 1965 (Consol. Law Ch. 40) § 70.15, Subd. 1

**Trial Magistrates Act**
Md. Ann. Code 1974, Art. CJ, § 4-101 et seq.

**Trial of Right of Property Act**
Ill. Rev. Stat. 1991, Ch. 110, § 12-201 et seq.

**Tribal Development Student Assistance Act**
July 23, 1992, P.L. 102-325, 25 U.S. Code §§ 3331 to 3338

**Tribal Economic Development and Technology Related Education Assistance Act of 1990**
Sept. 25, 1990, P.L. 101-392, 25 U.S. Code prec. § 1801 nt.
Oct. 7, 1998, P.L. 105-244, 25 U.S. Code § 1852

**Tribal Self-Governance Act**
Oct. 21, 1998, P.L. 105-277, 25 U.S. Code § 458ff

**Tribal Self-Governance Act of 1994**
Oct. 25, 1994, P.L. 103-413, 25 U.S. Code § 450 nt.

**Tribal Self-Governance Demonstration Project Act**
Dec. 4, 1991, P.L. 102-184, 25 U.S. Code § 450f nt.

**Tribal-State Cooperative Agreements Act**
Neb. Rev. Stat. 1943, 13-1501 et seq.

**Tribally Controlled College or University Assistance Act of 1978**
Oct. 17, 1978, P.L. 95-471, Act 92 Stat. 1325, 25 U.S. Code §§ 640a, nt., 640c, 640c-1, 1801 to 1815
Oct. 17, 1978, P.L. 95-471, 92 Stat. 1325, 25 U.S. Code §§ 640a nt., 640c, 640c-1, 1901 to 1915
Dec. 21, 1982, P.L. 97-375, 25 U.S. Code §§ 1807, 1808
Dec. 1, 1983, P.L. 98-192, 25 U.S. Code §§ 1801 to 1803, 1804a, 1805 to 1815, 1831 to 1836
Sept. 30, 1986, P.L. 99-428, 25 U.S. Code §§ 1801, 1810, 1836
April 28, 1988, P.L. 100-297, 25 U.S. Code §§ 1808, 1809
Sept. 9, 1988, P.L. 1004427, 25 U.S. Code § 1808
Sept. 25, 1990, P.L. 101-392, 25 U.S. Code §§ 1801 nt., 1812, 1851, 1852
Oct. 30, 1990, P.L. 101-477, 25 U.S. Code §§ 1808, 1810, 1811, 1832, 1832 nt., 1834 to 1836
July 23, 1992, P.L. 102-325, 25 U.S. Code §§ 1810, 1836, 1852
Oct. 20, 1994, P.L. 103-382, 25 U.S. Code § 1832

Oct. 7, 1998, P.L. 105-244, 25 U.S. Code §§ 1801, 1801 nt., prec. 1802 to 1804, 1804a, 1805 to 1813, prec. 1831, 1832 to 1836, 1851

**Tribally Controlled Community College Assistance Act of 1978**

See Tribally Controlled College or University Assistance of 1978

**Tribally Controlled Community College Assistance Amendments of 1986**

Sept. 30, 1986, P.L. 99-428, 25 U.S. Code § 1801 nt.

**Tribally Controlled Schools Act of 1988**

April 28, 1988, P.L. 100-297, 25 U.S. Code §§ 2501 et seq., 2501 nt.

Sept. 9, 1988, P.L. 100-427, 25 U.S. Code §§ 2503 to 2508

May 24, 1990, P.L. 101-301, 25 U.S. Code §§ 2504, 2508

Oct. 7, 1991, P.L. 102-119, 25 U.S. Code §§ 2503, 2504

Oct. 20, 1994, P.L. 103-382, 25 U.S. Code §§ 2503, 2504, 2507, 2508

Nov. 10, 1998, P.L. 105-362, 25 U.S. Code § 2505

**Tribally Controlled Vocational Institutions Support Act of 1990**

Sept. 25, 1990, P.L. 101-392, 20 U.S. Code § 2397 nt.

**Triborough Bridge and Tunnel Authority Act**

N.Y. Public Authorities Laws (Consol. Laws Ch. 43A) § 550 et seq.

**Tributyltin Antifoulant Paint Control Act**

R.I. Gen. Laws 1956, 46-17.2-1 et seq.

**Trichinosis Control Act**

Ill. Rev. Stat. 1991, Ch. 5, § 1801 et seq.

**Trimble Act (Highways; Condemnation)**

Ky. Rev. Stat. 1971, 416.540 et seq.

**Trimming and Preservation Act (Mangrove)**

Fla. Stat. Ann., 403.9321 et seq.

**Trinity River Basin Fish and Wildlife Management Act of 1984**

May 15, 1996, P.L. 104-143, 110 Stat. 1341

**Trinity River Basin Fish and Wildlife Management Reauthorization Act of 1995**

May 15, 1996, P.L. 104-143, 110 Stat. 1338

**Trip Tax Act**

N.M. Stat. Ann., 7-15-1.1 et seq.

**Triple Damage Act (Timber)**

Va. Code 1950, § 55-331 et seq.

**Tripp-Bonine Act (Labor Disputes)**

Mich. Comp. Laws Ann., 423.1 et seq.

**Trivette-Waggoner Act (Elections)**

Ky. Rev. Stat. 1948, 117.155, 117.541, 117.545

**Trivial Error Act**

N.D. Rules of Civil Procedure 1957, Rule 8, Subd. f

**Troll Act**

Ore. Code 1930, §§ 40-1109, 40-1110

**Troll Act (Salmon Fishing)**

Ore. Rev. Stat., 509.230

**Tropical Fruit Policy Act**

Fla. Stat. Ann., 603.201 et seq.

**Troup County Airport Authority Act**

Ga. Laws 1977, p. 3387

**Troup County Pension and Retirement Act**

Ga. Laws 1951, p. 2637

**Trout and Steelhead Conservation and Management Planning Act**

Cal. Fish and Game Code 1957, § 1725 et seq.

**Trout License Act (Commercial)**

Mich. Comp. Laws Ann., 308.1 et seq.

**Troy Budget Act (Cash Basis)**

N.Y. Laws 1949, Ch. 668

**Troy City Court Act**
N.Y. Laws 1939, Ch. 881

**Troy Industrial Development Authority Act**
N.Y. Public Authorities Law (Consol. Laws Ch. 43A) § 1950 et seq.

**Troy Parking Authority Act**
N.Y. Public Authorities Law (Consol. Laws Ch. 43A) § 1569a et seq.

**Truancy Act**
Cal. Education Code 1976, § 48260 et seq.
Iowa Code Ann., 299.1 et seq.
Kan. Stat. Ann., 72-1111
Ky. Rev. Stat. 1971, 159.150
Ore. Rev. Stat., 339.010 et seq.

**Truck Act**
N.C. Gen. Stat. 1943, § 62-259 et seq.
S.C. Code Ann. 1976, § 56-5-4010 et seq.

**Truck Act (Motor Carriers)**
Ill. Rev. Stat. 1953, Ch. 95 1/2, § 240 et seq.
Tex. Rev. Civ. Stat., Art. 6701d-11

**Truck and Bus Safety and Regulatory Reform Act of 1988**
Nov. 18, 1988, P.L. 100-690, 49 U.S. Code Appx. § 2501 nt.

**Truck and Bus Transportation Act**
Mo. Rev. Stat., 390.011 et seq.
Wis. Stat. Ann., 194.01 et seq.

**Truck Axle Loads Act**
Mo. Rev. Stat., 304.180

**Truck Drivers Act**
Mich. Comp. Laws Ann., 480.11 et seq.

**Truck Operators Law**
Iowa Code Ann., 327.1 et seq.

**Truck Overload Act**
Mich. Comp. Laws Ann., 257.722

**Truck Rental Permit Law**
Ore. Laws 1947, Ch. 467 § 9

**Truck Weight Act**
Me. Rev. Stat. Ann. 1964, Title 29, § 1651 et seq.
Wis. Stat. Ann., 348.01 et seq.

**Truckee-Carson-Pyramid Lake Water Rights Settlement Act**
Nov. 16, 1990, P.L. 101-618, 43 U.S. Code § 614 nt.

**Truckee-Tahoe Sanitation Agency Act**
Cal. Statutes 1971, Ch. 1560, p. 3084

**Truckers Compact (New England)**
N.H. Rev. Stat. 1955, 267:1

**Truckers' Fuel Use Tax Act**
N.C. Gen. Stat. 1943, § 105-449.37 et seq.

**Trucking Industry Regulatory Reform Act of 1994**
Aug. 26, 1994, P.L. 103-311, 49 U.S. Code § 10101 nt.

**Trucking Industry Self-funded Research and Development Act**
Okla. Stat. Ann., Title 47, § 1161 et seq.

**Trucking Reciprocity Act**
Cal. Statutes 1983, Ch. 1000

**Trucks Act (Communist Control)**
Mich. Comp. Laws 1970, 752.321 et seq.

**True-Ad Law**
Ky. Rev. Stat. 1971, 517.030, 517.040

**True Name Act**
Me. Rev. Stat. Ann. 1964, Title 30, § 2801 et seq.

**True Name Act (Lodging-Entry in Register)**
Mass. Gen. Laws Ann., 140:27 et seq.

**Truman-Hobbs Act**
June 21, 1940, Ch. 409, 54 Stat. 497, 33 U.S. Code §§ 511 to 523
July 16, 1952, Ch. 889, 66 Stat. 732, 33 U.S. Code §§ 511, 516, 523, 524

**Trunk Line Highway Act**
Mich. Comp. Laws Ann., 247.651 et seq.

**Truss Construction Fire Safety Act**
Ill. Comp. Stat. 1992, Ch. 425, § 68/1 et seq.

**Trust Accounting Act**
Fla. Stat. 1973, 737.01 et seq.
La. Rev. Stat. Ann., 9:2081 et seq.

**Trust Accounts Act (Interest on Lawyers')**
Pa. Purdon's Stat., Title 62, § 4021 et seq.

**Trust Accumulation Act**
Ill. Rev. Stat. 1991, Ch. 30, § 152.9, 153

**Trust Act**
Ga. Code Ann., 53-12-1
Nev. Rev. Stat. Ann., 163.010 et seq.
N.M. Stat. Ann., 46-2-11 et seq.
Okla. Stat. Ann., Title 60, § 175.1 et seq.
Tex. Property Code § 111.001 et seq.
Wash. Rev. Code Ann., 11.98.009 et seq.

**Trust Act (Business)**
Del. Code of 1974, Title 12, § 3815 et seq.
Ind. Code. Ann., 23-5-1-1 et seq.

**Trust Act (Cemetary Merchandise)**
Okla. Stat. Ann., Title 8, § 301 et seq.

**Trust Act (Charitable)**
Ill. Rev. Stat. 1991, Ch. 14, § 51 et seq.
Utah Code Ann. 1953, 59-18-101 et seq.

**Trust Act (Deed)**
N.M. Stat. Ann., 48-10-1 et seq.

**Trust Act (Education)**
Mich. Comp. Laws Ann., 390.1421 et seq.

**Trust Act (Executive Mansion)**
N.Y. Arts and Cultural Affairs Law (Consol. Laws Ch. 11C) § 54.01 et seq.

**Trust Act (Historical Records)**
R.I. Gen. Laws 1956, 42-8.1-20

**Trust Act (Income)**
N.Y. Estate, Powers, and Trusts Law (Consol. Law Ch. 17B) § 7-1.5

**Trust Act (Monopolies)**
Minn. Stat. 1980, 301.58

**Trust Act (Nonprofit Risk Indemnification)**
La. Rev. Stat. Ann., 22:1521 et seq., 22:2001 et seq.
Minn. Stat. Ann., 60A.29

**Trust Act (Real Estate Investment)**
Ill. Rev. Stat. 1991, Ch. 30, § 250 et seq.

**Trust Act (Spendthrift)**
Nev. Rev. Stat. 1979 Reprint, 166.010 et seq.

**Trust Administration Act**
Fla. Stat. Ann., 737.101 et seq.
N.D. Cent. Code, 59-04-01 et seq.

**Trust and Payable on Death Accounts Act**
Ill. Rev. Stat. 1987, Ch. 17, § 2131 et seq.

**Trust Apportionment Act**
Del. Code of 1974, Title 12, § 3710

**Trust Code**
Cal. Probate Code § 15000 et seq.
Ind. Code. Ann., 30-4-1-1 et seq.
La. Rev. Stat. Ann., 9:1721 et seq.
Mont. Laws 1989, Ch. 685, §§ 1 to 215

**Trust Commission Act (Health Insurance)**
N.C. Gen. Stat. 1943, § 58-68-1 et seq.

**Trust Company Act**
Cal. Financial Code § 1500 et seq.
Colo. Rev. Stat., 11-23-101 et seq.
Ill. Rev. Stat. 1991, Ch. 17, § 301 et seq.
Iowa Code Ann., 524A.1 et seq.
Kan. Stat. Ann., 17-2001 et seq.
Mass. Gen. Laws Ann., 172:1 et seq.
Mich. Comp. Laws 1948, 487.191 et seq.
Mo. Rev. Stat., 362.115 et seq.
N.H. Rev. Stat. 1955, 392:1 et seq.
N.J. Stat. Ann., 17:9A-1 et seq.
N.M. Stat. Ann., 58-9-1 et seq.
P.R. Laws Ann. 1954, Title 7, § 301 et seq.

*Continued*

S.D. Codified Laws 1967, 51-19-1 et seq.
Tex. Rev. Civ. Stat., Art. 342a-1.001 et seq.
Tex. Rev. Civ. Stat., 342a-1.001

**Trust Company and Bank Act**
Conn. Gen. Stat. Ann., § 36-53 et seq.

**Trust Company and Bank Insurance Powers Act**
Del. Laws, Vol. 67, Ch. 223

**Trust Company and Bank Merger Act**
N.J. Stat. Ann., 17:9A-133 et seq.

**Trust Company Shares Tax Act**
Pa. Purdon's Stat., Title 72, § 7801 et seq.

**Trust Deeds Act**
Neb. Rev. Stat. 1943, 76-1001 et seq.
Utah Code Ann. 1953, 57-1-19 et seq.
Wash. Rev. Code Ann., 61.24.010 et seq.

**Trust Deposits Act**
Mich. Comp. Laws Ann., 487.702
N.H. Rev. Stat. 1955, 384-D:1 et seq.

**Trust Fund Act**
Ariz. Rev. Stat. Ann. § 6-871 et seq.
N.J. Stat. Ann., 2A:44-148, 2A:102-12
W. Va. Code 1966, § 44-6-6 et seq.

**Trust Fund Act (Area of Critical State Concern Restoration)**
Fla. Stat. Ann., 380.0558

**Trust Fund Act (Children's)**
Del. Code of 1974, Title 31, § 401 et seq.
La. Rev. Stat. Ann., 46:2401 et seq.
Miss. Code Ann. 1972, § 93-21-301 et seq.
N.J. Stat. Ann. 9:6A-1 et seq., 54A-9-25.4, 54A-9-25.5
Pa. Purdon's Stat., Title 11, § 2231 et seq.
Wyo. Stat. Ann. Ann. 1977, § 14-8-101 et seq.

**Trust Fund Act (Common)**
See Common Trust Fund Act
See Uniform Common Trust Fund Act
Ill. Comp. Stat. 1992, Ch. 760, § 45/1 et seq.

**Trust Fund Act (Environmental Protection)**
Ill. Rev. Stat. 1991, Ch. 111 1/2, §§ 1060, 1061

**Trust Fund Act (Indigent Health Care)**
La. Rev. Stat. Ann., 40:2193 et seq.

**Trust Fund Act (Land Title)**
N.M. Stat. Ann., 58-28-1 to 58-28-8

**Trust Fund Act (Natural Resources)**
Mich. Comp. Laws Ann., 318.501 et seq.

**Trust Fund Act (Petroleum Storage Tank)**
Ark. Code Ann. 1987, No. 173

**Trust Fund Act (Public)**
Vt. Stat. Ann. 1959, Title 24, § 2431 et seq.

**Trust Fund Act (Remedial)**
Ark. Code Ann. 1987, 8-7-501 to 8-7-522

**Trust Fund Act (Shelter for Homeless)**
Neb. Laws 1992, L.B. 1192, §§ 1 to 8

**Trust Fund Act (Transportation)**
Del. Code of 1974, Title 2, § 1401 et seq.

**Trust Fund Act (Veterans)**
Mich. Comp. Laws Ann., 35.601 et seq.

**Trust Fund Act (Volunteer)**
Tenn. Code Ann., 49-3-401 et seq.

**Trust Fund Act (William B. Hoyt Memorial Children and Family)**
N.Y. Social Services Law (Consol. Laws Ch. 55) § 481a et seq.

**Trust Fund Administration and Enforcement Act (Local Government Investment Pool)**
Colo. Rev. Stat., 11-51-901 et seq.

**Trust Fund Code of 1981**
Dec. 29, 1981, P.L. 97-119, 26 U.S. Code § 9500 et seq.

**Trust Fund for Higher Education Act (Endowment)**
Fla. Stat. Ann., 240.598

**Trust Fund for the Prevention of Child Abuse Act**
Minn. Stat. Ann., 299A.20 et seq.

**Trust Fund Investment Act**
Wyo. Stat. Ann., § 2-3-101 et seq.

**Trust Fund Supplement to the General Appropriation Acts of 1973—1975 (Federal Revenue Sharing)**
Pa. 1974 Pamph. Laws No. 1334, No. 4A
Pa. 1974 Pamph. Laws No. 1418, No. 25A
Pa. 1975 Pamph. Laws No. 648, No. 7A

**Trust Funds Act (Health Care and State Veterans Homes)**
Miss. Laws 1999, H.B. 109

**Trust Indenture Act**
N.Y. Real Property Law (Consol. Laws Ch.50) § 124 et seq.

**Trust Indenture Act of 1939**
Aug. 3, 1939, Ch. 411, 53 Stat. 1149, 15 U.S. Code §§ 77aaa to 77bbbb
Aug. 10, 1954, Ch. 667, 68 Stat. 686, 15 U.S. Code §§ 77ccc, 77ddd, 77eee, 77fff, 77xxx
Aug. 21, 1958, P.L. 85-699, 72 Stat. 694, 15 U.S. Code § 77ddd
Sept. 13, 1960, P.L. 86-760, 74 Stat. 902, 15 U.S. Code § 77ddd
Nov. 3, 1966, P.L. 89-754, 80 Stat. 1278, 15 U.S. Code § 77ddd
Dec. 22, 1970, P.L. 91-567, 84 Stat. 1499, 15 U.S. Code § 77ddd
Nov. 6, 1978, P.L. 95-598, 15 U.S. Code § 77ccc
Dec. 4, 1987, P.L. 100-181, 15 U.S. Code § 77ccc
Nov. 15, 1990, P.L. 101-550, 15 U.S. Code §§ 77ccc to 77eee, 77iii to 77rrr, 77uuu
Oct. 11, 1996, P.L. 104-290, 15 U.S. Code § 77ddd
Nov. 3, 1998, P.L. 105-353, 15 U.S. Code §§ 77ccc, 77ddd, 77mmm, 77sss

**Trust Indenture Reform Act of 1990**
Nov. 15, 1990, P.L. 101-550, 15 U.S. Code § 77aaa nt.

**Trust Institutions Act**
Ark. Acts 1997, No. 940

**Trust Instruments Powers Act**
Conn. Gen. Stat. Ann., § 45a-450 et seq.

**Trust Interests and Bequest Act (Distributions in Kind)**
Mich. Comp. Laws Ann., 700.216

**Trust Investment Act**
Ind. Burns' 1933, 31-501 et seq.
La. Rev. Stat. Ann., 9:2127, 9:2128

**Trust Lands Act (School and Institutional)**
Utah Code Ann. 1953, 53C-1-101 et seq.

**Trust Law**
Cal. Probate Code § 15000 et seq.

**Trust Powers Act (Savings and Loan)**
Va. Code 1950, § 6.1-195.77 et seq.

**Trust Receipts Act**
See also Uniform Trust Receipts Act
Kan. Laws 1959, Ch. 241

**Trust Reporting Act**
Cal. Government Code § 12580 et seq.

**Trust Subsidiary Act**
Va. Code 1950, § 6.1-32.1 et seq.

**Trustee Act (Natural Resources)**
N.M. Stat. Ann., 75-7-1 et seq.

**Trustee Division of Trusts Act**
Ark. Code Ann. 1987, 28-69-701 et seq.

**Trustee Powers Act**
Neb. Rev. Stat. 1943, 30-2819 et seq.

**Trustee Process Act**
R.I. Gen. Laws 1956, 10-17-1 et seq.

**Trustee Registration Act**
Minn. Stat. Ann., 507.35

**Trustee Savings Act**
Ga. Code 1933, 109-701 et seq.

**Trustee Surety Release Act**
Ill. Rev. Stat. 1991, Ch. 103, §§ 20.9, 21

**Trustees' Accounting Act**
See also Uniform Trustees' Accounting Act
Conn. Gen. Stat. Ann., § 45a-175 et seq.
Wash. Rev. Code Ann., 11.106.010 et seq.

**Trustees Act (Educational)**
Ill. Rev. Stat. 1991, Ch. 144, § 7.9 et seq.

**Trustees Act (University of Illinois)**
Ill. Rev. Stat. 1991, Ch. 144, § 40m et seq.

**Trustees and Charitable Trusts Act (Supervision of)**
Minn. Stat. Ann., 501B.33 et seq.

**Trustees Emergency Act**
Ill. Rev. Stat. 1991, Ch. 17, § 1751 et seq.

**Trustees for Charitable Purposes Supervision Act**
See Uniform Supervision of Trustees for Charitable Purposes Act

**Trustees' Investment Act**
Ill. Rev. Stat. 1991, Ch. 17, § 1651 et seq.

**Trustees' Powers Act**
See also Uniform Trustees' Powers Act
Ill. Rev. Stat. 1991, Ch. 17, § 1654 et seq.
Ind. Code. Ann., 30-4-3-3(a)
Minn. Stat. Ann., 501B.79 et seq.
N.C. Gen. Stat. 1943, § 32-25 et seq.
Okla. Stat. 1981, Title 60, § 175.24
S.D. Codified Laws 1967, 55-1A-1 et seq.
Wash. Rev. Code Ann., 11.98.070 et seq.

**Trustees Powers Act (Charitable)**
Mich. Comp. Laws Ann., 14.271 et seq.

**Trustee's Supervision Act**
Cal. Government Code § 12580 et seq.

**Trusts Act**
See also Uniform Trusts Act
Ala. Code 1975, § 19-3-1 et seq.
Alaska Stat. 1962, § 13.36.105 et seq.
La. Rev. Stat. Ann., 9:1721 et seq.
N.C. Gen. Stat. 1943, § 36A-60 et seq.
N.J. Rev. Stat. 1937, 17:9A-35
Ore. Rev. Stat., 128.055 et seq.
P.R. Laws Ann. 1954, Title 31, § 2541 et seq.
S.C. Code Ann. 1976, § 62-7-101 et seq.
S.D. Codified Laws 1967, 55-4-1 et seq.

**Trusts Act (Pour-Over)**
See Pour-Over Act (Trusts)

**Trusts Act (Testamentary Additions)**
See Uniform Testamentary Additions to Trusts Act

**Trusts Administration Act (Charitable Remainder)**
N.C. Gen. Stat. 1943, § 36A-59.1

**Trusts and Dissolution of Marriage Act**
Ill. Rev. Stat. 1991, Ch. 148, §§ 300, 301

**Trusts and Powers Act**
Kan. Stat. Ann., 58-2401 et seq.

**Trusts and Trustees Act**
Ill. Rev. Stat. 1991, Ch. 17, § 1651 et seq.

**Trusts and Trustees Act (Supervision of Charitable)**
Minn. Stat. Ann., 501B.33 et seq.

**Trusts and Uses Act**
Wis. Stat. Ann., 701.01 et seq.

**Trusts for Employees Act**
Ill. Rev. Stat. 1991, Ch. 48, § 39s-90 et seq.

**Trusts, Pools and Combines Act**
Ill. Rev. Stat. 1959, Ch. 121 1/2, § 301 et seq.

**Trusts Receipts Act**
Ala. Code 1958, Title 39, § 191(4) et seq.
Ark. Stat. 1947, 68-1701 et seq.
N.Y. Commercial Code (Consol. Laws, Ch. 38), § 9-101 et seq.

**Trusts Receipts Act (Uniform Commercial Code)**
Tex. Business and Commerce Code, § 9-101 et seq.

**Truth and Deception Examiner's Licensing Act**
Neb. Rev. Stat. 1943, 81-1901 et seq.

**Truth in Advertising Act (Industrial Hygienist)**
N.J. Stat. Ann., 13:1L-17.1 et seq.

**Truth in Advertising Act (Workers' Compensation)**
Cal. Labor Code § 5430 et seq.
Ga. Official Code Ann., 34-9-30 to 34-9-32

**Truth in Construction Act (Residential)**
La. Rev. Stat. Ann., 9:4851 et seq.

**Truth in Construction and Consumer Protection Act**
Tenn. Code Ann., 66-11-201 et seq.

**Truth-in-Consumer Contact Warranty and Notice Act**
N.J. Stat. Ann. 56:12-14 et seq.

**Truth-in-Dialing Act**
N.Y. General Business Law (Consol. Laws Ch. 20) § 206e
N.Y. Public Service Law (Consol. Laws, Ch. 48) §§ 90, 92c, Subd. 3
N.Y. Public Service Law (Consol. Laws Ch. 48) § 90 et seq.

**Truth in Endorsements Law**
Cal. Election Code 1976, § 11700 et seq.

**Truth in Fabrics Act**
Colo. Stat. Ann. 1935, Ch. 178

**Truth in Heating Act**
N.Y. Energy Law (Consol. Laws Ch. 17A) §§ 17-101, 17-103

**Truth in Labeling Act (Organic Foods)**
Mont. Code Ann., 50-31-221 et seq.

**Truth in Lending Act**
May 29, 1968, P.L. 90-321, 82 Stat. 146, 15 U.S. Code §§ 1601 to 1613, 1631 to 1641, 1671 to 1677
Oct. 26, 1970, P.L. 91-508, 84 Stat. 1126, 15 U.S. Code §§ 1602, 1642 to 1644
Feb. 27, 1976, P.L. 94-222, 15 U.S. Code §§ 1666f et seq.
March 31, 1980, P.L. 96-221, 15 U.S. Code § 1601 et seq.
Oct. 15, 1982, P.L. 97-320, 15 U.S. Code §§ 1602, 1602 nt., 1603, 1603 nt.
Dec. 21, 1982, P.L. 97-375, 15 U.S. Code § 1613; 18 U.S. Code § 891 nt.
Nov. 3, 1988, P.L. 100-583, 15 U.S. Code §§ 1610, 1632, 1637, 1640, 1646
Nov. 23, 1988, P.L. 100-709, 15 U.S. Code §§ 1632, 1637, 1637a, 1647, 1655b
Aug. 9, 1989, P.L. 101-73, 15 U.S. Code § 1607
Dec. 19, 1991, P.L. 102-242, 15 U.S. Code § 1607
Oct. 28, 1992, P.L. 102-550, 15 U.S. Code § 1607
Sept. 23, 1994, P.L. 103-325, 15 U.S. Code §§ 1602, 1604, 1610, 1639, 1640, 1641, 1647, 1648, 1667c
May 18, 1995, P.L. 104-12, 15 U.S. Code § 1640
Sept. 30, 1995, P.L. 104-29, 15 U.S. Code §§ 1605, 1631, 1635, 1640, 1641, 1649
Sept. 30, 1996, P.L. 104-208, 15 U.S. Code §§ 1603, 1604, 1607, 1638, 1649, 1667c, 1667f
Conn. Gen. Stat. Ann., § 36-393 et seq.
Kan. Laws 1969, Ch. 112
Mass. Gen. Laws Ann., 140D:1 et seq.
N.H. Rev. Stat. 1955, Ch. 399-B:1 et seq.
N.Y. General Obligations Law (Consol. Laws Ch. 24A) § 6-101 et seq.
Tenn. Code Ann., 47-14-125
Tex. Finance Code, § 301.001 et seq.
Tex. Rev. Civ. Stat., Art. 5069-1.01 et seq.

**Truth in Lending Act (Consumer Credit Code)**
Me. Rev. Stat. Ann. 1964, Title 9-A, § 8-101 et seq.

**Truth in Lending Act Amendments of 1995**
Sept. 30, 1995, P.L. 104-29, 15 U.S. Code § 1601 nt.

**Truth in Lending and Retail Selling Act**
R.I. Gen. Laws 1956, 6-27-1 et seq.

**Truth in Lending Class Action Relief Act of 1995**
May 18, 1995, P.L. 104-12, 15 U.S. Code § 1601 nt.

**Truth in Lending Simplification and Reform Act**
March 31, 1980, P.L. 96-221, 15 U.S. Code §§ 1601 et seq., 1601 nt.

**Truth in Mileage Act of 1986**
Oct. 28, 1986, P.L. 99-579, 15 U.S. Code § 1901 nt.

**Truth in Motor Vehicles Leasing Act**
N.J. Stat. Ann., 56:12-50 et seq.

**Truth in Negotiations Act**
U.S. Code, also, Armed Forces
Sept. 10, 1962, P.L. 87-653, 76 Stat. 528, 10 U.S. Code §§ 2304(a), (a)(14), (g) 2; (a), (f), 2310(b), 2311

**Truth in Political Advertising Act**
Cal. Education Code 1976, § 20010

**Truth-in-Pricing Law**
N.Y. Adm. Code '85, § 20-707

**Truth in Renting Act**
Mich. Comp. Laws Ann., 554.631 et seq.
N.J. Stat. Ann., 46:8-43 et seq.

**Truth in Repairs Act**
Minn. Stat. Ann., 325F.56 et seq.

**Truth in Savings Act**
Dec. 19, 1991, P.L. 102-242, 12 U.S. Code § 4301 nt.
Oct. 28, 1992, P.L. 102-550, 12 U.S. Code § 4302
Sept. 23, 1994, P.L. 103-325, 12 U.S. Code § 4313
Sept. 30, 1996, P.L. 104-208, 12 U.S. Code §§ 4302, 4305, 4310, 4313
Mass. Gen. Laws Ann., 140E:14

**Truth in Securities Act**
See Securities Act of 1933

**Truth in Sentencing Act**
Del. Laws, Vol. 67, Ch. 130

**Truth in Sentencing Act (Davis-Areias)**
Cal. Penal Code § 1191.3

**Truth in Spending Act**
Wash. Rev. Code Ann., 43.01.130

**Truth-in-Storage Act**
N.Y. General Business Law (Consol. Laws, Ch. 20) § 605 et seq.

**Truth in Taxation Act**
Ill. Comp. Stat. 1992, Ch. 35, §§ 215/1 to 215/9.2
Ill. Rev. Stat. 1991, Ch. 120, § 861 et seq.
Tenn. Code Ann., 67-5-1701

**Truth in Testing Law**
N.Y. Education Law 1947 (Consol. Laws Ch. 16) § 340 et seq.

**Truth in Travel Act**
N.Y. General Business Law (Consol. Laws Ch. 20) § 155 et seq.

**Truth of Statutes Act**
Minn. Stat. Ann., 599.02

**Tuberculars Aid Act**
Colo. Rev. Stat. 1963, 119-2-1 et seq.

**Tuberculin Testing and Immunization Act (Children)**
Mich. Comp. Laws Ann., 333.9201 et seq.

**Tuberculosis Act**
Colo. Rev. Stat., 25-4-501 et seq.

**Tuberculosis Code**
Tex. Health and Safety Code, § 13.031 et seq.

**Tuberculosis Control Act**
Ariz. Rev. Stat. Ann., § 36-711 et seq.
Fla. Stat. Ann., 392.501 et seq.
Ky. Rev. Stat. 1971, 215.520 et seq.
Mich. Comp. Laws Ann., 333.5203 et seq.
S.D. Codified Laws 1967, 34-22-1 et seq.
Tenn. Code Ann., 68-9-101 et seq.

Vt. Stat. Ann., Title 18, § 1055 et seq.
Wash. Rev. Code Ann., 70.28.010 et seq.

**Tuberculosis Control Act (State)**
Ky. Rev. Stat. 1971, 215.520 to 215.600

**Tuberculosis Eradication Act (Bovine)**
Ill. Comp. Stat. 1992, Ch. 510, § 35/1 et seq.

**Tuberculosis Free Care Act**
Wis. Laws 1945, Ch. 104, § 4

**Tuberculosis Health Threat Act**
Minn. Stat. Ann., 144.4801 to 144.4813

**Tuberculosis Hospital Act (County)**
Ind. Code. Ann., 16-11-1-1 et seq.
Mo. Rev. Stat., 205.380 et seq.
N.J. Rev. Stat. 30:9-57 to 30;9-69
Pa. 1925 Pamph. Laws 65, No. 44

**Tuberculosis Hospital Act (Southern Indiana)**
Ind. Burns' 1933, 22-2118 et seq.

**Tuberculosis Prevention Act**
N.C. Gen. Stat. 1943, § 130A-177

**Tuberculosis Prevention Amendments of 1990**
Aug. 15, 1990, P.L. 101-368, 42 U.S. Code § 201 nt.

**Tuberculosis Registration Act (District of Columbia)**
May 13, 1908, Ch. 165, 35 Stat. 126

**Tuberculosis Research Institution Act**
Ill. Rev. Stat. 1991, Ch. 111 1/2, § 121.990 et seq.

**Tuberculosis Sanatorium Commission Act**
Mich. Comp. Laws Ann., 332.151 et seq.

**Tuberculosis Sanitarium Act**
Ill. Rev. Stat. 1991, Ch. 34, § 5-23001

**Tuberculosis Sanitarium Act (Municipal)**
Ill. Rev. Stat. 1991, Ch. 24, § 11-29-1 et seq.

**Tuberculosis Sanitarium District Act**
Ill. Rev. Stat. 1991, Ch. 23, § 1700 et seq.

**Tuberculosis Subsidy Act**
Cal. Health and Safety Code § 3279 et seq.

**Tuberculosis Treatment Act**
Wis. Stat. Ann., 149.01 et seq.

**Tuck Law (County Expenditures)**
Iowa Code Ann., 331.901, 331.476

**Tuckahoe Parking Authority Act**
N.Y. Public Authorities Law (Consol. Laws Ch. 43A) § 1545 et seq.

**Tucker Act (Admiralty-Limitations)**
June 30, 1932, Ch. 315, 47 Stat. 420, 46 U.S. Code § 745

**Tucker Act (Claims)**
March 3, 1887, Ch. 359, 24 Stat. 505 (U.S. Code 28 U.S. Code §§ 507, 1346, 1402, 1491, 1496, 1497, 1501, 1503, 2071, 2072, 2411, 2501, 2512)

**Tucker Health Care Coverage Act**
Cal. Labor Code § 2500 et seq.

**Tucquan Creek and Bear Run Scenic Rivers Act**
Pa. Purdon's Stat., Title 32, § 820.111 et seq.

**Tuition Account Program and College Savings Bond Act**
Pa. Purdon's Stat., Title 24, § 6901.101 et seq.

**Tuition Act**
Del. Code of 1974, Title 14, § 601 et seq.
S.D. Codified Laws 1967, 13-28-19 et seq.

**Tuition Act (Non-resident Attendance)**
N.Y. Education Law 1947 (Consol. Laws Ch. 16) § 2045

**Tuition Aid Act (Higher Education)**
Okla. Stat. Ann., Title 70, § 626.1 et seq.

**Tuition Assistance Act**
Tex. Education Code, § 56.101

**Tuition Assistance Act (Mathematics and Science Teacher)**
Neb. Laws 1984, L.B. 931

**Tuition Assistance Act (National Guard)**
N.C. Gen. Stat. 1943, § 127A-190 et seq.
S.C. Code Ann. 1976, § 59-114-10 et seq.

**Tuition Assistance Grant Act**
Va. Code 1950, § 23-38.11 et seq.

**Tuition Fund Act**
Ind. Burns' 1933, 28-912 et seq.

**Tuition Savings Program Act (Tax-Deferred)**
Ark. Code Ann. 1987, 6-83-101 et seq.

**Tuition Trust Act**
Okla. Stat. Ann., Title 70, § 6000 et seq.

**Tuition Trust Act (Higher Education)**
W. Va. Code 1966 § 18-30-1 et seq.

**Tuition Waiver Act (National Guard)**
N.D. Cent. Code, 37-07.1-01 et seq.

**Tulare County Flood Control District Act**
Cal. Water Code, Appx. § 111-1 et seq.

**Tulpehocken Creek and Yellow Breeches Creek Scenic River Act**
Pa. Purdon's Stat., Title 32, § 820.151 et seq.

**Tulsa County Registration Act**
Okla. Stat. 1971, Title 26, § 4-101 et seq.

**Tumor Registry Act**
Mont. Code Ann., 50-15-701 et seq.

**Tuna Conventions Act**
Oct. 26, 1992, P.L. 102-523, 16 U.S. Code §§ 952, 953
Aug. 15, 1997, P.L. 105-42, 16 U.S. Code §§ 952, 953, 962

**Tuna Conventions Act of 1950**
Sept. 7, 1950, Ch. 907, 64 Stat. 777, 16 U.S. Code §§ 951 to 961
Oct. 15, 1962, P.L. 87-814, 76 Stat. 923, 16 U.S. Code §§ 951, 955, 956, 957, 959
Oct. 9, 1972, P.L. 92-471, 86 Stat. 787, 16 U.S. Code § 954

**Tunnel Act**
N.Y. Railroad Law (Consol. Laws Ch. 49) § 28

**Tunnel Act (Municipal Corporation)**
Cal. Statutes 1951, Ch. 1347, p. 3248

**Tunnel and Bridge Unification Act (New York-New Jersey)**
N.Y. Unconsolidated Laws § 6501 et seq.

**Tunnel and Mine Safety Act (Tom Carrell Memorial)**
Cal. Labor Code § 7950 et seq.

**Tunnel Authority Act (El Dorado County)**
Cal. Streets and Highways Code § 31100 et seq.

**Tunnel Authority Act (Los Angeles County)**
Cal. Streets and Highways Code § 31300 et seq.

**Tunnel Authority Act (Municipal)**
Cal. Statutes 1951, Ch. 1347, p. 3248

**Tunnel Authority Act (New York City)**
N.Y. Public Authorities Law (Consol. Laws Ch. 43A) § 625 et seq.

**Tunnel District Act**
Wash. Rev. Code 1951, 47.57.230 et seq.

**Tuolumne County Road Facilities Improvement Act**
Cal. Public Utilities Code § 150000 et seq.

**Tuolumne County Water Agency Act**
Cal. Water Code, Appx. § 113-1 et seq.

**Turf Grass Law**
Md. Ann. Code 1974, Art. AG, § 9-101 et seq.

**Turkey Promotion Act**
N.D. Cent. Code, 4-13.1-01 et seq.

**Turlington Act (Intoxicating Liquor)**
N.C. Gen. Stat. 1943, § 18B-100 et seq.

**Turner Act (Drainage Districts)**
Ark. Code Ann. 1987, 14-121-101, 14-121-201 et seq.

**Turner-Jacobson Act (Taxation)**
Ark. Acts 1911, Ex. Sess., p. 495, No. 1

**Turnover Act (Property in Litigation)**
N.Y. Civil Practice Law and Rules (Consol. Laws Ch. 8) § 2701 et seq.

**Turnover Statute (Judgments and Decrees)**
Tex. Civil Practice and Remedies Code, § 31.002

**Turnpike Act**
Del. Code of 1974, Title 2, § 1401 et seq.
Fla. Stat. Ann., 338.22 et seq.
Mich. Comp. Laws 1948, 252.101 et seq.
Ohio Rev. Code 1953, 5537.01 et seq.
Pa. Purdon's Stat., Title 36, § 652a et seq.
W. Va. Code 1966, § 17-16A-1 et seq.

**Turnpike Act (Johnston Murray)**
Okla. Laws 1953, p. 508

**Turnpike Act (Keystone Shortway)**
Pa. Purdon's Stat., Title 36, § 666.1 et seq.

**Turnpike and Bridge Authority Act**
R.I. Gen. Laws 1956, 24-12-1 et seq.

**Turnpike Authority Act**
Ala. Code 1975, § 23-2-1 et seq.
Ark. Code Ann. 1987, 27-71-101 et seq.
Ga. Laws 1952, p. 430
Ga. Laws 1953 (Nov.-Dec. Sess.), p. 18
Kan. Stat. Ann., 68-2001 et seq.
Ky. Rev. Stat. 1971, 175.410 et seq.
Mass. Acts 1952, Ch. 354
Me. Private and Special Laws 1941, Ch. 69, § 1 et seq.
Mo. Rev. Stat. 1959, 225.010 et seq.
N.C. Gen. Stat. 1943, § 136-89.12 et seq.
N.J. Stat. Ann., 27:23-1 et seq.
Okla. Stat. Ann., Title 69, § 1701 et seq.

**Turnpike Commission Act**
Pa. Purdon's Stat., Title 36, § 652d

**Turnpike Control Act**
Ida. Code 1947, 40-2601 et seq.

**Turnpike Corporation Act**
Wis. Stat. Ann., 182.30 et seq.

**Turnpike Extension Act (Delaware River)**
Pa. Purdon's Stat., Title 36, § 658.1 et seq.

**Turnpike Extension Act (Erie)**
Pa. 1949 Pamph. Laws 1037, No. 301

**Turnpike Extension Act (Gettysburg)**
Pa. Purdon's Stat., Title 36, § 667.1 et seq.

**Turnpike Extension Act (Northeastern)**
Pa. Purdon's Stat., Title 36, § 660.1 et seq.

**Turnpike Extension Act (Northwestern)**
Pa. Purdon's Stat., Title 36, § 668.1 et seq.

**Turnpike Extension Act (Philadelphia Loop)**
Pa. Purdon's Stat., Title 36, § 652.1 et seq.

**Turnpike Extension Act (Philadelphia)**
Pa. Purdon's Stat., Title 36, § 653 et seq.

**Turnpike Extension Act (Scranton)**
Pa. 1949 Pamph. Laws 1050, No. 302

**Turnpike Extension Act (Southwestern)**
Pa. Purdon's Stat., Title 36, § 669.1 et seq.

**Turnpike Extension Act (Western Pennsylvania)**
Pa. Purdon's Stat., Title 36, § 654 et seq.

**Turnpike Financing Act**
Pa. Purdon's Stat., Title 36, § 659.1 et seq.

**Turnpike Law Enforcement Fund Act**
Okla. Stat. 1961, Title 69, § 693

**Turnpike Organization, Extension and Toll Road Conversion Act**
Pa. Purdon's Stat., Title 36, § 651.1 et seq.

**Turnpike Projects Act**
Ky. Rev. Stat. 1971, 177.390 et seq.
Tex. Rev. Civ. Stat., Art. 6674v

**Turnpike Raiders' Act**
Ky. Rev. Stat. 1971, Superseded Vols., 437.110 et seq.

**Turnpike System Act**
N.H. Rev. Stat. 1955, 237:1 et seq.

**Turnpike System Revenue Bond Act**
N.H. Rev. Stat. 1955, 237-A:1 et seq.

**Turtle Protection Act (Marine)**
Fla. Stat. Ann., 370.12

**Tuscaloosa Civil Service System Act**
Ala. Local Acts 1947, p. 174

**Tuscaloosa County Crime Stoppers Reward Compensation Fund Act**
Ala. Acts 1998, H.B. 704

**Tuthill-Kiper Act (Taxation)**
Ind. Laws 1920, Special Session, Ch. 45, p. 153

**Tutor-Scholars Program Act**
N.M. Stat. Ann., 22-2A-1 et seq.

**Tuttle Road Act (Counties)**
Ore. General Laws 1905, Ch. 230

**Tuxedo Interim Development Law**
N.Y. Local Laws 1971, Town of Tuxedo, p. 3544

**TVA Act (Tennessee Valley Authority)**
Ky. Rev. Stat. 1971, 96.550 et seq.

**Tweed Charter (New York City Reorganization)**
N.Y. Laws 1870, Ch. 137

**Tweed-New Haven Airport Authority Act**
Conn. Public Acts 1997, No. 271

**Twelve Month Statute of Limitations (Workmen's Compensation)**
N.Y. Workers' Compensation Law (Consol. Laws, Ch. 67), § 40

**Twentieth Amendment Adjustment Act**
June 5, 1934, Ch. 390, 48 Stat. 379, 2 U.S. Code §§ 1, 7 (U.S. Code 3 U.S. Code §§ 7, 12, 13, 15, 101) 48 U.S. Code § 891

**Twenty-Eight Hour Law (Transportation of Animals)**
See Live Stock Transportation Act

**Twenty-First Century Education Act**
N.M. Stat. Ann., 22-13B-1 et seq.
Ore. Rev. Stat., 326.705 et seq.

**Twenty-First Century Environmental Quality Bond Act**
N.Y. Laws 1990, Ch. 147

**Twenty-First Century Fund Investments Act**
Del. Code of 1974, Title 29, § 6102A

**Twenty-First Century Schools Act**
N.Y. Education Law 1947 (Consol. Laws Ch. 16) § 309a et seq.

**Twenty-First Century Workforce Commission Act**
Aug. 7, 1998, P.L. 105-220, Subtitle C, 29 U.S. Code § 2701 nt.

**Twenty Hook Law (Fishing)**
Ala. Code 1975, § 9-11-140 et seq.

**Twenty Hour Detention Act**
Mo. Rev. Stat., 544.170

**Twenty-One Year Act (Real Property Limitations)**
Pa. Cons. Stat., Title 42, § 5530

**Twenty Year Adverse Possession Act**
N.D. Cent. Code, 28-01-08

**Twenty Year Statute of Limitation (Debt and Covenant)**
R.I. Gen. Laws 1956, 9-1-17

**Twenty Year Statute of Limitation (Real Property)**
N.C. Gen. Stat. 1943, § 1-40

**Twenty Year Statute of Limitations**
Ga. Code Ann., 9-3-22
Ind. Code. Ann., 34-1-2-2, Subd. 6

**Twenty Year Statute of Limitations (Adverse Possession)**
N.D. Cent. Code, 28-01-08

**Twenty Year Statute of Limitations (Dower)**
N.Y. Real Property Actions and Proceedings Law (Consol. Laws,

**Twenty Year Statute of Limitations (Estate Tax Liens)**
N.Y. Tax Law (Consol. Laws, Ch. 60), § 24911

**Twenty Year Statute of Limitations (Judgments)**
N.Y. Civil Practice Law and Rules (Consol. Laws Ch. 8) § 211, Subd. b

**Twenty Year Statute of Limitations (Real Actions)**
Del. Code of 1974, Title 10, §§ 7901, 7902
Fla. Stat. Ann., 95.231

**Twenty Year Statute of Limitations (Real Estate Claims)**
Ill. Rev. Stat. 1991, Ch. 110, § 13-101 et seq.

**Twiggs County Recreation Authority Act**
Ga. Laws 1996, p. 4015

**Twin Cities Area Metropolitan Transit Commission Act**
Minn. Stat. Ann., 473.404 et seq.

**Twin County Peace Officers' Relief Act**
N.C. Laws 1949, Ch. 1186

**Twin Falls County Landfill Act of 1994**
July 22, 1994, P.L. 103-281, 108 Stat. 1420

**Two and Three Month Statutes of Limitations (Probate Claims)**
Cal. Probate Code § 714

**Two-cent Fare Act**
Minn. Laws 1907, Ch. 97

**Two Cent Passanger Rate Act**
Mo. Laws 1907, p. 170

**Two Cent Rate Act**
Ill. Rev. Stat. 1983, Ch. 114, § 154 et seq.

**Two Donee Law**
Miss. Laws 1856, Ch. 108, Art. 3, p. 273

**Two Hour Detaining Act**
Del. Code of 1974, Title 11, § 1902, Subsec. c

**Two Mile Limit Law (Sheep)**
Ida. Code 1947, 25-901 et seq.

**Two Mile Prohibitory Act**
Ky. Acts 1883-84 (Local and Private) Ch. 185

**Two Month Statute of Limitations (Probate Claims)**
Cal. Probate Code § 714

**Two Platoon Law (Fire Department)**
N.Y. City Adm. Code '38, Ch. 19, § 487a-11.0

**Two Quart Liquor Act**
Kan. Stat. Ann., 41-407

**Two Strikes and You're Off Act**
Ga. Official Code Ann., 49-4-15, Subd. d

**Two Term Act (Prosecutions)**
Ind. Code 1976, 35-1-26-2
Ohio Rev. Code 1953, 2945.71

**Two Term Discharge Act**
Ark. Stat. 1947, 16-89-101

**Two-Thirds Act (Insolvents)**
N.Y. Debtor and Creditor Law (Consol, Laws Ch. 12) § 50 et seq.

**Two Thousand (2000) Act (University of Connecticut)**
Conn. Public Acts 1995, No. 230

**Two Thousand (2000) Education Challenge Act**
Okla. Laws 1991, p. 1210

**Two Thousand (2000) Pilot Program (Youth-at-Risk)**
Fla. Stat. Ann., 446.001 et seq.

**Two Trial Act (Capital Offenses)**
Cal. Penal Code § 190.1

**Two Witnesses Act (Capital Cases)**
Conn. Gen. Stat. Ann., § 54-83

**Two Year College Maintenance Act**
N.M. Stat. Ann., 21-27-1 et seq.

**Two-Year Incontestability Act (Insurance)**
S.C. Code Ann. 1976, Superseded Vols., 1976, §§ 38-9-250, 38-9-260

**Two-Year Limitations Act (Torts)**
Ill. Rev. Stat. 1991, Ch. 110, § 13-202

**Two Year Separation Act (Divorce)**
La. Rev. Stat. Ann., 9:301 et seq.

**Two Year Statute of Limitations (Dower)**
N.Y. Real Property Actons and Proceedings Law (Consol. Laws, Ch. 81), § 1001

**Two Year Statute of Limitations (Misdemeanors)**
Ga. Code Ann., 17-13-1

**Two-Year Statute of Limitations (Personal Actions)**
Colo. Rev. Stat., 13-80-105

**Two Year Statute of Limitations Act**
Alaska Stat. 1962, § 09.10.070
Cal. Code of Civil Procedure, § 339
Del. Code of 1974, Title 10, § 8119
Fla. Stat. Ann. 95.11
Kan. Stat. Ann., 60-513
Me. Rev. Stat. Ann. 1964, Title 14, § 753
Minn. Stat. Ann., 541.07
N.C. Gen. Stat. 1943, § 1-53
Pa. Cons. Stat., Title 42, § 524 § 34
Wash. Rev. Code Ann., 4.16.130

**Tydings Amendment.**
Nov. 13, 1942, Ch. 638, 56 Stat. 1018

**Tydings-McDuffie Acts**
Jan. 17, 1933, Ch. 11, 47 Stat. 761
March 24, 1934, Ch. 84, 48 Stat. 456, 2 U.S. Code § 31

**Tyler Jaeger Act**
Cal. Penal Code § 273ab

**Tyson-Fitzgerald Act**
May 24, 1928, Ch. 735, 45 Stat. 735

## U

**U C D Act (Disability)**
Cal. Unemployment Insurance Code § 2601 et seq.

**U-Drive-It Act**
N.J. Stat. Ann., 45:21-1 et seq.

**UCC Fee and Corporation Bureau Law**
Pa. Cons. Stat., Title 15, § 151 et seq.

**Uintah and Ouray Reservation Termination Act of 1954**
Aug. 27, 1954, Ch. 1009, 68 Stat. 868, 25 U.S. Code §§ 677 to 677aa
Aug. 2, 1956, Ch. 880, 70 Stat. 936, 25 U.S. Code §§ 677d, 677g, 677p
Sept. 25, 1962, P.L. 87-698, 76 Stat. 597, 25 U.S. Code § 677i

**Ulster County Resource Recovery Agency Act**
N.Y. Public Authorities Law (Consol. Laws Ch. 43A) § 2050a et seq.

**Ulster Site Development Law**
N.Y. Local Laws 1971, Town of Ulster, p. 3552

**Ultimate Street Improvements Act**
N.C. Private Laws 1927, Ch. 156

**Umatilla Basin Project Act**
Oct. 28, 1988, P.L. 100-557, 102 Stat. 2791

**Umatilla Herd Law**
Ore. Code 1930, §§ 20-2077 to 20-2084

**Umstead Act (Government Sale of Merchandise)**
N.C. Gen. Stat. 1943, § 66-58

**UMTA**
See Urban Mass Transportation Act of 1964

**Unattended Motor Vehicle Act**
S.C. Code Ann. 1976, § 56-5-2570

**Unauthorized Attorney Compensation Act**
Tex. Government Code, § 84.001 et seq.

**Unauthorized Companies Act**
Pa. Purdon's Stat., Title 72, §§ 2265, 2266

**Unauthorized Compensation Law (Attorney)**
Tex. Government Code, § 84.001 et seq.

**Unauthorized Domestic Insurers Act**
N.C. Gen. Stat. 1943, § 58-14-1 et seq.

**Unauthorized Harvesting of Timber Act**
Tex. Natural Resources Code, § 151.101 et seq.

**Unauthorized Insurance Process Law**
Fla. Stat. Ann., 626.904 et seq.

**Unauthorized Insurance Regulation Act**
Colo. Rev. Stat., 10-3-901 et seq.

**Unauthorized Insurers Act**
See Uniform Unauthorized Insurers Act
Conn. Gen. Stat. 1983, § 38-263 et seq.
Ind. Code 1982, 37-4-4-1 et seq.
Neb. Rev. Stat. 1943, 44-2001 to 44-2008
N.M. Stat. Ann., 59A-15-21 et seq.
W. Va. Code 1966, § 33-3-18 et seq.

**Unauthorized Insurers False Advertising Process Act**
Cal. Insurance Code § 1620.1 et seq.
Ida. Code 1947, 41-1235 et seq.
Ill. Rev. Stat. 1991, Ch. 73, § 735.1
Ind. Code Ann., 27-4-6-1 et seq.
Kan. Stat. Ann., 40-2415 et seq.
La. Rev. Stat. Ann., 22:1231 et seq.
Md. Ann. Code 1957, Art. 48A, § 235 et seq.
Md. Ann. Code 1974, Art. IN, § 27-701 et seq.
Me. Rev. Stat. Ann. 1964, Title 24-A, § 2102, 2109 et seq.
Minn. Stat. Ann., 72A.33 et seq.
N.C. Gen. Stat. 1943, § 58-29-1 et seq.
N.D. Cent. Code, 26-09.1-01 et seq.
Neb. Rev. Stat. 1943, 44-1801 et seq.
Nev. Rev. Stat. 1979 Reprint, 685B.090 et seq.
*Continued*

N.H. Rev. Stat. 1955, 406-A:1 et seq.
N.M. Stat. Ann., S9A-15-11 et seq.
S.D. Codified Laws 1967, 58-33-47 et seq.
Tex. Insurance Code, Art. 21.21-1
Utah Code Ann. 1953, Miscellaneous Superseded Code Provisions, 31-36-1 et seq.
Wyo. Stat. Ann., § 26-12-301 et seq.

**Unauthorized Insurers Service of Process Act**
Ala. Code 1975, § 27-10-50 et seq.
Ark. Code Ann. 1987, 23-65-201 et seq.
Cal. Insurance Code § 1610 et seq.
Colo. Rev. Stat., 10-3-1001 et seq.
Fla. Stat. Ann., 626.904 et seq.
Ga. Code Ann., 33-5-50 et seq.
Haw. Rev. Stat. Ann., § 431-342
Ida. Code 1947, 41-1204 et seq.
Ill. Rev. Stat. 1991, Ch. 73, § 735
Ind. Code Ann., 27-4-4-1 et seq.
Iowa Code Ann., 507A.1 et seq.
Kan. Stat. Ann., 40-2001 et seq.
Mass. Gen. Laws Ann., 175B:1 et seq.
Md. Ann. Code 1957, Art. 48A, § 201 et seq.
Me. Rev. Stat. Ann. 1964, Title 24-A, § 2102 et seq.
Mich. Comp. Laws Ann., 500.1820 et seq.
Miss. Code Ann. 1972, § 83-21-17 et seq.
Mont. Code Ann., 33-1-611 et seq.
N.C. Gen. Stat. 1943, § 58-16-35
N.D. Cent. Code, 26.1-11-01 et seq.
Neb. Rev. Stat. 1943, 44-137.01 et seq.
N.H. Rev. Stat. 1955, 406-B:1 et seq.
N.J. Stat. Ann., 17B:33-1 et seq.
N.M. Stat. Ann., 38-1-7 et seq.
N.Y. Insurance Law (Consol. Laws Ch. 28) § 1213
Ohio Rev. Code 1953, 3901.17
Pa. Cons. Stat., Title 42, § 5322 et seq.
R.I. Gen. Laws 1956, 27-16-3 et seq.
S.D. Codified Laws 1967, 58-8-6 et seq.
Tenn. Code Ann., 56-2-601 et seq.
Utah Code Ann. 1953, Miscellaneous Superseded Code Provisions, x1-35-1 et seq.
Va. Code 1950, § 38.1-63 et seq.
Vt. Stat. Ann., Title 8, § 3381 et seq.
W. Va. Code 1966, § 33-4-13
Wyo. Stat. Ann., § 26-12-201 et seq.

**Unauthorized Nonresident Brokers and Agents Process Act**
Va. Code 1950, § 38.1-70.1 et seq.

**Unauthorized Practice of Law Act**
Cal. Business and Professions Code § 6125 et seq.
La. Rev. Stat. Ann., 37:213
Minn. Stat. Ann., 481.02 et seq.
N.H. Rev. Stat. 1955, 311:7a et seq.
Wis. Stat. 1981, 757.30 et seq.

**Unauthorized Recording Practices Act**
N.M. Stat. Ann., 30-16B-1 et seq.
Utah Code Ann. 1953, 13-10-1 et seq.

**Unauthorized Treatment of Cancer Act**
Ky. Rev. Stat. 1971, 211.182 et seq.

**Unbonded Agricultural Warehouse Act**
Iowa Code 1962, 544.1 et seq.
Ky. Rev. Stat. 1971, 251.010 et seq.

**UNCITRAL Model Law on International Commercial Arbitration**
Conn. Gen. Stat. 1983, § 50a-101 et seq.

**Unclaimed and Abandoned Property Disposition Act**
N.D. Cent. Code, 47-30-01 et seq.
Pa. Purdon's Stat., Title 72, § 1301.1 et seq.

**Unclaimed Funds Act for Life Insurance Companies**
Me. Rev. Stat. Ann. 1964, Title 24-A, § 4551 et seq.
Nev. Rev. Stat. 1979 Reprint, 697A.010 et seq.
N.Y. Abandoned Property Law (Consol. Laws Ch. 1) § 700 et seq.
Pa. Purdon's Stat., Title 27, § 461 et seq.
P.R. Laws Ann. 1954, Title 26, § 2601 et seq.
Tenn. Code Ann., Superseded Vol., 56-340 et seq.

**Unclaimed Funds Statute for Life Insurance Companies**
Tex. Insurance Code, Art. 4.08

**Unclaimed Money and Other Liquid Assets Act**
P.R. Acts 1989, No. 36

**Unclaimed Moneys Act (Municipal)**
Pa. Purdon's Stat., Title 27, § 491 et seq.

**Unclaimed Personal Property Disposition Act**
Tex. Property Code, § 72.001 et seq.

**Unclaimed Property Act**
See also Uniform Unclaimed Property Act
Cal. Code of Civil Procedure, § 1300 et seq.
Colo. Rev. Stat., 38-13-101 et seq.
Fla. Stat. Ann., 717.001 et seq.
Ind. Code Ann., 32-9-1-1 et seq.
Ind. Code 1982, 32-9-1.5-1 et seq.
Kan. Stat. Ann., 58-3901 et seq.
Me. Rev. Stat. Ann. 1964, Title 33, § 1801 et seq.
Minn. Stat. Ann., 345.31 et seq.
Utah Code Ann. 1953, 78-44-1 et seq.
Va. Code 1950, § 55.210.1 et seq.
Wash. Rev. Code Ann., 63.29.010 et seq.

**Unclaimed Property Act (Museum)**
Miss. Code Ann. 1972, § 39-19-1 et seq.

**Unclaimed Property Disposition Act**
See Uniform Disposition of Unclaimed Property Act

**Unclaimed Property Sale Act**
Ill. Rev. Stat. 1991, Ch. 141, § 0.01 et seq.

**Unclassified Cities Act**
Wash. Rev. Code Ann., 35.30.010 et seq.

**Uncollectable Tax Act**
Ill. Comp. Stat. 1992, Ch. 35, § 710/1 et seq.
Ill. Rev. Stat. 1991, Ch. 120, § 890 et seq.

**Unconscionable Pricing Act**
Ala. Code 1975, § 8-31-1 et seq.

**Uncontested Forfeiture Act**
Ark. Acts 1991, No. 859

**Uncultivable Public Lands Sales Law**
Cal. Public Resources Code § 7301 et seq.

**Undercover Officers Protection Act**
Ala. Code 1975, § 13A-5-40

**Undergraduate and Vocational Incentive Scholarship Program**
Va. Code 1950, § 23-38.19:3 et seq.

**Underground and Aboveground Storage Tank Trust Fund Act**
Ala. Code 1975, § 22-25-1 et seq.

**Underground and Strip Mine Reclamation Act**
Mont. Code Ann. 1947, 50-1034 et seq.

**Underground and Strip Mine Siting Act**
Mont. Code Ann. 1947, 50-1601 et seq.

**Underground Conversion of Utilities Act**
Colo. Rev. Stat., 29-8-101 et seq.
Ida. Code 1947, 50-2501 et seq.
Mont. Code Ann., 69-4-301 et seq.
Utah Code Ann. 1953, 54-8-1 et seq.
Wyo. Stat. Ann., § 37-13-101 et seq.

**Underground Damage Prevention Act**
N.C. Gen. Stat. 1943, § 87-100 et seq.

**Underground Excavation Enforcement Act**
D.C. Code Ann., §§ 7-620, 7-621

**Underground Facility Damage Prevention and Safety Act**
Fla. Stat. Ann., 556.101 et seq.
Ky. Rev. Stat. 1971, 367.4901 et seq.
Tex. Rev. Civ. Stat., Art. 9033 et seq.

**Underground Facility Protection Act**
N.J. Stat. Ann., 48:2-73 et seq.

**Underground Facility Safety and Damage Prevention Act**
Ark. Code Ann. 1987, No. 600
D.C. Code Ann., § 43-1701 et seq.
Del. Code of 1974, Title 26, § 801 et seq.
Mo. Rev. Stat., 319.010 et seq.
Okla. Stat. Ann., Title 63, § 142.1 et seq.

**Underground Gas Storage Act**
Ark. Stat. 1947, 15-72-601 et seq.
Ga. Code Ann., 46-4-50 et seq.
Mo. Rev. Stat., 393.410 et seq.
Wash. Rev. Code Ann., 49.24.010 et seq.

**Underground Mine Reclamation Act**
Mont. Code Ann., 82-4-201 et seq.

**Underground Mine Siting Act**
Mont. Code Ann., 82-4-101 et seq.

**Underground Mined Space Development Act**
Minn. Stat. 1986, 472B.01 et seq.

**Underground Natural Gas Storage Act**
Wash. Rev. Code Ann., 80.40.010 et seq.

**Underground Natural Gas Storage and Conservation Act**
Tex. Natural Resources Code, § 91.171 et seq.

**Underground Petroleum Environmental Response Bank Act**
S.C. Code Ann. 1976, § 44-2-10 et seq.

**Underground Safety Act**
Wash. Rev. Code Ann., 49.24.010 et seq.

**Underground Services Law**
N.Y. Local Laws 1969, Town of Erwin, p. 1202

**Underground Storage Act**
Pa. Purdon's Stat., Title 58, § 451 et seq.

**Underground Storage Act (Prince Georges' County)**
Md. Ann. Code 1974, Art. NR, § 6-201 et seq.

**Underground Storage Tank Act**
Ga. Code Ann., 12-13-1 et seq.
Mich. Comp. Laws Ann., 299.831 et seq.
Miss. Code Ann. 1972, § 49-17-401 et seq.
Mont. Code Ann., 75-11-501 et seq.
Utah Code Ann. 1953, 19-6-401 et seq.
W. Va. Code 1966, §§ 20-5H-1 et seq., 22-17-1 et eq.

**Underground Storage Tank and Wellhead Protection Act**
Ala. Code 1975, § 22-36-1 et seq.

**Underground Storage Tank Cleanup Act (Leaking Petroleum)**
N.C. Gen. Stat. 1943, § 143-215.94A et seq.

**Underground Storage Tank Cleanup Fund Act**
Mass. Gen. Laws 1984, 215:1 et seq.

**Underground Storage Tank Cleanup Trust Fund Act (Barry Keene)**
Cal. Health and Safety Code § 25299.10

**Underground Storage Tank Corrective Action Act (Water Pollution)**
Wyo. Stat. Ann., § 35-11-1414 et seq.

**Underground Storage Tank Economic and Environmental Assistance Act**
Wyo. Stat. Ann., § 35-11-1401 et seq.

**Underground Storage Tank Finance Act**
N.J. Stat. Ann., 58:10A-37.1 et seq.

**Underground Storage Tank Financial Assurance Act**
Mich. Comp. Laws Ann., 299.801 et seq.

**Underground Storage Tank Financial Responsibility Act**
R.I. Gen. Laws 1956, 46-12.9-1 et seq.

**Underground Storage Tank Installer Licensing and Permitting Act**
Mont. Laws 1991, Ch. 594

**Underground Storage Tank Maintenance Fee Bill of Rights**
Cal. Revenue and Taxation Code § 50156 et seq.

**Underground Storage Tank Maintenance Fee Law**
Cal. Revenue and Taxation Code § 50101 et seq.

**Underground Storage Tank Reform Act (Thompson-Richter)**
Cal. Health and Safety Code § 25289 et seq.

**Underground Storage Tank Regulation Act**
Okla. Stat. Ann., Title 17, § 301 et seq.

**Underground Storage Tank Regulatory Act**
Mich. Comp. Laws Ann., 299.701a et seq.
Okla. Stat. Ann., Title 17, § 301 et seq.

**Underground Storage Tank Technician Certification Act**
Ida. Code 1947, 41-276 et seq.

**Underground Storage Tank Trust Fund Act**
Ala. Acts 1988, No. 378

**Underground Transmission Law (Electric)**
Cal. Public Utilities Code § 8051 et seq.

**Underground Utilities and Facilities Damage Prevention Act**
La. Rev. Stat. Ann., 40:1749.11 et seq.

**Underground Utility Damage Prevention Act**
Kan. Stat. Ann., 66-1801 et seq.
S.C. Code Ann. 1976, § 58-35-10 et seq.
Tenn. Code Ann., 65-31-101 et seq.
Va. Code 1950, § 56-265.14 et seq.

**Underground Utility Damage Prevention and Safety Act**
Del. Code of 1974, Title 26, § 801 et seq.

**Underground Water Act**
Ariz. Rev. Stat. Ann., § 45-402 et seq.
Colo. Rev. Stat., 37-90-101 et seq.
Ida. Code 1947, 42-226 et seq.
Mont. Code Ann., 85-2-501 et seq.
N.M. Stat. Ann., 72-12-1 et seq.
Ore. Rev. Stat., 537.505 et seq.
Utah Code Ann. 1953, 73-3-22 et seq.
Wash. Rev. Code Ann., 90.44.020 et seq.
Wyo. Stat. Ann., § 41-3-901 et seq.

**Underground Water Appropriation Act**
Nev. Rev. Stat. 1979 Reprint, 534.010 et seq.

**Underground Water Conservation Act**
Tex. Water Code, § 52.001 et seq.

**Underground Water Storage Savings and Replenishment Act**
Fla. Laws 1994, Ch. 291

**Underground Workings Act (Eight Hour)**
Alaska Stat. 1962, § 23.10.405 et seq.

**Underinsured Motorist Insurance Coverage Act**
Neb. Rev. Stat. 1943, 60-571 et seq.
S.C. Code Ann. 1976, § 38-77-160 et seq.

**Undertakers Act**
Pa. 1931 Pamph. Laws 485, No. 153

**Undertakers Licensing Act**
Pa. Purdon's Stat., Title 63, § 479.1 et seq.

**Undertaking and Bond Law**
Cal. Code of Civil Procedure § 995.010 et seq.

**Underwater Antiquities Act**
S.C. Code Ann. 1976, § 54-7-610 et seq.

**Underwater Archaeological Sites and Resources Protection, Conservation and Study Act**
P.R. Laws Ann. 1954, Title 18, § 1501 et seq.

**Underwood Tariff Act**
Oct. 3, 1913, Ch. 16, 38 Stat. 114 (See 18 U.S. Code § 1905) 19 U.S. Code §§ 124, 128, 130 131; 46 U.S. Code § 146

**Underwriters Patrol Act**
Ill. Rev. Stat. 1973, Ch. 142

**Underwriting Act**
Ky. Rev. Stat. 1971, 304.40-010 et seq.

**Underwriting Association Act (Joint)**
Minn. Stat. Ann., 62I.01 et seq.

**Underwriting Association Act (Rural Risk)**
Miss. Code Ann. 1972, § 83-38-1 et seq.

**Underwriting Association Licensing Act (Joint)**
Tex. Insurance Code, Art. 21.49-3b

**Undetectable Firearms Act of 1988**

Nov. 10, 1988, P.L. 100-649, 18 U.S. Code § 921 nt.

Nov. 29, 1990, P.L. 101-647, 18 U.S. Code § 924

Oct. 21, 1998, P.L. 105-277, 18 U.S. Code § 922 nt.

**Undocumented Vessel Numbering and Registration Act**

Cal. Harbor and Navigation Code § 680 et seq.

Cal. Vehicle Code § 9850 et seq.

**Uneconomic Practices Act (Governmental)**

Ill. Rev. Stat. 1991, Ch. 121 1/2, § 205.9 et seq.

**Unemployment Benefit Pension Offset Refund Act (McAlister-Duffy-Greene)**

Cal. Statutes 1985, Ch. 1217, §§ 1, 7, 11, 16

**Unemployment Compensation Act**

Ala. Code 1975, § 25-4-1 et seq

Alaska Stat. 1962, § 23.20.005 et seq.

Ariz. Rev. Stat. Ann., § 23-601 et seq.

Ark. Code Ann. 1987, 11-10-102 et seq.

Cal. Statutes 1953, Ch. 308, p. 1457

Cal. Unemployment Insurance Code § 3501 et seq.

Colo. Rev. Stat., 8-70-101 et seq.

Conn. Gen. Stat. 1983, § 31-222 et seq.

D.C. Code Ann., § 46-101 et seq.

Del. Code of 1974, Title 19, § 3101 et seq.

Fla. Stat. Ann., 443.011 et seq.

Ga. Code Ann., 34-8-1 et seq.

Haw. Rev. Stat. Ann., § 383-1 et seq.

Ida. Code 1947, 72-1301 et seq.

Ill. Rev. Stat. 1991, Ch. 48, § 300 et seq.

Ind. Code Ann., 22-4-1-1 et seq.

Iowa Code Ann., 96.1 et seq.

Kan. Stat. Ann., 44-701 et seq.

Ky. Rev. Stat. 1971, 341.005 et seq.

La. Rev. Stat. Ann., 23:1471 et seq.

Mass. Gen. Laws Ann., 151A:1 et seq.

Md. Ann. Code 1974, Art. LE, § 8-101 et seq.

Me. Rev. Stat. Ann. 1964, Title 26, § 1041 et seq.

Mich. Comp. Laws Ann., 421.1 et seq.

Minn. Stat. Ann., 268.03 et seq.

Miss. Code Ann. 1972, § 71-5-1 et seq.

Mo. Rev. Stat., 288.010 et seq.

Mont. Code Ann., 39-51-101 et seq.

N.C. Gen. Stat. 1943, §§ 36A-90 et seq., 96-1 et seq.

N.D. Cent. Code, 52-01-01 et seq.

Neb. Rev. Stat. 1943, 48-601 et seq.

Nev. Rev. Stat. 1979 Reprint, 612.010 et seq.

N.H. Rev. Stat. 1955, 282-A:1 et seq.

N.J. Stat. Ann., 43:21-1 et seq.

N.M. Stat. Ann., 51-1-1 et seq.

N.Y. Labor Law (Consol. Laws Ch. 31) § 500 et seq.

Ohio Rev. Code 1953, 4141.01 et seq.

Okla. Stat. Ann., Title 40, § 1-101 et seq.

Ore. Rev. Stat., 657.005 et seq.

Pa. Purdon's Stat., Title 43, § 751 et seq.

R.I. Gen. Laws 1956, 28-42-1 et seq.

S.C. Code Ann. 1976, §§ 41-27-10 et seq., 41-35-120 et seq.

S.D. Codified Laws 1967, 61-1-1 et seq.

Tenn. Code Ann., 50-7-101 et seq.

Tex. Labor Code, § 201.001 et seq.

Tex. Rev. Civ. Stat., Art. 5221b-1 et seq.

Utah Code Ann. 1953, 35-4-1 et seq.

Va. Code 1950, § 60.2-100 et seq.

Vt. Stat. Ann., Title 21, § 1301 et seq.

Wash. Rev. Code Ann., 50.01.005 et seq.

Wis. Stat. 1975, 108.01 et seq.

W. Va. Code 1966, § 21A-4-1 et seq.

Wyo. Stat. Ann., § 27-3-101 et seq.

**Unemployment Compensation Act (Additional Benefits)**

Haw. Rev. Stat. Ann., § 385-1 et seq.

**Unemployment Compensation Amendments of 1976**

Oct. 10, 1979, P.L. 96-84, 26 U.S. Code § 3304 nt.

Aug. 22, 1996, P.L. 104-193, 42 U.S. Code § 603a

Aug. 7, 1998, P.L. 105-220, 42 U.S. Code § 655a

**Unemployment Compensation Amendments of 1992**
July 3, 1992, P.L. 102-318, 26 U.S. Code § 1 nt.
Aug. 20, 1996, P.L. 104-188, 26 U.S. Code §§ 691, 4973

**Unemployment Compensation Amendments of 1993**
Nov. 24, 1993, P.L. 103-152, 26 U.S. Code §§ 1 nt., 3304 nt.; 42 U.S. Code §§ 503, 503 nt., 504, 1105, 1108, 1382j; 45 U.S. Code § 352 nt.

**Unemployment Compensation Benefits Act**
Wash. Rev. Code Ann., 50.20.010 et seq.

**Unemployment Compensation Contributions Act**
Wash. Rev. Code Ann., 50.24.010 et seq.

**Unemployment Compensation Disability Benefits Law**
Cal. Unemployment Insurance Code § 2601 et seq.

**Unemployment Compensation Extension Act of 1977 (Emergency)**
Md. Ann. Code 1974, Art. LE, § 8-101 et seq.

**Unemployment Compensation Trust Fund Act**
Ore. Rev. Stat., 657.805 et seq.

**Unemployment Elimination Act**
P.R. Laws Ann. 1954, Title 28, § 661 et seq.

**Unemployment Relief Act**
March 31, 1933, Ch. 17, 48 Stat. 22
Cal. Labor Code § 2010 et seq.
Haw. Session Laws 1933, Act 209
Wash. Laws 1933, Ch. 8

**Unemployment Relief Bond Act**
Cal. Statutes 1933, p. 677

**Unemployment Relief Income Tax Act (Emergency)**
Wis. Laws 1931-32, Special Session, Ch. 29

**Unemployment Relief Tax Act**
N.Y. Laws 1933, 1st Ex. Sess., Ch. 815

**Unemployment Reserves Act**
Cal. Unemployment Insurance Code § 1025 et seq.
Utah Laws 1935, Ch. 38
Wis. Stat. 1981, 108.01 et seq.

**Unemployment Security Act**
Me. Rev. Stat. Ann. 1964, Title 26, § 1041 et seq.
Mich. Comp. Laws Ann., 421.1 et seq.
N.H. Rev. Stat. 1955, 282-A:1 et seq.
Tenn. Code Ann., 50-7-101 et seq.

**Unemployment Tax Act**
Mich. Comp. Laws Ann., 421.13

**Unemployment Tax Amnesty Program**
Ga. Code Ann., 34-8-270 et seq.

**Unfair Agricultural Marketing Practices Act**
Wash. Rev. Code Ann., 15.83.005 et seq., 15.83.900

**Unfair Business Practices Act**
Wash. Rev. Code Ann., 19.86.010 et seq.

**Unfair Cigarette and Tobacco Products Sales Act**
Ala. Code 1958, Title 57, § 83(1) et seq.
Ark. Code Ann. 1987, 4-75-701 et seq.
Colo. Rev. Stat., 6-5-101 et seq.
Conn. Gen. Stat. 1983, § 12-326a et seq.
Del. Code of 1974, title 6, § 2601 et seq.
Iowa Code Ann., 551A.1 et seq.
Ky. Rev. Stat. 1971, 365.260 et seq.
Mass. Acts 1941, Ch. 715
Md. Ann. Code 1974, Art. CL, § 11-501 et seq.
Minn. Stat. Ann., 325D.30 et seq.
Miss. Code Ann. 1972, § 75-23-1 et seq.
Mont. Code Ann., 16-10-101 et seq.
Neb. Rev. Stat. 1943, 59-1501 et seq.
N.J. Stat. Ann., 56:7-18 et seq.
N.M. Stat. Ann., 57-2-1 et seq.
Ohio Rev. Code 1953, 1333.11 et seq.
Okla. Stat. Ann., Title 68, § 326 et seq.
Ore. Laws 1951, Ch. 540

*Continued*

Pa. Purdon's Stat., Title 73, § 231.1 et seq.
S.D. Codified Laws 1967, 37-10-1 et seq.
Tenn. Code Ann., 47-25-301 et seq.
Wash. Rev. Code Ann., 19.91.010 et seq.
W. Va. Code 1966, §§ 11-12-6a, 11-12-6b

**Unfair Cigarette Sales Below Cost Act**
Wash. Rev. Code Ann., 19.91.010 et seq.

**Unfair Cigarette Sales Tax Act**
Ga. Code 1933, 84-2801 et seq.

**Unfair Claims Settlement Practices Act**
Ga. Code Ann., 33-6-30 et seq.
Mo. Rev. Stat., 375.1000 et seq.
Neb. Rev. Stat. 1943, 44-1536 et seq.
Okla. Stat. Ann., Title 36, §§ 1221 et seq.,1250.1 to 1250.16
Tex. Insurance Code, Art. 21.21-2

**Unfair Competition Act**
Sept. 8, 1916, Ch. 463, 39 Stat. 798, 15 U.S. Code §§ 71 to 77; See 18 U.S. Code § 1905; 19 U.S. Code §§ 1333, 1335
Conn. Gen. Stat. 1983, § 42-115e et seq.
Mass. Gen. Laws Ann., 93:14E et seq.
Mont. Code Ann. 1947, 94-1107 et seq.
N.J. Stat. Ann., 56:4-1 et seq.
Okla. Stat. Ann., Title 79, § 81 et seq.
Wash. Rev. Code Ann., 19.90.010 et seq.

**Unfair Competition Act (Trade Names)**
Ga. Code Ann., 10-1-451

**Unfair Competition and Discrimination Act**
Minn. Stat. Ann., 325D.01 et seq.
Wyo. Stat. Ann., § 40-4-106 et seq.

**Unfair Competition and Trade Practices Act**
Ind. Code Ann., 27-4-1-1 et seq.
Neb. Rev. Stat. 1943, 44-1522 et seq.

**Unfair Dairy Trade Practices Act**
Wis. Stat. Ann., 100.201

**Unfair Discrimination Act (Sales)**
Iowa Code Ann., 551.1 et seq.
Mont. Rev. Code 1947, 94-1107 et seq.

**Unfair Discrimination against Subjects of Abuse in Health Benefit Plans Act**
R.I. Gen. Laws 1956, 27-60-1 et seq.

**Unfair Employment Practices Act**
Iowa Code Ann., 601A.6

**Unfair Frozen Dessert Sales Law**
Tenn. Code Ann., 53-3-301 et seq.

**Unfair Home Improvement Loans Act**
Mo. Laws 1999, H.B. No. 52

**Unfair Home Improvement Loans for Senior Citizens Act**
R.I. Gen. Laws 1956, 6-28.1-1 et seq.

**Unfair Insurance Trade Practices Act**
Fla. Stat. Ann., 626.951 et seq.
Ill. Rev. Stat. 1991, Ch. 73, § 1028 et seq.
Ky. Rev. Stat. 1962, 304.924 et seq.
N.D. Cent. Code, 26.1-04-01 et seq.
N.H. Rev. Stat. 1955, 417:1 et seq.
N.M. Stat. Ann., 59-11-9 et seq.
Pa. Purdon's Stat., Title 40, § 1171.1 et seq.
S.D. Codified Laws 1967, 58-33-1 et seq.
Wash. Rev. Code Ann., 48.30.010 et seq.

**Unfair Milk Sales Act**
Miss. Code Ann. 1972, § 75-31-307 et seq.
Mo. Rev. Stat., 416.410 et seq.
Tenn. Code Ann., 53-3-201 et seq.

**Unfair Motor Fuels Practices Act**
N.J. Stat. Ann., 56:6-19 et seq.

**Unfair Practices Act**
Ariz. Rev. Stat. Ann., § 44-1421 et seq.
Ark. Code Ann. 1987, 4-75-207 et seq.
Cal. Business and Professions Code § 17000 et seq.
Colo. Rev. Stat., 6-2-101 et seq.
Haw. Rev. Stat. Ann., § 481-1 et seq.
Kan. Laws 1941, Ch. 277
Mont. Code Ann. 1987, 30-14-201 et seq.
Neb. Rev. Stat. 1943, 59-501 et seq.
N.M. Stat. Ann., 57-12-1 et seq.
Utah Code Ann. 1953, 13-5-1 et seq.
Wash. Rev. Code Ann., 19.90.010 et seq.
Wyo. Stat. Ann., § 40-4-101 et seq.

**Unfair Practices Act (Agricultural Marketing)**
Wash. Rev. Code Ann., 15.83.005 et seq.

**Unfair Practices Act (Insurance)**
See Insurance Unfair Trade Practices Act

**Unfair Profiteering Act**
P.R. Laws Ann. 1954, Title 13, § 2231 et seq.

**Unfair Sales Act for the Retail Sale of Motor Fuels**
Mass. Gen. Laws Ann., 94:295P et seq.

**Unfair Sales Practices Act**
Ariz. Rev. Stat. Ann., § 44-1461 et seq.
Conn. Gen. Stat. 1983, § 42-115e et seq.
Ida. Code 1947, 48-401 et seq.
La. Rev. Stat. Ann., 51:421 et seq.
Mass. Gen. Laws Ann., 93:14E et seq.
Md. Ann. Code 1974, Art. CL, § 11-401 et seq.
Me. Rev. Stat. Ann. 1964, Title 10, § 1201 et seq.
Mont. Rev. Code 1947, 51-101 et seq
Neb. Laws 1941, Ch. 123
N.H. Rev. Stat. 1955, 358:1 et seq.
N.J. Stat. Ann., 56-4-1 et seq.
Okla. Stat. Ann., Title 68, § 326 et seq.
Pa. Purdon's Stat., Title 73, § 211 et seq.
R.I. Gen. Laws 1956, 6-13-1 et seq.
Tenn. Code Ann., 47-25-201 et seq.
Va. Code 1950, § 59.1-10 et seq.
Wis. Stat. 1981, 100.30

**Unfair Trade Practices Act**
Conn. Gen. Stat. 1983, § 42-110a et seq.
Del. Code of 1974, Title 18, § 2301 et seq.
Fla. Stat. Ann., 501.201 et seq.
Ind. Code Ann., 24-3-1-1 et seq.
Kan. Stat. Ann., 40-2401 et seq., 50-148 et seq.
Ky. Rev. Stat. 1971, 365.020 et seq.
Me. Rev. Stat. Ann. 1964, Title 5, §§ 205-A et seq.,
Minn. Stat. Ann., 325D.08 et seq.
Mo. Rev. Stat. 1978, 375.930
N.D. Cent. Code, 51-10-01 et seq.
Nev. Rev. Stat. 1979 Reprint, 598A.010 et seq.
Ore. Rev. Stat., 646.010 et seq.
S.C. Code Ann. 1976, § 39-5-10 et seq.
Tenn. Code Ann., 47-25-901 et seq.
W. Va. Code 1966, § 47-11A-1 et seq.
Wyo. Stat. Ann., § 26-13-101 et seq.

**Unfair Trade Practices Act (Barbers)**
Okla. Stat. Ann., Title 68, § 340 et seq.

**Unfair Trade Practices Act (Dairy Industry)**
Minn. Stat. Ann., 32A.01 et seq.

**Unfair Trade Practices Act (Insurance)**
See also Insurance Unfair Trade Practices Act
Alaska Stat. 1962, Replaced Titles, § 21.10.865 et seq.
Ga. Code Ann., 33-6-1 et seq.
La. Rev. Stat. Ann., 22:771 et seq.
Minn. Stat. Ann., 72A.17 et seq.
S.C. Code Ann. 1976, § 38-55-10 et seq.
Utah Code Ann. 1953, 31A-23-302

**Unfair Trade Practices and Consumer Protection Act**
Fla. Stat. 1971, 817.76 et seq.
La. Rev. Stat. Ann., 51:1401 et seq.
Mont. Code Ann., 30-14-101 et seq.
Pa. Purdon's Stat., Title 73, § 201-1 et seq.
R.I. Gen. Laws 1956, 6-13.1-1 et seq.

**Unfair Trade Practices and Monopolies Anti-Trust Act**
Ariz. Rev. Stat. Ann., § 44-1401 et seq.

**Unfired Pressure Vessel Act**
N.H. Rev. Stat. 1955, 157-A:1 et seq.
Ore. Rev. Stat., 480.510 et seq.

**Unfired Pressure Vessel and Boiler Law**
Pa. 1998 Pamph. Laws, No. 85

**Unfit Parents Termination of Rights Act**
Miss. Code Ann. 1972, § 93-15-101 et seq.

**Unfit Residence Act**
Ind. Code Ann., 16-1-25-1 et seq.

**Unfunded Mandated Act (Federal)**
Miss. Code Ann. 1972, §§ 5-3-73, 5-3-79

**Unfunded Mandates Reform Act of 1995**
March 22, 1995, P.L. 104-4, 2 U.S. Code § 1501 nt.

**Unicoi County Massage Registration Act**
Tenn. Private Acts 1977, Ch. 20

**Unicoi County Road Law**
Tenn. Private Acts 1915, Ch. 248

**Unification Act**
Kan. Stat. Ann., 72-6734 et seq. (First)
Kan. Stat. Ann., 72-6764 et seq. (Second)
Kan. Stat. Ann., 72-6793 et seq. (Third)

**Unification Act (Judicial Employees)**
N.J. Stat. Ann., 2B:11-1 et seq.

**Unification Act (Railroads)**
N.Y. Rapid Transit Law (Consol. Laws Ch. 48A) § 90 et seq.

**Unification Acts (School)**
Kan. Stat. Ann., 72-6764 et seq.

**Unification and Financing Act (Port)**
N.J. Stat. Ann., 34:1B-144 et seq.

**Unification Commission and County Charter Act (Griffin-Spalding County)**
Ga. Laws 1995, p. 4429

**Unified Atlanta-Fulton County Water and Sewer System Act**
Ga. Laws 1978, p. 4637

**Unified Bond Ceiling Allocation Act**
Colo. Rev. Stat., 24-32-1601 et seq.

**Unified Community Mental Health Services Act**
Okla. Stat. 1981, Title 43A, § 3-301 et seq.

**Unified Investment Program**
Mont. Code Ann., 17-6-201 et seq.

**Unified Juvenile Code**
Ky. Rev. Stat. 1971, 600.010 et seq.

**Unified Juvenile Code (Mental Health Act)**
Ky. Rev. Stat. 1971, 645.010

**Unified License and Permit Bond Act (Contractor)**
Ill. Comp. Stat. 1992, Ch. 50, § 830/1 et seq.

**Unified Port District Act (San Diego)**
Cal. Statutes 1962, 1st Ex. Sess., Ch. 67, p. 362

**Unified School District Act**
Kan. Stat. Ann., 72-6734 et seq.

**Unified Sentencing Act**
Ida. Code 1947, 19-2513

**Unified State Case Registry and Disbursement Unit Act**
Tex. Family Code, § 234.001 et seq.

**Unified Trial Court Act**
Iowa Code 1983, 602.1 et seq.

**Unified Volume Cap Bond Allocation Plan Act**
Mont. Code Ann., 17-5-1301 et seq.

**Unified Volume Limitation Allocation Act**
Mich. Comp. Laws Ann., 12.111 et seq.

**Uniform Abandonment Act**
Wis. Stat. Ann., 767.08

**Uniform Absence as Evidence of Death and Absentees' Property Act**
Mont. Code Ann., 72-1-108
Tenn. Code Ann., 30-3-101 et seq.
Wis. Stat. Ann., 813.22 et seq.

**Uniform Accident Reporting Act**
Mont. Code Ann., 61-7-101 et seq.

**Uniform Accounting Act (Local Government)**
Colo. Rev. Stat., 29-1-501 et seq.

**Uniform Accounting and Auditing Practices for Community Agencies Act**
Me. Rev. Stat. Ann. 1964, Title 5, § 1660-C et seq.

**Uniform Accounting System Act (State and County)**

Mich. Comp. Laws Ann., 21.41 et seq.

**Uniform Acknowledgement Act**

Ariz. Rev. Stat. Ann., § 33-511 et seq.
Ark. Code Ann. 1987, 16-47-201 et seq.
Conn. Gen. Stat. 1983, § 1-28 et seq.
Haw. Rev. Stat. Ann., § 502-41 et seq.
Ida. Code 1947, 55-701 et seq.
La. Rev. Stat. Ann., 35:511 et seq.
Mass. Gen. Laws Ann., 183.29 et seq.
Mich. Comp. Laws Ann., 565.251 et seq.
Mont. Code Ann., 1-5-101 et seq.
N.D. Cent. Code, 47-19-13 et seq.
N.H. Rev. Stat. 1955, 456:1 et seq.
Pa. Purdon's Stat., Title 21, § 291. 1 et seq.
S.D. Codified Laws 1967, 18-5-1 et seq.
Utah Code Ann. 1953, 57-2-1 et seq.
Wis. Stat. Ann., 706.07
Wyo. Stat. Ann., § 34-2-114 et seq.

**Uniform Acknowledgments Act**

Md. Ann. Code 1974, Art. SG, § 19-101 et seq.

**Uniform Act Fixing Basis of Participation by Secured Creditors in Insolvent Estates**

N.Y. Debtor and Creditor Law (Consol. Laws Ch. 12) § 30 et seq.

**Uniform Act for Licensing Agencies**

N.C. Gen. Stat. 1943, § 150-9 et seq.

**Uniform Act for Out of State Parolee Supervision**

Ariz. Rev. Stat. Ann., § 31-461 et seq.
Ark. Code Ann. 1987, 16-93-901, 16-93-903
Cal. Penal Code § 11175 et seq.
Colo. Rev. Stat., 24-60-301 et seq.
Conn. Gen. Stat. 1983, § 54-133
Del. Code of 1974, Title 11, §§ 4358, 4359
Fla. Stat. Ann., 949.07 et seq.
Ga. Code Ann., 42-9-70, 42-9-71
Ida. Code 1947, 20-301, 20-302
Ind. Code Ann., 11-13-4-1, 11-13-4-2
Iowa Code 1977, 247.10
Kan. Stat. Ann., 22-4101 et seq.
Ky. Rev. Stat. 1971, 439.560
La. Rev. Stat. Ann., 15:574.14
Mass. Gen. Laws Ann., 127:151A et seq.
Md. Ann. Code 1957, Art. 41, § 4-801 et seq.
Me. Rev. Stat. Ann. 1964, Title 34-A, § 9801 et seq.
Minn. Stat. Ann., 243.16 et seq.
Miss. Code Ann. 1972, § 47-7-71
Mo. Rev. Stat., 217.810
Mont. Code Ann., 46-23-1101 et seq.
N.C. Gen. Stat. 1943, § 148-65.1 et seq.
N.D. Cent. Code, 12-56-01, 12-56-02
Neb. Rev. Stat. 1943, 29-2637, 29-2638
Nev. Rev. Stat. 1979 Reprint, 213.180 et seq.
N.H. Rev. Stat. 1955, 651-A:25 et seq.
N.J. Stat. Ann., 2A:168-14 et seq.
N.M. Stat. Ann., 31-5-1, 31-5-2
N.Y. Executive Law (Consol. Laws Ch. 18) 1977, § 259m
Ohio Rev. Code 1953, 2965. 34
Okla. Stat. Ann., Title 57, § 347 et seq.
Ore. Rev. Stat., 144.610
Pa. Purdon's Stat., Title 61, § 321 et seq.
R.I. Gen. Laws 1956, 13-9-1 et seq.
S.C. Code Ann. 1976, § 24-21-810 et seq.
S.D. Codified Laws 1967, 24-16-1 et seq.
Tenn. Code Ann., 40-28-401 et seq.
Tex. Code of Criminal Procedure, Art. 42.11
Utah Code Ann. 1953, 77-27-24 et seq.
Va. Code 1950, § 53.1-166 et seq.
Vt. Stat. Ann., Title 28, § 1301
Wash. Rev. Code Ann., 9.95.270
Wis. Stat. 1987, 57.13

**Uniform Act for the Application of Building and Fire Related Codes to Existing Buildings**

Ga. Code Ann., 8-2-200 et seq.

**Uniform Act for the Disposition of Unclaimed Property**

Vt. Stat. Ann., Title 27, § 1208 et seq.

**Uniform Act for the Extradition of Persons of Unsound Mind**

Alaska Stat. 1962, § 47.30.410 et seq.
Colo. Rev. Stat., 16-20-101 et seq.
Haw. Rev. Stat. Ann., § 337-1 et seq.
Ill. Rev. Stat. 1991, Ch. 91 1/2, § 121 et seq.
Ind. Code Ann., 16-13-9-1 et seq.

*Continued*

La. Rev. Stat. Ann., 28:501 et seq.
Md. Ann. Code 1957, Art. 41 § 2-301 et seq.
Nev. Rev. Stat. 1957 Ed., 434.010 et seq.
S.D. Codified Laws 1967, 27A-11-1 et seq.
Tenn. Code Ann., 33-9-101 et seq.
Va. Code 1950, § 37.1-172 et seq.
Vt. Stat. Ann., Title 18, § 9101 et seq.
Wis. Stat. Ann., 51.81 et seq.

**Uniform Act for the Extradition of Prisoners as Witnesses**
Wis. Stat. Ann., 976.01

**Uniform Act for the Extradition of Witnesses in Criminal Actions**
Wis. Stat. Ann., 976.02

**Uniform Act for Voting by New Residents in Presidential Elections**
Haw. Rev. Laws 1955, § 11-230 et seq.
Minn. Stat. 1974, 208.21 et seq.
Neb. Rev. Stat. 1943, 32-1301.01 et seq.

**Uniform Act Governing Secured Creditors' Dividends in Liquidation Proceedings**
Ind. Code Ann., 30-2-7-1 et seq.
N.J. Rev. Stat. 1937, 2A:46-1 et seq.
N.Y. Debtor and Creditor Law (Consol. Laws Ch. 12) § 30 et seq.
S.D. Codified Laws 1967, 54-10-1 et seq.
Wis. Stat. 1981, 128.25

**Uniform Act on Blood Tests to Determine Paternity**
Cal. Family Code § 7550 et seq.
Ill. Rev. Stat. 1991, Ch. 40, § 2511
La. Rev. Stat. Ann., 9:396 et seq.
N.H. Rev. Stat. 1955, 522:1 et seq.
Okla. Stat. Ann., Title 10, § 501 et seq.
Ore. Rev. Stat., 109.250 et seq.
Pa. Cons. Stat., Title 42, § 6131 et seq.

**Uniform Act on Fresh Pursuit**
Cal. Penal Code § 852 et seq.
Fla. Stat. Ann., 941.31 et seq.
La. Code of Crim. Proc. 1966, Arts. 231, 232
Me. Rev. Stat. Ann. 1964, Title 36, § 3981 et seq.
Mont. Code Ann., 46-6-411
N.Y. Criminal Procedure Law (Consol. Laws Ch. 11A) § 140.55
R.I. Gen. Laws 1956, 12-8-1 et seq.
Wis. Stat. Ann., 976.04

**Uniform Act on Interstate Arbitration of Death Taxes**
Cal. Revenue and Taxation Code § 13801 et seq.
Md. Ann. Code 1974, Art. TG, § 7-115
Me. Rev. Stat. Ann. 1964, Title 36. § 3911 et seq.
Vt. Stat. Ann., Title 32, § 7101 et seq.

**Uniform Act on Interstate Compromise and Arbitration of Inheritance Law**
Colo. Rev. Stat., 39-24-101 et seq.
Pa. Cons. Stat., Title 72, § 1701 et seq.

**Uniform Act on Interstate Compromise of Death Taxes**
Cal. Revenue and Taxation Code §§ 13801 et seq.
Md. Ann. Code 1974, Art. TG, § 7-122
Me. Rev. Stat. Ann. 1964, Title 15, § 151 et seq.
Vt. Stat. Ann., Title 32, § 7201 et seq.

**Uniform Act on Paternity**
Me. Rev. Stat. Ann. 1964, Title 19-A, § 1551 et seq.
Miss. Code Ann. 1972, § 93-9-1 et seq.
N.H. Rev. Stat. 1955, 168-A:1 et seq.
Utah Code Ann. 1953, 78-45a-1 et seq.

**Uniform Act on Regulating Traffic on Highways**
Mont. Code Ann. 1987, 61-8-101 et seq., 61-9-101 et seq.
N.D. Cent. Code, 29-06-05 et seq.
N.H. Rev. Stat. 1955, 614:1 et seq.
N.J. Stat. Ann., 2A:155-1 et seq.
N.M. Stat. Ann., 31-2-1 et seq.
N.Y. Criminal Procedure Law (Consol. Laws Ch. 11A) § 140.55
Ohio Rev. Code 1953, 2935.29 et seq.
Okla. Stat. Ann., Title 22, § 221 et seq.
Ore. Rev. Stat., 133.410 et seq.
S.D. Codified Laws 1967, Superseded Vol., 23-23-2 et seq.
Tenn. Code Ann., 40-7-201 et seq.
Vt. Stat. Ann., Title 13, § 5041 et seq.
Wash. Rev. Code Ann., 10.89.010 et seq.

W. Va. Code 1966, § 62-11-1 et seq.

**Uniform Act on Status of Convicted Persons**
Haw. Rev. Stat. Ann., § 831-1 et seq.
N.H. Rev. Stat. 1955, 607-A:1 et seq.

**Uniform Act Regulating Traffic on Highways**
Ariz. Rev. Stat. Ann., § 28-601 et seq.
Ark. Code Ann. 1987, 27-49-201 et seq.
Ill. Rev. Stat. 1991, Ch. 95 1/2, 11-100 et seq.
Ind. Code Ann., § 9-4-1-1 et seq.
Iowa Code Ann., 321.228 et seq.
Kan. Stat. Ann., 8-1401 et seq.
Miss. Code Ann. 1972, § 63-3-1 et seq.
Mont. Rev. Code 1947, 32-2101 et seq.
N.D. Cent. Code, 39-07-01 et seq.
Neb. Laws 1931, Ch. 110
N.M. Stat. Ann. 1953, 64-14-1 et seq.
S.C. Code Ann. 1976, § 56-5-10 et seq.
S.D. Codified Laws 1967, 32-14-1 et seq.
Tex. Rev. Civ. Stat., Art. 6701d
Wyo. Stat. Ann., § 31-5-101 et seq.

**Uniform Act to Provide for Appointment of Commissioners**
Ky. Rev. Stat. 1971, 7.110

**Uniform Act to Secure Rendition of Prisoners as Witnesses in Criminal Proceedings**
Iowa Code Ann., 819A.1 et seq.
Kan. Stat. Ann., 22-4207 et seq.

**Uniform Act to Secure Rendition of Prisoners in Criminal Proceedings**
Okla. Stat. Ann., Title 22, § 728 et seq.
Tex. Code of Criminal Procedure 1965, Art. 24.29

**Uniform Act to Secure the Attendance of Witnesses from Without a State in Criminal Cases**
Ala. Code 1975, 12-21-280 et seq.
Alaska Stat. 1962, § 12.50.010 et seq.
Ariz. Rev. Stat. Ann., § 13-4091 et seq.
Ark. Code Ann. 1987, 16-43-402 et seq.
Cal. Penal Code § 1334 et seq.
Colo. Rev. Stat., 16-9-201 et seq.
Conn. Gen. Stat. 1983, § 54-82i
D.C. Code Ann., § 23-1501 et seq.
Del. Code of 1974, Title 11, § 3521 et seq.
Fla. Stat. 1983, 942.01 et seq.
Ga. Code Ann., 24-10-90 et seq.
Haw. Rev. Stat. Ann., § 836-1 et seq.
Ida. Code 1947, 19-3005
Ind. Code Ann., 35-37-5-1 et seq.
Iowa Code Ann., 819.1 et seq.
Kan. Stat. Ann., 22-4201 et seq.
Ky. Rev. Stat. 1971, 421.230 et seq.
La. Code of Crim. Proc. 1966, Art. 741 et seq.
Mass. Gen. Laws Ann., 233:13A et seq.
Md. Ann. Code 1974, Art. CJ, § 9-301 et seq.
Me. Rev. Stat. Ann. 1964, Title 15, § 1411 et seq.
Mich. Comp. Laws Ann., 767.91 et seq.
Minn. Stat. Ann., 634.07 et seq.
Miss. Code Ann. 1972, § 99-9-27 et seq.
Mo. Rev. Stat., 491.400 et seq.
Mont. Code Ann., 46-15-111 et seq.
N.C. Gen. Stat. 1943, § 15A-811 et seq.
N.D. Cent. Code, 31-03-25 et seq.
Neb. Rev. Stat. 1943, 29-1906 et seq.
Nev. Rev. Stat. 1979 Reprint, 174.395 et seq.
N.H. Rev. Stat. 1955, 613:1 et seq.
N.J. Stat. Ann., 2A:81-18 et seq.
N.M. Stat. Ann., 31-8-1 et seq.
N.Y. Criminal Procedure Law (Consol. Laws Ch. 11A) § 640.10
Ohio Rev. Code 1953, 2939.25 et seq.
Okla. Stat. Ann., Title 22, § 721 et seq.
Ore. Rev. Stat., 136.623 et seq.
Pa. Cons. Stat., Title 42, § 5961 et seq.
P.R. Laws Ann. 1954, Title 34, § 1471 et seq.
R.I. Gen. Laws 1956, 12-16-1 et seq.
S.C. Code Ann. 1976, § 19-9-10 et seq.
S.D. Codified Laws 1967, 23A-14-14 et seq.
Tenn. Code Ann., 40-17-201 et seq.
Tex. Code of Criminal Procedure, Art. 24.28
Utah Code Ann. 1953, 77-21-1 et seq.
Va. Code 1950, § 19.2-272 et seq.
Vt. Stat. Ann., Title 13, § 6641 et seq.
Wash. Rev. Code Ann., 10.55.010 et seq.
Wis. Stat. Ann., 976.02
W. Va. Code 1966, § 62-6A-1 et seq.
Wyo. Stat. Ann., § 7-11-407 et seq.

**Uniform Act to Secure the Attendance of Witnesses from Without a State in Criminal Proceedings**
Haw. Rev. Stat. Ann., § 836-1 et seq.
Mass. Gen. Laws Ann., 233:13A to 233:13D

**Uniform Administration Act (Trusts)**
N.D. Cent. Code, 59-04-01 et seq.

**Uniform Administrative Agencies Practice Act**
N.D. Cent. Code, 28-32-01 et seq.

**Uniform Administrative Procedure Act**
See also Administrative Procedure Act
Ala. Code 1975, § 41-22-1 et seq.
Ariz. Rev. Stat. Ann., § 41-1001 et seq.
Ark. Code Ann. 1987, 25-15-201 et seq.
Conn. Gen. Stat. 1983, § 4-166 et seq.
D.C. Code Ann., § 1-1501 et seq.
Ga. Code Ann., 50-13-1 et seq.
Haw. Rev. Stat. 1985, § 91-1 et seq.
Ida. Code 1947, 67-5201 et seq.
Ill. Rev. Stat. 1991, Ch. 127, § 1001 et seq.
Iowa Code Ann., 17A.1 et seq.
La. Rev. Ann., 49:950 et seq.
Md. Ann. Code 1957, Art. SG, § 10-201 et seq.
Me. Rev. Ann. 1964, Title 5, § 8001 et seq.
Mich. Comp. Laws Ann., 24.201 et seq.
Miss. Code Ann. 1972, § 25-43-1 et seq.
Mo. Rev. Stat., 536.010 et seq.
Mont. Code Ann., 2-4-101 et seq.
Neb. Rev. Stat. 1943, 84-901 et seq.
Nev. Rev. Stat. 1987, 233B.010 et seq.
N.H. Rev. Stat. 1955, 541-A:1 et seq.
N.Y. State Administrative Procedure Act (Consol. Laws Ch. 82), § 100 et seq.
Ohio Rev. Code 1953, 119.01 et seq.
Okla. Stat. Ann., Title 75, §§ 250.3 et seq., 302 et seq.
Ore. Rev. Stat., 183.310 et seq.
R.I. Gen. Laws 1956, § 42-35-1 et seq.
S.D. Codified Laws 1967, § 1-26-1 et seq.
Tenn. Code Ann., 4-5-101 et seq.
Vt. Stat. Ann., Title 3, § 801 et seq.
Wash. Rev. Code Ann., 34.05.001 et seq.
Wis. Stat. Ann., 227.01 et seq.
W. Va. Code 1966, § 29A-1-1 et seq.
Wyo. Stat. Ann., § 16-3-101 et seq.

**Uniform Administrative Procedures Act**
P.R. Laws Ann. 1954, Title 3, § 2101 et seq.

**Uniform Adoption Act**
See also Adoption Act
Alaska Stat. 1962, § 25.23.005 et seq.
Ark. Code Ann. 1987, 9-9-201 et seq.
Mont. Code Ann. 1987, 40-8-101 et seq.
N.D. Cent. Code, 14-15-01 et seq.
Ohio Rev. Code 1953, 3107.01 et seq.

**Uniform Aeronautical Regulatory Act**
R.I. Gen. Laws 1956, 1-4-1 et seq.
Utah Code Ann. 1953, 2-1-1 et seq.

**Uniform Aeronautics Act**
Ariz. Rev. Stat. Ann., § 2-101 et seq.
Del. Code of 1974, Title 2, § 301 et seq.
Ga. Code Ann., 6-2-1 et seq.
Haw. Rev. Stat. Ann., § 263-1 et seq.
Ind. Code Ann., 8-21-4-1 et seq.
Mo. Rev. Stat., 305.010 et seq.
N.C. Gen. Stat. 1943, § 63-1 et seq.
N.J. Rev. Stat. 1937, 6:2-1 et seq.
Pa. 1929 Pamph. Laws 753, No. 317
S.C. Code Ann. 1976, § 55-3-10 et seq.

**Uniform Agricultural Cooperative Association Act**
Me. Rev. Stat. Ann. 1964, Title 13, § 1771 et seq.
Utah Code Ann. 1953, 3-1-1 et seq.

**Uniform Air Licensing Act**
Alaska Stat. 1962, § 02.35.010 et seq.
N.D. Cent. Code, 2-05-01 et seq.
Tenn. Public Acts 1931, Ch. 73

**Uniform Aircraft Financial Responsibility Act**
See also Aircraft Financial Responsibility Act
Cal. Public Utilities Code § 24230 et seq.
Conn. Gen. Stat. 1983, § 15-102 et seq.
Mass. Gen. Laws Ann., 90:49B et seq.
Mich. Comp. Laws Ann., 259.671 et seq.
N.H. Rev. Stat. 1955, 422-A:1 et seq.
S.C. Code Ann. 1976, § 55-8-10 et seq.

**Uniform Airport Zoning Act**
Minn. Stat. Ann., 360.061 et seq.

**Uniform Airports Act**
Fla. Laws 1937, Ch. 17708
Ga. Code Ann., 6-3-1 et seq.
La. Rev. Stat. Ann., 2:131 et seq.
Minn. Stat. Ann., 360.031 et seq.
S.C. Code Ann. 1976, § 55-9-10 et seq.
Utah Code Ann. 1953, 2-2-1 et seq.

**Uniform Alcoholism and Intoxication Treatment Act**
See also Alcoholism and Intoxication Treatment Act
Alaska Stat. 1962, § 47.37.010 et seq.
Colo. Rev. Stat., 25-1-301 et seq.
Del. Code of 1974, Title 16, § 2201 et seq.
Ga. Code Ann., 37-8-1 et seq.
Me. Rev. Stat. Ann. 1964, Title 22, § 1361 et seq.
Mont. Code Ann. 1987, 53-24-101 et seq.
R.I. Gen. Laws 1956, 40.1-4-1 et seq.
S.C. Code Ann. 1976, § 44-51-410 et seq.
S.D. Codified Laws 1967, 34-20A-1 et seq.
Wash. Rev. Code Ann., 70.96A.010 et seq.
Wis. Stat. Ann., 51.45

**Uniform Anatomical Gift Act**
See also Anatomical Gift Act
Ala. Code 1975, § 22-19-40 et seq.
Alaska Stat. 1962, § 13.50.010 et seq.
Ariz. Rev. Stat. Ann., § 36-841 et seq.
Ark. Code Ann. 1987, 20-17-402 et seq.
Cal. Health and Safety Code § 7150 et seq.
Colo. Rev. Stat., 12-34-101 et seq.
Conn. Gen. Stat. 1983, § 19a-279a et seq.
D.C. Code Ann., § 2-1501 et seq.
Del. Code of 1974, Title 24, § 1780 et seq.
Fla. Stat. Ann., 732.910 et seq.
Ga. Code Ann., 44-5-140 et seq.
Haw. Rev. Stat. Ann., § 327-1 et seq.
Ida. Code 1947, 39-3401 et seq.
Ill. Comp. Stat. 1992, Ch. 755, § 50/1 et seq.
Ind. Code Ann., 29-2-16-1 et seq.
Iowa Code Ann., 142A.1 et seq.
Iowa Code Ann., 142C.1 et seq.
Kan. Stat. Ann., 65-3209 et seq.
Ky. Rev. Stat. 1971, 311.165 et seq.
La. Rev. Stat. Ann., 17:2351 et seq.
Mass. Gen. Laws Ann., Ch. 113, § 7 et seq.
Md. Ann. Code 1974, § 4-501 et seq.
Me. Rev. Stat. Ann. 1964, Title 22, § 2901 et seq.
Mich. Comp. Laws Ann., 333.10101 et seq.
Minn. Stat. Ann., 525.921 et seq.
Miss. Code Ann. 1972, §§ 41-39-11, 41-39-31 et seq.
Mo. Rev. Stat., 194.210 et seq.
Mont. Code Ann., 72-17-101 et seq.
N.C. Gen. Stat. 1943, § 90-220.1 et seq.
N.D. Cent. Code, 23-06.1-01 et seq.
Neb. Rev. Stat. 1943, 71-4801 et seq.
Nev. Rev. Stat. 1979 Reprint, 451.500 et seq.
N.H. Rev. Stat. 1955, 291-A:1 et seq.
N.J. Stat. Ann., 26:6-57 et seq.
N.M. Stat. Ann., 24-6-1 et seq.
N.Y. Public Health Law 1953 (Consol. Laws Ch. 45) § 4301 et seq.
Ohio Rev. Code 1953, 2108.00 et seq.
Okla. Stat. Ann., Title 63, § 2201 et seq.
Ore. Rev. Stat., 97.250 et seq.
Pa. Cons. Stat., Title 20, § 8601 et seq.
R.I. Gen. Laws 1956, 23-18.5-1 et seq.
S.C. Code Ann. 1976, § 44-43-310 et seq.
S.D. Codified Laws 1967, 34-26-20 et seq.
Tenn. Code Ann., 53-42-101 et seq.
Tex. Rev. Civ. Stat., Art. 4590-2
Utah Code Ann. 1953, 26-28-1 et seq.
Va. Code 1950, § 32.1-289 et seq.
Vt. Stat. Ann., Title 18, § 5231 et seq.
Wash. Rev. Code Ann., 68-50-340 et seq.
Wis. Stat. Ann., 155.06
W. Va. Code 1966, § 16-19-1 et seq.
Wyo. Stat. Ann., § 35-5-101 et seq.

**Uniform Ancillary Administration of Estates Act**
See also Ancillary Administration of Estates Act
Mont. Code Ann., 53-24-101 et seq.
Wis. Stat. Ann., 868.03

**Uniform Appeals Act**
Fla. Stat. Ann., 59.04 et seq.

**Uniform Arbitration Act**
Alaska Stat. 1962, § 09.43.010 et seq.
Ariz. Rev. Stat. Ann., § 12-1501 et seq.
Ark. Code Ann. 1987, 16-108-201 et seq.
Colo. Rev. Stat., 13-22-201 et seq.
D.C. Code Ann., § 16-4301 et seq.
Del. Code of 1974, Title 10, § 5701 et seq.
Ida. Code 1947, 7-901 et seq.
Ill. Rev. Stat. 1991, Ch. 10, § 101 et seq.
Ind. Code Ann., 34-4-2-1 et seq.
Iowa Code Ann., 679A.1 et seq.
Kan. Stat. Ann., 5-401 et seq.
Ky. Rev. Stat. 1971, 417.045 et seq.
Mass. Gen. Laws Ann., 251:1 et seq.
Md. Ann. Code 1974, Art. CJ, § 3-201 et seq.
Me. Rev. Stat. Ann. 1964, Title 14, § 5927 et seq.
Mich. Comp. Laws Ann., 600.5001 et seq.
Minn. Stat. Ann., 572.08 et seq.
Mo. Rev. Stat., 435.350 et seq.
Mont. Code Ann., 27-5-111 et seq.
N.C. Gen. Stat. 1943, § 1-567.1 et seq.
N.D. Cent. Code, 32-29.2-01 et seq.
Neb. Rev. Stat. 1943, 25-2601 et seq.
Nev. Rev. Stat. 1979 Reprint, 38.015 et seq.
N.M. Stat. 1978, 44-7-1 et seq.
Okla. Stat. Ann., Title 15, § 801 et seq.
Pa. Cons. Stat., Title 42, § 7301 et seq.
S.C. Code Ann. 1976, § 15-48-10 et seq.
S.D. Codified Laws 1967, 21-25A-1 et seq.
Tenn. Code Ann., 29-5-301 et seq.
Tex. Civil Practice and Remedies Code, § 171.001 et seq.
Tex. Rev. Civ. Stat., Art. 224 et seq.
Utah Code Ann. 1953, 78-31a-1 et seq.
Wis. Stat. Ann., 788.01 et seq.
Wyo. Stat. Ann., § 1-36-101 et seq.

**Uniform Arrest Act**
Del. Code of 1974, Title 11, § 1901 et seq.
N.H. Rev. Stat. 1955, 594:1 et seq.
R.I. Gen. Laws 1956, 12-7-1 et seq.

**Uniform Arrest Ticket Act**
Miss. Code Ann. 1972, § 63-9-21

**Uniform Attendance and Leave Policy Act**
Ark. Code Ann. 1987, 21-4-201 et seq.

**Uniform Audio-Visual Deposition Act**
Va. Code 1950, § 8.01-412.2 et seq.

**Uniform Automobile Liability Security Act**
Pa. 1933 Pamph. Laws 553, No. 110

**Uniform Bank Collections Act**
N.J. Stat. Ann., 7:6-1 to 7:6-17
Pa. 1931 Pamph. Laws 568, No. 198

**Uniform Barber Law**
Ark. Code Ann. 1987, 17-18-301 et seq.

**Uniform Barbiturate Act**
Ohio Rev. Code 1953, 3719.23 et seq.

**Uniform Beer Tax Act**
Ga. Code Ann., 3-5-60, 3-5-61

**Uniform Billing and Electronic Data Exchange Act**
Colo. Rev. Stat., 10-1-131

**Uniform Bills of Lading Act**
See also Uniform Commercial Code—Documents of Title
Ala. Code 1958, Title 48, § 356 et seq.
Alaska Laws 1913, Ch. 59
Ariz. Laws 1921, Ch. 48
Ark. Stat. 1947, 68-1101 et seq.
Cal. Civil Code § 2126 et seq.
Del. Code of 1953, Title 6, § 7-301 et seq.
Ill. Rev. Stat. 1961, Ch. 27, § 2 et seq.
Iowa Code 1962, 487.1 et seq.
La. Acts 1912, No. 94
Mass. Gen. Laws Ann., 108:42 et seq.
Md. Ann. Code 1974, Art. CL, § 7-301
Me. Rev. Stat. 1954, Ch. 186, § 1 et seq.
Mich. Comp. Laws Ann., 440.7101 et seq.
Minn. Stat. 1961, 228.01 et seq.
Mo. Rev. Stat. 1959, 407.010 et seq.
N.C. Gen. Stat. 1943, §§ 21-1 et seq., 25-7-101 et seq.
Nev. Rev. Stat. 1957, 94.010 et seq.
N.H. Rev. Stat. 1955, Superseded Vols., 334:1 et seq.
N.J. Stat. Ann., 48:20-1 to 48:20-54

N.M. Stat. Ann. 1953, 50-12-1 et seq.
N.Y. Personal Property Law (Consol. Laws Ch. 41) § 187 et seq.
Pa. Cons. Stat., Title 13, § 7301 et seq.
R.I. Gen. Laws 1956, Superseded Vol., 6-24-1 et seq.
Vt. Acts 1915, No. 149
Wis. Stat. Ann., 407.301 et seq.

**Uniform Boat Titling Act**
R.I. Gen. Laws 1956, 46-22.1-1 et seq.

**Uniform Boiler and Pressure Vessel Act**
N.C. Gen. Stat. 1943, § 95-69.8 et seq.

**Uniform Boll Weevil Eradication Act**
N.C. Gen. Stat. 1943, § 106-65.67 et seq.

**Uniform Bond Act**
Ohio Rev. Code 1953, 133.01 et seq.

**Uniform Brain Death Act**
Mont. Code Ann., 50-22-101

**Uniform Budget Act**
Ohio Rev. Code 1953, 5705.01 et seq.
Tex. Rev. Civ. Stat., Art. 689a-1 et seq.

**Uniform Budgeting and Accounting Act**
Mich. Comp. Laws Ann., 141.421 et seq.

**Uniform Building Lines Act**
D.C. Code 1973, § 5-201 et seq.

**Uniform Business Corporation Act**
Ky. Rev. Stat. 1971, 271B.1-010 et seq.
La. Rev. Stat. Ann., 12:1 et seq.
Wash. Rev. Code Ann., 23A.04.010 et seq.

**Uniform Business License Tax Act (Highway Carriers)**
Cal. Public Utilities Code § 4301 et seq.

**Uniform Business Records Act**
Ala. Code 1975, § 12-21-42 et seq.

**Uniform Business Records as Evidence Act**
Ariz. Rev. Stat. Ann., § 12-2262
Ariz. Rules of Civil Procedure 1955, Rule 44(q)
Cal. Code of Civil Procedure § 1953e et seq.
Conn. Gen. Stat. Ann., § 52-180 et seq.
Del. Code of 1974, Title 10, § 4309
Fla. Stat. 1983, 92.36
Ga. Code Ann., 24-3-14
Haw. Rev. Stat. Ann., § 622-5
Ida. Code 1947, 9-413 et seq.
Minn. Stat. Ann., 600.02 et seq.
Mo. Rev. Stat., 490.660 et seq.
Mont. Rev. Code 1947, 93-801-1 et seq.
N.D. Cent. Code, 31-08-01 et seq.
Neb. Rev. Stat. 1943, 25-12, 194 et seq.
Nev. Rev. Stat. 1967 Reprint, Replaced Pages, 51.030
N.H. Rev. Stat. 1955, 521:1 et seq.
N.J. Stat. Ann., 2A:82-34 et seq.
N.Y. Civil Practice Law and Rules (Consol. Laws Ch. 8) Rule 4518
Ohio Rev. Code 1953, 2317.40 et seq.
Ore. Rev. Stat., 41.680 et seq.
Pa. Cons. Stat., Title 42, § 6108
S.C. Code Ann. 1976, § 19-5-510 et seq.
S.D. Codified Laws 1967, 19-16-10
Tenn. Code Ann., 24-7-111
Tex. Rules of Criminal Evidence, Rule 902
Vt. Stat. Ann., Title 12, § 1700
Wash. Rev. Code Ann., 5.45.010 et seq.
Wyo. Stat. 1957, § 1-170 et seq.

**Uniform Certificate of Title and Antitheft Act**
Ala. Code 1975, § 32-8-1 et seq.

**Uniform Certification of Questions of Law Act**
Ala. Rules of Appellate Procedure, Rule 18
Ariz. Rev. Stat. Ann., § 12-1861 et seq.
Colo. Appellate Rules, Rule 21.1
Conn. Gen. Stat. 1983, § 51-199a et seq.
Conn. Public Acts 1999, No. 107
D.C. Code Ann., § 11-723
Fla. Rules of Appellate Procedure, Rule 9.150
Ga. Code Ann., 15-2-9
Ind. Code Ann., 33-2-4-1
Iowa Code Ann., 684A.1 et seq.
Kan. Stat. Ann., 60-3201 et seq.
Ky. Rules of Civil Procedure, Rule 76.37
La. Rev. Stat. Ann., 13:72.1
La. Supreme Court Rules, Rule 12
Mass. Rules of Supreme Judicial Court 1981, Rule 1:03

*Continued*

Md. Ann. Code 1974, Art. CJ, § 12-601 et seq.
Me. Rules of Civil Procedure, Rule 76B
Mich. Rules of Appellate Procedure, Rule 407
Minn. Stat. Ann., 480.061
Miss. Rules of Supreme Court 1988, Rule 20
N.D. Rules of Appellate Procedure 1973, Rule 47
N.H. Supreme Court Rules, Rule 34
N.M. Stat. Ann., 34-2-8
N.M. Stat. Ann., 39-7-1 to 39-7-13
Ohio Supreme Court Rules of Practice, Rule XVI
Okla. Stat. Ann., Title 20, § 1601 et seq.
Ore. Rev. Stat., 28.200 et seq.
P.R. Supreme Court Rules, Rule 27
R.I. Supreme Court Rules, Rule 6
S.D. Codified Laws 1967, 15-24A-1 et seq.
S.D. Laws 1985, Ch. 412
Wash. Rev. Code Ann., 2.60.010 et seq.
Wis. Stat. Ann., 821.01 et seq.
W. Va. Code 1966, § 51-1A-1 et seq.

**Uniform Charitable Trusts Administration Act**
Md. Ann. Code 1974, Art. ET, § 14-302

**Uniform Chemical Test for Intoxication Act**
Iowa Code 1985, 321B.1 et seq.
Okla. Stat. Ann., Title 47, § 751 et seq.

**Uniform Chemical Test Implied Consent Act**
N.D. Cent. Code, 39-20-01 et seq.

**Uniform Child Custody Jurisdiction Act**
Ala. Code 1975, § 30-3-20 et seq.
Alaska Stat. 1962, § 25.30.010 et seq.
Ariz. Rev. Stat. Ann., § 8-401 et seq.
Ark. Code Ann. 1987, 9-13-201 et seq.
Cal. Family Code § 3400 et seq.
Colo. Rev. Stat., 14-13-101 et seq.
Conn. Gen. Stat. 1983, § 46b-90 et seq.
D.C. Code Ann., § 16-4501 et seq.
Del. Code of 1974, Title 13, § 1901 et seq.
Fla. Stat. Ann., 61.1302 et seq.
Ga. Code Ann., 19-9-40 et seq.
Haw. Rev. Stat. Ann., § 583-1 et seq.
Ida. Code 1947, 32-1101 et seq.
Ill. Comp. Stat. 1992, Ch. 750, § 351/1 et seq.
Ind. Code Ann., 31-1-11.6-1 et seq.
Iowa Code Ann., 598A.1 et seq.
Kan. Stat. Ann., 38-1301 et seq.
Ky. Rev. Stat. 1971, 403.400 et seq.
La. Rev. Stat. Ann., 13:1700 et seq.
Mass. Gen. Laws Ann., 209B:1 et seq.
Md. Ann. Code 1974, Art. FL, § 9-201 et seq.
Me. Rev. Stat. Ann. 1964, Title 19-A, § 1701 et seq.
Mich. Comp. Laws Ann., 600.651 et seq.
Minn. Stat. Ann., 518A.01 et seq.
Miss. Code Ann. 1972, § 93-23-1 et seq.
Mo. Rev. Stat., 452.440 et seq.
Mont. Code Ann., 40-7-101 et seq.
N.C. Gen. Stat. 1943, § 50A-1 et seq.
N.D. Cent. Code, 14-14-01 et seq.
Neb. Rev. Stat. 1943, 43-1201 et seq.
Nev. Rev. Stat. 1979 Reprint, 125A.010 et seq.
N.H. Rev. Stat. 1955, 458-A:1 et seq.
N.J. Stat. Ann., 2A:34-28 et seq.
N.M. Stat. Ann., 40-10-1 et seq.
N.Y. Domestic Relations Law (Consol. Laws Ch. 14) § 75a et seq.
Ohio Rev. Code 1953, 3109.21 et seq.
Okla. Stat. Ann., Title 43, § 501 et seq.
Ore. Rev. Stat., 109.700 et seq.
Pa. Cons. Stat., Title 42, § 5341 et seq.
R.I. Gen. Laws 1956, 15-14-1 et seq.
S.C. Code Ann. 1976, § 20-7-782 et seq.
S.D. Codified Laws 1967, 26-5A-1 et seq.
Tenn. Code Ann., 36-6-201 et seq.
Tex. Family Code, § 11.51 et seq.
Utah Code Ann. 1953, 78-45C-1 et seq.
Va. Code 1950, § 20-125 et seq.
Vt. Stat. Ann., Title 15, § 1031 et seq.
Wash. Rev. Code Ann., 26.27.010 et seq.
Wis. Stat. Ann., 822.01 et seq.
W. Va. Code 1966, § 48-10-1 et seq.
Wyo. Stat. Ann., § 20-5-101 et seq.

**Uniform Child Custody Jurisdiction and Enforcement Act**
Alaska Stat. 1962, § 25.30.010 et seq.
Conn. Public Acts 1999, No. 185

**Uniform Child Custody Jurisdiction and Marital or Parent and Child Long-Arm Jurisdiction Amendments Act**

D.C. Code Ann., § 16-4501 et seq.

**Uniform Choice of Forum Act**

Neb. Rev. Stat. 1943, 25-413 et seq.

**Uniform City Court Act**

N.Y. Uniform City Court Act, § 101 et seq.

**Uniform City Manager and Commission Charter**

Tenn. Code Ann. 1955, 6-1801 et seq.

**Uniform City Utility Users Tax Act**

Mich. Comp. Laws Ann., 141.801 et seq., 141.1151 et seq.

**Uniform City Utility Users Tax Ordinance**

Mich. Comp. Laws Ann., 141.821 et seq., 141.1161 et seq.

**Uniform Civil Liability for Support Act**

Cal. Civil Code § 241 et seq.

Me. Rev. Stat. Ann. 1964, Title 19, § 441 et seq.

N.H. Rev. Stat. 1955, 546-A:1 et seq.

R.I. Gen. Laws 1956, 31-10.3-1 et seq.

Utah Code Ann. 1953, 78-45-1 et seq.

**Uniform Classification and Compensation Act**

Ark. Code Ann. 1987, 21-5-201 et seq.

**Uniform Classified Commercial Driver's License Act**

Fla. Stat. Ann., 322.01 et seq.

Tenn. Code Ann., 55-7-101 et seq.

**Uniform Clerks of Superior Court Retirement Act**

N.C. Gen. Stat. 1943, §§ 135-84, 135-85

**Uniform Close Pursuit Act**

N.Y. Criminal Procedure Law (Consol. Laws Ch. 11A) § 140.55

**Uniform Code for the Anchoring of Mobile Homes**

Ala. Code 1975, § 24-5-30 et seq.

**Uniform Code of Construction and Installation Standards for Mobile Homes of the State of New York**

N.Y. Executive Law 1951 (Consol. Laws Ch. 18) § 400aa et seq.

**Uniform Code of Military Justice**

May 5, 1950, Ch. 169, 64 Stat. 108 (See 10 U.S. Code §§ 801 to 940)

March 2, 1955, Ch. 9, 69 Stat. 10 (See 10 U.S. Code § 867)

Aug. 1, 1956, Ch. 852, 70 Stat. 911, 50 U.S. Code § 552

Aug. 10, 1956, Ch. 1041, 70A Stat. 36, 10 U.S. Code §§ 801 to 940

Oct. 4, 1961, P.L. 87-385, 75 Stat. 814, 10 U.S. Code § 923a

Oct. 24, 1968, P.L. 90-632, 82 Stat. 1335, 10 U.S. Code §§ 801, 806, 816, 818 to 820 825, 826 to 829, 835 to 842, 845, 849, 851, 852, 854, 857, 865 to 871, 873, 936

Nov. 14, 1986, P.L. 99-661, 100 Stat. 3905

Ark. Code Ann. 1987, § 12-64-101 et seq.

Conn. Gen. Stat. 1983, § 27-141 et seq.

Ida. Code 1947, 46-1101 et seq.

Iowa Code Ann., 29B.1 et seq.

Kan. Stat. Ann., 48-2101 et seq.

La. Rev. Stat. Ann., 29:101 et seq.

Mich. Comp. Laws. 1979, 32.1001 et seq.

Minn. Stat. Ann., 192A.01 et seq.

Miss. Code Ann. 1972, § 33-13-1 et seq.

Mo. Rev. Stat., 40.005 et seq.

Neb. Rev. Stat. 1943, 55-401 et seq.

Nev. Rev. Stat. 1979 Reprint, 412.196 et seq.

N.H. Rev. Stat. 1955, 110-B:39 et seq.

N.M. Stat. Ann., 20-12-1 et seq.

Ohio Rev. Code 1953, 5924.01 et seq.

Okla. Stat. Ann., Title 44, § 2101 et seq.

Pa. Cons. Stat., Title 51, § 5100 et seq.

P.R. Laws Ann. 1954, Title 25, § 2301 et seq.

R.I. Gen. Laws 1956, 30-13-1 et seq.

Tex. Government Code, § 432.001 et seq.

Wash. Rev. Code Ann., 38.38.004 et seq.

Wis. Stat. Ann., 21.37

W. Va. Code 1966, § 15-1E-1 et seq.

**Uniform Code of Municipal Government**

Minn. Stat. Ann., 412.015 et seq.

**Uniform Cold Storage Act**
Ill. Rev. Stat. 1991, Ch. 56 1/2, § 79.1 et seq.
Md. Ann. Code 1974, Art. HG, § 21-501 et seq.

**Uniform College and University Employees Insurance Benefits Act**
Tex. Insurance Code, Art. 3.50-3

**Uniform Commercial Code**
Ala. Code 1975, § 7-1-101 et seq.
Alaska Stat. 1962, § 45.01.101 et seq.
Ariz. Rev. Stat. Ann., § 47-1101 et seq.
Ark. Code Ann. 1987, 4-4-101 et seq.
Cal. Commercial Code § 1101 et seq.
Colo. Rev. Stat., 4-1-101 et seq.
Conn. Gen. Stat. 1983, § 42a-1-101 et seq.
D.C. Code 1973, § 28:1-101 et seq.
Del. Code of 1974, Title 6, § 1-101 et seq.
Fla. Stat. Ann., 671.101 et seq.
Ga. Code Ann., 11-1-101 et seq.
Haw. Rev. Stat. Ann., § 490:1-101 et seq.
Ida. Code 1947, 28-1-101 et seq.
Ill. Rev. Stat. 1991, Ch. 26
Ind. Code Ann., 26-1-1-101 et seq.
Iowa Code Ann., 554.1101 et seq.
Kan. Stat. Ann., 84-1-101 et seq.
Ky. Rev. Stat. 1971, 355.1-101 et seq.
La. Rev. Stat. Ann., 10:1-101 et seq.
Mass. Gen. Laws Ann., 106:1-101 et seq.
Md. Ann. Code 1974, Art. CL, § 1-101 et seq.
Me. Rev. Stat. Ann. 1964, Title 11, § 1-101 et seq.
Mich. Comp. Laws Ann., 440.1101 et seq.
Minn. Stat. Ann., 336.1-101 et seq.
Miss. Code Ann. 1972, § 75-1-101 et seq.
Mo. Rev. Stat., 400.1-101 et seq.
Mont. Code Ann., 30-1-101 et seq.
N.C. Gen. Stat. 1943, § 25-1-101 et seq.
N.D. Cent. Code, 41-01-02 et seq.
Neb. Rev. Stat. 1943, § 1-101 et seq.
Nev. Rev. Stat. Ann., 104.1101 et seq.
N.H. Rev. Stat. 1955, 382-A:1-101 et seq.
N.J. Stat. Ann., 12A:1-101 et seq.
N.M. Stat. Ann., 55-1-101 et seq.
N.Y. Uniform Commercial Code (Consol. Laws Ch. 38) § 1-101 et seq.
Ohio Rev. Code 1953, 1301.01 et seq.
Okla. Stat. Ann., Title 12A, § 1-101 et seq.
Ore. Rev. Stat., 71.1010 et seq.
Pa. Cons. Stat., Title 13, § 1101 et seq.
R.I. Gen. Laws 1956, 6A-1-101 et seq.
S.C. Code Ann. 1976, § 36-1-101 et seq.
S.D. Codified Laws 1967, 57A-1-101 et seq.
Tenn. Code Ann. 1955, 47-1-101 et seq.
Tex. Business and Commerce Code, § 1.101 et seq.
Utah Code Ann. 1953, 70A-1-101 et seq.
Va. Code 1950, § 8.1-101 et seq.
Vt. Stat. Ann., Title 9A, § 1-101 et seq.
Wash. Rev. Code Ann., 62A.1-101 et seq.
Wis. Stat. Ann., 401.101 et seq.
W. Va. Code 1966, § 46-1-101 et seq.
Wyo. Stat. Ann., § 34.1-1-101 et seq.

**Uniform Commercial Code-Funds Transfers**
Ala. Code 1975, §§ 7-1-105, 7-4A-101 et seq.
Alaska Stat. 1962, § 45.14.101 et seq.
Del. Code of 1974, Title 6, § 4A-101 et seq.
Ga. Code Ann., 11-4A-101 et seq.
Ida. Code 1947, 28-4-601 et seq.
Iowa Code Ann., 554.12101 et seq.
Ky. Rev. Stat. 1971, 355.4A-101 et seq.
Mich. Comp. Laws. Ann., 440.4601 et seq.
Miss. Code Ann. 1972, § 75-4A-101 et seq.
N.C. Gen. Stat. 1943, § 25-4A-101 et seq.
N.D. Cent. Code, 41-04.1-01 et seq.
N.H. Rev. Stat. 1955, 382-A:4A-101 et seq.
N.J. Stat. Ann., 12A:4A-101 et seq.
N.M. Stat. Ann., 55-4A-101 et seq.
Pa. Cons. Stat., Title 13, § 4A101 et seq.
R.I. Gen. Laws 1956, 6A-4.1-101 et seq.
Tex. Business and Commerce Code, § 4A.101 et seq.
Wis. Laws 1991, Act 304
W. Va. Code 1966,§ 46-4A-101 et seq.

**Uniform Commercial Code Liability Act (Secretary of State)**
Ill. Rev. Stat. 1991, Ch. 124, §§ 13.9, 14

**Uniform Commercial Code Modernization Act**
Pa. 1992 Pamph. Laws, No. 97

**Uniform Commercial Code—Bank Deposits and Collections**
Ala. Code 1975, § 7-4-101 et seq.
Alaska Stat. 1962, § 45.04.101 et seq.
Ariz. Rev. Stat. Ann., § 47-4101 et seq.
Ark. Code Ann. 1987, 4-4-101 et seq.
Cal. Commercial Code § 4101 et seq.
Colo. Rev. Stat., 4-4-101 et seq.
Colo. Rev. Stat., 4-4-101 et seq.
Conn. Gen. Stat. 1983, § 42a-4-101 et seq.
D.C. Code 1973, § 28:4-101 et seq.
Del. Code of 1974, Title 6, § 4-101 et seq.
Del. Code of 1974, Title 6. § 4-101 et seq.
Fla. Stat. Ann., 674.101 et seq.
Ga. Code Ann., 11-4-101 et seq.
Ga. Code Ann., 11-4-101 et seq.
Haw. Rev. Stat. Ann., § 490:4-101 et seq.
Ida. Code 1947, 28-4-101 et seq.
Ill. Rev. Stat. 1991, Ch. 26, § 4-101 et seq.
Ind. Code Ann., 26-1-4-101 et seq.
Iowa Code 1983, 554.4101 et seq.
Kan. Stat. Ann., 84-4-101 et seq.
Ky. Rev. Stat. 1971, 355.4-101 et seq.
La. Rev. Stat. Ann., 10:4-101 et seq.
Mass. Gen. Laws Ann., 106:4-101 et seq.
Mass. Gen. Laws Ann., 106.4-101 et seq.
Md. Ann. Code 1974, Art. CL, § 4-101 et seq.
Me. Rev. Stat. Ann. 1964, Title 11, § 4-101 et seq.
Mich. Comp. Laws Ann., 440.4101 et seq.
Minn. Stat. Ann., 336.4-101 et seq.
Miss. Code Ann. 1972, § 75-4-101 et seq.
Mo. Rev. Stat., 400.4-101 et seq.
Mont. Code Ann., 30-4-101 et seq.
N.C. Gen. Stat. 1943, § 25-4-101 et seq.
N.D. Cent. Code, 41-04-01 et seq.
Neb. Rev. Stat. 1943, § 4-101 et seq.
Nev. Rev. Stat. 1979 Reprint, 104.4101 et seq.
N.H. Rev. Stat. 1955, 382-A:4-101 et seq.
N.J. Stat. Ann., 12A:4-101 et seq.
N.M. Stat. Ann., 55-4-101 et seq.
N.Y. Uniform Commercial Code (Consol. Laws Ch. 38) § 4-101 et seq.
Ohio Rev. Code 1953, 1304.01 et seq.
Okla. Stat. Ann., Title 12A, § 4-101 et seq.
Ore. Rev. Stat., 74.1010 et seq.
Pa. Cons. Stat., Title 13, § 4101 et seq.
R.I. Gen. Laws 1956, 6A-4-101 et seq.
S.C. Code Ann. 1976, § 36-4-101 et seq.
S.D. Codified Laws 1967, 57A-4-101 et seq.
Tenn. Code Ann. 1955, 47-4-101 et seq.
Tex. Business and Commerce Code, § 4.101 et seq.
Utah Code Ann. 1953, 70A-4-101 et seq.
Utah Code Ann. 1953, 70A-4-101 et seq.
Va. Code 1950, § 8.4-101 et seq.
Vt. Stat. Ann., Title 9A, § 4-101 et seq.
Wash. Rev. Code Ann., 62A.4-101 et seq.
Wis. Stat. Ann., 404.101 et seq.
W. Va. Code 1966, § 46-6-101 et seq.
Wyo. Stat. Ann., § 34.1-4-101 et seq.

**Uniform Commercial Code—Bulk Sales**
Fla. Stat. Ann., 670.101 et seq.
Haw. Rev. Stat. Ann., § 490:4A-101 et seq.
Ill. Rev. Stat. 1991, Ch. 26, § 4A-101 et seq.
Ind. Code Ann., 26-1-4.1-101 et seq.
Mass. Gen. Laws Ann., 106:4A-101 et seq.
Minn. Stat. Ann., 336.4A-101 et seq.
Neb. Rev. Stat. 1943, § 4A-101 et seq.
N.Y. Uniform Commercial Code (Consol. Laws Ch. 38) § 4-A-101 et seq.
Okla. Stat. Ann., Title 12A, § 4A-101 et seq.
Ore. Laws 1991, Ch. 442
S.D. Codified Laws 1967, 57A-4A-101 et seq.
Utah Code Ann. 1953, 70A-4a-101 et seq.
Va. Code 1950, § 8.4A-101 et seq.
Wash. Rev. Code Ann., 62A.4A-101 et seq.

**Uniform Commercial Code—Bulk Transfers**
Ala. Code 1975, § 7-6-101 et seq.
Alaska Stat. 1962, § 45.06.101 et seq.
Ariz. Rev. Stat. Ann., § 45.06.101 et seq.
Ark. Code Ann. 1987, 4-6-101 et seq.
Cal. Commercial Code § 6101 et seq.
Colo. Rev. Stat., 4-6-101 et seq.
Conn. Gen. Stat. 1983, § 42a-6-101 et seq.
D.C. Code 1973, § 28:6-101 et seq.
Del. Code of 1974, Title 6, § 6-101 et seq.
Fla. Stat. Ann., 676.101 et seq.

*Continued*

Ga. Code Ann., 11-6-101 et seq.
Haw. Rev. Stat. Ann., § 490:6-101 et seq.
Ida. Code 1947, 28-6-101 et seq.
Ill. Rev. Stat. 1991, Ch. 26, § 6-101 et seq.
Ind. Code Ann., 26-1-6-101 et seq.
Iowa Code Ann., 554.6101 et seq.
Kan. Stat. Ann., 84-6-101 et seq.
Ky. Rev. Stat. 1971, 355.6-101 et seq.
Mass. Gen. Laws Ann., 106:6-101 et seq.
Md. Ann. Code 1974, Art. CL, § 6-101 et seq.
Me. Rev. Stat. Ann. 1964, Title 11, § 6-101 et seq.
Mich. Comp. Laws Ann., 440.6101 et seq.
Minn. Stat. Ann., 336.6-101 et seq.
Miss. Code Ann. 1972, § 75-6-101 et seq.
Mo. Rev. Stat., 400.6-101 et seq.
Mont. Code Ann. 1989, 30-6-101 et seq.
N.C. Gen. Stat. 1943, § 25-6-101 et seq.
N.D. Cent. Code, 41-06-01 et seq.
Neb. Rev. Stat. 1943, § 6-101 et seq.
Nev. Rev. Stat. 1979 Reprint, 104.6101 et seq.
N.H. Rev. Stat. 1955, 382-A:6-101 et seq.
N.J. Stat. Ann., 12A:6-101 et seq.
N.M. Stat. Ann., 55-6-101 et seq.
N.Y. Uniform Commercial Code (Consol. Laws Ch. 38) § 6-101 et seq.
Ohio Rev. Code 1953, 1306.01 et seq.
Okla. Stat. Ann., Title 12A, § 6-101 et seq.
Ore. Rev. Stat., 76.1010 et seq.
Pa. Cons. Stat., Title 13, § 6101 et seq.
R.I. Gen. Laws 1956, 6A-6-101 et seq.
S.C. Code Ann. 1976, § 36-6-101 et seq.
S.D. Codified Laws 1967, 57A-6-101 et seq.
Tenn. Code Ann. 1955, 47-6-101 et seq.
Tex. Business and Commerce Code, § 6.101 et seq.
Utah Code Ann. 1953, 70A-6-101 et seq.
Va. Code 1950, § 8.6-101 et seq.
Vt. Stat. Ann., Title 9A, § 6-101 et seq.
Wash. Rev. Code Ann., 62A.6-101 et seq.
Wis. Stat. Ann., 406.101 et seq.
W. Va. Code 1966, § 46-6-101 et seq.
Wyo. Stat. Ann., § 34.1-6-101 et seq.

**Uniform Commercial Code—Commercial Paper**

See also Uniform Negotiable Intruments Law
Ala. Code 1975, § 7-3-101 et seq.
Alaska Stat. 1962, § 45.03.101 et seq.
Ariz. Rev. Stat. Ann., § 47-3101 et seq.
Ark. Code Ann. 1987, 4-3-101 et seq.
Cal. Commercial Code § 3101 et seq.
Colo. Rev. Stat., 4-3-101 et seq.
Conn. Gen. Stat. 1983, § 42a-3-101 et seq.
D.C. Code 1973, § 28:3-101 et seq.
Del. Code of 1974, Title 6, § 3-101 et seq.
Fla. Stat. Ann., 673.101 et seq.
Ga. Code Ann., 11-3-101 et seq.
Ga. Code Ann., 11-3-101 et seq.
Haw. Rev. Stat. Ann., § 490:3-101 et seq.
Ida. Code 1947, 28-3-101 et seq.
Ill. Rev. Stat. 1991, Ch. 26, § 3-101 et seq.
Ind. Code Ann., 26-1-3-101 et seq.
Iowa Code Ann., 554.3101 et seq.
Kan. Stat. Ann., 84-3-101 et seq.
Ky. Rev. Stat. 1971, 355.3-101 et seq.
La. Rev. Stat. Ann., 10:3-101 et seq.
Mass. Gen. Laws Ann., 106:3-101 et seq.
Md. Ann. Code 1974, Art. CL, § 3-101 et seq.
Me. Rev. Stat. Ann. 1964, Title 11, § 3-101 et seq.
Mich. Comp. Laws Ann., 440.3101 et seq.
Minn. Stat. Ann., 336.3-101 et seq.
Miss. Code Ann. 1972, § 75-3-101 et seq.
Mo. Rev. Stat., 400.3-101 et seq.
Mont. Code Ann., 30-3-101 et seq.
N.C. Gen. Stat. 1943, § 25-3-101 et seq.
N.D. Cent. Code, 41-03-01 et seq.
Neb. Rev. Stat. 1943, § 3-101 et seq.
Nev. Rev. Stat. 1979, Reprint, 104.3101 et seq.
N.H. Rev. Stat. 1955, 382-A:3-101 et seq.
N.J. Stat. Ann., 12A:3-101 et seq.
N.M. Stat. Ann., 55-3-101 et seq.
N.Y. Uniform Commercial Code (Consol. Laws Ch. 38) § 3-101 et seq.
Ohio Rev. Code 1953, 1303.01 et seq.
Okla. Stat. Ann., Title 12A, § 3-101 et seq.
Ore. Rev. Stat., 73.1010 et seq.
Pa. Cons. Stat., Title 13, § 3101 et seq.

R.I. Gen. Laws 1956, 6A-3-101 et seq.
S.C. Code Ann. 1976, § 36-3-101 et seq.
S.D. Codified Laws 1967, 57A-3-101 et seq.
Tenn. Code Ann. 1955, 47-3-101 et seq.
Tex. Business and Commerce Code, § 3.101 et seq.
Utah Code Ann. 1953, 70A-3-101 et seq.
Va. Code 1950, § 8.3-101 et seq.
Vt. Stat. Ann., Title 9A, § 3-101 et seq.
Wash. Rev. Code Ann., 62A.3-101 et seq.
Wis. Stat. Ann., 403.101 et seq.
W. Va. Code 1966, § 46-3-101 et seq.
Wyo. Stat. Ann., § 34.1-3-101 et seq.

**Uniform Commercial Code—Documents of Title**

See also Uniform Bills of Lading Act and Uniform Warehouse Reciepts Act
Ala. Code 1975, § 7-7-101 et seq.
Alaska Stat. 1962, § 45.07.101 et seq.
Ariz. Rev. Stat. Ann., § 47-7101 et seq.
Ark. Code Ann. 1987, 4-7-101 et seq.
Cal. Commercial Code § 7101 et seq.
Colo. Rev. Stat., 4-7-101 et seq.
Conn. Gen. Stat. 1983, § 42a-7-101 et seq.
D.C. Code 1973, § 28:7-101 et seq.
Del. Code of 1974, Title 6, § 7-101 et seq.
Fla. Stat. Ann., 677.101 et seq.
Ga. Code Ann., 11-7-101 et seq.
Haw. Rev. Stat. Ann., § 490:7-101 et seq.
Ida. Code 1947, 28-7-101 et seq.
Ill. Rev. Stat. 1991, Ch. 26, § 7-101 et seq.
Ind. Code Ann., 26-1-7-101 et seq.
Iowa Code Ann., 554.7101 et seq.
Kan. Stat. Ann., 84-7-101 et seq.
Ky. Rev. Stat. 1971, 355.7-101 et seq.
La. Rev. Stat. Ann., 10:7-101 et seq.
Mass. Gen. Laws Ann., 106:7-101 et seq.
Md. Ann. Code 1974, Art. CL, § 7-101 et seq.
Me. Rev. Stat. Ann. 1964, Title 11, § 7-101 et seq.
Mich. Comp. Laws Ann., 440.7101 et seq.
Minn. Stat. Ann., 336.7-101 et seq.
Miss. Code Ann. 1972, § 75-7-101 et seq.
Mo. Rev. Stat., 400.7-101 et seq.
Mont. Code Ann., 30-7-101 et seq.
N.C. Gen. Stat. 1943, § 25-1-101 et seq.
N.D. Cent. Code, 41-07-01 et seq.
Neb. Rev. Stat. 1943, § 7-101 et seq.
Nev. Rev. Stat. 1979 Reprint, 104.7101 et seq.
N.H. Rev. Stat. 1955, 382-A:7-101 et seq.
N.J. Stat. Ann., 12A:7-101 et seq.
N.M. Stat. Ann., 55-7-101 et seq.
N.Y. Uniform Commercial Code (Consol. Laws Ch. 38) § 7-101 et seq.
Ohio Rev. Code 1953, 1307.01 et seq.
Okla. Stat. 1981, Title 12A, § 7-101 et seq.
Ore. Rev. Stat., 77.1010 et seq.
Pa. Cons. Stat., Title 13, § 7101 et seq.
R.I. Gen. Laws 1956, 6A-7-101 et seq.
S.C. Code Ann. 1976, § 36-7-101 et seq.
S.D. Codified Laws 1967, 57A-7-101 et seq.
Tenn. Code Ann., 47-7-101 et seq.
Tex. Business and Commerce Code, § 7.101 et seq.
Utah Code Ann. 1953, 70A-7-101 et seq.
Va. Code 1950, § 8.7-101 et seq.
Vt. Stat. Ann., Title 9A, § 7-101 et seq.
Wash. Rev. Code Ann., 62A.7-101 et seq.
Wis. Stat. Ann., 407.101 et seq.
W. Va. Code 1966, § 46-7-101 et seq.
Wyo. Stat. Ann., § 34.1-7-101 et seq.

**Uniform Commercial Code—Funds Transfers**

Ariz. Rev. Stat. Ann., § 47-4A101 et seq.
Cal. Commercial Code § 11101 et seq.
Colo. Rev. Stat., 4-4.5-101 et seq.
Conn. Gen. Stat. Ann., 4-4.5-101 et seq.
Fla. Stat. Ann., 670.101 et seq.
Haw. Rev. Stat. Ann., § 490:4A-101 et seq.
Ill. Rev. Stat. 1991, Ch. 26, § 4A-101 et seq.
Ind. Code Ann., 26-1-4.1-101 et seq.
Kan. Stat. Ann., 84-4a-101 et seq.
La. Rev. Stat. Ann., 10:4A-101 et seq.
Mass. Gen. Laws Ann., 106:4A-101 et seq.
Minn. Stat. Ann., 336.4A-101 et seq.
Neb. Rev. Stat. 1943, § 4A-101 et seq.
N.Y. Uniform Commercial Code (Consol. Laws Ch. 38) § 4-A-101 et seq.
Okla. Stat. Ann., Title 12A, § 4A-101 et seq.
Ore. Laws 1991, Ch. 442
S.D. Codified Laws 1967, 57A-4A-101 et seq.
Utah Code Ann. 1953, 70A-4a-101 et seq.

*Continued*

Va. Code 1950, § 8.4A-101 et seq.
Wash. Rev. Code Ann., 62A.4A-101 et seq.

**Uniform Commercial Code—Investment Securities**

See also Uniform Commercial Code—Revised Article 8
See also Uniform Stock Transfer Act
Ala. Code 1975, § 7-8-101 et seq.
Alaska Stat. 1962, § 45.08.101 et seq.
Ariz. Rev. Stat. Ann., § 47-8101 et seq.
Ark. Code Ann. 1987, 4-8-101 et seq.
Cal. Commercial Code § 8101 et seq.
Colo. Rev. Stat., 4-8-101 et seq.
Conn. Gen. Stat. 1983, § 42a-8-101 et seq.
D.C. Code 1973, § 28:8-101 et seq.
Del. Code of 1974, Title 6, § 8-101 et seq.
Fla. Stat. Ann., 678.101 et seq.
Fla. Stat. Ann., 678.1011 et seq.
Ga. Code Ann., 11-8-101 et seq.
Haw. Rev. Stat. Ann., § 490:8-101 et seq.
Ida. Code 1947, 28-8-101 et seq.
Ill. Rev. Stat. 1991, Ch. 26, § 8-101 et seq.
Ind. Code Ann., 26-1-8-101 et seq.
Iowa Code Ann., 554.8101 et seq.
Kan. Stat. Ann., 84-8-101 et seq.
Ky. Rev. Stat. 1971, 355.8-101 et seq.
La. Rev. Stat. Ann., 10:8-101 et seq.
Mass. Gen. Laws Ann., 106:8-101 et seq.
Md. Ann. Code 1974, Art. CL, § 8-101 et seq.
Me. Rev. Stat. Ann. 1964, Title 8, § 1101 et seq.
Me. Rev. Stat. Ann. 1964, Title 11, § 8-100 et seq.
Mich. Comp. Laws Ann., 440.8101 et seq.
Minn. Stat. Ann., 336.8-101 et seq.
Miss. Code Ann. 1972, § 75-8-101 et seq.
Mo. Rev. Stat., 400.8-101 et seq.
Mont. Code Ann., 30-8-101 et seq.
N.C. Gen. Stat. 1943, § 25-8-101 et seq.
N.D. Cent. Code, 41-08-01 et seq.
Neb. Rev. Stat. 1943, § 8-101 et seq.
Nev. Rev. Stat. Ann., 104.8101 et seq.
N.H. Rev. Stat. 1955, 382-A:8-101 et seq.
N.J. Stat. Ann., 12A:8-101 et seq.
N.M. Stat. Ann., 55-8-101 et seq.
N.M. Stat. Ann., 55-8-101 et seq.
N.Y. Uniform Commercial Code (Consol. Laws Ch. 38) § 8-101 et seq.
Ohio Rev. Code 1953, 1308.01 et seq.
Okla. Stat. Ann., Title 12A, § 8-101 et seq.
Ore. Rev. Stat., 78.1010 et seq.
Pa. Cons. Stat., Title 13, § 8101 et seq.
R.I. Gen. Laws 1956, 6A-8-101 et seq.
S.C. Code Ann. 1976, § 36-8-101 et seq.
S.D. Codified Laws 1967, 57A-8-101 et seq.
S.D. Codified Laws 1967, 57A-8-101 et seq.
Tenn. Code Ann., 47-8-101 et seq.
Tex. Business and Commerce Code, § 8.101 et seq.
Utah Code Ann. 1953, 70A-8-101 et seq.
Va. Code 1950, § 8.8A-101 et seq.
Va. Code 1950, § 8.8-101 et seq.
Vt. Stat. Ann., Title 9A, § 8-101 et seq.
Wash. Rev. Code Ann., 62A.8-101 et seq.
Wis. Stat. Ann. 408.101 et seq.
Wis. Stat. Ann., 408.101 et seq.
W. Va. Code 1966, § 46-8-101 et seq.
Wyo. Stat. Ann., § 34.1-8-101 et seq.

**Uniform Commercial Code—Leases**

Ala. Code 1975, § 7-2A-101 et seq.
Alaska Stat. 1962, § 45.12.101 et seq.
Ariz. Rev. Stat. Ann., § 47-2A101 et seq.
Cal. Commercial Code § 10101 et seq.
Colo. Rev. Stat., 4-2.5-101 et seq.
Conn. Gen. Stat. 1983, § 2A-101 et seq.
Del. Code of 1974, Title 6, § 2A-101 et seq.
Fla. Stat. Ann., 680.1011 et seq.
Ga. Code Ann., 11-2A-101 et seq.
Haw. Rev. Stat. Ann., § 490:2A-101 et seq.
Ida. Code 1947, 28-12-101 et seq.
Ind. Code Ann., 26-1-2.1-101 et seq.
Iowa Code Ann., 554.13101 et seq.
Kan. Stat. Ann., 84-2a-101 et seq.
Ky. Rev. Stat. 1971, 355.2A-101 et seq.
Mass. Gen. Laws Ann., 106:2A-101 et seq.
Me. Rev. Stat. Ann. 1964, Title 11, § 2-1101 et seq.
Mich. Comp. Laws. Ann., 440.2801 et seq.
Minn. Stat. Ann., 336.2A-101 et seq.
Miss. Code Ann. 1972, § 75-2A-101 et seq.
Mont. Code Ann., 30-2A-101 et seq.
N.C. Gen. Stat. 1943, § 25-2A-101 et seq.
N.D. Cent. Code, 41-02.1-01 et seq.

Neb. Rev. Stat. 1943, § 2A-101 et seq.
N.H. Rev. Stat. 1955, 382-A:2A-101 et seq.
N.J. Stat. Ann., 12A:2A-101 et seq.
N.M. Stat. Ann., 55-2A-101 et seq.
N.Y. Uniform Commercial Code (Consol. Laws Ch. 38) § 2A-101 et seq.
Okla. Stat. Ann., Title 12A, § 2A-101 et seq.
Ore. Laws 1991, Ch. 676
Pa. Cons. Stat., Title 13, § 2A101 et seq.
Tenn. Code Ann., 47-2A-101 et seq.
Tex. Business and Commerce Code, § 2A.101 et seq.
Utah Code Ann. 1953, 70A-2a-101 et seq.
Va. Code 1950, § 8.2A-101 et seq.
Vt. Stat. Ann., Title 9A, § 2A-101 et seq.
Wash. Rev. Code Ann., 62A.2A-101 et seq.
Wyo. Stat. Ann., § 34.1-2A-101 et seq.

**Uniform Commercial Code—Letters of Credit**

See also Uniform Commercial Code—Revised Article 5
Ala. Code 1975, § 7-5-101 et seq.
Alaska Stat. 1962, § 45.05.101 et seq.
Ariz. Rev. Stat. Ann., § 47-5101 et seq.
Ark. Code Ann. 1987, 4-5-101 et seq.
Ark. Code Ann. 1987, 4-5-101 et seq.
Cal. Commercial Code § 5101 et seq.
Colo. Rev. Stat., 4-5-101 et seq.
Conn. Gen. Stat. 1983, § 42a-5-101 et seq.
D.C. Code 1973, § 28:5-101 et seq.
Del. Code of 1974, Title 6, § 5-101 et seq.
Fla. Stat. Ann., 675.101 et seq.
Ga. Code Ann., 11-5-101 et seq.
Haw. Rev. Stat. Ann., § 490:5-101 et seq.
Haw. Rev. Stat. Ann., § 490:5-101 et seq.
Ida. Code 1947, 28-5-101 et seq.
Ill. Rev. Stat. 1991, Ch. 26, § 5-101 et seq.
Ind. Code Ann., 26-1-5-101 et seq.
Iowa Code Ann., 554.5101 et seq.
Kan. Stat. Ann., 84-5-101 et seq.
Ky. Rev. Stat. 1971, 355.5-101 et seq.
La. Rev. Stat. Ann., 10:5-101 et seq.
Mass. Gen. Laws Ann., 106:5-101 et seq.
Mass. Gen. Laws Ann., 106:5-101 et seq.
Md. Ann. Code 1974, Art. CL, § 5-101 et seq.
Me. Rev. Stat. Ann. 1964, Title 11, § 5-1101 et seq.
Mich. Comp. Laws Ann., 440.5101 et seq.
Minn. Stat. Ann., 336.5-101 et seq.
Minn. Stat. Ann., 336.5-101 et seq.
Miss. Code Ann. 1972, § 75-5-101 et seq.
Mo. Rev. Stat., 400.5-101 et seq.
Mont. Code Ann., 30-5-101 et seq.
N.C. Gen. Stat. 1943, § 25-5-101 et seq.
N.D. Cent. Code, 41-05-01 et seq.
Neb. Rev. Stat. 1943, § 5-101 et seq.
Nev. Rev. Stat. Ann., 104.5101 et seq.
Nev. Rev. Stat. 1979 Reprint, 104.5101 et seq.
N.H. Rev. Stat. 1955, 382-A:5-101 et seq.
N.J. Stat. Ann., 12A:5-101 et seq.
N.M. Stat. Ann., 55-5-101 et seq.
N.M. Stat. Ann., 55-5-101 et seq.
N.Y. Uniform Commercial Code (Consol. Laws Ch. 38) § 5-101 et seq.
Ohio Rev. Code 1953, 1305.01 et seq.
Okla. Stat. Ann., Title 12A, § 5-101 et seq.
Ore. Rev. Stat., 75.1010 et seq.
Pa. Cons. Stat., Title 13, § 5101 et seq.
Pa. Cons. Stat., Title 13, § 5101 et seq.
R.I. Gen. Laws 1956, 6A-5-101 et seq.
S.C. Code Ann. 1976, § 36-5-101 et seq.
S.D. Codified Laws 1967, 57A-5-101 et seq.
S.D. Codified Laws 1967, 57A-5-101 et seq.
Tenn. Code Ann., 47-5-101 et seq.
Tex. Business and Commerce Code, § 5.101 et seq.
Utah Code Ann. 1953, 70A-5-101 et seq.
Va. Code 1950, § 8.5-101 et seq.
Vt. Stat. Ann., Title 9A, § 5-101 et seq.
Wash. Rev. Code Ann., 62A.5-101 et seq.
Wis. Stat. Ann., 405.101 et seq.
W. Va. Code 1966, § 46-5-101 et seq.
Wyo. Stat. Ann., § 34.1-5-101 et seq.

**Uniform Commercial Code—Negotiable Instruments**

Ala. Code 1975, § 7-3-101 et seq.
Ariz. Rev. Stat. Ann., § 47-31-1 et seq.
Ark. Code 1987, 4-3-101 et seq.
Cal. Commercial Code § 3101 et seq.
Colo. Rev. Stat., 4-3-101 et seq.
Conn. Gen. Stat. Ann., § 42a-3-101 et seq.
Del. Code of 1974, Title 6, § 3-101 et seq.
Fla. Stat. Ann., 673.1011 et seq.

*Continued*

Ga. Code Ann., 11-3-101 et seq.
Haw. Rev. Stat. Ann., § 490:3-101 et seq.
Ida. Code 1947, 28-3-101 et seq.
Iowa Code Ann., 554.3101 et seq.
La. Rev. Stat. Ann. 10:3-101 et seq.
Mass. Gen. Laws Ann., 106.3-101 et seq.
Mass. Gen. Laws 1984, 106:3-201 et seq.
Me. Rev. Stat. Ann. 1964, Title 11, § 3-1101 et seq.
Minn. Stat. Ann., 336.3-101 et seq.
Miss. Code Ann. 1972, § 75-3-101 et seq.
Mont. Code Ann., 30-3-101 et seq.
N.C. Gen. Stat. 1943, § 25-3-101 et seq.
N.D. Cent. Code, 41-03-01 et seq.
Neb. Rev. Stat. 1943, § 3-101 et seq.
N.H. Rev. Stat. 1955, 382-A:3-101 et seq.
N.M. Stat. Ann., 55-3-101 et seq.
Okla. Stat. Ann., Title 12A, § 3-101 et seq.
Ore. Rev. Stat., 73.0101 et seq.
Pa. Cons. Stat., Title 13, § 3101 et seq.
R.I. Gen. Laws 1956, 6A-2.1-101 et seq.
Tenn. Code Ann., 47-3-101 et seq.
Utah Code Ann. 1953, 70A-3-101 et seq.
Va. Code 1950, § 8.3:1-101 et seq.
Vt. Stat. Ann., Title 9A, § 3-301 et seq.
Wash. Rev. Code Ann., 62A.3-101 et seq.
W. Va. Code 1966,§ 46-3A-101 et seq.
Wyo. Stat. Ann., § 34.1-3-101 et seq.

**Uniform Commercial Code—Revised Article 5**
Ark. Acts 1997, No. 1070
Miss. Code Ann. 1972, § 75-5-101 et seq.
Pa. Cons. Stat., Title 13, § 5101 et seq.

**Uniform Commercial Code—Revised Article 8**
Miss. Code Ann. 1972, § 75-8-101 et seq.
Pa. Cons. Stat., Title 13, § 8101 et seq.

**Uniform Commercial Code—Sales**
See also Uniform Sales Act
Ala. Code 1975, § 7-2-101 et seq.
Alaska Stat. 1962, § 45.02.101 et seq.
Ariz. Rev. Stat. Ann., § 47-2101 et seq.
Ark. Code Ann. 1987, 4-2-101 et seq.
Cal. Commercial Code § 2101 et seq.
Colo. Rev. Stat., 4-2-101 et seq.
Conn. Gen. Stat. 1983, § 42a-2-101 et seq.
D.C. Code 1973, § 28:2-101 et seq.
Del. Code of 1974, Title 6, § 2-101 et seq.
Fla. Stat. Ann., 372.101 et seq.
Fla. Stat. Ann., 672.101 et seq.
Ga. Code Ann., 11-2-101 et seq.
Haw. Rev. Stat. Ann., § 490:2-101 et seq.
Ida. Code 1947, 28-2-101 et seq.
Ill. Rev. Stat. 1991, Ch. 26, § 2-101 et seq.
Ind. Code Ann., 26-1-2-101 et seq.
Iowa Code Ann., 554.2101 et seq.
Kan. Stat. Ann., 84-2-101 et seq.
Ky. Rev. Stat. 1971, 355.2-101 et seq.
Mass. Gen. Laws Ann., 106:2-101 et seq.
Md. Ann. Code 1974, Art. CL, § 2-101 et seq.
Me. Rev. Stat. Ann. 1964, Title 11, § 2-101 et seq.
Mich. Comp. Laws Ann., 440.2101 et seq.
Minn. Stat. Ann., 336.2-101 et seq.
Miss. Code Ann. 1972, § 75-2-101 et seq.
Mo. Rev. Stat., 400.2-101 et seq.
Mont. Code Ann., 30-2-101 et seq.
N.C. Gen. Stat. 1943, § 25-2-101 et seq.
N.D. Cent. Code, 41-02-01 et seq.
Neb. Rev. Stat. 1943, sect, 2-101 et seq.
Nev. Rev. Stat. 1979 Reprint, 104-2101 et seq.
N.H. Rev. Stat. 1955, 832-A:2-101 et seq.
N.J. Rev. Stat. 1937, 12A:2-101 et seq.
N.M. Stat. Ann., 55-2-101 et seq.
N.Y. Uniform Commercial Code (Consol. Laws Ch. 38) § 2-101 et seq.
Ohio Rev. Code 1953, 1302.01 et seq.
Okla. Stat. Ann., Title 12A, § 2-101 et seq.
Ore. Rev. Stat., 72.1010 et seq.
Pa. Cons. Stat., Title 13, § 2101 et seq.
R.I. Gen. Laws 1956, 6A-2-101 et seq.
S.C. Code Ann. 1976, § 36-2-101 et seq.
S.D. Codified Laws 1967, 57A-2-101 et seq.
Tenn. Code Ann., 47-2-101 et seq.
Tex. Business and Commerce Code, § 2.101 et seq.
Utah Code Ann. 1953, 70A-2-101 et seq.
Va. Code 1950, § 8.2-101 et seq.
Vt. Stat. Ann., Title 9A, § 2-101 et seq.
Wash. Rev. Code Ann., 62A.2-101 et seq.
Wis. Stat. Ann., 402.101 et seq.
W. Va. Code 1966, § 46-2-101 et seq.

Wyo. Stat. Ann., § 34.1-2-101 et seq.

**Uniform Commercial Code—Secured Transactions**

See also Uniform Conditional Sales Act and Uniform Trust Receipts Act
Ala. Code 1975, § 7-9-101 et seq.
Alaska Stat. 1962, § 45.09.101 et seq.
Ariz. Rev. Stat. Ann., § 47-9101 et seq.
Ark. Code Ann. 1987, 4-9-101 et seq.
Cal. Commercial Code § 9101 et seq.
Colo. Rev. Stat., 4-9-101 et seq.
Conn. Gen. Stat. 1983, § 42a-9-101 et seq.
D.C. Code 1973, § 28:9-101 et seq.
Del. Code of 1974, Title 6, § 9-101 et seq.
Fla. Stat. Ann., 679.101 et seq.
Ga. Code Ann., 11-9-101 et seq.
Haw. Rev. Stat. Ann., § 490:9-101 et seq.
Ida. Code 1947, 28-9-101 et seq.
Ill. Rev. Stat. 1991, Ch. 26, § 9-101 et seq.
Ind. Code Ann., 26-1-9-101 et seq.
Iowa Code Ann., 554.9101 et seq.
Kan. Stat. Ann., 84-9-101 et seq.
Ky. Rev. Stat. 1971, 355.9-101 et seq.
La. Rev. Stat. Ann., 10:9-101 et seq.
Mass. Gen. Laws Ann., 106:9-101 et seq.
Md. Ann. Code 1974, Art. CL, § 9-101 et seq.
Me. Rev. Stat. Ann. 1964, Title 11, § 9-101 et seq.
Mich. Comp. Laws Ann., 440.9101 et seq.
Minn. Stat. Ann., 336.9-101 et seq.
Miss. Code Ann. 1972, § 75-9-101 et seq.
Mo. Rev. Stat., 400.9-101 et seq.
Mont. Code Ann., 30-9-101 et seq.
N.C. Gen. Stat. 1943, § 25-9-101 et seq.
N.D. Cent. Code, 41-09-01 et seq.
Neb. Rev. Stat. 1943, § 9-101 et seq.
Nev. Rev. Stat. 1979 Reprint, 104.9101 et seq.
N.H. Rev. Stat. 1955, 382-A:9-101 et seq.
N.J. Stat. Ann., 12A:9-101 et seq.
N.M. Stat. Ann., 55-9-101 et seq.
N.Y. Uniform Commercial Code (Consol. Laws Ch. 38) § 9-101 et seq.
Ohio Rev. Code 1953, 1309.01 et seq.
Okla. Stat. Ann., Title 12A, § 9-101 et seq.
Ore. Rev. Stat., 79.1010 et seq.
Pa. Cons. Stat., Title 13, § 9101 et seq.
R.I. Gen. Laws 1956, 6A-9-101 et seq.
S.C. Code Ann. 1976, § 36-9-101 et seq.
S.D. Codified Laws 1967, 57A-9-101 et seq.
Tenn. Code Ann., 47-9-101 et seq.
Tex. Business and Commerce Code, § 9.101 et seq.
Utah Code Ann. 1953, 70A-9-101 et seq.
Va. Code 1950, § 8.9-101 et seq.
Vt. Stat. Ann., Title 9A, § 9-101 et seq.
Wash. Rev. Code Ann., 62A.9-101 et seq.
Wis. Stat. Ann., 409.101 et seq.
W. Va. Code 1966, § 46-9-101 et seq.
Wyo. Stat. Ann., § 34.1-9-101 et seq.

**Uniform Commercial Driver's License Act**

Utah Code Ann. 1953, 53-3-401 et seq.
W. Va. Code 1966,§ 17E-1-1 et seq.

**Uniform Commercial Drivers License Act**

Ala. Code 1975, § 32-6-49.1 et seq.
Ark. Code Ann. 1987, 27-23-101 1987, No. 241
Del. Code of 1974, Title 21, § 2601 et seq.
Ga. Code Ann., 40-5-140 et seq.
Mo. Rev. Stat., 302.700 et seq.
Pa. Cons. Stat., Title 75, § 1601 et seq.
Wash. Rev. Code Ann., 46.25.001 et seq.
Wyo. Stat. Ann., § 31-17-101 et seq.

**Uniform Commercial Paper Code**

See Uniform Commercial Code—Commercial Paper

**Uniform Common Interest Ownership Act**

Alaska Stat. 1962, § 34.08.010 et seq.
Colo. Rev. Stat., 38-33.3-101 et seq.
Nev. Stat. 1991, Ch. 245, p. 535, § 1 et seq.
W. Va. Code 1966, § 36B-1-101 et seq.

**Uniform Common Trust Fund Act**

Ala. Code 1975, § 5-12A-1 et seq.
Alaska Stat. 1962, § 06.35.010 et seq.
Ariz. Rev. Stat. Ann., § 6-871 et seq.
Ark. Code Ann. 1987, 28-69-203 et seq.
Cal. Financial Code § 1564
Colo. Rev. Stat., 11-24-101 et seq.
D.C. Code Ann., § 26-301 et seq.
Fla. Stat. 1951, 655.29 et seq.
Ida. Code 1947, 68-701 et seq.
*Continued*

Ill. Rev. Stat. 1987, Ch. 17, § 2101 et seq.
Iowa Code Ann., 633.126 et seq.
Kan. Stat. Ann., 9-1609
Mass. Gen. Laws Ann., 203A:1 et seq.
Mich. Comp. Laws Ann., 555.101 et seq.
Miss. Code Ann. 1972, § 81-5-37
Mo. Rev. Stat. 1959, 363.225
Mont. Code Ann., 32-1-701 et seq.
N.C. Gen. Stat. 1943, § 36A-90 et seq.
Neb. Rev. Stat. 1943, 24-601.01, 24-601.02
Nev. Rev. Stat. 1979 Reprint, 164.070 et seq.
N.H. Rev. Stat. 1955, 391:1 et seq.
N.M. Stat. Ann., 46-1-13 et seq.
Ohio Rev. Code 1953, 1109.20 et seq.
Okla. Stat. Ann., Title 60, § 162
Ore. Rev. Stat., 79.1010 et seq.
S.D. Codified Laws 1967, 55-6-1 et seq.
Tenn. Code Ann., 35-4-101 et seq.
Tex. Property Code, §§ 113.171, 113.172
Utah Code Ann. 1953, 7-5-13 et seq.
Wash. Rev. Code Ann., 11.102.010 et seq.
Wis. Stat. Ann., 223.055
W. Va. Code 1966, § 44-6-6 et seq.
Wyo. Stat. Ann., § 2-3-401 et seq.

**Uniform Community Development District Act**
Fla. Stat. Ann., 190.001 et seq.

**Uniform Comparative Fault Act**
Iowa Code Ann., § 668.1 et seq.
Wash. Rev. Code Ann., 4.22.005 et seq.

**Uniform Compensation Act**
P.R. Laws Ann. 1954, Title 3, § 760 et seq.

**Uniform Composite Reports as Evidence Act**
Neb. Rev. Stat. 1943, 25-12.115 et seq.
Ohio Rev. Code 1953, 2317.36 et seq.
S.D. Codified Laws 1967, 19-15-5 et seq.

**Uniform Condemnation Procedures Act**
Mich. Comp. Laws Ann., 213.51 et seq.

**Uniform Conditional Sales Act**
See also Uniform Commercial Code—Secured Transactions
Ariz. Laws 1919, Ch. 40
Del. Code of 1953, Title 6, § 9-901 et seq.
Haw. Rev. Stat. Ann., § 201-1 et seq.
Ind. Burns' 1933, 58-801 et seq.
Mich. Comp. Laws Ann., § 29-2-1 et seq.
N.H. Rev. Stat. 1955, Superseded Vol., 361:1 et seq.
N.J. Stat. Ann., 46:32-1 to 46:32-33
N.Y. Uniform Commercial Code (Consol. Laws Ch. 38) § 9-101 et seq.
Pa. 1925 Pamph. Laws 603, No. 325
S.D. Code 1939, 54.0201 et seq.
Wis. Stat. 1963, 122.01 et seq.
W. Va. Code 1966, § 46-2-101 et seq.

**Uniform Condominium Act**
Ala. Code 1975, § 35-8A-101 et seq.
Me. Rev. Stat. Ann. 1964, Title 33, § 1601-101 et seq.
Minn. Stat. Ann., 515A.1-101 et seq.
Mo. Rev. Stat., 448.1-101 et seq.
Neb. Rev. Stat. 1943, 76-825 et seq.
Pa. Cons. Stat., Title 68, § 3101 et seq.
Tex. Property Code, § 82.001 et seq.
Wash. Rev. Code Ann., 64.34.010 et seq.
W. Va. Code 1966, § 36B-1-101 et seq.

**Uniform Conflict of Laws—Limitations Act**
Ark. Code Ann. 1987, § 16-56-201 et seq.
Colo. Rev. Stat., 13-82-101 et seq.
Mont. Code Ann., 27-2-501 et seq.
N.D. Cent. Code, 28-01.2-01 et seq.
Ore. Rev. Stat., 12.410 et seq.
Wash. Rev. Laws 1989, 4.18.010 et seq.

**Uniform Consent Law (Medical Attendance and Care)**
La. Rev. Stat. Ann., 40:1299.40

**Uniform Conservation Easement Act**
Alaska Stat. 1962, § 34.17.010 et seq.
Ariz. Rev. Stat. Ann., § 33-271 et seq.
D.C. Code Ann., § 45-2601 et seq.
Del. Code of 1974, Title 7, § 6901 et seq.
Ga. Code Ann., 44-10-1 et seq.
Ida. Code 1947, § 55-2101 et seq.
Ind. Code Ann., 32-5-2.6-1 et seq.
Kan. Stat. Ann., 58-3810 et seq.
Ky. Rev. Stat. 1971, 382.800 et seq.
Me. Rev. Stat. Ann. 1964, Title 33, § 476 et seq.
Minn. Stat. Ann., 84C.01 et seq.

Miss. Code Ann. 1972, § 89-19-1 et seq.
Nev. Rev. Stat. 1987, 111.390 et seq.
N.M. Stat. Ann., § 47-12-1 et seq.
S.C. Code Ann. 1976, § 27-8-10 et seq.
Tex. Natural Resources Code § 183.001 et seq.
Va. Code 1950, § 10.1-1009 et seq.
Wis. Stat. Ann., 700.40

**Uniform Construction Code Act**
La. Rev. Stat. Ann., 40:1725 et seq.
N.J. Stat. Ann., 52:27D-119 et seq.

**Uniform Consumer Credit Code**
See also Consumer Credit Code
Ida. Code 1947, 28-31-101 et seq.
Iowa Code Ann., 537.1101 et seq.
Kan. Stat. Ann., 16a-1-101 et seq.
Me. Rev. Stat. Ann. 1964, Title 9-A, § 1-101 et seq.
Wis. Stat. Ann., 421.101 et seq.

**Uniform Consumer Credit Code (Revised)**
See Revised Uniform Comsumer Credit Code

**Uniform Consumer Credit Code-Deferred Presentment**
Ind. Code 1982, 24-4.5-7-101 et seq.

**Uniform Consumer Credit Code-Truth-in-Lending**
Me. Rev. Stat. Ann. 1964, Title 9-A, § 7-101 et seq.

**Uniform Consumer Credit Code—Administration**
See also Consumer Credit Code—Administration
Colo. Rev. Stat., 5-6-101 et seq.
Ida. Code 1947, 28-46-101 et seq.
Ind. Code Ann., 24-4.5-6-101 et seq.
Iowa Code Ann., 537.6101 et seq.
Kan. Stat. Ann., 16a-6-1 et seq.
Me. Rev. Stat. Ann. 1964, Title 9-A, § 6-101 et seq.
Okla. Stat. Ann., Title 14A, § 6-101 et seq.
Wyo. Stat. Ann., § 40-14-601 et seq.

**Uniform Consumer Credit Code—Administration (Revised)**
See Revised Uniform Consumer Credit Code—Administration

**Uniform Consumer Credit Code—Credit Sales**
Colo. Rev. Stat., 5-2-101 et seq.
Ida. Code 1947, 28-32-101 et seq.
Ind. Code Ann., 24-4.5-2-101 et seq.
Okla. Stat. Ann., Title 14A, § 2-101 et seq.
Wyo. Stat. Ann., § 40-14-201 et seq.

**Uniform Consumer Credit Code—Credit Service Organizations**
Me. Rev. Stat. Ann. 1964, Title 9-A, § 10-101 et seq.

**Uniform Consumer Credit Code—Finance Charges and Related Provisions**
Iowa Code Ann., 537.2101 et seq.
Me. Rev. Stat. Ann. 1964, Title 9-A, § 2-101 et seq.

**Uniform Consumer Credit Code—Finance Charges and Related Provisions (Revised)**
See Revised Uniform Consumer Credit Code—Finance Charges and Related Provisions

**Uniform Consumer Credit Code—Insurance**
Colo. Rev. Stat., 5-4-101 et seq.
Ida. Code 1947, 28-44-101 et seq.
Ind. Code Ann., 24-4.5-4-101 et seq.
Kan. Stat. Ann., 16a-4-101 et seq.
Me. Rev. Stat. Ann. 1964, Title 9-A, § 4-101 et seq.
Okla. Stat. Ann., Title 14A, § 4-101 et seq.
Utah Code Ann. 1953, 70C-6-101 et seq.
Wyo. Stat. Ann., § 40-14-401 et seq.

**Uniform Consumer Credit Code—Insurance (Revised)**
See Revised Uniform Consumer Credit Code—Insurance

**Uniform Consumer Credit Code—Loans**
Colo. Rev. Stat., 5-3-101 et seq.
Ida. Code 1947, 28-33-101 et seq.
*Continued*

Ind. Code Ann., 24-4.5-3-101 et seq.

Okla. Stat. Ann., Title 14A, § 3-101 et seq.

Utah Code Ann. 1953, Miscellaneous Superseded Code Provisions, 70B-3-101 et seq.

Wyo. Stat. Ann., § 40-14-301 et seq.

**Uniform Consumer Credit Code—Regulation of Agreements and Practices (Revised)**

See Revised Uniform Consumer Credit Code—Regulation of Agreements and Practices

**Uniform Consumer Credit Code—Regulations of Agreements and Practices**

Iowa Code Ann., 537.3101 et seq.

Me. Rev. Stat. Ann. 1964, Title 9-A, § 3-101 et seq.

**Uniform Consumer Credit Code—Remedies and Penalties**

See also Consumer Credit Code—Remedies and Penalties

Colo. Rev. Stat., 5-5-101 et seq.

Ida. Code 1947, 28-45-101 et seq.

Ind. Code Ann., 24-4.5-5-101 et seq.

Iowa Code Ann., 537.5101 et seq.

Kan. Stat. Ann., 16a-5-101 et seq.

Me. Rev. Stat. Ann. 1964, Title 9-A, § 5-101 et seq.

Okla. Stat. Ann., Title 14A, § 5-101 et seq.

Utah Code Ann. 1953, 70C-7-101 et seq.

Wyo. Stat. Ann., § 40-14-501 et seq.

**Uniform Consumer Credit Code—Remedies and Penalties (Revised)**

See Revised Uniform Consumer Credit Code—Remedies and Penalties

**Uniform Consumer Protection Act**

Fla. Special Laws 1973, Ch. 73-602 (Pinellas County)

Fla. Special Laws 1974, Ch. 74-573 (Pasco County)

Fla. Special Laws 1975, Ch. 75-394 (Hillsborough County)

Fla. Special Laws 1976, Ch. 76-471

**Uniform Consumer Sales Practices Act**

Kan. Stat. Ann., 50-623 et seq.

Ohio Rev. Code 1953, 1345.01 et seq.

Utah Code Ann. 1953, 13-11-1 et seq.

**Uniform Contraband Transportation Act**

Fla. Stat. Ann., 932.701 et seq.

**Uniform Contribution Among Joint Tortfeasors Act**

Md. Ann. Code 1974, Art. CJ, § 3-1401 et seq.

**Uniform Contribution Among Tortfeasors Act**

Alaska Stat. 1962, § 09.16.010 et seq.

Ariz. Rev. Stat. Ann., § 12-2501 et seq.

Ark. Code Ann. 1987, 16-61-201 et seq.

Colo. Rev. Stat., 13-50.5-101 et seq.

Del. Code of 1974, Title 10, § 6301 et seq.

Fla. Stat. Ann., 768.31 et seq.

Haw. Rev. Stat. Ann., § 663-11 et seq.

Ky. Rev. Stat. 1971, 412.030

Mass. Gen. Laws Ann., 231B:1 et seq.

Md. Ann. Code 1957, Art. 50, § 16 et seq.

Mich. Comp. Laws 1948, 600.2925a et seq.

Miss. Code Ann. 1972, § 85-5-5

Mo. Rev. Stat., 537.060

N.C. Gen. Stat. 1943, § 1 B-1 et seq.

N.D. Cent. Code, 32-38-01 et seq.

Nev. Rev. Stat. 1979 Reprint, 17.225 et seq.

N.J. Stat. Ann., 2A:53A-1 to 2A:53A-5

N.M. Stat. Ann., 41-3-1 et seq.

Ohio Rev. Code 1953, § 2307.31 et seq.

Okla. Stat. Ann., Title 12, § 832

Pa. Cons. Stat., Title 42, § 8321 et seq.

R.I. Gen. Laws 1956, 10-6-1 et seq.

S.C. Code Ann. 1976, § 15-38-10 et seq.

S.D. Codified Laws 1967, 15-8-11 et seq.

Tenn. Code Ann., § 29-11-101 et seq.

Tex. Civil Practice and Remedies Code, § 32.001 et seq.

W. Va. Code 1966, § 55-7-13

Wyo. Stat. Ann., § 1-1-110 et seq.

**Uniform Controlled Dangerous Substances Property Forfeiture Act (Seizure of)**

La. Rev. Stat. Ann., 40:2601 et seq.

**Uniform Controlled Substances Act**
Ala. Code 1975, § 20-2-1 et seq.
Alaska Stat. 1962, §§ 11.71.010 et seq., 17.30.010 et seq.
Ariz. Rev. Stat. Ann., § 36-2501 et seq.
Ark. Code Ann. 1987, 5-64-101 et seq.
Cal. Health and Safety Code § 11000 et seq.
Colo. Rev. Stat., 12-22-301 et seq., 18-18-101 et seq.
Conn. Gen. Stat. Ann., § 21a-240 et seq.
D.C. Code Ann., § 33-501 et seq.
Del. Code of 1974, Title 16, § 4701 et seq.
Fla. Stat. Ann., 893.01 et seq.
Ga. Code Ann., 16-13-20 et seq.
Haw. Rev. Stat. Ann., § 329-1 et seq.
Ida. Code 1947, 37-2701 et seq.
Ill. Comp. Stat. 1992, Ch. 720, § 570/100 et seq.
Ind. Code 1971, 35-24-1-1 et seq.
Iowa Code Ann., 124.101 et seq.
Kan. Stat. Ann., 63-4101 et seq.
Ky. Rev. Stat. 1971, 218A.010 et seq.
La. Rev. Stat. Ann., 40:961 et seq.
Mass. Gen. Laws Ann., 94C:1 et seq.
Md. Ann. Code 1957, Art. 27, § 276 et seq.
Me. Rev. Stat. Ann. 1964, Title 32, § 13702 et seq.
Mich. Comp. Laws Ann., 333.7101 et seq.
Minn. Stat. Ann., 152.01 et seq.
Miss. Code 1942, § 68-4-4 et seq.
Mo. Rev. Stat., 195.005 et seq.
Mont. Code Ann., 50-32-101 et seq.
N.C. Gen. Stat. 1943, § 90-86 et seq.
N.D. Cent. Code, 19-0.1-101 et seq.
Neb. Rev. Stat. 1943, 28-401 et seq.
Nev. Rev. Stat. 1979 Reprint, 453.011 et seq.
N.H. Rev. Stat. 1955, 318-B:1 et seq.
N.J. Stat. Ann., 24:21-1 et seq., 2C:35-1 et seq.
N.M. Stat. Ann., 30-31-1 et seq.
N.Y. Public Health Law 1953 (Consol. Laws Ch. 45) § 3300 et seq.
Ohio Rev. Code 1953, 3719.01 et seq.
Okla. Stat. Ann., Title 63, § 2-101 et seq.
Ore. Rev. Stat., 475.005 et seq.
Pa. Cons. Stat., Title 35, § 780-101 et seq.
P.R. Laws Ann. 1954, Title 24, § 2101 et seq.
R.I. Gen. Laws 1956, 21-28-1.01 et seq.
S.C. Code Ann. 1976, § 44-53-110 et seq.
S.D. Codified Laws 1967, § 39-16-1 et seq.
Tenn. Code Ann., 39-6-401 et seq.
Tex. Health and Safety Code, § 481.001 et seq.
Utah Code Ann. 1953, 58-37-1 et seq.
Va. Code 1950, § 54.1-3400 et seq.
Vt. Acts 1951, No. 170, §§ 135, 4141 et seq.
Wash. Rev. Code Ann., 69.50.101 et seq.
Wis. Stat. Ann., 161.001 et seq.
W. Va. Code 1966, Ch. 60A-1-101 et seq.
Wyo. Stat. Ann., § 5-7-1001 et seq.

**Uniform Conviction Information Act**
Conn. Gen. Stat. 1983, § 21a-240 et seq.
Del. Code of 1974, Title 16, § 4701 et seq.
Fla. Stat. Ann., 893.01 et seq.
Ga. Code Ann., 16-13-20 et seq.
Haw. Rev. Stat. Ann., § 329-1 et seq.
Ida. Code 1947, 37-2701 et seq.
Ill. Comp. Stat. 1992, Ch. 20, § 2635/1 et seq.
Ind. Code Ann., 35-48-1-1 et seq.
Iowa Code Ann., 204.101 et seq.
Kan. Stat. Ann., 65-4101 et seq.
Ky. Rev. Stat. 1971, 218A.010 et seq.
La. Rev. Stat. Ann., 40:961 et seq.
Mass. Gen. Laws Ann., 94C:1 et seq.
Md. Ann. Code 1957, Art. 27, § 276 et seq.
Mich. Comp. Laws Ann., 333.7101 et seq.
Minn. Stat. Ann., 152.01 et seq.
Miss. Code Ann. 1972, § 41-29-101 et seq.
Mo. Rev. Stat., 195.005 et seq.
Mont. Code Ann., 50-32-101 et seq.
N.C. Gen. Stat. 1943, § 90-86 et seq.
N.D. Cent. Code, 19-03.1-01 et seq.
Neb. Rev. Stat. 1943, 28-401 et seq.
Nev. Rev. Stat. 1979 Reprint, 453.011 et seq.
N.J. Stat. Ann., 24:21-1 et seq.
N.M. Stat. Ann., 30-31-1 et seq.
N.Y. Public Health Law 1953 (Consol. Laws Ch. 45) § 3300 et seq.
Ohio Rev. Code 1953, 3719.01 et seq.
Okla. Stat. Ann., Title 63, § 2-101 et seq.
Ore. Rev. Stat., 475.005 et seq.
Pa. Cons. Stat., Title 35, § 780-101 et seq.
P.R. Laws Ann. 1954, Title 24, § 2101 et seq.
R.I. Gen. Laws 1956, 21-281.01 et seq.
S.C. Code Ann. 1976, § 44-53-110 et seq.
*Continued*

S.D. Codified Laws 1967, 34-20B-1 et seq.
Tenn. Code Ann., 39-17-401 et seq.
Tex. Health and Safety Code, § 481.001 et seq.
Utah Code Ann. 1953, 58-37-1 et seq.
Va. Code 1950, § 54.1-3400 et seq.
Wash. Rev. Code Ann., 69.50.101 et seq.
Wis. Stat. Ann., 161.001 et seq.
W. Va. Code 1966, § 60A-1-101 et seq.
Wyo. Stat. Ann., § 35-7-1001 et seq.

**Uniform Cotton Classing Fees Act of 1987**
Aug. 20, 1987, P.L. 100-108, 7 U.S. Code §§ 471 nt., 473a, 473a nt.
Dec. 13, 1991, P.L. 102-237, 7 U.S. Code § 473a nt.

**Uniform County Bond Law**
Miss. Code Ann. 1972, § 19-9-1 et seq.

**Uniform County Budget Act**
Ky. Rev. Stat. 1971, 68.210 et seq.

**Uniform County Libraries Act**
S.C. Code Ann. 1976, § 4-9-35 et seq.

**Uniform Crime Victims Reparations Act**
See also Crime Victims Reparations Act
Kan. Stat. Ann., 74-7301 et seq.
La. Rev. Stat. Ann., 46:1801 et seq.
Mont. Code Ann., 53-9-101 et seq.
N.D. Cent. Code, 65-13-01 et seq.
Ohio Rev. Code 1953, 2743.51 et seq.
Tex. Rev. Civ. Stat., Art. 8309-1
Wyo. Stat. Ann., § 1-1-110 et seq.

**Uniform Criminal and Nonsupport Act**
Va. Code 1950, § 20-61 et seq.

**Uniform Criminal Extradition Act**
Ala. Code 1975, § 15-9-20 et seq.
Alaska Stat. 1962, § 12.70.010 et seq.
Ariz. Rev. Stat. Ann., § 13-3841 et seq.
Ark. Code Ann. 1987, 16-94-201 et seq.
Cal. Penal Code § 1547 et seq.
Colo. Rev. Stat., 16-19-101 et seq.
Conn. Gen. Stat. 1983, § 54-157 et seq.
Del. Code of 1974, Title 11, § 2501 et seq.
Fla. Stat. Ann., 941.01 et seq.
Ga. Code Ann., 17-13-20 et seq.
Haw. Rev. Stat. Ann., § 832-1 et seq.
Ida. Code 1947, 19-4501 et seq.
Ill. Rev. Stat. 1991, Ch. 60, § 18 et seq.
Ind. Code Ann., 35-33-10-3
Iowa Code Ann., 820.1 et seq.
Kan. Stat. Ann., 22-2701 et seq.
Ky. Rev. Stat. 1971, 440.150 et seq.
La. Code of Crim. Proc. 1966, Art. 261 et seq.
Mass. Gen. Laws Ann., 276:11 et seq.
Md. Ann. Code 1957, Art. 41, § 2-201 et seq.
Me. Rev. Stat. Ann. 1964, Title 15, § 201 et seq.
Mich. Comp. Laws Ann., 780.1 et seq.
Minn. Stat. Ann., 629.01 et seq.
Mo. Rev. Stat., 548.011 et seq.
Mont. Code Ann., 46-30-101 et seq.
N.C. Gen. Stat. 1943, § 15A-721 et seq.
N.D. Cent. Code, 29-30.3-01 et seq.
Neb. Rev. Stat. 1943, 29-729 et seq.
Nev. Rev. Stat. 1979 Reprint, 179.177 et seq.
N.H. Rev. Stat. 1955, 612:1 et seq.
N.J. Rev. Stat. 1937, 2A:160-6 et seq.
N.M. Stat. Ann., 31-4-1 et seq.
N.Y. Criminal Procedure Law (Consol. Laws Ch. 11A) § 570.02 et seq.
Ohio Rev. Code 1953, 2963.01 et seq.
Okla. Stat. Ann., Title 22, § 1141.1 et seq.
Ore. Rev. Stat., 133.743 et seq.
Pa. Cons. Stat., Title 42, § 9121 et seq.
P.R. Laws Ann. 1954, Title 34, § 1881 et seq.
R.I. Gen. Laws 1956, 12-9-1 et seq.
S.D. Codified Laws 1967, 23-24-1 et seq.
Tenn. Code Ann., 40-9-101 et seq.
Tex. Code of Criminal Procedure 1965, Art. 51.13
Utah Code Ann. 1953, 77-30-1 et seq.
Va. Code 1950, § 19.2-85 et seq.
Vt. Stat. Ann., Title 13, § 4941 et seq.
Wash. Rev. Code Ann., 10.88.200 et seq.
Wis. Stat. Ann., 976.03
W. Va. Code 1966, § 5-1-7 et seq.
Wyo. Stat. Ann., § 7-3-201 et seq.

**Uniform Criminal Interstate Rendition Act**
Mass. Gen. Laws Ann., 276:11 et seq.

**Uniform Criminal Responsibility and Post-Trial Disposition Act**
N.D. Cent. Code, 12.1-04.1-01 et seq.

**Uniform Criminal Statistics Act**
Cal. Penal Code § 13000 et seq.
Ky. Rev. Stat. 1971, 17.140 et seq.

**Uniform Custodial Trust Act**
Alaska Stat. 1962, § 13.60.010 et seq.
Ark. Code Ann. 1987, 28-72-401 et seq.
Haw. Rev. Stat. Ann., § 554B-1 et seq.
Ida. Code 1947, 68-1301 et seq.
Mass. Gen. Laws Ann., 203B:1 to 203B:19
Minn. Stat. Ann., 529.01 et seq.
Mo. Rev. Stat., 404.400 et seq.
Neb. Rev. Stat. 1943, 30-3501 to 30-3522
N.M. Stat. Ann., 45-7-501 et seq.
R.I. Gen. Laws 1956, 18-13-1 et seq.
Va. Code 1950, § 55-34.1 et seq.
Wis. Stat. Ann., 880.81 et seq.

**Uniform Dealer Tag Permit**
Miss. Code Ann. 1972, § 27-19-301 et seq.

**Uniform Deceptive Trade Practices Act**
Colo. Rev. Stat., § 6-1-101 et seq.
Del. Code of 1974, Title 6, § 2531 et seq.
Ga. Code Ann., 10-1-370 et seq.
Haw. Rev. Stat. Ann., § 481A-1 et seq.
Ill. Rev. Stat. 1991, Ch. 121 1/2, § 311 et seq.
Me. Rev. Stat. Ann. 1964, Title 10, § 1211 et seq.
Minn. Stat. Ann., 325D.43 et seq.
Neb. Rev. Stat. 1943, 87-301 et seq.
N.M. Stat. Ann. 1978, § 57-12-1 et seq.
Ohio Rev. Code 1953, § 4165.01 et seq.
Okla. Stat. Ann., Title 78, § 51 et seq.
Ore. Rev. Stat., 646.605 et seq.

**Uniform Declaratory Judgments Act**
Ala. Code 1975, § 6-6-220 et seq.
Ariz. Rev. Stat. Ann., § 12-1831 et seq.
Ark. Code Ann. 1987, 16-111-103 et seq.
Colo. Rev. Stat., 13-51-101 et seq.
Del. Code of 1974, Title 10, § 6501 et seq.
Fla. Stat. Ann., 86.011 et seq.
Ga. Code Ann., 9-4-1 et seq.
Ida. Code 1947, 10-1201 et seq.
Ill. Rev. Stat. 1991, Ch. 110, § 2-701
Ind. Code Ann., 34-4-10-1 et seq.
Iowa Rules of Civil Procedure, Rules 261 et seq.
La. Code of Civil Procedure Art. 1871 et seq.
Mass. Gen. Laws Ann., 231A:1 et seq.
Md. Ann. Code 1974, Art. CJ, § 3-401 et seq.
Me. Rev. Stat. Ann. 1964, Title 14, § 5951 et seq.
Minn. Stat. Ann., 555.01 et seq.
Mo. Rev. Stat., 527.010 et seq.
Mont. Code Ann., 27-8-101 et seq.
N.C. Gen. Stat. 1943, § 1-253 et seq.
N.D. Cent. Code, 32-23-01 et seq.
Neb. Rev. Stat. 1943, 25-21.149 et seq.
Nev. Rev. Stat. Ann., 30.010 et seq.
N.J. Stat. Ann., 2A:16-50 et seq.
N.M. Stat. Ann., 44-6-1 et seq.
Ohio Rev. Code 1953, 2721.01 et seq.
Okla. Stat. Ann., Title 12, § 1651 et seq.
Ore. Rev. Stat., 28.010 et seq.
Pa. Cons. Stat., Title 42, § 7531 et seq.
P.R. Laws Ann. 1954, Title 32, § 2991 et seq.
R.I. Gen. Laws 1956, 9-30-1 et seq.
S.C. Code Ann. 1976, § 15-53-10 et seq.
S.D. Codified Laws 1967, 21-24-1 et seq.
Tenn. Code Ann., 29-14-101 et seq.
Tex. Civil Practice and Remedies Code, § 37.001 et seq.
Utah Code Ann. 1953, 78-33-1 et seq.
Va. Code 1950, § 8.01-184 et seq.
Vt. Stat. Ann., Title 12, § 4711 et seq.
Wash. Rev. Code Ann., 7.24.010 et seq.
Wis. Stat. Ann., 806.04
W. Va. Code 1966, § 55-13-1 et seq.
Wyo. Stat. Ann., § 1-37-101 et seq.

**Uniform Delinquent Tax Enforcement Act**
N.Y. Real Property Tax Law (Consol. Laws Ch. 50A) § 1100 et seq.

**Uniform Depository Act**
Ohio Rev. Code 1953, 135.01 et seq.

**Uniform Desertion and Nonsupport Act**
Ala. Code 1975, § 30-4-50 et seq.
Alaska Stat. 1962, §§ 11.51.100, 11.51.120
Cal. Penal Code §§ 270e, 273h
Del. Code of 1974, Title 13, § 501 et seq.

*Continued*

Haw. Rev. Stat. Ann., § 575-1 et seq.
Ill. Rev. Stat. 1991, Ch. 40, § 1101 et seq.
Mass. Gen. Laws Ann., 273:1 et seq.
Miss. Code Ann. 1972, § 97-5-3
N.D. Cent. Code, 14-07-15, 14-07-16
Nev. Rev. Stat. 1979 Reprint, 201.015 et seq.
N.H. Rev. Stat. 1955, 460:23
N.J. Stat. Ann., 2C:24-5, 2C:62-1
Okla. Stat. Ann., Title 21, §§ 853, 854
S.D. Codified Laws 1967, 25-7-15
Utah Code Ann. 1953, Miscellaneous Superseded Code Provisions, 76-15-1, 76-15-2
Va. Code 1950, § 20-61 et seq.
Vt. Stat. Ann., Title 15, § 201 et seq.
Wash. Rev. Code Ann., 26.20.030 et seq.
Wis. Stat. Ann., 767.08 et seq.
W. Va. Code 1966, § 48-8-1 et seq.
Wyo. Stat. Ann., § 20-3-101 et seq.

**Uniform Detainer Act**

Pa. Cons. Stat., Title 42, § 9101 et seq.

**Uniform Determinate Sentencing Act**

Cal. Statutes 1976, Ch. 1139

**Uniform Determination of Death Act**

D.C. Code Ann., § 6-2401
Iowa Laws 1999, S.F. 12
Kan. Stat. Ann., 77-204 et seq.
Md. Ann. Code 1974, Art. HG, § 5-202
Me. Rev. Stat. Ann. 1964, Title 22, § 2811 et seq.
Minn. Stat. Ann., 145.135
Miss. Code Ann. 1972, §§ 41-36-1, 41-36-3
Mont. Code Ann., 50-22-101 et seq.
Neb. Laws 1992, L.B. 906
N.H. Rev. Stat. 1955, 141-D:1 et seq.
Okla. Stat. Ann., Title 63, § 3121 et seq.
Pa. Purdon's Stat., Title 35, § 10201 et seq.
S.C. Code Ann. 1976, §§ 44-43-450, 44-43-460
Vt. Stat. Ann., Title 18, § 5218
W. Va. Code 1966, § 16-10-1 et seq.
Wyo. Stat. Ann., § 35-19-101 et seq.

**Uniform Disability Insurance Policy Provisions Law**

Ida. Code 1947, 41-2101 et seq.
Mich. Comp. Laws Ann., 500.3400 et seq.
Wyo. Stat. Ann., § 26-18-101 et seq.

**Uniform Disciplinary Act**

Wash. Rev. Code Ann., 18.130.010 et seq.

**Uniform Disclaimer of Property Interests Act**

Ala. Code 1975, § 43-8-290 et seq.
Haw. Rev. Stat. Ann., § 560:2-801 et seq.
Md. Ann. Code 1974, Art. ET, § 9-201 et seq.
Me. Rev. Stat. Ann. 1964, Title 18A, § 2-801 et seq.
Miss. Code Ann. 1972, § 89-21-1 et seq.
N.H. Rev. Stat. 1955, 563-B:1 et seq.
W. Va. Code 1966, § 42-6-1 et seq.

**Uniform Disclaimer of Transfers by Will, Intestacy, or Appointment Act**

Alaska Stat. 1962, § 13.11.295
Ariz. Rev. Stat. Ann., § 14-2803
Colo. Rev. Stat., § 15-11-801
Del. Code of 1974, Title 12, § 601 et seq.
Fla. Stat. Ann., § 732-801
Haw. Rev. Stat. Ann., § 560:2-801
Ida. Code 1947, § 15-2-801
Ill. Rev. Stat. 1991, Ch. 110 1/2, § 2-7
Kan. Stat. Ann., 59-2291 et seq.
Ky. Rev. Stat. 1971, 394.610 et seq.
Me. Rev. Stat. Ann. 1964, Title 18A, § 2-801 et seq.
Minn. Stat. Ann., § 525.532
N.C. Gen. Stat. 1943, § 31B-1 et seq.
Neb. Rev. Stat. Ann. 1943, 3A:25-39 et seq.
N.J. Stat. Ann., § 45-2-801
Ore. Rev. Stat., 112.650 et seq.
Utah Code Ann. 1953, 75-2-801

**Uniform Disclaimer of Transfers under Nontestamentary Instruments Act**

Del. Code of 1974, Title 12, § 601 et seq.
Kan. Stat. Ann., 59-2291 et seq.
Ky. Rev. Stat. 1971, § 394.035
Me. Rev. Stat. Ann. 1964, Title 18A, § 2-801 et seq.
N.D. Cent. Code, 47-11.1-01 et seq.

Ore. Rev. Stat., 105.625 et seq.

**Uniform Disposition of Abandoned Property Act**
Md. Ann. Code 1974, Art. CL, § 17-101 et seq.

**Uniform Disposition of Community Property Rights at Death Act**
Alaska Stat. 1962, § 13.41.005 et seq.
Ark. Code Ann. 1987, 28-12-101 et seq.
Colo. Rev. Stat., 15-20-101 et seq.
Conn. Gen Stat. 1983, 45a-458 et seq.
Fla. Stat. Ann., 732.216 et seq.
Haw. Rev. Stat. Ann., § 510-21 et seq.
Ky. Rev. Stat. 1971, 391.210 et seq.
Mich. Comp. Laws Ann., 557.261 et seq.
Mont. Code Ann. 1987, 72-6-101 et seq.
N.Y. Estates, Powers and Trusts Law (Consol. Laws Ch. 17B) § 6-6.1 et seq.
Ore. Rev. Stat., 112.705 et seq.
Va. Code 1950, § 64.1-197 et seq.
Wyo. Stat. Ann., § 2-7-720 et seq.

**Uniform Disposition of Criminal Cases on the Merits Act**
Okla. Stat. Ann., Title 22, § 1145.1 et seq.

**Uniform Disposition of Traffic Infractions Act**
Fla. Stat. Ann., 318.11 et seq.

**Uniform Disposition of Unclaimed Property Act**
Ala. Code 1975, § 35-17-1 et seq.
Ariz. Rev. Stat. Ann., § 44-351 et seq.
Ark. Code Ann. 1987, 18-28-201 et seq.
Cal. Code of Civil Procedure § 1500 et seq.
Conn. Gen. Stat 1983, § 45-298a et seq.
D.C. Code Ann., § 42-201 et seq.
Fla. Stat. Ann., 717.001 et seq.
Ga. Code Ann., 44-12-190 et seq.
Haw. Rev. Stat. Ann., § 523-1 et seq.
Ida. Code 1947, 14-501 et seq.
Ill. Rev. Stat. 1991, Ch. 141, § 101 et seq.
Ind. Code Ann., 32-9-1-1 et seq.
Iowa Code Ann., 556.1 et seq.
Kan. Stat. Ann., 58-3901 et seq.
La. Rev. Stat. Ann., 9:151 et seq.
Md. Ann. Code 1974, Art. CL, § 17-101 et seq.
Me. Rev. Stat. 1964, Title 33, § 1301 et seq.
Minn. Stat. Ann., 345.31 et seq.
Miss. Code Ann. 1972, § 89-12-1 et seq.
Mo. Rev. Stat., 447.500 et seq.
Mont. Code Ann., 70-9-101 et seq.
N.D. Cent. Code, 47-30-01 et seq.
Neb. Rev. Stat. 1943, 69-1301 et seq.
Nev. Rev. Stat. 1979 Reprint, 122A.010 et seq.
N.H. Rev. Stat. 1955, 471-A:1 et seq.
N.M. Stat. Ann., 7-8-1 et seq.
Okla. Stat. Ann., Title 60, § 651 et seq.
Ore. Rev. Stat., 98.302 et seq.
R.I. Gen. Laws 1956, 33-21-11 et seq.
S.C. Code Ann. 1976, Superseded Vols., § 27-17-10 et seq.
S.D. Codified Laws 1967, 43-41A-1 et seq.
Tenn. Code Ann., 66-29-101 et seq.
Utah Code Ann. 1953, 78-44-1 et seq.
Va. Code 1950, § 55-210.1 et seq.
Vt. Stat. Ann., Title 27, § 1208 et seq.
Wash. Rev. Code Ann., 63.28.070 et seq.
Wis. Stat. Ann., 177.01 et seq.
W. Va. Code 1966, § 36-8-1 et seq.
Wyo. Stat. Ann., § 9-5-201 et seq.

**Uniform Dissolution of Marriage Act**
Colo. Rev. Stat., 14-10-101 et seq.

**Uniform District Court Act**
Mont. Code Ann. 1987, Title 25, Ch. 19
N.Y. Uniform District Court Act, § 101 et seq.

**Uniform District Election Law**
Cal. Elections Code 1976, § 23500 et seq.

**Uniform Division of Income for Tax Purposes Act**
Ala. Code 1975, § 40-27-1 et seq.
Alaska Stat. 1962, § 43.19.010 et seq.
Ariz. Rev. Stat. Ann., § 43-1131 et seq.
Ark. Code Ann. 1987, 26-51-701 et seq.
Cal. Revenue and Taxation Code § 25120 et seq.
Colo. Rev. Stat., 24-60-1301 et seq.
Haw. Rev. Stat. Ann., § 235-21 et seq.
Ida. Code 1947, 63-3027 et seq.
Kan. Stat. Ann., 79-3271 et seq.
*Continued*

Ky. Rev. Stat. 1971, 141.120 et seq.
Me. Rev. Stat. 1964, Title 36, §§ 5210, 5211
Mich. Comp. Laws Ann., 205.581 et seq.
Minn. Stat. Ann., 290.171 et seq.
Mo. Rev. Stat., § 32.200 et seq.
Mont. Code Ann., 15-31-301 et seq.
N.D. Cent. Code, 57-38.1-01 et seq.
Neb. Rev. Stat. 1943, § 77-2901 et seq.
Nev. Rev. Stat., 376.010 et seq.
N.M. Stat. Ann., 7-4-1 et seq.
Ore. Rev. Stat., 314.605 et seq.
S.C. Code Ann. 1976, § 12-7-1110 et seq.
S.D. Codified Laws 1967, 10-54-1 et seq.
Tex. Tax Code, § 141.001 et seq.
Utah Code Ann. 1953, 59-7-301 et seq.
Va. Code 1950, § 58.1-302 et seq.
Wash. Rev. Code 1951, 82.56.010 et seq.

**Uniform Divorce Recognition Act**
Cal. Family Code § 2090 et seq.
N.D. Cent. Code, 14-05-08.1
Neb. Rev. Stat. 1943, 42-341 et seq.
N.H. Rev. Stat. 1955, 459:1 et seq.
N.J. Stat. Ann., 2A:34-1 et seq.
R.I. Gen. Laws 1956, 15-6-1 et seq.
S.C. Code Ann. 1976, § 20-3-410 et seq.
Wis. Stat. Ann., 767.22

**Uniform Dormant Mineral Interests Act**
Conn. Gen. Stat. 1983, § 47-33m et seq.

**Uniform Drainage Law**
Del. Code of 1974, Title 7, § 4101 et seq.

**Uniform Driver's License Act**
N.C. Gen. Stat. 1943, § 20-5 et seq.
Utah Code Ann. 1953, 53-3-701 et seq.

**Uniform Drug, Device and Cosmetic Act**
Ill. Rev. Stat. 1965, Ch. 111 1/2, § 401 et seq.

**Uniform Durable Power of Attorney Act**
See also Durable Power of Attorney Act
Ala. Code 1975, § 26-1-2
Ariz. Rev. Stat. Ann., §§ 14-5501, 14-5502
Cal. Civil Code § 2400 et seq.
Colo. Rev. Stat., 15-14-501, 15-14-502
D.C. Code Ann., § 21-2081 et seq.
Del. Code of 1974, Title 12, § 4901 et seq.
Haw. Rev. Stat. Ann., § 551D-1 et seq.
Ida. Code 1947, 15-5-501 et seq.
Kan. Stat. Ann., 58-610 et seq.
Ky. Rev. Stat. 1971, 386.093
Mass. Gen. Laws Ann., 201B:1 et seq.
Me. Rev. Stat. Ann. 1964, Title 18A, §§ 5-501, 5-502
Mich. Comp. Laws Ann., 700.495, 700.497
Minn. Stat. Ann., 523.07, 523.08
Miss. Code Ann. 1972, §§ 87-3-5, 87-3-15, 87-3-101 et seq.
Mo. Rev. Stat., 404.700 et seq.
Mont. Code Ann. 1987, 72-5-501, 72-5-502
N.D. Cent. Code, 30.1-30-01 et seq.
Neb. Rev. Stat. 1943, 30-2664 et seq.
N.M. Stat. Ann., 45-5-501, 45-5-502
Okla. Stat. Ann., Title 58, § 1071 et seq.
Pa. Cons. Stat., Title 20, § 5604 et seq.
S.C. Code Ann. 1976, § 62-5-501 et seq.
Tenn. Code Ann., 34-6-101 et seq.
Tex. Probate Code, § 481 et seq.
Utah Code Ann. 1953, 75-5-501 75-5-502
Wis. Stat. Ann., 243.07
W. Va. Code 1966, § 39-4-1 et seq.

**Uniform Duties to Disabled Persons Act**
Colo. Rev. Stat., 25-20-101 et seq.
La. Rev. Stat. Ann., 40:1299.71 et seq.
Minn. Stat. Ann., 145.851 et seq.
N.D. Cent. Code, 23-28-01 et seq.
Okla. Stat. Ann., Title 63, § 2551 et seq.

**Uniform Election Code**
Colo. Rev. Stat., 1-1-101 et seq.

**Uniform Eminent Domain Act**
Ohio Rev. Code 1953, 163.01 et seq.

**Uniform Eminent Domain Procedural Act**
Neb. Rev. Stat. 1943, 76-701 et seq.

**Uniform Enforcement of Foreign Judgments Act**
See also Enforcement of Foreign Judgments Act
Alaska Stat. 1962, § 09.30.200 et seq.
Ariz. Rev. Stat. Ann., § 12-1701 et seq.
Colo. Rev. Stat., 13-53-101 et seq.
Conn. Gen. Stat. 1983, § 52-604 et seq.
Del. Code of 1974, Title 10, § 4781 et seq.

Fla. Stat. Ann., 55.501 et seq.
Ga. Code Ann., 9-12-130 et seq.
Haw. Rev. Stat. Ann., § 636C-1 et seq.
Ida. Code 1947. 10-1301 et seq.
Ill. Rev. Stat. 1991, Ch. 110, § 12-101 et seq.
Iowa Code Ann., 626A.1 et seq.
Kan. Stat. Ann., 60-3001 et seq.
Ky. Rev. Stat. 1971, 426.950 et seq.
La. Rev. Stat. Ann., 13:4241 et seq.
Md. Ann. Code 1974, Art. CJ, § 11-801 et seq.
Me. Rev. Stat. Ann. 1964, Title 14, § 8001 et seq.
Mich. Comp. Laws. Ann., 691.1171 et seq.
Minn. Stat. Ann., 548.26 et seq.
Miss. Code Ann. 1972, 11-7-301 et seq.
Mo. Rev. Stat., 511.760
Mont. Laws 1987, Ch. 66
Neb. Laws 1993, L.B. No. 458, §§ 1 to 9
Nev. Rev. Stat. Ann., 17.330 et seq.
N.H. Rev. Stat. 1955, 524-A:1 et seq.
N.J. Stat. Ann., 2A:49A-25 et seq.
N.M. Stat. Ann., 39-4A-1 et seq.
N.Y. Civil Practice Laws and Rules (Consol. Laws, Ch. 8) § 5401 et seq.
Ohio Rev. Code 1953, 2329.021 et seq.
Okla. Stat. Ann., Title 12, § 719 et seq.
Ore. Rev. Stat. 1953, 24.105 et seq.
Pa. Cons. Stat., Title 42, § 4306
R.I. Gen. Laws 1956, 9-32-1 et seq.
S.C. Code Ann. 1976, § 15-35-900 et seq.
S.D. Codified Laws 1967, 15-16A-1 et seq.
Tenn. Code Ann., 26-6-101 et seq.
Tex. Rev. Civ. Stat., Art. 2328b-5
Utah Code Ann. 1953, 78-22al et seq.
Va. Code 1950, § 8.01-465.1 et seq.
Wash. Rev. Code Ann., 6.36.010 et seq.
Wis. Stat. Ann., 806.24
W. Va. Code 1966, § 55-14-1 et seq.
Wyo. Stat. Ann., § 1-17-701 et seq.

**Uniform Enforcement of Support Act**
See Uniform Reciprocal Enforcement of Support Act
Ark. Code Ann. 1987, 9-14-301 et seq.
Fla. Stat. Ann., 88.011 et seq.
Wyo. Stat. 1957, § 20-77 et seq.

**Uniform Environmental Permitting Act**
Okla. Stat. Ann., Title 27A, § 2-14-101 et seq.

**Uniform Estate Tax Apportionment Act**
See also Estate Tax Apportionment Act
Alaska Stat. 1962, 13.16.610
Conn. Gen. Stat. 1983, § 12-400 et seq.
Fla. Stat. Ann., 733.817
La. Rev. Stat. Ann., 9:2431 et seq.
Mass. Gen. Laws Ann., 65A:5
Md. Ann. Code 1974, Arts. ET, § 11-109; TG, § 7-308
Mich. Comp. Laws Ann., 720.11 et seq.
Miss. Code Ann. 1972, § 27-10-1 et seq.
Mont. Code Ann., 72-16-601 et seq.
Neb. Rev. Stat. 1943, 77-2108
N.H. Rev. Stat. 1955, 88-A:1 et seq.
N.J. Stat. Ann., 3B:24-1 et seq.
N.Y. Estates, Powers and Trusts Law (Consol. Laws Ch. 17B) § 2-1.8
Ohio Rev. Code 1953, 2113.85 et seq.
Okla. Stat. 1961, Title 60, § 181 et seq.
Pa. Cons. Stat., Title 20, § 3701 et seq.
R.I. Gen. Laws 1956, 44-23.1-1 et seq.
S.D. Codified Laws 1967, 29-7-1 et seq.
Va. Code 1950, § 64.1-160 et seq.
Vt. Stat. Ann., Title 32, § 7301 et seq.
Wash. Rev. Code Ann., 83.110.010 et seq.
Wyo. Stat. Ann., § 2-10-101 et seq.

**Uniform Estate Tax Apportionment Act (Revised)**
See Revised Uniform Estate Tax Apportionment Act

**Uniform Evidence Act**
Ohio Rev. Code 1953, 2317.36 et seq.

**Uniform Execution of Wills Act**
Tenn. Code Ann. 1955, 32-101 et seq.

**Uniform Exemptions Act**
Alaska Stat. 1962, § 09.38.010 et seq.

**Uniform Expert Testimony Act**
S.D. Codified Laws 1967, 19-15-1 et seq.

**Uniform Extradition Act**
Ala. Code 1975, 15-9-20 et seq.
Ariz. Rev. Stat. Ann., § 13-3841 et seq.
Cal. Penal Code § 1548 et seq.
Colo. Stat. Ann. 1935, Ch. 72
Conn. Gen. Stat. 1983, § 54-157 et seq.
D.C. Code 1973, § 23-701 et seq.
Fla. Stat. Ann., 941.01 et seq.
Ga. Code Ann., 17-13-1 et seq.
Haw. Rev. Stat. Ann., § 832-1 et seq.
Ida. Code 1947, 19-4501 et seq.
Ill. Rev. Stat. 1991, Ch. 60, § 18 et seq.
Ind. Code Ann., 35-33-10-3
Kan. Stat. Ann., 22-2701 et seq.
Me. Rev. Stat. Ann. 1964, Title 15, § 201 et seq.
Mich. Comp. Laws Ann., 780.1 et seq.
Mont. Rev. Code 1947, 94-501-1 et seq.
N.D. Cent. Code, 29-30-01 et seq.
Neb. Rev. Stat. 1943, 29-729 et seq.
N.H. Rev. Stat. 1955, 612:1 et seq.
N.Y. Criminal Procedure Law (Consol. Laws Ch. 11A) § 570.02 et seq.
Ohio Rev. Code 1953, 2963.01 et seq.
Ore. Rev. Stat., 133.743 et seq.
Pa. Cons. Stat., Title 42, § 9121 et seq.
P.R. Laws Ann. 1954, Title 34, § 1881 et seq.
R.I. Gen. Laws 1956, 12-9-1 et seq.
Tex. Code of Criminal Procedure, § 51.13
Vt. Stat. Ann., Title 13, § 4941 et seq.
Wyo. Stat Ann., § 7-3-201

**Uniform Extradition and Rendition Act**
N.D. Cent. Code, 29-30.3-01 et seq.

**Uniform Extradition of Insane Persons Act**
Wis. Stat. Ann., 51.81 et seq.

**Uniform Extradition of Witnesses Act**
Utah Code Ann. 1953, 77-33-1 et seq.

**Uniform Facsimile Signature of Public Officials Act**
Ark. Code Ann. 1987, 12-10-101 et seq.
Cal. Government Code § 5500 et seq.
Colo. Rev. Stat., 11-55-101 et seq.
Del. Code of 1974, Title 29, § 5401 et seq.
Fla. Stat. Ann., 116.34
Ida. Code 1947, 59-1018 et seq.
Ill. Rev. Stat. 1991, Ch. 102, § 61 et seq.
Kan. Stat. Ann., 75-4001 et seq.
Md. Ann. Code 1974, Art. SF, § 2-301 et seq.
Mo. Rev. Stat., 105.273 et seq.
Mont. Code Ann., 2-16-114
N.D. Cent. Code, 44-08-12 et seq.
Nev. Rev. Stat. 1979 Reprint, 351.010 et seq.
N.H. Rev. Stat. 1955, 93-A:1 et seq.
N.M. Stat. Ann., 6-9-1 et seq.
Okla. Stat. Ann., Title 62, § 601 et seq.
Pa. Purdon's Stat., Title 65, § 301 et seq.
R.I. Gen. Laws 1956, 35-11-1 et seq.
Tex. Rev. Civ. Stat., Art. 717j-1
Wash. Rev. Code Ann., 39.62.010 et seq.
W. Va. Code 1966, § 6-14-1 et seq.
Wyo. Stat. Ann., 16-2-101 et seq.

**Uniform Federal Crime Reporting Act of 1988**
Nov. 18, 1988, P.L. 100-690, 28 U.S. Code § 534 nt.

**Uniform Federal Lien Registration Act**
Ala. Code 1975, § 35-11-42 et seq.
Alaska Stat. 1962, § 40.19.010 et seq.
Ariz. Rev. Stat. Ann., § 33-1031 et seq.
Ark. Code Ann. 1987, 18-47-201 et seq.
Ark. Code 1987, 18-47-201 et seq.
Cal. Code of Civil Procedure § 2100 et seq.
Colo. Rev. Stat., 38-25-101 et seq.
Conn. Gen. Stat. 1983, § 49-32a
Fla. Stat. Ann., 713.901
Ida. Code 1947, 45-201 et seq.
Ill. Rev. Stat. 1991, Ch. 82, § 401 et seq.
Iowa Code Ann., 331.609
Kan. Stat. Ann., 79-2613 et seq.
La. Rev. Stat. Ann., 52:51 et seq.
Md. Ann. Code 1974, Art. RP, § 3-401 et seq.
Me. Rev. Stat. Ann. 1964, Title 33, § 1901 et seq.
Mich. Comp. Laws Ann., 211.661 et seq.
Minn. Stat. Ann., 272.479, 272.481 et seq.
Miss. Code Ann. 1972, § 85-8-1 et seq.
Mont. Code Ann., 71-3-201 et seq.
N.C. Gen. Stat. 1943, § 44-68.10 et seq.
N.D. Cent. Code, 35-29-01 et seq.
Nev. Rev. Stat. 1979 Reprint, 108.825 et seq.

N.H. Rev. Stat. 1955, 454-B:1 et seq.
N.M. Stat. Ann., 48-1-1 et seq.
N.Y. Civil Practice Law and Rules (Consol. Laws Ch. 8) § 5401 et seq.
N.Y. Lien Law (Consol. Laws Ch. 33) § 240 et seq.
Okla. Stat. 1981, Title 68, § 3401 et seq.
Ore. Rev. Stat., 87.806 et seq.
Pa. Purdon's Stat., Title 74, § 157-1 et seq.
S.D. Codified Laws 1967, 44-7-1 et seq.
Tex. Property Code, § 14.001 et seq.
Va. Code 1950, § 55-142.1 et seq.
Wash. Rev. Code Ann., 60.68.005 et seq.
Wis. Stat. Ann., 779.97
Wyo. Stat. Ann., § 29-6-201 et seq.

**Uniform Federal Tax Lien Registration Act**
Ariz. Rev. Stat. Ann., § 11-485 et seq.
Colo. Rev. Stat., 38-25-101 et seq.
Conn. Gen. Stat. 1983, § 49-32a
Del. Code of 1974, Title 25, § 4801 et seq.
Ga. Code Ann., 44-14-570 et seq.
Iowa Code Ann., 331.609
Kan. Stat. Ann., 79-2608 et seq.
Ky. Rev. Stat. 1971, 382.480 et seq.
La. Rev. Stat. Ann., 52:51 et seq.
Minn. Stat. Ann., 272.479 et seq.
N.C. Gen. Stat. 1943, 44-68.1 et seq.
Neb. Rev. Stat. 1943, 52-1001 et seq.
N.H. Rev. Stat. Ann. 1955, § 48-1-1 et seq.
Okla. Stat. Ann., Title 68 § 24300 et seq.
S.C. Code Ann. 1976, § 12-57-10 et seq.
S.D. Codified Laws 1967, 44-7-1 et seq.
Tex. Tax Code, § 113.201 et seq.
Va. Code 1950, § 55-142.1 et seq.

**Uniform Federal Tax Lien Registration Act (Revised)**
See Revised Uniform Federal Tax Lien Registration Act

**Uniform Federal Voting Rights Compliance Act**
N.M. Stat. Ann., 1-21-1 et seq.

**Uniform Fiduciaries Act**
May 14, 1928, Ch. 545, 45 Stat. 509

**Uniform Fiduciary Act**
See also Fiduciaries Act
Ala. Code 1975, § 19-1-1 et seq.
Ariz. Rev. Stat. Ann., § 14-7501 et seq.
Colo. Rev. Stat., 15-1-101 et seq.
D.C. Code 1973, § 21-1701 et seq.
Haw. Rev. Stat. Ann., § 556-1 et seq.
Ida. Code 1947, 68-301 et seq.
Ill. Rev. Stat. 1991, Ch. 17, § 2001 et seq.
Ind. Code Ann., 30-2-4-1 et seq.
La. Rev. Stat. Ann., 9:3801 et seq.
Md. Ann. Code 1974, Art. ET, § 15-201 et seq.
Minn. Stat. Ann., 520.01 et seq.
Mo. Rev. Stat., 456.240 et seq.
N.C. Gen. Stat. 1943, § 32-1 et seq.
Nev. Rev. Stat. 1979 Reprint, 162.010 et seq.
N.J. Stat. Ann., 3B:14-52 et seq.
N.M. Stat. Ann., 46-1-1 et seq.
Ohio Rev. Code 1953, 1339.03 et seq.
Pa. Purdon's Stat., Title 7, § 6351 et seq.
R.I. Gen. Laws 1956, 18-4-15 et seq.
S.D. Codified Laws 1967, 55-7-2 et seq.
Tenn. Code Ann., 35-2-101 et seq.
Utah Code Ann. 1953, 22-1-1 et seq.
Wis. Stat. Ann., 112.01
Wyo. Stat. Ann., § 2-3-201 et seq.

**Uniform Film Permit Act**
Cal. Government Code § 14999.30 et seq.

**Uniform Fire Prevention and Building Code Act**
N.Y. Executive Law 1951 (Consol. Laws Ch. 18) § 370 et seq.

**Uniform Fire Safety Act**
N.J. Stat. 52:27D-192 et seq.

**Uniform Firearms Act**
Ala. Code 1975, § 13A-11-50 et seq.
Cal. Penal Code § 12000 et seq.
Ind. Code Ann., 35-47-1-1 et seq.
Mich. Comp. Laws Ann., 28.421 et seq., 750.222 et seq.
Okla. Stat. Ann., Title 21, § 1289.1 et seq.
Ore. Rev. Stat. 1953, 166.180 et seq.
Pa. Cons. Stat., Title 18, § 6101 et seq.
R.I. Gen. Laws 1956, 11-47-1 et seq.
*Continued*

S.D. Codified Laws 1967, 23-7-3 et seq.
Wash. Rev. Code Ann., 9.41.010 et seq.

**Uniform Firearms Act (Joe Carlucci)**
Fla. Stat. Ann., 790.33

**Uniform Fiscal Procedures Act for Cities, Counties and Towns**
Utah Code Ann. 1953, 10-5-101 et seq., 10-6-101 et seq., 17-36-1 et seq.

**Uniform Fiscal Procedures for Special Districts Act**
Utah Code Ann. 1953, 17A-1-401 et seq.

**Uniform Flag Act**
Ariz. Rev. Stat. Ann. 1956, § 41-853
Del. Code of 1953, Title 11, § 531 et seq.
La. Rev. Stat. Ann., 14:116, 14:117
Md. Ann. Code 1957, Art. 27, § 81 et seq.
Me. Rev. Stat. Ann. 1964, Title 1, § 251 et seq.
Mich. Comp. Laws Ann., 750.244 et seq.
Miss. Code Ann. 1972, § 97-7-39
N.Y. General Business Law (Consol. Laws Ch. 20), § 136
Pa. Cons. Stat., Title 18, § 2102
S.D. Codified Laws 1967, 22-9-1
Tenn. Code Ann., 39-5-841 et seq.
Va. Code 1950, § 18.2-486 et seq.
Vt. Stat. Ann., Title 13, § 1901 et seq.
Wash. Rev. Code Ann., 9.86.010 et seq.

**Uniform Flag Act (Exhibition or Display)**
N.Y. General Business Law (Consol. Laws Ch. 20) § 136

**Uniform Fluid Milk Act**
Wash. Rev. Code Ann., 15.36.005 et seq.

**Uniform Food Act**
Ill. Rev. Stat. 1991, Ch. 56 1/2, § 401 et seq.

**Uniform Food, Drug and Cosmetic Act**
Conn. Gen. Stat. 1983, § 21a-91 et seq.
Ind. Code Ann., 16-1-28-1 et seq.
Wash. Rev. Code Ann., 69.04.001 et seq.

**Uniform Foreign Depositions Act**
See also Foreign Depositions Act
Alaska Laws 1923, Ch. 13
Cal. Code of Civil Procedure § 2036a
Fla. Stat. Ann., 92.251
Ga. Code Ann., 24-10-110 et seq.
La. Rev. Stat. Ann., 13:3821, 13:3822
Md. Ann. Code 1974, Art. CJ, § 9-401 et seq.
Mich. Comp. Laws 1948, 691.631 et seq.
Neb. Rev. Stat. 1943, 25-1267.18
Nev. Rev. Stat. 1979 Reprint, 53.050 et seq.
Ohio Rev. Code 1953, 2329.09 et seq.
Okla. Stat. Ann., Title 12, § 719 et seq.
Ore. Rev. Stat., 45.250
Pa. Cons. Stat., Title 42, § 5326 et seq.
S.D. Codified Laws 1967, 19-5-4
Tenn. Code Ann., 24-9-103
Va. Code 1950, § 8.01-411 et seq.
Wyo. Stat. 1957, § 1-157 et seq.

**Uniform Foreign Depositions Law**
N.H. Rev. Stat. 1955, 17-A:1 et seq.

**Uniform Foreign Executed Wills Act**
Kan. Stat. Ann., 59-609
La. Rev. Stat. Ann., 9:2401
Mass. Gen. Laws Ann., 191:5
Minn. Stat. Ann., 524.4-101 et seq.
N.Y. Decedent Estate Law (Consol. Laws Ch. 13) § 22a
Wis. Stat. Ann., 853.05

**Uniform Foreign Law Evidence Act**
Pa. Cons. Stat., Title 42, § 5327

**Uniform Foreign Money Claims Act**
Cal. Code of Civil Procedure § 676 et seq.
Colo. Rev. Stat., 13-62.1-101 et seq.
Conn. Gen. Stat. 1983, § 50a-51 et seq.
Haw. Rev. Stat. Ann., § 658B-1 et seq.
Ill. Rev. Stat. 1991, Ch. 110, § 12-630 et seq.
Minn. Stat. Ann., 548.40 et seq.
N.D. Cent. Code, 32-41-01 et seq.
N.M. Stat. Ann., 39-4C-1 et seq.
Ore. Laws 1991, Ch. 202
Utah Code Ann. 1953, 78-22b-101 et seq.
Va. Code 1950, § 8.01-465.14 et seq.
Wash. Rev. Code Ann., 6.44.010 et seq.

**Uniform Foreign-Money Claims Act**
Mont. Code Ann., 25-9-701 et seq.
Nev. Stat. 1993., Ch. 113, p. 193

N.J. Stat. Ann., 2A:49A-1 et seq.
Okla. Stat. Ann., Title 12, § 729.1

**Uniform Foreign Money Judgments Recognition Act**
Alaska Stat. 1962, § 09.30.100 et seq.
Cal. Code of Civil Procedure § 1713 et seq.
Colo. Rev. Stat., 13-62.1-101 et seq.
Conn. Gen. Stat. 1983, § 52-610 et seq.
Fla. Stat. Ann., 55.601 to 55.607*
Ga. Code Ann., 9-12-110 et seq.
Haw. Session Laws 1996, Act 49
Ida. Code 1947, 10-1401 et seq.
Ill. Rev. Stat. 1991, Ch. 110, § 12-618 et seq.
Iowa Code Ann., 626B.1 et seq.
Mass. Gen. Laws Ann., 235:23A
Md. Ann. Code 1974, Art. CJ, § 10-701 et seq.
Me. Rev. Stat. Ann. 1964, Title 14, § 8501 et seq.
Mich. Comp. Laws Ann., 691.1151 et seq.
Minn. Stat. Ann., 548.35
Mo. Rev. Stat., 511.770 et seq.
Mont. Code Ann., 25-9-601 et seq.
N.M. Stat. Ann., 39-4B-1 et seq.
N.Y. Civil Practice Laws and Rules (Consol. Laws Ch. 8) § 5301 et seq.
Ohio Rev. Code 1953, 2329.90 et seq.
Okla. Stat. Ann., Title 12, § 710 et seq.
Ore. Rev. Stat., 24.200 et seq.
Pa. Purdon's Stat., Title 42, § 22001 et seq.
Tex. Civ. Practice and Remedies Code, § 36.001 et seq.
Va. Code 1950, 8.01-465.6 et seq.
Wash. Rev. Code Ann., 6.40.010 et seq.

**Uniform Foreign Probate Act**
Ill. Rev. Stat. 1991, Ch. 110 1/2, § 7-1 et seq.
Wyo. Stat. Ann., § 2-11-101 et seq.

**Uniform Foreign Probated Wills Act**
La. Rev. Stat. Ann., 9:2421 et seq.

**Uniform Fraternal Act**
N.H. Rev. Stat. 1955, 418:1 et seq.

**Uniform Fraudulent Conveyance Act**
Ala. Code 1975, § 8-9A-1 et seq.
Ariz. Rev. Stat. Ann., § 44-1001 et seq.
Cal. Civil Code § 3439 et seq.
Colo. Rev. Stat., 38-8-101 et seq.
Conn. Public Acts 1991, No. 297
Del. Code of 1974, Title 6, § 1301 et seq.
Fla. Stat. Ann., 726.101 et seq.
Haw. Rev. Stat. Ann., § 651c-1 et seq.
Ida. Code 1947, 55-910 et seq.
Ill. Rev. Stat. 1991, Ch. 59, § 101 et seq.
Mass. Gen. Laws Ann., 109A:1 et seq.
Md. Ann. Code 1974, Art. CL, § 15-101 et seq.
Me. Rev. Stat. Ann. 1964, Title 14, § 3571 et seq.
Mich. Comp. Laws Ann., 566.11 et seq.
Minn. Stat. Ann., 513.20 et seq.
Mont. Code Ann., 31-2-301 et seq.
N.D. Cent. Code, 13-02.1-01 et seq.
Neb. Rev. Stat. 1943, 36-601 et seq.
Nev. Rev. Stat. Ann., 112.140 et seq.
N.H. Rev. Stat. 1955, 545:1 et seq.
N.J. Stat. Ann., 25:2-7 et seq.
N.M. Stat. Ann., 56-10-1 et seq.
N.Y. Debtor and Creditor Law (Consol. Laws Ch. 12) § 270 et seq.
Ohio Rev. Code 1953, 1336.01 et seq.
Okla. Stat. Ann., Title 24, § 101 et seq.
Ore. Rev. Stat., 95.200 et seq.
Pa. Purdon's Stat., Title 39, § 351 et seq.
R.I. Gen. Laws 1956, 6-16-1 et seq.
S.D. Codified Laws 1967, 54-8-1 et seq.
Tenn. Code Ann., 66-3-301 et seq.
Tex. Business and Commerce Code, § 24-001 et seq.
Utah Code Ann. 1953, 6-1-2 et seq.
Wash. Rev. Code Ann., 19.40.011 et seq.
Wis. Stat. Ann., 242.01 et seq.
W. Va. Code 1966, § 40-1A-1 et seq.
Wyo. Stat. Ann., § 34-14-101 et seq.

**Uniform Fraudulent Transfer Act**
Colo. Rev. Stat., 38-8-101 et seq.
Conn. Gen. Stat. 1983, § 52-552a et seq.
Ga. Code Ann., 18-2-70 et seq.
Iowa Code Ann., 684.1 et seq.
Mass. Gen. Laws Ann., 109A:1 et seq.
Pa. Cons. Stat., Title 12, § 5101 et seq.

**Uniform Fresh Pursuit Act**
Ark. Code Ann. 1987, 16-81-401 et seq.
Cal. Penal Code § 852 et seq.
*Continued*

Colo. Rev. Stat., 16-3-104, Subd. 2
D.C. Code Ann., § 23-901 et seq.
Del. Code of 1974, Title 11, § 1931 et seq.
Fla. Stat. Ann., 941.31 et seq.
Ida. Code 1947, 19-701 et seq.
Ind. Code Ann., 35-33-3-1 et seq.
Iowa Code Ann., 806.1 et seq.
Kan. Stat. Ann., 22-2404
La. Code of Crim. Proc. 1966, Arts. 231, 232
Md. Ann. Code 1957, Art. 27, § 595 et seq.
Me. Rev. Stat. Ann. 1964, Title 15, § 151 et seq.
Mich. Comp. Laws Ann., 780.100 et seq.
Minn. Stat. Ann., 626.65 et seq.
Mo. Rev. Stat., 544.155
Neb. Rev. Stat. 1943, 29-416 et seq.
Nev. Rev. Stat. 1979 Reprint, 171.154 et seq.
N.H. Rev. Stat. 1955, 614:1 et seq.
N.J. Stat. Ann., 2A:155-1 et seq.
S.D. Codified Laws 1967, 23A-3-9 et seq.

**Uniform Gifts to Minors Act**
See also Gifts to Minors Act
Ala. Code 1975, § 35-5A-1 et seq.
Alaska Stat. 1962, § 45.60.011 et seq.
Ariz. Rev. Stat. Ann., § 44-2071 et seq.
Ark. Stat. 1947, 50-901 et seq.
Cal. Civil Code § 1154 et seq.
Colo. Rev. Stat., 11-50-101 et seq.
Conn. Gen. Stat. 1983, § 45-101 et seq.
D.C. Code Ann., § 21-301 et seq.
Del. Code of 1974, Title 12, § 4501 et seq.
Fla. Stat. Ann., 710.101 et seq.
Ga. Code Ann., 44-5-113 et seq.
Haw. Rev. Stat. Ann., § 553-1 et seq.
Ida. Code 1947, 68-801 et seq.
Ill. Rev. Stat. 1985, Ch. 110 1/2, § 201 et seq.
Ind. Code Ann., 30-2-8-1 et seq.
Iowa Code 1985, 565A.1 et seq.
Kan. Stat. Ann., 38-901 et seq.
Ky. Rev. Stat. 1971, 385.011 et seq.
La. Rev. Stat. Ann., 9:735 et seq.
Mass. Gen. Laws Ann., 201A:1 et seq.
Md. Ann. Code 1974, Art. ET, § 13-301 et seq.
Me. Rev. Stat. Ann. 1964, Title 33, § 1001 et seq.
Mich. Comp. Laws Ann., 554.451 et seq.
Minn. Stat. Ann., 527.01 et seq.
Miss. Code Ann. 1972, § 91-19-1 et seq.
Mo. Rev. Stat., 404.005 et seq.
Mont. Code Ann. 1985, 72-26-101 et seq.
N.C. Gen. Stat. 1943, § 33-68 et seq.
N.D. Cent. Code, 47-24-01 et seq.
Neb. Rev. Stat. 1943, 38-1001 et seq.
Nev. Rev. Stat. 1979 Reprint, 167.010 et seq.
N.H. Rev. Stat. 1955, 463-A:1 et seq.
N.J. Rev. Stat. 1937, 46:38-13 et seq.
N.M. Stat. Ann., 46-7-1 et seq.
N.Y. Estates, Powers and Trusts Law (Consol. Laws Ch. 17B) § 7-4.1 et seq.
Ohio Rev. Code 1953, 1339.31 et seq.
Okla. Stat. Ann., Title 60, § 401 et seq.
Ore. Rev. Stat., 126.805 et seq.
Pa. Cons. Stat., Title 20, § 5301 et seq.
R.I. Gen. Laws 1956, § 18-7-1 et seq.
S.C. Code Ann. 1976, § 20-7-140 et seq.
S.D. Codified Laws 1967, 55-10A-1 et seq.
Tenn. Code Ann., 35-7-101 et seq.
Tex. Property Code, § 141.001 et seq.
Utah Code Ann. 1953, 75-5-601 et seq.
Va. Code 1950, § 31-26 et seq.
Vt. Stat. Ann., Title 14, § 3201 et seq.
Wash. Rev. Code Ann., 21.24.010 et seq.
Wis. Stat. Ann., 880.61 et seq.
W. Va. Code 1966, § 36-7-1 et seq.
Wyo. Stat. Ann., § 34-13-101 et seq.

**Uniform Grant and Contract Management Act**
Tex. Government Code, § 783.001 et seq.

**Uniform Group Benefits Act (Political Subdivision Employees)**
Tex. Local Government Code, § 172.001 et seq.

**Uniform Guardianship Act (Veterans and Infant Wards)**
N.Y. Mental Hygiene Law 1972 (Consol. Laws Ch. 27) § 79.01 et seq.

**Uniform Guardianship and Protective Proceedings Act**
Ala. Code 1975, § 26-2A-1 et seq.
Colo. Rev. Stat., §§ 15-10-102, 15-14-201 et seq.
D.C. Code Ann., § 21-2001 et seq.

Haw. Rev. Stat. Ann., § 560:5-101 et seq.

Ida. Code 1947, § 15-5-101 et seq.

Me. Rev. Stat. Ann. 1964, Title 18-A, § 5-101 et seq.

Mich. Comp. Laws Ann., § 700.401 et seq.

Mont. Code Ann., 72-5-101 et seq.

N.D. Cent. Code, 30.1-26-01

Neb. Rev. Stat. 1943, § 30-2601 et seq.

N.M. Stat. Ann., 45-5-101 et seq.

S.C. Code Ann. 1976, § 62-5-101 et seq.

Utah Code Ann. 1953, 75-5-101 et seq.

**Uniform Hazardous Substances Labeling Act**

Ill. Rev. Stat. 1991, Ch. 111 1/2, § 251 et seq.

Me. Rev. Stat. Ann. 1964, Title 7, § 501 et seq.

**Uniform Health and Accident Law (Insurance Policies)**

Ark. Stat. 1947, 66-531 et seq.

**Uniform Health Care Decisions Act**

Me. Rev. Stat. Ann. 1964, Title 18-A, § 5-801 et seq.

Miss. Code Ann. 1972, §§ 41-41-201 to 41-41-229

N.M. Laws 1995, Ch. 182

**Uniform Health Care Information Act**

Mont. Code Ann., 15-16-101 et seq.

Wash. Rev. Code Ann., 70.02.005 et seq.

**Uniform Health Policy Provisions Act**

Ky. Rev. Stat. 1971, 304.17-010 et seq.

Me. Rev. Stat. Ann. 1964, Title 24-A, § 2701 et seq.

Nev. Rev. Stat. 1979 Reprint, 689A.010 et seq.

**Uniform Highway Traffic Regulation Act**

Kan. Stat. Ann., 8-1401 et seq.

Minn. Stat. Ann., 169.01 et seq.

**Uniform Highway Traffic Regulation Act—Equipment and Identification Regulations**

Miss. Code Ann. 1972, § 63-7-1 et seq.

**Uniform Highway Traffic Regulation Act—Rules of the Road**

Miss. Code Ann. 1972, § 63-3-1 et seq.

**Uniform Highway Traffic Regulation Act—Size, Weight and Load Regulations**

Miss. Code Ann. 1972, § 63-5-1 et seq.

**Uniform Highway Traffic Regulation Act—Traffic Violations Procedure**

Miss. Code Ann. 1972, § 63-9-1 et seq.

**Uniform Illegitimacy Act**

Iowa Code Ann., 675.1 et seq.

Nev. Rev. Stat. 1979 Reprint, 126.010 et seq.

N.M. Stat. Ann., 40-11-1 et seq.

S.D. Codified Laws 1967, 25-8-1 et seq.

Wyo. Stat. 1957, § 14-59 et seq.

**Uniform Income and Principal Act**

Ariz. Rev. Stat. Ann., § 14-7401 et seq.

Minn. Stat. Ann., 501B.59 et seq.

**Uniform Individual Accident and Health Insurance Minimum Standards Act**

Iowa Code Ann., 514D.1 et seq.

**Uniform Individual Accident and Sickness Act**

Iowa Code Ann., 514A.1 et seq.

**Uniform Individual Accident and Sickness Insurance Act**

Mo. Rev. Stat., 376.770 et seq.

**Uniform Individual Accident and Sickness Policy Provisions Act**

Cal. Insurance Code § 10320 et seq.

**Uniform Information Practices Act (Modified)**

Haw. Rev. Stat. Ann., § 92F-1 et seq.

**Uniform Insurance Benefits Act for College and University Employees**

Tex. Insurance Code, Art. 3.50-3

**Uniform Insurer's Liquidation Act**

Kan. Stat. Ann., 40-2605 et seq.

Md. Ann. Code 1974, Art. IN, § 9-101 et seq.

Me. Rev. Stat. Ann. 1964, Title 24-A, § 4363 et seq.

*Continued*

R.I. Gen. Laws 1956, 27-14.4-1 et seq.

**Uniform Insurers Liquidation Act**
Ala. Code 1975, § 27-32-1 et seq.
Alaska Stat. 1962, § 21.78.200 et seq.
Ariz. Rev. Stat. Ann., § 20-611 et seq.
Ark. Code Ann. 1987, 23-68-102, 23-68-104, 23-68-105, 23-68-113 et seq.
Cal. Insurance Code § 1064.1 et seq.
Colo. Rev. Stat., 10-3-501 et seq.
Del. Code of 1974, Title 18, §§ 5901 et seq., 5913 et seq.
Fla. Stat. Ann., 631.011, 631.031, 631.041, 631.141
Ga. Code Ann., 33-37-40 et seq.
Haw. Rev. Stat. Ann., § 431-661 et seq.
Ida. Code 1947, 41-3-301 et seq.
Ill. Rev. Stat. 1991, Ch. 73, § 833.1 et seq.
Ky. Rev. Stat. 1962, 304.960 et seq.
La. Rev. Stat. Ann., 22:757 et seq.
Mass. Gen. Laws Ann., 175:180A et seq.
Mich. Comp. Laws Ann., 500.7836 et seq.
Minn. Stat. Ann., 608.01 et seq.
Mo. Rev. Stat., 375.950 et seq.
Mont. Code Ann., 33-2-1301 et seq.
Mont. Rev. Code 1947, 40-5101, 40-5103, 40-5104, 40-5114 et seq.
N.C. Gen. Stat. 1943, Miscellaneous Superseded Code Provisions, § 58-155.10 et seq.
Nev. Rev. Stat. Ann., 696B.280 et seq.
N.J. Stat. Ann., 17:30C-1, 17:30C-4, 17:30C-5, 17:30C-15 et seq., 17B:32-1, 17B:32-4, 17B:32-5, 17B:32-15 et seq.
N.M. Stat. Ann., 59A-41-17 et seq.
N.Y. Insurance Law (Consol. Laws Ch. 28) § 7408 et seq.
Ohio Rev. Code 1953, 3903.01 et seq.
Okla. Stat. Ann., Title 36, § 1901 et seq.
Ore. Rev. Stat., 734.018, 734.030 et seq., 734.240 et seq.
P.R. Laws Ann. 1954, Title 26, § 4007 et seq.
S.D. Codified Laws 1967, 58-29-1 et seq.
Tenn. Code Ann., 56-9-101, 56-9-102, 56-9-104, 56-9-105, 56-9-115
Utah Code Ann. 1953, 31A-27-101 et seq.
Wash. Rev. Code Ann., 48.31.110 et seq.
Wis. Stat. Ann., 645.01 et seq.
W. Va. Code 1966, §§ 33-10-1, 33-10-3, 33-10-4, 33-10-14 et seq.
Wyo. Stat. Ann., § 26-28-101 et seq.

**Uniform International Wills Act**
Cal. Probate Code § 6380 et seq.
Colo. Rev. Stat., 15-11-1001 et seq.
Ill. Rev. Stat. 1991, Ch. 110 1/2, § 50 et seq.
Ore. Rev. Stat., 112.232

**Uniform Interparty Agreement Act**
Md. Ann. Code 1957, Art. 50, § 10 et seq.
Md. Ann. Code 1974, Art. CL, § 20-101 et seq.
Nev. Rev. Stat. 1979 Reprint, 102.010 et seq.
Pa. Purdon's Stat., Title 69, § 541 et seq.
Utah Code Ann. 1953, 15-3-1 et seq.

**Uniform Interstate Air Pollution Agreements Act**
Pa. Purdon's Stat., Title 35, § 4101 et seq.

**Uniform Interstate and International Procedure Act**
Ark. Code Ann. 1987, 16-4-108 et seq.
D.C. Code Ann., § 13-401 et seq.
Mass. Gen. Laws Ann., 223A:1 et seq.
Mich. Comp. Laws Ann., 600.1852, 600.2114a, 600.2118a
Okla. Stat. Ann., Title 12, § 1701.01 et seq.
Pa. Cons. Stat., Title 42, § 5321 et seq.

**Uniform Interstate Arbitration and Compromise of Death Taxes Act**
Cal. Revenue and Taxation Code § 13820 et seq.
Colo. Rev. Stat., 39-24-101 et seq.
Conn. Gen. Stat. 1983, § 12-372 et seq.
Mass. Gen. Laws Ann., 65B:1 et seq.
Md. Ann. Code 1974, Art. TG, § 7-104 et seq.
Me. Rev. Stat. Ann. 1964, Title 36, § 3911 et seq.
Mich. Comp. Laws Ann., 205.601 et seq.
Minn. Stat. Ann., 291.41 et seq.
Neb. Rev. Stat. 1943, 291.41 et seq.
N.H. Rev. Stat. 1955, 86:71
N.J. Stat. Ann., 54:38A-1, 54:38A-2
N.Y. Tax Laws (Consol. Laws Ch. 60) § 978
Pa. Cons. Stat., Title 72, § 1701 et seq.
S.C. Code Ann. 1976, § 12-16-210
Tenn. Code Ann., 67-8-501 et seq.

Va. Code 1950, § 58-217.1 et seq.
Vt. Stat. Ann., Title 32, § 7101 et seq.
Wis. Stat. Ann., 72.35
W. Va. Code 1966, § 11-11B-1 et seq.

**Uniform Interstate Arbitration of Death Taxes Act**
Me. Rev. Stat. Ann. 1964, Title 36, § 3711 et seq.

**Uniform Interstate Compact on Juveniles**
Me. Rev. Stat. Ann. 1964, Title 34-A, § 9001 et seq.
Miss. Code Ann. 1972, § 43-25-1 et seq.

**Uniform Interstate Compact on Juveniles Act**
Alaska Stat. 1962, § 47.15.010 et seq.
Ind. Code Ann., 31-6-10-1 et seq.
Tex. Family Code, § 25.01 et seq.

**Uniform Interstate Family Support Act**
Ala. Code 1975, § 30-3A-101 et seq.
Alaska Stat. 1962, § 25.25.101 et seq.
Ariz. Rev. Stat. Ann., § 12-1751 et seq.
Cal. Family Code § 4900 et seq.
Del. Code of 1974, Title 13, § 601 et seq.
Fla. Stat. Ann., 88.0011 et seq.
Haw. Rev. Stat. Ann., § 576B-101 et seq.
Ida. Code 1947, 7-1001 et seq.
Ill. Comp. Stat. 1992, Ch. 750, § 22/100
Ind. Code 1982, 31-18-9-1 et seq.
Iowa Code Ann., 252K.901 to 252K.904
Kan. Stat. Ann., 23-9,101 et seq.
Md. Ann. Code 1974, Art. FL, § 10-301 et seq.
Me. Rev. Stat. Ann. 1964, Title 19-A, § 2801 et seq.
Mich. Comp. Laws. Ann., 552.1101 et seq.
Minn. Stat. Ann., 518C.902
Miss. Code Ann. 1972, §§ 93-25-1 to 93-25-117
Mo. Rev. Stat., 454.850 to 454.997
Mont. Code Ann., 40-5-101 et seq.
Neb. Rev. Stat. 1943, 42-701 et seq.
N.H. Rev. Stat. 1955, 546-B:58
N.J. Stat. Ann., 2A:4-30.65
N.M. Stat. Ann., 40-6A-902 et seq.
N.Y. Family Court Act, § 580-101 et seq.
Okla. Stat. Ann., Title 43, § 601-101 et seq.
Ore. Laws 1993, Ch. 449
Pa. Cons. Stat., Title 23, § 7171 et seq.
S.C. Code Ann. 1976, § 20-7-960 et seq.
Tex. Family Code, § 21.01 et seq.
Va. Code 1950, §§ 20-88.32 to 20-88.82
Vt. Stat. Ann., Title 15B, § 101 et seq.
Wash. Rev. Code Ann., 26.21.005 et seq.
Wis. Stat. Ann., 769.101 et seq.
W. Va. Code 1966, § 48B-9-901 et seq.
Wyo. Stat.Ann., §§ 20-4-139 to 20-4-189

**Uniform Intrastate Family Support Act**
Pa. Cons. Stat., Title 23, § 8101 et seq.

**Uniform Joint Obligations Act**
Haw. Rev. Stat. Ann., § 483-1 et seq.
Me. Rev. Stat. Ann. 1964, Title 14, § 11 et seq.
Nev. Rev. Stat. 1979 Reprint, 101.010 et seq.
N.Y. General Obligations Law (Consol. Laws Ch. 24A) § 15-101 et seq.
Utah Code Ann. 1953, 15-4-1 et seq.
Wis. Stat. Ann., 113.01 et seq.

**Uniform Joint Tortfeasors Act**
Ark. Acts 1941, p. 188, No. 315

**Uniform Judicial Notice of Foreign Law Act**
Colo. Rev. Stat., 13-25-106
Del. Code of 1974, Title 10, §§ 4312, 4313
Fla. Stat. Ann., 90.201 et seq.
Haw. Rev. Stat. Ann., § 623-1 et seq.
Ill. Rev. Stat. 1991, Ch. 110, § 8-1003 et seq.
Ind. Code Ann., 34-3-2-1 et seq.
Ind. Code 1982, 34-38-4-1 et seq.
Kan. Stat. Ann., 60-409
Ky. Rev. Stat. 1971, 422.081 et seq.
La. Code of Civil Procedure Art. 1391
Md. Ann. Code 1974, Art. CJ, § 10-501 et seq.
Me. Rev. Stat. Ann. 1964, Title 16, § 401 et seq.
Minn. Stat. Ann., 599.04 et seq.
Mo. Rev. Stat., 490.070 et seq.
Mont. Rev. Code 1991, 93-501-1 et seq.
N.D. Cent. Code, 31-10-03 et seq.
Neb. Rev. Stat. 1943, 25-12.101 to 25-12.107
N.J. Stat. Ann., 2A:82-27 et seq.
Ohio Civ. Rule 44.1
*Continued*

Okla. Stat. 1981, Title 12, § 2201 et seq.
Ore. Rev. Stat. 1953, 41.420 et seq.
Pa. Cons. Stat., Title 42, § 5327
R.I. Gen. Laws 1956, 9-19-2 et seq.
S.C. Code Ann. 1976, § 19-3-110 et seq.
S.D. Codified Laws 1967, 19-8-1 et seq.
Tenn. Code Ann., 24-6-201 et seq.
Wash. Rev. Code Ann., 5.24.010 et seq.
Wis. Stat. Ann., 902.02
Wyo. Stat. Ann., § 1-12-301 et seq.

**Uniform Jury Law (Counties over One Million)**
N.Y. Judiciary Law (Consol. Laws Ch. 30) § 500 et seq.

**Uniform Jury Selection and Service Act**
Colo. Rev. Stat., 13-71-101 et seq.
Haw. Rev. Stat. Ann., § 612-1 et seq.
Ida. Code 1947, 2-201 et seq.
Ind. Code Ann., 33-4-5.5-1 et seq.
Me. Rev. Stat. Ann. 1964, Title 14, § 1211 et seq.
Minn. Stat. Ann., § 593.31 et seq.
Miss. Code Ann. 1972, 13-5-2 et seq.
N.D. Cent. Code, 27-09.1-01 et seq.

**Uniform Justice Court Act**
N.Y. Uniform Justice Court Act, § 101 et seq.

**Uniform Juvenile Court Act**
Ga. Code Ann., 15-11-1 et seq.
N.D. Cent. Code, 27-20-01 et seq.
Pa. Cons. Stat., Title 42, § 6301 et seq.

**Uniform Land and Timeshare Sales Practices Act**
Utah Code Ann. 1953, 57-11-1 et seq.

**Uniform Land Registration Act**
Va. Code 1950, § 55-112

**Uniform Land Sales Practices Act**
Alaska Stat. 1962, § 34.55.004 et seq.
Conn. Gen. Stat. 1983, § 20-329a et seq.
Fla. Stat. Ann., 489.001 et seq.
Haw. Rev. Stat. Ann., § 484-1 et seq.
Ida. Code 1947, 55-1801 et seq.
Kan. Stat. Ann., 58-3301 et seq.
Minn. Stat. Ann., 83.20 et seq.
Mont. Rev. Code 1991, 76-4-1201 et seq.
S.C. Code Ann. 1976, § 27-29-10 et seq.
Utah Code Ann. 1953, 57-11-1 et seq.

**Uniform Law Commissioners' Model Class Actions Act**
Iowa Rules of Civil Procedure, Rule 42.1 et seq.
N.D. Rules of Civil Procedure, Rule 23

**Uniform Law Commissioners' Model Eminent Domain Code**
Ala. Code 1975, § 18-1A-1 et seq.

**Uniform Law Commissioners' Model Healthcare Consent Act**
Ind. Code Ann., 16-8-12-1 et seq.

**Uniform Law Commissioners' Model Joint Obligations Act**
Haw. Rev. Stat. Ann., 483-1 et seq.
Me. Rev. Stat. Ann. 1964, Title 14, § 11 et seq.
Nev. Rev. Stat. 1979 Reprint, 101.010 et seq.
N.Y. General Obligations Law (Consol. Laws Ch. 23A) 15-101 et seq.
Utah Code Ann. 1953, 15-4-1 et seq.
Wis. Stat. Ann., 113.01 et seq.

**Uniform Law for Out-of-State Probation and Parole Supervision**
Fla. Stat. Ann., 949.07 et seq.

**Uniform Law for Transporting of Dangerous Articles by Motor Vehicle**
Pa. 1959 Pamph. Laws 58, No. 32, § 1117

**Uniform Law on Notarial Acts**
D.C. Code Ann., § 45-621 et seq.
Del. Code of 1974, Title 29, § 4321 et seq.
Iowa Code Ann., 77A.1 et seq.
Kan. Stat. Ann., 53-501 et seq.
Minn. Stat. Ann., 358.41 et seq.
Mont. Code Ann., 1-5-601 et seq.
Nev. Stat.s 1993, Ch. 115, p. 200, §§ 1 to 18
N.M. Stat. Ann., 14-14-11 et seq.
Okla. Stat. 1981, Title 49, § 111 et seq.
Ore. Rev. Stat., 194.505 et seq.
Wis. Stat. Ann., 706.07

**Uniform Law on Paternity**
Miss. Code Ann. 1972, § 93-9-1 et seq.
R.I. Gen. Laws 1956, 15-8-1 et seq.

**Uniform Laws Commission Act**
Ark. Code Ann. 1987, 6-401 et seq.
Cal. Government Code § 10400 et seq.

**Uniform Licensing Act**
N.M. Stat. Ann., 61-1-1 et seq.

**Uniform Licensing Law**
Neb. Rev. Stat. 1943, 71-101 et seq.

**Uniform Licensure Law**
Neb. Rev. Stat. 1943, 71-101 et seq.

**Uniform Limited Liability Company Act**
Haw. Rev. Stat. Ann., § 428-101 et seq.
S.C. Code Ann. 1976, § 33-44-101 et seq.
W. Va. Code 1966, § 31B-12-1201 et seq.

**Uniform Limited Partnership Act**
Alaska Stat. 1962, § 32.11.010 et seq.
Ariz. Rev. Stat. Ann., § 29-301 et seq.
Cal. Corporations Code §§ 15001 et seq., 15611 et seq.
Colo. Rev. Stat., 7-62-101 et seq.
Fla. Stat. Ann., 620.101 et seq.
Haw. Rev. Stat. Ann., § 425D to 1101 et seq.
Haw. Rev. Stat. Ann., 425D-101 et seq.
Ill. Rev. Stat. 1991, Ch. 106 1/2, § 151-1 et seq.
Kan. Stat. Ann., 56-1a01 et seq.
Mass. Acts 1932, Ch. 109
Mich. Comp. Laws. Ann., 449.1101 et seq.
Minn. Stat. Ann., 322A.01 et seq.
Miss. Code Ann. 1972, § 79-13-1 et seq.
Mont. Code Ann. 1987, 35-12-101 et seq.
N.D. Cent. Code, 45-10-01 et seq.
Neb. Rev. Stat. 1943, 67-201 et seq.
N.H. Rev. Stat. 1955, 304-B:1 et seq.
N.J. Stat. Ann., 42:2A-1 et seq.
N.Y. Partnership Law (Consol. Laws Ch. 39) § 90 et seq.
Okla. Stat. Ann., Title 54, §§ 141 et seq., 301 et seq.
Ore. Rev. Stat. 1953, 70.005 et seq.
R.I. Gen. Laws 1956, 7-13-1 et seq.
S.C. Code Ann. 1976, § 33-42-10 et seq.
Wash. Rev. Code Ann., 25.10.010 et seq.
Wis. Stat. Ann., 179.01 et seq.
W. Va. Code 1966, § 47-9-1 et seq.
Wyo. Stat. Ann., §§ 17-14-101 et seq., 17-14-201 et seq.

**Uniform Limited Partnership Act (Revised)**
See Revised Uniform Limited Partnership Act
Tex. Rev. Civ. Stat., Art. 6132a-1, § 1.01

**Uniform Limited Partnership Law (1976)**
N.J. Stat. Ann., 42:2A-1 et seq.

**Uniform Liquidation Act**
Cal. Insurance Code § 1064.1 et seq.

**Uniform Local Government Financial Management and Reporting Act**
Fla. Stat. Ann., 218.30 et seq.

**Uniform Local Sales and Use Tax Act**
Cal. Revenue and Taxation Code § 7200 et seq.
Utah Code Ann. 1953, 11-9-1 et seq.

**Uniform Machine Gun Act**
Ark. Code Ann. 1987, 5-73-201 et seq.
Md. Ann. Code 1957, Art. 27, § 372 et seq.
Mont. Rev. Code 1947, 94-3101 et seq.
S.D. Codified Laws 1967, 23-7-26 et seq.
Va. Code 1950, § 18.2-288 et seq.
Wis. Stat. Ann., 941.25 et seq.

**Uniform Management of Institutional Funds Act**
See also Management of Institutional Funds Act
Ala. Code 1975, § 16-61A-1 et seq.
Cal. Probate Code § 18500 et seq.
Colo. Rev. Stat., 15-1-1101 et seq.
Conn. Gen. Stat. 1983, § 45-100h et seq.
D.C. Code Ann., § 32-401 et seq.
Del. Code of 1974, Title 12, § 4701 et seq.
Fla. Stat. Ann., 237.41
Ga. Code Ann., 44-15-1 et seq.
Ill. Rev. Stat. 1991, Ch. 32, § 1101 et seq.
Ind. Code Ann., 30-2-12-1 et seq.
Iowa Code Ann., 122C.1 et seq.

*Continued*

Kan. Stat. Ann., 58-3601 et seq.
Ky. Rev. Stat. 1971, 273.510 et seq.
La. Rev. Stat. Ann., 9:2337.1 et seq.
Mass. Gen. Laws Ann., 180A:1 et seq.
Md. Ann. Code 1974, Art. ET, § 15-401 et seq.
Me. Rev. Stat. Ann. 1964, Title 13, § 4100 et seq.
Mich. Comp. Laws Ann., 451.1201 et seq.
Minn. Stat. Ann., 309.62 et seq.
Miss. Code Ann. 1972, §§ 79-11-601 to 79-11-617
Mo. Rev. Stat., 402.010 et seq.
Mont. Code Ann., 72-30-101 et seq.
N.C. Gen. Stat. 1943, § 36B-1 et seq.
N.D. Cent. Code, 15-67-01 et seq.
Neb. Rev. Stat. 1943, 58-601 to 58-609
N.H. Rev. Stat. 1955, 292-B:1 et seq.
N.J. Stat. Ann., 15:18-15 et seq.
N.M. Stat. Ann., 46-9-1 to 46-9-12
N.Y. Not-for-Profit Corporation Law (Consol. Laws Ch. 35) §§ 102, 512 et seq., 717
Ohio Rev. Code 1953, 1715.51 et seq.
Ore. Rev. Stat., 128.310 et seq.
R.I. Gen. Laws 1956, 18-12-1 et seq.
S.C. Code Ann. 1976, § 34-6-10 et seq.
Tenn. Code Ann., 35-10-101 et seq.
Tex. Property Code, § 163.001 et seq.
Va. Code 1950, § 55-268.1 et seq.
Vt. Stat. Ann., Title 14, § 3401 et seq.
Wash. Rev. Code Ann., 24.44.010 et seq.
Wis. Stat. Ann., 112.10
W. Va. Code 1966, § 44-6A-1 et seq.
Wyo. Stat. Ann., § 17-7-201 et seq.

**Uniform Mandatory Disposition of Detainers Act**
See also Mandatory Disposition of Detainers Act
Ala. Code 1975, § 15-9-80 et seq.
Ariz. Rules of Criminal Procedure 1973, Rule 8.3
Colo. Rev. Stat., 16-14-101 et seq.
Kan. Stat. Ann., 22-4301 et seq.
Minn. Stat. Ann., 629.292
Mo. Rev. Stat., 217.450 et seq.
N.D. Cent. Code, 29-33-01 et seq.

**Uniform Manufacturers or Dealers Registration Act**
Kan. Stat. Ann., 8-2401 et seq.

**Uniform Marital Property Act**
Wis. Stat. Ann., 766.001 et seq.

**Uniform Marriage and Divorce Act**
See also Marriage and Divorce Act
Ariz. Rev. Stat. Ann., § 25-311 et seq.
Colo. Rev. Stat., 14-10-101 et seq.
Ill. Rev. Stat. 1991, Ch. 40, § 101 et seq.
Ky. Rev. Stat. 1971, 403.010 et seq.
Minn. Stat. Ann., 518.002 et seq.
Mo. Rev. Stat., 452.300 et seq.
Mont. Rev. Code 1991, 40-1-101 et seq., 40-4-101 et seq.
Wash. Rev. Code Ann., 26.09.002 et seq.

**Uniform Marriage Evasion Act**
Ill. Rev. Stat. 1991, Ch. 40, § 216 et seq.
La. Rev. Stat. Ann., 9:221 et seq.
Mass. Gen. Laws Ann., 207:10 et seq., 207:50
Wis. Stat. Ann., 765.04

**Uniform Mechanics' Lien Law**
Fla. Stat. Ann., 713.56 et seq.

**Uniform Minor Student Capacity to Borrow Act**
Ariz. Rev. Stat. Ann., §§ 44-140, 44.140.01
Cal. Civil Code § 42.1 et seq.
Miss. Code Ann. 1972, § 37-49-1 et seq.
N.D. Cent. Code, 14-10.2-01 et seq.
Okla. Stat. Ann., Title 15, § 31 et seq.
Wash. Rev. Code Ann., 26.30.10 et seq.

**Uniform Mobile Homes and Recreational Vehicles Standards Act**
Kan. Stat. Ann., 75-1211 et seq.

**Uniform Mobile Homes Warranty Act**
Mich. Comp. Laws Ann., 125.991 et seq.

**Uniform Model Joint Obligations Act**
Me. Rev. Stat. Ann. 1964, Title 14, § 11 et seq.

**Uniform Model Real Estate Cooperative Act**
Va. Code 1950, § 55-424 et seq.

**Uniform Model Real Estate Time-Share Act**
Mass. Gen. Laws Ann., 183B:1 et seq.
R.I. Gen. Laws 1956, 34-41-1.01 et seq.
Wis. Stat. Ann., 707.02 et seq.

**Uniform Model State Administration Procedure Act**
Ala. Code 1975, § 41-22-1 et seq.
Ariz. Rev. Stat. Ann., § 41-1001 et seq.
Ark. Code Ann. 1987, 25-15-201 et seq.
Conn. Gen. Stat. 1983, § 4-166 et seq.
D.C. Code Ann., § 1-501 et seq.
Ga. Code Ann., 50-13-1 et seq.
Haw. Rev. Stat. Ann., § 91-1 et seq.
Ida. Code 1947, 67-5201 et seq.
Ill. Rev. Stat. 1991, Ch. 127, § 1001 et seq.
Iowa Code Ann., 17A.1 et seq.
La. Rev. Stat. Ann., 49:950 et seq.
Md. Ann. Code 1957, SG, § 10-201 et seq.
Me. Rev. Stat. Ann. 1964, Title 5, § 8001 et seq.
Mich. Comp. Laws Ann., 24.201 et seq.
Miss. Code Ann. 1972, § 25-43-1 et seq.
Mo. Rev. Stat., 536.010 et seq.
Mont. Code Ann., 2-4-101 et seq.
Neb. Rev. Stat. 1943, 84-901 et seq.
Nev. Rev. Stat. 1987, 233B.010 et seq.
N.H. Rev. Stat. 1955, 541-A:1 et seq.
N.Y. State Administrative Procedure Act (Consol. Laws Ch. 82) § 100 et seq.
Okla. Stat. Ann., Title 75, §§ 250.3 et seq., 302 et seq.
Ore. Rev. Stat., 183.310 et seq.
R.I. Gen. Laws 1956, 42-35-1 et seq.
S.D. Codified Laws 1967, 1-26-1 et seq.
Tenn. Code Ann., 4-5-101 et seq.
Vt. Stat. Ann., Title 3, § 801 et seq.
Wash. Rev. Code Ann., 34.05.001 et seq.
Wis. Stat. Ann., 227.01 et seq.
W. Va. Code 1966, § 29A-1-1 et seq.
Wyo. Stat. Ann., § 16-3-101 et seq.

**Uniform Motor Vehicle Accident Reparations Act**
Ky. Rev. Stat. 1971, 304-39.010 et seq.

**Uniform Motor Vehicle Act**
See also Motor Vehicle Act
Colo. Rev. Stat., 42-1-101 et seq.
N.D. Cent. Code, 39-01-01 et seq.

**Uniform Motor Vehicle Certificate of Title and Antitheft Act**
Ala. Code 1975, § 32-8-1 et seq.
Ark. Code Ann. 1987, 27-14-101 et seq.
Conn. Gen. Stat. 1983, § 14-165 et seq.
Ga. Code Ann., 40-3-1 et seq.
Ill. Rev. Stat. 1955, Ch. 95 1/2, § 74 et seq.
Mass. Gen. Laws Ann., 90D:1 et seq.
Me. Rev. Stat. Ann. 1964, Title 29, § 2350 et seq.
Minn. Stat. Ann., 168A.01 et seq.
Miss. Code Ann. 1972, § 63-21-1 et seq.
N.D. Cent. Code, 39-05-01 et seq.
N.H. Rev. Stat. 1955, 261:1 et seq.
N.Y. Vehicle and Traffic Law 1959 (Consol. Laws Ch. 71) § 2101 et seq.
R.I. Gen Laws 1956, 31-3.1-1 et seq.
Vt. Stat. Ann., Title 23, § 2001 et seq.

**Uniform Motor Vehicle Drivers' License Act**
Nev. Rev. Stat. 1979 Reprint, 483.010 et seq.

**Uniform Motor Vehicle Financial Responsibility Act**
N.D. Cent. Code, 39-16-01 et seq.

**Uniform Motor Vehicle Liability Security Act**
Haw. Rev. Stat. Ann., § 160-80 et seq.

**Uniform Motor Vehicle Operators' and Chauffeurs' License Act**
See also Motor Vehicle Operators' and Chauffeurs' License Act
Ariz. Rev. Stat. Ann., § 28-401 et seq.
Ark. Code Ann. 1987, 27-16-201 et seq.
Iowa Code 1991, 321.174 et seq.
Ky. Rev. Stat. 1971, 186.400 et seq.
Mich. Comp. Laws Ann., 257.301 et seq.
Mo. Rev. Stat., 302.010 et seq.
Mont. Rev. Code 1947, 31-117 et seq.
*Continued*

N.M. Stat. Ann. 1953, 64-13-31 et seq.
Okla. Stat. Ann., Title 47, § 6-101 et seq.

**Uniform Motor Vehicle Operators' License Act**
N.D. Cent. Code, 39-06-01 et seq.
Tenn. Code Ann., 55-7-101 et seq.
Wis. Stat. Ann., 343.01 et seq.

**Uniform Motor Vehicle Records Disclosure Act**
Neb. Rev. Stat. 1943, 60-2901 to 60-2913
W. Va. Code 1966, § 17A-2A-1 et seq.

**Uniform Motor Vehicle Registration Act**
Del. Code of 1974, Title 21, § 2101 et seq.
Kan. Stat. Ann., 8-126 et seq.

**Uniform Motor Vehicle Safety Responsibility Act**
Ariz. Rev. Stat. Ann., § 28-1101 et seq.
Colo. Rev. Stat., 42-7-101 et seq.
D.C. Code Ann., § 40-401 et seq.
Mont. Code Ann., 61-6-101 et seq.
Pa. 1945 Pamph. Laws 1340, No. 433
Wash. Rev. Code Ann., 46.29.010 et seq.

**Uniform Motor Vehicles Equipment and Identification Law**
Miss. Code Ann. 1972, § 63-7-1 et seq.

**Uniform Multiple-Person Accounts Act**
Ala. Code 1975, § 5-24-31 et seq.

**Uniform Municipal Bond Act**
Miss. Code Ann. 1972, § 21-33-301 et seq.

**Uniform Municipal Contracting Law**
Minn. Stat. Ann., 471.345

**Uniform Municipal Court Act**
Mich. Comp. Laws Ann., 730.501 et seq.
Ohio Rev. Code 1953, 1901.01 et seq.

**Uniform Municipal Election Law**
S.C. Code Ann. 1976, § 5-15-10 et seq.

**Uniform Municipal Fiscal Procedures Act**
Utah Code Ann. 1953, 10-6-101 et seq.
Wyo. Stat. Ann., § 16-4-101 et seq.

**Uniform Municipal Non-Ad Valorem Tax Law**
S.D. Codified Laws 1967, 10-52-1 et seq.

**Uniform Narcotic Drug Act**
See also Uniform Controlled Substances Act
Me. Rev. Stat. Ann. 1964, Title 17, § 1101 et seq., Title 22, § 2361 et seq

**Uniform Negotiable Instruments Act**
See also Uniform Commercial Code—Commercial Paper
Ala. Code 1958, Title 13, § 1 et seq.
Ariz. Rev. Stat. Ann., § 44-401 et seq.
Ark. Stat. 1947, 68-501 et seq.
Cal. Civil Code § 3082 et seq.
Colo. Rev. Stat., 95-1-1 et seq.
Del. Code of 1953, Title 6, § 101 et seq.
Fla. Stat. 1965, 674.01 et seq.
Ga. Code 1933, 14-101 et seq.
Haw. Rev. Stat. Ann., § 197-1 et seq.
Ida. Code 1947, 27-101 et seq.
Ill. Rev. Stat. 1991, Ch. 17, § 600 et seq.
Ind. Burns' 1933, 19-101 to 19-1807
Iowa Code 1962, 541.1 et seq.
Kan. Laws 1905, Ch. 310
Ky. Rev. Stat. 1953, 356.001 et seq.
La. Rev. Stat. Ann., 7:1 et seq.
Mass. Gen. Laws Ann., 106:3-201 et seq.
Me. Rev. Stat. Ann. 1964, Title 32, Ch. 891
Me. Rev. Stat. 1954, Ch. 188, § 1 et seq.
Mich. Comp. Laws Ann., 430.3101 et seq.
Minn. Stat. Ann., 335.01 et seq.
Miss. Code 1942, § 42 et seq.
Mo. Rev. Stat. 1959, 401.001 et seq.
Mont. Rev. Code 1947, 55-101 et seq.
N.C. Public Laws 1899, Ch. 733
N.D. Cent. Code, 41-01-01 et seq.
Neb. Rev. Stat. 1943, 62-101 et seq.
Nev. Rev. Stat. 1957, 92.001 et seq.
N.H. Rev. Stat. 1955, 337:1 et seq.
N.J. Stat. Ann., 7:1-1 et seq.
N.M. Stat. Ann. 1953, 50-1-1 et seq.
Ore. Code 1930, § 57-101 et seq.
Pa. Cons. Stat., Title 13, § 3101 et seq.
P.R. Laws Ann. 1954, Title 19, § 1 et seq.
R.I. Gen. Laws 1956, 6-18-1 et seq.
S.C. Code Ann. 1962, § 8-801 et seq.

S.D. Code 1939, 46.0101 et seq.
Tenn. Code 1932, § 7325 et seq.
Va. Code 1950, § 6-353 et seq.
Vt. Acts 1912, No. 99
W. Va. Code 1931, Miscellaneous Superseded Code Provisions, § 46-1-1 et seq.
Wyo. Stat. 1957, § 13-280 et seq.

**Uniform Nepotism Policy Act**
Tenn. Code Ann., 8-31-101 et seq.

**Uniform Nepotism Policy Act (Haywood County Employees)**
Tenn. Private Acts 1985, Ch. 27

**Uniform Nonpartisan Elections Law**
N.J. Stat. Ann., 40:45-5 et seq.

**Uniform Nonprobate Transfers on Death Act**
Wis. Stat. Ann., 705.20 et seq.

**Uniform Nonsupport and Desertion Act**
Miss. Code Ann. 1972, § 97-5-3
Okla. Stat. Ann., Title 21, §§ 853, 854

**Uniform Notary Act**
Cal. Government Code § 8200 et seq.
Colo. Rev. Stat., 12-55-101 et seq.
Del. Code of 1974, Title 29, § 4321 et seq.
Ida. Code 1947, 51-101 et seq.
Ill. Rev. Stat. 1991, Ch. 30, § 221 et seq.; Ch. 102, § 210-101 et seq.
Kan. Stat. Ann., 53-502 et seq.
La. Rev. Stat. Ann., 35:1 et seq.
Md. Ann. Code 1957, Art. 68
Mich. Comp. Laws Ann., 55.107 et seq.
Minn. Stat. Ann., 358.41 et seq.
Mo. Rev. Stat., 486.200 et seq.
Mont. Code Ann., 1-5-401 et seq.
N.C. Gen. Stat. 1943, § 10A-1 et seq.
N.H. Rev. Stat. 1955, 455:1 et seq.
N.J. Stat. Ann., 52:7-10 et seq.
Ore. Rev. Stat., 194.505 et seq.
Pa. Purdon's Stat., Title 57, § 147 et seq.
P.R. Laws Ann. 1954, Title 4, § 1001 et seq.
Tex. Government Code, § 406.001 et seq.
Va. Code 1950, § 47.1-1 et seq.
Wash. Rev. Code Ann., 42.44.010 et seq.
W. Va. Code 1966, § 29C-1-101 et seq.

**Uniform Official Reports as Evidence Act**
Ida. Code 1947, 9-316 et seq.
Mont. Rev. Code 1991, 93-901-1 et seq.
N.D. Cent. Code, 31-09-11, 31-09-12
Ohio Rev. Code 1953, 2317.42, 2317.43
Pa. Cons. Stat., Title 42, § 6104
Tex. Rules of Criminal Evidence, Rules 201, 901, 1001 et seq.
Wis. Stat. Ann., 889.18 et seq.
Wyo. Stat. 1957, § 1-165 et seq.

**Uniform Operation of Commercial Motor Vehicles Act**
Mass. Gen. Laws Ann., 90F:1 et seq.

**Uniform Out-of-Country Foreign Money-Judgment Recognition Act**
Fla. Stat. Ann., 55.601 to 55.607

**Uniform Out of State Incarceration Act**
N.J. Stat. Ann., 2A:168-18 et seq.

**Uniform Out-of-State Parolee Supervision Act**
Fla. Stat. Ann., 949.07, 949.08
Kan. Stat. Ann., 22-4101 et seq.
Md. Ann. Code 1974, Governor-Executive and Administrative Departments, § 4-803
Me. Rev. Stat. Ann. 1964, Title 34-A, § 9801 et seq.
Miss. Code Ann. 1972, § 47-7-71 et seq.
S.C. Code Ann. 1976, § 24-21-810 et seq.

**Uniform Owner-Resident Relations Act**
N.M. Stat. Ann., 47-8-1 to 47-8-51

**Uniform Owner-Resident Relationship Act**
N.M. Stat. Ann., 47-8-1 et seq.

**Uniform Parcel Identifier Law**
Pa. Purdon's Stat., Title 21, § 331 et seq.

**Uniform Parentage Act**
Ala. Code 1975, 26-17-1 et seq.
Cal. Family Code § 7600 et seq.
Colo. Rev. Stat., 19-4-101 et seq.
Del. Code of 1974, Title 13, § 801 et seq.
Haw. Rev. Stat. Ann., § 584-1 et seq.
Ill. Rev. Stat. 1991, Ch. 40, § 1451 et seq.

*Continued*

Kan. Stat. Ann., 38-1110 et seq.
Minn. Stat. Ann., 257.51 et seq.
Mo. Rev. Stat., 210.817 et seq.
Mont. Code Ann., 40-6-101 et seq.
N.D. Cent. Code, 14-17-01 et seq.
Nev. Rev. Stat. 1987, 126.011 et seq.
N.J. Stat. Ann., 9:17-38 et seq.
N.M. Stat. Ann., 40-11-1 et seq.
Ohio Rev. Code 1953, 3111.01 et seq.
R.I. Gen. Laws 1953, Superseded Vols., 15-8-1 et seq.
Wash. Rev. Code Ann., 26.26.010 et seq.
Wyo. Stat. Ann., § 14-2-101 et seq.

**Uniform Parish Court Jurisdiction and Procedure Act**
La. Rev. Stat. Ann., 13:1441 et seq.

**Uniform Partnership Act**
Ala. Code 1975, § 10-8A-101 et seq.
Alaska Stat. 1962, § 32.05.010 et seq.
Ariz. Rev. Stat. Ann., § 29-201 et seq.
Ark. Code Ann. 1987, 4-42-101 et seq.
Cal. Corporations Code § 15001 et seq.
Colo. Rev. Stat., 7-60-101 et seq.
Conn. Gen. Stat. 1983, § 34-39 et seq.
D.C. Code 1973, § 41-101 et seq.
Del. Code of 1974, Title 6, § 1501 et seq.
Fla. Stat. Ann., 620.56 et seq.
Ga. Code Ann., 14-8-1 et seq.
Haw. Rev. Stat. Ann., § 425-101 et seq.
Ida. Code 1947, 53-3-1201 et seq.
Ill. Rev. Stat. 1991, Ch. 106 1/2, § 1 et seq.
Ind. Code Ann., 23-4-1-1 et seq.
Iowa Code Ann., 486.1 et seq., 544/1 et seq.
Kan. Stat. Ann., 56-301 et seq.
Ky. Rev. Stat. 1971, 362.150 et seq.
La. Rev. Stat. Ann., 9:3401 et seq.
Mass. Gen. Laws Ann., 108A:1 et seq.
Md. Ann. Code 1974, Art. CA, § 9-101 et seq.
Me. Rev. Stat. Ann. 1964, Title 31, § 281 et seq.
Mich. Comp. Laws Ann., 449.1 et seq.
Minn. Stat. Ann., 323A.1-01 et seq.
Minn. Stat. Ann., 323.01 et seq.
Miss. Code Ann. 1972, § 79-12-1 et seq.
Mo. Rev. Stat., 358.010 et seq.
Mont. Code Ann., 35-10-101 et seq.
N.C. Gen. Stat. 1943, § 59-31 et seq.
N.D. Cent. Code, 45-05-01 et seq.
Neb. Laws 1997, L.B. 523
Neb. Rev. Stat. 1943, 67-301 et seq.
Nev. Rev. Stat. Ann., 87.010 et seq.
N.H. Rev. Stat. 1955, 304-A:1 et seq.
N.J. Stat. Ann., 42:1-1 et seq.
N.M. Stat. Ann., 54-1-1 et seq., 54-1A-101 et seq.
N.Y. Partnership Law (Consol. Laws Ch. 39) § 1 et seq.
Ohio Rev. Code 1953, 1775.01 et seq.
Okla. Stat. Ann., Title 54, § 201 et seq.
Ore. Rev. Stat., 68.010 et seq.
Pa. Cons. Stat., Title 15, § 8301 et seq.
R.I. Gen. Laws 1956, 7-12-12 et seq.
S.C. Code Ann. 1976, § 33-41-10 et seq.
S.D. Codified Laws 1967, 48-1-1 et seq.
Tenn. Code Ann., 61-1-101 et seq.
Tex. Rev. Civ. Stat., Art. 6132b
Utah Code Ann. 1953, 48-1-1 et seq.
Va. Code 1950, §§ 50-1 et seq., 50-73.79 et seq.
Vt. Stat. Ann., Title 11, § 1121 et seq.
Wash. Rev. Code Ann., 25.04.010 et seq.
Wis. Stat. Ann., 178.01 et seq.
W. Va. Code 1966, § 47-8A-1 et seq.
Wyo. Stat. Ann., §§ 17-13-101 et seq., 17-21-1001 et seq.

**Uniform Partnership Act (Revised)**
Fla. Stat. Ann., 620.81001 et seq.

**Uniform Paternity Act**
See also Paternity Act
Ky. Rev. Stat. 1971, 406.011 et seq.
Me. Rev. Stat. Ann. 1964, Title 19, § 271 et seq.
Miss. Code Ann. 1972, § 93-9-1 et seq.
N.H. Rev. Stat. 1955, 168-A:1 et seq.
R.I. Gen. Laws 1956, 15-8-1 et seq.
Utah Code Ann. 1953, 78-45a-1 et seq.

**Uniform Peace Officers' Disciplinary Act**
Ill. Rev. Stat. 1991, Ch. 85, § 2551 et seq.

**Uniform Penalty and Interest Act**
Ill. Comp. Stat. 1992, Ch. 35, § 735/3-1 et seq.

**Uniform Pension Act (Firemen and Policemen)**
Ohio Rev. Code 1953, 741.01 et seq.

**Uniform Perpetuation of Testimony Act**
Okla. Stat. Ann., Title 12, § 538.1 et seq.

**Uniform Pharmacy Continuing Professional Education Act**
Okla. Stat. Ann., Title 59, § 361 et seq.

**Uniform Photographic Copies of Business and Public Records as Evidence Act**
See also Photographic Copies of Business and Public Records as Evidence Act
Ala. Code 1975, § 12-21-44
Ark. Code Ann. 1987, 16-46-101
Cal. Evidence Code §§ 1550, 1551
Colo. Rev. Stat., 13-26-101 et seq.
Conn. Gen. Stat. 1983, § 52-180
Ga. Code Ann., 24-5-26
Ida. Code 1947, 9-417 et seq.
Iowa Code Ann., 622.30
Kan. Stat. Ann., 60-469
Ky. Rev. Stat. 1971, 422.105 et seq.
Mass. Gen. Laws Ann., 233:79E
Md. Ann. Code 1974, Art. CJ, § 10-102
Me. Rev. Stat. Ann. 1964, Title 16, § 456
Mich. Comp. Laws Ann., 600.2147
Minn. Stat. Ann., 600.135
N.C. Gen. Stat. 1943, § 8-45.1 et seq.
N.D. Cent. Code, 31-08-01.1
Neb. Rev. Stat. 1943, 25-12,112 et seq.
N.H. Rev. Stat. 1955, 520:1 et seq.
N.J. Stat. Ann., 2A:82-38 et seq.
N.Y. Civil Practice Laws and Rules (Consol. Laws Ch. 8) Rule 4539
Ohio Rev. Code 1953, 2317.41
Pa. Cons. Stat., Title 42, §§ 6108, 6109
S.C. Code Ann. 1976, § 19-5-610 et seq.
S.D. Codified Laws 1967, 19-7-12
Va. Code 1950, § 8.01-391
Vt. Stat. Ann., Title 12, § 1701
Wash. Rev. Code Ann., 5.46.010 et seq.
Wis. Stat. Ann., 889.29
W. Va. Code 1966, § 57-1-7a et seq.

**Uniform Planned Community Act**
Pa. Cons. Stat., Title 68, § 5101 et seq.

**Uniform Pleasure Boating Act**
La. Rev. Stat. Ann., 34:851.1 et seq.

**Uniform Plumbing Code**
Ariz. Rev. Stat. Ann., § 9-801 et seq.
Mo. Rev. Stat., 341.090 et seq.

**Uniform Policy Act**
Ore. Rev. Stat., 742.001

**Uniform Policy Act (Accident and Sickness)**
Kan. Stat. Ann., 40-2201 et seq.

**Uniform Post-Conviction Collateral Act**
Miss. Code Ann. 1972, § 99-39-1 et seq.

**Uniform Post-Conviction Collateral Relief Act**
Miss. Code Ann. 1972, § 99-39-1 et seq.

**Uniform Post-Conviction Procedure Act**
See also Post-Conviction Procedure Act
Ida. Code 1947, 19-4901 et seq.
Iowa Code Ann., 663A.1 et seq., 822.1 et seq.
Md. Ann. Code 1957, Art. 27, § 645A et seq.
Minn. Stat. Ann., 590.01 et seq.
Mont. Code Ann., 46-21-101 et seq.
N.D. Cent. Code, 29-32.1-01 et seq.
Nev. Rev. Stat. 1979 Reprint, 177.315 et seq.
Okla. Stat. Ann., Title 22, 1080 et seq.
Ore. Rev. Stat., 138.510 et seq.
R.I. Gen. Laws 1956, 10-9.1-1 et seq.
S.C. Code Ann. 1976, § 17-27-10 et seq.
S.D. Codified Laws 1967, 23A-34-1 et seq.

**Uniform Practice Act (Administrative Agencies)**
N.D. Cent. Code, 28-32-01 et seq.

**Uniform Practice Act of the Public Utilities Commissioner**
Ore. Rev. Stat., 756.050 et seq.

**Uniform Premarital Agreement Act**
Ariz. Rev. Stat. Ann., § 25-201 et seq.
Ark. Code Ann. 1987, 9-11-401 et seq.
*Continued*

Cal. Civil Code § 5300
Cal. Family Code § 1600 et seq.
Haw. Rev. Stat. Ann., 5720-1 et seq.
Ill. Rev. Stat. 1991, Ch. 40, § 2601 et seq.
Iowa Code Ann., 595A.1, et seq.
Kan. Stat. Ann., 23-801 et seq.
Me. Rev. Stat. Ann. 1964, Title 19-A, § 601 et seq.
Mont. Code Ann. 1983, 40-2-601 et seq.
N.C. Gen. Stat. 1943, § 52B-1 et seq.
N.D. Cent. Code, 14-03.1-01 et seq.
Neb. Rev. Stat. 1943, 42-1001 et seq.
N.J. Stat. Ann., 37:2-31 et seq.
N.M. Stat. Ann., 40-3A-1 et seq.
Ore. Rev. Stat., 108.700 et seq.
R.I. Gen. Laws 1956, § 15-17-1 et seq.
S.D. Codified Laws 1967, 25-2-16 et seq.
Tex. Family Code, §§ 4.001 et seq., 5.50 et seq.
Utah Code Ann. 1953, 30-8-1 et seq.
Va. Code 1950, § 20-147 et seq.

**Uniform Preservation of Private Business Records Act**
Ill. Rev. Stat. 1991, Ch. 116, § 59 et seq.
Md. Ann. Code 1974, Art. BR. § 1-307 et seq.
N.H. Rev. Stat. 1955, 337-A:1 et seq.
Okla. Stat. Ann., Title 67, § 251 et seq.

**Uniform Primaries Act**
Pa. 1906 Ex. Pamph. Laws 36, No. 10

**Uniform Principal and Income Act**
See also Principal and Income Act
Ala. Code 1975, § 19-3-270 et seq.
Alaska Stat. 1962, § 13.38.010 et seq.
Ariz. Rev. Stat. Ann., § 14-7401 et seq.
Ark. Code Ann. 1987, 28-70-101 et seq.
Cal. Probate Code § 16300 et seq.
Colo. Rev. Stat., 15-1-401 et seq.
Conn. Gen. Stat. 1983, § 45-350 et seq.
Fla. Stat. 1973, 738.01 et seq.
Ga. Code Ann., 53-12-210 et seq.
Haw. Rev. Stat. Ann., § 557-1 et seq.
Ida. Code 1947, 68-1001 et seq.
Ill. Rev. Stat. 1991, Ch. 30, § 501 et seq.
Ind. Code 1971, 30-4-5-1 et seq.
Kan. Stat. Ann., 58-901 et seq.
Ky. Rev. Stat. 1971, 386.190 et seq.
Md. Ann. Code 1974, Art. ET, § 14-201 et seq.
Mich. Comp. Laws Ann., 555.51 et seq.
Minn. Stat. Ann., 501B.59 et seq.
Miss. Code Ann. 1972, § 91-17-1 et seq.
Mont. Code Ann., 72-34-401 et seq.
N.C. Gen. Stat. 1943, § 37-16 et seq.
N.D. Cent. Code, 59-04.1-01 et seq.
Neb. Rev. Stat. 1943, 30-3101 et seq.
Nev. Rev. Stat. 1987, 164.140 et seq.
N.H. Rev. Stat. 1955, 464-B:1 et seq.
N.J. Stat. Ann., 3B:19A-1 et seq.
N.M. Stat. Ann., 46-3-1 et seq.
N.Y. Estates, Powers and Trusts Law (Consol. Laws Ch. 17B) § 11-2.1
Okla. Stat. Ann., Title 60, § 175.1 et seq.
Ore. Rev. Stat., 129.005 et seq.
Pa. 1945 Pamph. Laws 416, No. 171
S.C. Code Ann. 1976, § 62-7-401 et seq.
S.D. Codified Laws 1967, 55-13-1 et seq.
Tenn. Code Ann., 35-6-101 et seq.
Tex. Property Code, § 113.101 et seq.
Utah Code Ann. 1953, 22-3-1 et seq.
Va. Code 1950, §§ 55-253 et seq.,55-277.1 to 55-277.33
Vt. Stat. Ann., Title 14, § 3301 et seq.
Wash. Rev. Code Ann., 11.104.010 et seq.
Wis. Stat. 1981, 701.20
W. Va. Code 1966, § 36-6-1 et seq.
Wyo. Stat. Ann., § 2-3-601 et seq.

**Uniform Principal and Income Act (Revised)**
See Revised Uniform Principal and Income Act

**Uniform Probate Code**
See also Probate Code
Alaska Stat. 1962, § 13.06.005 et seq.
Ariz. Rev. Stat. Ann., § 14-1101 et seq.
Colo. Rev. Stat., 15-10-101 et seq.
Fla. Stat. Ann., §§ 731.005 et seq., 737.101 et seq.
Haw. Rev. Stat. Ann., § 560:1-101 et seq.
Ida. Code 1947, 15-1-101 et seq.
Ky. Rev. Stat. 1971, 386.650 et seq.
Me. Rev. Stat. Ann. 1964, Title 18-A, § 1-101 et seq.
Mich. Comp. Laws Ann., § 700.1 et seq.

Minn. Stat. Ann., 524.1-101 et seq.
Mont. Code Ann., 72-1-101 et seq.
N.D. Cent. Code, 30.1-01-01 et seq.
Neb. Rev. Stat. 1943, 30-2201 et seq.
N.M. Stat. Ann., 45-1-101 et seq.
S.C. Code Ann. 1976, § 62-1-100 et seq.
Utah Code Ann. 1953, 75-1-101 et seq.

**Uniform Probate of Foreign Wills Act**
See also Probate Act of Foreign Wills
Tex. Probate Code, § 100 et seq.
Wis. Stat. Ann., 868.01

**Uniform Procedure Act**
Ga. Code Ann., 23-3-1 et seq.

**Uniform Procedure for Licensing Boards Act**
N.C. Gen. Stat. 1943, § 150-9 et seq.

**Uniform Procurement Act**
Mass. Gen. Laws Ann., 30B:1 to 30B:19

**Uniform Professional and Vocational Licensing Act**
Haw. Rev. Stat. Ann., § 436B-1 et seq.

**Uniform Proof of Statutes Act**
Alaska Laws 1923, Ch. 4
Cal. Code of Civil Procedure § 1900
Del. Code of 1974, Title 10, § 4314
Haw. Rev. Stat. Ann., § 622-12
Ida. Code 1947, 9-304 et seq.
Ill. Rev. Stat. 1991, Ch. 110, §§ 8-1101, 8-1102
Ind. Code Ann., 34-3-1-1 et seq.
Ind. Code 1982, 34-38-3-1 et seq.
Kan. Gen. Stat. 1949, 60-2852
La. Rev. Stat. Ann., 13:3717, 13:3718
Md. Ann. Code 1974, Art. CJ, § 10-202
Mich. Comp. Laws Ann., 600.2114a, 600.2118a
Minn. Stat. Ann., 599.02
Mo. Rev. Stat., 490.010 et seq.
N.D. Cent. Code, 31-09-01 et seq.
Ohio Rev. Code 1953, 2317.08
Ore. Rev. Stat. 1953, 43.310
Pa. Cons. Stat., Title 42, § 5327
S.D. Codified Laws 1967, 19-7-1 et seq.
Tenn. Code Ann., 24-6-104
Wash. Rev. Code Ann., 5.44.050

**Uniform Property Act**
Neb. Rev. Stat. 1943, 76-101 et seq.

**Uniform Property Tax Act**
S.C. Constitution Article 10, §§ 1 to 15

**Uniform Prudent Investor Act**
Alaska Stat. 1992, §§ 13.36.200 to 13.36.275
Cal. Probate Code § 16045 et seq.
Colo. Rev. Stat., 15.1.1-101 et seq.
Conn. Public Acts 1997, No. 140
Haw. Rev. Stat. Ann., § 554C-1 et seq.
Ind. Code 1982, 30-4-3.5-1 to 30-4-3.5-13
Neb. Rev. Stat. 1943, 8-2201 to 8-2213
N.M. Stat. Ann., 45-7-601
Ohio Rev. Code 1953, 1339.52 to 1339.61
Va. Code 1950, §§ 26-45.3 to 26-45.14
W. Va. Code 1966, § 44-6C-1 et seq.

**Uniform Public Construction Cost Accounting Act**
Cal. Public Contract Code § 21000 et seq.

**Uniform Pulpwood Scaling and Practices Act**
Miss. Code Ann. 1972, § 75-79-1 et seq.

**Uniform Purchaser and Vendor Risk Act**
Wis. Stat. Ann., 706.12

**Uniform Purchasing Act**
Ark. Code Ann. 1987, 22-4-501 et seq.

**Uniform Rate Act (Fire Insurance)**
La. Rev. Stat. Ann., 22:1405

**Uniform Rate Revision and Modification Act**
P.R. Laws Ann. 1954, Title 27, § 261 et seq.

**Uniform Rebate Act (Insurance)**
N.C. Gen. Stat. 1943, § 58-44.5

**Uniform Recall Election Law**
N.J. Stat. Ann., 19:27A-1 et seq.

**Uniform Reciprocal Enforcement of Support Act**

See also Revised Uniform Reciprocal Enforcement of Support Act

Ala. Code 1975, § 30-4-80 et seq.

Alaska Stat. 1962, § 25.25.010 et seq.

Ariz. Rev. Stat. Ann., § 12-1651 et seq.

Cal. Family Code § 4800 et seq.

Conn. Gen. Stat. 1983, § 46b-180 et seq.

D.C. Code 1973, § 30-301 et seq.

Del. Code of 1974, Title 13, § 601 et seq.

Fla. Stat. Ann., 88.011 et seq.

Ind. Code Ann., 31-2-1-1 et seq.

La. Children's Code, Art. 1301 et seq.

Mass. Gen. Laws Ann., 273A:1 et seq.

Me. Rev. Stat. Ann. 1964, Title 19, § 331 et seq.

Mich. Comp. Laws. Ann., 780.151 et seq.

Miss. Code Ann. 1972, § 93-11-1 et seq.

Mo. Rev. Stat., 454.010 et seq.

N.H. Rev. Stat. 1955, 546:41

N.Y. Domestic Relations Law (Consol. Laws Ch. 14) § 30 et seq.

Okla. Stat. Ann., Title 12, § 1600.1 et seq.

Pa. Cons. Stat., Title 23, § 4501 et seq.

P.R. Laws Ann. 1954, Title 32, § 3311 et seq.

Tenn. Code Ann., 36-5-201 et seq.

Utah Code Ann. 1953, 77-31-1 et seq.

Wash. Rev. Code Ann., 26.21.010 et seq.

**Uniform Reciprocal Enforcement of Support Act (Revised)**

See Revised Uniform Reciprocal Enforcement of Support Act

**Uniform Reciprocal Enforcement of Support Act (Support of Dependent)**

N.Y. Domestic Relations Law (Consol. Laws Ch. 14) § 30 et seq.

**Uniform Reciprocal Liquidation Act**

Ill. Rev. Stat. 1991, Ch. 73, § 833.1 et seq.

Ohio Rev. Code 1953, 3903.24 et seq.

**Uniform Reciprocal Nonsupport Act**

Ala. Code 1975, § 30-4-80 et seq.

**Uniform Reciprocal Transfer Tax Act**

See also Reciprocal Transfer Tax Act

Alaska Stat. 1962, Replaced Titles, § 43.31.410

Colo. Rev. Stat., 39-23-104

Ida. Code 1947, 14-410

Iowa Code 1991, 450.91

Md. Ann. Code 1974, Art. TG, §§ 7-203, 7-303, 7-402

Mich. Comp. Laws Ann., 205.201

Mont. Code Ann., 72-16-801

Neb. Rev. Stat. 1943, 77-2007.01, 77-2007.02

Okla. Stat. Ann., Title 68, § 807

S.C. Code Ann. 1962, § 65-481 et seq.

S.D. Codified Laws 1967, 10-40-4 et seq.

W. Va. Code 1966, § 11-11-8

**Uniform Recognition of Acknowledgments Act**

See also Recognition of Acknowledgments Act

Ala. Stat 1962, § 09.63.050 et seq.

Ariz. Rev. Stat. Ann., § 33-501 et seq.

Colo. Rev. Stat., 12-55-201 et seq.

Conn. Gen. Stat. 1983, §§ 1-57 et seq.,1-65 et seq.

Ill. Rev. Stat. 1991, Ch. 30, § 221 et seq.

Ky. Rev. Stat. 1971, 423.110 et seq.

Me. Rev. Stat. Ann. 1964, Title 4, § 1011 et seq.

Mich. Comp. Laws Ann., 565.261 et seq.

N.D. Cent. Code, 47-19-14.1 et seq.

Neb. Rev. Stat. 1943, 64-201 et seq.

N.H. Rev. Stat. 1955, 456-A:1 et seq.

Ohio Rev. Code 1953, 147.51 et seq.

S.C. Code Ann. 1976, § 26-3-10 et seq.

Va. Code 1950, § 55-118.1 et seq.

W. Va. Code 1966, § 39-1A-1 et seq.

**Uniform Records Retention Act**

Colo. Rev. Stat., 6-17-101 et seq.

**Uniform Registration Act (Federal)**

Ariz. Rev. Stat. Ann., § 33-1031 et seq.

**Uniform Relocation Act Amendments of 1987**

April 2, 1987, P.L. 100-17, 42 U.S. Code sect. 4601 nt.

**Uniform Relocation Assistance Act**

Conn. Gen. Stat. 1983, § 8-266 et seq.

Ga. Code Ann., 32-8-1

Tenn. Code Ann., 13-11-101 et seq.

Wash. Rev. Code Ann., 8.26.010 et seq.

**Uniform Relocation Assistance and Real Property Acquisition Policies Act**

Kan. Stat. Ann., 58-3501 et seq.

N.C. Gen. Stat. 1943, § 133-5 et seq.

Nev. Rev. Stat. 1979 Reprint, 342.010 et seq.

S.D. Codified Laws 1967, 25-9A-1 et seq.

Va. Code 1950, § 25-235 et seq.

**Uniform Relocation Assistance and Real Property Acquisition Policies Act of 1970**

Jan. 2, 1971, P.L. 91-646, 84 Stat. 1894, 42 U.S. Code §§ 1415, 2473, 2307, 4601, 4602, 4621 to 4638, 4651 to 4655; 49 U.S. Code § 1606

April 2, 1987, P.L. 100-17, 42 U.S. Code §§ 4601, 4602, 4621 et seq.

Dec. 18, 1991, P.L. 102-240, 42 U.S. Code § 4633

Dec. 21, 1995, P.L. 104-66, 42 U.S. Code § 4604

Nov. 21, 1997, P.L. 105-117, 42 U.S. Code §§ 4605, 4633

**Uniform Rendition and Extradition Act**

N.D. Cent. Code, 29-30.3-01 et seq.

**Uniform Rendition of Accused Persons Act**

Colo. Rev. Stat., 16-4-301 et seq.

Haw. Rev. Stat. Ann., § 833-1 et seq.

Ida. Code 1947, 19-4530 et seq.

Ill. Rev. Stat. 1991, Ch. 38, § 157-21 et seq.

Mich. Comp. Laws Ann., 780.41 et seq.

Neb. Rev. Stat. 1943, 29-3101 et seq.

S.D. Codified Laws 1967, 23-26A-1 et seq.

Wash. Rev. Code Ann., 10.91.010 et seq.

**Uniform Rendition of Prisoners as Witn[illegible] in Criminal Proceedings Act**

Ark. Code Ann. 1987, 16-43-301 et seq.

Ga. Code Ann., 19-11-40 et seq.

Ida. Code 1947, 19-3013 et seq.

Ill. Rev. Stat. 1991, Ch. 38, § 157-1 et seq.

Kan. Stat. Ann., 22-4207 et seq.

Ky. Rev. Stat. 1971, 421.600 et seq.

Me. Rev. Stat. Ann. 1964, Title 15, § 1461 et seq.

Mich. Comp. Laws Ann., 780.111 et seq.

Neb. Rev. Stat. 1943, 29-3101 et seq.

N.H. Rev. Stat. 1955, 613-A:1 et seq.

Okla. Stat. 1981, Title 22, § 728 et seq.

Pa. Cons. Stat., Title 42, § 5971 et seq.

R.I. Gen. Laws 1956, 12-16.1-1 et seq.

Tex. Code of Criminal Procedure, Art. 24.29

Utah Code Ann. 1953, 77-33-1 et seq.

Wis. Stat. Ann., 976.01

**Uniform Reporters' Privilege Act**

Del. Code of 1974, Title 10, § 4320 et seq.

**Uniform Residential Landlord and Tenant Act**

See also Residential Landlord and Tenant Act

Alaska Stat. 1962, § 34.03.010 et seq.

Ariz. Rev. Stat. Ann., § 33-1301 et seq.

Fla. Stat. Ann., 83.40 et seq.

Haw. Rev. Stat. Ann., § 521-1 et seq.

Iowa Code Ann., 562A.1 et seq.

Kan. Stat. Ann., 58-2540 et seq.

Ky. Rev. Stat. 1971, 383.505 et seq.

Mont. Code Ann., 70-24-101 et seq.

Neb. Rev. Stat. 1943, 76-1401 et seq.

N.M. Stat. Ann., 47-8-1 et seq.

Ore. Rev. Stat., 90.105 et seq.

R.I. Gen. Laws 1956, 34-18-1 et seq.

S.C. Code Ann. 1976, § 27-40-10 et seq.

Tenn. Code Ann., 66-28-101

Va. Code 1950, § 55-248.2 et seq.

**Uniform Retail Food Facilities Law**

Cal. Health and Safety Code § 27500 et seq.

...46 Stat. 243 (See 5

... 85-861, 72 Stat. 1570 (See
§ 5532)

**U... Retirement System for Justices and ...dges Act**
Okla. Stat. Ann., Title 20, § 1101 et seq.

**Uniform Revenue Bond Act**
Ore. Rev. Stat., 288.805 et seq.

**Uniform Revenue Procedures and Taxpayers' Bill of Rights Act**
Ala. Code 1975, § 40-2A-1 et seq.

**Uniform Revised Partnership Act**
Fla. Stat. Ann., 620.81001 et seq.

**Uniform Rights of Terminally Ill Act**
Me. Rev. Stat. Ann. 1964, Title 18-A, § 5-701 et seq.

**Uniform Road Law (County)**
Tenn. Code Ann., 54-7-101 et seq.

**Uniform Rule Making Act (State Boards)**
Ind. Code Ann., 4-22-2-1 et seq.

**Uniform Rules of Appellate Procedure**
Mont. Code Ann. 1987, Title 25, Ch. 21

**Uniform Rules of Civil Procedure**
Mont. Code Ann. 1987, Title 25, Ch. 20

**Uniform Rules of Evidence**
Ark. Code Ann. 1987, 16-41-101
Mont. Code Ann. 1987, Title 12, Ch. 10

**Uniform Rules of the Road Act**
Ga. Code Ann., 40-6-1 et seq.

**Uniform Safety and Traffic Act**
Ark. Code Ann. 1987, 27-49-201 et seq.

**Uniform Safety Code**
Colo. Rev. Stat., 42-4-101 et seq.

**Uniform Salary Law (County Officers)**
Okla. Stat. Ann., Title 19, § 179.13 et seq.

**Uniform Sale of Goods Law**
N.J. Stat. Ann., 46:30-1 et seq.

**Uniform Sale of Securities Act**
Fla. Stat. 1953, 517.01 et seq.
Haw. Rev. Laws 1955, § 199-1 et seq.
Ore. Laws 1939, Ch. 397

**Uniform Sales Act**
See also Uniform Commercial Code—Sales
Ala. Code 1958, Title 57, § 1 et seq.
Ariz. Laws 1907, Ch. 99
Ark. Stat. 1947, 68-1401 et seq.
Cal. Civil Code § 1721 et seq.
Colo. Rev. Stat., 1963, 121-1-1 et seq.
Del. Code of 1953, Title 6, § 701 et seq.
Haw. Rev. Stat. Ann., § 476-1 et seq.
Ill. Rev. Stat. 1961, Ch. 121 1/2, § 1 et seq.
Ind. Burns' 1933, 58-101 et seq.
Iowa Code 1962, 554.1 et seq.
Ky. Rev. Stat. 1953, 361.010 et seq.
Mass. Gen. Laws Ann., 106:3 et seq.
Me. Rev. Stat. 1954, Ch. 185, § 1 et seq.
Mich. Comp. Laws Ann. 1949, § 29-1-1 et seq.
Minn. Stat. 1961, 512.01 et seq.
Mont. Code Ann., 30-11-101 et seq.
Nev. Rev. Stat. 1957, 96.010 et seq.
N.H. Rev. Stat. 1955, 382-A:8-101 et seq.
N.J. Stat. Ann., 46:30-1 et seq.
S.D. Code 1939, 54.0101 et seq.
Tenn. Code 1932, § 7194 et seq.
Vt. Acts 1921, No. 171
Wis. Stat. Ann., 121.01 et seq.
Wyo. Stat. 1957, § 34-157 et seq.

**Uniform School Act**
Miss. Code Ann. 1972, § 37-6-1 et seq.

**Uniform School Requirements Act**
Iowa Code Ann., 280.1 et seq.

**Uniform Securities Act**
See also Securities Act
Ala. Code 1975, § 8-6-1 et seq.
Alaska Stat. 1962, § 45.55.010 et seq.
Ark. Code Ann. 1987, 23-42-507 et seq.
Colo. Rev. Stat., 11-51-101 et seq.

Conn. Gen. Stat. 1983, § 36-470 et seq.
D.C. Code Ann., § 2-2601 et seq.
Del. Code of 1974, Title 6, § 7301 et seq.
Haw. Rev. Stat. Ann., § 485-1 et seq.
Iowa Code Ann., 502.101 et seq.
Kan. Stat. Ann., 17-1252 et seq.
Ky. Rev. Stat. 1971, 292.310 et seq.
Mass. Gen. Laws Ann., 110A:1 et seq.
Md. Ann. Code 1974, Art. CA, § 11-101 et seq.
Me. Rev. Stat. 1954, Title 32, § 10101 et seq.
Mich. Comp. Laws Ann., 451.501 et seq.
Minn. Stat. Ann., 80A.01 et seq.
Miss. Code Ann. 1972, § 75-71-101 et seq.
Mo. Rev. Stat., 409.101 et seq.
Mont. Code Ann., 30-10-101 et seq.
N.C. Gen. Stat. 1943, § 78A-1 et seq.
Neb. Rev. Stat. 1943, 8-1101 et seq.
Nev. Rev. Stat. 1957, 90-211 et seq.
N.H. Rev. Stat. 1955, 421-B:1 et seq.
N.J. Stat. Ann., 49:3-47 et seq.
N.M. Stat. Ann., 58-13A-1 et seq.
Okla. Stat. Ann., Title 71, § 101 et seq.
Ore. Stat. 1991, 59.005 et seq.
Pa. Purdon's Stat., Title 70, § 1-101 et seq.
P.R. Laws Ann. 1954, Title 10, § 851 et seq.
R.I. Gen. Laws 1956, 7-11-101 et seq.
S.C. Code Ann. 1976, § 35-1-10 et seq.
Utah Code Ann. 1953, 61-1-1 et seq.
Va. Code 1950, § 13.1-501 et seq.
Vt. Stat. Ann., Title 9, § 4201 et seq.
Wash. Rev. Code Ann., 21.20.940
Wis. Stat. Ann., 551.01 et seq.
W. Va. Code 1966, § 32-1-101 et seq.
Wyo. Stat. Ann., § 17-4-101 et seq.

**Uniform Securities Ownership by Minors Act**

Ala. Code 1975, § 8-6-90 et seq.
Ark. Code Ann. 1987, 9-26-305 et seq.
N.D. Cent. Code, 14-10.1-01 et seq.
Pa. Purdon's Stat., Title 70, § 101 et seq.
Wis. Stat. Ann., 880.75

**Uniform Seed Law**

Mo. Rev. Stat., 266.011 et seq.

**Uniform Seizure Act**

P.R. Laws Ann. 1954, Title 34, § 1723 et seq.

**Uniform Short Form Mortgage Act**

Minn. Stat. Ann., 507.15

**Uniform Simplification of Fiduciary Security Transfers Act**

See also Simplification of Fiduciary Security Transfers Act
Ala. Code 1975, § 8-6-70 et seq.
Ariz. Rev. Stat. Ann., § 14-7601 et seq.
Colo. Rev. Stat., 15-1-601 et seq.
D.C. Code 1961, § 28-2901 et seq.
Del. Code of 1974, Title 12, § 4301 et seq.
Fla. Stat. Ann., 610.011 et seq.
Ga. Code Ann., 53-12-320 et seq.
Ida. Code 1947, 68-901 et seq.
Ill. Rev. Stat. 1991, Ch. 32, § 439.49 et seq.
Ind. Code Ann., 30-2-5-1 et seq.
Iowa Code 1983, 633.130 et seq.
Kan. Stat. Ann., 17-4903 et seq.
La. Rev. Stat. Ann., 9:3831 et seq.
Md. Ann. Code 1974, Art. ET, § 15-301 et seq.
Me. Rev. Stat. Ann. 1964, Title 13, § 641 et seq.
Mich. Comp. Laws Ann., 441.101 et seq.
Minn. Stat. Ann., 520.21 et seq.
Miss. Code Ann. 1972, § 91-11-1 et seq.
Mo. Rev. Stat., 403.250 et seq.
Mont. Code Ann., 30-10-401 et seq.
N.C. Gen. Stat. 1943, § 32-14 et seq.
N.D. Cent. Code, 10-18.1-01 et seq.
Neb. Rev. Stat. 1943, 30-3301 et seq.
Nev. Rev. Stat. Ann., 162.150 et seq.
N.J. Stat. Ann., 14:18-1 et seq.
N.M. Stat. Ann., 46-8-1 et seq.
N.Y. General Business Law (Consol. Laws Ch. 20) § 359m et seq.
R.I. Gen. Laws 1956, 18-11-1 et seq.
S.C. Code Ann. 1976, § 35-7-10 et seq.
S.D. Codified Laws 1967, 55-8-1 et seq.
Tenn. Code Ann., 35-8-101 et seq.
Tex. Business and Commerce Code, § 33.01 et seq.
Utah Code Ann. 1953, 22-5-1 et seq.
Va. Code 1950, § 13.1-424 et seq.

*Continued*

...0 et seq.

...-4D-1 et seq.,

... § 2-3-701 et seq.

**...multaneous Death Act**

...o Simultaneous Death Act

... Code 1975, § 43-7-1 et seq.

Alaska Stat. 1962, Replaced Titles, § 13.43.010 et seq.

Ariz. Rev. Stat. Ann. § 14-2804 et seq.

Ark. Code Ann. 1987, 28-10-101 et seq.

Cal. Probate Code § 220 et seq.

Colo. Rev. Stat., 15-11-613 et seq.

Conn. Gen. Stat. 1983, § 45-287

D.C. Code Ann., § 19-501 et seq.

Del. Code of 1974, Title 12, § 701 et seq.

Fla. Stat. Ann., 732.601 et seq.

Ga. Code Ann., 53-10-1 et seq., 53-11-1 et seq.

Haw. Rev. Stat. Ann., § 534-1 et seq.

Haw. Session Laws 1993, Act 122

Ida. Code 1947, 15-2-613

Ill. Rev. Stat. 1991, Ch. 110 1/2, §§ 3-1, 3-2

Ind. Code Ann., 29-2-14-1 et seq.

Iowa Code Ann., 633.523 et seq.

Kan. Stat. Ann., 58-701 et seq.,58-708 et seq.

Ky. Rev. Stat. 1971, 397.010 et seq.

Mass. Gen. Laws Ann., 190A:1 et seq.

Md. Ann. Code 1974, Art. CJ, § 10-801 et seq.

Me. Rev. Stat. Ann. 1964, Title 18-A, § 2-805 et seq.

Mich. Comp. Laws Ann., 720.101 et seq.

Minn. Stat. Ann., 525.90

Miss. Code Ann. 1972, § 91-3-1 et seq.

Mo. Rev. Stat., 471.010 et seq.

N.C. Gen. Stat. 1943, § 28A-24-1 et seq.

N.D. Cent. Code, 31-12-01 et seq.

Neb. Rev. Stat. 1943, 30-121 et seq.

Nev. Rev. Stat. Ann., 135.010 et seq.

N.H. Rev. Stat. 1955, 563:1 et seq.

N.J. Stat. Ann., 3B:6-1 et seq.

N.M. Stat. Ann., 45-8-1 et seq.

N.Y. Estate, Powers, and Trusts Law (Consol. Laws, Ch. 17B), 2-1.6

Okla. Stat. Ann., Title 58, § 1001 et seq.

Ore. Rev. Stat., 112.575 et seq.

Pa. Cons. Stat., Title 20, § 8501 et seq.

R.I. Gen. Laws 1956, 33-2-1 et seq.

S.C. Code Ann. 1976, § 62-1-501 et seq.

S.D. Codified Laws 1967, 29-8-1 et seq.

Tenn. Code Ann., 31-3-101 et seq.

Tex. Probate Code, § 47

Utah Code Ann. 1953, 75-2-1001 et seq.

Va. Code 1950, § 64.1-97 et seq.

Vt. Stat. Ann., Title 14, § 621 et seq.

Wash. Rev. Code Ann. 11.05.010 et seq.

Wis. Stat. Ann., 851.55

W. Va. Code 1966, § 42-5-1 et seq.

Wyo. Stat. Ann., § 2-13-101 et seq.

**Uniform Single Publication Act**

Ariz. Rev. Stat. Ann., § 12-651

Cal. Civil Code § 3425.1 et seq.

Fla. Stat. 770.05 et seq.

Ida. Code 1947, 6-702 et seq.

Ill. Rev. Stat. 1991, Ch. 126, § 11 et seq.

N.D. Cent. Code, 14-02-10

N.M. Stat. Ann., 41-7-1 et seq.

Pa. Cons. Stat., Title 42, § 8341 et seq.

**Uniform Small Loan Act**

Haw. Rev. Stat. Ann., § 409-1 et seq.

**Uniform Small Loan Law**

Md. Ann. Code 1957, Art. 58A

**Uniform Solicitorial Retirement Act**

N.C. Gen. Stat. 1943, §§ 135-77, 135-78

**Uniform Special District Accountability Act**

Fla. Stat. Ann., 189.401 et seq.

**Uniform Standards Code for Factory Manufactured Homes Act**

La. Rev. Stat. Ann., 51:911.21 et seq.

N.C. Gen. Stat. 1943, § 143-144 et seq.

Neb. Rev. Stat. 1943, 71-1555 et seq.

N.Y. Executive Law 1951 (Consol. Laws Ch. 18) § 400a et seq.

S.C. Code Ann. 1976, 40-20-10 et seq.

Tenn. Code Ann., Superseded Vols., 53-4801 et seq.

**Uniform Standards Code for Factory Manufactured Mobile Homes Act**
Ala. Code 1975, § 24-5-1 et seq.
Ark. Stat. 1947, 82-3001 et seq.
Fla. Stat. 1983, 320.822 et seq.
Ga. Code Ann., 8-2-130 et seq.
La. Rev. Stat. Ann., 51:911.21 et seq.
Miss. Code Ann. 1972, § 75-49-1 et seq.
N.J. Laws 1972, Ch. 148
Okla. Stat. Ann., Title 63, § 2451 et seq.
S.C. Code Ann. 1976, Superseded Vols., § 31-17-10 et seq.
Tex. Rev. Civ. Stat., Art. 5221f

**Uniform Standards Code for Manufactured Housing Units Act**
Neb. Rev. Stat. 1943, 71-1555 et seq.

**Uniform Standards Code for Mobile Homes and Recreational Vehicles**
Kan. Stat. Ann., 75-1211 et seq.
Neb. Rev. Stat. 1943, 71-4601 et seq.
Tenn. Code Ann., 68-126-101 et seq.

**Uniform Standards Code for Remanufactured Housing**
La. Rev. Stat. Ann., 51:912 et seq.

**Uniform Standby Charge Procedures Act**
Cal. Government Code § 54984 et seq.

**Uniform State Accounting Law**
Ky. Rev. Stat. 1971, 46.010 et seq.

**Uniform State Aeronautical Regulatory Act**
S.C. Code Ann. 1976, § 55-5-10 et seq.

**Uniform State Aeronautics Department Act**
Ida. Code 1947, 21-101 et seq.
Minn. Stat. Ann., 360.011 et seq.

**Uniform State Antitrust Act**
Ariz. Rev. Stat. Ann., § 44-1401 et seq.
Del. Code of 1974, Title 6, § 2101 et seq.
Mich. Comp. Laws Ann., 445.771 et seq.
N.D. Cent. Code, 51-08.1-01 et seq.

**Uniform State Grading Act**
N.D. Laws 1917, Ch. 56

**Uniform State Law of Aeronautics**
Ariz. Rev. Stat. Ann., § 2-101 et seq.
Ind. Code Ann., 8-21-4-1 et seq.
Md. Laws 1927, Ch. 637
Mont. Code Ann., 67-1-201 et seq.
N.D. Cent. Code, 2-03-01 et seq.
Nev. Rev. Stat. 1979 Reprint, 493.010 et seq.
N.J. Rev. Stat. 1937, 6:2-1 to 6:2-12
Pa. 1929 Pamph. Laws 753, No. 317
S.C. Code Ann. 1976, § 55-3-10 et seq.
S.D. Codified Laws 1967, 50-1-1 et seq.
Tenn. Code Ann., 42-1-101 et seq.
Wyo. Stat. Ann., § 10-4-101 et seq.

**Uniform State Laws Commission Act**
Ala. Code 1975, § 41-9-370 et seq.
Ariz. Rev. Stat. Ann., §§ 41-1306, 41-1307
Ark. Code Ann. 1987, 6-401 et seq.
Cal. Government Code § 10400 et seq.
Conn. Gen. Stat. 1983, § 2-80
Tex. Rev. Civ. Stat., Art. 1273b

**Uniform State Pharmacy Act**
Wyo. Stat. Ann., § 33-24-101 et seq.

**Uniform State School Law**
Tenn. Code Ann., 49-1-101 et seq.

**Uniform State Tax Procedure Law**
N.J. Stat. Ann., 54:48-1 to 54:52-3

**Uniform Statewide Accounting Project Act**
Tex. Rev. Civ. Stat., Art. 4348f

**Uniform Status of Convicted Persons Act**
Mont. Code Ann. 1987, 46-18-801

**Uniform Statute and Rule Construction Act**
N.M. Stat. Ann., 12-2A-1 to 12-2A-20

**Uniform Statute of Limitations on Foreign Claims Act**
Mich. Comp. Laws Ann., 600.5861
Okla. Stat. Ann., Title 12, § 104 et seq.
Pa. Cons. Stat., Title 42, § 5521 et seq.
W. Va. Code 1966, § 55-2A-1 et seq.

**Uniform Statutory Construction Act**
See also Statutory Construction Act
Colo. Rev. Stat., 2-4-101 et seq.
*Continued*

Iowa Code 1962, 4.1 et seq.
Ohio Rev. Code 1953, 1.41 et seq.
Wis. Stat. Ann., 990.001 et seq.

**Uniform Statutory Form Power of Attorney Act**
See also Statutory Form Power of Attorney Act
Cal. Probate Code § 4400 et seq.
Colo. Rev. Stat., 15-1-1301 et seq.
Kan. Stat. Ann., 58-610 et seq.
N.M. Stat. Ann., 45-5-601 to 45-5-617
Wis. Stat. Ann., 243.10

**Uniform Statutory Rule against Perpetuities Act**
Alaska Stat. 1962, § 34.27.050 et seq.
Colo. Rev. Stat., 15-11-1101 et seq.
Conn. Public Acts 1991, No. 44
Fla. Stat. Ann., 689.225
Ga. Code Ann., 44-6-200 et seq.
Haw. Session Laws 1992, Act 262
Kan. Stat. Ann., 59-3401 et seq.
Mich. Comp. Laws Ann., 554.71 et seq.
Minn. Stat. Ann., 501A.01 et seq.
Mont. Code Ann., 70-1-801 et seq.
N.C. Gen. Stat. 1943, §§ 41-15 to 41-22
Neb. Rev. Stat. 1943, 76-2001 et seq.
N.J. Stat. Ann., 46:2F-1 et seq.
Ore. Rev. Stat. 105.950 et seq.
S.C. Code Ann. 1976, § 27-6-10 et seq.
W. Va. Code 1966,§ 36-1A-1 et seq.

**Uniform Statutory Will Act**
Mass. Gen. Laws 1984, 191B:1 et seq.
N.M. Stat. Ann., 45-2A-1 et seq.

**Uniform Stock Transfer Act**
See also Uniform Commercial Code—Investment Securities
Ala. Code 1958, Title 10, § 48 et seq.
Alaska Laws 1959, Ch. 148
Ark. Pope's Digest 1937, § 2150 et seq.
Cal. Corporations Code § 2450 et seq.
Colo. Rev. Stat., 1963, 31-11-1 et seq.
Conn. Pub. Acts 1917, p. 2453, Ch. 325
D.C. Code 1961, § 28-2901 et seq.
Del. Code of 1953, Title 8, § 181 et seq.
Fla. Stat. 1965, 614.01 et seq.
Ga. Code Ann., 14-6-1 et seq.
Haw. Rev. Laws 1955, § 172-60 et seq.
Ill. Rev. Stat. 1961, Ch. 32, § 416 et seq.
Ind. Burns' 1933, 25-701 et seq.
Iowa Code 1962, 493A.1 et seq.
Kan. Laws 1947, Ch. 186
Ky. Rev. Stat. 1953, 274.010 et seq.
La. Rev. Stat. Ann., 12:621 et seq.
Mass. Gen. Laws 1932, Ch. 155, § 24 et seq.
Md. Ann. Code 1974, Art. CA, § 11-101 et seq.
Me. Rev. Stat. 1954, Ch. 53, § 51 et seq.
Minn. Stat. 1961, 302.01 et seq.
Miss. Code 1942, § 5359-01 et seq.
Mo. Rev. Stat., 403.025 et seq.
Mont. Rev. Code 1947, 15-628 et seq.
N.C. Laws 1955, Ch. 1371
N.D. Cent. Code, (Superseded Vol.), 10-18-01 et seq.
Neb. Laws 1941, Ch. 42
Nev. Rev. Stat. 1957, 79.010 et seq.
N.H. Rev. Stat. 1955, 382-A:1-103 et seq.
N.J. Stat. Ann., Superseded Vol., 14:8-23 et seq.
N.M. Stat. Ann. 1953, 51-5-1 et seq.
Okla. Stat. Ann., Title 12A, § 8-308 et seq.
Ore. Rev. Stat., 59.005 et seq.
Pa. 1911 Pamph. Laws, No. 126
S.C. Code Ann. 1962, § 12-301 et seq.
S.D. Code 1939, 11.0501 et seq.
Tenn. Code Ann., 48-24-101 et seq.
Va. Code 1950, § 13.1-401 et seq.
Vt. Acts 1947, No. 103
W. Va. Code 1931, § 31-1-41 et seq.
Wyo. Stat. 1957, § 17-79 et seq.

**Uniform Supervision of International Student Exchange Visitor Placement Organizations Act**
Cal. Government Code § 12620 et seq.

**Uniform Supervision of Trustees for Charitable Purposes Act**
See also Supervision of Trustees for Charitable Purposes Act
Cal. Government Code § 12580 et seq.
Ill. Rev. Stat. 1991, Ch. 14, § 41 et seq.
Mich. Comp. Laws Ann., 14.251 et seq.
Ore. Rev. Stat., 128.610 et seq.

**Uniform Support Act**
D.C. Code 1973, § 30-301 et seq.
Pa. Purdon's Stat., Title 62, § 1971 et seq.

**Uniform Support of Dependents Act**
Fla. Stat. Ann., 88.01 et seq.
Ga. Laws 1951, p. 107
Ill. Rev. Stat. 1991, Ch. 40, § 1101 et seq.
Iowa Code Ann., 252A.1 et seq.
Ky. Rev. Stat. 1971, 407.010 et seq.
N.Y. Domestic Relations Law (Consol. Laws Ch. 14) § 30 et seq.
Ohio Rev. Code 1953, 3115.01 et seq.
Okla. Stat. Ann., Title 12, § 1601 et seq.
S.C. Code Ann. 1976, § 20-7-110 et seq.

**Uniform System of Accounting Act**
Ala. Code 1958, Title 41, § 3

**Uniform Tax and Budget Act**
Ohio Rev. Code 1953, 5705.01 et seq.

**Uniform Tax Levy Act**
Ohio Rev. Code 1953, 5705.01 et seq.

**Uniform Tax Lien Registration and Enforcement Act**
Neb. Rev. Stat. 1943, 77-3901 et seq.

**Uniform Tax Procedure Act**
La. Rev. Stat. Ann., 47:1 et seq.
Okla. Stat. Ann., Title 68, § 201 et seq.

**Uniform Testamentary Additions to Trusts Act**
Alaska Stat. 1962, § 13.11.200
Ariz. Rev. Stat. Ann., § 14-2511
Ark. Code Ann. 1987, 28-27-101 et seq.
Cal. Probate Code § 6300 et seq.
Colo. Rev. Stat., 1963, 15-11-511
Conn. Gen. Stat. 1983, § 45a-173a
D.C. Code Ann., § 18-306
Del. Code 1974, Title 12 § 211
Fla. Stat. Ann., § 732.513
Ga. Code Ann., 53-12-70 et seq.
Haw. Rev. Stat. 1968, § 437-1 et seq.
Ida. Code 1947, § 15-2-511
Ill. Rev. Stat. 1991, Ch. 110 1/2 § 4-4
Ind. Code Ann., § 24-1-5-9
Iowa Code Ann., 633.277 et seq.
Kan. Stat. Ann., 59-3101 et seq.
Ky. Rev. Stat. 1971, 394.075, 394.076
Mass. Gen. Laws Ann., 203:3B
Md. Ann. Code 1974, Art. ET, § 4-411 et seq.
Me. Rev. Stat. Ann. 1964, Title 18-A, § 2-511
Mich. Comp. Laws Ann., 555.461 et seq.
Minn. Stat. Ann., 525.223
Miss. Code Ann. 1972, § 91-5-11
Mont. Code Ann., § 72-2-314
N.C. Gen. Stat. 1943, § 31-47
N.D. Cent. Code, § 30.1-08-11
Neb. Rev. Stat. 1943, § 30-2336
Nev. Rev. Stat. 1979 Reprint, 163.220 et seq.
N.H. Rev. Stat. 1955, 563-A:1 et seq.
N.J. Stat. Ann., 3B:4-1 et seq.
N.M. Stat. Ann., 46-5-1 et seq.
N.Y. Estates, Powers and Trust Law (Consol. Laws Ch. 17B) § 3-3.7
Ohio Rev. Code 1953, 2107.63
Okla. Stat. Ann., Title 84, § 301 et seq.
Ore. Rev. Stat., 112.265
Pa. Cons. Stat., Title 20, § 2515
R.I. Gen. Laws 1956, 18-14-1 et seq.
S.C. Code Ann. 1976, § 62-2-510 et seq.
S.D. Codified Laws 1967, 29-2-18 et seq.
Tenn. Code Ann., 32-3-106
Tex. Probate Code, § 58a
Utah Code Ann. 1953, 75-2-511
Vt. Stat. Ann., Title 14, § 2329
Wash. Rev. Code Ann., § 11.12.250
W. Va. Code 1966, § 41-3-8 et seq.
Wyo. Stat. Ann., § 2-6-103

**Uniform Textbook Act**
Ala. Code 1975, § 16-36-1 et seq.
Ark. Code Ann. 1987, 6-21-401 et seq.
Ky. Rev. Stat. 1948, 156.260 et seq., 157.100 et seq.
Tenn. Acts 1937, Ch. 246

**Uniform Time Act of 1966**
April 13, 1966, P.L. 89-387, 80 Stat. 107, 15 U.S. Code §§ 260, 260a, 261 to 263, 266, 267
March 30, 1972, P.L. 92-267, 86 Stat. 116, 15 U.S. Code § 260a
July 8, 1986, P.L. 99-359, 15 U.S. Code § 260a
*Continued*

**Uniform TOD Security Registration Act**
Colo. Rev. Stat., 1990, § 15-15-301 et seq.
N.D. Cent. Code, § 30.1-31-21 et seq.
Ore. Laws 1991, Ch. 306
Wis. Stat. Ann., § 705.21 et seq.

**Uniform Trade Practices Act (Insurance)**
Mich. Comp. Laws Ann., 500.2001 et seq.

**Uniform Trade Secrets Act**
See also Trade Secrets Act
Ala. Code 1975, § 8-27-1 et seq.
Alaska Stat. 1962, Replaced Titles, § 45.50.910 et seq.
Ariz. Rev. Stat. Ann., § 44-401 et seq.
Ark. Code Ann. 1987, 4-75-601 et seq.
Cal. Civil Code § 3426 et seq.
Colo. Rev. Stat., 7-74-101 et seq.
Conn. Gen. Stat. 1983, § 35-50 et seq.
D.C. Code 1973, § 48-501 et seq.
Del. Code of 1974, Title 6, § 2001 et seq.
Fla. Stat. Ann., 688.001 et seq.
Haw. Rev. Stat. Ann., § 482B-1 et seq.
Ida. Code 1947, 48-801 et seq.
Ill. Rev. Stat. 1991, Ch. 140, § 351 et seq.
Ind. Code Ann., 24-2-3-1 et seq.
Iowa Code Ann., 550.1 et seq.
Kan. Stat. Ann., 60-3320 et seq.
Ky. Rev. Stat. 1971, 365.880 et seq.
La. Rev. Stat. Ann., 51:1431 et seq.
Md. Ann. Code 1974, Art. CL, § 11-1201 et seq.
Me. Rev. Stat. Ann. 1964, Title 10, § 1541 et seq.
Minn. Stat. Ann., 325C.01 et seq.
Miss. Code Ann. 1972, § 75-26-1 et seq.
Miss. Laws 1990, Ch. 442, p. 294
Mont. Code Ann., 30-14-401 et seq.
N.D. Cent. Code, 47-25.1-01 et seq.
Neb. Rev. Stat. 1943, § 87-501 et seq.
Nev. Rev. Stat. (1987 Reprint), 600A.010 et seq.
N.H. Rev. Stat. 1955, 350-B:1 et seq.
N.M. Stat. Ann., 57-3A-1 et seq.
Okla. Stat. Ann., Title 78, § 85 et seq.
Ore. Rev. Stat. 646.461 et seq.
R.I. Gen. Laws 1956, 6-41-1 et seq.
S.C. Code Ann. 1976, § 39-8-1 et seq.
S.D. Codified Laws 1967, 37-29-1 et seq.
Utah Code Ann. 1953, 13-24-1 et seq.
Va. Code 1950, § 59.1-336 et seq.
Wash. Rev. Code Ann., 19.108.010 et seq.
Wis. Stat. Ann., 134.90
W. Va. Code 1966, § 47-22-1 et seq.

**Uniform Trademark Act**
Ala. Code 1975, §§ 8-12-6 et seq, 4511.01 et seq.
Tex. Business and Commerce, § 16.01 et seq.

**Uniform Traffic Act**
Ill. Rev. Stat. 1991, Ch. 95 1/2, § 11-100 et seq.
Kan. Stat. Ann., 8-1401 et seq.
La. Rev. Stat. Ann., 51:1431 et seq.
Ohio Rev. Code 1953, 4511.01 et seq.
Okla. Stat. Ann., Title 47, § 1-101 et seq.
S.C. Code Ann. 1976, §§ 56-5-170, 56-5-740, 56-5-1810, 56-5-2120, 56-5-2510 et seq., 56-5-3110, 56-5-3810
Tex. Rev. Civ. Stat., Art. 6701d

**Uniform Traffic Control Act**
Conn. Gen. Stat. 1983, § 14-212 et seq.
Fla. Stat. Ann., 316.001 et seq.

**Uniform Traffic Laws Act**
Alaska Stat. 1962, §§ 28.01.010, 28.01.020

**Uniform Traffic Regulation Act**
Minn. Stat. Ann., 169.01 et seq.

**Uniform Traffic Ticket Act**
Miss. Code Ann. 1972, § 63-9-21

**Uniform Traffic Ticket Offenses Act**
S.C. Code Ann. 1976, § 56-7-10 et seq.

**Uniform Transboundary Pollution Reciprocal Access Act**
Colo. Rev. Stat., 13-1.5-101 et seq.
Conn. Gen. Stat. 1983, § 51-351 et seq.
Mich. Comp. Laws Ann., 3.871 et seq.
Mont. Code Ann., 75-16-101 et seq.
N.J. Stat. Ann., 2A:58A-1 et seq.
Ore. Laws 1991, Ch. 826
Wis. Stat. Ann., 144.995

**Uniform Transcript and Certificate Act**
N.Y. Judiciary Law (Consol. Laws Ch. 30) § 255c

**Uniform Transfer of Dependents Act**
Cal. Welfare and Institutions Code § 18400 et seq.
Colo. Rev. Stat., 26-4-101 et seq.
Del. Code of 1953, Title 31, § 119
Ida. Code 1947, 68-801 et seq.
La. Rev. Stat. Ann., 46:401 et seq.
Me. Rev. Stat. Ann. 1964, Title 22, § 3102
Minn. Stat. Ann., 261.25, 261.251
N.D. Cent. Code, 50-06-11, 50-06-12
Pa. 1941 Pamph. Laws 20, No. 12
S.D. Codified Laws 1967, Superseded Vol., 28-16-7
Va. Code 1950, § 63.1-99

**Uniform Transfer of Shares Act**
Pa. 1911 Pamph. Laws 126

**Uniform Transfer on Death (TOD) Security Registration Act**
Ala. Code 1975, § 8-6-150 et seq.
Cal. Probate Code § 5500 et seq.
Conn. Public Acts 1997, No. 42
Fla. Stat. Ann., 711.50 to 711.512
Ga. Code Ann., 53-5-60 et seq.
Haw. Session Laws 1998, Act 63
Ida. Code 1947, 15-6-301 et seq.
Ill. Comp. Stat. 1992, Ch. 815, § 10/1
Iowa Code Ann., 633.800 to 633.811
Kan. Stat. Ann., 17-49a01 et seq.
Ky. Rev. Stat. 1971, 292.6501 to 292.6512
Mass. Gen. Laws Ann., 201E:101 et seq.
Md. Ann. Code 1974, Art. ET, § 16-101 et seq.
Miss. Code Ann. 1972, § 91-21-1 et seq.
N.J. Stat. Ann., 3B:30-1 et seq.
Okla. Stat. Ann., Title 71, § 901 et seq.
S.C. Code Ann. 1976, § 35-6-10 et seq.
Tenn. Code Ann., 35-12-101 to 35-12-113
Tex. Probate Code, §§ 466 to 480
Wash. Rev. Code Ann., 21.35.900
W. Va. Code 1966, § 36-10-1 et seq.
Wyo. Stat. 1977, § 2-16-101 et seq.

**Uniform Transfers to Minors Act**
See also Transfers to Minors Act
Alaska Stat. 1962, Replaced Titles, § 13.46.010 et seq.
Ariz. Rev. Stat. Ann., § 14-7651 et seq.
Cal. Probate Code § 3900 et seq.
Colo. Rev. Stat., 11-50-101 et seq.
Conn. Public Acts 1995, No. 117
Fla. Stat. Ann., 710.101 et seq.
Ga. Code Ann., 44-5-110 et seq.
Haw. Rev. Stat. Ann., § 553A-1 et seq.
Ill. Rev. Stat. 1991, Ch. 110 1/2, § 251 et seq.
Ill. Rev. Stat. 1991, Ch. 127, § 155h et seq.
Iowa Code Ann., 565B.1 et seq.
Kan. Stat. Ann., 38-1701 et seq.
Mass. Gen. Laws Ann., 201A:1 et seq.
Md. Ann. Code 1974, Art. ET, § 13-301 et seq.
Me. Rev. Stat. Ann. 1964, Title 33, § 1651 et seq.
Minn. Stat. Ann., 527.21 et seq.
Miss. Code Ann. 1972, § 91-20-1 et seq.
Mo. Rev. Stat., 404.005 et seq.
Mont. Code Ann., 72-26-501 et seq.
N.C. Gen. Stat. 1943, § 333A-1 et seq.
Neb. Laws 1992, L.B. 907, §§ 1 to 24
N.H. Rev. Stat. 1955, 463-A:1 et seq.
N.J. Stat. Ann., 46:38A-1 et seq.
N.M. Stat. Ann., 46-7-11 et seq.
N.Y. Estates, Powers and Trusts Law (Consol. Laws Ch. 17B) § 7-6.1 et seq.
Okla. Stat. Ann., Title 58, § 1201 et seq.
Ore. Rev. Stat., 126.805 et seq.
Pa. Cons. Stat., Title 20, § 5301 et seq.
R.I. Gen. Laws 1956, 18-7-1 et seq.
Tenn. Code Ann., 35-7-101 et seq.
Tex. Property Code, § 141.001 et seq.
Utah Code Ann. 1953, 75-5a-101 et seq.
Wash. Rev. Code 1991, 11.114.010 et seq.
Wis. Stat. Ann., 880.61 et seq.
W. Va. Code 1966, § 36-7-1 et seq.

**Uniform Transportation Replacement Housing Relocation Act**
N.J. Stat. Ann., 27:7-72 et seq.

**Uniform Trust Act**
N.M. Stat. Ann., 46-2-1 et seq.

**Uniform Trust Administration Law**
Fla. Stat. 1973, 737.101 et seq.

**Uniform Trust Receipts Act**
See also Uniform Commercial Code—Secured Transactions
Ala. Code 1958, Title 39, § 191(4) et seq.
Ariz. Laws 1947, Ch. 72
Ark. Stat. 1947, 68-1701 et seq.
Cal. Civil Code § 3012 et seq.
Del. Code of 1974, Title 6, § 1-101 et seq.
Fla. Stat. 1965, 673.01 et seq.
Haw. Rev. Laws 1955, § 206-1 et seq.
Ill. Rev. Stat. 1961, Ch. 121 1/2, § 166 et seq.
Ind. Burns' 1933, 51-601 et seq.
Mass. Gen. Laws 1932, Ch. 255A
Md. Ann. Code 1957, Art. 79, § 7
Me. Rev. Stat. 1954, Ch. 189, § 1 et seq.
Mich. Comp. Laws Ann. 1949, Supp. 1957, § 31A-1-1 et seq.
Mich. Comp. Laws 1948, 555.401 et seq.
Minn. Stat. 1961, 522.01 et seq.
Miss. Code 1942, § 5080-01 et seq.
Mont. Rev. Code 1947, 65-201 et seq.
N.C. Gen. Stat. 1943, § 45-46 et seq.
N.D. Cent. Code, Superseded Vol., 41-18-01 et seq.
Neb. Rev. Stat. 1943, Superseded Vol., 69-701 et seq.
Nev. Rev. Stat. 1957, 93.010 et seq.
N.J. Rev. Stat. 1937, 46:35-1 et seq.
N.M. Stat. Ann. 1953, 50-13-1 et seq.
Ore. Rev. Stat., 126.805 et seq.
Pa. 1941 Pamph. Laws 307, No. 138
P.R. Laws Ann. 1954, Title 10, § 611 et seq.
S.D. Code 1939, 39.1801 et seq.
Tenn. Public Acts 1937, Ch. 89
Va. Code 1950, § 6-550 et seq.
Wis. Stat. 1963, 241.31 et seq.
W. Va. Code 1931, Ch. 38, Art. 15, § 1 et seq.
Wyo. Stat. 1957, § 34-296 et seq.

**Uniform Trustees' Accounting Act**
Ind. Code Ann., 30-4-5-12
Kan. Stat. Ann., 59-1601 et seq., 59-2253 et seq.
Nev. Rev. Stat. 1979 Reprint, 165.010 et seq.
N.M. Stat. Ann. 1953, 33-2-1 et seq.

**Uniform Trustees' Powers Act**
Ariz. Rev. Stat. Ann., § 14-7231 et seq.
Fla. Stat. Ann., 737.401 et seq.
Haw. Rev. Stat. Ann., § 554A-1 et seq.
Ida. Code 1947, 68-104 et seq.
Kan. Stat. Ann., 58-1201 et seq.
Ky. Rev. Stat. 1971, 386.800 et seq.
Me. Rev. Stat. Ann. 1964, Title 18-A, § 7-401 et seq.
Mich. Comp. Laws Ann., 700.821 et seq.
Miss. Code Ann. 1972, § 91-9-101 et seq.
Mont. Code Ann., 72-21-101 et seq.
Neb. Rev. Stat. 1943, § 30-2819 et seq.
N.H. Rev. Stat. 1955, 564-A:1 et seq.
N.M. Stat. Ann. 1953, 75-7-401
Ore. Rev. Stat., 128.003 et seq.
S.C. Code Ann. 1976, § 62-7-701 et seq.
Utah Code Ann. 1953, 75-7-401 et seq.
Wyo. Stat. Ann., § 4-8-101 et seq.

**Uniform Trusts Act**
La. Rev. Stat. Ann., 9:1791 et seq.
N.C. Gen. Stat. 1943, § 36A-60 et seq.
Nev. Rev. Stat. 1979 Reprint, 163.010 et seq.
N.M. Stat. Ann. 1953, 46-2-1 et seq.
Okla. Stat. Ann., Title 60, § 175.1 et seq.
S.D. Codified Laws 1967, 55-4-1 et seq.

**Uniform Unauthorized Insurers Act**
Ala. Code 1975, § 27-10-1 et seq.
Ark. Stat. 1947, 23-65-101 et seq.
Conn. Gen. Stat. 1983, § 38a-271 et seq.
Ida. Code 1947, 41-1201 et seq.
Ill. Rev. Stat. 1991, Ch. 73, § 733 et seq.
Ind. Code Ann., 27-4-5-1 et seq.
Iowa Code Ann., 507A.1 et seq.
Kan. Stat. Ann., 40-2701 et seq.
Ky. Rev. Stat. 1971, 304.11-010 et seq.
La. Rev. Stat. Ann., 22:1251 et seq.
N.C. Gen. Stat. 1943, § 58-28-45
Neb. Rev. Stat. 1943, 44-2001 et seq.

Nev. Rev. Stat. 1979 Reprint, 685B.020 et seq.
N.H. Rev. Stat. 1955, 406-B:1 et seq.
Okla. Stat. Ann., Title 36, § 1101 et seq.
R.I. Gen. Laws 1956, 27-16-1.1 et seq.
S.C. Code Ann. 1976, Superseded Vols., § 38-25-10 et seq.
S.D. Laws 1939, Ch. 129
Tex. Insurance Code, Art. 21.38
Utah Code Ann. 1953, 31A-15-102 et seq.
Wash. Rev. Code Ann., 48.15.020 et seq.
Wis. Stat. 1973, 201.42

**Uniform Unclaimed Property Act**
Alaska Stat. 1962, § 34.45.110 et seq.
Ariz. Rev. Stat. Ann., § 44-301 et seq.
Cal. Code of Civil Procedure § 1300 et seq.
Colo. Rev. Stat., 38-13-101 et seq.
Fla. Stat. Ann., 717.01 et seq.
Ga. Code Ann., 44-12-190, et seq.
Haw. Rev. Stat § 523A-1 et seq.
Ida. Code 1947, 14-501 et seq.
Ill. Rev. Stat. 1991, Ch. 141, § 0.01 et seq.
Iowa Code Ann., 556.1 et seq.
Kan. Stat. Ann., 58-3901 et seq.
La. Rev. Stat. Ann., 9:151 et seq.
Mass. Gen. Laws Ann., 200A:1 et seq.
Md. Ann. Code 1974, Art. CL, § 17-101
Me. Rev. Stat. Ann. 1964, Title 33, §§ 1801 et seq.,1951 et seq.
Mich. Comp. Laws. Ann., 567.221 et seq.
Minn. Stat. 1961, 345.31 et seq.
Miss. Code Ann. 1972, § 89-12-1 et seq.
Mont. Code Ann., 70-9-101 et seq.
N.D. Cent. Code, 47-30.1-01 et seq.
Nev. Rev. Stat. 1957, 120A.010 et seq.
N.H. Rev. Stat. 1955, Superseded Vols., 471-C:1 et seq.
N.J. Stat Ann., 46:30B-1 et seq.
N.M. Stat. Ann., 7-8-1 et seq., 7-8A-1 et seq.
Okla. Stat. Ann., Title 60, § 651 et seq.
Ore. Code 1991, 98.302 et seq.
R.I. Gen. Laws 1956, 33-21.1-1 et seq.
S.C. Code Ann. 1976, § 27-18-10 et seq.
Tenn. Code Ann., 66-29-101 et seq.
Va. Code 1950, § 55-210.1 et seq.
Vt. Stat. Ann., Title 27, § 1208 et seq.
Wash. Rev. Code Ann., 63.24.150 et seq.
Wis. Stat. Ann., 177.01 et seq.
W. Va. Code 1966, § 36-8-1 et seq.
Wyo. Stat. 1977, § 34-24-101 et seq.

**Uniform Unincorporated Nonprofit Association Act**
Ark. Code 1987, 4-28-501 et seq.
Colo. Rev. Stat., 7-30-115 et seq.
Ida. Code 1947, 53-715 et seq.
W. Va. Code 1966, § 36-11-1 et seq.

**Uniform Up-State Jury Law (Selection of Jurors)**
N.Y. Judiciary Law (Consol. Laws Ch. 30) § 500 et seq.

**Uniform Vehicle Certificate of Title Act**
N.Y. Vehicle and Traffic Law 1959 (Consol. Laws Ch. 71) § 2101 et seq.

**Uniform Vehicle Code**
Alaska Stat. 1962, § 28.01.010 et seq.
Okla. Stat. Ann., Title 47, § 1-101 et seq.
Tenn. Code Ann., 55-1-101 et seq.

**Uniform Vehicle Equipment Safety Act**
Mich. Comp. Laws Ann., 257.1001 et seq.

**Uniform Vehicle, Mount, Vessel and Plane Seizure Act**
P.R. Laws Ann. 1954, Title 34, §§ 1721, 1722

**Uniform Vendor and Purchaser Risk Act**
Cal. Civil Code § 1662
Haw. Rev. Stat. Ann., § 508-1
Ill. Rev. Stat. 1991, Ch. 29, § 8.1 et seq.
Mich. Comp. Laws Ann., 565.701 et seq.
N.C. Gen. Stat. 1943, § 39-37 et seq.
Nev. Rev. Stat. 1979 Reprint, 113.030 et seq.
N.M. Stat. Ann., 47-1A-1, 47-1A-2
N.Y. General Obligations Law (Consol. Laws Ch. 24A) § 5-1311
Okla. Stat. Ann., Title 16, § 201 et seq.
Ore. Rev. Stat., 93.290 et seq.
S.D. Codified Laws 1967, 43-26-5 et seq.
Tex. Property Code, § 5.007
Wis. Stat. Ann., 453.02 et seq., 706.12

**Uniform Vendors Reciprocity Act**
W. Va. Code 1966, § 5A-3-45

**Uniform Veterans' Guardianship Act**
See also Veterans' Guardianship Act
Ark. Code Ann. 1987, 28-66-101 et seq.
Colo. Rev. Stat., 28-5-201 et seq.
Fla. Stat. Ann., 744.602 et seq.
Ind. Code Ann., 29-1-19-1 et seq.
Kan. Stat. Ann., 73-501 et seq.
Ky. Rev. Stat. 1971, 388.190 et seq.
La. Rev. Stat. Ann., 29:351 et seq.
Mich. Comp. Laws. Ann., 35.88
Miss. Code Ann. 1972, § 35-5-3 et seq.
Mo. Rev. Stat., 475.380 et seq.
N.C. Gen. Stat. 1943, § 34-1 et seq.
N.H. Rev. Stat. 1955, 465:1 et seq.
Ohio Rev. Code 1953, 5905.01 et seq.
Okla. Stat. Ann., Title 72, § 126.1 et seq.
R.I. Gen. Laws 1956, 33-16-1 et seq.
S.D. Codified Laws 1967, 30-33-1 et seq.
S.D. Laws 1992, Ch. 312
Tenn. Code Ann., 34-5-101 et seq.
Vt. Stat. Ann., Title 14, § 3101 et seq.
Wash. Rev. Code Ann., 73.36.010 et seq.
Wis. Stat. Ann., 880.60

**Uniform Veteran's Guardianship Act 1972 (Mental Hygiene Law 1972)**
N.Y. General Obligations Law (Consol. Laws, Ch. 27), § 79.01 et seq.

**Uniform Vital Statistics Act**
Ark. Code Ann. 1987, 20-18-102 et seq.
Haw. Rev. Stat. Ann., § 338-1 et seq.
Ida. Code 1947, 39-240 et seq.
Kan. Stat. Ann., 65-2401 et seq.
La. Rev. Stat. Ann., 40:32 et seq.
Mich. Comp. Laws Ann. 1949, Supp. 1957, § 40-11-31 et seq.
Minn. Stat. Ann., 144.211 et seq.
Mo. Rev. Stat., 193.005 et seq.
Okla. Stat. Ann., Title 63, § 560.1 et seq.
Ore. Rev. Stat., 432.005 et seq.
Pa. 1943 Pamph. Laws 414, No. 192
Tenn. Code Ann., 68-3-101 et seq.
Wyo. Stat. 1957, § 35-36 et seq.

**Uniform Vocational and Professional Licensing Act**
Haw. Rev. Stat. Ann., § 436B-1 et seq.

**Uniform Wage Payment Law**
N.C. Gen. Stat. 1943, § 95-25.1 et seq.

**Uniform War Service Validation Act**
Wis. Stat. 1969, 235.255

**Uniform Warehouse Receipts Act**
See also Uniform Commercial Code—Documents of Title
Ala. Code 1958, Title 2, § 504 et seq.
Ariz. Laws 1921, Ch. 47
Ark. Stat. 1947, 68-1201 et seq.
Cal. Civil Code § 1858.01 et seq.
Colo. Rev. Stat., 1963, 147-1-1 et seq.
Conn. Gen. Stat. Ann., § 40-1 et seq.
Fla. Stat. 1965, 678.01 et seq.
Ga. Code 1933, 111-401 et seq.
Haw. Rev. Laws 1955, § 207-1 et seq.
Ida. Laws 1915, Ch. 31
Ill. Rev. Stat. 1981, Ch. 114, § 233 et seq.
Ind. Code Ann., 26-3-2-1 et seq.
Iowa Code Ann., 554.721 et seq.
Kan. Laws 1909, Ch. 262
Ky. Rev. Stat. 1953, 358.010 et seq.
La. Rev. Stat. Ann., 10:7-201 et seq.
Mass. Gen. Laws Ann., 106:7-501 et seq.
Md. Ann. Code 1974, Art. CL, § 7-601
Me. Rev. Stat. 1954, Ch. 187, § 1 et seq.
Mich. Comp. Laws Ann. 1949, § 31-1-1 et seq.
Minn. Stat. 1961, 227.01 et seq.
Miss. Code 1942, § 5012 et seq.
Mo. Rev. Stat. 1959, 406.010 et seq.
Mont. Rev. Code 1947, 88-150 et seq.
N.C. Gen. Stat. 1943, § 27-1 et seq.
Neb. Rev. Stat. 1943, 88-101 et seq.
Nev. Rev. Stat. 1957, 95.010 et seq.
N.H. Rev. Stat. 1955, Superseded Vols., 335:1 et seq.
N.J. Stat. Ann., Superseded Vol., 57:1-1 et seq.
N.M. Stat. Ann. 1953, 50-8-1 et seq.
Okla. Stat. Ann., Title 81, § 261 et seq.
Ore. Code 1930, § 71-201 et seq.

Pa. 1909 Pamph. Laws 19, No. 13
P.R. Laws Ann. 1954, Title 10, § 391 et seq.
R.I. Gen. Laws 1956, Superseded Vol., 6-25-1 et seq.
S.C. Code Ann. 1962, § 69-151 et seq.
S.D. Code 1939, 60.0401 et seq.
Tenn. Code Ann., Superseded Vol., 47-901 et seq.
Va. Code 1950, § 61-1 et seq.
Vt. Acts 1912, No. 186
W. Va. Code 1931, § 475-1 et seq.
Wyo. Stat. 1957, § 34-315 et seq.

**Uniform Warning Light Act**
Neb. Rev. Stat. 1943, 39-6, 148 et seq.

**Uniform Water District Regulations**
Neb. Rev. Stat. 1943, 39-6, 148 et seq.
N.Y. Local Laws 1969, Town of Skaneateles, p. 2081
N.Y. Local Laws 1970, Town of Lee, p. 2013

**Uniform Weights and Measures Act**
N.C. Gen. Stat. 1943, § 81A-37 et seq.
S.C. Code Ann. 1976, § 39-9-10 et seq.

**Uniform Weights and Measures Law**
S.C. Code Ann. 1976, § 39-9-10 et seq.

**Uniform Wildlife Regulatory Act**
Tex. Parks and Wildlife Code, § 61.001 et seq.

**Uniform Wills Act (Foreign Executed)**
La. Rev. Stat. Ann., 9:2401
Mass. Gen. Laws Ann., 191:5
Wis. Stat. Ann., 853.05

**Uniform Wills Act (Foreign Probated)**
La. Rev. Stat. Ann., 9:2421 et seq.
Pa. Purdon's Stat., Title 33, § 6 et seq.

**Uniform Witness Attendance Law**
Miss. Code Ann. 1972, § 99-9-27 et seq.

**Uniform Written Obligations Act**
Pa. Purdon's Stat., Title 33, § 6 et seq.

**Uniform Youth Court Systems and Procedures Act**
Miss. Code Ann. 1972, § 43-21-701 et seq.

**Uniformed and Overseas Citizens Absentee Voting Ac**
Aug. 28, 1986, P.L. 99-410, 42 U.S. Code §§ 1973ff nt., 1973ff-1 to 1973ff-6
Oct. 21, 1998, P.L. 105-277, 42 U.S. Code § 1973ff

**Uniformed Services Contingency Option Act of 1953**
Aug. 8, 1953, Ch. 393, 67 Stat. 501 (See 10 U.S. Code §§ 1431 to 1444)
April 29, 1954, Ch. 176, 68 Stat. 64 (See 10 U.S. Code §§ 1431 to 1433)
Aug. 1, 1956, Ch. 837, 70 Stat. 884 (See 10 U.S. Code § 1441)

**Uniformed Services Employment and Reemployment Rights Act of 1994**
Oct. 13, 1994, P.L. 103-353, 38 U.S. Code §§ 101 nt., 4301 et seq.
Oct. 9, 1996, P.L. 104-275, 38 U.S. Code § 4301 nt.

**Uniformed Services Former Spouses' Protection Act**
Sept. 8, 1982, P.L. 97-252, 10 U.S. Code § 1401 nt.

**Uniformed Services Health Professionals Special Pay Act of 1980**
June 28, 1980, P.L. 96-284, 37 U.S. Code §§ 101 nt., 302 et seq.

**Uniformed Services Health Professions Revitalization Act of 1972**
Sept. 21, 1972, P.L. 92-426, 86 Stat. 713, 10 U.S. Code §§ 2112 to 2117, 2120 to 2127
Nov. 16, 1990, P.L. 101-597, 10 U.S. Code § 2123

**Uniformed Services Pay Act of 1963**
Oct. 2, 1963, P.L. 88-132, 77 Stat. 210, 10 U.S. Code §§ 1401a, 1402, 3991, 6151, 6323, 6325 to 6327, 6381, 6383, 6390, 6394, 6396, 6398 to 6400, 6483, 8991; 14 U.S. Code § 423; 33 U.S. Code § 857a; 37 U.S. Code §§ 201, 203, 301, 302, 305, 310, 403, 421, 427; 42 U.S. Code § 213a

**Uniformed Services Pay Act of 1981**
Oct. 14, 1981, P.L. 97-60, 37 U.S. Code § 101 nt.

**Uniformed Services Survivor Benefits Amendments of 1980**
Oct. 9, 1980, P.L. 96-402, 10 U.S. Code § 1447 nt.

**Uniformed Services Survivors' Benefits Amendments of 1978**
Nov. 9, 1979, P.L. 96-107, 10 U.S. Code § 1447 nt.

**Uniformity Clause (Taxation)**
Minn. Const. 1857, Art. 9, § 1

**Uniforms Act**
La. Rev. Stat. Ann., 23:963 (Employees)
La. Rev. Stat. Ann., 29:18 et seq. (National Guard)
La. Rev. Stat. Ann., 40:1376 (Department of Public Safety)

**Unigov Act (Consolidated First Class Cities and Counties)**
Ind. Code Ann., 36-3-1-1 et seq.

**Unincorporated Area Certified Territory Law**
Pa. Cons. Stat., Title 15, § 7351 et seq.

**Unincorporated Association Act**
Ohio Rev. Code 1953, 1745.01 et seq.

**Unincorporated Associations Act (Legal Actions)**
Ga. Code Ann., 9-2-24 et seq.

**Unincorporated Associations Property Act**
Ill. Rev. Stat. 1991, Ch. 30, § 182.9 et seq.

**Unincorporated Business Franchise Tax Revision Act**
D.C. Code Ann., § 47-1803.3

**Unincorporated Business Tax Act**
N.J. Stat. Ann., 54:11B-1 et seq.
N.Y. Tax Law (Consol. Laws Ch. 60) § 386 et seq.
R.I. Gen. Laws 1956, 44-10-1 et seq.

**Unincorporated Nonprofit Association Act**
See also Uniform Unincorporated Nonprofit Association Act
Ala. Code 1975, § 10-3B-1 et seq.
Wyo. Stat. Ann., § 17-21-101 et seq.

**Unincorporated Professional Association Act**
Ala. Code 1975, § 10-10-1 et seq.
S.C. Code Ann. 1976, Superseded Vols., § 33-51-10 et seq.

**Unincorporated Territory Sewer Districts Act**
Cal. Health and Safety Code § 4659 et seq.

**Unincorporated Town Government Law**
Nev. Rev. Stat. 1979 Reprint, 269.500 et seq.

**Uninhabited Territory Annexation Act**
Cal. Government Code § 35300 et seq.

**Uninsurable Health Insurance Plan Act**
Colo. Rev. Stat., 10-8-501 et seq.
Kan. Stat. Ann., 40-2117 et seq.

**Uninsured Children's Program Act**
Ark. Code Ann. 1987, 22-77-601 et seq.

**Uninsured Motor Vehicle Accident Claims Act**
Mich. Comp. Laws Ann., 257.1101 et seq.

**Uninsured Motor Vehicle Registration Act**
Va. Code 1950, § 46.2-706 et seq.

**Uninsured Motorist Identification Database Program Act**
Colo. Rev. Stat., 42-7-601, 42-7-602
Utah Code Ann. 1953, 41-12a-801 et seq.

**Uninsured Motorists Act**
Ala. Code 1975, § 32-7-23
Ariz. Rev. Stat. Ann., § 20-259.01
Ark. Code Ann. 1987, 23-89-403, 23-89-404
Cal. Insurance Code § 11580.2
Fla. Stat. Ann., 627.727 et seq.
Ga. Code Ann., 33-7-11
Ill. Rev. Stat. 1991, Ch. 73, § 755a
Ind. Code Ann., 27-7-5-1 et seq.
Iowa Code Ann., 516A.1 et seq.

La. Rev. Stat. Ann., 22:1406
Md. Rules of Procedure, Rule BW 1 et seq.
Mich. Comp. Laws Ann., 257.1101 et seq.
N.H. Rev. Stat. 1955, 264:14
N.Y. Insurance Law (Consol. Laws Ch. 28) § 5201 et seq.
Ohio Rev. Code 1953, 3937.18
Ore. Rev. Stat., 742.500 et seq.
Pa. Purdon's Stat., Title 40, § 2000
S.C. Code Ann. 1976, Superseded Vols., § 56-9-810 et seq.
Tenn. Code Ann., 56-7-1201 et seq.
Tex. Insurance Code, Art. 5.06-1
Va. Code 1950, § 38.2-2206
Vt. Stat. Ann., Title 23, § 941 et seq.

**Union Act (Credit)**
Neb. Rev. Stat. 1943, 21-1760 et seq.

**Union Control Act**
S.D. Codified Laws 1967, 60-9-6 et seq.

**Union County Family Connection Commission Act**
Ga. Laws 1999, S.B. 151

**Union Depot Act (Railroads)**
Ill. Rev. Stat. 1991, Ch. 114, § 175 et seq.
N.C. Gen. Stat. 1943, § 62-231

**Union Depot Companies Act**
Mich. Comp. Laws Ann., 471.1 et seq.

**Union High School Law**
Ore. Rev. Stat., 335.210 et seq.

**Union-Jackson Counties Regional Port District Act**
Ill. Rev. Stat. 1991, Ch. 19, § 851 et seq.

**Union Label Act**
Conn. Gen. Stat. 1983, § 35-18a et seq.
Fla. Stat. Ann., 506.06 et seq.
Ida. Code 1947, 44-601 et seq.
Ill. Rev. Stat. 1991, Ch. 121 1/2, § 1301 et seq.
Ind. Burns' 1933, 66-101 et seq.
La. Rev. Stat. Ann., 51:211 et seq.
Me. Rev. Stat. Ann. 1964, Title 10, § 1521 et seq.
Nev. Rev. Stat. 1979 Reprint, 600.010 et seq.
N.Y. Labor Law (Consol. Laws Ch. 31) §§ 208, 209
Pa. Cons. Stat., Title 54 § 1311 et seq.

**Union Labor Act**
La. Rev. Stat. Ann., 51:211 et seq.

**Union Pacific Railroad Charter**
July 1, 1862, Ch. 120, 12 Stat. 489

**Union Regulation Act**
Fla. Stat. Ann., 447.01 et seq.
Kan. Stat. Ann., 44-801 et seq.
N.D. Cent. Code, 34-09-01 et seq.
Tex. Rev. Civ. Stat., Art. 5154a

**Union Reporting Act (Labor)**
Conn. Gen. Stat. 1983, § 31-77

**Union Responsibility Act**
Ga. Code Ann., 9-2-24 et seq.

**Union School District Act**
Vt. Stat. Ann., Title 16, § 701 et seq.

**Union Security Act**
Fla. Stat. 1983, 447.01 et seq.
Tex. Business and Commerce Code, § 15.03 et seq.
Wis. Stat. 1981, 111.06

**Union Station Redevelopment Act of 1981**
Dec. 29, 1981, P.L. 97-125, 40 U.S. Code § 801 nt.

**Union Station Tracks Act**
May 23, 1908, Ch. 190, 35 Stat. 246

**Unit Act (County Schools)**
Neb. Laws 1915, Ch. 233

**Unit Act (County)**
Ore. Rev. Stat., 333.005 et seq.

**Unit Development Act**
N.J. Stat. Ann., 40:55D-37 et seq.

**Unit of Assessment Law**
Ala. Code 1958, Title 51, § 78 et seq.

**Unit Operation Act**
Ala. Code 1975, § 9-17-80 et seq.
Mich. Comp. Laws Ann., 319.351 et seq.

**Unit Ownership Act**
Conn. Gen. Stat. 1983, § 47-68c et seq.
Me. Rev. Stat. 1964, Title 33, § 560 et seq.
Mont. Code Ann., 70-23-101 et seq.
N.C. Gen. Stat. 1943, § 47A-1 et seq.
N.H. Rev. Stat. 1955, 479-A:1 et seq.
Ore. Rev. Stat., 94.004 et seq.
Wis. Stat. Ann., 703.01 et seq.

**Unit Ownership Act (Building)**
N.M. Stat. Ann., 47-7-1 et seq.

**Unit Ownership Estate Act**
Okla. Stat. Ann., Title 60, § 501 et seq.

**Unit Price Disclosure Act**
N.J. Stat. Ann., 56:8-21 et seq.

**Unit Pricing Act**
Fla. Stat. Ann., 501.135
N.Y. Agriculture and Markets Law (Consol. Laws Ch. 69) §§ 214h, 214i
Ore. Rev. Stat., 616.850 et seq.
Vt. Stat. Ann., Title 6, § 681 et seq.

**Unit Primary Act**
Tenn. Code Ann., Superseded Vol., 26-801 et seq.

**Unit Property Act**
Del. Code of 1974, Title 25, § 2201 et seq.
Pa. Cons. Stat., Title 68, § 3101 et seq.
W. Va. Code 1966, § 36A-1-1 et seq.

**Unit System Act**
Ala. Code 1958, Title 51, § 78 et seq.
Ore. Rev. Stat., 333.005 et seq.

**Unitary Residence and Financial Responsibility Act**
Minn. Stat. Ann., 256G.01 et seq.

**Unitary Review Act (Capital)**
Pa. Cons. Stat., Title 42, § 9570 et seq.

**Unitary Wind Tunnel Plan Act of 1949**
Oct. 27, 1949, Ch. 766, 63 Stat. 936, 50 U.S. Code §§ 511, 511 nt., 512 to 515
July 29, 1958, P.L. 85-568, 72 Stat. 433, 50 U.S. Code §§ 511 to 513, 515

**United Companies Act**
N.J. Laws 1869, Ch. 386

**United Nations Palestine Refugee Aid Act of 1950**
June 5, 1950, Ch. 220, 64 Stat. 203

**United Nations Participation Act of 1945**
Dec. 20, 1945, Ch. 583, 59 Stat. 619, 22 U.S. Code §§ 287 to 287e
Oct. 10, 1949, Ch. 660, 63 Stat. 734, 22 U.S. Code §§ 287, 287c, 287d, 287d-1, 287e
Sept. 6, 1960, P.L. 86-707, 74 Stat. 797, 22 U.S. Code § 287e
Sept. 28, 1965, P.L. 89-206, 79 Stat. 841, 22 U.S. Code § 287
March 18, 1977, P.L. 95-12, 22 U.S. Code § 287c et seq.
Nov. 22, 1983, P.L. 98-164, 22 U.S. Code § 287e-1
Oct. 1, 1988, P.L. 100-459, 22 U.S. Code §§ 287e, 287e-1
April 30, 1994, P.L. 103-236, 22 U.S. Code § 287b

**United Nations Relief and Rehabilitation Administration Participation Act of 1946**
Dec. 14, 1945, Ch. 577, 59 Stat. 609

**United Nations Relief and Rehabilitation Administration Participation Appropriation Act, 1945**
June 30, 1944, Ch. 324, 58 Stat. 629

**United Services Organization's 50th Anniversary Commemorative Coin Act**
Oct. 2, 1990, P.L. 101-404, 31 U.S. Code § 5112 nt.

**United States Arbitration Act**
Feb. 12, 1925, Ch. 213, 43 Stat. 883 (See 9 U.S. Code §§ 1 to 14, 201 to 208)

**United States-Canada Free-Trade Agreement Act of 1988**

Aug. 20, 1990, P.L. 101-382, 19 U.S. Code §§ 1677f, 2112 nt.

**United States-Canada Free-Trade Agreement Implementation Act of 1988**

Dec. 7, 1989, P.L. 101-207, 19 U.S. Code § 2112 nt.

**United States-Canada Free-Trade Implementation Act of 1988**

Dec. 8, 1993, P.L. 103-182, 19 U.S. Code § 2112 nt.

Dec. 21, 1995, P.L. 104-66, 19 U.S. Code § 2112 nt.

July 22, 1998, P.L. 105-206, 19 U.S. Code § 2112 nt.

**United States Coast Guard Bicentennial Medal Act**

March 30, 1990, P.L. 101-260, 31 U.S. Code § 5111 nt.

**United States Coin Act of 1997**

Dec. 1, 1997, P.L. 105-124, 31 U.S. Code § 5101 nt.

**United States Commemorative Coin Act of 1996**

Oct. 20, 1996, P.L. 104-329, 31 U.S. Code § 5101 nt.

**United States Commission on Civil Rights Act of 1983**

Nov. 30, 1983, P.L. 98-183, 42 U.S. Code § 1975 et seq.

Nov. 28, 1989, P.L. 101-480, 42 U.S. Code §§ 1975e, 1975f

**United States Commission on Civil Rights Act of 1992**

Oct. 6, 1983, P.L. 102-400, 42 U.S. Code § 1975e

**United States Commission on Civil Rights Authorization Act of 1992**

Oct. 6, 1992, P.L. 102-400, 42 U.S. Code § 1975 nt.

**United States Commission on Civil Rights Reauthorization Act of 1983**

Nov. 26, 1991, P.L. 102-167, 42 U.S. Code §§ 1975, 1975a, 1975c, 1975d, 1975e, 1975f

**United States Commission on Civil Rights Reauthorization Act of 1991**

Nov. 26, 1991, P.L. 102-167, 42 U.S. Code § 1974 nt.

**United States Commissioners Act**

May 28, 1896, Ch. 252, 29 Stat. 140, 5 U.S. Code §§ 38, 92 (See 18 U.S. Code §§ 203, 3041, 3045, 3569) 20 U.S. Code § 3; 22 U.S. Code § 257 (See 28 U.S. Code 502, 505, 508 to 510, 541, 542, 550 to 553 631, 633, 636, 637, 751, 953, 958, 1918, 1922, 1923, 1929) 31 U.S. Code §§ 495, 670; 46 U.S. Code §§ 603, 604; 49 U.S. Code § 12

**United States Congress Commemorative Coin Act**

May 25, 1990, P.L. 101-302, 31 U.S. Code § 5112 nt.

**United States Constitution Amendment Act**

Ill. Rev. Stat. 1991, Ch. 1, §§ 300, 301

**United States Cotton Futures Act**

Oct. 4, 1976, P.L. 94-455, 7 U.S. Code § 15b

Dec. 13, 1991, P.L. 102-237, 7 U.S. Code § 15b

**United States Cotton Futures Acts**

Aug. 18, 1914, Ch. 255, 38 Stat. 693

Aug. 11, 1916, Ch. 313, 39 Stat. 453, 7 U.S. Code §§ 71 to 87, 111, 113, 241 to 273, 2209; 16 U.S. Code §§ 490, 683; 31 U.S. Code §§ 617, 638e

**United States Cotton Standards Act**

March 4, 1923, Ch. 288, 42 Stat. 1517, 7 U.S. Code §§ 51 to 65

Sept. 21, 1944, Ch. 412, 58 Stat. 734, 7 U.S. Code §§ 56, 57, 57a

Oct. 24, 1988, P.L. 100-518, 7 U.S. Code § 55

**United States Courthouse Cession Act (Chicago)**
Ill. Comp. Stat. 1992, Ch. 5, §§ 530/0.01, 530/1

**United States Fire Administration Authorization Act for Fiscal Years 1998 and 1999**
Nov. 20, 1997, P.L. 105-108, 15 U.S. Code § 2201 nt.

**United States Fishing Fleet Improvement Act**
June 12, 1960, P.L. 86-516, 74 Stat. 212, 46 U.S. Code §§ 1401 to 1413
Aug. 30, 1964, P.L. 88-498, 78 Stat. 614, 46 U.S. Code §§ 1401 to 1403, 1405, 1409, 1412, 1413
June 12, 1970, P.L. 91-279, 84 Stat. 307, 46 U.S. Code §§ 1402, 1403, 1405, 1407, 1409, 1411 to 1413

**United States Flood Control Receipts Fund Act**
Cal. Government Code § 16415 et seq.

**United States Friendship Treaty (1849)**
Haw. Session Laws 1850, p. 208, Dec. 20, 1849

**United States Grain Standards Act**
Aug. 11, 1916, Ch. 313, 39 Stat. 453, 7 U.S. Code §§ 71 to 87, 111, 113, 241 to 273, 2209; 16 U.S. Code §§ 490, 683; 31 U.S. Code §§ 617, 638e
July 18, 1940, Ch. 636, 54 Stat. 765, 7 U.S. Code § 74
Aug. 1, 1956, Ch. 812, 70 Stat. 780, 7 U.S. Code § 85
July 11, 1958, P.L. 85-509, 72 Stat. 352, 7 U.S. Code § 78
Aug. 15, 1968, P.L. 90-487, 82 Stat. 761, 7 U.S. Code §§ 71, 74 to 79, 84 to 87h
Oct. 15, 1970, P.L. 91-452, 84 Stat. 928, 7 U.S. Code § 87f
Sept. 29, 1977, P.L. 95-113, 7 U.S. Code §§ 79 et seq., 87a,.
Oct. 11, 1984, P.L. 98-469, 7 U.S. Code §§ 79, 79c, 79 nt., 87h
Dec. 23, 1985, P.L. 99-198, 7 U.S. Code § 76
Nov. 10, 1986, P.L. 99-641, 7 U.S. Code §§ 74, 87b, 86b nt.
Oct. 24, 1988, P.L. 100-518, 7 U.S. Code §§ 79, 79 nt., 79a, 79d, 87h, 87j
Nov. 28, 1990, P.L. 101-624, 7 U.S. Code §§ 74, 76, 77, 87b, 87k
Dec. 13, 1991, P.L. 102-237, 7 U.S. Code §§ 75, 87e, 87f-2
Nov. 24, 1993, P.L. 103-156, 7 U.S. Code § 75 et seq., 84 et seq.
Oct. 13, 1994, P.L. 103-354, 7 U.S. Code § 75 et seq.
Nov. 2, 1994, P.L. 103-437, 7 U.S. Code § 87

**United States Grain Standards Act Amendments of 1988**
Oct. 24, 1988, P.L. 100-518, 7 U.S. Code § 71 nt.
Nov. 24, 1993, P.L. 103-156, 7 U.S. Code § 79 nt.

**United States Grain Standards Act Amendments of 1993**
Nov. 24, 1993, P.L. 103-156, 7 U.S. Code §§ 71 nt., 75 et seq., 84 et seq.

**United States Grain Standards Act of 1976**
Oct. 21, 1976, P.L. 94-582, 7 U.S. Code § 71 et seq.
Sept. 29, 1977, P.L. 95-113, 7 U.S. Code §§ 74 nt., 75a nt., 79 nt .

**United States-Hong Kong Policy Act of 1992**
Oct. 5, 1992, P.L.102-383, 22 U.S. Code §§ 5701, 5701 nt., 5702, 5711 to 5715, 5721 to 5724, 5731, 5732
Feb. 12, 1996, P.L. 104-107, 22 U.S. Code § 5731
July 22, 1998, P.L. 105-206, 22 U.S. Code § 5713
June 25, 1999, P.L. 106-36, 22 U.S. Code § 5712.

**United States Housing Act**
February 5, 1988, P.L. 100-242, 42 U.S. Code § 1437l

**United States Housing Act of 1937**
Sept. 1, 1937, Ch. 896, 50 Stat. 888, 42 U.S. Code §§ 1401, 1402, 1404 to 1416, 1419 to 1422, 1427 to 1430
June 21, 1938, Ch. 554, 52 Stat. 820, 42 U.S. Code § 1420
Oct. 30, 1941, Ch. 467, 55 Stat. 759, 42 U.S. Code § 1420
July 31, 1947, Ch. 418, 61 Stat. 704, 42 U.S. Code § 1415

Feb. 27, 1948, Ch. 77, 62 Stat. 37
July 15, 1949, Ch. 338, 63 Stat. 422, 42 U.S. Code §§ 1401, 1402, 1406, 1409 to 1411, 1413 to 1416, 1420 to 1422, 1427 to 1430
April 20, 1950, Ch. 94, 64 Stat. 73, 42 U.S. Code § 1412, 1412 nt.
Oct. 26, 1951, Ch. 577, 65 Stat. 647, 42 U.S. Code § 1402
June 30, 1953, Ch. 170, 67 Stat. 128, 42 U.S. Code § 1402
Aug. 2, 1954, Ch. 649, 68 Stat. 630, 42 U.S. Code §§ 1407, 1410, 1415
June 30, 1955, Ch. 251, 69 Stat. 225, 42 U.S. Code § 1410
Aug. 11, 1955, Ch. 783, 69 Stat. 638, 42 U.S. Code § 1410, 1585
Aug. 7, 1956, Ch. 1029, 70 Stat. 1103, 42 U.S. Code § 1402, 1410, 1412, 1421
July 12, 1957, P.L. 85-104, 71 Stat. 301, 42 U.S. Code §§ 1402, 1415
Sept. 23, 1959, P.L. 86-372, 73 Stat. 679, 42 U.S. Code §§ 1401, 1402, 1410, 1415
June 30, 1961, P.L. 87-70, 75 Stat. 163, 42 U.S. Code §§ 1402, 1410, 1415, 1421, 1421a
Sept. 2, 1964, P.L. 88-560, 78 Stat. 784, 42 U.S. Code §§ 1402, 1410, 1415
Aug. 10, 1965, P.L. 89-117, 79 Stat. 455, 42 U.S. Code §§ 1402, 1410, 1412, 1415, 1421a, 1421b, 1422
Nov. 3, 1966, P.L. 89-754, 80 Stat. 1284, 42 U.S. Code §§ 1416, 1421b
May 25, 1967, P.L. 90-19, 81 Stat. 19, 42 U.S. Code §§ 1403 to 1407, 1410, 1413, 1415, 1416, 1421a
Aug. 1, 1968, P.L. 90-448, 82 Stat. 503, 42 U.S. Code §§ 1401 to 1403, 1410, 1415, 1417a, 1420, 1421b
Dec. 24, 1969, P.L. 91-152, 83 Stat. 388, 42 U.S. Code §§ 1402, 1409, 1410, 1414, 1415, 1421b
Dec. 31, 1970, P.L. 91-609, 84 Stat. 1776, 42 U.S. Code §§ 1401, 1402, 1410, 1415, 1421b
Oct. 18, 1972, P.L. 92-503, 86 Stat. 906, 42 U.S. Code §§ 1410, 1453
Oct. 2, 1973, P.L. 93-117, 87 Stat. 422, 42 U.S. Code § 1410
April 30, 1977, P.L. 95-24, 42 U.S. Code §§ 1437c et seq.
Oct. 12, 1977, P.L. 95-128, 42 U.S. Code §§ 1437c, 1437f et seq.
Oct. 31, 1978, P.L. 95-557, 42 U.S. Code §§ 1437a et seq.
Nov. 9, 1978, P.L. 95-619, 42 U.S. Code § 1437c
Dec. 21, 1979. P.L. 96-153, 42 U.S. Code §§ 1437a, 1437c, 1437d, 1437f, 1437g, 1437k
Nov. 30, 1983, P.L. 98-181, 42 U.S. Code §§ 1437a, 1437o to 1437q, 5307
Oct. 17, 1984, P.L. 98-479, 42 U.S. Code §§ 1437a, 1437d, 1437f
Nov. 25, 1985, P.L. 99-160, 42 U.S. Code § 1437d
April 7, 1986, P.L. 99-272, 42 U.S. Code § 1437b
July 2, 1986, P.L. 99-349, 100 Stat. 727
Nov. 6, 1986, P.L. 99-603, 42 U.S. Code § 1437r
Feb. 5, 1988, P.L. 100-242, 42 U.S. Code §§ 1437a, 1437c to 1437g, 1437j 1437l-p, 1437r, 1437s, 1485
April 28, 1988, P.L. 100-297, 20 U.S. Code §§ 238 et seq., 238 nt.
June 29, 1988, P.L. 100-358, 102 Stat. 676, 42 U.S. Code §§ prec. 1437, 1437a, 1437c, 1437aa to 1437ee
Nov. 7, 1988, P.L. 100-628, 42 U.S. Code §§ 1437 et seq .
Nov. 18, 1988, P.L. 100-690, 42 U.S. Code § 1437d
Nov. 9, 1989, P.L. 101-144, 42 U.S. Code § 1437d
Dec. 15, 1989, P.L. 101-235, 42 U.S. Code §§ 1437a, 1437f, 1437o
May 25, 1990, P.L. 101-302, 42 U.S. Code § 1437o
Nov. 5, 1990, P.L. 101-507, 42 U.S. Code § 1437o
Nov. 28, 1990, P.L. 101-625, 42 U.S. Code §§ 1437a et seq., 1437aa to 1437dd, 1437aaa-1 to 1437aaa-8, 1472 nt., 1479 nt., 1490 nt.
April 10, 1991, P.L. 102-27, 42 U.S. Code § 1437o
Oct. 28, 1991, P.L. 102-139, 42 U.S. Code §§ 1437d, 1437f, 1437l
Oct. 28, 1992, P.L. 102-550, 42 U.S. Code §§ 1437, 1437a, 1437c to 1437g, 1437l, 1437n to 1437w, 1437aa to 1437cc, 1437aaa to 1437aaa-2
April 11, 1994, P.L. 103-233, 42 U.S. Code §§ 1437a, 1437d, 1437f , 1437g, 1437l, 1437x

*Continued*

Sept. 28, 1994, P.L. 103-327, 42 U.S. Code § 1437f

July 27, 1995, P.L. 104-19, 42 U.S. Code §§ 1437c, 1437f, 1437l, 1437p, 1437aaa-3

Dec. 21, 1995, P.L. 104-66, 42 U.S. Code § 1437s

Jan. 26, 1996, P.L. 104-99, 42 U.S. Code §§ 1437a, 1437d, 1437e, 1437f, 1437n, 1437v

March 28, 1996, P.L. 104-120, 42 U.S. Code §§ 1437d, 1437e, 1437n

April 26, 1996, P.L. 104-134, 42 U.S. Code §§ 1437f, 1437g, 1437l, 1437p

Aug. 22, 1996, P.L. 104-193, 42 U.S. Code §§ 1437d, 1437f, 1437y, 1437z

Sept. 26, 1996, P.L. 104-204, 42 U.S. Code § 1437f

Oct. 19, 1996, P.L. 104-316, 42 U.S. Code §§ 1437h, 1437u

Oct. 26, 1996, P.L. 104-330, 42 U.S. Code §§ 1437 et seq., 1437a, 1437aa

June 12, 1997, P.L. 105-18, 42 U.S. Code § 1437f

Aug. 5, 1997, P.L. 105-33, 42 U.S. Code §§ 1437f, 1437y

Oct. 27, 1997, P.L. 105-65, 42 U.S. Code §§ 1437f, 1437z, 1437z-1

Oct. 21, 1998, P.L. 105-276, 42 U.S. Code §§ 1437, 1437a, 1437c, 1437c-1, 1437d to 1437g, 1437j to 1437l, 1437n, 1437p, 1437r to 1437w, 1437z-2 to 1437z-7, 1437aaa-2 to 1437aaa-4, 1437aaa-6, 1437bbb, 1437bbb-1 to 1437bbb-9

Oct. 21, 1998, P.L. 105-277, 42 U.S. Code § 1437u

**United States-India Fund for Cultural, Educational, and Scientific Cooperation Act**

Nov. 22, 1983, P.L. 98-164, 22 U.S. Code §§ 290j, 290j nt., 290j- 1

Aug. 16, 1985, P.L. 99-93, 22 U.S. Code § 290j-1

Dec. 22, 1987, P.L. 100-204, 22 U.S. Code § 290j-1

**United States Information Agency Authorization Act, Fiscal Years 1982 and 1983**

Aug. 24, 1982, P.L. 97-241, 22 U.S. Code §§ 1442, 1451 to 1453, 1461 nt., 1472, 1474, 1475c to 1475e, 2455 nt.

**United States Information and Educational Exchange Act of 1948**

Jan. 27, 1948, Ch. 36, 62 Stat. 6, 22 U.S. Code §§ 965, 966 nts., 1431 to 1440, 1446 to 1448, 1451 to 1453, 1456 to 1458, 1461, 1462, 1466 to 468, 1471 to 1473, 1476 to 1479

April 5, 1952, Ch. 159, 66 Stat. 43, 22 U.S. Code §§ 272b, 281b, 290a, 1434

Aug. 26, 1954, Ch. 937, 68 Stat. 862, 22 U.S. Code §§ 281b-2, 1442

July 18, 1956, Ch. 627, 70 Stat. 563, 22 U.S. Code § 1442

June 30, 1958, P.L. 85-477, 72 Stat. 274, 22 U.S. Code § 442

July 24, 1959, P.L. 86-108, 73 Stat. 257, 22 U.S. Code § 1442

Aug. 14, 1961, P.L. 87-139, 75 Stat. 341, 22 U.S. Code § 1471

Sept. 21, 1961, P.L. 87-256, 22 U.S. Code §§ 1431, 1434, 1439, 1440, 1448, 1466, 1467, 1468 nt.

Feb. 7, 1972, P.L. 92-226, 86 Stat. 35, 22 U.S. Code § 1476

March 30, 1972, P.L. 92-264, 86 Stat. 114, 22 U.S. Code § 1477a

July 13, 1972, P.L. 92-352, 86 Stat. 493, 22 U.S. Code §§ 1461, 1474 to 1476

Aug. 20, 1972, P.L. 92-394, 86 Stat. 577, 22 U.S. Code § 1477a

July 6, 1973, P.L. 93-59, 87 Stat. 142, 22 U.S. Code § 1477a

Nov. 29, 1973, P.L. 93-168, 87 Stat. 688, 22 U.S. Code § 1476

Aug. 15, 1979, P.L. 96-60, 22 U.S. Code §§ 1434 repealed, 1461, 1469, 1471, 1474, 1475a, 1477b

Aug. 24, 1982, P.L. 97-241, 22 U.S. Code §§ 1442, 1451 to 1453, 1472, 1474, 1475c to 1475e

Nov. 22, 1983, P.L. 98-164, 22 U.S. Code §§ 1471, 1477c

Aug. 16, 1985, P.L. 99-93, 22 U.S. Code § 1477c

Dec. 22, 1987, P.L. 100-204, 22 U.S. Code §§ 1464, 1469, 1471, 1475e, 1477c

Feb. 16, 1990, P.L. 101-246, 22 U.S. Code §§ 1461, 1464a, 1464b, 1469, 1474, 1475e, 1475f

Oct. 28, 1991, P.L. 102-138, 22 U.S. Code §§ 1471, 1474, 1475g, 1477c

Oct. 24, 1992, P.L. 102-499, 22 U.S. Code § 1476
April 30, 1994, P.L. 103-236, 22 U.S. Code §§ 1463, 1471, 1472, 1477b
Oct. 25, 1994, P.L. 103-415, 22 U.S. Code § 1476
Oct. 21, 1998, P.L. 105-277, 22 U.S. Code §§ 1440, 1464a, 1464b, 1469, 1471, 1475b, 1475c, 1475e, 1475f, 1475g, 1476, 1477b, 1477c

**United States Institute of Peace Act**
Oct. 19, 1984, P.L. 98-525, 22 U.S. Code §§ 4601 nt., 4601 to 4611
Oct. 17, 1986, P.L. 99-498, 22 U.S. Code § 4609, 4609 nt.
June 3, 1987, P.L. 100-50, 22 U.S. Code § 4604
Oct. 31, 1988, P.L. 100-569, 22 U.S. Code § 4606
Nov. 3, 1990, P.L. 101-520, 22 U.S. Code §§ 4603, 4604, 4606
July 23, 1992, P.L. 102-325, 22 U.S. Code §§ 4604, 4609
Oct. 7, 1998, P.L. 105-244, 22 U.S. Code §§ 4604, 4609, 4611
Oct. 21, 1998, P.L. 105-277, 22 U.S. Code § 4605

**United States Insular Areas Drug Abuse Act of 1986**
Oct. 27, 1986, P.L. 99-570, 48 U.S. Code § 1494
Nov. 18, 1988, P.L. 100-690, 48 U.S. Code §§ 1494 to 1494c

**United States International Broadcasting Act of 1994**
April 30, 1994, P.L. 103-236, 22 U.S. Code § 6201, 6201 et seq.
Oct. 21, 1998, P.L. 105-277, 22 U.S. Code §§ 6202 to 6207, 6209
Oct. 27, 1998, P.L. 105-292, 22 U.S. Code § 6202

**United States-Israel Free Trade Area Implementation Act of 1985**
June 11, 1985, P.L. 99-47, 19 U.S. Code §§ 2112, 2112 nt., 2462 to 2464, 2518
Oct. 2, 1996, P.L. 104-234, 19 U.S. Code § 2112 nt.

**United States-Japan Fishery Agreement Approval Act of 1987**
Dec. 29, 1987, P.L. 100-220, 16 U.S. Code § 1801 nt.; 33 U.S. Code §§ 883a, 1121 et seq. 1901 et seq., 2267 nt.; 42 U.S. Code § 6981 nt.

**United States-Mexico Border Health Commission Act**
Oct. 22, 1994, P.L. 103-400, 22 U.S. Code §§ 290n nt., 290n et seq.

**United States Mint Reauthorization and Reform Act of 1992**
Oct. 6, 1992, P.L. 102-390, 31 U.S. Code § 5101 nt.

**United States National Tourism Organization Act of 1996**
Oct. 11, 1996, P.L. 104-288, 22 U.S. Code § 2141 nt.

**United States Olympians Assistance Act**
Ill. Rev. Stat. 1991, Ch. 1, §§ 7061, 7062

**United States Olympic Committee Act**
Ill. Rev. Stat. 1987, Ch. 1, § 7051 et seq.

**United States Organization's 50th Anniversary Commemorative Coin Act**
Oct. 6, 1992, P.L. 102-390, 31 U.S. Code § 5112 nt.

**United States Patent and Trademark Office Reauthorization Act, Fiscal Year 1999**
Nov. 10, 1998, P.L. 105-358, 112 Stat. 3272, 35 U.S. Code § 1 nt.

**United States Public Vessel Medical Waste Anti-Dumping Act of 1988**
Nov. 11, 1988, P.L. 100-688, 33 U.S. Code §§ 2501 nt., 2501 to 2504

**United States Railway Association Amendments Act of 1978**
Nov. 1, 1978, P.L. 95-565, 43 U.S. Code §§ 975, 975 nt.; 45 U.S. Code §§ 701, 726, 747, 825

**United States Synthetic Fuels Corporation Act of 198**
June 30, 1980, P.L. 96-294, 42 U.S. Code § 8701 et seq., 8701 nt.
Oct. 12, 1984, P.L. 98-473, 42 U.S. Code §§ 8713, 8768

**United States Tax Lien Registration Act**
See Federal Tax Lien Registration Act

**United States Veterans' Bureau Act**
Aug. 9, 1921, Ch. 57, 42 Stat. 147

**United States Warehouse Act**
Aug. 11, 1916, Ch. 313, 39 Stat. 486, 7 U.S. Code §§ 71 to 87, 111, 113, 241 to 273, 2209; 16 U.S. Code §§ 490, 683; 31 U.S. Code §§ 617, 638e
Feb. 23, 1923, Ch. 106, 42 Stat. 1282, 7 U.S. Code §§ 242, 245, 247, 252, 253, 256, 257, 260, 269, 270
March 20, 1986, P.L. 99-260, 7 U.S. Code § 259
Nov. 28, 1990, P.L. 101-624, 7 U.S. Code §§ 259, 270
Dec. 13, 1991, P.L. 102-237, 7 U.S. Code § 259
Oct. 28, 1992, P.L. 102-553, 7 U.S. Code § 259

**Unitization Act (Oil and Gas)**
Ala. Code 1975, § 9-17-80 et seq.
Alaska Stat. 1962, § 31.05.110
Ariz. Rev. Stat. Ann., § 27-531 et seq.
Ark. Code Ann. 1987, 15-72-301, 15-72-303 et seq.
Colo. Rev. Stat., 34-60-118
Fla. Stat. 1983, 377.25
Ga. Code Ann., 12-4-40 et seq.
Kan. Stat. Ann., 55-1301 et seq.
La. Rev. Stat. Ann., 30:9 et seq.
Mich. Comp. Laws Ann., 319.351 et seq.
N.D. Cent. Code, 38-08-09.1 et seq.
Neb. Rev. Stat. 1943, 57-910 et seq.
Nev. Rev. Stat. 1979 Reprint, 522.082 et seq.
N.M. Stat. Ann., 70-7-1 et seq.
N.Y. Environmental Conservation Law 1972 (Consol. Laws Ch. 43B) §§ 23-0701, 23-0901 et seq.
Okla. Stat. Ann., Title 52, § 287.1 et seq.
Ore. Rev. Stat., 520.260
S.D. Codified Laws 1967, 45-9-20 et seq.
Wash. Rev. Code Ann., 78.52.330
Wyo. Stat. Ann., § 30-5-110

**Universal Good Samaritan Law**
N.Y. Public Health Law 1953 (Consol. Laws Ch. 45) § 3000a

**Universal Health Care Act**
Okla. Stat. Ann., Title 63, § 2521 et seq.

**Universal Military Training and Service Act**
See also Military Selective Service Act of 1967
June 19, 1951, Ch. 144, 65 Stat. 75, 50 U.S. Code Appx. §§ 451 to 454 , 455, 456, 459, 460 463, 466, 467, 471
July 9, 1952, Ch. 608, 66 Stat. 509, 50 U.S. Code Appx. § 454
June 29, 1953, Ch. 158, 67 Stat. 86, 50 U.S. Code Appx. §§ 454, 454e
March 15, 1954, Ch. 79, 68 Stat. 27
Aug. 21, 1954, Ch. 783, 68 Stat. 758 (See 10 U.S. Code § 3292)
June 30, 1955, Ch. 250, 69 Stat. 223, 50 U.S. Code Appx. §§ 456, 467
July 12, 1955, Ch. 327, 69 Stat. 295, 50 U.S. Code Appx. § 459
Aug. 9, 1955, Ch. 665, 69 Stat. 602, 50 U.S. Code Appx. §§ 454, 456
July 9, 1956, Ch. 523, 70 Stat. 509, 50 U.S. Code Appx. §§ 459, 459 nt.
Aug. 10, 1956, Ch. 1041, 70 A Stat. 630, 50 U.S. Code Appx. §§ 454 , 458
June 27, 1957, P.L. 85-62, 71 Stat. 206, 50 U.S. Code Appx. §§ 454, 455, 456
July 28, 1958, P.L. 85-564, 72 Stat. 424, 50 U.S. Code Appx. § 454
Aug. 21, 1958, P.L. 85-722, 72 Stat. 711, 50 U.S. Code Appx. § 456
Sept. 2, 1958, P.L. 85-861, 72 Stat. 1556, 50 U.S. Code Appx. § 454
March 23, 1959, P.L. 86-4, 73 Stat. 13, 50 U.S. Code Appx. § 467
June 25, 1959, P.L. 86-70, 73 Stat. 150, 50 U.S. Code Appx. § 466
July 12, 1960, P.L. 86-624, 74 Stat. 422, 50 U.S. Code Appx. § 466
July 12, 1960, P.L. 86-632, 74 Stat. 467, 50 U.S. Code Appx. § 459

Oct. 4, 1961, P.L. 87-378, 75 Stat. 807, 50 U.S. Code Appx. § 456
Oct. 4, 1961, P.L. 87-391, 75 Stat. 821, 50 U.S. Code Appx. § 459
July 18, 1962, P.L. 87-536, 76 Stat. 167, 50 U.S. Code Appx. § 456
Sept. 7, 1962, P.L. 87-651, 76 Stat. 524, 50 U.S. Code Appx. § 454
March 28, 1963, P.L. 88-2, 77 Stat. 4, 50 U.S. Code Appx. § 467
Sept. 3, 1963, P.L. 88-110, 77 Stat. 135, 50 U.S. Code Appx. §§ 456, 463
July 7, 1964, P.L. 88-360, 78 Stat. 296, 50 U.S. Code Appx. § 456
Aug. 30, 1965, P.L. 89-152, 79 Stat. 586, 50 U.S. Code Appx. § 462
June 30, 1967, P.L. 90-40, 81 Stat. 100, 50 U.S. Code Appx. §§ 451, 454 to 456, 460, 462, 467

**Universal Service Fund Act (Telecommunications)**
Neb. Rev. Stat. 1943, 86-1401 to 86-1411

**Universal Telephone Service Act**
Ark. Code Ann. 1987, 23-17-301 et seq.
Cal. Public Utilities Code § 871 et seq.
Cal. Revenue and Taxation Code § 44000 et seq.

**Universities Act (Vacated Grounds)**
Ill. Rev. Stat. 1991, Ch. 144, §§ 11.9, 12

**Universities and Private Colleges Authority Act**
Ga. Code Ann., 20-3-200 et seq.

**Universities and State Colleges Gasohol Use Act**
Ill. Rev. Stat. 1991, Ch. 144, § 2851 et seq.

**Universities Research Institutes Act**
Miss. Code Ann. 1972, § 57-55-1 et seq.

**University Airport Access Road Act**
Ill. Rev. Stat. 1991, Ch. 144, §§ 78b.9, 78c

**University and College Employees Uniform Insurance Benefits Act**
Tex. Insurance Code, Art. 3.50-3

**University and College Equipment Financing Act**
Miss. Code Ann. 1972, § 37-101-419 et seq.

**University and College Security Information Act**
Del. Code of 1974, Title 14, § 9001 et seq.
Pa. Purdon's Stat., Title 24, § 2502-1 et seq.
Tenn. Code Ann., 49-7-2201 et seq.

**University Athletics Act (Televised)**
D.C. Code Ann., § 31-1511 et seq.
Ill. Rev. Stat. 1991, Ch. 144, §§ 254, 255

**University-Based Research and Economic Development Act**
Iowa Code Ann., 262B.1 et seq.

**University Building Association Act**
Mass. Acts 1958, Ch. 603

**University Building Authority Leased Lands Act**
Ill. Rev. Stat. 1991, Ch. 144, § 70.10 et seq.

**University Building Transfer of Funds Act**
Ill. Rev. Stat. 1991, Ch. 127, §§ 167c.9, 167d

**University Chancellors Act**
Ill. Rev. Stat. 1991, Ch. 144, §§ 5m, 6

**University Civil Service System Act**
Ill. Rev. Stat. 1991, Ch. 24 1/2, § 38b.01 et seq.

**University Contract Act**
Cal. Education Code 1976, § 90100 et seq.

**University County Hospital Act**
Mich. Comp. Laws Ann., 331.251 et seq.

**University Education Authority Act**
Ga. Code Ann., 20-3-150 et seq.

**University Employees Custodial Accounts Act**
Ill. Rev. Stat. 1991, Ch. 144, § 1700 et seq.

**University Endowment Act**
N.M. Stat. Ann., 21-1A-1 et seq.

**University Facilities Revenue Bond Act (Winthrop)**
S.C. Code Ann. 1976, § 59-12-310 et seq.

**University Faculty Research and Consulting Act**
Ill. Rev. Stat. 1991, Ch. 144, § 215.9 et seq.

**University Hospital Psychiatry and Neurology Service Act**
Okla. Stat. Ann., Title 70, § 3307 et seq.

**University Hospitals Authority Act**
Okla. Stat. Ann., Title 63, § 3201 et seq.

**University Law**
N.Y. Laws 1892, Ch. 378

**University Military Inspection Act**
Ill. Rev. Stat. 1991, Ch. 144, § 17p et seq.

**University of Alaska Act**
Alaska Stat. 1962, § 14.40.010 et seq.

**University of California Building Bond Act**
Cal. Statutes 1915, No. 2, p. 1923

**University of California Dormitory Revenue Bond Act**
Cal. Education Code 1976, § 92400 et seq.
Cal. Statutes 1947, Ch. 1027, p. 2289

**University of California Health Science Facilities Construction Program Bond Act**
Cal. Statutes 1969, Ch. 1544, p. 3139

**University of California Pest Research Act**
Cal. Food and Agricultural Code § 576 et seq.

**University of Connecticut Health Center Finance Corporation Act**
Conn. Gen. Stat. 1983, § 10a-250 et seq.

**University of Connecticut 2000 Act**
Conn. Public Acts 1995, No. 230

**University of Illinois Act**
Ill. Rev. Stat. 1987, Ch. 120, §§ 404, 405 (Tax Levy)
Ill. Rev. Stat. 1991, Ch. 23, § 1370 et seq. (Hospital)
Ill. Rev. Stat. 1991, Ch. 144, §§ 47m, 48 (Name Change)
Ill. Rev. Stat. 1991, Ch. 144, §§ 48.7m, 48.8 (Facility Use Prohibition)
Ill. Rev. Stat. 1991, Ch. 144, §§ 60.9, 61 (Agricultural Experimental Station)
Ill. Rev. Stat. 1991, Ch. 144, § 21m et seq.
Ill. Rev. Stat. 1991, Ch. 144, § 40a.1 et seq. (At Chicago)
Ill. Rev. Stat. 1991, Ch. 144, § 40m et seq. (Trustees)
Ill. Rev. Stat. 1991, Ch. 144, § 63m et seq. (Works Projects)
Ill. Rev. Stat. 1991, Ch. 144, § 48.1 et seq. (Revenue Bond Financing Act for Auxiliary Facilities)
Ill. Rev. Stat. 1991, Ch. 144, § 57.9 et seq. (Veterinary College)
Ill. Rev. Stat. 1991, Ch. 144, § 67.9 et seq. (Construction Financing)
Ill. Rev. Stat. 1991, Ch. 144, § 78.9 et seq. (Airport)
Ill. Rev. Stat. 1991, Ch. 144, § 2650 et seq. (Institutes for Juvenile Research and Developmental Disabilities)
Ill. Rev. Stat. 1991, Ch. 144, § 54.01 et seq. (Gerontological Committee)
Ill. Rev. Stat. 1991, Ch. 144, § 54.90 et seq. (Mining Engineering)
Ill. Rev. Stat. 1991, Ch. 144, § 61.90 et seq. (Journalism College)
Ill. Rev. Stat. 1991, Ch. 144, § 70.01 et seq. (At Chicago Land Transfer)
Ill. Rev. Stat. 1991, Ch. 144, § 70.90 et seq. (Revenue Bond)

**University of Illinois at Springfield Law**
Ill. Comp. Stat. 1992, Ch. 110, § 327/40-1 et seq.

**University of Maine System Labor Relations Act**
Me. Rev. Stat. Ann. 1964, Title 26, § 1021 et seq.

**University of Medicine and Dentistry of New Jersey Flexibility Act**
N.J. Stat. Ann., 18A:64G-1 et seq.

**University of Minnesota Hospitals Act**
Minn. Stat. Ann., 158.01 et seq.

**University of Mississippi Research Authority Act**
Miss. Code Ann. 1972, § 37-147-1 et seq.

**University of Pennsylvania Act (Indiana)**
Pa. Purdon's Stat., Title 24, § 2510-101 et seq.

**University of Pittsburgh—Commonwealth Act**
Pa. Purdon's Stat., Title 24, § 2510-201 et seq.

**University of Puerto Rico Act**
P.R. Laws Ann. 1954, Title 18, § 601 et seq.

**University of Rhode Island Development Act**
R.I. Public Laws 1955, Ch. 3536

**University of Rhode Island Research Corporation Act**
R.I. Gen. Laws 1956, 35-12-1 et seq.

**University Religious Observances Act**
Ill. Rev. Stat. 1991, Ch. 144, §§ 2100, 2101

**University Research Center Act**
Miss. Code Ann. 1972, § 37-141-1

**University Research Park Act**
N.M. Stat. Ann., 21-28-1 et seq.

**University Retail Sales Act**
Ill. Rev. Stat. 1991, Ch. 144, §§ 251.9, 252

**University Retirement System of Illinois**
Ill. Rev. Stat. 1991, Ch. 108 1/2, § 15-101 et seq.

**University Securities Act**
Nev. Rev. Stat. 1979 Reprint, 396.809 et seq.
Wyo. Stat. Ann., § 21-17-402 et seq.

**University System Building Authority Act**
Ga. Code Ann., 20-3-150 et seq.

**Unjust Conviction and Imprisonment Act**
N.Y. Court of Claims Act §§ 8b, 9

**Unjust Conviction Law**
May 24, 1938, Ch. 266, 52 Stat. 438 (See 28 U.S. Code §§ 1495, 2513)

**Unjust Discrimination in Employment Because of Age Act**
Neb. Rev. Stat. 1943, 48-1001 et seq.

**Unjust Enrichment Act**
P.R. Laws Ann. 1954, Title 13, § 2231 et seq.

**Unknown or Nonresident Tax Foreclosure Act**
Tex. Rev. Civ. Stat., Art. 7342
Tex. Rules of Civil Procedure, Rule 117a

**Unknown Owner's Money Act**
La. Rev. Stat. Ann., 9:151 et seq.

**Unlawful Assembly Act**
Ala. Code 1975, § 13A-11-5 et seq.
Tex. Penal Code, § 42.02
Wash. Rev. Code 1974, 9.27.060 et seq.

**Unlawful Business Practices Act**
Minn. Stat. 1969, 325.81 et seq.

**Unlawful Cohabitation Act**
Ark. Stat. 1947, 41-805

**Unlawful Collection Agency Practices Act**
Pa. Cons. Stat., Title 18, § 7311

**Unlawful Death Act**
Pa. Cons. Stat., Title 42, §§ 5524, 8301

**Unlawful Detainer Act**
Cal. Code of Civil Procedure § 1160 et seq.
Colo. Rev. Stat., 13-40-101 et seq.
Minn. Stat. Ann., 566.02
Mo. Rev. Stat., 534.010 et seq.
P.R. Laws Ann. 1954, Title 32, § 2821 et seq.
Utah Code Ann. 1953, 78-36-3
Wash. Rev. Code Ann., 59.12.030 et seq., 59.16.010 et seq.
Wis. Stat. Ann., 799.40 et seq.
Wyo. Stat. Ann., § 1-21-1001 et seq.

**Unlawful Disturbances Act**
Wash. Rev. Code Ann., 9.27.015 et seq.

**Unlawful Entry and Detainer Act**
Okla. Stat. Ann., Title 39, § 391 et seq.

**Unlawful Liquor Sales Abatement Law**
Cal. Penal Code § 11200 et seq.

**Unlawful Practice of Law Act**
La. Rev. Stat. Ann., 37:213
N.J. Stat. Ann., 2A:170-78 et seq.

**Unlawful Trade Practices Act**
Mich. Comp. Laws Ann., 445.101 et seq.
Minn. Stat. Ann., 325D.09 et seq.
Ore. Rev. Stat. 646.608 et seq.

**Unlawful Trusts and Monopolies Act**
S.D. Codified Laws 1967, 37-1-3.1 et seq.

**Unlawful Use of Process Act**
S.D. Codified Laws 1967, 22-12-5 et seq.

**Unlicensed Insurers Process Act**
Va. Code 1950, § 38.2-800 et seq.

**Unlicensed Nonresident Brokers and Agents Process Act**
Va. Code 1950, § 38.2-808 et seq.

**Unlimited Tax Election Act**
Mich. Comp. Laws Ann., 141.161 et seq.

**Unlimited Time Act (Estates)**
Minn. Stat. Ann., 500.20, Subd. 2

**Unlimited Time Act (Real Property)**
Mass. Gen. Laws Ann., 184:23

**Unliquidated Damages Interest Act**
Ga. Code Ann., 51-12-14

**Unlisted Securities Trading Act**
May 27, 1936, Ch. 462, 49 Stat. 1375, 15 U.S. Code §§ 78ff, 78hh-1, 78l to 78ll, 78o to 78o-2, 78q, 78t, 78u, 78w,

**Unlisted Trading Privileges Act of 1994**
Oct. 22, 1994, P.L. 103-389, 15 U.S. Code § 78a nt.

**Unloading Act (Motor Vehicles)**
Tex. Rev. Civ. Stat., Art. 6701d-11, § 6

**Unmarked Human Burial and Human Skeletal Remains Protection Act**
N.C. Gen. Stat. 1943, § 70-26 et seq.
Neb. Rev. Stat. 1943, 12-1201 et seq.

**Unmarked Human Burial Sites Preservation Act**
Kan. Stat. Ann., 75-2741 et seq.
La. Rev. Stat. Ann., 8:671 et seq.

**Unoccupied Premises Standards Law (Town of Evans)**
N.Y. Local Laws 1967, Town of Evans, p. 1532

**Unpaid Wages Prohibition Act**
N.Y. Laws 1997, Ch. 605

**Unpledged Elector Act**
Miss. Code Ann. 1972, § 23-1-1 et seq.

**Unqualified Insurers Process Act**
Tenn. Code Ann., 56-2-601 et seq.

**Unreasonable Rent Defense Law**
N.Y. Laws 1920, Ch. 136

**Unredeemed Lands Resale Act**
Okla. Stat. 1981, Title 68, § 3125 et seq.

**Unrelated Business Income Act (Excise Tax)**
Ore. Rev. Stat., 317.910 et seq.

**Unretrieved Animal Act**
N.J. Stat. Ann., 45:16-13 et seq.

**Unruh Act (Credit Sales)**
Cal. Civil Code § 1801 et seq.

**Unruh-Cameron Beach, Park, Recreational and Historical Facilities Bond Act**
Cal. Public Resources Code § 5096.1 et seq.

**Unruh-Cameron Park and Recreation Bond Act**
Cal. Public Resources Code § 5095.1 et seq.

**Unruh Civil Rights Act**
Cal. Civil Code § 51
Cal. Civil Code § 51 et seq.

**Unruh-Collier Local Transportation Development Act**
Cal. Statutes 1963, Ch. 1852, p. 3805

**Unruh-Miller Basic Reading Act**
Cal. Education Code 1976, § 54100 et seq.

**Unsafe Building Act**
Ill. Rev. Stat. 1991, Ch. 24, § 11-31-1 et seq.

**Unsafe Buildings Demolition Bond Act (Urban and Rural Centers)**
N.J. Laws 1997, Ch. 125

**Unsafe Crossings Act**
Ga. Code Ann., 32-6-190 et seq.

**Unsafe Motor Vehicle Law**
Wyo. Stat. Ann., § 31-5-970 et seq.

**Unsatisfied Claim and Judgment Fund Act**
Md. Ann. Code 1957, Superseded Vol., Art. 66 1/2, § 7-601 et seq.
N.J. Stat. Ann., 39:6-61 et seq.

**Unsatisfied Judgment Fund Act**
Ill. Rev. Stat. 1955, Ch. 95 1/2, § 58c et seq.
N.D. Cent. Code, 26.1-23-01 et seq.

**Unsealed Instrument Validation Act**
Ill. Rev. Stat. 1991, Ch. 30, § 153m et seq.

**Unsold Bonds Sales Law**
Cal. Government Code §§ 53400, 53401

**Unsolicited Credit Card Act**
Ill. Rev. Stat. 1991, Ch. 17, § 6201 et seq.

**Unsolicited Merchandise Act**
Ill. Rev. Stat. 1991, Ch. 121 1/2, §§ 350, 351

**Unsolicited Telefacsimile Advertising Act**
Tenn. Code Ann., 47-18-1601 et seq.

**Unsworn Statement Act**
Ga. Code Ann., 17-7-28

**Untried Worker Placement and Employment Incentive Act**
Fla. Stat. Ann., 446.603

**Unwholesome Food Sale Act**
D.C. Code 1973, § 22-3416 et seq.

**Unwritten Lease Tenancy at Will**
Fla. Stat. Ann., 83.01

**Up State Jury Act**
N.Y. Judiciary Law (Consol. Laws Ch. 30) § 500 et seq.

**Updating of Vocational—Technical Equipment Act**
Pa. Cons. Stat., Title 24, § 5801 et seq.

**Upholstered Furniture, Quilted Clothing and Bedding Act**
Utah Code Ann. 1953, 4-10-1 et seq.

**Upholstery and Bedding Act**
La. Rev. Stat. Ann., 40:1191 et seq.
Ore. Rev. Stat. 1953, 433.405 et seq.
Pa. Purdon's Stat., Title 35, § 972 et seq.

**Upper Berth Act**
Wis. Laws 1911, Ch. 272

**Upper Colorado Act**
April 11, 1956, Ch. 203, 70 Stat. 105, 43 U.S. Code §§ 620 to 620o

**Upper Colorado River Authority Act**
Tex. General Laws 44th Leg., 1935, p. 336, Ch. 126

**Upper Colorado River Basin Compact**
Colo. Rev. Stat., 37-62-101 et seq.
N.M. Stat. Ann., 72-15-26
Utah Code Ann. 1953, 73-13-9 et seq.
Wyo. Stat. Ann., §§ 41-12-401, 41-12-402

**Upper Guadalupe River Authority Act**
Tex. General and Special Laws 46th Leg., 1939, p. 1062

**Upper Illinois River Valley Development Authority Act**
Ill. Rev. Stat. 1991, Ch. 85, § 7151 et seq.

**Upper Mississippi Land Acquisition Act**
Ill. Rev. Stat. 1991, Ch. 1, §§ 4000, 4001

**Upper Mississippi River Wild Life and Fish Refuge Act**
June 7, 1924, Ch. 346, 43 Stat. 650, 16 U.S. Code §§ 721 to 731
Oct. 30, 1998, P.L. 105-312, 16 U.S. Code §§ 721, 722

**Upper Mississippi Riverway Compact**
Iowa Code Ann., 27A.1 et seq.

**Upper Mohawk Valley Memorial Auditorium Authority Act**
N.Y. Public Authorities Law (Consol. Laws Ch. 43A) § 1940 et seq.

**Upper Mohawk Valley Regional Water Board**
N.Y. Public Authorities Law (Consol. Laws Ch. 43A) § 1226aa et seq.

**Upper Mohawk Valley Regional Water Finance Authority Act**
N.Y. Public Authorities Law (Consol. Laws Ch. 43A) § 1226a et seq.

**Upper Niobrara River Compact Act**
Wyo. Stat. Ann., §§ 41-12-701, 41-12-702

**Upper Santa Clara Valley Water Agency Act**
Cal. Statutes 1962, 1st Ex. Sess., Ch. 28, p. 208

**Upper Savannah River Development Authority Act**
Ga. Code Ann., 12-3-400 et seq.

**Upson County-Thomaston Airport Authority Act**
Ga. Laws 1988, p. 4225

**Upson County Water and Sewerage Authority Act**
Ga. Laws 1998, H.B. 1876

**Upton Water Loan Act**
Mass. Acts 1953, Ch. 202

**Uranium Act (Taxation)**
Okla. Stat. Ann., Title 68, § 1018 et seq.

**Uranium Exploration Act**
S.D. Codified Laws 1967, 45-6D-1 et seq.

**Uranium Mill Tailings Radiation Control Act of 1978**
Nov. 8, 1978, P.L. 95-604, 42 U.S. Code §§ 2014, 2021, 2022, 2111, 2113, 2114, 2201, 7901, 7901 nt., 7911 et seq.
Nov. 9, 1979, P.L. 96-106, 42 U.S. Code § 2021 nt.
Jan. 4, 1983, P.L. 97-415, 42 U.S. Code §§ 2021 nt., 7918, 7912
Nov. 5, 1988, P.L. 100-616, 42 U.S. Code §§ 7916, 7922
Oct. 24, 1992, P.L. 102-486, 42 U.S. Code § 7922

**Uranium Mill Tailings Remedial Action Amendments Act of 1988**
Nov. 5, 1988, P.L. 100-616, 42 U.S. Code § 7901 nt.

**Uranium Surface Mining and Reclamation Act**
Tex. Natural Resources Code, § 131.001 et seq.

**Urban American River Parkway Preservation Act**
Cal. Public Resources Code § 5840 et seq.
N.J. Stat. Ann., 32:27-1 et seq

**Urban and Rural Centers Unsafe Buildings Demolition Bond Act**
N.J. Laws 1997, Ch. 125

**Urban and Rural Enterprise Zone Act**
Colo. Rev. Stat., 39-30-101 et seq.

**Urban and Rural Teacher Loan Forgiveness Act**
Pa. Purdon's Stat., Title 24, § 5191 et seq.

**Urban Area Compact (Delaware Valley)**
N.J. Stat. Ann., 32:27-1 et seq.

**Urban Area Insurance Placement Facility Act**
Mass. Gen. Laws Ann., 175C:1 et seq.

**Urban Area Trade Mart and Coliseum Authority Act**
Ala. Acts 1975, p. 1863

**Urban Assistance Act**
Pa. Purdon's Stat., Title 71, § 1049.101 et seq.

**Urban Assistance Incentive Fund Act**
Va. Code 1950, § 15.1-1500 et seq.

**Urban Betterment and Elderly Housing Act**
Mass. Acts 1973, Ch. 1215

**Urban, Coastal, and State Park Bond Act**
Cal. Public Resources Code § 5096.111 et seq.

**Urban Community Conservation Act**
Ill. Rev. Stat. 1991, Ch. 67 1/2, § 91.8 et seq.

**Urban Cooperation Act**
Mich. Comp. Laws Ann., 124.501 et seq.

**Urban-County Government Act**
Ky. Rev. Stat. 1971, 67A.010 et seq.

**Urban County Law**
Nev. Rev. Stat. 1979 Reprint, 244A.010 et seq.

**Urban Creek Restoration and Flood Control Act**
Cal. Water Code § 7048

**Urban Cultural Park Commission Act (Hudson-Mohawk)**
N.Y. Public Authorities Law (Consol. Laws Ch. 43A) § 2630 et seq.

**Urban Cultural Parks Act**
N.Y. General Municipal Law (Consol. Laws Ch. 24) § 852, 854, 858
N.Y. Parks, Recreation and Historic Preservation Law (Consol. Laws Ch. 36b) §§ 33.01 et seq., 35.01 et seq.

**Urban Development Act**
Conn. Gen. Stat. 1983, § 12-406 et seq.
N.J. Stat. Ann., 55:19-20 et seq.
N.M. Stat. Ann., 3-46-1 et seq.

**Urban Development Action Area Act**
N.Y. General Municipal Law (Consol. Laws Ch. 24) § 690 et seq.

**Urban Development and Research Corporations Act (New York State)**
N.Y. Unconsolidated Laws, § 6301 et seq.

**Urban Development Corporation Act**
N.J. Stat. Ann., 55:19-1 et seq.
N.Y. Unconsolidated Laws, § 6251 et seq.

**Urban Development Corporation Act (State)**
N.Y. Laws 1998, Ch. 58

**Urban Development Guarantee Fund of New York Act**
N.Y. Unconsolidated Laws, § 6341 et seq.

**Urban Development Incentive Act**
Cal. Health and Safety Code § 56010 et seq.

**Urban Drainage and Flood Control Act**
Colo. Rev. Stat., 32-11-101 et seq.
Miss. Code Ann. 1972, § 51-35-301 et seq.

**Urban Enterprise Zone Act**
Ga. Laws 1988, p. 4164
N.J. Stat. Ann., 52:27H-60 et seq.
Va. Code 1950, § 59.1-270 et seq.

**Urban Environment Management Act**
Ariz. Rev. Stat. Ann., § 9-461 et seq.

**Urban Fishing Program Act**
Cal. Public Resources Code § 5670 et seq.

**Urban Fishing Program Act (Presley)**
Cal. Public Resources Code § 5670 et seq.

**Urban Flood and Drainage Control Act**
Miss. Code Ann. 1972, § 51-35-301 et seq.

**Urban Forestry Act**
Cal. Public Resources Code § 4799.06 et seq.

**Urban Forestry and Community Act**
Mont. Code Ann., 77-5-401 et seq.

**Urban Forestry Assistance Act**
Ill. Rev. Stat. 1991, Ch. 96 1/2, § 9301 et seq.

**Urban Growth and New Community Development Act of 1970**
Dec. 31, 1970, P.L. 91-609, 84 Stat. 1791, 12 U.S. Code §§ 371, 1464; 40 U.S. Code § 461; 42 U.S. Code §§ 1453, 1460, 1492, 4501 to 4503, 4511 to 4532
Oct. 12, 1977, P.L. 95-128, 42 U.S. Code §§ 4501 et seq.

**Urban Heavy Rescue Act**
Cal. Government Code §§ 8584, 8584.1

**Urban Homesteading Act**
N.J. Stat. Ann., 40A:12-31 et seq.

**Urban Land Assembly Act**
Mich. Comp. Laws Ann., 125.1851 et seq.

**Urban Land-Banking Law**
La. Rev. Stat. Ann., 40:592.1 et seq.

**Urban Mass Transportation Act**
Ind. Code Ann., 19-5-2-1 et seq.
Pa. Purdon's Stat., Title 74, § 1101 et seq.

**Urban Mass Transportation Act of 1964**
See also Federal Transit Act
July 9, 1964, P.L. 88-365, 78 Stat. 302, 49 U.S. Code §§ 1601 to 1611
Aug. 10, 1965, P.L. 89-117, 79 Stat. 475, 49 U.S. Code §§ 1605, 1608
Sept. 8, 1966, P.L. 89-562, 80 Stat. 715, 49 U.S. Code §§ 1602, 1603, 1605, 1607a to 1611
May 25, 1967, P.L. 90-19, 81 Stat. 25, 49 U.S. Code §§ 1602, 1603 , 1605 to 1610
June 28, 1967, P.L. 90-34, 81 Stat. 81, 49 U.S. Code § 1604
Dec. 1, 1967, P.L. 90-169, 81 Stat. 526, 49 U.S. Code § 1604
Aug. 1, 1968, P.L. 90-448, 82 Stat. 534, 49 U.S. Code §§ 1603 to 1605, 1608
Dec. 24, 1969, P.L. 91-152, 83 Stat. 392, 49 U.S. Code § 1604
Oct. 15, 1970, P.L. 91-453, 84 Stat. 962, 49 U.S. Code §§ 1602 to 1605, 1608, 1610 to 1612
Aug. 13, 1973, P.L. 93-87, 87 Stat. 295, 49 U.S. Code §§ 1603, 1607a, 1608, 1612
Nov. 16, 1977, P.L. 95-187, 49 U.S. Code §§ 1613, 1614
Nov. 6, 1978, P.L. 95-599, 49 U.S. Code §§ 1602 et seq.
Nov. 9, 1979, P.L. 96-106, 49 U.S. Code § 1604
Jan. 6, 1983, P.L. 97-424, 49 U.S. Code §§ 1607a, 1607a-1, 1602, 1603, 1607c, 1608, 1612, 1614, 1618
Aug. 22, 1984, P.L. 98-396, 49 U.S. Code Appx. § 1604
Dec. 19, 1985, P.L. 99-190, 49 U.S. Code Appx. §§ 1604, 1607a nt., , 1614
April 2, 1987, P.L. 100-17, 49 U.S. Code Appx. §§ 1602 nt., 1602 to 1604, 1607, 1607a, 1607a-2, 1607c, 1608, 1608 nt., 1612 to 1614, 1617, 1619 to 1621
Nov. 21, 1989, P.L. 101-164, 49 U.S. Code Appx. § 1619

**Urban Mass Transportation Assistance Act of 1970**
Oct. 15, 1970, P.L. 91-453, 84 Stat. 962, 49 U.S. Code §§ 1601a, 1602 to 1605, 1608, 1610 to 1612
July 2, 1986, P.L. 99-349, 100 Stat. 745

**Urban Mass Transportation Authority Act**
W. Va. Code 1966, § 8-27-1 et seq.

**Urban Open-Space and Recreation Program Act**
Cal. Public Resources Code § 5620 et seq.

**Urban Park and Recreation Recovery Act of 1978**
Nov. 10, 1978, P.L. 95-625, 16 U.S. Code § 2501 et seq.
Sept. 13, 1994, P.L. 103-322, 16 U.S. Code §§ 2502 et seq., 2512
Nov. 12, 1996, P.L. 104-333, 16 U.S. Code § 2514

**Urban Parks Recovery Grant Fund Act**
La. Rev. Stat. Ann., 56:1809

**Urban Property Protection and Reinsurance Act of 1968**

Aug. 1, 1968, P.L. 90-448, 82 Stat. 555, 5 U.S. Code §§ 5315, 7313 nt.; 12 U.S. Code §§ 1701s, 1709, 1735d, 1749bbb to 1749bbb-21; 15 U.S. Code § 2636; 42 U.S. Code §§ 1462, 3533a

Dec. 21, 1979, P.L. 96-153, 42 U.S. Code § 3533a

**Urban Redevelopment Act**

Conn. Gen. Stat. 1983, § 8-124 et seq.

N.H. Rev. Stat. 1955, 205:1 et seq.

N.Y. Laws 1941, Ch. 892

Okla. Stat. Ann., Title 11, § 1701 et seq.

**Urban Redevelopment Act (Cities Over 100,000)**

Okla. Stat. Ann., Title 11, § 1601 et seq.

**Urban Redevelopment Act (Cities Under 100,000)**

Okla. Stat. Ann., Title 11, § 1651 et seq.

**Urban Redevelopment Corporations Act**

Ark. Code Ann. 1987, 14-169-601 et seq.

Ga. Code Ann., 36-61-1 et seq.

Haw. Rev. Stat. Ann., § 53-1 et seq.

Ind. Code Ann., 18-7-7-1 et seq.

Mass. Gen. Laws Ann., 121A:1 et seq.

Mich. Comp. Laws Ann., 125.901 et seq.

Mo. Rev. Stat., 353.010 et seq.

N.C. Gen. Stat. 1943, § 160A-500 et seq.

N.H. Rev. Stat. 1955, 205:1 et seq.

N.J. Rev. Stat. 1937, 55:14E-1 et seq.

N.Y. Private Housing Finance Law (Consol. Laws Ch. 44B) § 200 et seq.

Ohio Rev. Code 1953, 725.01 et seq.

Ore. Rev. Stat., 457.010 et seq.

Pa. Purdon's Stat., Title 35, § 1701 et seq.

Va. Acts 1946, Ch. 190

Wis. Stat. Ann., 66.405 et seq.

**Urban Redevelopment Financing Act**

Mich. Comp. Laws 1970, 125.1501 et seq.

**Urban Redevelopment Limited Dividend Act**

Mass. Gen. Laws Ann., 121A:9

**Urban Renewal Act**

Ala. Code 1975, § 24-3-1 et seq.

Alaska Stat. 1962, § 18.55.680 et seq.

Colo. Rev. Stat., 31-25-101 et seq.

D.C. Code 1973, § 5-801 et seq.

Fla. Laws 1967, Ch. 67-734

Haw. Rev. Stat. Ann., § 53-51 et seq.

Ida. Code 1947, 50-2001 et seq.

Iowa Code Ann., 403.1 et seq.

Kan. Stat. Ann., 17-4742 et seq.

Mass. Gen. Laws Ann., 121 B:45 et seq.

Miss. Code Ann. 1972, § 43-35-1 et seq.

Mont. Code Ann., 7-15-4201 et seq.

N.D. Cent. Code, 40-58-01 et seq.

Nev. Rev. Stat. 1979 Reprint, 279.010 et seq.

N.M. Stat. Ann., 3-46-1 et seq.

Okla. Stat. Ann., Title 11, § 38-101 et seq.

S.C. Code Ann. 1976, Superseded Vols., § 31-7-10 et seq.

S.D. Codified Laws 1967, 11-8-1 et seq.

Tex. Local Government Code, § 374.001 et seq.

Utah Code Ann. 1953, 11-15-1 et seq.

Vt. Stat. Ann., Title 24, § 3201 et seq.

Wash. Rev. Code Ann., 35.81.010 et seq.

Wis. Stat. Ann., 66.435

Wyo. Stat. Ann., § 15-9-101 et seq.

**Urban Renewal Act of Florida**

Fla. Laws 1963, Ch. 63-1888 (Sarasota)

Fla. Laws 1965, Extra Session, Ch. 65-2457 (Fort Walton Beach)

Fla. Laws 1967, Ch. 67-734

Fla. Special Laws 1957, Ch. 57-1904 (Tampa)

Fla. Special Laws 1961, Ch. 61-1687 (Auburndale)

Fla. Special Laws 1961, Ch. 61-2020 (City of Cocoa)

Fla. Special Laws 1961, Ch. 61-2067 (Daytona Beach)

Fla. Special Laws 1961, Ch. 61-2165 (Fort Lauderdale)

Fla. Special Laws 1961, Ch. 61-2195 (Gainesville)

Fla. Special Laws 1961, Ch. 61-2382 (Lakeland)

Fla. Special Laws 1961, Ch. 61-2486 (Melbourne)

*Continued*

Fla. Special Laws 1961, Ch. 61-2603 (Orlando)
Fla. Special Laws 1961, Ch. 61-2693 (Plant City)
Fla. Special Laws 1961, Ch. 61-2781 (St. Petersburg)
Fla. Special Laws 1961, Ch. 61-3007 (Winter Haven)
Fla. Special Laws 1963, Ch. 63-1493 (Key West)
Fla. Special Laws 1965, Ch. 65-1793 (Lake Worth)
Fla. Special Laws 1965, Ch. 65-1860 (Live Oak)
Fla. Special Laws 1965, Ch. 65-2207
Fla. Special Laws 1967, Ch. 67-1362 (Eau Gallie)
Fla. Special Laws 1967, Ch. 67-1392 (Fort Pierce)
Fla. Special Laws 1967, Ch. 67-1596
Fla. Special Laws 1967, Ch. 67-1650
Fla. Special Laws 1967, Ch. 67-1767 (Niceville)
Fla. Special Laws 1967, Ch. 67-2137 (Titusville)
Fla. Special Laws 1969, Ch. 69-884 (Brooksville)
Md. Laws 1975, Ch. 380 (Kent County)

**Urban Renewal Agency Act**
N.Y. General Municipal Law (Consol. Laws Ch. 24) § 550 et seq.

**Urban Renewal and Community Development Act**
Ky. Rev. Stat. 1971, 99.330 et seq.

**Urban Renewal and Redevelopment Act**
Ky. Rev. Stat. 1971, 99.010 et seq.
Neb. Rev. Stat. 1943, 18-2101 et seq.

**Urban Renewal Authorities Act**
Me. Rev. Stat. Ann. 1964, Title 30, § 4801 et seq.
W. Va. Code 1966, § 16-18-1 et seq.

**Urban Renewal Authority for Slum Clearance (District Heights)**
Md. Laws 1999, Ch. 413

**Urban Renewal Authority Law**
W. Va. Code 1966, § 16-18-1 et seq.

**Urban Renewal Authority Law (Bangor)**
Me. Private and Special Laws 1957, Ch. 168

**Urban Renewal, Community Development Law**
Neb. Rev. Stat. 1943, 18-2101 et seq.

**Urban Renewal Consolidation Act**
Ill. Rev. Stat. 1991, Ch. 67 1/2, § 91-101 et seq.

**Urban Renewal Corporation and Association Law**
N.J. Rev. Stat. 1937, 40:55C-40 et seq.

**Urban Renewal Nonprofit Corporation Law**
N.J. Stat. Ann., 40:55C-77 et seq.

**Urban Renewal Projects State Aid Act**
N.J. Stat. Ann., 52:27D-44 et seq.

**Urban Residential Finance Authorities Act for Large Municipalities**
Ga. Code Ann., 36-41-1 et seq.

**Urban-Rural Recovery Act of 1983**
Aug. 22, 1996, P.L. 104-193, 42 U.S. Code § 602 nt.

**Urban School Construction Aid Law**
Cal. Education Code 1976, § 17300 et seq.

**Urban Transportation Districts Act**
Ill. Rev. Stat. 1983, Ch. 111 2/3, § 501 et seq.
Mont. Code Ann., 7-14-201 et seq.

**Urban Water Management Planning Act**
Cal. Water Code § 10610 et seq.

**Urban Waterfront Area Restoration Financing Authority Act**
Cal. Public Resources Code § 32000 et seq.

**Urban Waterfront Restoration Act**
Cal. Public Resources Code § 31300 et seq.

**Urban Woman Job Training Center Act**
N.J. Stat. Ann., 52:27D-288 et seq.

**Urgent Assistance for Democracy in Panama Act of 1990**
Feb. 14, 1990, P.L. 101-243, 104 Stat. 7

**Urgent Deficiencies Appropriation Acts**
June 30, 1939, Ch. 254, 53 Stat. 980
Feb. 12, 1940, Ch. 28, 54 Stat. 35
May 24, 1941, Ch. 132, 55 Stat. 197, 42 U.S. Code § 1523 nt.
May 7, 1943, Ch. 94, 57 Stat. 78
July 12, 1943, Ch. 218, 57 Stat. 431
March 22, 1947, Ch. 20, 61 Stat. 14
March 3, 1948, Ch. 91, 62 Stat. 59
March 27, 1950, Ch. 77, 64 Stat. 37
June 30, 1952, Ch. 532, 66 Stat. 313
Jan. 25, 1955, Ch. 3, 69 Stat. 4, 15 U.S. Code § 713a-10
Feb. 14, 1956, Ch. 34, 70 Stat. 13, 2 U.S. Code § 72a-2
May 14, 1958, P.L. 85-400, 72 Stat. 108

**Urgent Relief for the Homeless Supplemental Appropriations Act of 1987**
July 11, 1987, P.L. 100-71, 101 Stat. 468

**Urgent Supplemental Appropriations Act of 1982**
July 18, 1982, P.L. 97-216, 20 U.S. Code § 1221e nt., 23 U.S. Code § 104 nt., 26 U.S. Code §§ 162, 162 nt., 280A, 39 U.S. Code § 2401 nt., 45 U.S. Code §§ 543, 1015

**Urgent Supplemental Appropriations Act of 1986**
July 2, 1986, P.L. 99-349, 100 Stat. 750
Nov. 23, 1993, P.L. 103-149, 107 Stat. 1506

**Urgent Supplemental Appropriations Act of 1989**
Nov. 18, 1988, P.L. 100-690, 102 Stat. 4544

**Urstadt Law (Rent Control)**
N.Y. Unconsolidated Laws, § 8605

**Uruguay Round Agreements Act**
Dec. 8, 1994, P.L. 103-465, 19 U.S. Code § 3501 nt.
April 4, 1996, P.L. 104-127, 19 U.S. Code § 3611
Aug. 20, 1996, P.L. 104-188, 19 U.S. Code § 3551; 26 U.S. Code § 411 nt.
Oct. 11, 1996, P.L. 104-295, 19 U.S. Code §§ 1337, 1671b, 1673a, 1673d, 1677-1, 2192, 2416, 2465, 2578a, 3552, 3571, 3572, 3591, 3592, 3602
Aug. 5, 1997, P.L. 105-34, 26 U.S. Code § 411 nt.
July 22, 1998, P.L. 105-206, 19 U.S. Code § 3555
Nov. 10, 1998, P.L. 105-362, 19 U.S. Code § 3622

**U.S. Holocaust Assets Commission Act of 1998**
June 23, 1998, P.L. 105-186, 22 U.S. Code § 1621 nt.

**Usage Tax Act (Motor Vehicles)**
Ky. Rev. Stat. 1971, 138.450 et seq.

**Use Act (Narcotics)**
N.J. Stat. Ann., 2A:108-9

**Use Act (Safety Belt)**
Ala. Code 1975, § 32-5B-1 et seq.

**Use and Control of Fire Arms and Other Devices Law (Hamburg)**
N.Y. Local Laws 1966, Town of Hamburg, p. 1030

**Use and Excise Tax Act**
Tex. Tax Code, § 151.001 et seq.

**Use and Municipal Sales Tax Act**
Tex. Tax Code, § 321.001 et seq.

**Use and Occupation Tax Refund Act**
Ill. Comp. Stat. 1992, Ch. 35, § 150/1
Ill. Rev. Stat. 1991, Ch. 120, §§ 1500, 1501

**Use and Sale Tax**
Utah Code Ann. 1953, 59-12-101 et seq.

**Use and Sales Tax Act**
See Sales and Use Tax Act

**Use and Sales Tax Refund Act**
Iowa Code Ann., 422.45

**Use and Storage Tax Act**
Ohio Rev. Code 1953, 5741.01 et seq.
Pa. 1953 Pamph. Laws 377, No. 85

**Use Fuel Tax Act**
Ariz. Rev. Stat. Ann., § 28-1551 et seq.
Cal. Revenue and Taxation Code § 8601 et seq.
Ida. Code 1947, 63-2401 et seq.
La. Rev. Stat. Ann., 47:801 et seq.
Me. Rev. Stat. Ann. 1964, Title 36, § 3021 et seq.
Nev. Stat. 1939, Ch. 149, p. 193
Ore. Rev. Stat., 319.510 et seq.
Pa. Purdon's Stat., Title 72, § 2614.1 et seq.
Utah Code Ann. 1953, 59-13-101 et seq.
Va. Code 1950, § 58.1-2100 et seq.
Wash. Rev. Code 1951, 82.40.010 et seq.

**Use Fuel Tax Law (Bill of Rights)**
Cal. Revenue and Taxation Code § 9260 et seq.

**Use of Assisted Housing by Aliens Act of 1996**
Sept. 30, 1996, P.L. 104-208, Subtitle E, 42 U.S. Code § 1436a nt.

**Use of Intoxicating Compounds Act**
Ill. Rev. Stat. 1991, Ch. 38, § 81 et seq.

**Use of School Property Law**
Cal. Education Code 1976, §§ 40040 et seq., 82530 et seq.

**Use of University Stationery Act**
Ill. Rev. Stat. 1991, Ch. 38, § 70 et seq.

**Use or Compensating Tax Law**
Miss. Code Ann. 1972, § 27-67-1 et seq.

**Use Tax Act**
Ala. Code 1975, § 40-23-60 et seq.
Ariz. Rev. Stat. Ann., § 42-1401 et seq.
Ark. Code Ann. 1987, 26-53-101 et seq.
Cal. Revenue and Taxation Code § 6201 et seq.
Colo. Rev. Stat., 39-26-101 et seq.
D.C. Code Ann., § 47-2201 et seq.
Fla. Stat. Ann., 212.01 et seq.
Ga. Code Ann., 48-8-1 et seq.
Haw. Rev. Stat. Ann., § 238-1 et seq.
Ill. Comp. Stat. 1992, Ch. 35, § 105/1 et seq.
Ill. Rev. Stat. 1991, Ch. 120, § 439.1 et seq.
Ind. Code Ann., 6-2-1-41 et seq.
Iowa Code Ann., 432.1 et seq.
Kan. Stat. Ann., 79-3701 et seq.
La. Rev. Stat. Ann., 47:301 et seq.
Mass. Gen. Laws Ann., 64I:1 et seq.
Md. Ann. Code 1957, Art. 81, § 372 et seq.
Me. Rev. Stat. Ann. 1964, Title 36, § 1751 et seq.
Mich. Comp. Laws Ann., 205.91 et seq.
Miss. Code Ann. 1972, § 27-67-1 et seq.
Mo. Rev. Stat., 144.600 et seq.
N.C. Gen. Stat. 1943, § 105-164.1 et seq.
N.D. Cent. Code, 57-40.2-01 et seq.
Nev. Rev. Stat. 1979 Reprint, 372.010 et seq.
N.J. Stat. Ann., 54:32B-1 et seq.
N.M. Stat. Ann. 1953, 72-17-1 et seq.
Ohio Rev. Code 1953, 5741.01 et seq.
Okla. Stat. Ann., Title 68, § 1401 et seq.
S.C. Code Ann. 1976, § 12-36-1310 et seq.
S.D. Codified Laws 1967, 10-46-1 et seq.
Tenn. Code Ann., 67-6-101 et seq.
Wash. Rev. Code Ann., 82.12.010 et seq.
Wis. Stat. Ann., 77.51 et seq.
W. Va. Code 1966, § 11-15A-1 et seq.
Wyo. Stat. Ann., § 39-6-501 et seq.

**Use Tax Act (Beneficial)**
Tenn. Code Ann., 67-4-1501 et seq.

**Use Tax Act (Cigarette)**
Ill. Comp. Stat. 1992, Ch. 35, § 135/1 et seq.

**Use Tax Act (County Automobile Renting)**
Ill. Rev. Stat. 1991, Ch. 34, § 5-1033

**Use Tax Act (County)**
Ill. Rev. Stat. 1987, Ch. 34, § 409.10

**Use Tax Act (Importers)**
N.D. Cent. Code, 57-43.1-01 et seq.

**Use Tax Act (Motor Fuels)**
N.J. Stat. Ann., 54:39A-1 et seq.

**Use Tax Act (Motor Vehicles)**
Mo. Rev. Stat., 144.440 et seq.

**Use Tax Act (Municipal Automobile Renting)**
Ill. Rev. Stat. 1991, Ch. 24, § 8-11-8

**Use Tax Act (Municipal)**
Ill. Rev. Stat. 1991, Ch. 24, § 8-11-6

**Use Tax Act (Service)**
Ill. Comp. Stat. 1992, Ch. 35, § 110/1 et seq.

**Use Tax Act (Temporary)**
Mass. Acts 1966, Ch. 14, § 2

**Use Tax Exemption Act**
Ala. Code 1975, § 40-23-62
Mich. Comp. Laws Ann., 205.94

**USEC Privatization Act**
April 26, 1996, P.L. 104-134, 42 U.S. Code § 2011 nt.
Sept. 30, 1996, P.L. 104-206, 42 U.S. Code § 2297h-8
Oct. 13, 1997, P.L. 105-62, 42 U.S. Code § 2297h-5
Oct. 7, 1998, P.L. 105-245, 42 U.S. Code § 2297h-5

**Used Car Dealers' Registration Act**
Ga. Code Ann., 43-47-1 et seq.

**Used Car Lemon Law**
N.Y. General Business Law (Consol. Laws Ch. 20) § 198b

**Used Lubricant Act**
Ill. Rev. Stat. 1991, Ch. 96 1/2, § 5800 et seq.

**Used Merchandise Act**
N.M. Stat. Ann., 57-9-1 et seq.

**Used Motor Oil and Lead-Acid Battery Recycling Act**
Okla. Stat. Ann., Title 27A, § 2001 et seq.

**Used Motor Oil Recycling Act**
Ill. Rev. Stat. 1991, Ch. 96 1/2, § 7751 et seq.

**Used Motor Vehicle Dealers' and Used Motor Vehicle Parts Dealers' Registration Act**
Ga. Code Ann., 43-47-1 et seq.

**Used Motor Vehicle Dismantlers, Rebuilders, and Salvage Dealers Registration Act**
Ga. Code Ann., 43-48-1 et seq.

**Used Oil Collection Act**
Tenn. Code Ann., 68-211-1001 et seq.

**Used Oil Collection Demonstration Grant Program Act**
Cal. Public Resources Code § 3475 et seq.

**Used Oil Collection, Management, and Recycling Act**
Tex. Health and Safety Code, § 371.001 et seq.

**Used Oil Management Act**
Utah Code Ann. 1953, 19-6-701 et seq.

**Used Oil Recycling Act**
Cal. Public Resources Code § 3460 et seq.
Md. Ann. Code 1974, Art. EN, § 5-1001 et seq.
Mich. Comp. Laws Ann., 319.311 et seq.
Ore. Rev. Stat., 468.850 et seq.
Pa. Purdon's Stat., Title 58, § 471 et seq.
R.I. Gen. Laws 1956, 23-19.6-1 et seq.
Wash. Rev. Code Ann., 70.95I.005 et seq.

**Used Oil Recycling Act of 1980**
Oct. 15, 1980, P.L. 96-463, 42 U.S. Code § 6901 nt.
Nov. 10, 1998, P.L. 105-362, 42 U.S. Code § 6932 nt.

**Useless Public Records Act**
Ga. Code 1933, 40-809, 40-810

**Users Act (Agriculture Gas)**
Tex. Rev. Civ. Stat., Art. 6066g

**Uses Act (Stale Claims)**
Iowa Code Ann., 614.24

**Uses and Trusts Act**
Wis. Stat. Ann., 701.01 et seq.

**Usurpation Act**
Colo. Rules of Civil Procedure, Rule 106

**Usurpation Act (Public Office)**
Ark. Code Ann. 1987, 16-118-105 et seq.
Ida. Code 1947, 6-602, 6-610
La. Rev. Stat. Ann., 42:71 et seq.

**Usury Act**
Ala. Code 1975, § 8-8-1 et seq.
Alaska Stat. 1962, § 45.45.010 et seq.
Ariz. Rev. Stat. Ann., § 44-1202 et seq.
Ark. Code Ann. 1987, 4-57-106 et seq.
Cal. Const., Art. 20, § 22 (Usury)
Colo. Rev. Stat., 1963, 73-3-1 et seq.
Conn. Gen. Stat. 1983, § 37-1 et seq.
Del. Code of 1974, Title 16, § 2304
Fla. Stat. Ann., 687.01 et seq.
Ga. Code Ann., 7-4-1 et seq.
Haw. Rev. Stat. Ann., § 478-1 et seq.
Ida. Code 1947, 28-22-105, 28-22-107 et seq.
Ill. Rev. Stat. 1991, Ch. 17, § 6400 et seq.
Ind. Code Ann., 28-1-11-13 et seq.
Iowa Code Ann., 535.1 et seq.
Kan. Stat. Ann., 16-201 et seq.
Ky. Rev. Stat. 1971, 360.010 et seq.
La. Civil Code 1992, Art. 2924
Md. Ann. Code 1974, Art. CL, § 12-101 et seq.
Me. Rev. Stat. Ann. 1964, Title 9-A, §§ 2-201, 2-202, 2-401, 2-401
Mich. Comp. Laws Ann., 438.31 et seq.
Minn. Stat. Ann., 334.02 et seq.
Miss. Code Ann. 1972, § 75-17-1 et seq.
Mo. Rev. Stat., 408.030 et seq.
Mont. Code Ann., 31-1 108
N.C. Gen. Stat. 1943, § 24-2
N.D. Cent. Code, 47-14-09 et seq.
Neb. Rev. Stat. 1943, 45-101.02 et seq.
N.J. Stat. Ann., 31:1-1 et seq.
N.M. Stat. Ann., 56-8-1 et seq.
N.Y. General Obligations Law (Consol. Laws Ch. 24A) § 5-501 et seq.
Ohio Rev. Code 1953, 1343.04, 1343.05
Okla. Stat. Ann., Title 18, § 1129 et seq.
Ore. Rev. Stat., 82.010 et seq.
Pa. Purdon's Stat., Title 41, §§ 201 et seq., 501 et seq.
S.C. Code Ann. 1976, Superseded Vols., § 34-31-50 et seq.
Tenn. Code Ann., 47-14-101 et seq.
Tex. Rev. Civ. Stat., Art. 5069-1.01 et seq.
Utah Code Ann. 1953, 15-1-1 et seq.
Va. Code 1950, § 6.1-330.56 et seq.
Vt. Stat. Ann., Title 9, § 41 et seq.
Wash. Rev. Code Ann., 19.52.005 et seq.
Wis. Stat. Ann., 138.05, 138.06
W. Va. Code 1966, § 47-6-5 et seq.
Wyo. Stat. 1957, § 13-482 et seq.

**Usury and Interest Act**
D.C. Code 1973, § 28-3301 et seq.
N.Y. General Obligations Law (Consol. Laws Ch. 24A) § 5-501 et seq.
R.I. Gen. Laws 1956, 6-26-1 et seq.

**Usury Forfeiture Act**
Fla. Stat. Ann., 687.04, 687.07

**Usury Injunction Act**
Tex. Rev. Civ. Stat., Art. 5069-1.01 et seq.

**Utah Schools and Lands Exchange Act of 1998**
Oct. 31, 1998, P.L. 105-335, 112 Stat. 3139, 16 U.S. Code § 431 nt.

**Utah Schools and Lands Improvement Act of 1993**
Oct. 1, 1993, P.L. 103-93, 107 Stat. 995

**Utah Wilderness Act of 1984**
Sept. 28, 1984, P.L. 98-428, 98 Stat. 1657, 16 U.S. Code § 1132 nt.

**Ute Indian Water Compact Act**
Utah Code Ann. 1953, 73-21-1, 73-21-2

**Utica City Court Act**
N.Y. Laws 1882, Ch. 103
N.Y. Laws 1966, Ch. 443

**Utica Parking Authority Act**
N.Y. Public Authorities Law (Consol. Laws Ch. 43A) § 1590a et seq.

**Utilities Act**
Colo. Rev. Stat., 40-1-101 et seq.
Haw. Rev. Stat. Ann., § 269-1 et seq.
Ind. Code Ann., 8-1-1-1 et seq.
Me. Rev. Stat. Ann. 1964, Title 35-A, § 103 et seq.
Mich. Comp. Laws Ann., 460. 51 et seq.

Mont. Code Ann., 69-1-101 et seq.
N.C. Gen. Stat. 1943, § 62-1 et seq.
Nev. Rev. Stat. 1979 Reprint, 704.010 et seq.
N.H. Rev. Stat. 1955, 362:1 et seq.
N.J. Stat. Ann., 48:1-1 et seq.
Ore. Rev. Stat., 576.010 et seq.
Pa. Cons. Stat., Title 66, § 101 et seq.
Utah Code Ann. 1953, 54-1-1 et seq.

**Utilities Act (Electrical)**
S.C. Code Ann. 1976, § 58-27-10 et seq.

**Utilities Act (Municipal)**
Kan. Stat. Ann., 12-801 et seq.
Wash. Rev. Code Ann., 35.92.010 et seq.

**Utilities Act (State)**
Kan. Stat. Ann., 66-101 et seq.

**Utilities and Cooperatives Act (Electric)**
S.C. Code Ann. 1976, § 58-27-10 et seq.

**Utilities Assessment Act**
Wash. Rev. Code Ann., 84.12.200 et seq.

**Utilities Authority Act (Lee County)**
Ga. Laws 1992, p. 6419

**Utilities Authority Act (Lowndes County)**
Ga. Laws 1970, p. 3112

**Utilities Commission Act**
N.C. Gen. Stat. 1943, § 62-10 et seq.

**Utilities Commission Procedure Act**
N.C. Gen. Stat. 1943, § 62-60 et seq.

**Utilities Cut-Off Procedures Act**
Tenn. Code Ann., 65-32-101 et seq.

**Utilities Facilities Act (Excavations near Underground)**
Miss. Code Ann. 1972, § 77-13-1 et seq.

**Utilities Relocation Act**
Ind. Code Ann., 8-1-9-1 et seq.
N.D. Cent. Code, 24-01-41
Tex. Rev. Civ. Stat., Art. 6674w-4
Utah Code Ann. 1953, 27-12-11

**Utilities Revenue Bond Act**
S.C. Code Ann. 1976, § 6-21-10 et seq.

**Utilities Securities Act**
Mich. Comp. Laws Ann., 460.301 et seq.

**Utilities Service Taxes Act**
Fla. Stat. 1971, 167.431

**Utilities Underground Conversion Act**
Colo. Rev. Stat., 29-8-101 et seq.
Ida. Code 1947, 50-2501 et seq.
Mont. Code Ann., 69-4-301 et seq.
Utah Code Ann. 1953, 54-8-1 et seq.
Wyo. Stat. Ann., § 37-13-101 et seq.

**Utility Act (Public)**
N.M. Stat. Ann., 62-13-1 et seq.

**Utility Act of Escambia County**
Fla. Special Laws 1957, Ch. 57-1313

**Utility Advocate Act (Small Business)**
Ill. Rev. Stat. 1991, Ch. 11 2/3, § 1201 et seq.

**Utility and Farm Equipment Act**
Mich. Comp. Laws Ann., 445.1451 et seq.

**Utility Anti-Strike Act**
See Antistrike Act (Public Utilities)

**Utility Authority Act (Oconee)**
Ga. Laws 1986, p. 4123

**Utility Board Act (Citizens)**
Ill. Comp. Stat. 1992, Ch. 220, § 10/1 et seq.
Wis. Stat. Ann., 199.01 et seq.

**Utility Bond Act**
Fla. Special Laws 1945, Ch. 23-242 (Daytona Beach)
Fla. Special Laws 1947, Ch. 24-494 (Edgewater)
Fla. Special Laws 1963, Ch. 63-1598 (Manatee County)
Fla. Special Laws 1967, Ch. 67-2048 (Sarasota County)
Fla. Special Laws 1971, Ch. 71-804 (Orange County)

**Utility Consumers' Bill of Rights**
N.Y. Public Service Law (Consol. Laws Ch. 48) § 30 et seq.

**Utility Control Act (Solid Waste)**
N.J. Stat. Ann., 48:13A-1 et seq.

**Utility Damage Prevention Act (Underground)**
Kan. Stat. Ann., 66-1801 et seq.

**Utility Damage Prevention and Safety Act (Underground)**
Del. Code of 1974, Title 26, § 801 et seq.

**Utility District Act**
Ore. Rev. Stat., 261.005 et seq.
Tenn. Code Ann., 7-82-101 et seq.

**Utility District Act (Municipal)**
Cal. Public Utility Code § 11501 et seq.

**Utility Employees' Service Letter Law**
Cal. Labor Code §§ 1055, 1056

**Utility Environmental Protection Act**
Me. Rev. Stat. Ann. 1964, Title 35-A, § 2901 et seq.

**Utility Facilities Act**
Va. Code 1950, § 56-265.1 et seq.

**Utility Facility Environmental and Economic Protection Act**
Ark. Stat. 1947, 23-18-501 et seq.

**Utility Facility Siting and Environmental Protection Act**
S.C. Code Ann. 1976, § 58-33-10 et seq.

**Utility Financing Bank Act (Public)**
Me. Rev. Stat. Ann. 1964, Title 35-A, § 2901 et seq.

**Utility Holding Company Act**
See Public Utility Holding Company Act

**Utility Industry Restructuring and Customer Choice Act (Electric)**
Mont. Code Ann., 69-8-101 et seq.

**Utility Operators Certification Act**
N.M. Stat. Ann., 61-30-1 et seq.

**Utility Regulatory Reform Act**
Okla. Laws 1987, Ch. 17

**Utility Relief Act for Needy**
La. Rev. Stat. Ann., 46:191 et seq.

**Utility Relocation Act**
N.D. Cent. Code, 24-01-41

**Utility Relocation Assistance Act**
Wyo. Stat. Ann., § 24-13-101 et seq.

**Utility Restructuring and Customer Choice Act (Natural Gas)**
Mont. Code Ann., 69-3-1401 et seq.

**Utility Service Act (Rental Property)**
Ill. Rev. Stat. 1991, Ch. 80, § 61 et seq.

**Utility Service Tenants Rights Act**
Pa. Purdon's Stat., Title 68, § 399.1 et seq.

**Utility Services Interference Act**
Ill. Rev. Stat. 1991, Ch. 111 2/3, § 1500 et seq.

**Utility Siting Act**
Mont. Code Ann., 75-20-101 et seq.

**Utility Supplement Act**
N.M. Stat. Ann., 27-6-1 et seq.

**Utility Systems Act (Drainage)**
Tex. Government Code, § 402.041 et seq.

**Utility Tax Act**
Miss. Code Ann. 1972, § 21-33-201 et seq.
Wash. Rev. Code Ann., 82.16.010 et seq.
Wis. Stat. Ann., 76.01 et seq.

**Utility Transfers Act**
Va. Code 1950, § 56-88 et seq.

**Utility Users Tax Act (Cities)**
Miss. Code Ann. 1972, § 21-33-201 et seq.

**Utility Users Tax Ordinance (City)**
See also Uniform City Utility Users Tax Ordinance
Mich. Comp. Laws Ann., 141.801 et seq., 141.1151 et seq.

**Utilization and Conservation of Natural Energy and Water Resources Compact Act**
Tex. Natural Resources Code, § 142.001 et seq.

**Utilization Review Act**
Minn. Stat. 1986, 62M.01 et seq.

**Utilization Review Act (Health Care Service)**
Ala. Code 1975, § 27-3A-1 et seq.
Tenn. Public Acts 1992, Ch. 812

**Utilization Review Certification Act**
Neb. Laws 1992, L.B. 428 §§ 1 to 15

**Utilization Review Organization Act**
Kan. Stat. Ann., 40-2201 et seq.

## V

**Vacancies Act (Judicial)**
Ill. Rev. Stat. 1991, Ch. 37, § 72.41-1 et seq.

**Vacancy Act (Municipal)**
N.J. Stat. Ann., 49A:16-1 et seq.

**Vacancy Act (Public Lands)**
Tex. Natural Resources Code, § 51.171 et seq.

**Vacancy Decontrol Law**
Cal. Civil Code § 1954.50 et seq.

**Vacant Areas Development Act (Blighted)**
Ill. Comp. Stat. 1992, Ch. 315, § 10/1 et seq.

**Vacant Land Statute**
Wash. Rev. Code Ann., 7.28.080

**Vacated Grounds for Universities Act**
Ill. Rev. Stat. 1991, Ch. 144, §§ 11.9, 12

**Vacation Act (Courts)**
Me. Rev. Stat. Ann. 1964, Title 4, § 1051

**Vacation Club Act**
Fla. Stat. Ann., 721.50 et seq.
Tenn. Code Ann., 66-32-102, 66-32-201 to 66-32-204

**Vacation of Plats Act**
Ill. Rev. Stat. 1991, Ch. 109, § 6 et seq.

**Vacation Plan and Time Sharing Act**
Fla. Stat. Ann., 721.01 et seq.

**Vacation Time Act (State Employee)**
Ill. Rev. Stat. 1991, Ch. 127, §§ 63b120.01, 63b121

**Vacation Time Sharing Plans Act**
S.C. Code Ann. 1976, § 27-32-10 et seq.

**Vaccination Act**
Mass. Gen. Laws Ann., 76:15, 111:181 et seq.
N.Y. Public Health Law 1953 (Consol. Laws Ch. 45) § 2130 et seq.

**Vaccination Act (School Children)**
D.C. Code Ann., § 31-501 et seq.
Mont. Code Ann. 1979, 20-5-401 et seq.
N.H. Rev. Stat. 1955, 200.38 et seq.
N.Y. Public Health Law 1953 (Consol. Laws Ch. 45) § 2164
Ohio Rev. Code 1953, 3313.67
R.I. Gen. Laws 1956, 16-38-2

**Vaccination Assistance Act of 1962**
Oct. 23, 1962, P.L. 87-868, 76 Stat. 1155, 42 U.S. Code § 247b

**Vaccine and Immunization Amendments of 1990**
Nov. 3, 1990, P.L. 101-502, 42 U.S. Code § 201 nt.

**Vaccine Compensation Amendments of 1987**
Dec. 22, 1987, P.L. 100-203, 42 U.S. Code § 201 nt.

**Vaccine Injury Compensation Program Modification Act**
Oct. 21, 1998, P.L. 105-277, Division C, Title XV, 112 Stat. 2681, 26 U.S. Code § 1 nt.

**Vag Addict Act**
Ariz. Rev. Stat. Ann., § 13-3408

**Vagabonds Act**
Md. Ann. Code 1957, Art. 27, § 490

**Vagrancy Act**
Ala. Code 1958, Title 14, § 437 et seq.
Ariz. Rev. Stat. Ann., § 13-2905
Ark. Code Ann. 1987, 5-71-213
Cal. Penal Code § 647a
Colo. Rev. Stat. 1963, 40-8-19
Conn. Gen. Stat. Ann., § 53-340
D.C. Code 1973, § 22-3302 et seq.
Fla. Stat. Ann., 856.021, 856.031
Ga. Code 1933, 26-7001
Haw. Rev. Stat. Ann., § 772-1
Ill. Rev. Stat. 1991, Ch. 24, § 11-5-4
Ind. Code Ann., 35-1-110-2
Iowa Code 1977, 746.1 et seq.
La. Rev. Stat. Ann., 14:107
Mass. Gen. Laws Ann., 272:66

Md. Ann. Code 1957, Art. 27, § 581
Me. Rev. Stat. Ann. 1964, Title 17, § 3758
Minn. Stat. Ann., 609.725
Mont. Rev. Code 1947, 94-35-248
Neb. Laws 1879, Ch. 64
N.Y. Code of Criminal Procedure § 887 et seq.
Ore. Rev. Stat. 1953, 166.060
Pa. Purdon's Stat., Title 18, § 2032 et seq.
R.I. Gen. Laws 1956, Superseded Vol., 11-45-1 et seq.
Tenn. Code Ann., 39-17-301
Tex. Penal Code 1925, Art. 607 et seq.
Va. Code 1950, Misc. Superseded Code Provisions, § 63-338 et seq.
Vt. Stat. Ann., Title 13, § 3901 et seq.
Wash. Rev. Code Ann., 35.22.280 et seq.
Wis. Stat. 1989, 947.02

**Vail Act (Mortgage Foreclosure)**
N.J. Stat. Ann., 2A:50-1 et seq.

**Valatie Zoning Law**
N.Y. Local Laws 1972, Village of Valatie, p. 3967

**Valdosta-Lowndes County Conference Center and Tourism Authority Act**
Ga. Laws 1999, H.B. 899

**Valdosta-Lowndes County Industrial Authority Act**
Ga. Laws 1960, p. 2786

**Valdosta School Tax Act**
Ga. Laws 1949, p. 1392

**Valentine Act (Antitrust)**
Ohio Rev. Code 1953, 1331.01 et seq.

**Validating Act (Bonds, Municipal Securities)**
N.D. Cent. Code, 1-07-01 et seq.

**Validating Act (Bonds)**
N.C. Public Laws 1939, Ch. 117
N.D. Cent. Code, 21-09-01 et seq.
Wyo. Session Laws 1935, Ch. 102

**Validating Act (Divorce)**
Pa. 1909 Pamph. Laws 390, No. 219
Pa. 1927 Pamph. Laws 991, No. 478

**Validating Act (First School Bond)**
Cal. Statutes 1952, 2nd Ex. Sess., Ch. 23, p. 466

**Validating Act (First)**
Cal. Statutes 1951, Ch. 675, p. 1882
Cal. Statutes 1952, 2nd Ex. Sess., Ch. 31, p. 505
Cal. Statutes 1953, Ch. 1156, p. 2655
Cal. Statutes 1955, Ch. 11, p. 454
Cal. Statutes 1957, Ch. 133, p. 719
Cal. Statutes 1958, 1st Ex. Sess., Ch. 10, p. 191
Cal. Statutes 1959, Ch. 12, p. 1857
Cal. Statutes 1959, Ch. 30, p. 1875
Cal. Statutes 1961, Ch. 405, p. 1472
Cal. Statutes 1963, Ch. 7, p. 613
Cal. Statutes 1965, Ch. 95, p. 1035
Cal. Statutes 1967, Ch. 2, p. 4
Cal. Statutes 1968, Ch. 6, p. 145
Cal. Statutes 1970, Ch. 4, p. 6
Cal. Statutes 1971, Ch. 12, p. 17
Cal. Statutes 1972, Ch. 41, p. 53
Cal. Statutes 1973, Ch. 38
Cal. Statutes 1974, Ch. 12
Cal. Statutes 1976, Ch. 114
Cal. Statutes 1977, Ch. 33
Cal. Statutes 1978, Ch. 135
Cal. Statutes 1982, Ch. 617
Cal. Statutes 1984, Ch. 91
Cal. Statutes 1988, Ch. 95
Cal. Statutes 1990, Ch. 87
Cal. Statutes 1991, Ch. 17
Cal. Statutes 1991, Ch. 22

**Validating Act (General)**
Cal. Statutes 1946, 1st Ex. Sess., Ch. 17, p. 20

**Validating Act (Ideal Farms Drainage District)**
Fla. Special Laws 1925, Ch. 10699

**Validating Act (Incorporation of Cities and Towns of 5,000 or Less)**
Tex. Rev. Civ. Stat., Art. 966c
Tex. Rev. Civ. Stat., Art. 974d-2

**Validating Act (Municipal Obligations)**
Pa. Purdon's Stat., Title 53, § 5591 et seq.

**Validating Act (School District)**
Cal. Statutes 1957, Ch. 34, p. 589

**Validating Act (Second-Public Bodies)**
Cal. Statutes 1947, Ch. 492, p. 1473

**Validating Act (Second)**
Cal. Statutes 1946, 2nd Ex. Sess., Ch. 6, p. 336
Cal. Statutes 1949, Ch. 782, p. 1511
Cal. Statutes 1950, 1st Ex. Sess., Ch. 72, p. 541
Cal. Statutes 1951, Ch. 1445, p. 3404
Cal. Statutes 1953, Ch. 1886, p. 3680
Cal. Statutes 1956, 1st Ex. Sess., Ch. 16, p. 307
Cal. Statutes 1957, Ch. 134, p. 724
Cal. Statutes 1959, Ch. 31, p. 1880
Cal. Statutes 1961, Ch. 985
Cal. Statutes 1962, 1st Ex. Sess., Ch. 15, p. 168
Cal. Statutes 1970, Ch. 365, p. 776
Cal. Statutes 1971, Ch. 564, p. 1079
Cal. Statutes 1972, Ch. 314, p. 583
Cal. Statutes 1974, Ch. 689
Cal. Statutes 1975, Ch. 680
Cal. Statutes 1976, Ch. 724
Cal. Statutes 1978, Ch. 666
Cal. Statutes 1981, Ch. 568
Cal. Statutes 1985, Ch. 594
Cal. Statutes 1988, Ch. 756
Cal. Statutes 1990, Ch. 810
Cal. Statutes 1991, Ch. 398
Cal. Statutes 1991, Ch. 441
Cal. Statutes 1991, Ch. 619
N.C. Gen. Stat. 1943, § 39-37 et seq.

**Validating Act (Third)**
Cal. Statutes 1943, Ch. 458, p. 1993
Cal. Statutes 1967, Ch. 938, p. 2429
Cal. Statutes 1970, Ch. 1149, p. 2029
Cal. Statutes 1971, Ch. 712, p. 1379
Cal. Statutes 1972, Ch. 337, p. 632
Cal. Statutes 1974, Ch. 911
Cal. Statutes 1975, Ch. 681
Cal. Statutes 1976, Ch. 725
Cal. Statutes 1978, Ch. 667
Cal. Statutes 1981, Ch. 568
Cal. Statutes 1985, Ch. 590
Cal. Statutes 1988, Ch. 757
Cal. Statutes 1990, Ch. 811
Cal. Statutes 1991, Ch. 399
Cal. Statutes 1991, Ch. 442
Cal. Statutes 1991, Ch. 777

**Validating Act of 1931-1948**
Cal. Statutes 1931, Ch. 70, p. 77
Cal. Statutes 1939, Ch. 593, p. 2004
Cal. Statutes 1940, 1st Ex. Sess., p. 40
Cal. Statutes 1947, Ch. 17, p. 491
Cal. Statutes 1948, Ch. 35, p. 146
Cal. Statutes 1949, Ch. 781, p. 1508
Del. Rev. Code 1935, § 6265 et seq.
Mont. Laws 1935, Ch. 99
N.Y. Laws 1935, Ch. 663
N.Y. Laws 1940, Ch. 500
Okla. Stat. Ann., Title 62, § 381 et seq.
Tenn. Public Acts 1937, Ch. 238
Tenn. Public Acts 1939, Ch. 57
Va. Code 1950, Misc. Superseded Code Provisions, § 15-663 et seq.

**Validating Act of 1935**
Okla. Stat. Ann., Title 62, § 381 et seq.

**Validating Act of 1992 (Second)**
Cal. Statutes 1992, Ch. 568

**Validating Act of 1992 (Third)**
Cal. Statutes 1992, Ch. 567

**Validating Act of 1995 (Second)**
Cal. Statutes 1995, Ch. 851

**Validating Act of 1995 (Third)**
Cal. Statutes 1995, Ch. 688

**Validating Act of 1996 (Second)**
Cal. Statutes 1996, Ch. 479

**Validating Act of 1996 (Third)**
Cal. Statutes 1996, Ch. 172

**Validation Act (Acknowledgment)**
Ill. Comp. Stat. 1992, Ch. 765, § 25/1 et seq.
Ill. Rev. Stat. 1991, Ch. 30, §§ 155a, 155a.1

**Validation Act (Assignment of Accounts Receivable)**
Ark. Code Ann. 1987, 4-58-105
Ind. Burns' 1933, 19-2101 et seq.
Mich. Comp. Laws Ann., 565.651 et seq.

**Validation Act (Banking Practice)**
Ill. Rev. Stat. 1991, Ch. 17, § 311 et seq.

**Validation Act (City Election)**
Ill. Rev. Stat. 1991, Ch. 46, §§ 700, 701

**Validation Act (Conservation District Organization)**
Ill. Rev. Stat. 1991, Ch. 96 1/2, §§ 7200, 7201

**Validation Act (Home Rule County)**
N.M. Stat. Ann., 4-37-10 et seq.

**Validation Act (Mayoral Election)**
Ill. Rev. Stat. 1991, Ch. 24, §§ 808d.01, 808d.1

**Validation Act (Municipal and School Tax Levy)**
Ill. Rev. Stat. 1991, Ch. 122, §§ 407.41h, 407.42

**Validation Act (Municipal Tax)**
Ill. Rev. Stat. 1991, Ch. 24, §§ 1650, 1651

**Validation Act (Religious Corporation)**
Ill. Rev. Stat. 1991, Ch. 32, §§ 188.3, 188.4

**Validation Act (Representative Districts)**
Mich. Comp. Laws Ann., 565.651

**Validation Act (River Conservancy District)**
Ill. Rev. Stat. 1991, Ch. 42, §§ 410.01, 410.1

**Validation Act (Township Library Bond)**
Ill. Rev. Stat. 1991, Ch. 81, §§ 16.1h, 16.2
Ill. Rev. Stat. 1991, Ch. 81, §§ 16.2h, 16.3

**Validation Act (Township Library Bond) 1963, 1969**
Ill. Rev. Stat. 1991, Ch. 24, § 808d.12h et seq.

**Validation Act (Unsealed Instrument)**
Ill. Rev. Stat. 1991, Ch. 30, § 153m et seq.

**Validation Act (Village Election)**
Ill. Rev. Stat. 1991, Ch. 24, §§ 808d.10, 808d.11

**Validation Act (Village Incorporation)**
Ill. Rev. Stat. 1991, Ch. 24, §§ 808d.11m, 808d.12
N.M. Stat. Ann., 59A-8-5

**Validation Act (War Service)**
Wis. Stat. 1969, 235.255

**Validation of Bonds Act**
Fla. Stat. Ann., 75.01 et seq.
Miss. Code Ann. 1972, § 31-13-1 et seq.

**Vallejo Sanitation and Flood Control District Act**
Cal. Statutes 1952, 1st Ex. Sess., Ch. 17, p. 351
Cal. Water Code, Appendix, § 67-1 et seq.

**Valley Falls Trailer Law**
N.Y. Local Laws 1972, Village of Valley Falls, p. 4010

**Valley Greenway Act (Hudson River)**
N.Y. Environmental Conservation Law 1972 (Consol. Laws Ch. 43B) § 44-0101 et seq.

**Valuables Not Deposited in Safe Act**
Pa. Purdon's Stat., Title 37, § 61 et seq.

**Valuation Act (District of Columbia Public Utilities)**
March 4, 1913, Ch. 150, 37 Stat. 978

**Valuation Act (Interstate Commerce)**
March 1, 1913, Ch. 92, 37 Stat. 701, 49 U.S. Code § 19a

**Valuation Act (Land)**
Ky. Rev. Stat. 1971, 426.200 et seq.

**Valuation Act (Life Insurance)**
Colo. Rev. Stat., 10-7-301 et seq.
Fla. Stat. Ann., 625.121
Haw. Rev. Stat. Ann., § 431-269
Ida. Code 1947, 41-612
Iowa Code Ann., 508.36
Me. Rev. Stat. Ann. 1964, Title 24-A, § 951 et seq.
Minn. Stat. 1965, 61.261 et seq.
Miss. Code Ann. 1972, § 83-7-23
Mo. Rev. Stat., 376.380
N.H. Rev. Stat. 1955, 410:1 et seq.
N.J. Stat. Ann., 17B:19-8
S.D. Codified Laws 1967, 58-26-13 et seq.
Tex. Insurance Code, Art. 3.28
Utah Code Ann. 1953, 31A-17-403
Vt. Stat. Ann., Title 8, § 3781 et seq.

**Valuation Act (Public Utilities)**
D.C. Code Ann., § 43-505 et seq.

**Valuation Law (Standard)**
Ariz. Rev. Stat. Ann., § 20-510
Miss. Code Ann. 1972, § 83-7-23
R.I. Gen. Laws 1956, 27-4.5-1 et seq.
Utah Code Ann. 1953, 31A-17-501 et seq.

**Valuation of Reserve Liabilities Law-Life Insurance (Standard)**
Mont. Code Ann., 33-2-521

**Valued Policy Act**
Miss. Code Ann. 1972, §§ 81-13-1, 83-13-5

**Valued Policy Act (Insurance)**
Ark. Code Ann. 1987, 23-88-101
Del. Code of 1953, Title 18, § 1102
Fla. Stat. Ann., 627.702
Kan. Stat. Ann., 40-905
Ky. Rev. Stat. 1948, 298.120 et seq.
La. Rev. Stat. Ann., 22:695
Minn. Stat. 1965, 65.05
Miss. Code Ann. 1972, § 83-13-5
Mo. Rev. Stat., 379.160
N.D. Cent. Code, 26.1-39-04
Neb. Rev. Stat. 1943, 44-380
Ohio Rev. Code 1953, 3929.26
S.C. Code Ann. 1976, § 38-75-20
S.D. Code 1939, 31.2213
Tenn. Code Ann., 56-7-801 et seq.
Tex. Insurance Code, Art. 6.13
Wis. Stat. 1975, 203.21

**Valued Policy Law (Livestock)**
Ky. Rev. Stat. 1962, 304.907

**Valued Policy Law (Real Property)**
Ky. Rev. Stat. 1962, 304.905

**Van Alstyne Act (Public Parking)**
N.J. Stat. Ann., 40:56-1.1 et seq.

**Van Eenenaam-Watson-Tomlin Act (State Bridge Commission)**
Mich. Comp. Laws Ann., 254.151 et seq.

**Van Hare Act (Zoning; Municipal Boundary)**
N.Y. General Municipal Law (Consol. Laws Ch. 24) § 239m

**Van Hoose-Warinner Act (Public Assistance)**
Ky. Rev. Stat. 1971, 205.010 et seq.

**Van Ness Act (Intoxicating Liquor)**
N.J. Laws 1921, Ch. 103

**Van Ness-Henley Act (Elections)**
Ind. Laws 1944, 1st Special Session, Ch. 3, p. 11

**Van Ness Ordinance Act (San Francisco)**
Cal. Statutes 1858, p. 52

**Van Norstrand, R.E., Neighborhood Assistance Act**
Conn. Gen. Stat. 1983, § 120631 et seq.

**Van Nuys Anti-Trust Act**
Oct. 10, 1942, Ch. 589, 56 Stat. 781, 15 U.S. Code § 16 nt.

**Van Zandt Patent Act**
Aug. 7, 1939, Ch. 568, 53 Stat. 1264 (See 35 U.S. Code §§ 133, 267 )

**Vance, Robinson and Blake Act (Soil Conservation)**
Ky. Rev. Stat. 1971, 262.010 et seq.

**Vandalism Act**
Ill. Rev. Stat. 1991, Ch. 38, § 21-1 et seq.

**Vandalism Act (Liability)**
Cal. Civil Code § 1714.1

**Vander Werp-Emunson Act (Fishing)**
Mich. Comp. Laws 1948, 308.131

**Vander Werp-MacKay Act (Hunting)**
Mich. Comp. Laws Ann., 312.11, 314.19a, 314.26

**Variable Annuities Act**
Neb. Rev. Stat. 1943, 44-2201 et seq.

**Variable Contract Act**
Mont. Code Ann., 33-20-601 et seq.
N.M. Stat. Ann., 59A-20-30
Wash. Rev. Code Ann., 48.18A.010 et seq.

**Variable Licensing Periods Act**
D.C. Code Ann., §§ 1-351, 47-2805

**Variable School Calendar Act**
N.M. Stat. Ann., 22-22-1 et seq.

**Varser Act (Injunction Pending Appeal)**
N.C. Gen. Stat. 1943, § 1-500

**Vault Charge Enabling Act**
N.Y. Unconsolidated Laws § 9445

**Veazy Water and Sewer Authority Act**
Ga. Laws 1972, p. 4108

**Vector Control Act**
Ill. Rev. Stat. 1991, Ch. 111 1/2, § 7801 et seq.

**Vegetable and Fresh Fruit Marketing Act**
Ill. Rev. Stat. 1991, Ch. 5, § 138z et seq.

**Vegetable and Fruit Container Act**
Ind. Code Ann., 24-6-6-1 et seq.

**Vegetable and Fruit Standardization Act**
Ariz. Rev. Stat. Ann., § 3-481 et seq.
N.M. Stat. Ann., 76-15-1 et seq.

**Vegetable Ink Printing Act of 1994**
Oct. 6, 1994, P.L. 103-348, 44 U.S. Code § 501 nt.

**Vegetable Plant Law**
N.C. Gen. Stat. 1943, § 106-284.14 et seq.
Okla. Stat. Ann., Title 2, § 3-201 et seq.

**Vegetable Seed Act**
Tenn. Code Ann., Superseded Vol., 43-1001 et seq.
Wash. Rev. Code Ann., 15.49.005 et seq.

**Vegetables and Fruits Standardization and Inspection Act**
Fla. Stat. Ann., 603.11 et seq.

**Vehicle Accident Reporting Act**
Mont. Code Ann. 1991, 61-7-101 et seq.

**Vehicle Act**
Alaska Stat. 1962, § 28.01.010 et seq.
Ariz. Rev. Stat. Ann., § 28-101 et seq.
Ark. Code Ann. 1987, 27-14-201 et seq.
Cal. Statutes 1959, Ch. 3, p. 1523, § 2
Ill. Rev. Stat. 1991, Ch. 95 1/2, § 1-100 et seq.
Md. Ann. Code 1974, Art. TR, § 11-101 et seq.
Me. Rev. Stat. Ann. 1964, Title 29, § 1 et seq.
Mich. Comp. Laws Ann., 257.1 et seq.
Mont. Code Ann. 1991, 61-1-101 et seq.
Okla. Stat. Ann., Title 47, § 1-101 et seq.
Ore. Rev. Stat., 801.010 et seq.
Pa. Cons. Stat., Title 75, § 101 et seq.
Tenn. Code Ann., 55-1-101 et seq.
Wis. Stat. 1989, 340.01 et seq.

**Vehicle Act (Motor)**
Neb. Rev. Stat. 1943, 60-101 et seq.

**Vehicle Advertising Sign Law**
N.Y. Local Laws 1973, Village of Greenwood Lake, p. 3395

**Vehicle and Traffic Law**
N.Y. Consol. Laws Ch. 71
P.R. Laws Ann. 1954, Title 9, § 301 et seq.

**Vehicle Antitheft Act**
Nev. Rev. Stat. 1979 Reprint, 205.272 et seq.

**Vehicle Carrier Safety Act (Motor)**
N.M. Stat. Ann., 65-3-1 et seq.

**Vehicle Certificate of Title Act**
La. Rev. Stat. Ann., 32:701 et seq.
N.Y. Vehicle and Traffic Law 1959 (Consol, Laws Ch. 71) § 2101 et seq.

**Vehicle Certificate of Title and Antitheft Act (Motor)**
Me. Rev. Stat. Ann. 1964, Title 29-A, § 601 et seq.

**Vehicle Code**
Okla. Stat. Ann., Title 47, § 1-101 et seq.

**Vehicle Dealer Tag Permit Law**
See Uniform Dealer Tag Permit Law

**Vehicle Dealers and Manufacturers Licensing Act**
Kan. Stat. Ann., 8-2401 et seq.

**Vehicle Dealers and Salesmen Licensing Act**
Vt. Stat. Ann., Title 32, § 5931 et seq.

**Vehicle Emissions Inspection Act**
Ill. Rev. Stat. 1991, Ch. 95 1/2, § 13A-101 et seq.

**Vehicle Emissions Inspection and Maintenance Act**
Mich. Comp. Laws Ann., 257.1051 et seq.

**Vehicle Equipment Safety Compact Act**
Ariz. Rev. Stat. Ann., § 28-1611 et seq.
Cal. Vehicle Code 1959, § 28100 et seq.
Conn. Gen. Stat. Ann., § 14-369 et seq.
Del. Code of 1974, Title 21, § 8001 et seq.
Fla. Stat. Ann., 325.01 et seq.
Haw. Rev. Stat. Ann., § 286A-1, § 286A-2
Ida. Code 1947, 49-2001 et seq.
Ill. Rev. Stat. 1991, Ch. 95 1/2, § 14-101 et seq.
Ind. Code Ann., 9-8-5-1 et seq.
Iowa Code Ann., 321D.1, 321D.2
Kan. Stat. Ann., 8-1201 et seq.
Ky. Rev. Stat. 1971, Superseded Vols., 189.760
La. Rev. Stat. Ann., 32:1401 et seq.
Md. Ann. Code 1974, Art. TR, § 22-501 et seq.
Mich. Comp. Laws Ann., 257.1001 et seq.
Minn. Stat. 1969, 169.991 et seq.
Mo. Rev. Stat. 1976, 307.250 et seq.
Mont. Code Ann. 1991, 61-2-201 et seq.
Nev. Rev. Stat. 1967 Reprint, Replaced Pages, 484.645 et seq.
N.H. Rev. Stat. 1955, 266:90 et seq.
N.J. Stat. Ann., 32:26-1 et seq.
N.M. Stat. Ann., 66-3-876 et seq.
Okla. Stat. Ann., Title 47, § 721
Ore. Rev. Stat., 815.010 et seq.
Pa. Cons. Stat., Title 75, § 8111 et seq.
R.I. Gen. Laws 1956, 31-23.1-1 et seq.
S.D. Codified Laws 1967, Superseded Vol., 32-16-1 et seq.
Tenn. Code Ann., 55-9-501 et seq.
Utah Code Ann. 1953, 41-15-1 et seq.
Vt. Stat. Ann., Title 23, § 1801 et seq.
Wyo. Stat. Ann., § 31-15-101 et seq.

**Vehicle-Equipment Television Act**
Ky. Rev. Stat. 1971, Superseded Vols., 189.025

**Vehicle Excise Tax Code**
Okla. Stat. Ann., Title 68, § 2101 et seq.

**Vehicle Financial Responsibility Act**
See also Financial Responsibility Act (Motor Vehicles)
Fla. Stat. Ann., 324.011 et seq.
Ga. Official Code Ann., 40-9-1 et seq.
Iowa Code Ann., 321A.1 et seq.
N.C. Gen. Stat. 1943, § 20-309 et seq.

**Vehicle Forfeiture Law**
Cal. Health and Safety Code § 11610 et seq.

**Vehicle Gross Receipts Tax Act (Leased)**
N.M. Stat. Ann., 7-14A-1 et seq.

**Vehicle Identification Act**
Ill. Rev. Stat. 1991, Ch. 127, § 133e et seq.

**Vehicle Inspection Act**
N.Y. Vehicle and Traffic Law 1959 (Consol. Laws Ch. 71) § 301 et seq.

**Vehicle Joy Ride Act**
Iowa Code Ann., 714.7

**Vehicle Law (Snowmobile and All-Terrain)**
Pa. Cons. Stat., Title 75, § 7701 et seq.

**Vehicle Leasing Act**
Cal. Civil Code § 2985.7

**Vehicle License and Registration Act**
Nev. Rev. Stat. 1979 Reprint, 482.010 et seq.
Okla. Stat. Ann., Title 47, § 1101 et seq.
Wis. Stat. 1989, 343.01 et seq.

**Vehicle License Fee Law**
Cal. Revenue and Taxation Code § 10701 et seq.

**Vehicle Manufacturers, Distributors and Dealers Regulation of Business Practices Act**
Me. Rev. Stat. Ann. 1964, Title 10, § 1431 et seq.

**Vehicle Mileage Act**
Ill. Rev. Stat. 1991, Ch. 127, § 132.500 et seq.
N.C. Gen. Stat. 1943, § 20-340 et seq.

**Vehicle, Mount, Vessel and Plane Seizure Act**
P.R. Laws Ann. 1954, Title 34, § 1721, § 1722

**Vehicle Park Occupancy Law (Recreational)**
Cal. Civil Code § 799.20 et seq.

**Vehicle Parking District Law**
Cal. Streets and Highways Code § 31500 et seq.

**Vehicle Parking Law**
N.Y. Local Laws 1972, Town of New Lebanon, p. 2161

**Vehicle Privilege Tax Law**
Nev. Rev. Stat. 1979 Reprint, 371.010 et seq.

**Vehicle Quality Assurance Act (Motor)**
N.M. Stat. Ann., 57-16A-1

**Vehicle Races Act (Motor)**
Vt. Stat. Ann., Title 31, § 301 et seq.

**Vehicle Recycling Fund Transfer Act**
Ill. Rev. Stat. 1991, Ch. 95 1/2, §§ 239.40, 239.41

**Vehicle Registration Act**
See also Motor Vehicle Registration Act
La. Rev. Stat. Ann., 47:501 et seq.
N.Y. Vehicle and Traffic Law 1959 (Consol. Laws Ch. 71) § 401

**Vehicle Registration License Tax Act**
La. Rev. Stat. Ann., 47:451 et seq.

**Vehicle Rental Industry Act (Motor)**
Dec. 21, 1995, P.L. 104-66, 109 Stat. 717, Title 1, Subtitle E
Haw. Rev. Stat. Ann., § 437D-1 et seq.

**Vehicle Retail Installment Sales Finance Act (Motor)**
Vt. Stat. Ann., Title 9, § 2351 et seq.

**Vehicle Safety Act (All-Terrain)**
Ill. Rev. Stat. 1989, Ch. 95 1/2, § 1201-1 et seq.

**Vehicle Safety Act (Private Passenger)**
Cal. Vehicle Code 1959, § 27315

**Vehicle Safety Responsibility Act**
See Motor Vehicle Safety Responsibility Act

**Vehicle Speed Act**
See Speed Act (Motor Vehicles)

**Vehicle Storage Facility Act**
Tex. Rev. Civ. Stat., Art. 6687-9a

**Vehicle Taking Act**
Ind. Burns' 1933, 10-3010

**Vehicle Tax Act**
Ill. Laws 1907, p. 510

**Vehicle Title Act**
Mich. Comp. Laws Ann., 257.201 et seq.

**Vehicle Weight Limit Act (Collier-Porter)**
Cal. Vehicle Code 1959, § 35551

**Vehicle Weight Tax Act**
Mich. Comp. Laws Ann., 257.801

**Vehicles Speed Act**
Mont. Code Ann. 1991, 61-8-303 et seq.

**Vehicular Homicide Act**
Md. Ann. Code 1957, Art. 27, § 388
N.Y. Penal Law 1965 (Consol. Laws Ch. 40) §§ 125.10, 125.15, Subd. 1
Ohio Rev. Code 1953, 2903.06 et seq.

**Vehicular Traffic Act**
N.J. Stat. Ann., 39:1-1 et seq.

**Vehicular Visible Emission Control Act**
Ga. Code Ann., 40-8-180 et seq.

**Venango Act**
Pa. 1851 Pamph. Laws 216, No. 163

**Vender and Purchaser Risk Act**
See also Uniform Vendor and Purchaser Risk Act
Cal. Civil Code § 1662
Nev. Rev. Stat. Ann., 113.030 et seq.
Tex. Property Code, § 5.007
Wis. Stat. 1989, 706.12

**Vending Devices Decal Act**
Ark. Acts 1997, No. 928

**Vending Facilities Act (Blind Persons Operating)**
Ill. Comp. Stat. 1992, Ch. 20, § 2420/0.01

**Vending Machine Act (Postage Stamp)**
Ill. Comp. Stat. 1992, Ch. 35, §§ 815/1 to 815/3
Ill. Rev. Stat. 1989, Ch. 121 1/2, § 910 et seq.

**Vending Machine License Act**
Conn. Gen. Stat. Ann., § 21a-34 et seq.

**Vending Machine Protection Act (Water)**
Fla. Stat. Ann., 381.0071, 500.459
Okla. Stat. Ann., Title 16, § 201 et seq.

**Vending Machine Tax Law**
Tex. Taxation-General, Art. 13.01 et seq.

**Vending Stand Act**
Ga. Code Ann., 49-9-40 et seq.

**Venditioni Exponas Act**
Pa. Cons. Stat., Title 42, § 5529

**Vendor Act (Responsible)**
Ala. Code 1975, § 28-10-1

**Vendor Act (WIC)**
S.C. Code Ann. 1976, § 43-5-910 et seq.

**Vendor and Purchaser Risk Act**
See Uniform Vendor and Purchaser Risk Act

**Vendor Assessment Plan Act**
Colo. Rev. Stat., 26-4-415 to 26-4-419

**Vendor Management Act (WIC)**
Ill. Rev. Stat. 1991, Ch. 111 1/2, § 7551 et seq.

**Vendor Purchaser Act (Tax Liens)**
Iowa Code Ann., 445.30

**Vendors and Hawkers Act (Drugs-Tolet Preparations)**
Mich. Comp. Laws 1970, 446.301 et seq.

**Vendors License Act**
Colo. Rev. Stat., 12-51-101 et seq.

**Vendor's Lien Act**
Ark. Code Ann. 1987, 16-118-104 et seq.
Ore. Rev. Stat. 1953, 689.350
S.D. Codified Laws 1967, 44-6-1 et seq.

**Vendors Reciprocity Act**
See Uniform Vendors Reciprocity Act

**Vendors Regulation Amendments Act of 1978**
D.C. Code Ann., § 1-315

**Veneman Act (Child Protection)**
Cal. Welfare and Institutions Code § 16500 et seq.

**Venereal Disease Act**
Cal. Health and Safety Code §§ 3001, 3180 et seq.
Iowa Code Ann., 140.1 et seq.
Me. Rev. Stat. Ann. 1964, Title 22, § 1091 et seq.
Ore. Rev. Stat. 1953, 434.005 et seq.
Pa. 1945 Pamph. Laws 577, No. 236
Tex. Health and Safety Code, § 81.001 et seq.
Wash. Rev. Code Ann., 70.24.010 et seq.
W. Va. Code 1966, § 16-4-1 et seq.

**Venereal Disease Prevention Device Act**
Ore. Rev. Stat. 1953, 435.010 et seq.

**Venice Sewer Revenue Bond Act**
Fla. Special Laws 1945, Ch. 23586

**Ventilation, Air Conditioning, Refrigeration, and Heating Contractors Act**
Md. Ann. Code 1974, Art. BR, § 9A-601 et seq.

**Ventilation, Heating and Air Conditioning Act**
Mont. Code Ann. 1981, 37-70-101 et seq.

**Ventura County Court Services Consolidation Act**
Cal. Government Code § 26630 et seq.

**Ventura County Flood Control Act**
Cal. Water Code, Appendix, § 46-1 et seq.

**Ventura County Harbor District Act**
Cal. Statutes 1927, p. 1819

**Ventura County Waste Management Authority Act**
Cal. Public Resources Code § 60200 et seq.

**Venture Capital Act**
Kan. Stat. Ann., 74-8301 et seq.
Miss. Code Ann. 1972, §§ 27-7-22.11, 57-77-1 et seq.

**Venture Capital Company Act**
Kan. Stat. Ann., 74-8301 et seq.

**Venture Capital Investment Act**
Iowa Code Ann., 28.111 et seq.
N.M. Stat. Ann., 7-2D-1 et seq.

**Venture Capital Network Act**
La. Rev. Stat. Ann., 51:1141 et seq.
Neb. Rev. Stat. 1943, 81-1265 et seq.

**Venture Fund Act**
Ky. Rev. Stat. 1971, 155.400 et seq.

**Venue Act**
Ill. Rev. Stat. 1991, Ch. 110, § 2-101 et seq.

**Venue Act (Actions against State Officers)**
Pa. Cons. Stat., Title 42, § 761

**Venue Act (Civil)**
Ala. Code 1975, § 6-3-1 et seq.
Ariz. Rev. Stat. Ann., § 12-401 et seq.
Ark. Code Ann. 1987, 16-60-101 et seq.
Cal. Code of Civil Procedure § 392 et seq.
Conn. Gen. Stat. Ann., § 52-1 et seq.
Fla. Stat. Ann., 47.011 et seq.
Ga. Code Ann., 9-10-30 et seq.
Ind. Burns' 1933, 2-701 et seq.
Iowa Code Ann., 616.1 et seq.
La. Rev. Stat. Ann., 13:3231 et seq.
Md. Ann. Code 1974, Art. CJ, § 6-201 et seq.
Mich. Comp. Laws Ann., 600.1601 et seq.
Minn. Stat. Ann., 542.01 et seq.
Miss. Code Ann. 1972, § 11-11-51 et seq.
Mo. Rev. Stat., 508.010 et seq.
Mont. Code Ann. 1991, 25-2-101 et seq.
N.C. Gen. Stat. 1943, § 1-76 et seq.
Nev. Rev. Stat. 1979 Reprint, 13.010 et seq.
N.H. Rev. Stat. 1955, 507:9 et seq.
N.M. Stat. Ann., 38-3-1 et seq.
N.Y. Civil Practice Law and Rues (Consol, Laws Ch. 8) § 501 et seq.
Ohio Civ. Rule 3(B)(5)
Okla. Stat. Ann., Title 12, § 131 et seq.
Ore. Rev. Stat., 14.040 et seq.
R.I. Gen. Laws 1956, 9-4-2 et seq.
S.C. Code Ann. 1976, § 15-7-10 et seq.
Tenn. Code Ann., 20-4-101 et seq.

*Continued*

Tex. Civ. Prac. and Rem., § 15.001 et seq.
Va. Code 1950, § 8.01-257 et seq.
Wash. Rev. Code Ann., 4.12.010 et seq.
Wis. Stat. 1989, 801.50 et seq.
W. Va. Code 1966, § 56-1-1 et seq.

**Venue Act (Criminal)**
Miss. Code Ann. 1972, § 99-15-35 et seq.
Mont. Code Ann. 1989, 46-3-201 et seq.
N.C. Gen. Stat. 1943, § 15A-131 et seq.
N.H. Rev. Stat. 1955, 602:1
R.I. Gen. Laws 1956, 12-3-1 et seq., 12-21-3
Tex. Code of Criminal Procedure, Art. 13.01 et seq.
Wash. Rev. Code Ann., 10.25.065 et seq.

**Venue Act (Double)**
Mont. Code Ann. 1991, 46-3-111 et seq.

**Venue Act (General)**
Utah Code Ann. 1953, 78-13-1 et seq.

**Venue Act (Motor Vehicle Accidents)**
Ohio Rev. Code 1953, 4515.01
Wash. Rev. Code Ann., 4.12.020

**Venue Transfer Act**
N.D. Cent. Code, 28-04-07
Nev. Rev. Stat. 1979 Reprint, 13.050
S.D. Codified Laws 1967, 15-5-11 et seq.

**Verdier Act (Home Rule Cities)**
Mich. Comp. Laws Ann., 117.1 et seq.

**Verified Pleading Law**
Tex. Rules of Civil Procedure 1984, Rule 93

**Vermillion and Decatur Civic Centers Act**
Ill. Rev. Stat. 1991, Ch. 85, § 1551 et seq.

**Vermillion County Seat Act**
Ind. Laws 1919, Ch. 47, p. 103

**Vermillion River Middle Fork Act**
Ill. Rev. Stat. 1991, Ch. 19, § 1300 et seq.

**Vermont-New Hampshire Interstate School Compact Act**
N.H. Rev. Stat. 1955, 200-B:1
Vt. Stat. Ann. 1959, Title 16, § 771 et seq.

**Vermont-New Hampshire Interstate Sewage and Waste Disposal Facilities Compact Act**
N.H. Rev. Stat. 1955, 149-J:1
Vt. Stat. Ann. 1959, Title 10, § 1201 et seq.

**Vermont-New Hampshire Solid Waste Compact Act**
N.H. Rev. Stat. 1955, 53-D:1
Vt. Stat. Ann., Title 10, § 1222 et seq.

**Vermont-New York Interstate School Compact Act**
Vt. Stat. Ann. 1959, Title 16, § 791 et seq.

**Vermont Wilderness Act of 1984**
June 19, 1984, P.L. 98-322, 16 U.S. Code §§ 460nn-460nn-3, 1132 nt.

**Verplanck Act (Insurance Corporations)**
N.Y. Insurance Law (Consol. Laws Ch. 28) § 52

**Vesicular Exanthema Act**
N.M. Stat. Ann., 77-7-16 et seq.

**Vessel and Motor Excise Tax Act**
Okla. Stat. Ann., Title 63, § 4101 et seq.

**Vessel and Motor Registration Act**
Okla. Stat. Ann., Title 63, § 4001 et seq.

**Vessel Bridge-to-Bridge Radiotelephone Act**
Aug. 4, 1971, P.L. 92-63, 85 Stat. 164, 33 U.S. Code §§ 1201 to 1208
Oct. 19, 1996, P.L. 104-324, 33 U.S. Code § 1203

**Vessel Bridge-to-Bridge Radiotelephone Act of 1971**
Dec. 19, 1991, P.L. 102-241, 33 U.S. Code § 1203

**Vessel Documentation Act**
Dec. 24, 1980, P.L. 96-594, 46 U.S. Code § 65 nt.

**Vessel Hull Design Protection Act**
Oct. 28, 1998, P.L. 105-304, Title V, 112 Stat. 2905, 17 U.S. Code § 101 nt.

**Vessel Registration and Safety Law**
Fla. Stat. 1981, 327.01 et seq.

**Vessel Safety Act (Boiler and Pressure)**
Ill. Comp. Stat. 1992, Ch. 430, § 75/1 et seq.
Va. Code 1950, § 40.1-51.5 et seq.

**Vessels Act (Boilers and Pressure)**
Me. Rev. Stat. Ann. 1964, Title 26, § 141 et seq.

**Vessels Lien Law**
Wash. Rev. Code Ann., 60.36.010 et seq.

**Vessels Manufacturing Act**
Miss. Code Ann. 1972, § 59-21-41 et seq.

**Vessels Quarantine Law**
Wash. Rev. Code Ann., 70.16.010 et seq.

**Vessels Registration Law**
Cal. Revenue and Taxation § 43101 et seq.

**Vessels Regulation Act**
Wash. Rev. Code Ann., 88.04.010 et seq.

**Vestal Code**
N.Y. Local Laws 1966, Town of Vestal, p. 1606

**Vestibule Act (Street Railroad)**
Ill. Rev. Stat. 1991, Ch. 131 1/4, § 5.9 et seq.

**Vesting of Perpetuities Act**
Ill. Rev. Stat. 1989, Ch. 30, §§ 153a.1, 153a

**Vestry Act**
Md. Ann. Code 1974, Art. CA, § 5-301 et seq.

**Veterans Act**
N.Y. Civil Service Law 1958 (Consol. Laws Ch. 7) § 85 et seq.

**Veterans Act (Children of Deceased)**
Ill. Rev. Stat. 1989, Ch. 126 1/2, § 26

**Veterans Act (Korea and Vietnam)**
Alaska Stat. 1962, § 26.15.160

**Veterans Act (Peddler's License)**
Mich. Comp. Laws Ann., 35.441 et seq.

**Veterans Act (State Lands)**
Colo. Rev. Stat., 36-5-101 et seq.

**Veterans Act (World War II)**
Alaska Stat. 1962, § 26.15.010 et seq.

**Veterans' Additional Compensation Act**
Wash. Laws 1949, Ch. 4

**Veterans' Adjusted Compensation Act**
Minn. Stat. 1961, 197.80 et seq.
N.D. Laws 1949, Ch. 236

**Veterans' Adjusted Compensation Act (Vietnam Conflict)**
N.D. Cent. Code, 37-25-01 et seq.

**Veterans Adjusted Compensation Act, 1936**
See Adjusted Compensation Payment Act

**Veterans' Administration and Department of Defense Health Resources Sharing and Emergency Operations Act**
May 4, 1982, P.L. 97-174, 38 U.S. Code §§ 101 nt., 1786(a), 5001, 5011, 5011A

**Veterans' Administration Guardianship Act**
Ind. Code Ann., 29-1-19-1 et seq.

**Veteran's Administration Health-Care Amendments of 1980**
Aug. 26, 1980, P.L. 96-330, 38 U.S. Code § 101 nt.

**Veterans' Administration Health-Care Amendments of 1985**
Dec. 3, 1985, P.L. 99-166, 38 U.S. Code § 101 nt., 210, 230, 601, 610, 612-612B, 620, 620A, 767, 777, 3203 nt., 3305, 4101, 4110, 4114, 4151, 4152, 5004, 5007, 5035
April 7, 1986, P.L. 99-272, 38 U.S. Code §§ 601, 603

**Veterans' Administration Health-Care Programs Improvement and Extension Act of 1982**
Sept. 8, 1982, P.L. 97-251, 38 U.S. Code § 101 nt.

**Veterans' Administration Medical School Assistance and Health Manpower Training Act of 1972**
Oct. 24, 1972, P.L. 92-541, 86 Stat. 1100, 38 U.S. Code §§ 4121 to 4124, 5070 to 5074, 5081 to 5083, 5091 to 5093, 5096

**Veterans' Administration Physician and Dentist Pay Comparability Act of 1975**
Aug. 26, 1980, P.L. 96-330, 38 U.S. Code §§ 4104 nt., 4118 nt., 38 U.S. Code § 4101 et seq.

**Veterans' Administration Physician and Dentist Pay Comparability Amendments of 1977**
Nov. 23, 1977, P.L. 95-201, 38 U.S. Code § 101 nt.

**Veterans' Administration Programs Extension Act of 1978**
Oct. 26, 1978, P.L. 95-520, 38 U.S. Code §§ 101 nt., 230, 601, 601 nt., 632, 2012, 2014, 4118 nt., 5082

**Veterans' Administration Records Act**
Ill. Rev. Stat. 1991, Ch. 116, § 28.9 et seq.

**Veterans' Administration Retrocession Act**
Ill. Rev. Stat. 1991, Ch. 1, § 4550 et seq.

**Veterans' Advocate Office Act**
P.R. Laws Ann. 1954, Title 29, § 823 et seq.

**Veterans' Affairs Act**
Ind. Code Ann., 10-5-1-1 et seq.
Iowa Code Ann., 35.7 et seq.
La. Rev. Stat. Ann., 29:251 et seq.
N.C. Gen. Stat. 1943, § 165-1 et seq.
Utah Code Ann. 1953, 71-8-1 et seq.

**Veterans' Affairs Commission Act**
Tex. Gov. Code, § 434.001 et seq.

**Veterans Affairs Construction Fund Act**
Cal. Military and Veterans Code § 996.13 et seq.

**Veterans' Affairs Department Act**
Ill. Rev. Stat. 1991, Ch. 126 1/2, § 65.9 et seq.

**Veterans Affairs Nurse Pay Act of 1990**
Nov. 2, 1994, P.L. 103-452, 38 U.S. Code § 1720C nt.

**Veterans' Aid Fund Act**
Neb. Rev. Stat. 1943, 80-401 et seq.

**Veterans and Exempt Volunteer Firemen's Act**
N.Y. Civil Services Law (Consol. Laws Ch. 7) § 85 et seq.

**Veterans' and Handicapped Persons Employment Preference Act**
Mont. Laws 1983, Sp. Sess., Ch. 1, § 1 et seq.

**Veterans and Military Act**
N.J. Stat. Ann., 38A:1-1 et seq.

**Veterans' and State Nursing Homes Act**
Colo. Rev. Stat., 26-12-101 et seq.

**Veterans' and Survivors Pension Adjustment Act of 1977**
Dec. 2, 1977, P.L. 95-204, 38 U.S. Code §§ 101 nt., 521 et seq.

**Veterans' and Survivors' Pension Improvement Act of 1978**
Nov. 4, 1978, P.L. 95-588, 38 U.S. Code §§ 101, 101 nt., 415, 501 , 503, 506, 508, 512, 521, 522, 536, 541 to 543, 612, 3012, 3104, 3112, 3203
Aug. 6, 1991, P.L. 102-83, 38 U.S. Code § 1321 nt.

**Veterans and Survivors Pension Interim Adjustment Act of 1975**
Dec. 23, 1975, P.L. 94-169, 89 Stat. 1013, 38 U.S. Code §§ 45, 101, 322, 415, 501 to 503, 505 to 507, 510 to 512, 521, 531, 532, 534 to 537, 541 to 544, 560 to 562, 583

**Veterans and Volunteer Firemen's Act**
N.Y. Civil Service Law 1958 (Consol. Laws Ch. 7) § 85 et seq.

**Veterans' Appreciation Act**
Cal. Military and Veterans Code § 975.5

**Veterans' Assistance Act (Indigent)**
Ill. Rev. Stat. 1991, Ch. 23, § 3080 et seq.

**Veterans' Benefits**

Aug. 27, 1958, P.L. 85-782, 72 Stat. 936, 38 U.S. Code § 314

Sept. 2, 1958, P.L. 85-857, 72 Stat. 1105, 38 U.S. Code §§ 101 to 5228

Sept. 2, 1958, P.L. 85-896, 72 Stat. 1716, 38 U.S. Code § 723

June 25, 1959, P.L. 86-70, 73 Stat. 148, 38 U.S. Code §§ 903, 2007

June 30, 1959, P.L. 86-73, 73 Stat. 156, 38 U.S. Code §§ 1802, 1803, 1804, 1823

July 23, 1959, P.L. 86-103, 73 Stat. 224, 38 U.S. Code § 230

July 28, 1959, P.L. 86-109, 73 Stat. 258, 38 U.S. Code § 4202

July 28, 1959, P.L. 86-113, 73 Stat. 262, 38 U.S. Code § 3103

July 28, 1959, P.L. 86-116, 73 Stat. 265, 38 U.S. Code § 235

Aug. 7, 1959, P.L. 86-146, 73 Stat. 297, 38 U.S. Code §§ 3202, 3203

Aug. 11, 1959, P.L. 86-150, 73 Stat. 332, 38 U.S. Code § 1622

Aug. 11, 1959, P.L. 86-152, 73 Stat. 332, 38 U.S. Code § 624

Aug. 25, 1959, P.L. 86-187, 73 Stat. 418, 38 U.S. Code § 312

Aug. 25, 1959, P.L. 86-188, 73 Stat. 418, 38 U.S. Code § 312

Aug. 25, 1959, P.L. 86-195, 73 Stat. 424, 38 U.S. Code § 101

Aug. 29, 1959, P.L. 86-211, 73 Stat. 432, 38 U.S. Code §§ 503, 506, 521, 522, 541 to 543, 617, 3203

Sept. 1, 1959, P.L. 86-212, 73 Stat. 436, 38 U.S. Code § 358

Sept. 1, 1959, P.L. 86-222, 73 Stat. 452, 38 U.S. Code §§ 3503 to 3505

Sept. 8, 1959, P.L. 86-236, 73 Stat. 471, 38 U.S. Code § 1701

Sept. 8, 1959, P.L. 86-239, 73 Stat. 472, 38 U.S. Code § 801

June 8, 1960, P.L. 86-490, 74 Stat. 161, 38 U.S. Code § 3011

June 8, 1960, P.L. 86-491, 74 Stat. 161, 38 U.S. Code § 302

June 8, 1960, P.L. 86-492, 74 Stat. 161, 38 U.S. Code § 402

June 8, 1960, P.L. 86-495, 74 Stat. 163, 38 U.S. Code § 3104

June 8, 1960, P.L. 86-497, 74 Stat. 164, 38 U.S. Code § 712

June 8, 1960, P.L. 86-499, 74 Stat. 165, 38 U.S. Code § 315

June 10, 1960, P.L. 86-501, 74 Stat. 195, 38 U.S. Code § 359

June 11, 1960, P.L. 86-507, 74 Stat. 202, 38 U.S. Code §§ 784, 5226

July 1, 1960, P.L. 86-568, 74 Stat. 300, 38 U.S. Code §§ 4103, 4107, 4108

July 5, 1960, P.L. 86-590, 74 Stat. 329, 38 U.S. Code § 111

July 7, 1960, P.L. 86-598, 74 Stat. 335, 38 U.S. Code § 601

July 12, 1960, P.L. 86-624, 74 Stat. 418, 38 U.S. Code §§ 624, 903, 2007

July 12, 1960, P.L. 86-625, 74 Stat. 424, 38 U.S. Code § 641

July 12, 1960, P.L. 86-639, 74 Stat. 472, 38 U.S. Code §§ 601, 612

July 14, 1960, P.L. 86-663, 74 Stat. 528, 38 U.S. Code § 314

July 14, 1960, P.L. 86-665, 74 Stat. 531, 38 U.S. Code §§ 1803, 1804, 1806, 1811, 1814, 1823 to 1825

July 14, 1960, P.L. 86-670, 74 Stat. 545, 38 U.S. Code §§ 511, 512.

Sept. 8, 1960, P.L. 86-721, 74 Stat. 820, 38 U.S. Code § 1502

Sept. 14, 1960, P.L. 86-785, 74 Stat. 1023, 38 U.S. Code §§ 1701, 1723

July 6, 1961, P.L. 87-84, 75 Stat. 201, 38 U.S. Code §§ 1802, 1803, 1811, 1814, 1823

July 20, 1961, P.L. 87-97, 75 Stat. 215, 38 U.S. Code § 4004

July 21, 1961, P.L. 87-99, 75 Stat. 218, 38 U.S. Code § 903

July 21, 1961, P.L. 87-101, 75 Stat. 218, 38 U.S. Code § 521

July 21, 1961, P.L. 87-102, 75 Stat. 219, 38 U.S. Code § 106

Aug. 14, 1961, P.L. 87-138, 75 Stat. 338, 38 U.S. Code §§ 560 to 562

Sept. 13, 1961, P.L. 87-223, 75 Stat. 495, 38 U.S. Code § 723

Sept. 14, 1961, P.L. 87-240, 75 Stat. 512, 38 U.S. Code § 901

Sept. 21, 1961, P.L. 87-268, 75 Stat. 566, 38 U.S. Code §§ 107, 411, 412, 415, 422, 503

Sept. 26, 1961, P.L. 87-314, 75 Stat. 675, 38 U.S. Code § 5011

Oct. 4, 1961, P.L. 87-377, 75 Stat. 806, 38 U.S. Code §§ 612, 1712 nt.

*Continued*

July 25, 1962, P.L. 87-544, 76 Stat. 208, 38 U.S. Code § 3203
July 25, 1962, P.L. 87-546, 76 Stat. 216, 38 U.S. Code § 1723
July 25, 1962, P.L. 87-549, 76 Stat. 219, 38 U.S. Code § 742
July 27, 1962, P.L. 87-556, 76 Stat. 245, 38 U.S. Code § 3203
July 27, 1962, P.L. 87-557, 76 Stat. 245, 38 U.S. Code § 718
Aug. 6, 1962, P.L. 87-572, 76 Stat. 307, 38 U.S. Code § 216
Aug. 6, 1962, P.L. 87-574, 76 Stat. 308, 38 U.S. Code §§ 233, 618 , 4103, 4105, 4108, 4114
Aug. 14, 1962, P.L. 87-583, 76 Stat. 381, 38 U.S. Code §§ 610, 612
Aug. 16, 1962, P.L. 87-591, 76 Stat. 393, 38 U.S. Code § 1502A
Aug. 28, 1962, P.L. 87-610, 76 Stat. 406, 38 U.S. Code § 360
Sept. 7, 1962, P.L. 87-645, 76 Stat. 441, 38 U.S. Code §§ 312, 314, 3203
Sept. 19, 1962, P.L. 87-666, 76 Stat. 553, 38 U.S. Code §§ 4005 to 4007
Sept. 19, 1962, P.L. 87-671, 76 Stat. 557, 38 U.S. Code §§ 3301, 4009
Sept. 19, 1962, P.L. 87-674, 76 Stat. 558, 38 U.S. Code §§ 101, 103, 3010
Sept. 19, 1962, P.L. 87-675, 76 Stat. 558, 38 U.S. Code §§ 2001 to 2005
Oct. 11, 1962, P.L. 87-793, 76 Stat. 859, 38 U.S. Code §§ 4103, 4107, 4108, 4111
Oct. 15, 1962, P.L. 87-815, 76 Stat. 926, 38 U.S. Code §§ 101, 230, 235, 624, 1502, 1613, 1712
Oct. 15, 1962, P.L. 87-819, 76 Stat. 935, 38 U.S. Code §§ 641, 1712
Oct. 15, 1962, P.L. 87-825, 76 Stat. 948, 38 U.S. Code §§ 110, 351, 359, 3010, 3012, 3110
Oct. 23, 1962, P.L. 87-850, 76 Stat. 1126, 38 U.S. Code § 619
April 2, 1963, P.L. 88-3, 77 Stat. 4, 38 U.S. Code § 904
May 8, 1963, P.L. 88-18, 77 Stat. 15, 38 U.S. Code § 4103
May 15, 1963, P.L. 88-20, 77 Stat. 17, 38 U.S. Code § 314
May 15, 1963, P.L. 88-21, 77 Stat. 17, 38 U.S. Code §§ 411, 413, 414, 415
May 15, 1963, P.L. 88-22, 77 Stat. 18, 38 U.S. Code § 314
June 13, 1963, P.L. 88-40, 77 Stat. 66, 38 U.S. Code § 632
July 25, 1963, P.L. 88-77, 77 Stat. 95, 38 U.S. Code §§ 560 to 562
Sept. 23, 1963, P.L. 88-126, 77 Stat. 158, 38 U.S. Code §§ 1735 to 1737, 1771 to 1778
Oct. 5, 1963, P.L. 88-134, 77 Stat. 223, 38 U.S. Code § 411
Oct. 17, 1963, P.L. 88-151, 77 Stat. 271, 38 U.S. Code § 1820
Dec. 17, 1963, P.L. 88-207, 77 Stat. 402, 38 U.S. Code § 4110
Feb. 29, 1964, P.L. 88-274, 78 Stat. 147, 38 U.S. Code § 1823
July 7, 1964, P.L. 88-355, 78 Stat. 272, 38 U.S. Code § 715
July 7, 1964, P.L. 88-359, 78 Stat. 296, 38 U.S. Code § 902
July 7, 1964, P.L. 88-361, 78 Stat. 297, 38 U.S. Code §§ 1643, 1701, 1711, 1712, 1741, 1762
July 7, 1964, P.L. 88-364, 78 Stat. 302, 38 U.S. Code § 712
Aug. 4, 1964, P.L. 88-401, 78 Stat. 380, 38 U.S. Code § 801
Aug. 4, 1964, P.L. 88-402, 78 Stat. 380, 38 U.S. Code § 1811
Aug. 14, 1964, P.L. 88-426, 78 Stat. 409, 38 U.S. Code §§ 210, 4103, 4107
Aug. 14, 1964, P.L. 88-430, 78 Stat. 438, 38 U.S. Code § 612
Aug. 14, 1964, P.L. 88-433, 78 Stat. 441, 38 U.S. Code § 216
Aug. 19, 1964, P.L. 88-445, 78 Stat. 464, 38 U.S. Code § 110
Aug. 19, 1964, P.L. 88-448, 78 Stat. 495, 38 U.S. Code § 4103 nt.
Aug. 19, 1964, P.L. 88-450, 78 Stat. 500, 38 U.S. Code §§ 101, 612, 617, 620, 641, 3203, 5001, 5031 to 5037
Aug. 22, 1964, P.L. 88-481, 78 Stat. 593, 38 U.S. Code § 601
Sept. 2, 1964, P.L. 88-560, 78 Stat. 800, 38 U.S. Code §§ 1820, 1823
Oct. 2, 1964, P.L. 88-616, 78 Stat. 994, 38 U.S. Code § 106
Oct. 13, 1964, P.L. 88-651, 78 Stat. 1078, 38 U.S. Code § 560
Oct. 13, 1964, P.L. 88-664, 78 Stat. 1094, 38 U.S. Code §§ 502, 503, 506, 521, 541, 542, 612, 704, 725, 3104
June 14, 1965, P.L. 89-40, 79 Stat. 130, 38 U.S. Code § 725

June 24, 1965, P.L. 89-50, 79 Stat. 173, 38 U.S. Code § 2104
July 24, 1965, P.L. 89-88, 79 Stat. 264, 38 U.S. Code § 112
Aug. 10, 1965, P.L. 89-117, 79 Stat. 460, 38 U.S. Code §§ 1084, 1816
Aug. 26, 1965, P.L. 89-137, 79 Stat. 576, 38 U.S. Code §§ 315, 1504
Aug. 26, 1965, P.L. 89-138, 79 Stat. 577, 38 U.S. Code §§ 1502, 1503, 1511
Sept. 29, 1965, P.L. 89-214, 79 Stat. 880, 38 U.S. Code §§ 211, 765 to 776
Sept. 30, 1965, P.L. 89-222, 79 Stat. 896, 38 U.S. Code §§ 1701, 1732, 1742
Oct. 28, 1965, P.L. 89-300, 79 Stat. 1110, 38 U.S. Code §§ 235, 236
Oct. 29, 1965, P.L. 89-301, 79 Stat. 1117, 38 U.S. Code § 4107
Oct. 31, 1965, P.L. 89-311, 79 Stat. 1154, 38 U.S. Code §§ 101, 106, 314, 315, 360, 414, 560, 4116, 5001, 5033, 5034, 5035
Nov. 8, 1965, P.L. 89-349, 79 Stat. 1313, 38 U.S. Code § 1701
March 3, 1966, P.L. 89-358, 80 Stat. 12, 38 U.S. Code §§ 101, 102 , 111, 211, 337, 610, 901, 903, 1651, 1652, 1661 to 1663, 1670 to 1676, 1681 to 1686, 1701, 1711, 1731, 1734 to 1736, 1761, 1762, 1770 to 1776, 1781 to 1790, 1803, 1811, 1818, 1822, 1826, 2001 to 2004, 3013
March 7, 1966, P.L. 89-360, 80 Stat. 29, 38 U.S. Code § 902
March 7, 1966, P.L. 89-361, 80 Stat. 29, 38 U.S. Code §§ 210, 212
March 7, 1966, P.L. 89-362, 80 Stat. 30, 38 U.S. Code § 3203
June 18, 1966, P.L. 89-455, 80 Stat. 208, 38 U.S. Code § 111
June 22, 1966, P.L. 89-466, 80 Stat. 217, 38 U.S. Code § 412
June 22, 1966, P.L. 89-467, 80 Stat. 218, 38 U.S. Code § 507
July 18, 1966, P.L. 89-504, 80 Stat. 291, 38 U.S. Code § 4107
July 18, 1966, P.L. 89-506, 80 Stat. 307, 38 U.S. Code § 4116
Sept. 30, 1966, P.L. 89-612, 80 Stat. 859, 38 U.S. Code §§ 622, 632, 634
Sept. 30, 1966, P.L. 89-613, 80 Stat. 861, 38 U.S. Code §§ 1765, 1766
Oct. 11, 1966, P.L. 89-641, 80 Stat. 885, 38 U.S. Code § 107
Nov. 2, 1966, P.L. 89-705, 80 Stat. 1099, 38 U.S. Code § 216
Nov. 2, 1966, P.L. 89-730, 80 Stat. 1157, 38 U.S. Code §§ 413 to 415, 776 nt., 3012
Nov. 6, 1966, P.L. 89-769, 80 Stat. 1316, 38 U.S. Code § 1820
Nov. 7, 1966, P.L. 89-785, 80 Stat. 1368, 38 U.S. Code §§ 210, 213, 233, 610, 4101 to 4107, 4111 to 4114, 4117, 5004, 5012, 5051 to 5057
May 25, 1967, P.L. 90-19, 81 Stat. 28, 38 U.S. Code §§ 1802, 1804
Aug. 31, 1967, P.L. 90-77, 81 Stat. 178, 38 U.S. Code §§ 101, 103 , 302, 314, 404, 502, 503, 511, 512, 521, 531, 532, 534, 536, 541, 542, 544, 602, 612, 617, 901, 1652, 1661, 1662, 1673, 1677, 1678, 1682 to 1687, 1712, 1777 to 1779, 1784, 1802, 1803, 1811, 1901, 1905
Dec. 16, 1967, P.L. 90-206, 81 Stat. 631, 38 U.S. Code § 4107
March 28, 1968, P.L. 90-275, 82 Stat. 64, 38 U.S. Code §§ 415, 521, 541, 3012
May 7, 1968, P.L. 90-301, 82 Stat. 113, 38 U.S. Code §§ 1810, 1811, 1822, 1827
July 26, 1968, P.L. 90-429, 82 Stat. 446, 38 U.S. Code § 620
July 26, 1968, P.L. 90-431, 82 Stat. 447, 38 U.S. Code § 1504
July 26, 1968, P.L. 90-432, 82 Stat. 448, 38 U.S. Code §§ 641, 5033
Aug. 1, 1968, P.L. 90-448, 82 Stat. 545, 38 U.S. Code § 1820
Aug. 19, 1968, P.L. 90-493, 82 Stat. 808, 38 U.S. Code §§ 314, 356 nt., 617, 1682 nt.
Oct. 21, 1968, P.L. 90-612, 82 Stat. 1202, 38 U.S. Code §§ 601, 620
Oct. 23, 1968, P.L. 90-631, 82 Stat. 1331, 38 U.S. Code §§ 1502, 1661, 1677, 1682, 1700, 1701, 1711, 1712, 1720, 1774, 1791
June 6, 1969, P.L. 91-22, 83 Stat. 32, 38 U.S. Code §§ 801 to 803, 1811
June 11, 1969, P.L. 91-24, 83 Stat. 33, 38 U.S. Code §§ 101, 104, 213, 351, 401, 411, 560, 625, 631, 632, 904, 1503, 1701, 1711, 1765, 1789, 3203 , 3301, 3401, 3402, 3503, 3504
June 23, 1969, P.L. 91-32, 83 Stat. 38, 38 U.S. Code § 110
Oct. 27, 1969, P.L. 91-96, 83 Stat. 144, 38 U.S. Code §§ 322, 401 to 403, 411, 421
Oct. 30, 1969, P.L. 91-101, 83 Stat. 167, 38 U.S. Code § 620

*Continued*

Oct. 30, 1969, P.L. 91-102, 83 Stat. 168, 38 U.S. Code § 612

Dec. 30, 1969, P.L. 91-178, 83 Stat. 836, 38 U.S. Code §§ 641, 644

March 26, 1970, P.L. 91-219, 84 Stat. 76, 38 U.S. Code §§ 240 to 244, 1504, 1652, 1661, 1673, 1677, 1681 to 1684, 1690 to 1693, 1695 to 1697, 1712, 1723, 1732, 1733, 1742, 1763, 1772, 1777, 1781

May 7, 1970, P.L. 91-241, 84 Stat. 203, 38 U.S. Code § 361

May 21, 1970, P.L. 91-262, 84 Stat. 256, 38 U.S. Code §§ 101, 413 , 414

June 25, 1970, P.L. 91-291, 84 Stat. 326, 38 U.S. Code §§ 417, 705, 707, 717, 745, 752, 765, 767 to 770, 774

July 16, 1970, P.L. 91-338, 84 Stat. 437, 38 U.S. Code § 230

Aug. 12, 1970, P.L. 91-376, 84 Stat. 787, 38 U.S. Code §§ 103, 211, 312, 314, 315, 3010, 3104, 3111

Oct. 22, 1970, P.L. 91-496, 84 Stat. 1092, 38 U.S. Code §§ 4107, 4114, 5053

Oct. 22, 1970, P.L. 91-500, 84 Stat. 1096, 38 U.S. Code §§ 610, 612, 622

Oct. 23, 1970, P.L. 91-506, 84 Stat. 1108, 38 U.S. Code §§ 802, 1802 to 1804, 1810, 1811, 1818, 1819

Dec. 24, 1970, P.L. 91-584, 84 Stat. 1575, 38 U.S. Code §§ 1652, 1681 to 1684, 1701, 1711, 1712, 1720, 1733, 1801, 1802, 3010

Dec. 24, 1970, P.L. 91-588, 84 Stat. 1580, 38 U.S. Code §§ 101, 322, 411, 415, 503, 506 and others

Dec. 31, 1970, P.L. 91-606, 84 Stat. 1753, 38 U.S. Code § 1820

Dec. 31, 1970, P.L. 91-621, 84 Stat. 1864, 38 U.S. Code §§ 101, 3105

Jan. 11, 1971, P.L. 91-666, 84 Stat. 1998, 38 U.S. Code §§ 1901 to 1903

Aug. 5, 1971, P.L. 92-66, 85 Stat. 173, 38 U.S. Code § 1811

Aug. 6, 1971, P.L. 92-69, 85 Stat. 178, 38 U.S. Code § 5055

Aug. 11, 1971, P.L. 92-95, 85 Stat. 320, 38 U.S. Code § 806

**Veterans' Benefits Act (Under Age)**

Ill. Rev. Stat. 1991, Ch. 126 1/2, § 45.9, 46

**Veterans' Benefits Act of 1957**

June 17, 1957, P.L. 85-56, 71 Stat. 83, 10 U.S. Code §§ 1218 to 1220, 6159, 6160; 26 U.S. Code § 121; generally distributed in 38 U.S. Code

Aug. 27, 1957, P.L. 85-168, 71 Stat. 425 (See 38 U.S. Code §§ 314 , 315, 334, 335)

Aug. 28, 1957, P.L. 85-171, 71 Stat. 440 (See 38 U.S. Code § 3020)

Aug. 28, 1957, P.L. 85-194, 71 Stat. 472 (See 38 U.S. Code § 5207)

Aug. 28, 1957, P.L. 85-209, 71 Stat. 485 (See 38 U.S. Code §§ 103 , 302, 532, 534, 536, 541, 543)

Sept. 7, 1957, P.L. 85-311, 71 Stat. 632 (See 38 U.S. Code §§ 102 , 503)

April 11, 1958, P.L. 85-376, 72 Stat. 86 (See 38 U.S. Code § 3105)

May 23, 1958, P.L. 85-425, 72 Stat. 133 (See 38 U.S. Code §§ 510, 531 to 537)

June 18, 1958, P.L. 85-461, 72 Stat. 200 (See 38 U.S. Code §§ 107 , 622, 624)

June 20, 1958, P.L. 85-462, 72 Stat. 209 (See 38 U.S. Code §§ 4103 to 4105, 4107, 4108, 4111)

July 7, 1958, P.L. 85-507, 72 Stat. 338 (See 38 U.S. Code § 4113)

Aug. 14, 1958, P.L. 85-652, 72 Stat. 608 (See 38 U.S. Code § 314)

Aug. 14, 1958, P.L. 85-655, 72 Stat. 611

Aug. 18, 1958, P.L. 85-674, 72 Stat. 624 (See 38 U.S. Code §§ 902 , 903)

Aug. 27, 1958, P.L. 85-782, 72 Stat. 936 (See 38 U.S. Code §§ 314 )

Sept. 2, 1958, P.L. 85-857, 72 Stat. 1268 (See 38 U.S. Code §§ 103, 111, 351, 352, 3001, 3010, 3021)

**Veterans' Benefits Act of 1992**

Oct. 29, 1992, P.L. 102-568, 38 U.S. Code § 101 nt.

Nov. 2, 1994, P.L. 103-446, 38 U.S. Code § 3102 nt.

**Veterans' Benefits Act of 1997**

Nov. 21, 1997, P.L. 105-114, 38 U.S. Code § 101 nt.

**Veterans Benefits Act of 1998**
June 9, 1998, P.L. 105-178, 38 U.S. Code § 101 nt.

**Veterans' Benefits Amendments of 1989**
Dec. 18, 1989, P.L. 101-237, 38 U.S. Code § 101 nt.

**Veterans' Benefits and Programs Improvement Act**
Oct. 21, 1998, P.L. 105-277, 29 U.S. Code § 1721 nt.

**Veterans' Benefits and Programs Improvement Act of 1988**
Nov. 18, 1988, P.L. 100-689, 38 U.S. Code § 101 nt.

**Veterans' Benefits and Services Act of 1988**
May 20, 1988, P.L. 100-322, 102 Stat. 487, 38 U.S. Code § 101 nt.
Nov. 18, 1988, P.L. 100-687, 38 U.S. Code § 5025 nt.
Aug. 6, 1991, P.L. 102-83, 38 U.S. Code §§ 210 nt., 1712 nt., 7333 nt.
Nov. 5, 1991, P.L. 102-151, 105 Stat. 983
Oct. 9, 1992, P.L. 102-405, 38 U.S. Code § 1712 nt.
Oct. 27, 1992, P.L. 102-531, 38 U.S. Code § 303 nt.
Nov. 2, 1994, P.L. 103-452, 38 U.S. Code § 1712 nt.
Feb. 13, 1996, P.L. 104-110, 38 U.S. Code § 1712 nt.
Oct. 9, 1996, P.L. 104-275, 38 U.S. Code § 1712 nt.
Nov. 21, 1997, P.L. 105-114, 38 U.S. Code § 1712 nt.

**Veterans' Benefits Improvement Act of 1984**
Oct. 24, 1984, P.L. 98-543, 38 U.S. Code §§ 101 nt., 314, 314 nt. , 315, 411, 413, 414, 1508, 1682, 1732, 1742, 1798
Oct. 28, 1986, P.L. 99-576, 38 U.S. Code § 413

**Veterans' Benefits Improvement Act of 1988**
Nov. 18, 1988, P.L. 100-687, 38 U.S. Code § 101 nt.
Feb. 6, 1991, P.L. 102-4, 38 U.S. Code § 241 nt.
Aug. 6, 1991, P.L. 102-83, 38 U.S. Code §§ 210 nt., 241 nt.

**Veterans' Benefits Improvement and Health-Care Authorization Act of 1986**
Oct. 28, 1986, P.L. 99-576, 38 U.S. Code § 101 nt.
Aug. 6, 1991, P.L. 102-83, 38 U.S. Code § 354 nt.

**Veterans' Benefits Improvements Act of 1994**
Nov. 2, 1994, P.L. 103-446, 38 U.S. Code § 101 nt.
Oct. 9, 1996, P.L. 104-275, 38 U.S. Code § 5101 nt.
Nov. 21, 1997, P.L. 105-114, 38 U.S. Code § 7721 nt.

**Veterans' Benefits Improvements Act of 1996**
Oct. 9, 1996, P.L. 104-275, 38 U.S. Code § 101 nt.
Nov. 11, 1998, P.L. 105-368, 38 U.S. Code §§ 545 nt., 4104 nt.

**Veterans' Benefits Programs Improvement Act of 1991**
Aug. 14, 1991, P.L. 102-86, 38 U.S. Code § 101 nt.
Nov. 2, 1994, P.L. 103-446, 36 U.S. Code § 493

**Veterans' Bill of Rights**
P.R. Laws Ann. 1954, Title 29, §§ 761, 811 et seq.

**Veterans' Bill of Rights for Employment and Training Services (New York State)**
N.Y. Laws 1994, Ch. 553

**Veterans Bond Act**
Cal. Military and Veterans Code §§ 990 et seq., 993 et seq., 995.01 et seq., 996 et seq., 997.001 et seq., 998.001 et seq.
Cal. Statutes 1921, p. 959

**Veterans' Bonus Act**
Ind. Code Ann., 10-5-14-1 et seq.
Ky. Rev. Stat. 1971, 40.005 et seq.
Mass. Acts 1945, Ch. 731
Mont. Code Ann. 1947, 84-5606 et seq.
N.Y. Laws 1920, Ch. 872
N.Y. Laws 1921, Chs. 315, 344
*Continued*

R.I. Public Laws 1946, January Session, Ch. 1721
Vt. Stat. Ann., Title 20, § 1544
Wash. Rev. Code 1976, 73.32.020 et seq., 73.33.010 et seq.
W. Va. Acts 1951, Ch. 197

**Veterans' Bonus Act (Korean War)**
Ind. Code Ann., 10-5-16-1 et seq.
Iowa Code 1977, 35B.1 et seq.
Mich. Comp. Laws Ann., 35.971 et seq.
R.I. Public Laws 1955, Ch. 3608

**Veterans' Bonus Act (Vietnam)**
Mich. Comp. Laws Ann., 35.1021 et seq.

**Veterans' Bonus Act (World War II)**
Mich. Comp. Laws Ann., 35.921 et seq.

**Veterans' Bonus Sales and Use Tax Law**
Ky. Rev. Stat. 1971, 139.010 et seq.

**Veterans Bonus Tax Law**
N.J. Stat. Ann., 54:10C-1

**Veterans Bureau Interest Act**
Pa. Purdon's Stat., Title 20, §§ 8411, 8412

**Veterans' Burial Act**
Cal. Military and Veterans Code § 940 et seq.
Ill. Rev. Stat. 1991, Ch. 21, § 59.9 et seq.
Mich. Comp. Laws Ann., 35.801

**Veterans' Cemetery Protection Act of 1997**
Nov. 19, 1997, P.L. 105-101, 28 U.S. Code § 994 nt.

**Veterans' Children Act**
Ill. Rev. Stat. 1991, Ch. 126 1/2, § 25.9 et seq.

**Veterans' Commission Act**
Ill. Rev. Stat. 1973, Ch. 126 1/2, § 36 et seq.

**Veterans' Compensation Act**
Ill. Rev. Stat. 1991, § 57.70 et seq.
Pa. Cons. Stat., Title 51, § 20001 et seq.

**Veteran's Compensation Act (Vietnam)**
Ill. Rev. Stat. 1991, Ch. 126 1/2, § 57.51 et seq.
Pa. Cons. Stat., Title 51, § 20121 et seq.

**Veterans' Compensation Amendments of 1991**
Feb. 6, 1991, P.L. 102-3, 38 U.S. Code §§ 101 nt., 314, 315, 362 , 411, 413, 414

**Veterans' Compensation and Bond Act (Persian Gulf Conflict)**
Pa. 1992 Pamph. Laws, No. 106

**Veterans' Compensation and Program Improvements Amendments of 1984**
March 2, 1984, P.L. 98-223, 38 U.S. Code §§ 101 nt., 312, 314, 315, 355, 362, 411, 413, 414, 1781, 1795, 3011, 3202, 4002

**Veterans' Compensation and Relief Act of 1972**
June 30, 1972, P.L. 92-328, 86 Stat. 393, 38 U.S. Code §§ 210, 314, 315, 334, 335, 362, 536, 1817, 1820, 3021, 3102, 3202, 3203, 3503

**Veterans Compensation Bond Act (Korean Conflict)**
Pa. Cons. Stat., Title 51, § 20107 et seq.

**Veterans' Compensation Cost-of-Living Adjustment Act of 1987**
Dec. 31, 1987, P.L. 100-227, 38 U.S. Code §§ 101 nt., 314, 315, 362, 411, 414, 524

**Veterans' Compensation Cost-of-Living Adjustment Act of 1992**
Oct. 24, 1992, P.L. 102-510, 38 U.S. Code §§ 101 nt.

**Veterans' Compensation Cost-of-Living Adjustment Act of 1994**
Oct. 25, 1994, P.L. 103-418, 38 U.S. Code §§ 101 nt., 1114 nt.

**Veterans' Compensation Cost-of-Living Adjustment Act of 1995**
Nov. 22, 1995, P.L. 104-57, 38 U.S. Code § 101 nt.

**Veterans' Compensation Cost-of-Living Adjustment Act of 1996**
Oct. 9, 1996, P.L. 104-263, 38 U.S. Code § 101 nt.

**Veterans' Compensation, Education, and Employment Amendments of 1982**
Oct. 14, 1982, P.L. 97-306, 38 U.S. Code § 101 nt.

**Veterans' Compensation Rate Amendments of 1991**
Nov. 12, 1991, P.L. 102-152, 38 U.S. Code § 101 nt.

**Veterans' Compensation Rate Amendments of 1997**
Nov. 19, 1997, P.L. 105-98, 38 U.S. Code § 101 nt.

**Veterans' Compensation Rate Increase and Job Training Amendments of 1985**
Jan. 13, 1986, P.L. 99-238, 29 U.S. Code § 1721 nt., 38 U.S. Code § 101 nt., 314, 315, 362, 411, 413, 414, 1516 nt.
Aug. 6, 1991, P.L. 102-83, 38 U.S. Code § 3116 nt.

**Veterans' Compensation Rates Amendments of 1993**
Nov. 11, 1993, P.L. 103-140, 38 U.S. Code §§ 101 nt., 1114, 1114nt., 1115, 1162, 1311, 1313, 1314

**Veterans' Corporation Land Act**
Ill. Rev. Stat. 1991, Ch. 32, § 392.9 et seq.

**Veterans' County Service Office Act**
Tex. Gov. Code, § 434.031 et seq.

**Veterans Curators Act**
Kan. Stat. Ann., 73-501 et seq.

**Veterans' Day**
See Armistice Day Act

**Veterans' Day Act**
Ill. Rev. Stat. 1991, Ch. 1, § 3051-90

**Veterans' Dioxin and Radiation Exposure Compensation Standards Act**
Oct. 24, 1984, P.L. 98-542, 38 U.S. Code § 354 nt.
April 20, 1988, P.L. 100-321, 38 U.S. Code § 354 nt.
Oct. 30, 1992, P.L. 102-578, 38 U.S. Code § 1154 nt.

**Veterans' Disability Compensation and Housing Benefits Amendments of 1980**
Oct. 7, 1980, P.L. 96-385, 38 U.S. Code § 101 nt.

**Veterans Disability Compensation and Survivor Benefits Act of 1974**
May 31, 1974, P.L. 93-295, 88 Stat. 180, 38 U.S. Code §§ 301 nt., 314, 315, 322, 337, 342, 411, 413, 414, 1701, 3202

**Veterans Disability Compensation and Survivor Benefits Act of 1977**
Oct. 3, 1977, P.L. 95-117, 38 U.S. Code §§ 101 nt., 314 et seq., 314 nt.

**Veterans' Disability Compensation and Survivors' Benefits Act of 1978**
Oct. 18, 1978, P.L. 95-479, 24 U.S. Code § 295a nt.; 36 U.S. Code § 121; 38 U.S. Code §§ 101 nt., 314, 314 nt., 315, 362, 410 et seq., 562, 902 et seq., 1902

**Veterans' Disability Compensation and Survivors' Benefits Amendments of 1979**
Nov. 28, 1979, P.L. 96-128, 26 U.S. Code § 6103 nt., 38 U.S. Code §§ 101 nt., 314, 314 nt., 315, 362, 411, 413, 414, 611, 612A, 633, 718, 725, 726, 753, 761, 5005
Dec. 20, 1979, P.L. 96-151, 38 U.S. Code § 314 nt.
Aug. 6, 1991, P.L. 102-83, 26 U.S. Code § 6103 nt.

**Veterans' Disability Compensation, Housing, and Memorial Benefits Amendments of 1981**
Oct. 17, 1981, P.L. 97-66, 38 U.S. Code § 101 nt.

**Veterans' Discharges Recording Act**
Wash. Rev. Code Ann., 73.04.030 et seq.

**Veterans' Domiciliary Home of Florida Act**
Fla. Stat. Ann., 296.01 et seq.

**Veterans' Education Act**
Ga. Laws 1947, p. 1143
Ore. Rev. Stat., 408.010 et seq.
Pa. Purdon's Stat., Title 24, § 5171 et seq.

**Veterans Education and Employment Amendments of 1989**
Dec. 18, 1989, P.L. 101-237, 38 U.S. Code § 101 nt.
Dec. 21, 1995, P.L. 104-66, 38 U.S. Code § 4100 nt.

**Veterans' Education and Training Act**
Colo. Stat. Ann. 1935, Ch. 170A, § 11 et seq.

**Veterans' Education and Training Amendments Act of 1970**
March 26, 1970, P.L. 91-219, 84 Stat. 76, 38 U.S. Code §§ 240 to 244, 1504, 1652, 1661, 1673, 1677, 1681 to 1684, 1690 to 1693, 1695 to 1697, 1712, 1723, 1732, 1733, 1742, 1763, 1772, 1777, 1781

**Veterans' Education and Training Amendments of 1950**
July 13, 1950, Ch. 461, 64 Stat. 336

**Veterans' Education Reorganization Act**
Ga. Code Ann., 38-4-30 et seq.

**Veterans' Educational Assistance Act of 1984**
See Montgomety GI Bill Act of 1984

**Veterans' Educational Assistance Amendments of 1991**
Oct. 19, 1991, P.L. 102-127, 10 U.S. Code §§ 2131, 2133; 38 U.S. Code §§ 101 nt., 2131, 2133, 3013, 3231, 3511, 3680, 3680 nt., 4211, 4214

**Veterans' Educational Assistance Law**
Cal. Military and Veterans Code § 870 et seq. (World War I)
Cal. Military and Veterans Code § 981 et seq. (World War II)

**Veterans' Emergency Housing Act**
N.J. Stat. Ann., 55:14G-1 et seq.
Ohio Rev. Code 1953, 3735.58 et seq.

**Veterans' Emergency Housing Act of 1946**
May 22, 1946, Ch. 268, 60 Stat. 207, 12 U.S. Code §§ 1738, 1739, 1743
Aug. 10, 1946, Ch. 951, 60 Stat. 993

**Veterans' Employment Act**
R.I. Gen. Laws 1956, 30-21-1 et seq.
Wash. Rev. Code Ann., 73.16.010 et seq.

**Veterans Employment Act (Vietnam)**
Cal. Government Code § 7280 et seq.

**Veterans' Employment and Readjustment Act of 1972**
Oct. 24, 1972, P.L. 92-540, 86 Stat. 1094, 38 U.S. Code §§ 2001 to 2008, 2011 to 2013

**Veterans Employment Opportunities Act of 1998**
Oct. 31, 1998, P.L. 105-339, 112 Stat. 3182, 5 U.S. Code § 2101 nt.

**Veterans Employment Preference Act**
N.C. Gen. Stat. 1943, § 128-15
N.D. Cent. Code, 37-19.1-01 et seq.

**Veterans' Employment Representative Act**
Ill. Comp. Stat. 1992, Ch. 330, § 50/1 et seq.
Ill. Rev. Stat. 1991, Ch. 48, § 186a et seq.

**Veterans' Employment, Training, and Counseling Amendments of 1988**
May 20, 1988, P.L. 100-323, 102 Stat. 556, 38 U.S. Code § 101 nt., generally 38 U.S. Code § 2001 et seq.

**Veterans Enabling Act (Minors)**
N.C. Gen. Stat. 1943, § 165-12 et seq.

**Veterans' Equalized Compensation Act**
Wash. Laws 1920, Extra Session, Ch. 1

**Veterans' Exemption Act**
Nev. Rev. Stat. 1979 Reprint, 361.090

**Veterans' Facility Act**
Mich. Comp. Laws Ann., 36.1 et seq.

**Veterans' Farm and Home Purchase Act**
Cal. Military and Veterans Code § 987.50 et seq.
Miss. Code Ann. 1972, § 35-7-1 et seq.

**Veterans' Farm and Home Purchase Act (World War I)**
Cal. Military and Veterans Code § 800 et seq.

**Veterans' Farm and Home Purchase Act (World War II)**
Cal. Military and Veterans Code § 985 et seq.

**Veterans' Fishing License Act**
Ind. Burns' 1933, 11-1405, Subd. c

**Veterans Flag Act**
July 11, 1939, Ch. 263, 53 Stat. 999

**Veterans' Graves Law**
Cal. Military and Veterans Code § 960 et seq.

**Veterans' Guardianship Act**
See also Uniform Veterans' Guardianship Act
Ala. Code 1975, § 26-9-1 et seq.
Ariz. Rev. Stat. Ann. §§ 41-603, 41-605
Cal. Probate Code § 1400 et seq.
Fla. Stat. Ann., 744.602 et seq.
Haw. Rev. Stat. Ann., § 552-1 et seq.
Ida. Code 1947, Superseded Vols., 15-1901 et seq.
Iowa Code Ann., 633.614 et seq.
Md. Ann. Code 1957, Art. 96 1/2 § 19 et seq.
Me. Rev. Stat. Ann. 1964, Title 18-A, § 5-101 et seq.
Mich. Comp. Laws Ann., 35.71 et seq.
Miss. Code Ann. 1972, § 35-5-1 et seq.
Mont. Rev. Code 1947, 91-4801 et seq.
Neb. Laws 1929, Ch. 76
Nev. Rev. Stat. 1979 Reprint, 160.010 et seq.
N.J. Stat. Ann., 3B:13-1 et seq.
N.M. Stat. Ann. 1953, 74-6-1 et seq.
N.Y. Mental Hygiene Law 1972 (Consol. Laws Ch. 27) § 79.01 et seq.
P.R. Laws Ann. 1954, Title 31 § 861 et seq.
S.C. Code Ann. 1976, § 62-5-601 et seq.
Utah Code Ann. 1953, 75-5-314, 75-5-315
W. Va. Code 1966, § 44-15-1 et seq.
Wyo. Stat. Ann., § 3-6-101 et seq.

**Veterans' Hawking and Peddling License Act**
Okla. Stat. Ann., Title 72, § 1 et seq.

**Veterans Health Care Act of 1992**
Nov. 4, 1992, P.L. 102-585, 38 U.S. Code § 101 nt.
April 12, 1993, P.L. 103-18, 38 U.S. Code § 8126
Nov. 2, 1994, P.L. 103-446, 38 U.S. Code § 8111 nt.
Nov. 2, 1994, P.L. 103-452, 38 U.S. Code §§ 1710 nt., 1720D nt., 7303 nt.
Oct. 9, 1996, P.L. 104-262, 38 U.S. Code § 8111 nt.
Nov. 11, 1998, P.L. 105-368, 38 U.S. Code §§ 7601 to 7604, 7632, 7636

**Veterans' Health Care Amendments of 1979**
June 13, 1979, P.L. 96-22, 38 U.S. Code §§ 101, 101 nt., 230, 235 , 601, 601 nt., 606, 610, 611, 612, 612 nt., 612A, 612A nt., 620A, 634, 661 to 664, 4107, 4108, 5001 et seq.
Aug. 6, 1991, P.L. 102-83, 38 U.S. Code § 1712A nt.

**Veterans' Health Care Amendments of 1983**
Nov. 21, 1983, P.L. 98-160, 38 U.S. Code § 101 nt.
Oct. 28, 1986, P.L. 99-576, 38 U.S. Code § 612A nt.
Aug. 6, 1991, P.L. 102-83, 38 U.S. Code § 1701 nt.

**Veterans' Health-Care Amendments of 1986**
April 7, 1986, P.L. 99-272, 38 U.S. Code § 101 nt.
May 7, 1986, P.L. 102-40, 38 U.S. Code § 610 nt.
May 20, 1992 P.L. 102-291, 38 U.S. Code § 1710 nt.

**Veterans' Health Care Eligibility Reform Act of 1996**
Oct. 9, 1996, P.L. 104-262, 38 U.S. Code § 101 nt.

**Veterans' Health Care, Training, and Small Business Loan Act of 1981**
Nov. 3, 1981, P.L. 97-72, 38 U.S. Code § 101 nt.

**Veterans' Health Initiative Act (Vietnam)**
Pa. Cons. Stat., Title 51, § 20201 et seq.

**Veterans Health Programs Extension Act of 1994**
Nov. 2, 1994, P.L. 103-452, 38 U.S. Code §§ 101 nt., 1710, 1712, 1720C, 1720D, 7303, 8169

**Veterans Health Programs Extension and Improvement Act of 1979**
Dec. 20, 1979, P.L. 96-151, 38 U.S. Code §§ 101 nt., 111, 111 nt. , 219 nt., 314 nt., 601, 612 to 614, 628, 641, 641 nt., 4104 to 4106, 4112, 5010, 5033, 5053 to 5055, 5070, 5082, 5083
Oct. 24, 1984, P.L. 98-542, 38 U.S. Code § 219 nt.

**Veterans' Home Act (Anna)**
Ill. Rev. Stat. 1991, Ch. 23, § 5050 et seq. (Quincy)
Ill. Rev. Stat. 1991, Ch. 126 1/2, § 500 et seq. (Manteno)
Ill. Rev. Stat. 1991, Ch. 126 1/2, § 600 et seq. (La Salle)
Ill. Rev. Stat. 1991, Ch. 126 1/2, § 700 et seq. (Anna)

**Veterans' Home Law (Aged and Disabled Veterans)**
Cal. Military and Veterans Code § 1010 et seq.

**Veterans Home Loan Indemnity and Restructuring Act of 1989**
Dec. 18, 1989, P.L. 101-237, 38 U.S. Code § 101 nt.

**Veterans Home Loan Program Amendments of 1992**
Oct. 28, 1992, P.L. 102-547, 38 U.S. Code § 101 nt.
Nov. 2, 1994, P.L. 103-446, 38 U.S. Code § 3703 nt.

**Veterans' Home Loan Program Emergency Amendments of 1988**
Feb. 29, 1988, P.L. 100-253, 102 Stat. 20, 38 U.S. Code §§ 101 nt., 1803 nt., 1816, 1819

**Veterans' Home Loan Program Improvements and Property Rehabilitation Act of 1987**
Dec. 21, 1987, P.L. 100-198, 38 U.S. Code §§ 101 nt., 113, 113 nt., 1803, 1803 nt., 1804, 1804 nt., 1810, 1817A, 1829
Aug. 6, 1991, P.L. 102-83, 38 U.S. Code § 3720 nt.

**Veterans Home of Florida Act**
Fla. Stat. Ann., 296.01 et seq.

**Veterans' Home Purchase Law**
Miss. Code Ann. 1972, § 35-7-1 et seq.

**Veterans Homestead Act**
Fla. Stat. 1969, 253.351 et seq.

**Veterans' Homestead Tax Exemption Act**
Mich. Comp. Laws Ann., 211.7b

**Veterans' Honorarium Act**
Mont. Code Ann. 1947, 84-5606 et seq.

**Veterans Hospitalization and Medical Services Modernization Amendments of 1966**
Nov. 7, 1966, P.L. 89-785, 80 Stat. 1368, 38 U.S. Code §§ 210, 213, 233, 610, 4101 to 4107, 4111 to 4114, 4117, 5004, 5012, 5051 to 5057

**Veterans' Housing Act of 1970**
Oct. 23, 1970, P.L. 91-506, 84 Stat. 1108, 38 U.S. Code §§ 802, 1802 to 1804, 1810, 1811, 1818, 1819

**Veterans' Housing Act of 1970-1974**
Mass. Gen. Laws Ann., 121B:34 et seq.
Miss. Code 1942, § 7516.7-01 et seq.
N.J. Stat. Ann., 55:14G-1 et seq.
Wis. Stat. 1989, 66.39, 66.92, 67.015

**Veterans Housing Amendment of 1976**
June 30, 1976, P.L. 94-324, 12 U.S. Code § 1709-1a

**Veterans Housing Authority Act**
Pa. Purdon's Stat., Title 35, § 1590.1 et seq.

**Veterans' Housing Benefits Act of 1978**
Oct. 18, 1978, P.L. 95-476, 38 U.S. Code §§ 101 nt., 802, 902, 903, 906, 1008, 1798, 1802 et seq.

**Veterans' Incentive Program Act**
W. Va. Code 1966, § 21A-2C-1 et seq.

**Veterans Insignia Law**
Cal. Military and Veterans Code § 1820

**Veterans' Insurance Act of 1974**
May 24, 1974, P.L. 93-289, 88 Stat. 165, 38 U.S. Code §§ 707, 723 , 765, 767 to 771, 774, 777 to 779

**Veterans' Insurance Reform Act of 1996**
Oct. 9, 1996, P.L. 104-275, Title IV, 38 U.S. Code § 101 nt.

**Veterans' Job Training Act**
Oct. 24, 1984, P.L. 98-543, 29 U.S. Code § 1721 nt.
Sept. 30, 1985, P.L. 99-108, 29 U.S. Code § 1721 nt.
Jan. 13, 1986, P.L. 99-238, 29 U.S. Code § 1721 nt.
July 2, 1986, P.L. 99-349, 100 Stat. 730
July 22, 1987, P.L. 100-77, 29 U.S. Code § 1721 nt.
Dec. 21, 1987, P.L. 100-198, 38 U.S. Code § 1820 nt.
Dec. 31, 1987, P.L. 100-227, 29 U.S. Code § 1721 nt.
Oct. 21, 1998, P.L. 105-277, 29 U.S. Code § 1721 nt.

**Veterans' Judicial Review Act**
Nov. 18, 1988, P.L. 100-687, 38 U.S. Code § 101 nt.
Aug. 16, 1989, P.L. 101-94, 38 U.S. Code §§ 4004 nt., 4051 nt.
Pa. Purdon's Stat., Title 71, § 1190.45a et seq.

**Veterans' Land Act**
Tex. Natural Resources Code, § 161.001 et seq.

**Veterans' Land Fund Act**
Tex. Natural Resources Code, § 161.171 et seq.

**Veterans Leadership Program Act (Vietnam)**
Ill. Rev. Stat. 1991, Ch. 126 1/2, § 201 et seq.

**Veterans' License Act**
Ga. Code Ann., 43-12-1

**Veterans' Loan Act**
N.J. Rev. Stat. 1937, 38:23B-1 et seq.
Okla. Stat. Ann., Title 72, § 261 et seq.
Ore. Rev. Stat., 407.085 et seq.

**Veterans Loan Act (World War)**
N.C. Public Laws 1923, Ch. 190
N.C. Public Laws 1925, Ch. 155
N.C. Public Laws 1927, Ch. 97
N.C. Public Laws 1929, Ch. 298

**Veterans' Loan Insurance Act**
Wash. Rev. Code Ann., 73.12.010 et seq.

**Veterans' Medical Programs Amendments of 1992**
Oct. 9, 1992, P.L. 102-405, 38 U.S. Code §§ 101 nt., prec. 301, 305, 305 nt., 306, 306 nt., prec. 501, 527 nt., 541-543, 543 nt., 709, 1710, 1712 nt., 1712A, 1712A nt., 1717, 1717 nt., 1718, 1720, 3902, 3904, 5904, 5904 nt., prec. 7301, 7301, 7303, 7303 nt., 7304, 7305, 7306, 7311, 7311 nt., 7312 to 7315, 7331, 7363, 7364, 7401 to 7405, 7407, 7410, 7423, 7424, 7431, 7432, 7433, 7435, 7437, 7437 nt., 7451, 7455, 7458, 7461, 7462, 7472, 7473, 7474, 7612, 7612 nt., 7616, 7701, prec. 8101, 8104, 8104 nt., 8105, 8107, 8110, 8111, 8111A, 8125, 8155, 8157, 8158
Nov. 21, 1997, P.L. 105-114, 38 U.S. Code § 527 nt.

**Veterans' Memorial Act**
Ohio Rev. Code 1953, 345.01 et seq.

**Veterans Memorial Commission Act**
Pa. Cons. Stat., Title 71, § 1901 et seq.

**Veterans Memorial School Construction Act**
Ind. Code Ann., 21-1-11-1 et seq.

**Veterans Military Affairs Act**
Alaska Stat. 1962, § 26.05.010 et seq.

**Veterans' Military Pay Act**
Del. Laws Vol. 47, p. 1047, 1st Sp. Sess., Ch. 1
Mich. Comp. Laws Ann., 35.921 et seq.

**Veterans' Military Pay Act No. II**
Del. Laws Vol. 50, p. 977, Ch. 449

**Veterans' Military Pay Act No. III**
Del. Laws Vol. 56, p. 885, Ch. 250

**Veterans' Military Pay Fund Act**
Mich. Comp. Laws Ann., 35.971 et seq.

**Veterans' Mortgage Fund Act**
W. Va. Code 1966, § 31-18C-1 et seq.

**Veterans' Mortgage Loan Extension Act**
N.H. Rev. Stat. 1955, 479:18-a et seq.

**Veterans' Nursing Home of Florida Act**
Fla. Stat. Ann., 296.31 et seq.

**Veterans of World War II Bonus Act**
Ill. Rev. Stat. 1991, Ch. 126 1/2, § 47 et seq.

**Veterans of World War II Temporary Housing Act**
Conn. Public Acts 1991, May Special Session, p. 7, No. 3

**Veterans Omnibus Health Care Act of 1976**
Aug. 6, 1991, P.L. 102-83, 38 U.S. Code § 1718 nt.

**Veterans' Paralysis Act**
July 19, 1939, Ch. 329, 53 Stat. 1067

**Veterans' Pension Act**
N.J. Stat. Ann., 43:4-1 et seq.

**Veterans' Pension Act of 1959**
Aug. 29, 1959, P.L. 86-211, 73 Stat. 432, 10 U.S. Code § 1441; 38 U.S. Code §§ 503, 506, 521, 522, 541 to 543, 617, 3203; 45 U.S. Code § 228s-1

**Veterans Pension and Readjustment Assistance Act of 1967**
Aug. 31, 1967, P.L. 90-77, 81 Stat. 178, 38 U.S. Code §§ 101, 103 , 302, 314, 404, 502, 503, 511, 512, 521, 531, 532, 534, 536, 541, 542, 544, 602, 612 and others

**Veterans' Preference Act**
Ark. Code Ann. 1987, 21-3-304 et seq.
Ill. Rev. Stat. 1991, Ch. 126 1/2, § 22.9 et seq.
Iowa Code Ann., 70.1 et seq., 400.10
Kan. Stat. Ann., 73-201 et seq.
Ky. Rev. Stat. 1971, 18A.150
Mass. Gen. Laws Ann., 31:3
Mass. Gen. Laws Ann., 31:26
Md. Ann. Code 1957, Art. 64A, § 18
Mich. Comp. Laws Ann., 35.401 et seq.
Minn. Stat. Ann., 197.455 et seq.
Mont. Code Ann. 1991, 10-2-201 et seq.
N.H. Rev. Stat. 1955, 283:4 et seq.
N.J. Stat. Ann., 11A:5-1 et seq.
Pa. Cons. Stat., Title 51, § 7101 et seq.
Pa. Consol. Stat., Title 51, § 7101
S.D. Codified Laws 1967, 3-3-1 et seq.
Tex. Rev. Civ. Stat., Art. 4413(31)
Vt. Stat. Ann., Title 20, § 1543

**Veterans' Preference Act (Land Settlement)**
Wash. Rev. Code 1951, 89.04.080

**Veterans' Preference Act of 1944**
June 27, 1944, Ch. 287, 58 Stat. 387 (See 5 U.S. Code §§ 1302, 2108, 3305, 3306, 3308 to 3320, 3351, 3363, 3364, 3501 to 3504, 7512, 7701)
Aug. 4, 1947, Ch. 447, 61 Stat. 723 (See 5 U.S. Code § 7701)
Jan. 19, 1948, Ch. 1, 62 Stat. 3 (See 5 U.S. Code §§ 2108, 3305, 3309)
June 22, 1948, Ch. 604, 62 Stat. 575 (See 5 U.S. Code § 7701)
July 2, 1948, Ch. 816, 62 Stat. 1233 (See 5 U.S. Code § 2108)
Aug. 26, 1949, Ch. 513, 63 Stat. 666 (See 5 U.S. Code § 2108)
Dec. 27, 1950, Ch. 1151, 64 Stat. 1117 (See 5 U.S. Code §§ 2108, 3305, 3309)
July 14, 1952, Ch. 728, 66 Stat. 626 (See 5 U.S. Code §§ 2108, 3309)
Aug. 14, 1953, Ch. 485, 67 Stat. 581 (See 5 U.S. Code §§ 3309, 3310, 3313, 3318)
Aug. 19, 1964, P.L. 88-448, 78 Stat. 486 (See 5 U.S. Code §§ 3501 to 3503)
March 3, 1966, P.L. 89-358, 80 Stat. 28 (See 5 U.S. Code § 2108)

**Veterans Preference Amendment**
N.Y. Const. 1894, Art. 5, § 6

**Veterans' Preference Enforcement Act (Political Subdivision)**
Colo. Rev. Stat., 29-5.5-101 et seq.

**Veterans' Preferential Public Employment Act**
Alaska Stat. 1962, § 39.25.150, Subd. 23
Wash. Rev. Code Ann., 73.16.010, 73.16.020

**Veterans Programs Enhancement Act of 1998**
Nov. 11, 1998, P.L. 105-368, 112 Stat. 3315, 38 U.S. Code § 101 nt.

**Veteran's Public Retirement Act**
N.J. Stat. Ann., 43:4-1 et seq.

**Veterans' Radiation Exposure Amendment of 1992**
Oct. 30, 1992, P.L. 102-578, 38 U.S. Code § 101 nt.

**Veterans' Re-employment Act**
Md. Ann. Code 1957, Art. 96 1/2, § 8 et seq.
Mont. Code Ann. 1991, 10-2-211 et seq.
Wash. Rev. Code Ann., 73.16.031 et seq.

**Veterans' Readjustment Assistance Act of 1952**
July 16, 1952, Ch. 875, 66 Stat. 553
Aug. 20, 1954, Ch. 779, 68 Stat. 755 (See 38 U.S. Code §§ 1612, 1613)
Feb. 15, 1955, Ch. 7, 69 Stat. 8 (See 38 U.S. Code §§ 1601, 1611 to 1613)
July 26, 1955, Ch. 384, 69 Stat. 376 (See 38 U.S. Code § 2009)
July 26, 1955, Ch. 388, 69 Stat. 380 (See 38 U.S. Code § 2104)
Aug. 9, 1955, Ch. 640, 69 Stat. 558 (See 38 U.S. Code § 1632)
July 30, 1956, Ch. 791, 70 Stat. 730 (See 38 U.S. Code § 1625)
June 17, 1957, P.L. 85-56, 71 Stat. 159 (See 38 U.S. Code §§ 111, 213, 1601, 1661)
June 18, 1958, P.L. 85-460, 72 Stat. 200 (See 38 U.S. Code § 1601)
Aug. 14, 1958, P.L. 85-638, 72 Stat. 593 (See 38 U.S. Code § 2104)
Aug. 28, 1958, P.L. 85-807, 72 Stat. 975 (See 38 U.S. Code §§ 1612, 1613)

**Veterans' Readjustment Benefits Act of 1966**
March 3, 1966, P.L. 89-358, 80 Stat. 12, 38 U.S. Code §§ 101, 102 , 111, 211, 337, 610, 901, 903, 1651, 1652, 1661 to 1663, 1670 to 1676 and others; 50 U.S. Code Appx. § 530

**Veterans Reconciliation Act of 1993**
Aug. 10, 1993, P.L. 103-66, 38 U.S. Code § 101 nt.

**Veterans Reconciliation Act of 1997**
Aug. 5, 1997, P.L. 105-33, 38 U.S. Code § 101 nt.

**Veterans' Recreation Authorities Law**
N.C. Gen. Stat. 1943, § 165-23 et seq.

**Veterans Referral Program Act**
Fla. Laws 1979, Ch. 79-154

**Veterans' Rehabilitation and Education Amendments of 1980**
Oct. 17, 1980, P.L. 96-466, 38 U.S. Code § 101 nt.
Oct. 21, 1998, P.L. 105-277, 38 U.S. Code § 4101 nt.

**Veterans' Rehabilitation Loan Act**
Wis. Stat. 1987, 45.35

**Veterans' Reimbursement Act**
Ga. Code Ann., 48-1-10

**Veterans' Relief Act**
Mich. Comp. Laws Ann., 35.21 et seq.
N.Y. Laws 1922, Ch. 589
Wash. Rev. Code Ann., 73.08.010 et seq.

**Veterans' Relief Act (Indigent)**
Cal. Military and Veterans Code § 920 et seq.

**Veterans' Relief Act (Spanish War)**
Minn. Laws 1931, Ch. 405

**Veterans' Resettlement Act**
Ga. Laws 1945, p. 170

**Veterans' Retirement Act**
Mass. Gen. Laws Ann., 32:56 et seq.

**Veterans Revenue Debenture Act**
Cal. Military and Veterans Code § 1001.1 et seq.

**Veterans' Right to Employment Services Act**
Mich. Comp. Laws Ann., 35.1091 et seq.

**Veterans' Service Act**
N.M. Stat. Ann., 28-13-1 et seq.

**Veterans' Service Office Act**
Ark. Stat. 1947, 11-1401 et seq.

**Veterans' Services Fund Loan Act**
Mass. Acts 1953, Ch. 440

**Veterans' Small Business Loan Act**
Me. Rev. Stat. Ann. 1964, Title 10, § 1100A et seq.
Me. Rev. Stat. Ann. 1964, Title 37-B, § 551 et seq.

**Veterans' Small Business Loan Act of 1981**
Nov. 3, 1981, P.L. 97-72, 38 U.S. Code § 101 nt.

**Veterans' State Aid Act**
Ore. Rev. Stat., 406.310 et seq.

**Veterans' Statistics Commission Act**
Wash. Laws 1945, Ch. 258

**Veterans' Tax Exemption Act**
Iowa Code Ann., 427.3
N.H. Rev. Stat. 1955, 72:28 et seq.
Wyo. Stat. Ann., § 39-1-202

**Veterans' Tenure Act**
Mass. Gen. Laws Ann., 30:9A
Mass. Gen. Laws Ann., 31:21 et seq.
N.J. Rev. Stat. 1937, 38:16-1 et seq.

**Veterans' Trust Fund Act**
Mich. Comp. Laws Ann., 35.601 et seq.

**Veterans' Welfare Act**
Cal. Military and Veterans Code § 690 et seq.
Ga. Code Ann., 43-50-1 et seq.
Mont. Rev. Code 1947, 77-1001

**Veterans' Welfare Bond Act**
Cal. Statutes 1933, p. 1758

**Veterinarians Licensing Act**
N.Y. Education Law 1947 (Consol. Laws Ch. 16) § 6701 et seq.

**Veterinarian's Lien Act**
Iowa Code Ann., 581.1 et seq.

**Veterinarians Practicing and Licensing Act**
Ala. Code 1975, § 34-29-20 et seq.
Ariz. Rev. Stat. Ann., § 32-2201 et seq.
Ark. Code Ann. 1987, 17-99-101 et seq.
Cal. Business and Professions Code § 4800 et seq.
Colo. Rev. Stat., 12-64-101 et seq.
Conn. Gen. Stat. Ann., § 20-196 et seq.
D.C. Code Ann., § 2-2721 et seq.
Del. Code of 1974, Title 24, § 3301 et seq.
Fla. Stat. Ann., 474.201 et seq.
Ga. Code Ann., 43-50-1 et seq.
Haw. Rev. Stat. Ann., § 471-1 et seq.
Ida. Code 1947, 54-2101 et seq.
Ill. Rev. Stat. 1991, Ch. 111, § 7001 et seq.
Ind. Code Ann., 15-5-1.1-1 et seq.
Iowa Code Ann., 169.1 et seq.
Kan. Stat. Ann., 47-814 et seq.
Ky. Rev. Stat. 1971, 321.180 et seq.
La. Rev. Stat. Ann., 37:151 et seq.
Md. Ann. Code 1974, Art. AG, § 2-301 et seq.
Me. Rev. Stat. Ann. 1964, Title 32, § 4852 et seq.
Mich. Comp. Laws Ann., 333.18801 et seq.
Minn. Stat. Ann., 156.001 et seq.
Miss. Code Ann. 1972, § 73-39-1 et seq.
Mo. Rev. Stat., 340.010 et seq.
Mont. Code Ann. 1991, 37-18-101 et seq.
N.C. Gen. Stat. 1943, § 90-179 et seq.
N.D. Cent. Code, 43-29-01 et seq.
Neb. Rev. Stat. 1943, 71-1, 153 et seq.
Nev. Rev. Stat. 1979 Reprint, 638.010 et seq.
N.H. Rev. Stat. 1955, 332-B:1 et seq.
N.J. Stat. Ann., 45:16-9.1 et seq.
N.M. Stat. Ann., 61-14-1 et seq.
N.Y. Educaton Law 1947 (Consol. Laws Ch. 16) § 6701 et seq.

Ohio Rev. Code 1953, 4741.01 et seq.
Ore. Rev. Stat., 686.010 et seq.
Pa. Purdon's Stat., Title 63, § 485.1 et seq.
P.R. Laws Ann. 1954, Title 20, § 2951 et seq.
R.I. Gen. Laws 1956, 5-25-1 et seq.
S.C. Code Ann. 1976, § 40-69-10 et seq.
S.D. Codified Laws 1967, 36-12-1 et seq.
Tenn. Code Ann. 63-12-101 et seq.
Tex. Rev. Civ. Stat., Art. 8890
Utah Code Ann. 1953, 58-28-1 et seq.
Va. Code 1950, § 54-1-3800 et seq.
Vt. Stat. Ann., Title 26, § 2351 et seq.
Wash. Rev. Code Ann., 18.92.010 et seq.
Wis. Stat. Ann., 453.02 et seq.
W. Va. Code 1966, § 30-10-1 et seq.
Wyo. Stat. Ann., § 33-30.101 et seq.

**Veterinarian's Professional Corporation Act**
Minn. Stat. Ann., 319A.01 et seq.

**Veterinarians' Registration Act**
Mass. Gen. Laws Ann., 112:54 et seq.

**Veterinary College Act (University of Illinois)**
Ill. Rev. Stat. 1991, Ch. 144, § 57.9 et seq.

**Veterinary Corporation Act**
S.D. Codified Laws 1967, 47-13-1 et seq.

**Veterinary Good Samaritan Law**
N.J. Stat. Ann., 45:16-9.10, 45:16-9.11

**Veterinary Medical Education Act of 1966**
Nov. 2, 1966, P.L. 89-709, 80 Stat. 1103, 42 U.S. Code §§ 293, 293a, 293d, 293e, 294 to 294b

**Veterinary Medical Practice Act**
Okla. Stat. Ann., Title 59 § 698.1 et seq.
Pa. Purdon's Stat., Title 63, § 485.1 et seq.

**Veterinary Medicine Corporations Act**
La. Rev. Stat. Ann., 12:1151 et seq.

**Veterinary Medicine School Act**
Tenn. Code Ann., 49-9-801

**Veterinary Surgery Act**
Ark. Stat. 1947, 72-1117 et seq.

**Vexatious Delay Act (Insurance)**
Mo. Rev. Stat., 375.420

**Vexatious Litigants Act**
Tex. Civil Practice and Remedies Code, § 11.001 et seq.

**Vexatious Litigation Act**
Cal. Code of Civil Procedure § 391 et seq.

**Viable Neighborhood Maintenance Act**
N.J. Stat. Ann., 52:27D-142 et seq.

**Viatical Settlement Act**
Ark. Code Ann. 1987, 23-81-501 et seq.
Ill. Comp. Stat. 1992, Ch. 215, § 158/1 et seq.
Me. Rev. Stat. Ann. 1964, Title 24-A, § 6801 et seq.
Mont. Code Ann., 33-20-1301 et seq.
N.Y. Civil Practice Laws and Rules (Consol. Laws Ch. 8) § 5205
N.Y. Insurance Law 1984 (Consol. Laws Ch. 28) §§ 3220, 7801 et seq.
N.Y. Public Health Law 1953 (Consol. Laws Ch. 45) § 20
N.Y. Social Services Law (Consol. Laws Ch. 55) § 366
N.Y. Tax Law (Consol. Laws Ch. 60) § 612
Wash. Rev. Code Ann., 48.102.005 et seq.

**Vicarious Liability Act (Crimes)**
Wis. Stat. Ann., 939.05

**Vicarious Liability Law (Automobile Use)**
N.Y. Vehicle and Traffic Law 1959 (Consol. Laws Ch. 71) § 388

**Vice and Immorality Act (Sunday Closing)**
N.J. Stat. Ann., 2A:171-1 et seq.

**Victim Advocate Law**
Pa. Purdon's Stat., Title 71, § 2301 et seq.

**Victim and Witness Advisory Council Act**
Minn. Stat. Ann., 611A.70, 611A.71

**Victim and Witness Protection Act**
Colo. Rev. Stat., 18-8-701 et seq.
Fla. Laws 1984, Ch. 84-363
Iowa Code Ann., 910A.1 et seq.

**Victim and Witness Protection Act of 1982**
Oct. 12, 1982, P.L. 97-291, 18 U.S. Code §§ 1501 nt., 1512 et seq., 3579 et seq.
Oct. 12, 1984, P.L. 98-473, 18 U.S. Code § 1512 nt.

**Victim Counselor Confidentiality Act**
Ala. Acts 1991, p. 1040
N.M. Stat. Ann., 31-25-1 et seq.

**Victim Impact Statement Act**
Miss. Code Ann. 1972, § 99-19-151 et seq.
N.Y. Criminal Procedure Law (Consol. Laws Ch. 11A) §§ 390.30, Subds. 3, 5, 390.50, Subd. 2, 440.50, Subd. 2
N.Y. Executive Law 1951 (Consol. Laws Ch. 18) § 623, Subd. 20
N.Y. Penal Law 1965 (Consol. Laws Ch. 40) § 60.27, Subd. 1
Tenn. Code Ann., 40-38-201 et seq.

**Victim-Offender Mediation Center Act**
Tenn. Code Ann., 16-20-101 et seq.

**Victim Ombudsman Act (Crime)**
Minn. Stat. Ann., 611 A.72 et seq.

**Victim Protection Act (Child Physical and Sexual Abuse)**
Ala. Code 1975, § 15-25-30 et seq.

**Victim Protection and Domestic Violence Prevention Act**
Alaska Stat. 1962, § 18.66.010 et seq.

**Victim Restitution Program (Crime)**
Cal. Penal Code §§ 1202.4, 11225
Cal. Welfare and Institutions Code §§ 656.2, 729.6, 729.7

**Victim Restitution Work Program (Juvenile Offender)**
Okla. Stat. Ann., Title 10, § 1404.1

**Victim—Witness Assistance Programs Act**
S.C. Code Ann. 1976, § 16-3-1110 et seq.

**Victim's and Witness' Bill of Rights Act**
S.C. Code Ann. 1976, § 16-3-1510 et seq.

**Victims' and Witnesses' Bill of Rights Act**
Alaska Laws 1991, Ch. 57
Cal. Const. 1879, Art. 1, § 28
Cal. Penal Code §§ 25, 667, 1191-1, 1192-7, 3043
Cal. Welfare and Institutions Code §§ 1732-5, 1767, 6331
Fla. Stat. Ann., 775.089 et seq.
Ill. Rev. Stat. 1991, Ch. 38, § 1401 et seq.
Mich. Comp. Laws Ann., 780.751 et seq.
Ore. Rev. Stat., 147.405 et seq.
R.I. Gen. Laws 1956, 12-28-1 et seq.
S.C. Code Ann. 1976, § 16-3-1510 et seq.
Tenn. Code Ann., 40-38-101 et seq.
Wyo. Stat. Ann., § 1-40-201 et seq.

**Victims' Asset Discovery Act (Criminal)**
Ill. Comp. Stat. 1992, Ch. 725, § 145/1 et seq.

**Victims Bill of Rights**
Cal. Const. 1979, Art. 1, § 28

**Victim's Bill of Rights (Drunk Driving)**
N.J. Stat. Ann., 39:4-50.9 et seq.

**Victims' Bill of Rights Act (Campus Sexual Assault)**
N.J. Stat. Ann., 18A:61E-1 et seq.

**Victims' Compensation Act**
Ill. Comp. Stat. 1992, Ch. 740, § 45/1 et seq.
Miss. Code Ann. 1972, § 99-41-1 et seq.

**Victims Compensation Act (Murrah Crime)**
Okla. Stat. Ann., Title 21, § 142.31 et seq.

**Victims Compensation Act (Therapist Sexual Misconduct)**
Tenn. Code Ann., 29-26-201 et seq.

**Victims' Compensation from the Proceeds of the Crime Act**
Tenn. Code Ann., 29-13-401 et seq.

**Victims of and Witnesses to Crimes and Aid to Law Enforcement Assistance Act**
Colo. Rev. Stat., 24-4.2-101 et seq.

**Victims of Child Abuse Act of 1990**
Nov. 29, 1990, P.L. 101-647, 18 U.S. Code §§ 403, 2258, 3509, 42 U.S. Code §§ 13001 to 13004, 13011 to 13014, 13021 to 13024, 13031, 13041, 13051 to 13055
Nov. 4, 1992, P.L. 102-586, 42 U.S. Code §§ 13001, 13001a, 13002 to 13004
Sept. 13, 1994, P.L. 103-322, 42 U.S. Code §§ 10601, 10602, 13012, 13014, 13021, 13024
Oct. 3, 1996, P.L. 104-235, 42 U.S. Code § 13004

**Victims of Crime Act**
Cal. Government Code § 13959 et seq.
Kan. Stat. Ann., 74-7333
Mont. Code Ann., 53-9-101 et seq.
N.M. Stat. Ann., 31-26-1 et seq.

**Victims of Crime Act of 1984**
Oct. 12, 1984, P.L. 98-473, 42 U.S. Code §§ 10601 nt., 10601- 10603
Aug. 27, 1986, P.L. 99-401, 42 U.S. Code §§ 10601, 10603, 10603a
Nov. 10, 1986, P.L. 99-646, 18 U.S. Code § 3150a; 42 U.S. Code §§ 10601, 10603, 10604
Nov. 18, 1988, P.L. 100-690, 42 U.S. Code §§ 10601 to 10605
Nov. 29, 1990, P.L. 101-647, 42 U.S. Code § 10601
Oct. 29, 1992, P.L. 102-572, 42 U.S. Code § 10601
Oct. 27, 1993, P.L. 103-121, 42 U.S. Code §§ 10601, 10603
Aug. 26, 1994, P.L. 103-317, 42 U.S. Code § 10603
Sept. 13, 1994, P.L. 103-322, 42 U.S. Code §§ 10601 et seq.
April 24, 1996, P.L. 104-132, 42 U.S. Code §§ 10601 to 10603, 10603b
July 3, 1996, P.L. 104-155, 42 U.S. Code § 10602
Sept. 30, 1996, P.L. 104-208, 42 U.S. Code § 10601
Oct. 3, 1996, P.L. 104-235, 42 U.S. Code § 10603a

**Victims of Crime Assistance Act**
Tenn. Public Acts 1986, Ch. 880

**Victims of Criminal Sexual Offenses Privacy Act (Children)**
Ill. Rev. Stat. 1991, Ch. 38, § 1451 et seq.

**Victims of Sexual Assault Act**
Wash. Rev. Code Ann., 70.125.010 et seq.

**Victims of Terrorism Compensation Act**
Aug. 27, 1986, P.L. 99-399, 5 U.S. Code §§ 5569, 5569 nt., 5570, 6325; 10 U.S. Code § 1051, 1051 nt., 1095, 1095 nt., 2181 to 2185; 37 U.S. Code §§ 559, 559 nt., 1013

**Victims of Violent Crime Compensation Act**
D.C. Code Ann., § 3-401 et seq.
Ind. Code Ann., 16-7-3.6-1 et seq.

**Victims' Reimbursement Act**
Ga. Code Ann., 48-1-10

**Victims Reparation Act (Crime)**
N.M. Stat. Ann., 31-24-1 et seq.

**Victims' Rights Act**
Alaska Laws 1991, Ch. 57
Okla. Stat. Ann., Title 21, § 142A et seq.

**Victim's Rights Act (Speedy Trial)**
Ga. Code Ann., 17-7-173

**Victims Rights and Restitution Act of 1990**
Nov. 29, 1990, P.L. 101-647, 42 U.S. Code §§ 10601 nt., 10606, 10606 nt., 10607
Sept. 13, 1994, P.L. 103-322, 42 U.S. Code §§ 10607, 14011

**Victims Rights Clarification Act of 1997**
March 19, 1997, P.L. 105-6, 18 U.S. Code § 3481 nt.

**Victims' Rights Implementation Act**
Ariz. Rev. Stat. Ann., § 13-4401 et seq.

**Victor Code of Ethics Local Law**
N.Y. Local Laws 1970, Town of Victor, p. 2904

**Victor Partial Exemption from Taxation of Certain Real Property Owned by Persons Sixty-Five Years of Age or Over Local Law**
N.Y. Local Laws 1971, Town of Victor, p. 3635

**Victor Retention of Assessors Local Law**
N.Y. Local Laws 1971, Town of Victor, p. 3637

**Victor Sign Law**
N.Y. Local Laws 1969, Town of Victor, p. 2154

**Victory Liberty Loan Acts**
March 3, 1919, Ch. 100, 40 Stat. 1309, 31 U.S. Code §§ 750, 753, 754, 763, 767, 774, 802, 803
March 2, 1923, Ch. 179, 42 Stat. 1427, 31 U.S. Code § 767

**Victory Motor Vehicle Act**
Wash. Laws 1943, Ch. 281

**Vidalia Onion Act**
Ga. Code Ann., 2-14-130 et seq.

**Video Consumer Privacy Act**
N.Y. General Business Law (Consol. Laws Ch. 20) § 670 et seq.

**Video Customer Service Act**
Cal. Government Code § 53088 et seq.

**Video Draw Poker Devices Control Law**
La. Rev. Stat. Ann., 33:4862.1 et seq.

**Video Draw Poker Machine Control Law**
Mont. Laws 1985, Ch. 720

**Video Game Machine Act**
S.C. Code Ann. 1976, § 12-21-2770 et seq.

**Video Movie Sales and Rentals Act**
Ill. Comp. Stat. 1992, Ch. 720, § 395/1 et seq.
Ill. Rev. Stat. 1991, Ch. 121 1/2, § 1351 et seq.

**Video Piracy Act**
N.M. Stat. Ann., 30-16B-1 et seq.

**Video Privacy Protection Act of 1988**
Nov. 5, 1988, P.L. 100-618, 18 U.S. Code § 2701 nt.

**Video Programming Municipal Tax Authorization Act**
Pa. Purdon's Stat., Title 72, § 6171 et seq.

**Video Provider and Cable Television Customer Service and Information Act**
Cal. Government Code § 53054 et seq.

**Vienna Parking Authority Act**
Va. Acts 1991, Ch. 446

**Vietnam Conflict Prisoners of War Compensation Act**
Pa. Cons. Stat., Title 51, § 20151 et seq.

**Vietnam Conflict Veterans' Adjusted Compensation Act**
N.D. Cent. Code, 37-25-01 et seq.

**Vietnam Conflict Veterans' Compensation Act**
Pa. Cons. Stat., Title 51, § 20121 et seq.

**Vietnam Era Veterans' Readjustment Assistance Act of 1972**
Oct. 24, 1972, P.L. 92-540, 86 Stat. 1074, 38 U.S. Code §§ 101, 102, 240, 241, 1502, 1504, 1507; 50 U.S. Code Appx. §§ 511, 591

**Vietnam Herbicides Information Act**
Pa. Cons. Stat., Title 51, § 20201 et seq.

**Vietnam Veteran Benefits Act**
Ore. Rev. Stat., 408.300 et seq.

**Vietnam Veterans' Act**
Ill. Rev. Stat. 1991, Ch. 126 1/2, § 201 et seq.

**Vietnam Veterans Bonus Act**
Alaska Stat. 1962, § 26.15.160
Conn. Gen. Stat. Ann., § 27-140a et seq.
Mich. Comp. Laws Ann., 35.1021 et seq.
R.I. Public Laws 1976, Ch. 81
S.D. Codified Laws 1967, 33-17-16 et seq.

**Vietnam Veterans Compensation Act**
Ill. Rev. Stat. 1991, Ch. 126 1/2, § 57.51 et seq.

**Vietnam Veterans Education Loan Act**
Neb. Rev. Stat. 1943, 80-801 et seq.

**Vietnam Veterans Employment Act (Burton-Stull)**
Cal. Government Code § 7280 et seq.

**Vietnam Veterans Health Initiative Act**
Pa. Cons. Stat., Title 51, § 20201 et seq.

**Vietnam Veterans Leadership Program Act**
Ill. Rev. Stat. 1991, Ch. 126 1/2, § 201 et seq.

**Vietnam Veterans' Memorial Act**
Fla. Stat. Ann., 240.258
Mich. Comp. Laws Ann., 35.1051 et seq.

**Vietnam Veterans National Medal Act**
Oct. 30, 1984, P.L. 98-566, 98 Stat. 2923

**Vietnam War Veterans Act**
Ill. Rev. Stat. 1987, Ch. 126 1/2, § 251 et seq.

**View by Jury Act**
Wash. Rev. Code Ann., 10.58.080

**Viewers Act**
Pa. 1911 Pamph. Laws 1123

**Village Act**
Mich. Comp. Laws Ann., 61.1 et seq.
Minn. Stat. Ann., 412.013 et seq.
N.J. Stat. Ann., 40:157-1 et seq.
N.Y. Consol. Laws, Ch. 64
Wis. Stat. 1989, 61.187 et seq.

**Village and City Planning Act**
Mich. Comp. Laws Ann., 125.31 et seq.

**Village and City Zoning Act**
Mich. Comp. Laws Ann., 125.581 et seq.

**Village and Township Public Improvements Act**
Mich. Comp. Laws Ann., 41.411 et seq.

**Village, City and Municipal Corporation Ground Water Permit Act**
Neb. Rev. Stat. 1943, 46-638 et seq.

**Village Election Validation Act**
Ill. Rev. Stat. 1991, Ch. 24, §§ 808d.10, 808d.11

**Village General Law Act**
Mich. Comp. Laws Ann., 74.1 et seq.

**Village Home Rule Act**
Mich. Comp. Laws Ann., 78.1 et seq.
N.Y. Municipal Home Rule Law (Consol. Laws Ch. 36A) § 1 et seq.

**Village Incorporation Act**
Alaska Stat. 1962, § 29.25.010 et seq.
Ill. Rev. Stat. 1991, Ch. 24, § 2-3-1 et seq.

**Village Incorporation Validation Act**
Ill. Rev. Stat. 1991, Ch. 24, §§ 808d.11m, 808d.12

**Village Library Act**
Ill. Rev. Stat. 1991, Ch. 81, § 16b.9 et seq.

**Village Library and Gymnasium Tax Act**
Ill. Rev. Stat. 1991, Ch. 81, § 73.9 et seq.

**Village Library Conversion Act**
Ill. Rev. Stat. 1991, Ch. 81, §§ 27.31h, 27.32

**Village of Nyack Parking Authority Act**
N.Y. Public Authorities Law (Consol. Laws Ch. 43A) § 1622a et seq.

**Village of Port Chester Parking Authority Act**
N.Y. Public Authorities Law (Consol. Laws Ch. 43A) § 1620a et seq.

**Village of Suffern Parking Authority Act**
N.Y. Public Authorities Law (Consol. Laws Ch. 43A) § 1600 et seq.

**Village Organization Act**
Minn. Stat. Ann., 412.013 et seq.

**Village Safe Water Act**
Alaska Stat. 1962, § 46.07.010 et seq.

**Village Zoning Act**
Neb. Rev. Stat. 1943, 19-901 et seq.

**Villages, Second and First Class Cities Combined Improvements Act**
Neb. Rev. Stat. 1943, 19-2408 et seq.

**Vincent-Strange Act (National Parks)**
Ky. Rev. Stat. 1962, 148.90 et seq.

**Vinegar Act**
W. Va. Code 1966, § 19-22-1 et seq.

**Vineyard Act**
Ohio Rev. Code 1953, 927.34 et seq.

**Vinous and Spirituous Liquor Floor Tax Law**
Pa. 1933 Ex. Pamph. Laws 5, No. 1

**Vinous and Spirituous Liquor Tax Law**
Pa. Purdon's Stat., Title 47, § 745 et seq.

**Vinson Naval Expansion Acts**
See Naval Expansion Acts

**Vinson Naval Parity Act**
See Naval Parity Act

**Vinson-Patman-McCormack Act**
See Adjusted Compensation Payment Act

**Vinson Priorities Act**
See Army Reorganization Acts

**Vinson-Trammel Parity Act**
March 27, 1934, Ch. 95, 48 Stat. 503 (See 10 U.S. Code §§ 2382, 7300, 7342, 7343; 40 U.S. Code § 474)
June 25, 1936, Ch. 812, 49 Stat. 1926 (See 10 U.S. Code §§ 2382, 7300)
April 3, 1939, Ch. 35, 53 Stat. 560 (See 10 U.S. Code §§ 2382, 7300)
Aug. 7, 1946, Ch. 770, 60 Stat. 867 (See 10 U.S. Code §§ 2382, 7300)

**Violation Disclosure Act**
N.J. Stat. Ann., 55:13A-20.1, 55:13A-20.2

**Violation Notice Posting Act (Building Code)**
Ill. Comp. Stat. 1992, Ch. 50, § 81-/0.01 et seq.

**Violence Against Women Act of 1994**
Sept. 13, 1994, P.L. 103-322, 42 U.S. Code § 13701 nt.

**Violence Prevention Act (Domestic)**
Cal. Family Code § 6200 et seq.
N.Y. Social Services Law (Consol. Laws Ch. 55) § 459a et seq.

**Violence Protection and School Safety Act**
Cal. Education Code 1976, § 32228 et seq.

**Violence Reduction and Extended Schoolday Activities Act**
Cal. Education Code 1976, § 58750 et seq.

**Violent and Sexual Offenders Act (DNA Detection of)**
Pa. Purdon's Stat., Title 35, § 7651.101 et seq.

**Violent Crime Control and Law Enforcement Act of 1994**
Sept. 13, 1994, P.L. 103-322, 42 U.S. Code § 13701 nt.
April 24, 1996, P.L. 104-132, 8 U.S. Code § 1252 nt.
April 26, 1996, P.L. 104-134, 18 U.S. Code § 3626 nt.; 42 U.S. Code §§ prec. 13701, 13701 to 13712, 14092
May 17, 1996, P.L. 104-145, 42 U.S. Code § 14071
Sept. 30, 1996, P.L. 104-208, 8 U.S. Code §§ 1158 nt., 1252 nt., 1258, 1324; 28 U.S. Code, Fed. R. Evid., Rule 413 nt.
Oct. 3, 1996, P.L. 104-236, 42 U.S. Code §§ 14071, 14072
Oct. 11, 1996, P.L. 104-294, 18 U.S. Code §§ 922, 924, 3553
Oct. 19, 1996, P.L. 104-316, 42 U.S. Code § 13753
Nov. 26, 1997, P.L. 105-119, 42 U.S. Code §§ 14071, 14072
Oct. 21, 1998, P.L. 105-277, 42 U.S. Code §§ 13705, 13823, 14072
Oct. 30, 1998, P.L. 105-314, 42 U.S. Code §§ 5601 nt., 5776a, 5776a nt., 5777, 14071

**Violent Crime Control Appropriations Act, 1995**

Aug. 26, 1994, P.L. 103-317, 108 Stat. 1777

**Violent Crime Victims Assistance Act**

Ill. Rev. Stat. 1991, Ch. 70, § 501 et seq.

**Violent Felony Offender Law**

N.Y. Criminal Procedure Law (Consol. Laws Ch. 11A) §§ 1.20, 100.15, 180.50, 180.70, 180.75, 190.60, 190.71, 200.50, 220.10, 220.30, 300.50, 310.85, 330.20, 400.15, 400.16, 510.15, 720.10, 720.15, 725.00 et seq.

N.Y. Executive Law 1951 (Consol. Laws Ch. 18) 510a, 510b, 530, 837, 837a

N.Y. Family Court Act §§ 249, 254a, 712, 731, 733, 734, 734A, 739, 744, 746

N.Y. Penal Law 1965 (Consol. Laws Ch. 40) §§ 10.00, Subd. 18, 30.00, 60.00, 60.05, 60.10, 70.00, 70.02, 70.04, 70.05, 70.06, 70.08, 70.10, 70.25, 70.30, 70.40

**Violent Persons Commitment Act (Sexually)**

Ill. Comp. Stat. 1992, Ch. 725, § 207/1 et seq.

**Violent Predator Act (Sexually)**

Iowa Code Ann., 709C.1 et seq.

**Violent Predator Incapacitation Act**

N.J. Stat. Ann., 2C:43-6.4

**Virgin Islands Acquisition Act**

March 3, 1917, Ch. 171, 39 Stat. 1132, 48 U.S. Code §§ 1391, 1392, 1394 to 1396

**Virgin Islands Corporation Act**

June 30, 1949, Ch. 285, 63 Stat. 350, 31 U.S. Code § 846; 48 U.S. Code §§ 1407 to 1407i

Oct. 4, 1961, P.L. 87-382, 75 Stat. 812, 48 U.S. Code § 1407e

**Virgin Islands Elective Governor Act**

Aug. 23, 1968, P.L. 90-496, 82 Stat. 837, 10 U.S. Code § 336; 48 U.S. Code §§ 1541, 1561, 1572 to 1575, 1591, 1593, 1595, 1597, 1599, 1641

**Virgin Islands Nonimmigrant Alien Adjustment Act of 1982**

Sept. 30, 1982, P.L. 97-271, 8 U.S. Code § 1255 nt.

Nov. 29, 1990, P.L. 101-649, 8 U.S. Code § 1255 nt.

**Virgin Islands Organic Act Amendments of 1959**

Sept. 16, 1959, P.L. 86-289, 73 Stat. 568, 48 U.S. Code §§ 1572, 1573, 1597, 1617

**Virgin Islands Permanent Government Act**

See Organic Act of the Virgin Islands of the United States

**Virginia Agricultural Foundation**

Va. Code 1950, § 31-22 et seq.

**Virginia City Charter**

Nev. Statutes 1862, Ch. 83, p. 84

Nev. Statutes 1865, Ch. 68, p. 209

**Virginia Compact of 1785**

Md. Laws 1785-86, Ch. 1

**Virginia Wilderness Act of 1984**

Oct. 30, 1984, P.L. 98-586, 98 Stat. 3105

**Virginians with Disabilities Act**

Va. Code 1950, § 51.01-1 et seq.

**Virus-Serum-Toxin Act**

March 4, 1913, Ch. 145, 21 U.S. Code §§ 151 et seq.

Dec. 23, 1985, P.L. 99-198, 21 U.S. Code §§ 151, 154, 154a, 157, 159

**Vision and Hearing Test Act (Child)**

Ill. Comp. Stat. 1992, Ch. 410, § 205/1 et seq.

**Vision Care Act (Consumer Access to)**

Wash. Rev. Code Ann., 18.195.900

**Vision Service Corporations Act**

N.D. Cent. Code, 26.1-17-01 et seq.

**Vision Service Plan Act**

Ill. Rev. Stat. 1991, Ch. 32, § 651 et seq.

Tenn. Code Ann., 56-31-101 et seq.

**Visionary Disabled Persons Law (Print Access Aids for)**
Tex. Government Code, § 441.111 et seq.

**Visitation Act (Grandparents)**
Me. Rev. Stat. Ann. 1964, Title 19, § 1001 et seq.
S.C. Code Ann. 1976, § 20-7-420 et seq.

**Visitation Privileges Act (Grandparents)**
N.M. Stat. Ann., 40-9-1 et seq.

**Visitation Program Act (Youthful Drunk Driver)**
Fla. Stat. Ann., 322.0602

**Visitation Rights Law (Grandparents)**
Miss. Code Ann. 1972, § 93-16-1 et seq.

**Visitor Travel and Hospitality Act**
La. Rev. Stat. Ann., 51:1252 et seq.

**Visitors Bureau and Convention Authority Act (Kingsland Area)**
Ga. Laws 1991, p. 4101

**Visitors Bureau and Convention Authority Act (Thomasville)**
Ga. Laws 1991 Ex. Sess., p. 434

**Visitors' Development Act**
Neb. Rev. Stat. 1943, 81-1245 et seq.

**Visual Artists Rights Act of 1990**
Dec. 1, 1990, P.L. 101-650, 17 U.S. Code §§ 101 et seq. generally, 301, 411, 412, 501, 506

**Visual Tag Act (Vehicles)**
Mass. Gen. Laws Ann., 90:20C

**Visually Impaired, Auditorily Impaired, and Learning Disabled Students Act**
N.J. Stat. Ann., 18A:72H-1 et seq.

**Visually Impaired Voter Assistance Act**
Cal. Elections Code § 225 et seq.

**Vital Areas Law**
Ga. Laws 1973, p. 935

**Vital Records Act**
Ill. Rev. Stat. 1991, Ch. 111 1/2, § 73-1 et seq.
Md. Ann. Code 1974, Art. HG, § 4-201 et seq.
Tenn. Code Ann., 68-3-101 et seq.
Wyo. Stat. Ann., § 35-1-401 et seq.

**Vital Statistics Act**
See also Uniform Vital Statistics Act
Alaska Stat. 1962, § 18.50.010 et seq.
Ariz. Rev. Stat. Ann., § 36-301 et seq.
Ark. Code Ann. 1987, 20-18-102 et seq.
Cal. Health and Safety Code § 10000 et seq.
Colo. Rev. Stat., 25-2-101 et seq.
Conn. Gen. Stat. Ann., § 7-36 et seq.
Del. Code of 1974, Title 16, § 3101 et seq.
Fla. Stat. Ann., 382.001 et seq.
Ga. Code Ann., 31-10-1 et seq.
Haw. Rev. Stat. Ann., § 338-1 et seq.
Ida. Code 1947, 39-240 et seq.
Ill. Rev. Stat. 1991, Ch. 111 1/2, § 73-1 et seq.
Iowa Code Ann., 144.1 et seq.
Kan. Stat. Ann., 65-2401 et seq.
Ky. Rev. Stat. 1971, 213.011 et seq.
La. Rev. Stat. Ann., 40:32 et seq.
Md. Ann. Code 1974, Art. H6, § 4-201 et seq.
Mich. Comp. Laws Ann., 333.2801 et seq.
Minn. Stat. Ann., 144.111 et seq.
Mo. Rev. Stat., 193.005 et seq.
Mont. Code Ann. 1991, 50-15-101 et seq.
N.C. Gen. Stat. 1943, § 130A-90 et seq.
N.D. Cent. Code, 23-02.1-01 et seq.
N.H. Rev. Stat. 1955, 126:1 et seq.
N.J. Stat. Ann., 26:8-1
N.M. Stat. Ann., 24-14-1 et seq.
N.Y. Public Health Law 1953 (Consol. Laws Ch. 45) § 4100 et seq.
Ohio Rev. Code 1953, 3705.01 et seq.
Okla. Stat. Ann., Title 63, § 1-301 et seq.
Ore. Rev. Stat., 432.005 et seq.
Pa. Purdon's Stat., Title 35, § 450.101 et seq.
P.R. Laws Ann. 1954, Title 24, § 1041 et seq.
R.I. Gen. Laws 1956, 23-3-1 et seq.
S.D. Codified Laws 1967, 34-25-1 et seq.
Tex. Health and Safety Code, § 191.001 et seq.

Utah Code Ann. 1953, 26-2-1 et seq.
Vt. Stat. Ann., Title 18, § 5001 et seq.
Wash. Rev. Code Ann., 70.58.005 et seq.
W. Va. Code 1966, § 16-5-1 et seq.
Wyo. Stat. Ann., § 35-1-401 et seq.

**Vital Statistics Registry Act**
P.R. Laws Ann. 1954, Title 24, § 1041

**Viticulture Act**
Del. Code of 1974, Title 3, § 501 et seq.

**Viticulture Policy Act**
Fla. Stat. Ann., 599.0005, 599.001 et seq.
Tenn. Code Ann., 43-30-101 et seq.

**Vivisection Act**
Mich. Comp. Laws Ann., 333.2671 et seq.

**Vocational and Private Business Schools Act**
Ill. Rev. Stat. 1991, Ch. 144, § 136 et seq.

**Vocational and Professional Licensing Act**
See also Uniform Vocational and Professional Licensing Act

**Vocational and Technical Education Act**
Cal. Education Code 1976, § 52380 et seq.

**Vocational and Technical Institute Act**
N.M. Stat. Ann., 21-16-1 et seq.

**Vocational and Technical Training Law (Junior College)**
Miss. Code Ann. 1972, § 37-29-161 et seq.

**Vocational and Trade School Act (Regional)**
Ala. Code 1975, § 16-60-190 et seq.

**Vocational and Training Act**
Cal. Education Code 1976, § 12051 et seq.

**Vocational Capital Improvements Act**
N.M. Stat. Ann. 1953, 73-43-1 et seq.

**Vocational Education Act (Council on)**
Ill. Comp. Stat. 1992, Ch. 105, § 420/0.01 et seq.

**Vocational Education Act (Federal)**
Miss. Code Ann. 1972, § 37-33-157

**Vocational Education Act of 1917**
Feb. 23, 1917, Ch. 114, 39 Stat. 929, 20 U.S. Code §§ 11 to 15, 16 to 28
June 25, 1959, P.L. 86-70, 73 Stat. 144, 20 U.S. Code § 14
July 12, 1960, P.L. 86-624, 74 Stat. 414, 20 U.S. Code §§ 12, 14
Dec. 21, 1995, P.L. 104-66, 20 U.S. Code § 28

**Vocational Education Act of 1917-1963**
Colo. Rev. Stat. 1963, 146-1-1 et seq.
Ill. Rev. Stat. 1991, Ch. 122, § 693h et seq.
Ind. Code Ann., 20-10.1-6-1 et seq.
Mich. Comp. Laws Ann., 395.1 et seq.
S.D. Codified Laws 1967, 13-39-3 et seq.
Tex. Education Code, § 31.01 et seq.
Wyo. Stat. Ann., § 21-12-101 et seq.

**Vocational Education Act of 1936**
See also, Vocational Education Act of 1946;
June 8, 1936, Ch. 541, 49 Stat. 1488 (See 20 U.S. Code §§ 1241 et seq.)

**Vocational Education Act of 1946**
See also Vocational Education Act Of 1936
See Vocational Education Act of 1946
Aug. 1, 1946, Ch. 725, 60 Stat. 775 (See 20 U.S. Code §§ 1241 et seq.)
Aug. 2, 1956, Ch. 871, 70 Stat. 925 (See 20 U.S. Code §§ 1241 et seq.)
Aug. 8, 1956, Ch. 1039, 70 Stat. 1126
Sept. 2, 1958, P.L. 85-864, 72 Stat. 1597
June 25, 1959, P.L. 86-70, 73 Stat. 144
July 12, 1960, P.L. 86-624, 74 Stat. 414
April 24, 1961, P.L. 87-22, 75 Stat. 44
Oct. 3, 1961, P.L. 87-344, 75 Stat. 760
Dec. 18, 1963, P.L. 88-210, 77 Stat. 411

**Vocational Education Act of 1963**
See Carl D. Perkins Vocational Education Act
Dec. 18, 1963, P.L. 88-210, 77 Stat. 403 (See 20 U.S. Code §§ 1241 et seq.)
Oct. 16, 1968, P.L. 90-576, 82 Stat. 1064, 20 U.S. Code §§ 1241 to 1248, 1261 to 1264, 1281 to 1284, 1301 to 1305, 1321 to 1323, 1341, 1352 to 1355, 1371 to 1374, 1391
April 13, 1970, P.L. 91-230, 84 Stat. 188, 20 U.S. Code §§ 1242 to 1244, 1322, 1323, 1341, 1371, 1373, 1391

*Continued*

June 3, 1977, P.L. 95-40, 20 U.S. Code § 2301 et seq.
Oct. 17, 1979, P.L. 96-88, 20 U.S. Code § 2390

**Vocational Education Amendments of 1958**
Oct. 19, 1984, P.L. 98-524, 20 U.S. Code § 11 nt.

**Vocational Education Amendments of 1968**
Oct. 16, 1968, P.L. 90-576, 82 Stat. 1064, 20 U.S. Code §§ 6, 11 nt., 15i nt., 240, 241c, 611, 886 nt., 1119c to 1119c-4, 1202, 1221, 1226, 1241- -1248 and others; 42 U.S. Code § 2809 nt.
April 13, 1970, P.L. 91-230, 84 Stat. 189, 20 U.S. Code § 11 nt.
June 3, 1977, P.L. 95-40, 20 U.S. Code § 11 nt.
Oct. 30, 1998, P.L. 105-332, 20 U.S. Code § 11 nt.

**Vocational Education and Private Postsecondary Reform Act**
Cal. Education Code 1976, § 94700 et seq.

**Vocational Education and Rehabilitation Act**
N.D. Cent. Code, 15-20.1-01 et seq.

**Vocational Education Expansion and Development Act**
R.I. Public Laws 1963, Ch. 199

**Vocational Education Loan Guarantee Act**
Colo. Rev. Stat., 23-3-101 et seq.

**Vocational Educational Act**
Aug. 6, 1979, P.L. 96-46, 20 U.S. Code §§ 2308, 2310

**Vocational Educational Act of 1934**
May 21, 1934, Ch. 324, 48 Stat. 792

**Vocational Educational Authorization Act (Private)**
Neb. Rev. Stat. 1943, 79-2801 et seq.

**Vocational Evaluation and Work Adjustment Act**
Cal. Welfare and Institutions Code §§ 19325, 19326

**Vocational Improvement Fund Act**
Fla. Stat. Ann., 233.069

**Vocational Nurse Act**
Tex. Rev. Civ. Stat., Art. 4528c

**Vocational Nursing Practice Act**
Cal. Business and Professions Code § 2840 et seq.

**Vocational Rehabilitation Act**
Ark. Code Ann. 1987, 20-79-201 et seq.
Fla. Stat. Ann., 413.20 et seq.
Ga. Code Ann., 49-9-1 et seq.
Haw. Rev. Stat. Ann., § 348-1 et seq.
Iowa Code Ann., 259.1 et seq.
Ky. Rev. Stat. 1971, 163.020 et seq.
Me. Rev. Stat. Ann. 1964, Title 20, § 3051 et seq.
Mich. Comp. Laws Ann., 395.81 et seq.
Miss. Code Ann. 1972, § 37-33-11 et seq.
Mont. Rev. Code 1947, 41-801 et seq.
N.D. Cent. Code, 50-06.1-01 et seq.
N.J. Rev. Stat. 1937, 34:16-20 et seq.
N.Y. Education Law 1947 (Consol. Laws Ch. 16) § 1001 et seq.
Ore. Rev. Stat., 344.511 et seq.
Pa. Purdon's Stat., Title 43, § 681.1 et seq.
P.R. Laws Ann. 1954, Title 18, § 1046 et seq.
R.I. Gen. Laws 1956, 42-12-8 et seq.
S.C. Code Ann. 1976, § 43-31-10 et seq.
S.D. Codified Laws 1967, 28-9-23 et seq.
Tenn. Code Ann., 49-11-601 et seq.
Utah Code Ann. 1953, 53a-24-101 et seq.
Vt. Stat. Ann., Title 16, § 3011 et seq.
Wash. Rev. Code Ann., 74.29.005 et seq.
Wis. Stat. 1989, 47.01

**Vocational Rehabilitation Act (Endowment for)**
Fla. Stat. Ann., 413.615

**Vocational Rehabilitation Acts**
June 27, 1918, Ch. 107, 40 Stat. 617
July 11, 1919, Ch. 12, 41 Stat. 158
June 2, 1920, Ch. 219, 41 Stat. 735, 29 U.S. Code §§ 31 to 41
July 6, 1943, Ch. 190, 57 Stat. 374, 29 U.S. Code §§ 31 to 41

Aug. 3, 1954, Ch. 655, 68 Stat. 662, 29 U.S. Code §§ 31 to 42

Aug. 1, 1956, Ch. 852, 70 Stat. 910, 29 U.S. Code § 41

Aug. 3, 1956, Ch. 903, 70 Stat. 956, 29 U.S. Code § 34

Aug. 28, 1957, P.L. 85-198, 71 Stat. 473, 29 U.S. Code §§ 34, 37

Aug. 28, 1957, P.L. 85-213, 71 Stat. 488, 29 U.S. Code § 34

June 25, 1959, P.L. 86-70, 73 Stat. 147, 29 U.S. Code § 41

July 12, 1960, P.L. 86-624, 74 Stat. 416, 29 U.S. Code § 41

Sept. 10, 1965, P.L. 89-178, 79 Stat. 676, 29 U.S. Code § 42

Nov. 8, 1965, P.L. 89-333, 79 Stat. 1282, 29 U.S. Code §§ 31 to 35, 37, 38, 41 to 41d, 42

Oct. 3, 1967, P.L. 90-99, 81 Stat. 250, 29 U.S. Code §§ 31, 34, 35, 41, 42a, 42b

July 7, 1968, P.L. 90-391, 82 Stat. 298, 29 U.S. Code §§ 31 to 35, 37, 41 to 41b, 42-1 to 42b

Dec. 31, 1970, P.L. 91-610, 84 Stat. 1817, 29 U.S. Code §§ 31, 34 , 41a, 41b, 42-1

**Vocational Rehabilitation and Industrial Aid for the Blind Act**

Ind. Code Ann., 16-7-9-1 et seq.

**Vocational Rehabilitation of the Blind Act**

Miss. Code Ann. 1972, 37-33-51 et seq.

Tenn. Code Ann., 71-4-601 et seq.

Tex. Human Resources Code, § 91.051 et seq.

**Vocational School Act**

Ill. Rev. Stat. 1991, Ch. 122, § 694 et seq.

Iowa Code Ann., 280A.1 et seq.

Wis. Stat. 1989, 38.001 et seq.

**Vocational School Act (Private)**

Colo. Rev. Stat., 12-59-101 et seq.

**Vocational School Licensing Law**

Ore. Rev. Stat., 345.010 et seq.

**Vocational Schools and Salesmen Act**

Ore. Rev. Stat., 345.010 et seq.

**Vocational-Technical Education Act**

Tex. Education Code § 31.01 et seq.

**Vocational-Technical Equipment Act (Updating)**

Pa. Cons. Stat., Title 24, § 5801 et seq.

**Vocational-Technical High School Construction Act**

Del. Laws Vol. 59, p. 891, Ch. 259

**Vocational Trade School Building Authority Act**

Ga. Code Ann., 20-20-544

**Voight Filled Milk Act**

Wis. Stat. 1989, 97.48

**Voir Dire Act (Prospective Jurors)**

Ga. Code Ann., 15-12-164

**Volker-Metcalf Act (Drug Addiction)**

N.Y. Mental Hygiene Law 1972 (Consol. Laws Ch. 27) § 19.01 et seq.

**Volstead Act**

Oct. 28, 1919, Ch. 85, 41 Stat. 305

**Volstead Act (Drainage under State Laws)**

May 20, 1908, Ch. 181, 35 Stat. 169, 43 U.S. Code §§ 1021 to 1027

**Volume Cap Allocation Act**

Utah Code Ann. 1953, Miscellanous Superseded Code Provisions, 11-7a-1 et seq.

Utah Code Ann. 1953, 9-4-501 et seq.

**Voluntary Action Act (Governor's Office)**

Ill. Rev. Stat. 1991, Ch. 127, § 3800 et seq.

**Voluntary Admission Procedures Act (Mental Hospital)**

Okla. Stat. Ann., Title 43A, § 5-301 et seq.

**Voluntary Alternative Dispute Resolution Act**

Del. Code of 1974, Title 6, § 7701 et seq.

**Voluntary Appraisal Standards and Appraiser Certification Law**
Iowa Code Ann., 117B.1 et seq.

**Voluntary Apprenticeship Act**
La. Rev. Stat. Ann., 23:381 et seq.
Me. Rev. Stat. Ann. 1964, Title 26, § 1001 et seq.
Nev. Rev. Stat. 1979 Reprint, 610.010 et seq.
S.C. Code Ann. 1976, § 41-21-10 et seq.

**Voluntary Arbitration Act**
Cal. Code of Civil Procedure § 1280 et seq.

**Voluntary Assignment Act**
Ill. Rev. Stat. 1937, Ch. 10 3/4

**Voluntary Basic Health Insurance Coverage Act**
Miss. Code Ann. 1972, § 83-61-1 et seq.

**Voluntary Basic Health Insurance Coverage Law**
Miss. Code Ann. 1972, § 83-61-1 et seq.

**Voluntary Certification Act (Real Estate Appraisal)**
Ky. Rev. Stat. 1971, 324A.010 et seq.

**Voluntary Cleanup and Redevelopment Act**
Mont. Code Ann., 75-10-730 et seq.

**Voluntary Cleanup and Redevelopment Act (Voluntary)**
Miss. Code Ann. 1972, § 49-35-1 et seq.

**Voluntary Community Property Act**
Okla. Laws 1939, p. 356

**Voluntary Conservation Easement Act**
Mont. Code Ann. 1991, 76-6-101 et seq.

**Voluntary Consolidation and Annexation Incentive Plan**
Mont. Code Ann. 1991, 20-6-401 et seq.

**Voluntary Declaration of Paternity Act**
Utah Code Ann. 1953, 78-45e-1 et seq.

**Voluntary Disclosure and Exchange of Y2K Readiness Information**
Va. Laws 1999, Ch. 859

**Voluntary Dissolution Act (Corporations)**
Ill. Rev. Stat. 1991, Ch. 32, § 12.05 et seq.

**Voluntary Education Service Agencies Act**
Va. Code 1950, § 22-351 et seq.

**Voluntary Employee Commute Options Emission Reduction Credit Act**
Ill. Comp. Stat. 1992, Ch. 625, § 33/1 et seq.

**Voluntary Environmental Audit Act**
Mont. Code Ann., 75-1-1201 et seq.

**Voluntary Fish Products Inspection Act**
Me. Rev. Stat. Ann. 1964, Title 12, § 4681 et seq.

**Voluntary Health Facility and Clinic Philanthropic Support Act**
Cal. Health and Safety Code § 448 et seq.

**Voluntary Health Services Plan Act**
Ill. Rev. Stat. 1991, Ch. 32, § 595 et seq.

**Voluntary Home Mortgage Credit Act**
Aug. 2, 1954, Ch. 649, 68 Stat. 637, 12 U.S. Code §§ 1750a to 1750jj
June 29, 1957, P.L. 85-66, 71 Stat. 209, 12 U.S. Code § 1750jj
July 12, 1957, P.L. 85-104, 71 Stat. 304, 12 U.S. Code § 1750jj
Sept. 2, 1958, P.L. 85-857, 72 Stat. 1266, 12 U.S. Code §§ 1750bb , 1750gg
July 31, 1959, P.L. 86-119, 73 Stat. 266, 12 U.S. Code § 1750jj

**Voluntary Inspection of Meat, Meat Products and Meat By-Products Law**
N.C. Gen. Stat. 1943, § 106-549.15 et seq.

**Voluntary Nonprofit Health Service Act**
Pa. Purdon's Stat., Title 40, § 1551 et seq.

**Voluntary Payroll Deductions Act**
Ill. Rev. Stat. 1985, Ch. 15, § 501 et seq.

**Voluntary Poultry Inspection Act**
N.C. Gen. Stat. 1943, § 106-549.1 et seq.
Ore. Rev. Stat. 1953, 619.410 et seq.

**Voluntary Pupil Integration Act**
Cal. Education Code 1976, §§ 42248, 42249

**Voluntary Redevelopment Act (Brownfields)**
Okla. Stat. Ann., Title 27A, § 2-15-101 et seq.

**Voluntary Remediation Act**
N.J. Stat. Ann., 74-4G-1 to 74-4G-12

**Voluntary Retirement Pension Act**
N.J. Stat. Ann., 43:12-1.12 et seq.

**Voluntary School Consolidation Act**
Okla. Stat. Ann., Title 70, § 7-201 et seq.

**Voluntary Separation Act**
Md. Ann. Code 1974, Art. CJ, § 3-601 et seq.

**Voluntary Service Acts**
May 1, 1884, Ch. 37, 23 Stat. 15
March 3, 1905, Ch. 1484, 33 Stat. 1257, 31 U.S. Code § 665; 44 U.S. Code § 219a
Feb. 27, 1906, Ch. 510, 34 Stat. 49, 31 U.S. Code § 665

**Voluntary Sterilization Act**
Ga. Code Ann., 31-20-1 et seq.
Mont. Rev. Code 1947, 69-6401 et seq.
N.C. Gen. Stat. 1943, § 90-271 et seq.

**Voluntary Trade Tribunal Act**
Pa. Cons. Stat., Title 42, § 7341 et seq.

**Voluntary Zoning Law**
Mont. Code Ann., 76-2-101 et seq., 76-2-201 et seq.

**Volunteer Ambulance Workers' Benefit Law**
N.Y. Volunteer Firemen's Benefit Law (Consol. Laws Ch. 64B) § 1 et seq.

**Volunteer and Mentor Service Act (Academic)**
Cal. Government Code § 96100 et seq.

**Volunteer Army Act**
April 22, 1898, Ch. 187, 30 Stat. 361

**Volunteer Employment Act (Civil War)**
July 22, 1861, Ch. 9, 12 Stat. 268

**Volunteer Fire Company Ambulance Service and Rescue Squad Assistance Act**
Pa. Purdon's Stat., Title 72, § 3943.1 et seq.

**Volunteer Fire Protection Association Act**
Ill. Rev. Stat. 1991, Ch. 127 1/2, § 901 et seq.

**Volunteer Firefighter and Rescue Squad Worker Protection Act**
Del. Code of 1974, Title 19, § 1621 et seq.

**Volunteer Firefighters Act**
Okla. Stat. Ann., Title 11, § 29-201 et seq.

**Volunteer Firefighters' Compensation Act**
Mont. Code Ann. 1991, 19-12-101 et seq.

**Volunteer Firefighters Length of Service Award Act**
Cal. Government Code § 50950 et seq.

**Volunteer Firefighters Relief Association Act**
Pa. Purdon's Stat., Title 53, § 8501 et seq.

**Volunteer Firefighters Retirement Act**
Minn. Stat. Ann., 424A.01 et seq.
N.M. Stat. 1978, 10-11A-1 et seq.

**Volunteer Firefighters Retirement Act (Statewide)**
Tex. Rev. Civ. Stat., Art. 6243e.3

**Volunteer Firefighting Rescue Unit Use Act**
Ill. Rev. Stat. 1989, Ch. 127, § 288.9 et seq.

**Volunteer Firemen's Benefit Act**
N.Y. Consol. Laws, Ch. 64A

**Volunteer Firemen's Dependents Act**
Ohio Rev. Code 1953, 146.01 et seq.

**Volunteer Firemen's Pension Fund Act**
Wyo. Stat. Ann., § 35-9-601 et seq.

**Volunteer Firemen's Relief and Pension Act**
Wash. Rev. Code Ann., 41.24.010 et seq.

**Volunteer Firemen's Relief Association Act**
Pa. Purdon's Stat., Title 53, § 8501 et seq.

**Volunteer Firemen's Relief Association Guidelines Act**
Minn. Stat. Ann., 69.771 et seq.

**Volunteer Health Services Act**
Pa. Purdon's Stat., Title 35, § 449.41 et seq.
Tenn. Code Ann., 63-6-701 et seq.

**Volunteer Immunity Act**
Ark. Code Ann. 1987, No. 390

**Volunteer Leave Act (Disaster Service)**
Del. Code of 1974, Title 29, § 6001 et seq.
Fla. Stat. Ann., 110.120
Kan. Stat. Ann., 75-5546 et seq.
R.I. Gen. Laws 1956, 28-49-1 et seq.

**Volunteer Medical Professional Act**
Ala. Acts 1998, No. 297

**Volunteer Protection Act**
Fla. Stat. Ann., 768.1355
Mont. Code Ann., 27-1-732

**Volunteer Protection Act of 1997**
June 18, 1997, P.L. 105-19, 42 U.S. Code § 14501 nt.

**Volunteer Public Education Trust Fund Act**
Tenn. Code Ann., 49-3-401 et seq.

**Volunteer Services Act**
Ala. Code 1975, § 6-5-336
Ala. Code 1975, § 6-5-336
Colo. Rev. Stat., 13-21-115.5
D.C. Code Ann., § 1-304 et seq.
Md. Ann. Code 1974, Art. CJ, § 5-407

**Volunteer State Workers Act**
Utah Code Ann. 1953, 67.20-1 et seq.

**Volunteer Workers' Compensation Act (Civil Defense)**
N.Y. Workers' Compensation Law (Consol. Laws Ch. 67) § 300 et seq.

**Volunteerism Act**
Okla. Stat. Ann., Title 74, § 8001 et seq.

**Volunteerism and Citizens Service Act (Center for)**
Wash. Rev. Code Ann., 43.150.020

**Volunteers Act (Government)**
Cal. Government Code § 3110 et seq.
S.C. Code Ann. 1976, § 8-25-10 et seq.

**Volunteers Act (Service Corps)**
P.R. Laws Ann. 1954, Title 18, § 1411 et seq.

**Volunteers for Children Act**
Oct. 9, 1998, P.L. 105-251, Title II, Subtitle B, 112 Stat. 1885, 42 U.S. Code § 5101 nt.

**Volunteers in Medicine Health Care Act**
Ga. Code Ann., 43-34-45.1

**Volunteers in the National Forest Act of 1972**
May 18, 1972, P.L. 92-300, 16 U.S. Code § 588a nt.
May 9, 1990, P.L. 101-286, 16 U.S. Code § 588c

**Volunteers in the Parks Act of 1969**
July 29, 1970, P.L. 91-357, 84 Stat. 472, 16 U.S. Code §§ 18g to 18j
Oct. 24, 1984, P.L. 98-540, 16 U.S. Code §§ 18j, 18y
May 9, 1990, P.L. 101-286, 16 U.S. Code § 18i
Nov. 12, 1996, P.L. 104-333, 16 U.S. Code § 18j

**Volunteers Program Act (Registered)**
Ark. Code Ann. 1987, 6-22-101 et seq.

**Volusia County-Daytona Beach Improvement Authority Act**
Fla. Special Laws 1951, Ch. 51-27963

**Volusia County Permanent Registration Act**
Fla. Laws 1949, Ch. 49-25460

**Volusia County School Building Authority Act**
Fla. Special Laws 1951, Ch. 27950

**Volusia County Waste Collection and Disposal System Act**
Fla. Special Laws 1965, Ch. 65-2357

**Volusia County Water and Sewer District Law**
Fla. Special Laws 1970, Ch. 70-971

**Volusia County Water District Act**
Fla. Special Laws 1951, Ch. 27960

**Voorhees Act (Referendum)**
N.J. Stat. Ann., 40:123-1 et seq.

**Voorhees Franchise Tax Act**
N.J. Stat. Ann., 54:30A-16 et seq.

**Voorhis Anti-Propaganda Act**
Oct. 17, 1940, Ch. 897, 54 Stat. 1201 (See 18 U.S. Code § 2386)

**Vorys Act (Budget)**
Ohio Laws Vol. 111, p. 371

**Vote Act (County Unit)**
Ga. Code 1933, 34-1501 et seq.

**Vote Corruption Act**
La. Rev. Stat. Ann., 15:468

**Voter Law (Confined)**
Neb. Rev. Stat. 1943, 32-1241

**Voter Protection Act**
Fla. Stat. Ann., 97.012, Subsec. 5, 97.021, Subsec. 26, 97.021, Subsec. 27, 101.015 et seq.

**Voter Records System Act (Automated)**
N.M. Stat. Ann., 1-5-1 et seq.

**Voter Registration Act**
Fla. Stat. Ann., 97.032 et seq.
Pa. Purdon's Stat., Title 25, § 961.101 et seq.

**Voter Registration Act of 1975 (Moscone-Keysor)**
Cal. Statutes 1950, 3rd. Ex. Sess., Ch. 12, p. 19

**Voter Registration by Mail Act**
S.C. Code Ann. 1976, § 7-5-155 et seq.

**Voters Act**
S.C. Code Ann. 1976, § 7-5-10 et seq.

**Voters Act (Absentee)**
Me. Rev. Stat. Ann. 1964, Title 21-A, § 751 et seq.
Mont. Code Ann. 1991, 13-13-201 et seq.
S.C. Code Ann. 1976, § 7-15-10 et seq.
Vt. Stat. Ann., Title 17, § 2531 et seq.

**Voter's Bill of Rights**
P.R. Laws Ann. 1954, Title 16, § 3051

**Voters Law (War)**
Cal. Statutes 1950, 3rd Ex. Sess., Ch. 12, p. 19

**Voters' Qualification Act**
Alaska Stat. 1962, § 15.05.010 et seq.
D.C. Code Ann., § 1-1302
La. Rev. Stat. Ann., 18:101
Okla. Stat. Ann., Title 26, § 4-101 et seq.

**Voters' Qualification Amendment**
Ala. General Acts 1951, p. 760, No. 426

**Voters' Registration Act**
Ala. Code 1975, § 17-4-120 et seq.
Alaska Stat. 1962, § 15.07.010 et seq.
Ariz. Rev. Stat. Ann., § 16-101 et seq.
Cal. Elections Code 1976, § 300 et seq.
Colo. Rev. Stat., 1-2-201 et seq.
Conn. Gen. Stat. Ann., § 9-12 et seq.
D.C. Code Ann., § 1-1311
Del. Code of 1974, Title 15, § 1101 et seq.
Fla. Stat. Ann., 97.011 et seq.
Ga. Code Ann., 21-2-210 et seq.
Haw. Rev. Stat. Ann., § 11-11 et seq.
Ida. Code 1947, 34-401 et seq.
Ind. Code Ann., 3-1-7-1 et seq.
Iowa Code Ann., 48.1 et seq.
Kan. Stat. Ann., 25-2301 et seq.
*Continued*

Ky. Rev. Stat. 1971, 116.013 et seq.
La. Rev. Stat. Ann., 18:101 et seq.
Mass. Gen. Laws Ann., 51:1 et seq.
Md. Ann. Code 1957, Art. 33, § 3-1 et seq.
Me. Rev. Stat. Ann. 1964, Title 21, § 41 et seq.
Mich. Comp. Laws Ann., 168.491 et seq.
Minn. Stat. Ann., 201.01 et seq.
Miss. Code Ann. 1972, § 23-5-1 et seq.
Mo. Rev. Stat. 115.132 et seq.
Mont. Code Ann. 1991, 13-2-102 et seq.
N.C. Gen. Stat. 1943, § 163-65 et seq.
N.D. Cent. Code, 40-21-10
Neb. Rev. Stat. 1943, 32-216 et seq.
Nev. Rev. Stat. 1979 Reprint, 293.485 et seq.
N.H. Rev. Stat. 1955, 654:7 et seq.
N.J. Stat. Ann., 19:31-1 et seq.
N.M. Stat. Ann., 1-4-1 et seq.
N.Y. Election Law 1976 (Consol. Laws Ch. 17) § 5-100 et seq.
Ohio Rev. Code 1953, 3503.06 et seq.
Okla. Stat. Ann., Title 26, § 4-101 et seq.
Ore. Rev. Stat., 247.012 et seq.
P.R. Laws Ann. 1954, Title 16, § 2181 et seq.
R.I. Gen. Laws 1956, 17-9-1 et seq.
S.C. Code Ann. 1976, § 7-5-10 et seq.
S.D. Codified Laws 1967, 12-4-1 et seq.
Tenn. Code Ann., 2-2-101 et seq.
Tex. Election Code Art., § 12.001 et seq.
Utah Code Ann. 1953, 20-2-1 et seq.
Va. Code 1950, § 24.1-41 et seq.
Vt. Stat. Ann., Title 17, § 2121 et seq.
Wash. Rev. Code Ann., 29.07.010 et seq.
Wis. Stat. 1989, 6.26 et seq.
W. Va. Code 1966, § 3-2-1 et seq.
Wyo. Stat. Ann., § 22-3-101 et seq.

**Voting Accessibility for the Elderly and Handicapped Act**
Sept. 28, 1984, P.L. 98-435, 98 Stat. 1678, 42 U.S. Code § 1973ee et seq.

**Voting Act (Armed Forces)**
R.I. Gen. Laws 1956, 17-21.1-1 et seq.

**Voting Act (Corporate Stockholders)**
Ga. Code Ann., 14-2-117

**Voting Act (Mail-in)**
Mo. Rev. Stat., 115.650 et seq.

**Voting Act (New Residents)**
Neb. Rev. Stat. 1943, 32-1301.01 et seq.

**Voting Act (Youth)**
Mont. Laws 1991, Ch. 348

**Voting and Registration of Electors Act (Military Services)**
Utah Code Ann. 1953, 20-17-1 et seq.

**Voting Assistance Act**
N.M. Stat. Ann., 1-12-12 et seq.

**Voting Boundary Commission Act**
Wash. Rev. Code Ann., 29.70.010 et seq.

**Voting by New or Former Residents in Presidential Elections Act**
Neb. Rev. Stat. 1943, 32-1302 et seq.

**Voting by New Residents in Presidential Elections Act**
Haw. Rev. Laws 1955, § 11-230 et seq.
Neb. Rev. Stat. 1943, 32-1301.01 et seq.

**Voting Device Act (House)**
Ill. Rev. Stat. 1991, Ch. 63, § 100.9 et seq.

**Voting Equipment Acquisition Act**
Fla. Stat. Ann., 101.292 et seq.

**Voting Machine Act**
Ala. Code 1975, § 17-9-1 et seq.
Ark. Stat. 1947, 3-1201 et seq.
Cal. Elections Code 1976, § 15300 et seq.
Del. Code of 1974, Title 15, § 5001 et seq.
Ill. Rev. Stat. 1991, Ch. 46, § 24-1 et seq.
Ind. Code Ann., 3-11-12-1 et seq.
Ky. Rev. Stat. 1971, 117.105 et seq.
La. Rev. Stat. Ann., 18:1351 et seq.
Md. Ann. Code 1957, Art. 33, § 16-1 et seq.
Mich. Comp. Laws Ann., 168.770 et seq.
Mo. Rev. Stat., 115.225 et seq.
Mont. Code Ann. 1991, 13-17-101 et seq.
N.D. Cent. Code, 16.1-06-10 et seq.
N.H. Rev. Stat. 1955, 656:40
N.J. Stat. Ann., 19:48-1 et seq.

N.M. Stat. Ann., 1-9-1 et seq.
Ore. Rev. Stat., 258.005 et seq.
Pa. Purdon's Stat., Title 25, § 3001 et seq.
R.I. Gen. Laws 1956, 17-19-1 et seq.
S.D. Codified Laws 1967, 12-17-1 et seq.
Tex. Election Code, Art. 7.14
Vt. Stat. Ann., Title 17, § 2491 et seq.
Wash. Rev. Code Ann., 29.33.010 et seq.

**Voting Reform Act**
R.I. Gen. Laws 1956, 17-1-3 et seq.

**Voting Rights Act Amendments of 1970**
June 22, 1970, P.L. 91-285, 84 Stat. 314, 42 U.S. Code §§ 1973 nt., 1973b, 1973c, 1973aa to 1973bb-4

**Voting Rights Act Amendments of 1982**
May 30, 1908, Ch. 229, 35 Stat. 546, 12 U.S. Code § 104
June 29, 1982, P.L. 97-205, 42 U.S. Code §§ 1973b, 1973aa,

**Voting Rights Act of 1965**
Aug. 6, 1965, P.L. 89-110, 79 Stat. 437, 42 U.S. Code §§ 1971, 1973 to 1973p
April 11, 1968, P.L. 90-284, 82 Stat. 75, 42 U.S. Code § 1973j
June 22, 1970, P.L. 91-285, 84 Stat. 315, 42 U.S. Code §§ 1973b, 1973c, 1973aa to 1973bb-4
Sept. 22, 1970, P.L. 91-405, 84 Stat. 853, 42 U.S. Code § 1973i
Aug. 6, 1975, P.L. 94-73, 89 Stat. 400, 42 U.S. Code §§ 1973a et seq., 1973aa et seq., 1973bb, 1973bb-1
June 29, 1982, P.L. 97-205, 42 U.S. Code §§ 1973b, 1973aa
Aug. 26, 1992, P.L. 102-344, 42 U.S. Code § 1973aa-1a
Oct. 6, 1993, P.L. 103-94, 42 U.S. Code § 1973d

**Voting Rights Compliance Act (Federal)**
N.M. Stat. Ann., 1-21-1 et seq.

**Voting Rights Language Assistance Act of 1992**
Aug. 26, 1992, P.L. 102-344, 42 U.S. Code § 1971 nt.

**Voting Time Act**
Alaska Stat. 1962, § 15.56.100
Nev. Rev. Stat. 1979 Reprint, 293.463
Wyo. Stat. Ann., § 22-2-111

**Voting Time Act (Employees')**
Ariz. Rev. Stat. Ann., § 16-402
Ark. Stat. 1947, 3-1306
Cal. Elections Code 1976, § 14350 et seq.
Colo. Rev. Stat., 1-7-102
Ga. Code 1933, 89-923
Haw. Rev. Stat. Ann., § 11-95
Ill. Rev. Stat. 1991, Ch. 46, § 17-15
Ind. Code Ann., 3-5-4-2, 3-5-4-3
Iowa Code Ann., 49.109
Kan. Stat. Ann., 25-418
Ky. Rev. Stat. 1971, Superseded Vols., 118.340
Mass. Gen. Laws Ann., 149:178
Md. Ann. Code 1957, Art. 100, § 81 et seq.
Minn. Stat. 1974, 204.15
Mo. Rev. Stat. 1969, 129.060
Neb. Rev. Stat. 1943, 32-1046
Nev. Rev. Stat. 1979 Reprint, 293.463
N.M. Stat. Ann., 1-12-42
N.Y. Election Law 1976 (Consol. Laws Ch. 17) § 3-110
Ohio Rev. Code 1953, 3599.06
Okla. Stat. Ann., Title 26, § 7-101
S.D. Codified Laws 1967, 12-3-5
Tenn. Code Ann., 2-1-106
Tex. Election Code, Art. 15.14
Utah Code Ann. 1953, 20-13-18
Wis. Stat. 1989, 6.76
W. Va. Code 1966, § 3-1-42
Wyo. Stat. 1957, § 22.1-14

**Voting Trust Act (Corporations)**
Cal. Corporations Code § 706 § 2230, § 2231
Del. Code of 1974, Title 8, § 218
Ill. Rev. Stat. 1991, Ch. 32, § 7.65
Ind. Code Ann., 23-3-31-1 et seq.
Kan. Stat. Ann., 17-6508 et seq.
Ky. Rev. Stat. 1971, Supeseded Vols., 271A.170
Mich. Comp. Laws Ann., 450.1466, 450.1467
N.C. Gen. Stat. 1943, § 55-7-30

*Continued*

S.C. Code Ann. 1976, Superseded Vols., § 33-11-160

**Voting Trusts Act**
N.H. Rev. Stat. 1955, 293-A:34 et seq.

**Voucher Act (Public Disbursements)**
Wash. Rev. Code 1951, 42.24.035 et seq.

**Vrooman Act (Street Improvements)**
Cal. Statutes 1885, p. 147
Cal. Streets and Highways Code § 5100 et seq.

**Vulnerable Adults Act**
Miss. Code Ann. 1972, § 43-47-1 et seq.

## W

**W.A.A.C**
See W.A.C. Act
May 14, 1942, Ch12, 56 Stat. 278
Oct. 26, 1942, Ch. 627, 56 Stat. 988

**Wabash and Ohio Rivers Improvement Act**
Ill. Rev. Stat. 1991, Ch. 1, § 3550 et seq.

**Wabash Valley Compact Act**
Ill. Rev. Stat. 1991, Ch. 127, § 63t et seq.
Ind. Code 1976, 13-5-1-1 et seq.

**W.A.C. Act**
July 1, 1943, Ch. 187, 57 Stat. 371

**Wachusett Regional School District Athletic Field Loan Act**
Mass. Acts 1967, Ch. 84

**Wadlin-Condon Act (Strikes by Public Employees)**
N.Y. Civil Service Law 1967 (Consol. Laws Ch. 7) § 210

**Wadsworth Act (Emergency Relief)**
N.Y. Social Services Law (Consol. Laws Ch. 55) §§ 5 et seq., 160 et seq.

**Wadsworth-Burke Bill**
See Selective Training and Service Act of 1940

**Wadsworth-Kahn Act**
March 15, 1920, Ch. 100, 41 Stat. 530 (See 40 U.S. Code §§ 483, 484)

**Wadsworth-Livingston Act (Emergency Relief)**
N.Y. Laws 1937, Ch. 358

**Wage Act (Attorney's Fees)**
Ill. Rev. Stat. 1991, Ch. 13, §§ 12.9, 13

**Wage Act (Fisheries)**
Me. Rev. Stat. Ann. 1964, Title 26, § 491 et seq.

**Wage Act (Forty Four Hours)**
Pa. 1937 Pamph. Laws 2766, No. 567

**Wage Act (Minimum)**
See Minimum Wage Act

**Wage Act (Minors')**
Wash. Rev. Code Ann., 49.12.121

**Wage Act (Paydays)**
Colo. Rev. Stat., 8-4-101 et seq.

**Wage Act (Weekly Payment)**
Me. Rev. Stat. Ann. 1964, Title 26, § 621

**Wage Actions Act (Attorneys Fees)**
Ill. Comp. Stat. 1992, Ch. 705, § 225/0.01 et seq.

**Wage Acts (Prevailing Rate)**
N.Y. Labor Law (Consol. Laws Ch. 31) § 220 et seq.

**Wage and Hour Act**
Alaska Stat. 1962, § 23.10.050 et seq.
Cal. Labor Code § 1171 et seq.
Haw. Rev. Stat. Ann., § 387-1 et seq.
Ky. Rev. Stat. 1971, 337.010 et seq.
Mass. Gen. Laws Ann., 151:1 et seq.
Md. Ann. Code 1957, Art. 100, § 81 et seq.
Mont. Code Ann., 39-3-401 et seq.
N.C. Gen. Stat. 1943, § 95-25.1 et seq.
N.D. Cent. Code 34-06-01 et seq.
Neb. Rev. Stat. 1943, 48-1201 et seq.
N.J. Stat. Anno, 34:11-56a et seq.
N.M. Stat. Ann., 50-4-1 et seq.
Ore. Rev. Stat., 652.010 et seq., 653.010 et seq.
P.R. Laws Ann. 1954, Title 29, § 245 et seq.
S.D. Codified Laws 1967, 60-11-1 et seq.
Wash. Rev. Code Ann. 49.46.005 et seq.
Wyo. Stat. Ann., § 27-4-101 et seq.

**Wage Assignment Act**
Conn. Gen. Stat. Ann., § 52-361a
Ill. Rev. Stat. 1991, Ch. 48. § 39.01 et seq.
Mass. Gen. Laws Ann., 154:1 et seq.
Md. Ann. Code 1974, Art. CL, § 15-301 et seq.
Mo. Rev. Stat., 432.030
*Continued*

N.Y. Personal Propert Law (Consol. Laws Ch. 41) § 46 et seq.
Ohio Rev. Code 1953, 1321.31 et seq.
R.I. Gen. Laws 1956, 28-15-1 et seq.
Wash. Rev. Code Ann., 49.48.090 et seq.

**Wage Assignment Act (Involuntary)**
Ill. Rev. Stat. 1991, Ch. 39m

**Wage Attachment Act**
Md. Ann. Code 1974, Art. CL, § 15-601 et seq.

**Wage Brokers Act**
Mont. Code Ann., 31-1-301 et seq.

**Wage Claims Preference Act**
Mont. Code Ann., 80-5-201 et seq.
Wash. Rev. Code Ann. 49.56.010 et seq.

**Wage Deduction Act**
Ill. Rev. Stat. 1991, Ch. 110, § 12-801 et seq.

**Wage Discrimination Act**
Ida. Code 1947, 44-1701 et seq.

**Wage Discrimination Act (Sex)**
Ida. Code 1947, 44-1701 et seq.
Ill. Rev. Stat. 1991, Ch. 48, 4a et seq.
Mich. Comp. Laws Ann., 750.556
R.I. Gen. Laws 1956, 28-6-17 et seq.

**Wage Earner Receivership Act**
R.I. Gen. Laws 1956, 10-18-1 et seq.

**Wage Exemption Act**
D.C. Code 1973, § 15-503
Del. Code of 1974, Title 10, § 4913
Fla. Stat. Ann., 222.11
Iowa Code 1971, 627.10 et seq.
Md. Ann. Code 1974, Art. CL, § 15-602
Wash. Rev. Code Ann. 6.27.150

**Wage Garishment Law**
Cal. Code of Civil Procedure § 706.010 et seq.

**Wage Garnishment Exemption Act**
Fla. Stat. Ann., 222.11

**Wage-Hour Bill**
See Fair Labor Standards Act of 1938

**Wage Kickback Act**
Wash. Rev. Code Ann. 49.52.050 et seq.

**Wage Law (Minimum)**
Ga. Code Ann., 34-4-1 et seq.

**Wage Levy Act (Taxes)**
Md. Ann. Code 1974, Art. TG, §§ 13-805, 13-1007

**Wage Loan Corporation Act**
Ill. Rev. Stat. 1947, Ch. 32, § 348 et seq.

**Wage Payment Act**
Cal. Labor Code § 200 et seq.
Colo. Rev. Stat. 1973, 8-4-101 et seq.
Conn. Gen. Stat. Ann., § 31-71a et seq.
Ida. Code 1947, 45-601 et seq.
Ind. Code Ann., 22-2-5-1 et seq.
Mass. Gen. Laws Ann., 149:148 et seq.
Mont. Code Ann., 39-3-101 et seq.
N.H. Rev. Stat. 1955, 275:42 et seq.
N.J. Rev. Stat. 1937, 34:11-4.1 et seq.
N.M. Stat. Ann., 50-4-1 et seq.
N.Y. Labor Law (Consol. Laws Ch. 31) § 192 et seq.
Okla. Stat. Title 40, § 1-219 et seq.
R.I. Gen. Laws 1956, 28-14-1 et seq.
S.C. Code Ann. 1976, § 41-11-10 et seq.
Tex. Rev. Civ. Stat., Art. 5155 et seq.

**Wage Payment Act (Miners)**
Ark. Code Ann. 1987, 11-7-319

**Wage Payment Act (Semi-Monthly)**
Mich. Comp. Laws Ann., 408.471 et seq.
Pa. Purdon's Stat., Title 43, § 251 et seq.

**Wage Payment Act (Weekly)**
See Weekly Wage Payment Act

**Wage Payment and Collection Act**
Alaska Stat. 1962, § 23.05.140 et seq.
Del. Code of 1974, Title 19, § 1101 et seq.
Ill. Rev. Stat. 1991, Ch. 48, § 39m-1 et seq.
Iowa Code Ann., 91A.1 et seq.
Kan. Stat. Ann., 44-313 et seq.

Md. Ann. Code 1974, Art. LE, § 3-501 et seq.
N.D. Cent. Code 34-14-01 et seq.
Neb. Rev. Stat. 1943, 48-1228 et seq.
Ore. Rev. Stat., 652.110 et seq.
Pa. Purdon's Stat., Title 43, § 260.1 et seq.
Wash. Rev. Code Ann. 49.48.010 et seq.

**Wage Penalty Act**
Mo. Rev. Stat., 290.110

**Wage Preference Act**
Pa. Purdon's Stat., Title 43, § 221 et seq.

**Wage Protection Act-Restaurant, Bar, and Tavern**
Mont. Code Ann., 39-3-601 et seq.

**Wage Record Conversion Act (DeLange, Geake, Cherry, Murphy)**
Mich. Comp. Laws Ann., 421.1 et seq.

**Wage Refund Act (Personal Service)**
Ill. Rev. Stat. 1991, Ch. 48, § 216a et seq.

**Wage Reporting Act**
N.J. Stat. Ann. 54:1-55 et seq.

**Wage Scale Act**
Ind. Code Ann., 5-16-7-1 et seq.

**Wage Subsidy Program for Eligible Farmers Act**
P.R. Acts 1989, No. 46

**Wagering Act (Pari-Mutuel)**
Fla. Stat. Ann., 550.001 et seq.

**Wagering and Racing Board Act**
N.Y. Laws 1973, Ch. 346, § 3

**Wagering Stamp Act**
Fla. Stat. Ann., 849.051

**WAGES Act (Work and Gain Economic Self-Sufficiency)**
Fla. Stat. Ann., 414.015 et seq.

**Wages Claims Act (Preference)**
Ill. Rev. Stat. 1991, Ch. 82, § 62.9 et seq.

**Wages Collection Reciprocal Agreement Act**
Mont. Code Ann., 39-3-301 et seq.

**Wages-Hours Act Amendment.**
Aug. 9, 1939, Ch. 605, 53 Stat. 1266, 29 U.S. Code § 213
Oct. 29, 1941, Ch. 461, 55 Stat. 756, 29 U.S. Code § 207

**Wages Law (Kick-Back)**
N.Y. Labor LAw (Consol. Laws Ch. 31) § 198b

**Wages of Women and Minors Act**
Ill. Rev. Stat. 1991, Ch. 48, § 198 et seq.

**Wages Tax Ordinance**
Pa. Philadelphia Code § 19-1504

**Wageworkers' Preference Act**
Mont. Code Ann., 71-3-301 et seq.

**Waggoner-Trivette Act (Elections)**
Ky. Rev. Stat. 1948, 117.155, 117.541, 117.545

**Wagner Act (Advance Planning of Public Works)**
Feb. 10, 1931, Ch. 117, 46 Stat. 1084

**Wagner Act (Labor Relations)**
Conn. Gen. Stat. Ann., § 31-101 et seq.

**Wagner Act (Rapid Transit)**
N.Y. Laws 1912, Ch. 226

**Wagner-Cole Act**
See Trust Indenture Act of 1939

**Wagner-Connery Labor Relations Act**
See National Labor Relations Act

**Wagner-Connery Wages and Hours Act**
See Fair Labor Standards Act, 1938

**Wagner Foreign Credits Act**
May 7, 1940, Ch. 185, 54 Stat. 179, 12 U.S. Code §§ 95 nt., 95a; 50 U.S. Code Appx. § 5

**Wagner-Lea Act**
See Investment Advisors Act of 1940 and Investment Company Act of 1940

**Wagner-Lewis 500,000,000 Dollar Emergency Relief Act**
See A.A.A. Farm Relief and Inflation Act

**Wagner-O'Day Act**
June 25, 1938, Ch. 697, 52 Stat. 1196, 41 U.S. Code §§ 46 to 48
June 23, 1971, P.L. 92-28, 85 Stat. 77, 41 U.S. Code §§ 46 to 48c
June 13, 1991, P.L. 102-54, 41 U.S. Code § 46
Oct. 29, 1992, P.L. 102-569, 41 U.S. Code § 46
Aug. 11, 1993, P.L. 103-73, 41 U.S. Code § 46

**Wagner-Peyser Act**
June 6, 1933, Ch. 49, 48 Stat. 113, 29 U.S. Code §§ 49, 49c, 49d, 49g, 49h, 49j, 49k, 557
Oct. 13, 1982, P.L. 97-300, 29 U.S. Code §§ 49 et seq.
Dec. 31, 1982, P.L. 97-404, 28 U.S. Code § 49l
Dec. 23, 1985, P.L. 99-198, 29 U.S. Code § 49b
Sept. 25, 1990, P.L. 101-392, 29 U.S. Code § 49f
Aug. 22, 1996, P.L. 104-193, 29 U.S. Code § 49b
Aug. 7, 1998, P.L. 105-220, 29 U.S. Code §§ 49 nt., 49a to 49g, 49j, 49k, 49l-2
Oct. 21, 1998, P.L. 105-277, 29 U.S. Code § 49l-2
Oct. 31, 1998, P.L. 105-332, 29 U.S. Code § 49l-2

**Wagner-Peyser National Employment System Act**
June 6, 1933, Ch. 49, 48 Stat. 113, 29 U.S. Code §§ 49, 49c, 49d, 49h, 49j, 49k, 557

**Wagner-Steagall Housing Act**
See United States Housing Act of 1937

**Wagstaff Act (Water Appropriation)**
Tex. Water Code, § 11.024 et seq.

**Wait and See Act (Perpetuities)**
Conn. Gen. Stat. Ann., § 45a-503 et seq.
Ky. Rev. Stat. 1971, 381.216
Mass. Gen. Laws Ann. 184A:1 et seq.
Md. Ann. Code 1974, Art. ET, § 11-103
Me. Rev. Stat. Ann. 1964, Title 33, § 101 et seq.
Ohio Rev. Code 1953, 2131.08
Pa. Cons. Stat., Title 20, § 6104
Vt. Stat. Ann., Title 27, § 501 et seq.
Wash. Rev. Code Ann. 11.98.130 et seq.

**Waiver Act (Collision Damage)**
Kan. Stat. Ann., 50-654 et seq.

**Waiver Act (Demurrers and Answers)**
Cal. Code of Civil Procedure § 430.80 § 430.10

**Waiver Act (Jury Trial)**
Ariz. Rules of Civil Procedure 1955, Rule 38(d)
Wash. Rev. Code Ann. 4.48.010

**Waiver of Immunity Act**
N.Y. Criminal Procedure Law (Consol. Laws Ch. 11A) § 50.10 et seq.

**Waiver of Indictment Act**
Me. Rev. Stat. Ann. 1964, Title 15, § 811
Ohio Rev. Code 1953, 2941.021
S.C. Code Ann. 1976, § 17-23-120 et seq.

**Walden-Norman Act (Local Option Stock)**
Ala. Code 1975, § 3-5-2 et seq.

**Waldie Act (Handicapped Minors)**
Cal. Education Code 1976, § 56600 et seq.

**Waldie-Lanterman-Gibson Act (Legislative Organization)**
Cal. Government Code § 8900 et seq.

**Wales Act (Immoral Plays)**
N.Y. Penal Law 1965 (Consol. Lawss Ch. 40) § 235.05, Subd. 2

**Walhalla National Fish Hatchery Conveyance Act**
Oct. 9, 1996, P.L. 104-265, 110 Stat. 3288

**Walk-On-The-Left-Side Act**
Mich. Comp. Laws Ann., 257.655

**Walker Act (2.75 Beer)**
N.Y. Laws 1920, Ch. 911

**Walker Act (Electrical Systems)**
Ala. General Acts 1935, p. 201

**Walker Act (K. K. K.)**
N.Y. Civil Rights Law (Consol. Law Ch. 6) § 53 et seq.

**Walker Act (Tax Refund)**
N.Y. Laws 1923, Ch. 896

**Walker-Barr Act (Sex Offender Sentencing)**
Pa. Cons. Stat., Title 42, § 9721 et seq.

**Walker Baseball Act (Sunday Baseball)**
N.Y. General Business Law (Consol. Laws Ch. 20) § 7

**Walker Boxing Act (Commission)**
N.Y. Laws 1920, Ch. 912
N.Y. Laws 1921, Ch. 714

**Walker Boxing Laws (Sports)**
N.Y. Unconsolidated Laws, § 8901 et seq.

**Walker County Water and Sewer Utility Authority Act**
Ga. Laws 1991, p. 3796

**Walker County Water and Sewerage Authority Act**
Ga. Laws 1977, p. 3303

**Walker-Foley Act (Workmen's Compensation)**
N.Y. Laws 1913, Ch. 816
N.Y. Laws 1914, Ch. 41

**Walker Tariff Act**
July 30, 1846, Ch. 74, 9 Stat. 42

**Walker-Waters Act (Intoxicating Liquors)**
N.Y. Laws 1920, Ch. 911

**Wallace Act (Free Toll Bridges)**
Ala. General Acts 1935, p. 785

**Wallace Act (Industrial Promotion)**
Ala. Code 1975, § 11-54-20 et seq.

**Wallace-Dickey Memorial Burial Plot Act**
Ill. Rev. Stat. 1991, Ch. 21, §§ 65.9, 66

**Wallace-Folsom Prepaid College Tuition Act**
Ala. Acts 1991, p. 1717

**Wallace—Cater Act (Industrial Development Board)**
Ala. Code 1975, § 11-54-80 et seq.

**Wallkill River National Wildlife Refuge Act**
Nov. 16, 1990, P.L. 101-593, 16 U.S. Code § 668dd nt.

**Walmsley Act (Game)**
Mo. Laws 1905, p. 158

**Walnutgrove-Youth Water Authority Act**
Ga. Laws 1972, p. 3623

**Walsh Act**
July 3, 1926, Ch. 762, 44 Stat. 835 (See 28 U.S. Code §§ 1783, 1784)

**Walsh Act (Additional Federal Judges)**
Sept. 14, 1922, Ch. 306, 42 Stat. 837 (See 28 U.S. Code §§ 44, 132, 291, 292, 295, 296, 331, 456)

**Walsh Act (Commission Government)**
N.J. Stat. Anno, 40:70-1 to 40:76-27

**Walsh Act (Labor Relations)**
N.Y. Labor Law (Consol. Laws Ch. 31) § 700 et seq.

**Walsh Act (Municipal Government)**
N.J. Stat. Ann., 40:72-1 et seq.

**Walsh-Bonn Act (Air Pollution Control)**
Ky. Rev. Stat. 1971, 77.005 et seq.

**Walsh-Healey Act**

June 30, 1936, Ch. 881, 49 Stat. 2036, 29 U.S. Code § 557; 41 U.S. Code §§ 35 to 45

May 13, 1942, Ch. 306, 56 Stat. 277, 41 U.S. Code § 35

June 30, 1952, Ch. 530, 66 Stat. 308, 41 U.S. Code §§ 43a, 44, 45

Nov. 8, 1985, P.L. 99-145, 41 U.S. Code § 35

Oct. 13, 1994, P.L. 103-355, 41 U.S. Code §§ 35, 35 nt., 43a, 43b

Feb. 10, 1996, P.L. 104-106, 41 U.S. Code §§ 35 nt., 43a, 43b, 44, 45

**Walsh-Quimby Act (Indecent Exposure)**

Cal. Penal Code § 318.5

**Walter-Logan Act**

See Administrative Procedure Act

**Walter S. Reickert Act (Falls of the Ohio Interstate Park Compact)**

Ky. Rev. Stat. 1971, 148.241

**Walter Stiern Act**

Cal. Education Code 1976, § 70900.5

**Walter Thomas and Ronald McCurdy Act**

Ala. Acts 1990, No. 339

**Walters Act (Cancellation of War Contracts)**

N.Y. Laws 1918, Ch. 585

**Waltham Incinerator Loan Act**

Mass. Acts 1958, Ch. 517

**Wampanoag Tribal Council of Gay Head, Inc., Indian Claims Settlement Act of 1987**

Aug. 18, 1987, P.L. 100-95, 25 U.S. Code §§ 1771 nt., 1771 to 1771i

**War Ballot Act**

N.Y. Election Law 1976 (Consol. Laws Ch. 17) §§ 3-600, 7-124, 10-100 et seq.

**War Bonus Extension Act**

Ill. Rev. Stat. 1991, Ch. 126 1/2, § 57.70 et seq.

**War Claims Act of 1948**

July 3, 1948, Ch. 826, 62 Stat. 1240, 42 U.S. Code § 1702; 50 U.S. Code Appx. §§ 39, 2001 to 2010, 2012, 2013

May 27, 1949, Ch. 145, 63 Stat. 112, 50 U.S. Code Appx. §§ 2001, 2007

Sept. 30, 1950, Ch. 1116, 64 Stat. 1090, 50 U.S. Code Appx. § 2005

April 5, 1951, Ch. 27, 65 Stat. 29, 50 U.S. Code Appx. § 2001, 2001 nt.

April 9, 1952, Ch. 167, 66 Stat. 47, 50 U.S. Code Appx. §§ 2005, 2006

April 9, 1952, Ch. 168, 66 Stat. 49, 50 U.S. Code Appx. §§ 2004, 2005

Aug. 21, 1954, Ch. 784, 68 Stat. 759, 50 U.S. Code Appx. §§ 2001, 2004, 2005

Aug. 6, 1956, Ch. 985, 70 Stat. 1063, 50 U.S. Code Appx. § 2006

Aug. 31, 1962, P.L. 87-617, 76 Stat. 413, 50 U.S. Code Appx. § 2004

Oct. 22, 1962, P.L. 87-846, 76 Stat. 1107, 50 U.S. Code Appx. §§ 2001, 2003 to 2010, 2012, 2013 to 2016, 2017 to 2017p

June 24, 1970, P.L. 91-289, 84 Stat. 323, 50 U.S. Code Appx. §§ 2004, 2005

Dec. 24, 1970, P.L. 91-571, 84 Stat. 1503, 50 U.S. Code Appx. § 2017l

March 14, 1980, P.L. 96-209, 50 U.S. Code Appx. § 2001

Oct. 19, 1996, P.L. 104-316, 50 U.S. Code Appx. § 2017l

**War Contracts Relief Act**

Aug. 7, 1946, Ch. 864, 60 Stat. 902, 41 U.S. Code § 106 nt.

**War Council Act**

Ill. Rev. Stat. 1949, Ch. 127, §§ 63j to 63q.

Mich. Comp. Laws 1948, 30.1 et seq.

Wash. Laws 1943, Ch. 200

**War Crimes Act of 1996**

Aug. 21, 1996, P.L. 104-192, 18 U.S. Code § 2401 nt.

**War Damage Insurance Act**

March 27, 1942, Ch. 198, 56 Stat. 174

**War Declaration Against Germany**
Dec. 11, 1941, Ch. 564, 55 Stat. 796, 50 U.S. Code Appx. prec. § 1 nt.

**War Declaration Against Italy**
Dec. 11, 1941, Ch. 565, 55 Stat. 797, 50 U.S. Code Appx. prec. § 1 nt.

**War Declaration Against Japan**
Dec. 8, 1941, Ch. 561, 55 Stat. 795, 50 U.S. Code Appx. prec. § 1 nt.

**War Department Civil Appropriation Acts**
July 19, 1937, Ch. 511, 50 Stat. 515, 24 U.S. Code §§ 46b, 290; 33 U.S. Code § 701h
June 11, 1938, Ch. 348, 52 Stat. 667, 24 U.S. Code §§ 289, 290
June 28, 1939, Ch. 246, 53 Stat. 856, 24 U.S. Code §§ 289, 290
June 24, 1940, Ch. 415, 54 Stat. 505, 24 U.S. Code §§ 289, 290
May 23, 1941, Ch. 130, 55 Stat. 190, 24 U.S. Code §§ 289, 290
April 28, 1942, Ch. 246, 56 Stat. 220, 24 U.S. Code § 290; 41 U.S. Code § 6b
June 2, 1943, Ch. 115, 57 Stat. 93, 24 U.S. Code § 290; 33 U.S. Code § 701b-5; 41 U.S. Code § 6b.
June 26, 1944, Ch. 275, 58 Stat. 327, 24 U.S. Code § 290; 33 U.S. Code § 701b-5; 41 USC. § 6b
March 31, 1945, Ch. 45, 59 Stat. 39, 24 U.S. Code § 290; 33 U.S. Code § 701b-5; 41 U.S. Code § 6b
Dec. 28, 1945, Ch. 589, 59 Stat. 632
May 2, 1946, Ch. 247, 60 Stat. 160, 24 U.S. Code § 290; 41 U.S. Code § 6b
July 31, 1947, Ch. 411, 61 Stat. 686, 24 U.S. Code §§ 45 nt., 290; 41 U.S. Code § 6b

**War Duration Appointment Act**
Pa. 1943 Pamph. Laws 870, No. 363

**War Emergency Act**
Minn. Laws 1943, Ch. 600
N.Y. Laws 1942, Ch. 445

**War Emergency Compensation Act (Judiciary)**
N.Y. Laws 1945, Ch. 303

**War Emergency Dispensation Act**
N.Y. Laws 1942, Ch. 4

**War Estate Tax Act**
Oct. 3, 1917, Ch. 63, 40 Stat. 324

**War Excess Profits Tax Act**
Oct. 3, 1917, Ch. 63, 40 Stat. 302

**War Finance Corporation Acts**
April 5, 1918, Ch. 45, 40 Stat. 512, 12 U.S. Code § 82
Aug. 24, 1921, Ch. 80, 42 Stat. 181
March 4, 1923, Ch. 252, 42 Stat. 1480

**War Hazards Compensation Act**
Dec. 2, 1942, Ch. 668, 56 Stat. 1035, 42 U.S. Code §§ 1651, 1701 to 1706, 1711 to 1717
Dec. 23, 1943, Ch. 380, 57 Stat. 626, 42 U.S. Code §§ 1701, 1705
Aug. 7, 1946, Ch. 805, 60 Stat. 899, 42 U.S. Code § 1701
July 3, 1948, Ch. 826, 62 Stat. 1242, 42 U.S. Code § 1702
June 30, 1953, Ch. 176, 67 Stat. 134, 42 U.S. Code §§ 1701, 1711
June 30, 1954, Ch. 431, 68 Stat. 336, 42 U.S. Code § 1711
June 30, 1955, Ch. 257, 69 Stat. 241, 42 U.S. Code § 1711
July 9, 1956, Ch. 537, 70 Stat. 519, 42 U.S. Code § 1711
June 30, 1958, P.L. 85-477, 72 Stat. 273, 42 U.S. Code § 1701
June 25, 1959, P.L. 86-70, 73 Stat. 151, 42 U.S. Code §§ 1701, 1704, 1711
Sept. 4, 1961, P.L. 87-195, 75 Stat. 463, 42 U.S. Code § 1701

**War Housing Act**
Cal. Statutes 1943, Ch. 798, p. 2590
Conn. Gen. Stat. Ann., § 8-38 et seq.

**War Housing Appropriation Act**
July 2, 1942, Ch. 478, 56 Stat. 633

**War Labor Disputes Act**
June 25, 1943, Ch. 144, 57 Stat. 163

**War Manpower Commission Appropriation Acts**
July 12, 1943, Ch. 221, 57 Stat. 517, 29 U.S. Code §§ 50, 50b
June 28, 1944, Ch. 302, 58 Stat. 570
July 3, 1945, Ch. 263, 59 Stat. 380

**War Memorial Act**
Ind. Code Ann., 10-7-1-1 et seq.

**War Memorial Act (Living)**
Ill. Rev. Stat. 1991, Ch. 105, § 255.26h et seq.

**War Memorial Authority Act**
N.Y. Public Authorities Law (Consol. Laws Ch. 43A) § 1375 et seq.

**War Minerals Relief Act**
March 2, 1919, Ch. 94, 40 Stat. 1274

**War Mobilization and Reconversion Act of 1944**
Oct. 3, 1944, Ch. 480, 58 Stat. 785.
Aug. 6, 1947, Ch. 510, 61 Stat. 794

**War Orphans Education Assistance Act of 1956**
June 29, 1956, Ch. 476, 70 Stat. 411 (See 18 U.S. Code §§ 1001, 1621; 38 U.S. Code §§ 111, 213, 1662, 1701, 1710 to 1714, 1720, 1721 to 1726, 1731 to 1736, 1740 to 1743, 1761 to 1768)
June 17, 1957, P.L. 85-56, 71 Stat. 160 (See 38 U.S. Code §§ 111, 213, 1662, 1701, 1761)
June 18, 1958, P.L. 85-460, 72 Stat. 200 (See 38 U.S. Code §§ 111 , 213, 1662, 1701, 1723, 1731, 1761)
Sept. 2, 1958, P.L. 85-871, 72 Stat. 1695 (See 38 U.S. Code §§ 1712, 1735)

**War Overtime Pay Act of 1943**
May 7, 1943, Ch. 93, 57 Stat. 75
Sept. 30, 1944, Ch. 450, 58 Stat. 758

**War Pay and Allowances Act of 1942**
March 7, 1942, Ch. 166, 56 Stat. 143, 50 U.S. Code Appx. §§ 1001 to 1012, 1013 to 1016
Dec. 24, 1942, Ch. 828, 56 Stat. 1092, 50 U.S. Code Appx. §§ 1003 to 1006, 1015

**War Powers Act (Emergency)**
Mont. Laws 1943, Ch. 155
N.C. Gen. Stat. 1943, § 147-33.1 et seq.

**War Powers Act of 1916 - 1942**
Cal. Military and Veterans Code § 1500 et seq.

**War Powers Resolution**
Nov. 7, 1973, P.L. 93-148, 87 Stat. 555, 50 U.S. Code §§ 1541 to 1548

**War Production Act**
Cal. Statutes 1943, p. 124

**War Profits and Excess Profits Tax**
Feb. 24, 1919, Ch. 18, 40 Stat. 1088

**War Profits Tax Act**
Oct. 3, 1917, Ch. 63, 40 Stat. 302
Nov. 23, 1921, Ch. 136, 42 Stat. 271

**War Revenue Acts**
See Revenue Acts
June 13, 1898, Ch. 448, 30 Stat. 448, 31 U.S. Code § 756
Oct. 22, 1914, Ch. 331, 38 Stat. 745
Feb. 24, 1919, Ch. 18, 40 Stat. 1057

**War Risk Contributions Act**
Minn. Stat. Ann., 268.06 et seq.

**War Risk Insurance Acts**
Sept. 2, 1914, Ch. 293, 38 Stat. 711.
June 12, 1917, Ch. 26, 40 Stat. 102
Oct. 6, 1917, Ch. 105, 40 Stat. 398
May 20, 1918, Ch. 77, 40 Stat. 555
June 25, 1918, Ch. 104, 40 Stat. 609
July 11, 1918, Ch. 145, 40 Stat. 897
Feb. 25, 1919, Ch. 36, 40 Stat. 1160
Aug. 6, 1919, Ch. 33, 41 Stat. 274
Dec. 24, 1919, Ch. 16, 41 Stat. 371
Aug. 9, 1921, Ch. 57, 42 Stat. 152
Dec. 18, 1922, Ch. 10, 42 Stat. 1064
March 2, 1923, Ch. 173, 42 Stat. 1374
March 4, 1923, Ch. 291, 42 Stat. 1521
April 11, 1942, Ch. 240, 56 Stat. 214
Sept. 7, 1950, Ch. 906, 64 Stat. 773, 46 U.S. Code §§ 1281 to 1294

**War-Risk Insurance Fund Act**
June 5, 1942, Ch. 332, 56 Stat. 310

**War Service Validation Act**
Wis. Stat. 1969, 235.255

**War Time Act**
Jan. 20, 1942, Ch. 7, 56 Stat. 9, 15 U.S. Code § 261 nt.

**War Time Passport Act**
May 22, 1918, Ch. 81, 40 Stat. 559

**War Time Prohibition Act**
Nov. 21, 1918, Ch. 212, 40 Stat. 1046

**War Veterans Act (Relief)**
Ill. Rev. Stat. 1991, Ch. 23, § 3080 et seq.

**War Veterans Act (Vietnam)**
Ill. Rev. Stat. 1987, Ch. 126 1/2, § 251 et seq.

**War Veterans' Tenure Act**
Mass. Gen. Laws Ann., 31:9A

**War Veterans Tenure of Office Act**
N.J. Stat. Ann., 38:16-1

**War Voters Act**
Cal. Statutes 1950, 3rd Ex. Sess., Ch. 12, p. 19
Va. Code 1950, § 24-345.1 et seq.

**Ward-Gillen Act (Criminal Courts)**
Ohio Rev. Code 1953, 2931.01 et seq.

**Ward-Ratliff Textbook Act**
Ky. Rev. Stat. 1971, 156.405, 156.447, 156.474, 156.475, 157.100, 157.110

**Ware Act (Education of Exceptional Children)**
Ky. Rev. Stat. 1971, 157.200 et seq.

**Ware School Loan Act**
Mass. Acts 1951, Ch. 627

**Warehouse Act**
See United States Warehouse Act
Ala. Code 1975, 8-15-1 et seq.
Ga. Code Ann., 10-4-1 et seq.
Ill. Rev. Stat. 1953, Ch. 114, § 189 et seq.
Ind. Code Ann., 26-3-1-1 et seq.
Kan. Stat. Ann., 34-223 et seq.
Ky. Rev. Stat. 1971, 359.010 et seq.
Mo. Rev. Stat. 415.010 et seq.
N.D. Cent. Code 60-01-01 et seq.
P.R. Laws Ann. 1954, Title 10, § 341 et seq.
S.C. Code Ann. 1976, § 39-21-10 et seq.
S.D. Codified Laws 1967, 49-42-1 et seq.

**Warehouse Act (Agricultural)**
Cal. Agricultural 1967, § 54601 et seq.

**Warehouse Act (Bonded)**
N.H. Rev. Stat. 1955, 348:1 et seq.

**Warehouse Act (Farm Storage of Grain)**
S.D. Code 1939, 60.0601 et seq.

**Warehouse Act (Food)**
Cal. Public Utilities Code § 2501 et seq.

**Warehouse Act (Grain)**
Neb. Rev. Stat. 1943, 88-501 et seq.
Wash. Rev. Code Ann., 22.09.011 et seq.

**Warehouse Act (Public)**
Minn. Stat. 1961, 230.01 et seq.
Ore. Rev. Stat., 586.210 et seq.
S.D. Codified Laws 1967, 49-42-1 et seq.

**Warehouse Act (Storage)**
Wash. Rev. Code 1979, 81.92.010 et seq.

**Warehouse Act (Terminal)**
Wash. Rev. Code Ann., 22.09.011 et seq.

**Warehouse and Commodity Dealer Law**
Tenn. Code Ann., 43-32-101 et seq.

**Warehouse and Grain Act**
Minn. Stat. Ann., 232.01 et seq.

**Warehouse, Commodity Dealer, and Grain Standards Act (Agricultural)**
Mont. Code Ann., 80-4-401 et seq.

**Warehouse Endorsement Act (Motor Vehicles)**
Minn. Stat. Ann., 168.81

**Warehouse Exemption Act (Taxation)**
N.J. Stat. Anno, 54:4-3.20

**Warehouse Inspection Act (Grain)**
Ky. Rev. Stat. 1971, 359.100

**Warehouse Receipts Act**
See Uniform Warehouse Receipts Act

**Warehouse Receipts Act (District of Columbia)**
April 15, 1910, Ch. 167, 36 Stat. 301

**Warehouse Receipts Act (Foreign)**
Cal. Civil Code § 1858.90 et seq.

**Warehouse Receipts Act (UCC)**
Mont. Code Ann., 30-7-101

**Warehouse Receipts Act (Uniform)**
Ariz. Laws 1921, Ch. 47
Cal. Civil Code § 1858.01 et seq.
N.D. Cent. Code 41-07-07 et seq.

**Warehouseman's Lien Act**
N.J. Stat. Anno, 12A:7-209, 12A:7-210

**Warehousemen Act**
Mich. Comp. Laws Ann., 444.1 et seq.
Tex. Agriculture Code § 14.201

**Warehousemen Act (Grain)**
Mont. Code Ann., 80-4-101 et seq.

**Warehousemen Act (Seeds)**
Mont. Code Ann., 80-5-201 et seq.

**Warehousemen and Dealers of Agricultural Products Act**
Colo. Rev. Stat., 12-16-101 et seq.

**Warehousemen Licensing Act**
Iowa Code Ann., 543.1
N.J. Stat. Ann. 45:14D-1 et seq.

**Warehousing Act (Farm)**
Neb. Rev. Stat. 1943, 88-601 et seq.

**Wariner-Van Hoose Act (Public Assistance)**
Ky. Rev. Stat. 1971, 117.275, 118.025, 118.035
Ky. Rev. Stat. 1971, 205.010 et seq.

**Warinner-Bates Act (Alcoholic Beverages)**
Ky. Rev. Stat. 1971, 244.195

**Warinner-Hilton Act (Elections)**
Ky. Rev. Stat. 1971, Superseded Vols., 118.040, 118.350, 118.370, 119.040

**Warm Air Heating Contractors Act**
Ga. Code Ann., 43-14-1 et seq.

**Warm Springs Study Act of 1988**
Oct. 28, 1988, P.L. 100-559, 102 Stat. 2801

**WARN ACT**
See Worker Adjustment and Retraining Notification Act

**Warner Canyon Ski Hill Land Exchange Act of 1997**
Aug. 11, 1997, P.L. 105-40, 111 Stat. 1117

**Warnes Act (Assessment Districts)**
Ohio Laws Vol. 103, p. 786

**Warning Board Act (Railroad Crossings)**
Ark. Code Ann. 1987, 23-12-411

**Warning Light Act**
Neb. Rev. Stat. 1943, 39-6,148 et seq.

**Warrant Act**
Ill. Rev. Stat. 1991, Ch. 146 1/2, § 1
Ky. Rev. Stat. 1971, 41.130 et seq.

**Warrant Act (Excise Tax)**
Wash. Rev. Code Ann. 82.32.210 et seq.

**Warrant Cancellation Act**
N.M. Stat. Ann., 6-10-55 et seq.

**Warrant Officer Act of 1954**
May 29, 1954, Ch. 249, 68 Stat. 157

**Warrant Officer Management Act**
Dec. 5, 1991, P.L. 102-190, 10 U.S. Code § 571 nt.

**Warranties for Facilitative Technology Act**
Colo. Rev. Stat., 6-1-501 to 6-1-511

**Warrants and Jurors Certificates Act**
Ill. Rev. Stat. 1991, Ch. 146 1/2, § 0.01 et seq.

**Warrants Escheat Act (State)**
Ill. Rev. Stat. 1971, Ch. 15, § 210.14 et seq.

**Warranty Act (Assistive Technology Device)**
Fla. Stat. Ann., 427.801 et seq.

**Warranty Act (Consumers)**
Cal. Civil Code § 1790 et seq.

**Warranty Act (Farm Tractor)**
Ga. Code Ann., 10-1-810 et seq.

**Warranty Act (Insurance Contracts)**
Mass. Gen. Laws Ann., 175:186

**Warranty Act (Motorized Wheelchair)**
Pa. Purdon's Stat., Title 73, § 2231 et seq.

**Warranty Act (New Home)**
La. Rev. Stat. Ann., 9:2789.1 et seq.

**Warranty Disclosure Act (Grey Markets Merchandise)**
N.Y. General Business Law (Consol. Laws Ch. 20) § 218aa

**Warranty Enforcement Act (Motor Vehicle)**
Fla. Stat. Ann., 681.110 et seq.
Miss. Code Ann. 1972, § 63-17-151 et seq.
Va. Code 1950, § 59.1-207.9 et seq.

**Warranty Extension Act (Consumer Protection)**
Tenn. Code Ann., 47-18-1401 et seq.

**Warranty of Habitability Act**
N.Y. Real Property Law (Consol. Laws Ch. 48A) § 235b

**Warranty Practices Act (Motor Vehicle)**
Ga. Code Ann., 10-1-640 et seq.

**Warranty Rights Act (Homeowner's)**
Ga. Code Ann., 10-1-910 et seq.

**Warranty Rights Act (Motor Vehicle)**
Ga. Code Ann., 10-1-780 et seq.

**Warren Act (Livestock at Large)**
Fla. Stat. Ann., 588.12 et seq.

**Warren Act (Reclamation)**
Feb. 21, 1911, Ch. 141, 36 Stat. 925, 43 U.S. Code §§ 523 to 525

**Warren-Alquist State Energy Resources Conservation and Development Act**
Cal. Public Resources Code § 25000 et seq.

**Warren-Miller Energy Lifeline Act**
Cal. Public Utilities Code § 739

**Warren Public Parking Act**
R.I. Public Laws 1968, Ch. 204

**Warren S. Henderson Wetlands Protection Act**
Fla. Stat. Ann., 403.91 et seq.

**Warren-911-Emergency Assistance Act**
Cal. Government Code § 53100 et seq.

**Warriner-Shields-Webb Act (Married Woman's Property)**
Ky. Rev. Stat. 1971, 404.010

**Warrington Charter**
Fla. Laws 1976, Ch. 76-499

**Warrington Incorporation Act**
Fla. Special Laws 1975, Ch. 518, 1976, Ch. 76-499

**Warsaw Convention (International Air Transportation)**
Oct. 12, 1929, 49 Stat. 3000, 49 U.S. Code § 1502 nt.

**Wartime Substitution Law (Fiduciaries')**
Cal. Probate Code § 350 et seq.

**Warwick Minimum Standards Housing Act**
R.I. Public Laws 1958, Ch. 99

**Washburn Act (Workmen's Compensation and Labor Violations)**
N.Y. Labor Law (Consol. Laws Ch. 31) § 213
N.Y. Workmen's Compensation Law (Consol. Laws Ch. 67) § 132

**Washington and Martin Counties Peace Officers' Relief Act**
N.C. Laws 1953, Ch. 402

**Washington Conference for Limitation of Armaments**
July 12, 1921, Ch. 45, 42 Stat. 141

**Washington Convention Center Management Act**
D.C. Code Ann., § 9-601 et seq.

**Washington County Development Authority Act**
Fla. Special Laws 1961, Ch. 61-2988

**Washington County Government Administrative Procedure Act**
Md. Ann. Code 1957, Art. 25, § 237 et seq.

**Washington County Salary Act**
Ark. 1954 Initiated Acts of Washington County

**Washington County School Bond Act of 1967 - 1971**
Md. Laws 1967, Ch. 352
Md. Laws 1971, Ch. 343

**Washington-Maryland Regional District Act**
Md. Laws 1943, Ch. 992

**Washington Metropolitan Area Transit Authority Compact**
Md. Ann. Code 1974, Art. TR, § 10-204

**Washington Metropolitan Area Transit Authority Stable and Reliable Source of Revenues Act**
D.C. Code Ann., §§ 1-2466, 1-2467

**Washington Metropolitan Area Transit Regulation Compact Act**
D.C. Code Ann., § 1-2411 et seq.
Md. Ann. Code 1974, Art. TR, § 10-203

**Washington Metropolitan Region Development Act**
D.C. Code Ann., § 1-2101 et seq.

**Washington National Airport Act**
June 29, 1940, Ch. 444, 49 U.S. Code § 2401 et seq.
May 15, 1947, Ch. 82, 49 U.S. Code §§ 2404 to 2407
Aug. 23, 1958, P.L. 85-726, 72 Stat. 807

**Washington Park Wilderness Act of 1988**
Nov. 16, 1988, P.L. 100-668, 16 U.S. Code § 90 nt.

**Washington Serves Act**
Wash. Laws 1993, Ch. 7

**Washington State Health Care Reform Act**
Wash. Rev. Code 1989, 41.05.011 et seq.

**Washington State Wilderness Act of 1984**
July 3, 1984, P.L. 98-339, 16 U.S. Code §§ 460pp, 1132 nt.
Nov. 7, 1986, P.L. 99-635, 100 Stat. p. 3527

**Washoe County Airport Authority Act**
Nev. Statutes 1977, Ch. 474, p. 968

**Washoe County Metropolitan Water Authority Law**
Nev. Statutes 1983, Ch. 487, p. 1309

**Washroom Act**
Ill. Rev. Stat. 1991, Ch. 48, § 97.9 et seq.

**Washroom Act (Employee)**
Ill. Rev. Stat. 1991, Ch. 48, § 97.9 et seq.

**Waste Act**
Mich. Comp. Laws Ann., 600.2919
Wash. Rev. Code Ann., 64.12.010 et seq.

**Waste Act (High Level Radioactive)**
N.H. Rev. Stat. 1955, 125-G:1 et seq.

**Waste Act (Oil and Gas)**
See Oil and Gas Conservation Act

**Waste Act (Solid)**
Haw. Rev. Stat. § 340A-1 et seq.

**Waste Activity Law (Nuclear)**
Me. Rev. Stat. Ann. 1964, Title 38, § 1451 et seq.

**Waste and Estrepement**
Mich. Comp. Laws Ann., 600.2919
R.I. Gen. Laws 1956, 34-14-1 et seq.
Wash. Rev. Code Ann. 64.12.010 et seq.

**Waste and Sewage Disposal Facilities Compact (New Hampshire—Vermont)**
N.H. Rev. Stat. 1955, 252-B:1

**Waste and Underground Storage Tank Act (Hazardous)**
Mont. Code Ann., 75-10-401 et seq.

**Waste Authority Act (Low-Level Radioactive)**
Me. Rev. Stat. Ann. 1964, Title 38, § 1501 et seq.

**Waste Collection and Disposal System Act (Broward County)**
Fla. Special Laws 1963, Ch. 63-1172

**Waste Collection and Disposal System Act (Volusia County)**
Fla. Special Laws 1965, Ch. 65-2357

**Waste Collection Regulatory Reform Act (Solid)**
N.J. Stat. Ann., 48:13A-7.1 et seq.

**Waste Compact Act**
Vt. Stat. Ann., Title 10, § 1201 et seq.

**Waste Control Act**
N.J. Stat. Ann., 13:1 1-1 et seq.

**Waste Control Act (Infectious)**
Minn. Stat. Ann., 116.76 et seq.

**Waste Control Law**
Ga. Code Ann., 16-7-50 et seq.

**Waste Disposal Act**
N.H. Rev. 1955, 485-A:1 et seq.

**Waste Disposal Act (Low-Level Radioactive)**
Ariz. Rev. Stat. Ann., § 30-721 et seq.
Me. Rev. Stat. Ann. 1964, Title 38, § 1481 et seq.
Neb. Rev. Stat. 1943, 81-1578 et seq.
Pa. Purdon's Stat., Title 35, § 7130.101 et seq.

**Waste Disposal Act (Metropolitan Area)**
Miss. Code Ann. 1972, § 21-27-161 et seq.

**Waste Disposal Act (PCB)**
Ida. Code 1947, 39-6201 et seq.

**Waste Disposal Act (Regional)**
Tex. Health and Safety Code, § 361.001 et seq.

**Waste Disposal Act (Solids)**
Ala. Code 1975, § 22-27-1 et seq.
Mass. Gen. Laws Ann., 18 et seq.
Miss. Code Ann. 1972, § 17-17-1 et seq.
Tenn. Code Ann., 68-21-101 et seq.
Tex. Rev. Civ. Stat., Art. 4477-7

**Waste Disposal and Pollution Abatement Facilities Financing Act**
Ark. Code Ann. 1987, No. 686

**Waste Disposal and Resources Recovery Authority Act**
W. Va. Code 1966, § 16-26-1 et seq.

**Waste Disposal Authority Act (Gulf Coast)**
Tex. Rev. Civ. Stat. 1925, Art. 7621d-2

**Waste Disposal Authority Act (Northeast Maryland)**
Md. Ann. Code 1974, Art. NR, § 3-901 et seq.

**Waste Disposal Compact Act (New Hampshire-Massachusetts)**
N.H. Rev. Stat. 1955, 149-K:1

**Waste Disposal Compact Act (New Hampshire—Vermont)**
N.H. Rev. Stat. 1955, 149-J:1

**Waste Disposal District Act**
Ill. Rev. Stat. 1991, Ch. 85, § 1651 et seq.

**Waste Disposal Facility Siting Act (Regional Low-Level Radioactive)**
N.J. Stat. Ann., 13:1E-177 et seq.

**Waste Disposal System Construction Act**
Ark. Acts 1983, p. 1119, No. 535

**Waste Dumping Elimination Act (Ocean Solid)**
Del. Code of 1974, Title 7, § 6070 et seq.

**Waste Enforcement (Hazardous)**
Cal. Health and Safety Code § 25192
Cal. Statutes 1986, Ch. 1187

**Waste Facility Siting Act (Hazardous)**
Mass. Gen. Laws Ann., 21D:1 et seq.
Utah Code Ann. 1953, 19-6-201 et seq.

**Waste Facility Siting Act (Statewide Multipurpose Hazardous)**
Fla. Stat. Ann., 403.78 et seq.

**Waste Feasibility Study Act (Hazardous)**
N.M. Stat. Ann., 74-4C-1 et seq.

**Waste from Mines Act**
Fla. Stat. 1983, 533.01 et seq.

**Waste Fund Act (Hazardous)**
Okla. Stat. Ann., Title 27A, § 2-7-301 et seq.

**Waste Funding Act (Household Hazardous)**
Pa. Purdon's Stat., Title 35, § 6025.1 et seq.

**Waste Haulers Act (Oil and Gas)**
Tex. Natural Resources, § 91.111 et seq.
Tex. Water Code, § 29.001 et seq.

**Waste Isolation Pilot Plant Land Withdrawal Amendment Act**
Sept. 23, 1996, P.L. 104-201, Title XXXI, Subtitle F, 110 Stat 2851

**Waste Isolation Pilot Plant Land Withdrawals Act**
Oct. 30, 1992, P.L. 102-579, 106 Stat. 4777

**Waste Management Act**
Haw. Rev. Stat. Ann., § 342-51 et seq.
Minn. Stat. Ann., 115A.01 et seq.
N.C. Gen. Stat. 1943, § 143B-216.10 et seq.
Okla. Stat. Ann., Title 63, § 1-2300 et seq.
Va. Code 1950, § 10.1-1400 et seq.

**Waste Management Act (Hazardous)**
Cal. Health and Safety Code § 25179.1 et seq.
Mass. Gen. Laws Ann., 21C:1 et seq.
Mich. Comp. Laws Ann., 324.11101 et seq.
N.Y. Environmental Conservation Law 1972 (Consol. Laws Ch. 43B) §§ 71-2701, 71-2703, 71-2705
Okla. Stat. Ann., Title 27A, § 2-7-101 et seq.
S.C. Code Ann. 1976, § 44-96-240

**Waste Management Act (Infectious)**
Mont. Laws 1991, Ch. 483

**Waste Management Act (Integrated)**
Cal. Public Resources Code § 40050 et seq.
Mont. Laws 1991, Ch. 222, §§ 1 to 7

**Waste Management Act (Medical)**
Cal. Health and Safety Code § 25015 et seq.
N.J. Stat. Ann. 13:1E-48.1 et seq.

**Waste Management Act (Metallic Minerals)**
Mo. Rev. Stat., 444.352 et seq.

**Waste Management Act (Solid)**
Okla. Stat. Ann., Title 27A, § 2-10-101 et seq.
Utah Code Ann. 1953, 19-6-501 et seq.

**Waste Management Act (Solids)**
See Solid Waste Management Act

**Waste Management Act (Trauma Scene)**
Cal. Health and Safety Code § 118321 et seq.

**Waste Management and Resource Recovery Finance Act**
Mich. Comp. Laws Ann., 123.311 et seq.

**Waste Management Authority Act**
Iowa Code Ann., 455B.480 et seq.

**Waste Management Authority Act (Low-Level Radioactive)**
N.C. Gen. Stat. 1943, § 104G-1 et seq.

**Waste Management Authority Act (Ventura County)**
Cal. Public Resources Code § 60200 et seq.

**Waste Management Commission Act (Hazardous)**
N.C. Gen. Stat. 1943, § 130B-1 et seq.

**Waste Management Compact (Northeast Interstate Low Level Radioactive)**
Conn. Gen. Stat. Ann., § 22a-161

**Waste Management Compact Act (Radioactive)**
N.J. Stat. Ann. 32:31-1

**Waste Management Fee Law (Integrated)**
Cal. Revenue and Taxation Code § 45001 et seq.

**Waste Management Institute at Cornell University Act (New York State)**
N.Y. Environmental Conservation Law 1972 (Consol. Laws Ch. 43B) § 27-0403 nt.

**Waste Management Reform Act (Hazardous)**
Cal. Statutes 1995, Ch. 638

**Waste Management Services Act (Solid)**
Conn. Gen. Stat. Ann., § 20-7a

**Waste Minimization Act**
Mich. Comp. Laws Ann., 299.731 et seq.

**Waste Minimization Act (Comprehensive Multimedia)**
Miss. Code Ann. 1972, § 49-31-1 et seq.

**Waste Minimization—Pollution Prevention Act**
Del. Code of 1974, Title 7, § 7801 et seq.

**Waste Oil Recovery Act**
Ill. Rev. Stat. 1991, Ch. 96 1/2, § 7701 et seq.

**Waste Pesticide Disposal Act**
Miss. Code Ann. 1972, § 69-23-301 et seq.

**Waste Planning, Recycling and Waste Reduction Act (Municipal)**
Pa. Purdon's Stat., Title 53, § 4000.101 et seq.

**Waste Reduction Act (Hazardous)**
Tenn. Code Ann., 68-212-301 et seq.

**Waste Reduction Assistance Act**
Mich. Comp. Laws Ann., 324.14501

**Waste Reduction Law**
La. Rev. Stat. Ann., 30:2291 et seq.

**Waste Reduction Policy Act of 1991**
Tex. Laws, 1991, p. 1235, Ch. 296

**Waste Reduction Program (Hazardous)**
Okla. Stat. Ann., Title 27A, § 2-11-201 et seq.

**Waste Reduction, Recycling and Model Litter Control Act**
Wash. Rev. Code Ann., 70.93.010

**Waste Reduction, Recycling, and Treatment Research and Demonstration Act (Hazardous)**
R.I. Gen. Laws 1956, 23-19.10-1 et seq.

**Waste Regulatory Act (Medical)**
Mich. Comp. Laws Ann., 333.13801 et seq.

**Waste Siting Act**
Colo. Rev. Stat. 25-15-200.1 et seq.

**Waste Source Reduction and Management Review Act (Hazardous)**
Cal. Health and Safety Code § 25244.12 et seq.

**Waste Systems Operators Act**
Md. Ann. Code 1974, Art. EN, § 12-101 et seq.

**Waste Tire Recycling Act**
Okla. Stat. Ann., Title 27A, § 2-11-401 et seq.
Okla. Stat. Ann., Title 68, § 53001 et seq.
Pa. Purdon's Stat., Title 35, § 6029.201 et seq.
Utah Code Ann. 1953, 26-32a-101 et seq.

**Waste Transportation and Disposal Act (Radioactive)**
S.C. Code Ann. 1976, § 48-48-10 et seq.

**Waste Treatment Act (Solid and Hazardous)**
Miss. Code Ann. 1972, § 17-17-101 et seq.

**Waste Treatment Cost Efficiency Act**
Fla. Laws 1986, Ch. 213

**Waste Water and Sewage Act (County)**
Nev. Rev. Stat. 1979 Reprint, 244A.455 et seq.

**Waste Water Facilites Act**
Tenn. Public Act 1991, Ch. 299

**Waste Water Reuse Act**
Cal. Water Code § 460 et seq.

**Wastewater and Public Water Environmental Health Act**
Tenn. Code Ann., 68-211-301 et seq.

**Wastewater and Water Operators Certification Act**
Fla. Stat. Ann., 468.540 et seq.

**Wastewater and Water Supply Operators Licensing Act**
N.J. Stat. Ann., 58:11-64 et seq.

**Wastewater and Water System Regulatory Law**
Fla. Stat. Ann., 367.011 et seq.

**Wastewater Authority Act (Gulf Coast Regional)**
Miss. Code Ann. 1972, § 49-17-303 et seq.

**Wastewater Disposal System Law (Individual On-Site)**
Miss. Code Ann. 1972, § 41-67-1

**Wastewater Disposal Zones Act (Municipal)**
Ill. Rev. Stat. 1991, Ch. 24, § 1400 et seq.

**Wastewater Facility Construction Act**
N.M. Stat. Ann., 74-6A-1 et seq.

**Wastewater Land Treatment Site Regulation Act**
Ill. Rev. Stat. 1991, Ch. 111 1/2, § 581 et seq.

**Wastewater Management District Act (San Diego Area)**
Cal. Statutes 1992, Ch. 803

**Wastewater Management Plans**
Kan. Stat. Ann., 65-3308

**Wastewater Reclamation and Reuse Law**
Cal. Water Code § 13500 et seq.

**Wastewater Transmission Authority Act (South Seminole and North Orange County)**
Fla. Special Laws 1978, Ch. 78-617

**Wastewater Treatment Bond Act**
N.J. Laws 1985, Ch. 329

**Wastewater Treatment Districts Act**
Ark. Code Ann. 1947, 14-250-101 et seq.

**Wastewater Treatment Facility Construction Assistance Act**
Neb. Rev. Stat. 1943, 81-15, 147 et seq.

**Wastewater Treatment Operator Certification Act**
Neb. Rev. Stat. 1943, 81-15, 128 et seq.

**Wastewater Treatment Privatization Act**
N.J. Stat. Ann., 58:27-1

**Wastewater Treatment Public-Private Contracting Act**
N.J. Stat. Ann., 58:27-19 et seq.

**Wastewater Treatment Revolving Fund Act**
Mont. Laws 1991, Ch. 678

**Wastewater Treatment Trust Act**
N.J. Stat. Ann., 58:11B-1 et seq.

**Wastewater Treatment Works Construction Grant Act**
Tenn. Code Ann., 68-211-801 et seq.

**Watch Act (Second-hand)**
Ill. Rev. Stat. 1991, Ch. 121 1/2, § 191.1 et seq.

**Watch Dog Act (Public Funds)**
Ohio Rev. Code 1953, 309.12

**Watch Sales Act (Secondhand)**
Cal. Business and Professions Code § 21500 et seq.

**Watchmaking Act**
La. Rev. Stat. Ann., 37:1581 et seq.
N.C. Gen Stat. 1943, § 96C-1 et seq.
Okla. Stat., Title 59, § 771 et seq.

**Water Act**
Iowa Code Ann., 455B.171 et seq., 455B.261 et seq.
Mont. Code Ann., 85-1-101 et seq.
N.D. Cent. Code 61-01-01 et seq.
Nev. Rev. Stat. 1979, Reprint, 533.010 et seq.
N.M. Stat. Ann., 72-1-1 et seq.
Okla. Stat., Title 59, § 1101 et seq.
Ore. Rev. Stat., 537.010 et seq.
P.R. Laws Ann. 1954, Title 12, § 501 et seq.
Utah Code Ann. 1953, 73-1-1 et seq.
Wyo. Stat. Ann., § 41-3-101 et seq.

**Water Act (Binghamton)**
N.Y. Laws 1867, Ch. 780

**Water Act (Bottled)**
Fla. Stat. Ann., 381.007

**Water Act (Mount Vernon)**
N.Y. Laws 1911, Ch. 127

**Water Act (Municipal Corporations)**
Ark. Code Ann. 1987, 14-234-204 et seq.

**Water Act (Safe Drinking)**
Neb. Rev. Stat. 1943, 71-5301 et seq.
S.C. Code Ann. 1976, § 40-23-150 et seq.
Wash. Rev. Code Ann., 70.119A.020 et seq.

**Water Act (Underground)**
Mont. Code Ann., 85-2-501 et seq.
Wyo. Stat. Ann., § 41-3-901 et seq.

**Water Adjudication Act**
Colo. Rev. Stat. 1963, 148.9-1 et seq.
Utah Code Ann. 1953, 73-4-1 et seq.

**Water Agency Act (Alpine County)**
Cal. Statutes 1961, Ch. 1896
Cal. Water Code, Appx., § 102-1 et seq.

**Water Agency Act (Amador County)**
Cal. Statutes 1959, Ch. 2137, p. 5061
Cal. Water Code, Appx., § 95-1 et seq.

**Water Agency Act (Antelope Valley-East Kern)**
Cal. Statutes 1959, Ch. 2146, p. 5114 § 49 et seq.

**Water Agency Act (Big Horn Mountains)**
Cal. Water Code, Appx., § 112-1 et seq.

**Water Agency Act (Central Delta)**
Cal. Statutes 1973, Ch. 1133

**Water Agency Act (Contra Costa County)**
Cal. Statutes 1957, Ch. 518, p. 1553
Cal. Water Code, Appx., § 80-1 et seq.

**Water Agency Act (Crestline-Lake Arrowhead)**
Cal. Statutes 1962, 1st Ex. Sess., Ch. 40, p. 278
Cal. Water Code, Appx., § 104-1 et seq.

**Water Agency Act (Desert)**
Cal. Statutes 1961, Ch. 1069
Cal. Water Code, Appx., § 100-1 et seq.

**Water Agency Act (El Dorado County)**
Cal. Statutes 1959, Ch. 2139, p. 5084

**Water Agency Act (Kern County)**
Cal. Statutes 1961, Ch. 1003
Cal. Water Code, Appx., § 99-1 et seq.

**Water Agency Act (Mariposa County)**
Cal. Statutes 1959, Ch. 2036, p. 4685
Cal. Water Code, Appx., § 85-1 et seq.

**Water Agency Act (Mojave)**
Cal. Statutes 1959, Ch. 2146, p. 5114, §§ 1-48

**Water Agency Act (Nevada County)**
Cal. Statutes 1959, Ch. 2122, p.4966
Cal. Water Code, Appx., § 90-1 et seq.
*Continued*

**Water Agency Act (North Delta)**
Cal. Statutes 1973, Ch. 283

**Water Agency Act (Placer County)**
Cal. Statutes 1957, Ch. 1234, p. 2519
Cal. Water Code, Appx., § 81-1 et seq.

**Water Agency Act (Sacramento County)**
Cal. Statutes 1952, 1st Ex. Sess., Ch. 10, p. 315
Cal. Water Code, Appx., § 66-1 et seq.

**Water Agency Act (San Gorgonia Pass)**
Cal. Water Code, Appx., § 101-1 et seq.

**Water Agency Act (San Gorgonio Pass)**
Cal. Statutes 1961, Ch. 1435, p. 3239

**Water Agency Act (Santa Barbara County)**
Cal. Statutes 1945, Ch. 1501, p. 2780
Cal. Water Code, Appx., § 51-1 et seq.

**Water Agency Act (Santa Clara Valley)**
Cal. Water Code, Appx., § 60-1 et seq.

**Water Agency Act (Shasta County)**
Cal. Statutes 1957, Ch. 1512, p. 2844
Cal. Water Code, Appx., § 83-1 et seq.

**Water Agency Act (Shelby County)**
Cal. Water Code, Appx., § 83-1 et seq.

**Water Agency Act (Solano County)**
Cal. Statutes 1991, Ch. 573

**Water Agency Act (South Delta)**
Cal. Statutes 1973, Ch. 1089
Cal. Water Code, Appx., § 116-1.1

**Water Agency Act (Sutter County)**
Cal. Statutes 1959, Ch. 2088, p. 4819
Cal. Water Code, Appx., § 86-1 et seq.

**Water Agency Act (Tuolumne County)**
Cal. Water Code, Appx., § 113-1 et seq.

**Water Agency Act (Upper Santa Clara Valley)**
Cal. Statutes 1962, 1st Ex. Sess., Ch. 28, p. 208

**Water Agency Act (Yuba County)**
Cal. Statutes 1959, Ch. 788, p. 2780
Cal. Water Code, Appx., § 84-1 et seq.

**Water and Air Pollution Control Act**
Ark. Code Ann. 1987, 8-4-101 et seq.
Fla. Stat. Ann., 403.011 et seq.
Miss. Code Ann. 1972, 49-17-1 et seq.

**Water and Air Pollution Control Tax Refund Act**
Neb. Rev. Stat. 1943, 77-27, 149 et seq.

**Water and Air Quality Reporting Act**
N.C. Gen. Stat. 1943, § 143-215.63 et seq.

**Water and Air Resources Act**
N.C. Gen. Stat. 1943, § 143-211 et seq.

**Water and Irrigation Act**
Utah Code Ann. 1953, 73-1-1 et seq.

**Water and Land Conservation and Reclamation Act**
Pa. Purdon's Stat., Title 32, § 5101 et seq.

**Water and Land Resources Compact Act (Northeastern)**
N.H. Rev. Stat. 1955, 489-A:1 et seq.

**Water and Navigation Control Act (Brevard County)**
Fla. Special Laws 1963, Ch. 63-1145

**Water and Power Board Act**
Utah Code Ann. 1953, 73-10-1 et seq.

**Water and Power Plan Act**
Ariz. Rev. Stat. Ann., § 45-1701 et seq.

**Water and Related Land Resources Compact Act (Northeastern)**
Conn. Gen. Stat. Ann., §§ 25-120 et seq.

**Water and Sanitary Sewerage Authority Act (Duval County)**
Fla. Special Laws 1959, Ch. 59-1248

**Water and Sanitation District Act (Three Lakes)**
Colo. Rev. Stat., 32-10-101 et seq.

**Water and Sanitation Systems Act**
Colo. Rev. Stat., 32-4-101 et seq.

**Water and Sewage System Training Institute Act**
Ill. Rev. Stat. 1991, Ch. 144, § 690 et seq.

**Water and Sewer Act (Broward County)**
Fla. Special Laws 1963, Ch. 63-1181

**Water and Sewer Act (Escambia County)**
Fla. Special Laws 1971, Ch. 71-629

**Water and Sewer Act (Palm Beach County)**
Fla. Special Laws 1967, Ch. 67-1880

**Water and Sewer Act (Pickens County)**
Ga. Laws 1969, p. 2764

**Water and Sewer Assistance Authority Act**
Va. Code 1950, § 62.1-197 et seq.

**Water and Sewer Authorities Act**
Md. Ann. Code 1974, Art. EN, § 9-901 et seq.
N.C. Gen. Stat. 1943, § 162A-1 et seq.
Va. Code 1950, § 15.1-1239 et seq.

**Water and Sewer Authority Act (Cayuga County)**
N.Y. Public Authorities Law (Consol. Laws Ch. 43A) § 1199aaaa et seq.

**Water and Sewer Authority Act (Clayton-Rabun County)**
Ga. Laws 1992, p. 6403

**Water and Sewer Authority Act (Hall County)**
Ga. Laws 1992, p. 6986

**Water and Sewer Authority Act (Jasper County)**
Ga. Laws 1999, H.B. 972

**Water and Sewer Authority Act (Joint Wilkinson-McIntyre-Irwinton-Toomsboro)**
Ga. Laws 1990, p. 4685

**Water and Sewer Authority Act (Lamar County)**
Ga. Laws 1991, p. 3942

**Water and Sewer Authority Act (Rensselaer County)**
N.Y. Public Authorities Law (Consol. Laws Ch. 43A) § 1199 et seq.

**Water and Sewer Authority Act (Scott)**
Ga. Laws 1972, p. 2831

**Water and Sewer Authority Act (Veazy)**
Ga. Laws 1972, p. 4108

**Water and Sewer Authority Act (Wilton)**
N.Y. Public Authorities Law (Consol. Laws Ch. 43A) § 1121 et seq.

**Water and Sewer Department Accounting Act**
Ark. Code Ann. 1947, 14-237-101 et seq.

**Water and Sewer District Act**
Ida. Code 1947, 42-3201 et seq.
Wyo. Stat. Ann., § 41-10-101 et seq.

**Water and Sewer District Act (County)**
Fla. Stat. Ann., 153.50 et seq.
Mont. Rev. Code 1947, 16-4501 et seq.

**Water and Sewer District Act (Eastpoint)**
Fla. Special Laws 1967, Ch. 67-1399

**Water and Sewer District Act (Regional)**
Ohio Rev. Code 1953, 6119.01 et seq.

**Water and Sewer District Act (Rural)**
Okla. Stat. Title 82, § 1324.1 et seq.

**Water and Sewer District Act (Volusia County)**
Fla. Special Laws 1970, Ch. 70-971

**Water and Sewer District Revenue Bond Act**
Ida. Code 1947, 42-4101 et seq.

**Water and Sewer Districts Act (Immokalee)**
Fla. Special Laws 1978, Ch. 78-494

**Water and Sewer Facilities Act (County)**
N.C. Gen. Stat. 1943, § 153A-283 et seq.

**Water and Sewer Facilities Act (Municipal)**
Wash. Rev. Code Ann. 35.91.010 et seq.

**Water and Sewer Improvement Districts Act**
Utah Code Ann. 1953, 17a-2-301 et seq.

**Water and Sewer Reorganization Act (Model)**
Mass. Gen. Laws. Ann., 40N:2

**Water and Sewer Repair and Compensation Act**
D.C. Code Ann., § 6-405

**Water and Sewer Revenue Act (Port Orange)**
Fla. Special Laws 1951, Ch. 27832

**Water and Sewer Revenue Bond Act**
Nev. Rev. Stat. 1979 Reprint, 350.350 et seq.
N.M. Stat. Ann., 3-31-1 et seq.

**Water and Sewer System Regulatory Act**
Fla. Stat. Ann., 367.011 et seq.

**Water and Sewer Utility Authority Act (Hart County)**
Ga. Laws 1992, p. 6828

**Water and Sewerage Authority Act**
Ga. Code Ann., 12-5-540 to 12-5-555, 12-5-560 to 12-5-564

**Water and Sewerage Authority Act (Alcony Shores)**
Ga. Laws 1979, p. 3177

**Water and Sewerage Authority Act (Atlanta-Fulton County)**
Ga. Laws 1978, p. 4637

**Water and Sewerage Authority Act (Atlanta)**
Ga. Laws 1998, H.B. 1898

**Water and Sewerage Authority Act (Bald Mountain)**
Ga. Laws 1983, p. 4466

**Water and Sewerage Authority Act (Barrow County)**
Ga. Laws 1991, p. 4444

**Water and Sewerage Authority Act (Bibb County)**
Ga. Laws 1966, p. 2737

**Water and Sewerage Authority Act (Butts County, City of Flovilla, City of Jackson, City of Jenkinsburg)**
Ga. Laws 1986, p. 5457

**Water and Sewerage Authority Act (Douglasville-Douglas County)**
Ga. Laws 1985, p. 3584

**Water and Sewerage Authority Act (Ellijay-Gilmer County)**
Ga. Laws 1991, p. 5424

**Water and Sewerage Authority Act (Forsyth County)**
Ga. Laws 1975, p. 3767
Ga. Laws 1996, p. 4084

**Water and Sewerage Authority Act (Franklin County)**
Ga. Laws 1980, p. 4388

**Water and Sewerage Authority Act (Gilmer County)**
Ga. Laws 1984, p. 5215

**Water and Sewerage Authority Act (Gwinnett County)**
Ga. Laws 1970, p. 2827

**Water and Sewerage Authority Act (Jackson County)**
Ga. Laws 1986, p. 5473

**Water and Sewerage Authority Act (Lowndes County)**
Ga. Laws 1973, p. 3285
Ga. Laws 1974, p. 2678

**Water and Sewerage Authority Act (Lumpkin County)**
Ga. Laws 1984, p. 4500

**Water and Sewerage Authority Act (Macon-Bibb County)**
Ga. Laws 1966, p. 2757
Ga. Laws 1973, p. 2603

**Water and Sewerage Authority Act (Meriwether County)**
Ga. Laws 1975, p. 3194

**Water and Sewerage Authority Act (Multi-City)**
Ga. Laws 1975, p. 3033

**Water and Sewerage Authority Act (Murray County)**
Ga. Laws 1980, p. 3447

**Water and Sewerage Authority Act (Newton County)**
Ga. Laws 1970, p. 2449

**Water and Sewerage Authority Act (Oak Ridge)**
Ga. Laws 1991, p. 4310

**Water and Sewerage Authority Act (Peach County)**
Ga. Laws 1986, p. 4664

**Water and Sewerage Authority Act (Peachtree City)**
Ga. Laws 1991, p. 5085

**Water and Sewerage Authority Act (Pike County)**
Ga. Laws 1991, p. 4180

**Water and Sewerage Authority Act (Quitman County)**
Ga. Laws 1998, H.B. 1574

**Water and Sewerage Authority Act (Rockdale County)**
Ga. Laws 1996, p. 3994

**Water and Sewerage Authority Act (Stewart County)**
Ga. Laws 1988, p. 4498

**Water and Sewerage Authority Act (Taylor County)**
Ga. Laws 1996, p. 3589

**Water and Sewerage Authority Act (Tift County)**
Ga. Laws 1972, p. 2808

**Water and Sewerage Authority Act (Towns County)**
Ga. Laws 1972, p. 3407

**Water and Sewerage Authority Act (Upson County)**
Ga. Laws 1998, H.B. 1876

**Water and Sewerage Authority Act (Walker County)**
Ga. Laws 1977, p. 3303

**Water and Sewerage Authority Act (White County)**
Ga. Laws 1984, p. 4920

**Water and Sewerage Facilities Act (Spalding County)**
Ga. Laws 1982, p. 4987

**Water and Soil Conservation District Act**
Ark. Code Ann. 1987, 14-125-101 et seq.
D.C. Code Ann., § 1-2801 et seq.
Ga. Code Ann., 2-6-28 et seq.
Ill. Rev. Stat. 1991, Ch. 5, § 106 et seq.
Ind. Code Ann., 13-3-1-1 et seq.
Ky. Rev. Stat. 1971, 262.010 et seq.
Me. Rev. Stat. Ann. 1964, Title 12, § 1 et seq.
Miss. Code Ann. 1972, § 69-27-1 et seq.
Neb. Rev. Stat. 1943, 2-1575 et seq.
N.M. Stat. Ann., 73-20-1 et seq.
S.C. Code Ann. 1976, § 48-9-10 et seq.
S.D. Codified Laws 1967, 38-8-1 et seq.
Wash. Rev. Code 1983, 89.08.005 et seq.
Wyo. Stat. Ann., § 11-16-101 et seq.

**Water and Soil Conservation Districts Law**
Me. Rev. Stat. Ann. 1964, Title 12, § 1 et seq.
Minn. Stat. 1986, 103C.005 et seq.

**Water and Wastewater Authority Act (Dutchess County)**
N.Y. Public Authorities Law (Consol. Laws Ch. 43A) § 1121 et seq.

**Water and Wastewater Operators Certification Act**
Fla. Stat. Ann., 468.540 et seq.

**Water and Wastewater System Regulatory Law**
Fla. Stat. Ann., 367.011 et seq.

**Water and Wastewater Systems Operators Certification Act (Municipal and Domestic)**
Miss. Code Ann. 1972, § 21-27-201 et seq.

**Water and Wastewater Treatment Authority Act**
Tenn. Code Ann., 68-211-601 et seq.

**Water and Wastewater Treatment Plant Operators Act**
Ga. Code Ann., 43-51-1 et seq.

**Water Appropriation Act**
Cal. Water Code § 1200 et seq.
Kan. Stat. Ann., 82a-701 et seq.
Mont. Code Ann., 85-2-301 et seq.
Nev. Rev. Stat. 1979 Reprint, 533.350 et seq.
N.M. Stat. Ann., 72-5-1 et seq.
Tex. Water Code, § 11.024 et seq.
Utah Code Ann. 1953, 73-3-1 et seq.
Wash. Rev. Code Ann. 90.03.010 et seq.

**Water Assurance Program Act**
Kan. Stat. Ann., 82a-1330 et seq.

**Water Authorities Act**
Ill. Rev. Stat. 1991, Ch. 111 2/3, § 222.9 et seq.

**Water Authority Act (Appling)**
Ga. Laws 1975, p. 2605

**Water Authority Act (Butts County)**
Ga. Laws 1971, p. 3568

**Water Authority Act (Charter)**
Mich. Comp. Laws Ann., 121.1 et seq.

**Water Authority Act (Clifton Park)**
N.Y. Public Authorities Law (Consol. Laws Ch. 43A) § 1120 et seq.

**Water Authority Act (Cobb County-Marietta)**
Ga. Laws 1951, p. 497

**Water Authority Act (Coosa)**
Ga. Laws 1972, p. 3926

**Water Authority Act (County)**
Cal. Water Code, Appx., § 45-1 et seq.

**Water Authority Act (Dade County)**
Ga. Laws 1958, p. 3260

**Water Authority Act (Douglasville-Douglas County)**
Ga. Laws 1974, p. 3376

**Water Authority Act (Echols County)**
Ga. Laws 1972, p. 2981

**Water Authority Act (Erie County)**
N.Y. Public Authorities Law (Consol. Laws Ch. 43A) § 1050 et seq.

**Water Authority Act (Fayette County)**
Ga. Laws 1991, p. 4026

**Water Authority Act (Forsyth-Etowah)**
Ga. Laws 1984, p. 4779

**Water Authority Act (Franklin-Heard County)**
Ga. Laws 1984, p. 4613

**Water Authority Act (Grayson)**
Ga. Laws 1991, p. 4195

**Water Authority Act (Great Neck North)**
N.Y. Public Authorities Law (Consol. Laws Ch. 43A) § 1197a et seq.

**Water Authority Act (Great Neck)**
N.Y. Public Authorities Law (Consol. Laws Ch. 43A) § 1230 et seq.

**Water Authority Act (Haralson County)**
Ga. Laws 1971, p. 3258

**Water Authority Act (Hinsonton)**
Ga. Laws 1974, p. 2997

**Water Authority Act (Macon)**
Ga. Laws 1992, p. 4991

**Water Authority Act (Monroe County)**
N.Y. Public Authorities Law (Consol. Laws Ch. 43A) § 1093 et seq.

**Water Authority Act (Morgan County)**
Ga. Laws 1991, p. 4670

**Water Authority Act (Mountville)**
Ga. Laws 1982, p. 4452

**Water Authority Act (Nicholson)**
Ga. Laws 1972, p. 3964

**Water Authority Act (Nolta)**
Ga. Laws 1972, p. 3385

**Water Authority Act (North Smithfield)**
R.I. Laws 1993, Ch. 218

**Water Authority Act (Oglethorpe County)**
Ga. Laws 1991, p. 3605

**Water Authority Act (Onondaga County)**
N.Y. Public Authorities Law (Consol. Laws Ch. 43A) § 1150 et seq.

**Water Authority Act (Orange County)**
N.Y. Public Authorities Law (Consol. Laws Ch. 43A) § 1199aa et seq.

**Water Authority Act (Paulding County)**
Ga. Laws 1961, p. 2837

**Water Authority Act (Perkins)**
Ga. Laws 1972, p. 3604

**Water Authority Act (Powersville)**
Ga. Laws 1972, p. 3724

**Water Authority Act (Saratoga County)**
N.Y. Public Authorities Law (Consol. Laws Ch. 43A) § 1199aaa et seq.

**Water Authority Act (Suffolk County)**
N.Y. Public Authorities Law (Consol. Laws Ch. 43A) § 1074 et seq

**Water Authority Act (Tri-County)**
Ga. Laws 1986, p. 5318

**Water Authority Act (Walnutgrove-Youth)**
Ga. Laws 1972, p. 3623

**Water Authority Act (Wayne County)**
N.Y. Public Authorities Law (Consol. Laws Ch. 43A) § 1199aa et seq.

**Water Authority Act (West Georgia)**
Ga. Laws 1988, p. 4926

**Water Authority of Great Neck North Act**
N.Y. Public Authorities Law (Consol. Laws Ch. 43A) § 1197a et seq.

**Water Authority of Southeastern Nassau County Act**
N.Y. Public Authorities Law (Consol. Laws Ch. 43A) § 1174a et seq.

**Water Authority of Western Nassau County Act**
N.Y. Public Authorities Law (Consol. Laws Ch. 43A) § 1198a et seq.

**Water Bank Act**
Dec. 13, 1970, P.L. 91-559, 84 Stat. 1468, 16 U.S. Code §§ 1301 to 1311
Dec. 19, 1971, P.L. 91-559, 16 U.S. Code § 1301 nt.
Jan. 2, 1980, P.L. 96-182, 16 U.S. Code §§ 1302, 1304, 1310

**Water Bank Extension Act of 1994**
Oct. 22, 1994, P.L. 103-393, 16 U.S. Code § 1305 nt.

**Water Board Act (Albany)**
N.Y. Public Authorities Law (Consol. Laws Ch. 43A) §§ 1116, 1118
N.Y. Public Authorities Law (Consol. Laws Ch. 43A) §§ 1116, 1118

**Water Bond Act**
N.J. Laws 1958, Ch. 35

**Water Bond Law of 1984 (Clean)**
Cal. Water Code § 13985 et seq.
Cal. Water Code § 13999 et seq.

**Water Bond Law of 1984 (Safe Drinking)**
Cal. Water Code § 13810 et seq.

**Water Carriers Act**
Haw. Rev. Stat. Ann., § 271G-1 et seq.
Mich. Comp. Laws Ann., 460.201 et seq.

**Water Closet Act (Railroads)**
Tex. Rev. Civ. Stat., Arts. 6396 to 6398

**Water Code**
Ariz. Rev. Stat. Ann., § 45-101 et seq.
Cal. Statutes 1943, Ch. 368, p. 1604
Ore. Rev. Stat., 537.010 et seq.
Wash. Rev. Code Ann., 90.03.005 et seq.

**Water Commission Act**
Cal. Water Code § 100 et seq.
Cal. Water Code § 150 et seq. § 100 et seq.
Ill. Rev. Stat. 1991, Ch. 24, § 11-135-2 et seq.

**Water Commissioners Act**
Kan. Laws 1917, Ch. 172
Mont. Code Ann., 85-5-101 et seq.
N.Y. Laws 1905, Ch. 723
W. Va. Code 1931, Ch. 16, Art. 11, § 1 et seq.

**Water Compact Act (Ute Indian)**
Utah Code Ann. 1953, 73-21-1, 73-21-2

**Water Company Act**
Cal. Public Utilities Code § 2701 et seq.
N.J. Stat. Anno, 48:19-1 et seq.
Wash. Rev. Code 1983, 80.28.010 et seq.

**Water Company Invested Capital Tax Act**
Ill. Comp. Stat. 1992, Ch. 35, § 625/1 et seq.
Ill. Rev. Stat. 1991, Ch. 120, § 1411 et seq.

**Water Company Merger Act**
Pa. 1907 Pamph. Laws 455, No. 307

**Water Conservancy Act**
Colo. Rev. Stat., 37-45-101 et seq.
Utah Code Ann. 1953, 17A-2-1402

**Water Conservancy District Act**
Colo. Rev. Stat., 37-45-101 et seq.
Nev. Rev. Stat. 1979 Reprint, 541.010 et seq.
Ohio Rev. Code 1953, 6101.01 et seq.
Okla. Stat. Title 82, § 531 et seq.
Wyo. Stat. Ann., § 41-3-701 et seq.

**Water Conservancy Districts Law**
S.D. Codified Laws 1967, 46A-9-1 et seq.

**Water Conservation Act**
Cal. Statutes 1927, p. 160
Cal. Statutes 1929, p. 307
Cal. Statutes 1931, p. 2045
Cal. Water Code, Appx., § 34-1 et seq.
Colo. Rev. Stat., 37-60-101, et seq.
D.C. Code Ann., § 1-2801 et seq.
Fla. Stat. 1983, 553.14
Ind. Code 1976, 19-3-2-1 et seq.
Ky. Rev. Stat. 1971, Superseded Vols., 262.670 et seq.
Miss. Code Ann. 1972, § 51-3-1 et seq.
Mont. Code Ann., 85-1-101 et seq.
N.D. Cent. Code 61-02-01 et seq.
Neb. Rev. Stat. 1943, 2-1575 et seq.
Nev. Rev. Stat. 1979 Reprint, 541.010 et seq.
Ohio Rev. Code 1953, 6101.01 et seq.
Okla. Stat. Title 82, § 531 et seq.
Utah Code Ann. 1953, 73-9-1 et seq.
Wyo. Stat. Ann., § 41-3-701 et seq.

**Water Conservation Act (Ground)**
Ind. Code Ann., 13-2-2-1 et seq.

**Water Conservation and Agricultural Management Act**
Cal. Water Code § 10520 et seq.

**Water Conservation and Control Act (Nassau County)**
Fla. Special Laws 1961, Ch. 61-2525

**Water Conservation and Control Act (Orange County)**
Fla. Special Laws 1961, Ch. 61-2581

**Water Conservation and Control Act (Seminole County)**
Fla. Laws 1963, Ch. 63-1936

**Water Conservation and Flood Control District Act**
Cal. Statutes 1931, Ch. 641 p. 1369

**Water Conservation and Flood Control District Act (San Benito County)**
Cal. Statutes 1953, Ch. 1598, p. 3279
Cal. Water Code, Appx., § 70-1 et seq.

**Water Conservation and Flood Control District Merger Act (San Benito County)**
Cal. Statutes 1961, Ch. 203

**Water Conservation and Landscaping Act**
Cal. Government Code § 65591 et seq.

**Water Conservation and Utilization Act**
Oct. 31, 1994, P.L. 103-434, 108 Stat. 4549

**Water Conservation and Water Quality Act**
Cal. Water Code § 15200 et seq.

**Water Conservation and Water Quality Bond Law**
Cal. Water Code § 13450 et seq.

**Water Conservation Bond Act**
N.J. Laws 1969, Ch. 127

**Water Conservation Bond Interest Rate Ceiling Elimination Act**
N.J. Laws 1981, Ch. 233

**Water Conservation Bond Law**
Cal. Water Code § 12879 et seq.

**Water Conservation District and Flood Control Act (Colusa County)**
Cal. Statutes 1983, Ch. 926

**Water Conservation District Law**
Cal. Water Code § 74000 et seq.

**Water Conservation Districts Act**
Cal. Statutes 1923, p. 978
Colo. Rev. Stat., 37-45-101 et seq.
Ga. Code Ann., 2-6-20 et seq.
N.D. Cent. Code 61-16-01 et seq.
Ore. Rev. Stat., 552.020 et seq.
S.C. Code Ann. 1976, § 48-9-10 et seq.
Wash. Rev. Code Ann., 89.08.005 et seq.

**Water Conservation Fund Act of 1965**
June 9, 1998, P.L. 105-178, 16 U.S. Code § 460l-11

**Water Conservation in Landscaping Act (State Projects)**
Colo. Rev. Stat., 37-96-101 et seq.

**Water Conservation Projects Act**
Cal. Water Code § 11950 et seq.

**Water Control Act**
La. Rev. Stat. Ann., 30:1091 et seq.
Va. Code 1950, § 62.1-44.2 et seq.

**Water Control Act (Park Commission)**
Ill. Rev. Stat. 1991, Ch. 105, § 91.9 et seq.

**Water Control and Drainage Act**
Fla. Stat. Ann., 298.001

**Water Control and Improvement District Act**
Tex. Water Code, § 51.001 et seq.

**Water Dam Use Act**
Ill. Rev. Stat. 1991, Ch. 96 1/2, §§ 8150, 8151

**Water Desalination Act of 1996**
Oct. 11, 1996, P.L. 104-298, 42 U.S. Code § 10301 nt.

**Water Development Act**
Kan. Stat. Ann., 82a-701 et seq.

**Water Development Act (Omnibus)**
S.D. Codified Laws 1967, 46A-1-60 et seq.
S.D. Laws 1982, Ch. 316
S.D. Laws 1983, Ch. 315

**Water Development Authority Act**
W. Va. Code 1966, § 20-5C-1 et seq.
W. Va. Code 1966, § 22C-1-1 et seq.

**Water Development Board Act**
Tex. Water Code, § 6.001 et seq.

**Water Development Bonding Law**
Mont. Code Ann., 90-2-101 et seq.

**Water Distribution Act**
Ida. Code 1947, 42-607

**Water Distribution District Act**
Wash. Rev. Code 1951, 87.60.010 et seq.

**Water Distribution District Act (Regional)**
Ark. Code Ann. 1947, 14-116-101 et seq.

**Water District Act**
Cal. Public Contracts Code § 20930
Cal. Water Code § 34000 et seq.
Me. Rev. Stat. Ann. 1964, Title 35-A, § 6301 et seq.
Minn. Stat. 1988, 112.34 et seq.
Tenn. Code Ann., 7-82-101 et seq.
Wash. Rev. Code Ann., 57.02.010 et seq.
Wis. Stat. Ann., 198.22

**Water District Act (Brevard County)**
Fla. Special Laws 1951, Ch. 27419

**Water District Act (Brisbane County)**
Cal. Statutes 1950, 1st Ex. Sess., Ch. 13, p. 447
Cal. Water Code, Appx., § 57-1 et seq.

**Water District Act (County)**
Cal. Water Code § 30000 et seq. § 34000 et seq.
Mont. Code Ann., 7-13-2201 et seq.

**Water District Act (Madera)**
Cal. Statutes 1991, Ch. 735

**Water District Act (Metropolitan)**
Cal. Stat. 1969, Ch. 209, p. 492
Cal. Water Code, Appx., § 109-1 et seq.
Mo. Rev. Stat., 247.230 et seq.
Utah Code Ann. 1953, 73-8-1 et seq.

**Water District Act (Metropoliton)**
Utah Code Ann. 1953, 17A-2-801 et seq.

**Water District Act (Odessa)**
Cal. Statutes 1991, Ch. 533

**Water District Act (Orange County)**
Cal. Statutes 1933, Ch. 924, p. 2400
Cal. Water Code, Appx., § 40-1 et seq.

**Water District Act (Rural)**
Neb. Rev. Stat. 1943, 46-1001 et seq.

**Water District Act (Santa Clara Valley)**
Cal. Statutes 1973, Ch. 56
Cal. Water Code, Appx., 60-1 et seq.

**Water District Act (Volusia County)**
Fla. Special Laws 1951, Ch. 27960

**Water District Addition Loan Act**
Mass. Acts 1962, Ch. 654

**Water District Conservation Act (Collier County)**
Fla. Special Laws 1961, Ch. 61-2037

**Water District Enabling Act (Standard)**
Me. Rev. Stat. Ann. 1964, Title 35-A, § 6401 et seq.

**Water District Improvement Loan Act (West Boylston)**
Mass. Acts 1951, Ch. 739

**Water District Loan Act (Boylston)**
Mass. Acts 1951, Ch. 421
Mass. Acts 1955, Ch. 537

**Water District Loan Act (Byfield)**
Mass. Acts 1954, Ch. 470
Mass. Acts 1956, Ch. 251

**Water District Loan Act (Dighton)**
Mass. Acts 1967, Ch. 500

**Water District Loan Act (Griswoldville)**
Mass. Acts 1962, Ch. 470

**Water District Loan Act (Kalmia Woods)**
Mass. Acts 1953, Ch. 357

**Water District Loan Act (Montague Center)**
Mass. Acts 1953, Ch. 107

**Water District Loan Act (Mount Pleasant)**
Mass. Acts 1955, Ch. 664

**Water District Loan Act (Westhampton)**
Mass. Acts 1953, Ch. 105

**Water District Management Act (Hendry County)**
Fla. Special Laws 1967, Ch. 67-1443

**Water District Sewer Bond Urgency Validating Act**
Cal. Statutes 1964, 1st Ex. Sess., Ch. 43, p. 178

**Water District Sewer Bond Validating Act**
Cal. Statutes 1964, 1st Ex. Sess., Ch. 42, p. 176

**Water Districts Act Public Services Districts for Water and Sewerage Services Act)**
W. Va. Code 1966, § 16-13A-1 et seq.

**Water Diversion Policy Act**
Conn. Gen. Stat. Ann., § 22a-365 et seq.

**Water Drainage Utility Act (Surface)**
Wyo. Stat. 1977, §§ 16-10-101 to 16-10-110

**Water Environmental Health Act**
Tenn. Code Ann., 68-221-301

**Water Facilities Act**
Aug. 28, 1937, Ch. 870, 50 Stat. 869, 16 U.S. Code §§ 590r to 590x
Aug. 17, 1954, Ch. 751, 68 Stat. 734, 16 U.S. Code §§ 590r, 590s, 590x-1 to 590x-3
Aug. 25, 1958, P.L. 85-748, 72 Stat. 841, 16 U.S. Code § 590x-4
Cal. Water Code § 12950 et seq.

**Water Facilities Assistance Program Act**
R.I. Gen. Laws 1956, 46-15.2-1 et seq.

**Water Facilities Restoration Act**
Pa. Cons. Stat., Title 32, § 7501 et seq.

**Water Finance Authority Act (Albany)**
N.Y. Public Authorities Law (Consol. Laws Ch. 43A) § 1115 et seq.

**Water Finance Authority Act (Upper Mohawk Valley)**
N.Y. Public Authorities Law (Consol. Laws Ch. 43A) § 1226a et seq.

**Water for Drinking Act**
S.C. Code Ann. 1976, § 44-55-10 et seq.

**Water Fund Act**
Cal. Water Code § 12900 et seq.

**Water Improvement and Management Act (Surface)**
Fla. Stat. Ann., 373.451 et seq.

**Water Improvement District Accounting Act**
Ark. Code Ann. 1947, 14-119-101 et seq.

**Water Improvement District Act**
Ore. Rev. Stat., 552.020 et seq.

**Water Law**
Minn. Stat. Ann., 103A.001 et seq.
Minn. Stat. 1986, 103A.201 et seq.
Mo. Rev. Stat. 1978, 644.006 et seq.

**Water Lien Act**
Mass. Gen. Laws Ann., 40:42A et seq.

**Water Loan Act (Brewster)**
Mass. Acts 1965, Ch. 552

**Water Loan Act (Brockton)**
Mass. Acts 1953, Ch. 147

**Water Loan Act (Clarksburg)**
Mass. Acts 1951, Ch. 651

**Water Loan Act (Dartsmouth)**
Mass. Acts 1955, Ch. 22

**Water Loan Act (Fitchburg)**
Mass. Acts 1951, Ch. 732

**Water Loan Act (Holyoke)**
Mass. Acts 1953, Ch. 659

**Water Loan Act (Lynnfield Water District)**
Mass. Acts 1956, Ch. 616

**Water Loan Act (Marlborough)**
Mass. Acts 1959, Ch. 518

**Water Loan Act (Mattapoisett)**
Mass. Acts 1952, Ch. 331

**Water Loan Act (Metropolitan District)**
Mass. Acts 1950, Ch. 660
Mass. Acts 1952, Ch. 619
Mass. Acts 1956, Ch. 685

**Water Loan Act (North Brookfield)**
Mass. Acts 1951, Ch. 140

**Water Loan Act (Orleans)**
Mass. Acts 1953, Ch. 418

**Water Loan Act (Pepperell)**
Mass. Acts 1950, Ch. 702

**Water Loan Act (Provincetown)**
Mass. Acts 1952, Ch. 439

**Water Loan Act (Rowley)**
Mass. Acts 1954, Ch. 204

**Water Loan Act (Somerset)**
Mass. Acts 1957, Ch. 622

**Water Loan Act (South Hadley Fire District No. 2)**
Mass. Acts 1954, Ch. 412

**Water Loan Act (Taunton)**
Mass. Acts 1953, Ch. 540

**Water Loan Act (Upton)**
Mass. Acts 1953, Ch. 202

**Water Main Loan Act (Metropolitan District)**
Mass. Acts 1954, Ch. 278

**Water Management Act**
Ala. Code 1975, § 9-9-1 et seq.
Mass. Gen. Laws Ann., 21G:1 et seq.
Mich. Comp. Laws Ann., 280.551 et seq.
N.D. Cent. Code 61-16-01 et seq.

**Water Management Act (Comprehensive Local)**
Minn. Stat. 1986, 103B.301 et seq.

**Water Management Act (Local)**
Minn. Stat. Ann., 103B.301 et seq.

**Water Management District Act (Pinallas Park)**
Fla. Special Laws 1975, Ch. 491

**Water Management Planning Act (Agricultural)**
Cal. Water Code § 10800 et seq.

**Water Management Planning Act (Urban)**
Cal. Water Code § 10610 et seq.

**Water Management Practices Act (Efficient Agricultural Water Suppliers)**
Cal. Water Code § 10900 et seq.

**Water Measurement Law**
Cal. Water Code § 500 et seq.

**Water Meter Law (Violations)**
Ky. Rev. Stat. 1962, 433.570 et seq.

**Water Metering Act**
Colo. Rev. Stat., 37-97-101 et seq.

**Water Mill Act**
Me. Rev. Stat. Ann. 1964, Title 38, § 651 et seq.

**Water Partnership Law (Clean)**
Minn. Stat. Ann., 103F.701 et seq.

**Water Permit Act**
Iowa Code Ann., 455B.171 et seq.
Tex. Rev. Water Code, § 11.121 et seq.

**Water Plan Act**
Kan. Stat. Ann., 82a-901 et seq.
Mont. Code Ann., 85-1-203
Tex. Water Code, § 11.001 et seq.

**Water Plan Storage Act**
Kan. Stat. Ann., 82a-1301 et seq.

**Water Pollutant Discharge Act**
Ill. Rev. Stat. 1991, Ch. 85, § 1700 et seq.

**Water Pollution Abatement Projects Administration Fund Act**
Mass. Gen. Laws. Ann., 21:27a, 29:2w

**Water Pollution Act (Dickey)**
Cal. Statutes 1949, Ch. 1549, p. 2782, § 1
Cal. Water Code § 13000 et seq.

**Water Pollution Agency Act**
Nev. Rev. Stat. 1967 Reprint, Replaced Pages, 445.040 et seq.

**Water Pollution Commission Act**
Del. Code of 1974, Title 7, § 1112 et seq.

**Water Pollution Control Act**
See also Water Quality Control Act
Ala. Code 1975, § 22-22-1 et seq.
Alaska Stat. 1962, § 46.03.050 et seq.
Ariz. Rev. Stat. Ann., § 36-1851 et seq.
Ark. Stat. 1947, 8-4-101 et seq.
Cal. Statutes 1965, Ch. 1351, p. 3239
Colo. Rev. Stat. 25-8-101 et seq.
Conn. Gen. Stat. Ann., § 22a-416 et seq.
Fla. Stat. Ann., 387.01 et seq.
Ga. Code Ann., 12-5-20 et seq.
Haw. Rev. Stat. Ann., § 321-16
Iowa Code 1983, 455B.171 et seq.
Kan. Stat. Ann., 12-3101 et seq., 65-161 et seq.
Ky. Rev. Stat. 1971, 224.01-060 et seq.
Mass. Gen. Laws Ann., 21:26 et seq.
Md. Ann. Code 1974, Art. EN, § 4-401 et seq.
Me. Rev. Stat. Ann. 1964, Title 38, § 361 et seq.
Minn. Stat. Ann., 115.01 et seq.
Mont. Code Ann., 75-5-101 et seq.
N.D. Cent. Code 61-28-01 et seq.
Neb. Rev. Stat. 1943, 81-1501 et seq.
Nev. Rev. Stat. 1979 Reprint, 445.131 et seq.
N.H. Rev. Stat. 1955, 485-A:1 et seq.
N.J. Stat. Ann. 58:10A-1 et seq.
N.Y. Environmental Conservation Law 1972 (Consol. Laws Ch. 438) § 17-0101 et seq.
Ohio Rev. Code 1953, 6111.01 et seq.
Okla. Stat. Ann., Title 82, § 926.1 et seq.
Ore. Rev. Stat., 468B.005 et seq.
Pa. Purdon's Stat., Title 35, § 691.1 et seq.
R.I. Gen. Laws 1956, 46-12-1 et seq.
S.C. Code Ann. 1976, § 48-1-10 et seq.
S.D. Codified Laws 1967, 34A-2-1 et seq.
Tex. Water Code, § 26.121 et seq.
Utah Code Ann. 1953, 26-11-1 et seq.
Vt. Stat. Ann., Title 10, § 1251 et seq.; Title 18, § 1201 et seq.
Wash. Rev. Code Ann., 90.48.010 et seq.
Wis. Stat. Ann., 144.01 et seq.
W. Va. Code 1966, §§ 20-5A-1 et seq., 22-11-1 et seq.

**Water Pollution Control Act Amendment of 1956**
July 9, 1956, Ch. 518, 70 Stat. 498 (See 33 U.S. Code §§ 1151 et seq.)

**Water Pollution Control Act of 1966**
Colo. Rev. Stat. 1963, 66-28-1 et seq.

**Water Pollution Control and Sewage Treatment Plant Grant Act**
Fla. Stat. Ann., 403.1821 et seq.

**Water Pollution Control Commission Act (Interstate)**
Also known as New England Interstate Water Pollution Control Compact
Me. Rev. Stat. Ann. 1964, Title 38, § 491 et seq.

**Water Pollution Control Compact**
Tex. Water Code, § 26.043

**Water Pollution Control Compact (New England Interstate)**
Conn. Gen. Stat. Ann., § 22a-308 et seq.
Me. Rev. Stat. Ann. 1964, Title 38, § 491 et seq.
N.H. Rev. Stat. 1955, 488:1 et seq.
R.I. Gen. Laws 1956, 46-16-1 et seq.
Vt. Stat. Ann., Title 10, § 1331 et seq.

**Water Pollution Control Revolving Fund Act**
Miss. Code Ann. 1972, § 49-17-81 et seq.

**Water Pollution Control Revolving Fund and Emergency Loan Fund Act**
Miss. Code Ann. 1972, §§ 49-17-81 to 49-17-89

**Water Pollution Control State Grant Act**
Ark. Code Ann. 1947, 82-1915 to 8-5-401

**Water Pollution Control Tax Refund Act**
Neb. Rev. Stat. 1943, 77-27,149 et seq.

**Water Pollution from Underground Storage Tank Corrective Action Act**
Wyo. Stat. Ann., § 35-11-1414 et seq.

**Water Power Act**
See Federal Power Act and Federal Water Power Act
N.Y. Environmental Conservation Law 1972 (Consol. Laws Ch. 43B) §§ 15-1701 et seq., 71-1117, 71-1119
Va. Code 1950, § 62.1-80 et seq.
Wis. Stat. Ann., 31.01 et seq.
W. Va. Code 1966, § 31-9-1 et seq.

**Water Power Act (Chicago Sanitary District)**
Ill. Rev. Stat. 1989, Ch. 42, § 369.9 et seq.

**Water Power Companies Act**
Mich. Comp. Laws Ann., 486.1 et seq.

**Water Power Generation Act**
Cal. Statutes 1911, Ex. Sess., Ch. 41, p. 175

**Water Project Revenue Bonding Act**
Neb. Rev. Stat. 1943, 2-4501 et seq.

**Water Projects Act (Davis-Dolwig)**
Cal. Water Code § 11900 et seq.

**Water Projects Assistance Act**
Cal. Water Code § 15050 et seq.

**Water Projects Environmental Coordination Act**
Kan. Stat. Ann., 82a-325 et seq.

**Water Protection Act (Ground)**
N.M. Stat. Ann., 74-6B-1 et seq.

**Water Protection District Act**
Cal. Statutes 1880, Ch. 63, p. 55
Cal. Statutes 1895, Ch. 201, p. 247
Cal. Statutes 1907, Ch. 25, p. 16

**Water Protection District Act (Surface)**
Ill. Rev. Stat. 1991, Ch. 42, § 447.99 et seq.

**Water Protection Fund Act**
Ariz. Rev. Stat. Ann., § 45-2101 et seq.

**Water Purification Finance Authority Act (Utica)**
N.Y. Public Authorities Law (Consol. Laws Ch. 43A) § 1226 et seq.

**Water Quality Act**
Utah Code Ann. 1953, 19-5-101 et seq.

**Water Quality Act of 1965**
Oct. 2, 1965, P.L. 89-234, 79 Stat. 903 (See 33 U.S. Code §§ 1151 et seq.)

**Water Quality Act of 1987**
Feb. 4, 1987, P.L. 100-4, 33 U.S. Code §§ 251 et seq., 1251 nt.
Dec. 21, 1995, P.L. 104-66, 33 U.S. Code §§ 1342, 1375 nt.

**Water Quality and Water Conservation Act**
Cal. Water Code § 15200 et seq.

**Water Quality Assurance Act**
Fla. Laws 1983, Ch. 83-310

**Water Quality Authority Act (San Gabriel Basin)**
Cal. Statutes 1992, Ch. 776

**Water Quality Control Act**
See also Water Pollution Control Act
Cal. Water Code § 13000 et seq.
Colo. Rev. Stat., 25-8-101 et seq.
Ga. Code Ann., 12-5-20 et seq.
Iowa Code Ann., 455B.291 et seq.
N.M. Stat. Ann., 74-6-1 et seq.
Tenn. Code Ann., 69-3-101 et seq.
Tex. Water Code, § 26.001 et seq.

**Water Quality Financing Administration Act**
Md. Ann. Code 1974, Art. EN, § 9-1601 et seq.

**Water Quality Improvement Act**
N.J. Laws 1971, Ch. 173

**Water Quality Improvement Act of 1970**
April 3, 1970, P.L. 91-224, 84 Stat. 91, 33 U.S. Code §§ 1151 nts., 1152, 1155, 1156, 1158, 1160 to 1175

**Water Quality Joint Development Act**
Wash. Rev. Code Ann., 70.150.010 et seq.

**Water Quality Laboratory Certification Act**
Md. Ann. Code 1974, Art. HE, § 9-1001 et seq.

**Water Quality Loan Act**
Md. Laws 1968, Ch. 445

**Water Quality Monitoring Act**
Neb. Rev. Stat. 1943, 46-1301 et seq.

**Water Quality Planning Act**
N.J. Stat. Ann. 58:11A-1 et seq.

**Water Quality Protection Act (Ground)**
Ida. Code 1947, 39-120 et seq.

**Water Quality Protection Act (Puget Sound)**
Wash. Rev. Code Ann., 90.71.900

**Water Quality Revolving Fund Authority Act**
S.C. Code Ann. 1976, § 48-5-10 et seq.

**Water Quality Standard Approval Act**
D.C. Code Ann., § 1-319

**Water Rates Regulation Act**
Wash. Rev. Code Ann. 80.28.010 et seq.

**Water Reclamation Act**
Cal. Water Code § 13500 et seq.

**Water Reclamation and Clean Water Bond Law**
Cal. Water Code § 14050 et seq.

**Water Reclamation District Act (Metropolitan)**
Ill. Rev. Stat. 1987, Ch. 42, § 3245 et seq.

**Water Recordation Act**
Cal. Water Code § 4999 et seq.

**Water Recreation Act**
Ga. Code 1933, 17-1201 et seq.

**Water Recreational Areas Act**
Iowa Code Ann., 111.59 et seq.

**Water Recycling Act**
Cal. Water Code § 13575 et seq.

**Water Replenishment District Act**
Cal. Water Code § 60000 et seq.

**Water Rescue Act**
Ill. Comp. Stat. 1992, Ch. 50, § 755/1 et seq.

**Water Research, Conservation and Development Act**
N.M. Stat. Ann., 75-2-1 et seq.

**Water Research Planning Act**
Aug. 20, 1972, P.L. 92-396, 86 Stat. 578, 42 U.S. Code § 1962d
July 1, 1973, P.L. 93-55, 87 Stat. 140, 42 U.S. Code § 1962d
Oct. 16, 1975, P.L. 94-112, 89 Stat. 575, 42 U.S. Code §§ 1962a, 1962a-4, 1962b-4, 1962c, 1962d

**Water Resource Bond Act**
N.J. Laws 1975, Ch. 202

**Water Resource Districts Act**
N.D. Cent. Code 61-16.1-01 et seq.

**Water Resource Planning Act**
Kan. Stat. Ann., 82a-901 et seq.

**Water Resources Act**
Oct. 31, 1992, P.L. 102-580, 106 Stat. 4797
Ala. Code 1975, § 9-10B-1 et seq.
Fla. Stat. Ann., 373.013 et seq.
Ind. Code Ann., 13-2-1-1 et seq.
Mich. Comp. Laws Ann., 323.1 et seq.
Mo. Rev. Stat., 640.400 et seq.
*Continued*

Mont. Code Ann., 85-1-101 et seq.
N.Y. Environmental Conservation Law 1972 (Consol. Laws Ch. 43B) § 15-0101 et seq.
P.R. Laws Ann. 1954, Title 12, § 1501 et seq.
Va. Code 1950, § 62.1-44.45 et seq.
Wash. Rev. Stat. 1976, 90.54.010 et seq.
Wis. Stat. Ann., 144.01 et seq.

**Water Resources Act (Alligator Point)**
Fla. Special Laws 1963, Ch. 63-1350

**Water Resources and Power Development Authority Act**
Colo. Rev. Stat. 37-95-101 et seq.

**Water Resources Authority Act**
P.R. Laws Ann. 1954, Title 22, § 191 et seq.

**Water Resources Board Act**
Ore. Rev. Stat., 536.210 et seq.
Utah Code Ann. 1953, 73-10-1 et seq.
W. Va. Code 1931, Ch. 20, Art. 5, § 1 et seq.

**Water Resources Bond Act**
Cal. Water Code § 15000 et seq.

**Water Resources Commission Act**
Mich. Comp. Laws Ann., 323.1 et seq.

**Water Resources Committee Act**
R.I. Gen. Laws 1956, 22-7.1-1 et seq.

**Water Resources Conservation, Development and Use Act**
P.R. Laws Ann. 1954, Title 12, § 1501 et seq.

**Water Resources Cost Share Finance Act**
Ark. Code Ann. 1987, No. 257

**Water Resources Department Act**
N.C. Gen. Stat. 1943, § 143-350 et seq.

**Water Resources Development Act**
Ark. Code Ann. 1987, 15-22-601 et seq.
Miss. Code Ann. 1972, § 51-3-1 et seq.

**Water Resources Development Act (Federal)**
N.C. Gen. Stat. 1943, § 143-215.38 et seq.

**Water Resources Development Act of 1974**
March 7, 1974, P.L. 93-251, 88 Stat. 49, 42 U.S. Code § 1962d-5c nt.
Oct. 22, 1976, P.L. 94-587, 90 Stat. 2928, 2932, 2933, 2936
Aug. 15, 1985, P.L. 99-88, 99 Stat. 316
Nov. 17, 1986, P.L. 99-662, 16 U.S. Code § 460ee; 42 U.S. Code § 1962d-16
July 11, 1987, P.L. 100-71, 101 Stat. 404
Nov. 17, 1988, P.L. 100-676, 102 Stat. 4031
Nov. 23, 1988, P.L. 100-707, 102 Stat. 4715
Nov. 15, 1990, P.L. 101-561, 16 U.S. Code § 460ee
Nov. 28, 1990, P.L. 101-640, 33 U.S. Code § 579, 42 U.S. Code § 1962d-16
Oct. 31, 1992, P.L. 102-580, 42 U.S. Code § 1962d-16
Oct. 12, 1996, P.L. 104-303, 42 U.S. Code § 1962d-16

**Water Resources Development Act of 1976**
Oct. 22, 1976, P.L. 94-587, 42 U.S. Code § 1962d-5d
June 28, 1980, P.L. 96-292, 42 U.S. Code § 1962d-11a
Dec. 29, 1981, P.L. 97-140, 95 Stat. 1717
July 30, 1983, P.L. 98-63, 97 Stat. 312
Nov. 17, 1986, P.L. 99-662, 33 U.S. Code §§ 426j, 426m; 42 U.S. Code §§ 1962d-5d, 1962d-5f
Nov. 17, 1988, P.L. 100-676, 33 U.S. Code § 426j
Oct. 31, 1992, P.L. 102-580, 33 U.S. Code § 426j
Nov. 2, 1994, P.L. 103-437, 42 U.S. Code §§ 1962d-5g, 1962d-14a
Feb. 10, 1996, P.L. 104-106, 33 U.S. Code § 544c

**Water Resources Development Act of 1986**
Aug. 20, 1987, P.L. 100-109, 101 Stat. p. 730
Nov. 14, 1988, P.L. 100-653, 102 Stat. 3834
Nov. 17, 1988, P.L. 100-676, 33 U.S. Code §§ 701b-12, 2211, 2239, 2280, 2291, 2294, 2294 nt.
Sept. 29, 1989, P.L. 101-101, 103 Stat. 649

**Water Resources Development Act of 1988**
Nov. 17, 1986, P.L. 99-662, 100 Stat. 4082
Nov. 17, 1988, P.L. 100-676, 33 U.S. Code § 2201 nt.

June 30, 1989, P.L. 101-45, 103 Stat. 99, 100

Sept. 29, 1989, P.L. 101-101, 103 Stat. 649, 650

Nov. 5, 1990, P.L. 101-514, 104 Stat. 2081

Nov. 28, 1990, P.L. 101-640, 16 U.S. Code §§ 460d nt., 470tt, 33 U.S. Code §§ 579a, 652, 2213, 2215, 2232, 2238, 2239, 2294 nt., 2281, 2309a

Nov. 28, 1990, P.L. 101-640, 33 U.S. Code §§ 2314 nt., 2314a

Oct. 31, 1992, P.L. 102-580, 16 U.S. Code § 460tt; 33 U.S. Code §§ 652, 2211, 2213, 2283, 2309a

Oct. 31, 1992, P.L. 102-580, 106 Stat. 4859

Dec. 21, 1995, P.L. 104-66, 33 U.S. Code § 2236

Oct. 12, 1996, P.L. 104-303, 33 U.S. Code §§ 579a nt., 2313

Oct. 12, 1996, P.L. 104-303, 33 U.S. Code §§ 579a, 701b-12, 701n , 2211, 2213, 2215, 2241, 2263, 2281, 2309a

**Water Resources Development Act of 1990**

Nov. 28, 1990, P.L. 101-640, 33 U.S. Code §§ 59bb, 426e nt., 701n, 1252 nt., 1268 nt., 2201 nt., 2213 nts., 2232 nt., 2239 nt., 2313 nt., 2316 to 2324, 48 U.S. Code § 1405c nt.

Oct. 31, 1992, P.L. 102-580, 106 Stat. 4807, 4847, 4861

Oct. 12, 1996, P.L. 104-303, 33 U.S. Code §§ 2319, 1252 nt., 1268 nt.

**Water Resources Development Act of 1992**

Oct. 31, 1992, P.L. 102-580, 33 U.S. Code § 2201 nt.

Nov. 13, 1995, P.L. 104-46, 109 Stat. 407

Oct. 12, 1996, P.L. 104-303, 33 U.S. Code §§ 426i-1, 2267 nt., 2239 nt., 2325, 2326, 2328

Oct. 19, 1996, P.L. 104-316, 33 U.S. Code § 2281 nt.

**Water Resources Development Act of 1996**

Oct. 12, 1996, P.L. 104-303, 33 U.S. Code § 2201 nt.

**Water Resources Development Bond Act**

Cal. Water Code § 12930 et seq.

**Water Resources Impoundment Site Loan Act**

Mass. Gen. Laws. Ann., 21:9A

**Water Resources Management Act**

S.D. Codified Laws 1967, 46A-1-1 et seq.

**Water Resources Planning Act**

July 22, 1965, P.L. 89-80, 79 Stat. 244, 42 U.S. Code §§ 1962, 1962-1, 1962a, 1962a-1. to 1962a-4, 1962b, 1962b-1 to 1962b-6, 1962c, 1962c-1 to 1962c-6, 1962d-1 to 1962d-3

Oct. 2, 1968, P.L. 90-547, 82 Stat. 935, 42 U.S. Code § 1962d

June 17, 1971, P.L. 92-227, 85 Stat. 77, 42 U.S. Code § 1962d

June 6, 1977, P.L. 95-41, 42 U.S. Code § 1962

Conn. Gen. Stat. Ann., § 22a-352 et seq.

Kan. Stat. Ann., 82a-901 et seq.

**Water Resources Planning and Coordination Act**

S.C. Code Ann. 1976, § 49-3-10 et seq.

**Water Resources Protection and Management Program (Local)**

Minn. Stat. Ann., 103B.3361 et seq.

**Water Resources Research Act**

Ind. Code Ann., 13-2-7-1 et seq.

**Water Resources Research Act of 1964**

July 17, 1964, P.L. 88-379, 78 Stat. 329, 42 U.S. Code §§ 1961 to 1961c-6

April 19, 1966, P.L. 89-404, 80 Stat. 129, 42 U.S. Code §§ 1961a- 4, 1961b, 1961c-7

**Water Resources Research Act of 1984**

March 22, 1984, P.L. 98-242, 42 U.S. Code §§ 7801, 7802, 7811 to 7819, 7831 to 7835, 7836, 7851 to 7853, 7871 to 7883, 10301 to 10309

Sept. 28, 1990, P.L. 101-397, 42 U.S. Code §§ 10301 nt., 10302 to 10305, 10307

Dec. 21, 1995, P.L. 104-66, 42 U.S. Code § 10301 nt.

May 24, 1996, P.L. 104-147, 42 U.S. Code §§ 10301 to 10303

**Water Resources Restoration and Preservation Act**
Fla. Stat. Ann., 403.0615

**Water Revenue Bond Act (Daytona Beach)**
Fla. Special Laws 1945, Ch. 45-23237

**Water Right Determination and Administration Act**
Colo. Rev. Stat., 37-92-101 et seq.

**Water Rights Act**
Ind. Code Ann., 13-2-1-1 et seq.
Mont. Rev. Code 1947, 89-801 et seq.
Ore. Rev. Stat., 536.050, 536.070, 537.120, 537.130, 537.140 to 537.250, 537.280 to 537.300, 538.410, 538.420, 539.010 to 539.220, 540.010 to 540.130, 540.210 to 540.230, 540.310 to 540.430, 540.510 to 540.530, 540.710 to 540.750
S.D. Codified Laws 1967, 46-1-1 et seq.
Tex. Water Code, § 1.001 et seq.
Wash. Rev. Code Ann. 90.03.010 et seq.

**Water Rights Adjudication Act**
Colo. Rev. Stat., 37-92-101 et seq.
Tex. Water Code, § 11.301 et seq.
Utah Code Ann. 1953, 73-4-1 et seq.

**Water Rights Commission Act**
Haw. Rev. Stat. Ann., § 664-31 et seq.
Tex. Water Code, § 35.001 et seq.

**Water Rights Permitting Reform Act**
Cal. Water Code § 1228 et seq.

**Water Rules and Regulations Act (Town of Farmington)**
N.Y. Local Laws 1968, Town of Farmington, p. 2381

**Water Safety Act**
Ala. Code 1975, § 33-5-1 et seq.
N.C. Gen. Stat. 1943, § 75A-1 et seq.
Tex. Parks and Wildlife Code, § 31.001 et seq.

**Water, Sanitation and Sewer Revenue Bond Act**
Cal. Government Code § 54300 et seq.

**Water Sanitation Compact Act (Ohio River Valley)**
Ill. Rev. Stat. 1991, Ch. 111 1/2, § 116.990 et seq.

**Water Service District Act**
Ill. Rev. Stat. 1991, Ch. 111 2/3, § 212.90 et seq.

**Water Service Regulation Act**
Neb. Rev. Stat. 1943, 75-1002 et seq.

**Water, Sewage, and Solid Waste Authority Act (Polk County)**
Ga. Laws 1967, p. 3108
Ga. Laws 1994, p. 3876
Ga. Laws 1996, p. 4052

**Water, Sewer and Solid Waste Management Systems Finance Act**
Ark. Code Ann. 1947, 14-230-101 et seq.

**Water, Sewer and Solid Waste Service Assistance Act (Low Income)**
N.M. Stat. Ann., 27-6A-1 et seq.

**Water, Sewer, Gas, and Solid Waste Management Districts Act (Rural)**
Okla. Stat. Ann., Title 82, § 1324.1 et seq.

**Water, Sewerage and Recreational Authority Act (Peachtree)**
Ga. Laws 1973, p. 2989

**Water Shortage Emergency Act**
Cal. Water Code § 350 et seq.

**Water Stock Transfer Act**
Cal. Civil Code § 330.26

**Water Storage Act**
Cal. Water Code § 1242
Kan. Stat. Ann., 82a-405 et seq.

**Water Storage and Conservation District Act**
Cal. Statutes 1941, p. 3139

**Water Storage District Act**
Cal. Water Code § 39000 et seq.

**Water Storage Policy Act**
Mont. Laws 1991, Ch. 659, §§ 1 to 4

**Water Storage, Savings and Replenishment Act (Underground)**
Fla. Laws 1994, Ch. 291

**Water Study Act**
Colo. Rev. Stat. 1963, 148-2-9 et seq.

**Water Supply Act**
Ind. Code Ann., 16-1-26-1 et seq.
N.J. Rev. Stat. 1937, 58:19-1 et seq., 58-22-1 et seq.
N.Y. City Adm. Code 1938, Ch. 51, § K51-1.0 et seq.
Pa. Purdon's Stat., Title 35, § 691.1 et seq.

**Water Supply Act (Bristol County)**
R.I. Gen. Laws 1956, 45-15.5-1 et seq.

**Water Supply Act (Metropolitan)**
Mass. Gen. Laws Ann., 92:1 et seq.
Miss. Code Ann. 1972, § 51-9-189 et seq.

**Water Supply Act of 1958**
July 3, 1958, P.L. 85-500, 72 Stat. 319, 43 U.S. Code § 390b
July 20, 1961, P.L. 87-88, 75 Stat. 210, 43 U.S. Code § 390b

**Water Supply and Sewage Act**
Kan. Stat. Ann., 65-161 et seq.

**Water Supply and Sewage Disposal Districts Act**
Mich. Comp. Laws Ann., 324.4701 et seq.

**Water Supply and Wastewater Operators Licensing Act**
N.J. Stat. Ann. 58:11-64 et seq.

**Water Supply Associations Act**
N.M. Stat. Ann., 3-28-1 et seq.

**Water Supply Authorities Act (Municipal)**
Mich. Comp. Laws Ann., 124.251 et seq.

**Water Supply Authority Act**
N.J. Stat. Ann. 58:1B-1 et seq.

**Water Supply Bond Act**
N.J. Laws 1981, Ch. 261

**Water Supply Construction Act**
N.M. Stat. Ann., 75-1-1 et seq.

**Water Supply Damage Loan Act (Westborough)**
Mass. Acts 1957, Ch. 515

**Water Supply District Act**
Pa. Purdon's Stat., Title 53, § 3001 et seq.

**Water Supply District Improvement Loan Act (Leicester)**
Mass. Acts 1954, Ch. 363

**Water Supply Financing Law (Counties)**
N.J. Stat. Ann. 40:55D-97

**Water Supply Management Act**
N.J. Stat. Ann. 58:1A-1 et seq.

**Water Supply Operations Act (Public)**
Ill. Rev. Stat. 1991, Ch. 111 1/2, § 500 et seq.

**Water Supply Permit Act**
Cal. Water Code § 1390 et seq.

**Water Supply Planning Act**
N.C. Gen. Stat. 1943, § 162A-20 et seq.

**Water Supply Privatization Act**
N.J. Stat. 58:26-1 et seq.

**Water Supply Public-Private Contracting Act**
N.J. Stat. Ann., 58:26-10 et seq.

**Water Supply Regulation Act**
Ill. Rev. Stat. 1991, Ch. 111 1/2, § 121a et seq.

**Water Supply Systems Act**
Okla. Stat. Ann., Title 27A, § 2-6-301 et seq.

**Water Surplus Act**
Mich. Comp. Laws Ann., 281.301 et seq.

**Water System Act (Cities)**
Ky. Rev. Stat. 1971, 96.350 et seq.

**Water System Act (Township)**
Mich. Comp. Laws Ann., 486.501 et seq.

**Water System and Sanitary Sewer Financing Act (County)**
Fla. Stat. Ann., 153.01 et seq.

**Water System Coordination Act (Public)**
Wash. Rev. Code Ann., 70.116.010 et seq.

**Water System Investment and Consolidation Act (Public)**
Cal. Public Utilities Code § 2718 et seq.

**Water Systems and Lighting Act (Municipal)**
N.H. Rev. Stat. 1955, 38:2 et seq.

**Water Systems Assistance Act (Small)**
Pa. Purdon's Stat., Title 35, § 724.1 et seq.
Pa. 1992 Pamph. Laws, No. 5

**Water Tank Act (Livestock)**
Colo. Rev. Stat., 35-49-101 et seq.

**Water Transfer Act**
Kan. Stat. Ann., 82a-1501 to 82a-1506

**Water Transfer Act (Costa-Isenberg)**
Cal. Water Code § 470 et seq.

**Water Transmission Facilities Act**
N.J. Stat. Anno, 58:5-31 et seq.

**Water Transportation Act**
Okla. Stat. Ann., Title 17, § 159.11 et seq.

**Water Treatment Units Act**
Haw. Rev. Stat. Ann., § 481H-1 et seq.

**Water Use Act**
Alaska Stat. 1962, § 46.15.010 et seq.
Ill. Rev. Stat. 1991, Ch. 5, § 1601 et seq.
Mont. Code Ann., 85-2-101 et seq.
N.C. Gen. Stat. 1943, § 143-215.11 et seq.

**Water Use Leasing Act**
N.M. Stat. Ann., 72-6-1 et seq.

**Water Use Reporting and Coordination Act**
S.C. Code Ann. 1976, § 49-4-10 et seq.

**Water User District Act**
S.D. Codified Laws 1967, 46A-9-1 et seq.

**Water Utility Infrastructure Improvement Act**
Cal. Public Utilities Code § 789 et seq.

**Water Vending Machine Protection Act**
Fla. Stat. Ann., 500.459

**Water Well and Pump Installation Contractor's License Act**
Ill. Rev. Stat. 1991, Ch. 111, § 7101 et seq.

**Water Well Construction Act**
Ark. Code Ann. 1987, 17-43-101 et seq.
Wash. Rev. Code Ann. 18.104.005 et seq.

**Water Well Contractors' License Act**
Mont. Code Ann., 37-43-101 et seq.
N.C. Gen. Stat. 1943, § 87-65 et seq.
N.D. Cent. Code 43-35-01 et seq.

**Water Well Drillers' Act**
Mo. Rev. Stat. 256.600 et seq.
N.M. Stat. Ann., 72-13-1 et seq.
Pa. Purdon's Stat., Title 32, § 645.1 et seq.
Tenn. Code Ann., 69-11-101 et seq.
Tex. Rev. Civ. Stat., Art. 7621e

**Water Well Pump Installers Act**
Tex. Rev. Civ. Stat., Art. 8905

**Water Well Standards Act**
Ga. Code Ann., 12-5-120 et seq.

**Water Well Standards and Contractors' Licensing Act**
Neb. Rev. Stat. 1943, 46-1201 et seq.
Neb. Rev. Stat. 1943, 46-1202 et seq.

**Watercourse Protection Act**
N.Y. Local Laws 1971, Town of New Castle, p. 2881
N.Y. Local Laws 1972, Town of North Castle, p. 2224

**Watercourses and Wetlands Act (Inland)**
Conn. Gen. Stat. Ann., § 22a-36 et seq.

**Watercraft Act**
Mich. Comp. Laws Ann., 281.1001 et seq.
Ohio Rev. Code 1953, 1547.01 et seq.
Wyo. Stat. Ann., § 41-13-101 et seq.

**Watercraft Act (Railroads)**
Ill. Rev. Stat. 1991, Ch. 114, § 46.9 et seq.

**Watercraft Act (Service of Process)**
La. Rev. Stat. Ann., 13:3479 et seq.

**Watercraft Dealer Licensing Act**
Va. Code 1950, §§ 29.1-747 et seq.

**Watercraft, Fish and Game Law**
S.C. Code Ann. 1976, § 50-1-10 et seq.

**Watercraft Lien Act**
Mich. Comp. Laws Ann., 570.401 et seq.
Ohio Rev. Code 1953, 4585.01 et seq.

**Watercraft Pollution Control Act**
Mich. Comp. Laws Ann., 323.331 et seq.

**Watercraft Registration and Safety Act**
Ill. Rev. Stat. 1991, Ch. 111 2/3, § 242
Me. Rev. Stat. Ann. 1964, Title 12, § 7791 et seq.

**Watercraft Regulation Act**
Wyo. Stat. Ann., § 41-13-101 et seq.

**Watercraft Safety Act (Personal)**
La. Rev. Stat. Ann., 34:855.1 et seq.
Okla. Stat. Ann., Title 63, § 4220 et seq.

**Watercraft Sales and Use Tax Act**
Va. Code 1950, § 58.1-1400 et seq.

**Watercraft Tax Act**
Mich. Comp. Laws Ann., 281.1031 et seq.

**Watercraft Titling Act**
N.C. Gen. Stat. 1943, § 75A-32 et seq.

**Watered Stock Act**
N.C. Gen. Stat. 1943, § 55-6-22

**Waterfowl Stamp Act**
N.J. Stat. Ann., 23:3-75 et seq.

**Waterfront and Airport Commission Act**
N.Y. Unconsolidated Laws, § 9801 et seq.

**Waterfront and Airport Commission Compact Act**
N.J. Rev. Stat. Ann., 32:23-1 et seq.
N.Y. Laws 1953, Ch. 882
N.Y. Laws 1970, Ch. 951

**Waterfront Area Restoration Financing Authority Act (Urban)**
Cal. Public Resources Code § 32000 et seq.

**Waterfront Development Act (Bradenton)**
Fla. Special Laws 1963, Ch. 63-1129

**Waterfront Development Act (Municipal)**
Ohio Rev. Code 1953, 721.11

**Watermelon Marketing Act**
Fla. Stat. Ann., 573.801 et seq.

**Watermelon Research and Promotion Act**
June 30, 1948, Ch. 758, 62 Stat. 1155 (See 33 U.S. Code §§ 1151 et seq.)
July 17, 1952, Ch. 927, 66 Stat. 755
July 9, 1956, Ch. 518, 70 Stat. 498
Dec. 23, 1985, P.L. 99-198, 7 U.S. Code §§ 4901 et seq., 4901. nt.
Dec. 14, 1993, P.L. 103-189, 7 U.S. Code § 4901 et seq.

**Watermelon Research and Promotion Improvement Act of 1993**
Dec. 14, 1993, P.L. 103-189, 7 U.S. Code § 4901 nt.

**Waters Act (Recreational)**
S.C. Code Ann. 1976, § 44-55-2320 et seq.

**Waters Child Abuse Prevention Training Act**
Cal. Welfare and Institutions Code § 18975 et seq.

**Waters-Nielsen-Vuich-Berryhill Foreign Market Development Export Incentive Program for California Agriculture Act**
Cal. Food and Agriculture Code 1967, § 58551 et seq.

**Waters Protection Act**
Wis. Stat. Ann., 144.01

**Waters-Walker Act (Intoxicating Liquors)**
N.Y. Laws 1920, Ch. 911

**Watershed Act**
Minn. Stat. Ann., 103D.011 et seq., 112.34 et seq.
S.D. Codified Laws 1967, 46A-14-1 et seq.

**Watershed and Basin Act (Kaskaskia River)**
Ill. Rev. Stat. 1991, Ch. 19, §§ 41.09, 41.1

**Watershed Conservation Districts Act**
S.C. Code Ann. 1976, § 48-11-10 et seq.

**Watershed Cooperation Act (Interstate)**
Ark. Code Ann. 1947, 14-115-101 et seq.

**Watershed District Act**
Kan. Stat. Ann., 24-1201 et seq.
N.M. Stat. Ann., 73-20-1 et seq.
Tenn. Code Ann., 69-7-101 et seq.

**Watershed Diversion Act**
Tex. Water Code, § 11.085 et seq.

**Watershed Enhancement Act (Inland Bays)**
Del. Code of 1974, Title 7, § 7601 et seq.

**Watershed Improvement Act**
Ill. Rev. Stat. 1991, Ch. 19, § 128.01 et seq.

**Watershed Improvement Districts Act**
Ida. Code 1947, 42-3701 et seq.
N.C. Gen. Stat. 1943, 139-16 et seq.
W. Va. Code 1966, § 19-21B-1 et seq.

**Watershed Improvement, Irrigation and Drainage District Act**
Ark. Code Ann. 1947, 14-117-101 et seq.

**Watershed Law**
Minn. Stat. Ann., 103D.011 et seq.

**Watershed Management Planning Act**
Cal. Statutes 1996, Ch. 166

**Watershed of Origin Act**
Cal. Water Code § 11460 et seq.

**Watershed Operation and Maintenance Act (Kaskaskia River)**
Ill. Rev. Stat. 1991, Ch. 105, §§ 540, 541

**Watershed Project Act (Broad Brook)**
Mass. Acts 1963, Ch. 563

**Watershed Project Act (Clam River)**
Mass. Acts 1963, Ch. 563

**Watershed Protection Act**
P.R. Laws Ann. 1954, Title 12, § 232 et seq.

**Watershed Protection and Flood Prevention Act**
Aug. 4, 1954, Ch. 656, 68 Stat. 666, 16 U.S. Code §§ 1001 to 1007; 33 U.S. Code § 701b
July 19, 1956, Ch. 639, 70 Stat. 580, 16 U.S. Code § 1005
Aug. 7, 1956, Ch. 1027, 70 Stat. 1088, 16 U.S. Code §§ 1001 nt., 1002 to 1005, 1006a, 1006b
Aug. 12, 1958 P.L. 85-624, 72 Stat. 567, 16 U.S. Code § 1008
Sept. 2, 1958, P.L. 85-865, 72 Stat. 1605, 16 U.S. Code § 1004
May 13, 1960, P.L. 86-468, 74 Stat. 131, 16 U.S. Code §§ 1006a, 1007
June 29, 1960, P.L. 86-545, 74 Stat. 254, 16 U.S. Code § 1004
Aug. 30, 1961, P.L. 87-170, 75 Stat. 408, 16 U.S. Code § 1002
Sept. 27, 1962, P.L. 87-703, 76 Stat. 608, 16 U.S. Code §§ 1004, 1005
Nov. 8, 1965, P.L. 89-337, 79 Stat. 1300, 16 U.S. Code § 1002
June 27, 1968, P.L. 90-361, 82 Stat. 250, 16 U.S. Code § 1005
Aug. 30, 1972, P.L. 92-419, 86 Stat. 667, 16 U.S. Code §§ 1001 to 1005
Sept. 29, 1977, P.L. 95-113, 16 U.S. Code §§ 1002, 1005 et seq.

April 4, 1996, P.L. 104-127, 16 U.S. Code § 1006a
Cal. Water Code § 12850 et seq.
Cal. Water Code § 20066
Nev. Rev. Stat. 1973 Reprint, Replaced Pages, 542.010 et seq.

**Watershed Protection and Flood Prevention Act of 1954**
Nov. 28, 1990, P.L. 101-624, 16 U.S. Code §§ 1002, 1003, 1003a, 1010
Nov. 2, 1994, P.L. 103-437, 16 U.S. Code § 1002

**Watershed Reparations Act**
Cal. Water Code § 1245 et seq.

**Watershed Restoration Act (Illinois River)**
Ill. Comp. Stat. 1992, Ch. 20, § 3967/1 et seq.

**Watertown, Boston & Brighton Incinerator Loan Act**
Mass. Acts 1954, Ch. 523

**Waterway Act**
Ill. Rev. Stat. 1991, Ch. 19, § 78.9 et seq.

**Waterway Development and Conservation Act**
Me. Rev. Stat. Ann. 1964, Title 38, § 630 et seq.

**Waterway Development Compact**
Ky. Rev. Stat. 1971, 182.300 et seq.

**Waterway Districts Act**
Wash. Rev. Code 1951, 91.04.010 et seq.

**Waterways Act**
Wash. Rev. Code Ann. 91.08.010 et seq.

**Waterways and Canals Act**
Ill. Rev. Stat. 1991, Ch. 19

**Waterways Commission Act**
Mich. Comp. Laws Ann., 281.501 et seq.

**Waterways Development Authority Act (Monroe County)**
Fla. Special Laws 1963, Ch. 63-1657

**Waterways Improvement Loan Act (Woburn)**
Mass. Acts 1956, Ch. 407

**Waterways Structures Act (Town of Hempstead)**
N.Y. Local Laws 1967, Town of Hempstead, p. 1702

**Waterworks Act**
S.C. Code Ann. 1976, § 5-31-10 et seq.

**Waterworks Act (Municipal)**
Ark. Code Ann. 1947, 19-4201 et seq.
Mich. Comp. Laws Ann., 486.301 et seq.
S.C. Code Ann. 1976, § 5-31-10 et seq.
Vt. Stat. Ann., Title 24, § 3301 et seq.

**Waterworks Act (Township)**
Ill. Rev. Stat. 1991, Ch. 139, § 160.30h et seq.

**Waterworks and Sewage Disposal Act**
Mich. Comp. Laws Ann., 325.201 et seq.

**Waterworks and Sewage Treatment Plant Operators' Certification Act**
Pa. Purdon's Stat., Title 63, § 1001 et seq.

**Waterworks and Waste Systems Operators Act**
Md. Ann. Code 1974, Art. EN, § 12-101 et seq.

**Waterworks and Waste Waterworks Operator Certification Act**
Okla. Stat. Ann., Title 59, § 1101 et seq.

**Waterworks Construction Loan Act**
Tenn. Code Ann., 68-221-501 et seq.

**Waterworks District Act (County)**
Cal. Water Code § 55100 et seq.

**Waterworks Districts Securities Commission Act**
Cal. Water Code § 20000 et seq.

**Waterworks Improvement Lease Act (Park)**
Ill. Rev. Stat. 1989, Ch. 105, § 327w9 et seq.

**Watson-O'Connell Fire Prevention Act**
Cal. Health and Safety Code § 13132.7

**Watson-Roosevelt Act (Land Contract Moratorium)**
Mich. Public Acts 1937, No. 1

**Watson-Tomlin-Van Eenenaam Act (State Bridge Commission)**
Mich. Comp. Laws Ann., 254.151 et seq.

**Waukegan Civic Center Law**
Ill. Rev. Stat. 1991, Ch. 85, § 7007-1 et seq.

**Waukegan, Pontiac, Randolph County, Carbondale, Riverside, Matteson, Ottawa, and Illinois Valley Civic Centers Act**
Ill. Rev. Stat. 1991, Ch. 85, § 7000-1 et seq.

**Waukegan Port District Act**
Ill. Rev. Stat. 1991, Ch. 19, § 179 et seq.

**Waveland Regional Wastewater Management Act**
Miss. Code Ann. 1972, § 49-17-161 et seq.

**Waxman-Duffy Prepaid Health Plan Act**
Cal. Welfare and Institutions Code § 14200 et seq.

**Waxman-Dymally Campaign Disclosure Act**
N.Y. Public Authorities Law (Consol. Laws Ch. 43A) § 1199aa et seq.

**Waycross Street Improvement Act**
Ga. Laws 1925, p. 1557

**Wayland School Building Loan Act**
Mass. Acts 1952, Ch. 49

**Wayne County Civil Service Act**
Mich. Comp. Laws Ann., 38.401 et seq.

**Wayport Authority Act**
Miss. Code Ann. 1972, § 61-4-1 et seq.

**Ways and Means Act (Civil War)**
March 3, 1863, Ch. 73, 12 Stat. 709

**Wayward Minors Act**
Mich. Comp. Laws Ann., 712A.1 et seq.
N.Y. Code of Criminal Procedure § 913a et seq.
N.Y. Family Court Act, § 711 et seq.

**Weak-minded Persons Act**
Pa. 1895 Pamph. Laws 300, No. 220
Pa. 1907 Pamph. Laws 292, No. 222

**Weapon Act (Boarding Aircraft)**
Ill. Rev. Stat. 1991, Ch. 38, § 84-0.1 et seq.

**Weapon-Free Schools Act**
Kan. Stat. Ann., 72-89a01 et seq.

**Weapons Act**
Cal. Penal Code § 12000 et seq.
Ga. Code Ann., 16-11-120 et seq.
Iowa Code Ann., 724.1 et seq.
Mich. Comp. Laws Ann., 28.421 et seq.
N.J. Stat. Ann. 2C:58-1 et seq.
Pa. Cons. Stat., Title 18, § 6101
P.R. Laws Ann. 1954, Title 25, § 411 et seq.
Wash. Rev. Code Ann., 9.41.010 et seq.

**Weapons Act (Concealed)**
See Concealed Weapons Act

**Weapons of Mass Destruction Control Act of 1992**
Oct. 23, 1992, P.L. 102-484, 106 Stat. 2567
Feb. 10, 1996, P.L. 104-106, 22 U.S. Code § 5859a
Sept. 23, 1996, P.L. 104-201, 22 U.S. Code § 5859a
Nov. 18, 1997, P.L. 105-85, 22 U.S. Code § 5859a
Oct. 17, 1998, P.L. 105-261, 22 U.S. Code § 5859a

**Weather Control Act**
N.M. Stat. Ann., 75-3-1 et seq.
S.D. Codified Laws 1967, 46-3A-1 et seq.

**Weather Control District Act**
Neb. Rev. Stat. 1943, 2-2428 et seq.

**Weather Information Act**
Tenn. Code Ann., 7-6-201

**Weather Modification Act**
Colo. Rev. Stat., 36-20-101 et seq.
Ill. Rev. Stat. 1991, Ch. 111, § 7301 et seq.
Kan. Stat. Ann., 82a-1401 et seq.
Mich. Comp. Laws Ann., 295.101 et seq.
Minn. Stat. Ann., 42.01 et seq.
Mont. Code Ann., 85-3-101 et seq.
N.D. Cent. Code 61-04.1-01 et seq.
Neb. Rev. Stat. 1943, 2-2401 et seq.
Okla. Stat. Ann., Title 82, § 1087.1 et seq.
Tex. Water Code, § 18.001 et seq.

**Weather Modification Research Act**
Nev. Rev. Stat. 1979 Reprint, 544.010 et seq.

**Weather Resources Management Act**
Cal. Water Code § 400 et seq.

**Weather Service Modernization Act**
Oct. 29, 1992, P.L. 102-567, 15 U.S. Code § 313 nt.

**Webb-Crawford Act (Apportionment)**
Ala. Acts 1962, Sp. Sess., p. 121

**Webb Exporter Combination Act**
April 10, 1918, Ch. 50, 40 Stat. 516, 15 U.S. Code §§ 63 to 65

**Webb-Kenyon Act**
March 1, 1913, Ch. 90, 37 Stat. 699, 27 U.S. Code § 122

**Webb-Martin Act (Fraudulent Practices with Securities)**
N.Y. General Business Law (Consol. Laws Ch. 20 § 352 et seq.

**Webb-Pomerene Act (Export Trade)**
See Export Trade Act

**Webb-Shields-Warriner Act (Married Woman's Property)**
Ky. Rev. Stat. 1971, 404.010

**Webster Drainage Control Act**
N.Y. Local Laws 1969, Town of Webster, p. 2259

**Webster Interim Development Act**
N.Y. Local Laws 1969, Town of Webster, p. 2266

**Webster Land Filling Act**
N.Y. Local Laws 1971, Town of Webster, p. 3680

**Webster Refuse Disposal Act**
N.Y. Local Laws 1967, Town of Webster, p. 2005

**Webster Sign Act**
N.Y. Local Laws 1969, Town of Webster, p. 2268

**Wedworth-Townsend Paramedic Act**
Cal. Health and Safety Code § 1480 et seq.

**Weed Act (Exotic)**
Ill. Rev. Stat. 1991, Ch. 5 § 931 et seq.

**Weed and Pest Control Act**
Wyo. Stat. Ann., § 11-5-101 et seq.

**Weed Control Act**
Cal. Government Code § 39560 et seq.
Colo. Rev. Stat., 35-5.5-101 et seq.
Iowa Code Ann., 317.1 et seq.
Kan. Stat. Ann., 2-1314 et seq.
Minn. Stat. Ann., 18.331 et seq.
Mont. Code Ann., 80-7-701 et seq.
N.D. Cent. Code 63-01.1-01 et seq.
N.M. Stat. Ann., 76-7-1 et seq., 76-7-23 et seq.
Ore. Rev. Stat., 570.505 et seq.
S.D. Codified Laws 1967, 38-22-1.1 et seq.
Utah Code Ann. 1953, 4-17-1 et seq.
Va. Code 1950, § 3.1-296.11 et seq.
Wash. Rev. Code Ann. 17.04.010 et seq.

**Weed Control Act (Aquatic)**
Fla. Stat. Ann., 369.20 et seq.
N.C. Gen. Stat. 1943, §§ 113A-220 to 113A-227

**Weed Control Act (Noxious)**
Neb. Rev. Stat. 1943, 2-945.01 et seq.

**Weed Control Law (Noxious)**
Pa. Purdon's Stat., Title 3, § 255.1 et seq.

**Weed Free Area Act**
Cal. Food and Agricultural Code 1967, § 7201 et seq.

**Weed-Free Forage Crop Certification Act**
Colo. Rev. Stat., 35-27.5-101 to 35-27.5-108

**Weekly Wage Payment Act**
Ind. Code Ann., 22-2-5-1 et seq.
Mass. Gen. Laws Ann., 149:148 et seq.
Me. Rev. Stat. Ann. 1964, Title 26, § 621 et seq.
N.Y. Labor Law (Consol. Laws Ch. 31) § 191
R.I. Public Laws 1941, Ch. 1069
Vt. Stat. Ann., Title 21, § 341 et seq.

**Weeks Law**
March 1, 1911, Ch. 186, 36 Stat. 961, 16 U.S. Code §§ 480, 500, 513 to 519, 521, 552, 563

**Weigher Law (Model State Public)**
Conn. Gen. Stat. Ann., § 43-16a et seq.

**Weighmaster Act**
Ida. Code 1947, 71-401 et seq.
Nev. Rev. Stat. 1979 Reprint, 582.010 et seq.
N.M. Stat. Ann., 57-18-1 et seq.
S.C. Code Ann. 1976, § 39-11-10 et seq.
Tenn. Code Ann., 47-26-401 et seq.

**Weighmasters Act (Public)**
S.C. Code Ann. 1976, § 39-11-10 et seq.

**Weight Act (Maximum)**
Tenn. Code Ann., 55-7-203

**Weight Act (Truck)**
Me. Rev. Stat. Ann. 1964, Title 29, § 1651 et seq.

**Weight Distance Tax Act**
N.M. Stat. Ann., 7-15A-1 et seq.

**Weight-Distance Tax Act (Motor Vehicles)**
N.Y. Tax Law (Consol. Laws Ch. 60) § 501 et seq.

**Weight Limit Act (Vehicles)**
Conn. Gen. Stat. Ann., § 14-266 et seq.
Mo. Rev. Stat., 304.180 et seq.
N.J. Rev. Stat. 1937, 39:3-84 et seq.
N.M. Stat. Ann. 1953, 64-23-1 et seq.
Ohio Rev. Code 1953, 5577.01 et seq.

**Weight-Loss Practices Act (Commercial)**
Fla. Stat. Ann., 501.057 et seq.

**Weight, Size and Load Regulations**
Miss. Code Ann. 1972, § 63-5-1

**Weight Tax Act (Motor Vehicles)**
Mich. Comp. Laws Ann., 257.801
Wis. Stat. Ann., 341.25, 341.26

**Weighted Vote Act**
N.Y. Optional County Government Law (Consol. Laws Ch. 11A) § 1006a

**Weights and Measures Act**
Alaska Stat. 1962, §§ 45.75.010, 45.75.020
Ark. Code Ann. 1987, 4-18-202 et seq.
Cal. Business and Professions Code § 12001 et seq.
Colo. Rev. Stat. Replaced Vols., 35-14-101 et seq.
D.C. Code Ann., § 10-101 et seq.
Del. Code of 1974, Title 6, § 5101 et seq.
Fla. Stat. Ann., 531.36 et seq.
Ga. Code Ann., 10-2-1 et seq.
Ida. Code 1947, 71-101 et seq.
Ill. Rev. Stat. 1991, Ch. 147, § 101 et seq.
Iowa Code Ann., 210.1 et seq.
Ky. Rev. Stat. 1971, 363.510 et seq.
Mass. Gen. Laws Ann., 98:1 et seq.
Md. Ann. Code 1974, Art. AG, § 11-301 et seq.
Me. Rev. Stat. Ann. 1964, Title 10, § 2301 et seq.
Mich. Comp. Laws Ann., 290.601 et seq.
Miss. Code Ann. 1972, § 75-27-1 et seq.
Mont. Code Ann., 30-12-101 et seq.
N.C. Gen. Stat. 1943, § 81A-1 et seq.

N.D. Cent. Code 64-01-01 et seq.
Neb. Rev. Stat. 1943, 89-182.01 et seq.
N.H. Rev. Stat. 1955, 438:1 et seq.
N.J. Stat. Anno, 51:1-1 to 51:9-21
Ohio Rev. Code 1953, 901.10 et seq., 1327.46 et seq.
Pa. Purdon's Stat., Title 73, § 1651 et seq.
P.R. Laws Ann. 1954, Title 23, § 901 et seq.
R.I. Gen. Laws 1956, 47-1-1 et seq.
S.C. Code Ann. 1976, § 39-9-10 et seq.
S.D. Codified Laws 1967, 37-20-1 et seq.
Tenn. Code Ann., 47-26-201 et seq.
Tex. Agricultural Code, § 13.001 et seq.
Utah Code Ann. 1953, 4-9-1 et seq.
Va. Code 1950, 3.1-919 et seq.
Vt. Stat. Ann. Title 9, § 2631 et seq.
Wash. Rev. Code Ann., 19.94.010 et seq.
Wis. Stat. Ann., 98.01 et seq.
W. Va. Code 1966, § 47-1-1 et seq.

**Weights and Measures Act (Consolidated)**
Pa. Cons. Stat., Title 3, § 4101 et seq.

**Weights and Measures Act (District of Columbia)**
March 3, 1921, Ch. 118, 41 Stat. 1217

**Weights and Measures Act (Penal)**
Ind. Code Ann., 35-18-6-1 et seq.

**Weights and Measures Inspection Act**
S.D. Codified Laws 1967, 37-21-1 et seq.

**Weights and Measures Law**
See Uniform Weights and Measures Law

**Weir-Dunipace Act (Probate Code)**
Ohio Rev. Code 1953, 2101.01 et seq.

**Weir Farm National Historic Site Act of 1990**
Nov. 10, 1998, P.L. 105-363, 16 U.S. Code § 461 nt.

**Weir Farm National Historic Site Establishment Act of 1990**
Oct. 31, 1990, P.L. 101-485, 16 U.S. Code § 461 nt.
Nov. 10, 1998, P.L. 105-363, 16 U.S. Code § 461 nt.

**Weir Farm National Historic Site Expansion Act of 1994**
Nov. 2, 1994, P.L. 103-449, 16 U.S. Code § 461 nt.

**Weisinger Act (Married Women's Property)**
Ky. Rev. Stat. 1971, 404.010 et seq.

**Wekiva River Protection Act**
Fla. Stat. Ann., 369.301 et seq., 564.301 et seq.

**Welch Act**
May 28, 1928, Ch. 814, 45 Stat. 776

**Welding Act**
Okla. Stat. Ann., Title 59, § 1624 et seq.

**Weldon Act**
Tenn. Code Ann., 49-10-101, 49-10-801, 49-10-901

**Welfare Abuse Hotline Act**
Kan. Stat. Ann., 39-760

**Welfare Act**
Ala. Code 1975, § 38-1-1 et seq.
Alaska Stat. 1962, § 47.05.010 et seq.
Ariz. Rev. Stat. Ann., § 46-101 et seq.
Del. Code of 1974, Title 31, § 501 et seq.
Fla. Stat. 1983, 409.01 et seq.
Haw. Session Laws 1933, Act 209
Ind. Code Ann., 12-1-1-1 et seq.
Kan. Stat. Ann., 39-701 et seq.
Ky. Rev. Stat. 1971, 205.010 et seq.
La. Rev. Stat. Ann., 46:1 et seq.
Me. Rev. Stat. Ann. 1964, Title 22, § 1 et seq.
Mich. Comp. Laws Ann., 400.1 et seq.
Mont. Code Ann., 53-1-101 et seq.
Nev. Rev. Stat. 1979 Reprint, 422.005 et seq.
N.M. Stat. Ann. 1953, 13-1-1 et seq.
Okla. Stat. Ann., Title 56, § 26.3 et seq.
Ore. Rev. Stat., 411.010 et seq.
S.C. Code Ann. 1976, § 43-1-10 et seq.
Tenn. Code Ann., 71-1-101 et seq.
Tex. Human Resources Code, § 11.001 et seq.
Vt. Stat. Ann., Title 33, § 2501 et seq.
Wash. Rev. Code Ann., 74.04.005 et seq.
W. Va. Code 1966, §§ 9-1-1 et seq., 49-1-1 et seq.

*Continued*

**Welfare Act (Child)**
Miss. Code Ann. 1972, § 43-15-5 et seq.

**Welfare Act (Children)**
Ind. Code Ann., 31-6-1-1 et seq.
Iowa Code Ann., 235.1 et seq.
N.C. Gen. Stat. 1943, § 110-20.1 et seq.

**Welfare Act (Veterans)**
Mont. Rev. Code 1947, 71-1011 et seq.

**Welfare Agency Licensing Act (Child)**
Ark. Acts 1997, No. 1041

**Welfare and Assistance Act**
Va. Code 1950, § 63.1-86 et seq.

**Welfare and Institutions Code**
Cal. Statutes 1965, Ch. 1784, p. 3977

**Welfare and Pension Plans Disclosure Act**
Aug. 28, 1958, P.L. 85-836, 72 Stat. 997, 29 U.S. Code §§ 301 to 309
July 12, 1960, P.L. 86-624, 74 Stat. 417, 29 U.S. Code § 302
March 20, 1962, P.L. 87-420, 76 Stat. 35, 29 U.S. Code §§ 301 nts. 302 to 309

**Welfare and Rehabilitation Services Planning Act**
Ill. Rev. Stat. 1991, Ch. 127, § 951 et seq.

**Welfare Arrangement Act (Multiple Employer)**
Fla. Stat. Ann., 624.436 et seq.

**Welfare Arrangement Regulation Act (Self-Funded Multiple Employer)**
Mont. Code Ann., 33-35-101 et seq.

**Welfare Benefits Act**
Colo. Rev. Stat. 1963, 119-1-1 et seq.

**Welfare Board Act**
D.C. Code 1973, § 3-101 et seq.

**Welfare Board Act (Animal)**
Me. Rev. Stat. Ann. 1964, Title 7, § 3901 et seq., Title 17, § 1011 et seq.

**Welfare Compact Act (New England)**
See New England Welfare Compact Act

**Welfare Corporation Act**
Tenn. Code Ann. 1955, 48-1101 et seq.

**Welfare District Loan Act (Northern Worcester County)**
Mass. Acts 1958, Ch. 653

**Welfare, Education and Public Health Tax Act**
Conn. Gen. Stat. Ann., § 12-406 et seq.

**Welfare Employment Act**
Del. Code of 1974, Title 31, § 1501 et seq.

**Welfare Employment Skills Training Act**
Cal. Welfare and Institutions Code § 11340 et seq.

**Welfare Exemption Act**
Cal. Revenue and Taxation Code § 214 et seq.

**Welfare Fund Act (Employees)**
Conn. Gen. Stat. Ann., § 31-78 et seq.

**Welfare Fund Disclosure Act (Employee)**
Mass. Gen. Laws. Ann., 151D:11 et seq.

**Welfare Funds Disclosure Act**
Cal. Insurance Code § 10640 et seq.
Mass. Gen. Laws Ann., 151D:1 et seq.
N.Y. Insurance Law (Consol. Laws Ch. 28) § 4401 et seq.

**Welfare Home Act (State)**
Del. Code of 1953, Title 31, § 701 et seq.

**Welfare Law (Municipal Corporations)**
Ark. Code Ann. 1987, 14-54-105

**Welfare Organization Law of 1936**
Colo. Rev. Stat. 1963, 119-1-1 et seq.

**Welfare Reform Act**
Cal. Statutes 1979, Ch. 1170
Del. Laws Vol. 70, Ch. 65
Ky. Rev. Stat. 1971, 205.010 et seq.
La. Rev. Stat. Ann., 46:460 et seq.

Neb. Rev. Stat. 1943, 68-1708 et seq.
N.H. Rev. Stat. 1955, 126-A:4c
N.Y. Social Services Law (Consol. Laws Ch. 55) § 2 et seq.

**Welfare Reform Act (Child)**
N.Y. Social Services Law (Consol. Laws Ch. 55) §§ 22, 153d, 153e, 358a, 358b, 372b, 372c, 372e, 383, 387, 398b, 407, 409d et seq., 442

**Welfare Reform and Self-Sufficiency Act**
Colo. Rev. Stat., 26-2-401 et seq.

**Welfare Reorganization Act**
Ga. Code Ann., 49-1-1 et seq.

**Welfare Restructuring Program Act**
Miss. Code Ann. 1972, § 43-49-1 et seq.

**Welfare Services Act (Child)**
Vt. Stat. Ann., Title 33, § 4901 et seq.

**Welfare Services Compact Act**
Me. Rev. Stat. Ann. 1964, Title 22, § 4101 et seq.

**Welfare Services Interstate Compact Act**
Conn. Gen. Stat. Ann., § 17-16 et seq.

**Welfare-to-Work Act (Thompson-Maddy-Ducheny-Ashburn)**
Cal. Education Code 1976, § 8208 et seq.

**Welfare-to-Work Grant Program**
Cal. Unemployment Insurance Code § 10000 et seq.

**Welfare-to-Work Tax Credit Act**
Ga. Code Ann., 48-7-42

**Welfare Work Incentive Program Act**
N.C. Gen. Stat. 1943, § 108-39.1

**Well Abandonment Act**
Ill. Rev. Stat. 1991, Ch. 96 1/2, § 5200 et seq.

**Well Act (High Capacity)**
Wis. Stat. Ann., 144.025, Subsec. 2, Subd. e

**Well Construction Act**
N.C. Gen. Stat. 1943, § 87-83 et seq.

**Well Driller Registration Act**
N.C. Gen. Stat. 1943, § 143-355, Subsec. e

**Well Drillers Act**
Md. Ann. Code 1974, Art. EN, § 13-101 et seq.

**Well Drillers Act (Water)**
See Water Well Drillers' Act

**Well Drilling Code**
Conn. Gen. Stat. Ann., § 25-126 et seq.

**Well Drilling Lien Act**
Tenn. Code Ann., 66-11-141

**Well Fund Act (Orphan)**
Mich. Comp. Laws Ann., 319.41 et seq.

**Well Plugging Fund Act (Coalbed Methane Gas)**
Ala. Code 1975, § 9-17-130 et seq.

**Well Protection Act**
Mich. Comp. Laws Ann., 750.493b

**Well Site Location Law**
Cal. Public Resources Code § 3600 et seq.

**Well Spacing Act (Oil and Gas)**
Cal. Public Resources Code § 3600 et seq.
Okla. Stat. Ann., Title 52, § 87.1

**Wellhead Protection Area Act**
Neb. Laws 1997, L.B. 1161, §§ 2 to 10

**Wellness and Physical Fitness Act**
Cal. Government Code § 12040 et seq.

**Wellness Program Act**
Okla. Stat. Ann., Title 74, § 1381 et seq.

**Wells Act (Ticket Sellers, Money Deposits)**
N.Y. General Business Law (Consol. Laws Ch. 20) § 150 et seq.

**Wells Charter**
Nev. Statutes 1927, Ch. 104, p. 141
Nev. Statutes 1967, Ch. 159, p. 284
Nev. Statutes 1971, Ch. 275, p. 457

**Wells-Gilbert Tobacco Control Act**
Ky. Rev. Stat. 1971, 248.010, 248.280 et seq.

**Wells on Public Lands Act (Oil and Gas)**
Ill. Rev. Stat. 1991, Ch. 96 1/2, § 5000 et seq.

**Werts Act (Intoxicating Liquor)**
N.J. Laws 1889, Ch. 53

**West Barnstable Fire District Water Loan Act**
Mass. Acts 1966, Ch. 315

**West Bay Rapid Transit Authority**
Cal. Public Utilities Code, Appx. 2, § 1.1 et seq.

**West Bay Rapid Transit Authority Act**
Cal. Statutes 1964, 1st Ex. Sess., Ch. 104, p. 324

**West Boylston Water District Improvement Loan Act**
Mass. Acts 1951, Ch. 739

**West Frankfort Civic Center Law**
Ill. Rev. Stat. 1991, Ch. 85, § 6101 et seq.

**West Georgia Airport Authority Act**
Ga. Laws 1968, p. 2769

**West Georgia Regional Water Authority Act**
Ga. Laws 1988, p. 4926

**West Kentucky Economic Revitalization Act**
Ky. Rev. Stat. 1971, 154.85-010c et seq.

**West Monroe, Louisiana Redevelopment Agency Act**
La. Acts 1968, No. 439

**West Palm Beach Downtown Development Authority Act**
Fla. Special Laws 1967, Ch. 67-2170

**West Palm Beach Police Pension Act**
Fla. Special Laws 1947, Ch. 24981

**West Palm Beach Transportation Act**
Fla. Special Laws 1947, Ch. 24979

**West Point Act**
Oct. 1, 1942, Ch. 573, 56 Stat. 763
July 16, 1943, Ch. 242, 57 Stat. 566, 16 U.S. Code §§ 590y, 590z-1 to 590z-3

**West Point Cadet Act**
June 7, 1935, Ch. 201, 49 Stat. 332 (See 10 U.S. Code §§ 4342, 9342)

**West Valley Demonstration Project Act**
Oct. 1, 1980, P.L. 96-368, 42 U.S. Code § 2021a nt.

**West Virginia Admission Act**
Dec. 31, 1862, Ch. 6, 12 Stat. 633

**West Virginia Centennial Commission Act**
W. Va. Acts 1959, Ch. 175

**West Virginia National Interest River Conservation Act of 1987**
Oct. 26, 1988, P.L. 100-534, 16 U.S. Code § 460m-15 nt.
Nov. 2, 1994, P.L. 103-437, 16 U.S. Code § 460ww
Nov. 12, 1996, P.L. 104-333, 16 U.S. Code §§ 460ww-1, 460ww-4

**West Virginia-Ohio Interstate Compact on Air Pollution**
See Air Pollution Compact Act (Ohio-West Virginia)

**West Virginia WORKS Act**
W. Va. Code 1966, § 9-9-1 et seq.

**Westborough Water Supply Damage Loan Act**
Mass. Acts 1957, Ch. 515

**Westchester County Administrative Code**
N.Y. Laws 1948, Ch. 852

**Westchester County Annexation Act**
N.Y. Laws 1895, Ch. 934

**Westchester County Charter**
N.Y. Laws 1937, Ch. 617

**Westchester County Cross Parkway Authority Act**
N.Y. Public Authorities Law (Consol. Laws Ch. 43A) § 300 et seq.

**Westchester County Handgun Recordkeeping and Accountability Act**
N.Y. Laws 1997, Ch. 446

**Westchester County Health Care Corporation Act**
N.Y. Public Authorities Law (Consol. Laws Ch. 43A) § 3300 et seq.

**Westchester County Park Act**
N.Y. Laws 1922, Ch. 292

**Westchester County Park Commission Act**
N.Y. Laws 1948, Ch. 852, § 471 et seq.

**Westchester County Parkway Authority Act**
N.Y. Public Authorities Law (Consol. Laws Ch. 43A) § 400 et seq.

**Westchester County Playland Authorities Act**
N.Y. Laws 1940, Ch. 826

**Westchester County Playland Commission Act**
N.Y. Laws 1941, Ch. 777

**Westchester County Property Tax Stabilization and Relief Act**
N.Y. Tax Law (Consol. Laws Ch. 60) § 1262b

**Westchester County Sanitary Sewer Act**
N.Y. Laws 1926, Ch. 603
N.Y. Laws 1948, Ch. 852, § 161 et seq.
N.Y. Local Laws 1971, County of Westchester, p. 947

**Westchester County Special Police Act**
N.Y. Unconsolidated Laws § 5711 (q)(1).

**Westchester County Spending Limitation Act**
N.Y. Tax Law (Consol. Laws Ch. 60) § 1262 nt.

**Westchester County Stream Control Act**
N.Y. Laws 1948, Ch. 852, § 191 et seq.
N.Y. Laws 1956, Ch. 853

**Westchester County Tax Act**
N.Y. Laws 1874, Ch. 610
N.Y. Laws 1914, Ch. 510
N.Y. Laws 1916, Ch. 105
N.Y. Laws 1948, Ch. 852, § 521 et seq.

**Westchester County Toll Act**
N.Y. Public Authorities Law (Consol. Laws Ch. 43A) § 404, Subd. 9

**Westchester Cross County Parkway Authority Act**
N.Y. Public Authorities Law (Consol. Laws Ch. 43A) § 300 et seq.

**Westchester Parkway Rehabilitation Act**
N.Y. State Finance Law 1940 (Consol. Laws Ch. 56) § 92K
N.Y. Transportation Law (Consol. Laws Ch. 61A) §§ 70 et seq., 310 et seq.

**Westerly Minimum Nonresidential Standards Act**
R.I. Public Laws 1968, Ch. 67

**Western Finger Lakes Solid Waste Authority Act**
N.Y. Public Authorities Law (Consol. Laws Ch. 43A) § 2725 et seq.

**Western Gateway Act**
N.Y. Laws 1917, Ch. 735

**Western Hemisphere Drug Elimination Act**
Oct. 21, 1998, P.L. 105-277, Division C, Title VIII, 112 Stat 2681, 21 U.S. Code § 801 nt.

**Western Hemisphere Drug Elimination Technical Corrections Act**
June 15, 1999, P.L. 106-35, 113 Stat. 126

**Western Illinois University Act**
Ill. Rev. Stat. 1991, Ch. 144, §§ 900, 902a, 902b

**Western Illinois University Law**
Ill. Comp. Stat. 1992, Ch. 110, § 690/35-1 et seq.

**Western Illinois University Name Change Act**
Ill. Rev. Stat. 1991, Ch. 144, §§ 899, 900

**Western Illinois University Objects Act**
Ill. Rev. Stat. 1991, Ch. 144, § 902.01 et seq.

**Western Illinois University Revenue Bond Law**
Ill. Comp. Stat. 1992, Ch. 110, § 691/36-1 et seq.

**Western Illinois University Television Act**
Ill. Rev. Stat. 1991, Ch. 144, § 919 et seq.

**Western Interstate Commission for Higher Education**
Mont. Code Ann., 20-25-801 et seq.

**Western Interstate Corrections Compact Act**
Alaska Stat. 1962, § 33.36.060 et seq.
Ariz. Rev. Stat. Ann., § 31-471 et seq.
Cal. Penal Code § 11190 et seq.
Colo. Rev. Stat., 24-60-801 et seq.
Haw. Rev. Stat. Ann., § 355-1 et seq.
Ida. Code 1947, 20-701 et seq.
Mont. Code Ann., 46-19-301
Mont. Rev. Code 1947, 95-2308
N.M. Stat. Ann., 31-5-4 et seq.
Ore. Rev. Stat., 421.282 et seq.
Utah Code Ann. 1953, 77-28-1 et seq.
Wash. Rev. Code 1983, 72.70.010 et seq.
Wyo. Stat. Ann., § 7-3-401 et seq.

**Western Interstate Nuclear Compact Act**
Alaska Stat. 1962, § 41.98.110 et seq.
Ariz. Rev. Stat. Ann., § 30-701 et seq.
Cal. Government Code §§ 67400, 67401
Colo. Rev. Stat., 24-60-1401 et seq.
Ida. Code 1947, 39-3020 et seq.
Mont. Code Ann., 90-5-201
Nev. Rev. Stat. 1979 Reprint, 459.001 et seq.
N.M. Stat. 1978, 11-9-1 et seq.
Ore. Rev. Stat. 1953, 453.810 et seq.
Utah Code Ann. 1953, 63-41-1 et seq.
Wash. Rev. Code 1983, 43.21F.010 et seq.
Wyo. Stat. Ann., § 9-6-101 et seq.

**Western Low-Level Waste Disposal Compact Act**
Ariz. Rev. Stat. Ann., § 30-721 et seq.

**Western Nassau County Water Authority Act**
N.Y. Public Authorities Law (Consol. Laws Ch. 43A) § 1198a et seq.

**Western Pennsylvania Turnpike Extension Act**
Pa. Purdon's Stat., Title 36, § 654 et seq.

**Western Regional Cooperation in Higher Education Compact Act**
Ariz. Rev. Stat. Ann., § 15-1741 et seq.

**Western Regional Higher Education Compact Act**
Alaska Stat. 1962, § 14.44.010 et seq.
Mont. Code Ann., 20-25-801 et seq.
N.M. Stat. Ann., 11-10-1 et seq.
Ore. Rev. Stat., 351.770 et seq.
Wash. Rev. Code Ann., 28B.70.010 et seq.
Wyo. Stat. Ann., §§ 21-16-201, 21-16-202

**Western Water Policy Review Act of 1992**
Oct. 30, 1992, P.L. 102-575, 43 U.S. Code § 371 nt.

**Westfield Flood Control Act**
Mass. Acts 1939, Ch. 278

**Westfield Flood Protection Loan Act**
Mass. Acts 1962, Ch. 638

**Westfield Junk Yards Licensing and Regulating Act**
N.Y. Local Laws 1969, Town of Westfield, p. 2281

**Westford Home Rule Charter Act**
Mass. Acts 1991, Ch. 480

**Westhampton Water District Loan Act**
Mass. Acts 1953, Ch. 105

**Westlands Water District Merger Act**
Cal. Water Code § 37800 et seq.

**Westminster Playground Improvement Loan Act**
Mass. Acts 1957, Ch. 208

**Westside Freeway Park and Development Act**
Cal. Government Code §§ 7000 et seq., 66400 et seq.
Cal. Public Resources Code §§ 5006.3, 5093

**Wetback Act**
See Mexican Agricultural Workers Importation Act

**Wetland Conservation Act**
Minn. Laws 1991, Ch. 354

**Wetland Policy Act (Interagency)**
Ill. Rev. Stat. 1991, Ch. 96 1/2, § 9701-1 et seq.

**Wetlands Act**
Del. Code of 1974, Title 7, § 6601 et seq.
Fla. Stat. Ann., 403.91 et seq.
Mass. Gen. Laws Ann., 131:40, 131:40A
Md. Ann. Code 1974, Art. NR, § 9-101 et seq.
Me. Rev. Stat. Ann. 1964, Title 38, § 480-C et seq.
Mich. Comp. Laws Ann., 281.701 et seq.
Miss. Code Ann. 1972, § 49-27-1 et seq.
N.J. Stat. Ann., 13:9A-1 et seq.
N.Y. Environmental Conservation Law 1972 (Consol. Laws Ch. 43B) §§ 11-2101, Subd. 1, g; 11-2307
N.Y. Laws 1959, Ch. 545
Tex. Water Code, § 11.501 et seq.
Wyo. Stat. Ann., § 35-11-308 et seq.

**Wetlands Act (Freshwater)**
N.J. Stat. Ann., 13:9B-1 et seq.
N.Y. Environmental Conservation Law 1972 (Consol. Laws Ch. 43B) § 24-0101 et seq.

**Wetlands Act (Tidal)**
N.Y. Environmental Conservation Law 1972 (Consol. Laws Ch. 43B) § 25-0101 et seq.

**Wetlands Act of 1961**
Oct. 4, 1961, P.L. 87-383, 75 Stat. 813, 16 U.S. Code §§ 715k-3 to 715k-5

**Wetlands and Coastal Tidelands Act**
S.C. Code Ann. 1976, § 48-39-270 et seq.

**Wetlands and Drainage Act**
N.Y. Local Laws 1973, Town of North Castle, p. 2663

**Wetlands and Watercourses Act (Inland)**
Conn. Gen. Stat. Ann., § 22a-36 et seq.

**Wetlands and Wildlife Enhancement Act of 1998**
Oct. 30, 1998, P.L. 105-312, Title III, 112 Stat. 2958, 16 U.S. Code § 4401 nt.

**Wetlands Conservation Act (Keene-Nejedly)**
Cal. Public Resources Code § 5810 et seq.

**Wetlands Conservation and Restoration Act (Coastal)**
La. Rev. Stat. Ann., 49:214.1 et seq.

**Wetlands Loan Extension Act of 1976**
Feb. 17, 1976, P.L. 94-215, 16 U.S. Code §§ 715K-3 et seq.

**Wetlands Mitigation Bank Act**
Ore. Rev. Stat. 1989, 196.600

**Wetlands Mitigation Bank Act (Sacramen-to-San Joaquin Valley)**
Cal. Fish and Game Code 1957, § 1775 et seq.

**Wetlands Preservation Act**
Cal. Public Resources Code § 5810 et seq.

**Wetlands Protection Act**
Miss. Code Ann. 1972, § 49-27-1 et seq.

**Wetlands Protection Act (Warren S. Henderson)**
Fla. Stat. Ann., 403.91 et seq.

**Wewahitchka Development Authority Act**
Fla. Laws 1965, Extra Session, Ch. 65-2458

**Weymouth Drainage and Stream Improvement Loan Act**
Mass. Acts 1958, Ch. 481

**Weymouth Sewerage Loan Act**
Mass. Acts 1960, Ch. 412

**Whale Conservation and Protection Study Act**
Oct. 17, 1976, P.L. 94-532, 16 U.S. Code §§ 917 et seq.

**Whaling Convention Act of 1949**
Aug. 8, 1950, Ch. 653, 64 Stat. 421, 16 U.S. Code §§ 916 to 916l

**Whaling Treaty Act**
May 1, 1936, Ch. 251, 49 Stat. 1246, 16 U.S. Code §§ 901 to 915

**Wharf Loan Act (Provincetown)**
Mass. Acts 1955, Ch. 139

**Wharfinger Act**
Wash. Rev. Code 1979, 81.94.010 et seq.

**Wharves Act**
N.J. Laws 1851, p. 335
Wash. Rev. Code Ann., 88.24.010 et seq.

**Wheat Acreage Act**
See Agricultural Adjustment Act of 1938

**Wheat Act**
Kan. Stat. Ann., 2-2601 et seq.

**Wheat and Wheat Foods Research and Nutrition Education Act**
Sept. 29, 1977, P.L. 95-113, 7 U.S. Code §§ 3401, 3401 nt., 3402- -3417

**Wheat Commission Act**
N.D. Cent. Code 4-28-01 et seq.

**Wheat Development Act**
Ill. Comp. Stat. 1992, Ch. 505, § 145/1 et seq.

**Wheat Development and Utilization Act**
Neb. Laws 1951, Ch. 2

**Wheat Research and Marketing Act**
Mont. Code Ann., 80-11-201 et seq.

**Wheat Research and Promotion Act**
Sept. 26, 1970, P.L. 91-430, 84 Stat. 885, 7 U.S. Code § 1292 nt.

**Wheat Resources Act**
Neb. Rev. Stat. 1943, 2-2301 et seq.
Okla. Stat. Ann., Title 2, § 1021 et seq.
S.D. Codified Laws 1967, 38-10-1 et seq.

**Wheatland Excavation Act**
N.Y. Local Laws 1971, Town of Wheatland, p. 3708

**Wheatland Parks Act**
N.Y. Local Laws 1971, Town of Wheatland, p. 3702

**Wheelchair Lemon Law**
N.Y. General Business Law (Consol. Laws Ch. 20) § 670

**Wheelchair Warranty Act**
Mont. Code Ann., 30-14-1201 et seq.

**Wheelchair Warranty Act (Motorized)**
Md. Ann. Code 1974, Art. CL, § 14-2701 et seq.
Pa. Purdon's Stat., Title 73, § 2231 et seq.

**Wheeler Act**
Ore. Code 1991, §§ 35-4001 to 35-4008

**Wheeler Act (Motor Vehicle Revenues Distribution)**
Ohio Rev. Code 1953, 4501.04

**Wheeler-Case Act**
July 16, 1943, Ch. 242, 57 Stat. 566, 16 U.S. Code §§ 590y, 590z-1 to 590z-3

**Wheeler Coal-Miners Act**
See Railroad Retirement Act of 1937

**Wheeler-Howard Act**
June 18, 1934, Ch. 576, 48 Stat. 984, 25 U.S. Code §§ 461 to 479

**Wheeler-Lea Act**
March 21, 1938, Ch. 49, 52 Stat. 111, 15 U.S. Code § 41, 44, 45, 52 to 58

**Wheeler-Lea Transportation Act**
See Transportation Act of 1940

**Wheeling Creek Watershed Protection and Flood Prevention District Compact**
Pa. Purdon's Stat., Title 32, § 819.1 et seq.

**Wherry Act (Housing Near Military Establishments)**
Aug. 8, 1949, Ch. 403, 63 Stat. 570, 12 U.S. Code §§ 1702, 1706, 1715c, 1716, 1748 to 1748g

**Whetmore Musician Booking Agency Act of 1975**
Cal. Business and Professions Code § 9999 et seq.

**Whey Pollution Abatement Authority Act**
Vt. Stat. Ann., Title 10, § 1701 et seq.

**Whiskey Export Act**
Ark. Stat. 1947, 48-328 et seq.

**Whisky Act**
Ga. Code Ann., 3-1-1 et seq.

**Whistle and Bell Act**
Ark. Code Ann. 1947, 23-12-410

**Whistleblower Act**
Colo. Rev. Stat., 24-50.5-101 et seq., 24-114-101 et seq.
N.Y. Civil Service Law (Consol. Laws Ch. 7) § 75b
N.Y. Labor Law (Consol. Laws Ch. 31) § 740
Tex. Government Code, § 554.001 et seq.
W. Va. Code 1966, § 6C-1-1 et seq.

**Whistleblower Protection Act**
Alaska Stat. 1962. Replaced Titles § 39.90.100 et seq.
Fla. Stat. Ann., 112.3187
Haw. Rev. Stat. 378-61 et seq.
Ill. Rev. Stat. 1991, Ch. 127, §§ 63b90.9, 63b91
Kan. Stat. Ann., 75-2973
Me. Rev. Stat. Ann. 1964, Title 26, § 831 et seq.
Mich. Comp. Laws Ann., 15.361 et seq.
N.H. Rev. Stat. 1955, 275-E:1 et seq.
N.Y. Civil Services Law (Consol. Laws Ch. 7) 75b
N.Y. Labor Law (Consol. Laws Ch. 31) § 1425 et seq.
Ore. Rev. Stat. 659.545 et seq.
Pa. Purdon's Stat., Title 43, § 1421 et seq.
R.I. Gen. Laws 1956, 36-15-1 et seq.
S.C. Code Ann. 1976, § 8-27-10 et seq.

**Whistleblower Protection Act of 1989**
April 10, 1989, P.L. 101-12, 5 U.S. Code § 1201 nt.
Oct. 29, 1994, P.L. 103-424, 5 U.S. Code § 5509 nt.
Sept. 30, 1996, P.L. 104-208, 5 U.S. Code § 5509 nt.

**White Act (Collisions on Great Lakes)**
Feb. 8, 1895, Ch. 64, 28 Stat. 645, 33 U.S. Code §§ 241 to 244, 251 to 262, 271, 272, 281 to 294, 301; 46 U.S. Code § 381

**White Act (Fisheries)**
Alaska Stat. 1962, § 16.10.010 et seq.

**White Cane Law**
Ill. Rev. Stat. 1991, Ch. 23, § 3361 et seq.
Kan. Stat. Ann., 39-1101 et seq.
La. Rev. Stat. Ann., 46:1951 et seq.
Md. Ann. Code 1957, Art. 30, § 33
Me. Rev. Stat. Ann. 1964, Title 17, § 1311 et seq.
Minn. Stat. Ann., 256C.01 et seq.
Mont. Code Ann., 49-4-202 et seq.
N.H. Rev. Stat. 1955, 167-C:1 et seq.
N.M. Stat. Ann., 28-7-1 et seq.
Pa. Cons. Stat., Title 75, § 3549
S.C. Code Ann. 1976, § 43-33-10 et seq.
Wash. Rev. Code Ann. 70.84.010 et seq.
W. Va. Code 1966, § 5-15-1 et seq.

**White Cane Safety Day Act**
Oct. 6, 1964, P.L. 88-628, 78 Stat. 1003, 36 U.S. Code § 169d

**White Cap Law (Conspiracy)**
Tenn. Code Ann., 39-1-606, 39-1-612, 40-12-102, 40-13-216

**White Charger Act**
July 12, 1960, P.L. 86-616, 74 Stat. 395, 10 U.S. Code § 3297 nt.

**White Charter (2nd Class Cities)**
N.Y. Laws 1898, Ch. 182

**White Civil Service Act**
N.Y. Laws 1899, Ch. 370

**White Clay Creek Study Act**
Dec. 11, 1991, P.L. 102-215, 16 U.S. Code § 1271 nt.

**White Collar Crimes and Theft Act**
D.C. Code Ann., §§ 22-711 et seq., 22-2511 et seq., 22-3801 et seq.
Tenn. Code Ann., 40-3-201

**White County Port District Act**
Ill. Rev. Stat. 1991, Ch. 19, § 750 et seq.

**White County Soil Erosion and Sedimentation Control Ordinance**
Ga. Laws 1978, p. 4729

**White County Water and Sewerage Authority Act**
Ga. Laws 1973, p. 3752
Ga. Laws 1984, p. 4920

**White Earth Reservation Land Settlement Act of 1985**
March 24, 1986, P.L. 99-264, 25 U.S. Code § 331 nt.
Nov. 5, 1987, P.L. 100-153, 24 U.S. Code § 331 nt.
Dec. 24, 1987, P.L. 100-212, 25 U.S. Code § 331 nt.
May 24, 1990, P.L. 101-301, 25 U.S. Code § 331 nt.
May 31, 1994, P.L. 103-263, 25 U.S. Code § 331 nt.

**White House Conference for a Drug Free America**
Oct. 27, 1986, P.L. 99-570, 20 U.S. Code § 4601 nt.
Oct. 23, 1987, P.L. 101-138, 20 U.S. Code § 4701 nts.

**White House Conference on Aging Act, 1981**
Oct. 18, 1978, P.L. 95-478, 42 U.S. Code § 3001 nt.

**White House Conference on Productivity Act**
Oct. 25, 1982, P.L. 97-367, 15 U.S. Code § 2401 nt.

**White House Conference on Small Business Authorization Act**
May 8, 1984, P.L. 98-276, 15 U.S. Code § 631 nt.
Oct. 5, 1990, P.L. 101-409, 15 U.S. Code § 631 nt.
Aug. 13, 1993, P.L. 103-81, 15 U.S. Code § 631 nt.

**White House Conference on the Arts Act, 1979**
May 3, 1978, P.L. 95-272, 20 U.S. Code § 951 nt.

**White House Conference on the Humanities Act, 1979**
May 3, 1978, P.L. 95-272, 20 U.S. Code § 951 nt.

**White House Police Act**
April 22, 1940, Ch. 133, 54 Stat. 156 (See 3 U.S. Code § 203)

**White Man's Primary Act**
Tex. General Laws 38th Leg., 1923, 2nd C.S., p. 74, Ch. 32, § 1

**White-Mulcahy Act (Highways)**
Ohio Laws, 106, p. 69

**White Phosphorous Matches Act**
April 9, 1912, Ch. 75, 37 Stat. 81

**White Pine Blister Rust Act**
Mich. Comp. Laws Ann., 286.101 et seq.
Pa. Purdon's Stat., Title 3, § 215 et seq.

**White Plains City Court Act**
N.Y. Laws 1915, Ch. 356, §§ 239-256
N.Y. Laws 1944, Ch. 783

**White Plains Parking Authority Act**
N.Y. Public Authorities Law (Consol. Laws Ch. 43A) § 1425 et seq.

**White Potato Industry Promotion and Tax Act**
N.J. Rev. Stat. 1937, 54:47B-1 et seq.

**White Primary Act**
Tex. Election Code, Art. 13.01 et seq.

**White Russian Act**
June 8, 1934, Ch. 429, 48 Stat. 926

**White Slave Act**
Kan. Stat. Ann., 21-3513, 21-3514
Mont. Rev. Code 1947, 94-4109
Ohio Rev. Code 1953, 2907.21 et seq.
Va. Code 1950, § 18.2-355 et seq.
Vt. Stat. Ann., Title 13, § 2635 et seq.

**White-Slave Laws**
March 26, 1910, Ch. 128, 36 Stat. 263
June 25, 1910, Ch. 395, 36 Stat. 825 (See 18 U.S. Code §§ 2421 to 2424)

**White-Slave Traffic Act**
See White-Slave Laws

**White Slough Protection and Development Act**
Cal. Government Code § 66670 et seq.

**Whitecap Act (Intimidation)**
Ind. Code 1971, 35-1-77-2
Tex. Penal Code 1925, Art. 1303

**Whiteface Mountain Authority Act**
N.Y. Public Authorities Law (Consol. Laws Ch. 43A) § 100 et seq.

**Whiteface Mountain Highway Commission Act**
N.Y. Public Authorities Law (Consol. Laws Ch. 43A) § 100 et seq.

**Whiteley Act (Intoxicating Liquor)**
Nev. Statutes 1923, Ch. 37, p. 43

**Whitlock-Hickerson Act (Abandoned Cemeteries)**
Ky. Rev. Stat. 1971, 381.720 et seq.

**Whitman Mission National Historic Site**
May 31, 1962, P.L. 87-471, 76 Stat. 90, 16 U.S. Code § 433n

**Whitman Sewerage Loan Act**
Mass. Acts 1961, Ch. 460

**Whitney Act (Drug Maintenance Treatment)**
N.Y. Laws 1917, Ch. 431

**Whitney Act (Police Courts)**
Cal. Statutes 1885, Ch. 164, p. 213

**Whittemore Act (Delinquent Real Estate Taxes)**
Ohio Rev. Code 1953, 323.41 et seq.

**Whittemore Act (Foreign Corporations)**
Ohio Rev. Code 1953, 1703.01 et seq.

**Whittemore Act (Private Corporations)**
Ohio Rev. Code 1953, 1701.05 et seq.

**Who Gave It-Who Got It Act**
Fla. Stat. 1983, 106.011 et seq.

**Wholesale Beer Tax Act**
Tenn. Code Ann., 57-6-101 et seq.

**Wholesale Compensating Tax Act**
Miss. Code Ann. 1972, § 27-67-301 et seq.

**Wholesale Competition and Economic Development Act (Electric Energy)**
Va. Code 1950, §§ 56-576 to 56-591

**Wholesale Distributor—Supplier Equity Agreement Act**
Wash. Rev. Code Ann., 19.126.010 et seq.

**Wholesale Drug Distributor Licensing Act**
Minn. Stat. Ann., 151.42 et seq.
N.C. Gen. Stat. 1943, § 106-145.1 et seq.
Neb. Laws 1992, L.B. 1019, §§ 1 to 26
*Continued*

Pa. Purdon's Stat., Title 63, § 391.1 et seq.
W. Va. Code 1966, § 60A-8-1 et seq.

**Wholesale Fishing and Other Equipment Revenue Act**
Fla. Stat. 1965, 212.50 et seq.

**Wholesale License Agreement Act**
Me. Rev. Stat. Ann. 1964, Title 28-A, § 1451 et seq.

**Wholesale Licensee and Certificate of Approval Holder Agreement Act**
Me. Rev. Stat. Ann. 1964, Title 28-A, § 1451 et seq.

**Wholesale Meat Act**
P.R. Laws Ann. 1954, Title 24, § 771

**Wholesale Merchants' License Tax Act**
Va. Code 1950, § 58-304 et seq.

**Wholesale Minnow Dealers Act**
Miss. Code Ann. 1972, § 49-7-29

**Wholesale or Franchise Insurance Act**
Cal. Insurance Code § 10200.5

**Wholesale Potato Dealers Act**
Mich. Comp. Laws Ann., 290.451 et seq.

**Wholesale Prescription Drug Distributors License Act**
Pa. 1992 Pamph. Laws, No. 145

**Wholesale Produce Dealers Act**
Cal. Food and Agricultural Code 1967, § 43601 et seq.
Minn. Stat. Ann., 27.01 et seq.

**Wholesale Water Supply District Act**
Kan. Stat. Ann., 19-3545 et seq.

**Wholesome Eggs and Eggs Products Act**
Wash. Rev. Code Ann., 69.25.010 et seq.

**Wholesome Food and Animal Drug Act**
Utah Code Ann. 1953, 4-5-1 et seq.

**Wholesome Meat Act**
Dec. 15, 1967, P.L. 90-201, 81 Stat. 584, 19 U.S. Code § 1306; 21 U.S. Code §§ 601 to 623, 641 to 645, 661, 671 to 680, 691
Nov. 2, 1994, P.L. 103-437, 21 U.S. Code § 691
Md. Ann. Code 1974, Art. AG, § 4-101 et seq.
P.R. Laws Ann. 1954, Title 24, § 771 et seq.
Wyo. Stat. Ann., § 35-7-701 et seq.

**Wholesome Poultry and Poultry Products for Human Comsumption Act**
P.R. Laws Ann. 1954, Title 24, § 741 et seq.

**Wholesome Poultry Products Act**
Aug. 18, 1968, P.L. 90-492, 82 Stat. 791, 21 U.S. Code §§ 451 to 461, 463 to 465, 467, 467a to 467f, 470
Wash. Rev. Code Ann., 16.74.010 et seq.

**Whooping Cough Immunization Act**
N.C. Gen. Stat. 1943, § 130A-152 et seq.

**WIC Farmers' Market Nutrition Act of 1992**
July 7, 1992, P.L. 102-314, 42 U.S. Code §§ 1771 nt., 1786, 1786 nt.

**WIC Infant Formula Procurement Act of 1992**
Oct. 24, 1992, P.L. 102-512, 42 U.S. Code § 1771 nt.
Nov. 2, 1994, P.L. 103-448, 42 U.S. Code § 1786

**WIC Program Act**
Mass. Gen. Laws. Ann., 111i:1 et seq.

**WICHE**
Mont. Code Ann., 20-25-801 et seq.

**WICHE Loan for Service Act (Western Interstate Commission on Higher Education)**
N.M. Stat. Ann., 21-29-1 to 21-29-6

**Wichita City Court Act**
Kan. Laws 1899, Ch. 130

**Wichita County Hospital District Act**
Tex. Rev. Civ. Stat. 1925, Art. 4494q-5

**Wicks Act (Emergency Relief)**
N.Y. Laws 1931, Ex. Sess., Ch. 798

**Wicks Act (Prevailing Rate of Wages)**
N.Y. Labor Law (Consol. Laws Ch. 31) § 220d

**Wicks Act (Transit Employees' Civil Service)**
N.Y. Laws 1939, Ch. 927

**Wicks-Austin Act (Public Housing Discrimination)**
N.Y. Civil Rights Law (Consol. Laws Ch. 6) § 18a et seq.

**Wicks Grade Crossing Elimination Act**
N.Y. Laws 1939, Ch. 289

**Wicks Law (Bidding on Public Construction Contracts)**
N.Y. General Municipal Law (Consol. Laws Ch. 24) § 101
N.Y. Public Housing Law (Consol. Laws Ch. 44A) § 151a
N.Y. State Finance Law 1940 (Consol. Laws Ch. 56) § 135

**Wicks Law (Prevailing Rate of Wages)**
N.Y. Labor Law (Consol. Laws Ch. 31) § 220 et seq.

**Wide Tire and Maximum Load Law**
Ky. Rev. Stat. 1971, 189.200

**Widow's Allowance Act (Probate)**
Alaska Stat. 1962, § 13.11.125 et seq.
Colo. Rev. Stat., 15-11-402 et seq.
Ga. Code Ann., 53-4-1 et seq.

**Widows' and Orphan's Exemption Act**
Nev. Rev. Stat. 1979 Reprint, 361.080

**Widow's Election Act**
Mich. Comp. Laws Ann., 700.281 et seq.
Wis. Stat. Ann., 861.03 et seq.

**Widows' Exemption Act**
Pa. Cons. Stat., Title 20, § 3121 et seq.

**Widows' Homestead Act**
La. Civil Code, Art. 3252

**Widows' Pension Act**
April 19, 1908, Ch. 147, 35 Stat. 64
Iowa Laws 1904 (30th G. A.) Ch. 11, § 8
Iowa Laws 1913 (35th G. A.), Ch. 31, § 1
N.Y. Social Services Law (Consol. Laws Ch. 55) § 169
Ore. Code 1930, §§ 27-1301 to 27-1321

**Width and Weight Act (Motor Vehicles)**
N.M. Stat. Ann. 1953, 64-23-12 et seq.

**Wife Abandonment Act**
See Nonsupport Act
Ill. Rev. Stat. 1991, Ch. 40, § 1101 et seq.

**Wilcox Air Base Act**
Aug. 12, 1935, Ch. 511, 49 Stat. 610 (See 10 U.S. Code § 9774)

**Wild and Scenic Designation and Preservation of Myakka River Act**
Fla. Stat. Ann., 258.501

**Wild and Scenic River Act (Lower St. Croix)**
Minn. Stat. Ann., 103F.301 et seq.

**Wild and Scenic River Act (Stony Creek)**
Pa. Purdon's Stat., Title 32, § 820.71 et seq.

**Wild and Scenic Rivers Act**
Oct. 2, 1968, P.L. 90-542, 82 Stat. 906, 16 U.S. Code §§ 1271 to 1287
May 10, 1974, P.L. 93-279, 88 Stat. 122, 16 U.S. Code §§ 1274 to 1276, 1278, 1286, 1287
Oct. 12, 1976, P.L. 94-486, 16 U.S. Code § 1274 et seq.
Nov. 10, 1978, P.L. 95-625, 16 U.S. Code § 1273 et seq.
Oct. 12, 1979, P.L. 96-87, 16 U.S. Code § 1276
March 5, 1980, P.L. 96-199, 16 U.S. Code § 1276
July 23, 1980, P.L. 96-312, 16 U.S. Code § 1274
Sept. 8, 1980, P.L. 96-344, 16 U.S. Code § 1274
June 19, 1984, P.L. 98-323, 16 U.S. Code § 1276
*Continued*

Aug. 28, 1984, P.L. 98-406, 16 U.S. Code § 1274
Sept. 28, 1984, P.L. 98-425, 98 Stat. 1632, 16 U.S. Code § 1274
Oct. 4, 1984, P.L. 98-444, 98 Stat. 1714, 16 U.S. Code § 1274
Oct. 17, 1984, P.L. 98-484, 16 U.S. Code § 1276
Oct. 19, 1984, P.L. 98-494, 16 U.S. Code §§ 1274, 1276
Oct. 27, 1986, P.L. 99-530, 16 U.S. Code § 1274
Oct. 30, 1986, P.L. 99-590, 16 U.S. Code §§ 1274 to 1280, 1282, 1283 , 1286
Nov. 17, 1986, P.L. 99-663, 16 U.S. Code §§ 1274, 1276
May 7, 1987, P.L. 100-33, 16 U.S. Code § 1276
Nov. 2, 1987, P.L. 100-149, 16 U.S. Code §§ 1274, 1276
Nov. 3, 1987, P.L. 100-150, 16 U.S. Code § 1274
Nov. 23, 1987, P.L. 100-173, 16 U.S. Code § 1274
Oct. 26, 1988, P.L. 100-534, 16 U.S. Code § 1274
Oct. 28, 1988, P.L. 100-547, 16 U.S. Code § 1274
Oct. 28, 1988, P.L. 100-554, 16 U.S. Code § 1274
Oct. 28, 1988, P.L. 100-557, 16 U.S. Code §§ 1274, 1276
Nov. 7, 1988, P.L. 100-633, 16 U.S. Code § 1274
June 20, 1989, P.L. 101-40, 16 U.S. Code §§ 1274, 1276
June 6, 1990, P.L. 101-306, 16 U.S. Code § 1274
Aug. 10, 1990, P.L. 101-356, 16 U.S. Code § 1276
Aug. 10, 1990, P.L. 101-357, 16 U.S. Code § 1276
Aug. 15, 1990, P.L. 101-364, 16 U.S. Code § 1276
Nov. 8, 1990, P.L. 101-538, 16 U.S. Code § 1276
Nov. 16, 1990, P.L. 101-612, 16 U.S. Code § 1274
Nov. 28, 1990, P.L. 101-628, 16 U.S. Code §§ 1274, 1276
May 24, 1991, P.L. 102-50, 16 U.S. Code §§ 1274, 1276
Dec. 11, 1991, P.L. 102-214, 16 U.S. Code § 1276
Dec. 11, 1991, P.L. 102-215, 16 U.S. Code § 1276
March 3, 1992, P.L. 102-249, 16 U.S. Code §§ 1274, 1276
April 20, 1992, P.L. 102-271, 16 U.S. Code §§ 1274, 1274 nt., 1276
April 22, 1992, P.L. 102-275, 16 U.S. Code § 1274
June 19, 1992, P.L. 102-301, 16 U.S. Code §§ 1274, 1276
Oct. 23, 1992, P.L. 102-432, 16 U.S. Code §§ 1274, 1276
Oct. 23, 1992, P.L. 102-460, 16 U.S. Code § 1276
Oct. 26, 1992, P.L. 102-525, 16 U.S. Code § 1276
Oct. 27, 1992, P.L. 102-536, 16 U.S. Code § 1274
Dec. 1, 1993, P.L. 103-162, 16 U.S. Code § 1274
May 4, 1994, P.L. 103-242, 16 U.S. Code §§ 1274, 1276
Aug. 26, 1994, P.L. 103-313, §§ 1274, 1274 nt.
Nov. 2, 1994, P.L. 103-437, 16 U.S. Code §§ 1274, 1278
Sept. 30, 1996, P.L. 104-208, 16 U.S. Code § 1274
Oct. 19, 1996, P.L. 104-311, 16 U.S. Code § 1276
Oct. 19, 1996, P.L. 104-314, 16 U.S. Code § 1274
Nov. 12, 1996, P.L. 104-333, 16 U.S. Code §§ 1274, 1276
April 9, 1999, P.L. 106-20, 16 U.S. Code § 1274
Cal. Public Resources Code § 5093.50 et seq.
Ill. Rev. Stat. 1991, Ch. 105, § 491.90 et seq.
Ky. Rev. Stat. 1971, 146.200 et seq.
N.J. Stat. Ann. 13:8-45 et seq.

**Wild and Scenic Rivers Act (Minnesota)**
Minn. Stat. 1986, 103F.301 et seq.

**Wild and Scenic Rivers Additions Act (East Fork of the Jemez River and the Pecos River)**
N.J. Stat. Ann. 13:8-45 et seq.

**Wild Animal and Pest Control in Counties Act**
Ida. Code 1947, 25-2601 et seq.

**Wild Animal Bounty Law**
Colo. Rev. Stat., 35-40-107 et seq.

**Wild Animals Act (Domesticated)**
Ill. Rev. Stat. 1991, Ch. 8, § 23y et seq.

**Wild Bird Conservation Act of 1992**
Oct. 23, 1992, P.L. 102-440, 16 U.S. Code §§ 4901, 4901 nt., 4902 to 4916

**Wild Flower Conservation Act**
Ore. Rev. Stat., 564.010 et seq.

**Wild Flower Preservation Act**
Ga. Code Ann., 12-6-170 et seq.

**Wild Free-Roaming Horses and Burros Act**
Dec. 15, 1971, P.L. 92-195, 16 U.S. Code §§ 1331 to 1340

**Wild Life Conservation Act**
March 10, 1934, Ch. 55, 48 Stat. 401, 16 U.S. Code §§ 661 to 666

**Wild Life Restoration Act**
Sept. 2, 1937, Ch. 889, 50 Stat. 917, 16 U.S. Code 669 to 669b, 669c to 669i
Aug. 18, 1941, Ch. 367, 55 Stat. 632, 16 U.S. Code § 669g-1
July 24, 1946, Ch. 605, 60 Stat. 656, 16 U.S. Code §§ 669c, 669g
Aug. 3, 1950, Ch. 523, 64 Stat. 399, 16 U.S. Code § 669g-1
Aug. 12, 1955, Ch. 861, 69 Stat. 698, 16 U.S. Code § 669g
July 2, 1956, Ch. 489, 70 Stat. 473, 16 U.S. Code §§ 669a, 669g-1
Aug. 1, 1956, Ch. 852, 70 Stat. 908, 16 U.S. Code § 669g-1
Oct. 23, 1970, P.L. 91-503, 84 Stat. 1097, 16 U.S. Code §§ 669b to 669g-1
July 9, 1984, P.L. 98-347, 16 U.S. Code § 669g-1

**Wild Plant Conservation Act**
Ill. Rev. Stat. 1991, Ch. 5, § 230 et seq.

**Wild Resource Conservation Act**
Pa. Purdon's Stat., Title 32, § 5301 et seq.

**Wilderness Act**
Oct. 31, 1994, P.L. 103-433, 16 U.S. Code § 1132 nt.
Cal. Public Resources Code § 5093.30 et seq.

**Wilderness Act of 1964**
Sept. 3, 1964, P.L. 88-577, 78 Stat. 890, 16 U.S. Code §§ 1131- 1136
Oct. 21, 1978, P.L. 95-495, 16 U.S. Code § 1133
Sept. 8, 1982, P.L. 97-250, 16 U.S. Code § 1132 nt.
Dec. 22, 1982, P.L. 97-384, 16 U.S. Code § 1132 nt.
Jan. 13, 1983, P.L. 97-466, 16 U.S. Code § 1132 nt.
Oct. 16, 1986, P.L. 99-490, 16 U.S. Code § 1132 nt.
June 7, 1988, P.L. 100-326, 102 Stat. 584, 16 U.S. Code § 1132 nt.

**Wilderness and Natural Areas Act**
Mich. Comp. Laws Ann., 322.751 et seq.

**Wilderness System Act (State)**
Fla. Stat. Ann., 258.17 et seq.

**Wildfire Act**
Minn. Stat. Ann., 88.02 to 88.22

**Wildfire Disaster Recovery Act of 1989**
May 9, 1990, P.L. 101-286, 16 U.S. Code §§ 551 nt., 551b, 551b nt., 551c

**Wildfire Suppression Aircraft Transfer Act of 1996**
Oct. 14, 1996, P.L. 104-307, 10 U.S. Code § 2576 nt.

**Wildfire Suppression Assistance Act**
April 7, 1989, P.L. 101-11, 42 U.S. Code §§ 1856m nt., 1856p

**Wildflower Seed Revolving Fund**
Miss. Code Ann. 1972, § 69-27-14

**Wildland Fire Protection and Resources Management Act**
Cal. Public Resources Code § 4461 et seq.

**Wildlands Act**
Me. Rev. Stat. Ann. 1964, Title 12, § 681 et seq.

**Wildlife Act**
Ill. Rev. Stat. 1991, Ch. 61, § 1.1 et seq.
Ohio Rev. Code 1953, 1531.01 et seq.
Ore. Rev. Stat. 496.002 et seq.
P.R. Laws Ann. 1954, Title 12, § 81 et seq.

**Wildlife and Agricultural Damage Prevention Act**
Utah Code Ann. 1953, 4-23-1 et seq.

**Wildlife and Fish Act**
Ind. Code Ann., 14-2-1-1 et seq.
La. Rev. Stat. Ann., 56:1 et seq.
Mont. Code Ann., 87-1-101 et seq.

**Wildlife and Fish Crimestoppers Act**
Mont. Code Ann., 87-5-601 et seq.

**Wildlife and Fish Habitat Enhancement Act**
Cal. Fish and Game Code 1957, § 2600 et seq.

**Wildlife and Fish Law**
N.Y. Environmental Conservation Law 1972 (Consol. Laws Ch. 43B) § 11-0101 et seq.

**Wildlife and Fish Management Act**
Miss. Code Ann. 1972, § 49-3-1 et seq.

**Wildlife and Forestry Act**
Mo. Rev. Stat., 252.010 et seq.

**Wildlife and Natural Areas Conservation Act**
Cal. Fish and Game Code 1957, § 2700 et seq.

**Wildlife and Recreation Lands Management Act (State)**
Wash. Rev. Code Ann., 43.98A.010 et seq.

**Wildlife, Coastal and Parkland Conservation Act**
Cal. Public Resources Code § 5900 et seq.

**Wildlife Code**
Pa. Cons. Stat., Title 34, § 101 et seq.
Wash. Rev. Code Ann., 77.04.010 et seq.

**Wildlife Conservation Act**
N.M. Stat. Ann., 17-2-37 to 17-2-46

**Wildlife Conservation Code**
Cal. Fish and Game Code 1959, § 1300 et seq.
Mich. Comp. Laws Ann., 300.251 et seq.
N.M. Stat. Ann., 17-2-37 et seq.
Okla. Stat. Ann., Title 29, § 1-101 et seq.
Tex. Parks and Wildlife Code, § 61.001 et seq.

**Wildlife Enhancement Bond Act**
Cal. Water Code § 11922 et seq.

**Wildlife Habitat Management Areas Act**
Ill. Rev. Stat. 1991, Ch. 61, § 217.9 et seq.

**Wildlife Heritage Act**
Utah Code Ann. 1953, 23-26-1 et seq.

**Wildlife Management Law**
Miss. Code Ann. 1972, § 49-3-1 et seq.

**Wildlife Prairie Park Act**
Ill. Comp. Stat. 1992, Ch. 20, § 4029/1 et seq.

**Wildlife Protection Act**
Cal. Fish and Game Code 1957, § 2780 et seq.
Tenn. Code Ann., 70-1-101 et seq.

**Wildlife Recodification Acts**
S.C. Code Ann. 1976, §§ 50-11-10 et seq., 50-17-10 et seq.

**Wildlife Refuge Designation Act**
Ga. Laws 1988, p. 4498

**Wildlife Regulatory Act**
Tex. Parks and Wildlife Code, § 61.001 et seq.

**Wildlife Resources Act**
N.C. Gen. Stat. 1943, § 143-237 et seq.
Tenn. Code Ann., 70-1-101 et seq.
Utah Code Ann. 1953, 23-13-1 et seq.

**Wildlife Resources Conservation Act (Nongame)**
Vt. Acts 1985, No. 191

**Wildlife Restoration Act**
Mich. Comp. Laws Ann., 299.201

**Wildlife Restoration Cooperation Act**
Ill. Rev. Stat. 1991, Ch. 61, § 132.9 et seq.

**Wildlife Violator Compact**
Ariz. Rev. Stat. Ann., § 17-501 et seq.
Colo. Rev. Stat., 24-60-2601 et seq.

**Wildlife Violator Compact (Interstate)**
Mont. Laws 1995, Ch. 122
Utah Code Ann. 1953, 23-25-1 et seq.

**Wildman-Keeley-Solis Exemplary Teacher Training Act**
Cal. Education Code 1976, § 44391 et seq.

**Wiley Act (Food and Drugs)**
June 30, 1906, Ch. 3915, 34 Stat. 768

**Wiley Act (Homestead Lands, Alabama)**
March 3, 1903, Ch. 1013, 32 Stat. 1222

**Will Act (Living)**
S.C. Code Ann. 1976, § 44-77-10 et seq.

**Will County and Lake County Metropolitan Exposition and Auditorium Authority Act**
Ill. Rev. Stat. 1991, Ch. 85, § 1580-1 et seq.

**Will-Kankakee Regional Development Authority Law**
Ill. Rev. Stat. 1989, Ch. 85, § 7451 et seq.

**Will Sanitary District Act (Eastern)**
Ill. Comp. Stat. 1992, Ch. 70, § 3020/1 et seq.

**Willard Act (Foreign Insurance Companies)**
N.C. Gen. Stat. 1943, § 58-16-1 et seq.

**Willful Neglect Act (Wrongful Death)**
Ky. Rev. Stat. 1971, 411.130

**William and Budd Bell Prevention and Protection Act**
Fla. Stat. Ann., 39.001 et seq.

**William B. Hoyt Memorial Children and Family Trust Fund Act**
N.Y. Social Services Law (Consol. Laws Ch. 55) § 481a et seq.

**William E. Sadowski Affordable Housing Act**
Fla. Laws 1992, Ch. 317

**William F. Goodling Child Nutrition Reauthorization Act of 1998**
Oct. 31, 1998, P.L. 105-336, 112 Stat. 3143, 42 U.S. Code § 1751 nt.

**Williams Act (Rural Electrification Transfer)**
S.C. Acts 1940, p. 2059, No. 1030

**Williams, J. Howard-Abshire-Maloney-John McCarthy-Murdy Bill (Average Annual Earnings)**
Cal. Labor Code §§ 4452, 4453, 4455, 4460, 4702

**Williams-Moorman Anti-Daylight Saving Time Act**
Ky. Rev. Stat. 1962, 2.160

**Williams Rule (Evidence)**
Fla. Stat. Ann., 90.404

**Williams-Steiger Occupational Safety and Health Act of 1970**
See Occupational Saftey and Health Act of 1970

**Williamsburg Bridge Act**
N.Y. Laws 1895, Ch. 789

**Williamson Act (Bank Deposits)**
N.Y. Banking Law (Consol. Laws Ch. 2) § 134, Subds. 5, 7, §§ 138, 171

**Williamson Act (False Advertising)**
N.Y. Penal Law 1965 (Consol. Laws Ch. 40) § 190.20

**Williamson Act (Land Conservation)**
Cal. Government Code § 51200 et seq.

**Williamson Act (Veterans' Administration)**
July 3, 1930, Ch. 863, 46 Stat. 1016

**Williamson, Beatty, Love Act (Trucks)**
Ky. Rev. Stat. 1971, 189.340

**Willie L. Brown, Jr., Bill Lockyer Civil Liability Reform Act**
Cal. Business and Professions Code § 6146
Cal. Civil Code §§ 1714.45, 2860, 3294, 3295
Cal. Code of Civil Procedure § 425.13

**Willis-Campbell Act**
Nov. 23, 1921, Ch. 134, 42 Stat. 222

**Williston Park Demolition Act**
N.Y. Local Laws 1972, Village of Williston Park, p. 4065

**Willow Creek Valley Groundwater Basin Act**
Cal. Water Code, Appx., § 135-101 et seq.

**Wills Act**
Ala. Code 1975, § 43-8-130 et seq.
Alaska Stat. 1962, § 13.11.005 et seq.
Ariz. Rev. Stat. Ann., § 14-2501 et seq.
Ark. Code Ann. 1987, 28-40-301 et seq.
Ark. Stat. 1947, 60-101 et seq.
Cal. Probate Code § 20 et seq.
Colo. Rev. Stat. 15-10-201 et seq.
Conn. Gen. Stat. Ann., § 45a-250 et seq.
D.C. Code 1973, § 18-101 et seq.
Del. Code 1974, Title 12, § 101 et seq.
Fla. Stat. Ann., 732.501 et seq., 732.502
Ga. Code Ann., 53-2-1 et seq.
Haw. Rev. Stat. Ann., § 560:2-501 et seq.
Ida. Code 1947, 15-2-501 et seq.
Ill. Rev. Stat. 1991, Ch. 110 1/2, § 4-1 et seq.
Ind. Code Ann., 29-1-5-1 et seq.
Iowa Code Ann., 633.264 et seq.
Kan. Stat. Ann., 59-601 et seq.
Ky. Rev. Stat. 1971, 394.010 et seq.
La. Rev. Stat. Ann., 9:2401
Mass. Gen. Laws Ann., 191:1 et seq.
Md. Ann. Code 1974, Art. ET, § 4-101 et seq.
Me. Rev. Stat. Ann. 1964, Title 18A, § 2-501 et seq.
Mich. Comp. Laws Ann., 700.121 et seq.
Minn. Stat. Ann., 524.2-101 et seq.
Minn. Stat. 1974, 525.18 et seq.
Miss. Code Ann. 1972, § 91-5-1 et seq.
Mo. Rev. Stat., 474.310 et seq.
Mont. Code Ann., 72-2-301 et seq., 72-12-101 et seq.
N.C. Gen. Stat. 1943, § 31-1 et seq.
N.D. Cent. Code 30.1-08-01 et seq.
Neb. Rev. Stat. 1943, 30-2326 et seq.
Nev. Rev. Stat. 1979 Reprint, 133.010 et seq.
N.H. Rev. Stat. 1955, 551:1 et seq.
N.J. Stat. Ann. 3B:3-1 et seq.
N.M. Stat. Ann., 45-2-501 et seq.
N.Y. Estates, Powers and Trusts Law (Consol. Laws Ch. 17B) § 1-1.1 et seq.
Ohio Rev. Code 1953, 2107.01 et seq.
Okla. Stat. Ann., Title 84, § 41 et seq.
Ore. Rev. Stat., 112.575 et seq.
Pa. Cons. Stat., Title 20, § 2501 et seq.
R.I. Gen. Laws 1956, 33-5-1 et seq.
S.C. Code Ann. 1976, Superseded Vols., § 21-7-10 et seq.
S.D. Codified Laws 1967, 29-2-1 et seq.
Tenn. Code Ann., 32-1-101 et seq.
Tex. Probate Code, § 57 et seq.
Utah Code Ann. 1953, 75-1-101 et seq.
Va. Code 1950, § 64.1-45 et seq.
Vt. Stat. Ann., Title 14, § 1 et seq.
Wash. Rev. Code Ann., 11.12.010 et seq.
Wis. Stat. Ann., 853.01 et seq.
W. Va. Code 1966, § 41-1-1 et seq.
Wyo. Stat. Ann., § 2-6-101 et seq.

**Wills Act (International)**
Cal. Probate Code § 60 et seq.
Ill. Rev. Stat. 1991, Ch. 110 1/2, § 50 et seq.

**Wills Act (Living)**
La. Rev. Stat. Ann., 40:1299.58.1 et seq.

**Wills Act (Lost or Destroyed)**
N.Y. Surrogates Court Procedure Act (Consol. Laws Ch. 59A) § 1407

**Wills Act, Foreign Executed**
See Foreign Executed Wills Act

**Wills Act, Foreign Probated**
Kan. Stat. Ann., 59-2229 et seq.
La. Rev. Stat. Ann., 9:2401 et seq.
Nev. Rev. Stat. 1979 Reprint, 136.260 et seq.
Tenn. Code Ann., 32-5-101 et seq.

**Wills and Administrations Tax Act**
Va. Code 1950, § 58.1-1711 et seq.

**Wills and Powers of Attorney Act (Special Military)**
P.R. Laws Ann. 1954, Title 25, § 2901 et seq.

**Wills Contest Act**
Ohio Rev. Code 1953, 2107.71 et seq.
Wash. Rev. Code Ann., 11.24.010 et seq.
Wyo. Stat. Ann., § 2-6-303 et seq.

**Wills Registry Act**
Conn. Gen. Stat. Ann., § 51-11a

**Wills Revocation Act**
N.C. Gen. Stat. 1943, § 31-5.1 et seq.
N.Y. Estates, Powers and Trusts Law (Consol. Laws Ch. 17B) §§ 3-4.1 et seq., 5-1.3

**Wilmington Athletic Field Loan Act**
Mass. Acts 1955, Ch. 200

**Wilmington Employees' Retirement Act**
Del. Laws Vol. 46, p. 637, Ch. 237

**Wilmington Firemen's Pension Act**
Del. Laws Vol. 33, p. 303, Ch. 118
Del. Laws Vol. 45, p. 634, Ch. 168

**Wilmington Marine Terminal Bond Act**
Del. Laws Vol. 50, p. 996, Ch. 457

**Wilmington Public Parks Act**
Del. Laws Vol. 17, p. 404, Ch. 204

**Wilmington Sewer Revenue Bond Act**
Del. Laws Vol. 47, p. 581, Ch. 269

**Wilmot Proviso (Slavery in Territories)**
June 19, 1862, Ch. 111, 12 Stat. 432

**Wilson Act (Northern Pacific Railroad)**
July 1, 1898, Ch. 546, 30 Stat. 597

**Wilson Act (Original Packages)**
Aug. 8, 1890, Ch. 728, 26 Stat. 313, 27 U.S. Code § 121

**Wilson Act (Review of Liquor Authority Decisions)**
N.Y. Alcoholic Beverage Law (Consol. Laws Ch. 3B) § 121

**Wilson Act (State Liquor Authority Review)**
N.Y. Alcoholic Beverage Control Law (Consol. Laws Ch. 3B) § 121, Subd. 1

**Wilson Act (Tariff)**
Aug. 27, 1894, Ch. 349, 28 Stat. 509, 15 U.S. Code §§ 8 to 11

**Wilson-Pakula Act (Party Candidates)**
N.Y. Election Law 1976 (Consol. Laws Ch. 17) § 6-120

**Wilson Police Department Benefit Fund Act**
N.C. Laws 1969, Ch. 892

**Wilton Water and Sewer Authroity Act**
N.Y. Public Authorities Law (Consol. Laws Ch. 43A) § 1121 et seq.

**WIN Demonstration Program Extension Act of 1988**
July 11, 1988, P.L. 100-364, 102 Stat. 822, 42 U.S. Code §§ 645, 1305 nt.

**Winchester Regional Airport Authority Act**
Va. Acts 1991, Ch. 687

**Wind Energy Systems Act of 1980**
Sept. 8, 1980, P.L. 96-345, 42 U.S. Code § 9201 et seq., 9201 nt.
Aug. 22, 1986, P.L. 99-386, 42 U.S. Code § 9210
Dec. 21, 1995, P.L. 104-66, 42 U.S. Code § 9208

*Continued*

**Wind Erosion Act**
N.M. Stat. Ann., 73-22-1

**Wind Erosion Conservation Districts Act**
Tex. Agriculture Code, § 202.001 et seq.

**Wind Erosion Control Act**
Colo. Rev. Stat., 35-72-101 et seq.
Okla. Stat. 1961, Title 82, § 521 et seq.

**Wind Erosion District Act**
N.M. Stat. Ann. 1953, 45-6-1 et seq.

**Winder Public Facilities Authority Act**
Ga. Laws 1998, H.B. 1768

**Windfall Tax Act (Estate Transfer)**
La. Rev. Stat. Ann., 47:2431 et seq.

**Windfall Tax Extension Act**
March 13, 1937, Ch. 40, 50 Stat. 29

**Winding Stair Mountain National Recreation and Wilderness Area Act**
Oct. 18, 1988, P.L. 100-499, 102 Stat. 2491, 16 U.S. Code §§ 460vv nt., 460vv to 460vv-19
Nov. 2, 1994, P.L. 103-437, 16 U.S. Code § 460vv-11

**Window of Opportunity Act**
Mont. Code Ann., 15-35-201 et seq.

**Windstorm Insurance Association Act**
Tex. Insurance Code, Art. 21.49 et seq.

**Windstorm Underwriting Association Act**
Miss. Code Ann. 1972, § 83-34-1 et seq.

**Wine Act (Clerget)**
Ark. Code Ann. 1947, 3-5-401 et seq.

**Wine Act (Domestic)**
Ga. Code Ann., 3-6-1 et seq.
N.M. Stat. 1978, 60-6A-21 et seq.

**Wine Act-Kitchen and Table Wine (County Option)**
Ida. Code 1947, 23-1301 et seq.

**Wine and Beer Act**
Miss. Code Ann. 1972, § 67-3-1 et seq.
S.C. Code Ann. 1976, § 61-9-10 et seq.

**Wine and Beer Local Option Act**
N.C. Gen. Stat. 1943, § 18A-51 et seq.

**Wine and Grape Act**
Tenn. Code Ann., 57-3-207

**Wine, Beer, Ale and Porter Act**
S.C. Code Ann. 1976, § 61-9-10 et seq.

**Wine, Beer and Liquor Control Act**
Iowa Code Ann., 123.1 et seq.

**Wine Control Act (Fortified)**
N.C. Gen. Stat. 1943, § 18-94 et seq.

**Wine Equity and Export Expansion Act of 1984**
Oct. 30, 1984, P.L. 98-573, 19 U.S. Code § 2801

**Wine Franchise Act**
Va. Code 1950, § 4-118.21 et seq.

**Wine Industry Development Act**
Colo. Rev. Stat., 35-29.5-101 et seq.

**Wine Industry Disaster Relief Act**
Ark. Code Ann. 1947, 3-5-801 et seq.

**Wine Regulation Act**
Ga. Code Ann., 3-6-20 et seq.

**Wine Sampling Act**
Tex. Alcoholic Beverage Code, § 16.07

**Wine Tax Act**
Ga. Code Ann., 3-6-50 et seq.

**Wine—Grape Foundation Act**
N.Y. Laws 1985, Ch. 80, §§ 1 to 9

**Winegrape Local Commission Act (Doctor Bill Filante)**
Cal. Statutes 1989, Ch. 854
Cal. Statutes 1992, Ch. 998

**Winegrape Pest and Disease Control District Law**
Cal. Food and Agricultural Code 1967, § 6200 et seq.

**Winegrowers Joint Commission Act (Dills-Bronzan)**
Cal. Food and Agricultural Code 1967, § 74001 et seq.

**Winery and Small Brewery Act (Domestic)**
N.M. Stat. Ann., 60-6A-21 et seq.

**Winery Signage Act (Limited)**
Pa. Purdon's Stat., Title 73, § 411 et seq.

**Wingo Act (Foreign Corporations)**
Ark. Code Ann. 1947, 4-27-104 et seq.

**Winnemucca Charter**
Nev. Statutes 1913, Ch. 77, p. 66

**Winnings Withholding Act**
Ark. Code Ann. 1987, No. 899

**Winslow Act**
March 4, 1923, Ch. 285, 42 Stat. 1511

**Winslow Partial Payment Act (Railroads)**
See Partial Payments Act (Railroads)

**Winter Haven Downtown Development Act**
Fla. Special Laws 1980, Ch. 80-618

**Winter Haven Downtown Development Authority Act**
Fla. Special Laws 1979, Ch. 79-581

**Winter Haven Downtown Development Board Act**
Fla. Special Laws 1970, Ch. 70-987

**Winter Haven Urban Renewal Act**
Fla. Special Laws 1961, Ch. 61-3007

**Winter Run Chinook Salmon Captive Broodstock Act of 1993**
Aug. 11, 1994, P.L. 103-292, 108 Stat. 1458

**Winter 1979-1980 Home Heating Oil Emergency Credit Act**
N.Y. Laws 1979, Ch. 728

**Winthrop University Facilities Revenue Bond Act**
S.C. Code Ann. 1976, § 59-12-310 et seq.

**Winton Act (School Employment Relations)**
Cal. Education Code 1959, § 13080 et seq.
Cal. Government Code, § 3501

**Wiping Rags Act**
Cal. Health and Safety Code § 3900 et seq.

**WIPO Copyright and Performances and Phonograms Treaties Implementation Act of 1998**
Oct. 28, 1998, P.L. 105-304, Title I, 112 Stat. 2861, 17 U.S. Code § 101 nt.

**Wireless Services Theft Prevention Law**
Ark. Code Ann. 1987, 5-36-301 et seq.
Ill. Comp. Stat. 1992, Ch. 720, § 16F-1 et seq.

**Wireless Telephone Protection Act**
April 24, 1998, P.L. 105-172, 18 U.S. Code § 1001 nt.

**Wiretap Act (Presley-Felando-Eaves)**
Cal. Penal Code § 629 et seq.

**Wiretapping and Electronic Surveillance Acts**
Ariz. Rev. Stat. Ann., § 13-3004 et seq.
Cal. Penal Code § 631 § 640
Colo. Rev. Stat. 18-9-301 et seq.
Fla. Stat. Ann., 934.01 et seq.
Ill. Rev. Stat. 1991, Ch. 38, §§ 14-1 et seq., 108A-1 et seq.
Md. Ann. Code 1974, Art. CJ, § 10-401 et seq.
Mich. Comp. Laws Ann., 750.540
N.C. Gen. Stat. 1943, § 14-155
Nev. Rev. Stat. 1979 Reprint, 200.610 et seq.
N.J. Stat. Ann., 2A:156A-1 et seq.
N.Y. Criminal Procedure Law (Consol. Laws Ch. 11A) § 700.05 et seq.
N.Y. Penal Law 1965 (Consol. Laws Ch. 40) §§ 145.20, 250.00 et seq.
*Continued*

Pa. Cons. Stat., Title 18, § 5701 et seq.
R.I. Gen. Laws 1956, 11-35-12, 11-35-13
Tenn. Code Ann., 39-3-1324
Wash. Rev. Code Ann., 9.73.030 et seq.
W. Va. Code 1966, § 62-1D-1 et seq.

**Wisconsin Wilderness Act of 1984**
June 19, 1984, P.L. 98-321, 16 U.S. Code § 1132 nt.

**Withdrawal Act (Public Lands)**
N.C. Gen. Stat. 1943, § 136-96

**Withdrawal of Life Support Mechanisms Act**
Miss. Code Ann. 1972, § 41-41-101 et seq.

**Withholding Act (Income Tax)**
Ga. Code Ann., 48-7-100 et seq.
Ky. Rev. Stat. 1971, 141.310 et seq.
Mass. Gen. Laws Ann., 62B:1 et seq.
Md. Ann. Code 1974, Art. TG, 10-701 et seq.
Mont. Code Ann., 15-30-201 et seq.
N.M. Stat. Ann., 7-3-1 et seq.
Ore. Rev. Stat., 316.162 et seq.
Vt. Stat. Ann., Title 32, § 5841 et seq.

**Withholding Act (Income)**
Kan. Stat. Ann., 23-4,105 et seq.

**Withholding Act (Interstate Income)**
Kan. Stat. Ann., 23-4,125 et seq.

**Withholding Act (Model Interstate Income)**
Tex. Family Code, § 14.61 et seq.

**Withholding Act (State Employees)**
Ill. Rev. Stat. 1991, Ch. 127, § 351 et seq.

**Withholding and Declaration of Estimated Tax Act**
Kan. Stat. Ann., 79-3294 et seq.
Mass. Gen. Laws Ann., 62B:1 et seq.

**Withholding for Support Act (Income)**
Ill. Comp. Stat. 1992, Ch. 750, § 28/1 et seq.

**Withholding of Wages Act**
Mo. Rev. Stat., 290.110

**Witness Act (Adverse Party)**
Md. Ann. Code 1974, Art. CJ, § 9-113

**Witness and Crime Victim Advisory Coucil Act**
Minn. Stat. Ann., 611A.70, 611A.71

**Witness and Victim Protection Act**
Colo. Rev. Stat. 18-8-701 et seq.
Fla. Stat. Ann., 960.001 et seq.
Iowa Code Ann., 910A.1 et seq.

**Witness' and Victim's Bill of Rights Act**
S.C. Code Ann. 1976, § 16-3-1510 et seq.

**Witness Attendance Act (Nonresident)**
W. Va. Code 1966, § 62-6A-1 et seq.

**Witness Competency Act**
Ark. Code Ann. 1987, 16-43-501
Conn. Gen. Stat. Ann., § 54-84
D.C. Code 1973, § 14-301 et seq.
Del. Code of 1974, § 4302 et seq.
Ind. Code Ann., 34-1-14-4
Iowa Code Ann., 622.1 et seq.
Mass. Gen. Laws. Ann., 233:20
Pa. Cons. Stat., Title 42, § 5911 et seq.
Va. Code 1950, § 8.01-396 et seq.
Wash. Rev. Code Ann., 5.60.020 et seq.
Wash. Rev. Code Ann., 10.52.020 et seq.

**Witness Disquualification Act**
Ala. Code 1975, 12-21-162

**Witness from Within or Without a State, Attendance in Criminal Proceedings Act**
Fla. Stat. Ann., 942.06

**Witness from without a State in Criminal Proceedings Act**
Va. Code 1950, § 19.2-272 et seq.

**Witness Immunity Act**
Fla. Stat. Ann., 914.04 et seq.
Fla. Stat. Ann., 914.04, 914.05
Ill. Rev. Stat. 1991, Ch. 38, § 106-1 et seq.
Me. Rev. Stat. Ann. 1964, Title 15, § 1314-A
Mich. Comp. Laws Ann., 750.560, 767.91 et seq.
N.Y. Criminal Procedure Law (Consol. Laws Ch. 11A) § 190.40

Ohio Rev. Code 1953, 101.44, 2945.44
Pa. Cons. Stat., Title 18, § 5513
Pa. Cons. Stat., Title 42, § 8331
P.R. Laws Ann. 1954, Title 34, § 1476 et seq.
Vt. Stat. Ann., Title 12, § 1664
Wash. Rev. Code 1983, 10.52.090

**Witness Immunity Act (Gambling)**
D.C. Code Ann., § 22-1514

**Witness Outside the State Attendance Act**
Wash. Rev. Code Ann., 10.55.010 et seq.

**Witness Pilot and Demonstration Programs (Child Victim)**
Cal. Penal Code § 14000 et seq.

**Witness Privileges Act**
N.J. Stat. Anno, 2A:81-4 et seq.

**Witness Protection Act**
Ill. Rev. Stat. 1991, Ch. 38, § 155-21 et seq.

**Witness Protection Act (Child Victim)**
Mo. Rev. Stat., 491.675

**Witness Protection Act (Gang Crime)**
Ill. Comp. Stat. 1992, Ch. 725, § 172/5-1 et seq.

**Witness Protection Act (Hayden and Frusetta)**
Cal. Penal Code § 1054.2

**Witness Protection Act (Hertzberg-Leslie)**
Cal. Penal Code § 14020 et seq.

**Witness Security Reform Act of 1984**
Oct. 12, 1984, P.L. 98-473, 18 U.S. Code §§ 3521 nt., 3521 to 3528

**Witness Trauma Reduction Act (Child)**
Ill. Comp. Stat. 1992, Ch. 705, §§ 80/0.01, 80/1

**Witness—Victim Assistance Programs Act**
S.C. Code Ann. 1976, § 16-3-1510 et seq.

**Witnesses Act**
Ga. Code Ann., 24-10-1 et seq.
Mo. Rev. Stat., 491.010 et seq.
N.C. Gen. Stat. 1943, § 8-49 et seq.
N.H. Rev. Stat. 1955, 516:1 et seq.
Pa. Cons. Stat., Title 42, § 5911 et seq.
R.I. Gen. Laws 1956, 9-17-1 et seq.
Wyo. Stat. 1957, § 1-138 et seq.

**Witnesses Act (Expert)**
See Expert Testimony Act

**Witnesses Act (Husband and Wife)**
Pa. Cons. Stat., Title 42, § 5923 et seq.

**Witnesses' and Crime Victims' Bill of Rights Act**
N.M. Stat. Ann., 31-24-1 et seq.

**Witnesses' Attendance Act**
Tenn. Code Ann., 24-2-101 et seq.

**Witnesses Attendance in Criminal Cases Act**
P.R. Laws Ann. 1954, Title 34 § 1471 et seq.

**Witnesses' Compensation Act**
Pa. Cons. Stat., Title 42, § 5903

**Witnesses' Disqualification Act**
Ala. Code 1975, 12-21-162
Wash. Rev. Code Ann., 5.60.060

**Witnesses from Within or Without a State, Attendance in Criminal Proceedings Act**
See Uniform Act to Secure the Attendance of Witnesses from Within or Without a State in Criminal Proceedings

**Witnesses in Criminal Actions Extradition Act**
Wis. Stat. Ann., 976.02

**Witnesses in Criminal Proceedings Act (Prisoners)**
See Uniform Rendition of Prisoners as Witnesses in Criminal Proceedings Act

**Witnesses in Criminal Proceedings Act (Rendition of Prisoners as)**
See Uniform Rendition of Prisoners as Witnesses in Criminal Proceedings Act
Me. Rev. Stat. Ann. 1964, Title 15, § 1461 et seq.

**Witnesses Privileged Communications Act**
Ore. Rev. Stat., 40.225

**Witnesses to and Victims of Crimes and Aid to Law Enforcement Assistance Act**
Colo. Rev. Stat. 24-4.2-101 et seq.

**Woburn Off-Street Parking Loan Act**
Mass. Acts 1956, Ch. 276

**Woburn Waterways Improvement Loan Act**
Mass. Acts 1956, Ch. 407

**Wolf Bounty Act**
S.D. Code 1939, 25.1001 et seq.

**Wolf Trap Farm Park Act**
Oct. 15, 1966, P.L. 89-671, 80 Stat. 950, 16 U.S. Code §§ 284 to 284b
Oct. 14, 1982, P.L. 97-310, 16 U.S. Code §§ 284 et seq.
Dec. 19, 1985, P.L. 99-190, 16 U.S. Code § 284c nt.
Nov. 28, 1990, P.L. 101-636, 16 U.S. Code §§ 284, 284 nt., 284c, 284c nt., 284d
Nov. 2, 1994, P.L. 103-437, 16 U.S. Code § 284c, 284h

**Wolfner Library Trust Fund Act**
Mo. Rev. Stat., 181.150

**Wolverine Bounty Act**
Alaska Stat. 1962, § 16.35.050 et seq.

**Wolves and Coyotes Bounty Act**
Alaska Stat. 1962, § 16.35.050 et seq.

**Woman Suffrage Act**
Tex. Election Code, Art. 11.001 et seq.

**Women and Minority Business Assistance Act**
Ore. Rev. Stat. 200.005 et seq.

**Women and Minority Owned Businesses Assistance Act (Omnibus)**
Wash. Laws 1993, Ch. 512

**Women Doctors' Bill**
April 16, 1943, Ch. 63, 57 Stat. 65
Nov. 8, 1943, Ch. 297, 57 Stat. 587

**Women in Apprenticeship and Nontraditional Occupations Act**
Oct. 27, 1992, P.L. 102-530, 29 U.S. Code §§ 2501, 2501 nt., 2502 to 2509

**Women Jurors Act**
Ill. Laws 1929, p. 539, § 1, Subsec. 1

**Women-Owned Businesses Assistance and Omnibus Minority Act**
Wash. Laws 1993, Ch. 512

**Women Veterans Health Programs Act of 1992**
Nov. 4, 1992, P.L. 102-585, 38 U.S. Code § 101 nt.
Dec. 20, 1993, P.L. 103-210, 38 U.S. Code § 1720D nt.

**Women's Access to Health Care Act**
Ala. Code 1975, § 27-49-1 et seq.
Ga. Code Ann., 33-24-58

**Womens Alternative Sentencing Program Act (Pregnant and Parenting)**
Cal. Penal Code § 1174 et seq.

**Womens and Minority Business Enterprise Act**
La. Rev. Stat. Ann., 36:1951 et seq.

**Women's and Minors' Employment Act**
Cal. Labor Code § 1171 et seq.
Ky. Rev. Stat. 1971, Superseded Vols., 337.210 et seq.

**Women's and Minors Hours of Work Act**
Cal. Labor Code § 1350 et seq.

**Women's and Minors' Minimum Wage Act**
Ill. Rev. Stat. 1991, Ch. 48, § 198.1 et seq.
Okla. Stat. Ann., Title 40, § 261 et seq.
Ore. Rev. Stat., 653.010 et seq.
Wis. Stat. Ann., 104.01 et seq.

**Women's and Minors' Ten Hour Act**
N.H. Rev. Stat. 1955, 275:15

**Women's and Minors' Wages Act**
Ill. Rev. Stat. 1991, Ch. 48, § 198 et seq.

**Women's Armed Services Integration Act of 1948**
June 12, 1948, Ch. 449, 62 Stat. 356
June 15, 1956, Ch. 393, 70 Stat. 285

**Women's Business Center Amendments Act of 1999**
April 6, 1999, P.L. 106-17, 113 Stat. 27, 15 U.S. Code § 631 nt.

**Women's Business Development Act of 1991**
Dec. 5, 1991, P.L. 102-191, 15 U.S. Code § 631 nt.

**Women's Business Ownership Act**
Cal. Government Code § 15365.40 et seq.
Ill. Comp. Stat. 1992, Ch. 20, § 705/1

**Women's Business Ownership Act of 1988**
Oct. 25, 1988, P.L. 100-533, 15 U.S. Code § 631 nt.
Dec. 5, 1991, P.L. 102-191, 15 U.S. Code § 631 nt.
Aug. 13, 1993, P.L. 103-81, 15 U.S. Code § 631 nt.
Oct. 22, 1994, P.L. 103-403, 15 U.S. Code § 631 nt.
Dec. 2, 1997, P.L. 105-135, 15 U.S. Code § 631 nt.; 41 U.S. Code § 417a

**Women's Demonstration Resource Centers Act (Hispanic)**
N.J. Laws 1991, Ch. 378

**Women's Educational Equity Act of 1978**
Nov. 1, 1978, P.L. 95-561, 20 U.S. Code § 3341 et seq.
April 1, 1988, P.L. 100-297, 102 Stat. 234, 20 U.S. Code §§ 3041 et seq.

**Women's Educational Equity Amendments of 1984**
Oct. 19, 1984, P.L. 98-511, 20 U.S. Code §§ 2701 nt., 3341 et seq .

**Women's Eight Hour Day Act**
Colo. Rev. Stat. 1963, 80-14-10, 80-14-11
Wyo. Stat. Ann., § 27-6-101

**Women's Emancipation Act**
See also Women's Rights Act
Ind. Code Ann., 31-7-10-1 et seq.
La. Rev. Stat. Ann., 9:101 et seq.
Wash. Rev. Code Ann., 26.16.150 et seq.

**Women's Equal Pay Act**
N.H. Rev. Stat. 1955, 275:36 et seq.
N.J. Stat. Ann., 34:11-56.2
Pa. Purdon's Stat., Title 43, § 336.1 et seq.

**Women's Health and Cancer Rights Act of 1998**
Oct. 21, 1998, P.L. 105-277, 101(f), Title IX, 112 Stat. 2681

**Women's Health Research and Prevention Amendments of 1998**
Oct. 31, 1998, P.L. 105-340, 112 Stat. 3191, 42 U.S. Code § 201 nt.

**Women's Home Guard Act**
Okla. Stat. Ann., Title 44, § 261 et seq.

**Women's Hours of Work Act**
Mont. Rev. Code 1947, 41-1118 et seq.
N.J. Stat. Anno, 34:2-28
N.Y. Labor Law (Consol. Laws Ch. 31) § 172 et seq.
Tex. Rev. Civ. Stat., Art. 5172a
Wis. Stat. Ann., 103.01 et seq.

**Women's, Infants and Children Program Act**
Mass. Gen. Laws. Ann., 111i:1 et seq.

**Women's, Infant's, and Children's Nutrition Improvement Act**
Pa. Purdon's Stat., Title 62, § 2951

**Women's Informed Consent Act**
Ga. Code Ann., 16-12-150

**Women's Intercollegiate Athletics Equity Act**
Fla. Stat. Ann., 240.533

**Women's Jurors Law**
N.Y. Judiciary Law (Consol. Laws Ch. 30) §§ 502, Subds. 1, 3;546, 635, 686, Subds. 1, 3;720

**Women's Labor Act**
D.C. Code 1973, § 36-301 et seq.
Pa. Purdon's Stat., Title 43, § 101 et seq.

*Continued*

Wash. Rev. Code Ann., 49.12.175 et seq.

**Women's Maximum Hour Act**
Mont. Code Ann. 1947, 41-1118 et seq.

**Women's Minimum Wage Act**
La. Rev. Stat. Ann., 23:371 et seq.
Wash. Rev. Code Ann., 49.12.175

**Women's Naval Reserve Act**
July 30, 1942, Ch. 538, 56 Stat. 730

**Women's Preventative Health Services Act**
Pa. Purdon's Stat., Title 40, § 1571 et seq.

**Women's Progress Commemoration Act**
Oct. 31, 1998, P.L. 105-341, 112 Stat. 3196, 16 U.S. Code § 470a nt.

**Women's Rest Period Act**
Ky. Rev. Stat. 1962, 337.365

**Women's Right to Health Care Act**
Ga. Code Ann., 33-24-59.1

**Women's Right-to-Know Act**
Ga. Code Ann., 16-12-150 et seq.
Mont. Code Ann., 50-20-301 et seq.
S.C. Code Ann. 1976, § 44-41-310 et seq.

**Women's Rights Act**
See also Women's Emancipation Act
Ala. Code 1975, § 30-4-1 et seq.
Conn. Gen. Stat. Ann., § 46b-36 seq.
Fla. Stat. Ann., 708.08 et seq.

**Women's Status Act**
Haw. Rev. Stat. Ann., § 367-1 et seq.

**Women's Suffrage Act**
Ill. Laws 1913, p. 333
Tenn. Public Acts 1919, Ch. 139

**Women's Ten Hour Act**
Ill. Rev. Stat. 1975, Ch. 48, § 5 et seq.

**Woner Act (Liquor Control)**
Pa. 1921 Pamph. Laws 407, No. 192

**Wood Act**
Mo. Laws 1887, p. 179

**Wood Act (Security)**
N.Y. Business Corporation Law 1961 (Consol. Laws Ch. 4) § 627, 720b

**Wood County Court Act**
Wis. Laws 1951, Ch. 197

**Wood Products Labeling Act of 1939**
Sept. 24, 1984, P.L. 98-417, 98 Stat. 1604, 1605, 15 U.S. Code §§ 68b, 68c

**Wood Residue Utilization Act of 1980**
Dec. 19, 1980, P.L. 96-554, 16 U.S. Code § 1600 nt.

**Wood River Reservoir Site Acquisition Act**
R.I. Public Laws 1962, Ch. 91
R.I. Public Laws 1964, Ch. 133

**Wood-Stockfish Act (Costs and Fees)**
Mich. Comp. Laws Ann., 600.2576

**Woodland Management Act**
Ore. Rev. Stat., 526.450 et seq.

**Woodland Tax Act**
Wis. Stat. Ann., 77.16

**Woodland Transactions and Use Tax Act**
Cal. Revenue and Taxation Code § 7286.52

**Woodrow Wilson Bridge and Tunnel Revenue Bond Act**
Md. Ann. Code 1974, Art. TR, § 10-301 et seq.

**Woodrow Wilson Memorial Act of 1968**
Oct. 24, 1968, P.L. 90-637, 82 Stat. 1356, 20 U.S. Code §§ 80e to 80j
May 26, 1978, P.L. 95-286, 20 U.S. Code §§ 80g-1 et seq.
April 9, 1990, P.L. 101-268, 20 U.S. Code § 80f.
Oct. 21, 1998, P.L. 105-277, 20 U.S. Code § 80f

**Woodrow Wilson Memorial Bridge Authority Act of 1995**
Nov. 28, 1995, P.L. 104-59, Title IV, 109 Stat. 627

**Woods Act (Delinquent Taxes)**
N.D. Laws 1897, Ch. 67

**Woods Act (Local Option)**
Mo. Laws 1907, p. 231, No. 2

**Wool and Sheep Authority Act**
Colo. Rev. Stat., 35-57.5-101 et seq.

**Wool and Sheep Production Development and Marketing Act**
Ill. Rev. Stat. 1991, Ch. 5, § 1051 et seq.

**Wool and Woolens Act (Tariff)**
March 2, 1867, Ch. 197, 14 Stat. 559

**Wool Products Labeling Act of 1939**
Oct. 14, 1940, Ch. 871, 54 Stat. 1128, 15 U.S. Code §§ 68 to 68j
May 5, 1980, P.L. 96-242, 15 U.S. Code §§ 68, 68 nt., 68b

**Wool Promotion, Research, and Education Act (Sheep, Lamb and)**
Ida. Code 1947, 25-153 to 25-160

**Woonsocket Minimum Nonresidential Standards Act**
R.I. Public Laws 1970, Ch. 40

**Woonsocket Minimum Standards Housing Act**
R.I. Public Laws 1961, Ch. 76

**Worcester County Court House Loan Act**
Mass. Acts 1932, Ch. 98

**Worcester County Jail Farm Barn Loan Act**
Mass. Acts 1970, Ch. 266

**Worcester County Reconciliation Act**
Mass. Acts 1961, Ch. 620

**Worcester Diversion Loan Act**
Mass. Acts 1956, Ch. 15

**Worcester Flood Protection Loan Act**
Mass. Acts 1956, Ch. 235

**Worcester Incinerator Loan Act**
Mass. Acts 1952, Ch. 164

**Worcester Industrial School Building Loan Act**
Mass. Acts 1952, Ch. 273

**Worcester Municipal Airport Loan Act**
Mass. Acts 1941, Ch. 24

**Worcester Off-Street Parking Facilities Loan Act**
Mass. Acts 1955, Ch. 365

**Worcester Retirement Act**
Mass. Acts 1923, Ch. 410

**Worcester School Building Loan Act**
Mass. Acts 1950, Ch. 643
Mass. Acts 1952, Ch. 568

**Worcester Street Improvement Loan Act**
Mass. Acts 1951, Ch. 385

**Words Act (Insulting)**
Miss. Code Ann. 1972, § 95-1-1

**Work Act**
Tenn. Public Acts 1983, Ch. 400

**Work and Gain Economic Self-Sufficiency Act (WAGES)**
Fla. Stat. Ann., 414.015 et seq.

**Work-Based—Youth Apprenticeship Learning Act**
Ark. Code Ann. 1987, 6-50-501 et seq.

**Work First New Jersey Act**
N.J. Stat. Ann., 44:10-55 et seq.

**Work First Program**
Minn. Stat. 1986, 256K.01 to 256K.09

**Work First Temporary Assistance for Needy Families Act**
Wash. Rev. Code Ann., 74.08A.010 et seq.

**Work Force Development Implementation Act**
Fla. Laws 1998, Ch. 58

**Work Force Education Act**
Ark. Code Ann. 1987, 6-51-904, 25-6-301 et seq.
Miss. Code Ann. 1972, §§ 37-153-1 et seq.

**Work Furlough Act (Cobey)**
Cal. Penal Code § 1208

**Work Furlough Rehabilitation Law**
Cal. Penal Code § 1208

**Work Hours Act of 1962**
Aug. 13, 1962, P.L. 87-581, 76 Stat. 357, 28 U.S. Code § 1499; 40 U.S. Code §§ 327 to 332

**Work Incentive Act**
N.M. Stat. Ann., 27-2-37 et seq.

**Work Incentive Employment and Training Act**
N.J. Stat. Ann., 34:15B-5 et seq.

**Work Incentive Programs**
Cal. Unemployment Insurance Code § 5000 et seq.

**Work Interference Act**
N.H. Rev. Stat. 1955, Superseded Volume, 572:35

**Work Law (Right to)**
Neb. Rev. Stat. 1943, 48-217 et seq.

**Work or Don't Eat Act (Moffat)**
N.Y. Labor Law (Consol. Laws Ch. 31) § 21c
N.Y. Social Welfare Law (Consol. Laws Ch. 55) § 158a

**Work Permit Act (Minors)**
Ky. Rev. Stat. 1971, Superseded Vols., 339.280 et seq.

**Work Practice Act (Social Workers Board Certified Social)**
La. Rev. Stat. Ann., 37:2701 et seq.

**Work Prevention Act**
R.I. Gen. Laws 1956, 11-11-4

**Work Programs Act (Joint State and County)**
Miss. Code Ann. 1972, § 47-5-451 et seq.

**Work Release Act (County Prisoners)**
Ala. Code 1975, § 14-8-30 et seq.

**Work-Release Act (Prisoners)**
Alaska Stat. 1962, § 33.30.250
Cal. Penal Code § 2910
D.C. Code 1973, § 24-461 et seq.
Fla. Stat. 1983, 945.091
Iowa Code 1985, 247A.1 et seq.
Minn. Stat. Ann., 241.26
Neb. Rev. Stat. 1943, 83-184
N.Y. Correction Law (Consol. Laws Ch. 43) § 852
Pa. Purdon's Stat., Title 61, § 1051 et seq.
Tex. Rev. Civ. Stat. 1974, Art. 6166x-3
Wis. Stat. 1987, 56.065

**Work Release Act (State Penitentiary)**
Wyo. Stat. Ann., § 7-13-717 et seq.

**Work Release Program Act**
S.C. Code Ann. 1976, §§ 24-3-30 et seq., 24-13-610 et seq.

**Work Relief Act**
See Emergency Relief Appropriation Acts

**Work Relief and Public Works Appropriation Act of 1938**
June 21, 1938, Ch. 554, 52 Stat. 809
June 27, 1942, Ch. 450, 56 Stat. 392
June 26, 1943, Ch. 145, 57 Stat. 180

**Work-Site Education and Training Act**
Cal. Unemployment Insurance Code § 9900 et seq.

**Work-Study Act**
N.M. Stat. 1978, 21-21B-1 et seq.

**Work Study Program Act (Cooperative)**
Ill. Comp. Stat. 1992, Ch. 110, § 225/1 et seq.

**Work Under Compressed Air Act**
Ill. Rev. Stat. 1985, Ch. 48, § 261 et seq.

**Worker Adjustment Act**
N.Y. Labor Law (Consol. Laws Ch. 31) § 835 et seq.

**Worker Adjustment and Retraining Notification Act**
Aug. 4, 1988, P.L. 100-379, 29 U.S. Code § 2101 et seq.
Oct. 21, 1998, P.L. 105-277, 29 U.S. Code § 2102

**Worker and Community Right to Know Act**
N.J. Stat. Ann. 34:5A-1 et seq.
Pa. Purdon's Stat., Title 35, § 7301 et seq.
Wash. Rev. Code Ann., 49.70.010 et seq.

**Worker Cooperative Corporations Act**
Conn. Gen. Stat. Ann., § 33-418f
Conn. Gen. Stat. Ann., 33-418f et seq., No. 430 §§ 1 to 12
Vt. Stat. Ann., Title 11, § 1081 et seq.

**Worker Health and Safety Act**
Mich. Comp. Laws Ann., 408.1002 et seq.
N.J. Stat. Anno, 34:6A-1 et seq.

**Worker Owned Corporation Study Act**
N.J. Stat. Ann. 34:1B-30 et seq.

**Worker Safety Act (Agricultural)**
Fla. Stat. Ann., 487.201 to 487.207

**Worker Training Act**
Ohio Rev. Code 1953, 3304.01 et seq.

**Workermens' Compensation Insurance Minimum Rating Law**
Cal. Insurance Code § 11730 et seq.

**Workers' Bill of Rights (Displaced Defense)**
Conn. Public Acts 1994, May Special Session No. 2, § 192

**Workers' Compensation Act**
Ala. Code 1975, § 25-5-1 et seq.
Alaska Stat. 1962, § 23.30.005 et seq.
Ariz. Rev. Stat. Ann., § 23-901 et seq.
Ark. Code Ann. 1987, 81-1301 et seq.
Ark. Stat. 1947, 11-9-101 et seq.
Cal. Labor Code § 3200 et seq.
Colo. Rev. Stat., 8-40-101 et seq.
Conn. Gen. Stat. Ann., § 31-275 et seq.
D.C. Code Ann., § 36-301 et seq.
Del. Code of 1974, Title 19, § 2301 et seq.
Fla. Stat. Ann., 440.01 et seq.
Ga. Code Ann., 34,9,1 et seq.
Haw. Rev. Stat. Ann., § 386-1 et seq.
Ida. Code 1947, 72-101 et seq.
Ill. Rev. Stat. 1991, Ch. 48, § 138.1 et seq.
Ind. Code Ann., 22-3-2-1 et seq.
Iowa Code Ann., 85.1 et seq.
Kan. Stat. Ann., 44-501 et seq.
Ky. Rev. Stat. 1971, 342.012 et seq.
La. Rev. Stat. Ann., 23:1021 et seq.
Mass. Gen. Laws Ann., 152:1 et seq.
Md. Ann. Code 1974, Art. LE, § 9-101 et seq.
Me. Rev. Stat. Ann. 1964, Title 39, § 1 et seq.
Me. Rev. Stat. Ann. 1964, Title 39-A, §§ 101 to 111
Mich. Comp. Laws Ann., 418.101 et seq.
Minn. Stat. Ann., 176.011 et seq.
Miss. Code Ann. 1972, § 71-3-1 et seq.
Mo. Rev. Stat., 287.010 et seq.
Mont. Code Ann., 39-71-101 et seq.
N.C. Gen. Stat. 1943, § 97-1 et seq.
N.D. Cent. Code 65-01-01 et seq.
Neb. Rev. Stat. 1943, 48-101 et seq.
Nev. Rev. Stat. 1979 Reprint, 616.010 et seq.
N.H. Rev. Stat. 1955, 281-A:1 et seq.
N.J. Stat. Anno, 34:15-1 et seq.
N.M. Stat. Ann., 52-1-1 et seq.
N.Y. Consol. Laws, Ch. 67
Ohio Rev. Code 1953, 4123.01 et seq.
Okla. Stat. Ann., Title 85, § 1 et seq.
Ore. Rev. Stat., 656.001 et seq.
Pa. Purdon's Stat., Title 77, § 1 et seq.
P.R. Laws Ann. 1954, Title 11, § 1 et seq.
R.I. Gen. Laws 1956, 28-29-1 et seq.
S.C. Code Ann. 1976, § 42-1-10 et seq.
S.D. Codified Laws 1967, 62-1-1 et seq.
Tenn. Code Ann., 50-6-101 et seq.
Tex. Labor Code, § 401.001 et seq.
Tex. Rev. Civ. Stat., Arts. 8306 et seq., 8308-1.01
Utah Code Ann. 1953, 35-1-1 et seq.
Va. Code 1950, §§ 65.1-1 et seq., 65.2-100 et seq.
Vt. Stat. Ann., Title 21, § 601 et seq.
Wash. Rev. Code Ann., 51.04.010 et seq.

*Continued*

Wis. Stat. Ann., 102.01 et seq.
W. Va. Code 1966, § 23-1-1 et seq.
Wyo. Stat. Ann., § 27-14-101 et seq.

**Workers' Compensation Act (Extra-Territorial)**
Okla. Stat. Ann., Title 85, § 4

**Workers Compensation Act (Public Employee)**
Ark. Code Ann. 1947, 21-5-603 et seq.

**Workers' Compensation Act for Civil Defense Volunteers**
N.Y. Workers' Compensation Law (Consol. Laws Ch. 67) § 300 et seq.

**Workers' Compensation Administration Act**
N.M. Stat. Ann., 52-5-1.1 et seq.

**Workers' Compensation Apportionment Act**
Cal. Labor Code § 4663
Ky. Rev. Stat. 1971, 342.120 et seq.
Miss. Code Ann. 1972, § 71-3-7

**Workers' Compensation Assigned Risk Pool Law**
N.M. Stat. Ann., 59A-33-1 et seq.

**Workers Compensation Competition Rating Act**
Me. Rev. Stat. Ann. 1964, Title 24-A, § 2361 et seq.

**Workers' Compensation Contractor-Under Act**
Ga. Code Ann., 34-9-8

**Workers' Compensation Cost Containment Act**
Colo. Rev. Stat., 8-14.5-101 et seq.
La. Rev. Stat. Ann., 23:1175 et seq.

**Workers' Compensation Death Benefit Act**
Mich. Comp. Laws Ann., 318.321
Ohio Rev. Code 1953, 4123.59 et seq.

**Workers' Compensation Estoppel Act**
Okla. Stat. 1981, Title 85, § 65.2

**Workers' Compensation Health Care Provider Organization Act**
Cal. Labor Code § 5150 et seq.

**Workers' Compensation Insurance Act**
Cal. Insurance Code § 11630 et seq.

**Workers' Compensation Insurance Fraud Reporting Act**
Cal. Insurance Code § 1877 et seq.

**Workers' Compensation Insurance Fund Act**
Tenn. Code Ann., 50-6-601 et seq.

**Workers' Compensation Insurance Guaranty Association Act**
Fla. Stat. Ann., 631.901 et seq.

**Workers' Compensation Insurance Plan**
Ark. Code Ann. 1987, 23-67-101 et seq.

**Workers' Compensation Insurance Rating Act**
Cal. Insurance Code § 11730 et seq.

**Workers' Compensation-Occupational Diseases Act**
R.I. Gen. Laws 1956, 28-34-1 et seq.

**Workers Compensation or Occupational Diseases Insurance for Rejected Employers**
Ill. Rev. Stat. 1981, Ch. 73, § 1081 et seq.

**Workers' Compensation Premium Reduction Act (Drug-Free Workplace)**
Miss. Code Ann. 1972, §§ 71-3-201 to 71-3-225

**Workers' Compensation Rating Act**
Me. Rev. Stat. Ann. 1964, Title 24-A, §§ 2381 to 2387-B

**Workers Compensation Rating Act**
La. Rev. Stat. Ann., 23:1851 et seq.
Me. Rev. Stat. Ann. 1964, Title 24, § 2361

**Workers' Compensation Reform Act**
Cal. Government Code § 50920
Tenn. Public Acts 1992, Ch. 900

**Workers Compensation Reform Act (Margolin-Bill Greene)**
Cal. Statutes 1991, Ch. 892

**Workers' Compensation Residual Market Deficit Resolution and Recovery Act**
Me. Rev. Stat. Ann. 1964, Title 24-A, § 2391 et seq.

**Workers' Compensation Security Fund Act**
N.J. Stat. Ann. 34:15-103 et seq.
Pa. Purdon's Stat., Title 77, § 1051 et seq.

**Workers' Compensation Self-Insurer Guaranty Association Act**
Miss. Code Ann. 1972, § 71-3-151 et seq.

**Workers' Compensation Special Fund Act**
Minn. Stat. Ann., 176.131

**Workers' Compensation Statute of Limitations**
Cal. Labor Code § 5400 et seq.
Iowa Code 1991, 85.26

**Workers' Compensation Subrogation Act**
Vt. Stat. Ann., Title 21, § 624

**Workers' Compensation Truth in Advertising Act**
Cal. Labor Code § 5430 et seq.
Ga. Code Ann., 34-9-30 to 34-9-32

**Workers' Cooperative Corporation Law**
Pa. Cons. Stat., Title 15, § 7701 et seq.

**Workers' Disability Compensation Act**
Mich. Comp. Laws Ann., 418.101 et seq.

**Workers' Family Protection Act**
Oct. 26, 1992, P.L. 102-522, 29 U.S. Code § 671a

**Workers' Licensing Act (Social)**
N.J. Laws 1991, Ch. 134
N.J. Stat. Ann., 2A:162-11 et seq.

**Workers' Medical Aid Act**
Wash. Rev. Code Ann., 51.36.010 et seq.

**Workers' Medical Aid Contracts Act**
Wash. Rev. Code Ann., 51.40.010 et seq.

**Workers' Occupational Diseases Act**
Ill. Rev. Stat. 1991, Ch. 48, § 172.36 et seq.
Ind. Code Ann., 22-3-7-1 et seq.
Iowa Code Ann., 85A.1 et seq.

**Workers' Right to Know Law (Toxic Substances)**
N.H. Rev. Stat. 1955, 277-A:1 et seq.
N.Y. Labor Law (Consol. Laws Ch. 31) 875 et seq.
N.Y. Public Health Laws 1953 (Consol. Laws Ch. 45) § 4800 et seq.

**Workers Technology Skill Development Act**
Oct. 20, 1994, P.L. 103-382, 29 U.S. Code §§ 2701 nt., 2701 et seq.

**Workfare Act**
La. Rev. Stat. Ann., 23:1851 et seq.
S.C. Code Ann. 1976, § 43-5-510 et seq.

**Workfare Policy Act**
Fla. Stat. Ann., 409.029 et seq.

**Workforce and Economics Competitiveness Act**
Tex. Laws 1993, p. 2468, Ch. 668

**Workforce Development Fund Program**
Iowa Code 1995, 15.341 et seq.

**Workforce Drug and Alcohol Testing Act**
Mont. Code Ann., 39-2-205 et seq.

**Workforce Education Act**
Ark. Code Ann. 1987, 6-5-904, 25-6-301 et seq.

**Workforce Florida Act**
Fla. Stat. Ann., 446.601 et seq.

**Workforce Investment Act of 1998**
Aug. 7, 1998, P.L. 105-220, 20 U.S. Code § 9201 nt.
Oct. 7, 1998, P.L. 105-244, 29 U.S. Code §§ 2801, 9202
Oct. 21, 1998, P.L. 105-277, 29 U.S. Code §§ 760 to 765, 2701 nt., 2821, 2822, 2831, 2832, 2864, 2899, 2911, 2912, 2915, 2916, 2918, 2939, 2940, 2942, 9271, 9275, 9276

*Continued*

Oct. 31, 1998, P.L. 105-332, 29 U.S. Code §§ 2801, 2841

**Workforce Preparation Act (Immigrant)**
Cal. Education Code 1976, § 52651 et seq.

**Workforce Preparation Evaluation Act**
N.Y. Executive Law 1951 (Consol. Laws Ch. 18) § 980 et seq.

**Workforce Quality Act**
Ore. Laws 1991, Ch. 667

**Workforce Reinvestment Act**
Ga. Code Ann., 34-8-151, 34-8-155, 34-8-156, 34-8-180, 34-8-181, 34-8-185, 34-8-193

**Workhouse Act (County)**
Del. Code of 1953, Title 11, § 6701 et seq.
Tenn. Code Ann., 41-2-101 et seq.

**Workhouse Act (Municipal)**
Tenn. Code Ann., 41-3-101 et seq.

**Working Act (Penal)**
Ky. Rev. Stat. 1971, 431.140

**Working Cash Fund Act**
Ill. Rev. Stat. 1991, Ch. 122, § 34-1 et seq.

**Working Family Income Tax Credit**
Minn. Stat. Ann., 290.0671

**Working Hours Act**
Cal. Labor Code § 510 et seq.

**Working Parents Support Act**
N.H. Laws 1993, Ch. 269

**Working Poor Families Assistance Act**
N.J. Laws 1971, Ch. 209

**Workingmen's Union Label Act**
N.Y. Labor Law (Consol. Laws Ch. 31) § 208 et seq.

**Workmen Recreation and Rest Development Corporation Act**
P.R. Laws Ann. 1954, Title 29, § 1301 et seq.

**Workmen's Accident Compensation Act**
P.R. Laws Ann. 1954, Title 11, § 1 et seq.

**Workmen's Compensation Act (Creation of Bureau)**
Pa. 1915 Pamph. Laws 758, No. 339

**Workmen's Compensation Acts**
May 30, 1908, Ch. 236, 35 Stat. 556
Sept. 7, 1916, Ch. 458, 39 Stat. 742 (See 5 U.S. Code §§ 8101 et seq.)
April 11, 1940, Ch. 79, 54 Stat. 105
July 18, 1940, Ch. 633, 54 Stat. 762

**Workmen's Compensation Administrative Reform Act**
Tex. Rev. Civ. Stat., Arts. 8306, 8307, 8309, 8309a

**Workmen's Compensation Amendments of 1945**
N.J. Stat. Ann., 34:15-10 et seq.

**Workmen's Compensation Apportionment Act**
Ida. Code 1947, 72-406
Ind. Code Ann., 22-3-3-12 et seq.
Ky. Rev. Stat. 1971, 342.120 et seq.
Miss. Code Ann. 1972, § 71-3-7

**Workmen's Compensation Bureau Act**
N.J. Stat. Anno, 34:1-57 et seq.

**Workmen's Compensation Death Benefit Act**
Ind. Code Ann., 22-3-3-16 et seq.

**Workmen's Compensation Rating Bureau Act**
Ind. Code Ann., 27-7-2-1 et seq.

**Workmen's Compensation Safety Act**
N.M. Stat. Ann., 52-1-10

**Workmen's Compensation Security Fund Act**
N.C. Gen. Stat. 1943, § 97-105 et seq.
N.J. Stat. Anno, 34:15-103 et seq.
Pa. Purdon's Stat., Title 77, § 1051 et seq.

**Workmen's Compensation Special Disability Trust Fund Act**
Fla. Stat. Ann., 440.49

**Workmen's Compensation Statute of Limitations**
Neb. Rev. Stat. 1943, 48-137

**Workmen's Compensation Subsequent Injury Act**
N.M. Stat. Ann., 52-2-1 et seq.

**Workmen's Insurance Board Act**
Pa. Purdon's Stat., Title 77, § 201 et seq.

**Workmen's Occupational Diseases Act**
See Occupational Disease Act

**Workmen's Safety Act**
Cal. Labor Code § 6300 et seq.

**Workplace Drug and Alcohol Testing Standards Act**
Okla. Stat. Ann., Title 40, § 551 et seq.

**Workplace Right to Privacy Act**
Ill. Rev. Stat. 1989, Ch. 48, § 2851 et seq.

**Workplace Smoking Act**
Haw. Rev. Stat. Ann., § 32K-11 et seq.
Me. Rev. Stat. Ann. 1964, Title 22, § 1580-A

**Workplace Smoking Pollution Control Act**
R.I. Gen. Laws 1956, 23-20.7-1 et seq.

**Workplace Violence Safety Act**
Cal. Code of Civil Procedure § 527.8

**Works Act (Youth)**
Minn. Stat. 1986, 121.701 to 121.710

**Works Mediation Act (Public)**
N.M. Stat. Ann., 13-14c-1 et seq.

**Works Projects Act (University of Illinois)**
Ill. Rev. Stat. 1991, Ch. 144, § 63m et seq.

**Workshop and Factory Inspection Act**
Tenn. Code Ann., 50-3-101 et seq.

**Workshops and Factories Act**
Ohio Rev. Code 1953, 4107.01 et seq.

**World Congress Center Act**
Ga. Code Ann., 10-9-1 et seq.

**World Cup USA 1994 Commemorative Coin Act**
May 13, 1992, P.L. 102-281, 31 U.S. Code § 5112 nt.
Oct. 6, 1992, P.L. 102-390, 31 U.S. Code § 5112 nt.
Dec. 21, 1995, P.L. 104-66, 31 U.S. Code § 5112 nt.

**World Trade Center Authorities Act**
Cal. Statutes 1947, Ch. 1508, p. 3106

**World Trade Center Authority Act (San Francisco)**
Cal. Government Code § 8320 et seq.

**World Trade Center Authority Act (Southern California)**
Cal. Government Code § 8420 et seq.

**World Trade Corporation Act**
N.Y. Public Authorities Law (Consol. Laws Ch. 43A) § 1450 et seq.

**World Trade Development Act**
Okla. Stat. Ann., Title 74, § 2050 et seq.
Tex. Rev. Civ. Stat., Art. 4413(301)
Tex. Rev. Civ. Stat., Art. 5190.8

**World War Adjusted Compensation Act**
May 19, 1924, Ch. 157, 43 Stat. 121

**World War I Bonus Act**
Iowa Code 1977, 35.1 et seq.

**World War II Bonus Act**
Conn. Public Acts 1991, p. 17, No. 13
Ill. Rev. Stat. 1981, Ch. 126 1/2, § 47 et seq.
Iowa Code 1977, 35A.1 et seq.
Mont. Rev. Code. 1947, 84-5606 et seq.
S.D. Laws 1949, Ch. 158

**World War II Veterans Act, 1924**
Alaska Stat. 1962, § 26.15.010 et seq.

**World War II Veterans' Compensation Act**
Pa. Cons. Stat., Unconsol. Stat., Title 51, § 20041 et seq.

**World War II Veterans Compensation Bond Act (Supplemental)**
Pa. Cons. Stat., Unconsol. Title 51, § 20072 et seq.

**World War II 50th Anniversary Commemorative Coins Act**
Oct. 14, 1992, P.L. 102-414, 31 U.S. Code § 5112 nt.

**World War Memorial Act**
Ind. Code Ann., 10-7-1-1 et seq.

**World War Memorial Authority Act**
N.Y. Public Authorities Law (Consol. Laws Ch. 43A) § 1375 et seq.

**World War Pension Act**
July 19, 1939, Ch. 331, 53 Stat. 1068

**World War Veterans' Act, 1924**
June 7, 1924, Ch. 320, 43 Stat. 607
June 1, 1937, Ch. 285, 50 Stat. 241
Oct. 17, 1940, Ch. 893, 54 Stat. 1193
March 23, 1943, Ch. 19, 57 Stat. 41
Aug. 1, 1946, Ch. 728, 60 Stat. 789
April 15, 1947, Ch. 34, 61 Stat. 39
Aug. 2, 1951, Ch. 286, 65 Stat. 151
July 12, 1952, Ch. 703, 66 Stat. 595
July 23, 1953, Ch. 240, 67 Stat. 186
March 16, 1954, Ch. 97, 68 Stat. 28
July 26, 1955, Ch. 389, 69 Stat. 380
Aug. 1, 1956, Ch. 837, 70 Stat. 883
June 17, 1957, P.L. 85-56, 71 Stat. 158

**World War Veterans' Compensation Act**
Pa. 1923 Pamph. Laws 236, No. 156

**World War Veterans' Loan Act**
N.C. Public Laws 1923, Ch. 190
N.C. Public Laws 1925, Ch. 155
N.C. Public Laws 1927, Ch. 97
N.C. Public Laws 1929, Ch. 298

**World War Veterans' State Aid Act**
Ore. Code 1930, §§ 66-101 to 66-124

**World's Fair Act**
April 29, 1939, Ch. 106, 53 Stat. 625

**World's Fair Act (New York)**
N.Y. Laws 1936, Chs. 543, 544, 866
N.Y. Laws 1937, Chs. 40, 58, 125, 686, 727, 786

**World's Fair Commission Act**
Ill. Rev. Stat. 1991, Ch. 127, § 167f9 et seq.

**World's Fair—1992 Authority Act (Chicago)**
Ill. Rev. Stat. 1983, Ch. 127, § 2101.01 et seq.

**Worthier Title Doctrine Abolishment Act**
Ill. Rev. Stat. 1991, Ch. 30, § 187.9 et seq.

**Worthless Check Abatement Act**
Kan. Laws 1915, Ch. 92, § 3

**Worthless Check Act**
Ala. Code 1975, § 13A-9-13.1 et seq.
Alaska Stat. 1962, § 11.46.280
Ariz. Laws 1919, Ch. 33
Ark. Stat. 1947, 67-714 et seq.
Colo. Rev. Stat., 18-5-205
D.C. Code 1973, § 22-1410
Del. Code of 1974, Title 11, § 900
Fla. Stat. Ann., 832.05
Ga. Code Ann., 16-9-20 et seq.
Haw. Rev. Stat. Ann., § 708-857
Ill. Rev. Stat. 1991, Ch. 38, § 17-1,
Ind. Code Ann., 35-43-5-5
Kan. Stat. Ann., 21-3707 et seq.
Ky. Rev. Stat. 1971, 514.040
La. Rev. Stat. Ann., 14:71
Mass. Gen. Laws Ann., 266:37
Md. Ann. Code 1957, Art. 27, § 141 et seq.
Mich. Comp. Laws Ann., 750.131 et seq.
Mont. Code Ann., 45-6-316
N.C. Gen. Stat. 1943, §§ 14-106, 14-107
N.D. Cent. Code 6-08-16 et seq.
Neb. Rev. Stat. 1943, 28-611
Nev. Rev. Stat. 1979 Reprint, 205.130

N.H. Rev. Stat. 1955, 507:7
N.J. Stat. Anno, 2C:21-5
N.M. Stat. Ann., 30-36-1 et seq.
N.Y. Penal Law 1965 (Consol. Laws Ch. 40) §§ 155.05, Subd. 2, + c; 190.00 et seq.
Ohio Rev. Code 1953, 2913.11
Ore. Rev. Stat. 1953, 165.065
Pa. Cons. Stat., Title 18, § 4105
S.C. Code Ann. 1976, § 34-11-60 et seq.
Tenn. Code Ann., 39-14-121 et seq.
Utah Code Ann. 1953, 76-6-505
Va. Code 1950, § 18.2-181 et seq.
Vt. Stat. Ann., Title 9, § 2311; Title 13, § 2002
Wash. Rev. Code Ann., 9A.56.060
Wis. Stat. Ann., 943.24
W. Va. Code 1966, § 61-3-39
Wyo. Stat. Ann., § 6-3-701 et seq.

**WPA Compliance Act**
Mont. Laws 1937, Ch. 115

**Wreck Commissioner Act**
Va. Code 1950, Misc. Superseded Code Provisions, § 63-158

**Wrecking Act (Motor Vehicles)**
Ore. Rev. Stat. 1953, 481.345 et seq.

**Wrestling Act**
Pa. Cons. Stat., Title 5, § 301 et seq.

**Wrestling and Boxing Act**
Colo. Rev. Stat., 12-10-101 et seq.
Ill. Rev. Stat. 1991, Ch. 111, § 5001 et seq.
Tex. Rev. Civ. Stat., Art. 8501-1
Wash. Rev. Code Ann. 67.08.001 et seq.

**Wrestling and Boxing Commission Act**
D.C. Code Ann., § 2-601 et seq.

**Wright Act (Irrigation Districts Bonds)**
Cal. Statutes 1887, Ch. 34, p. 29

**Wright Act (Prohibition)**
Cal. Statutes 1921, p. 79

**Wright Amendment.**
Feb. 15, 1980, P.L. 96-192, 94 Stat. 48

**Wright-Barnes Study Act**
Tex. Education Code, § 21.501 et seq.

**Wright Bone Dry Act**
Ind. Laws 1917, Ch. 4, p. 15

**Wright-Bridgeford Act (Irrigation Districts)**
Cal. Statutes 1897, p. 254
Cal. Water Code § 20500 et seq.

**Wright Brothers Day Act**
Dec. 17, 1963, P.L. 88-209, 77 Stat. 402, 36 U.S. Code § 169

**Wright, McCorquodale, and Bronzan Act**
Cal. Welfare and Institutions Code § 5800 et seq.

**Wright-Polanco-Lempert Hazardous Waste Treatment Permit Reform Act**
Cal. Statutes 1992, Ch. 1345

**Writ of Error Act**
Haw. Rev. Stat. 1968, § 641-11 et seq.

**Writ of Prohibition Act**
Mont. Code Ann., 27-27-101 et seq.

**Writing Skills Act**
Fla. Stat. Ann., 236.1223

**Written Obligations Act**
Pa. Purdon's Stat., Title 33, § 6 et seq.

**Wrongful Death Act (Lord Campbell's Act)**
Ala. Code 1975, § 6-5-410
Alaska Stat. 1962, Replaced Titles, § 13.20.340
Ariz. Rev. Stat. Ann., § 12-61 et seq.
Ark. Code Ann. 1987, 16-62-102 et seq.
Cal. Code of Civil Procedure § 377
Colo. Rev. Stat., 13-21-201 et seq.
Conn. Gen. Stat. Ann., § 52-555
D.C. Code 1973, § 16-2701 et seq.
Del. Code of 1974, Title 10, § 8107 et seq.
Fla. Stat. Ann., 768.16 et seq.
Ga. Code Ann., 51-4-1 et seq.
Haw. Rev. Stat. Ann., § 663-3
Ida. Code 1947, 5-310, 5-311
Ill. Rev. Stat. 1991, Ch. 70, § 0.01 et seq.
*Continued*

Ind. Code Ann., 34-1-1-2
Iowa Code Ann., 633.336
Kan. Stat. Ann., 60-1901 et seq.
Ky. Rev. Stat. 1971, 411.130
La. Civil Code, Art. 2315
Mass. Gen. Laws Ann., 229:1 et seq.
Md. Ann. Code 1974, Art. CJ, § 3-901 et seq.
Me. Rev. Stat. Ann. 1964, Title 18A, § 2-804 et seq.
Mich. Comp. Laws Ann., 600.2922
Mich. Comp. Laws 1948, 691.581 et seq.
Minn. Stat. Ann., 573.02
Miss. Code Ann. 1972, § 11-7-13
Mo. Rev. Stat., 537.080 et seq.
Mont. Code Ann., 27-1-512, 27-1-513
N.C. Gen. Stat. 1943, § 28A-18-2
N.D. Cent. Code 32-21-01 et seq.
Neb. Rev. Stat. 1943, 30-809, 30-810
Nev. Rev. Stat. 1979 Reprint, 41.085
N.H. Rev. Stat. 1955, 556:12 et seq.
N.J. Stat. Anno, 2A:31-1 et seq.
N.M. Stat. Ann., 41-2-1 et seq.
N.Y. Estates, Powers and Trusts Law (Consol. Laws Ch. 17B) § 5-4.1 et seq.
Ohio Rev. Code 1953, 2125.01 et seq.
Okla. Stat. Ann., Title 12, §§ 1053, 1054
Ore. Rev. Stat. 1953, 30.020
Pa. Cons. Stat., Title 42, §§ 5524, 8301
P.R. Laws Ann. 1954, Title 32, § 311
R.I. Gen. Laws 1956, 10-7-1 et seq.
S.C. Code Ann. 1976, § 15-51-10 et seq.
S.D. Codified Laws 1967, 21-5-1 et seq.
Tenn. Code Ann., 20-5-106 et seq.
Tex. Prac. and Rem. Code, § 71.001 et seq.
Utah Code Ann. 1953, 78-11-6, 78-11-7
Va. Code 1950, §§ 8.01-50, 8.01-244
Vt. Stat. Ann., Title 14, §§ 1491, 1492
Wash. Rev. Code Ann., 4.20.005 et seq.
Wis. Stat. Ann., 895.03 et seq.
W. Va. Code 1966, §§ 55-7-5, 55-7-6
Wyo. Stat. Ann., §§ 1-38-101, 1-38-102

**Wrongful Death Act (Railroad Employees)**
Ga. Code Ann., 34-7-40 et seq.

**Wrongful Death Act (Willful Neglect)**
Ky. Rev. Stat. 1971, 411.130

**Wrongful Death of Minors Act**
Ala. Code 1975, § 6-5-391
Fla. Stat. Ann., 768.041
Fla. Stat. 1971, 768.03
Ida. Code 1947, 5-310
Mont. Rev. Code 1947, 93-2809

**Wrongful Discharge from Employment Act**
Mont. Code Ann., 39-2-901 et seq.
Mont. Laws 1991, Ch. 641, §§ 1 to 9

**Wrongful Tree Cutting Act**
Ill. Rev. Stat. 1991, Ch. 96 1/2, § 9400 et seq.

**Wrongs to Children Act**
Ill. Rev. Stat. 1991, Ch. 23, § 2350 et seq.

**Wunderlich Act**
May 11, 1954, Ch. 199, 68 Stat. 81, 41 U.S. Code §§ 321, 322
May 11, 1954, P.L. 83-356, 41 U.S. Code §§ 321 et seq.

**Wylie Fair Trade Act**
Ky. Rev. Stat. 1971, Superseded Vols., 365.080, 365.090

**Wyllie Local Option Law**
Cal. Statutes 1911, Ch. 351, p. 599

**Wyoming Land Act**
May 29, 1908, Ch. 220, 35 Stat. 465, 43 U.S. Code §§ 82, 224

**Wyoming Wilderness Act of 1984**
Oct. 30, 1984, P.L. 98-550

**Wytheville and Pulaski Parking Authority Act**
Va. Acts 1968, Ch. 682

## X

**X-Ray Diagnostic Facility Act**
Okla. Stat. Ann., Title 63, §§ 1-1501.1 to 1-1505

**X-Ray Retention Act**
Ill. Rev. Stat. 1991, Ch. 111 1/2, §§ 157-10, 157-11

**X-Ray Technicians Act**
N.J. Stat. Ann., 26:2D-24 et seq.

## Y

**Y2K Act**
July 20, 1999, P.L. 106-37, 113 Stat. 185, 15 U.S. Code § 6601 nt.

**Yacht and Ship Brokers Act**
Cal. Harbors and Navigation Code § 700 et seq.
Fla. Stat. Ann., 326.001 et seq.

**Yacht Club Association Act**
Ala. Code 1975, § 10-4-360 et seq.

**Yacht Tax Acts**
Aug. 5, 1909, Ch. 6, 36 Stat. 112
Feb. 24, 1919, Ch. 18, 40 Stat. 1129
Nov. 23, 1921, Ch. 136, 42 Stat. 297

**Yasmin Paleso's Memorial Swimming Pool Safety Law**
Cal. Health and Safety Code § 116049.1

**Yavapai-Prescott Indian Tribe Water Rights Settlement Act of 1994**
Oct. 31, 1994, P.L. 103-434, 108 Stat. 4526
Jan. 6, 1996, P.L. 104-91, 110 Stat. 14

**Year-Around High School Experiment Act**
Cal. Education Code 1976, § 7475 et seq.

**Year 2000 Health Objectives Planning Act**
Nov. 15, 1990, P.L. 101-582, 42 U.S. Code § 246 nt.
Oct. 27, 1992, P.L. 102-531, 42 U.S. Code § 246 nt.

**Year 2000 Information and Readiness Disclosure Act**
Oct. 19, 1998, P.L. 105-271, 112 Stat. 2386, 15 U.S. Code § 1 nt.

**Year 2000 Readiness Information and Voluntary Disclosure Act**
Va. Acts 1999, Ch. 859

**Year 2000 Technology Task Force Act**
Ill. Comp. Stat. 1992, Ch. 20, § 4035/1 et seq.

**Year's Support Act (Estates)**
Tenn. Code Ann., 30-2-101

**Yellow Breeches Creek and Tulpehocken Creek Scenic River Act**
Pa. Purdon's Stat., Title 32, § 820.151 et seq.

**Yellow Breeches Creek Scenic River Act**
Pa. Purdon's Stat., Title 32, § 820.141 et seq.

**Yellow Creek Project Area Fund**
Miss. Code Ann. 1972, § 57-75-1 et seq.

**Yellow Dog Contracts Act**
Ida. Code 1947, 44-901
Kan. Laws 1903, Ch. 222
Mass. Gen. Laws Ann., 149:20A
Md. Ann. Code 1957, Art. 100, § 63 et seq.
N.H. Rev. Stat. 1955, 275:1 et seq.
N.Y. General Obligations Law (Consol. Laws Ch. 24A) § 5-301
N.Y. Labor Law (Consol. Laws Ch. 31) § 704
Ohio Rev. Code 1953, 4113.02

**Yellow Line Act**
N.H. Rev. Stat. 1955, 265:22

**Yellowstone Moratorium**
Mont. Code Ann., 85-2-601 et seq.

**Yellowstone National Park Protection Act**
May 7, 1894, Ch. 72, 28 Stat. 73, 16 U.S. Code §§ 24 to 31

**Yellowstone River Compact Act**
Mont. Code Ann., 85-20-101
N.D. Cent. Code 61-23-01, 61-23-02
Wyo. Stat. Ann., §§ 41-12-601, 41-12-602

**Yerington Charter**
Nev. Stat. 1971, Ch. 465, p. 901

**Yield Right of Way Act**
Cal. Vehicle Code 1959, § 21800 et seq.

**Yoder-Pollock Act (Elections)**
Ohio Laws Vol. 114, p. 679

**Yolo County Flood Control and Water Conservation Act**
Cal. Water Code, Appendix, § 65-1 et seq.

**Yolo County Flood Control and Water Conservation District Act**
Cal. Statutes 1951, Ch. 1657, p. 3772

**Yonkers City Court Act**
N.Y. Laws 1893, Ch. 416

**Yonkers Earnings Tax on Nonresidents Act**
N.Y. Laws 1987, Ch. 333, § 167

**Yonkers Educational Construction Fund Act**
N.Y. Education Law 1947 (Consol. Laws Ch. 16) § 475 et seq.

**Yonkers Financial Emergency Act**
N.Y. Laws 1975, Ex. Sess., Ch. 871, § 2
N.Y. Laws 1984, Ch. 103, § 2

**Yonkers Income Tax Surcharge Act**
N.Y. Laws 1987, Ch. 333, § 167

**Yonkers Parking Authority Act**
N.Y. Public Authorities Law (Consol. Laws Ch. 43A) § 1596a et seq.

**York County Act (Roads and Bridges)**
Pa. 1860 Pamph. Laws 61, No. 77

**York County Government Act**
S.C. Code Ann. 1962, § 14-3601 et seq.

**York County Road Bond Act**
S.C. Acts 1955, p. 1493, Ch. 604

**Young Act (Stabilization of Fluid Milk and Cream)**
Cal. Food and Agricultural Code 1967, §§ 61801 et seq., 62730

**Young Adult Act**
Aug. 25, 1958, P.L. 85-752, 72 Stat. 846, 18 U.S. Code § 4209

**Young Adult Delayed Sentencing Program**
Okla. Stat. Ann., Title 22, § 996 et seq.

**Young Astronaut Program Medal Act**
May 12, 1986, P.L. 99-295, 31 U.S. Code § 5111 nt.
Dec. 24, 1987, P.L. 100-210, 31 U.S. Code § 5111 nt.
Sept. 20, 1988, P.L. 100-437, 31 U.S. Code § 5111 nt.

**Young Drivers Safety Act**
Ga. Code Ann., 40-5-21 et seq.

**Young Family Housing Act**
Minn. Stat. 1986, 290.08, Subd. 25

**Young-La Follette Self-Insurers Security Act**
Cal. Labor Code § 3740 et seq.

**Youth Access to Tobacco Act (Prevention of)**
La. Rev. Stat. Ann., 14:91.8
Miss. Code Ann. 1972, §§ 45-37-1 et seq., 97-5-25, 97-5-43 to 97-5-47, 97-27-35
Okla. Stat. Ann., Title 37, § 600.1 et seq.

**Youth Access to Tobacco Products Control Act**
Mont. Code Ann., 16-11-301 et seq.

**Youth Act**
Ind. Burns' 1933, 63-2601 et seq.

**Youth Act (Homeless and Runaway)**
N.Y. Executive Law 1951 (Consol. Laws Ch. 18) § 532 et seq.

**Youth Affairs Advisory Council Act**
P.R. Laws Ann. 1954, Title 3, § 1601 et seq.

**Youth and Adult Offender Education and Crime Prevention Act**
Cal. Statutes 1991, Ch. 1358

**Youth and Children Act**
Ga. Code Ann., 49-5-1 et seq.

**Youth and Children Commission Act**
Tenn. Code Ann., 37-3-101 et seq.

**Youth and Children Services Act (Community)**
Ore. Rev. Stat., 417.400 et seq.

**Youth and Young Adult Employment Act**
Ill. Rev. Stat. 1991, Ch. 48, § 2551 et seq.

**Youth Apprenticeship/Work-Based Learning Act**
Ark. Code Ann. 1987, 6-50-501 et seq.

**Youth-at-Risk 2000 Pilot Program**
Fla. Stat. Ann., 446.21 et seq., 446.001 et seq.

**Youth Authority Act**
Ariz. Laws 1951, Ch. 92
Cal. Welfare and Institutions Code § 1700 et seq.
Ind. Code Ann., 11-1-2-1 et seq.
Ky. Rev. Stat. 1971, Superseded Vols., 208.010 et seq.
Mass. Gen. Laws Ann., 120:1 et seq.
N.M. Stat. Ann., 9-20-1 et seq.

**Youth Camp Act**
Ga. Code Ann., 49-5-280 et seq.
Ill. Rev. Stat. 1991, Ch. 111 1/2, § 549.1 et seq.
Md. Ann. Code 1974, Art. HG, § 14-401 et seq.

**Youth Camp Health and Safety Act**
Ill. Rev. Stat. 1991, Ch. 111 1/2, § 541 et seq.
Miss. Code Ann. 1972, § 75-74-1 et seq.
N.J. Stat. Ann., 26:12-1 et seq.
Tex. Health and Safety Code, § 141.001 et seq.

**Youth Career Development Act (High Risk)**
Ill. Rev. Stat. 1991, Ch. 23, §§ 6550, 6551

**Youth Center and Youth Shelter Bond Act**
Cal. Welfare and Institutions Code § 2000 et seq.

**Youth Challenge Program**
Miss. Laws 1994, Ch. 652

**Youth, Children and Families Department Act**
N.M. Stat. Ann., 9-2A-1 et seq.

**Youth Commission Act**
Ill. Rev. Stat. 1991, Ch. 23, § 2501 et seq.
La. Rev. Stat. Ann., 46:271 et seq.
N.Y. Executive Law 1951 (Consol. Laws Ch. 18) § 410 et seq.

**Youth Community Services Act**
Okla. Stat. Ann., Title 70, § 11-108 et seq.

**Youth Conservation and Service Corps Act**
Mass. Gen. Laws Ann., 78A:1 to 78A:7

**Youth Conservation Corps Act**
Cal. Public Resources Code § 14000 et seq.
Fla. Stat. Ann., 369.105
N.M. Stat. Ann., 9-5B-1 et seq.

**Youth Conservation Corps Act of 1970**
Aug. 13, 1970, P.L. 91-378, 16 U.S. Code § 1701 et seq.
Sept. 21, 1993, P.L. 103-82, 16 U.S. Code §§ 1701 nt., 1701 et seq.

**Youth Conservation Project Act**
Ida. Code 1947, 56-601 et seq.

**Youth Corps Act**
Mich. Comp. Laws Ann., 409.221 et seq.
N.J. Stat. Ann., 9:25-1 et seq.

**Youth Corps Litter Control and Incentive Employment Program**
La. Rev. Stat. Ann., 23:1821 et seq.

**Youth Correction Act**
Minn. Stat. Ann., 242.37
Nev. Rev. Stat. 1979 Reprint, 62.010 et seq.

**Youth Correction Authority Act**
Mass. Gen. Laws Ann., 120:1 et seq.

**Youth Council Act**
N.C. Gen. Stat. 1943, § 143B-385 et seq.
Nev. Rev. Stat. 1979 Reprint, 2330.020 et seq.

**Youth Court Act**
Miss. Code Ann. 1972, § 43-21-101 et seq.
Mont. Code Ann., 41-5-101 et seq.
N.Y. Laws 1956, Ch. 838

**Youth Crime Prevention Consortium Act**
Ill. Comp. Stat. 1992, Ch. 110, § 125/1 et seq.

**Youth Development Act (Agriculture and Rural)**
Pa. 1991 Pamph. Laws, No. 33

**Youth Development Act (Community)**
Okla. Stat. Ann., Title 10, § 601.61 et seq.

**Youth Education Service Programs**
Kan. Stat. Ann., 74-32108 et seq.

**Youth Emotional Development and Suicide Prevention Act**
Fla. Laws 1984, Ch. 317, §§ 24 to 26

**Youth Employment Act**
N.H. Rev. Stat. 1955, 276-A:1 et seq.

**Youth Employment and Demonstration Projects Act of 1977**
Aug. 5, 1977, P.L. 95-93, 29 U.S. Code §§ 801 nt., 802 et seq.

**Youth Employment and Development Act**
Cal. Unemployment Insurance Code § 9800 et seq.

**Youth Employment and Neighborhood Improvement Act**
Kan. Laws 1994, Ch. 264, §§ 1 to 8

**Youth Employment Clearinghouse Act**
Mich. Comp. Laws Ann., 409.201 et seq.

**Youth Employment Demonstration Amendments of 1981**
June 16, 1981, P.L. 97-14, 29 U.S. Code § 801 nt.

**Youth Employment Opportunity Act**
Colo. Rev. Stat., 8-12-101 et seq.

**Youth Employment Standards Act**
Mich. Comp. Laws Ann., 409.101 et seq.

**Youth Facilities Improvement Act**
N.Y. Social Services Law (Consol. Laws Ch. 55) § 410d et seq.

**Youth Futures Authority Act (Chatham-Savannah)**
Ga. Laws 1988, p. 3743

**Youth Guidance Council Act**
N.J. Stat. Ann., 9:22-1 et seq.

**Youth in Community Service Corps Act**
N.J. Stat. Ann., 9:24-1 et seq.

**Youth Incentive Employment Program**
La. Rev. Stat. Ann., 23:1821 et seq.

**Youth Investment Act**
Tenn. Code Ann., 37-3-401 et seq.

**Youth Law (Runaway and Homeless)**
La. Rev. Stat. Ann., 46:1351 et seq.

**Youth Leadership Academy Act**
Neb. Rev. Stat. 1943, 50-1001 et seq.

**Youth Mentor Act**
S.C. Code Ann. 1976, § 20-7-1331 et seq.

**Youth Mentoring Services Act**
Colo. Rev. Stat., 24-32-2801, 24-32-2805

**Youth Opportunity Program Act**
N.Y. Laws 1990, Ch. 174

**Youth Rehabilitation Services Act**
Mich. Comp. Laws Ann., 803.301 et seq.

**Youth Service Corps Act**
Wash. Rev. Code Ann., 50.48.010 et seq.

**Youth Services Act**
D.C. Code Ann., § 1-2601 et seq.
La. Rev. Stat. Ann., 46:1941.1 et seq.
S.C. Code Ann. 1976, § 20-7-3100 et seq.
Wis. Stat. 1975, 54.01 et seq.

**Youth Services Act (Comprehensive)**
Cal. Welfare and Institutions Code § 18220 et seq.

**Youth Services Amendments Act**
D.C. Code Ann., §§ 1-2604, 1-2606

**Youth Services and State Prison Facilities Bond Act**
N.C. Laws 1991, Ch. 935

**Youth Tobacco Act**
Mich. Comp. Laws Ann., 722.645

**Youth Voting Act**
Mont. Laws 1991, Ch. 348

**Youth Works Act**
Minn. Stat. Ann., 121.701 to 121.710

**Youthbuild Act**
Ga. Code Ann., 49-2-30 et seq.
Ill. Comp. Stat. 1992, Ch. 20, § 1315/1 et seq.

**Youthful Drunk Driver Visitation Program Act**
Cal. Vehicle Code 1959, §§ 23145 et seq., 23509 et seq.
Fla. Stat. Ann., 322.0602

**Youthful Offender Act**
Ala. Code 1975, § 15-19-1 et seq.
Conn. Gen. Stat. Ann., § 54-76b et seq.
Fla. Stat. 1983, 958.011 et seq.
Ga. Code Ann., 42-7-1 et seq.
Mont. Code Ann., 52-5-101 et seq.
N.C. Gen. Stat. 1943, § 148-49.10 et seq.
N.Y. Criminal Procedure Law (Consol. Laws Ch. 11A) § 720.10 et seq.
S.C. Code Ann. 1976, § 24-19-10 et seq.
Wis. Stat. Ann., 54.01 et seq.

**Youthful Offender Alternative Service Act**
Ark. Code Ann. 1987, 12-27-104, 12-27-105, 16-93-501 et seq., 16-93-601

**Youthful Trainee Act**
Mich. Comp. Laws Ann., 762.11 et seq.

**Ysleta Del Sur Pueblo and Alabama and Coushatta Indian Tribes of Texas Restoration Act**
Aug. 18, 1987, P.L. 100-89, 25 U.S. Code §§ 731, 731 nt., 732-737, 1300g-1300g-7
Nov. 2, 1994, P.L. 103-437, 25 U.S. Code § 734

**Yuba-Bear River Basin Authority Act**
Cal. Statutes 1959, Ch. 2131, p. 5032

**Yuba County Water Agency Act**
Cal. Statutes 1959, Ch. 788, p. 2780
Cal. Water Code, Appendix, § 84-1 et seq.

**Yugoslav Emergency Relief Assistance Act of 1950**
Dec. 29, 1950, Ch. 1182, 64 Stat. 1122

**Yukon River Salmon Act of 1995**
Nov. 3, 1995, P.L. 104-43, Title VII, 16 U.S. Code § 5701 et seq.

**Yuma Reclamation Project Act**
Mont. Code Ann., 53-30-202 et seq.

## Z

**Zachary and New Iberia Community Improvement Act**
La. Acts 1972, No. 32

**Z'berg-Bagley-Nejedly Suisun Marsh Preservation Act**
Cal. Fish and Game Code 1957, § 1850 et seq.

**Z'berg-Collier Highway Beautification Act**
Cal. Business and Professions Code § 5208 et seq.

**Z'berg-Collier Outdoor Advertising Act**
Cal. Business and Professions Code § 5405 et seq.

**Z'berg-Collier Park Bond Act**
Cal. Public Resources Code § 5096.71 et seq.

**Z'berg-Collier State Seashore Act**
Cal. Public Resources Code, §§ 5001.6, 5019.62

**Z'berg-Dills-Nejedly Solid Waste Management and Resource Recovery**
Cal. Government Code § 66700 et seq.

**Z'berg-Kapiloff Solid Waste Control Act**
Cal. Government Code § 66795 et seq.

**Z'berg-Nejedly Forest Practice Act**
Cal. Public Resources Code, § 4511 et seq.

**Z'berg-Roberti Urban Open-Space and Recreation Program Act**
Cal. Public Resources Code § 5620 et seq.

**Z'berg-Warren-Keene-Collier Forest Taxation Reform Act**
Cal. Statutes 1976, Ch. 176

**Zenovich-Dunlap-Berman-Alatarre Agricultural Labor Relations Act**
Cal. Labor Code § 1140 et seq.

**Zenovich-Maddy-Dixon California Arts Act**
Cal. Government Code § 8750 et seq.

**Zenovich-Moscone-Chacon Housing and Home Finance Act**
Cal. Health and Safety Code § 50000 et seq.

**Zero Tolerance for Guns Act**
N.J. Stat. Ann., 18A:37-7 et seq.

**Zero Tolerance Law**
N.Y. Criminal Procedure Law (Consol. Laws Ch. 11A) § 160.55
N.Y. Vehicle and Traffic Law 1959 (Consol. Laws Ch. 71) §§ 201, 216a, 503, 511, 1192 to 1194a, 1196, 1197, 1803
Ore. Rev. Stat. 813.300 et seq.

**Zollie M. Maunard, Sr., Education for Handicapped Adults Act**
Fla. Stat. Ann., 228.0727

**Zone Act (Enterprise)**
Kan. Stat. Ann., 74-50,113 et seq.
Neb. Rev. Stat. 1943, 13-2101 to 13-2112
S.C. Code Ann. 1976, § 11-11-410 et seq.
Tex. Government Code, § 2303.001 et seq.
Tex. Rev. Civ. Stat., Art. 5190.7
Utah Code Ann. 1953, 9-2-401 et seq.

**Zone Act (Environmental Opportunity)**
N.J. Stat. Ann., 54:4-3.150 et seq.

**Zone Act (Job Development)**
Vt. Stat. Ann., Title 10, § 691 et seq.

**Zone Act (Renaissance)**
Mich. Comp. Laws Ann., 125.2681 et seq.

**Zone Employment Act (Enterprise)**
Ga. Code Ann., 36-88-1 et seq.

**Zone Liquor Act (Military Camps)**
Tex. General Laws 35th Leg., 1918, 4th C. S., p. 18, Ch. 12

**Zones Act (Job Opportunity)**
Me. Rev. Stat. Ann. 1964, Title 5, § 15131 et seq.

**Zoning Act**
See also Municipal Zoning Act, Planning Act, Planning and Zoning Act, Zoning and Planning Act
Ala. Code 1975, 11-52-70 et seq.
Ark. Code Ann. 1987, 14-56-301 et seq.
Cal. Government Code §§ 65800 et seq., 65000, 38690
Colo. Rev. Stat., 31-23-301 et seq.
D.C. Code Ann. 1973, § 5-412 et seq.
Del. Code of 1974, Title 22, § 301 et seq.
Fla. Stat. Ann., 163.205 et seq., 333.01 et seq.
Ky. Rev. Stat. 1971, 100.201 et seq.
Mass. Gen. Laws Ann., 40A:1 et seq.
Md. Ann. Code 1957, Art. 66B, § 1.00 et seq.
Minn. Stat. Ann., 462.12 et seq.
Miss. Code Ann. 1972, § 17-1-1 et seq.
N.D. Cent. Code, 40-47-01 et seq.
N.H. Rev. Stat. 1955, 672:1 et seq.
N.J. Stat. Ann. 40:55D-62, 40:55D-65, 40:55D-67
N.M. Stat. Ann., 3-21-1 et seq.
N.Y. Local Laws 1972, Village of Geneseo, p. 3276
R.I. Gen. Laws 1956, 45-24-1 et seq.
S.C. Code Ann. 1976, §§ 5-23-10 et seq., 6-7-710 et seq.
Tex. Government Code, § 241.001 et seq.
Tex. Rev. Civ. Stat., Art. 1011a et seq.
Va. Code 1950, § 15.1-486 et seq.
Vt. Stat. Ann. Title 24, § 4401 et seq.
W. Va. Code 1966, § 8-24-1 et seq.

**Zoning Act (Airport)**
Ala. Code 1975, 4-6-1 et seq.
Alaska Stat. 1962, § 02.25.010 et seq.
Haw. Rev. Stat. Ann., § 262-1 et seq.
Ida. Code 1947, 21-501 et seq.
Ill. Rev. Sat. 1991, Ch. 15 1/2, § 48.1 et seq.
Mass. Gen. Laws Ann., 90:40A et seq.
Me. Rev. Stat. Ann. 1964, Title 6, § 241 et seq.
Mich. Comp. Laws Ann., 259.431 et seq.
Miss. Code Ann. 1972, § 61-7-1 et seq.
Mont. Code Ann., 67-6-101 et seq.
N.C. Gen. Stat. 1943, § 63-30 et seq.
Neb. Rev. Stat. 1943, 3-301 et seq.
Nev. Rev. Stat. Ann., 497.010 et seq.
N.H. Rev. Stat. 1955, 424:1 et seq.
Okla. Stat. Ann., Title 3, § 65.19 et seq.
Ore. Rev. Stat., 492.510 et seq.
R.I. Gen. Laws 1956, 1-3-1 et seq.
S.D. Codified Laws 1967, 50-10-1 et seq.
Vt. Stat. Ann., Title 5, § 1001 et seq.

**Zoning Act (Boston)**
Mass. Acts 1924, Ch. 488

**Zoning Act (Buildings)**
Okla. Stat. Ann., Title 11, § 47-122 et seq.

**Zoning Act (Cities of First and Second Class and Villages)**
Neb. Rev. Stat. 1943, 19-901 et seq.

**Zoning Act (City and Village)**
Mich. Comp. Laws Ann., 125.581 et seq., 125.593 et seq.
N.Y. Village Law 1972 (Consol. Laws Ch. 64) § 7-700 et seq.

**Zoning Act (City - County)**
Ill. Rev. Stat. 1991, Ch. 24, § 11-13-1 et seq.; Ch. 34, § 5-12001 et seq
Kan. Stat. Ann., 12-715b et seq.
Nev. Rev. Stat. Ann., 268.230 et seq.
Okla. Stat. Ann., Title 19, § 863.1 et seq.
Ore. Rev. Stat., 215.010 et seq., 227.210 et seq
Tenn. Code Ann., 13-7-101 et seq.
Wash. Rev. Code Ann., 35.63.010 et seq.

**Zoning Act (County Rural)**
Mich. Comp. Laws Ann., 125.201 et seq.
Ohio Rev. Code 1953, 303.01 et seq.

**Zoning Act (County)**
Iowa Code Ann., 335.1 et seq.

**Zoning Act (First Class Cities)**
Mo. Rev. Stat. 1969, 89.150 et seq.
Neb. Rev. Stat. 1943, 15-901 et seq.
Pa. Purdon's Stat., Title 53, § 14751 et seq.

**Zoning Act (Metropolitan Class Cities)**
Neb. Rev. Stat. 1943, 14-401 et seq.

**Zoning Act (Municipal and Parish Co-ordination)**
La. Rev. Stat. Ann., 33:119

**Zoning Act (Municipal)**
See Municipal Zoning Act

**Zoning Act (New Castle County)**
Del. Code of 1974, Title 9, § 2601 et seq.

**Zoning Act (Rural)**
S.D. Code 1939, 12.20A01 et seq.

**Zoning Act (Second Class Cities and Villages)**
Neb. Rev. Stat. 1943, 19-901 et seq.

**Zoning Act (Second Class Cities)**
Pa. Purdon's Stat., Title 53, § 25051 et seq.

**Zoning Act (Third Class Cities)**
Pa. Purdon's Stat., Title 53, § 10601 et seq.

**Zoning Act (Township)**
Ill. Rev. Stat. 1991, Ch. 139, § 301 et seq.
Ind. Code Ann., 36-7-4-100 et seq.
Mich. Comp. Laws Ann., 125.271 et seq.
Ohio Rev. Code 1953, 519.01 et seq.

**Zoning Act (Zoning and Planning Act)**
Cal. Government Code, § 65000 et seq.
Haw. Rev. Stat. Ann., § 226-1 et seq.
Ky. Rev. Stat. 1971, 100.111 et seq.
Pa. Purdon's Stat., Title 71, § 1049.1 et seq.
S.C. Code Ann. 1976, § 6-7-10 et seq.

**Zoning and Manufactured Housing Act**
N.M. Stat. Ann., 3-21A-1 et seq.

**Zoning and Planning Act (Cities of the First Class)**
Ky. Rev. Stat. 1962, 100.031 et seq.

**Zoning and Planning Act (Cities of the Second Class)**
Ky. Rev. Stat. 1962, 100.320 et seq.

**Zoning and Planning Act (Cities of the Third through Sixth Classes)**
Ky. Rev. Stat. 1962, 100.850 et seq.

**Zoning and Planning Act (Cobb County)**
Ga. Laws 1956, p. 2006

**Zoning and Planning Act (County)**
See also Planning Act (County), Zoning Act (County)
Ariz. Rev. Stat. Ann., § 11-801 et seq.
Kan. Stat. Ann., 19-2901 et seq.
Miss. Code Ann. 1972, § 17-1-1 et seq.
Mo. Rev. Stat., 64.010 et seq.
S.C. Code Ann. 1976, § 4-27-10 et seq.
S.D. Codified Laws 1967, 11-2-1 et seq.
Utah Code Ann. 1953, 17-27-1 et seq.
Wash. Rev. Code Ann., 36.70.010 et seq.
Wis. Stat. Ann., 59.97 et seq.

**Zoning and Planning Act (Enabling)**
See also Planning Act, Planning and Zoning Act, Zoning Enabling Act
Md. Ann. Code 1957, Art. 66B
Miss. Code Ann. 1972, § 17-1-1 et seq.
Mo. Rev. Stat., 89.010 et seq.
Pa. Purdon's Stat., Title 53, § 10101 et seq.

**Zoning and Planning Act (Municipalities)**
Ariz. Rev. Stat. Ann., § 9-461 et seq.
Ga. Code 1933, 69-801 et seq.
Mo. Rev. Stat., 89.300 et seq.

**Zoning and Planning Act (Town)**
N.Y. Town Law (Consol. Laws Ch. 62) § 261 et seq.

**Zoning and Planning Commission Act**
Md. Ann. Code 1957, Art. 66B, § 3.01 et seq.

**Zoning and Planning District Act (County)**
Mont. Rev. Code 1947, 16-4101 et seq.

**Zoning and Street Improvement Act (Greensboro)**
N.C. Private Laws 1921, Extra Session, Ch. 130

**Zoning Appeals Act**
Mass. Gen. Laws 1932, Ch. 40B, § 20 et seq.

**Zoning Approval Act (Municipal Boundary)**
N.Y. General Municipal Law (Consol. Laws Ch. 24) § 239m

**Zoning Commission and Board of Zoning Adjustment Compensation Act**
D.C. Code Ann, § 5-430 et seq.

**Zoning District Act (Counties)**
Mont. Code Ann., 76-2-101 et seq.

**Zoning District Act (Special)**
N.M. Stat. Ann., 3-21-15 et seq.

**Zoning Enabling Act (Baltimore County)**
Md. Laws 1941, Ch. 247

**Zoning Enabling Act (Liberty County)**
Ga. Laws 1941, p. 903

**Zoning Enabling Act (Villages)**
N.Y. Village Law 1972 (Consol. Laws Ch. 64) § 7-700 et seq.

**Zoning Enabling Acts**
See also Municipal Zoning Act, Planning Act, Planning and Zoning Act, Zoning and Planning Act

**Zoning Law**
Cal. Government Code § 65000 et seq. § 65800

**Zoning Law (Municipalities)**
Iowa Code Ann., 414.1 et seq.

**Zoning Law (Rural)**
Mont. Code Ann., 76-2-101 et seq., 76-2-201 et seq.

**Zoning Law (Voluntary)**
Mont. Code Ann., 76-2-101 et seq., 76-2-201 et seq.

**Zoning Procedures Act**
Ga. Code Ann., 36-66-1 et seq.

**Zoning Regulations Act (Municipal)**
La. Rev. Stat. Ann., 33:4721 et seq.
Ohio Rev. Code 1953, 713.06 et seq.

**Zoning to Eliminate Airport Hazards Act**
Ill. Comp. Stat. 1992, Ch. 620, § 30/0.01 et seq.
Ill. Rev. Stat. 1991, Ch. 15 1/2, § 48.100 et seq.

**Zoological Park Act**
Ill. Rev. Stat. 1991, Ch. 96 1/2, § 6800 et seq.

**Zoological Park and Garden District Act**
Miss. Code Ann. 1972, § 55-21-1 et seq.

**Zoological Parks Act (Forest Preserve)**
Ill. Rev. Stat. 1991, Ch. 96 1/2, § 6800 et seq.

**Zoul Act (Cuyahoga County Juvenile Court)**
Ohio Rev. Code 1953, 2153.01 et seq.

**Zoul Act (Taxation)**
Ohio Laws Vol. 117, p. 32

**Zuni-Cibola National Historical Park Establishment Act of 1988**
Oct. 31, 1988, P.L. 100-567, 16 U.S. Code §§ 410pp, 410pp nt.
June 27, 1990, P.L. 101-313, 16 U.S. Code § 410pp
Nov. 2, 1994, P.L. 103-437, 16 U.S. Code §§ 410pp-1, 410pp-5, 410pp-6

**Zuni Land Conservation Act of 1990**
Oct. 31, 1990, P.L. 101-486, 104 Stat. 1174

**Zuni River Watershed Act of 1992**
Aug. 11, 1992, P.L. 102-338, 106 Stat. 866

# FEDERAL AND STATE CASES
# CITED BY POPULAR NAMES

A – Z

## A

**A & P. Case**
78 F. Supp. 388, 77 U.S.P.Q. (BNA) 343; 179 F.2d 636, 84 U.S.P.Q. (BNA) 209; 339 U.S. 947, 94 L. Ed. 1361, 70 S. Ct. 803; 340 U.S. 147, 95 L. Ed. 162, 71 S. Ct. 127, 87 U.S.P.Q. (BNA) 303; 340 U.S. 918, 95 L. Ed. 663, 71 S. Ct. 349

**AAA Cases**
297 U.S. 1, 80 L. Ed. 477, 56 S. Ct. 312
297 U.S. 110, 80 L. Ed. 513, 56 S. Ct. 82
43 F. Supp. 1017; 317 U.S. 111, 87 L. Ed. 122, 63 S. Ct. 82

**Aaron Burr Case**
F. Cas. Nos. 14,692; 14,692a to 14,692h; 14,693; 14,694; 14,694a

**Abandoned Child Case**
344 Ill. App. 266, 100 N.E.2d 497; 412 Ill. 488, 107 N.E.2d 696

**Abandoned Property Case**
204 F. 641; 231 U.S. 423, 58 L. Ed. 296, 34 S. Ct. 125

**Abercrombie Case**
162 F.2d 338; 7 T.C. 120

**Abie's Irish Rose Case**
34 F.2d 145; 45 F.2d 119; 282 U.S. 902, 75 L. Ed. 795, 51 S. Ct. 216

**Abilene Cotton Oil Case**
38 Tex. Civ. App. 366, 85 S.W. 1052; 204 U.S. 426, 51 L. Ed. 553, 27 S. Ct. 350

**Abolition of Office Case**
249 Ala. 14, 29 So. 2d 411; 249 Ala. 32, 29 So. 2d 418

**Abortion Cases**
410 U.S. 113, 35 L. Ed. 2d 147, 93 S. Ct. 705; 410 U.S. 179, 35 L. Ed. 2d 147, 35 L. Ed. 201, 93 S. Ct. 739
428 U.S. 52, 49 L. Ed. 2d 788, 96 S. Ct. 2831
428 U.S. 132, 49 L. Ed. 2d 844, 96 S. Ct. 2331
462 U.S. 416, 76 L. Ed. 2d 687, 103 S. Ct. 2481
492 U.S. 490, 1036 L. Ed. 2d 410, 109 S. Ct. 3040
500 U.S. 173, 114 L. Ed. 2d 233, 111 S. Ct. 1759

**Abortion Clinic Access Case**
519 U.S. 357, 137 L. Ed. 2d 1, 117 S. Ct. 855 (1997)

**Abortion Clinic Obstruction Case**
506 U.S. 263, 122 L. Ed. 2d 34, 113 S. Ct. 753 (1993)

**Abortion Notification Case**
450 U.S. 398, 67 L. Ed. 2d 388, 101 S. Ct. 1164

**Abortion Parental Notification Cases**
497 U.S. 417, 111 L. Ed. 2d 344, 110 S. Ct. 2926
497 U.S. 502, 111 L. Ed. 2d 405, 110 S. Ct. 2972

**Abortion Protest Injunction Case**
512 U.S. 753, 129 L. Ed. 2d 593, 114 S. Ct. 2516 (1994)

**Abrams Case**
250 U.S. 616, 63 L. Ed. 1173, 40 S. Ct. 17

**Abscam Case**
635 F.2d 945

**Absent Judge Murder Case**
74 So. 2d 74 (Fla.)

**A.C.A. Cases**
101 U.S. 51, 25 L. Ed. 993
2 Sand. Ch. (4 N.Y. Super. Ct.) 599

**Acceleration Disclosure Case**
444 U.S. 555, 63 L. Ed. 2d 22, 100 S. Ct. 790

**Accidental Sunstroke Case**
158 Ohio St. 394; 49 Ohio Op. 273, 109 N.E.2d 649

**Accommodation Note Case**
173 N.E. 289; 203 Ind. 427, 178 N.E. 685

**Accountants' RICO Liability Case**
507 U.S. 170, 122 L. Ed. 2d 525, 113 S. Ct. 1163 (1993)

**Accounting of Illegal Partnership Case**
85 Ohio App. 328, 40 Ohio Op. 222, 88 N.E.2d 429; 153 Ohio St. 574, 42 Ohio Op. 41, 93 N.E.2d 5; 156 Ohio St. 52, 45 Ohio Op. 60, 99 N.E.2d 898

**Acetylene Cases**
152 F. 642; 159 F. 935; 166 F. 907
188 F. 85; 197 F. 908; 203 F. 276
188 F. 89; 192 F. 321, 112 C.C.A. 573
190 F. 201
198 F. 650, 117 C.C.A. 354; 227 U.S. 677, 57 L. Ed. 700, 33 S. Ct. 405; 239 U.S. 156, 60 L. Ed. 191, 36 S. Ct. 86

**Actual Innocence/Death-Sentence Case**
506 U.S. 390, 122 L. Ed. 2d 203, 113 S. Ct. 853 (1993)

**Adair Case**
208 U.S. 161, 52 L. Ed. 436, 28 S. Ct. 277

**Adamite Case**
248 F. 705

**Adams Cases**
176 N.Y. 351, 68 N.E. 636; 85 A.D. 390, 83 N.Y.S. 481; 44 Misc 550, 90 N.Y.S. 134; 192 U.S. 585, 48 L. Ed. 575, 24 S. Ct. 372
100 Ohio St. 348, 126 N.E. 300
257 Wis. 433, 43 N.W.2d 446

**Adamson Case**
332 U.S. 46, 91 L. Ed. 1903, 67 S. Ct. 1672; 27 Cal. 2d 478, 165 P.2d 3; 34 Cal. 2d 320, 210 P.2d 13; 167 F.2d 996; 332 U.S. 784, 92 L. Ed. 367, 68 S. Ct. 27

**Adamson Eight-Hour Law Case**
243 U.S. 332, 61 L. Ed. 755, 37 S. Ct. 298

**Addington Case**
17 S.C.L. (1 Bail.) 310, 18 S.C.L. (2 Bail.) 516

**Addyston Pipe Case**
78 F. 712; 85 F. 271; 175 U.S. 211, 44 L. Ed. 136, 20 S. Ct. 96

**Adkins Case (Minimum Wage Law)**
284 F. 613; 52 App. D.C. 109, 261 U.S. 525, 67 L. Ed. 785, 43 S. Ct. 394; 130 W. Va. 645, 46 S.E.2d 81; 127 W. Va. 786, 34 S.E.2d 585

**Administrative Segregation Right to Counsel Case**
467 U.S. 180, 81 L. Ed. 2d 146, 104 S. Ct. 2292

**Admission Tickets Case**
302 F. Supp. 1339

**Admissions to Probation Officer Case**
79 L. Ed. 2d 409, 104 S. Ct. 1136

**Adopted Child Collateral Inheritance Case**
220 Miss. 691, 71 So. 2d 783

**Adoption Annulment Case**
186 Tenn. 294, 209 S.W.2d 859

**Adrenalin Case**
189 F. 95; 196 F. 496

**Adult Child Support Case**
227 N.C. 614, 44 S.E.2d 31

**Adult Theater Zoning Case**
475 U.S. 41, 89 L. Ed. 2d 29, 106 S. Ct. 925

**Adulterated Food Case**
421 U.S. 658, 44 L. Ed. 2d 489, 96 S. Ct. 1903

**Advanced Funding Case**
455 U.S. 720, 71 L. Ed. 2d 580, 102 S. Ct. 1373

**Advancing Wave Case**
107 U.S. 192, 27 L. Ed. 438, 2 S. Ct. 225

**Adverse Possession of Minerals Case**
206 Okla. 13, 240 P.2d 757

**Adverse Spousal Testimony Case**
445 U.S. 40, 63 L. Ed. 2d 186, 100 S. Ct. 906

**Advertising Card Case**
170 F. 91

**Advisory Jury Death Penalty Case**
513 U.S. 504, 130 L. Ed. 2d 1004, 115 S. Ct. 1031 (1995)

**AFDC Notice Relief Case**
474 U.S. 64, 88 L. Ed. 2d 371, 106 S. Ct. 423

**Affirmative Action Cases**
478 U.S. 421, 92 L. Ed. 2d 344, 106 S. Ct. 3019

**Age Discrimination After-Acquired Evidence Case**
513 U.S. 352, 130 L. Ed. 2d 852, 115 S. Ct. 879 (1995)

**Age Discrimination Case**
517 U.S. 308, 134 L. Ed. 2d 433, 116 S. Ct. 1307 (1996)

**Age Discrimination in Employment Act Case**
460 U.S. 226, 75 L. Ed. 2d 18, 103 S. Ct. 1054

**Agency Shop Case**
188 Kan. 11, 360 P.2d 456; 368 U.S. 829, 7 L. Ed. 2d 32, 82 S. Ct. 51

**Agency Shop Clause Case**
431 U.S. 209, 52 L. Ed. 2d 261, 97 S. Ct. 1782

**Agency-Shop Service Fee Case**
431 U.S. 209, 52 L. Ed. 2d 261, 97 S. Ct. 1782
475 U.S. 292, 89 L. Ed. 2d 232, 106 S. Ct. 1066

**Agent Orange Manufacturers Case**
516 U.S. 417,134 L. Ed. 2d 47, 116 S. Ct. 981 (1996)

**Aggravating Circumstances Case**
456 U.S. 410, 72 L. Ed. 2d 222, 102 S. Ct. 1856

**Agricultural Debt Relief Act Case**
295 U.S. 555, 79 L. Ed. 1593, 55 S. Ct. 854; 296 U.S. 661, 80 L. Ed. 471, 56 S. Ct. 82

**Agricultural Marketing Agreement Act Cases**
26 F. Supp. 534; 59 S. Ct. 646; 59 S. Ct. 776; 307 U.S. 533, 83 L. Ed. 1446, 59 S. Ct. 993; 308 U.S. 631, 84 L. Ed. 526, 60 S. Ct. 66; 308 U.S. 631, 84 L. Ed. 526, 60 S. Ct. 67

**Agricultural Prorate Case**
39 F. Supp. 895; 62 S. Ct. 946; 86 L. Ed. 1778, 62 S. Ct. 1266; 317 U.S. 341, 87 L. Ed. 315, 63 S. Ct. 307

**Aid to Parochial Students Case**
521 U.S. 203, 138 L. Ed. 2d 391, 117 S. Ct. 1997 (1997)

**Aiello Dairy Farms Case**
110 N.L.R.B. 1365, No. 205

**Air Ban Case**
108 F. Supp. 315; 204 F.2d 446; 346 U.S. 832, 98 L. Ed. 355, 74 S. Ct. 48

**Air Brake Case**
170 U.S. 537, 42 L. Ed. 1136, 18 S. Ct. 707, 83 Off. Gaz. Pat. Office 1067

**Air Carrier Liability Case**
470 U.S. 392, 84 L. Ed. 2d 289, 105 S. Ct. 1338

**Air Pollution Case**
421 U.S. 60, 43 L. Ed. 2d 731, 95 S. Ct. 1470

**Airline Pilots Case**
469 U.S. 111, 83 L. Ed. 2d 523, 105 S. Ct. 613

**Airline Taxation Case**
78 L. Ed. 2d 10, 104 S. Ct. 291

**Airlines and the Handicapped Case**
477 U.S. 597, 91 L. Ed. 2d 494, 106 S. Ct. 2705

**Airport Cases**

369 U.S. 84, 7 L. Ed. 2d 585, 82 S. Ct. 531; 369 U.S. 857, 8 L. Ed. 2d 16, 82 S. Ct. 931; 402 Pa. 411, 168 A.2d 123

321 Mo. 514, 11 S.W.2d 1045

321 Mo. 536, 11 S.W.2d 1054

**Alabama Death Sentence Case**

447 U.S. 625, 65 L. Ed. 2d 392, 100 S. Ct. 2382

**Alabama Freight Lines Case**

64 Ariz. 101, 166 P.2d 816

**Alabama Labor Contract Law Case**

158 Ala. 18, 48 So. 498; 211 U.S. 452, 53 L. Ed. 278, 29 S. Ct. 141; 161 Ala. 75, 49 So. 886; 219 U.S. 219, 55 L. Ed. 191, 31 S. Ct. 145

**Alabama N.A.A.C.P. Case**

357 U.S. 449, 2 L. Ed. 2d 1488, 78 S. Ct. 1163; 360 U.S. 240, 3 L. Ed. 2d 1205, 79 S. Ct. 1001; 361 U.S. 856, 4 L. Ed. 2d 96, 80 S. Ct. 43; 265 Ala. 349, 91 So. 2d 214; 265 Ala. 699, 91 So. 2d 221; 268 Ala. 531, 109 So. 2d 138; 271 Ala. 33, 122 So. 2d 396

**Alabama Peonage Cases**

213 F. 345; 235 U.S. 133, 59 L. Ed. 162, 35 S. Ct. 86; 213 F. 352; 235 U.S. 133, 59 L. Ed. 162, 35 S. Ct. 86

**Alabama Power Company Cases**

10 F. Supp. 854; 12 F. Supp. 70; 79 F.2d 995; 81 F.2d 986; 298 U.S. 651, 80 L. Ed. 1379, 56 S. Ct. 941; 299 U.S. 259, 81 L. Ed. 178, 57 S. Ct. 202; 19 F. Supp. 932; 91 F.2d 665

302 U.S. 485, 82 L. Ed. 381, 58 S. Ct. 306

91 F.2d 303; 301 U.S. 681, 81 L. Ed. 1339, 57 S. Ct. 946; 302 U.S. 464, 82 L. Ed. 374, 58 S. Ct. 300

**Alabama Preclusion Clause Case**

456 U.S. 605, 72 L. Ed. 2d 357, 102 S. Ct. 2049

**Alabama Unemployment Insurance Act Case**

17 F. Supp. 225; 300 U.S. 644, 81 L. Ed. 858, 57 S. Ct. 668; 300 U.S. 644, 81 L. Ed. 858, 57 S. Ct. 672; 300 U.S. 644, 81 L. Ed. 858, 57 S. Ct. 674; 301 U.S. 495, 81 L. Ed. 1245, 57 S. Ct. 868

**Alabama Voting Rights Case**

502 U.S. 491, 117 L. Ed. 2d 51, 112 S. Ct. 820 (1992)

**Alaska Case**

19 I.C.C. 105; 37 App. D.C. 266; 224 U.S. 474, 56 L. Ed. 849, 32 S. Ct. 556; 25 I.C.C. 136

**Alaska Packers Case**

1 Cal. 2d 250, 34 P.2d 716; 55 S. Ct. 145; 294 U.S. 532, 79 L. Ed. 1044, 55 S. Ct. 518

**Alaska Pipeline Rate Case**

436 U.S. 631, 56 L. Ed. 2d 591, 98 S. Ct. 2053

**Alaskan Case**

197 U.S. 516, 49 L. Ed. 862, 25 S. Ct. 514

**Albany Bridge Case**

F. Cas. No. 12,851; F. Cas. No. 12,852; 66 U.S. 582, 17 L. Ed. 81; F. Cas. No. 2,983; 69 U.S. 403, 17 L. Ed. 8786

**Albea's Case**

113 N.C. 214, 18 S.E. 389; 41 L. Ed. 1187, 17 S. Ct. 1002

**Albertini Case**

206 F. 133

**Album Case**

33 F. 457; 144 U.S. 35, 36 L. Ed. 336, 12 S. Ct. 607

**Alcatraz Cases**

304 U.S. 458, 82 L. Ed. 1461, 58 S. Ct. 1019

312 U.S. 275, 85 L. Ed. 830, 61 S. Ct. 574

313 U.S. 342, 85 L. Ed. 1392, 61 S. Ct. 1015

313 U.S. 538, 85 L. Ed. 1507, 61 S. Ct. 834

**Alcoa Cases**
44 F. Supp. 97; 320 U.S. 708, 88 L. Ed. 415, 64 S. Ct. 73; 322 U.S. 716, 88 L. Ed. 1557, 64 S. Ct. 1281; 148 F.2d 416, 65 U.S.P.Q. (BNA) 6; 91 F. Supp. 333; 153 F. Supp. 132; 164 F.2d 159, 75 U.S.P.Q. (BNA) 190; 171 F.2d 285, 79 U.S.P.Q. (BNA) 434; 333 U.S. 841, 92 L. Ed. 1125, 68 S. Ct. 659, 76 U.S.P.Q. (BNA) 621; 334 U.S. 258, 92 L. Ed. 1351, 68 S. Ct. 1035, 77 U.S.P.Q. (BNA) 436
285 F.2d 911

**Alemite Cases**
13 F.2d 463
19 F.2d 937
19 F.2d 939; 19 F.2d 944
22 F.2d 331
23 F.2d 92
26 F.2d 722; 39 F.2d 904; 52 F.2d 36; 54 F.2d 285; 285 U.S. 531, 76 L. Ed. 926, 52 S. Ct. 312; 286 U.S. 567, 76 L. Ed. 1298, 52 S. Ct. 495
26 F.2d 724
40 F.2d 549
50 F.2d 592; 53 F.2d 470; 73 F.2d 543; 295 U.S. 726, 79 L. Ed. 1677, 55 S. Ct. 833; 298 U.S. 415, 80 L. Ed. 1251, 56 S. Ct. 767; 56 S. Ct. 944

**Alger Case**
323 Mich. 523, 35 N.W.2d 669

**Alger Hiss Case**
88 F. Supp. 559; 185 F.2d 822; 340 U.S. 948, 95 L. Ed. 683, 71 S. Ct. 532; 107 F. Supp. 128; 201 F.2d 372; 345 U.S. 942, 97 L. Ed. 1368, 73 S. Ct. 830

**Alien Commuters Case**
419 U.S. 65, 42 L. Ed. 2d 231, 95 S. Ct. 272

**Alien Exclusion Cases**
194 U.S. 279, 48 L. Ed. 979, 24 S. Ct. 719
344 U.S. 590, 97 L. Ed. 576, 73 S. Ct. 472
345 U.S. 206, 97 L. Ed. 956, 73 S. Ct. 625

**Alien Free Public Education Case**
457 U.S. 202, 72 L. Ed. 2d 786, 102 S. Ct. 2382

**Alien Land Law Cases**
274 F. 841; 263 U.S. 197, 68 L. Ed. 255, 44 S. Ct. 15
279 F. 114; 263 U.S. 225, 68 L. Ed. 278, 44 S. Ct. 21
279 F. 117; 263 U.S. 313, 68 L. Ed. 318, 44 S. Ct. 112
281 F. 407; 263 U.S. 326, 68 L. Ed. 323, 44 S. Ct. 115
195 Cal. 71, 231 P. 554
29 Cal. 2d 164, 173 P.2d 794; 330 U.S. 818, 91 L. Ed. 1270, 67 S. Ct. 1093; 332 U.S. 633, 92 L. Ed. 249, 68 S. Ct. 269

**Alien Passenger Case**
48 U.S. 283, 12 L. Ed. 702

**Aliens Right To Civil Service Employment Case**
426 U.S. 88, 48 L. Ed. 2d 495, 96 S. Ct. 1895

**Alighting Passenger Liability Case**
225 Minn. 274, 30 N.W.2d 523

**Alimony after Death Case**
195 Va. 102, 77 S.E.2d 471

**Alimony after Desertion Case**
2 Ill. 2d 451, 118 N.E.2d 433

**Alimony Case**
440 U.S. 268 , 59 L. Ed. 2d 306, 99 S. Ct. 1102

**Alimony Pension Case**
38 Wash. 2d 207, 228 P.2d 470

**Allen Bradley Case**
325 U.S. 797, 89 L. Ed. 1939, 65 S. Ct. 1533; 145 F.2d 215; 159 F.2d 669; 164 F.2d 71; 41 F. Supp. 727; 51 F. Supp. 36; 323 U.S. 706, 89 L. Ed. 569, 65 S. Ct. 430, 65 S. Ct. 431; 323 U.S. 707, 89 L. Ed. 570, 65 S. Ct. 433; 326 U.S. 803, 90 L. Ed. 489, 66 S. Ct. 11

**Allen Case**
164 U.S. 492, 41 L. Ed. 528, 17 S. Ct. 154; 150 U.S. 551, 37 L. Ed. 1179, 14 S. Ct. 196; 157 U.S. 675, 39 L. Ed. 854, 15 S. Ct. 720

**Allergic Dermatitis Case**
120 Utah 474, 235 P.2d 525

**Alligator-Man Case**
134 Mo. App. 696, 115 S.W. 459; 163 Mo. App. 697, 147 S.W. 497

**Allis-Chalmers Case**
243 Wis. 332, 10 N.W.2d 197; 320 U.S. 776, 88 L. Ed. 466, 64 S. Ct. 90

**Allison Estate Cases**
99 N.J. Eq. 572, 134 A. 81; 101 N.J. Eq. 252, 137 A. 582; 276 U.S. 625, 72 L. Ed. 738, 48 S. Ct. 304
106 N.J. Eq. 55, 150 A. 52; 107 N.J. Eq. 197, 152 A. 6

**All's Over Case**
377 Pa. 109, 103 A.2d 708

**Altered Check Case**
240 Minn. 484, 62 N.W.2d 344

**Alternative to Imprisonment Case**
471 U.S. 606, 85 L. Ed. 2d 636, 105 S. Ct. 2254

**Alton Post Robbery Case**
24 F.2d 82

**Aluminum Cases**
44 F. Supp. 97; 320 U.S. 708, 88 L. Ed. 415, 64 S. Ct. 73; 322 U.S. 716, 88 L. Ed. 1557, 64 S. Ct. 1281; 148 F.2d 416, 65 U.S.P.Q. (BNA) 6; 91 F. Supp. 333; 153 F. Supp. 132; 164 F.2d 159, 75 U.S.P.Q. (BNA) 190; 171 F.2d 285, 79 U.S.P.Q. (BNA) 434; 334 U.S. 258, 92 L. Ed. 1351, 68 S. Ct. 1035, 77 U.S.P.Q. (BNA) 436
285 F.2d 911

**Aluminum Workers Cases**
230 F.2d 515
112 N.L.R.B. 619, No. 80

**Alvin Case**
155 Tex. 502, 289 S.W.2d 559

**Alyea-Nichols Case**
12 F.2d 998; 21 F.2d 501; 276 U.S. 617, 72 L. Ed. 733, 48 S. Ct. 208

**Amalgamated Clothing Workers' Case**
181 N.Y.S. 161; 111 Misc. 284, 181 N.Y.S. 165; 112 Misc. 395, 183 N.Y.S. 195

**Ambrose Light Case**
25 F. 408

**Ambulance-Chaser Case**
338 Ill. App. 552, 88 N.E.2d 364

**Amelia Island Case**
F. Cas. No. 15,227; 31 U.S. 404, 8 L. Ed. 443

**American Bank Note Company Case**
129 N.Y. 252, 29 N.E. 302

**American Beverage Case**
42 F.2d 488, 6 U.S.P.Q. (BNA) 67
59 F.2d 1051

**American Buslines Case**
221 F. Supp. 958

**American Casualty Insurance Company Case**
82 Md. 535, 34 A. 778; 86 Md. 254, 37 A. 646

**American Cousin Case**
F. Cas. No. 7,644

**American Creosoting Case**
257 U.S. 247, 66 L. Ed. 217, 42 S. Ct. 80

**American Fruit Growers Case**
35 F.2d 106; 281 U.S. 709, 74 L. Ed. 112, 50 S. Ct. 249; 283 U.S. 1, 75 L. Ed. 801, 51 S. Ct. 328

**American Iron and Machine Works Case**
115 N.L.R.B. 800, No. 121

**American Manufacturing Case**
363 U.S. 564, 4 L. Ed. 2d 1403, 4 L. Ed. 2d 1432, 80 S. Ct. 1343, 80 S. Ct. 1363; 264 F.2d 624; 269 F.2d 327; 269 F.2d 633; 168 F. Supp. 308; 168 F. Supp. 702; 361 U.S. 881, 4 L. Ed. 2d 118, 80 S. Ct. 152; 363 U.S. 574, 4 L. Ed. 2d 1409, 80 S. Ct. 1347; 363 U.S. 593, 4 L. Ed. 2d 1424, 80 S. Ct. 1358

**American Medical Association Case**
26 F. Supp. 429

**American Navel Stores Company Case**
172 F. 455; 186 F. 489, 108 C.C.A. 467; 186 F. 592; 219 U.S. 587, 55 L. Ed. 348, 31 S. Ct. 471; 229 U.S. 373, 57 L. Ed. 1232, 33 S. Ct. 780

**American News Company Case**
58 F.T.C. 10

**American Oil Company Case**
325 F.2d 101; 377 U.S. 954, 12 L. Ed. 2d 498, 84 S. Ct. 1631

**American Potash Case**
107 N.L.R.B. 1418, No. 290

**American Roll Gold Leaf Company Case**
212 F. 720

**American Steel Foundries Case**
257 U.S. 184, 66 L. Ed. 189, 42 S. Ct. 72; 238 F. 728; 245 U.S. 670, 62 L. Ed. 539, 38 S. Ct. 190; 42 S. Ct. 271

**American Sugar Case**
152 F. Supp. 387; 259 F.2d 524; 143 F. Supp. 100; 19 F.R.D. 396

**American Tobacco Company Case**
221 F. Supp. 387; 259 F.2d 524; 143 F. Supp. 100; 19 F.R.D. 396

**American Tragedy Case**
191 N.Y. 107, 83 N.E. 680

**American Unhairing Machine Company Case**
98 F. 297; 99 F. 1003, 39 C.C.A. 677; 108 F. 82; 115 F. 498, 53 C.C.A. 230

**American Washboard Case**
103 F. 281

**Ames Case**
64 F. 165; 169 U.S. 466, 42 L. Ed. 819, 18 S. Ct. 418; 171 U.S. 361, 43 L. Ed. 197, 18 S. Ct. 888; 100 F. 235; 102 F. 197; 110 F. 3

**Amter Case (Ballot Exclusion)**
275 N.Y. 396, 9 N.E.2d 975

**Amtrack Case**
414 U.S. 453, 38 L. Ed. 2d 646, 94 S. Ct. 690
470 U.S. 451, 84 L. Ed. 2d 432, 105 S. Ct. 1441

**Amusement Park Cases**
187 Cal. 323, 202 P. 34
159 Ill. App. 110; 250 Ill. 452, 95 N.E. 445
97 Me. 108, 53 A. 979

**Anamoose Bank Case**
190 F. 336; 206 F. 374, 124 C.C.A. 256

**Anarchist Case**
122 Ill. 1, 12 N.E. 865, 17 N.E. 898, 123 U.S. 131, 31 L. Ed. 80, 8 S. Ct. 22

**Anastaplo's Bar Admission Case**
18 Ill. 2d 182, 163 N.E.2d 429; 366 U.S. 82, 6 L. Ed. 2d 135, 81 S. Ct. 978; 348 U.S. 946, 99 L. Ed. 740, 75 S. Ct. 436, 755 S. Ct. 439; 429 U.S. 903, 99 L. Ed. 1240, 75 S. Ct. 575; 364 U.S. 806, 81 S. Ct. 41; 368 U.S. 869, 7 L. Ed. 2d 69, 82 S. Ct. 21; 3 Ill. 2d 471, 121 N.E.2d 826

**Androscoggin County Election Cases**
118 Me. 101, 106 A. 115

**Anesthesiologist Exclusive Contract Case**
80 L. Ed. 2d 2, 104 S. Ct. 1551

**Angeline Case**
401 U.S. 715, 28 L. Ed. 2d 434, 91 S. Ct. 1041

273 F. 848; 259 U.S. 156, 66 L. Ed. 871, 42 S. Ct. 540

**Anheuser-Busch Case**
265 F.2d 677; 363 U.S. 536, 4 L. Ed. 2d 1385, 80 S. Ct. 1267; 361 U.S. 880, 4 L. Ed. 2d 117, 80 S. Ct. 151; 364 U.S. 170, 4 L. Ed. 2d 1639, 80 S. Ct. 1388; 364 U.S. 856, 5 L. Ed. 2d 80, 81 S. Ct. 32; 266 F.2d 222; 364 U.S. 137, 4 L. Ed. 2d 1639, 80 S. Ct. 1405

**Anheuser-Busch Labor Case**
364 Mo. 573, 265 S.W.2d 325; 348 U.S. 808, 99 L. Ed. 638, 75 S. Ct. 32; 348 U.S. 468, 99 L. Ed. 546, 75 S. Ct. 480

**Animal Sacrifice Case**
508 U.S. 520, 124 L. Ed. 2d 472, 113 S. Ct. 2217 (1993)

**Anneke Jans Cases**
44 F.2d 716; 283 U.S. 827, 75 L. Ed. 1441, 51 S. Ct. 351; 49 F.2d 908
1 Abb. Pr. 385
179 A.D. 621, 167 N.Y.S. 107
4 Paige Ch. 178; 15 Wend. 111; 4 Sand. Ch. 369; 4 Sand. Ch. 633
7 Paige Ch. 195; 24 Wend. 587; 30 Barb. 537; 22 N.Y. 44
83 N.Y. 348

**Annette Islands Case**
240 F. 274, 4 Alaska Fed. 533; 5 Alaska 484; 4 Alaska Fed. 709; 248 U.S. 78, 63 L. Ed. 138, 39 S. Ct. 40

**Annexation Cases of Baltimore**
133 Md. 247, 104 A. 540

**Anonymous Campaign Literature Case**
514 U.S. 334, 131 L. Ed. 2d 426, 115 S. Ct. 1511 (1995)

**Anonymous Informants Tip Case**
76 L. Ed. 2d 527, 103 S. Ct. 2317

**Anthracite Cases**
183 F. 427; 226 U.S. 324, 57 L. Ed. 243, 33 S. Ct. 90; 228 U.S. 158, 58 L. Ed. 779, 33 S. Ct. 509
225 F. 399; 254 U.S. 255, 65 L. Ed. 246, 41 S. Ct. 110; 254 U.S. 617, 65 L. Ed. 440, 41 S. Ct. 149
226 F. 229; 253 U.S. 26, 64 L. Ed. 760, 40 S. Ct. 425; 253 U.S. 478, 64 L. Ed. 1022, 40 S. Ct. 585

**Anthracite Coal Tax Case**
274 Pa. 448, 118 A. 394; 260 U.S. 245, 67 L. Ed. 237, 43 S. Ct. 83

**Anti-Alien Labor Law of Arizona Case**
219 F. 273; 239 U.S. 33, 60 L. Ed. 131, 36 S. Ct. 7

**Anti-Fee Bill Case**
152 Tenn. 258, 277 S.W. 71

**Anti-Public Utility Strike Case**
142 N.J. Eq. 785, 61 A.2d 570; 2 N.J. 335, 66 A.2d 616

**Anti-Saloon League Contempt Case**
200 Ind. 623, 157 N.E. 769, 162 N.E. 441, 163 N.E. 272; 200 Ind. 716, 164 N.E. 408

**Anti-Trust Civil Liability Case**
456 U.S. 556, 72 L. Ed. 2d 330, 102 S. Ct. 1935

**Antibiotic Drug Cases**
404 U.S. 548, 30 L. Ed. 2d 721, 92 S. Ct. 731; 426 F.2d 32; 281 F. Supp. 837
52 F.R.D. 131
295 F. Supp. 1402; 297 F. Supp. 1126; 299 F. Supp. 1403; 301 F. Supp. 1158
314 F. Supp. 710
320 F. Supp. 586
333 F. Supp. 267
333 F. Supp. 274
333 F. Supp. 278
333 F. Supp. 291
333 F. Supp. 299
333 F. Supp. 310

**Antiquarian Book Store Case**
39 Cal. 501

**Anvil Creek Cases**
106 F. 775
109 F. 710

**Apalachin Case**
177 F. Supp. 106; 178 F. Supp. 62; 180 F. Supp. 71; 285 F.2d 408

**Apex Cases**
66 F. 212
88 F. 986, 31 C.C.A. 592; 171 U.S. 55, 43 L. Ed. 72, 18 S. Ct. 895; 97 F. 981, 38 C.C.A. 691
108 F.2d 71; 309 U.S. 644, 84 L. Ed. 997, 60 S. Ct. 589; 310 U.S. 469, 84 L. Ed. 1311, 60 S. Ct. 982

**Apex Hosiery Case**
310 U.S. 469, 84 L. Ed. 1311, 60 S. Ct. 982

**Appalachian Coal Case**
288 U.S. 344, 77 L. Ed. 825, 53 S. Ct. 471

**Appam Cases**
234 F. 389; 240 F. 676, 153 C.C.A. 474; 243 U.S. 124, 61 L. Ed. 633, 37 S. Ct. 337
243 F. 230

**Appointed Counsel Immunity Case**
444 U.S. 193, 62 L. Ed. 2d 355, 100 S. Ct. 402

**Aqueduct Cases**
14 N.Y.S. 785
58 Hun 609, 12 N.Y.S. 269
27 Jones & S. 583 (59 N.Y.S. Ct.), 13 N.Y.S. 887; 128 N.Y. 117, 28 N.E. 19

**Archer County Case**
3 F.2d 160; 269 U.S. 396, 70 L. Ed. 330, 46 S. Ct. 141

**Architect's Certificate for Payment Case**
221 Miss. 190, 72 So. 2d 424

**Ardmore Case**
383 Pa. 253, 118 A.2d 561

**Arizona Death Sentence Case**
81 L. Ed. 2d 164, 104 S. Ct. 2305

**Arizona Employers' Liability Cases**
19 Ariz. 151, 166 P. 278; 250 U.S. 400, 63 L. Ed. 1058, 39 S. Ct. 553
19 Ariz. 182, 165 P. 1101; 250 U.S. 400, 63 L. Ed. 1058, 39 S. Ct. 553

**Arizona Grazing Lease Condemnation Case**
424 U.S. 295, 47 L. Ed. 2d 1, 96 S. Ct. 910

**Arkansas Anti-Removal Case**
257 U.S. 529, 66 L. Ed. 352, 42 S. Ct. 188

**Arkansas Bates Case**
261 U.S. 516, 4 L. Ed. 2d 480, 80 S. Ct. 412; 229 Ark. 819, 319 S.W.2d 37

**Arkansas Cotton Cases**
12 Ct. Cl. 638

**Arkansas Rate Case**
163 F. 141; 168 F. 720; 187 F. 290; 230 U.S. 553, 57 L. Ed. 1625, 33 S. Ct. 1030; 211 F. 172; 220 F. 8786, 136 C.C.A. 442; 244 U.S. 368, 61 L. Ed. 1200, 37 S. Ct. 611

**Arkansas River Bed Case**
40 Okla. 479, 139 P. 943

**Arkansas Road District Case**
257 U.S. 547, 66 L. Ed. 364, 42 S. Ct. 250

**Arlington Case**
F. Cas. No. 8,191; F. Cas. No. 8,192; 106 U.S. 196, 27 L. Ed. 171, 1 S. Ct. 240

**Armstrong Case**
113 Ohio St. 93, 148 N.E. 584

**Army Data Bank Case**
444 F.2d 947

**Arredondo Case**
31 U.S. 691, 8 L. Ed. 547

**Arson Investigation Case**
78 L. Ed. 2d 477, 104 S. Ct. 641

**Arson Search Case**
436 U.S. 499, 56 L. Ed. 2d 486, 98 S. Ct. 1942

**Art Collection Case**
71 F. Supp. 357, 108 Ct. Cl. 650; 177 F.2d 73, 85 App. D.C. 227; 339 U.S. 905, 94 L. Ed. 1334, 70 S. Ct. 513

**Art Museum Case**
241 Mo. 231, 145 S.W. 801

**Arthur Case**
54 F. 730; 150 U.S. 393, 37 L. Ed. 1120, 14 S. Ct. 123

**Arthur Kill Case**
32 F. 9; 140 U.S. 699, 35 L. Ed. 603, 11 S. Ct. 1028

**Artificial Lard Case**
256 F. 23; 249 U.S. 598, 63 L. Ed. 795, 39 S. Ct. 390; 254 U.S. 156, 65 L. Ed. 196, 41 S. Ct. 75

**Arzner Case**
57 F.2d 488; 287 U.S. 583, 77 L. Ed. 510, 53 S. Ct. 21; 53 S. Ct. 290; 287 U.S. 470, 77 L. Ed. 436, 53 S. Ct. 238

**ASCAP Cases**
307 U.S. 66, 83 L. Ed. 1111, 59 S. Ct. 725
313 U.S. 406, 85 L. Ed. 1426, 61 S. Ct. 969
24 F. Supp. 541, 37 U.S.P.Q. (BNA) 676; 59 S. Ct. 97; 305 U.S. 569, 83 L. Ed. 358, 59 S. Ct. 145; 313 U.S. 387, 85 L. Ed. 1416, 61 S. Ct. 962; 36 F. Supp. 405, 48 U.S.P.Q. (BNA) 316
33 F. Supp. 377, 46 U.S.P.Q. (BNA) 354; 33 F. Supp. 1014, 47 U.S.P.Q. (BNA) 18; 313 U.S. 387, 85 L. Ed. 1416, 61 S. Ct. 962
34 F. Supp. 510

**Ashbacker Case**
326 U.S. 327, 90 L. Ed. 108, 66 S. Ct. 148

**Ashwander Case**
297 U.S. 288, 80 L. Ed. 688, 56 S. Ct. 466

**Aspirin Cases**
171 F. 887; 179 F. 701, 103 C.C.A. 243; 220 U.S. 622, 55 L. Ed. 613, 31 S. Ct. 724
197 F. 894, 117 C.C.A. 133; 203 F. 476, 121 C.C.A. 598
272 F. 505

**Assateague Island Condemnation Cases**
324 F. Supp. 1170
354 F. Supp. 1233

**Assault by Servant Case**
329 Mich. 556, 46 N.W.2d 382

**Assertion of Right to Counsel Case**
475 U.S. 625, 89 L. Ed. 2d 631, 106 S. Ct. 1404

**Assessment Covenant Case**
14 N.J. 186, 101 A.2d 855

**Assigned Car Case**
9 F.2d 429; 274 U.S. 564, 71 L. Ed. 1204, 47 S. Ct. 727; 80 I.C.C. 520; 93 I.C.C. 701

**Associated Press Cases**
301 U.S. 103, 81 L. Ed. 953, 57 S. Ct. 650
240 F. 983; 245 F. 244, 157 C.C.A. 436; 25 U.S. 644, 62 L. Ed. 528, 38 S. Ct. 10; 248 U.S. 215, 63 L. Ed. 211, 39 S. Ct. 68

**Assurance Case**
76 S.C. 76, 56 S.E. 654

**At-Large Electoral Systems Case**
446 U.S. 55, 64 L. Ed. 2d 47, 100 S. Ct. 1490

**Atlanta Gas Rate Case**
278 F. 242; 262 U.S. 625, 67 L. Ed. 1144, 43 S. Ct. 680

**Atlanta School Case**
377 U.S. 263, 12 L. Ed. 2d 288, 84 S. Ct. 1235

**Atlanten Case**
22 F. 403; 252 U.S. 313, 64 L. Ed. 586, 40 S. Ct. 332; 250 F. 935; 248 U.S. 553, 63 L. Ed. 418, 39 S. Ct. 8

**Atlantic Case**
120 S.W.2d 543 (Tex.)

**Atlantic Coast Line Dividend Case**
102 Md. 73, 61 A. 295, 296, 297

**Atlantic, Mississippi and Ohio Railroad Case**
F. Cas. No. 12,922

**Atlas Case**
269 F.2d 950; 363 U.S. 843, 4 L. Ed. 2d 1727, 80 S. Ct. 1608

**Atmos Clock Case**
119 F. Supp. 209; 221 F.2d 464; 350 U.S. 832, 100 L. Ed. 743, 76 S. Ct. 67; 350 U.S. 897, 100 L. Ed. 789, 76 S. Ct. 149; 123 U.S.P.Q. (BNA) 381

**Atomic Spy Case**
108 F. Supp. 798; 195 F.2d 583; 10 F.R.D. 521; 200 F.2d 666; 344 U.S. 838, 97 L. Ed. 652, 73 S. Ct. 20; 344 U.S. 889, 97 L. Ed. 687, 73 S. Ct. 134; 345 U.S. 965, 97 L. Ed. 1384, 73 S. Ct. 949; 345 U.S. 989, 97 L. Ed. 1397, 73 S. Ct. 1151; 345 U.S. 1003, 97 L. Ed. 1408, 73 S. Ct. 1151; 346 U.S. 271, 97 L. Ed. 1607, 73 S. Ct. 1152; 346 U.S. 313, 97 L. Ed. 1629, 73 S. Ct. 1173; 346 U.S. 322, 97 L. Ed. 1633, 73 S. Ct. 1178

**Attorney Area of Practice Advertising Case**
455 U.S. 191, 71 L. Ed. 2d 64, 102 S. Ct. 929

**Attorney Business Solicitation Case**
471 U.S. 626, 85 L. Ed. 2d 652, 105 S. Ct. 2265

**Attorney-Client Privilege Case**
141 L. Ed. 2d 379, 118 S. Ct. 2081 (1998)

**Attorney Contemp Case**
419 U.S. 449, 42 L. Ed. 2d 574, 95 S. Ct. 584

**Attorney Discrimination Case**
81 L. Ed. 2d 59, 104 S. Ct. 2229

**Attorney General Immunity Case**
472 U.S. 511, 86 L. Ed. 2d 411, 105 S. Ct. 2806

**Attorney Solicitation Case**
436 U.S. 412, 56 L. Ed. 2d 417, 98 S. Ct. 1893

**Attorneys' Client-Solicitation Case**
515 U.S. 618, 132 L. Ed. 2d 541, 115 S. Ct. 2371 (1995)

**Auction without Reserve Case**
264 Wis. 286, 58 N.W.2d 693

**Auditorium Tax Case**
211 S.C. 77, 44 S.E.2d 88

**Aunt Jemima Case**
234 F. 804; 247 F. 407, 159 C.C.A. 461; 245 U.S. 672, 62 L. Ed. 540, 38 S. Ct. 222

**Austrian Bond Cases**
147 U.S. 449, 37 L. Ed. 237, 13 S. Ct. 409

**Auto Club Cases**
495 U.S. 930, 109 L. Ed. 2d 497, 110 S. Ct. 2168
706 F. Supp. 264; 887 F.2d 417

**Automatic Fire Door Case**
151 I.C.C. 448

**Automobile Guest Law Case**
108 Conn. 371, 143 A. 240; 73 L. Ed. 1014, 49 S. Ct. 342; 280 U.S. 117, 74 L. Ed. 221, 50 S. Ct. 57

**Automobile Inventory Search Case**
428 U.S. 364, 49 L. Ed. 2d 1000, 96 S. Ct. 3092

**Automobile Passing Cut-Back Case**
242 Minn. 60, 64 N.W.2d 9

**Automobile Passive Restraints Case**
77 L. Ed. 2d 443, 103 S. Ct. 2856

**AVCO Case**
11 F.C.C. 3

**Awning Cases**
74 N.Y. 264
120 N.Y. 98, 24 N.E. 389

**Axman Case**
167 F. 922, 93 C.C.A. 322; 193 F. 644, 113 C.C.A. 512; 215 U.S. 617, 54 L. Ed. 350, 30 S. Ct. 408; 234 U.S. 36, 58 L. Ed. 1198, 34 S. Ct. 736

## B

**B R T Case**
377 U.S. 1, 12 L. Ed. 2d 89, 84 S. Ct. 1113; 377 U.S. 960, 12 L. Ed. 2d 505, 84 S. Ct. 1625

**Babcock and Wilcox Case**
351 U.S. 105, 100 L. Ed. 975, 76 S. Ct. 679; 222 F.2d 316; 222 F.2d 543; 222 F.2d 858; 350 U.S. 818, 100 L. Ed. 731, 76 S. Ct. 78; 350 U.S. 894, 100 L. Ed. 786, 76 S. Ct. 156

**Baby Doe Case**
476 U.S. 610, 90 L. Ed. 2d 584, 106 S. Ct. 2101

**Baby Lenore Case**
28 N.Y.2d 185, 269 N.E.2d 787, 321 N.Y.S.2d 65

**Baby Scarpetta Case**
28 N.Y.2d 185, 269 N.E.2d 787, 321 N.Y.S.2d 65

**Bache Denman Coal Company Cases**
235 F. 1, 148 C.C.A. 495; 242 U.S. 653, 61 L. Ed. 547, 37 S. Ct. 246; 258 F. 829, 169 C.C.A. 549; 259 U.S. 344, 66 L. Ed. 975, 42 S. Ct. 570; 66 L. Ed. 1079, 42 S. Ct. 587; 300 F. 972; 268 U.S. 295, 69 L. Ed. 963, 45 S. Ct. 551
300 F. 965; 266 U.S. 630, 69 L. Ed. 477, 45 S. Ct. 195; 28 F.2d 851; 279 U.S. 841, 73 L. Ed. 987, 49 S. Ct. 263

**Bad Check Law Case**
109 Ohio St. 393, 142 N.E. 897

**Bad Egg Case**
220 U.S. 45, 55 L. Ed. 364, 31 S. Ct. 364

**Bad Faith Insurance Case**
471 U.S. 202, 85 L. Ed. 2d 206, 105 S. Ct. 1904

**Badger Will Case**
18 Mass. (1 Pick.) 192

**Bahia de Nipe Case**
197 F. Supp. 710; 295 F.2d 24

**Bail Out Procedure Case**
446 U.S. 156, 64 L. Ed. 2d 119, 100 S. Ct. 1548

**Baird Case**
123 F. 969; 194 U.S. 25, 48 L. Ed. 860, 24 S. Ct. 563

**Bakelite Case**
Treas. Dec. 42827, 16 C.C.P.A. 191; Treas. Dec. 43964, 17 C.C.P.A. 494; 39 F.2d 247; 282 U.S. 852, 75 L. Ed. 755, 51 S. Ct. 29

**Baker Case**
24 F.2d 766

**Bakeshop Case**
73 A.D. 120, 16 N.Y. Crim. 520, 76 N.Y.S. 396; 177 N.Y. 145, 69 N.E. 373; 198 U.S. 45, 49 L. Ed. 937, 25 S. Ct. 539

**Bakke Case**
438 U.S. 265, 57 L. Ed. 2d 750, 98 S. Ct. 2733

**Baldwinsville Homicide Case**
67 Barb. 548, 5 Hun 104; 63 N.Y. 143

**Ball Rent Law Case**
267 F. 614, 50 App. D.C. 56; 254 U.S. 640, 65 L. Ed. 452, 41 S. Ct. 13; 267 F. 631, 50 App. D.C. 73; 256 U.S. 135, 65 L. Ed. 865, 41 S. Ct. 458

**Ballistics Case**
221 Ky. 648, 299 S.W. 553; 230 Ky. 411, 19 S.W.2d 1091

**Balloon Tire Case**
27 F.2d 427; 42 F.2d 406

**Balm of Thousand Flowers Cases**
4 Abb. Pr. 156
13 How. Pr. 385, 4 Abb. Pr. 144

**Baltic Ship Cases**
145 F.2d 431
342 U.S. 816, 96 L. Ed. 617, 72 S. Ct. 30; 80 F. Supp. 683; 188 F.2d 1000

**Baltimore Club Whiskey Case**
171 F. 125; 183 F. 22, 105 C.C.A. 314

**Baltimore Street Railway Case**
280 U.S. 234, 74 L. Ed. 390, 50 S. Ct. 123

**Banana Cases**
196 Misc. 798, 95 N.Y.S.2d 202; 276 A.D. 1006, 95 N.Y.S.2d 871; 8 A.D.2d 310, 188 N.Y.S.2d 62; 7 N.Y.2d 752, 193 N.Y.S.2d 664, 162 N.E.2d 748; 8 N.Y.2d 430, 209 N.Y.S.2d 289, 171 N.E.2d 443
237 Miss. 141, 112 So. 2d 529
252 Miss. 693, 173 So. 2d 603

**Bank Building Cases**
239 F. Supp. 613; 365 F.2d 641
247 F. Supp. 547; 362 F.2d 857

**Bank Credit Card Interest Rate Case**
439 U.S. 299, 58 L. Ed. 2d 534, 99 S. Ct. 540

**Bank Deposit Tax Case**
277 Ky. 343, 126 S.W.2d 463; 60 S. Ct. 80; 308 U.S. 525, 84 L. Ed. 444, 60 S. Ct. 593; 309 U.S. 83, 84 L. Ed. 590, 60 S. Ct. 406

**Bank Guarantee Cases**
175 F. 365; 179 F. 461, 102 C.C.A. 607; 218 U.S. 673, 54 L. Ed. 1205, 31 S. Ct. 223; 219 U.S. 121, 55 L. Ed. 123, 31 S. Ct. 189; 228 U.S. 1, 57 L. Ed. 707, 33 S. Ct. 409
22 Okla. 48, 97 P. 590; 219 U.S. 104, 55 L. Ed. 112, 31 S. Ct. 186; 219 U.S. 575, 55 L. Ed. 341, 31 S. Ct. 299

**Bank Holding Company Case**
450 U.S. 46, 67 L. Ed. 2d 36, 101 S. Ct. 973

**Bank Night Cases**
86 F.2d 597
86 F.2d 958
11 F. Supp. 566
54 Ga. App. 738, 188 S.E. 925
366 Ill. 256, 8 N.E.2d 648
220 Iowa 1369, 264 N.W. 608
144 Kan. 687, 62 P.2d 929
276 Mich. 127, 267 N.W. 602
160 Misc. 174, 289 N.Y.S. 649; 273 N.Y. 475, 6 N.E.2d 410
338 Mo. 597, 92 S.W.2d 141
87 N.H. 477, 183 A. 590
128 N.J.L. 311, 25 A.2d 892
41 N.M. 258, 67 P.2d 286
170 Tenn. 351, 95 S.W.2d 310
129 Tex. 40, 100 S.W.2d 695

**Bank of Greencastle's Case**
15 Ct. Cl. 225

**Bank of Kentucky Case**
70 F.2d 819

**Bank Secrecy Case**
416 U.S. 21, 39 L. Ed. 2d 812, 94 S. Ct. 1494

**Bank Stock Tax Cases**
18 F.2d 269
214 Iowa 1229, 232 N.W. 445; 283 U.S. 813, 75 L. Ed. 1430, 51 S. Ct. 353; 75 L. Ed. 1474, 51 S. Ct. 652; 284 U.S. 239, 73 L. Ed. 265, 52 S. Ct. 133; 244 N.W. 309
109 Neb. 753, 192 N.W. 322

**Bank Stockholder's Double Liability Cases**
203 Ind. 9, 179 N.E. 1
203 Ind. 655, 178 N.E. 449; 181 N.E. 589; 185 N.E. 273

**Bank Tax Cases (Kentucky)**
174 U.S. 428, 43 L. Ed. 1034, 19 S. Ct. 874
174 U.S. 435, 43 L. Ed. 1037, 19 S. Ct. 874
174 U.S. 436, 43 L. Ed. 1037, 19 S. Ct. 874
174 U.S. 439, 43 L. Ed. 1039, 19 S. Ct. 753
88 F. 383; 174 U.S. 799, 43 L. Ed. 1187, 19 S. Ct. 881
88 F. 398; 174 U.S. 412, 43 L. Ed. 1028, 19 S. Ct. 747
88 F. 407; 174 U.S. 429, 43 L. Ed. 1034, 19 S. Ct. 875
88 F. 409; 174 U.S. 438, 43 L. Ed. 1038, 19 S. Ct. 876; 109 F. 1056, 47 C.C.A. 679
88 F. 985; 174 U.S. 799, 43 L. Ed. 1187, 19 S. Ct. 881
88 F. 986; 174 U.S. 800, 43 L. Ed. 1187, 19 S. Ct. 881
88 F. 987; 174 U.S. 409, 43 L. Ed. 1027, 19 S. Ct. 880
88 F. 988; 174 U.S. 799, 43 L. Ed. 1187, 19 S. Ct. 881
88 F. 988; 174 U.S. 800, 43 L. Ed. 1187, 19 S. Ct. 881

*Continued*

88 F. 990; 174 U.S. 432, 43 L. Ed. 1035, 19 S. Ct. 759

103 F. 523; 185 U.S. 270, 46 L. Ed. 906, 22 S. Ct. 645

129 F. 792; 198 U.S. 100, 49 L. Ed. 963, 25 S. Ct. 562

97 Ky. 590, 17 Ky. Law Rep. 465, 31 S.W. 1013; 102 Ky. 174, 19 Ky. Law Rep. 248, 39 S.W. 1030; 173 U.S. 636, 43 L. Ed. 840, 19 S. Ct. 530, 571; 173 U.S. 662, 43 L. Ed. 850, 19 S. Ct. 875; 173 U.S. 663, 43 L. Ed. 850, 19 S. Ct. 875; 21 Ky. Law Rep. 1611, 55 S.W. 1080; 108 Ky. 766, 22 Ky. Law Rep. 466, 57 S.W. 787; 22 Ky. Law Rep. 1384, 60 S.W. 19; 111 Ky. 950, 23 Ky. Law Rep. 1285, 65 S.W. 10; 23 Ky. Law Rep. 1704, 66 S.W. 186; 120 F. 165; 124 F. 18, 59 C.C.A. 538; 191 U.S. 499, 48 L. Ed. 276, 24 S. Ct. 154

108 Ky. 427, 22 Ky. Law Rep. 70, 56 S.W. 683, 19 Ky. Law Rep. 247, 39 S.W. 1116; 173 U.S. 664, 43 L. Ed. 850, 19 S. Ct. 537

44 S.W. 1131; 43 L. Ed. 1178, 19 S. Ct. 877

**Bank Tax Cases (New York)**

154 U.S. 551, 18 L. Ed. 229, 14 S. Ct. 1215

40 Barb. 334; 26 N.Y. 163; 67 U.S. 620, 17 L. Ed. 451; 25 How. Pr. 9; 69 U.S. 200, 17 L. Ed. 793

43 Barb. 550; 33 N.Y. 161; 70 U.S. 573, 18 L. Ed. 229; 154 U.S. 550, 18 L. Ed. 229, 14 S. Ct. 1198; 31 How. Pr. 288

18 How. Pr. 245; 32 Barb. 509, 20 How. Pr. 182; 23 N.Y. 192; 17 L. Ed. 456

**Bankers Life Case**

346 U.S. 379, 98 L. Ed. 106, 74 S. Ct. 145; 199 F.2d 593; 345 U.S. 933, 97 L. Ed. 1361, 73 S. Ct. 796

**Bankhead Cotton Act Case**

305 U.S. 61, 83 L. Ed. 41, 59 S. Ct. 41

**Banking Stock Assessment Case**

134 A.D. 966, 119 N.Y.S. 1139; 198 N.Y. 503, 92 N.E. 1096; 231 U.S. 373, 58 L. Ed. 274, 34 S. Ct. 114

**Bankruptcy Courts Case**

458 U.S. 50, 73 L. Ed. 2d 598, 102 S. Ct. 2858

**Bankruptcy Rent Cases**

291 U.S. 320, 78 L. Ed. 825, 54 S. Ct. 385; 292 U.S. 607, 78 L. Ed. 1468, 54 S. Ct. 771

69 F.2d 90; 292 U.S. 620, 78 L. Ed. 1476, 54 S. Ct. 778; 293 U.S. 307, 79 L. Ed. 379, 55 S. Ct. 150

**Baptist Church Case**

108 U.S. 317, 27 L. Ed. 739, 2 S. Ct. 719

**Bar Admission Case**

470 U.S. 274, 84 L. Ed. 2d 205, 105 S. Ct. 1272

**Barbed Wire Patent Case**

33 F. 261; 143 U.S. 275, 36 L. Ed. 154, 12 S. Ct. 443; 143 U.S. 293, 36 L. Ed. 161, 12 S. Ct. 450

**Barber Shop Price Fixing Cases**

174 Tenn. 178, 124 S.W.2d 253

236 Wis. 414, 295 N.W. 718

237 Wis. 85, 294 N.W. 796, 296 N.W. 622

**Barenblatt Case**

354 U.S. 930, 1 L. Ed. 2d 1533, 77 S. Ct. 1394; 240 F.2d 875; 252 F.2d 129; 356 U.S. 929, 2 L. Ed. 2d 760, 78 S. Ct. 771; 360 U.S. 109, 3 L. Ed. 2d 1115, 79 S. Ct. 1081

**Bargain City Case**

407 Pa. 129, 179 A.2d 439

**Barker Brothers Case**

138 N.L.R.B. 478, No. 54; 328 F.2d 431

**Barneson Case**

133 F.2d 428; 44 B.T.A. 1348

**Barney Google Case**

299 F. 533

**Barnhart Island Case**
5 N.Y.2d 24, 152 N.E.2d 411, 177 N.Y.S.2d 289; 5 N.Y.2d 793; 5 A.D.2d 117; 5 N.Y.2d 874, 155 N.E.2d 870; 154 N.E.2d 574, 180 N.Y.S.2d 322; 168 N.Y.S.2d 894; 170 N.Y.S.2d 1010; 6 A.D.2d 854, 175 N.Y.S.2d 1010; 4 Misc. 2d 110, 158 N.Y.S.2d 540; 359 U.S. 910, 3 L. Ed. 2d 573, 79 S. Ct. 586; 359 U.S. 982, 3 L. Ed. 2d 982, 79 S. Ct. 1127; 359 U.S. 1015, 3 L. Ed. 2d 1039, 79 S. Ct. 1146

**Barry Case**
23 F. 712; 131 U.S. 100, 33 L. Ed. 60, 9 S. Ct. 755

**Baseball Peonage Case**
172 F.2d 402

**Basing Point Price Cases**
147 F.2d 589; 157 F.2d 533; 330 U.S. 815, 91 L. Ed. 1268, 67 S. Ct. 967, 67 S. Ct. 968, 67 S. Ct. 969; 333 U.S. 683, 92 L. Ed. 1010, 68 S. Ct. 793; 334 U.S. 839, 92 L. Ed. 1764, 68 S. Ct. 1492

**Bath Tub Trust Cases**
187 F. 229
187 F. 232
191 F. 172; 226 U.S. 20, 57 L. Ed. 107, 33 S. Ct. 9

**Bathhouse Case**
403 F.2d 800

**Bathing Doll Case**
265 F. 268

**Bathing Resort Drowning Liability Case**
364 Mo. 849, 269 S.W.2d 52

**Baton Rouge Black Muslim Cases**
365 So. 2d 1361 (La.)

**Battle Creek Case**
31 I.C.C. 559

**Battle Creek Fourth Section Case**
24 I.C.C. 604

**Batture Cases**
3 La. Ann. 230; 3 La. Ann. 239
2 Mart. (n.s.) 545; 4 Mart. (n.s.) 68
6 Mart. (o.s.) 19
6 Mart. (o.s.) 281

**Baugh Case**
149 U.S. 368, 37 L. Ed. 772, 13 S. Ct. 914

**Bear Case**
21 Ky. (5 T.B. Mon.) 4

**Beaver Lake Case**
106 Ind. 435, 7 N.E. 379

**Beck Loan Case**
365 U.S. 146, 5 L. Ed. 2d 476, 81 S. Ct. 547; 365 U.S. 875, 5 L. Ed. 2d 864, 81 S. Ct. 899; 196 F. Supp. 198

**Becker Case**
210 N.Y. 274, 104 N.E. 396; 215 N.Y. 126, 109 N.E. 127; 215 N.Y. 721, 109 N.E. 1086; 91 Misc. 329, 33 N.Y. Crim. 439, 155 N.Y.S. 107

**Bedding Together Case**
199 Ga. 81, 33 S.E.2d 325

**Bedford Cut Stone Cases**
9 F.2d 40; 273 U.S. 677, 71 L. Ed. 835, 47 S. Ct. 97; 274 U.S. 37, 71 L. Ed. 916, 47 S. Ct. 522

**Bee Case**
114 W. Va. 40, 171 S.E. 539

**Beech-Nut Case**
264 F. 885; 253 U.S. 482, 64 L. Ed. 1024, 40 S. Ct. 584; 257 U.S. 441, 66 L. Ed. 307, 42 S. Ct. 150

**Beecher Case**
48 How. Pr. 175; 59 N.Y. 176

**Beechwood Avenue Sewer Case**
179 Pa. 494, 36 A. 210

**Beef Trust Cases**
122 F. 529; 196 U.S. 375, 49 L. Ed. 518, 25 S. Ct. 276
142 F. 808
*Continued*

**Beeper Monitoring Case**
460 U.S. 276, 75 L. Ed. 2d 55, 103 S. Ct. 1081

**Beer Sales Sex Discrimination Case**
429 U.S. 190, 50 L. Ed. 2d 397, 97 S. Ct. 451

**Behrens Case**
233 U.S. 473, 58 L. Ed. 1051, 34 S. Ct. 646

**Beirne Initiative Case**
595 P.2d 1 (Alk.)

**Belknap Hardware Case**
264 F. 676; 271 F. 144; 285 F. 379; 264 U.S. 572, 68 L. Ed. 856, 44 S. Ct. 402

**Bell Avenue Case**
253 N.Y. 345, 171 N.E. 565; 230 A.D. 797, 244 N.Y.S. 780; 233 A.D. 324, 253 N.Y.S. 345

**Bell-Ringer Case**
65 F.2d 112

**Bell Telephone Company Case**
282 U.S. 133, 75 L. Ed. 255, 51 S. Ct. 65; 283 U.S. 808, 75 L. Ed. 1427, 51 S. Ct. 646; 98 F.2d 930

**Bellicose Bull Case**
58 Wash. 2d 709, 364 P.2d 500

**Belmont Case**
301 U.S. 324, 81 L. Ed. 1134, 57 S. Ct. 758; 85 F.2d 542; 299 U.S. 537, 81 L. Ed. 396, 57 S. Ct. 313; 300 U.S. 641, 81 L. Ed. 856, 57 S. Ct. 505

**Belt Line Cases**
165 F. 459; 165 F. 472; 176 F. 470
166 F. 569; 168 F. 937; 170 F. 625; 170 F. 626; 171 F. 1014; 177 F. 925, 101 C.C.A. 205; 177 F. 1001

**Ben Avon Case**
68 Pa. Super. 561; 260 Pa. 289, 103 A. 744; 251 U.S. 542, 64 L. Ed. 405, 40 S. Ct. 583; 253 U.S. 287, 64 L. Ed. 908, 40 S. Ct. 527; 75 Pa. Super. 290; 271 Pa. 346, 114 A. 369

**Benny Case**
239 F.2d 532; 131 F. Supp. 165, 105 U.S.P.Q. (BNA) 302; 356 U.S. 43, 2 L. Ed. 2d 583, 78 S. Ct. 667; 116 U.S.P.Q. (BNA) 479; 353 U.S. 946, 1 L. Ed. 2d 856, 77 S. Ct. 824, 113 U.S.P.Q. (BNA) 549; 356 U.S. 934, 2 L. Ed. 2d 764, 78 S. Ct. 770

**Bensenville Case**
408 Ill. 480, 97 N.E.2d 463

**Bercu Case**
299 N.Y. 728, 87 N.E.2d 451; 273 A.D. 524, 78 N.Y.S.2d 209; 188 Misc. 406, 69 N.Y.S.2d 730

**Berea College Case**
123 Ky. 209, 29 Ky. Law Rep. 284, 94 S.W. 623; 211 U.S. 45, 53 L. Ed. 81, 29 S. Ct. 33

**Bergdoll Cases**
107 F.2d 897
274 F. 458

**Bering Sea Cases**
24 F.2d 933; 33 F.2d 241

**Berlin and Jones Envelope Company Case**
9 A.D. 425, 41 N.Y.S. 345; 38 A.D. 499, 56 N.Y.S. 588; 166 N.Y. 292, 59 N.E. 906

**Berman Case**
277 A.D. 560, 101 N.Y.S. 206

**Bernel Foam Case**
146 N.L.R.B. 1277, No. 161

**Bernstein Case**
163 F.2d 246; 173 F.2d 71; 210 F.2d 375

**Berry Will Case**
93 Md. 560, 49 A. 401; 2 B.C.R. 233; 2 B.C.R. 235

**Bertie Kay Case**
106 F. Supp. 244; 201 F.2d 736, 1953 App. D.C. 337

**Bertoldi Naturalization Case**
178 F.2d 977; 86 App. D.C. 1

**Berwind-White Case**
255 A.D. 961, 8 N.Y.S.2d 668; 281 N.Y. 610, 22 N.E.2d 173; 308 U.S. 546, 84 L. Ed. 459, 60 S. Ct. 261; 281 N.Y. 670, 22 N.E.2d 764; 309 U.S. 33, 84 L. Ed. 565, 60 S. Ct. 388

**Bess Case**
357 U.S. 51, 2 L. Ed. 2d 1135, 78 S. Ct. 1054; 243 F.2d 675; 134 F. Supp. 467

**Bethlehem Baby Case**
151 Pa. Super. 522, 30 A.2d 726; 347 Pa. 418, 32 A.2d 565; 346 Pa. 438, 31 A.2d 11; 320 U.S. 782, 88 L. Ed. 469, 64 S. Ct. 192

**Betts Cadillac Case**
96 N.L.R.B. 268, No. 46

**Betts Case**
316 U.S. 455, 86 L. Ed. 1595, 62 S. Ct. 1252; 315 U.S. 791, 86 L. Ed. 1194, 62 S. Ct. 639

**Betty Boop Case**
5 F. Supp. 808; 73 F.2d 276; 294 U.S. 717, 79 L. Ed. 1250, 55 S. Ct. 516; 14 F. Supp. 401

**Bevans Case**
F. Cas. No. 14,589; 16 U.S. 336, 4 L. Ed. 404

**Bevin Case**
64 F. 859; 73 F. 469, 19 C.C.A. 534

**Beyer Case**
145 F. 353; 146 F. 1022, 76 C.C.A. 678

**Biased Juror Case**
256 Ala. 673, 57 So. 2d 103

**Bible Reading Case**
374 U.S. 203, 10 L. Ed. 2d 844, 83 S. Ct. 1560; 364 U.S. 298, 5 L. Ed. 2d 89, 81 S. Ct. 268; 177 F. Supp. 398; 184 F. Supp. 381; 195 F. Supp. 518; 201 F. Supp. 815; 228 Md. 239, 179 A.2d 698; 371 U.S. 807, 9 L. Ed. 2d 52, 83 S. Ct. 25; 371 U.S. 809, 9 L. Ed. 2d 52, 83 S. Ct. 21

**Bicycle Tax Case**
175 Ill. 445, 51 N.E. 907

**Big Interest Cases**
1 Minor 209 (Ala.)
1 Stew. 81 (Ala.)
1 Stew. 556 (Ala.)

**Big John Case**
372 U.S. 658, 10 L. Ed. 2d 52, 83 S. Ct. 984; 379 U.S. 642, 13 L. Ed. 2d 550, 85 S. Ct. 610
318 I.C.C. 641; 321 I.C.C. 582; 325 I.C.C. 752

**Big Vein Coal Case**
17 I.C.C. 149; 174 F. 687

**Biggs Case**
157 F. 264; 211 U.S. 507, 53 L. Ed. 305, 29 S. Ct. 181

**Bilder Case**
289 F.2d 291; 33 T.C. 155; 369 U.S. 499, 8 L. Ed. 2d 65, 82 S. Ct. 881

**Bilged Barrel Case**
36 App. D.C. 104, 1911 C.D. 274

**Bill of Rights for the Disabled Case**
451 U.S. 1, 67 L. Ed. 2d 694, 101 S. Ct. 1531

**Billboard Banning Case**
453 U.S. 571, 69 L. Ed. 2d 800, 101 S. Ct. 2882

**Billboard Cases**
202 Ind. 85, 172 N.E. 309
289 Mass. 149, 193 N.E. 799; 296 U.S. 543, 80 L. Ed. 385, 56 S. Ct. 95; 297 U.S. 725, 80 L. Ed. 1008, 56 S. Ct. 495; 297 U.S. 725, 80 L. Ed. 1008, 56 S. Ct. 496
140 Misc. 42, 249 N.Y.S. 495; 234 A.D. 896, 254 N.Y.S. 542; 259 N.Y. 327, 182 N.E. 5

**Billiard Cue Rack Case**
135 U.S. 227, 34 L. Ed. 122, 10 S. Ct. 822

**Billing Envelope Freedom of Speech Case**
475 U.S. 1, 89 L. Ed. 2d 1, 106 S. Ct. 903

**Billposter Case**
271 F. 140; 67 L. Ed. 1221, 43 S. Ct. 97; 260 U.S. 501, 67 L. Ed. 368, 43 S. Ct. 167

**Billy Rose Case**
280 A.D. 785, 113 N.Y.S.2d 661; 280 A.D. 864, 114 N.Y.S.2d 255

**Binding Evidence Case**
227 N.C. 80, 40 S.E.2d 609

**Binghamton Bridge Case**
27 N.Y. 87, 26 How. Pr. 124; 70 U.S. 51, 18 L. Ed. 137; 30 How. Pr. 346

**Bird Man of Alcatraz Case**
139 F.2d 171; 163 F.2d 312; 321 U.S. 796, 88 L. Ed. 1085, 64 S. Ct. 846

**Birth Control Case**
367 U.S. 497, 6 L. Ed. 2d 989, 81 S. Ct. 1752; 362 U.S. 987, 4 L. Ed. 2d 1020, 80 S. Ct. 1077; 368 U.S. 869, 7 L. Ed. 2d 69, 82 S. Ct. 21, 82 S. Ct. 22; 381 U.S. 479, 14 L. Ed. 2d 510, 85 S. Ct. 1678; 17 Conn. 48, 156 A.2d 508

**Bisbee Deportation Case**
254 F. 611; 254 U.S. 281, 65 L. Ed. 270, 41 S. Ct. 133

**Bischoff Case**
170 A.D. 679, 156 N.Y.S. 563; 218 N.Y. 106, 112 N.E. 759

**Bishop Case**
81 Misc. 19, 142 N.Y.S. 83; 159 A.D. 279, 144 N.Y.S. 373; 161 A.D. 904, 145 N.Y.S. 1113; 211 N.Y. 174, 105 N.E. 213; 211 N.Y. 609, 105 N.E. 1081; 166 A.D. 952, 151 N.Y.S. 1105

**Bituminous Coal Case**
298 U.S. 238, 80 L. Ed. 1160, 56 S. Ct. 855

**Black and White Scotch Case**
390 F.2d 117

**Black Diamond Collieries Case**
144 Tenn. 465, 234 S.W. 322

**Black Diamond Steamship Case**
167 F.2d 308, 1948 A.M.C. 815; 336 U.S. 386, 93 L. Ed. 754, 69 S. Ct. 622

**Black Hand Cases**
278 Pa. 1, 122 A. 88; 278 Pa. 7, 122 A. 90

**Black Muslim Cases**
206 F. Supp. 370; 295 F.2d 171, 111 App. D.C. 184
291 F.2d 196; 304 F.2d 670
293 F.2d 233; 319 F.2d 844; 212 F. Supp. 865
57 Cal. 2d 860, 22 Cal. Rptr. 478, 372 P.2d 310
10 N.Y.2d 531, 225 N.Y.S.2d 497, 180 N.E.2d 791; 13 A.D.2d 668, 215 N.Y.S.2d 1017

**Black Tom Cases**
92 N.J.L. 467, 105 A. 206; 249 U.S. 600, 63 L. Ed. 796, 39 S. Ct. 258
94 N.J.L. 213, 109 A. 309; 253 U.S. 482, 64 L. Ed. 1024, 40 S. Ct. 482
94 N.J.L. 228, 109 A. 745; 253 U.S. 483, 64 L. Ed. 1024, 40 S. Ct. 482
94 N.J.L. 236, 109 A. 743; 253 U.S. 483, 64 L. Ed. 1024, 40 S. Ct. 482
94 N.J.L. 260, 109 A. 745; 253 U.S. 483, 64 L. Ed. 1024, 40 S. Ct. 482
96 N.J.L. 25, 114 A. 242
97 N.J.L. 474, 117 A. 598

**Black Watch Case**
376 F. Supp. 1154

**Blackbird Creek Case**
27 U.S. 245, 7 L. Ed. 412

**Blaisdell Case**
189 Minn. 422, 249 N.W. 334; 189 Minn. 448, 249 N.W. 893; 290 U.S. 398, 78 L. Ed. 413, 54 S. Ct. 231

**Blake and Johnson Case**
161 F. 134

**Blanchard Case**
389 P.2d 951 (Okla.)

**Bleached Flour Cases**
168 F. 911
202 F. 615, 121 C.C.A. 23; 229 U.S. 619, 57 L. Ed. 1354, 33 S. Ct. 778; 232 U.S. 399, 58 L. Ed. 658, 34 S. Ct. 337

**Bleistein Case**
188 U.S. 239, 47 L. Ed. 460, 23 S. Ct. 298; 104 F. 993

**Blighted Area Case**
99 N.H. 161, 106 A.2d 571

**Blockburger Case**
284 U.S. 299, 76 L. Ed. 306, 52 S. Ct. 180; 50 F.2d 795; 284 U.S. 607, 76 L. Ed. 520, 52 S. Ct. 40

**Blood-Alcohol Test Case**
459 U.S. 553, 74 L. Ed. 2d 748, 103 S. Ct. 916
382 U.S. 971

**Blood Grouping Paternity Cases**
114 F.2d 479, 72 App. D.C. 318
18 N.J. Misc. 633, 16 A.2d 80
62 S.D. 123, 252 N.W. 7
64 S.D. 309, 266 N.W. 667
59 Ohio App. 191, 17 N.E.2d 428; 135 Ohio St. 187, 20 N.E.2d 229
63 Ohio App. 16, 24 N.E.2d 962
67 P.2d 1059; 10 Cal. 2d 428, 74 P.2d 1043
123 Pa. Super. 161, 186 A. 298
227 Wis. 279, 278 N.W. 535; 231 Wis. 616, 286 N.W. 3

**Blood Hound Case**
70 Neb. 395, 97 N.W. 593

**Blood Test Paternity Case**
98 N.H. 481, 103 A.2d 188

**Bloody Shorts Case**
386 U.S. 1, 17 L. Ed. 2d 690, 87 S. Ct. 785

**Blue Baby Case**
252 S.W.2d 97 (Mo)

**Blue Flash Case**
109 N.L.R.B. 591, No. 85

**Blue Law Cases**
366 U.S. 420, 6 L. Ed. 2d 393, 81 S. Ct. 1101, 81 S. Ct. 1153, 81 S. Ct. 1218; 362 U.S. 959, 4 L. Ed. 2d 874, 80 S. Ct. 874; 368 U.S. 869, 7 L. Ed. 2d 69, 7 L. Ed. 2d 70, 82 S. Ct. 21, 82 S. Ct. 22; 176 F. Supp. 466; 220 Md. 117, 151 A.2d 156
366 U.S. 582, 6 L. Ed. 2d 551, 81 S. Ct. 1135; 362 U.S. 960, 4 L. Ed. 2d 875, 80 S. Ct. 876, 368 U.S. 869, 7 L. Ed. 2d 69, 81 S. Ct. 21; 266 F.2d 427; 273 F.2d 954; 179 F. Supp. 944
366 U.S. 599, 6 L. Ed. 2d 563, 81 S. Ct. 1144; 362 U.S. 987, 4 L. Ed. 2d 1020, 80 S. Ct. 1078; 184 F. Supp. 352; 368 U.S. 869, 7 L. Ed. 2d 70, 82 S. Ct. 22
366 U.S. 617, 6 L. Ed. 2d 536, 81 S. Ct. 1122; 362 U.S. 960, 4 L. Ed. 2d 875, 80 S. Ct. 876; 176 F. Supp. 466; 178 F. Supp. 336

**Blue Ribbon Case**
284 F. 110

**Blue River Case**
130 Colo. 375, 276 P.2d 992

**Blue Shoe Case**
326 U.S. 310, 90 L. Ed. 95, 66 S. Ct. 154; 22 Wash. 2d 146, 154 P.2d 801; 65 S. Ct. 1579

**Blue Sky Cases**
228 F. 805; 242 U.S. 568, 61 L. Ed. 498, 37 S. Ct. 227
230 F. 233; 242 U.S. 539, 61 L. Ed. 480, 37 S. Ct. 217
230 F. 236; 242 U.S. 559, 61 L. Ed. 493, 37 S. Ct. 224

**Bluefield Case**
89 W. Va. 736, 110 S.E. 205; 258 U.S. 622, 66 L. Ed. 796, 42 S. Ct. 315; 262 U.S. 679, 67 L. Ed. 1176, 43 S. Ct. 675

**Bluestone Reservoir Case**
33 F. Supp. 756; 39 F. Supp. 540; 122 F.2d 733; 314 U.S. 683, 86 L. Ed. 547, 62 S. Ct. 187; 56 F. Supp. 298

**Board of Control Case**
275 U.S. 519, 72 L. Ed. 404, 48 S. Ct. 122; 277 U.S. 189, 72 L. Ed. 845, 48 S. Ct. 480

**Board of Equalization Case**
49 Ark. 518, 6 S.W. 1

**Boatwright Cases**
130 F. 905
147 F. 321, 77 C.C.A. 499
195 Mo. 693, 93 S.W. 934

**Bob-Lo Case**
317 Mich. 686, 27 N.W.2d 139; 333 U.S. 28, 92 L. Ed. 455, 68 S. Ct. 358

**Bob-Tail Case**
339 Pa. 353, 14 A.2d 438

**Bobsled Case**
228 A.D. 73, 239 N.Y.S. 31; 253 N.Y. 234, 170 N.E. 902

**Bohemian Oat Cases**
125 Ind. 265, 25 N.E. 281
68 Mich. 303, 36 N.W. 79
68 Mich. 389, 36 N.W. 187
68 Mich. 454, 36 N.W. 218
77 Mich. 598, 43 N.W. 994
80 Mich. 317, 45 N.W. 181
80 Mich. 396, 45 N.W. 337

**Bohnen Case**
232 F.2d 406; 345 U.S. 946, 97 L. Ed. 1371, 73 S. Ct. 863; 345 U.S. 978, 97 L. Ed. 1392, 73 S. Ct. 1120; 199 F.2d 492; 127 F. Supp. 232

**Boisdore Case**
52 U.S. 63, 13 L. Ed. 605

**Bollingers Champagne Case**
70 U.S. 560, 18 L. Ed. 78

**Bond Cases**
3 F. 673; 114 U.S. 663, 29 L. Ed. 281, 5 S. Ct. 974, 5 S. Ct. 1098
4 F. 97; 114 U.S. 663, 29 L. Ed. 281, 5 S. Ct. 974, 5 S. Ct. 1098

**Bond Debt Case**
12 S.C. 200

**Bonded Products Case**
13 F.2d 417; 21 F.2d 419; 275 U.S. 572, 72 L. Ed. 432, 48 S. Ct. 204

**Bone Rose Case**
Treas. Dec. 44446; Treas. Dec. 44576; Treas. Dec. 45259, 19 C.C.P.A. (Customs) 137; Abs. (n.s.) No. 18994

**Bongo Drum Cases**
12 N.Y.2d 826, 236 N.Y.S.2d 347, 187 N.E.2d 360; 16 A.D.2d 420, 228 N.Y.S.2d 514; 32 Misc. 2d 801, 223 N.Y.S.2d 940
14 N.Y.2d 498, 248 N.Y.S.2d 223, 197 N.E.2d 620; 19 A.D.2d 600, 240 N.Y.S.2d 624

**Bonnie Gray Case**
64 So. 2d 650 (Fla.)

**Bonwit Teller Case**
96 N.L.R.B. 608, No. 73; 197 F.2d 640; 345 U.S. 905, 97 L. Ed. 1342, 73 S. Ct. 644

**Bookie Entrapment Case**
139 Conn. 1, 89 A.2d 219

**Bootleg Coal Cases**
164 Misc. 803, 299 N.Y.S. 606; 166 Misc. 430, 2 N.Y.S.2d 545; 254 A.D. 388, 5 N.Y.S.2d 778; 279 N.Y. 16, 17 N.E.2d 407
168 Misc. 45, 6 N.Y.S.2d 103; 279 N.Y. 389, 18 N.E.2d 633

**Bootstrap Cases**
305 U.S. 165, 83 L. Ed. 104, 59 S. Ct. 134
308 U.S. 371, 84 L. Ed. 329, 60 S. Ct. 317
330 U.S. 258, 91 L. Ed. 884, 67 S. Ct. 677

**Borden Condensed Milk Case**
201 F. 510

**Borden Milk Case**
297 U.S. 251, 80 L. Ed. 669, 56 S. Ct. 453

**Border Divisions Case**
208 F. Supp. 661; 371 U.S. 26, 9 L. Ed. 2d 95, 83 S. Ct. 117

**Border Patrol Cases**
422 U.S. 873, 45 L. Ed. 2d 607, 95 S. Ct. 2574
422 U.S. 891, 45 L. Ed. 2d 623, 95 S. Ct. 2585
422 U.S. 916, 45 L. Ed. 2d 641, 95 S. Ct. 2569, 95 S. Ct. 2590

**Border Point Case**
269 I.C.C. 33; 270 I.C.C. 81; 270 I.C.C. 93; 270 I.C.C. 403; 272 I.C.C. 695; 276 I.C.C. 9; 279 I.C.C. 303

**Borg-Warner Cases**
356 U.S. 342, 2 L. Ed. 2d 823, 78 S. Ct. 718; 236 F.2d 898; 259 F.2d 270; 353 U.S. 907, 1 L. Ed. 2d 662, 77 S. Ct. 661
113 N.L.R.B. 1288, No. 120

**Boston and Maine Cases**
202 A.D. 54, 195 N.Y.S. 402; 234 N.Y. 629, 138 N.E. 475
227 A.D. 361, 238 N.Y.S. 27; 254 N.Y. 513, 173 N.E. 844

**Boston Bank Case**
10 Ct. Cl. 519; 13 Ct. Cl. 523; 96 U.S. 30, 24 L. Ed. 647

**Boston Milk Marketing Case**
136 F.2d 786; 320 U.S. 723, 88 L. Ed. 426, 64 S. Ct. 58, 64 S. Ct. 188; 321 U.S. 288, 88 L. Ed. 733, 64 S. Ct. 559; 82 F. Supp. 614; 185 F.2d 871; 341 U.S. 908, 95 L. Ed. 1346, 71 S. Ct. 621; 342 U.S. 451, 96 L. Ed. 497, 72 S. Ct. 433

**Bothick Cases**
43 La. Ann. 547, 9 So. 477; 44 La. Ann. 1037, 11 So. 712; 45 La. Ann. 1382, 14 So. 293, 47 La. Ann. 613, 17 So. 198; 52 La. Ann. 1863, 28 So. 458; 109 La. 1, 33 So. 47; 110 La. 109, 34 So. 163

**Botta Case**
26 N.J. 82, 138 A.2d 713; 42 N.J. Super. 95, 126 A.2d 32

**Bottle Law Case**
77 Ohio St. 438, 83 N.E. 797

**Bottle-Stopper Case**
4 F. 411

**Bouknight Case**
70 F. 442, 17 C.C.A. 181

**Boulder Dam Case**
283 U.S. 423, 75 L. Ed. 1154, 51 S. Ct. 522; 292 U.S. 341, 78 L. Ed. 1298, 54 S. Ct. 735

**Boulevard Case**
107 N.J.L. 223, 152 A. 175; 108 N.J.L. 282, 156 A. 772

**Bounty Hunter Case**
83 U.S. 366, 21 L. Ed. 287

**Bower Case**
74 F. 235, 20 C.C.A. 161

**Bowsky Case**
95 F. 474; 113 F. 698; 113 F. 699; 143 F. 508, 74 C.C.A. 617

**Boy Scout Case**
119 Vt. 378, 125 A.2d 835

**Boyd Case**
228 U.S. 482, 57 L. Ed. 931, 33 S. Ct. 554

**Boyden Brake Case**
66 F. 997; 70 F. 816, 17 C.C.A. 430; 170 U.S. 537, 42 L. Ed. 1136, 18 S. Ct. 707

**Boynton Cab Company Case**
237 Wis. 249, 296 N.W. 636

**Brackenridge Will Contest Case**
245 S.W. 786; 114 Tex. 418, 267 S.W. 244; 270 S.W. 1001 (Tex.)

**Bradley's Case**
224 F. Supp. 557

**Brady Handgun Act Case**
521 U.S. 898, 138 L. Ed. 2d 914, 117 S. Ct. 2365 (1997)

**Brake Beam Cases**
99 F. 758; 106 F. 693, 45 C.C.A. 544
99 F. 777; 106 F. 693, 45 C.C.A. 544

**Bramwell Case**
295 F. 331; 299 F. 705; 269 U.S. 483, 70 L. Ed. 368, 46 S. Ct. 176

**Branch Bank Case**
297 Mo. 397, 249 S.W. 619; 262 U.S. 732, 67 L. Ed. 1205, 43 S. Ct. 700; 263 U.S. 640, 68 L. Ed. 486, 44 S. Ct. 213

**Bread Cases**
12 La. Ann. 432

24 Misc. 745, 53 N.Y.S. 968; 39 A.D. 432, 57 N.Y.S. 347

86 Mich. 594, 49 N.W. 609

108 Neb. 674, 189 N.W. 383; 261 U.S. 608, 67 L. Ed. 824, 43 S. Ct. 433; 261 U.S. 625, 67 L. Ed. 833, 43 S. Ct. 359; 262 U.S. 728, 67 L. Ed. 1203, 43 S. Ct. 520; 264 U.S. 504, 68 L. Ed. 813, 44 S. Ct. 412

124 Neb. 464, 247 N.W. 39; 54 S. Ct. 63; 290 U.S. 570, 78 L. Ed. 505, 54 S. Ct. 277

**Bred Spred Cases**
35 F.2d 183

49 F.2d 87

**Breward Case**
41 U.S. 143, 10 L. Ed. 916

**Brewery Cases**
26 F. 178

247 N.Y. 176, 159 N.E. 902

**Bribery Cases**
291 F. 958; 263 U.S. 716, 68 L. Ed. 522, 44 S. Ct. 137; 263 U.S. 719, 68 L. Ed. 523, 44 S. Ct. 181

291 F. 972

291 F. 975; 263 U.S. 716, 68 L. Ed. 522, 44 S. Ct. 137

291 F. 988; 263 U.S. 716, 68 L. Ed. 522, 263 U.S. 719, 68 L. Ed. 523, 44 S. Ct. 181

**Bridge Election Case**
14 N.J.L. 222

**Briggs-Stratton Case**
250 Wis. 550, 27 N.W.2d 875, 28 N.W.2d 254; 333 U.S. 853, 92 L. Ed. 1134, 68 S. Ct. 734; 336 U.S. 245, 93 L. Ed. 651, 69 S. Ct. 516; 336 U.S. 970, 93 L. Ed. 1121, 69 S. Ct. 935

**Bright Case**
10 Ill. 2d 178, 139 N.E.2d 270

**Brimson Case**
53 F. 476; 154 U.S. 447, 38 L. Ed. 1047, 14 S. Ct. 1125; 155 U.S. 3, 39 L. Ed. 49, 15 S. Ct. 19

**Brimstone Division Case**
13 F.2d 914; 17 F.2d 165; 276 U.S. 104, 72 L. Ed. 487, 48 S. Ct. 282

**Brink's Robbery Cases**
209 F.2d 209

209 F.2d 219

209 F.2d 223

209 F.2d 225

209 F.2d 232

209 F.2d 234

292 F.2d 244

339 Mass. 487, 159 N.E.2d 870; 361 U.S. 895, 4 L. Ed. 2d 152, 80 S. Ct. 200

**Bristol Cabbage Seed Case**
7 Hun 427; 71 N.Y. 118; 78 N.Y. 393

**Britton Cases**
107 U.S. 655, 27 L. Ed. 520, 2 S. Ct. 512

108 U.S. 192, 27 L. Ed. 703, 2 S. Ct. 525

108 U.S. 193, 27 L. Ed. 701, 2 S. Ct. 526

108 U.S. 199, 27 L. Ed. 698, 2 S. Ct. 531

**Broadcast Coverage of Trials Case**
449 U.S. 560, 66 L. Ed. 2d 740, 101 S. Ct. 802

**Broadway Railway Case**
111 N.Y. 1, 18 N.E. 692

**Brogan Case**
228 F. 577, 143 C.C.A. 99; 246 U.S. 257, 62 L. Ed. 703, 38 S. Ct. 250

**Broken Bottles Case**

269 S.W.2d 761; 281 S.W.2d 9 (Mo)

**Broken Engagement Case**

96 N.H. 177, 71 A.2d 785

**Broken Plumbing Fixtures Case**

71 Ariz. 21, 222 P.2d 994

**Brokerage Commission Case**

422 U.S. 659, 45 L. Ed. 2d 463, 95 S. Ct. 2598

**Broker's Case**

77 Ga. 64

**Bronx County Case**

207 N.Y. 533, 101 N.E. 442

**Brooklyn Bridge Cases**

10 F. 513; 109 U.S. 385, 27 L. Ed. 971, 3 S. Ct. 228

76 N.Y. 475, 5 Abb. N. Cas. 383

**Browder Case**

113 F.2d 97

**Brower and Sturgeon Bay Company Case**

219 Wis. 434, 263 N.W. 376

**Brown and Patton Case**

334 F.2d 539

**Brown-Bagging Case**

268 N.C. 577, 151 S.E.2d 241; 268 N.C. 720, 152 S.E.2d 199

**Brown-Olds Case**

115 N.L.R.B. 594, No. 90

**Brown School Admissions Case**

32 Del. Ch. 343, 87 A.2d 862; 91 A.2d 137; 98 F. Supp. 529; 342 U.S. 350, 96 L. Ed. 342, 72 S. Ct. 327; 98 F. Supp. 797; 103 F. Supp. 337; 103 F. Supp. 920; 344 U.S. 1, 97 L. Ed. 3, 73 S. Ct. 1; 344 U.S. 141, 97 L. Ed. 152, 73 S. Ct. 124; 344 U.S. 891, 97 L. Ed. 689, 73 S. Ct. 213; 345 U.S. 972, 97 L. Ed. 1388, 73 S. Ct. 1118; 347 U.S. 483, 98 L. Ed. 873, 74 S. Ct. 686; 348 U.S. 886, 75 S. Ct. 210; 349 U.S. 294, 99 L. Ed. 1083, 75 S. Ct. 753; 349 U.S. 914, 75 S. Ct. 602

**Brown Shoe Case**

370 U.S. 294, 8 L. Ed. 2d 510, 82 S. Ct. 1502; 363 U.S. 825, 4 L. Ed. 2d 1521, 80 S. Ct. 1595; 365 U.S. 825, 81 S. Ct. 711; 179 F. Supp. 721

**Brown's Iron Bitters Case**

31 F. Supp. 453; 139 U.S. 540, 35 L. Ed. 247, 11 S. Ct. 625

**Brundage Mortgage Clause Case**

49 Misc. 262, 97 N.Y.S. 376; 113 A.D. 903, 98 N.Y.S. 1101; 114 A.D. 905, 100 N.Y.S. 1114; 54 Misc. 223, 104 N.Y.S. 423

**Bucket Shop Case**

2 Ga. App. 1, 58 S.E. 401

**Buckeye Case**

203 Wis. 248, 234 N.W. 342

**Buckeye State Case**

F. Cas. No. 13,445

**Buckfoot Gang Cases**

147 F.2d 321

77 Ark. 279, 91 S.W. 546

195 Mo. 693, 93 S.W. 934

257 P.2d 1049 (Okla.)

**Buckingham Hotel Annex Cases**

330 Mo. 1020, 51 S.W.2d 1033

331 Mo. 636, 56 S.W.2d 120; 337 Mo. 475, 85 S.W.2d 48; 343 Mo. 841, 123 S.W.2d 149

**Buckly Case**

110 Cal. 339, 42 P. 900

**Buck's Stove and Range Case**
221 U.S. 418, 55 L. Ed. 797, 31 S. Ct. 492; 233 U.S. 604, 58 L. Ed. 1115, 34 S. Ct. 693

**Buffalo Bill Circus Case**
229 F. 644, 144 C.C.A. 54; 241 U.S. 669, 60 L. Ed. 1229, 36 S. Ct. 553

**Buffalo Grain Case**
13 I.C.C. 31; 14 I.C.C. 398; 19 I.C.C. 128

**Buffalo Linen Supply Company Case**
353 U.S. 87, 1 L. Ed. 2d 676, 77 S. Ct. 643; 231 F.2d 110; 32 U.S. 818, 1 L. Ed. 2d 44, 77 S. Ct. 36

**Bug-Bite Case**
86 Ohio Abs 1, 173 N.E.2d 382; 372 U.S. 108, 9 L. Ed. 2d 618, 83 S. Ct. 659; 23 Ohio Op. 2d 53; 172 Ohio St. 488, 18 Ohio Op. 2d 6, 178 N.E.2d 597; 369 U.S. 848, 8 L. Ed. 2d 8, 82 S. Ct. 935

**Buggy Case**
67 N.C. 40

**Buick Case**
217 N.Y. 382, 111 N.E. 1050; 153 A.D. 474, 138 N.Y.S. 224; 160 A.D. 55, 145 N.Y.S. 462

**Building Height Cases**
181 Wis. 519, 195 N.W. 544

**Building Permit Takings Case**
512 U.S. 374, 129 L. Ed. 2d 304, 114 S. Ct. 2309 (1994)

**Bull Case**
295 U.S. 247, 79 L. Ed. 1421, 55 S. Ct. 695

**Bullet Case**
221 Ky. 648, 299 S.W. 553; 230 Ky. 411, 19 S.W.2d 1091

**Bund Case**
172 Misc. 1097, 15 N.Y.S.2d 1005

**Burco Holding Company Case**
81 F.2d 721; 297 U.S. 724, 80 L. Ed. 1008, 56 S. Ct. 670; 12 F. Supp. 667

**Bureau of Census Disclosure Case**
455 U.S. 345, 71 L. Ed. 2d 199, 102 S. Ct. 1103

**Buried Children Case**
78 R.I. 505, 82 A.2d 893

**Burned Baby Case**
186 Va. 746, 43 S.E.2d 882

**Burnham Hanna Munger Case**
14 I.C.C. 299; 171 F. 680; 218 U.S. 88, 54 L. Ed. 946, 30 S. Ct. 651

**Burns Brothers Case**
108 N.J. Eq. 275, 155 A. 28

**Burr Case**
F. Cas. Nos. 14,692; 14,692a to 14,692h; 14,693; 14,694; 14,694a

**Bus Employees Case**
340 U.S. 383, 95 L. Ed. 364, 71 S. Ct. 359; 257 Wis. 43, 42 N.W.2d 471; 258 Wis. 1, 44 N.W.2d 547; 340 U.S. 874, 95 L. Ed. 636, 71 S. Ct. 124; 340 U.S. 903, 95 L. Ed. 653, 71 S. Ct. 283

**Bus Passenger Search Case**
501 U.S. 429, 115 L. Ed. 2d 389, 111 S. Ct. 2382

**Bus Regulation Cases**
274 U.S. 554, 71 L. Ed. 1199, 47 S. Ct. 702
11 F.2d 161; 273 U.S. 45, 71 L. Ed. 530, 47 S. Ct. 298
19 F.2d 256; 276 U.S. 245, 72 L. Ed. 551, 48 S. Ct. 230
198 Ind. 563, 153 N.E. 504, 154 N.E. 369; 277 U.S. 163, 72 L. Ed. 833, 48 S. Ct. 502; 200 Ind. 162, 162 N.E. 54

**Business Activities Tax Case**
193 Wash. 451, 75 P.2d 1017; 305 U.S. 434, 83 L. Ed. 272, 59 S. Ct. 325

**Busing Case**
418 U.S. 717, 41 L. Ed. 2d 1069, 94 S. Ct. 3112

**Buster Brown Case**
146 F. 205

**Butcher Cases**
30 Tex. 508
30 Tex. 511
30 Tex. 514

**Butchers' Union Case**
111 U.S. 746, 28 L. Ed. 585, 4 S. Ct. 652; 120 U.S. 141, 30 L. Ed. 614, 7 S. Ct. 472

**Butler Case**
8 F. Supp. 552; 78 F.2d 1; 296 U.S. 561, 80 L. Ed. 396, 56 S. Ct. 144; 297 U.S. 1, 80 L. Ed. 477, 56 S. Ct. 312; 56 S. Ct. 438

**Butte City Smoke-House Lode Cases**
6 Mont. 397, 12 P. 858

**Butter Regulation Case**
116 F.2d 227; 313 U.S. 551, 85 L. Ed. 1515, 61 S. Ct. 834; 315 U.S. 148, 86 L. Ed. 754, 62 S. Ct. 491; 315 U.S. 786, 86 L. Ed. 1223, 62 S. Ct. 491; 315 U.S. 828, 86 L. Ed. 1223, 62 S. Ct. 491

**Butterfield Patent Cases**
385 U.S. 1009, 17 L. Ed. 2d 547, 87 S. Ct. 717
366 F.2d 338

**Butterfly Jewel Case**
225 F. 537

**Button-Fastener Case**
65 F. 619; 77 F. 288, 25 C.C.A. 267

**Buzzard Roost Case**
10 F. Supp. 854; 12 F. Supp. 70; 79 F.2d 995; 81 F.2d 986; 298 U.S. 651, 80 L. Ed. 1379, 56 S. Ct. 941; 299 U.S. 259, 81 L. Ed. 178, 57 S. Ct. 202; 19 F. Supp. 932; 91 F.2d 995; 302 U.S. 675, 82 L. Ed. 521, 58 S. Ct. 120; 302 U.S. 485, 82 L. Ed. 381, 58 S. Ct. 306; 25 F. Supp. 419; 25 F. Supp. 963; 107 F.2d 484; 309 U.S. 667, 84 L. Ed. 1014, 60 S. Ct. 608

**By-Products Recovery Cases**
288 F. 401
2 F.2d 664; 267 U.S. 599, 69 L. Ed. 807, 45 S. Ct. 354; 32 F.2d 502

## C

**Cab Curtain Cases**
188 Wis. 232, 205 N.W. 932; 272 U.S. 605, 71 L. Ed. 432, 47 S. Ct. 207; 192 Wis. 240, 212 N.W. 425
192 Wis. 241, 212 N.W. 425

**Cable Case**
40 Hun 1; 104 N.Y. 1, 10 N.E. 332; 45 Hun 153; 109 N.Y. 32, 15 N.E. 882

**Cable Television Case**
440 U.S. 689, 59 L. Ed. 2d 692, 99 S. Ct. 1435

**Cable TV Franchise Case**
476 U.S. 488, 90 L. Ed. 2d 480, 106 S. Ct. 2034

**Cable TV Indecent Programming Case**
518 U.S. 727, 135 L. Ed. 2d 888, 116 S. Ct. 2374 (1996)

**Cable TV Installation Case**
458 U.S. 419, 73 L. Ed. 2d 868, 102 S. Ct. 3164

**Calderon Case**
207 F.2d 377; 347 U.S. 1008, 98 L. Ed. 1133, 74 S. Ct. 863; 348 U.S. 160, 99 L. Ed. 202, 75 S. Ct. 186

**Caldwell Cases**
242 F. 177; 272 F. 356; 44 S. Ct. 135; 266 U.S. 85, 69 L. Ed. 178, 45 S. Ct. 22
8 Ct. Cl. 334; 86 U.S. 264, 22 L. Ed. 114

**California Billiard Hall Case**
225 U.S. 623, 56 L. Ed. 1229, 32 S. Ct. 697

**California Caravan Case**
23 F. Supp. 946; 306 U.S. 583, 83 L. Ed. 1001, 59 S. Ct. 744; 306 U.S. 620, 83 L. Ed. 1026, 59 S. Ct. 640; 59 S. Ct. 362

**California Case**
122 Tex. 377, 61 S.W.2d 807

**California Death Penalty Factors Case**
512 U.S. 967, 129 L. Ed. 2d 750, 114 S. Ct. 2630 (1994)

**California Land Law Cases**
279 F. 114; 263 U.S. 225, 68 L. Ed. 278, 44 S. Ct. 21
279 F. 117; 263 U.S. 313, 68 L. Ed. 318, 44 S. Ct. 112
281 F. 407; 263 U.S. 326, 68 L. Ed. 323, 44 S. Ct. 115
195 Cal. 71, 231 P. 554
29 Cal. 2d 164, 173 P.2d 794; 330 U.S. 818, 91 L. Ed. 1270, 67 S. Ct. 1093; 332 U.S. 633, 92 L. Ed. 249, 68 S. Ct. 269

**California Pipe Line Case**
204 F. 798; 234 U.S. 548, 58 L. Ed. 1459, 34 S. Ct. 956

**California Railroad Tax Cases**
13 F. 722; 116 U.S. 138, 29 L. Ed. 589, 6 S. Ct. 317
18 F. 385; 118 U.S. 394, 30 L. Ed. 118, 6 S. Ct. 1132

**California Red Flag Case**
283 U.S. 359, 75 L. Ed. 1117, 51 S. Ct. 532

**California Tidelands Case**
166 Cal. 630, 138 P. 100; 240 U.S. 142, 60 L. Ed. 569, 36 S. Ct. 338

**California Wine Pricing Case**
445 U.S. 97, 63 L. Ed. 2d 233, 100 S. Ct. 937

**Call House Madam Case**
49 A.D. 1, 63 N.Y.S.2d 227

**Calorite Case**
212 F. 422; 224 F. 464, 140 C.C.A. 150

**Calumet Contractors Boycott Case**
130 N.L.R.B. 78, No. 17; 133 N.L.R.B. 512, No. 57

**Cambuston Case**
F. Cas. No. 14,712; 61 U.S. 59, 15 L. Ed. 828; F. Cas. No. 14,713; 95 U.S. 285, 24 L. Ed. 448

**Campbell Case**
47 F.2d 227; 283 U.S. 818, 75 L. Ed. 1433, 51 S. Ct. 654; 284 U.S. 582, 76 L. Ed. 504, 52 S. Ct. 39

**Campbell Estate Tax Case**
117 N.E.2d 45 (Ohio); 162 Ohio St. 203, 55 Ohio Op. 102, 122 N.E.2d 695; 349 U.S. 911, 99 L. Ed. 1246, 75 S. Ct. 600; 349 U.S. 948, 99 L. Ed. 1274, 75 S. Ct. 870

**Canadian River Gas Case**
324 U.S. 581, 89 L. Ed. 1206, 65 S. Ct. 829; 142 F.2d 943; 323 U.S. 807, 89 L. Ed. 644, 65 S. Ct. 427, 65 S. Ct. 428; 324 U.S. 831, 89 L. Ed. 1397, 65 S. Ct. 1019, 65 S. Ct. 1020; 325 U.S. 891, 89 L. Ed. 2004, 65 S. Ct. 1082

**Cancerophobia Case**
5 N.Y.2d 16, 176 N.Y.S.2d 996, 152 N.E.2d 249; 5 N.Y.2d 793, 180 N.Y.S.2d 322, 154 N.E.2d 574; 3 A.D. 2d 829, 161 N.Y.S.2d 832

**Candelaria Case**
271 U.S. 432, 70 L. Ed. 1023, 46 S. Ct. 561

**Canned Heat Patent Case**
14 F.2d 629; 25 F.2d 387; 278 U.S. 608, 73 L. Ed. 534, 49 S. Ct. 12

**Cannelton Case**
364 U.S. 76, 4 L. Ed. 2d 1581, 80 S. Ct. 1581; 268 F.2d 334

**Canneries Case**
279 U.S. 553, 73 L. Ed. 838, 49 S. Ct. 423

**Cannery Workers' Disparate Impact Case**
490 U.S. 642, 104 L. Ed. 2d 733, 109 S. Ct. 2115

**Cannon Case**
267 U.S. 333, 69 L. Ed. 634, 45 S. Ct. 250; 292 F. 169

**Canteen Case**
346 U.S. 61, 97 L. Ed. 1454, 73 S. Ct. 1017; 194 F.2d 433; 344 U.S. 809, 97 L. Ed. 630, 73 S. Ct. 16

**Canvassing Regulation Case**
425 U.S. 610, 48 L. Ed. 2d 243, 96 S. Ct. 1755

**Cape Girardeau Case**
336 F.2d 920

**Capital Punishment Jury Exclusion Case**
477 U.S. 168, 91 L. Ed. 2d 144, 106 S. Ct. 2464

**Capital Punishment Scruples Case**
211 F.2d 171; 347 U.S. 963, 98 L. Ed. 1106, 74 S. Ct. 713; 347 U.S. 1022, 98 L. Ed. 1142, 74 S. Ct. 876; 348 U.S. 853, 99 L. Ed. 672, 75 S. Ct. 20; 122 F. Supp. 775; 214 F.2d 821

**Capital Removal Case**
35 N.D. 34, 159 N.W. 281

**Capital Sentencing Procedure Case**
430 U.S. 349, 51 L. Ed. 2d 393, 97 S. Ct. 1197

**Capitol Commission Case**
14 N.D. 532, 105 N.W. 724; 15 N.D. 205, 106 N.W. 293

**Capitol Graft Case**
40 Pa. Super. 546

**Capitol Police Case**
14 Ct. Cl. 78; 14 Ct. Cl. 145

**Car-Brake Case**
F. Cas. No. 6,560

**Car Coupler Case**
77 F. 739

**Car Distribution Cases**
200 F. 989
13 I.C.C. 451; 173 F. 930; 215 U.S. 452, 54 L. Ed. 280, 30 S. Ct. 155; 215 U.S. 479, 54 L. Ed. 291, 30 S. Ct. 163
14 I.C.C. 86; 215 U.S. 216, 54 L. Ed. 164, 30 S. Ct. 86
19 I.C.C. 356; 20 I.C.C. 52; 23 I.C.C. 186; 193 F. 81; 237 F. 267; 244 F. 53, 156 C.C.A. 481; 250 U.S. 368, 63 L. Ed. 1039, 39 S. Ct. 531

*Continued*

241 Pa. 509, 88 A. 761; 242 U.S. 298, 61 L. Ed. 316, 37 S. Ct. 118

**Car Unloading Case**
114 F. Supp. 420; 347 U.S. 645, 98 L. Ed. 1015, 74 S. Ct. 826; 347 U.S. 902, 98 L. Ed. 1062, 74 S. Ct. 427

**Carasso Case**
34 T.C. 1139; 292 F.2d 367; 369 U.S. 874, 8 L. Ed. 2d 277, 82 S. Ct. 1144

**Caravan Case of California**
300 U.S. 290, 81 L. Ed. 653, 57 S. Ct. 439

**Carbice Case**
283 U.S. 27, 75 L. Ed. 819, 51 S. Ct. 334; 283 U.S. 420, 75 L. Ed. 1153, 51 S. Ct. 496; 283 U.S. 794, 75 L. Ed. 1419, 51 S. Ct. 483

**Carbide Case**
112 F. 417; 117 F. 495, 55 C.C.A. 230

**Carboloy Case**
80 F. Supp. 989

**Carbon Black Case**
300 U.S. 258, 81 L. Ed. 632, 57 S. Ct. 447

**Cardiff Giant Case**
122 Mass. 235

**Carhook Case**
55 N.Y. 108; 4 Jones & S. 195

**Carnegie Steel Case**
89 F. 721; 96 F. 850, 37 C.C.A. 593; 175 U.S. 727, 44 L. Ed. 339, 20 S. Ct. 1031; 185 U.S. 403, 46 L. Ed. 968, 22 S. Ct. 698

**Carolene Products Case**
304 U.S. 144, 82 L. Ed. 1234, 58 S. Ct. 778; 7 F. Supp. 500; 58 S. Ct. 411; 104 F.2d 969

**Carolina Coach Company Case**
207 F.2d 408; 111 F. Supp. 329

**Carpenter Case**
180 F. 896; 209 F. 471

**Carpenter Case (Eminent Domain)**
126 Tex. 604, 89 S.W.2d 194

**Carpenter Receivership Case**
218 F. 273; 235 F. 17; 250 F. 668; 264 F. 772

**Carpet Cases**
118 U.S. 10, 30 L. Ed. 63, 6 S. Ct. 946

10 F. 385; 114 U.S. 439, 29 L. Ed. 177, 5 S. Ct. 945

**Carriage Spring Cases**
122 U.S. 121, 30 L. Ed. 1110, 7 S. Ct. 1057

145 U.S. 156, 36 L. Ed. 658, 12 S. Ct. 825

**Carrier's Dark Door Case**
63 A.2d 878 (D.C.); 68 A.2d 207

**Carrier's Open Door Liability Case**
189 Va. 258, 52 S.E.2d 129

**Carrollton Case**
231 Mo. 547, 133 S.W. 44

**Carter Coal Case**
298 U.S. 238, 80 L. Ed. 1160, 56 S. Ct. 855

**Carterfone Case**
250 F. Supp. 188; 365 F.2d 486

**Casale Case**
26 T.C. 1020; 247 F.2d 440

**Cash Bonus Case**
170 Wis. 218, 175 N.W. 589; 170 Wis. 251, 176 N.W. 224

**Cash Letter Case**
240 Iowa 1074, 38 N.W.2d 622

**Cash Register Cases**
45 F. 481; 156 U.S. 502, 39 L. Ed. 511, 15 S. Ct. 434; 159 U.S. 261, 40 L. Ed. 142, 15 S. Ct. 1041

47 F. 212; 53 F. 367, 3 C.C.A. 559

**Cash Register Trust Case**
201 F. 697; 205 F. 292; 222 F. 599, 138 C.C.A. 123; 238 U.S. 635, 59 L. Ed. 1499, 35 S. Ct. 939

**Cashman Case**
130 W Va. 430, 43 S.E.2d 805

**Cashmere Bouquet Soap Case**
88 F. 899

**Castine Case**
17 U.S. 246, 4 L. Ed. 562

**Castor Oil Case**
132 F.2d 902

**Casualty Insurance Company Case**
82 Md. 535, 34 A. 778; 86 Md. 254, 37 A. 646

**Catco Case**
360 U.S. 378, 3 L. Ed. 2d 1312, 79 S. Ct. 1246; 257 F.2d 717; 358 U.S. 926, 3 L. Ed. 2d 300, 79 S. Ct. 317; 361 U.S. 801, 4 L. Ed. 2d 53, 80 S. Ct. 42

**Catron Case**
133 W. Va. 610, 57 S.E.2d 465

**Catskill Case**
94 F. 868; 110 F. 377; 121 F. 83, 58 C.C.A. 167

**Cattle Raisers Case**
103 F. 249, 43 C.C.A. 209; 186 U.S. 320, 46 L. Ed. 1182, 22 S. Ct. 824

**CATV Cases**
415 U.S. 336, 39 L. Ed. 2d 370, 94 S. Ct. 1146;
415 U.S. 345, 39 L. Ed. 2d 370, 39 L. Ed. 2d 383, 94 S. Ct. 1151, 94 S. Ct. 1155; 415 U.S. 394, 39 L. Ed. 2d 415, 94 S. Ct. 1129

**Causa Mortis Check Case**
222 Ark. 97, 257 S.W.2d 369

**Causby Chicken Farm Case**
60 F. Supp. 751, 104 Ct. Cl. 342; 75 F. Supp. 262, 109 Ct. Cl. 768; 327 U.S. 775, 90 L. Ed. 1004, 66 S. Ct. 896, 66 S. Ct. 485; 328 U.S. 256, 90 L. Ed. 1206, 66 S. Ct. 1062, 106 Ct. Cl. 854

**Cause of Action Case**
460 U.S. 719, 75 L. Ed. 2d 413, 103 S. Ct. 1483

**Cawood Patent Case**
F. Cas. Nos. 14,270 to 14,272; 94 U.S. 695, 24 L. Ed. 238; 20 F. 912; 110 U.S. 301, 28 L. Ed. 154, 4 S. Ct. 5

**CBS Cases**
316 U.S. 407, 86 L. Ed. 1563, 62 S. Ct. 1194; 44 F. Supp. 688; 47 F. Supp. 940; 319 U.S. 190, 87 L. Ed. 1344, 63 S. Ct. 997; 62 S. Ct. 908
364 U.S. 573, 5 L. Ed. 2d 302, 81 S. Ct. 330; 272 F.2d 713

**Cedar Grove Refining Company Case**
178 La. 810, 152 So. 531

**Cedar Rapids Gas Rate Case**
144 Iowa 426, 120 N.W. 966; 223 U.S. 655, 56 L. Ed. 594, 32 S. Ct. 389

**Cedarville Cases**
436 F.2d 1256
479 F.2d 489

**Celanese Corporation Case**
95 N.L.R.B. 664, No. 83

**Celebrated Mule Case**
262 Mo. 353, 171 S.W. 352

**Cellophane Cases**
351 U.S. 377, 100 L. Ed. 1264, 76 S. Ct. 994; 107 F. Supp. 324; 118 F. Supp. 41, 99 U.S.P.Q. (BNA) 462; 348 U.S. 806, 99 L. Ed. 637, 75 S. Ct. 41, 103 U.S.P.Q. (BNA) 425
85 F.2d 75; 6 F. Supp. 859; 22 U.S.P.Q. (BNA) 145, 299 F.2d 601; 81 L. Ed. 443, 57 S. Ct. 194; 304 U.S. 575, 82 L. Ed. 1539, 58 S. Ct. 1047

**Celluloid Case**
32 F. 94

**Celotex Company Cases**
49 F.2d 1048
49 F.2d 1051
49 F.2d 1053

**Cement Cases**
147 F.2d 589; 334 U.S. 839, 92 L. Ed. 1764, 68 S. Ct. 1492
157 F.2d 533; 330 U.S. 815, 91 L. Ed. 1268, 67 S. Ct. 967, 67 S. Ct. 968, 67 S. Ct. 969; 333 U.S. 683, 92 L. Ed. 1010, 68 S. Ct. 793

**Cement Trust Case**
294 F. 390; 268 U.S. 563, 69 L. Ed. 1093, 45 S. Ct. 592; 268 U.S. 588, 69 L. Ed. 1104, 45 S. Ct. 586

**Cemetery Lot Restriction Case**
189 Md. 363, 56 A.2d 24

**Cemetery Trust Case**
98 N.H. 300, 100 A.2d 157

**Census Case**
517 U.S. 1, 134 L. Ed. 2d 167, 116 S. Ct. 1091 (1996)

**Census Sampling Case**
142 L. Ed. 2d 797, 119 S. Ct. 765

**Centr-O-Cast Case**
100 N.L.R.B. 1507, No. 253

**Central Kentucky Lunatic Asylum Cases**
97 Ky. 458, 17 Ky. Law Rep. 320, 30 S.W. 971; 110 Ky. 282, 22 Ky. Law Rep. 1722, 61 S.W. 283
103 Ky. 562, 20 Ky. Law Rep. 246, 45 S.W. 890
108 Ky. 357, 21 Ky. Law Rep. 1820, 56 S.W. 525
23 Ky. Law Rep. 1016, 64 S.W. 643

**Century Case**
130 Tex. 484, 109 S.W.2d 967; 127 S.W.2d 230

**Century Freeway Case**
352 F. Supp. 1324

**Chain Broadcasting Regulations Cases**
44 F. Supp. 688; 316 U.S. 407, 86 L. Ed. 1563, 62 S. Ct. 1194
47 F. Supp. 940; 62 S. Ct. 908; 316 U.S. 407, 86 L. Ed. 1563, 62 S. Ct. 1194; 316 U.S. 447, 86 L. Ed. 1586, 62 S. Ct. 1214; 63 S. Ct. 267; 318 U.S. 740, 87 L. Ed. 120, 63 S. Ct. 560; 318 U.S. 743, 87 L. Ed. 1121, 63 S. Ct. 772; 319 U.S. 190, 87 L. Ed. 1344, 63 S. Ct. 997

**Chain Institute Case**
63 F. Supp. 229; 334 U.S. 110, 92 L. Ed. 1245, 68 S. Ct. 947; 334 U.S. 830, 92 L. Ed. 1758, 68 S. Ct. 1343

**Chain Lightning Case**
267 F.2d 439

**Chain Store Tax Cases**
301 U.S. 412, 81 L. Ed. 1193, 57 S. Ct. 772; 302 U.S. 772, 82 L. Ed. 599, 58 S. Ct. 3
38 F.2d 652; 51 S. Ct. 39; 75 L. Ed. 1474, 51 S. Ct. 651; 283 U.S. 527, 75 L. Ed. 1248, 51 S. Ct. 540
58 F.2d 991; 284 U.S. 584, 76 L. Ed. 506, 52 S. Ct. 127
6 F. Supp. 494; 294 U.S. 87, 79 L. Ed. 780, 55 S. Ct. 333; 294 U.S. 732, 79 L. Ed. 1261, 55 S. Ct. 511
12 F. Supp. 760; 299 U.S. 32, 81 L. Ed. 22, 57 S. Ct. 56
103 Fla. 1269, 141 So. 172; 104 Fla. 609, 141 So. 153; 53 S. Ct. 6; 53 S. Ct. 315; 288 U.S. 517, 77 L. Ed. 929, 53 S. Ct. 481; 109 Fla. 477, 147 So. 463, 149 So. 8; 126 Fla. 359, 171 So. 326
196 N.C. 145, 144 S.E. 701
199 N.C. 433, 154 S.E. 838; 51 S. Ct. 352, 284 U.S. 575, 76 L. Ed. 500, 52 S. Ct. 26
107 Vt. 215, 177 A. 423
218 Wis. 506, 261 N.W. 20; 296 U.S. 625, 80 L. Ed. 444, 56 S. Ct. 148

**Chamberlain Case**
132 U.S. 304, 33 L. Ed. 341, 10 S. Ct. 87

**Chambers-Hiss Case**
185 F.2d 822; 340 U.S. 948, 95 L. Ed. 683, 71 S. Ct. 532; 107 F. Supp. 128; 201 F.2d 372; 345 U.S. 942, 97 L. Ed. 1368, 73 S. Ct. 830; 88 F. Supp. 559; 9 F.R.D. 515

**Champaign County School Case**
396 Ill. 14, 71 N.E.2d 161; 67 S. Ct. 1524; 68 S. Ct. 148; 68 S. Ct. 204; 68 S. Ct. 215; 68 S. Ct. 260; 333 U.S. 203, 92 L. Ed. 649, 68 S. Ct. 461

**Champertous Assignee Case**
77 N.D. 698, 45 N.W.2d 206

**Chandler-Dunbar Cases**
229 U.S. 53, 57 L. Ed. 1063, 33 S. Ct. 667
152 F. 25; 209 U.S. 447, 52 L. Ed. 881, 28 S. Ct. 579

**Changed Neighborhood Case**
189 Md. 73, 54 A.2d 331

**Charitable Trust Case**
74 N.E.2d 833; 227 Ind. 571, 86 N.E.2d 450

**Chariton Case**
256 F. 929; 255 U.S. 539, 65 L. Ed. 764, 41 S. Ct. 400; 257 U.S. 662, 66 L. Ed. 423, 42 S. Ct. 45

**Chariton Press Case**
182 F. Supp. 788

**Charles River Bridge Case**
23 Mass. (6 Pick.) 376; 24 Mass. (7 Pick.) 344; 36 U.S. (11 Pet.) 420, 9 L. Ed. 773, 9 L. Ed. 938

**Charleston Truck Farmers Case**
6 I.C.C. 295; 74 F. 70; 83 F. 611, 27 C.C.A. 631

**Chartreuse Cases**
221 U.S. 580, 55 L. Ed. 863, 31 S. Ct. 669; 156 F. 1016; 164 F. 25

**Chase National Bank Case**
65 N.L.R.B. 827, No. 145

**Chase National Bank Fund Case**
229 F. 349; 241 U.S. 661, 60 L. Ed. 1226, 36 S. Ct. 448

**Chattanooga Board of Trade Cases**
2 I.C. 798; 3 I.C. 106; 4 I.C. 213; 85 F. 107; 99 F. 52, 39 C.C.A. 413; 181 U.S. 1, 45 L. Ed. 719, 21 S. Ct. 516
10 I.C.C. 111

**Chatterbox Cases**
21 F. 189
22 F. 822
27 F. 22; 29 F. 91
30 F. 465
31 F. 154; 145 U.S. 662, 36 L. Ed. 854, 12 S. Ct. 991

**Chautauqua Land Condemnation Case**
199 Ind. 95, 155 N.E. 465

**Cheaters' Retribution Case**
208 Okla. 570, 257 P.2d 1049

**Checkoff Case**
359 U.S. 326, 3 L. Ed. 2d 854, 79 S. Ct. 847; 256 F.2d 429; 155 F. Supp. 315; 358 U.S. 812, 3 L. Ed. 2d 56, 79 S. Ct. 60

**Cheer Up Case**
148 F.2d 909; 153 F.2d 231, 68 U.S.P.Q. (BNA) 250; 326 U.S. 727, 90 L. Ed. 431, 66 S. Ct. 32, 67 U.S.P.Q. (BNA) 360; 329 U.S. 717, 91 L. Ed. 622, 67 S. Ct. 47, 71 U.S.P.Q. (BNA) 328

**Chemical Foundation Case**
272 U.S. 1, 72 L. Ed. 131, 48 S. Ct. 12

**Cherokee Indian Cases**
30 U.S. 1, 8 L. Ed. 25
179 F. 13; 224 U.S. 413, 56 L. Ed. 820, 32 S. Ct. 424

**Cherokee Intermarriage Case**
40 Ct. Cl. 411; 203 U.S. 76, 51 L. Ed. 96, 27 S. Ct. 29

**Cherokee Tobacco Case**
78 U.S. 616, 20 L. Ed. 227

**Cherokee Trust Funds Case**
20 Ct. Cl. 449; 117 U.S. 288, 29 L. Ed. 880, 6 S. Ct. 718

**Chesapeake and Ohio Coal Case**
128 F. 59; 200 U.S. 361, 50 L. Ed. 515, 26 S. Ct. 272

**Chessman Case**
35 Cal. 2d 455, 218 P.2d 769; 340 U.S. 840, 95 L. Ed. 616, 71 S. Ct. 29; 341 U.S. 929, 95 L. Ed. 1359, 71 S. Ct. 800; 38 Cal. 2d 166, 238 P.2d 1001; 343 U.S. 915, 96 L. Ed. 1330, 72 S. Ct. 650; 343 U.S. 937, 96 L. Ed. 1344, 72 S. Ct. 773; 205 F.2d 128; 346 U.S. 916, 98 L. Ed. 42, 74 S. Ct. 278; 347 U.S. 908, 98 L. Ed. 1066, 74 S. Ct. 430; 273 P.2d 936 (Cal.); 273 P.2d 263; 43 Cal. 2d 391, 43 Cal. 2d 408, 274 P.2d 645; 348 U.S. 864, 99 L. Ed. 681, 75 S. Ct. 85; 219 F.2d 162; 128 F. Supp. 600; 221 F.2d 276; 350 U.S. 3, 100 L. Ed. 2, 76 S. Ct. 34; 44 Cal. 2d 1, 279 P.2d 24; 138 F. Supp. 761; 354 U.S. 156, 1 L. Ed. 2d 1253, 77 S. Ct. 1127; 239 F.2d 205

**Chevaux Kid Case**
16 F.2d 886; 274 U.S. 746, 71 L. Ed. 1327, 47 S. Ct. 658; 71 L. Ed. 1341, 47 S. Ct. 763

**Chewelah Case**
187 Wash. 309, 60 P.2d 263

**Chicago Anarchists Case**
122 Ill. 1, 17 N.E. 898; 123 U.S. 131, 31 L. Ed. 80, 8 S. Ct. 22

**Chicago Auditorium Case**
240 U.S. 581, 60 L. Ed. 811, 36 S. Ct. 412

**Chicago Board of Trade Case**
246 U.S. 231, 62 L. Ed. 683, 38 S. Ct. 242

**Chicago Bridge Case**
12 F. 777; 107 U.S. 678, 27 L. Ed. 442, 2 S. Ct. 185

**Chicago Conspiracy Case**
461 F.2d 389

**Chicago Drainage Canal Cases**
266 U.S. 405, 69 L. Ed. 352, 45 S. Ct. 176
278 U.S. 367, 73 L. Ed. 426, 49 S. Ct. 163

**Chicago Film Censorship Case**
365 U.S. 43, 5 L. Ed. 2d 403, 81 S. Ct. 391; 365 U.S. 856, 5 L. Ed. 2d 820, 81 S. Ct. 798; 272 F.2d 90; 180 F. Supp. 843

**Chicago Gas Case**
121 Ill. 530, 13 N.E. 169

**Chicago Junction Cases**
264 U.S. 258, 68 L. Ed. 667, 44 S. Ct. 317
71 I.C.C. 631; 150 I.C.C. 32

**Chicago Lake Front Case**
33 F. 730; 146 U.S. 387, 36 L. Ed. 1018, 13 S. Ct. 110; 154 U.S. 225, 38 L. Ed. 971, 14 S. Ct. 1015; 91 F. 955, 34 C.C.A. 138; 176 U.S. 683, 44 L. Ed. 638, 20 S. Ct. 1026; 184 U.S. 77, 46 L. Ed. 440, 22 S. Ct. 300

**Chicago Live Stock Case**
141 F. 1003; 209 U.S. 108, 52 L. Ed. 705, 28 S. Ct. 493

**Chicago No Parking Law Case**
336 Ill. 573, 168 N.E. 661

**Chicago Proportional Rates Case**
22 I.C.C. 62

**Chicago Rate Refund Case**
269 U.S. 531, 70 L. Ed. 397, 46 S. Ct. 22; 282 U.S. 133, 75 L. Ed. 255, 51 S. Ct. 65; 292 U.S. 151, 78 L. Ed. 1178, 54 S. Ct. 634; 98 F.2d 930; 102 F.2d 58

**Chicago Riot Case**
237 Ill. 46, 86 N.E. 683; 222 U.S. 313, 56 L. Ed. 215, 32 S. Ct. 92

**Chicago River Case**
353 U.S. 30, 1 L. Ed. 2d 622, 77 S. Ct. 635; 229 F.2d 926; 352 U.S. 865, 1 L. Ed. 2d 73, 77 S. Ct. 97; 353 U.S. 948, 1 L. Ed. 2d 857, 77 S. Ct. 823

**Chicago Sanitary District Diversion Case**
266 U.S. 405, 69 L. Ed. 352, 45 S. Ct. 176; 46 S. Ct. 16; 46 S. Ct. 208; 46 S. Ct. 636; 270 U.S. 634, 70 L. Ed. 772, 46 S. Ct. 354; 271 U.S. 650, 70 L. Ed. 1132, 46 S. Ct. 636; 273 U.S. 637, 71 L. Ed. 816, 47 S. Ct. 247; 273 U.S. 640, 71 L. Ed. 817, 47 S. Ct. 102; 273 U.S. 642, 71 L. Ed. 818, 47 S. Ct. 235; 273 U.S. 644, 71 L. Ed. 819, 47 S. Ct. 235; 274 U.S. 488, 71 L. Ed. 1164, 47 S. Ct. 661; 274 U.S. 712, 71 L. Ed. 1340, 47 S. Ct. 573; 72 L. Ed. 1015, 48 S. Ct. 123; 278 U.S. 367, 73 L. Ed. 426, 49 S. Ct. 163; 279 U.S. 820, 73 L. Ed. 976, 49 S. Ct. 353; 279 U.S. 821, 73 L. Ed. 976, 49 S. Ct. 349; 74 L. Ed. 1179, 50 S. Ct. 151; 281 U.S. 179, 74 L. Ed. 799, 50 S. Ct. 266; 281 U.S. 696, 74 L. Ed. 1123, 50 S. Ct. 331; 52 S. Ct. 5; 52 S. Ct. 197; 287 U.S. 568, 77 L. Ed. 500, 53 S. Ct. 4; 287 U.S. 578, 77 L. Ed. 506, 53 S. Ct. 210; 288 U.S. 587, 77 L. Ed. 967, 53 S. Ct. 316; 288 U.S. 594, 77 L. Ed. 971, 53 S. Ct. 505; 289 U.S. 395, 77 L. Ed. 1283, 53 S. Ct. 671; 289 U.S. 710, 77 L. Ed. 1465, 53 S. Ct. 671, 53 S. Ct. 788; 309 U.S. 569, 84 L. Ed. 953, 60 S. Ct. 789; 309 U.S. 636, 84 L. Ed. 992, 60 S. Ct. 791; 311 U.S. 107, 85 L. Ed. 73, 61 S. Ct. 154; 61 S. Ct. 831; 61 S. Ct. 832; 313 U.S. 547, 85 L. Ed. 1513, 61 S. Ct. 1090, 61 S. Ct. 1091; 340 U.S. 858, 95 L. Ed. 628, 71 S. Ct. 85, 71 S. Ct. 86

**Chicago Seven Cases**
461 F.2d 389
472 F.2d 340

**Chicago Sunday Closing Case**
238 Ill. 593, 87 N.E. 840

**Chicago Terminal Switching Cases**
164 F. 638; 215 U.S. 98, 54 L. Ed. 112, 30 S. Ct. 66
7 I.C.C. 513; 7 I.C.C. 555a; 94 F. 272; 98 F. 173; 103 F. 249, 43 C.C.A. 209; 186 U.S. 320, 46 L. Ed. 1182, 22 S. Ct. 824; 10 I.C.C. 83; 11 I.C.C. 277; 12 I.C.C. 6; 12 I.C.C. 507
10 I.C.C. 385

**Chicago Warehouse Cases**
94 U.S. 113, 24 L. Ed. 77

**Chickasaw Freedmen Case**
38 Ct. Cl. 558; 193 U.S. 115, 48 L. Ed. 640, 24 S. Ct. 411

**Chickasaw Indian Cases**
179 F. 13, 103 C.C.A. 1; 224 U.S. 448, 56 L. Ed. 834, 32 S. Ct. 494
199 F. 811

**Chicken Case**
76 F.2d 617; 295 U.S. 495, 79 L. Ed. 1570, 55 S. Ct. 837; 295 U.S. 723, 79 L. Ed. 1676, 55 S. Ct. 651

**Chicken of the Sea Case**
50 F.2d 976; 3 U.S.P.Q. (BNA) 206

**Chicken Plucking Machine Case**
185 F.2d 722; 188 F.2d 880

**Chicken Salad Case**
187 S.W. 367 (Tex.); 108 Tex. 14, 191 S.W. 1138, 193 S.W. 139

**Child Abuse Confrontation Cases**
497 U.S. 805, 111 L. Ed. 2d 638, 110 S. Ct. 3139 (1990)
497 U.S. 836, 111 L. Ed. 2d 666, 110 S. Ct. 3157 (1990)

**Child Abuse Liability Case**
489 U.S. 189, 103 L. Ed. 2d 249, 109 S. Ct. 998

**Child Labor Case**
247 U.S. 251, 62 L. Ed. 1101, 38 S. Ct. 529

**Child Labor Tax Cases**
259 U.S. 20, 66 L. Ed. 817, 42 S. Ct. 449
274 F. 639; 259 U.S. 16, 66 L. Ed. 816, 42 S. Ct. 419
276 F. 452; 259 U.S. 20, 66 L. Ed. 817, 42 S. Ct. 449
250 Ill. 303, 95 N.E. 204; 231 U.S. 320, 58 L. Ed. 245, 34 S. Ct. 60

**Child Pornography Possession Case**
495 U.S. 103, 109 L. Ed. 2d 98, 110 S. Ct. 1691

**Child Pornography Cases**
458 U.S. 747, 73 L. Ed. 2d 1113, 102 S. Ct. 3348
573 U.S. 64, 130 L. Ed. 2d 372, 115 S. Ct. 464 (1994)

**Child Support Tax-Refund Intercept Case**
475 U.S. 851, 89 L. Ed. 2d 855, 106 S. Ct. 1600

**Child Support Venue Case**
218 Miss. 459, 67 So. 2d 459

**Children's Books Cases**
297 F. Supp. 385; 297 F. Supp. 1352; 299 F. Supp. 1139
376 F. Supp. 602

**Child's Contributory Negligence Case**
269 A.D. 997, 58 N.Y.S.2d 382; 269 A.D. 1050, 59 N.Y.S.2d 281; 295 N.Y. 436, 68 N.E.2d 431

**Child's Deposition Case**
156 Ohio St. 525, 103 N.E.2d 552

**Chinchilla Case**
70 Cal. App. 2d 103, 160 P.2d 846

**Chinese Cabin Waiter Case**
13 F. 286

**Chinese Cases**
140 U.S. 676, 35 L. Ed. 599, 11 S. Ct. 1018
140 U.S. 676, 35 L. Ed. 602, 11 S. Ct. 1018

**Chinese Copy Case**
269 F.2d 255; 361 U.S. 915, 4 L. Ed. 2d 185, 80 S. Ct. 259, 123
U.S.P.Q. (BNA) 590; 287 F.2d 417, 128 U.S.P.Q. (BNA) 408

**Chinese Exclusion Cases**
149 U.S. 698, 37 L. Ed. 905, 13 S. Ct. 1016
36 F. 431; 130 U.S. 581, 32 L. Ed. 1068, 9 S. Ct. 623

**Chinese Fisherman Case**
2 F. 733

**Chinese Laborer Case**
21 F. 791; 112 U.S. 536, 28 L. Ed. 770, 5 S. Ct. 255

**Chinese Laborers on Shipboard Case**
13 F. 291

**Chinese Laundry Cases**
68 Cal. 294, 9 P. 139; 26 F. 471; 118 U.S. 356, 30 L. Ed. 220, 6 S. Ct. 1064

**Chinese Merchant Case**
13 F. 605

**Chinese Pigtail Case**
F. Cas. No. 6,546

**Chinese Tax Case**
14 F. 338

**Chinese Wash-Houses Case**
4 Haw. 335

**Chinese Wife Case**
21 F. 785; 21 F. 808; 113 U.S. 216, 28 L. Ed. 983, 5 S. Ct. 431

**Chippewa Falls Gas Rate Case**
183 Wis. 96, 197 N.W. 359

**Chloromycetin Case**
38 Cal. Rptr. 183

**Chocolate Case**
316 Pa. 300, 175 A. 697

**Choctaw Indian Cases**
179 F. 13, 103 C.C.A. 1; 224 U.S. 448, 56 L. Ed. 834, 32 S. Ct. 494
199 F. 811

**Christian Science Publishing Society Cases**
240 Mass. 55, 132 N.E. 852
240 Mass. 88, 132 N.E. 865
240 Mass. 93, 132 N.E. 865

**Christie Case**
48 Ct. Cl. 293; 237 U.S. 234, 59 L. Ed. 933, 35 S. Ct. 565

**Chromium Plating Case**
53 F.2d 390; 60 F.2d 913; 288 U.S. 600, 77 L. Ed. 976, 53 S. Ct. 319

**Church Access to School Case**
508 U.S. 384, 124 L. Ed. 2d 352, 113 S. Ct. 2141 (1993)

**Church Case**
49 R.I. 269, 141 A. 703

**CIA Case**
471 U.S. 159, 85 L. Ed. 2d 173, 105 S. Ct. 1881

**Cigarette-Cancer Cases**
234 F.2d 170; 358 U.S. 875, 3 L. Ed. 2d 105, 79 S. Ct. 112; 256 F.2d 464; 158 F. Supp. 22
295 F.2d 292; 134 F. Supp. 829
328 F.2d 3; 164 F. Supp. 683
154 So. 2d 169 (Fla.)

**Cigarette Liability Case**
505 U.S. 504, 120 L. Ed. 2d 407, 112 S. Ct. 2608

**Cigarworkers Case**
98 N.Y. 98

**Cinmino's Case**
251 Mass. 158, 146 N.E. 245

**Circus Cases**
280 F. 959; 299 F. 142; 266 U.S. 582, 69 L. Ed. 452, 45 S. Ct. 94; 266 U.S. 610, 69 L. Ed. 466, 45 S. Ct. 94
56 Mich. 111, 22 N.W. 215
12 Wend. 383

**Circus Poster Case**
188 U.S. 239, 47 L. Ed. 460, 23 S. Ct. 298; 104 F. 993

**Citizenship Requirement Case**
454 U.S. 432, 70 L. Ed. 2d 677, 102 S. Ct. 735

**Citrus Fruit Case**
9 I.C.C. 182; 123 F. 597; 132 F. 829; 137 F. 606; 10 I.C.C. 590; 200 U.S. 536, 50 L. Ed. 585, 26 S.Ct. 330

**City and County Consolidation Case**
70 Mont. 355, 225 P. 1007

**City Antitrust Liability Case**
435 U.S. 389, 55 L. Ed. 2d 364, 98 S. Ct. 1123 (1978)

**City Bond Case**
89 Mont. 109, 89 Mont. 128, 297 P. 455

**City Manager Cases**
201 Ind. 88, 166 N.E. 270
201 Ind. 123, 166 N.E. 281
201 Ind. 286, 168 N.E. 10

**City of Dawson Case**
130 F. 152; 197 U.S. 178, 49 L. Ed. 713, 25 S. Ct. 420

**City Rent Ceiling Case**
475 U.S. 260, 89 L. Ed. 2d 206, 106 S. Ct. 1045

**City Slip Cases**
16 Cal. 591
18 Cal. 590
21 Cal. 351
23 Cal. 314
33 Cal. 134

**Civil Rights Act Retroactivity Cases**
511 U.S. 244, 128 L. Ed. 2d 229, 114 S. Ct. 1483 (1994)
511 U.S. 298, 128 L. Ed. 2d 274, 114 S. Ct. 1510 (1994)

**Civil Rights Attorney's Fee Case**
461 U.S. 424, 76 L. Ed. 2d 40, 103 S. Ct. 1933
471 U.S. 234, 85 L. Ed. 2d 233, 105 S. Ct. 1923

**Civil Rights Cases**
109 U.S. 3, 27 L. Ed. 835, 3 S. Ct. 18
27 Cal. 2d 478, 165 P.2d 3
332 U.S. 46, 91 L. Ed. 1903, 67 S. Ct. 1672

*Continued*

332 U.S. 784, 92 L. Ed. 367, 68 S. Ct. 27
333 U.S. 831, 92 L. Ed. 1115, 68 S. Ct. 610
167 F.2d 996
334 U.S. 834, 92 L. Ed. 1761, 68 S. Ct. 1342
378 U.S. 226, 12 L. Ed. 2d 822, 84 S. Ct. 1814
33 Cal. 2d 286, 201 P.2d 537
34 Cal. 2d 320, 210 P.2d 13
470 F. Supp. 664

**Civil Rights Lateral Estoppel Case**
449 U.S. 90, 66 L. Ed. 2d 308, 101 S. Ct. 411

**Civil Rights Trespass Cases**
373 U.S. 244, 10 L. Ed. 2d 323, 83 S. Ct. 1119, 83 S. Ct. 1133
373 U.S. 267, 10 L. Ed. 2d 338, 83 S. Ct. 1122
378 U.S. 153, 12 L. Ed. 2d 771, 84 S. Ct. 1693

**Civil Servant's Tax Liability Cases**
304 U.S. 405, 82 L. Ed. 1427, 58 S. Ct. 969
306 U.S. 466, 83 L. Ed. 927, 59 S. Ct. 595

**Civil Service Cases**
171 Ill. 44, 49 N.E. 229; 170 U.S. 182, 42 L. Ed. 998, 18 S. Ct. 550
416 U.S. 134, 40 L. Ed. 2d 15, 94 S. Ct. 163

**Claflin Cases**
19 F. 599; 62 F. 453; 66 F. 7, 13 C.C.A. 281, 76 F. 227, 22 C.C.A. 138; 82 F. 744, 27 C.C.A. 255, 166 U.S. 721, 41 L. Ed. 1187, 17 S. Ct. 992
86 F. 964; 88 F. 122, 31 C.C.A. 419

**Clapper Case**
51 F.2d 992; 284 U.S. 221, 76 L. Ed. 254, 52 S. Ct. 118; 286 U.S. 145, 76 L. Ed. 1026, 52 S. Ct. 571

**Clark Case**
66 Ill. App. 284; 171 Ill. 235, 49 N.E. 481

**Class Action Case**
417 U.S. 156, 40 L. Ed. 2d 732, 94 S. Ct. 2140

**Clay Case**
133 So. 2d 735 (Ala)

**Clayton College Case**
30 Colo. 231, 70 P. 429

**Clear and Present Danger Case**
253 F. 212; 249 U.S. 47, 63 L. Ed. 470, 39 S. Ct. 247

**Clear Channel Case**
284 F.2d 222

**Clearfield Case**
130 F.2d 93; 318 U.S. 363, 87 L. Ed. 838, 63 S. Ct. 573; 317 U.S. 619, 87 L. Ed. 502, 63 S. Ct. 258

**Clergy Disqualification Case**
435 U.S. 618, 55 L. Ed. 2d 593, 98 S. Ct. 1322

**Cleveland Passenger Terminal Cases**
70 I.C.C. 342; 56 F.2d 720
70 I.C.C. 659; 56 F.2d 721

**Cleveland Strike Case**
90 F. 598; 90 F. 608

**Clifford Case**
309 U.S. 331, 84 L. Ed. 788, 60 S. Ct. 554; 105 F.2d 586; 111 F.2d 896; 38 B.T.A. 1532; 308 U.S. 542, 84 L. Ed. 457, 60 S. Ct. 139

**Clinton Bridge Case**
F. Cas. No. 2,900; 77 U.S. 454, 19 L. Ed. 969

**Cliquot's Champagne Case**
70 U.S. 114, 18 L. Ed. 116

**Closed Shop Cases**
172 F. 963; 176 F. 549, 100 C.C.A. 137; 202 F. 512; 214 F. 685, 131 C.C.A. 425; 221 F. 1022, 136 C.C.A. 665; 241 U.S. 644, 60 L. Ed. 1218, 36 S. Ct. 450; 245 U.S. 229, 62 L. Ed. 260, 38 S. Ct. 65
219 F. 719, 135 C.C.A. 417; 221 F. 1022, 136 C.C.A. 664; 245 U.S. 275, 62 L. Ed. 286, 38 S. Ct. 80

**Closure Order Case**
448 U.S. 555, 65 L. Ed. 2d 973, 100 S. Ct. 2814

**Cloth Cases**

F. Cas. No. 2,902

**Clothing Wool Cases**

Treas. Dec. 39473, Gen. Appraisers 8613; Treas. Dec. 40019, 12 Ct. Cust. 62

Treas. Dec. 40368, Gen. Appraisers 8842; Treas. Dec. 40784, 12 Ct. Cust. 557; 269 U.S. 542, 70 L. Ed. 402, 46 S. Ct. 20; 274 U.S. 225, 71 L. Ed. 1013, 47 S. Ct. 616

Treas. Dec. 44460; Treas. Dec. 45388, 19 C.C.P.A. (Customs) 259; Treas. Dec. 45514; Treas. Dec. 45575; 56 F.2d 892, 19 C.C.P.A. (Patents) 1079; Abs. (n.s.) No. 20471; 287 U.S. 619, 77 L. Ed. 538, 53 S. Ct. 20

**Club Cracker Case**

7 F. Supp. 211

**Club House Gin Case**

7 Bosw. (20 N.Y. Super.Ct.) 222

**Coach Company Case**

28 N.J. Eq. 145

29 N.J. Eq. 299

31 N.J. Eq. 525

33 N.J. Eq. 267

**Coal Creek Case**

22 I.C.C. 233; 197 F. 66

**Coal Dust Nuisance Case**

254 Wis. 194, 36 N.W.2d 97

**Coal Hole Cases**

78 Vt. 349, 62 A. 1019

184 N.Y.S. 337

194 A.D. 696, 186 N.Y.S. 278

195 A.D. 942, 186 N.Y.S. 938

232 N.Y. 220, 133 N.E. 567

**Coal Movement Rates Case**

459 U.S. 131, 74 L. Ed. 2d 311, 103 S. Ct. 514

**Coal Rate Cases**

19 N.D. 45, 120 N.W. 869; 19 N.D. 57, 120 N.W. 874; 216 U.S. 579, 54 L. Ed. 624, 30 S. Ct. 423; 216 U.S. 581, 54 L. Ed. 1212, 30 S. Ct. 698, 31 S. Ct. 218; 26 N.D. 438, 145 N.W. 135; 236 U.S. 585, 59 L. Ed. 735, 35 S. Ct. 429

19 N.D. 57, 120 N.W. 874; 216 U.S. 581, 54 L. Ed. 1212, 30 S. Ct. 698, 31 S. Ct. 218

35 N.D. 331, 160 N.W. 140; 254 U.S. 376, 65 L. Ed. 312, 41 S. Ct. 142

40 N.D. 69, 168 N.W. 684; 254 U.S. 370, 65 L. Ed. 310, 41 S. Ct. 140

**Coal Severance Tax Case**

453 U.S. 609, 69 L. Ed. 2d 884, 101 S. Ct. 2946

**Coast Line Dividend Cases**

102 Md. 73, 61 A. 295

**Coastal Bend Case**

234 F.2d 686; 231 F.2d 498, 97 App. D.C. 339

**Coastal Highway Case**

137 S.C. 496, 135 S.E. 538

**Coca Cola Cases**

191 F. 431; 215 F. 535, 132 C.C.A. 47; 241 U.S. 265, 60 L. Ed. 995, 36 S. Ct. 573

269 F. 796

16 A.D.2d 196, 226 N.Y.S.2d 464

**Cocoanut Oil Processing Tax Case**

301 U.S. 308, 81 L. Ed. 1122, 57 S. Ct. 764

**Coconspirator Statement Case**

475 U.S. 387, 89 L. Ed. 2d 390, 106 S. Ct. 1121

**Codefendant's Confession Case**

442 U.S. 62, 60 L. Ed. 2d 713, 99 S. Ct. 2132

476 U.S. 530, 90 L. Ed. 2d 514, 106 S. Ct. 2056

**Coerced Confession Harmless Error Case**

499 U.S. 279, 113 L. Ed. 2d 302, 111 S. Ct. 1246

**Coffee Grinder Case**
68 Mass. 15, 46 N.E. 115

**Coffee Mill Case**
124 F. 923; 131 F. 240, 65 C.C.A. 587

**Coffee Urn Case**
247 A.D. 895, 287 N.Y.S. 118; 273 N.Y. 485, 6 N.E.2d 415; 271 N.Y. 664

**Coffee Urn Explosion Case**
125 A.D. 69, 109 N.Y.S. 172; 195 N.Y. 478, 88 N.E. 1063

**Cohan Case**
39 F.2d 540; 20 B.T.A. 1260; 11 B.T.A. 743

**Cohen Case**
264 F. 218; 255 U.S. 81, 65 L. Ed. 516, 41 S. Ct. 298

**Cohn Cases**
112 F. 1009; 119 F. 505, 56 C.C.A. 185
38 T.C. 387

**Cold Sunday Case**
78 Miss. 140, 28 So. 807

**Colgate Case**
253 F. 522; 250 U.S. 300, 63 L. Ed. 992, 39 S. Ct. 465

**Collective Bargaining Agreement Rejection Case**
465 U.S. 513, 79 L. Ed. 2d 482, 104 S. Ct. 1188

**Collective Bargaining Unit Case**
469 U.S. 490, 83 L. Ed. 2d 986, 105 S. Ct. 984

**Collins Cases**
245 F. 811; 259 F. 172, 170 C.C.A. 240; 250 U.S. 637, 63 L. Ed. 1183, 39 S. Ct. 490; 253 U.S. 77, 64 L. Ed. 790, 40 S. Ct. 450
36 Va. (9 Leigh) 666

**Collision Damage Insurance Case**
213 Miss. 520, 57 So. 2d 158; 220 Miss. 740, 71 So. 2d 765

**Colorado Anti-Trust Law Case**
9 F.2d 176; 274 U.S. 445, 71 L. Ed. 1146, 47 S. Ct. 681

**Colorado Gay Rights Case**
517 U.S. 620, 134 L. Ed. 2d 855, 116 S. Ct. 1620 (1996)

**Colorado Products Case**
83 Colo. 329, 266 P. 214

**Colorado River Water Case**
373 U.S. 546, 10 L. Ed. 2d 542, 83 S. Ct. 1468; 344 U.S. 919, 97 L. Ed. 708, 73 S. Ct. 385; 347 U.S. 985, 98 L. Ed. 1121, 74 S. Ct. 848; 350 U.S. 114, 100 L. Ed. 125, 76 S. Ct. 188; 350 U.S. 812, 100 L. Ed. 728, 76 S. Ct. 43; 364 U.S. 940, 81 S. Ct. 457; 374 U.S. 819, 83 S. Ct. 1860; 375 U.S. 892, 11 L. Ed. 2d 122, 84 S. Ct. 144; 376 U.S. 340, 11 L. Ed. 2d 757, 84 S. Ct. 755; 377 U.S. 921, 12 L. Ed. 2d 214, 84 S. Ct. 1218

**Colored Passenger Cases**
4 F. 37; 5 F. 499; 7 F. 51
11 F. 683
38 F. 226
186 F. 966, 109 C.C.A. 110; 235 U.S. 151, 59 L. Ed. 169, 35 S. Ct. 69
1 I.C. 314; 1 I.C. 493; 1 I.C. 719
2 I.C. 392,
12 I.C.C. 247
229 I.C.C. 703; 313 U.S. 80, 85 L. Ed. 1201, 61 S. Ct. 873
125 Ky. 299, 30 Ky. L. Rep. 1332, 101 S.W. 386; 218 U.S. 71, 54 L. Ed. 936, 30 S. Ct. 667

**Columbia Broadcasting Case**
121 N.L.R.B. 1207, No. 158; 272 F.2d 713; 364 U.S. 573, 5 L. Ed. 2d 302, 81 S. Ct. 330; 119 N.L.R.B. 594, No. 71

**Columbia College Case**
87 N.Y. 311

**Columbia Digger Company Case**
227 F. 780, 142 C.C.A. 304

**Columbian Case**

96 F.2d 948; 305 U.S. 583, 83 L. Ed. 368, 59 S. Ct. 86; 306 U.S. 292, 83 L. Ed. 660, 59 S. Ct. 501

**Commission Dealers Case**

124 Mich. 664, 83 N.W. 594

**Commodities Clause Cases**

164 F. 215; 213 U.S. 366, 53 L. Ed. 836, 29 S. Ct. 527; 176 F. 1015; 220 U.S. 257, 55 L. Ed. 458, 31 S. Ct. 387

225 F. 399; 254 U.S. 255, 65 L. Ed. 253, 41 S. Ct. 104; 254 U.S. 617, 65 L. Ed. 440, 41 S. Ct. 149

**Commodity Exchange Act Case**

456 U.S. 353, 72 L. Ed. 2d 182, 102 S. Ct. 1825

**Common Purchaser Case**

59 F.2d 750

**Communications Dual Property Pre-Emption Case**

476 U.S. 355, 90 L. Ed. 2d 369, 106 S. Ct. 1890

**Communist Cases**

203 F.2d 20, 91 App. D.C. 344; 347 U.S. 1008, 98 L. Ed. 1133, 94 S. Ct. 861; 349 U.S. 155, 99 L. Ed. 964, 75 S. Ct. 668

95 F. Supp. 1010; 95 F. Supp. 1012; 203 F.2d 54, 91 App. D.C. 378; 346 U.S. 809, 98 L. Ed. 338, 74 S. Ct. 23; 347 U.S. 1006, 98 L. Ed. 1132, 74 S. Ct. 861; 349 U.S. 190, 99 L. Ed. 997, 75 S. Ct. 687

203 F.2d 45, 91 App. D.C. 370; 347 U.S. 1011, 98 L. Ed. 1134, 74 S. Ct. 872; 349 U.S. 219, 99 L. Ed. 1016, 75 S. Ct. 712

**Communist Conspiracy Case**

79 F. Supp. 422; 80 F. Supp. 479; 81 F. Supp. 280; 170 F.2d 632; 81 F. Supp. 281; 83 F. Supp. 197; 176 F.2d 78; 9 F.R.D. 367, 183 F.2d 201; 184 F.2d 280; 340 U.S. 863, 95 L. Ed. 630, 71 S. Ct. 691; 340 U.S. 887, 95 L. Ed. 644, 71 S. Ct. 133; 341 U.S. 494, 95 L. Ed. 1137, 71 S. Ct. 857; 342 U.S. 842, 95 L. Ed. 636, 72 S. Ct. 20

**Communist Deportation Cases**

95 F.2d 976; 96 F.2d 1020; 305 U.S. 587, 83 L. Ed. 371, 59 S. Ct. 102; 307 U.S. 22, 83 L. Ed. 1082, 59 S. Ct. 694

90 F. Supp. 397; 90 F. Supp. 431; 187 F.2d 137; 342 U.S. 580, 96 L. Ed. 586, 72 S. Ct. 512; 343 U.S. 936, 96 L. Ed. 1344, 72 S. Ct. 767, 72 S. Ct. 768

**Communist Party Case**

367 U.S. 1, 6 L. Ed. 2d 625, 81 S. Ct. 1357; 351 U.S. 115, 100 L. Ed. 1003, 76 S. Ct. 663; 361 U.S. 951, 4 L. Ed. 2d 536, 80 S. Ct. 502; 367 U.S. 203, 6 L. Ed. 2d 782, 81 S. Ct. 1469; 367 U.S. 290, 6 L. Ed. 2d 836, 81 S. Ct. 1517; 367 U.S. 389, 6 L. Ed. 2d 919, 81 S. Ct. 1465; 368 U.S. 871, 7 L. Ed. 2d 72, 82 S. Ct. 20; 223 F.2d 531; 254 F.2d 314; 277 F.2d 78; 96 F. Supp. 47

**Communist Schoolteacher Case**

96 Misc. 873, 95 N.Y.S.2d 114; 276 A.D. 527, 96 N.Y.S.2d 466; 301 N.Y. 476, 95 N.E.2d 806; 342 U.S. 485, 96 L. Ed. 517, 72 S. Ct. 380

**Communist's Lawyer Contempt Case**

9 F.R.D. 394; 182 F.2d 416; 341 U.S. 952, 95 L. Ed. 1374, 71 S. Ct. 1010; 342 U.S. 858, 96 L. Ed. 646, 72 S. Ct. 84; 343 U.S. 1, 96 L. Ed. 717, 72 S. Ct. 451; 343 U.S. 931, 96 L. Ed. 1341, 72 S. Ct. 756, 93 S. Ct. 756, 93 S. Ct. 762

**Community Antenna Case**

211 F. Supp. 47; 335 F.2d 348, 142 U.S.P.Q. (BNA) 249

**Community Income Tax Case**

282 U.S. 101, 75 L. Ed. 239, 51 S. Ct. 58

**Commutation Rate Cases**

21 I.C.C. 428

27 I.C.C. 549

126 Md. 59, 94 A. 330; 245 U.S. 6, 62 L. Ed. 117, 38 S. Ct. 2

**Compania General Case**

249 U.S. 425, 63 L. Ed. 687, 39 S. Ct. 332

**Complaining Officer Immunity Case**
475 U.S. 335, 89 L. Ed. 2d 271, 106 S. Ct. 1092

**Compulsory Medical Care Case**
411 Ill. 618, 104 N.E.2d 769; 344 U.S. 824, 97 L. Ed. 642, 73 S. Ct. 24

**Compulsory Pension Plan Case**
439 U.S. 551, 58 L. Ed. 2d 808, 99 S. Ct. 790

**Compulsory School Law Case**
296 F. 928; 268 U.S. 510, 69 L. Ed. 1070, 45 S. Ct. 571

**Conatser Case**
61 Ark. 560, 33 S.W. 1057

**Concealed Purchaser Case**
171 F.2d 613; 336 U.S. 925, 93 L. Ed. 1086, 69 S. Ct. 656

**Concealment Case**
84 Off. Gaz. Pat. Office 147, 13 App. D.C. 86, 1898 C.D. 510

**Concealment Limitations Case**
321 Mass. 195, 72 N.E.2d 410

**Condemned Laundry Case**
166 F.2d 856; 335 U.S. 807, 93 L. Ed. 363, 69 S. Ct. 30; 338 U.S. 1, 93 L. Ed. 1765, 69 S. Ct. 1434

**Conditional Gift Deduction Case**
2 T.C. 1268; 151 F.2d 592; 327 U.S. 788, 90 L. Ed. 1014, 66 S. Ct. 807

**Conductor's Report Case**
241 Minn. 15, 62 N.W.2d 688

**Coney Island Park Case**
171 A.D. 834, 157 N.Y.S. 1015

**Confederate Money Case**
31 Tex. 675

**Confederate Note Case**
86 U.S. 548, 22 L. Ed. 196

**Confidential Proceedings Publishing Case**
435 U.S. 929, 56 L. Ed. 2d 1, 98 S. Ct. 1535

**Confiscation Case**
74 U.S. 454, 19 L. Ed. 196

**Confiscation Cases (Land)**
F. Cas. No. 3,097; 87 U.S. 92, 22 L. Ed. 320; 87 U.S. 114, 22 L. Ed. 327; 87 U.S. 115, 22 L. Ed. 328

**Confiscation Cases (Ships)**
74 U.S. 454, 19 L. Ed. 196

**Conflict of Interest in Representation Case**
435 U.S. 475, 55 L. Ed. 2d 426, 98 S. Ct. 1173

**Confrontation Clause and Harmless Error Case**
475 U.S. 673, 89 L. Ed. 2d 674, 106 S. Ct. 1431

**Confusion of Goods Case**
1 Utah 2d 180, 264 P.2d 283

**Congressional Reapportionment Case**
184 Minn. 228, 238 N.W. 494; 184 Minn. 647, 238 N.W. 792; 186 Minn. 331, 243 N.W. 133; 284 U.S. 616, 76 L. Ed. 526, 52 S. Ct. 266; 285 U.S. 355, 76 L. Ed. 795, 52 S. Ct. 397

**Congressional Redistricting Cases**
515 U.S. 737, 132 L. Ed. 2d 635, 115 S. Ct. 2431 (1995)
515 U.S. 900, 132 L. Ed. 2d 762, 115 S. Ct. 2475 (1995)
517 U.S. 899, 135 L. Ed. 2d 207, 116 S. Ct. 1894 (1996)
517 U.S. 952, 135 L. Ed. 2d 248, 116 S. Ct. 1941 (1996)

**Congressional Veto Case**
462 U.S. 919, 77 L. Ed. 2d 317, 103 S. Ct. 2764

**Conrod-Forgay Case**
47 U.S. 201, 12 L. Ed. 404

**Consent to Adoption Case**
441 U.S. 380, 60 L. Ed. 2d 297, 99 S. Ct. 1760

**Consolidated Edison Case**
305 U.S. 197, 83 L. Ed. 126, 59 S. Ct. 206

**Consolidated Gas Cases**
146 F. 150
157 F. 849; 212 U.S. 19, 53 L. Ed. 382, 29 S. Ct. 192
256 F. 238; 260 F. 1022; 250 U.S. 671, 63 L. Ed. 1199, 40 S. Ct. 15; 253 U.S. 219, 64 L. Ed. 870, 40 S. Ct. 511; 267 F. 231; 274 F. 986; 258 U.S. 165, 66 L. Ed. 538, 42 S. Ct. 264; 259 U.S. 101, 66 L. Ed. 844, 42 S. Ct. 438
260 F. 244
291 F. 704; 264 U.S. 571, 68 L. Ed. 855, 44 S. Ct. 401; 265 U.S. 78, 68 L. Ed. 909, 44 S. Ct. 481
6 F.2d 243; 6 F.2d 281; 272 U.S. 576, 71 L. Ed. 420, 47 S. Ct. 198

**Consolidated Shipment Case**
14 I.C.C. 422; 21 I.C.C. 300

**Consolidated Southwestern Cases**
123 I.C.C. 203; 139 I.C.C. 535; 144 I.C.C. 630; 147 I.C.C. 165; 148 I.C.C. 282; 148 I.C.C. 613; 155 I.C.C. 504; 159 I.C.C. 93; 164 I.C.C. 565; 169 I.C.C. 789; 173 I.C.C. 263; 179 I.C.C. 17; 183 I.C.C. 405; 183 I.C.C. 665; 185 I.C.C. 357; 185 I.C.C. 799; 188 I.C.C. 307; 191 I.C.C. 236; 194 I.C.C. 381

**Consortium Limitations Case**
75 N.D. 418, 28 N.W.2d 530

**Constance Case**
215 F.2d 571; 348 U.S. 913, 99 L. Ed. 716, 75 S. Ct. 294

**Constitutional Language Case**
107 Neb. 657, 187 N.W. 100; 262 U.S. 390, 67 L. Ed. 1042, 43 S. Ct. 625

**Constructive Desertion Case**
207 Miss. 500, 42 So. 2d 720

**Constructive Eviction Case**
196 S.W.2d 954 (Tex.); 146 Tex. 66, 202 S.W.2d 832

**Consumer Anti-Trust Case**
442 U.S. 330, 60 L. Ed. 2d 931, 99 S. Ct. 2326

**Contagious Disease as Handicap Case**
480 U.S. 273, 94 L. Ed. 2d 307, 107 S. Ct. 1123

**Contaminated Kerosene Cases**
139 Mich. 18, 102 N.W. 227
198 Mich. 222, 164 N.W. 668,
225 Mich. 344, 196 N.W. 339; 235 Mich. 53, 209 N.W.118
235 Mich. 15, 209 N.W. 172
265 Mich. 19, 251 N.W. 402
273 Mich. 536, 263 N.W. 875

**Contempt Cases**
220 F. 458; 237 F. 986, 150 C.C.A. 636; 247 U.S. 402, 62 L. Ed. 1186, 38 S. Ct. 560
266 F. 230; 279 F. 900; 274 F. 177; 282 F. 138; 263 U.S. 255, 68 L. Ed. 293, 44 S. Ct. 103

**Contempt-Pardon Case**
44 S. Ct. 634; 267 U.S. 87, 69 L. Ed. 527, 45 S. Ct. 332

**Continental Employee Bargaining Unit**
54 U.S. 170, 70 L. Ed. 2d 323, 102 S. Ct. 21

**Continental Oil Case**
256 U.S. 642, 65 L. Ed. 1139, 41 S. Ct. 606

**Contingent Marriage Trust Case**
169 Pa. Super. 226, 82 A.2d 262

**Continuity of Possession Case**
95 Ohio App. 93, 117 N.E.2d 489

**Contraceptive Advertising Case**
431 U.S. 678, 52 L. Ed. 2d 675, 97 S. Ct. 2010

**Contract Doctor's Monopoly Case**
95 F. Supp. 103; 71 S. Ct. 615; 343 U.S. 326, 96 L. Ed. 978, 72 S. Ct. 690

**Contract Price Limitation Cases**
58 Ark. 7, 22 S.W. 884
77 Ark. 156, 93 S.W. 67
85 Ark. 407, 108 S.W. 509
87 Ark. 56, 112 S.W. 174
107 Ark. 245, 154 S.W. 952

**Contributions Guest Case**
152 Ohio St. 50, 87 N.E.2d 87

**Conveyance to Debtor's Spouse Case**
194 Va. 191, 72 S.E.2d 349

**Convict Labor Cases**
Also Known as Convict-Made Goods Cases
297 U.S. 431, 80 L. Ed. 778, 56 S. Ct. 532
299 U.S. 334, 81 L. Ed. 270, 57 S. Ct. 277; 299 U.S. 525, 81 L. Ed. 386, 57 S. Ct. 19

**Conway's Express Case**
195 F.2d 906; 87 N.L.R.B. 972, No. 130

**Cook-Danelon Cases**
29 F.2d 314; 30 F.2d 242; 279 U.S. 850, 73 L. Ed. 993, 49 S. Ct. 346
31 F.2d 785; 24 F.2d 649; 278 U.S. 607, 73 L. Ed. 534, 49 S. Ct. 12; 278 U.S. 594, 73 L. Ed. 525, 49 S. Ct. 78; 279 U.S. 231, 73 L. Ed. 677, 49 S. Ct. 274

**Cookingham Case**
87 F. Supp. 203; 184 F.2d 213, 1950 A.M.C. 1793; 340 U.S. 935, 95 L. Ed. 675, 71 S. Ct. 495

**Cook's Goldblume Case**
441 F.2d 675

**Cook's Point Case**
98 F. Supp. 730; 198 F.2d 812; 204 F.2d 238

**Cooley Case**
72 Mass. (6 Gray) 350

**Cooper Will Case**
53 N.J. Eq. 682, 33 A. 1050; 56 N.J. Eq. 759, 36 A. 281; 61 N.J.L. 368, 39 A. 679; 61 N.J.L. 687, 40 A. 599, 41 A. 251, 59 N.J. Eq. 204, 45 A. 381

**Cooperative Member Expulsion Case**
472 U.S. 284, 86 L. Ed. 2d 202, 105 S. Ct. 2613

**Cooper's Case**
138 U.S. 404, 34 L. Ed. 993, 11 S. Ct. 289; 143 U.S. 472, 36 L. Ed. 232, 12 S. Ct. 453

**Copley Square Case**
174 Mass. 476, 55 N.E. 77; 178 Mass. 330, 59 N.E. 812; 188 U.S. 491, 47 L. Ed. 559, 23 S. Ct. 440

**Coplon Case**
84 F. Supp. 472; 88 F. Supp. 910; 88 F. Supp. 912; 88 F. Supp. 915; 88 F. Supp. 921; 89 F. Supp. 142; 89 F. Supp. 664; 91 F. Supp. 867; 185 F.2d 629; 191 F.2d 749; 342 U.S. 920, 96 L. Ed. 688, 72 S. Ct. 362; 342 U.S. 926, 96 L. Ed. 690, 72 S. Ct. 363

**Coppage Case**
87 Kan. 752, 125 P. 8; 236 U.S. 1, 59 L. Ed. 441, 35 S. Ct. 240

**Corcoran Case**
68 U.S. 604, 17 L. Ed. 619

**Corn Planter Patent Case**
F. Cas. No. 2,030; 90 U.S. 181, 23 L. Ed. 161

**Corn Products Cases**
11 Ga. App. 588, 75 S.E. 918; 236 U.S. 165, 59 L. Ed. 520, 35 S. Ct. 398
144 F.2d 211; 324 U.S. 726, 89 L. Ed. 1320, 65 S. Ct. 961; 323 U.S. 706, 89 L. Ed. 569, 65 S. Ct. 313

**Corn Products Taxation Case**
16 T.C. 395; 20 T.C. 503; 215 F.2d 513; 348 U.S. 911, 99 L. Ed. 714, 75 S. Ct. 298; 350 U.S. 46, 100 L. Ed. 29, 76 S. Ct. 20

**Corned Beef Sandwich Case**
135 Conn. 243, 63 A.2d 158

**Cornice Leakage Case**
231 Minn. 451, 44 N.W.2d 481

**Cornwell's Estate Case**
37 T.C. 688

**Corona Tire Case**
276 U.S. 358, 72 L. Ed. 610, 48 S. Ct. 380

**Coronado Coal Cases**
235 F. 1, 148 C.C.A. 495; 242 U.S. 653, 61 L. Ed. 547, 37 S. Ct. 246; 258 F. 829, 169 C.C.A. 549; 259 U.S. 344, 66 L. Ed. 975, 42 S. Ct. 570; 66 L. Ed. 1079, 42 S. Ct. 587; 300 F. 972; 268 U.S. 295, 69 L. Ed. 963, 45 S. Ct. 551
300 F. 965; 266 U.S. 630, 69 L. Ed. 477, 45 S. Ct. 195; 28 F.2d 851; 279 U.S. 841, 73 L. Ed. 987, 49 S. Ct. 263

**Corporate Debt Assumption Case**
194 Va. 324, 73 S.E.2d 385

**Corporate Distributions Income Tax Case**
66 F. Supp. 47; 163 F.2d 316

**Corporation Donation Case**
26 N.J. Super. 106, 97 A.2d 186; 13 N.J. 145, 98 A.2d 581; 346 U.S. 861, 98 L. Ed. 373, 74 S. Ct. 107

**Corporation Tax Cases**
220 U.S. 107, 55 L. Ed. 389, 31 S. Ct. 342
220 U.S. 187, 55 L. Ed. 428, 31 S. Ct. 361
192 F. 670; 228 U.S. 295, 57 L. Ed. 842, 33 S. Ct. 419
198 F. 242; 237 U.S. 28, 59 L. Ed. 825, 35 S. Ct. 499

**Corporations Freedom of Speech Case**
435 U.S. 765, 55 L. Ed. 2d 707, 98 S. Ct. 1407

**Corporeal Identification at Preliminary Hearing Case**
434 U.S. 220, 54 L. Ed. 2d 424, 98 S. Ct. 458

**Corpse Reburial Case**
275 A.D. 933, 91 N.Y.S.2d 624; 300 N.Y. 162, 90 N.E.2d 18

**Cortland City Case**
66 Misc. 2, 121 N.Y.S. 6

**Cossatat Case**
325 F. Supp. 728; 325 F. Supp. 749; 342 F. Supp. 1211

**Costello Case**
221 F.2d 668, 350 U.S. 359, 100 L. Ed. 397, 76 S. Ct. 406; 350 U.S. 819, 100 L. Ed. 732, 76 S. Ct. 48; 351 U.S. 904, 100 L. Ed. 1440, 76 S. Ct. 692; 352 U.S. 988, 1 L. Ed. 2d 367, 77 S. Ct. 388; 232 F.2d 958; 255 F.2d 876; 146 F. Supp. 63; 157 F. Supp. 461; 222 F.2d 656; 119 F. Supp. 159; 16 F.R.D. 428; 352 U.S. 1028, 1 L. Ed. 2d 591, 77 S. Ct. 642; 353 U.S. 978, 1 L. Ed. 2d 1140, 77 S. Ct. 1281; 239 F.2d 177; 355 U.S. 834, 2 L. Ed. 2d 45, 78 S. Ct. 53; 244 F.2d 21; 357 U.S. 937, 2 L. Ed. 2d 1551, 78 S. Ct. 1385, 358 U.S. 858, 3 L. Ed. 2d 93, 79 S. Ct. 16; 356 U.S. 256, 2 L. Ed. 2d 741, 78 S. Ct. 714; 350 U.S. 847, 100 L. Ed. 755, 76 S. Ct. 62; 247 F.2d 384; 144 F. Supp. 779; 145 F. Supp. 892; 247 F.2d 123; 247 F.2d 378; 115 F. Supp. 261; 149 F. Supp. 952; 150 F. Supp. 85; 19 F.R.D. 319; 362 U.S. 973, 4 L. Ed. 2d 1009, 80 S. Ct. 1058

**Cotney Case**
104 So. 2d 346 (Fla.)

**Cotton Bill Lading Case**
187 F. 686; 210 F. 810, 127 C.C.A. 360

**Cotton Compress Case**
151 U.S. 368, 38 L. Ed. 195, 14 S. Ct. 367

**Cotton Corner Case**
187 F. 664, 106 C.C.A. 600; 226 U.S. 525, 57 L. Ed. 333, 33 S. Ct. 141

**Cotton Gin Case**
257 U.S. 129, 66 L. Ed. 166, 42 S. Ct. 42; 121 Miss. 615, 83 So. 680

**Cotton Linter Cases**
79 Ct. Cl. 783
80 Ct. Cl. 855

**Cotton Plant Case**
77 U.S. 577, 19 L. Ed. 983

**Cotton Tie Case**
F. Cas. No. 293; 106 U.S. 89, 27 L. Ed. 79, 1 S. Ct. 52, 1882 C.D. 507, 22 Off. Gaz. Pat. Office 1976

**Cotton Trading Case**
172 F. 250; 185 F. 692, 107 C.C.A. 640; 206 F. 683; 211 F. 972, 128 C.C.A. 470; 217 F. 51, 133 C.C.A. 170; 223 F. 385, 138 C.C.A. 621; 241 U.S. 657, 60 L. Ed. 1225, 36 S. Ct. 286

**Cotton Yarn Rules Case**
281 A.D. 831, 118 N.Y.S.2d 569; 306 N.Y. 288, 118 N.E.2d 104; 281 A.D. 983, 121 N.Y.S.2d 261; 307 N.Y. 689, 120 N.E.2d 859

**Coughlin Case**
203 F.2d 307; 18 T.C. 528

**Count Joannes Cases**
87 Mass. (5 Allen) 169
88 Mass. (6 Allen) 236
88 Mass. (6 Allen) 240
88 Mass. (6 Allen) 241
88 Mass. (6 Allen) 243
88 Mass. (6 Allen) 245

**Countervailing Duty Cases**
113 F. 144, 51 C.C.A. 100; 186 U.S. 485, 46 L. Ed. 1261, 23 S. Ct. 856; 187 U.S. 496, 47 L. Ed. 275, 23 S. Ct. 222
Treas. Dec 35595, Gen. Appraisers 7758; Treas. Dec. 36426, 7 Ct. Cust. 97; 249 U.S. 34, 63 L. Ed. 461, 39 S. Ct. 218

**Court-Martial Counsel Case**
425 U.S. 25, 47 L. Ed. 2d 556, 96 S. Ct. 1281

**Courtroom Exclusion Case**
457 U.S. 596, 73 L. Ed. 2d 248, 102 S. Ct. 2613

**Covenant Against Competition Case**
138 Conn. 51, 82 A.2d 155

**Covert Entry Case**
441 U.S. 238, 60 L. Ed. 2d 177, 99 S. Ct. 1682

**Cow Case**
66 Mich. 568, 33 N.W. 919

**Cowlitz River Case**
207 F.2d 391; 347 U.S. 936, 98 L. Ed. 1087, 74 S. Ct. 626

**Cracking Patents Case**
33 F.2d 617; 283 U.S. 163, 75 L. Ed. 926, 51 S. Ct. 421, 9 U.S.P.Q. (BNA) 6; 51 S. Ct. 39

**Cramer Treason Case**
137 F.2d 888; 320 U.S. 730, 88 L. Ed. 431, 64 S. Ct. 192; 88 L. Ed. 1598, 64 S. Ct. 1149; 325 U.S. 1, 89 L. Ed. 1441, 65 S. Ct. 918

**Crane Elevator Cases**
56 F. 718, 6 C.C.A. 100
76 F. 767, 22 C.C.A. 549; 43 L. Ed. 1184, 19 S. Ct. 879

**Cream of Wheat Case**
224 F. 566; 227 F. 46

**Creamery Package Case**
179 F. 115, 102 C.C.A. 413; 227 U.S. 8, 57 L. Ed. 393, 33 S. Ct. 202

**Creation Science Case**
482 U.S. 578, 96 L. Ed. 2d 510, 107 S. Ct. 2573

**Creche and Menorah Case**
492 U.S. 573, 106 L. Ed. 2d 472, 109 S. Ct. 3086

**Credible and Reliable Identification Case**
461 U.S. 352, 75 L. Ed. 2d 903, 103 S. Ct. 1855

**Credit Card Late-Payment Fees Case**
517 U.S. 735, 135 L. Ed. 2d 25, 116 S. Ct. 1730 (1996)

**Credit Mobilier Case**
67 Pa. 233

**Credit Report Libel Case**
194 F.2d 160; 344 U.S. 821, 97 L. Ed. 639, 73 S. Ct. 18; 345 U.S. 960, 97 L. Ed. 1380, 73 S. Ct. 935

**Creek Indian Cases**
179 F. 13, 103 C.C.A. 1; 224 U.S. 448, 56 L. Ed. 834, 32 S. Ct. 494
199 F. 811

**Crefeld Mills Case**
57 F. 221

**Crime in Two Counties Case**
278 A.D. 512, 105 N.Y.S.2d 752; 106 N.Y.S.2d 372; 303 N.Y. 311, 101 N.E.2d 753

**Criminal Contempt Case**
421 U.S. 309, 44 L. Ed. 2d 186, 95 S. Ct. 1802

**Croker Case**
115 Fla. 733, 156 So. 146

**Crompton Case**
87 F. 731; 95 F. 987, 37 C.C.A. 351

**Crop Case**
165 S.C. 316, 163 S.E. 777

**Cropping Contract Cases**
279 F. 117; 263 U.S. 313, 68 L. Ed. 318, 44 S. Ct. 112
281 F. 407; 263 U.S. 326, 68 L. Ed. 323, 44 S. Ct. 115

**Crosby Stores Case**
109 N.J. Eq. 450, 158 A. 380

**Cross Burning Case**
505 U.S. 377, 120 L. Ed. 2d 305, 112 S. Ct. 2538 (1992)

**Cross-District Busing Case**
418 U.S. 717, 41 L. Ed. 2d 1069, 94 S. Ct. 3112

**Crossett Lumber Company Case**
8 N.L.R.B. 440, No. 51

**Crossing Whistle Cases**
167 S.W.2d 105 (Mo); 352 Mo. 44, 175 S.W.2d 889; 357 Mo. 1062, 212 S.W.2d 584
167 S.W.2d 96 (Mo); 175 S.W.2d 903

**Croswell Case**
3 Johns. Cas. 337, 3 Wheel. Crim. Cas. 330

**Croton Lake Case**
134 N.Y. 355, 31 N.E. 865; 32 N.E. 1014

**Crovo Case**
220 U.S. 364, 55 L. Ed. 498, 31 S. Ct. 399

**Crow Dog Case**
109 U.S. 556, 27 L. Ed. 1030, 3 S. Ct. 396; 3 Dakota 106, 14 N.W. 437

**Crowded Customer Case**
339 Ill. App. 501, 90 N.E.2d 500

**Crown Cafeteria Case**
130 N.L.R.B. 570, No. 68; 135 N.L.R.B. 1183, No. 124; 327 F.2d 351; 307 F.2d 197

**Crown Cork and Seal Company Case**
217 F. 381

**Crown Zellerback Cases**
416 F.2d 980
281 F. Supp. 337
282 F. Supp. 39

**Crucible Steel Cases**
132 F. 269; 137 F. 384, 69 C.C.A. 576, Treas. Dec. 26157
Treas. Dec. 26870, Gen. Appraisers 6213; 147 F. 537, Treas. Dec. 27446; 154 F. 1005, 83 C.C.A. 679, Treas. Dec. 28106

**Cruikshank Case**
F. Cas. No. 14, 897; 92 U.S. 542, 23 L. Ed. 588

**Crumady Case**
358 U.S. 423, 3 L. Ed. 2d 413, 79 S. Ct. 445; 249 F.2d 818, 1957 A.M.C. 2156, 1958 A.M.C. 225; 272 F.2d 396, 1962 A.M.C. 471; 142 F. Supp. 389, 1956 A.M.C. 2082; 176 F. Supp. 595, 1960 A.M.C. 802

**Cuba Railroad Case**
298 F. 664; 268 U.S. 628, 69 L. Ed. 1124, 45 S. Ct. 614

**Cuban Travel Case**
468 U.S. 222, 82 L. Ed. 2d 171, 104 S. Ct. 3026

**Cuban Treaty Case**
Treas. Dec. 43740; Treas. Dec. 44851, 19 C.C.P.A. (Customs) 88; Abs. (n.s.) No. 20289; 284 U.S. 634, 76 L. Ed. 539, 52 S. Ct. 18

**Culberson Case**
79 Tex. 65, 15 S.W. 219

**Curley Case**
189 Tenn. 397, 225 S.W.2d 550; 339 U.S. 952, 94 L. Ed. 1365, 70 S. Ct. 839

**Currens Case**
290 F.2d 751

**Curtis Brothers Case**
119 N.L.R.B. 232, No. 33; 274 F.2d 551; 359 U.S. 965, 3 L. Ed. 2d 833, 79 S. Ct. 876; 362 U.S. 274, 4 L. Ed. 2d 710, 80 S. Ct. 706

**Curtis Case**
362 U.S. 274, 4 L. Ed. 2d 710, 80 S. Ct. 706; 274 F.2d 551; 359 U.S. 965, 3 L. Ed. 2d 833, 79 S. Ct. 876

**Cusick's Election Case**
136 Pa. 459, 20 A. 574

**Custody of Illegitimate Case**
246 P.2d 147 (Cal.); 255 P.2d 761; 42 Cal. 2d 91, 265 P.2d 888

**Customs Forfeiture Remission Case**
474 U.S. 242, 88 L. Ed. 2d 587, 106 S. Ct. 610

**Cutler Case**
85 Iowa 516, 52 N.W. 490

**Cutler Hammer Case**
271 A.D. 917, 67 N.Y.S.2d 317; 297 N.Y. 519, 74 N.E.2d 464

**Cutter Polio Vaccine Case**
182 Cal. App. 2d 602, 6 Cal. Rptr. 320

**Cuyahoga Bridge Case**
F. Cas. No. 8,016

**Cyclone Case**
97 Miss. 622, 54 So. 310

## D

**Dagenhart Case**
247 U.S. 251, 62 L. Ed. 1101, 38 S. Ct. 529, 38 S. Ct. 581

**Dago Case**
31 F. 574

**Dairy Cases**
318 U.S. 261, 87 L. Ed. 748, 63 S. Ct. 617; 344 Pa. 635, 26 A.2d 431; 148 Pa. Super. 261, 24 A.2d 717
318 U.S. 285, 87 L. Ed. 761, 63 S. Ct. 628; 318 U.S. 801, 87 L. Ed. 1165, 63 S. Ct. 849; 19 Cal. 2d 818, 123 P.2d 442

**Dairy Queen Cases**
250 F.2d 503
305 F.2d 800; 310 F.2d 782
307 F.2d 816
354 F.2d 757
150 Me. 294, 110 A.2d 605

**Dake Case**
357 Mich. 20, 97 N.W.2d 748

**Dalkon Shield Cases**
62 Cal. App. 3d 484, 133 Cal. Rptr. 115

**Damaged Package Search Case**
80 L. Ed. 2d 85, 104 S. Ct. 1652

**Danann Case**
5 N.Y.2d 317, 184 N.Y.S.2d 599, 157 N.E.2d 597; 6 A.D.2d 674, 174 N.Y.S.2d 219

**Danbury Hatters' Cases**
130 F. 633; 142 F. 216; 148 F. 924; 208 U.S. 274, 52 L. Ed. 488, 28 S. Ct. 301; 187 F. 522, 109 C.C.A. 288; 223 U.S. 729, 56 L. Ed. 633, 32 S. Ct. 527; 209 F. 721, 126 C.C.A. 445; 235 U.S. 522, 59 L. Ed. 341, 35 S. Ct. 170
236 F. 444

**Dance Hall Nuisance Case**
57 N.M. 697, 262 P.2d 981

**Dangerous Trip Cases**
138 So. 2d 114 (La)
124 So. 2d 646 (La)
122 So. 2d 845 (La)

**Danner's Case**
38 S.C.L. 329

**Danville Brick Case**
320 Ill. 214, 150 N.E. 678

**Danville Case**
117 F. 741; 122 F. 800, 60 C.C.A. 540; 195 U.S. 639, 49 L. Ed. 356, 25 S. Ct. 790

**Daoust Case**
197 F. 678; 206 F. 434, 124 C.C.A. 316

**Darkey Stop Allotment Case**
206 F. 145, 124 C.C.A. 211

**Darlington Manufacturing Company Case**
139 N.L.R.B. 241, No. 23; 325 F.2d 682; 119 N.L.R.B. 1069, No. 116

**Dartmouth College Case**
1 N.H. 111; 65 N.H. 473; 17 U.S. 518, 4 L. Ed. 629

**Daubert Case (Scientific Evidence)**
509 U.S. 579, 125 L. Ed. 2d 469, 113 S. Ct. 2786 (1993)

**Daukus Case**
157 F.2d 267; 170 F.2d 364, 80 U.S.P.Q. (BNA) 36; 61 F. Supp. 139, 66 U.S.P.Q. (BNA) 400; 329 U.S. 799, 91 L. Ed. 683, 67 S. Ct. 491, 72 U.S.P.Q. (BNA) 529; 329 U.S. 835, 91 L. Ed. 707, 67 S. Ct. 631, 72 U.S.P.Q. (BNA) 529; 331 U.S. 796, 91 L. Ed. 1823, 67 S. Ct. 1726; 331 U.S. 860, 91 L. Ed. 1866, 67 S. Ct. 1756; 331 U.S. 869, 91 L. Ed. 1872, 67 S. Ct. 1749; 335 U.S. 911, 93 L. Ed. 444, 69 S. Ct. 482

**Davidson Chevrolet Case**
137 Colo. 575, 328 P.2d 377; 138 Colo. 171, 330 P.2d 1116; 359 U.S. 926, 3 L. Ed. 2d 629, 79 S. Ct. 609

**Davis Will Case**
10 Mont. 228, 25 P. 105; 11 Mont. 196, 28 P. 645

**Dawes Case**
278 Ill. 409, 116 N.E. 273; 216 Ill. App. 397

**Dayton Fan and Motor Cases**
106 F. 724; 118 F. 562, 55 C.C.A. 390
106 F. 729

**De Jure Segregation Case**
413 U.S. 189, 37 L. Ed. 2d 548, 93 S. Ct. 2686; 445 F.2d 990
303 F. Supp. 279; 303 F. Supp. 289; 313 F. Supp. 61;
313 F. Supp. 90

**De Lacy Case**
66 F. 450; 72 F. 726, 19 C.C.A. 157, 44 U.S. App. D.C. 257; 79 F. 1000, 24 C.C.A. 686, 44 U.S. App. D.C. 760; 174 U.S. 622, 43 L. Ed. 1111, 19 S. Ct. 791

**Dead Spouse Annulment Case**
99 N.H. 335, 111 A.2d 194

**Deaf Parochial Student's Interpreter Case**
509 U.S. 1, 125 L. Ed. 2d 1, 113 S. Ct. 2462 (1993)

**Dean Case**
111 F. 380

**Death Penalty Cases**
408 U.S. 238, 33 L. Ed. 2d 346, 92 S. Ct. 2726
58 U.S.L.W. 2475
428 U.S. 153, 49 L. Ed. 2d 859, 96 S. Ct. 2909,
428 U.S. 242, 49 L. Ed. 2d 913, 96 S. Ct. 2960
428 U.S. 262, 49 L. Ed. 2d 929, 96 S. Ct. 2950
428 U.S. 280, 49 L. Ed. 2d 944, 96 S. Ct. 2978
428 U.S. 325, 49 L. Ed. 2d 974, 96 S. Ct. 3001
458 U.S. 782, 73 L. Ed. 2d 1140, 102 S. Ct. 3368; 77 L. Ed. 2d 235, 103 S. Ct. 2733

**Death Penalty for Minors Case**
492 U.S. 361, 106 L. Ed. 2d 306, 109 S. Ct. 2969

**Death Penalty Qualified Jury Case**
476 U.S. 162, 90 L. Ed. 2d 137, 106 S. Ct. 1758

**Death Sentence Case**
79 L. Ed. 2d 29, 104 S. Ct. 871

**Debris Case**
16 F. 25; 18 F. 753; 27 F. 795; 45 F. 129

**Debs Cases**
158 U.S. 564, 39 L. Ed. 1092, 15 S. Ct. 900
249 U.S. 211, 63 L. Ed. 566, 39 S. Ct. 252

**Debt Cases**
206 U.S. 290, 51 L. Ed. 1068, 27 S. Ct. 732; 209 U.S. 514, 52 L. Ed. 914, 28 S. Ct. 614; 220 U.S. 1, 55 L. Ed. 353, 31 S. Ct. 330; 222 U.S. 17, 56 L. Ed. 71, 32 S. Ct. 4; 231 U.S. 89, 58 L. Ed. 135, 34 S. Ct. 29; 234 U.S. 117, 58 L. Ed. 1243, 34 S. Ct. 889; 238 U.S. 202, 59 L. Ed. 1272, 35 S. Ct. 795; 241 U.S. 531, 60 L. Ed. 1147, 36 S. Ct. 719; 246 U.S. 565, 62 L. Ed. 883, 38 S. Ct. 400
300 F. 737; 6 F.2d 372

**Debt Collecting Assault Case**
204 Okla. 394, 230 P.2d 483

**Debt Collection Attorneys Case**
514 U.S. 291, 131 L. Ed. 2d 395, 115 S. Ct. 1489 (1995)

**Deciduous Fruit Case**
30 F.2d 940; 72 L. Ed. 1018, 48 S. Ct. 561; 49 S. Ct. 20; 281 U.S. 658, 74 L. Ed. 1098, 50 S. Ct. 444

**Deep Rock Oil Case**
96 F.2d 693, 36 Am. B.R. (n.s.) 1088; 305 U.S. 584, 83 L. Ed. 369, 59 S. Ct. 96; 306 U.S. 618, 83 L. Ed. 1025, 59 S. Ct. 427; 38 Am. B.R. (n.s.) 692; 306 U.S. 307, 83 L. Ed. 669, 59 S. Ct. 543; 59 S. Ct. 550; 117 F.2d 615, 45 Am. B.R. (n.s.) 469

**Defective Brakes Case**
25 Wash. 2d 956, 172 P.2d 596; 190 P.2d 732

**Defective Hospital Bed Case**
125 Colo. 25, 240 P.2d 917

**Defective Search Warrant Case**
43 So. 2d 856 (Fla.)

**Defective Steering Case**
191 Va. 107, 60 S.E.2d 4

**Del Monte Cases**
66 F. 212; 88 F. 986, 31 C.C.A. 592; 171 U.S. 55, 43 L. Ed. 72, 18 S. Ct. 895; 97 F. 981, 38 C.C.A. 691
40 F. 108

**Delavan Avenue Case**
128 A.D. 373, 112 N.Y.S. 997; 200 N.Y. 113, 93 N.E. 520

**Delaware Indians Due Process Case**
430 U.S. 73, 51 L. Ed. 2d 173, 97 S. Ct. 911

**Delaware Railroad Tax Case**
F. Cas. No. 9,645; 85 U.S. 206, 21 L. Ed. 888

**Delaware River Aqueduct Case**
179 Misc. 475, 39 N.Y.S.2d 208; 291 N.Y. 81, 50 N.E.2d 552, 265 A.D. 989, 40 N.Y.S.2d 334; 290 N.Y. 932; 182 Misc 264, 44 N.Y.S.2d 402

**Delaware River Diversion Case**
279 U.S. 823, 73 L. Ed. 1016, 49 S. Ct. 478; 280 U.S. 514, 74 L. Ed. 585, 50 S. Ct. 15; 280 U.S. 528, 74 L. Ed. 595, 50 S. Ct. 151; 280 U.S. 533, 74 L. Ed. 598, 50 S. Ct. 161; 51 S. Ct. 332; 283 U.S. 336, 75 L. Ed. 1104, 51 S. Ct. 478; 283 U.S. 805, 75 L. Ed. 1425, 51 S. Ct. 562

**Delayed Telegram Case**
44 Del. 477, 61 A.2d 660; 45 Del. 345, 74 A.2d 77

**Delayed Warrantless Search Case**
469 U.S. 478, 83 L. Ed. 2d 890, 105 S. Ct. 881

**Delmonico Case**
144 Misc 832, 258 N.Y.S. 905; 236 A.D. 777, 258 N.Y.S. 1086; 236 A.D. 794, 258 N.Y.S. 1086

**Delta Avenue Case**
36 Ohio App. 251, 173 N.E. 45; 123 Ohio St. 174, 33 Ohio Law Rep. 486, 174 N.E. 586

**Deluxe Metal Case**
121 N.L.R.B. 995, No. 135

**Delvin Unemployment Compensation Case**
165 Pa. Super. 153, 67 A.2d 639

**Dema Realty Company Case**
168 La. 172, 121 So. 613; 168 La. 752, 123 So. 314; 280 U.S. 556, 74 L. Ed. 612, 50 S. Ct. 16

**Demand Case**
78 Ariz. 74, 275 P.2d 887

**Dempster Case**
265 F.2d 666; 162 F. Supp. 585; 361 U.S. 819, 4 L. Ed. 2d 65, 80 S. Ct. 63

**Denaturalization Case**
33 F. Supp. 510; 119 F.2d 500; 314 U.S. 597, 86 L. Ed. 481, 62 S. Ct. 98; 320 U.S. 118, 87 L. Ed. 1796, 63 S. Ct. 1333; 320 U.S. 807, 88 L. Ed. 488, 64 S. Ct. 24

**Denison Dam Case**
313 U.S. 508, 85 L. Ed. 1487, 61 S. Ct. 1050; 37 F. Supp. 93; 61 S. Ct. 831

**Dennett Case**
39 F.2d 564

**Dennis Case**
20 Ct. Cl. 119; 23 Ct. Cl. 324

**Dennis Communist Conspiracy Case**
79 F. Supp. 422; 80 F. Supp. 479; 81 F. Supp. 280; 170 F.2d 632; 81 F. Supp. 281; 83 F. Supp. 197; 176 F.2d 78; 9 F.R.D. 367; 183 F.2d 201; 184 F.2d 280; 340 U.S. 863; 95 L. Ed. 630, 71 S. Ct. 691; 340 U.S. 887, 95 L. Ed. 644, 71 S. Ct. 133; 341 U.S. 494, 95 L. Ed. 1137, 71 S. Ct. 857; 342 U.S. 842, 95 L. Ed. 636, 72 S. Ct. 20

**Denno Case**
378 U.S. 368, 12 L. Ed. 2d 908, 84 S. Ct. 1774

**Dental Company Case**
F. Cas. No. 5,598; 93 U.S. 486, 23 L. Ed. 952

**Denver Buick Case**
136 Colo. 482, 319 P.2d 490

**Denver Building Trades Case**
341 U.S. 675, 95 L. Ed. 1284, 71 S. Ct. 943; 186 F.2d 326

**Denver Water Company Cases**
246 U.S. 178, 62 L. Ed. 649, 38 S. Ct. 278
187 F. 890, 110 C.C.A. 24; 225 U.S. 707, 56 L. Ed. 1266, 32 S. Ct. 839; 229 U.S. 123, 57 L. Ed. 1101, 33 S. Ct. 657

**Dependent Children's Case**
421 U.S. 707, 44 L. Ed. 2d 525, 95 S. Ct. 1893

**Deportation Suspension Case**
471 U.S. 444, 85 L. Ed. 2d 452, 105 S. Ct. 2098

**Des Moines Proportional Rate Case**
17 I.C.C. 54

**Des Moines River Grant Cases**
72 U.S. 681, 18 L. Ed. 689
84 U.S. 144, 21 L. Ed. 561
84 U.S. 153, 21 L. Ed. 622
101 U.S. 755, 25 L. Ed. 915
101 U.S. 773, 25 L. Ed. 925
109 U.S. 329, 27 L. Ed. 952, 3 S. Ct. 188

**Des Plaines River Case**
256 F. 792, 168 C.C.A. 138; 256 U.S. 113, 65 L. Ed. 847, 41 S. Ct. 409

**Desegregation Cases**
32 Del. Ch. 343, 87 A.2d 862; 33 Del. Ch. 144, 91 A.2d 137; 344 U.S. 891, 97 L. Ed. 689, 73 S. Ct. 213; 345 U.S. 972, 97 L. Ed. 1388, 73 S. Ct. 1118; 347 U.S. 483, 98 L. Ed. 873, 74 S. Ct. 686; 348 U.S. 886, 75 S. Ct. 210; 349 U.S. 294, 99 L. Ed. 1083, 75 S. Ct. 753; 349 U.S. 914, 75 S. Ct. 602
98 F. Supp. 529; 342 U.S. 350, 96 L. Ed. 392, 72 S. Ct. 327; 103 F. Supp. 920; 344 U.S. 1, 97 L. Ed. 3, 73 S. Ct. 1; 345 U.S. 972, 97 L. Ed. 1388, 73 S. Ct. 1118; 347 U.S. 483, 98 L. Ed. 873, 74 S. Ct. 686; 348 U.S. 886, 75 S. Ct. 210; 349 U.S. 294, 99 L. Ed. 1083, 75 S. Ct. 753; 349 U.S. 914, 75 S. Ct. 602
98 F. Supp. 797; 344 U.S. 1, 97 L. Ed. 3, 73 S. Ct. 1; 344 U.S. 141, 97 L. Ed. 152, 73 S. Ct. 124; 345 U.S. 972, 97 L. Ed. 1388, 73 S. Ct. 1118; 347 U.S. 483, 98 L. Ed. 873, 74 S. Ct. 686; 348 U.S. 886, 75 S. Ct. 210; 349 U.S. 294, 99 L. Ed. 1083, 75 S. Ct. 753
103 F. Supp. 337; 344 U.S. 1, 97 L. Ed. 3, 73 S. Ct. 1; 345 U.S. 972, 97 L. Ed. 1388, 73 S. Ct. 1118, 347 U.S. 483, 98 L. Ed. 873, 74 S. Ct. 686; 348 U.S. 886, 75 S. Ct. 210; 349 U.S. 294, 99 L. Ed. 1083, 75 S. Ct. 753
132 F. Supp. 776
344 U.S. 873, 97 L. Ed. 676, 73 S. Ct. 173; 345 U.S. 972, 97 L. Ed. 1388, 73 S. Ct. 1114; 347 U.S. 497, 98 L. Ed. 884, 74 S. Ct. 693; 348 U.S. 886, 75 S. Ct. 210; 349 U.S. 294, 99 L. Ed. 1083, 75 S. Ct. 753; 75 S. Ct. 289

**Detroit Banking Cases**
7 F. Supp. 271; 86 F.2d 510

**Detroit Busing Case**
418 U.S. 717, 41 L. Ed. 2d 1069, 94 S. Ct. 3112

**Detroit Case**
340 U.S. 231, 95 L. Ed. 239, 71 S. Ct. 240; 173 F.2d 210; 233 F.2d 649; 337 U.S. 293, 93 L. Ed. 1371, 69 S. Ct. 1051; 338 U.S. 865, 94 L. Ed. 530, 70 S. Ct. 140; 339 U.S. 975, 94 L. Ed. 1381, 70 S. Ct. 1018; 340 U.S. 231, 95 L. Ed. 239, 71 S. Ct. 240; 355 U.S. 396, 2 L. Ed. 2d 359, 78 S. Ct. 369

**Detroit Park Case**
28 Mich. 228; McGrath No. 1695

**Detroit Reconsigning Case**
25 I.C.C. 392; 37 I.C.C. 274; 46 I.C.C. 231

**Detroit Switching Case**
198 F. 1009; 231 U.S. 457, 58 L. Ed. 310, 34 S. Ct. 152

**Deviating Carrier Case**
116 Vt. 266, 73 A.2d 321

**Devil's Law Case**
22 Wis. 2d 665, 126 N.W.2d 536

**Di Biasi Case**
7 N.Y.2d 544, 200 N.Y.S.2d 21, 166 N.E.2d 825; 12 A.D.2d 746, 201 N.Y.S.2d 754

**Dial a Porn Case**
492 U.S. 115, 106 L. Ed. 2d 93, 109 S. Ct. 2829

**Diamond Match Company Case**
106 N.Y. 473, 13 N.E. 419

**Diamond Rings Case**
183 U.S. 176, 46 L. Ed. 138, 22 S. Ct. 59

**Dictionary Case**
159 F. 638; 170 F. 167; 209 U.S. 551, 52 L. Ed. 922, 28 S. Ct. 761

**Diet Coke Cases**
563 F. Supp. 1122; 637 F. Supp. 1220; 696 F. Supp. 57; 769 F. Supp. 599
107 F.R.D. 288; 110 F.R.D. 363; 123 F.R.D. 97

**Dillard Case**
308 F.2d 920; 374 U.S. 827, 10 L. Ed. 2d 1051, 83 S. Ct. 1864

**Dillon Rule Case**
25 Iowa 163

**Dining Car Case**
110 Me. 105, 85 A. 396

**Director's Shutdown Case**
271 A.D. 326, 65 N.Y.S.2d 421; 297 N.Y. 52, 74 N.E.2d 305; 297 N.Y. 604, 75 N.E.2d 274; 75 N.E.2d 275; 113 N.Y.S.2d 181

**Dirty Stock Case**
227 F.2d 737; 127 F. Supp. 790; 351 U.S. 919, 100 L. Ed. 1451, 76 S. Ct. 712

**Disability Benefits for Pregnancies Case**
417 U.S. 484, 41 L. Ed. 2d 256, 94 S. Ct. 2485

**Disabled Child Social Security Case**
434 U.S. 47, 54 L. Ed. 2d 228, 98 S. Ct. 95

**Discounted Salt Case**
162 F.2d 949; 332 U.S. 850, 92 L. Ed. 420, 68 S. Ct. 355; 334 U.S. 37, 92 L. Ed. 1196, 68 S. Ct. 822

**Discrimination Law Case**
116 N.Y.S.2d 264; 282 A.D. 353, 122 N.Y.S.2d 721; 307 N.Y. 38, 119 N.E.2d 581

**Discriminatory Landlord Case**
190 Misc. 187, 74 N.Y.S.2d 220; 274 A.D. 992, 85 N.Y.S.2d 313; 299 N.Y. 512, 87 N.E.2d 541; 339 U.S. 981, 94 L. Ed. 1385, 70 S. Ct. 1019; 70 S. Ct. 243

**Disenfranchisement Case**
471 U.S. 222, 85 L. Ed. 2d 222, 105 S. Ct. 1916

**Disenfranchisement Ex-Felons Case**
418 U.S. 24, 41 L. Ed. 2d 551, 94 S. Ct. 2655

**Dispensary Cases**
41 S.C. 220, 19 S.E. 458

**Distilled Spirits Case**
78 U.S. 356, 20 L. Ed. 167

**District Court Case**
34 Ohio St. 431

**Ditty Case**
286 Ky. 395, 150 S.W.2d 672

**Dividend Cancellation Case**
335 Ill. App. 106, 80 N.E.2d 548; 403 Ill. 260, 85 N.E.2d 722

**Divisible Building Contract Case**
274 A.D. 901, 83 N.Y.S.2d 253; 299 N.Y. 303, 86 N.E.2d 757

**Divorce Default Fraud Case**
89 Ohio App. 47, 92 N.E.2d 275; 155 Ohio St. 226, 98 N.E.2d 401

**Divorce Residency Case**
419 U.S. 393, 42 L. Ed. 2d 532, 95 S. Ct. 553

**Divorced Parent Adoption Case**
94 App. D.C. 131, 214 F.2d 844

**Dixie Finance Company Case**
265 Ala. 267, 90 So. 2d 732

**Dixon Case**
104 Ky. 608, 20 Ky. Law Rep. 792, 47 S.W. 615; 20 Ky. Law Rep. 1883, 50 S.W. 252; 179 U.S. 131, 45 L. Ed. 121, 21 S. Ct. 67

**Dixon-Yates Case**
364 U.S. 520, 5 L. Ed. 2d 268, 81 S. Ct. 294; 365 U.S. 855, 5 L. Ed. 2d 820, 81 S. Ct. 798; 175 F. Supp. 505, 147 Ct. Cl. 1

**Dock Board Case**
49 La. Ann. 114, 21 So. 179

**Doctor-Nurse Interference Case**
322 Mass. 356, 77 N.E.2d 318

**Dodge Case**
105 F. 357; 111 F. 164, 49 C.C.A. 287; 131 F. 849, 65 C.C.A. 603; 195 U.S. 632, 49 L. Ed. 353, 25 S. Ct. 790

**Dodge-Morse Case**
105 A.D. 598, 94 N.Y.S. 1037; 184 N.Y. 30, 76 N.E. 732

**Dollar Savings Bank Case**
3 F. 817

**Dollar Steamship Case**
154 F.2d 307; 329 U.S. 700, 91 L. Ed. 611, 67 S. Ct. 62, 1946 A.M.C. 1496; 330 U.S. 731, 91 L. Ed. 1209, 67 S. Ct. 1009; 1947 A.M.C. 560; 82 F. Supp. 919; 184 F.2d 245, 87 App. D.C. 214, 1950 A.M.C. 1753; 340 U.S. 884, 95 L. Ed. 641, 71 S. Ct. 198; 188 F.2d 629, 88 App. D.C. 162; 340 U.S. 948, 95 L. Ed. 684, 71 S. Ct. 530, 71 S. Ct. 533; 341 U.S. 741, 95 L. Ed. 1331, 71 S. Ct. 987, 1951 A.M.C. 1059; 97 F. Supp. 50; 190 F.2d 366, 88 App. D.C. 311, 1951 A.M.C. 817; 190 F.2d 547; 100 F. Supp. 881; 193 F.2d 114; 196 F.2d 551; 344 U.S. 807, 97 L. Ed. 628, 73 S. Ct. 4; 343 U.S. 973, 96 L. Ed. 1367, 72 S. Ct. 1069; 100 F. Supp. 881

**Dollarway School Case**
176 F. Supp. 242; 271 F.2d 132; 181 F. Supp. 504; 183 F. Supp. 389; 282 F.2d 256; 194 F. Supp. 112; 196 F. Supp. 944

**Domes of Silence Cases**
201 F. 686; 209 F. 207, 126 C.C.A. 301
291 F. 594; 297 F. 619
13 F.2d 146; 16 F.2d 999

**Domicile Cases**
113 F.2d 25, 72 App. D.C. 30; 310 U.S. 631, 84 L. Ed. 1402, 60 S. Ct. 1082
119 F.2d 449; 313 U.S. 556, 85 L. Ed. 1518, 61 S. Ct. 1104; 314 U.S. 441, 86 L. Ed. 329, 62 S. Ct. 303
119 F.2d 451; 313 U.S. 556, 85 L. Ed. 1517, 61 S. Ct. 1103; 314 U.S. 441, 86 L. Ed. 329, 62 S. Ct. 303

**Donor Liability Case**
257 S.W.2d 604 (Ky.)

**Dooley Cases**
182 U.S. 222, 45 L. Ed. 1074, 21 S. Ct. 762
183 U.S. 151, 46 L. Ed. 128, 22 S. Ct. 62

**Door Case**
51 Cal. 2d 558, 334 P.2d 881

**Dope Peddler Entrapment Case**
198 F.2d 760

**Dorado Case**
62 Cal. 2d 338, 42 Cal. Rptr. 169, 398 P.2d 361

**Double Jeopardy Capital Sentencing Case**
476 U.S. 147, 90 L. Ed. 2d 123, 106 S. Ct. 1749

**Double Jeopardy Cases**
429 U.S. 1, 50 L. Ed. 2d 1, 97 S. Ct. 24
429 U.S. 5, 50 L. Ed. 2d 5, 97 S. Ct. 26
429 U.S. 14, 50 L. Ed. 2d 17, 97 S. Ct. 20
430 U.S. 564, 51 L. Ed. 2d 642, 97 S. Ct. 1349
437 U.S. 1, 57 L. Ed. 2d 1, 98 S. Ct. 2141; 459 U.S. 359, 74 L. Ed. 2d 535, 103 S. Ct. 673

**Double Jeopardy-Death Penalty Case**
451 U.S. 430, 68 L. Ed. 2d 270, 101 S. Ct. 1852

**Dougherty Case**
54 F.2d 721

**Dover Case**
39 N.J.L. 173

**Dover Church Case**
74 A. 841 (Del)

**Downe's Estate Case**
2 T.C. 967

**Down's Case**
336 F.2d 988

**Doyle Case**
234 A.D. 613, 251 N.Y.S. 802, 867; 234 A.D. 614, 251 N.Y.S. 868; 257 N.Y. 244, 177 N.E. 489; 257 N.Y. 545, 178 N.E. 788; 141 Misc. 141, 252 N.Y.S. 387; 234 A.D. 843, 253 N.Y.S. 1065; 258 N.Y. 437, 180 N.E. 110

**Dr. Miles Case**
164 F. 803, 90 C.C.A. 579; 212 U.S. 575, 53 L. Ed. 657, 29 S. Ct. 683; 220 U.S. 373, 55 L. Ed. 502, 31 S. Ct. 376

**Dr. Mudd's Case**
F. Cas. No. 9,899

**Dr. Townsend's Case**
95 F.2d 352; 303 U.S. 664, 82 L. Ed. 1121, 58 S. Ct. 830

**Draft Cases (World War II)**
36 F. Supp. 915
120 F.2d 236
131 F.2d 818
318 U.S. 749, 87 L. Ed. 1125, 63 S. Ct. 758
319 U.S. 33, 87 L. Ed. 1194, 63 S. Ct. 912
319 U.S. 785, 87 L. Ed. 1728, 63 S. Ct. 1323
132 F.2d 348
318 U.S. 754, 87 L. Ed. 1129, 63 S. Ct. 980
319 U.S. 484, 87 L. Ed. 1534, 63 S. Ct. 1206

**Draft Registration Case**
82 L. Ed. 2d 632, 104 S. Ct. 3348
468 U.S. 841, 82 L. Ed. 2d 632, 104 S. Ct. 3348

**Drainage Commission Case**
49 La. Ann. 1199, 22 So. 623

**Draining Company Case**
11 La. Ann. 338

**Drake Bakeries Case**
370 U.S. 254, 8 L. Ed. 2d 474, 82 S. Ct. 1346; 287 F.2d 155; 294 F.2d 399; 196 F. Supp. 148

**Dram Shop Case**
9 Ill. App. 2d 96, 132 N.E.2d 427

**Draper Case**
145 F.2d 199

**Dravo Case**
16 F. Supp. 527; 301 U.S. 665, 81 L. Ed. 1331, 57 S. Ct. 787; 301 U.S. 672, 57 S. Ct. 947; 302 U.S. 134, 82 L. Ed. 155, 58 S. Ct. 208; 114 F.2d 242; 312 U.S. 678, 85 L. Ed. 1117, 61 S. Ct. 450; 312 U.S. 714, 85 L. Ed. 1144, 61 S. Ct. 620

**Dred Scott Case**
60 U.S. 393, 15 L. Ed. 691

**Drinkhouse Gambling Case**
15 Misc. 2d 425, 183 N.Y.S.2d 679

**Drive-It-Yourself Case**
144 Md. 223, 125 A. 69

**Driven-Well Cases**
8 F. 269
15 F. 109; 122 U.S. 40, 30 L. Ed. 1064, 7 S. Ct. 1073
16 F. 387; 123 U.S. 267, 31 L. Ed. 160, 8 S. Ct. 101; 124 U.S. 694, 31 L. Ed. 557, 8 S. Ct. 676
F. Cas. No. 371

**Driver's License Revocation Case**
187 P.2d 421 (Cal.); 32 Cal. 2d 226, 195 P.2d 792

**Driver's License Stop Case**
440 U.S. 648, 59 L. Ed. 2d 660, 99 S. Ct. 1391

**Drover's Pass Cases**
84 U.S. 357, 21 L. Ed. 627
95 U.S. 655, 24 L. Ed. 535
67 F. 209, 14 C.C.A. 368
73 F. 519, 19 C.C.A. 551
200 F. 197, 118 C.C.A. 383
40 Ark. 298
6 Del. 469
160 Ill. 40, 43 N.E. 809; 57 Ill. App. 538
174 Ill. 13, 50 N.E. 1019; 69 Ill. App. 363
184 Ill. 294, 56 N.E. 331; 81 Ill. App. 137
47 Ind. 471
71 Ind. 271
139 Mich. 590, 102 N.W. 1037
88 Mo. 239
24 N.Y. 222
29 Barb. 132
78 Hun 387; 149 N.Y. 610, 44 N.E. 1120
19 Ohio St. 1
51 Pa. 315
208 Pa. 623, 57 A. 1125
13 Utah 275, 44 P. 932, 15 Utah 334, 49 P. 646
122 Wis. 423, 99 N.W. 1034

**Drowned Child Liability Case**
200 S.W.2d 699 (Tex.); 146 Tex. 434, 208 S.W.2d 843

**Drug Courier Profile Case**
490 U.S. 1, 104 L. Ed. 2d 1, 109 S. Ct. 1581

**Drug Forfeiture Case**
510 U.S. 43, 126 L. Ed. 2d 490, 114 S. Ct. 492,2 (1993)

**Drug Possession Life Imprisonment Case**
115 L. Ed. 2d 836, 111 S. Ct. 2680

**Drug Proceeds Forfeiture Cases**
491 U.S. 600; 105 L. Ed. 2d 512, 109 S. Ct. 2657; 491 U.S. 617, 105 L. Ed. 2d 528, 109 S. Ct. 2667

**Druggists Case**
85 Tenn. 449, 3 S.W. 490

**Drugless Healer Case**
36 Wash. 2d 482, 219 P.2d 79; 340 U.S. 892, 95 L. Ed. 646, 71 S. Ct. 208

**Drummer Cases**
217 U.S. 91, 54 L. Ed. 678, 30 S. Ct. 481
16 D.C. 489; 129 U.S. 141, 32 L. Ed. 637, 9 S. Ct. 256
95 Ark. 464, 130 S.W. 569; 227 U.S. 389, 57 L. Ed. 565, 33 S. Ct. 294
102 Ark. 314, 144 S.W. 211; 227 U.S. 401, 57 L. Ed. 569, 33 S. Ct. 298
57 Md. 251; 120 U.S. 502, 30 L. Ed. 699, 7 S. Ct. 655
167 Mich. 417, 132 N.W. 1071; 232 U.S. 665, 58 L. Ed. 786, 34 S. Ct. 476
127 N.C. 521, 37 S.E. 138; 187 U.S. 622, 47 L. Ed. 336, 23 S. Ct. 229
143 Pa. 642, 22 A. 893; 153 U.S. 289, 38 L. Ed. 719, 14 S. Ct. 829
81 Tenn. 303; 120 U.S. 489, 30 L. Ed. 694, 7 S. Ct. 592
105 Tenn. 412, 58 S.W. 1061; 185 U.S. 27, 46 L. Ed. 785, 22 S. Ct. 576
23 Tex. Crim. 662, 5 S.W. 91; 128 U.S. 129, 32 L. Ed. 368, 9 S. Ct. 1
113 Va. 562, 75 S.E. 1135; 236 U.S. 697, 59 L. Ed. 795, 35 S. Ct. 479
183 Va. 689, 33 S.E.2d 206; 327 U.S. 416, 90 L. Ed. 760, 66 S. Ct. 586; 65 S. Ct. 1557

**Dry Ice Case**
25 F.2d 730; 38 F.2d 62; 281 U.S. 711, 74 L. Ed. 1133, 50 S. Ct. 347; 283 U.S. 27, 75 L. Ed. 819, 51 S. Ct. 334; 283 U.S. 794, 75 L. Ed. 1419, 51 S. Ct. 483; 283 U.S. 420, 75 L. Ed. 1153, 51 S. Ct. 496

**Du Pont Cellophane Case**
351 U.S. 377, 100 L. Ed. 1264, 76 S. Ct. 994; 107 F. Supp. 324; 118 F. Supp. 41, 99 U.S.P.Q. (BNA) 462; 348 U.S. 806, 99 L. Ed. 637, 75 S. Ct. 41, 103 U.S.P.Q. (BNA) 425

**Du Pont-General Motors Case**
353 U.S. 586, 1 L. Ed. 2d 1057, 77 S. Ct. 872; 126 F. Supp. 235; 167 F. Supp. 957; 177 F. Supp. 1; 350 U.S. 815, 100 L. Ed. 729, 76 S. Ct. 61

**Du Pont Trust Case**
188 F. 127; 273 F. 869

**Dual Sovereignty Double Jeopardy Case**
474 U.S. 82, 88 L. Ed. 2d 387, 106 S. Ct. 433

**Duberstein Case**
363 U.S. 278, 4 L. Ed. 2d 1218, 80 S. Ct. 1190; 265 F.2d 28; 268 F.2d 727; 283 F.2d 949; 137 F. Supp. 803; 186 F. Supp. 393; 361 U.S. 923, 4 L. Ed. 2d 239, 80 S. Ct. 291; 364 U.S. 925, 5 L. Ed. 2d 265, 81 S. Ct. 352

**Dubilier Case**
289 U.S. 178, 77 L. Ed. 1114, 53 S. Ct. 554; 49 F.2d 306, 9 U.S.P.Q. (BNA) 131; 59 F.2d 381, 13 U.S.P.Q. (BNA) 337; 287 U.S. 588, 77 L. Ed. 513, 53 S. Ct. 88; 289 U.S. 706, 77 L. Ed. 1462, 53 S. Ct. 687

**Duck Lake Case**
223 La. 47, 64 So. 2d 839

**Ducros Case**
30 T.C. 1337; 272 F.2d 49

**Dud Fireworks Bomb Case**
273 A.D. 939, 78 N.Y.S.2d 4; 298 N.Y. 409, 84 N.E.2d 38

**Dude Ranch Horse Injury Case**
75 Idaho 24, 265 P.2d 988

**Due-On-Sale Clause Case**
458 U.S. 141, 73 L. Ed. 2d 664, 102 S. Ct. 3014

**Duke Power Company Cases**
10 F. Supp. 854; 12 F. Supp. 70; 79 F.2d 995; 81 F.2d 986; 298 U.S. 651, 80 L. Ed. 1379, 56 S. Ct. 941; 299 U.S. 259, 81 L. Ed. 178, 57 S. Ct. 202; 19 F. Supp. 932; 91 F.2d 665; 302 U.S. 485, 82 L. Ed. 381, 58 S. Ct. 306

91 F.2d 303; 301 U.S. 681, 81 L. Ed. 1339, 57 S. Ct. 946; 302 U.S. 464, 82 L. Ed. 374, 58 S. Ct. 300

**Dulles Case**
123 F. 371, 59 C.C.A. 499; 139 F. 510; 139 F. 513, 71 C.C.A. 500

**Duncan Iron Works Case**
136 Pa. 478, 20 A. 647

**Duplex Case**
247 F. 192; 252 F. 722, 164 C.C.A. 562; 254 U.S. 443, 65 L. Ed. 349, 41 S. Ct. 172

**Durfey Bird Cage Case**
265 Mich. 97, 251 N.W. 356

**Durham Case**
214 F.2d 862; 130 F 445, 94 App. D.C. 228; 237 F.2d 760, 99 App. D.C. 132

**Durham Smoking Tobacco Case**
F. Cas. No. 1,475

**Dutch Church Case**
41 U.S. 455, 10 L. Ed. 1029

**Dutcher Case**
F. Cas. No. 15,014

**Duty-to-Warn Case**
296 F.2d 623

**Dyanshine Case**
29 F.2d 474

**Dyer Case**
36 T.C. 456

**Dynamite Trap Case**
156 Ohio St. 120, 45 Ohio Op. 128, 100 N.E.2d 237

## E

**Eagle Snuff Case**
206 F. 420, 124 C.C.A. 302

**Earl Irwins Case**
121 Iowa 667, 92 N.W. 113, 97 N.W. 86

**East Indian Remedy Case**
128 Mass. 477

**East of the Rockies Concrete Pipe Case**
302 F. Supp. 244

**East Peoria Bridge Cases**
8 Ill. Ct. Cl. 609
8 Ill. Ct. Cl. 686
8 Ill. Ct. Cl. 724
8 Ill. Ct. Cl. 734

**Eastman Kodak Case**
207 F. 351; 213 F. 231, 129 C.C.A. 575; 213 F. 239; 216 F. 831; 222 F. 249, 138 C.C.A. 71

**Eau Claire Gas Rate Case**
183 Wis. 104, 197 N.W. 363

**Eaves Encroachment Case**
69 So. 2d 331 (Fla.)

**Ebasco Case**
75 F. Supp. 672

**Eclipse Oil Company Case**
47 W. Va. 84, 34 S.E. 923

**Edison Lamp Cases**
47 F. 454; 52 F. 300; 59 F. 501

**Editorial Process Case**
441 U.S. 153, 60 L. Ed. 2d 115, 99 S. Ct. 1635

**Edmondson Island Case**
42 F. 15

**Educational Bonds Cases**
68 Mont. 526, 219 P. 637
70 Mont. 90, 223 P. 832

**EEOC Class Action Case**
446 U.S. 318, 64 L. Ed. 2d 319, 100 S. Ct. 1698

**EEOC Notice Case**
80 L. Ed. 2d 41, 104 S. Ct. 1621

**EEOC Public Disclosure Case**
449 U.S. 590, 66 L. Ed. 2d 762, 101 S. Ct. 817

**Effective Assistance of Counsel Case**
466 U.S. 648, 80 L. Ed. 2d 657, 104 S. Ct. 2039
469 U.S. 387, 83 L. Ed. 2d 821, 105 S. Ct. 830

**Egg Coal Case**
41 Ind. App. 658, 84 N.E. 776

**Eibel Process Case**
267 F. 847; 274 F. 540; 257 U.S. 628, 66 L. Ed. 405, 42 S. Ct. 57; 261 U.S. 45, 67 L. Ed. 522, 43 S. Ct. 322

**Eight-Hour Law Cases**
243 U.S. 332, 61 L. Ed. 755, 37 S. Ct. 298
14 Utah 96, 46 P. 1105; 169 U.S. 366, 42 L. Ed. 780, 18 S. Ct. 383

**Eighteenth Amendment Cases**
251 U.S. 311, 64 L. Ed. 280, 40 S. Ct. 154
267 U.S. 132, 69 L. Ed. 543, 45 S. Ct. 280
257 F. 860; 252 U.S. 465, 64 L. Ed. 665, 40 S. Ct. 364
260 F. 486; 251 U.S. 210, 64 L. Ed. 229, 40 S. Ct. 139
264 F. 186; 253 U.S. 350, 64 L. Ed. 946, 40 S. Ct. 486, 588
268 F. 864; 260 U.S. 377, 67 L. Ed. 314, 43 S. Ct. 141
284 F. 596; 251 U.S. 146, 64 L. Ed. 194, 40 S. Ct. 106; 251 U.S. 264, 64 L. Ed. 260, 40 S. Ct. 141
156 Ga. 488, 119 S.E. 302; 267 U.S. 188, 69 L. Ed. 568, 45 S. Ct. 264
100 Ohio St. 385, 126 N.E. 400; 253 U.S. 221, 64 L. Ed. 871, 40 S. Ct. 495
100 Ohio St. 540, 127 N.E. 924; 253 U.S. 231, 64 L. Ed. 877, 40 S. Ct. 498

**Eisler Case**
75 F. Supp. 634; 75 F. Supp. 640; 176 F.2d 21; 337 U.S. 912, 93 L. Ed. 1723, 69 S. Ct. 1150; 337 U.S. 958, 93 L. Ed. 1758, 69 S. Ct. 1534; 83 App. D.C. 315, 170 F.2d 273; 335 U.S. 857, 93 L. Ed. 404, 69 S. Ct. 130; 338 U.S. 189, 93 L. Ed. 1897, 69 S. Ct. 1453; 69 S. Ct. 477; 69 S. Ct. 744; 338 U.S. 883, 94 L. Ed. 542, 70 S. Ct. 181

**Ekiu Case**
142 U.S. 651, 35 L. Ed. 1146, 12 S. Ct. 336

**El Dorado Cases**
308 U.S. 422, 84 L. Ed. 361, 60 S. Ct. 325; 309 U.S. 694, 84 L. Ed. 1035, 60 S. Ct. 465; 104 F.2d 903; 308 U.S. 533, 84 L. Ed. 449, 60 S. Ct. 85; 328 U.S. 12, 90 L. Ed. 1053, 66 S. Ct. 43
59 F. Supp. 738

**El Dorado School Case**
352 F.2d 14

**El Paso Natural Gas Case**
281 F.2d 567; 366 U.S. 912, 6 L. Ed. 2d 236, 81 S. Ct. 1083; 366 U.S. 955, 6 L. Ed. 2d 1247, 81 S. Ct. 1901

**Elder Case**
163 Minn. 457, 204 N.W. 557; 269 U.S. 544, 70 L. Ed. 403, 46 S. Ct. 26; 270 U.S. 611, 70 L. Ed. 757, 46 S. Ct. 420

**Elected Judges Cases**
234 F. Supp. 575
249 F. Supp. 860
256 F. Supp. 35
260 F. Supp. 318
267 F. Supp. 148
275 F. Supp. 937
311 F. Supp. 126
30 A.D.2d 432, 293 N.Y.S.2d 829

**Election Cases**
65 Pa. 20; 77 Pa. 295

**Election Solicitation Case**
459 U.S. 197, 74 L. Ed. 2d 364, 103 S. Ct. 552

**Electoral College Case**
F. Cas. No. 4,336

**Electric Bond and Share Case**
18 F. Supp. 131; 92 F.2d 580; 302 U.S. 681, 82 L. Ed. 526, 58 S. Ct. 411; 303 U.S. 419, 82 L. Ed. 936, 58 S. Ct. 678; 303 U.S. 617, 58 S. Ct. 766

**Elevated Railroad Cases**
104 N.Y. 268, 4 N.Y. St. Rep. 340, 10 N.E. 528; 7 N.Y. St. Rep. 870
7 Hun 239; 70 N.Y. 327, 3 Abb. N. Cas. 401
9 Hun 303; 70 N.Y. 361, 3 Abb. N. Cas. 434; 24 Hun 385; 38 Hun 438
7 Daly 174, 3 Abb. N. Cas. 347
9 Jones & S. (41 N.Y. Super. Ct.) 489; 71 N.Y. 430; 11 Jones & S. (43 N.Y. Super. Ct.) 292, 3 Abb. N. Cas. 372
18 Jones & S. (50 N.Y. Super. Ct.) 311
3 Abb. N. Cas. 301
3 Abb. N. Cas. 306; 67 N.Y. 484
3 Abb. N. Cas. 467
3 Abb. N. Cas. 478; 90 N.Y. 122, 11 Abb. N. Cas. 236
19 Abb. N. Cas. 261

**Elevator Allowance Cases**
249 F. 827, 162 C.C.A. 61
10 I.C.C. 309; 12 I.C.C. 85; 13 I.C.C. 498; 14 I.C.C. 315; 176 F. 409; 222 U.S. 42, 56 L. Ed. 83, 32 S. Ct. 22
14 I.C.C. 317; 14 I.C.C. 510; 14 I.C.C. 551; 22 I.C.C. 496

**Elevator Cases**
17 F. 200
69 Ill. 80; 94 U.S. 113, 24 L. Ed. 77
117 N.Y. 1, 22 N.E. 670, 682; 143 U.S. 517, 36 L. Ed. 247, 12 S. Ct. 468

**Elevator Leg Case**
81 F. 201

**Eleven Count Case**
88 N.J.L. 377, 96 A. 587

**Elgee Cotton Cases**
7 Ct. Cl. 605; 89 U.S. 180, 22 L. Ed. 863, 10 Ct. Cl. 181

**Elgin Case**
89 F. 487; 94 F. 667, 35 C.C.A. 237; 179 U.S. 665, 45 L. Ed. 365, 21 S. Ct. 270

**Elk Hills Cases**
249 F. 785, 162 C.C.A. 19; 251 U.S. 1, 64 L. Ed. 97, 40 S. Ct. 47
6 F.2d 43; 9 F.2d 761; 24 F.2d 206; 270 U.S. 640, 70 L. Ed. 775, 46 S. Ct. 356; 273 U.S. 456, 71 L. Ed. 734, 47 S. Ct. 416

**Ellis Cases**
2 Ohio 89
167 Wis. 392, 167 N.W. 1048
264 F.2d 325; 154 F. Supp. 32

**Elmira Reformatory Case**
120 A.D. 338, 105 N.Y.S. 554

**Elmira Savings Bank Case**
73 Hun 357, 55 N.Y. St. Rep. 912, 26 N.Y.S. 200; 37 N.E. 568; 142 N.Y. 590, 37 N.E. 646; 161 U.S. 275, 40 L. Ed. 700, 16 S. Ct. 502

**Emancipation Proclamation Cases**
31 Tex. 504

**Embezzlement Gambling Case**
268 S.W.2d 290 (Tex.)

**Embroidered Hosiery Case**
165 F. 902

**Emergency Rent Cases**
267 F. 614, 50 App. D.C. 56; 254 U.S. 640, 65 L. Ed. 452, 41 S. Ct. 13; 267 F. 631, 50 App. D.C. 73; 256 U.S. 135, 65 L. Ed. 865, 41 S. Ct. 458
269 F. 306; 256 U.S. 170, 65 L. Ed. 877, 41 S. Ct. 465
113 Misc. 527, 185 N.Y.S. 632; 194 A.D. 523, 186 N.Y.S. 58; 230 N.Y. 429, 130 N.E. 601; 257 U.S. 665, 66 L. Ed. 424, 42 S. Ct. 47
113 Misc. 536, 185 N.Y.S. 638; 195 A.D. 280, 186 N.Y.S. 63, 230 N.Y. 429, 130 N.E. 601

**Emergency School Aid Act Case**
444 U.S. 130, 62 L. Ed. 2d 275, 100 S. Ct. 363

**Emerys Case**
107 Mass. 172

**Emperor Field Case**
335 S.W.2d 425 (Tex. Civ. App.)

**Empire State Railroad Case**
22 Dep't Rep. 346

**Employee Defamation Case**
205 S.W.2d 887 (Mo.); 358 Mo. 674, 216 S.W.2d 523

**Employee Drug Testing Case**
489 U.S. 656, 103 L. Ed. 2d 685, 109 S. Ct. 1384

**Employees Sex Harassment Liability Case**
477 U.S. 57, 91 L. Ed. 2d 49, 106 S. Ct. 2399

**Employers' Liability Cases**
224 U.S. 547, 56 L. Ed. 879, 32 S. Ct. 603
250 U.S. 400, 63 L. Ed. 1058, 39 S. Ct. 553
148 F. 986; 207 U.S. 463, 52 L. Ed. 297, 28 S. Ct. 141
148 F. 997; 207 U.S. 463, 52 L. Ed. 297, 28 S. Ct. 141
173 F. 494; 223 U.S. 1, 56 L. Ed. 327, 32 S. Ct. 169
82 Conn. 373, 73 A. 762; 223 U.S. 1, 56 L. Ed. 327, 32 S. Ct. 169
7 A.D.2d 686, 179 N.Y.S.2d 270
9 A.D.2d 551, 189 N.Y.S.2d 456
57 N.J. Super. 470, 155 A.2d 129
106 U.S. 629, 27 L. Ed. 295, 1 S. Ct. 601; 265 U.S. 310, 68 L. Ed. 1031, 44 S. Ct. 529

**Employment Agency Law Case**
221 F. 694; 244 U.S. 590, 61 L. Ed. 1336, 37 S. Ct. 662

**Employment Agency Questionaire Case**
116 N.Y.S.2d 264; 282 A.D. 353, 122 N.Y.S.2d 721; 307 N.Y. 38, 119 N.E.2d 581

**Enameling Case**
201 U.S. 156, 50 L. Ed. 707, 26 S. Ct. 404

**Endangered Species Act Case**
437 U.S. 153, 57 L. Ed. 2d 117, 98 S. Ct. 2279

**Endangered Species Habitat Case**
515 U.S. 687, 132 L. Ed. 2d 597, 115 S. Ct. 2407 (1995)

**Engel Case**
18 Misc. 2d 659, 191 N.Y.S.2d 453; 11 A.D.2d 340, 206 N.Y.S.2d 183; 10 N.Y.2d 174, 218 N.Y.S.2d 659, 176 N.E.2d 579; 370 U.S. 421, 8 L. Ed. 2d 601, 82 S. Ct. 1261; 12 N.Y.2d 712, 233 N.Y.S.2d 766, 186 N.E.2d 124; 368 U.S. 982, 82 S. Ct. 597; 369 U.S. 809, 82 S. Ct. 686

**Engine Valve Case**
113 U.S. 679, 28 L. Ed. 1070, 5 S. Ct. 692

**Engineer's Case**
71 F. Supp. 797; 168 F.2d 722; 335 U.S. 851, 93 L. Ed. 399, 69 S. Ct. 80; 338 U.S. 96, 93 L. Ed. 1836, 69 S. Ct. 1377

**Enterprise Case**
363 U.S. 593, 4 L. Ed. 2d 1424, 80 S. Ct. 1358; 269 F.2d 327; 168 F. Supp. 308; 361 U.S. 929, 4 L. Ed. 2d 352, 80 S. Ct. 371; 363 U.S. 564, 4 L. Ed. 2d 1432, 80 S. Ct. 1363

**Entrapment Case**
287 U.S. 435, 77 L. Ed. 413, 53 S. Ct. 210; 287 U.S. 584, 77 L. Ed. 511, 53 S. Ct. 19

**Equal Access to Justice Act Case**
101 L. Ed. 2d 490, 108 S. Ct. 2541

**Erie Bribery Cases**
178 Pa. Super. 434, 115 A.2d 826
178 Pa. Super. 447, 115 A.2d 833; 350 U.S. 1005, 100 L. Ed. 868, 76 S. Ct. 649

**Erie-Lackawanna Merger Case**
366 U.S. 169, 6 L. Ed. 2d 206, 81 S. Ct. 913; 365 U.S. 809, 5 L. Ed. 2d 690, 81 S. Ct. 700; 366 U.S. 916, 6 L. Ed. 2d 240, 81 S. Ct. 1092; 366 U.S. 955, 6 L. Ed. 2d 1247, 81 S. Ct. 1901; 189 F. Supp. 942

**Erie Pass Case**
213 F. 391; 236 U.S. 259, 59 L. Ed. 567, 35 S. Ct. 396

**Erie Railroad Company Case**
90 F.2d 603; 302 U.S. 671, 82 L. Ed. 518, 58 S. Ct. 50; 304 U.S. 64, 82 L. Ed. 1188, 58 S. Ct. 817; 98 F.2d 49; 305 U.S. 637, 83 L. Ed. 410, 59 S. Ct. 108; 305 U.S. 673, 83 L. Ed. 436, 59 S. Ct. 229

**Erie Railroad Tax Case**
64 N.J.L. 123, 44 A. 976

**Erie Resistor Case**
303 F.2d 359; 371 U.S. 810, 9 L. Ed. 2d 53, 83 S. Ct. 48; 373 U.S. 221, 10 L. Ed. 2d 308, 83 S. Ct. 1139; 328 F.2d 723

**ERISA Plan Amendment Case**
142 L. Ed. 2d 881, 119 S. Ct. 755

**Erlanger Case**
136 Misc. 784, 242 N.Y.S. 257; 136 Misc. 792, 242 N.Y.S. 255; 136 Misc. 793, 242 N.Y.S. 249; 229 A.D. 778, 242 N.Y.S. 910; 231 A.D. 70, 246 N.Y.S. 275; 234 A.D. 34, 254 N.Y.S. 246; 145 Misc. 1, 259 N.Y.S. 610; 148 Misc. 339, 265 N.Y.S. 393

**Escobedo Case**
378 U.S. 478, 12 L. Ed. 2d 977, 84 S. Ct. 1758

**Espionage Cases**
245 F. 878; 245 F. 888; 247 U.S. 523, 62 L. Ed. 1247, 38 S. Ct. 428; 39 S. Ct. 12; 252 U.S. 239, 64 L. Ed. 542, 40 S. Ct. 205
247 F. 708; 248 F. 290; 254 F. 135; 251 U.S. 466, 64 L. Ed. 360, 40 S. Ct. 259
253 F. 212; 249 U.S. 47, 63 L. Ed. 470, 39 S. Ct. 247
248 U.S. 540, 63 L. Ed. 411, 39 S. Ct. 132; 249 U.S. 204, 63 L. Ed. 561, 39 S. Ct. 249
249 U.S. 211, 63 L. Ed. 566, 39 S. Ct. 252
250 U.S. 616, 63 L. Ed. 1173, 40 S. Ct. 17

*Continued*

**Esposito Case**
249 F. Supp. 308

**Esso Case**
98 F.2d I

**Estate Bond Limitations Case**
268 P.2d 897 (Okla.)

**Estate Tax Exemption Case**
267 P.2d 834 (Cal.); 43 Cal. 2d 594, 275 P.2d 467

**Estin Case**
334 U.S. 541, 92 L. Ed. 1561, 68 S. Ct. 1213; 332 U.S. 840, 92 L. Ed. 412, 68 S. Ct. 260; 296 N.Y. 308, 73 N.E.2d 113; 296 N.Y. 828, 72 N.E.2d 18; 271 A.D. 829, 66 N.Y.S.2d 421; 273 A.D. 901, N.Y.S.2d 240, 63 N.Y.S.2d 476

**Estray Cases**
28 Tex. 632
30 Tex. 515
30 Tex. 517
30 Tex. 518

**Ethnic Discrimination Cases**
481 U.S. 615, 95 L. Ed. 2d 594, 107 S. Ct. 2019; 481 U.S. 604, 95 L. Ed. 2d 582, 107 S. Ct. 2022

**Ethyl Gas Monopoly Case**
27 F. Supp. 959, 41 U.S.P.Q. (BNA) 772; 60 S. Ct. 296; 309 U.S. 436, 84 L. Ed. 852, 60 S. Ct. 618

**Etlah Case**
95 U.S. 61, 24 L. Ed. 371

**Eubank Case**
184 U.S. 27, 46 L. Ed. 416, 22 S. Ct. 277

**Eureka County Bank Habeas Corpus Cases**
35 Nev. 80, 126 P. 655, 129 P. 308; 35 Nev. 30, 126 P. 679

**Evasion of the Spirit of the Deal Cases**
121 F. 298
124 F.2d 147
130 F.2d 471
144 F.2d 720
245 F.2d 633
234 Md. 521, 200 A.2d 166
377 Pa. Super. 549, 105 A.2d 580
65 S.W. 689( Tex.)

**Evening News Case**
371 U.S. 195, 9 L. Ed. 2d 246, 83 S. Ct. 267; 362 Mich. 350, 106 N.W.2d 785

**Everson Case**
330 U.S. 1, 91 L. Ed. 711, 67 S. Ct. 504; 132 N.J.L. 98, 39 A.2d 75; 133 N.J.L. 350, 44 A.2d 333; 330 U.S. 855, 91 L. Ed. 1297, 67 S. Ct. 962

**Evidence of Subversiveness Case**
169 Pa. Super. 326, 82 A.2d 699; 369 Pa. 72, 85 A.2d 425

**Evolution Teaching Case**
152 Tenn. 424, 278 S.W. 57; 154 Tenn. 105, 289 S.W. 363

**Ex Parte 74 Case**
58 I.C.C. 220

**Ex Parte 103 Case**
178 I.C.C. 539; 179 I.C.C. 215; 191 I.C.C. 361

**Exchange Bank Tax Cases**
21 F. 99; 122 U.S. 154, 30 L. Ed. 1088, 7 S. Ct. 1244

**Exclusion Cases**
149 U.S. 698, 37 L. Ed. 905, 13 S. Ct. 1016
36 F. 431; 130 U.S. 581, 32 L. Ed. 1068, 9 S. Ct. 623
189 U.S. 86, 47 L. Ed. 721, 23 S. Ct. 611

**Exclusion from Restricted Areas Cases**
51 F. Supp. 383
52 F. Supp. 189; 55 F. Supp. 186

**Exclusion of Blacks from Juries Case**
476 U.S. 79, 90 L. Ed. 2d 69, 106 S. Ct. 1712

**Exclusionary Rule Case**
82 L. Ed. 2d 599, 104 S. Ct. 3380

**Executive Budget Case**
252 N.Y. 27, 168 N.E. 817

**Exemption from Jury Service Case**
439 U.S. 357, 58 L. Ed. 2d 579, 99 S. Ct. 664

**Exhaust Fumes Case**
234 S.W.2d 474 (Tex.)

**Expanded Metal Cases**
136 F. 870; 146 F. 984, 77 C.C.A. 230; 206 U.S. 561, 51 L. Ed. 1189, 27 S. Ct. 795; 214 U.S. 366, 53 L. Ed. 1034, 29 S. Ct. 652
157 F. 564; 164 F. 849, 90 C.C.A. 611; 212 U.S. 577, 53 L. Ed. 658, 30 S. Ct. 698; 214 U.S. 366, 53 L. Ed. 1034, 29 S. Ct. 652; 247 F. 899; 272 F. 1021

**Expatriation Cases**
99 F.2d 408, 69 App. D.C. 175; 305 U.S. 591, 83 L. Ed. 373, 59 S. Ct. 245; 307 U.S. 325, 83 L. Ed. 1320, 59 S. Ct. 884

**Expiration Case**
135 F. 368; 201 U.S. 529, 50 L. Ed. 854, 26 S. Ct. 513

**Express Company Case**
10 F. 210; 10 F. 869; 108 U.S. 24, 27 L. Ed. 638, 2 S. Ct. 6; 108 U.S. 30, 27 L. Ed. 640, 2 S. Ct. 9; 117 U.S. 1, 29 L. Ed. 791, 6 S. Ct. 542, 628

**Express Messenger Case**
176 U.S. 498, 44 L. Ed. 560, 20 S. Ct. 385

**Exterior Advertising Case**
194 N.Y. 19, 86 N.E. 824; 221 U.S. 467, 55 L. Ed. 815, 31 S. Ct. 709

**Extraterritorial Dramshop Act Case**
342 Ill. App. 151, 95 N.E.2d 512

## F

**Faber India Rubber Pencil Case**
F. Cas. No. 11,625; 92 U.S. 347, 23 L. Ed. 719

**Factory Surveys Case**
80 L. Ed. 2d 247, 104 S. Ct. 1758

**Failing Awning Case**
232 P.2d 20 (Cal.); 38 Cal. 2d 392, 240 P.2d 276

**Failing Car Doors Case**
356 Mo. 633, 202 S.W.2d 904; 358 Mo. 1100, 219 S.W.2d 322; 338 U.S. 823, 94 L. Ed. 499, 70 S. Ct. 69

**Failing Company Case**
280 U.S. 291, 74 L. Ed. 431, 50 S. Ct. 89; 29 F.2d 518; 279 U.S. 849, 73 L. Ed. 993, 49 S. Ct. 346

**Failing Monument Case**
28 N.J. Super. 266, 100 A.2d 558; 15 N.J. 608, 105 A.2d 841

**Fair Labor Standards Act Case**
469 U.S. 528, 83 L. Ed. 2d 1016, 105 S. Ct. 1005

**Fair Trade Cases**
299 U.S. 183, 81 L. Ed. 109, 57 S. Ct. 139
299 U.S. 198, 81 L. Ed. 122, 57 S. Ct. 147
184 F.2d 11; 340 U.S. 928, 95 L. Ed. 669, 71 S. Ct. 491; 341 U.S. 384, 95 L. Ed. 1035, 71 S. Ct. 745; 341 U.S. 956, 95 L. Ed. 1377, 71 S. Ct. 1011

**Fair Use Case**
471 U.S. 539, 85 L. Ed. 2d 588, 105 S. Ct. 2218

**Faircloth Will Case**
132 N.C. 476, 44 S.E. 47; 44 S.E. 1007

**Fall River Case**
202 Cal. 56, 259 P. 444

**Fallbrook Cases**
101 F. Supp. 298; 108 F. Supp. 72; 109 F. Supp. 281, 10 F. Supp. 767

**False Promise Case**
225 Mass. 435, 114 N.E. 681

**Falwell Parody Case**
485 U.S. 46, 99 L. Ed. 2d 41, 108 S. Ct. 876

**Family Home Sale Case**
76 L. Ed. 2d 236, 103 S. Ct. 2132

**Family Partnership Case**
19 B.T.A. 621; 51 F.2d 7; 284 U.S. 608, 76 L. Ed. 521, 52 S. Ct. 43; 285 U.S. 136, 76 L. Ed. 665, 52 S. Ct. 345

**Fanny Hill Case**
383 U.S. 413, 16 L. Ed. 2d 1, 86 S. Ct. 975

**Fansteel Case**
306 U.S. 240, 83 L. Ed. 627, 59 S. Ct. 490

**Farm Hand Prosecution Case**
240 Iowa 561, 36 N.W.2d 739

**Farm Loan Case**
255 U.S. 180, 65 L. Ed. 577, 41 S. Ct. 243

**Farm Moratorium Case**
8 F. Supp. 489, 26 Am. B.R. (n.s.) 473; 74 F.2d 576, 27 Am. B.R. (n.s.) 200; 294 U.S. 702, 79 L. Ed. 1238, 55 S. Ct. 547; 295 U.S. 555, 79 L. Ed. 1593, 55 S. Ct. 854; 55 S. Ct. 918; 55 S. Ct. 919; 296 U.S. 661, 80 L. Ed. 471, 56 S. Ct. 82

**Farm Roller Case**
88 A.D. 309, 84 N.Y.S. 622; 183 N.Y. 78, 75 N.E. 1098

**Farmworkers Unionization Case**
416 U.S. 802, 40 L. Ed. 2d 566, 94 S. Ct. 2191

**Farra Case**
66 F. 496, 13 C.C.A. 602

**Farragut Prize Cases**
89 U.S. 406, 22 L. Ed. 879
7 D.C. 94

**Fashion Originator's Case**
114 F.2d 80; 311 U.S. 641, 85 L. Ed. 409, 61 S. Ct. 175; 312 U.S. 457, 85 L. Ed. 949, 61 S. Ct. 703; 312 U.S. 668, 85 L. Ed. 949, 61 S. Ct. 703

**Fashion Park Cases**
3 F.2d 682; 7 F.2d 962
10 F.2d 904
49 F.2d 830, 18 C.C.P.A. (Patents) 1399

**Fat Acid Case**
F. Cas. No. 14,042; 86 U.S. 287, 22 L. Ed. 125

**Fayerweather Will Cases**
103 F. 548; 118 F. 943; 195 U.S. 276, 49 L. Ed. 193, 25 S. Ct. 58
91 Hun 509, 36 N.Y.S. 576; 151 N.Y. 282, 45 N.E. 876; 152 N.Y. 641, 46 N.E. 1152

**F.C.C. Minority Preference Case**
111 L. Ed. 2d 445, 110 S. Ct. 2997

**FDIC Insured Letter of Credit Case**
476 U.S. 426, 90 L. Ed. 2d 428, 106 S. Ct. 1931

**Federal Agencies Garnishment Case**
289 Mich. 91, 286 N.W. 169; 308 U.S. 541, 84 L. Ed. 456, 60 S. Ct. 129; 309 U.S. 242, 84 L. Ed. 726, 60 S. Ct. 488

**Federal Aid to Nonpublic Schools Case**
417 U.S. 402, 41 L. Ed. 2d 159, 94 S. Ct. 2274

**Federal Baseball Case**
269 F. 681; 50 App. D.C. 165; 259 U.S. 200, 66 L. Ed. 898, 42 S. Ct. 465; 42 S. Ct. 587

**Federal Bribery Statute Case**
79 L. Ed. 2d 458, 104 S. Ct. 1172

**Federal Common Law Case**
451 U.S. 304, 68 L. Ed. 2d 114, 101 S. Ct. 1784

**Federal Contract Sales Tax Cases**
241 Ala. 557, 3 So. 2d 572; 314 U.S. 1, 86 L. Ed. 3, 62 S. Ct. 43
241 Ala. 569, 3 So. 2d 582; 314 U.S. 14, 86 L. Ed. 9, 62 S. Ct. 48; 314 U.S. 599, 86 L. Ed. 482, 62 S. Ct. 118

**Federal-Contracting Affirmative-Action Case**
515 U.S. 200, 132 L. Ed. 2d 158, 115 S. Ct. 2097 (1995)

**Federal Control Cases**
53 F.2d 904; 286 U.S. 563, 76 L. Ed. 1296, 52 S. Ct. 645
5 B.T.A. 15
5 B.T.A. 108
6 B.T.A. 436
8 B.T.A. 225; 10 B.T.A. 1347
9 B.T.A. 365
16 B.T.A. 264

**Federal Election Campaign Act Case**
454 U.S. 27, 70 L. Ed. 2d 23, 102 S. Ct. 38

**Federal Employee Pay System Case**
454 U.S. 555, 70 L. Ed. 2d 768, 102 S. Ct. 805

**Federal Employers' Liability Cases**
224 U.S. 547, 56 L. Ed. 879, 32 S. Ct. 603
352 U.S. 500, 1 L. Ed. 2d 493, 77 S. Ct. 443
375 U.S. 253, 11 L. Ed. 2d 307, 84 S. Ct. 316; 113 F.2d 721; 140 F.2d 865; 204 F.2d 461; 289 F. Supp. 374
148 F. 986; 207 U.S. 463, 52 L. Ed. 297, 28 S. Ct. 141
148 F. 997; 207 U.S. 463, 52 L. Ed. 297, 28 S. Ct. 141
173 F. 494; 223 U.S. 1, 56 L. Ed. 327, 32 S. Ct. 169
82 Conn. 373, 73 A. 762; 223 U.S. 1, 56 L. Ed. 327, 32 S. Ct. 169

**Federal Estate Tax Case**
175 Misc. 489, 23 N.Y.S.2d 943; 287 N.Y. 61, 38 N.E.2d 131, 39 N.E.2d 308; 287 N.Y. 764, 40 N.E.2d 46; 315 U.S. 795, 86 L. Ed. 1197, 62 S. Ct. 918; 289 N.Y. 601, 43 N.E.2d 831; 317 U.S. 95, 87 L. Ed. 106, 63 S. Ct. 109; 289 N.Y. 760, 46 N.E.2d 361

**Federal Gas Rate Case**
134 F.2d 287; 319 U.S. 735, 87 L. Ed. 1695, 63 S. Ct. 1165; 320 U.S. 591, 88 L. Ed. 333, 64 S. Ct. 281

**Federal Housing Inspection Case**
173 F.2d 790; 337 U.S. 958, 93 L. Ed. 1757, 69 S. Ct. 1533

**Federal Islands Case**
12 Ill. 2d 218, 145 N.E.2d 637

**Federal Land Bank Case**
126 Conn. 132, 9 A.2d 819

**Federal Maternity Act Case**
288 F. 252; 262 U.S. 447, 67 L. Ed. 1078, 43 S. Ct. 597

**Federal Metal Bed Case**
110 N.J. Eq. 217, 159 A. 698

**Federal Radio Commission Cases**
289 U.S. 266, 77 L. Ed. 1166, 53 S. Ct. 627; 292 U.S. 613, 78 L. Ed. 1472, 54 S. Ct. 856

**Federal Shop Crafts Case**
283 F. 479; 286 F. 228; 290 F. 978

**Federal Skywalk Case**
680 F.2d 1175

**Federal Sugar Case**
20 I.C.C. 200; 225 U.S. 306, 56 L. Ed. 1100, 32 S. Ct. 817; 200 F. 779; 231 U.S. 274, 58 L. Ed. 218, 34 S. Ct. 75

**Federal Tax Lien Case**
210 La. 78, 26 So. 2d 361

**Federal Torts Claim Act Accrual Case**
44 U.S. 111, 62 L. Ed. 2d 259, 100 S. Ct. 35

**Feeder Case**
55 F. 490; 63 F. 588, 11 C.C.A. 342

**Felony-Murder Death Penalty Case**
481 U.S. 137, 95 L. Ed. 2d 127, 107 S. Ct. 1676

**Feltman Case**
230 A.D. 299, 243 N.Y.S. 625; 256 N.Y. 156, 176 N.E. 5

**Female-Promotion Affirmative-Action Case**
480 U.S. 616, 94 L. Ed. 2d 615, 107 S. Ct. 1442

**Fennerstein's Champagne Case**
70 U.S. 145, 18 L. Ed. 121

**Ferreira Case**
54 U.S. 40, 14 L. Ed. 42

**Ferro-Phosphorated Elixir of Calisaya Bark Case**
4 Abb. Pr. (n.s.) 6, 35 How. Pr. 76; 58 N.Y. 223

**Fertilizer Case**
301 U.S. 178, 81 L. Ed. 990, 57 S. Ct. 748

**Fetal Protection Sex Discrimination Case**
113 L. Ed. 2d 158, 111 S. Ct. 1196

**Fibreboard Case**
130 N.L.R.B. 1558, No. 161; 138 N.L.R.B. 550, No. 67

**Fifield Manor Tax Refund Case**
188 Cal. App. 2d 1, 10 Cal. Rptr. 242

**Fifteen Per Cent Cases**
290 U.S. 70, 78 L. Ed. 181, 54 S. Ct. 28
45 I.C.C. 303
178 I.C.C. 539; 179 I.C.C. 215; 191 I.C.C. 361
226 I.C.C. 41; 226 I.C.C. 746

**Fighting Ship Cases**
200 F. 806
216 F. 971; 239 U.S. 466, 60 L. Ed. 387, 36 S. Ct. 212
220 F. 230; 242 U.S. 537, 61 L. Ed. 479, 37 S. Ct. 233

**Fighting Words and Offensive Speech Case**
438 U.S. 726, 47 L. Ed. 2d 1073, 98 S. Ct. 3026

**Filbert Street Cases**
111 Pa. 353, 5 A. 742; 132 U.S. 75, 33 L. Ed. 267, 10 S. Ct. 34

**Filing Fee Case**
415 U.S. 709, 39 L. Ed. 2d 702, 94 S. Ct. 1315

**Filled Milk Case**
304 U.S. 144, 82 L. Ed. 1234, 58 S. Ct. 778, 104 F.2d 969

**Financial Responsibility Case**
156 Neb. 215, 55 N.W.2d 620

**Fine School Case**
96 N.J.L. 334, 115 A. 342

**Finn Case**
181 F.2d 845; 341 U.S. 6, 95 L. Ed. 702, 71 S. Ct. 534; 347 U.S. 912, 98 L. Ed. 1069, 74 S. Ct. 476; 207 F.2d 113

**Finnish Sailing Vessel Cases**
94 Ct. Cl. 315; 1941 A.M.C. 105; 315 U.S. 815, 86 L. Ed. 1213, 62 S. Ct. 804
96 Ct. Cl. 127
1956 A.M.C. 1409

**Fire Escape Case**
70 N.Y. 126

**Fire Extinguisher Case**
21 F. 40

**Fire Insurance Case**
189 F. 769; 233 U.S. 389, 58 L. Ed. 1011, 34 S. Ct. 612

**Fire Insurance Rate Case**
342 Mo. 139, 113 S.W.2d 795

**Fire Investigation Cases**
436 U.S. 499, 56 L. Ed. 2d 486, 98 S. Ct. 1942

**Firearms Disabilities Case**
460 U.S. 103, 74 L. Ed. 2d 845, 103 S. Ct. 986

**Firearms Transportation Cases**
28 F. Supp. 900; 36 F. Supp. 273; 42 F. Supp. 252; 131 F.2d 261; 217 U.S. 623, 87 L. Ed. 504, 63 S. Ct. 441; 319 U.S. 463, 87 L. Ed. 1519, 63 S. Ct. 1241
131 F.2d 614; 318 U.S. 748, 87 L. Ed. 1124, 63 S. Ct. 664; 319 U.S. 463, 87 L. Ed. 1519, 63 S. Ct. 1241

**Firefighters' Job Discrimination Case**
104 L. Ed. 2d 835, 109 S. Ct. 2180

**Firestone Cases**
147 F. 739; 151 F. 237, 80 C.C.A. 589
79 F.2d 948; 298 U.S. 679, 80 L. Ed. 1399, 56 S. Ct. 945; 298 U.S. 679, 80 L. Ed. 1399, 56 S. Ct. 946

**Firestone Estate Case**
45 So. 2d 681; 76 So. 2d 665 (Fla.)

**First Amendment Election Case**
456 U.S. 45, 71 L. Ed. 2d 732, 102 S. Ct. 1523

**First Amendment in Shopping Centers Case**
447 U.S. 74, 64 L. Ed. 2d 741, 100 S. Ct. 2035

**First Boston and Maine Case**
202 A.D. 54, 195 N.Y.S. 402; 234 N.Y. 629, 138 N.E. 475

**First Carpenter Case**
218 F. 273; 264 F. 772

**First Commodities Clause Case**
164 F. 215; 213 U.S. 366, 53 L. Ed. 836, 29 S. Ct. 527, 176 F. 1015; 220 U.S. 257, 55 L. Ed. 458, 31 S. Ct. 387

**First Coronado Coal Case**
259 U.S. 344, 66 L. Ed. 975, 42 S. Ct. 570; 268 U.S. 295, 69 L. Ed. 963, 45 S. Ct. 551

**First Crack Case**
84 Okla. Crim. 352, 182 P.2d 523; 77 F. Supp. 553; 172 F.2d 668; 337 U.S. 923, 93 L. Ed. 1731, 69 S. Ct. 1169; 339 U.S. 200, 94 L. Ed. 761, 70 S. Ct. 587

**First Employers' Liability Cases**
207 U.S. 463, 52 L. Ed. 297, 28 S. Ct. 141; 148 F. 986; 148 F. 997
239 U.S. 556, 60 L. Ed. 436, 36 S. Ct. 188
284 U.S. 415, 76 L. Ed. 370, 52 S. Ct. 205; 284 U.S. 604, 76 L. Ed. 517, 52 S. Ct. 24

**First Mutoscope Case**
114 F. 926

**First National Bank of Lexington Case**
208 F. Supp. 457; 374 U.S. 824, 10 L. Ed. 2d 1049, 83 S. Ct. 1864; 376 U.S. 935, 11 L. Ed. 2d 657, 84 S. Ct. 790; 376 U.S. 665, 12 L. Ed. 2d 1, 84 S. Ct. 1033

**First Pan-American Case**
6 F.2d 43; 9 F.2d 761; 24 F.2d 206; 273 U.S. 456, 71 L. Ed. 734, 47 S. Ct. 416

**First School Prayer Case**
18 Misc. 2d 659, 191 N.Y.S.2d 453; 11 A.D.2d 340, 206 N.Y.S.2d 183; 10 N.Y.2d 174, 218 N.Y.S.2d 659, 176 N.E.2d 579; 370 U.S. 421, 8 L. Ed. 2d 601, 82 S. Ct. 1261; 12 N.Y.2d 712, 233 N.Y.S.2d 766, 186 N.E.2d 124; 368 U.S. 982, 82 S. Ct. 597; 369 U.S. 809, 82 S. Ct. 686

**First United Mine Workers' Case**
259 U.S. 344, 66 L. Ed. 975, 42 S. Ct. 570; 268 U.S. 295, 69 L. Ed. 963, 45 S. Ct. 551

**Fish Hatcheries Case**
232 Pa. 504, 81 A. 544

**Fish Meal Case**
9 F.2d 940; 9 F.2d 622, 1926 A.M.C. 32; 271 U.S. 666, 70 L. Ed. 1140, 46 S. Ct. 482

**Fish Net Case**
152 U.S. 133, 38 L. Ed. 385, 14 S. Ct. 499

**Fish Refrigerator Case**
F. Cas. 11,180; 91 U.S. 37, 23 L. Ed. 200

**Fish-Wheel Case**
19 F. 643

**Fishgold Case**
62 F. Supp. 25; 154 F.2d 785; 328 U.S. 275, 90 L. Ed. 1230, 66 S. Ct. 1105; 327 U.S. 775, 90 L. Ed. 1004; 66 S. Ct. 904

**Fishing Rights Case**
241 Mo. App. 839, 263 S.W.2d 221; 364 Mo. 835, 269 S.W.2d 17

**Five Cent Fare Case**
25 F.2d 164; 26 F.2d 912; 279 U.S. 159, 73 L. Ed. 652, 49 S. Ct. 282; 73 L. Ed. 1011, 49 S. Ct. 338; 32 F.2d 1015

**Five Per Cent Cases**
110 U.S. 471, 28 L. Ed. 198, 4 S. Ct. 210

31 I.C.C. 351; 32 I.C.C. 325

**Five Per Cent Discount Cases**
Treas. Dec. 35508, 6 Ct. Cust. 291; 238 U.S. 637, 59 L. Ed. 1500, 35 S. Ct. 940; 243 U.S. 97, 61 L. Ed. 617, 37 S. Ct. 346

**Five-Person Jury Case**
55 L. Ed. 2d 234, 98 S. Ct. 1029

**Flag Burning Cases**
491 U.S. 397, 105 L. Ed. 2d 342, 109 S. Ct. 2533

496 U.S. 310, 110 L. Ed. 2d 287, 110 S. Ct. 2404

**Flag Desecration Cases**
394 U.S. 576, 22 L. Ed. 2d 572, 89 S. Ct. 1354; 415 U.S. 566, 39 L. Ed. 2d 605, 94 S. Ct. 1242; 418 U.S. 405, 41 L. Ed. 2d 842, 94 S. Ct. 2727

**Flag Misuse Case**
415 U.S. 566, 39 L. Ed. 2d 605, 94 S. Ct. 1242

**Flag Salute Cases**
316 U.S. 584, 86 L. Ed. 1691, 62 S. Ct. 1231; 319 U.S. 103, 87 L. Ed. 1290, 63 S. Ct. 890; 314 U.S. 593, 86 L. Ed. 478, 62 S. Ct. 93; 314 U.S. 651, 86 L. Ed. 522, 62 S. Ct. 99; 315 U.S. 782, 86 L. Ed. 1189, 62 S. Ct. 630, 315 U.S. 793, 86 L. Ed. 1196, 62 S. Ct. 903; 316 U.S. 649, 62 S. Ct. 1312; 318 U.S. 796, 87 L. Ed. 1161, 63 S. Ct. 658, 319 U.S. 105, 87 L. Ed. 1292, 63 S. Ct. 891, 320 U.S. 719, 88 L. Ed. 423, 64 S. Ct. 423

21 F. Supp. 581; 24 F. Supp. 271; 108 F.2d 683; 309 U.S. 645, 84 L. Ed. 998, 60 S. Ct. 609; 310 U.S. 586, 84 L. Ed. 1375; 60 S. Ct. 1010

47 F. Supp. 251; 319 U.S. 624, 87 L. Ed. 1628, 63 S. Ct. 1178

30 Ala. App. 142, 3 So. 2d 74

241 Ala. 279, 3 So. 2d 76

242 Ala. 549, 7 So. 2d 503

202 Ark. 614, 151 S.W.2d 1000

58 Ariz. 144, 118 P.2d 97

**Flagstaff Case**
98 U.S. 463, 25 L. Ed. 253

**Flash Money Case**
469 U.S. 70, 83 L. Ed. 2d 472, 105 S. Ct. 479

**Flat Tax Case**
34 Colo. 240, 82 P. 531; 204 U.S. 103, 51 L. Ed. 393, 27 S. Ct. 198

**Flaxseed Cases**
44 F. 258; 157 U.S. 183, 39 L. Ed. 665, 15 S. Ct. 583
15 I.C.C. 47

**Fleming Case**
24 Misc. 88, 53 N.Y.S. 291; 34 A.D. 627, 54 N.Y.S. 1112; 158 N.Y. 175, 52 N.E. 1113

**Fletcher Cases**
11 F. 377; 12 F. 557; 13 F. 526; 14 F. 846; 117 U.S. 519, 29 L. Ed. 934, 6 S. Ct. 837
166 F. 782, 173 F. 471, 97 C.C.A. 477; 215 U.S. 600, 54 L. Ed. 343, 30 S. Ct. 400

**Flexible Tariff Cases**
Treas. Dec. 42030, 14 Ct. Cust. 350; 276 U.S. 394, 72 L. Ed. 624, 48 S. Ct. 348
Treas. Dec. 45674, 20 C.C.P.A. (Customs) 27
Treas. Dec. 45675, 20 C.C.P.A. (Customs) 38
Treas. Dec. 45676, 20 C.C.P.A. (Customs) 45
Treas. Dec. 45677, 20 C.C.P.A. (Customs) 49

**Floating Zone Case**
214 Md. 48, 133 A.2d 83

**Florida Case (Citrus Fruit Rates)**
144 I.C.C. 603; 177 I.C.C. 735; 181 I.C.C. 251; 188 I.C.C. 229

**Florida Citrus Growers Guarantee Case**
28 F. Supp. 44; 60 S. Ct. 107; 309 U.S. 310, 84 L. Ed. 774, 60 S. Ct. 517

**Florida Fertilizer Case**
47 F. Supp. 552; 63 S. Ct. 764; 319 U.S. 441, 87 L. Ed. 1504, 63 S. Ct. 1137; 320 U.S. 810, 88 L. Ed. 489, 64 S. Ct. 27

**Florida Log Case**
30 F.2d 116; 31 F.2d 580; 74 L. Ed. 1179, 50 S. Ct. 161; 282 U.S. 194, 75 L. Ed. 291, 51 S. Ct. 119

**Florida Slot Machine Case**
121 Fla. 93, 163 So. 486

**Florida State Gasoline Tax Case**
99 Fla. 1, 99 Fla. 65, 115, 126 So. 308

**Flowers Case**
148 F.2d 163; 326 U.S. 465, 90 L. Ed. 203, 66 S. Ct. 250; 326 U.S. 812, 90 L. Ed. 496, 66 S. Ct. 482; 326 U.S. 701, 90 L. Ed. 413, 66 S. Ct. 31; 3 T.C. 1292

**Floyd Acceptances Case**
1 Ct. Cl. 270; 74 U.S. 666, 19 L. Ed. 169

**Flume Case**
177 N.C. 520, 99 S.E. 407

**Fly Wheel Case**
5 F. Supp. 32, 19 U.S.P.Q. (BNA) 249; 72 F.2d 53, 22 U.S.P.Q. (BNA) 8, 22 U.S.P.Q. (BNA) 244; 293 U.S. 528, 79 L. Ed. 638, 55 S. Ct. 139; 293 U.S. 587, 79 L. Ed. 682, 55 S. Ct. 101; 294 U.S. 477, 79 L. Ed. 1005, 55 S. Ct. 455; 294 U.S. 734, 79 L. Ed. 1262, 55 S. Ct. 634

**Flying School Liability Case**
44 So. 2d 504 (La.)

**Folding Bed Case**
37 F. 693; 41 F. 51; 157 U.S. 659, 39 L. Ed. 848, 15 S. Ct. 738, 1895 C.D. 294, 71 Off. Gaz. Pat. Office 451

**Foodstamp Fraud Case**
471 U.S. 419, 85 L. Ed. 2d 434, 105 S. Ct. 2084

**Football Admissions Tax Case**
304 U.S. 439, 82 L. Ed. 1448, 58 S. Ct. 980

**For Sale Sign Case**
431 U.S. 85, 52 L. Ed. 2d 155, 97 S. Ct. 1614

**Ford-Canton Case**
355 Mich. 103, 94 N.W.2d 407

**Ford Case**
37 La. Ann. 443

**Ford Dividend Cases**
20 F.2d 395
204 Mich. 459, 170 N.W. 668

**Ford-Ferguson Patent Case**
77 F. Supp. 425, 77 U.S.P.Q. (BNA) 464; 8 F.R.D. 414, 79 U.S.P.Q. (BNA) 205; 89 F. Supp. 45; 182 F.2d 329; 92 F. Supp. 868; 340 U.S. 851, 95 L. Ed. 624, 71 S. Ct. 79

**Ford Motor Case**
278 F. 373; 257 U.S. 658, 66 L. Ed. 421, 42 S. Ct. 185

**Foreign-Built Yacht Tax Cases**
190 F. 359; 232 U.S. 261, 58 L. Ed. 596, 34 S. Ct. 421; 232 U.S. 289, 58 L. Ed. 608, 34 S. Ct. 428; 232 U.S. 290, 58 L. Ed. 609, 34 S. Ct. 427; 232 U.S. 292, 58 L. Ed. 610, 34 S. Ct. 427; 232 U.S. 293, 58 L. Ed. 610, 34 S. Ct. 431; 232 U.S. 299, 58 L. Ed. 612, 34 S. Ct. 433; 232 U.S. 308, 58 L. Ed. 616, 34 S. Ct. 437; 232 U.S. 310, 58 L. Ed. 617, 34 S. Ct. 429
190 F. 372; 214 F. 67, 130 C.C.A. 507

**Foreign Divorce Recognition Case**
6 N.J. 380, 78 A.2d 896

**Foreign Domiciled Child Case**
203 S.W.2d 979 (Tex.); 146 Tex. 489, 208 S.W.2d 876; 210 S.W.2d 275

**Foreign Flag Vessel Case**
10 N.Y.2d 218, 219 N.Y.S.2d 21, 176 N.E.2d 719; 371 U.S. 804, 83 S. Ct. 18; 372 U.S. 24, 9 L. Ed. 2d 557, 83 S. Ct. 611; 11 A.D.2d 177, 202 N.Y.S.2d 692; 8 L. Ed. 2d 496, 82 S. Ct. 1552; 13 N.Y.2d 754, 242 N.Y.S.2d 57, 192 N.E.2d 26

**Foreign-Held Bond Case**
82 U.S. 300, 21 L. Ed. 179

**Foreign Languages in Schools Cases**
11 F.2d 710; 273 U.S. 677, 71 L. Ed. 835, 47 S. Ct. 99; 273 U.S. 284, 71 L. Ed. 646, 47 S. Ct. 406
191 Iowa 1060, 181 N.W. 508; 262 U.S. 404, 67 L. Ed. 1047, 43 S. Ct. 628
104 Neb. 93, 175 N.W. 531
107 Neb. 657, 187 N.W. 100; 262 U.S. 390, 67 L. Ed. 1042, 43 S. Ct. 625
108 Neb. 448, 187 N.W. 927; 262 U.S. 404, 67 L. Ed. 1047, 43 S. Ct. 628
102 Ohio St. 474, 132 N.E. 20; 262 U.S. 404, 67 L. Ed. 1047, 43 S. Ct. 628

**Foreign Realty Tort Case**
220 Ark. 521, 249 S.W.2d 994

**Foreign Source Dividend Income Tax Case**
445 U.S. 425, 63 L. Ed. 2d 510, 100 S. Ct. 1223

**Foreign Sovereign Immunities Act Case**
461 U.S. 480, 76 L. Ed. 2d 81, 103 S. Ct. 1962

**Forest Reserve Cases**
264 F. 898; 256 U.S. 51, 65 L. Ed. 825, 41 S. Ct. 439
311 U.S. 317, 85 L. Ed. 210, 61 S. Ct. 264; 309 U.S. 626, 84 L. Ed. 987, 60 S. Ct. 585; 310 U.S. 615, 84 L. Ed. 1391, 60 S. Ct. 1092; 311 U.S. 613, 85 L. Ed. 389, 61 S. Ct. 57; 41 F. Supp. 273

**Forestry Cases**
144 N.W. 1123 (Wis.); 160 Wis. 21, 151 N.W. 331; 162 Wis. 609, 157 N.W. 794
163 Wis. 283, 158 N.W. 81
163 Wis. 292, 158 N.W. 84; 166 Wis. 111, 164 N.W. 848

**Forfeiture of Currency Case**
461 U.S. 555, 76 L. Ed. 2d 143, 103 S. Ct. 2005

**Forgay-Conrad Case**
47 U.S. 201, 12 L. Ed. 404

**Forrest Divorce Case**
3 Code Rep. 121; 3 Code Rep. 141; 10 Barb. 46, 5 How. Pr. 125; 2 Edm. Sel. Cas. 171; 2 Edm. Sel. Cas. 180; 3 Code Rep. 254; 6 Duer (13 N.Y. Super. Ct.) 102, 3 Abb. Pr. 144; 3 Bosw. (16 N.Y. Super. Ct.) 650; 3 Bosw. (16 N.Y. Super. Ct.) 661, 9 Abb. Pr. 289; 5 Bosw. (18 N.Y. Super. Ct.) 672; 8 Bosw. (21 N.Y. Super. Ct.) 640; 25 N.Y. 501; 9 Bosw. (22 N.Y. Super. Ct.) 686

**Fort Smith School Case**
382 U.S. 198, 15 L. Ed. 2d 265, 86 S. Ct. 358

**Fort Street Case**
172 Mich. 136, 137 N.W. 645; 229 U.S. 39, 57 L. Ed. 1056, 33 S. Ct. 697; 255 U.S. 171, 65 L. Ed. 570, 41 S. Ct. 285

**Forty-Eight-Hour Detention Case**
114 L. Ed. 2d 49, 111 S. Ct. 1661

**Forty-Three Gallons of Cognac Brandy Case**
11 F. 47; 14 F. 539

**Forwarding Case**
220 U.S. 235, 55 L. Ed. 448, 31 S. Ct. 392

**Fossat Case**
61 U.S. 413, 15 L. Ed. 944; 62 U.S. 445, 16 L. Ed. 185; 69 U.S. 649, 17 L. Ed. 739

**Four-Wheel Scooter Case**
108 Cal. App. 2d 849, 240 P.2d 351

**Fourteen Diamond Rings Case**
183 U.S. 176, 46 L. Ed. 138, 22 S. Ct. 59

**Fourth Amendment Habeas Corpus Case**
428 U.S. 465, 49 L. Ed. 2d 1067, 96 S. Ct. 3037

**Fourth Amendment Rights Case**
439 U.S. 128, 58 L. Ed. 2d 387, 99 S. Ct. 421

**Fourth and First National Bank Case**
153 Tenn. 176, 281 S.W. 785

**Fowler Hotel Case**
181 F. Supp. 738

**Fox Case**
232 A.D. 308, 249 N.Y.S. 623; 257 N.Y. 305, 178 N.E. 289

**Frank-Georgia Mob Case**
141 Ga. 243, 80 S.E. 1016; 142 Ga. 617, 83 S.E. 233; 142 Ga. 741, 83 S.E. 645; 235 U.S. 694, 59 L. Ed. 429, 35 S. Ct. 208; 237 U.S. 309, 59 L. Ed. 969, 35 S. Ct. 582

**Frankensteinian Cases**
112 Kan. 616, 212 P. 69
140 Kan. 171, 34 F.2d 102
141 Kan. 533, 41 P.2d 1042
180 Kan. 168, 302 P.2d 542

**Frankie and Johnnie Case**
233 A.D. 704, 249 N.Y.S. 958, 258 N.Y. 451; 180 N.E. 169

**Franklin Bank Case**
11 G. & J. 28 (Md.)

**Franklin Knitting Mills Case**
15 F.2d 375; 273 U.S. 761, 71 L. Ed. 878, 47 S. Ct. 476; 7 F.2d 381

**Frazier-Lemke Act Cases**
295 U.S. 555, 79 L. Ed. 1593, 55 S. Ct. 854; 296 U.S. 661, 80 L. Ed. 471, 56 S. Ct. 82
300 U.S. 440, 81 L. Ed. 736, 57 S. Ct. 556
77 F.2d 9; 83 F.2d 493
79 F.2d 887
83 F.2d 322
83 F.2d 1013
12 F. Supp. 30
12 F. Supp. 206; 13 F. Supp. 893
12 F. Supp. 297
12 F. Supp. 625
13 F. Supp. 1
13 F. Supp. 221
13 F. Supp. 249; 90 F.2d 98
13 F. Supp. 283
13 F. Supp. 353; 299 U.S. 606, 81 L. Ed. 447, 57 S. Ct. 16; 299 U.S. 606, 81 L. Ed. 447, 57 S. Ct. 17
13 F. Supp. 371
13 F. Supp. 375
13 F. Supp. 645; 85 F.2d 1013
14 F. Supp. 72

*Continued*

**Free Appropriate Public Education Case**
458 U.S. 176, 73 L. Ed. 2d 690, 102 S. Ct. 3034

**Free Cartage Case**
2 I.C. 152, 2 I.C. 185, 3 I.C. 60; 57 F. 1005; 74 F. 803, 21 C.C.A. 103, 43 U.S. App. D.C. 308; 167 U.S. 633, 42 L. Ed. 306, 17 S. Ct. 986

**Free Text Book Case**
230 Ky. 287, 18 S.W.2d 1114

**Freedom of Speech Cases**
253 F. 212; 249 U.S. 47, 63 L. Ed. 470, 39 S. Ct. 247
91 N.H. 310, 18 A.2d 754; 91 N.H. 527, 31 A.2d 49; 62 S. Ct. 89; 315 U.S. 568, 86 L. Ed. 1031, 62 S. Ct. 766

**Freedom of the Press Cases**
283 U.S. 697, 75 L. Ed. 1357, 51 S. Ct. 625
10 F. Supp. 161; 56 S. Ct. 129; 297 U.S. 233, 80 L. Ed. 660, 56 S. Ct. 444
303 U.S. 444, 82 L. Ed. 949, 58 S. Ct. 666

**Freehand Map Admissibility Case**
212 Ark. 773, 207 S.W.2d 609; 214 Ark. 523, 217 S.W.2d 357

**Freight and Passenger Rates Case**
210 F. 902; 239 U.S. 655, 60 L. Ed. 488, 36 S. Ct. 167

**Freight Association Case**
53 F. 440, 3 C.C.A. 426; 58 F. 58, 7 C.C.A. 15, 19 U.S. App. D.C. 36; 166 U.S. 290, 41 L. Ed. 1007, 17 S. Ct. 540

**Freight Discrimination Cases**
95 N.C. 428
95 N.C. 434

**Freight Tax Case**
82 U.S. 232, 21 L. Ed. 146

**French Bank Case**
53 Cal. 495

**French Spoliation Cases**
21 Ct. Cl. 340
21 Ct. Cl. 434; 22 Ct. Cl. 1; 26 Ct. Cl. 249; 26 Ct. Cl. 290

**Frequent Flyer Case**
513 U.S. 219, 130 L. Ed. 2d 715, 115 S. Ct. 817 (1995)

**Freshman Case**
46 F.2d 792; 65 F.2d 1

**Freshwater Wetlands Case**
474 U.S. 121, 88 L. Ed. 2d 419, 106 S. Ct. 455

**Friars Club Case**
432 F.2d 879

**Friedman-Marks Case**
301 U.S. 58, 81 L. Ed. 893, 57 S. Ct. 645

**Fries Case**
3 U.S. 515, 1 L. Ed. 701

**Frisco Case**
229 F. 103, 143 C.C.A. 379

**Frisco Rate Case**
207 F. 287, 125 C.C.A. 31; 231 U.S. 755, 58 L. Ed. 468, 34 S. Ct. 323

**Fronizer Case**
15 Ohio Dec. 1, 2 Ohio N.P. (n.s.) 373; 15 Ohio Dec. 146, 2 Ohio N.P. (n.s.) 476; 5 Ohio C.C. (n.s.) 621, 17 Ohio C.D. 16; 15 Ohio Dec. 613, 3 Ohio N.P. (n.s.) 303; 72 Ohio St. 642, 3 Ohio Law Rep. 11, 50 Wkly. L. Bull. 146, 76 N.E. 1132; 8 Ohio C.C. (n.s.) 216, 18 Ohio C.D. 709; 77 Ohio St. 7, 5 Ohio Law Rep. 452, 52 Wkly. L. Bull. 550, 82 N.E. 518

**Front Street Case**
68 A.D. 488, 74 N.Y.S. 343; 81 A.D. 655, 81 N.Y.S. 1120; 114 A.D. 915, 99 N.Y.S. 1049; 176 N.Y. 308, 68 N.E. 587; 176 N.Y. 594, 68 N.E. 1115; 178 N.Y. 561, 70 N.E. 1097; 190 N.Y. 84, 82 N.E. 513

**Frothingham Case**
262 U.S. 447, 67 L. Ed. 1078, 43 S. Ct. 597; 288 F. 252

**Fruehauf Case**
301 U.S. 49, 81 L. Ed. 893, 57 S. Ct. 642

**Fruit-of-the-Poisonous-Tree Case**
251 U.S. 385, 64 L. Ed. 319, 40 S. Ct. 182; 39 S. Ct. 491; 39 S. Ct. 493, 265 F. 859

**Fruit Rind Case**
283 U.S. 1, 75 L. Ed. 801, 51 S. Ct. 328; 21 F.2d 110; 35 F.2d 106, 3 U.S.P.Q. (BNA) 69; 281 U.S. 709, 74 L. Ed. 1132, 50 S. Ct. 249

**Fruit Tree Doctrine Case**
281 U.S. 111, 74 L. Ed. 731, 50 S. Ct. 241; 30 F.2d 898; 10 B.T.A. 723; 280 U.S. 538, 74 L. Ed. 600, 50 S. Ct. 16; 50 S. Ct. 13

**Fugitive Slave Law Case**
59 U.S. 479, 15 L. Ed. 465; 62 U.S. 506, 16 L. Ed. 169

**Fulenweider Case**
9 Ct. Cl. 403

**Full Faith and Credit Clause Case**
456 U.S. 461, 72 L. Ed. 2d 262, 102 S. Ct. 1883

**Full Hearing Case**
304 U.S. 1, 82 L. Ed. 1129, 58 S. Ct. 773, 58 S. Ct. 999; 24 F. Supp. 214; 307 U.S. 183, 83 L. Ed. 1211, 59 S. Ct. 795; 32 F. Supp. 546

**Fund Impoundment Cases**
420 U.S. 35, 43 L. Ed. 2d 1, 95 S. Ct. 839; 420 U.S. 136, 43 L. Ed. 2d 82, 95 S. Ct. 847

## G

**Gag Law Case**
174 Minn. 457, 219 N.W. 770; 179 Minn. 40, 228 N.W. 326; 283 U.S. 697, 75 L. Ed. 1357, 51 S. Ct. 625

**Gag Order Case**
427 U.S. 539, 49 L. Ed. 2d 683, 96 S. Ct. 2791

**Gaines-New Orleans Case**
73 U.S. 642, 18 L. Ed. 950

**Gaines Will Case**
73 U.S. 642, 18 L. Ed. 950
104 U.S. 386, 26 L. Ed. 757

**Gainsville 8 Case**
384 F. Supp. 1229

**Galbraith Case**
63 U.S. 89, 16 L. Ed. 321; F. Cas. No. 15,182; 67 U.S. 394, 17 L. Ed. 448

**Galveston Case (Rates)**
258 U.S. 388, 66 L. Ed. 678, 42 S. Ct. 351

**Galveston Truck Line Case**
73 I.C.C. 617

**Galveston Wharfage Case**
14 I.C.C. 250; 166 F. 134; 219 U.S. 498, 55 L. Ed. 310, 31 S. Ct. 279; 28 I.C.C. 584

**Gambler's Pledge Case**
148 Ohio St. 89, 73 N.E.2d 513

**Gambler's Telephone Case**
136 Conn. 210, 70 A.2d 118

**Garbage Ordinance Case**
202 Ind. 138, 171 N.E. 199

**Garbage Search Case**
486 U.S. 35, 100 L. Ed. 2d 30, 108 S. Ct. 1625

**Gargill Case**
218 F.2d 556

**Garland Case**
112 Md. 83, 75 A. 631

**Garment Makers Strike Case**
204 A.D. 513, 198 N.Y.S. 128

**Garmon Case**
45 Cal. 2d 657, 291 P.2d 1; 353 U.S. 26, 1 L. Ed. 2d 618, 77 S. Ct. 607; 49 Cal. 2d 595, 320 P.2d 473; 359 U.S. 236, 3 L. Ed. 2d 775, 79 S. Ct. 773; 353 U.S. 951, 1 L. Ed. 2d 860, 77 S. Ct. 858; 354 U.S. 919, 1 L. Ed. 2d 1434, 77 S. Ct. 1374

**Garner Case**
373 Pa. 19, 94 A.2d 893; 346 U.S. 485, 98 L. Ed. 228, 74 S. Ct. 161

**Gary Case**
213 F. Supp. 819; 324 F.2d 209; 377 U.S. 924, 12 L. Ed. 2d 216, 84 S. Ct. 1223

**Gary Steel Supply Company Case**
144 N.L.R.B. 470, No. 45

**Gas Burner Cases**
106 U.S. 178, 27 L. Ed. 138, 1 S. Ct. 198
F. Cas. No. 2,906; 106 U.S. 166, 27 L. Ed. 134, 1 S. Ct. 188

**Gas Company's Cases**
101 Md. 541, 61 A. 532
105 Md. 43, 65 A. 628

**Gas Filed Rate Doctrine Case**
453 U.S. 571, 69 L. Ed. 2d 856, 101 S. Ct. 2925

**Gas Heater Case**
214 La. 145, 36 So. 2d 704

**Gas Light Case**
131 F. Supp. 165; 239 F.2d 532, 112 U.S.P.Q. (BNA) 11; 356 U.S. 43, 2 L. Ed. 2d 583, 78 S. Ct. 667; 356 U.S. 934, 2 L. Ed. 2d 764, 78 S. Ct. 770; 116 U.S.P.Q. (BNA) 479
480 F. Supp. 454

**Gas Rate Cases**
417 U.S. 283, 41 L. Ed. 2d 72, 94 S. Ct. 2328; 417 U.S. 380, 41 L. Ed. 2d 141, 94 S. Ct. 2315

**Gas Sign Cases**
238 La. 636, 116 So. 2d 277
238 La. 936, 117 So. 2d 64
375 Pa. 547, 101 A.2d 634

**Gasoline Cracking Case**
221 U.S. 1, 55 L. Ed. 619, 31 S. Ct. 502

**Gasoline Pump Cases**
273 F. 478; 261 U.S. 463, 67 L. Ed. 746, 43 S. Ct. 450
274 F. 571; 261 U.S. 463, 67 L. Ed. 746, 43 S. Ct. 450
276 F. 686; 257 U.S. 631, 66 L. Ed. 407, 42 S. Ct. 183; 261 U.S. 463, 67 L. Ed. 746, 43 S. Ct. 450
282 F. 81; 260 U.S. 718, 67 L. Ed. 479, 43 S. Ct. 97; 261 U.S. 463, 67 L. Ed. 746, 43 S. Ct. 450

**Gasoline Tax Case**
280 U.S. 78, 74 L. Ed. 175, 50 S. Ct. 63
138 S.W.2d 924 (Tex.); 313 U.S. 554, 85 L. Ed. 1516, 61 S. Ct. 1085; 314 U.S. 480, 86 L. Ed. 356, 62 S. Ct. 350; 159 S.W.2d 214 (Tex.)
19 Cal. 2d 104, 119 P.2d 329; 316 U.S. 481, 86 L. Ed. 1611, 62 S. Ct. 1037, 62 S. Ct. 1168

**Gay's Gold Case**
F. Cas. No. 15, 194; 80 U.S. 358, 20 L. Ed. 606

**Gazette Case**
7 Haw. 31

**Geer Case**
82 N.Y. 575

**Gelb Case**
298 F.2d 544; 34 T.C. 1161

**Gender-Based Peremptory Challenge Case**
511 U.S. 127, 128 L. Ed. 2d 89, 114 S. Ct. 1419 (1994)

**General American Investors Company Case**
19 T.C. 581; 211 F.2d 522; 348 U.S. 812, 99 L. Ed. 641, 75 S. Ct. 35; 348 U.S. 434, 99 L. Ed. 504, 75 S. Ct. 478

**General Brick Case**
68 I.C.C. 213; 80 I.C.C. 179; 203 I.C.C. 777

**General Commodity Rate Increases Case**
223 I.C.C. 657; 229 I.C.C. 435

**General Electric Case**
123 N.L.R.B. 1547, No. 180; 278 F.2d 282; 366 U.S. 667, 6 L. Ed. 2d 592, 81 S. Ct. 1285; 138 N.L.R.B. 342, No. 38

**General Electric Firemen's Case**
208 F.2d 805; 347 U.S. 951, 98 L. Ed. 1097, 74 S. Ct. 676; 347 U.S. 975, 98 L. Ed. 1115, 74 S. Ct. 787

**General Electric Lamp Case**
15 F.2d 715; 272 U.S. 476, 71 L. Ed. 362, 47 S. Ct. 192

**General Electric X-Ray Case**
67 N.L.R.B. 997, No. 121

**General Extrusion Company Case**
121 N.L.R.B. 1165, No. 147

**General Legacy Ademption Case**
210 Miss. 74, 48 So. 2d 845

**General Motors Corporation Case**
120 N.L.R.B. 1215, No. 162

**General Tire & Rubber Case**
160 Ohio St. 559, 117 N.E.2d 329

**Genet Case**
59 N.Y. 80

**Genuine Yankee Soap Case**
2 Bosw. (15 N.Y. Super. Ct.) 1

**Georgia Blow Post Cases**
217 U.S. 524, 54 L. Ed. 868, 30 S. Ct. 594
244 U.S. 310, 61 L. Ed. 1160, 37 S. Ct. 640

**Georgia Chiropractic Case**
151 Ga. 371, 106 S.E. 792

**Georgia Commission Case**
4 I.C. 120; 88 F. 186; 93 F. 83, 35 C.C.A. 217; 181 U.S. 29, 45 L. Ed. 729, 21 S. Ct. 512

**Georgia County Unit Case (Schools)**
372 U.S. 368, 9 L. Ed. 2d 821, 83 S. Ct. 801

**Georgia Death Penalty Case**
446 U.S. 420, 64 L. Ed. 2d 398, 100 S. Ct. 1759

**Georgia Indian Case**
31 U.S. 515, 8 L. Ed. 483

**Georgia Poll Tax Case**
183 Ga. 189, 188 S.E. 140; 57 S. Ct. 671; 58 S. Ct. 133; 302 U.S. 277, 82 L. Ed. 252, 58 S. Ct. 205

**Georgia Syndicalism Cases**
295 U.S. 441, 79 L. Ed. 1530, 55 S. Ct. 794; 296 U.S. 661, 80 L. Ed. 471, 56 S. Ct. 82
301 U.S. 242, 81 L. Ed. 1066, 57 S. Ct. 732

**Gerard Case**
37 T.C. 826

**Geritol Case**
381 F.2d 884
68 F.T.C. 481

**German Language School Cases**
191 Iowa 1060, 181 N.W. 508; 262 U.S. 404, 67 L. Ed. 1047, 43 S. Ct. 628
104 Neb. 93, 175 N.W. 531
107 Neb. 657, 187 N.W. 100; 262 U.S. 390, 67 L. Ed. 1042, 43 S. Ct. 625
108 Neb. 448, 187 N.W. 927; 262 U.S. 404, 67 L. Ed. 1047, 43 S. Ct. 628
102 Ohio St. 474, 132 N.E. 20; 262 U.S. 404, 67 L. Ed. 1047, 43 S. Ct. 628

**German Saboteur Cases**
47 F. Supp. 431; 317 U.S. 1, 87 L. Ed. 3, 63 S. Ct. 1, 63 S. Ct. 2, 63 S. Ct. 22

**German Ship Case**
277 U.S. 610, 72 L. Ed. 1014, 48 S. Ct. 434

**Gerrymander Cases**
81 Wis. 440, 51 N.W. 724
83 Wis. 90, 53 N.W. 35

**Gerson Cases**
255 A.D. 48, N.Y.S.2d 813
255 A.D. 50, 5 N.Y.S.2d 831
167 Misc. 77, 2 N.Y.S.2d 714

**Getaway Car Insurance Case**
113 Colo. 546, 160 P.2d 356; 118 Colo. 445, 195 P.2d 728

**Getty Case**
142 Wash. 270, 253 P. 115

**Gettysburg Park Case**
67 F. 869; 160 U.S. 668, 40 L. Ed. 576, 16 S. Ct. 427

**Gibbons Case**
25 F.2d 363

**Gideon Bible Case**
14 N.J. 31, 100 A.2d 857; 348 U.S. 816, 99 L. Ed. 644, 75 S. Ct. 25

**Gideon Case**
370 U.S. 908, 8 L. Ed. 2d 403, 80 S. Ct. 1259; 370 U.S. 932, 82 S. Ct. 1587; 135 So. 2d 746 (Fla.); 371 U.S. 857, 83 S. Ct. 115; 372 U.S. 335, 9 L. Ed. 2d 799, 83 S. Ct. 792

**Gift Tax Exemption Case**
476 U.S. 558, 90 L. Ed. 2d 538, 106 S. Ct. 2071

**Gift to Class Error Case**
211 Ark. 1091, 204 S.W.2d 543

**Giles Case**
229 Md. 370, 183 A.2d 359

**Gilt Edge Claim Case**
14 F.2d 77; 118 U.S. 196, 30 L. Ed. 98, 6 S. Ct. 1177

**Girard Cases**
103 Vt. 330, 154 A. 666
354 U.S. 524, 1 L. Ed. 2d 1544, 77 S. Ct. 1409; 152 F. Supp. 21; 354 U.S. 928, 1 L. Ed. 2d 1532, 77 S. Ct. 1390

**Girard College Cases**
43 U.S. 127, 11 L. Ed. 205
353 U.S. 230, 1 L. Ed. 2d 792, 77 S. Ct. 806
392 F.2d 120; 270 F. Supp. 782
391 Pa. 434, 138 A.2d 844; 357 U.S. 570, 2 L. Ed. 2d 1546, 78 S. Ct. 1383

**Girard Trust Case**
386 Pa. 548, 127 A.2d 287; 353 U.S. 230, 1 L. Ed. 2d 792, 77 S. Ct. 806

**Girard Will Case**
43 U.S. 127, 11 L. Ed. 205

**Gitlow Cases**
195 A.D. 773, 39 N.Y. Crim. 120, 187 N.Y.S. 783, 234 N.Y. 132, 40 N.Y. Crim. 44, 136 N.E. 317; 234 N.Y. 539, 138 N.E. 438; 260 U.S. 703, 67 L. Ed. 472, 43 S. Ct. 163; 268 U.S. 652, 69 L. Ed. 1138, 45 S. Ct. 625
268 U.S. 652, 69 L. Ed. 1138, 45 S. Ct. 625; 234 N.Y. 132, 136 N.E. 317; 195 A.D. 773, 187 N.Y.S. 783; 260 U.S. 703, 67 L. Ed. 472, 43 S. Ct. 163; 234 N.Y. 539, 138 N.E. 438

**Glass Wax Case**
129 F. Supp. 928; 352 U.S. 829, 1 L. Ed. 2d 51, 77 S. Ct. 41

**Glen Iris Case**
78 F. 511

**Gleneagles Case**
95 B.R. 992

**Glenshaw Case**
18 T.C. 860; 19 T.C. 637; 211 F.2d 928; 348 U.S. 813, 99 L. Ed. 641, 75 S. Ct. 50; 348 U.S. 426, 99 L. Ed. 483, 75 S. Ct. 473; 349 U.S. 925, 99 L. Ed. 1256, 75 S. Ct. 657

**Glidden Case**
288 F.2d 99; 185 F. Supp. 441; 370 U.S. 530, 8 L. Ed. 2d 671, 82 S. Ct. 1459; 216 F. Supp. 476; 368 U.S. 814, 7 L. Ed. 2d 22, 82 S. Ct. 56; 368 U.S. 885, 82 S. Ct. 140; 368 U.S. 973, 82 S. Ct. 476; 371 U.S. 854, 9 L. Ed. 2d 93, 83 S. Ct. 14; 327 F.2d 944; 216 F. Supp. 476; 28 F.R.D. 346

**Globe Case**
3 N LRB 294, No. 25

**Globe-Wernicke Case**
119 F. 696; 194 U.S. 634, 48 L. Ed. 1160, 24 S. Ct. 858

**Glucose Cases**
144 F.2d 211; 323 U.S. 706, 89 L. Ed. 569, 65 S. Ct. 313; 324 U.S. 726, 89 L. Ed. 1320, 65 S. Ct. 961
144 F.2d 221; 323 U.S. 702, 89 L. Ed. 567, 65 S. Ct. 189; 324 U.S. 746, 89 L. Ed. 1338, 65 S. Ct. 971

**Goat Case**
224 U.S. 458, 56 L. Ed. 841, 32 S. Ct. 544

**God's Little Acre Cases**
326 Mass. 281, 93 N.E.2d 819
147 Misc. 813, 264 N.Y.S. 534

**Gold Bond Stamp Company Case**
221 F. Supp. 391; 325 F.2d 1018

**Gold Clause Cases**
270 U.S. 280, 70 L. Ed. 585, 46 S. Ct. 253
294 U.S. 240, 79 L. Ed. 885, 55 S. Ct. 407
294 U.S. 317, 79 L. Ed. 907, 55 S. Ct. 428
294 U.S. 330, 79 L. Ed. 912, 55 S. Ct. 432

**Gold Dust Twin Case**
71 F. 295; 77 F. 869

**Gold Issue Mining Case**
267 Mo. 524, 184 S.W. 999; 243 U.S. 93, 61 L. Ed. 610, 37 S. Ct. 344

**Gold Leaf Case**
218 F. 170; 234 F. 895

**Gold Medal Case**
3 F.2d 321; 7 F.2d 304; 268 U.S. 706, 69 L. Ed. 1168, 45 S. Ct. 640

**Gold Mining Case**
2 Cal. App. 2d 370, 36 P.2d 40

**Gold Standard Case**
300 U.S. 324, 81 L. Ed. 678, 57 S. Ct. 485

**Goldbrick Case**
129 N.C. 584, 40 S.E. 71; 191 U.S. 126, 48 L. Ed. 121, 24 S. Ct. 49

**Golden Guernsey Case**
238 Wis. 379, 299 N.W. 31; 316 U.S. 668, 86 L. Ed. 1744, 62 S. Ct. 1035

**Golden Rocket Case**
51 Me. 465

**Golden Rule Argument Case**
130 So. 2d 74 (Fla.)

**Golden Rule Case**
360 S.W.2d 283 (Mo.)

**Good Humor Cases**
274 Minn. 110, 142 N.W.2d 628
397 S.W.2d 33 (Ky.)
63 Ohio App. 147, 16 Ohio Op. 422, 25 N.E.2d 700;
136 Ohio St. 340, 16 Ohio Op. 469, 25 N.E.2d 680
88 Ohio App. 52, 54 Ohio Law Abs. 307, 43 Ohio Op. 446, 85 N.E.2d 419; 153 Ohio St. 14, 41 Ohio Op. 109, 90 N.E.2d 851
75 Ohio Law Abs. 358, 141 N.E.2d 245
35 Ohio Op. 234, 72 N.E.2d 477
35 Ohio Op. 238, 70 N.E.2d 378

**Good Samaritan Case**
121 Fla. 173, 163 So. 476

**Gooding Case**
25 U.S. 460, 6 L. Ed. 693

**Goodman Case**
10 F.2d 58; 271 U.S. 658, 70 L. Ed. 1136, 46 S. Ct. 632; 275 U.S. 66, 72 L. Ed. 167, 48 S. Ct. 24

**Goose Creek Cases**
97 Ky. 458, 17 Ky. Law Rep. 320, 30 S.W. 971; 110 Ky. 282, 22 Ky. Law Rep. 1722, 61 S.W. 283
103 Ky. 562, 20 Ky. Law Rep. 246, 45 S.W. 890

**Gould and Preisner Case**
82 N.L.R.B. 1195, No. 137; 186 F.2d 326; 341 U.S. 675, 95 L. Ed. 1284, 71 S. Ct. 943

**Gove Cases**
138 Minn. 204, 164 N.W. 815; 147 Minn. 24, 179 N.W. 569
161 Minn. 66, 200 N.W. 833

**Government Contractor Affirmative Action Case**
488 U.S. 469, 102 L. Ed. 2d 854, 109 S. Ct. 706,

**Government-Contractor First Amendment Cases**
518 U.S. 668, 135 L. Ed. 2d 843, 116 S. Ct. 2342, 116 S. Ct. 2361 (1996)
518 U.S. 712, 135 L. Ed. 2d 874, 116 S. Ct. 2353 (1996)

**Grabow Case**
120 F. 258, 57 C.C.A. 39

**Graduation Prayers Case**
505 U.S. 577, 120 L. Ed. 2d 467, 112 S. Ct. 2649 (1992)

**Graef Case**
205 Wis. 597, 238 N.W. 377

**Grain Elevator Case**
94 U.S. 113, 24 L. Ed. 77

**Grain Rate Cases**
7 I.C.C. 33
205 I.C.C. 301
258 I.C.C. 337
259 I.C.C. 629
293 I.C.C. 479

**Grain Shipment Cases**
300 F. Supp. 1402; 304 F. Supp. 457

**Gramercy Park Case**
139 A.D. 83, 124 N.Y.S. 36; 200 N.Y. 518, 93 N.E. 1129; 200 N.Y. 519, 93 N.E. 1129

**Gramm-Rudman Case**
478 U.S. 714, 92 L. Ed. 2d 583, 106 S. Ct. 3181

**Granary Definition Case**
167 Kan. 17, 204 P.2d 773

**Grand Jury Discrimination Case**
474 U.S. 254, 88 L. Ed. 2d 598, 106 S. Ct. 617

**Grand Jury Miranda Warnings Case**
425 U.S. 564, 48 L. Ed. 2d 212, 96 S. Ct. 1768

**Grand Jury Right Case**
471 U.S. 130, 85 L. Ed. 2d 99, 105 S. Ct. 1811

**Grand Jury Testimony Case**
431 U.S. 174, 52 L. Ed. 2d 231, 97 S. Ct. 1823

**Grand Jury Testimony Impeachment Case**
440 U.S. 450, 59 L. Ed. 2d 501, 99 S. Ct. 1292

**Grand Jury Transcript Case**
441 U.S. 211, 60 L. Ed. 2d 156, 99 S. Ct. 1667

**Grand Rapids Street Railway Case**
48 Mich. 433, 12 N.W. 643

**Grand Trunk Case**
102 Me. 206, 66 A. 393

**Grandfather Clause Case (Licensing)**
226 Minn. 458, 33 N.W.2d 56

**Grandfather Clause Case (Voting)**
238 U.S. 347, 59 L. Ed. 1340, 35 S. Ct. 926

**Granger Cases**
F. Cas. No. 2,666; 94 U.S. 155, 24 L. Ed. 94
F. Cas. No. 11,138; 94 L. Ed. 164, 24 L. Ed. 97
68 Ill. 385; 135 F. 67, 67 C.C.A. 541
69 Ill. 80; 94 U.S. 113, 24 L. Ed. 77
91 Ill. 256; 105 U.S. 526, 27 L. Ed. 812, 2 S. Ct. 832
105 Ill. 236; 118 U.S. 557, 30 L. Ed. 244, 7 S. Ct. 4
19 Minn. 418 (Gil. 362); 94 U.S. 180, 24 L. Ed. 99
38 Minn. 281, 37 N.W. 782; 134 U.S. 418, 33 L. Ed. 970,
10 S. Ct. 462, 702
117 N.Y. 1, 22 N.E. 670, 682; 143 U.S. 517, 36 L. Ed. 247, 12 S. Ct. 468
26 Ohio St. 86; 95 U.S. 319, 24 L. Ed. 357, 4 Ohio Fed. Dec. 471
36 Wis. 252; 94 U.S. 179, 24 L. Ed. 99
37 Wis. 204; 94 U.S. 181, 24 L. Ed. 102

**Grant Park Cases**
169 Ill. 392, 48 N.E. 927
198 Ill. 104, 64 N.E. 705
241 Ill. 496, 89 N.E. 731
248 Ill. 299, 93 N.E. 910

**Grant Tire Cases**
91 F. 978
116 F. 363, 53 C.C.A. 583; 187 U.S. 641, 47 L. Ed. 345, 23 S. Ct. 842
116 F. 629
123 F. 85, 59 C.C.A. 215
142 F. 531; 154 F. 358, 83 C.C.A. 336; 207 U.S. 589, 52 L. Ed. 354, 28 S. Ct. 255
147 F. 739; 151 F. 237, 80 C.C.A. 589
157 F. 677, 85 C.C.A. 349; 162 F. 892, 89 C.C.A. 582; 212 U.S. 574, 58 L. Ed. 657, 29 S. Ct. 683; 220 U.S. 428, 55 L. Ed. 527, 31 S. Ct. 444
189 F. 591; 191 F. 832
195 F. 764; 202 F. 1021
195 F. 768; 202 F. 1021
197 F. 756; 203 F. 998
215 F. 106, 131 C.C.A. 323

**Granville Consolidation Case**
274 Wis. 50, 79 N.W.2d 340; 2 Wis. 2d 441, 86 N.W.2d 487

**Grape Sugar Company Case**
10 F. 835; 18 F. 638; 20 F. 505; 24 F. 604; 35 F. 212; 42 F. 455

**Graphic Arts Cases**

359 Ill. 427, 194 N.E. 565

364 Ill. 342, 4 N.E.2d 481

364 Ill. 360, 4 N.E.2d 476

15 Ill. 2d 485, 155 N.E.2d 574

**Grave Desecration Case**

304 Ky. 708, 202 S.W.2d 394

**Gravel-Pit Cases**

68 Minn. 184, 70 N.W. 978; 73 Minn. 103, 75 N.W. 1033

72 Minn. 225, 75 N.W. 219

**Graves Case**

253 A.D. 91, 1 N.Y.S.2d 195; 278 N.Y. 691, 16 N.E.2d 404; 305 U.S. 592, 83 L. Ed. 374, 59 S. Ct. 252; 306 U.S. 466, 83 L. Ed. 927, 59 S. Ct. 595

**Gray Market Case**

486 U.S. 281, 100 L. Ed. 2d 313, 108 S. Ct. 1811

**Great Lakes Diversion Case**

266 U.S. 405, 69 L. Ed. 352, 45 S. Ct. 176; 46 S. Ct. 16; 46 S. Ct. 208; 46 S. Ct. 636; 270 U.S. 634, 70 L. Ed. 772, 46 S. Ct. 354; 271 U.S. 650, 70 L. Ed. 1132, 46 S. Ct. 636; 273 U.S. 637, 71 L. Ed. 816, 47 S. Ct. 247; 273 U.S. 640, 71 L. Ed. 817, 47 S. Ct. 102; 273 U.S. 642, 71 L. Ed. 818, 47 S. Ct. 235; 273 U.S. 644, 71 L. Ed. 819, 47 S. Ct. 235; 274 U.S. 488, 71 L. Ed. 1164, 47 S. Ct. 661; 274 U.S. 712, 71 L. Ed. 1340, 47 S. Ct. 573; 72 L. Ed. 1015, 48 S. Ct. 123; 278 U.S. 367, 73 L. Ed. 426, 49 S. Ct. 163; 279 U.S. 820, 73 L. Ed. 976, 49 S. Ct. 353; 279 U.S. 821, 73 L. Ed. 976, 49 S. Ct. 349; 74 L. Ed. 1179, 50 S. Ct. 151; 281 U.S. 179, 74 L. Ed. 799, 50 S. Ct. 266; 281 U.S. 696, 74 L. Ed. 1123, 50 S. Ct. 331; 52 S. Ct. 5; 52 S. Ct. 197; 287 U.S. 568, 77 L. Ed. 500, 53 S. Ct. 4; 287 U.S. 578, 77 L. Ed. 506, 53 S. Ct. 210; 288 U.S. 587, 77 L. Ed. 967, 53 S. Ct. 316; 288 U.S. 594, 77 L. Ed. 971, 53 S. Ct. 505; 289 U.S. 395, 77 L. Ed. 1283, 53 S. Ct. 671; 289 U.S. 710, 77 L. Ed. 1465, 53 S. Ct. 671, 53 S. Ct. 788; 309 U.S. 569, 84 L. Ed. 953, 60 S. Ct. 789; 309 U.S. 636, 84 L. Ed. 992, 60 S. Ct. 791; 311 U.S. 107, 85 L. Ed. 73, 61 S. Ct. 154; 61 S. Ct. 831; 61 S. Ct. 832; 313 U.S. 547, 85 L. Ed. 1513, 61 S. Ct. 1090, 61 S. Ct. 1091; 340 U.S. 858, 95 L. Ed. 628, 71 S. Ct. 85, 71 S. Ct. 86

**Greek Case**

27 Idaho 797, 152 P. 280; 246 U.S. 343, 62 L. Ed. 763, 38 S. Ct. 323

**Green Giant Case**

263 Wis. 353, 57 N.W.2d 376

**Green River Cases**

60 F.2d 613

65 F.2d 112

50 Wyo. 52, 58 P.2d 456; 300 U.S. 638, 81 L. Ed. 854, 57 S. Ct. 510; 300 U.S. 688, 81 L. Ed. 889, 57 S. Ct. 572

217 La. 820, 47 So. 2d 553; 71 S. Ct. 282; 71 S. Ct. 488; 71 S. Ct. 504; 342 U.S. 622, 95 L. Ed. 1233, 71 S. Ct. 920; 342 U.S. 843, 96 L. Ed. 637, 72 S. Ct. 21

**Greene County Case**

292 Pa. 304, 141 A. 27

**Greenhouse Farmer Case**
66 F. Supp. 667; 158 F.2d 882

**Greenhouse Zoning Case**
330 Mass. 95, 111 N.E.2d 453

**Greer County Case**
162 U.S. 1, 40 L. Ed. 867, 16 S. Ct. 725

**Gregory Case**
293 U.S. 465, 79 L. Ed. 596, 55 S. Ct. 266; 69 F.2d 809; 293 U.S. 538, 79 L. Ed. 645, 55 S. Ct. 82

**Greyhound Cases**
303 U.S. 261, 82 L. Ed. 831, 58 S. Ct. 571
303 U.S. 272, 82 L. Ed. 838, 58 S. Ct. 577

**Griffin Cases**
60 F.2d 339
F. Cas. No. 2,783; F. Cas. No. 5,815
7 I.C.C. 224; 84 F. 258
351 U.S. 12, 100 L. Ed. 891, 76 S. Ct. 585; 349 U.S. 949, 99 L. Ed. 1274, 75 S. Ct. 885; 351 U.S. 958, 100 L. Ed. 1480, 76 S. Ct. 844; 9 Ill. 2d 164, 137 N.E.2d 485

**Griffin School Case**
8 N.C. 96

**Griffith's Case**
376 U.S. 315, 11 L. Ed. 2d 732, 84 S. Ct. 748

**Grimm Case**
45 F. 558; 50 F. 528; 156 U.S. 604, 39 L. Ed. 550, 15 S. Ct. 470

**Gross Income Tax Case**
167 Ark. 557, 271 S.W. 720

**Gross Receipts Tax Cases**
82 U.S. 284, 21 L. Ed. 164
112 F.2d 39, 72 App. D.C. 131; 122 F.2d 61, 74 App. D.C. 284
180 Tenn. 688, 177 S.W.2d 841

**Gross Revenue Tax of Oklahoma Case**
235 U.S. 292, 59 L. Ed. 234, 35 S. Ct. 27

**Group Discrimination Cases**
313 U.S. 545, 85 L. Ed. 1511, 61 S. Ct. 956; 314 U.S. 160, 86 L. Ed. 113, 62 S. Ct. 164
322 U.S. 385, 88 L. Ed. 1341, 64 S. Ct. 1101; 322 U.S. 718, 88 L. Ed. 1558, 64 S. Ct. 1047; 323 U.S. 809, 89 L. Ed. 645, 65 S. Ct. 27; 323 U.S. 809, 89 L. Ed. 645, 65 S. Ct. 28
131 F.2d 593; 319 U.S. 738, 87 L. Ed. 1697, 63 S. Ct. 1325; 321 U.S. 649, 88 L. Ed. 987, 64 S. Ct. 757; 322 U.S. 718, 88 L. Ed. 1558, 64 S. Ct. 1047; 322 U.S. 769, 88 L. Ed. 1594, 64 S. Ct. 1052
140 F2d289; 321 U.S. 760, 88 L. Ed. 1058, 64 S. Ct. 786; 323 U.S. 214, 89 L. Ed. 194, 65 S. Ct. 193; 324 U.S. 885, 89 L. Ed. 1435, 65 S. Ct. 674
140 F.2d 662; 322 U.S. 718, 88 L. Ed. 1558, 64 S. Ct. 946; 325 U.S. 91, 89 L. Ed. 1495, 65 S. Ct. 1031
162 F.2d 233, 82 App. D.C. 180; 332 U.S. 789, 92 L. Ed. 371, 68 S. Ct. 100; 334 U.S. 24, 92 L. Ed. 1187, 68 S. Ct. 847
46 F. Supp. 657; 63 S. Ct. 860; 320 U.S. 81, 87 L. Ed. 1774, 63 S. Ct. 1375
47 F. Supp. 251; 319 U.S. 624, 87 L. Ed. 1628, 63 S. Ct. 1178
229 I.C.C. 703; 313 U.S. 80, 85 L. Ed. 1201, 61 S. Ct. 873
229 Ala. 226, 156 So. 556; 287 U.S. 45, 77 L. Ed. 158, 53 S. Ct. 55; 293 U.S. 552, 79 L. Ed. 655, 55 S. Ct. 345; 294 U.S. 587, 79 L. Ed. 1074, 55 S. Ct. 579
245 Ala. 113, 16 So. 2d 416; 322 U.S. 722, 88 L. Ed. 1560, 64 S. Ct. 1260; 323 U.S. 192, 89 L. Ed. 173, 65 S. Ct. 226
189 La. 764, 180 So. 630; 305 U.S. 586, 83 L. Ed. 370, 59 S. Ct. 100; 306 U.S. 354, 83 L. Ed. 757, 59 S. Ct. 536
316 Mich. 614, 25 N.W.2d 638; 331 U.S. 804, 91 L. Ed. 1826, 67 S. Ct. 1754; 334 U.S. 1, 92 L. Ed. 1161, 68 S. Ct. 836
317 Mich. 686, 27 N.W.2d 139; 333 U.S. 28, 92 L. Ed. 455, 68 S. Ct. 358
201 Miss. 410, 29 So. 2d 96; 331 U.S. 804, 91 L. Ed. 1826, 67 S. Ct. 1757; 203 Miss. 265, 33 So. 2d 456; 332 U.S. 463, 92 L. Ed. 76, 68 S. Ct. 184; 338 U.S. 855, 94 L. Ed. 523, 70 S. Ct. 104
342 Mo. 121, 113 S.W.2d 783; 305 U.S. 337, 83 L. Ed. 208, 59 S. Ct. 232; 305 U.S. 580, 83 L. Ed. 365, 59 S. Ct. 65; 305 U.S. 676, 83 L. Ed. 437, 59 S. Ct. 356

*Continued*

355 Mo. 814, 198 S.W.2d 679; 331 U.S. 803, 91 L. Ed. 1826, 67 S. Ct. 1751; 334 U.S. 1, 92 L. Ed. 1161, 68 S. Ct. 836, 358 Mo. 364, 214 S.W.2d 525

180 Misc. 868, 44 N.Y.S.2d 601; 267 A.D. 470, 47 N.Y.S.2d 404; 293 N.Y. 315, 56 N.E.2d 721; 326 U.S. 88, 89 L. Ed. 2072, 65 S. Ct. 1483

199 Okla. 36, 180 P.2d 135; 332 U.S. 814, 92 L. Ed. 391, 68 S. Ct. 156; 332 U.S. 631, 92 L. Ed. 247, 68 S. Ct. 299; 199 Okla. 586, 190 P.2d 437

145 Tex. Crim. 289, 167 S.W.2d 758; 324 U.S. 836, 89 L. Ed. 1400, 65 S. Ct. 865; 325 U.S. 398, 89 L. Ed. 1692, 65 S. Ct. 1276

**Group Home Zoning Case**

514 U.S. 725, 131 L. Ed. 2d 801, 115 S. Ct. 1776 (1995)

**Grove Street Case**

62 Minn. 450, 64 N.W. 1140

**Growing Crop Damages Case**

211 Ark. 951, 203 S.W.2d 398

**Grunewald Case**

233 F.2d 556; 162 F. Supp. 626; 164 F. Supp. 640; 164 F. Supp. 644; 352 U.S. 866, 1 L. Ed. 2d 74, 77 S. Ct. 91; 353 U.S. 391, 1 L. Ed. 2d 931, 77 S. Ct. 963

**Guano Island Cases**

137 U.S. 202, 34 L. Ed. 691, 11 S. Ct. 80

137 U.S. 224, 34 L. Ed. 700, 11 S. Ct. 88

137 U.S. 647, 34 L. Ed. 825, 11 S. Ct. 242

**Guenzel Case**

28 T.C. 59; 258 F.2d 248

**Guest Interference Auto Case**

226 Minn. 491, 33 N.W.2d 821; 234 Minn. 221, 48 N.W.2d 169

**Guffey Coal Act Case**

12 F. Supp. 570; 298 U.S. 238, 80 L. Ed. 1160, 56 S. Ct. 855

**Guilty Plea Cases**

395 Mich. 96, 235 N.W.2d 132

**Guiteau's Case**

10 F. 161

**Gulf Company Case**

60 F. 966

**Gully Case**

299 U.S. 109, 81 L. Ed. 70, 57 S. Ct. 96; 81 F.2d 502; 298 U.S. 650, 80 L. Ed. 1378, 56 S. Ct. 939

**Gummed Products Company Case**

112 N.L.R.B. 1092, No. 141

**Gun-Free School Zone Case**

514 U.S. 549, 131 L. Ed. 2d 626, 115 S. Ct. 1624 (1995)

**Gunnison Company Case**

74 F. 335; 83 F. 230, 27 C.C.A. 522; 168 U.S. 708, 42 L. Ed. 1218, 18 S. Ct. 939

**Gunnison Tunnel Cases**

51 Colo. 425, 118 P. 996; 64 Colo. 421, 174 P. 808; 262 P. 514

65 Colo. 156, 174 P. 816

65 Colo. 157, 174 P. 816

65 Colo. 158, 174 P. 816

65 Colo. 159, 174 P. 816

67 Colo. 602, 174 P. 816

**Guss Case**

353 U.S. 1, 1 L. Ed. 2d 601, 77 S. Ct. 598, 77 S. Ct. 609; 5 Utah 2d 68, 296 P.2d 733; 352 U.S. 817, 1 L. Ed. 2d 44, 77 S. Ct. 65

**Gye Case**

207 F. 247, 124 C.C.A. 517; 231 U.S. 755, 58 L. Ed. 468, 34 S. Ct. 323

**Gypsum Monopoly Case**
51 F. Supp. 613; 53 F. Supp. 889, 59 U.S.P.Q. (BNA) 318; 67 F. Supp. 397, 70 U.S.P.Q. (BNA) 48; 69 S. Ct. 371, 71 U.S.P.Q. (BNA) 329; 333 U.S. 364, 92 L. Ed. 746, 68 S. Ct. 525, 76 U.S.P.Q. (BNA) 430; 333 U.S. 869, 92 L. Ed. 1147, 68 S. Ct. 788; 85 U.S.P.Q. (BNA) 37; 339 U.S. 959, 94 L. Ed. 1370, 70 S. Ct. 995; 339 U.S. 960, 94 L. Ed. 1370, 70 S. Ct. 996; 340 U.S. 76, 95 L. Ed. 89, 71 S. Ct. 160, 87 U.S.P.Q. (BNA) 276; 340 U.S. 909, 95 L. Ed. 657, 71 S. Ct. 289; 124 F. Supp. 573

**Gypsum Wallboard Cases**
297 F. Supp. 1350; 302 F. Supp. 794; 303 F. Supp. 510

## H

**Habeas Corpus Abuse of Writ Case**
114 L. Ed. 2d 49, 111 S. Ct. 1661

**Habeas Corpus Exhauston of Remedies Case**
455 U.S. 509, 71 L. Ed. 2d 379, 102 S. Ct. 1198

**Habitual Criminal Sterilization Case**
189 Okla. 235, 115 P.2d 123; 315 U.S. 789, 86 L. Ed. 1193, 62 S. Ct. 488; 316 U.S. 535, 86 L. Ed. 1655, 62 S. Ct. 1110

**Hachey Case**
173 F. 784, 97 C.C.A. 508

**Hadenfeldt Case**
157 Wash. 563, 289 P. 533

**Hague Case (Judge)**
103 N.J. Eq. 505, 143 A. 836; 104 N.J. Eq. 31, 144 A. 546; 104 N.J. Eq 369, 145 A. 618; 105 N.J. Eq. 134, 147 A. 220; 9 N.J. Misc. 89, 150 A. 322

**Hague Free Speech Case**
25 F. Supp. 127; 101 F.2d 774; 306 U.S. 624, 83 L. Ed. 1028, 59 S. Ct. 486; 307 U.S. 496, 83 L. Ed. 1423, 59 S. Ct. 954

**Haitian High Seas Case**
509 U.S. 155, 125 L. Ed. 2d 128, 113 S. Ct. 2549 (1993)

**Hall-Mills Case**
102 N.J.L. 537, 134 A. 733

**Hall Safe Cases**
143 F. 231, 74 C.C.A. 361; 203 U.S. 591, 51 L. Ed. 331, 27 S. Ct. 780; 208 U.S. 267, 52 L. Ed. 481, 28 S. Ct. 288
146 F. 37, 76 C.C.A. 495; 203 U.S. 591, 51 L. Ed. 331, 27 S. Ct. 780; 208 U.S. 554, 52 L. Ed. 616, 28 S. Ct. 350
31 App. D.C. 498
31 App. D.C. 506

**Hallgarten Will Case**
40 Hun 542; 110 N.Y. 678, 18 N.E. 482

**Halliburton Oil Well Cementing Company Case**
373 U.S. 64, 10 L. Ed. 2d 202, 83 S. Ct. 1201; 368 U.S. 809; 7 L. Ed. 2d 19, 82 S. Ct. 60; 369 U.S. 835, 7 L. Ed. 2d 841, 82 S. Ct. 865; 374 U.S. 858, 10 L. Ed. 2d 1082, 83 S. Ct. 1861; 241 La. 67, 127 So. 2d 502

**Halverstodt Case**
12 F.2d 995

**Hamburg-American Case**
216 F. 971; 239 U.S. 466, 60 L. Ed. 387, 36 S. Ct. 212

**Hamilton Case**
134 U.S. 296, 33 L. Ed. 905, 10 S. Ct. 546

**Hamilton Park Case**
67 Hun 495, 51 N.Y. St. Rep. 230, 22 N.Y.S. 497; 139 N.Y. 240, 34 N.E. 883; 35 N.E. 892

**Hampton Case**
120 F. 934, 57 C.C.A. 224; 195 U.S. 638, 49 L. Ed. 356, 25 S. Ct. 789

**Hamtramck Conspiracy Case**
13 F.2d 599; 273 U.S. 735, 71 L. Ed. 865, 47 S. Ct. 243

**Handbill Boycott Case**
132 N.L.R.B. 901, No. 67

**Handbill Cases (Non-Religious)**
299 Mass. 353, 13 N.E.2d 18
301 Mass. 584, 18 N.E.2d 166
25 F. Supp. 127; 101 F.2d 774; 306 U.S. 624, 83 L. Ed. 1028, 59 S. Ct. 486; 307 U.S. 496, 83 L. Ed. 1423, 59 S. Ct. 954; 307 U.S. 661
230 Wis. 131, 283 N.W. 301
33 Cal. App. 2d 747, 85 P.2d 231
34 F. Supp. 596; 122 F.2d 511; 314 U.S. 604, 86 L. Ed. 486, 62 S. Ct. 301; 316 U.S. 52, 86 L. Ed. 1262, 62 S. Ct. 920

**Handbill Cases (Religious)**
55 Ga. App. 609, 191 S.E. 152; 303 U.S. 444, 82 L. Ed. 949, 58 S. Ct. 666; 58 S. Ct. 52
120 N.J.L. 460, 200 A. 799; 121 N.J.L. 542, 3 A.2d 609; 308 U.S. 147, 84 L. Ed. 155, 60 S. Ct. 146

39 F. Supp. 30

39 F. Supp. 32; 130 F.2d 652; 318 U.S. 749, 87 L. Ed. 1125, 63 S. Ct. 660, 319 U.S. 166, 87 L. Ed. 1330, 63 S. Ct. 882; 319 U.S. 157, 87 L. Ed. 1324, 63 S. Ct. 877; 319 U.S. 782, 87 L. Ed. 1726, 63 S. Ct. 1170

30 Ala. App. 142, 3 So. 2d 74; 241 Ala. 279, 3 So. 2d 76; 30 Ala. App. 416, 242 Ala. 549, 7 So. 2d 503; 314 U.S. 593, 86 L. Ed. 478, 62 S. Ct. 93; 315 U.S. 782, 86 L. Ed. 1189, 62 S. Ct. 630; 316 U.S. 584, 86 L. Ed. 1691, 62 S. Ct. 1231; 318 U.S. 796, 87 L. Ed. 1161, 63 S. Ct. 658; 319 U.S. 103, 87 L. Ed. 1290, 63 S. Ct. 890

202 Ark. 614, 151 S.W.2d 1000; 314 U.S. 651, 86 L. Ed. 522, 62 S. Ct. 99; 315 U.S. 793, 86 L. Ed. 1196, 62 S. Ct. 903; 316 U.S. 584, 86 L. Ed. 1691, 62 S. Ct. 1231; 318 U.S. 796, 87 L. Ed. 1161, 63 S. Ct. 658; 319 U.S. 103, 87 L. Ed. 1290, 63 S. Ct. 890; 135 F.2d 981

58 Ariz. 144, 118 P.2d 97; 316 U.S. 584, 86 L. Ed. 1691, 62 S. Ct. 1231; 318 U.S. 796, 87 L. Ed. 1161, 63 S. Ct. 658; 319 U.S. 103, 87 L. Ed. 1290, 63 S. Ct. 890; 320 U.S. 719, 88 L. Ed. 423, 62 S. Ct. 423

139 Ohio St. 372, 40 N.E.2d 154; 317 U.S. 589, 87 L. Ed. 483, 63 S. Ct. 49; 318 U.S. 739, 87 L. Ed. 739, 63 S. Ct. 528; 319 U.S. 141, 87 L. Ed. 1313, 63 S. Ct. 862; 319 U.S. 166, 87 L. Ed. 1330, 63 S. Ct. 882; 64 S. Ct. 255

149 Pa. Super. 175, 27 A.2d 666; 316 U.S. 584, 86 L. Ed. 1691, 62 S. Ct. 1231; 318 U.S. 748, 87 L. Ed. 1125, 63 S. Ct. 660, 63 S. Ct. 661, 63 S. Ct. 662; 319 U.S. 105, 87 L. Ed. 1292, 63 S. Ct. 870

**Hands Around Case**

230 A.D. 200, 243 N.Y.S. 193; 254 N.Y. 373, 173 N.E. 227; 255 N.Y. 576, 175 N.E. 320

**Hanks Case**

101 F. 306; 111 F. 916; 122 F. 74, 58 C.C.A. 180; 194 U.S. 303, 48 L. Ed. 989, 24 S. Ct. 700; 130 F. 1022, 63 C.C.A. 684

**Hanson Case**

351 U.S. 225, 100 L. Ed. 1112, 76 S. Ct. 714; 160 Neb. 669, 71 N.W.2d 526; 350 U.S. 910, 100 L. Ed. 798, 76 S. Ct. 195; 351 U.S. 979, 100 L. Ed. 1494, 76 S. Ct. 1044; 352 U.S. 859, 1 L. Ed. 2d 69, 77 S. Ct. 22

**Happy Thought Case**

251 F. 301

**Harbor Tunnel Case**

214 Md. 266, 134 A.2d 312

**Hardwood Lumber Case**

263 F. 147; 40 S. Ct. 588; 41 S. Ct. 623, 257 U.S. 377, 66 L. Ed. 284, 42 S. Ct. 114

**Harlem Riot Case**

157 Misc. 157, 283 N.Y.S. 335

**Harmless Error Case**

460 U.S. 73, 74 L. Ed. 2d 823, 103 S. Ct. 969

**Harper County Case**

21 Kan. 210

**Harper's Ferry Arsenal Case**

F. Cas. No. 2,013

**Harriman Case**

12 I.C.C. 277; 157 F. 432; 211 U.S. 407, 53 L. Ed. 253, 29 S. Ct. 115

**Harry Thaw Case**

See Thaw Cases

**Hart Case**

7 F.R.D. 43, 74 U.S.P.Q. (BNA) 82; 73 F. Supp. 146, 75 U.S.P.Q. (BNA)210; 169 F.2d 580, 78 U.S.P.Q. (BNA) 310

**Hartwell Case**

73 U.S. 385, 18 L. Ed. 830

**Harvester Cases**

214 F. 987; 248 U.S. 587, 63 L. Ed. 434, 39 S. Ct. 5; 10 F.2d 827; 274 U.S. 693, 71 L. Ed. 1302, 47 S. Ct. 748

124 Ky. 543, 30 Ky. Law Rep. 716, 99 S.W. 637

131 Ky. 551, 115 S.W. 703

131 Ky. 768, 115 S.W. 755

*Continued*

137 Ky. 668, 126 S.W. 352; 144 Ky. 403, 138 S.W. 248
147 Ky. 557, 144 S.W. 1070
147 Ky. 564, 144 S.W. 1064; 234 U.S. 216, 58 L. Ed. 1284, 34 S. Ct. 853
147 Ky. 573, 144 S.W. 1068
147 Ky. 655, 145 S.W. 393; 234 U.S. 579, 58 L. Ed. 1479, 34 S. Ct. 944
147 Ky. 735, 145 S.W. 400
147 Ky. 795, 146 S.W. 12; 234 U.S. 216, 58 L. Ed. 1284, 34 S. Ct. 853
148 Ky. 37, 145 S.W. 1132
148 Ky. 572, 147 S.W. 1199; 234 U.S. 216, 58 L. Ed. 1284, 34 S. Ct. 853
148 Ky. 829, 147 S.W. 760; 234 U.S. 589, 58 L. Ed. 1484, 34 S. Ct. 947
170 Ky. 41, 185 S.W. 102
237 Mo. 369, 141 S.W. 672; 234 U.S. 199, 58 L. Ed. 1276, 34 S. Ct. 859

**Hashish Llama Case**
441 F.2d 295

**Hass Case**
141 F.2d 122; 141 F.2d 127

**Hat Cases**
17 F.T.C. 352; 17 F.T.C. 369; 17 F.T.C. 373
17 F.T.C. 378; 17 F.T.C. 382; 17 F.T.C. 386
17 F.T.C. 390; 17 F.T.C. 394; 17 F.T.C. 399

**Hat Trimming Cases**
49 F. 19; 49 F. 26; 49 F. 32; 89 F. 963, 32 C.C.A. 456; 172 U.S. 648, 19 S. Ct. 883
131 F. 574

**Hatch Act Case**
413 U.S. 548, 37 L. Ed. 2d 796, 93 S. Ct. 2880
56 F. Supp. 621; 330 U.S. 75, 91 L. Ed. 754, 67 S. Ct. 556
341 F. Supp. 578

**Hate Crimes/Sentence-Enhancement Case**
508 U.S. 476, 124 L. Ed. 2d 436, 113 S. Ct. 2194 (1993)

**Hauptmann Case**
115 N.J.L. 412, 180 A. 809; 296 U.S. 649, 80 L. Ed. 461, 56 S. Ct. 310

**Hawaiian Martial Law Case**
327 U.S. 304, 90 L. Ed. 688, 66 S. Ct. 606

**Hawkins Point Lighthouse Case**
39 F. 77; 155 U.S. 102, 39 L. Ed. 85, 15 S. Ct. 34

**Hawthorne Case**
279 F.2d 699; 165 F. Supp. 600

**Hay Classification Cases**
18 F. 584
9 I.C.C. 264; 134 F. 942; 202 U.S. 613, 50 L. Ed. 1171, 26 S. Ct. 766
19 I.C.C. 34

**Hayes Case**
341 S.W.2d 240 (Ky.)

**Haymaker Case**
279 F.2d 607, 125 U.S.P.Q. (BNA) 607; 117 F. Supp. 548, 100 U.S.P.Q. (BNA) 17; 171 F. Supp. 293, 121 U.S.P.Q. (BNA) 397

**Haymarket Riot Case**
122 Ill. 1, 12 N.E. 865, 17 N.E. 898; 123 U.S. 131, 31 L. Ed. 80, 8 S. Ct. 21, 8 S. Ct. 22

**Head Money Cases**
18 F. 135; 112 U.S. 580, 28 L. Ed. 798, 5 S. Ct. 247
18 F. 147; 112 U.S. 580, 28 L. Ed. 798, 5 S. Ct. 247

**Heard Case**
30 T.C. 1093; 269 F.2d 911

**Hearse Case**
169 N.C. 41, 85 S.E. 35

**Heavy Tailed Aircraft Case**
155 Neb. 749, 53 N.W.2d 902

**Hefley Case**
158 U.S. 98, 39 L. Ed. 910, 15 S. Ct. 802

**Heifer-Milch-Cow Case**
142 S.W. 18 (Tex.)

**Heilbron Case**
156 Cal. 408, 104 P. 979

**Henderson Will Cases**
250 Ala. 456, 34 So. 2d 835
258 Ala. 238, 61 So. 2d 817

**Henderson's Distilled Spirits Case**
F. Cas. No. 15,948; 81 U.S. 44, 20 L. Ed. 815

**Henderson's Tobacco Case**
78 U.S. 652, 20 L. Ed. 235

**Henfield's Case**
F. Cas. No. 6,360

**Henningsen Case**
143 F. 810, 74 C.C.A. 484; 208 U.S. 404, 52 L. Ed. 547, 28 S. Ct. 389

**Henze Case**
181 F.2d 196

**Herminghaus Case**
200 Cal. 81, 252 P. 607; 274 U.S. 728, 71 L. Ed. 1315, 47 S. Ct. 575; 275 U.S. 486, 72 L. Ed. 387, 48 S. Ct. 27

**Herndon Cases**
295 U.S. 441, 79 L. Ed. 1530, 55 S. Ct. 794; 296 U.S. 661, 80 L. Ed. 471, 56 S. Ct. 82
301 U.S. 242, 81 L. Ed. 1066, 57 S. Ct. 732

**Hesper Case**
18 F. 692; 18 F. 696; 122 U.S. 256, 30 L. Ed. 1175, 7 S. Ct. 1177

**Hess Case**
274 U.S. 352, 71 L. Ed. 1091, 47 S. Ct. 632

**Hetch-Hetchy Case**
310 U.S. 16, 84 L. Ed. 1050, 60 S. Ct. 749; 106 F.2d 569; 23 F. Supp. 40; 309 U.S. 642, 84 L. Ed. 996, 60 S. Ct. 467

**Hetland Case**
19 S.D. 1, 101 N.W. 1078

**Hever Case**
32 T.C. 947, 283 F.2d 865

**Hialeah Case**
129 Fla. 686, 176 So. 789

**Hickman-Parker Case**
204 Cal. 470, 268 P. 909,

**Hidden Rings Auction Case**
31 Tenn. App. 85, 212 S.W.2d 683

**High Mountain Sheep Case**
387 U.S. 428, 18 L. Ed. 2d 869, 87 S. Ct. 1712

**High School Religious Club Case**
496 U.S. 226, 110 L. Ed. 2d 191, 110 S. Ct. 2356

**Highland Park Case**
341 U.S. 322, 95 L. Ed. 969, 71 S. Ct. 758; 184 F.2d 98

**Highway Debenture Cases**
89 Mont. 205, 296 P. 1033
90 Mont. 152, 300 P. 549

**Hillmon Case**
145 U.S. 285, 36 L. Ed. 706, 12 S. Ct. 909; 105 F. 1003, 44 C.C.A. 684; 107 F. 834, 46 C.C.A. 668; 181 U.S. 620, 45 L. Ed. 1031, 22 S. Ct. 946; 188 U.S. 208, 47 L. Ed. 446, 23 S. Ct. 294

**Hindering of Performance Case**
93 F. Supp. 620
187 A.D. 280, 175 N.Y.S. 670
204 N.Y. St. Rep. 96, 97 N.E. 472

**Hines Case**
168 Misc. 453, 6 N.Y.S.2d 2, 15; 258 A.D. 466, 17 N.Y.S.2d 141; 12 N.Y.S.2d 454

**Hip-Pocket Law Cases**
5 F. Supp. 639; 71 F.2d 8; 293 U.S. 539, 79 L. Ed. 645, 55 S. Ct. 83, 55 S. Ct. 102; 293 U.S. 388, 79 L. Ed. 446, 55 S. Ct. 241
5 F. Supp. 633; 71 F. 2d 1; 293 U.S. 539, 79 L. Ed. 645, 55 S. Ct. 83, 55 S. Ct. 102; 293 U.S. 388, 79 L. Ed. 446, 55 S. Ct. 241

**Hiss Case**
185 F.2d 822; 340 U.S. 948, 95 L. Ed. 683, 71 S. Ct. 532; 107 F. Supp. 128; 201 F.2d 372; 345 U.S. 942, 97 L. Ed. 1368, 73 S. Ct. 830

**Hitaffer Case**
183 F.2d 811; 340 U.S. 852, 95 L. Ed. 624, 71 S. Ct. 80

**Hitchman Case**
245 U.S. 229, 62 L. Ed. 260, 38 S. Ct. 65

**HIV Disability Case**
141 L. Ed. 2d 540, 118 S. Ct. 2196 (1998)

**Hoarding Cases (Gold)**
5 F. Supp. 156

**Hoarding Cases (Necessaries)**
264 F. 870; 255 U.S. 567, 65 L. Ed. 789, 41 S. Ct. 375; 255 U.S. 579, 65 L. Ed. 795, 41 S. Ct. 375
264 F. 1016

**Hoboken Railroad Tax Case**
63 N.J.L. 561, 41 A. 728

**Hockey Players Case**
282 A.D. 634, 126 N.Y.S.2d 115

**Hoelzel's Case**
28 T.C. 384

**Hoffman Case**
363 U.S. 335, 4 L. Ed. 2d 1254, 80 S. Ct. 1084; 361 U.S. 809, 4 L. Ed. 2d 58, 80 S. Ct. 50; 260 F.2d 317, 119 U.S.P.Q. (BNA) 202; 261 F.2d 467

**Hoffman House Case**
61 N.Y. 123; 84 N.Y. 556

**Hoffman Kidnapping Case**
329 Mo. 306, 44 S.W. 2d 146

**Hole-in-the-Wall Case**
232 N.C. 333, 60 S.E.2d 322

**Holeproof Hoisery Case**
172 F. 859; 190 F. 606; 192 F. 534

**Holiday-Pay Case**
25 N.J. Super. 601, 96 A.2d 720; 29 N.J. Super. 68, 101 A.2d 592; 15 N.J. 79, 104 A.2d 94; 16 N.J. 280, 108 A.2d 409

**Holladay Case**
22 F. 13; 27 F. 830; 28 F. 117; 29 F. 226

**Holland Case**
348 U.S. 121, 99 L. Ed. 150, 75 S. Ct. 127; 209 F. 516; 347 U.S. 1008, 98 L. Ed. 1133, 74 S. Ct. 863; 348 U.S. 932, 99 L. Ed. 731, 75 S. Ct. 334

**Hollerbach Case**
47 Ct. Cl. 236; 233 U.S. 165, 58 L. Ed. 898, 34 S. Ct. 553

**Hollow Tree Case**
91 N.L.R.B. 635, No. 113

**Hollywood Case**
92 Fla. 187, 109 So. 228

**Holmes Case**
F. Cas. No. 15,383

**Holographic Will Incorporation Case**
305 Ky. 340, 204 S.W.2d 367

**Holt Case**
117 Tenn. 618, 100 S.W. 705

**Holy Trinity Church Case**
143 U.S. 457, 36 L. Ed. 226, 12 S. Ct. 511; 36 F. 303

**Home-Office Tax-Deduction Case**
506 U.S. 168, 121 L. Ed. 2d 634, 113 S. Ct. 701 (1993)

**Home Owners'Loan Act Case**
296 U.S. 315, 80 L. Ed. 251, 56 S. Ct. 235

**Home Port Cases**
89 A.D. 127, 84 N.Y.S. 1088; 177 N.Y. 584, 69 N.E. 1129; 183 N.Y. 575, 76 N.E. 1104; 183 N.Y. 576, 76 N.E. 1104; 202 U.S. 584, 50 L. Ed. 1155, 26 S. Ct. 714
213 Minn. 395, 7 N.W.2d 691; 319 U.S. 734, 87 L. Ed. 1695, 63 S. Ct. 1157; 322 U.S. 292, 88 L. Ed. 1283, 64 S. Ct. 950; 323 U.S. 809, 69 L. Ed. 645, 65 S. Ct. 26
406 Ill. 286, 94 N.E.2d 195; 341 U.S. 913, 95 L. Ed. 1349, 73 S. Ct. 734; 409 Ill. 480, 101 N.E.2d 205; 343 U.S. 940, 96 L. Ed. 1346, 72 S. Ct. 1033; 344 U.S. 574, 97 L. Ed. 559, 73 S. Ct. 460; 1 Ill. 2d 311, 115 N.E.2d 785

56 Cal. 2d 11, 14 Cal. Rptr. 25, 363 P.2d 25; 368 U.S. 899, 7 L. Ed. 2d 94, 82 S. Ct. 175

**Home Trust Company Robbery—Murder Case**

326 Mo. 661, 32 S.W.2d 596

**Homestead Cases**

31 Tex. 677

31 Tex. 681

31 Tex. 688

63 Va. (22 Gratt.) 266

**Homestead Murders Case**

46 Ore. 287, 80 P. 655

**Hominy Franchise Case**

2 F. Supp. 849

**Honolulu Smith Act Case**

251 F.2d 342

**Hood River Case**

114 Ore. 112, 227 P. 1065; 273 U.S. 647, 71 L. Ed. 821, 47 S. Ct. 245

**Hoop-Skirt Case**

F. Cas. No. 4,028; F. Cas. No. 4,030

**Hoosac Mills Cases**

297 U.S. 1, 80 L. Ed. 477, 56 S. Ct. 312

297 U.S. 110, 80 L. Ed. 513, 56 S. Ct. 374

**Hope Natural Gas Company Case**

319 U.S. 735, 87 L. Ed. 1695, 63 S. Ct. 1165; 134 F.2d 287; 320 U.S. 591, 88 L. Ed. 333, 64 S. Ct. 281

**Horace Mann Case**

242 Md. 645, 220 A.2d 51; 385 U.S. 97, 17 L. Ed. 2d 195, 87 S. Ct. 317

**Horicon Marsh Case**

200 Wis. 271, 228 N.W. 140

**Horse Collar Case**

33 F. 284; 141 U.S. 419, 35 L. Ed. 800, 12 S. Ct. 76

**Horse Nail Case**

172 F.2d 826

**Horseheads Case**

69 F. 257; 71 F. 886, 71 F. 396, 18 C.C.A. 145; 163 U.S. 685, 41 L. Ed. 315, 16 S. Ct. 1201

**Horseplay Cases**

208 Ky. 618, 271 S.W. 687

87 N.J.L. 103, 93 A. 79; 88 N.J.L. 161, 95 A. 1007

**Horseshoe Case**

14 F. 377; 118 U.S. 196, 30 L. Ed. 98, 6 S. Ct. 1177

**Horton Motor Lines Case**

170 Misc. 507, 10 N.Y.S.2d 580

**Hosiery Mills Case**

294 F. 587; 297 F. 897; 268 U.S. 325, 69 L. Ed. 982, 45 S. Ct. 525

**Hospital Medicaid Reimbursement Case**

496 U.S. 498, 110 L. Ed. 2d 455, 110 S. Ct. 2510

**Hostage Release Agreement Case**

453 U.S. 654, 69 L. Ed. 2d 918, 101 S. Ct. 2972

**Hot Cargo Cases**

241 F.2d 147; 355 U.S. 808, 2 L. Ed. 2d 27, 78 S. Ct. 13, 78 S. Ct. 42, 78 S. Ct. 56; 357 U.S. 93, 2 L. Ed. 2d 1186, 78 S. Ct. 1011

247 F.2d 71

**Hot Oil Case**

293 U.S. 388, 79 L. Ed. 446, 55 S. Ct. 241

**Hot Potato Case**

321 I.C.C. 238

**Hot Springs Cases**

10 Ct. Cl. 289; 10 Ct. Cl. 433; 92 U.S. 698, 23 L. Ed. 690

**Hound Dog Case**

77 Okla.Crim. 17, 138 P.2d 11S

**Hours of Labor Cases**

206 U.S. 246, 51 L. Ed. 1047, 27 S. Ct. 600

221 U.S. 612, 55 L. Ed. 878, 31 S. Ct. 621

236 U.S. 385, 59 L. Ed. 632, 35 S. Ct. 345

*Continued*

162 Cal. 687, 124 P. 427; 236 U.S. 373, 59 L. Ed. 628, 35 S. Ct. 342
210 Mass. 387, 97 N.E. 367; 232 U.S. 671, 58 L. Ed. 788, 34 S. Ct. 469
22 Ohio Dec. 39, 12 Ohio N.P. (n.s.) 1; 85 Ohio St. 494, 9 Ohio Law Rep. 571, 57 Wkly. L. Bull. 55, 98 N.E. 1126; 232 U.S. 718, 58 L. Ed. 813, 34 S. Ct. 479
48 Ore. 252, 85 P. 855; 208 U.S. 412, 52 L. Ed. 551, 28 S. Ct. 324
71 Ore. 259, 139 P. 731; 243 U.S. 426, 61 L. Ed. 830, 37 S. Ct. 435

**House Arrest Case**
445 U.S. 573, 63 L. Ed. 2d 639, 100 S. Ct. 1371

**House Leasing Cases**
258 U.S. 242, 66 L. Ed. 595, 42 S. Ct. 289
264 U.S. 543, 68 L. Ed. 841, 44 S. Ct. 405

**House of David Case**
1 F.2d 266; 266 U.S. 617, 69 L. Ed. 470, 45 S. Ct. 98

**Houseman Case**
93 U.S. 130, 23 L. Ed. 833

**Housing Authority Act Cases**
235 Ala. 485, 179 So. 535
239 Ala. 280, 195 So. 256
201 Ark. 263, 144 S.W.2d 49
14 Cal. 2d 437, 94 P.2d 794
106 Colo. 61, 101 P.2d 21
133 Fla. 590, 183 So. 145
186 Ga. 673, 199 S.E. 43
370 Ill. 356, 19 N.E.2d 193
215 Ind. 330, 19 N.E.2d 741
268 Ky. 97, 103 S.W.2d 651
190 La. 710, 182 So. 725
304 Mass. 288, 23 N.E.2d 665
304 Mass. 507, 24 N.E.2d 333
107 Mont. 512, 86 P.2d 656
270 N.Y. 333, 1 N.E.2d 153; 155 Misc. 681, 279 N.Y.S. 299
213 N.C. 744, 197 S.E. 693
136 Ohio St. 328, 25 N.E.2d 844
188 S.C. 377, 199 S.E. 425
174 Tenn. 76, 123 S.W.2d 1085
135 Tex. 158, 143 S.W.2d 79; 143 S.W.2d 95

**Housing Cases**
258 U.S. 242, 66 L. Ed. 595, 42 S. Ct. 289
264 U.S. 543, 68 L. Ed. 841, 44 S. Ct. 405
267 F. 614, 50 App. D.C. 56; 254 U.S. 640, 65 L. Ed. 452, 41 S. Ct. 13; 267 F. 631, 50 App. D.C. 73; 256 U.S. 135, 65 L. Ed. 865, 41 S. Ct. 458
269 F. 306; 256 U.S. 170, 65 L. Ed. 877, 41 S. Ct. 465
113 Misc. 527, 185 N.Y.S. 632; 194 A.D. 523, 186 N.Y.S. 58, 230 N.Y. 429, 130 N.E. 601; 257 U.S. 665, 66 L. Ed. 424, 42 S. Ct. 47
113 Misc. 536, 185 N.Y.S. 638; 195 A.D. 280, 186 N.Y.S. 63; 230 N.Y. 429, 130 N.E. 601; 257 U.S. 665, 66 L. Ed. 424, 42 S. Ct. 47

**Houston Telephone Rate Case**
268 F. 878; 259 U.S. 318, 66 L. Ed. 961, 42 S. Ct. 486

**Howe's Bakery Case**
6 Bosw. (19 N.Y. Super. Ct.) 354, 19 How. Pr. 14, 10 Abb. Pr. 264; 6 Bosw. (19 N.Y. Super. Ct.) 684, 11 Abb. Pr. 28

**Huey Long Case**
69 F.2d 386; 292 U.S. 619, 78 L. Ed. 1476, 54 S. Ct. 774; 293 U.S. 76, 79 L. Ed. 208, 55 S. Ct. 21

**Huggett Case**
167 So. 147 (La.)

**Hulbert Case**
124 Misc. 273, 207 N.Y.S. 710; 213 A.D. 865, 209 N.Y.S. 850; 241 N.Y. 525, 150 N.E. 539

**Human Jettison Case**
F. Cas. No. 15,383

**Hummel Cases**
49 Misc. 136, 20 N.Y. Crim. 239, 98 N.Y.S. 713; 119 A.D. 153, 21 N.Y. Crim. 162, 104 N.Y.S. 308
112 A.D. 866, 20 N.Y. Crim. 67, 98 N.Y.S. 399; 186 N.Y. 164, 78 N.E. 860
115 A.D. 346, 101 N.Y.S. 507; 188 N.Y. 49, 38 Civ. P. Rep. 217, 80 N.E. 570

**Humphrey Case**
295 U.S. 602, 79 L. Ed. 1611, 55 S. Ct. 869

**Huntley Hearing Case**
15 N.Y.2d 72, 255 N.Y.S.2d 838, 204 N.E.2d 179

**Hunyadi Janos Case**
88 F. 61; 91 F. 536, 33 C.C.A. 291, 63 U.S. App. D.C. 139; 173 U.S. 704, 19 S. Ct. 886, 179 U.S. 19, 45 L. Ed. 60, 21 S. Ct. 7; 179 U.S. 42, 45 L. Ed. 77, 21 S. Ct. 16; 127 F. 1023; 138 F. 22, 70 C.C.A. 452
88 F. 71; 91 F. 1004, 34 C.C.A. 690; 173 U.S. 704, 19 S. Ct. 886; 179 U.S. 43, 45 L. Ed. 77, 21 S. Ct. 16
140 F. 938; 147 F. 189, 77 C.C.A. 417; 203 U.S. 591, 51 L. Ed. 331, 27 S. Ct. 778

**Hurford Case**
317 Ill. 203, 148 N.E. 69

**Hurn Case**
289 U.S. 238, 77 L. Ed. 1148, 53 S. Ct. 586; 61 F.2d 1031; 288 U.S. 595, 77 L. Ed. 972, 53 S. Ct. 319

**Hutcheson Case**
32 F. Supp. 600; 60 S. Ct. 898; 312 U.S. 219, 85 L. Ed. 788, 61 S. Ct. 463

**Hutchinson Municipal Airport Case**
161 Kan. 502, 169 P.2d 615

**Hydroelectric Power Rates Case**
475 U.S. 657, 89 L. Ed. 2d 661, 106 S. Ct. 1422

**Hygrade Case**
295 U.S. 193, 79 L. Ed. 1382, 55 S. Ct. 748

**Hypophosphites and Borax Cases**
41 Minn. 74, 42 N.W. 781

## I

**Ice Cases**
285 U.S. 262, 76 L. Ed. 747, 52 S. Ct. 371
127 F.2d 165; 317 U.S. 634, 87 L. Ed. 511, 63 S. Ct. 29
40 F. Supp. 654; 131 F.2d 518
43 F. Supp. 424; 136 F.2d 353; 320 U.S. 761, 88 L. Ed. 454, 64 S. Ct. 72
62 Cal. App. 2d 357, 144 P.2d 896

**Ice Cream Cases**
168 Iowa 1, 147 N.W. 195
245 Pa. 554, 91 A. 922; 242 U.S. 153, 61 L. Ed. 217, 37 S. Ct. 28

**Ice Machine Case**
172 S.W. 206 (Tex.); 247 U.S. 21, 62 L. Ed. 963, 38 S. Ct. 430

**Idaho Farmer's Case**
332 U.S. 380, 92 L. Ed. 51, 62 S. Ct. 1

**Identification of Class Member for Notice Case**
437 U.S. 340, 57 L. Ed. 2d 253, 98 S. Ct. 2380

**Illegal Detention Case**
460 U.S. 491, 75 L. Ed. 2d 229, 103 S. Ct. 1319

**Illegitimate Childrens Benefit Case**
417 U.S. 628, 41 L. Ed. 2d 363, 94 S. Ct. 2496

**Illinois Bond Cases**
105 U.S. 667, 26 L. Ed. 1204

**Illinois Central Case**
173 F. 930; 215 U.S. 452, 54 L. Ed. 280, 30 S. Ct. 155; 215 U.S. 479, 54 L. Ed. 291, 30 S. Ct. 163

**Illinois Classification Case**
55 I.C.C. 290; 56 I.C.C. 202; 56 I.C.C. 687

**Illinois Coal Cases**
62 I.C.C. 741; 64 I.C.C. 751

**Illinois Dram Shop Case**
272 Ill. 127, 111 N.E. 735; 246 U.S. 97, 62 L. Ed. 596, 38 S. Ct. 298

**Illinois-Indiana Coal Cases**
128 I.C.C. 265

**Illinois Railroad Tax Cases**
92 U.S. 575, 23 L. Ed. 663

**Imbrie Case**
290 F. 33

**Immigration Cases**
10 I.C.C. 13

**Immigration Judicial Review Cases**
112 L. Ed. 2d 866, 111 S. Ct. 807; 112 L. Ed. 2d 1005, 111 S. Ct. 888

**Immunized Testimony Case**
459 U.S. 248, 74 L. Ed. 2d 430, 103 S. Ct. 608

**Impeachment Pardon Case**
91 F. Supp. 323; 192 F.2d 602, 89 App. D.C. 354; 342 U.S. 946, 96 L. Ed. 703, 72 S. Ct. 560; 343 U.S. 921, 96 L. Ed. 1334, 72 S. Ct. 676; 212 F.2d 453, 94 App. D.C. 85

**Import Case**
5 I.C. 405

**Import-Export Clause Case**
423 U.S. 276, 46 L. Ed. 2d 495, 96 S. Ct. 535

**Import Rate Case**
2 I.C. 660, 734, 755, 800, 3 I.C. 417; 4 I.C. 62; 52 F. 187; 4 I.C. 114, 57 F. 948, 6 C.C.A. 653, 20 U.S. App. D.C. 1; 4 I.C. 408; 162 U.S. 197, 40 L. Ed. 940, 16 S. Ct. 666

**Improper Loading Case**
209 F.2d 442; 347 U.S. 952, 98 L. Ed. 1098, 74 S. Ct. 677

**In-er-Seal Case**
127 F. 160; 127 F. 116, 62 C.C.A. 116; 195 U.S. 630, 49 L. Ed. 352, 25 S. Ct. 788

**In re: Belated Appeals in Criminal Cases**
265 Ark. 964, 761 S.W.2d 606

**In re: Federal Skywalk Case**
98 F.R.D. 462

**In re: President and Directors of Georgetown College**
331 F.2d 1000 (D.C. Cir.)

**Incandescent Lamp Case**
82 F. Supp. 753; 115 F. Supp. 835

**Incandescent Lamp Monopoly Case**
10 F.2d 715; 272 U.S. 476, 71 L. Ed. 362, 47 S. Ct. 192

**Incandescent Lamp Patent Cases**
40 F. 21, 49 Off. Gaz. Pat. Office 1536; 159 U.S. 465, 40 L. Ed. 221, 16 S. Ct. 75, 73 Off. Gaz. Pat. Office 1289
44 F. 294; 45 F. 55; 47 F. 454; 52 F. 300, 3 C.C.A. 83; 59 F. 501, 8 C.C.A. 200
53 F. 592, 3 C.C.A. 605; 149 U.S. 785, 37 L. Ed. 967, 13 S. Ct. 1052

**Income Tax Cases**
78 U.S. 113, 20 L. Ed. 122
157 U.S. 429, 39 L. Ed. 759, 15 S. Ct. 673; 158 U.S. 601, 39 L. Ed. 1108, 15 S. Ct. 912
5 App. D.C. 413; 163 U.S. 696, 41 L. Ed. 310, 16 S. Ct. 1204
148 Wis. 456, 134 N.W. 673, 135 N.W. 164; 231 U.S. 616, 58 L. Ed. 400, 34 S. Ct. 272

**Inconsistent Statements Case**
50 Ohio Law Abs. 577, 78 N.E.2d 395; 150 Ohio St 448, 38 Ohio Op. 314, 83 N.E.2d 222

**Increased Rates Case**
58 I.C.C. 220; 58 I.C.C. 302; 58 I.C.C. 489; 272 F. 758

**Independent Candidates Cases**
415 U.S. 724, 39 L. Ed. 2d 714, 94 S. Ct. 1274
415 U.S. 767, 39 L. Ed. 2d 744, 94 S. Ct. 1296

**Independent Case**
200 F. 411, 118 C.C.A. 563

**Independent Counsel Case**
487 U.S. 654, 101 L. Ed. 2d 569, 108 S. Ct. 2597

**Index Book Case**
60 F. 618

**Indian Burial Case**
102 F. Supp. 658; 245 Iowa 147, 60 N.W.2d 110; 347 U.S. 942, 98 L. Ed. 1091, 74 S. Ct. 638; 348 U.S. 880, 99 L. Ed. 693, 75 S. Ct. 122; 349 U.S. 70, 99 L. Ed. 897, 75 S. Ct. 614

**Indian Canoe Case**
240 Mo. App. 818, 219 S.W.2d 665

**Indian Country Cases**
93 U.S. 188, 23 L. Ed. 846; F. Cas. 15,136; 108 U.S. 491, 27 L. Ed. 803, 2 S. Ct. 906
234 U.S. 422, 58 L. Ed. 1383, 34 S. Ct. 794; 183 F. 611

**Indian Gaming Jurisdiction Case**
517 U.S. 44, 134 L. Ed. 2d 252, 116 S. Ct. 1114 (1996)

**Indian Hunting Rights Case**
420 U.S. 194, 43 L. Ed. 2d 129, 95 S. Ct. 944

**Indian Land Severance Tax Case**
455 U.S. 130, 71 L. Ed. 2d 21, 102 S. Ct. 894

**Indian Towing Case**
211 F.2d 886, 1954 A.M.C. 887; 348 U.S. 810, 99 L. Ed. 639, 75 S. Ct. 60, 1954 A.M.C. 2233; 349 U.S. 902, 99 L. Ed. 1239, 75 S. Ct. 575; 349 U.S. 926, 99 L. Ed. 1257, 75 S. Ct. 769, 1955 A.M.C. 1422; 350 U.S. 61, 100 L. Ed. 48, 76 S. Ct. 122

**Indiana Bus Cases**
201 Ind. 59, 163 N.E. 489
201 Ind. 66, 163 N.E. 483
201 Ind. 78, 166 N.E. 153

**Indiana Express Tax Cases**
166 U.S. 185, 41 L. Ed. 965, 17 S. Ct. 604
144 Ind. 549, 42 N.E. 483; 165 U.S. 255, 41 L. Ed. 707, 17 S. Ct. 991

*Continued*

47 N.E. 1113 (Ind.)

**Indiana Gross Income Tax Case**
212 Ind. 343, 7 N.E.2d 941; 58 S. Ct. 477; 304 U.S. 307, 82 L. Ed. 1365, 58 S. Ct. 913; 214 Ind. 707, 15 N.E.2d 1016

**Indiana Headlight Case**
182 Ind. 382, 101 N.E. 85; 242 U.S. 255, 61 L. Ed. 276, 37 S. Ct. 93

**Indiana Rate Case**
231 U.S. 1, 58 L. Ed. 97, 34 S. Ct. 7

**Indiana Teacher Tenure Case**
214 Ind. 347, 5 N.E.2d 531, 5 N.E.2d 913, 7 N.E.2d 777, 13 N.E.2d 955; 58 S. Ct. 2; 302 U.S. 678, 82 L. Ed. 524, 58 S. Ct. 262; 303 U.S. 95, 82 L. Ed. 685, 58 S. Ct. 443; 303 U.S. 667, 82 L. Ed. 1123, 58 S. Ct. 641

**Indianapolis Water Company Case**
272 U.S. 400, 71 L. Ed. 316, 47 S. Ct. 144

**Indigent Defendant Assistance Case**
470 U.S. 68, 84 L. Ed. 2d 53, 105 S. Ct. 1087

**Indigent's Parental-Rights Appeal Case**
519 U.S. 102, 136 L. Ed. 2d 473, 117 S. Ct. 555 (1996)

**Indirect Purchasers Antitrust Case**
490 U.S. 93, 104 L. Ed. 2d 86, 109 S. Ct. 1661

**Indoctrinated Jurors Case**
399 Ill. 527, 78 N.E.2d 245

**Indorsement Cases**
31 Tex. 693

**Industrial Institute and College Case**
81 Miss. 174, 32 So. 314

**Industrial Railways Case**
29 I.C.C. 212

**Industrial Siding Case**
140 N.C. 239, 52 S.E. 941

**Inevitable Discovery of Evidence Case**
467 U.S. 431, 81 L. Ed. 2d 377, 104 S. Ct. 2501

**Ingalls Case**
45 B.T.A. 787; 132 F.2d 862

**Ingersoll Case**
127 F. 418; 132 F. 168; 133 F. 226, 66 C.C.A. 280; 136 F. 689; 148 F. 169, 78 C.C.A. 303; 203 U.S. 596, 51 L. Ed. 333, 27 S. Ct. 785; 211 U.S. 335, 53 L. Ed. 208, 29 S. Ct. 92; 174 F. 666; 176 F. 194, 99 C.C.A. 548

**Ingot Molds Case**
392 U.S. 571, 20 L. Ed. 2d 1289, 88 S. Ct. 2105

**Inheritance from Illegitimate Case**
269 S.W.2d 227 (Ky.)

**Inheritance Tax Cases**
170 U.S. 283, 42 L. Ed. 1037, 18 S. Ct. 594
46 S. Ct. 634; 273 U.S. 12, 71 L. Ed. 511, 47 S. Ct. 265
55 Ct. Cl. 430; 255 U.S. 257, 65 L. Ed. 617, 41 S. Ct. 256
166 Iowa 617, 147 N.W. 1098; 245 U.S. 170, 62 L. Ed. 225, 38 S. Ct. 109
168 Iowa 511, 151 N.W. 66; 245 U.S. 176, 62 L. Ed. 228, 38 S. Ct. 111

**Injured Person Statement Case**
233 Minn. 1, 45 N.W.2d 776

**Ink and Paper Use Tax Case**
460 U.S. 575, 75 L. Ed. 2d 295, 103 S. Ct. 1365

**Inland Lakes Cases**
192 Mich. 319, 158 N.W. 951
197 Mich. 512, 163 N.W. 993
235 Mich. 174, 209 N.W. 152

**Inland Steel Case**
339 U.S. 382, 94 L. Ed. 925, 70 S. Ct. 674; 170 F.2d 247; 79 F. Supp. 563; 335 U.S. 910, 93 L. Ed. 443, 69 S. Ct. 480; 339 U.S. 382, 94 L. Ed. 925, 70 S. Ct. 674;339 U.S. 990, 94 L. Ed. 1391, 70 S. Ct. 1017

**Innocent Owner Drug Proceeds Forfeiture Case**
507 U.S. 111, 122 L. Ed. 2d 469, 113 S. Ct. 1126 (1993)

**Insanity Murder Case**
29 Wash. 2d 52, 185 P.2d 486

**Insanity Rape Case**
267 S.W.2d 642 (Mo.)

**Insider Short-Swing Profits Case**
208 F.2d 600

**Insular Cases**
182 U.S. 1, 45 L. Ed. 1041, 21 S. Ct. 743
182 U.S. 221, 45 L. Ed. 1065, 21 S. Ct. 742
182 U.S. 222, 45 L. Ed. 1074, 21 S. Ct. 762
182 U.S. 243, 45 L. Ed. 1086, 21 S. Ct. 827
182 U.S. 244, 45 L. Ed. 1088, 21 S. Ct. 770
183 U.S. 151, 46 L. Ed. 128, 22 S. Ct. 69
183 U.S. 176, 46 L. Ed. 138, 22 S. Ct. 59
190 U.S. 197, 47 L. Ed. 1016, 23 S. Ct. 787
195 U.S. 138, 49 L. Ed. 128, 24 S. Ct. 808
197 U.S. 516, 49 L. Ed. 862, 25 S. Ct. 514
103 F. 72; 182 U.S. 221, 45 L. Ed. 1065, 21 S. Ct. 742
105 F. 74; 182 U.S. 392, 45 L. Ed. 1146, 21 S. Ct. 827
105 F. 608; 182 U.S. 221, 45 L. Ed. 1065, 21 S. Ct. 742

**Insull Extradition Case**
8 F. Supp. 310

**Insurance Appraiser Case**
159 Ohio St. 237, 50 Ohio Op. 269, 112 N.E.2d 1

**Insurance Reinstatement Case**
134 N.J.L. 254, 47 A.2d 1

**Insurance Tax Cases**
160 Kan. 300, 161 P.2d 726

**Insured's Release of Tortfeasor Case**
235 N.C. 544, 70 S.E.2d 570

**Insurgents' Cases**
2 U.S. 335, 1 L. Ed. 404, F. Cas. No. 15,443
2 U.S. 343, 1 L. Ed. 408
2 U.S. 345, 1 L. Ed. 409
2 U.S. 346, 1 L. Ed. 409
2 U.S. 348, 1 L. Ed. 410
3 U.S. 513, 1 L. Ed. 700, F. Cas. No. 15,442
3 U.S. 515, 1 L. Ed. 701, F. Cas. No. 15,126
F. Cas. No. 15,127

**Inter-State National Bank of Kansas Case**
221 F.2d 382; 350 U.S. 944, 100 L. Ed. 823, 76 S. Ct. 297; 225 F.2d 499

**Interborough Metropolitan Case**
56 Misc. 128, 106 N.Y.S. 416; 125 A.D. 804, 110 N.Y.S. 186

**Interest on Funds in Court Case**
150 Neb. 272, 34 N.W.2d 331

**Interested Agent Case**
204 Okl. 138, 227 P.2d 670

**Interior Advertising Case**
95 Misc. 366, 158 N.Y.S. 750; 228 N.Y. 577, 127 N.E. 910; 182 A.D. 887, 168 N.Y.S. 1104

**Interlineated Will Case**
206 Okla. 174, 242 P.2d 135; 268 P.2d 236

**Interlocking Directorates Case**
76 L. Ed. 2d 456, 103 S. Ct. 2266

**Intermingled Cotton Cases**
3 Ct. Cl. 384
10 Ct. Cl. 502; 92 U.S. 651, 23 L. Ed. 756

**Intermountain Rate Cases**
191 F. 856; 234 U.S. 476, 58 L. Ed. 1408, 34 S. Ct. 986; 234 U.S. 495, 58 L. Ed. 1426, 34 S. Ct. 995
19 I.C.C. 148; 182 F. 189; 20 I.C.C. 106; 190 F. 591, 22 I.C.C. 149; 203 F. 56; 231 U.S. 736, 58 L. Ed. 460, 34 S. Ct. 316
19 I.C.C. 162; 21 I.C.C. 400; 23 I.C.C. 454
19 I.C.C. 218
19 I.C.C. 238; 21 I.C.C. 329; 23 I.C.C. 456
19 I.C.C. 257; 23 I.C.C. 456

**Internal Security Case**
421 U.S. 491, 44 L. Ed. 2d 324, 95 S. Ct. 1813

**International Boundaries Dispute Case**
27 U.S. 253, 7 L. Ed. 415

**International Boxing Club Case**
123 F. Supp. 575; 348 U.S. 236, 99 L. Ed. 290, 75 S. Ct. 259

**International Harvester Company Case**
234 U.S. 579, 58 L. Ed. 1479, 34 S. Ct. 944

**International News Cases**
248 U.S. 215, 63 L. Ed. 211, 39 S. Ct. 68; 240 F. 983; 245 F. 244; 245 U.S. 644, 62 L. Ed. 528, 38 S. Ct. 10
35 F.2d 279

**International Shoe Cases**
22 Wash. 2d 146, 154 P.2d 801; 65 S. Ct. 1579; 326 U.S. 310, 90 L. Ed. 95, 66 S. Ct. 154
280 U.S. 291, 74 L. Ed. 431, 50 S. Ct. 89; 97 F.2d 515; 279 U.S. 832, 73 L. Ed. 982, 49 S. Ct. 478; 279 U.S. 849, 73 L. Ed. 993, 49 S. Ct. 346

**International Yacht Cases**
90 Misc. 370, 153 N.Y.S. 264; 154 N.Y.S. 1109; 170 A.D. 484, 156 N.Y.S. 179

**Internet Free Speech Case**
521 U.S. 844, 138 L. Ed. 2d 874, 117 S. Ct. 2329 (1997)

**Intersection Right of Way Case**
225 Minn. 107, 29 N.W.2d 883

**Interterritorial Case**
151 I.C.C. 613

**Intoxicating Liquor Cases**
284 F. 890; 285 F. 79; 262 U.S. 100, 67 L. Ed. 894, 43 S. Ct. 504
25 Kan. 751

**Intoximeter Case**
179 Pa. Super. 134, 115 A.2d 820; 383 Pa. 461, 119 A.2d 211

**Intrastate Transfer of Aircraft Case**
78 Ga. App. 537, 51 S.E.2d 610

**Invalid Tax Title Case**
190 Okla. 382, 124 P.2d 409; 199 Okla. 312, 185 P.2d 452

**Inventory Cases**
17 Ariz. App. 64, 495 P.2d 504
17 Ariz. App. 76, 495 P.2d 516
18 Ariz. App. 110, 500 P.2d 641

**Inverse Condemnation of Indian Lands Case**
445 U.S. 253, 63 L. Ed. 2d 373, 100 S. Ct. 1127

**Investigatory Records Case**
456 U.S. 615, 72 L. Ed. 2d 376, 102 S. Ct. 2054

**Investment Advisers Act Case**
444 U.S. 11, 62 L. Ed. 2d 146, 100 S. Ct. 242

**Investment Banker's Case**
10 F.R.D. 240; 11 F.R.D. 445; 13 F.R.D. 300; 118 F. Supp. 621

**Iolanthe Case**
15 F. 439

**Iowa Cities Case**
256 F. 929; 255 U.S. 539, 65 L. Ed. 764, 41 S. Ct. 400; 257 U.S. 662, 66 L. Ed. 423, 42 S. Ct. 45

**Iron Hall Case**
83 Md. 83, 34 A. 839

**Iron Rate Case**
6 I.C.C. 488; 74 F. 42; 101 F. 779, 42 C.C.A. 12; 46 L. Ed. 1264, 22 S. Ct. 934

**Iron Silver Cases**
116 U.S. 687, 29 L. Ed. 774, 6 S. Ct. 601; 33 F. 354; 124 U.S. 374, 31 L. Ed. 466, 8 S. Ct. 598
16 F. 810; 24 F. 568; 128 U.S. 673, 32 L. Ed. 571, 9 S. Ct. 195
16 F. 829; 109 U.S. 550, 27 L. Ed. 1028, 3 S. Ct. 339; 143 U.S. 431, 36 L. Ed. 214, 12 S. Ct. 555

**Iroquois Theatre Fire Case**
1 Ill. Cir. Ct. 245; 2 Ill. Cir. Ct. 395

**Irrigation Cases**
200 U.S. 527, 50 L. Ed. 581, 26 S. Ct. 301
27 Utah 158, 75 P. 371; 198 U.S. 361, 49 L. Ed. 1085, 25 S. Ct. 676

**IRS Handwriting Exemplars Case**
444 U.S. 707, 63 L. Ed. 2d 141, 100 S. Ct. 874

**Irving House Case**
3 Sandf. (5 N.Y. Super. Ct.) 725

**Isis Case**
290 U.S. 333, 78 L. Ed. 348, 54 S. Ct. 162; 290 U.S. 609, 78 L. Ed. 533, 54 S. Ct. 50

**Isis Plumbing and Heating Company Case**
138 N.L.R.B. 716, No. 97; 322 F.2d 913

**Ivanhoe Case**
47 Cal. 2d 597, 306 P.2d 824; 357 U.S. 275, 2 L. Ed. 2d 1313, 78 S. Ct. 1174; 53 Cal. 2d 692, 3 Cal. Rptr. 317, 350 P.2d 69; 355 U.S. 803, 2 L. Ed. 2d 26, 78 S. Ct. 12, 78 S. Ct. 13; 356 U.S. 917, 78 S. Ct. 697, 78 S. Ct. 698; 358 U.S. 805, 3 L. Ed. 2d 94, 3 L. Ed. 2d 95, 79 S. Ct. 10, 79 S. Ct. 11

**Ives Case**
35 F. 176; 144 U.S. 408, 36 L. Ed. 485, 12 S. Ct. 679

## J

**Jack Case**
231 S.W. 1033 (Mo.)

**Jack O'Lantern Cases**
266 F. 562; 258 U.S. 96, 66 L. Ed. 482, 42 S. Ct. 243
282 F. 899

**Jackass Case**
31 So. 201 (Miss.)

**Jackson Case**
24 F.2d 981; 34 F.2d 241; 280 U.S. 549, 74 L. Ed. 608, 50 S. Ct. 86; 281 U.S. 344, 74 L. Ed. 891, 50 S. Ct. 294

**Jackson Hole Case**
58 F. Supp. 890

**Jacob's Will Case**
9 Cow. 437, 1 Hopk. Ch. 106; 1 Hopk. Ch. 372; 1 Hopk. Ch. 429

**Jaime Case**
61 Ariz. 387, 149 P.2d 687

**Jamaica Water Supply Cases**
128 A.D. 13, 112 N.Y.S. 392; 193 N.Y. 649, 86 N.E. 1130; 196 N.Y. 39, 89 N.E. 581; 197 N.Y. 33, 90 N.E. 112
57 Misc. 475, 109 N.Y.S. 948; 65 Misc. 630, 122 N.Y.S. 366

**James Case**
90 Ga. 254, 16 S.E. 83; 162 U.S. 650, 40 L. Ed. 1105, 16 S. Ct. 934

**Jamestown Builders Exchange Case**
93 N.L.R.B. 386, No. 51

**Jamestown College Case**
172 N.Y. 291, 64 N.E. 952

**Jane Froman Case**
299 N.Y. 88, 85 N.E.2d 880; 274 A.D. 767, 80 N.Y.S.2d 735; 190 Misc. 974, 77 N.Y.S.2d 257

**Jans Litigation Cases**
44 F.2d 716; 283 U.S. 827, 75 L. Ed. 1441, 51 S. Ct. 351; 49 F.2d 908
83 N.Y. 348
4 Paige 178; 15 Wend. 111; 4 Sandf. Ch. 369; 4 Sandf. Ch. 633
7 Paige 195; 24 Wend. 587
30 Barb. 537; 22 N.Y. 44
179 A.D. 621, 167 N.Y.S. 107
1 Abb. Pr. 385

**Japanese Curfew Case**
46 F. Supp. 657; 63 S. Ct. 860; 320 U.S. 81, 87 L. Ed. 1774, 63 S. Ct. 1375

**Japanese Electronic Products Antitrust Case**
475 U.S. 574, 89 L. Ed. 2d 538, 106 S. Ct. 1348

**Japanese Exclusion Case**
323 U.S. 214, 89 L. Ed. 194, 65 S. Ct. 193; 140 F.2d 289; 321 U.S. 760, 88 L. Ed. 1058, 64 S. Ct. 786; 324 U.S. 885, 89 L. Ed. 1435, 65 S. Ct. 674

**Japanese Immigrant Case**
189 U.S. 86, 47 L. Ed. 721, 23 S. Ct. 611

**Japanese Language School Case**
11 F.2d 710; 273 U.S. 677, 71 L. Ed. 835, 47 S. Ct. 99; 273 U.S. 284, 71 L. Ed. 646, 47 S. Ct. 406

**Japanese Naturalization Case**
260 U.S. 178, 67 L. Ed. 199, 43 S. Ct. 65

**Japanese Relocation Cases**
320 U.S. 81, 87 L. Ed. 1774, 63 S. Ct. 1375
323 U.S. 214, 89 L. Ed. 194, 65 S. Ct. 193; 140 F.2d 289; 321 U.S. 760, 88 L. Ed. 1058, 64 S. Ct. 786; 324 U.S. 885, 89 L. Ed. 1435, 65 S. Ct. 674

**Jaybird Case**
90 F. Supp. 595; 193 F.2d 600; 344 U.S. 883, 97 L. Ed. 684, 73 S. Ct. 180; 345 U.S. 461, 97 L. Ed. 1152, 73 S. Ct. 809; 345 U.S. 1003, 97 L. Ed. 1408, 73 S. Ct. 1128

**Jaycees Case**
468 U.S. 609, 82 L. Ed. 2d 462, 104 S. Ct. 3244

**Jefferson Davis Case**
F. Cas. No. 3,621a

**Jefferson Standard Broadcasting Case**
346 U.S. 464, 98 L. Ed. 195, 74 S. Ct. 172

**Jeffrey Case**
101 F. 121, 41 C.C.A. 247; 144 F. 130

**Jehovah's Witness Cases**
319 U.S. 103, 87 L. Ed. 1290, 63 S. Ct. 890; 241 Ala. 279, 3 So. 2d 76, 242 Ala. 549, 7 So. 2d 503; 30 Ala. App. 416, 7 So. 2d 503; 202 Ark. 614, 151 S.W.2d 1000; 58 Ariz. 144, 118 P.2d 97; 135 F.2d 981; 315 U.S. 793, 86 L. Ed. 1196, 62 S. Ct. 903; 316 U.S. 584, 86 L. Ed. 1691, 62 S. Ct. 1231; 318 U.S. 796, 87 L. Ed. 1161, 63 S. Ct. 658; 320 U.S. 719, 88 L. Ed. 423, 64 S. Ct. 423
319 U.S. 105, 87 L. Ed. 1292, 63 S. Ct. 870, 63 S. Ct. 891; 149 Pa. Super. 175, 27 A.2d 666; 316 U.S. 584, 86 L. Ed. 1691, 62 S. Ct. 1231; 318 U.S. 748, 87 L. Ed. 1125, 63 S. Ct. 660, 63 S. Ct. 661, 63 S. Ct. 662; 319 U.S. 157, 87 L. Ed. 1324, 63 S. Ct. 877
319 U.S. 141, 87 L. Ed. 1313, 63 S. Ct. 862; 139 Ohio St. 372, 40 N.E.2d 154; 317 U.S. 589, 87 L. Ed. 483, 63 S. Ct. 49; 318 U.S. 739, 87 L. Ed. 1119, 63 S. Ct. 528
319 U.S. 157, 87 L. Ed. 1324, 63 S. Ct. 877; 130 F.2d 652; 39 F. Supp. 32; 318 U.S. 749, 87 L. Ed. 1125, 63 S. Ct. 660; 319 U.S. 782, 87 L. Ed. 1726, 63 S. Ct. 1170
331 F.2d 1000 (D.C. Cir.)

**Jehovah's Witness Induction Cases**
115 F. Supp. 19; 213 F.2d 95; 348 U.S. 812, 99 L. Ed. 640, 75 S. Ct. 42
213 F.2d 911; 348 U.S. 812, 99 L. Ed. 640, 75 S. Ct. 59
213 F.2d 901; 348 U.S. 812, 99 L. Ed. 640, 75 S. Ct. 59
120 F. Supp. 730; 212 F.2d 71; 348 U.S. 811, 99 L. Ed. 640, 75 S. Ct. 27

**Jehovah's Witness Public Park Case**
97 N.H. 352, 88 A.2d 860; 345 U.S. 395, 97 L. Ed. 1105, 73 S. Ct. 760; 345 U.S. 978, 97 L. Ed. 1392, 73 S. Ct. 1119

**Jelke Case**
125 N.Y.S.2d 244; 284 A.D. 211, 130 N.Y.S.2d 662; 308 N.Y. 56, 123 N.E.2d 769

**Jencks Case**
353 U.S. 657, 1 L. Ed. 2d 1103, 77 S. Ct. 1007; 226 F.2d 540; 226 F.2d 553; 350 U.S. 980, 100 L. Ed. 849, 76 S. Ct. 467

**Jenkins Case**
18 F.2d 707; 275 U.S. 515, 72 L. Ed. 401, 48 S. Ct. 84, 277 U.S. 258, 72 L. Ed. 874, 48 S. Ct. 445

**Jennings Case**
161 F.2d 74; 63 F. Supp. 834

**Jerka Case**
126 Ill. App. 365; 227 Ill. 95, 81 N.E. 7

**Jig Saw Puzzle Case**
302 U.S. 16, 82 L. Ed. 20, 58 S. Ct. 95

**Jim Crow Cases**
186 F. 966, 109 C.C.A. 110; 235 U.S. 151, 59 L. Ed. 169, 35 S. Ct. 69
45 La. Ann. 80, 11 So. 948, 163 U.S. 537, 41 L. Ed. 256, 16 S. Ct. 1138

**Jim Crow Oil Company Case**
40 Okla. 479, 139 P. 943

**Jim-Jam-Jems Case**
211 F. 916, 128 C.C.A. 294

**Jitney Cases**
Tex. 489, 241 S.W. 994
170 Cal. 519, 150 P. 348
268 Ill. 175, 108 N.E. 991
137 La. 552, 68 So. 951
89 Misc. 230, 153 N.Y.S. 461; 167 A.D. 907, 151 N.Y.S. 1129; 168 A.D. 915, 152 N.Y.S. 1127; 168 A.D. 944, 153 N.Y.S. 1128
77 Tex. Crim. 72, 178 S.W. 537
95 S.W. 749 (Tex.); 175 S.W. 444; 183 S.W. xvi

*Continued*

178 S.W. 6 (Tex.); 185 S.W. xv
85 Wash. 294, 147 P. 1159
76 W. Va. 576, 85 S.E. 781

**John Barth Company Case**
27 F.2d 782; 278 U.S. 597, 73 L. Ed. 527, 49 S. Ct. 178; 279 U.S. 370, 73 L. Ed. 743, 49 S. Ct. 366

**John Deere Case**
383 U.S. 1, 15 L. Ed. 2d 545, 86 S. Ct. 649, 383 U.S. 39, 15 L. Ed. 2d 572, 86 S. Ct. 708

**John L's Case**
67 Miss. 346, 7 So. 275

**John's Island Case**
19 S.C. Eq. 192

**Johnson Case**
Treas. Dec. 24494, Gen. Appraisers 5352; 143 F. 915; 152 F. 164, 81 C.C.A. 416

**Johnson Grass Case**
194 U.S. 267, 48 L. Ed. 971, 24 S. Ct. 638

**Joint Anti-Fascist Case**
341 U.S. 123, 95 L. Ed. 817, 71 S. Ct. 624; 177 F.2d 79; 182 F.2d 368; 215 F.2d 870; 88 F. Supp. 873; 104 F. Supp. 567; 339 U.S. 910, 94 L. Ed. 1337, 70 S. Ct. 573, 339 U.S. 956, 94 L. Ed. 1367, 70 S. Ct. 978; 340 U.S. 805, 95 L. Ed. 592, 71 S. Ct. 39; 341 U.S. 918, 95 L. Ed. 1352, 71 S. Ct. 669; 345 U.S. 911, 97 L. Ed. 1346, 73 S. Ct. 649

**Joint Traffic Case**
76 F. 895; 89 F. 1020, 32 C.C.A. 491, 45 U.S. App. D.C. 762; 171 U.S. 505, 43 L. Ed. 259, 19 S. Ct. 25

**Joliet Case**
118 F.2d 174; 314 U.S. 591, 86 L. Ed. 476, 62 S. Ct. 70; 315 U.S. 44, 86 L. Ed. 658, 62 S. Ct. 442

**Jones and Laughlin Case**
301 U.S. 1, 81 L. Ed. 893, 57 S. Ct. 615; 90 F.2d 678

**Jones Cases**
95 U.S. 439, 24 L. Ed. 506
95 F. 370, 37 C.C.A. 106

**Jones County Calf Case**
63 Iowa 529, 17 N.W. 34; 19 N.W. 310; 69 Iowa 562, 29 N.W. 743, 82 Iowa 693, 47 N.W. 903, 48 N.W. 1081; 93 Iowa 165, 61 N.W. 422

**Jones Island Cases**
82 F. 160; 170 U.S. 41, 42 L. Ed. 941, 18 S. Ct. 503
106 Wis. 499, 81 N.W. 1027, 82 N.W. 534
109 Wis. 418, 84 N.W. 855, 85 N.W. 402; 160 Wis. 218, 151 N.W. 258
109 Wis. 449, 84 N.W. 1119; 119 Wis. 122, 95 N.W. 97, 123 Wis. 419, 101 N.W. 399
115 Wis. 68, 90 N.W. 1019
119 Wis. 580, 97 N.W. 166
133 Wis. 561, 113 N.W. 51
139 Wis. 281, 119 N.W. 935, 121 N.W. 362
164 Wis. 247, 159 N.W. 908

**Jonesboro Case**
110 N.L.R.B. 481, No. 67

**Joralemon Street Subway Case**
197 N.Y. 81, 90 N.E. 456; 197 N.Y. 613, 91 N.E. 1110; 208 N.Y. 25, 101 N.E. 706

**Journeymen Cordwainers' Case**
Yates Sel. Cas. 112, 2 Wheel. Crim. Cas. 262

**Joy Silk Mills Case**
85 N.L.R.B. 1263, No. 211; 185 F.2d 732; 341 U.S. 914, 95 L. Ed. 1350, 71 S. Ct. 734

**J.P. False Imprisonment Case**
299 Ky. 470, 185 S.W.2d 954

**J.P. Malicious Prosecution Case**
224 Minn. 224, 28 N.W.2d 780

**Judd Murder Case**
41 Ariz. 176, 16 P.2d 720; 39 Ariz. 242, 5 P.2d 192

**Judges' Cases**
102 Tenn. 509, 53 S.W. 134

**Judge's Income Tax Case**
307 U.S. 277, 83 L. Ed. 1289, 59 S. Ct. 838

**Judges' Salary Cases**
110 Tenn. 370, 75 S.W. 1061

**Judicial Review of Medicare Regulations Case**
476 U.S. 667, 90 L. Ed. 2d 623, 106 S. Ct. 2133

**Judicial Rule Making Case**
5 N.J. 240, 74 A.2d 406; 340 U.S. 877, 95 L. Ed. 638, 71 S. Ct. 123

**Judiciary Amendments Case**
77 Miss. 543, 27 So. 927

**Julien Case**
41 F. 679

**Jumel Litigation Case**
98 U.S. 254, 25 L. Ed. 47

**Junction Railroad Case**
88 Pa. 428

**Juneau Spruce Corporation Case**
82 N.L.R.B. 650, No. 71

**Junk Business Regulation Case**
140 Conn. 637, 103 A.2d 195

**Juror Bias Due Process Case**
455 U.S. 209, 71 L. Ed. 2d 78, 102 S. Ct. 940

**Juror Selection Case**
469 U.S. 412, 83 L. Ed. 2d 841, 105 S. Ct. 844

**Juvenile Pretrial Detention Case**
467 U.S. 253, 81 L. Ed. 2d 207, 104 S. Ct. 2403

## K

**Kahriger Case**
105 F. Supp. 322; 345 U.S. 22, 97 L. Ed. 754, 73 S. Ct. 510; 345 U.S. 931, 97 L. Ed. 1360, 73 S. Ct. 778; 210 F.2d 565

**Kaibab Case**
19 F.2d 634; 278 U.S. 96, 73 L. Ed. 200, 49 S. Ct. 38

**Kalasanckas Case**
38 F.2d 389, 282 U.S. 837, 75 L. Ed. 744, 51 S. Ct. 29

**Kalem Case**
169 F. 61, 94 C.C.A. 429; 222 U.S. 55, 56 L. Ed. 92, 32 S. Ct. 20

**Kalyton Case**
45 Ore. 116, 74 P. 491, 78 P. 332; 204 U.S. 458, 51 L. Ed. 566, 27 S. Ct. 346

**Kansas City Stockyards Case**
79 F. 679; 82 F. 839; 82 F. 850; 183 U.S. 79, 46 L. Ed. 92, 22 S. Ct. 30

**Kansas-Colorado Water Rights Case**
185 U.S. 125, 46 L. Ed. 838, 22 S. Ct. 552

**Kansas Highway Tax Case**
55 F.2d 347; 52 S. Ct. 410; 286 U.S. 352, 76 L. Ed. 1155, 52 S. Ct. 595

**Kansas Indians Cases**
3 Kan. 299; 3 Kan. 364; 72 U.S. 737, 18 L. Ed. 667, 18 L. Ed. 673, 18 L. Ed. 674

**Kansas Industrial Relations Court Case**
109 Kan. 629, 201 P. 418; 111 Kan. 501, 207 P. 806, 262 U.S. 522, 67 L. Ed. 1103, 43 S. Ct. 630; 114 Kan. 304, 219 P. 259; 114 Kan. 487, 227 P. 249; 267 U.S. 552, 69 L. Ed. 785, 45 S. Ct. 441

**Kansas Insurance Case**
189 F. 769; 233 U.S. 389, 58 L. Ed. 1011, 34 S. Ct. 612

**Kansas Prohibition Cases**
24 Kan. 700
88 Kan. 589, 128 P. 1114; 236 U.S. 568, 59 L. Ed. 721, 35 S. Ct. 419

**Kardon Case**
69 F. Supp. 512; 73 F. Supp. 798

**Karo Syrup Case**
143 Wis. 18, 126 N.W. 888; 228 U.S. 115, 57 L. Ed. 754, 33 S. Ct. 431; 154 Wis. 333, 145 N.W. 1103

**Kawakita Treason Case**
96 F. Supp. 824; 190 F.2d 506; 342 U.S. 932, 96 L. Ed. 694, 72 S. Ct. 378; 343 U.S. 717, 96 L. Ed. 1249, 72 S. Ct. 950; 344 U.S. 850, 97 L. Ed. 660, 73 S. Ct. 5; 108 F. Supp. 627

**Kean Taylor Case**
213 A.D. 750, 210 N.Y.S. 105; 241 N.Y. 252, 149 N.E. 849; 242 N.Y. 495, 152 N.E. 399

**Kearney Case**
8 I.C.C. 481

**Keary Case**
3 Ohio St. 201

**Keith Case**
89 Ind. App. 233, 146 N.E. 872

**Kelley Cases**
71 Minn. 172, 73 N.W. 642
71 Minn. 430, 74 N.W. 163
76 Minn. 413, 79 N.W. 394
78 Minn. 286, 80 N.W. 1125

**Kemper Military School Case**
214 Mo. 656, 113 S.W. 1083

**Kennon Case**
7 Ohio St. 546

**Kent Case**
416 U.S. 232, 40 L. Ed. 2d 90, 94 S. Ct. 1683
36 F.2d 401

**Kentucky Bank Tax Cases**
174 U.S. 428, 43 L. Ed. 1034, 19 S. Ct. 874
174 U.S. 435, 43 L. Ed. 1037, 19 S. Ct. 874

74 U.S. 436, 43 L. Ed. 1037, 19 S. Ct. 874
174 U.S. 439, 43 L. Ed. 1039, 19 S. Ct. 753
88 F. 383; 174 U.S. 799, 43 L. Ed. 1187, 19 S. Ct. 881
88 F. 398; 174 U.S. 412, 43 L. Ed. 1028, 19 S. Ct. 747
88 F. 407; 174 U.S. 429, 43 L. Ed. 1034, 19 S. Ct. 875
88 F. 409; 174 U.S. 438, 43 L. Ed. 1038, 19 S. Ct. 876; 109 F. 1056, 47 C.C.A. 679
88 F. 985; 174 U.S. 799, 43 L. Ed. 1187, 19 S. Ct. 881
88 F. 986; 174 U.S. 800, 43 L. Ed. 1187, 19 S. Ct. 881
88 F. 987; 174 U.S. 409, 43 L. Ed. 1027, 19 S. Ct. 880
88 F. 988; 174 U.S. 800, 43 L. Ed. 1187, 19 S. Ct. 881
88 F. 988; 174 U.S. 799, 43 L. Ed. 1187, 19 S. Ct. 881
88 F. 990; 174 U.S. 432, 43 L. Ed. 1035, 19 S. Ct. 759
103 F. 523; 185 U.S. 270, 46 L. Ed. 906, 22 S. Ct. 645
129 F. 792, 198 U.S. 100, 49 L. Ed. 963, 25 S. Ct. 562
97 Ky. 590, 17 Ky. Law Rep. 465, 31 S.W. 1013; 102 Ky. 174, 19 Ky. Law Rep. 248, 39 S.W. 1030; 173 U.S. 636, 43 L. Ed. 840, 19 S. Ct. 530, 19 S. Ct. 571; 173 U.S. 662, 43 L. Ed. 850, 19 S. Ct. 875; 173 U.S. 663, 43 L. Ed. 850, 19 S. Ct. 875; 21 Ky. Law Rep. 1611, 55 S.W. 1080; 108 Ky. 766, 22 Ky. Law Rep. 466, 57 S.W. 787; 22 Ky. Law Rep. 1384, 60 S.W. 19; 111 Ky. 950, 23 Ky. Law Rep. 1285, 65 S.W. 10; 23 Ky. Law Rep. 1704, 66 S.W. 186; 120 F. 165, 124 F. 18, 59 C.C.A. 538; 191 U.S. 499, 48 L. Ed. 276, 24 S. Ct. 154
108 Ky. 427, 22 Ky. Law Rep. 70, 56 S.W. 683
19 Ky. Law Rep. 247, 39 S.W. 1116; 173 U.S. 664, 43 L. Ed. 850, 19 S. Ct. 537
44 S.W. 1131; 43 L. Ed. 1178, 19 S. Ct. 877

**Kentucky Railroad Tax Case**
81 Ky. 492; 115 U.S. 321, 29 L. Ed. 414, 6 S. Ct. 57

**Kentucky Salary Case**
291 Ky. 109, 163 S.W.2d 33

**Kentucky Streetcar Cases**
157 Ky. 620, 163 S.W. 739
161 Ky. 44, 170 S.W. 499; 174 Ky. 679, 192 S.W. 656
175 Ky. 694, 194 S.W. 1048

**Kentucky Whip and Collar Case**
299 U.S. 334, 81 L. Ed. 270, 57 S. Ct. 277; 299 U.S. 525, 81 L. Ed. 386, 57 S. Ct. 19

**Keokuk Case**
41 I.C.C. 13; 41 I.C.C. 503; 245 U.S. 493, 62 L. Ed. 425, 38 S. Ct. 170; 49 I.C.C. 713

**Kepner Case**
195 U.S. 100, 49 L. Ed. 114, 24 S. Ct. 797

**Keppel Case**
291 U.S. 304, 78 L. Ed. 814, 54 S. Ct. 423

**Kernan Case**
355 U.S. 426, 2 L. Ed. 2d 382, 78 S. Ct. 394; 141 F. Supp. 582, 1956 A.M.C. 383; 231 F. Supp. 339

**Kesler Case**
369 U.S. 153, 7 L. Ed. 2d 641, 82 S. Ct. 807

**Keuka College Case**
167 N.Y. 96, 60 N.E. 325

**Key-in-Ignition Case**
209 Tenn. 55, 348 S.W.2d 332, 349 S.W.2d 793

**Keystone Case**
121 N.L.R.B. 880, No. 125

**Keystone Watch Case**
218 F. 502; 257 U.S. 664, 66 L. Ed. 424, 42 S. Ct. 45

**Kickback Case**
134 F.2d 847; 320 U.S. 543, 88 L. Ed. 300, 64 S. Ct. 315; 320 U.S. 720, 88 L. Ed. 424, 64 S. Ct. 33

**Kickback Tax Deduction Case**
14 T.C. 1066; 188 F.2d 269; 342 U.S. 808, 96 L. Ed. 611, 72 S. Ct. 45, 343 U.S. 90, 96 L. Ed. 769, 72 S. Ct. 497

**Kicked Can Case**
80 Cal. App. 2d 500, 182 P.2d 234

**Kilberg Case**
9 N.Y.2d 34, 211 N.Y.S.2d 133, 172 N.E.2d 526; 10 A.D.2d 261, 198 N.Y.S.2d 679

**Kilgore Case**
291 Ill. 256, 126 N.E. 144

**Killitts Case**
242 U.S. 27, 61 L. Ed. 129, 37 S. Ct. 72

**Killum Dead Trading Stamp Case**
141 Mont. 382, 378 P.2d 220

**Kimbell-Diamond Case**
14 T.C. 74; 187 F.2d 718; 342 U.S. 827, 96 L. Ed. 626, 72 S. Ct. 50

**King Cases**
106 F. 471; 114 F. 417, 52 C.C.A. 219; 186 U.S. 482, 46 L. Ed. 1260, 22 S. Ct. 941; 129 F. 1005, 62 C.C.A. 681

144 Tex. 583, 192 S.W.2d 260

**King-Townsend-Remillard Trilogy Cases**
392 U.S. 309, 20 L. Ed. 2d 2018, 88 S. Ct. 2128; 404 U.S. 282, 30 L. Ed. 2d 448, 92 S. Ct. 502; 406 U.S. 598, 32 L. Ed. 2d 352, 92 S. Ct. 1932

**King's Estate Case**
37 T.C. 973

**Kinsey Institute for Sex Research Case**
156 F. Supp. 350

**Kintner Case**
107 F. Supp. 976; 216 F.2d 418

**Kirby Lumber Company Case**
44 F.2d 885, 71 Ct. Cl. 290; 283 U.S. 814, 75 L. Ed. 1431, 51 S. Ct. 486; 284 U.S. 1, 76 L. Ed. 131, 52 S. Ct. 4

**Kirchner Case**
60 Cal. 2d 716, 36 Cal. Rptr. 488, 388 P.2d 720

**Kirk Soap Case**
68 F. 791, 15 C.C.A. 540

**Kissinger Tapes Case**
445 U.S. 136, 63 L. Ed. 2d 267, 100 S. Ct. 960

**Kitty Kelly Case**
51 Pa. D. & C. 383

**KKK Cross Display Case**
515 U.S. 753, 132 L. Ed. 2d 650, 115 S. Ct. 2440 (1995)

**Klauder Case**
318 U.S. 434, 87 L. Ed. 884, 63 S. Ct. 679; 129 F.2d 894, 50 Am. B.R. (n.s.) 345; 317 U.S. 617, 87 L. Ed. 500, 63 S. Ct. 161

**Klaxon Case**
23 F. Supp. 351, 37 U.S.P.Q. (BNA) 401; 28 F. Supp. 665, 42 U.S.P.Q. (BNA) 352; 30 FS

425, 43 U.S.P.Q. (BNA) 430; 115 F.2d 268, 47 U.S.P.Q. (BNA) 193; 312 U.S. 674, 85 L. Ed. 1115, 61 S. Ct. 734; 313 U.S. 487, 85 L. Ed. 1477, 61 S. Ct. 1020; 125 F.2d 820, 52 U.S.P.Q. (BNA) 404; 316 U.S. 685, 86 L. Ed. 1757, 62 S. Ct. 1284, 53 U.S.P.Q. (BNA) 685

**Klesner Case**
280 U.S. 19, 74 L. Ed. 138, 50 S. Ct. 1; 6 F.2d 701, 56 App. D.C. 3; 25 F.2d 524, 58 App. D.C. 100; 269 U.S. 545, 70 L. Ed. 404, 46 S. Ct. 102; 274 U.S. 145, 71 L. Ed. 972, 47 S. Ct. 557, 278 U.S. 591, 73 L. Ed. 524, 49 S. Ct. 30

**Klimas Case**
10 N.Y.2d 209, 219 N.Y.S.2d 14, 176 N.E.2d 714; 12 A.D.2d 551, 207 N.Y.S.2d 72

**Klumpp Case**
124 F. 554

**Knabe Piano Case**
211 F. 271, 127 C.C.A. 639

**Knight Cases**
66 U.S. 227, 17 L. Ed. 76

60 F. 306; 60 F. 934, 9 C.C.A. 297, 17 U.S. App. 466; 156 U.S. 1, 39 L. Ed. 325, 15 S. Ct. 249

**Knitting Company Cases**

250 F. 278; 265 F. 177; 253 U.S. 498, 64 L. Ed. 1031, 40 S. Ct. 588

250 F. 288; 265 F. 177; 253 U.S. 498, 64 L. Ed. 1032, 40 S. Ct. 588

**Knock-and-Announce Case**

514 U.S. 927, 131 L. Ed. 2d 976, 115 S. Ct. 1914 (1995)

**Knoxville Water Case**

212 U.S. 1, 53 L. Ed. 371, 29 S. Ct. 148

**Koehler and Heinrichs Case**

115 F. 648

**Kohler Cases**

351 U.S. 266, 100 L. Ed. 1162, 76 S. Ct. 794; 269 Wis. 578, 70 N.W.2d 191; 350 U.S. 957, 100 L. Ed. 833, 76 S. Ct. 346

116 N.L.R.B. 267, No. 37; 117 N.L.R.B. 321, No. 42; 128 N.L.R.B. 1062, No. 122; 300 F.2d 699

**Konigsberg Case**

52 Cal. 2d 769, 344 P.2d 777; 353 U.S. 252, 1 L. Ed. 2d 810, 77 S. Ct. 722; 366 U.S. 36, 6 L. Ed. 2d 105, 81 S. Ct. 997; 364 U.S. 805, 81 S. Ct. 40; 364 U.S. 806, 81 S. Ct. 40; 364 U.S. 858, 81 S. Ct. 101; 368 U.S. 869, 7 L. Ed. 2d 69, 82 S. Ct. 21

**Konstovich Case**

17 F.2d 84

**Korean Bonus Case**

134 Mont. 1, 328 P.2d 907

**Kosher Law Case**

266 U.S. 497, 69 L. Ed. 402, 45 S. Ct. 141

**Kramer Case**

230 A.D. 407, 245 N.Y.S. 121; 231 A.D. 758, 246 N.Y.S. 825; 231 A.D. 759, 246 N.Y.S. 824; 256 N.Y. 555, 177 N.E. 138

**Kszepka's Case**

408 Mass. 843, 563 N.E.2d 1357

**Ku Klux Cases**

110 U.S. 651, 28 L. Ed. 274, 4 S. Ct. 152 F. Cas. No. 7,946

F. Cas. Nos. 14,700, 14,701

F. Cas. No. 14,893

F. Cas. No. 15,790

278 U.S. 63,73 L. Ed. 184, 49 S. Ct. 61; 241 N.Y. 405, 150 N.E. 497; 213 A.D. 414, 210 N.Y.S. 269

**Kuhn Bund Case**

172 Misc. 1097, 15 N.Y.S.2d 1005

## L

**La Ronde Case**
305 N.Y. 336, 113 N.E.2d 502; 346 U.S. 587, 98 L. Ed. 329, 74 S. Ct. 286, 306 N.Y. 850, 118 N.E.2d 908; 280 A.D. 260, 114 N.Y.S.2d 561; 346 U.S. 863, 98 L. Ed. 374, 74 S. Ct. 104

**Labor Board Cases**
301 U.S. 1, 81 L. Ed. 893, 57 S. Ct. 615; 90 F.2d 678
301 U.S. 49, 81 L. Ed. 893, 57 S. Ct. 642
301 U.S. 58, 81 L. Ed. 893, 57 S. Ct. 645
301 U.S. 103, 81 L. Ed. 953, 57 S. Ct. 650
301 U.S. 142, 81 L. Ed. 965, 57 S. Ct. 648
282 F. 693; 282 F. 701; 260 U.S. 718, 67 L. Ed. 479, 43 S. Ct. 98; 261 U.S. 72, 67 L. Ed. 536, 43 S. Ct. 278

**Labor Dispute Unemployment Case**
231 Minn. 68, 42 N.W.2d 576

**Labor Union Antitrust Immunity Case**
421 U.S. 616, 44 L. Ed. 2d 418, 95 S. Ct. 1830

**LaBuy Case**
226 F.2d 703; 352 U.S. 249, 1 L. Ed. 2d 290, 77 S. Ct. 309; 352 U.S. 1019, 1 L. Ed. 2d 560, 77 S. Ct. 553

**Lackawanna Coal Case**
F. Cas. No. 3,764; 80 U.S. 311, 20 L. Ed. 581

**Lackawanna Coal Sales Case**
213 F. 240; 238 U.S. 516, 59 L. Ed. 1438, 35 S. Ct. 873

**Lady Duff-Gordon Case**
177 A.D. 624, 164 N.Y.S. 576; 222 N.Y. 88, 118 N.E. 214; 222 N.Y. 643, 118 N.E. 1082

**LaGrange Cases**
102 F. 709; 101 F. 146; 108 F. 988, 46 C.C.A. 685; 190 U.S. 273, 47 L. Ed. 1047, 23 S. Ct. 687
7 I.C.C. 431

**Laidlaw Case**
158 N.Y. 73, 52 N.E. 679

**Lake Cargo Coal Cases**
22 I.C.C. 604
22 I.C.C. 640; 24 I.C.C. 129
46 I.C.C. 159
101 I.C.C. 513; 126 I.C.C. 309
139 I.C.C. 367; 25 F.2d 462; 279 U.S. 812, 73 L. Ed. 971, 49 S. Ct. 262
181 I.C.C. 37

**Lake Chelan Case**
77 Wash. 2d 306, 462 P.2d 232

**Lake Dock Coal Cases**
89 I.C.C. 170; 234 I.C.C. 679

**Lake Front Cases**
16 F. 881; 33 F. 730; 146 U.S. 387, 36 L. Ed. 1618, 13 S. Ct. 110; 154 U.S. 225, 38 L. Ed. 971, 14 S. Ct. 1015; 91 F. 955, 34 C.C.A. 138; 176 U.S. 683, 44 L. Ed. 638, 20 S. Ct. 1026; 184 U.S. 77, 46 L. Ed. 440, 22 S. Ct. 300
33 F. 721
169 Ill. 392, 48 N.E. 927
198 Ill. 104, 64 N.E. 705
241 Ill. 496, 89 N.E. 731
248 Ill. 299, 93 N.E. 910
331 Ill. 514, 163 N.E. 418
339 Ill. 463, 171 N.E. 550; 282 U.S. 875, 75 L. Ed. 773, 51 S. Ct. 79

**Lake Jackson Case**
58 Fla. 398, 50 So. 826

**Lake-Level Case**
281 U.S. 179, 74 L. Ed. 799, 50 S. Ct. 266

**Lake Street Pharmacy Case**
68 Nev. 269, 229 P.2d 908

**Lakeland Cases**
20 F.2d 619

**L'Amerique Case**
35 F. 835

**Lamp Case**
82 F. Supp. 753

**Land Case**
203 F. 410, 121 C.C.A. 520; 235 U.S. 72, 59 L. Ed. 137, 35 S. Ct. 14

**Land Grant Case**
309 U.S. 626, 84 L. Ed. 987, 60 S. Ct. 585; 310 U.S. 615, 84 L. Ed. 1391, 60 S. Ct. 1092; 311 U.S. 613, 85 L. Ed. 389, 61 S. Ct. 57; 311 U.S. 317, 85 L. Ed. 210, 61 S. Ct. 264; 41 F. Supp. 273

**Land Trust Tax Case**
295 U.S. 422, 79 L. Ed. 1520, 55 S. Ct. 800

**Landed Aircraft Insurance Case**
72 S.D. 509, 37 N.W.2d 192

**Landis Case**
41 F.2d 700; 282 U.S. 872, 75 L. Ed. 770, 51 S. Ct. 77; 16 Am. B.R. (n.s.) 526

**Landon Case**
234 F. 152; 242 F. 658; 245 F. 950; 249 U.S. 236, 63 L. Ed. 577, 39 S. Ct. 268; 249 U.S. 590, 63 L. Ed. 791, 39 S. Ct. 389; 269 F. 411; 269 F. 423; 269 F. 433

**Lansingburgh Goose Case**
8 John. Cas. 428

**Lapham Case**
156 Mass. 480, 31 N.E. 638

**Larrison Case**
24 F.2d 82

**Las Palmas Trademark Case**
146 F. Supp. 594; 245 F.2d 874, 114 U.S.P.Q. (BNA) 473; 355 U.S. 927, 2 L. Ed. 2d 357, 78 S. Ct. 384, 110 U.S.P.Q. (BNA) 525

**Laundry Cases**
26 F. 471; 118 U.S. 356, 30 L. Ed. 220, 6 S. Ct. 1064
68 Cal. 294, 9 P. 139; 118 U.S. 356, 30 L. Ed. 220, 6 S. Ct. 1064

**Laundry License Case**
22 F. 701

**Laundry Ordinance Case**
13 F. 229

**Lawyers' Tax Cases**
8 Heisk. (55 Tenn.) 565

**Layoff of Minority Teachers Case**
476 U.S. 267, 90 L. Ed. 2d 260, 106 S. Ct. 1842

**Lead Pencil Case**
92 U.S. 347, 23 L. Ed. 719

**Leader Store Case**
238 Ind. 667, 154 N.E.2d 107

**Leadville Beer Cases**
13 I.C.C. 329; 187 F. 485, 109 C.C.A. 337; 233 U.S. 479, 58 L. Ed. 1055, 34 S. Ct. 641
17 I.C.C. 225; 195 F. 968

**Leake Case**
20 N.J.L. 31

**Leasehold Lien Case**
191 Ore. 1, 228 P.2d 216

**Leather Workers Case**
265 U.S. 457, 68 L. Ed. 1104, 44 S. Ct. 623

**Leet Case**
31 A.D. 248, 52 N.Y.S. 950; 157 N.Y. 90, 51 N.E. 431

**Legal Advertising Case**
433 U.S. 350, 53 L. Ed. 2d 810, 97 S. Ct. 2691

**Legal Tender Cases**
75 U.S. 603, 19 L. Ed. 513
78 U.S. 682
79 U.S. 457, 20 L. Ed. 287
80 U.S. 604, 20 L. Ed. 547
110 U.S. 421, 28 L. Ed. 204, 4 S. Ct. 122
157 U.S. 429, 39 L. Ed. 759, 15 S. Ct. 673; 158 U.S. 601, 39 L. Ed. 1108, 15 S. Ct. 912
294 U.S. 240, 79 L. Ed. 885, 55 S. Ct. 407
7 F.2d 330; 269 U.S. 547, 70 L. Ed. 405, 46 S. Ct. 106; 272 U.S. 517, 71 L. Ed. 383, 47 S. Ct. 166

*Continued*

14 Allen (96 Mass.) 94; 79 U.S. 457, 20 L. Ed. 287

52 Pa. 9

**Leghorn Seizures Case**

27 Ct. Cl. 224

**Legislative Pay Case**

199 Ind. 436, 156 N.E. 394, 157 N.E. 723

**Lehman Case**

109 F.2d 99; 310 U.S. 637, 84 L. Ed. 1406, 60 S. Ct. 1080, 39 B.T.A. 17

**Lemon Cases**

175 F. 141; 191 F. 101, 111 C.C.A. 581

19 I.C.C. 148; 182 F. 189; 20 I.C.C. 106; 190 F. 591; 22 I.C.C. 149; 203 F. 56; 231 U.S. 736, 58 L. Ed. 460, 34 S. Ct. 316

**Lenders Service Mail Fraud Case**

236 F. Supp. 424; 317 F.2d 249; 340 F.2d 63; 375 U.S. 838, 11 L. Ed. 2d 65, 84 S. Ct. 77

**Lent Servant Case**

165 F.2d 473

**Leo Frank Case**

141 Ga. 243, 80 S.E. 1016; 142 Ga. 617, 83 S.E. 233, 142 Ga. 741, 83 S.E. 645; 235 U.S. 694, 59 L. Ed. 429, 35 S. Ct. 208; 237 U.S. 309, 59 L. Ed. 969, 35 S. Ct. 582

**Leopold Tax Assessment Case**

118 Pa. Super. 158, 179 A. 904

**Lerner Case**

241 N.Y. 153, 149 N.E. 334; 212 A.D. 747, 209 N.Y.S. 698

**Lester Case**

279 F.2d 354; 366 U.S. 299, 6 L. Ed. 2d 306, 81 S. Ct. 1343; 364 U.S. 890, 5 L. Ed. 2d 186, 81 S. Ct. 220; 32 T.C. 1156

**Lethal Gas Case**

46 Nev. 418, 211 P. 676, 217 P. 587; 218 P. 1118

**Letter Carrier Cases**

27 Ct. Cl. 244; 148 U.S. 124, 37 L. Ed. 392, 13 S. Ct. 567, 28 Ct. Cl. 555, 148 U.S. 134, 37 L. Ed. 396, 13 S. Ct. 570

**Letty Lynton Case**

81 F.2d 49; 106 F.2d 45, 42 U.S.P.Q. (BNA) 540, 7 F. Supp. 837; 26 F. Supp. 134, 40 U.S.P.Q. (BNA) 238; 298 U.S. 669, 80 L. Ed. 1392, 56 S. Ct. 835; 308 U.S. 545, 84 L. Ed. 459, 60 S. Ct. 261; 308 U.S. 617, 84 L. Ed. 515, 60 S. Ct. 263, 43 U.S.P.Q. (BNA) 521; 309 U.S. 390, 84 L. Ed. 825, 60 S. Ct. 681, 44 U.S.P.Q. (BNA) 607

**Lewis (John L.) Contempt Case**

70 F. Supp. 42; 329 U.S. 708, 91 L. Ed. 616, 67 S. Ct. 359; 329 U.S. 709, 91 L. Ed. 617, 67 S. Ct. 373; 329 U.S. 710, 91 L. Ed. 618, 67 S. Ct. 485; 330 U.S. 258, 91 L. Ed. 884, 67 S. Ct. 677; 91 L. Ed. 1298, 67 S. Ct. 975; 91 L. Ed. 1298, 67 S. Ct. 976; 91 L. Ed. 1298, 67 S. Ct. 977

**Lexington Bank Case**

376 U.S. 665, 12 L. Ed. 2d 1, 84 S. Ct. 1033

**Lexington Mill Case**

232 U.S. 399, 58 L. Ed. 658, 34 S. Ct. 337; 202 F. 615, 229 U.S. 619, 57 L. Ed. 1354, 33 S. Ct. 778

**LHWCA Permanent Partial Disability Case**

449 U.S. 268, 66 L. Ed. 2d 446, 101 S. Ct. 509

**Libel of Litigants Case**

424 U.S. 448, 47 L. Ed. 2d 154, 96 S. Ct. 958

**Liberty Bond Gold Clause Case**

294 U.S. 330, 79 L. Ed. 912, 55 S. Ct. 432

**Libson Case**

353 U.S. 382, 1 L. Ed. 2d 924, 77 S. Ct. 990; 354 U.S. 943, 1 L. Ed. 2d 1542, 77 S. Ct. 1390; 229 F.2d 220

**License Cases**

41 Mass. (24 Pick.) 374; 46 U.S. 504, 12 L. Ed. 256

13 N.H. 536; 46 U.S. 504, 12 L. Ed. 256

1 R.I. 193; 46 U.S. 504, 12 L. Ed. 256

**License Plate Case**
430 U.S. 705, 51 L. Ed. 2d 752, 97 S. Ct. 1428

**License Tax Cases**
72 U.S. 462, 18 L. Ed. 497
72 U.S. 475, 18 L. Ed. 608

**Lie Detector Cases**
167 Misc. 51, 3 N.Y.S.2d 348
167 Misc. 868, 4 N.Y.S.2d 913; 277 N.Y. 440, 14 N.E.2d 783; 279 N.Y. 204, 18 N.E.2d 31; 279 N.Y. 788, 18 N.E.2d 870

**Lieberman Case**
81 A.D. 128, 80 N.Y.S. 1108; 175 N.Y. 440, 67 N.E. 913; 199 U.S. 552, 50 L. Ed. 305, 26 S. Ct. 144

**Lien Avoidance Retroactivity Case**
459 U.S. 70, 74 L. Ed. 2d 235, 103 S. Ct. 407

**Life Employment Case**
198 Md. 526, 84 A.2d 870

**Life Insurance Cases**
93 U.S. 24, 23 L. Ed. 789

**Life Insurance Gift Case**
213 Miss. 826, 58 So. 2d 18

**Lighter Case**
F. Cas. No. 5,307

**Lighterage Cases**
14 I.C.C. 619; 200 F. 652; 207 F. 733, 125 C.C.A. 251
17 I.C.C. 40
20 I.C.C. 200; 225 U.S. 306, 56 L. Ed. 1100, 32 S. Ct. 817; 200 F. 779; 231 U.S. 274, 58 L. Ed. 218, 34 S. Ct. 75

**Lightning Rod Case**
11 Ga. App. 46, 74 S.E. 564; 233 U.S. 16, 58 L. Ed. 828, 34 S. Ct. 578

**Lignite Coal Rate Cases**
19 N.D. 45, 120 N.W. 869; 19 N.D. 57, 120 N.W. 874; 216 U.S. 579, 54 L. Ed. 624, 30 S. Ct. 423; 216 U.S. 581, 54 L. Ed. 1212, 30 S. Ct. 698, 31 S. Ct. 218; 26 N.D. 438, 145 N.W. 135; 236 U.S. 585, 59 L. Ed. 735, 35 S. Ct. 429
19 N.D. 57, 120 N.W. 874; 216 U.S. 581, 54 L. Ed. 1212, 30 S. Ct. 698, 31 S. Ct. 218
35 N.D. 331, 160 N.W. 140; 254 U.S. 376, 65 L. Ed. 312, 41 S. Ct. 142
40 N.D. 69, 168 N.W. 684; 254 U.S. 370, 65 L. Ed. 310, 41 S. Ct. 140

**Lincoln Conspirators Cases**
F. Cas. No. 9,899
F. Cas. No. 16,423
6 D.C. 306

**Lincoln Mills Case**
230 F.2d 81; 352 U.S. 821, 1 L. Ed. 2d 46, 77 S. Ct. 54; 353 U.S. 448, 1 L. Ed. 2d 972, 77 S. Ct. 912, 77 S. Ct. 923

**Lincoln Park Case**
44 Minn. 299, 46 N.W. 355

**Lindbergh Kidnapping Case**
115 N.J.L. 412, 180 A. 809; 296 U.S. 649, 80 L. Ed. 461, 56 S. Ct. 310

**Line Item Veto Case**
141 L. Ed. 2d 393, 118 S. Ct. 2091 (1998)

**Linseed Case**
F. Cas. No. 12,589; 66 U.S. 108, 17 L. Ed. 35

**Linseed Oil Case**
275 F. 939; 262 U.S. 371, 67 L. Ed. 1035, 43 S. Ct. 607

**Lint Case**
140 Cal. App. 2d 967, 295 P.2d 154

**Liquid Sugar Case**
Treas. Dec. 46061, 20 C.C.P.A. (Customs) 272

**Liquor Sales to Women Case**
33 Wash. 2d 688, 206 P.2d 1209

**Liquor Transportation Cases**
140 Tenn. 582, 205 S.W. 423

**Listerine Case**
280 F.2d 197, 126 U.S.P.Q. (BNA) 3; 178 F. Supp. 655, 123 U.S.P.Q. (BNA) 431

**Litigating Partners Case**
108 Colo. 562, 120 P.2d 644

**Little Ivy Case**
46 Misc. 2d 233, 259 N.Y.S.2d 874

**Little Rock School Case**
358 U.S. 1, 3 L. Ed. 2d 3, 3 L. Ed. 2d 5, 3 L. Ed. 2d 19, 78 S. Ct. 1399, 78 S. Ct. 1401; 257 F.2d 33; 163 F. Supp. 13; 169 F. Supp. 325; 173 F. Supp. 944; 357 U.S. 566, 2 L. Ed. 2d 1544, 78 S. Ct. 1189; 358 U.S. 27, 3 L. Ed. 2d 1, 78 S. Ct. 1397; 358 U.S. 28, 3 L. Ed. 2d 3, 78 S. Ct. 1399; 358 U.S. 29, 3 L. Ed. 2d 3, 78 S. Ct. 1398

**Little Watchman Case**
50 Ga. App. 829, 179 S.E. 571; 296 U.S. 561, 80 L. Ed. 396, 56 S. Ct. 144; 297 U.S. 398, 80 L. Ed. 740, 56 S. Ct. 504; 297 U.S. 729, 80 L. Ed. 1011, 56 S. Ct. 667; 57 Ga. App. 53, 194 S.E. 602; 305 U.S. 619, 83 L. Ed. 395, 59 S. Ct. 78

**Livery Stable Case**
19 Colo. 179, 34 P. 902

**Livestock Cases**
190 I.C.C. 611; 194 I.C.C. 315; 194 I.C.C. 637; 197 I.C.C. 83; 200 I.C.C. 535; 201 I.C.C. 795

**Livingston Case**
42 F.2d 347

**Livingston Manor Case**
8 Barb. 253

**Livingston Shirt Case**
107 N.L.R.B. 400, No. 109

**Livingstone Cases**
304 F.2d 766; 332 F.2d 463
328 F.2d 634; 39 T.C. 1124; 39 T.C. 1128

**Lo Bue Case**
351 U.S. 243, 100 L. Ed. 1142, 76 S. Ct. 800; 223 F.2d 367; 256 F.2d 735; 22 T.C. 440; 28 T.C. 1317; 350 U.S. 893, 100 L. Ed. 786, 76 S. Ct. 151; 352 U.S. 859, 1 L. Ed. 2d 69, 77 S. Ct. 21

**Local Option Case**
50 N.J.L. 585, 15 A. 272

**Local Telephone Services Case**
142 L. Ed. 2d 834, 119 S. Ct. 721

**Lochner Case**
198 U.S. 45, 49 L. Ed. 937, 25 S. Ct. 539; 177 N.Y. 145, 69 N.E. 373; 73 A.D. 120, 76 N.Y.S. 396

**Locker Club Tax Case**
5 Ga. App. 750, 64 S.E. 807

**Lockout Cases**
353 U.S. 87, 1 L. Ed. 2d 676, 77 S. Ct. 643
380 U.S. 300, 13 L. Ed. 2d 855, 85 S. Ct. 955

**Locomotive Sander Case**
249 S.W.2d 335 (Mo.)

**Locomotive Truck Company Case**
2 F. 677; 110 U.S. 490, 28 L. Ed. 222, 4 S. Ct. 220

**Locust Street Subway Case**
319 Pa. 161, 179 A. 741

**Lofland's Brickyard Crossing Cases**
28 Del. (5 Boyce) 150, 91 A. 285; 29 Del. (6 Boyce) 145, 97 A. 418

**Logansport Electric Light Case**
202 Ind. 523, 177 N.E. 249

**Lohman Sales Company Case**
132 N.L.R.B. 901, No. 67

**Loitering Case**
421 U.S. 426, 44 L. Ed. 2d 274, 95 S. Ct. 1691

**Lone Ranger Case**
79 F. Supp. 190

**Lonely Hearts Murder Case**
195 Misc. 95, 89 N.Y.S.2d 421; 300 N.Y. 646, 90 N.E.2d 499; 301 N.Y. 302, 93 N.E.2d 859; 301 N.Y. 690, 95 N.E.2d 49; 340 U.S. 914, 95 L. Ed. 660, 71 S. Ct. 285; 340 U.S. 940, 95 L. Ed. 678, 71 S. Ct. 501; 202 Misc. 190, 109 N.Y.S.2d 569

**Long and Short Haul Case**
191 F. 856; 234 U.S. 476, 58 L. Ed. 1408, 34 S. Ct. 986; 234 U.S. 495, 58 L. Ed. 1426, 34 S. Ct. 995

**Long Arm Statute Case**
114 F. Supp. 914

**Long Case**
59 F.2d 602

**Long Island Lighting Company Case**
27 Dep't Rep. 44

**Long Term Compensation Tax Case**
11 T.C. 552; 188 F.2d 254

**Looper Case**
215 Ga. 27, 108 S.E.2d 796; 213 Ga. 279, 99 S.E.2d 101; 361 U.S. 807, 4 L. Ed. 2d 54, 80 S. Ct. 84; 363 U.S. 825, 4 L. Ed. 2d 1521; 364 U.S. 805, 81 S. Ct. 40; 81 S. Ct. 686

**Lorimer Bank Cases**
278 Ill. 409, 116 N.E. 273; 212 Ill. App. 665; 216 Ill. App. 397
297 Ill. 555, 131 N.E. 103
224 Ill. App. 474; 312 Ill. 396, 144 N.E. 165

**Los Angeles Gas Rate Case**
58 F.2d 256; 53 S. Ct. 116; 289 U.S. 287, 77 L. Ed. 1180, 53 S. Ct. 637

**Los Angeles Switching Case**
18 I.C.C. 310; 188 F. 229; 188 F. 929; 234 U.S. 294, 58 L. Ed. 1319, 34 S. Ct. 814

**Los Angeles Terminal Cases**
100 I.C.C. 421; 142 I.C.C. 489; 34 F.2d 228; 279 U.S. 830, 73 L. Ed. 980, 49 S. Ct. 349; 280 U.S. 52, 74 L. Ed. 163, 50 S. Ct. 53
190 Cal. 214, 211 P. 460; 262 U.S. 737, 67 L. Ed. 1207, 43 S. Ct. 522; 264 U.S. 331, 68 L. Ed. 713, 44 S. Ct. 376
209 Cal. 460, 288 P. 775; 51 S. Ct. 101; 283 U.S. 380, 75 L. Ed. 1128, 51 S. Ct. 553

**Lost Boundaries Case**
89 F. Supp. 596; 183 F.2d 562; 340 U.S. 853, 95 L. Ed. 625, 71 S. Ct. 80

**Lost Will Case**
249 S.W.2d 389 (Mo.)

**Lot of Whalebone Case**
51 F. 916

**Lottery Cases**
164 U.S. 676, 41 L. Ed. 595, 17 S. Ct. 219
188 U.S. 321, 47 L. Ed. 492, 23 S. Ct. 321
106 F. 896, 46 C.C.A. 25; 181 U.S. 619, 45 L. Ed. 1031, 22 S. Ct. 945; 188 U.S. 375, 47 L. Ed. 508, 23 S. Ct. 334

**Louisiana Bread Case**
12 La. Ann. 432

**Louisiana Rate Case**
23 I.C.C. 31; 205 F. 380; 205 F. 391; 234 U.S. 342, 58 L. Ed. 1341, 34 S. Ct. 833

**Louisiana Shrimp Act Case**
278 U.S. 1, 73 L. Ed. 147, 49 S. Ct. 1

**Louisville Condemnation Case**
9 F. Supp. 137; 78 F.2d 684; 294 U.S. 735, 79 L. Ed. 1263, 55 S. Ct. 548; 296 U.S. 567, 80 L. Ed. 400, 56 S. Ct. 154, 297 U.S. 726, 80 L. Ed. 1009, 56 S. Ct. 594

**Louisville Contest Cases**
125 Ky. 750, 31 Ky. Law Rep. 335, 102 S.W. 248; 32 Ky. Law Rep. 538, 105 S.W. 980

**Louisville Race Segregation Case**
165 Ky. 559, 177 S.W. 472; 245 U.S. 60, 62 L. Ed. 149, 38 S. Ct. 16

**Louisville Telephone Case**
279 F. 949

**Low Bridge Case**
218 F. 625

**Low Case**
41 U.S. 162, 10 L. Ed. 923

**Low Cost Housing Case**
9 F. Supp. 137; 78 F.2d 684; 294 U.S. 735, 79 L. Ed. 1263, 55 S. Ct. 548; 296 U.S. 567, 80 L. Ed. 400, 56 S. Ct. 154; 297 U.S. 726, 80 L. Ed. 1009, 56 S. Ct. 594

**Low Fare Case**
94 F. 385; 194 U.S. 517, 48 L. Ed. 1102, 24 S. Ct. 756; 194 U.S. 538, 48 L. Ed. 1109, 24 S. Ct. 764

**Loyalty Board Case**
348 U.S. 882, 99 L. Ed. 694, 75 S. Ct. 124, 349 U.S. 903, 75 S. Ct. 578; 349 U.S. 926, 75 S. Ct. 769; 349 U.S. 331, 99 L. Ed. 1129, 75 S. Ct. 790

**Loyalty Oath Case**
414 U.S. 441, 38 L. Ed. 2d 635, 94 S. Ct. 656

**Lucas Flour Case**
369 U.S. 95, 7 L. Ed. 2d 593, 82 S. Ct. 571; 57 Wash. 2d 95, 356 P.2d 1

**Lucille Miller Case**
131 F. Supp. 88; 233 F.2d 171

**Lukens Steel Case**
310 U.S. 113, 84 L. Ed. 1108, 60 S. Ct. 869

**Lullaby Swing Case**
243 A.D. 522, 277 N.Y.S. 143; 267 N.Y. 204, 196 N.E. 27

**Lumber Rate Case**
206 U.S. 428, 51 L. Ed. 1124, 27 S. Ct. 709; 138 F. 753; 159 F. 555

**Lund Case**
97 Cal. App. 2d 380, 217 P.2d 992, 15 Cal. Comp. Cas. 141

**Lusitania Case**
251 F. 715

**Lusthaus Case**
3 T.C. 540; 326 U.S. 702, 90 L. Ed. 414, 66 S. Ct. 48; 149 F.2d 232; 327 U.S. 293, 90 L. Ed. 679, 66 S. Ct. 539

**Lutheran Mutual Life Case**
242 Wis. 598, 9 N.W.2d 82

**Lutheran Synod Cases**
506 F.2d 796
576 F.2d 983

**Lynah Case**
106 F. 121; 188 U.S. 445, 47 L. Ed. 539, 23 S. Ct. 349

**Lynchburg Case**
295 F.2d 109

**Lynn-Lane Case**
29 Okla. 523, 118 P. 259

**Lyon County Case**
44 F. 329; 159 U.S. 245, 40 L. Ed. 144, 15 S. Ct. 1037; 82 F. 929; 95 F. 325

**Lyons Case**
24 Dep't Rep. 438

**Lyons Sedition Case**
F. Cas. No. 8,646

## M

**Macaroni Case**
190 F.2d 120

**Mackay Radio Case**
304 U.S. 333, 82 L. Ed. 1381, 58 S. Ct. 904; 87 F.2d 611; 92 F.2d 761; 303 U.S. 630, 82 L. Ed. 1090, 58 S. Ct. 644

**Macomber Case**
252 U.S. 189, 64 L. Ed. 521, 40 S. Ct. 189

**Macon County Case**
41 Mo. 453

**MacPherson Case**
153, A.D. 474, 138 N.Y.S. 224; 160 A.D. 55, 145 N.Y.S. 462; 161 A.D. 906, 145 N.Y.S. 1132; 217 N.Y. 382, 111 N.E. 1050

**Macy-Doubleday Case**
269 N.Y. 272, 199 N.E. 409

**Madison Oil Cases**
101 F.2d 870; 307 U.S. 620, 83 L. Ed. 1499, 59 S. Ct. 1044; 308 U.S. 519, 84 L. Ed. 441, 60 S. Ct. 177; 310 U.S. 150, 84 L. Ed. 1129, 60 S. Ct. 811
23 F. Supp. 531
23 F. Supp. 937; 24 F. Supp. 575; 105 F.2d 809; 308 U.S. 540, 84 L. Ed. 455, 60 S. Ct. 124; 310 U.S. 150, 84 L. Ed. 1129, 60 S. Ct. 811

**Magazine Gross Receipts Tax Case**
41 N.M. 141, 65 P.2d 863; 41 N.M. 288, 67 P.2d 505; 58 S. Ct. 45; 303 U.S. 250, 82 L. Ed. 823, 58 S. Ct. 546

**Magazine Libel Action Case**
79 L. Ed. 2d 790, 104 S. Ct. 1473

**Magazine Monopoly Case**
270 F. 881; 256 U.S. 688, 65 L. Ed. 1172, 41 S. Ct. 625; 260 U.S. 568, 67 L. Ed. 408, 43 S. Ct. 210

**Magic Ruffle Case**
F. Cas. No. 8,948

**Maginnis Case**
31 Pub. Lands Dec. 222

**Magnolia Blossom Case**
90 Fla. 207, 105 So. 330

**Mahon Company Case**
118 N.L.R.B. 1537, No. 207

**Mahone's Case**
63 Md. 141

**Mail Bag Cases**
90 Ark. 378, 119 S.W. 280
237 U.S. 625, 59 L. Ed. 1151, 35 S. Ct. 710

**Mail Box Case**
453 U.S. 114, 69 L. Ed. 2d 517, 101 S. Ct. 2676

**Mail Divisor Case**
53 Ct. Cl. 258; 251 U.S. 326, 64 L. Ed. 290, 40 S. Ct. 162

**Mail-Order Use Tax Case**
504 U.S. 298, 119 L. Ed. 2d 91, 112 S. Ct. 1904 (1992)

**Mail Robbery Case**
207 F. 18, 125 C.C.A. 102

**Mailman's Case**
118 Me. 172, 106 A. 606

**Maine Central Case**
77 N.H. 425, 92 A. 837

**Maine Cosmetic Case**
301 U.S. 183, 81 L. Ed. 1027, 57 S. Ct. 691

**Mallory Bushyhead Case**
237 F. 526, 150 C.C.A. 408; 248 U.S. 545, 63 L. Ed. 414, 39 S. Ct. 135

**Mallory Case**
236 F.2d 701; 352 U.S. 877, 1 L. Ed. 2d 79, 77 S. Ct. 103, 354 U.S. 449, 1 L. Ed. 2d 1479, 77 S. Ct. 1356

**Malott Case**
89 Mont. 37, 296 P. 1

**Maltese Falcon Case**
102 F. Supp. 141; 216 F.2d 945, 104 U.S.P.Q. (BNA) 103; 348 U.S. 971, 99 L. Ed. 756, 75 S. Ct. 532

**Malverne Case**
41 Misc. 2d 200, 245 N.Y.S.2d 682; 21 A.D.2d 561, 251 N.Y.S.2d 480; 14 N.Y.2d 965, 253 N.Y.S.2d 1002, 202 N.E.2d 381

**Manahan Case**
8 T.C. 1159

**Mandatory Death Penalty Case**
431 U.S. 633, 52 L. Ed. 2d 637, 97 S. Ct. 1993

**Mandatory Life Sentence Case**
445 U.S. 263, 63 L. Ed. 2d 382, 100 S. Ct. 1133

**Mandatory Retirement Case**
434 U.S. 192, 54 L. Ed. 2d 402, 98 S. Ct. 444

**Mandel Case**
266 F.2d 321

**Mangrove Prize Money Case**
188 U.S. 720, 47 L. Ed. 664, 23 S. Ct. 343

**Manila Prize Case**
188 U.S. 254, 47 L. Ed. 463, 23 S. Ct. 415

**Mankichi Case**
190 U.S. 197, 47 L. Ed. 1016, 23 S. Ct. 787

**Mann Act Cases**
227 U.S. 326, 57 L. Ed. 528, 33 S. Ct. 285
187 F. 992; 227 U.S. 308, 57 L. Ed. 523, 33 S. Ct. 281

**Maple Flooring Manufacturers Case**
268 U.S. 563, 69 L. Ed. 1093, 45 S. Ct. 578, 45 S. Ct. 592

**Mapp Case**
367 U.S. 643, 6 L. Ed. 2d 1081, 81 S. Ct. 1684; 364 U.S. 868, 5 L. Ed. 2d 90, 81 S. Ct. 111; 368 U.S. 871, 7 L. Ed. 2d 72, 82 S. Ct. 23; 170 Ohio St. 427, 11 Ohio Op. 2d 169, 166 N.E.2d 387

**Marbury Case**
5 U.S. 137, 2 L. Ed. 60

**Marchetti Trilogy Cases**
390 U.S. 39, 19 L. Ed. 2d 889, 88 S. Ct. 697; 390 U.S. 62, 19 L. Ed. 2d 906, 88 S. Ct. 709; 390 U.S. 85, 19 L. Ed. 2d 923, 88 S. Ct. 722

**Marchie Tiger Case**
21 Okla. 630, 96 P. 602; 221 U.S. 286, 55 L. Ed. 738, 31 S. Ct. 578

**Marconi Wireless Case**
320 U.S. 1, 87 L. Ed. 1731, 63 S. Ct. 1393; 81 Ct. Cl. 671, 27 U.S.P.Q. (BNA) 234; 99 Ct. Cl. 1; 100 Ct. Cl. 566; 53 U.S.P.Q. (BNA) 246; 317 U.S. 620, 87 L. Ed. 503, 63 S. Ct. 263, 55 U.S.P.Q. (BNA) 492; 320 U.S. 809, 88 L. Ed. 489, 64 S. Ct. 25

**Margrat Case**
51 Ohio St. 130, 37 N.E. 11

**Marihuana Tax Case**
340 U.S. 42, 95 L. Ed. 47, 71 S. Ct. 108

**Marina Case**
195 Cal. 426, 233 P. 965

**Maritime Employment Case**
459 U.S. 297, 74 L. Ed. 2d 465, 103 S. Ct. 634

**Mark Twain Case**
14 F. 728

**Market Street Railway Case**
45 Cal. R. Com. 53; 45 Cal. R. Com. 162; 24 Cal. 2d 378, 150 P.2d 196; 324 U.S. 548, 89 L. Ed. 1171, 65 S. Ct. 131, 65 S. Ct. 770; 324 U.S. 890, 89 L. Ed. 1438, 65 S. Ct. 1020; 28 Cal. 2d 363, 171 P.2d 875; 329 U.S. 793, 91 L. Ed. 678, 67 S. Ct. 370; 329 U.S. 833, 91 L. Ed. 705, 67 S. Ct. 501

**Married Conspirators Case**
350 Ill. App. 196, 112 N.E.2d 526; 4 Ill. 2d 105, 122 N.E.2d 245

**Marsh Foundation Case**
116 Ohio St 1, 155 N.E. 791

**Masonic Hall Case**
210 F. 169; 218 F. 642, 133 C.C.A. 663

**Massachusetts Foreign Corporation Tax Cases**
218 Mass. 558, 106 N.E. 310; 246 U.S. 147, 62 L. Ed. 632, 38 S. Ct. 295
228 Mass. 101, 117 N.E. 246; 246 U.S. 135, 62 L. Ed. 624, 38 S. Ct. 292
228 Mass. 117, 117 N.E. 5; 246 U.S. 146, 62 L. Ed. 631, 38 S. Ct. 298
232 Mass. 7, 121 N.E. 510
232 Mass. 16, 121 N.E. 513

**Massachusetts Trust Cases**
265 U.S. 144, 68 L. Ed. 949, 44 S. Ct. 462

**Massachusetts Unemployment Compensation Law Case**
296 Mass. 275, 5 N.E.2d 720; 300 U.S. 657, 81 L. Ed. 867, 57 S. Ct. 434

**Masses Case**
244 F. 535; 245 F. 102; 246 F. 24

**Mastro Plastics Case**
350 U.S. 270, 100 L. Ed. 309, 76 S. Ct. 349; 214 F.2d 462; 261 F.2d 147; 348 U.S. 910, 99 L. Ed. 714, 75 S. Ct. 297; 351 U.S. 980, 100 L. Ed. 1495, 76 S. Ct. 1043

**Match King Case**
96 F.2d 768
20 F. Supp. 964

**Maternity Act Case**
262 U.S. 447, 67 L. Ed. 1078, 43 S. Ct. 597

**Matzoon Cases**
72 F. 1010
90 F. 812; 98 F. 872, 39 C.C.A. 321

**Maximum Hours of Labor Cases**
73 A.D. 120, 16 N.Y. Crim. 520, 76 N.Y.S. 396; 177 N.Y. 145, 69 N.E. 373; 198 U.S. 45, 49 L. Ed. 937, 25 S. Ct. 539

**Maximum Price Fixing Case**
139 L. Ed. 2d 199, 118 S. Ct. 275 (1997)

**Maximum Rate Cases**
56 F. 925, 9 C.C.A. 689; 162 U.S. 184, 40 L. Ed. 935, 16 S. Ct. 700
69 F. 227; 74 F. 715, 21 C.C.A. 51, 41 U.S. App. D.C. 453, 5 I.C. 685; 168 U.S. 144, 42 L. Ed. 414, 18 S. Ct. 45
76 F. 183; 104 F. 1005, 43 C.C.A. 682; 167 U.S. 479, 42 L. Ed. 243, 17 S. Ct. 896

**Maxwell Land-Grant Cases**
21 F. 19
26 F. 118; 121 U.S. 325, 30 L. Ed. 949, 7 S. Ct. 1015; 122 U.S. 365, 30 L. Ed. 1211, 7 S. Ct. 1271

**Maybelline Case**
110 F.2d 989

**Mayor-Judge Kinship Case**
310 Ky. 483, 220 S.W.2d 858

**McAllister Transfer Case**
110 N.L.R.B. 1769, No. 224

**McAnnulty Case**
102 F. 565; 187 U.S. 94, 47 L. Ed. 90, 23 S. Ct. 33

**McCardel House Case**
28 How. Pr. 120

**McClennan Case**
131 F.2d 165; 46 B.T.A. 35

**McCollum Case**
333 U.S. 203, 92 L. Ed. 649, 68 S. Ct. 461; 396 Ill. 14, 71 N.E.2d 161

**McCown Case**
31 F.2d 334, 13 Am. B.R. (n.s.) 587; 35 F.2d 851, 14 Am. B.R. (n.s.) 619

**McCulloch Case**
17 U.S. 316, 4 L. Ed. 579

**McDonald Case**
16 Serg. & Rawle 390

**McIntire Cases**
9 Ohio 203
20 Ohio 483
17 Ohio St. 352

**McIntyre Case**
143 Minn. 77, 172 N.W. 902

**McLean Case**
8 Heisk. (55 Tenn.) 22

**McMann Trilogy Cases**
397 U.S. 742, 25 L. Ed. 2d 747, 90 S. Ct. 1463; 397 U.S. 759, 25 L. Ed. 2d 763, 80 S. Ct. 1441; 397 U.S. 790, 25 L. Ed. 2d 785, 90 S. Ct. 1458

**McMillin Case**
112 U.S. 244, 28 L. Ed. 702, 5 S. Ct. 218

**McNab Case**
9 Cal. 2d 126, 69 P.2d 985

**McNabb Moonshine Murder Case**
123 F.2d 848; 316 U.S. 658, 86 L. Ed. 1736, 62 S. Ct. 1305; 318 U.S. 332, 87 L. Ed. 819, 63 S. Ct. 608, 319 U.S. 784, 87 L. Ed. 1727, 63 S. Ct. 1322; 142 F.2d 904, 323 U.S. 771, 89 L. Ed. 616, 65 S. Ct. 114

**McNichol's Estate Case**
29 T.C. 1179; 265 F.2d 667; 361 U.S. 829, 4 L. Ed. 2d 71, 80 S. Ct. 78

**Meadows Case**
29 F.2d 739; 32 F.2d 440; 280 U.S. 550, 74 L. Ed. 608, 50 S. Ct. 152; 74 L. Ed. 1178, 50 S. Ct. 19; 281 U.S. 271, 74 L. Ed. 852, 50 S. Ct. 279

**Meat and Guano Inspection Cases**
41 F. 867; 136 U.S. 313, 34 L. Ed. 455, 10 S. Ct. 862; 43 F. 609; 138 U.S. 78, 34 L. Ed. 862, 11 S. Ct. 213

**Meat Market Covenant Case**
135 Conn. 195, 63 A.2d 161; 135 Conn. 413, 65 A.2d 171

**Mechanicville Bank Case**
241 A.D. 261, 271 N.Y.S. 842

**Media Right of Access Case**
438 U.S. 1, 57 L. Ed. 2d 553, 98 S. Ct. 2588

**Medicaid Abortion Case**
448 U.S. 297, 65 L. Ed. 2d 784, 100 S. Ct. 2671

**Medicaid and Mental Institutions Case**
450 U.S. 221, 67 L. Ed. 2d 186, 101 S. Ct. 1074

**Medical Education Exclusion Case**
441 U.S. 677, 260 L. Ed. 2d 560, 99 S. Ct. 1946

**Medical Monopoly Case**
26 F. Supp. 429; 28 F. Supp. 752; 308 U.S. 599, 84 L. Ed. 502, 60 S. Ct. 131; 110 F.2d 703, 72 App. D.C. 12; 310 U.S. 644, 84 L. Ed. 1411, 60 S. Ct. 1096; 130 F.2d 233, 76 App. D.C. 70; 317 U.S. 613, 87 L. Ed. 497, 63 S. Ct. 44; 317 U.S. 519, 87 L. Ed. 434, 63 S. Ct. 326

**Meeker Coal Cases**
162 F. 354; 175 F. 320; 183 F. 548

21 I.C.C. 129; 190 F. 1023; 23 I.C.C. 480; 204 F. 986; 211 F. 785, 128 C.C.A. 311; 234 U.S. 749, 58 L. Ed. 1576, 34 S. Ct. 674; 236 U.S. 412, 59 L. Ed. 644, 35 S. Ct. 328; 236 U.S. 434, 59 L. Ed. 659, 35 S. Ct. 337

**Meeting Competition Case**
460 U.S. 428, 75 L. Ed. 2d 174, 103 S. Ct. 1282

**Mein Kampf Case**
104 F.2d 306

**Melancholy Baby Case**
73 F. Supp. 165; 158 F.2d 759; 161 F.2d 406, 73 U.S.P.Q. (BNA) 5; 67 U.S.P.Q. (BNA) 12; 331 U.S. 820, 91 L. Ed. 1837, 67 S. Ct. 1310, 71 U.S.P.Q. (BNA) 286

**Membership Fees Tax Cases**
30 F. Supp. 142; 117 F.2d 146; 313 U.S. 555, 85 L. Ed. 1517, 61 S. Ct. 1104; 315 U.S. 32, 86 L. Ed. 619, 62 S. Ct. 425

119 F.2d 578; 314 U.S. 589, 86 L. Ed. 475, 62 S. Ct. 59; 315 U.S. 42, 86 L. Ed. 656, 62 S. Ct. 430

**Memoirs of Hecate County Case**
335 U.S. 848, 93 L. Ed. 398, 69 S. Ct. 79; 297 N.Y. 687, 77 N.E.2d 6; 272 A.D. 799, 71 N.Y.S.2d 736

**Memphis Cases**
223 Mo. 1, 122 S.W. 1008
250 F.2d 402; 355 U.S. 938, 2 L. Ed. 2d 420, 78 S. Ct. 429, 78 S. Ct. 430; 355 U.S. 949, 2 L. Ed. 2d 527, 78 S. Ct. 537, 78 S. Ct. 538; 358 U.S. 103, 3 L. Ed. 2d 153, 79 S. Ct. 194; 358 U.S. 802, 79 S. Ct. 18, 79 S. Ct. 19; 358 U.S. 942, 3 L. Ed. 2d 350, 79 S. Ct. 344

**Memphis Censors Case**
189 Tenn. 397, 225 S.W.2d 550; 339 U.S. 952, 94 L. Ed. 1365, 70 S. Ct. 839

**Memphis Parks Case**
373 U.S. 526, 10 L. Ed. 2d 529, 83 S. Ct. 1314; 303 F.2d 863

**Memphis Street Railway Cases**
133 Tenn. 99, 179 S.W. 635
138 Tenn. 594, 198 S.W. 890

**Mental Retardation Death Penalty Case**
106 L. Ed. 2d 256, 109 S. Ct. 2934

**Mercer Street Case**
4 Cow. 423

**Merchants' Elevator Case**
259 U.S. 285, 66 L. Ed. 943, 42 S. Ct. 477

**Meredith Case**
199 F. Supp. 754; 298 F.2d 696; 371 U.S. 828, 9 L. Ed. 2d 66, 83 S. Ct. 49; 372 U.S. 916, 9 L. Ed. 2d 723, 83 S. Ct. 722; 9 L. Ed. 2d 43, 83 S. Ct. 10; 305 F.2d 341; 305 F.2d 343; 306 F.2d 374; 313 F.2d 532; 313 F.2d 534; 328 F.2d 586; 202 F. Supp. 224

**Meretricious Relations Insurance Case**
321 Mass. 507, 73 N.E.2d 840

**Merger Cases**
370 U.S. 294, 8 L. Ed. 2d 510, 82 S. Ct. 1502
120 F. 721; 193 U.S. 197, 48 L. Ed. 679, 24 S. Ct. 436; 128 F. 808
188 F. 102; 226 U.S. 61, 57 L. Ed. 124, 33 S. Ct. 53; 226 U.S. 470, 57 L. Ed. 306, 33 S. Ct. 162

**Meriden Free Speech Case**
96 Conn. 190, 113 A. 385

**Meridian Rate Case**
66 I.C.C. 179; 92 I.C.C. 439

**Merrill Case**
75 F. 148, 21 C.C.A. 282, 41 U.S. App. D.C. 529; 78 F. 208, 24 C.C.A. 63, 41 U.S. App. D.C. 645; 173 U.S. 131, 43 L. Ed. 640, 19 S. Ct. 360

**Merry-Go-Round Case**
98 F.2d 245; 140 F.2d 465; 78 App. D.C. 287; 2 S.D.C. (n.s.) 17, 60 U.S.P.Q. (BNA) 224; 32 U.S.P.Q. (BNA) 113; 305 U.S. 583, 83 L. Ed. 368, 59 S. Ct. 85, 25 U.S.P.Q. (BNA) 83; 306 U.S. 30, 83 L. Ed. 470, 59 S. Ct. 397, 40 U.S.P.Q. (BNA) 190; 306 U.S. 668, 83 L. Ed. 1063, 59 S. Ct. 588

**Merrycow Case**
105 U.S.P.Q. (BNA) 392
182 U.S.P.Q. (BNA) 134

**Merryman Case**
F. Cas. No. 9,487

**Mesta Case**
347 Pa. 191, 32 A.2d 236; 322 U.S. 174, 88 L. Ed. 1209, 64 S. Ct. 908

**Methodist Book Concern Case**
F. Cas. No. 13,112; 57 U.S. 288, 14 L. Ed. 942

**Methodist Church Case**
F. Cas. No. 1,089

**Metro Case**
161 Kan. 683, 171 P.2d 784

**Metropolis Case**
217 F. 80; 241 U.S. 693, 60 L. Ed. 1239, 36 S. Ct. 724

**Metropolitan Building Company Case**
62 Wash. 409, 113 P. 1114; 64 Wash. 615, 117 P. 495; 72 Wash. 47, 129 P. 883; 144 Wash. 469, 258 P. 473

**Metropolitan Opera Case**
199 Misc. 786, 101 N.Y.S.2d 483; 279 A.D. 632, 107 N.Y.S.2d 795; 279 A.D. 646, 108 N.Y.S.2d 977; 279 A.D. 790, 110 N.Y.S.2d 282

**Metropolitan Police Case**
24 Barb. 187, 4 Abb. Pr. 322; 24 Barb. 265, 14 How. Pr. 233, 4 Abb. Pr. 333; 25 Barb. 344; 15 N.Y. 532

**Metropolitan Receivership Cases**
208 U.S. 90, 52 L. Ed. 403, 28 S. Ct. 219

**Mexican Abduction Case**
504 U.S. 655, 119 L. Ed. 2d 441, 112 S. Ct. 2188 (1992)

**Miami Case**
83 Fla. 81, 90 So. 854

**Michigan Dog Law Case**
219 Mich. 442, 189 N.W. 197

**Michigan Industrial Accident Board Cases**
214 Mich. 626, 183 N.W. 798
214 Mich. 636, 183 N.W. 913
214 Mich. 646, 183 N.W. 916
214 Mich. 652, 183 N.W. 902
214 Mich. 660, 183 N.W. 767

**Michigan Liquor Case**
204 Mich. 559, 171 N.W. 557

**Michigan Obscenity Case**
352 U.S. 380, 1 L. Ed. 2d 412, 77 S. Ct. 524, 350 U.S. 963, 100 L. Ed. 837, 76 S. Ct. 432

**Michigan Railroad Tax Cases**
138 F. 223; 201 U.S. 245, 50 L. Ed. 744, 26 S. Ct. 459

**Michigan Telephone Tax Cases**
185 F. 634; 229 U.S. 322, 57 L. Ed. 1206, 33 S. Ct. 833; 229 U.S. 335, 57 L. Ed. 1215, 33 S. Ct. 837

**Micky Will Cases**
46 Colo. 79, 102 P. 1075
46 Colo. 100, 102 P. 1088
50 Colo. 610, 115 P. 526
54 Colo. 510, 131 P. 422
57 Colo. 246, 141 P. 489; 58 Colo. 295, 144 P. 891
63 Colo. 506, 168 P. 404
68 Colo. 556, 191 P. 106
73 Colo. 1, 213 P. 131

**Middle South Broadcasting Company Case**
133 N.L.R.B. 1698, No. 165

**Middlesborough Beer Case**
4 I.C. 267

**Midget Injury Case**
217 S.C. 212, 60 S.E.2d 305

**Midland Carbon Company Case**
254 U.S. 300, 65 L. Ed. 276, 41 S. Ct. 118

**Midnight Judges Case**
5 U.S. 137, 2 L. Ed. 60

**Midwest Piping Case**
63 N.L.R.B. 1060, No. 163

**Migratory Bird Treaty Cases**
214 F. 154; 248 U.S. 594, 63 L. Ed. 438, 39 S. Ct. 134
221 F. 288
258 F. 479; 252 U.S. 416, 64 L. Ed. 641, 40 S. Ct. 382
96 Kan. 786, 153 P. 557
113 Me. 458, 94 A. 886

**Mikado Case**
25 F. 183

**Mileage and Commutation Cases**
11 Ct. Cl. 691; 94 U.S. 225, 24 L. Ed. 118
12 Ct. Cl. 98; 94 U.S. 219, 24 L. Ed. 116

**Military Death Penalty Case**
517 U.S. 748, 135 L. Ed. 2d 36, 116 S. Ct. 1737 (1996)

**Military Jurisdiction Cases**
50 F. Supp. 929
53 F. Supp. 80

**Military Justice Case**
417 U.S. 733, 41 L. Ed. 2d 439, 94 S. Ct. 2547

**Military Pension Case**
453 U.S. 210, 69 L. Ed. 2d 589, 101 S. Ct. 2728

**Military Service Registration Case**
453 U.S. 57, 69 L. Ed. 2d 478, 101 S. Ct. 2646

**Military Training Case**
293 U.S. 245, 79 L. Ed. 343, 55 S. Ct. 197; 293 U.S. 633, 79 L. Ed. 717, 55 S. Ct. 345

**Milk and Cream Case**
300 U.S. 608, 81 L. Ed. 835, 57 S. Ct. 549

**Milk Control Cases**
306 U.S. 619, 83 L. Ed. 1026, 59 S. Ct. 640
306 U.S. 669, 83 L. Ed. 1063, 59 S. Ct. 773
308 U.S. 188, 84 L. Ed. 181, 60 S. Ct. 182; 28 F. Supp. 177; 60 S. Ct. 125
318 U.S. 261, 87 L. Ed. 748, 63 S. Ct. 617
318 U.S. 285, 87 L. Ed. 761, 63 S. Ct. 628
318 U.S. 801, 87 L. Ed. 1165, 63 S. Ct. 849
21 F. Supp. 321; 97 F.2d 677; 26 F. Supp. 672; 306 U.S. 627, 83 L. Ed. 1031, 59 S. Ct. 647; 306 U.S. 629, 83 L. Ed. 1032, 59 S. Ct. 791, 307 U.S. 588, 83 L. Ed. 1478, 59 S. Ct. 1019
123 F.2d 100; 314 U.S. 605, 86 L. Ed. 486, 62 S. Ct. 362; 62 S. Ct. 413; 62 S. Ct. 414; 315 U.S. 110, 86 L. Ed. 726, 62 S. Ct. 523
127 F.2d 907
262 N.Y. 259, 186 N.E. 694; 291 U.S. 502, 78 L. Ed. 940, 54 S. Ct. 505; 54 S. Ct. 104
332 Pa. 34, 200 A. 854; 305 U.S. 589, 83 L. Ed. 372, 59 S. Ct. 229; 306 U.S. 346, 83 L. Ed. 752, 59 S. Ct. 528

**Milk, Cream and Butter-Fat Case**
117 Minn. 186, 134 N.W. 496

**Milk Drivers Case**
116 N.L.R.B. 1408, No. 195; 245 F.2d 817; 357 U.S. 345, 2 L. Ed. 2d 1367, 78 S. Ct. 1367

**Milk License Cases**
74 F.2d 695
8 F. Supp. 379
8 F. Supp. 403

**Milkshake Mary Case, The**
45 Ill. 2d 573, 262 N.E.2d 446

**Mill B Case**
40 N.L.R.B. 346, No. 57

**Miller Act Cases**
184 F. Supp. 520
195 F. Supp. 177
270 F. Supp. 215

**Miller Cases**
113 F. Supp. 80; 221 F.2d 62, 95 App. D.C. 189; 239 F.2d 25, 99 App. D.C. 205; 350 U.S. 907, 100 L. Ed. 796, 76 S. Ct. 192; 350 U.S. 911, 100 L. Ed. 799, 76 S. Ct. 192; 350 U.S. 962, 100 L. Ed. 835, 76 S. Ct. 429; 353 U.S. 942, 1 L. Ed. 2d 760, 77 S. Ct. 816
317 U.S. 369, 87 L. Ed. 336, 63 S. Ct. 276; 316 U.S. 657, 86 L. Ed. 1736, 62 S. Ct. 1290; 318 U.S. 798, 87 L. Ed. 1162, 63 S. Ct. 557; 125 F.2d 75

**Milligan Case**
71 U.S. 2, 18 L. Ed. 281

**Million Dollar Road Bond Case**
207 Iowa 923, 223 N.W. 737

**Milner Case**
F. Cas. No. 740, 35 Ga. 330

**Milwaukee County Case**
296 U.S. 268, 80 L. Ed. 220, 56 S. Ct. 229; 81 F.2d 753; 17 F. Supp. 759

**Milwaukee Park Land Case**
92 Wis. 236, 65 N.W. 1025

**Mimeographic Case**
224 U.S. 1, 56 L. Ed. 645, 32 S. Ct. 364

**Mine Workers Case**
70 F. Supp. 42; 329 U.S. 708, 91 L. Ed. 616, 67 S. Ct. 359; 329 U.S. 709, 91 L. Ed. 617, 67 S. Ct. 373, 329 U.S. 710, 91 L. Ed. 618, 67 S. Ct. 485; 330 U.S. 258, 91 L. Ed. 884, 67 S. Ct. 677; 91 L. Ed. 1298, 67 S. Ct. 975; 91 L. Ed. 1298, 67 S. Ct. 976; 91 L. Ed. 1298, 67 S. Ct. 977

**Mineral Interest Partition Case**
162 Kan. 474, 178 P.2d 235

**Mineral King Case**
405 U.S. 727, 31 L. Ed. 2d 636, 92 S. Ct. 1361

**Minerals Separation Case**
242 U.S. 261, 61 L. Ed. 286, 37 S. Ct. 82

**Minimum Wage Cases**
284 F. 613, 52 App. D.C. 109; 261 U.S. 525, 67 L. Ed. 785, 43 S. Ct. 394
300 F. 991
1 Ill. 2d 108, 115 N.E.2d 306; 347 U.S. 949, 98 L. Ed. 1096, 74 S. Ct. 680
156 Misc. 522, 282 N.Y.S. 576; 270 N.Y. 233, 200 N.E. 799; 297 U.S. 702, 80 L. Ed. 991, 56 S. Ct. 670; 298 U.S. 587, 80 L. Ed. 1347, 56 S. Ct. 918; 299 U.S. 619, 81 L. Ed. 456, 57 S. Ct. 4
185 Wash. 581, 55 P.2d 1083; 300 U.S. 379, 81 L. Ed. 703, 57 S. Ct. 578

**Mining Claims Forfeiture Case**
471 U.S. 84, 85 L. Ed. 2d 64, 105 S. Ct. 1785

**Mining Debris Cases**
16 F. 25; 18 F. 753; 45 F. 129
27 F. 795

**Mink Case**
53 N.H. 398; 57 N.H. 104

**Minneapolis Grain Rate Case**
4 I.C. 44, 230

**Minneapolis Milk Rate Case**
38 Minn. 281, 37 N.W. 782; 134 U.S. 418, 33 L. Ed. 970, 10 S. Ct. 462, 10 S. Ct. 702

**Minneapolis Rate Case**
285 F. 818

**Minnehaha Ditch Cases**
276 U.S. 567, 72 L. Ed. 703, 48 S. Ct. 396
282 F. 364; 297 F. 710; 266 U.S. 622, 69 L. Ed. 473, 45 S. Ct. 122; 45 S. Ct. 229; 270 U.S. 378, 70 L. Ed. 641, 46 S. Ct. 236
46 S.D. 374, 193 N.W. 132; 267 U.S. 584, 69 L. Ed. 799, 45 S. Ct. 461
51 S.D. 336, 213 N.W. 952
56 S.D. 569, 229 N.W. 932
57 S.D. 152, 231 N.W. 531; 58 S.D. 414, 236 N.W. 372

**Minnesota Blue Sky Case**
25 F. Supp. 948; 110 F.2d 601; 312 U.S. 666, 85 L. Ed. 1110, 61 S. Ct. 823; 142 F.2d 449

**Minnesota Bonds Case**
280 U.S. 204, 74 L. Ed. 371, 50 S. Ct. 98

**Minnesota Corporation Cases**
206 U.S. 516, 51 L. Ed. 1163, 27 S. Ct. 755; 234 U.S. 652, 58 L. Ed. 1518, 34 S. Ct. 926

**Minnesota Gag Law Case**
283 U.S. 697, 75 L. Ed. 1357, 51 S. Ct. 625

**Minnesota Income Tax Case**
191 Minn. 254, 253 N.W. 102

**Minnesota Milk Case**
38 Minn. 281, 37 N.W. 782; 134 U.S. 418, 33 L. Ed. 970, 10 S. Ct. 462, 10 S. Ct. 702

**Minnesota Milk Company Case**
133 N.L.R.B. 1314, No. 123; 314 F.2d 761

**Minnesota Minimum Wage Case**
139 Minn. 32, 165 N.W. 495, 166 N.W. 504

**Minnesota Mortgage Moratorium Case**
189 Minn. 422, 249 N.W. 334; 189 Minn. 448, 249 N.W. 893; 290 U.S. 398, 78 L. Ed. 413, 54 S. Ct. 231; 54 S. Ct. 80

**Minnesota Occupation Tax Case**
262 U.S. 172, 67 L. Ed. 929, 43 S. Ct. 526

**Minnesota Psychopathic Personality Case**
205 Minn. 545, 287 N.W. 297; 308 U.S. 515, 84 L. Ed. 439, 60 S. Ct. 140; 309 U.S. 270, 84 L. Ed. 744, 60 S. Ct. 523

**Minnesota Rate Cases**
134 U.S. 418, 33 L. Ed. 970, 10 S. Ct. 462, 10 S. Ct. 702
209 U.S. 123, 52 L. Ed. 714, 28 S. Ct. 441
155 F. 445
184 F. 765; 230 U.S. 352, 57 L. Ed. 1511, 33 S. Ct. 729

**Minnesota Reciprocal Demurrage Law Case**
110 Minn. 25, 124 N.W. 819; 226 U.S. 426, 57 L. Ed. 284, 33 S. Ct. 174

**Minnesota Soldiers' Bonus Case**
144 Minn. 415, 175 N.W. 903

**Minnesota Tea Company Case**
296 U.S. 378, 80 L. Ed. 284, 56 S. Ct. 269; 296 U.S. 562, 80 L. Ed. 397, 56 S. Ct. 107; 302 U.S. 609, 82 L. Ed. 474, 58 S. Ct. 393; 89 F.2d 711; 302 U.S. 665, 82 L. Ed. 513, 58 S. Ct. 16

**Minnesota Unfair Trade Practice Act Case**
23 F. Supp. 70

**Minnick Case**
57 F. 362, 6 C.C.A. 387; 61 F. 635, 10 C.C.A. 1

**Minor Case**
26 F. 672; 114 U.S. 233, 29 L. Ed. 110, 5 S. Ct. 836

**Minor Crimes Two-Tiered System Case**
80 L. Ed. 2d 311, 104 S. Ct. 1805

**Minor Party Campaign Disclosure Case**
459 U.S. 87, 74 L. Ed. 2d 250, 103 S. Ct. 416

**Minor Privilege Case**
131 Md. 600, 102 A. 1014

**Minority Business Enterprise Case**
448 U.S. 448, 65 L. Ed. 2d 902, 100 S. Ct. 2758

**Minshull Case**
141 Wash. 440, 252 P. 147

**Miracle Case**
343 U.S. 495, 96 L. Ed. 1098, 72 S. Ct. 777; 303 N.Y. 242, 101 N.E.2d 665; 304 N.Y. 718, 107 N.E.2d 658; 278 A.D. 253, 104 N.Y.S.2d 740; 105 N.Y.S.2d 384

**Miranda Case**
384 U.S. 436, 16 L. Ed. 2d 694, 86 S. Ct. 1602

**Miranda Interrogation Case**
446 U.S. 291, 64 L. Ed. 2d 297, 100 S. Ct. 1682

**Miranda Warnings Case**
470 U.S. 298, 84 L. Ed. 2d 222, 105 S. Ct. 1285

**Miranda Warnings Exception Case**
467 U.S. 649, 81 L. Ed. 2d 550, 104 S. Ct. 2626

**Miscegenation Inheritance Case**
203 Miss. 824, 36 So. 2d 140

**Misrouting Case**
15 I.C.C. 170; 17 I.C.C. 9; 187 F. 874; 191 F. 705, 112 C.C.A. 295

**Mississippi Milk Case**
424 U.S. 366, 47 L. Ed. 2d 55, 96 S. Ct. 923

**Mississippi Southern Bell Case**
127 So. 2d 404 (Miss.)

**Missouri Bridge Case**
79 Mo. 478; 125 U.S. 260, 31 L. Ed. 731, 8 S. Ct. 874

**Missouri Insurance Case**
189 S.W. 609 (Mo.); 246 U.S. 357, 62 L. Ed. 772, 38 S. Ct. 337

**Missouri Law School Case**
342 Mo. 121, 113 S.W.2d 783; 305 U.S. 580, 83 L. Ed. 365, 59 S. Ct. 65; 305 U.S. 337, 83 L. Ed. 208, 59 S. Ct. 232; 305 U.S. 676, 83 L. Ed. 437, 59 S. Ct. 356; 344 Mo. 1238, 131 S.W.2d 217

**Missouri Library Case**
318 Mo. 870, 2 S.W.2d 713

**Missouri Rate Cases**
155 F. 220; 161 F. 419, 92 C.C.A. 171; 168 F. 317; 230 U.S. 474, 57 L. Ed. 1571, 33 S. Ct. 975; 230 U.S. 509, 57 L. Ed. 1595, 33 S. Ct. 984; 230 U.S. 512, 57 L. Ed. 1596, 33 S. Ct. 983

**Missouri Test Oath Cases**
71 U.S. 277, 18 L. Ed. 356
71 U.S. 333, 18 L. Ed. 366
*Continued*

**Missouri Voting Time Case**
220 S.W.2d 782 (Mo.); 362 Mo. 299, 240 S.W.2d 886; 342 U.S. 421, 96 L. Ed. 469, 72 S. Ct. 405; 343 U.S. 921, 96 L. Ed. 1334, 72 S. Ct. 674

**Mistaken Ad Case**
207 Miss. 78, 41 So. 2d 30; 207 Miss. 91, 41 So. 2d 746; 211 Miss. 523, 52 So. 2d 35

**Mistaken Indentity Arrest Case**
253 Wis. 66, 33 N.W.2d 215

**Mistaken Payment of Insurance Case**
208 S.C. 6, 36 S.E.2d 860

**Misused CETA Funds Case**
476 U.S. 253, 90 L. Ed. 2d 248, 106 S. Ct. 1834

**Mitchell Cases**
2 U.S. 348, 1 L. Ed. 410
151 N.Y. 107, 45 N.E. 354; 77 Hun 607, 28 N.Y.S. 1136; 4 Misc. 575, 25 N.Y. Supp 744

**Mitigation of Punishment Evidence Case**
476 U.S. 1, 90 L. Ed. 2d 1, 106 S. Ct. 1669

**Mixed Acids Case**
Treas. Dec. 37927, Gen. Appraisers 8235; Treas. Dec. 38238, 9 Ct. Cust. 298; 253 U.S. 481, 64 L. Ed. 1023, 40 S. Ct. 483; 256 U.S. 402, 65 L. Ed. 1013, 41 S. Ct. 513

**Mobil Trilogy Cases**
610 F.2d 796; 647 F.2d 142; 678 F.2d 1083

**Moisture Case**
188 F. 157; 195 F. 657, 115 C.C.A. 463

**Moldy Tomato Paste Case**
111 F. Supp. 478; 113 F. Supp. 114; 212 F.2d 567

**Moline Plow Case**
54 Ill. 439

**Moline Properties Case**
45 B.T.A. 647; 131 F.2d 388; 318 U.S. 751, 87 L. Ed. 1127, 63 S. Ct. 768; 319 U.S. 436, 87 L. Ed. 1499, 63 S. Ct. 1132

**Molineux Case**
26 Misc. 589, 13 N.Y. Crim. 544, 57 N.Y.S. 643; 27 Misc. 60, 14 N.Y. Crim. 1, 57 N.Y.S. 936; 27 Misc. 79, 14 N.Y. Crim. 6, 58 N.Y.S. 155; 168 N.Y. 264, 61 N.E. 286; 36 Misc. 435, 16 N.Y. Crim. 245, 73 N.Y.S. 806

**Molitor and Perine Case**
8 F. 821; 113 U.S. 609, 28 L. Ed. 1106, 5 S. Ct. 618

**Molly Maguire Cases**
259 U.S. 344, 66 L. Ed. 975, 42 S. Ct. 570; 268 U.S. 295, 69 L. Ed. 963, 45 S. Ct. 551
84 Pa. 107
84 Pa. 187
85 Pa. 139
91 Pa. 57

**Monan Case**
174 U.S. 674, 43 L. Ed. 1130, 19 S. Ct. 827

**Money Bequest Case**
140 N.J. Eq. 433, 55 A.2d 14

**Moneyed Capital Tax Case**
123 Misc. 399, 205 N.Y.S. 870; 124 Misc. 27, 207 N.Y.S. 188; 213 A.D. 677, 211 N.Y.S. 85; 213 A.D. 702, 211 N.Y.S. 107; 213 A.D. 706, 211 N.Y.S. 110; 213 A.D. 710, 211 N.Y.S. 114; 213 A.D. 713, 211 N.Y.S. 117; 213 A.D. 715, 211 N.Y.S. 119; 213 A.D. 716, 211 N.Y.S. 120; 213 A.D. 719, 211 N.Y.S. 122; 242 N.Y. 277, 151 N.E. 452; 242 N.Y. 540, 152 N.E. 418; 242 N.Y. 541, 152 N.E. 418; 242 N.Y. 542, 152 N.E. 419; 242 N.Y. 543, 152 N.E. 419; 242 N.Y. 544, 152 N.E. 420; 242 N.Y. 545, 152 N.E. 420; 242 N.Y. 546, 152 N.E. 420

**Monroe Paper Products Case**
154 F. Supp. 263; 232 F.2d 458; 235 F.2d 129; 249 F.2d 797; 356 U.S. 935, 2 L. Ed. 2d 810, 78 S. Ct. 795; 356 U.S. 936, 2 L. Ed. 2d 812, 78 S. Ct. 778

**Montgomery Bus Case**
142 F. Supp. 707; 146 F. Supp. 127; 352 U.S. 903, 1 L. Ed. 2d 114, 77 S. Ct. 145; 352 U.S. 950, 1 L. Ed. 2d 245, 77 S. Ct. 323; 352 U.S. 955, 1 L. Ed. 2d 245, 77 S. Ct. 323

**Montgomery Ward Seizure Case**
58 F. Supp. 408; 324 U.S. 858, 89 L. Ed. 1416, 65 S. Ct. 862; 324 U.S. 888, 89 L. Ed. 1436, 65 S. Ct. 867; 150 F.2d 369; 326 U.S. 690, 90 L. Ed. 406, 66 S. Ct. 140

**Montpelier Dynamiting Case**
200 Ind. 88, 161 N.E. 375

**Mooney Case**
175 Cal. 666, 166 P. 999; 176 Cal. 105, 167 P. 696; 177 Cal. 642, 171 P. 690; 178 Cal. 525, 174 P. 325; 248 U.S. 579, 63 L. Ed. 430, 39 S. Ct. 21; 294 U.S. 103, 79 L. Ed. 791, 55 S. Ct. 511; 294 U.S. 732, 79 L. Ed. 1261, 55 S. Ct. 511; 296 U.S. 541, 80 L. Ed. 385, 56 S. Ct. 83

**Moor Case**
75 F.2d 386; 297 U.S. 101, 80 L. Ed. 509, 56 S. Ct. 372

**Moore Dry Dock Case**
92 N.L.R.B. 547, No. 93

**Moral Obligation Contract Case**
172 F.2d 495

**Morena Case**
245 U.S. 392, 62 L. Ed. 359, 38 S. Ct. 151

**Morey Case**
80 A.D. 280, 80 N.Y.S. 309; 175 N.Y. 394, 67 N.E. 620

**Morgan Envelope Case**
40 F. 577; 152 U.S. 425, 38 L. Ed. 500, 14 S. Ct. 627

**Mormon Case**
4 Utah 280, 9 P. 501; 4 Utah 295, 9 P. 686; 4 Utah 313, 9 P. 697; 118 U.S. 346, 30 L. Ed. 207, 6 S. Ct. 1059; 120 U.S. 274, 30 L. Ed. 658, 7 S. Ct. 556

**Morris and Essex Company Case**
95 U.S. 104, 24 L. Ed. 352

**Morris' Cotton Case**
75 U.S. 507, 19 L. Ed. 481

**Morse Case**
161 F. 429; 164 F. 1023, 90 C.C.A. 668; 168 F. 49, 93 C.C.A. 471; 169 F. 1021, 94 C.C.A. 667; 174 F. 539, 98 C.C.A. 321; 215 U.S. 605, 54 L. Ed. 346, 30 S. Ct. 406

**Morse Telegraph Case**
F. Cas. No. 9,859; 56 U.S. 61, 14 L. Ed. 601

**Mortgage Milking Case**
193 Wis. 503, 213 N.W. 304, 215 N.W. 571

**Mortgage Moratorium Cases**
187 Ark. 641, 61 S.W.2d 686
218 Iowa 339, 252 N.W. 507
189 Minn. 412, 249 N.W. 330
189 Minn. 450, 249 N.W. 672
63 N.D. 514, 249 N.W. 118
167 Okla. 53, 29 P.2d 22
167 Okla. 187, 29 P.2d 1
167 Okla. 208, 29 P.2d 21
167 Okla. 209, 29 P2.d 24
61 S.D. 356, 249 N.W. 631
122 Tex. 553, 62 S.W.2d 641
122 Tex. 575, 62 S.W.2d 652
122 Tex. 577, 62 S.W.2d 655
122 Tex. 580, 62 S.W.2d 654
122 Tex. 582, 62 S.W.2d 652
61 S.W.2d 1033 (Tex.)
57 S.W.2d 327 (Tex.); 62 S.W.2d 348
210 Wis. 489, 246 N.W. 556

**Mortgage Tax Case**
24 F. 197; 140 U.S. 690, 35 L. Ed. 593, 11 S. Ct. 1025

**Morton Salt Case**
162 F.2d 949; 332 U.S. 850, 92 L. Ed. 420, 68 S. Ct. 355; 334 U.S. 37, 92 L. Ed. 1196, 68 S. Ct. 822

**Motion Picture Free Speech Case**
103 N.Y.S.2d 657; 278 A.D. 253, 104 N.Y.S.2d 740; 105 N.Y.S. 2d 384; 303 N.Y. 242, 101 N.E.2d 665; 304 N.Y. 718, 107 N.E.2d 658; 343 U.S. 495, 96 L. Ed. 1098, 72 s. Ct. 777

**Motion Picture Monopoly Cases**
263 U.S. 291, 68 L. Ed. 308, 44 S. Ct. 96
20 F. Supp. 868; 58 S. Ct. 523; 304 U.S. 55, 82 L. Ed. 1146, 58 S. Ct. 768; 306 U.S. 208, 83 L. Ed. 610, 59 S. Ct. 467
66 F. Supp. 323, 69 U.S.P.Q. (BNA) 573; 70 F. Supp. 53, 72 U.S.P.Q. (BNA) 46; 67 S. Ct. 1752, 67 S. Ct. 1753, 73 U.S.P.Q. (BNA) 551; 75 S. Ct. 1002, 76 U.S.P.Q. (BNA) 296; 334 U.S. 131, 92 L. Ed. 1260, 68 S. Ct. 915; 85 F. Supp. 881, 82 U.S.P.Q. (BNA) 291; 338 U.S. 802, 94 L. Ed. 486, 70 S. Ct. 61; 339 U.S. 974, 94 L. Ed. 1380, 70 S. Ct. 1031, 70 S. Ct. 1032; 340 U.S. 803, 95 L. Ed. 590, 71 S. Ct. 16; 340 U.S. 857, 95 L. Ed. 627, 71 S. Ct. 69, 71 S, Ct. 70

**Motion Picture Patent Cases**
200 F. 411, 118 C.C.A. 563
235 F. 398, 148 C.C.A. 660; 242 U.S. 637, 61 L. Ed. 540, 37 S. Ct. 21; 243 U.S. 502, 61 L. Ed. 871, 37 S. Ct. 416

**Motor Boat Case**
116 F.2d 789, 1941 A.M.C. 31; 313 U.S. 554, 85 L. Ed. 1517, 61 S. Ct. 1087, 1941 A.M.C. 824; 314 U.S. 716, 86 L. Ed. 570, 62 S. Ct. 477

**Motor Home Warranties Search Case**
471 U.S. 386, 85 L. Ed. 2d 406, 105 S. Ct. 2066

**Motor Vehicle Accession Case**
70 So.2d 360 (Fla.)

**Motor Vehicle Tampering Case**
364 Mo. 684, 266 S.W.2d 626

**Mount Laurel Cases**
290 A.2d 465 (N.J.)
336 A.2d 713
391 A.2d 935
456 A.2d 390

**Mountain Meadow Massacre Case**
2 Utah 441

**Mounting and Finishing Case**
268 A.D. 901, 51 N.Y.S.2d 638; 294 N.Y. 104, 60 N.E.2d 825

**Mouse Case**
230 Mo. App. 275, 90 S.W.2d 445

**Moxie Cases**
152 F. 493; 153 F. 487; 155 F. 304; 162 F. 649, 89 C.C.A. 441; 179 F. 415
197 F. 678; 206 F. 434, 124 C.C.A. 316

**Mrs. Alexander's Cotton Case**
69 U.S. 404, 17 L. Ed. 915

**Mrs. Munsey's Case**
71 N.H. 594, 53 A. 1086, 72 N.H. 178, 55 A. 554, 196 U.S. 364, 49 L. Ed. 515, 25 S. Ct. 282

**Mt. Clemens Pottery Case**
328 U.S. 680, 90 L. Ed. 1515, 66 S. Ct. 1187; 326 U.S. 706, 90 L. Ed. 416, 66 S. Ct. 91; 329 U.S. 822, 91 L. Ed. 699, 67 S. Ct. 25; 331 U.S. 784, 91 L. Ed. 1815, 67 S. Ct. 1191; 149 F.2d 461; 60 F. Supp. 146; 69 F. Supp. 710

**Mt. Gilead Case**
338 U.S. 864, 94 L. Ed. 530, 70 S. Ct. 148; 87 F. Supp. 324

**Muffler Case**
17 N.Y.2d 64, 268 N.Y.S.2d 24, 215 N.E. 2d 345

**Mugg Case**
98 Tex. 352, 83 S.W. 800; 202 U.S. 242, 50 L. Ed. 1011, 26 S. Ct. 628

**Mugler Cases**
123 U.S. 623, 31 L. Ed. 205, 8 S. Ct. 273

**Mule Cases**
156 Mo. App. 427, 136 S.W. 760; 262 Mo. 353, 171 S.W. 352
165 S.C. 316, 163 S.E. 777
220 S.W.2d 196 (Tex.); 148 Tex. 565, 226 S.W.2d 996

**Multiple Dwelling Law Case**
251 N.Y. 467, 167 N.E. 705; 252 N.Y. 574, 170 N.E. 148; 252 N.Y. 615, 170 N.E. 164

**Muncie Gear Case**
315 U.S. 759, 86 L. Ed. 1171, 62 S. Ct. 865; 119 F.2d 404, 48 U.S.P.Q. (BNA) 411; 314 U.S. 594, 86 L. Ed. 479, 62 S. Ct. 100, 51 U.S.P.Q. (BNA) 545

**Munday Case**
204 Ill. App. 24; 280 Ill. 32, 117 N.E. 286; 215 Ill. App. 356; 293 Ill. 191, 127 N.E. 364; 254 U.S. 638, 65 L. Ed. 451, 41 S. Ct. 13

**Munich Case**
265 F. 477; 265 F. 481; 254 U.S. 554, 65 L. Ed. 403, 41 S. Ct. 214

**Municipal Bankruptcy Cases**
298 U.S. 513, 80 L. Ed. 1309, 56 S. Ct. 892; 298 U.S. 648, 80 L. Ed. 1377, 56 S. Ct. 683; 299 U.S. 619, 81 L. Ed. 457, 57 S. Ct. 5; 304 U.S. 27, 82 L. Ed. 1137, 58 S. Ct. 811

**Municipal Claim Notice Case**
364 Mo. 679, 265 S.W.2d 342

**Municipal Destruction of Buildings Case**
220 S.W.2d 320 (Tex.); 148 Tex. 391, 224 S.W.2d 871

**Municipal Falling Tree Case**
324 Mass. 327, 86 N.E.2d 511

**Municipal Incinerator Ash Case**
511 U.S. 328, 128 L. Ed. 2d 302, 114 S. Ct. 1588 (1994)

**Municipal Liability under Section 1983 Case**
475 U.S. 469, 89 L. Ed. 2d 452, 106 S. Ct. 1292

**Municipal Off-Street Parking Case**
323 Mich. 592, 36 N.W.2d 157

**Municipal Railway Election Case**
255 U.S. 171, 65 L. Ed. 570, 41 S. Ct. 285

**Municipalities' Civil-Rights Liability Case**
436 U.S. 658, 56 L. Ed. 2d 611, 98 S. Ct. 2018

**Munsingwear Case**
63 F. Supp. 933; 162 F.2d 125; 178 F.2d 204; 339 U.S. 941, 94 L. Ed. 1357, 70 S. Ct. 795, 70 S. Ct. 796; 340 U.S. 36, 95 L. Ed. 36, 71 S. Ct. 104

**Murarka Case**
108 F. Supp. 597; 215 F.2d 547; 111 F. Supp. 295

**Murchison Case**
349 U.S. 133, 99 L. Ed. 942, 75 S. Ct. 623; 340 Mich. 140, 65 N.W.2d 296; 340 Mich. 151, 65 N.W.2d 301

**Murder by Fright Case**
273 S.W.2d 380 (Ky.)

**Murder Scene Exception Case**
437 U.S. 385, 57 L. Ed. 2d 290, 98 S. Ct. 2408

**Murderer's Right to Succession Case**
40 Wash. 2d 850, 246 P.2d 445

**Murderous Legatee Case**
139 Conn. 491, 95 A.2d 71

**Murdock Case**
51 F.2d 389; 284 U.S. 141, 76 L. Ed. 210, 52 S. Ct. 63; 62 F.2d 926

**Murphy Motor Freight Case**
231 F.2d 654

**Murray Case**
374 U.S. 203, 10 L. Ed. 2d 844, 83 S. Ct. 1560; 228 Md. 239, 179 A.2d 698

**Music as You Ride Case**
191 F.2d 450, 89 App. D.C. 94; 342 U.S. 848, 96 L. Ed. 640, 72 S. Ct. 77, 72 S. Ct. 80; 72 S. Ct. 164; 72 S. Ct. 165; 72 S. Ct. 228; 72 S. Ct. 229; 343 U.S. 451, 96 L. Ed. 1068, 72 S. Ct. 813

**Music Masters Case**
22 App. D.C. 250; 194 U.S. 106, 48 L. Ed. 894, 24 S. Ct. 595

**Musical Parody Copyright Case**
510 U.S. 569, 127 L. Ed. 2d 500, 114 S. Ct. 1164 (1994)

**Musicians' Social Security Case**
59 F. Supp. 84; 157 F.2d 295; 329 U.S. 711, 91 L. Ed. 618, 67 S. Ct. 494; 332 U.S. 126, 91 L. Ed. 1947, 67 S. Ct. 1547

**Muskogee Cases**
31 I.C.C. 289; 31 I.C.C. 347; 57 I.C.C. 125

**Muskrat Case**
44 Ct. Cl. 137; 219 U.S. 346, 55 L. Ed. 246, 31 S. Ct. 250

**Mustang Case**
363 P.2d 835 (Okla.)

**Mutt and Jeff Cases**
91 Misc. 640, 155 N.Y.S. 782; 160 N.Y.S. 689; 188 A.D. 964, 176 N.Y.S. 923; 231 N.Y. 606, 132 N.E. 907; 257 U.S. 654, 66 L. Ed. 419, 42 S. Ct. 94
160 N.Y.S. 693; 188 A.D. 694, 176 N.Y.S. 899; 231 N.Y. 414, 132 N.E. 133; 257 U.S. 654, 66 L. Ed. 419, 42 S. Ct. 94
220 F. 359

**Mutual Fund Case**
422 U.S. 694, 45 L. Ed. 2d 486, 95 S. Ct. 2427

**Myers Case**
58 Ct. Cl. 199; 45 S. Ct. 350; 272 U.S. 52, 71 L. Ed. 160, 47 S. Ct. 21

## N

**Narcotic Drug Cases**
274 U.S. 289, 71 L. Ed. 1052, 47 S. Ct. 634
246 F. 958; 249 U.S. 86, 63 L. Ed. 493, 39 S. Ct. 214
4 F.2d 781
7 F.2d 553; 276 U.S. 332, 72 L. Ed. 600, 48 S. Ct. 388; 27 F.2d 1019

**Narcotics Delay Cases**
335 F.2d 982
349 F.2d 210
351 F.2d 817
353 F.2d 897

**Narrow Bridge Case**
246 Iowa 466, 68 N.W.2d 89

**Nashville-Atlanta Grain Case**
16 I.C.C. 590; 18 I.C.C. 280; 21 I.C.C. 186; 191 F. 37; 197 F. 58; 235 U.S. 314; 59 L. Ed. 245, 35 S. Ct. 113; 234 F. 699

**Nashville Coal Case**
28 I.C.C. 533; 216 F. 672; 238 U.S. 1, 59 L. Ed. 1177, 35 S. Ct. 696

**Nashville Reshipping Case**
16 I.C.C. 590; 18 I.C.C. 280; 21 I.C.C. 186; 191 F. 37; 197 F. 58; 235 U.S. 314, 59 L. Ed. 245, 35 S. Ct. 113; 234 F. 699

**Nashville Switching Cases**
24 I.C.C. 228; 207 F. 591; 238 U.S. 642, 59 L. Ed. 1502, 35 S. Ct. 602
28 I.C.C. 533; 216 F. 672; 238 U.S. 1, 59 L. Ed. 1177, 35 S. Ct. 696
33 I.C.C. 76; 227 F. 258; 227 F. 273; 242 U.S. 60, 61 L. Ed. 152, 37 S. Ct. 61

**Nassak Diamond Case**
Treas. Dec. 42943; Treas. Dec. 43494; Treas. Dec. 44093; 18 C.C.P.A. 117; 283 U.S. 828, 75 L. Ed. 1442, 51 S. Ct. 353; Abs. (n.s.) No. 16218

**Nassau Case**
118 N.L.R.B. 174, No. 19

**Nathans Case**
2 Clark 458, 4 Pa. L.J. 249; 2 Brewst. 149, 3 Clark 139, 5 Pa. L.J. 1; 2 Pa. 138

**National Bank Tax Cases**
154 U.S. 551, 18 L. Ed. 229, 14 S. Ct. 1215
130 F.2d 356; 317 U.S. 618, 87 L. Ed. 501, 63 S. Ct. 201; 318 U.S. 357, 87 L. Ed. 834, 63 S. Ct. 587
40 Barb. 334; 26 N.Y. 163; 67 U.S. 620, 17 L. Ed. 451; 25 How. Pr. 9; 69 U.S. 200, 17 L. Ed. 793
43 Barb. 550; 33 N.Y. 161; 70 U.S. 573, 18 L. Ed. 229; 154 U.S. 550, 18 L. Ed. 229, 14 S. Ct. 1198; 31 How. Pr. 288
124 Va. 522, 98 S.E. 643; 256 U.S. 635, 65 L. Ed. 1135, 41 S. Ct. 619

**National Bank Venue Case**
434 U.S. 35, 54 L. Ed. 2d 218, 98 S. Ct. 88

**National Cash Register Trust Case**
201 F. 697; 205 F. 292; 222 F. 599, 138 C.C.A. 123; 238 U.S. 635, 59 L. Ed. 1499, 35 S. Ct. 939

**National Docks Cases**
51 F. 858; 56 F. 697; 58 F. 929
52 N.J.L. 90, 18 A. 574; 53 N.J.L. 217, 21 A. 570; 54 N.J.L. 180, 23 A. 686
52 N.J. Eq. 58, 28 A. 71; 52 N.J. Eq. 590, 33 A. 50
52 N.J. Eq. 366, 28 A. 673; 52 N.J. Eq. 555, 30 A. 580
52 N.J. Eq. 552, 30 A. 581; 30 A. 1102; 53 N.J. Eq. 178, 32 A. 220; 54 N.J. Eq. 10, 33 A. 219
54 N.J. Eq. 142, 33 A. 860; 54 N.J. Eq. 167, 33 A. 936; 54 N.J. Eq. 647, 35 A. 433; 55 N.J. Eq. 820, 41 A. 1116
57 N.J.L. 265, 31 A. 462; 57 N.J.L. 637, 32 A. 274

**National Endowment for Arts Case**
141 L. Ed. 2d 500, 118 S. Ct. 2168 (1998)

**National Labor Relations Act Pre-Emption Case**
460 U.S. 669, 75 L. Ed. 2d 368, 103 S. Ct. 1453

**National Labor Relations Board Cases**
301 U.S. 1, 81 L. Ed. 893, 57 S. Ct. 615; 90 F.2d 678
301 U.S. 49, 81 L. Ed. 893, 57 S. Ct. 642
301 U.S. 58, 81 L. Ed. 893, 57 S. Ct. 645
301 U.S. 103, 81 L. Ed. 953, 57 S. Ct. 650
301 U.S. 142, 81 L. Ed. 965, 57 S. Ct. 648

**National Lead Case**
332 U.S. 319, 91 L. Ed. 2077, 67 S. Ct. 1634

**National Prohibition Cases**
251 U.S. 311, 64 L. Ed. 280, 40 S. Ct. 154
267 U.S. 132, 69 L. Ed. 543, 45 S. Ct. 280
257 F. 860; 252 U.S. 465, 64 L. Ed. 665, 40 S. Ct. 364
260 F. 486; 251 U.S. 210, 64 L. Ed. 229, 40 S. Ct. 139
264 F. 186; 253 U.S. 350, 64 L. Ed. 946, 40 S. Ct. 486, 588
268 F. 864; 260 U.S. 377, 67 L. Ed. 314, 43 S. Ct. 141
284 F. 596; 251 U.S. 146, 64 L. Ed. 194, 40 S. Ct. 106; 251 U.S. 264, 64 L. Ed. 260, 40 S. Ct. 141
156 Ga. 488, 119 S.E. 302; 267 U.S. 188, 69 L. Ed. 568, 45 S. Ct. 264
100 Ohio St. 385, 126 N.E. 400; 253 U.S. 221, 64 L. Ed. 871, 40 S. Ct. 495
100 Ohio St. 540, 127 N.E. 924; 253 U.S. 231, 64 L. Ed. 877, 40 S. Ct. 498

**National Radiator Case**
290 U.S. 504, 78 L. Ed. 465, 54 S. Ct. 298

**National Tube Case**
76 N.L.R.B. 1199, No. 169

**Nativity Scene Case**
79 L. Ed. 2d 604, 104 S. Ct. 1355

**Natural Carbonic Gas Case**
162 F. 954; 170 F. 1023; 220 U.S. 61, 55 L. Ed. 369, 31 S. Ct. 337

**Natural Gas Act Cases**
120 F.2d 625; 314 U.S. 593, 86 L. Ed. 478, 62 S. Ct. 91; 315 U.S. 575, 86 L. Ed. 1037, 62 S. Ct. 736; 129 F.2d 515; 141 F.2d 27; 324 U.S. 138, 89 L. Ed. 805, 65 S. Ct. 565
375 Ill. 634, 32 N.E.2d 157; 314 U.S. 498, 86 L. Ed. 371, 62 S. Ct. 384

**Natural Gas Regulation Case**
459 U.S. 400, 74 L. Ed. 2d 569, 103 S. Ct. 697

**Natural Gas Tax Case**
451 U.S. 725, 68 L. Ed. 2d 576, 101 S. Ct. 2114

**Naval Paymaster Cases**
8 F.2d 669; 270 U.S. 652, 70 L. Ed. 782, 46 S. Ct. 351

**Naval Stores Case**
121 F. 645, 57 C.C.A. 671; 128 F. 1020, 62 C.C.A. 681; 194 U.S. 634, 48 L. Ed. 1160, 24 S. Ct. 861; 198 U.S. 483, 49 L. Ed. 1135, 25 S. Ct. 745

**NBC—Westinghouse Case**
158 F. Supp. 333; 21 F.R.D. 103; 357 U.S. 918, 2 L. Ed. 2d 1362, 78 S. Ct. 1359; 358 U.S. 334, 3 L. Ed. 2d 354, 79 S. Ct. 457

**NCAA Television Case**
468 U.S. 85, 82 L. Ed. 2d 70, 104 S. Ct. 2948

**Near Case**
283 U.S. 697, 75 L. Ed. 1357, 51 S. Ct. 625; 179 Minn. 40, 228 N.W. 326

**Near-Sighted Engineer Case**
178 U.S. 373, 44 L. Ed. 1108, 20 S. Ct. 957; 82 F. 255; 91 F. 28; 173 U.S. 704, 19 S. Ct. 886

**Nebbia Case**
262 N.Y. 259, 186 N.E. 694; 291 U.S. 502, 78 L. Ed. 940, 54 S. Ct. 505

**Nebraska Bread Cases**
108 Neb. 674, 189 N.W. 383; 261 U.S. 608, 67 L. Ed. 824, 43 S. Ct. 433; 261 U.S. 625, 67 L. Ed. 833, 43 S. Ct. 359; 262 U.S. 728, 67 L. Ed. 1203, 43 S. Ct. 520; 264 U.S. 504, 68 L. Ed. 813, 44 S. Ct. 412
124 Neb. 464, 247 N.W. 39; 290 U.S. 570, 78 L. Ed. 505, 54 S. Ct. 277; 54 S. Ct. 63

**Nebraska Rate Case**
64 F. 165; 68 F. 726, 15 C.C.A. 671; 169 U.S. 466, 42 L. Ed. 819, 18 S. Ct. 418; 171 U.S. 361, 43 L. Ed. 197, IS S. Ct. 888; 100 F. 235; 102 F. 197, 42 C.C.A. 254

**Neff Case**
F. Cas. No. 10,083, 95 U.S. 714, 24 L. Ed. 565

**Neglected Child Case**
205 S.W.2d 812 (Tex.)

**Negligent Attorney Case**
239 N.C. 517, 80 S.E.2d 144

**Negligent Church Case**
116 Vt. 124, 70 A.2d 230

**Negligent Hunters' Joint Liability Case**
190 P.2d 963 (Cal.); 33 Cal. 2d 80, 199 P.2d 1

**Negligent Parent Case**
189 Ore. 282, 218 P.2d 445

**Negro Boy Case**
4 Denio 464

**Neill Case**
21 S.W.2d 532 (Tex.)

**Nelson Case**
350 U.S. 497, 100 L. Ed. 640, 76 S. Ct. 477; 377 Pa. 58, 104 A.2d 133; 172 Pa. Super. 125, 92 A.2d 431; 348 U.S. 814, 99 L. Ed. 642, 75 S. Ct. 58; 350 U.S. 922, 100 L. Ed. 807, 76 S. Ct. 218; 351 U.S. 934, 100 L. Ed. 1462, 76 S. Ct. 785

**Neon Cases**
31 F.2d 983; 31 F.2d 988; 21 F.2d 846; 27 F.2d 702; 278 U.S. 634, 73 L. Ed. 551, 49 S. Ct. 32; 31 F.2d 991; 33 F.2d 300; 33 F.2d 910; 36 F.2d 574; 40 F.2d 222; 281 U.S. 741, 74 L. Ed. 1155, 50 S. Ct. 347; 47 F.2d 345; 58 F.2d 384
32 F.2d 1008; 37 F.2d 1010
33 F.2d 949
34 F.2d 711
35 F.2d 263; 36 F.2d 998; 39 F.2d 548
39 F.2d 487; 36 F.2d 827; 38 F.2d 233
39 F.2d 907; 49 F.2d 886
40 F.2d 708; 48 F.2d 176
48 F.2d 824; 52 F.2d 1085
52 F.2d 169
54 F.2d 793

**Neponset Cases**
300 F. 981; 4 F.2d 132; 13 F.2d 808

**Net Worth Case**
209 F.2d 516; 347 U.S. 1008, 98 L. Ed. 1133, 74 S. Ct. 863; 348 U.S. 121, 99 L. Ed. 150, 75 S. Ct. 127; 348 U.S. 932, 99 L. Ed. 731, 75 S. Ct. 334

**Network Cases**
316 U.S. 407, 86 L. Ed. 1563, 62 S. Ct. 1194; 316 U.S. 447, 86 L. Ed. 1586, 62 S. Ct. 1214; 47 F. Supp. 940; 318 U.S. 743, 87 L. Ed. 1121, 63 S. Ct. 772; 319 U.S. 190, 87 L. Ed. 1344, 63 S. Ct. 997

**Nevada Train Limit Case**
18 F. Supp. 393

**New Bedford Bridge Case**
F. Cas. No. 15,867

**New Castle Case**
29 I.C.C. 114; 214 F. 445; 236 U.S. 351, 59 L. Ed. 616, 35 S. Ct. 370

**New Deal Cases**
293 U.S. 388, 79 L. Ed. 446, 55 S. Ct. 241
295 U.S. 495, 79 L. Ed. 1570, 55 S. Ct. 837
298 U.S. 238, 80 L. Ed. 1160, 56 S. Ct. 855; 12 F. Supp. 570; 296 U.S. 571, 80 L. Ed. 403, 56 S. Ct. 371; 296 U.S. 572, 80 L. Ed. 403, 56 S. Ct. 371; 296 U.S. 636, 80 L. Ed. 452, 56 S. Ct. 175; 56 S. Ct. 944; 56 S. Ct. 945; 56 S. Ct. 950; 56 S. Ct. 951
300 U.S. 324, 81 L. Ed. 678, 57 S. Ct. 485; 83 F.2d 398; 11 F. Supp. 518; 299 U.S. 526, 81 L. Ed. 387, 57 S. Ct. 24
301 U.S. 1, 81 L. Ed. 893, 57 S. Ct. 615; 83 F.2d 998; 90 F.2d 678; 299 U.S. 534, 81 L. Ed. 393, 57 S. Ct. 119; 299 U.S. 535, 81 L. Ed. 394, 57 S. Ct. 120
301 U.S. 548, 81 L. Ed. 1279, 57 S. Ct. 883; 89 F.2d 207; 300 U.S. 652, 81 L. Ed. 863, 57 S. Ct. 673; 57 S. Ct. 755

**New Dexedrine Case**
207 F.2d 190

**New Drug Marketing Case**
460 U.S. 453, 75 L. Ed. 2d 198, 103 S. Ct. 1298

**New England Divisions Case**
282 F. 306; 261 U.S. 184, 67 L. Ed. 605, 43 S. Ct. 270

**New Haven Inclusion Cases**
399 U.S. 392, 26 L. Ed. 2d 691, 90 S. Ct. 2054

**New Haven Wire Company Cases**
57 Conn. 352, 18 A. 266

**New Jersey Jockey Club Case**
63 N.J.L. 515, 44 A. 207

**New Jersey Rule Making Case**
5 N.J. Super. 30, 68 A.2d 332; 5 N.J. 240, 74 A.2d 406; 340 U.S. 877, 95 L. Ed. 638, 71 S. Ct. 123

**New Jersey Spill Fund Tax Case**
475 U.S. 335, 89 L. Ed. 2d 364, 106 S. Ct. 1103

**New Jersey Teacher's Case**
300 U.S. 319, 81 L. Ed. 674, 57 S. Ct. 483

**New Mexico Horse Cases**
16 Ct. Cl. 550
16 Ct. Cl. 559

**New Orleans Board of Trade Case**
17 I.C.C. 231; 184 F. 118; 195 F. 541; 227 U.S. 88, 57 L. Ed. 431, 33 S. Ct. 185

**New River Case**
311 U.S. 377, 85 L. Ed. 243, 61 S. Ct. 291; 107 F.2d 769; 23 F. Supp. 83; 309 U.S. 636, 84 L. Ed. 992, 60 S. Ct. 720; 309 U.S. 638, 84 L. Ed. 994, 60 S. Ct. 806; 309 U.S. 646, 84 L. Ed. 999, 60 S. Ct. 608; 312 U.S. 712, 85 L. Ed. 1143, 61 S. Ct. 548

**New Rockford Case**
35 N.D. 34, 159 N.W. 281

**New York Bank Tax Cases**
154 U.S. 551, 18 L. Ed. 229, 14 S. Ct. 1215
40 Barb. 334; 26 N.Y. 163; 67 U.S. 620, 17 L. Ed. 451; 25 How. Pr. 9; 69 U.S. 200, 17 L. Ed. 793
43 Barb. 550; 33 N.Y. 161; 70 U.S. 573, 18 L. Ed. 229; 154 U.S. 550, 18 L. Ed. 229, 14 S. Ct. 1198; 31 How. Pr. 288
18 How. Pr. 245; 32 Barb. 509, 20 How. Pr. 182; 23 N.Y. 192

**New York City Ferry Franchise Case**
115 U.S. 248, 29 L. Ed. 388, 6 S. Ct. 28

**New York City Sales Tax Cases**
254 A.D. 237, 4 N.Y.S.2d 661; 279 N.Y. 192, 18 N.E.2d 28; 280 N.Y. 691, 21 N.E.2d 199; 307 U.S. 620, 83 L. Ed. 1499, 59 S. Ct. 1043; 309 U.S. 430, 84 L. Ed. 849, 60 S. Ct. 670
254 A.D. 246, 4 N.Y.S.2d 615; 279 N.Y. 678, 18 N.E.2d 311; 280 N.Y. 688, 21 N.E.2d 198; 307 U.S. 620, 83 L. Ed. 1499, 59 S. Ct. 1044; 309 U.S. 70, 84 L. Ed. 584, 60 S. Ct. 404
255 A.D. 961, 8 N.Y.S.2d 668; 281 N.Y. 610, 22 N.E.2d 173, 281 N.Y. 670, 22 N.E.2d 764; 308 U.S. 546, 84 L. Ed. 459, 60 S. Ct. 261; 309 U.S. 33, 84 L. Ed. 565, 60 S. Ct. 388

**New York Electric Case**
107 N.Y. 593, 14 N.E. 820; 145 U.S. 175, 36 L. Ed. 666, 12 S. Ct. 880

**New York Elevated Railroad Cases**
90 N.Y. 122
104 N.Y. 268, 10 N.E. 528

**New York Estate Tax Case**
175 Misc. 489, 23 N.Y.S.2d 943; 287 N.Y. 61, 38 N.E.2d 131; 287 N.Y. 764, 40 N.E.2d 46; 178 Misc. 325, 34 N.Y.S.2d 254, 315 U.S. 795, 82 L. Ed. 1197, 62 S. Ct. 918; 264 A.D. 718, 34 N.Y.S.2d 831; 264 A.D. 755, 35 N.Y.S.2d 711; 289 N.Y. 601, 43 N.E.2d 831; 317 U.S. 95, 87 L. Ed. 106, 63 S. Ct. 109; 289 N.Y. 760, 46 N.E.2d 361

**New York Gas Case**
256 F. 238; 260 F. 244; 260 F. 1022, 171 C.C.A. 669; 250 U.S. 671, 63 L. Ed. 1199, 40 S. Ct. 15; 253 U.S. 219, 64 L. Ed. 870, 40 S. Ct. 511; 267 F. 231; 274 F. 986; 258 U.S. 165, 66 L. Ed. 538, 42 S. Ct. 264; 259 U.S. 101, 66 L. Ed. 844, 42 S. Ct. 438; 291 F. 704; 264 U.S. 571, 68 L. Ed. 855, 44 S. Ct. 401; 265 U.S. 78, 68 L. Ed. 909, 44 S. Ct. 481

**New York Housing Act Cases**
269 F. 306; 256 U.S. 170, 65 L. Ed. 877, 41 S. Ct. 465
194 A.D. 482, 186 N.Y.S. 5; 194 A.D. 521, 186 N.Y.S. 56; 230 N.Y. 634, 130 N.E. 923; 230 N.Y. 652, 130 N.E. 931; 258 U.S. 242, 66 L. Ed. 595, 42 S. Ct. 289

**New York Indians Case**
23 N.Y. 420; 72 U.S. 761, 18 L. Ed. 708

**New York Milk Case**
262 N.Y. 259, 186 N.E. 694; 291 U.S. 502, 78 L. Ed. 940, 54 S. Ct. 505

**New York Passenger Fare Case**
272 F. 758; 257 U.S. 591, 66 L. Ed. 385, 42 S. Ct. 239

**New York Port Authority Case**
304 U.S. 405, 82 L. Ed. 1427, 58 S. Ct. 969

**New York Rent Case**
269 F. 306; 256 U.S. 170, 65 L. Ed. 877, 41 S. Ct. 465

**New York Steamboat Case**
22 U.S. 1, 6 L. Ed. 23; 17 Johns. 488, 4 Johns. Ch 150; 19 U.S. 448, 5 L. Ed. 302

**New York Tax Cases**
274 F. 975, 260 U.S. 708, 67 L. Ed. 474, 43 S. Ct. 166; 261 U.S. 1, 67 L. Ed. 505, 43 S. Ct. 313; 266 U.S. 265, 69 L. Ed. 279, 45 S. Ct. 80
198 A.D. 963, 189 N.Y.S. 952; 232 N.Y. 42, 133 N.E. 122; 266 U.S. 271, 69 L. Ed. 282, 45 S. Ct. 82

**New York Telephone Rate Case**
36 F.2d 54

**New York Theatre Ticket Case**
273 U.S. 418, 71 L. Ed. 718, 47 S. Ct. 426

**New York Unemployment Insurance Case**
271 N.Y. 1, 2 N.E.2d 22; 299 U.S. 515, 81 L. Ed. 380, 57 S. Ct. 122

**Newark Case**
56 A. 471 (N.J.)

**Newcomb Motor Case**
30 App. D.C. 464, 133 Off. Gaz. Pat. Office 1680; 216 U.S. 608, 54 L. Ed. 636, 30 S. Ct. 575

**Newgold Case**
99 F. 567; 108 F. 957; 113 F. 877, 51 C.C.A. 501

**Newport News Cases**
23 I.C.C. 345; 204 F. 465
153 Va. 789, 151 S.E. 417
159 Va. 571, 166 S.E. 570, 167 S.E. 583

**Newport Water Works Case**
106 Ky. 434, 21 Ky. Law Rep. 42, 50 S.W. 845, 51 S.W. 433

**Newsboy Cases**
212 Ky. 366, 279 S.W. 339
213 Ky. 618, 281 S.W. 805
322 U.S. 111, 83 L. Ed. 1170, 64 S. Ct. 851, 320 U.S. 728, 88 L. Ed. 429, 88 L. Ed. 430, 64 S. Ct. 88, 64 S. Ct. 89; 322 U.S. 769, 88 L. Ed. 1595, 64 S. Ct. 1148; 322 U.S. 770, 88 L. Ed. 1595, 64 S. Ct. 1148; 322 U.S. 770, 88 L. Ed. 1595, 64 S. Ct. 1149; 136 F.2d 608

**Newspaper Invasion of Privacy Case**
419 U.S. 245, 42 L. Ed. 2d 419, 95 S. Ct. 465

**Newspaper Monopoly Cases**
180 F.2d 28
10 F.R.D. 487; 92 F. Supp. 794; 71 S. Ct. 743; 342 U.S. 143, 96 L. Ed. 162, 72 S. Ct. 181

**Newspaper Search Case**
56 L. Ed. 2d 525, 98 S. Ct. 1970
436 U.S. 547, 56 L. Ed. 2d 525, 98 S. Ct. 1970

*Continued*

**Newspaper Tax Case**
297 U.S. 233, 80 L. Ed. 660, 56 S. Ct. 444

**Newspaper-TV Joint Ownership Case**
436 U.S. 775, 56 L. Ed. 2d 697, 98 S. Ct. 2096

**Ng Hen Case**
220 F. 538

**Ng Ka Py Case**
24 F.2d 772

**Niagara Falls Railway Company Case**
108 N.Y. 375, 15 N.E. 429

**Nicholson Pavement Case**
F. Cas. No. 312; F. Cas. No. 311; F. Cas. No. 309; F. Cas. No.310; 97 U.S. 126, 24 L. Ed. 1000; 131 U.S. Appx. 138, 24 L. Ed. 1059

**Nick Carter Case**
204 F. 398; 231 U.S. 348, 58 L. Ed. 262, 34 S. Ct. 73, 1914 C.D. 353; 231 U.S. 755, 58 L. Ed. 468, 34 S. Ct. 323; 232 U.S. 724, 58 L. Ed. 815, 34 S. Ct. 602

**Nickel Plate Case**
331 F.2d 865
129 N.Y. 474, 129 N.Y. 654, 29 N.E. 959; 133 N.Y. 239, 30 N.E. 1011

**Nickle Case**
60 F.2d 372

**Nicolay Case**
51 F.2d 170

**Night Blooming Cereus Case**
5 Phila. 464

**Night Rider Cases**
192 F. 1, 112 C.C.A. 423
121 Tenn. 684, 120 S.W. 816

**Nine-Mile Halfway Drain Case**
257 Mich. 135, 241 N.W. 237

**Nipsco Case**
140 Ind. App. 79, 221 N.E.2d 442

**Nitro-Glycerine Case**
82 U.S. 524, 21 L. Ed. 206

**Nitro-Tungsten Case**
261 F. 606; 266 F. 994

**Nixon Cases**
273 U.S. 536, 71 L. Ed. 759, 47 S. Ct. 446
34 F.2d 464; 49 F.2d 1012; 284 U.S. 601, 76 L. Ed. 516, 52 S. Ct. 24; 76 L. Ed. 1301, 52 S. Ct. 202; 286 U.S. 73, 76 L. Ed. 984, 52 S. Ct. 484

**Nixon Tape Cases**
360 F. Supp. 1; 487 F.2d 700; 418 U.S. 683, 41 L. Ed. 2d 1039, 94 S. Ct. 3090

**NLRA Faculty Members Case**
444 U.S. 672, 63 L. Ed. 2d 115, 100 S. Ct. 856

**NLRB Cases**
301 U.S. 1, 81 L. Ed. 893, 57 S. Ct. 615; 90 F.2d 678
301 U.S. 49, 81 L. Ed. 893, 57 S. Ct. 642
301 U.S. 58, 81 L. Ed. 893, 57 S. Ct. 645
301 U.S. 103, 81 L. Ed. 953, 57 S. Ct. 650
301 U.S. 142, 81 L. Ed. 965, 57 S. Ct. 648

**No Damage Clause Case**
76 R.I. 87, 68 A.2d 32

**Noble State Bank Case**
219 U.S. 104, 55 L. Ed. 112, 31 S. Ct. 186; 22 Okla. 48, 97 P. 590; 219 U.S. 575, 55 L. Ed. 341, 31 S. Ct. 299

**Noe Case**
F. Cas. No. 10,285; F. Cas. No. 10, 286; 64 U.S. 312, 16 L. Ed. 462

**Noerr-Pennington Doctrine**
365 U.S. 127, 5 L. Ed. 2d 464, 81 S. Ct. 523 (1961)
381 U.S. 657, 14 L. Ed. 2d 626, 85 S. Ct. 1585 (1965)

**Non-Profit Private School Tax Exemption Case**
76 L. Ed. 2d 157, 103 S. Ct. 2017

**Nonemployees Picketing Case**
361 Pa. 246, 64 A.2d 834

**Nonforfeiture Insurance Case**
189 S.W. 609 (Mo.); 246 U.S. 357, 62 L. Ed. 772, 38 S. Ct. 337

**Nonpartisan Case**
44 N.D. 395, 176 N.W. 11; 253 U.S. 233, 64 L. Ed. 878, 40 S. Ct. 499

**Nonrecourse Mortgage Case**
461 U.S. 300, 75 L. Ed. 2d 863, 103 S. Ct. 1826

**Nonresident Alien Tax Cases**
166 Iowa 617, 147 N.W. 1098; 245 U.S. 170, 62 L. Ed. 225, 38 S. Ct. 109
168 Iowa 511, 151 N.W. 66; 245 U.S. 176, 62 L. Ed. 228, 38 S. Ct. 111

**Nonresident Annulment Case**
127 Colo. 359, 257 P.2d 581

**Nonresident Enemy Alien Case**
84 App. D.C. 396, 174 F.2d 961; 338 U.S. 877, 94 L. Ed. 538, 70 S. Ct. 158; 339 U.S. 763, 94 L. Ed. 1255, 70 S. Ct. 936

**Nonresident Insurers Service Case**
206 F.2d 518; 346 U.S. 877, 98 L. Ed. 384, 74 S. Ct. 125

**Nonresident Service Case**
185 F.2d 276

**Nonresident Trustee Service Case**
163 F.2d 809

**Nonresident Witness Case**
200 Ore. 35, 264 P.2d 419; 203 Ore. 487, 280 P.2d 414; 347 U.S. 962, 98 L. Ed. 1105, 74 S. Ct. 711

**Nonunion Employees Voting Case**
475 U.S. 192, 89 L. Ed. 2d 151, 106 S. Ct. 1007

**Norfolk School Teachers Case**
112 F.2d 992; 311 U.S. 693, 85 L. Ed. 448, 61 S. Ct. 75

**Normanna Case**
162 Tex. 274, 346 S.W.2d 801

**Norris-La Guardia Act Cases**
303 U.S. 323, 82 L. Ed. 872, 58 S. Ct. 578
303 U.S. 552, 82 L. Ed. 1012, 58 S. Ct. 703

**North Carolina Railroad Tax Case**
259 U.S. 576, 66 L. Ed. 1071, 42 S. Ct. 585; 289 F. 301; 260 U.S. 519, 67 L. Ed. 375, 43 S. Ct. 192; 261 U.S. 609, 67 L. Ed. 825, 43 S. Ct. 518; 262 U.S. 413, 67 L. Ed. 1051, 43 S. Ct. 620

**North Carolina Redistricting Case**
509 U.S. 630, 125 L. Ed. 2d 511, 113 S. Ct. 2816 (1993)

**North Dakota Coal Rate Cases**
19 N.D. 45, 120 N.W. 869; 19 N.D. 57, 120 N.W. 874; 216 U.S. 579, 54 L. Ed. 624, 30 S. Ct. 423; 216 U.S. 581, 54 L. Ed. 1212, 30 S. Ct. 698, 31 S. Ct. 218; 26 N.D. 438, 145 N.W. 135; 236 U.S. 585, 59 L. Ed. 735, 35 S. Ct. 429
35 N.D. 331, 160 N.W. 140; 254 U.S. 376, 65 L. Ed. 312, 41 S. Ct. 142
40 N.D. 69, 168 N.W. 684; 254 U.S. 370, 65 L. Ed. 310, 41 S. Ct. 140

**North Dakota Grain Cases**
258 U.S. 50, 66 L. Ed. 458, 42 S. Ct. 244
258 U.S. 65, 66 L. Ed. 467, 42 S. Ct. 250
268 U.S. 189, 69 L. Ed. 909, 45 S. Ct. 481

**North Jersey Street Railway Case**
68 N.J.L. 486, 53 A. 219

**North Shore Case**
175 A.D. 869, 162 N.Y.S. 405

**North Star Case**
73 F. 597; 83 F. 658, 28 C.C.A. 333; 171 U.S. 687, 18 S. Ct. 940

**Northern Central Dividend Cases**
126 Md. 16, 94 A. 338; 127 Md. 610, 96 A. 766

**Northern Fertilizer Case**
120 I.C.C. 361; 146 I.C.C. 419, 197 I.C.C. 70

**Northern Great Plains Coal Case**
427 U.S. 390, 49 L. Ed. 2d 576, 96 S. Ct. 2718

**Northern Securities Cases**
120 F. 721; 193 U.S. 197, 48 L. Ed. 679, 24 S. Ct. 436
132 F. 464; 134 F. 331; 196 U.S. 641, 49 L. Ed. 631, 25 S. Ct. 796; 197 U.S. 244, 49 L. Ed. 739, 25 S. Ct. 493

**Northway Case**
120 U.S. 327, 30 L. Ed. 664, 7 S. Ct. 580

**Northwestern Lumber Cases**
157 F. 588; 14 I.C.C. 41
157 F. 845; 165 F. 25, 91 C.C.A. 63; 16 I.C.C. 164
14 I.C.C. 1, 165 F. 13, 91 C.C.A. 51
14 I.C.C. 23; 165 F. 1, 91 C.C.A. 39; 222 U.S. 541, 56 L. Ed. 308, 32 S. Ct. 108

**Northwestern States Portland Cement Company Case**
358 U.S. 450, 3 L. Ed. 2d 421, 79 S. Ct. 357; 355 U.S. 911, 2 L. Ed. 2d 272, 78 S. Ct. 341; 213 Ga. 713, 101 S.E.2d 197; 214 Ga. 803, 108 S.E.2d 314; 250 Minn. 32, 84 N.W.2d 373; 258 Minn. 162, 103 N.W.2d 225

**Nose of Wax Case**
119 U.S. 47, 30 L. Ed. 303, 7 S. Ct. 72

**Notice of Alibi Case**
261 Wis. 70, 51 N.W.2d 495

**Notre Dame Case**
152 F. Supp. 269; 258 F.2d 256, 118 U.S.P.Q. (BNA) 431

**NRA Case**
295 U.S. 495, 79 L. Ed. 1570, 55 S. Ct. 837; 295 U.S. 723, 79 L. Ed. 1676, 55 S. Ct. 651

**Nuclear Energy Preemption Case**
78 L. Ed. 2d 443, 104 S. Ct. 615

**Nude Dancing Case**
115 L. Ed. 2d 504, 111 S. Ct. 2456

**Nugent Case**
1 Mart. (o.s.) 103, 1 Mart. (o.s.) 108; 1 Mart. (o.s.) 169

**Nujol Case**
28 F.2d 283

**Nuremberg Trial Cases**
6 F.R.D. 69

**Nurse Communication Case**
76 Ohio App. 483, 65 N.E.2d 300; 147 Ohio St. 416, 34 Ohio Op. 350, 72 N.E.2d 245

**Nurse's Testimony Case**
242 Minn. 265, 65 N.W.2d 185

**Nursing Home Case**
447 U.S. 773, 65 L. Ed. 2d 506, 100 S. Ct. 2467

**Nut Margarine Case**
284 U.S. 498, 76 L. Ed. 422, 52 S. Ct. 260

**Nutley Case**
98 N.J.L. 712, 121 A. 783, 99 N.J.L. 389, 125 A. 121

**Nylon Spinners Case**
100 F. Supp. 504; 8 F.R.D. 551, 81 U.S.P.Q. (BNA) 67; 105 F. Supp. 215, 93 U.S.P.Q. (BNA) 360

## O

**Oak Grove Cases**
56 Ore. 468, 105 P. 709, 109 P. 273; 229 U.S. 397, 57 L. Ed. 1248, 33 S. Ct. 820
57 Ore. 126, 105 P. 715; 229 U.S. 414, 57 L. Ed. 1259, 33 S. Ct. 827

**Oak Street Viaduct Case**
324 Mo. 882, 25 S.W.2d 1055

**Oakley Case**
338 U.S. 278, 94 L. Ed. 87, 70 S. Ct. 119; 170 F.2d 1008; 171 F.2d 128; 336 U.S. 943, 93 L. Ed. 1100, 69 S. Ct. 812; 336 U.S. 964, 93 L. Ed. 1115, 69 S. Ct. 937

**Oates Case**
18 T.C. 570; 207 F.2d 711

**Oberlin Rescue Case**
8 Ohio St. 599; 9 Ohio St. 77

**Obscenity Cases**
413 U.S. 15, 37 L. Ed. 2d 419, 93 S. Ct. 2607
413 U.S. 49, 37 L. Ed. 2d 446, 93 S. Ct. 2628
413 U.S. 115, 37 L. Ed. 2d 492, 93 S. Ct. 2680
413 U.S. 123, 37 L. Ed. 2d 500, 93 S. Ct. 2665
413 U.S. 139, 37 L. Ed. 2d 513, 93 S. Ct. 2674

**Obscenity Search Warrant Case**
475 U.S. 868, 89 L. Ed. 2d 871, 106 S. Ct. 1610

**Obstructed Crossing Case**
190 F.2d 917

**Oconto Water Cases**
52 F. 43; 52 F. 29; 59 F. 19, 7 C.C.A. 603, 18 U.S. App. D.C. 380; 61 F. 782, 10 C.C.A. 60; 68 F. 1006; 73 F. 516, 19 C.C.A. 548; 76 F. 166, 22 C.C.A. 110, 46 U.S. App. D.C. 281; 77 F. 774, 23 C.C.A. 454, 46 U.S. App 619; 166 U.S. 721, 41 L. Ed. 1188, 17 S. Ct. 996; 88 F. 613, 32 C.C.A. 57; 113 F. 793, 51 C.C.A. 465
89 Wis. 264, 60 N.W. 1004
105 Wis. 48, 81 N.W. 125; 183 U.S. 216, 46 L. Ed. 157, 22 S. Ct. 111

**Of Thee I Sing Case**
2 F. Supp. 73

**O'Fallon Case**
22 F.2d 980; 279 U.S. 461, 73 L. Ed. 798, 49 S. Ct. 384

**Office Car Cases**
282 U.S. 740, 75 L. Ed. 672, 51 S. Ct. 297
282 U.S. 760, 75 L. Ed. 684, 51 S. Ct. 304

**Offshore Rights Cases**
420 U.S. 515, 43 L. Ed. 2d 363, 95 S. Ct. 1155
420 U.S. 529, 43 L. Ed. 2d 373, 95 S. Ct. 1180
420 U.S. 531, 43 L. Ed. 2d 375, 95 S. Ct. 1162

**O'Gara Coal Case**
22 I.C.C. 341

**Oh, Mamma! Case**
232 Mass. 138, 122 N.E. 168

**Ohio Express Case**
69 F. 546, 16 C.C.A. 305, 37 U.S. App. D.C. 378; 165 U.S. 194, 41 L. Ed. 683, 17 S. Ct. 305; 166 U.S. 185, 41 L. Ed. 965, 17 S. Ct. 604

**Ohio-Michigan Coal Cases**
80 I.C.C. 663

**Ohio Penalty Cases**
438 U.S. 586, 57 L. Ed. 2d 973, 98 S. Ct. 2954; 438 U.S. 637, 57 L. Ed. 2d 1010, 98 S. Ct. 2977

**Ohio River Bridge Case**
54 U.S. 518, 14 L. Ed. 249; 59 U.S. 421, 15 L. Ed. 435; 59 U.S. 460, 15 L. Ed. 449

**Ohio Tax Cases**
203 F. 537; 232 U.S. 576, 58 L. Ed. 737, 34 S. Ct. 372

**Ohio Valley Case**
68 Pa. Super. 561; 260 Pa. 289, 103 A. 744; 260 Pa. 310, 103 A. 750; 251 U.S. 542, 64 L. Ed. 405, 40 S. Ct. 583; 253 U.S. 287, 64 L. Ed. 908, 40 S. Ct. 527; 75 Pa. Super. 290; 271 Pa. 346, 114 A. 369

**O.I.C. Swine Case**
289 F. 985; 292 F. 752

**Oil and Gas Waste Case**
210 S.W.2d 553 (Tex.); 146 Tex. 575, 210 S.W.2d 558; 216 S.W.2d 824

**Oil Company Multibillion-Dollar Abstention Case**
481 U.S. 1, 95 L. Ed. 2d 1, 107 S. Ct. 1519

**Oil Jobber Cases**
119 F.2d 747; 314 U.S. 644, 86 L. Ed. 516, 62 S. Ct. 84
133 F.2d 101
138 F.2d 967, 321 U.S. 792, 88 L. Ed. 1081, 64 S. Ct. 790
148 F.2d 580
37 F. Supp. 831
42 F. Supp. 369; 130 F.2d 535
64 F. Supp. 12

**Oil Permit Cases**
46 F.2d 217, 60 App. D.C. 11; 283 U.S. 414, 75 L. Ed. 1148, 51 S. Ct. 502; 283 U.S. 811, 75 L. Ed. 1429, 51 S. Ct. 343
46 F.2d 224; 283 U.S. 414, 75 L. Ed. 1148, 51 S. Ct. 502; 283 U.S. 811, 75 L. Ed. 1429, 51 S. Ct. 343

**Oil Shale Deposits Case**
446 U.S. 657, 64 L. Ed. 2d 593, 100 S. Ct. 1932

**Oil Tank Car Case**
34 I.C.C. 179; 227 F. 911; 242 U.S. 208, 61 L. Ed. 251, 37 S. Ct. 95

**Oilers Case**
176 F. Supp. 53; 271 F.2d 87; 364 U.S. 278, 4 L. Ed. 2d 1719, 80 S. Ct. 1609

**Oklahoma Death Penalty Case**
455 U.S. 104, 71 L. Ed. 2d 1, 102 S. Ct. 869

**Oklahoma Furniture Case**
368 U.S. 370, 7 L. Ed. 2d 360, 82 S. Ct. 408; 365 U.S. 839, 5 L. Ed. 2d 807, 81 S. Ct. 800; 193 F. Supp. 275

**Oklahoma Ice Case**
42 F.2d 913; 52 F.2d 349; 52 S. Ct. 140; 52 S. Ct. 310; 285 U.S. 262, 76 L. Ed. 747, 52 S. Ct. 371

**Oklahoma Oil Proration Case**
51 F.2d 823; 52 S. Ct. 15; 286 U.S. 210, 76 L. Ed. 1062, 52 S. Ct. 559

**Oklahoma Rate Case**
174 F. 59; 177 F. 493; 185 F. 321, 107 C.C.A. 403; 220 U.S. 618, 55 L. Ed. 612, 31 S. Ct. 721

**Oklahoma State Capitol Removal Case**
28 Okla. 121, 113 P. 944; 221 U.S. 559, 55 L. Ed. 853, 31 S. Ct. 688

**Olaa Sugar Case**
242 F.2d 714

**Olah Case**
300 N.Y. 96, 89 N.E.2d 329; 275 A.D. 319, 89 N.Y.S.2d 660

**Olathe Case**
156 F. 624

**Old Age Pension Cases**
301 U.S. 619, 81 L. Ed. 1307, 57 S. Ct. 904
209 Minn. 29, 295 N.W. 75
282 Pa. 440, 128 A. 80

**Old Bay Mare Case**
87 S.W.2d 316 (Tex.)

**Old Burying Grounds Case**
42 N.J. Eq. 531, 9 A. 203; 44 N.J. Eq. 179, 14 A. 630

**Old Cement Case**
294 F. 390; 268 U.S. 563, 69 L. Ed. 1093, 45 S. Ct. 578; 268 U.S. 586, 69 L. Ed. 1112, 45 S. Ct. 592; 268 U.S. 588, 69 L. Ed. 1104, 45 S. Ct. 586

**Old Dearborn Case**
363 Ill. 610, 2 N.E.2d 940; 57 S. Ct. 31; 299 U.S. 183, 81 L. Ed. 109, 57 S. Ct. 139

**Old Dominion Copper Cases**
210 U.S. 206, 52 L. Ed. 1035, 28 S. Ct. 634
203 Mass. 159, 89 N.E. 193

**Old Gray Mare Case**
65 Miss. 385, 4 So. 121

**Old Ironsides Case**
30 F.2d 402

**Old Maestro Case**
9 F. Supp. 754

**Old Rocking Chair Whiskey Case**
115 Mont. 278, 142 P.2d 229

**Old Settlers' Case**
27 Ct. Cl. 1; 28 Ct. Cl. 557; 148 U.S. 427, 37 L. Ed. 509, 13 S. Ct. 650

**Olds Motor Case**
145 Ky. 616, 140 S.W. 1047

**Oleomargarine Cases**
127 U.S. 678, 32 L. Ed. 253, 8 S. Ct. 992, 8 S. Ct. 1257
195 U.S. 27, 49 L. Ed. 78, 24 S. Ct. 769
292 U.S. 40, 78 L. Ed. 1109, 54 S. Ct. 599
156 Mass. 236, 30 N.E. 1127; 154 U.S. 506, 38 L. Ed. 1083, 14 S. Ct. 1147; 155 U.S. 461, 39 L. Ed. 223, 15 S. Ct. 154
99 N.Y. 377, 2 N.E. 29
156 Pa. 201, 27 A. 30, 4 I.C. 488; 170 Pa. 296, 33 A. 85; 189 Pa. 559, 42 A. 1117; 171 U.S. 1, 43 L. Ed. 49, 18 S. Ct. 757
170 Pa. 284, 33 A. 82, 5 I.C. 506; 189 Pa. 559, 42 A. 1117; 171 U.S. 1, 43 L. Ed. 49, 18 S. Ct. 757
170 Pa. 296, 33 A. 85; 189 Pa. 559, 42 A. 1117; 171 U.S. 1, 43 L. Ed. 49, 18 S. Ct. 757

**Olmstead Case**
5 F.2d 712; 7 F.2d 756; 7 F.2d 760; 19 F.2d 842; 275 U.S. 557, 72 L. Ed. 424, 48 S. Ct. 117; 276 U.S. 609, 72 L. Ed. 729, 48 S. Ct. 207; 72 L. Ed. 1017, 48 S. Ct. 212; 277 U.S. 438, 72 L. Ed. 944, 48 S. Ct. 564

**Omaha Bridge Cases**
47 F. 15; 51 F. 309, 2 C.C.A. 174, 10 U.S. App. D.C. 98; 163 U.S. 564, 41 L. Ed. 265, 16 S. Ct. 1173; 163 U.S. 611, 41 L. Ed. 282, 16 S. Ct. 1207
57 Ill. App. 430; 164 Ill. 88, 45 N.E. 488

**Omaha Rate Case**
29 F.2d 750; 73 L. Ed. 1015, 49 S. Ct. 350; 280 U.S. 420, 74 L. Ed. 524, 50 S. Ct. 220

**Omaha Waterworks Case**
210 U.S. 432, 52 L. Ed. 1136, 28 S. Ct. 762; 218 U.S. 180, 54 L. Ed. 991, 30 S. Ct. 615

**One Hundred and Sixteenth Street Case**
77 Misc. 487, 136 N.Y.S. 720

**One Hundred and Ten Thousand Bushels of Wheat Case**
120 F. 432

**One-Man Grand Jury Cases**
340 Mich. 140, 65 N.W.2d 296; 348 U.S. 894, 99 L. Ed. 703, 75 S. Ct. 216; 349 U.S. 133, 99 L. Ed. 942, 75 S. Ct. 623
340 Mich. 151, 65 N.W.2d 301; 348 U.S. 894, 99 L. Ed. 703, 75 S. Ct. 216; 349 U.S. 133, 99 L. Ed. 942, 75 S. Ct. 623

**One Man One Vote Case**
369 U.S. 186, 7 L. Ed. 2d 663, 82 S. Ct. 691; 179 F. Supp. 824

**One Million Case**
50 How. Pr. 280; 11 Hun 195

**Open Fields Case**
80 L. Ed. 2d 214, 104 S. Ct. 1735

**Open Primary Election Case**
450 U.S. 107, 67 L. Ed. 2d 82, 101 S. Ct. 1010

**Optical Rebating Case**
97 F. Supp. 66

**Optometry Case**
249 Pa. 253, 94 A. 1091

**Oral Brokers-Contract**
215 S.W.2d 201 (Tex.); 147 Tex. 536, 218 S.W.2d 842

**Oral Surrender Trust Case**
138 N.J. Eq. 287, 48 A.2d 397; 140 N.J. Eq. 575, 53 A.2d 805

**Orange County Case**
119 F. 365

**Orange Crush Case**
297 F. 892, 327 Off. Gaz. Pat. Office 687

**Orange Routing Case**
9 I.C.C. 182; 123 F. 597; 132 F. 829; 137 F. 606; 200 U.S. 536, 50 L. Ed. 585, 26 S. Ct. 330

**Ordinance Emergency Clause Case**
196 Ore. 157, 248 P.2d 324

**Oregon Bottle Case**
15 Ore. App. 618, 517 P.2d 691

**Oregon Criminal Syndicalism Case**
299 U.S. 353, 81 L. Ed. 278, 57 S. Ct. 255

**Oregon Frozen Foods Case**
254 F.2d 116; 264 F.2d 599; 145 F. Supp. 157; 359 U.S. 958, 3 L. Ed. 2d 765, 79 S. Ct. 797; 361 U.S. 231, 4 L. Ed. 2d 267, 80 S. Ct. 365

**Oregon Initiative and Referendum Case**
53 Ore. 162, 99 P. 427; 223 U.S. 118, 56 L. Ed. 377, 32 S. Ct. 224

**Oregon Land Grant Case**
238 U.S. 393, 59 L. Ed. 1360, 35 S. Ct. 908; 243 U.S. 549, 61 L. Ed. 890, 37 S. Ct. 443

**Oregon Methodist Homes Case**
226 Ore. 298, 360 P.2d 293

**Oregon Minimum Wage Cases**
69 Ore. 519, 139 P. 743; 243 U.S. 629, 61 L. Ed. 937, 37 S. Ct. 475
70 Ore. 261, 141 P. 158; 243 U.S. 629, 61 L. Ed. 937, 37 S. Ct. 475

**Oregon Postmaster Case**
58 Ct. Cl. 199; 45 S. Ct. 350; 272 U.S. 52, 71 L. Ed. 160, 47 S. Ct. 21

**Oregon Rate Case**
189 F. 182; 230 U.S. 537, 57 L. Ed. 1610, 33 S. Ct. 1027

**Oregon School Case**
296 F. 928; 268 U.S. 510, 69 L. Ed. 1070, 45 S. Ct. 571

**Oregon Ten-Hour Day for Women Workers Case**
208 U.S. 412, 52 L. Ed. 551, 28 S. Ct. 324; 48 Ore. 252, 85 P. 855

**Orient Divisions Case**
288 F. 102; 265 U.S. 274, 68 L. Ed. 1016, 44 S. Ct. 565

**Original Package Case**
78 Iowa 286, 43 N.W. 188; 135 U.S. 100, 34 L. Ed. 128, 10 S. Ct. 681

**Oscar Wilde Case**
17 F. 591; 111 U.S. 53, 28 L. Ed. 349, 4 S. Ct. 279

**OSHA Case**
448 U.S. 607, 65 L. Ed. 2d 1010, 100 S. Ct. 2844

**OSHA Warrantless Inspection Case**
436 U.S. 307, 56 L. Ed. 2d 305, 98 S. Ct. 1816

**O'Sullivan Rubber Case**
269 F.2d 694; 362 U.S. 329, 4 L. Ed. 2d 768, 80 S. Ct. 759

**Ouachita Cotton Cast**
73 U.S. 521, 18 L. Ed. 935

**Ouija Board Cases**
280 F. 658; 259 U.S. 587, 66 L. Ed. 1077, 42 S. Ct. 590; 262 F. 680
48 Ariz. 61, 59 P.2d 312

**Out of State Bank Holding Company Case**
472 U.S. 159, 86 L. Ed. 2d 112, 105 S. Ct. 2545

**Out-of-State Sales Tax Credit Case**
472 U.S. 14, 86 L. Ed. 2d 11, 105 S. Ct. 2465

**Outer Continental Shelf Lands Bidding Case**
454 U.S. 151, 70 L. Ed. 2d 309, 102 S. Ct. 205

**Owl Drug Company Case**
21 F. Supp. 907

**Owosso Case**
166 F. 309, 92 C.C.A. 227; 214 U.S. 525, 53 L. Ed. 1067, 29 S. Ct. 703

**Oyster Bed Case**
198 N.Y. 287, 91 N.E. 846; 229 U.S. 82, 57 L. Ed. 1083, 33 S. Ct. 679

**Oyster Cases**
94 Ct. Cl. 397

**Oyster Inspection Case**
117 Md. 335, 82 A. 380; 232 U.S. 494, 58 L. Ed. 698, 34 S. Ct. 377

## P

**Pacific Coast Terminals Case**
231 F. 292; 242 U.S. 178, 61 L. Ed. 233, 37 S. Ct. 24

**Pacific Intermountain Express Case**
107 N.L.R.B. 837, No. 158; 225 F.2d 343

**Pacific National Case**
304 U.S. 191, 82 L. Ed. 1282, 58 S. Ct. 857; 91 F.2d 590; 302 U.S. 679, 82 L. Ed. 524, 58 S. Ct. 281

**Pacific Railroad Removal Cases**
16 F. 292; 115 U.S. 1, 29 L. Ed. 319, 5 S. Ct. 1113
31 Kan. 388, 2 P. 605; 115 U.S. 1, 29 L. Ed. 319, 5 S. Ct. 1113
59 Tex. 349, 115 U.S. 1, 29 L. Ed. 319, 5 S. Ct. 1113
62 Tex. 227, 115 U.S. 1, 29 L. Ed. 319, 5 S. Ct. 1113

**Pacific Railway Cases**
127 U.S. 1, 32 L. Ed. 150, 8 S. Ct. 1073
12 F. 641; 111 U.S. 505, 28 L. Ed. 498, 4 S. Ct. 583

**Packard Foremen's Case**
157 F.2d 80; 329 U.S. 707, 91 L. Ed. 615, 67 S. Ct. 357; 67 S. Ct. 490; 330 U.S. 485, 91 L. Ed. 1040, 67 S. Ct. 789

**Packard Motor Case**
330 U.S. 485, 91 L. Ed. 1040, 67 S. Ct. 789; 157 F.2d 80; 329 U.S. 707, 91 L. Ed. 615, 67 S. Ct. 357

**Packers Consent Decree Case**
286 U.S. 106, 76 L. Ed. 999, 52 S. Ct. 460; 276 U.S. 311, 72 L. Ed. 587, 48 S. Ct. 311; 52 S. Ct. 201; 158 F. Supp. 551; 189 F. Supp. 885

**Packing Company Cases**
9 F. 547; 105 U.S. 566, 26 L. Ed. 1172
142 F. 808; 207 U.S. 590, 52 L. Ed. 354, 28 S. Ct. 256
153 F. 1, 82 C.C.A. 135; 209 U.S. 56, 52 L. Ed. 681, 28 S. Ct. 428

**Paddy's Market Case**
167 Misc. 815, 4 N.Y.S.2d 837; 254 A.D. 672, 4 N.Y.S.2d 844; 254 A.D. 720, 4 N.Y.S.2d 997; 278 N.Y. 667, 16 N.E.2d 394

**Padlocked Door Support Case**
134 Conn. 354, 57 A.2d 622

**Pain-Killer Case**
2 R.I. 566

**Painesville Case**
42 F.2d 413

**Palace Car Cases**
76 N.Y. 402
120 N.Y. 117, 24 N.E. 319

**Palisades Park Cases**
99 N.J. Eq. 572, 134 A. 81; 101 N.J. Eq. 252, 137 A. 582; 276 U.S. 625, 72 L. Ed. 738, 48 S. Ct. 304
106 N.J. Eq. 55, 150 A. 52; 107 N.J. Eq. 197, 152 A. 6

**Palmetto Trade-Mark Case**
1893 C.D. 622, 65 Off. Gaz. Pat. Office 1221

**Palsgraf Case**
222 A.D. 166, 225 N.Y.S. 412; 248 N.Y. 339, 162 N.E. 99; 249 N.Y. 511, 164 N.E. 564

**Pan-American Case**
6 F.2d 43; 9 F.2d 761; 24 F.2d 206; 273 U.S. 456, 71 L. Ed. 734, 47 S. Ct. 416

**Panama Canal Pay Case**
117 Ct. Cl. 221

**Panama Tolls Case**
143 F. Supp. 539; 243 F.2d 844, 1957 A.M.C. 1102; 355 U.S. 810, 2 L. Ed. 2d 29, 78 S. Ct. 37; 356 U.S. 309, 2 L. Ed. 2d 788, 78 S. Ct. 752, 1958 A.M.C. 1005; 356 U.S. 916, 78 S. Ct. 698; 357 U.S. 923, 2 L. Ed. 2d 1369, 78 S. Ct. 1367; 1 L. Ed. 2d 903, 77 S. Ct. 854

**Panhandle Case**
147 Miss. 663, 112 So. 584; 277 U.S. 218, 72 L. Ed. 857, 48 S. Ct. 451

**Panhandle Eastern Pipe Line Rate Case**
230 F.2d 810; 352 U.S. 829, 1 L. Ed. 2d 48, 77 S. Ct. 34, 77 S. Ct. 37; 352 U.S. 919, 1 L. Ed. 2d 125, 77 S. Ct. 211

**Panhandle-Indiana Case**
224 Ind. 662, 71 N.E.2d 117; 332 U.S. 507, 92 L. Ed. 128, 68 S. Ct. 190

**Paper Bag Cases**
105 U.S. 766, 26 L. Ed. 959

142 F. 479; 150 F. 741; 205 U.S. 542, 51 L. Ed. 922, 27 S. Ct. 789; 210 U.S. 405, 52 L. Ed. 1122, 28 S. Ct. 748

**Paper Bag Patent Cases**
142 F.2d 479; 150 F. 741; 80 C.C.A. 407; 205 U.S. 542, 51 L. Ed. 922, 27 S. Ct. 789; 210 U.S. 405, 52 L. Ed. 1122, 28 S. Ct. 748

175 F. 101; 177 F. 1002, 100 C.C.A. 420

**Paper Collar Cases**
F. Cas. No. 14,395; 90 U.S. 530, 23 L. Ed. 128

**Paper Hangers' Case**
170 Md. 251, 183 A. 354

**Paper Roll Case**
40 F. 577; 152 U.S. 425, 38 L. Ed. 500, 14 S. Ct. 627, 1894 C.D. 238, 67 Off. Gaz. Pat. Office 271

**Papermakers Case**
116 N.L.R.B. 267, No. 37

**Par Clearance Case**
183 N.C. 546, 112 S.E. 252; 262 U.S. 649, 67 L. Ed. 1157, 43 S. Ct. 651; 261 U.S. 610, 67 L. Ed. 825, 43 S. Ct. 361

**Parade Ordinance Case**
207 Va. 665, 152 S.E.2d 259

**Paraffine Tank Car Case**
34 I.C.C. 179; 227 F. 911; 242 U.S. 208, 61 L. Ed. 251, 37 S. Ct. 95

**Parental Consent to Abortion Case**
443 U.S. 622, 61 L. Ed. 2d 797, 99 S. Ct. 3035

**Parental-Rights Indigent's Appeal Case**
519 U.S. 102, 136 L. Ed. 2d 473, 117 S. Ct. 555 (1996)

**Parental Rights Termination Case**
455 U.S. 745, 71 L. Ed. 2d 599, 102 S. Ct. 1388

**Pari-Mutuel Bettor Case**
28 Del. Ch. 161, 39 A.2d 212; 28 Del. Ch. 532, 45 A.2d 547

**Parish Will Case**
4 Bradf. 24; 1 Redf. 1; 42 Barb. 274, 16 Abb. Pr. 397; 25 N.Y. 9, 1 Redf. 130

**Park and Shop Case**
176 Kan. 240, 270 P.2d 270

**Park Cases**
51 Ill. 37
51 Ill. 58
80 Ill. 423
90 Ill. 558
96 Ill. 331
107 Ill. 372

**Park Commission Case**
107 N.J.L. 223, 152 A. 175; 108 N.J.L. 282, 156 A. 772

**Parked Auto Injury Case**
312 Ky. 536, 228 S.W.2d 432

**Parker Case**
294 Pa. 144, 143 A. 904

**Parker Dam Case**
295 U.S. 174, 79 L. Ed. 1371, 55 S. Ct. 666

**Parking Lot Injury Case**
363 Pa. 168, 69 A.2d 65

**Parochial School Bus Case**
164 Misc. 889, 300 N.Y.S. 1037; 253 A.D. 907, 3 N.Y.S.2d 394; 278 N.Y. 200, 15 N.E.2d 576; 278 N.Y. 712, 17 N.E.2d 134

**Parochial Schools Tax Deduction Case**
77 L. Ed. 2d 721, 103 S. Ct. 3062

**Parole Procedure Case**
442 U.S. 1, 60 L. Ed. 2d 668, 99 S. Ct. 2100

**Parole Revocation Hearing Case**
429 U.S. 78, 50 L. Ed. 2d 236, 97 S. Ct. 274

**Parrish Minimum Wage Case**
185 Wash. 581, 55 P.2d 1083; 57 S. Ct. 40; 300 U.S. 379, 81 L. Ed. 703, 57 S. Ct. 578

**Parrott's Chinese Case**
1 F. 481

**Parsee Merchants Case**
11 Abb. Pr. (n.s.) 209, 3 Daly 529

**Parsons Case**
81 Ala. 577, 2 So. 854

**Partnership Constructive Trust Case**
72 Ariz. 345, 236 P.2d 28

**Partnership Larceny Case**
63 Nev. 463, 175 P.2d 430

**Partnership Residence Case**
240 Iowa 547, 37 N.W.2d 16

**Party Delegates Case**
419 U.S. 477, 42 L. Ed. 2d 595, 95 S. Ct. 541

**Party Rate Cases**
2 I.C. 572, 2 I.C. 729; 3 I.C. 192; 43 F. 37; 145 U.S. 263, 36 L. Ed. 699, 12 S. Ct. 844, 4 I.C. 92
12 I.C.C. 95

**Party Will Case**
194 Md. 546, 71 A.2d 292; 197 Md. 331, 79 A.2d 382

**Passaic Bridge Case**
F. Cas. No. 9, 620; 70 U.S. 782, 16 L. Ed. 799

**Passaic-Paterson Gas Case**
84 N.J.L. 463, 87 A. 651; 87 N.J.L. 581, 92 A. 606, 94 A. 634, 95 A. 1079, 87 N.J.L. 705, 95 A. 127; 242 U.S. 666, 61 L. Ed. 552, 37 S. Ct. 243; 242 U.S. 667, 61 L. Ed. 552, 37 S. Ct. 243

**Passavant Case**
169 U.S. 16, 42 L. Ed. 644, 18 S. Ct. 219

**Passed Dividends Case**
91 F. Supp. 285; 189 F.2d 927; 342 U.S. 867, 96 L. Ed. 652, 72 S. Ct. 107

**Passenger Cases**
45 Mass.(4 Met.) 282; 48 U.S. 283, 12 L. Ed. 702

**Passenger Fare Case**
41 I.C.C. 13; 14 I.C.C. 503; 245 U.S. 493, 62 L. Ed. 425, 38 S. Ct. 170; 49 I.C.C. 713

**Passenger Position Case**
203 Md. 426, 101 A.2d 213

**Passport Cases**
357 U.S. 116, 2 L. Ed. 2d 1204, 78 S. Ct. 1113
378 U.S. 500, 12 L. Ed. 2d 992, 84 S. Ct. 1659
381 U.S. 1, 14 L. Ed. 2d 179, 85 S. Ct. 1271
383 U.S. 745, 16 L. Ed. 2d 239, 86 S. Ct. 1170

**Patdown-Search/Plain Feel Case**
508 U.S. 333, 124 L. Ed. 2d 306, 113 S. Ct. 2112 (1993)

**Patent Estoppel Cases**
317 U.S. 173, 87 L. Ed. 165, 63 S. Ct. 172; 316 U.S. 652, 86 L. Ed. 1733, 62 S. Ct. 946; 53 U.S.P.Q. (BNA) 685; 63 S. Ct. 151; 122 F.2d 124, 50 U.S.P.Q. (BNA) 405; 125 F.2d 322, 52 U.S.P.Q. (BNA) 117
326 U.S. 249, 90 L. Ed. 47, 66 S. Ct. 101; 326 U.S. 811, 90 L. Ed. 495, 66 S. Ct. 263, 105 Ct. Cl. 823; 147 F.2d 608, 64 U.S.P.Q. (BNA) 320; 54 F. Supp. 105, 60 U.S.P.Q. (BNA) 174; 67 U.S.P.Q. (BNA) 193
329 U.S. 394, 91 L. Ed. 374, 67 S. Ct. 416, 1948 C.D. 652, 72 U.S.P.Q. (BNA) 18; 323 U.S. 761, 89 L. Ed. 609, 65 S. Ct. 90, 63 U.S.P.Q. (BNA) 359; 327 U.S. 758, 90 L. Ed. 992, 66 S. Ct. 527, 68 U.S.P.Q. (BNA) 121; 328 U.S. 826, 90 L. Ed. 1605, 66 S. Ct. 981, 69 U.S.P.Q. (BNA) 631; 329 U.S. 402, 91 L. Ed. 380, 67 S. Ct. 421, 67 S. Ct. 424, 1948 C.D. 643, 72 U.S.P.Q. (BNA) 21; 330 U.S. 853, 91 L. Ed. 1296, 67 S. Ct. 768; 123 F.2d 518, 51 U.S.P.Q. (BNA) 492; 139 F.2d 291, 60 U.S.P.Q. (BNA) 54; 153 F.2d 149, 68 U.S.P.Q. (BNA) 102; 57 U.S.P.Q. (BNA) 58; 62 U.S.P.Q. (BNA) 365; 66 U.S.P.Q. (BNA) 335

329 U.S. 402, 91 L. Ed. 380, 67 S. Ct. 421, 67 S. Ct. 424,1948 C.D. 643, 72 U.S.P.Q. (BNA) 21; 327 U.S. 812, 90 L. Ed. 1037, 66 S. Ct. 801; 67 S. Ct. 619; 350 Pa. 333, 38 A.2d 244, 62 U.S.P.Q. (BNA) 170; 352 Pa. 443, 43 A.2d 332, 66 U.S.P.Q. (BNA) 335

333 U.S. 364, 92 L. Ed. 746, 68 S. Ct. 525; 333 U.S. 869, 92 L. Ed. 1147, 68 S. Ct. 788; 339 U.S. 960, 94 L. Ed. 1370, 70 S. Ct. 996; 340 U.S. 76, 95 L. Ed. 89, 71 S. Ct. 160, '51 C.D. 580, 87 U.S.P.Q. (BNA) 276; 67 S. Ct. 371, 71 U.S.P.Q. (BNA) 329; 53 F. Supp. 889, 59 U.S.P.Q. (BNA) 318; 67 F. Supp. 397, 70 U.S.P.Q. (BNA) 48; 124 F. Supp. 573, 103 U.S.P.Q. (BNA) 343; 134 F. Supp. 69, 106 U.S.P.Q. (BNA) 216; 85 U.S.P.Q. (BNA) 37

**Patentability of Microorganism Case**

447 U.S. 303, 65 L. Ed. 2d 144, 100 S. Ct. 2204

**Paternity Limitations Case**

456 U.S. 91, 71 L. Ed. 2d 770, 102 S. Ct. 1549

**Paternity Presumption Case**

105 L. Ed. 2d 91, 109 S. Ct. 2333

**Paterson Strike Case**

63 N.J. Eq. 443, 52 A. 152; 64 N.J. Eq. 371, 51 A. 774; 191 U.S. 558, 48 L. Ed. 302, 24 S. Ct. 844

**Patrick Case**

182 N.Y. 131, 74 N.E. 843; 183 N.Y. 52, 75 N.E. 963; 183 N.Y. 537, 76 N.E. 1102; 203 U.S. 602, 51 L. Ed. 335, 27 S. Ct. 783

**Pattern Monopoly Case**

254 F. 493; 251 F. 559, 163 C.C.A. 553; 259 F. 793, 170 C.C.A. 593; 250 U.S. 658, 63 L. Ed. 1193, 40 S. Ct. 54; 258 U.S. 346, 66 L. Ed. 653, 42 S. Ct. 360

**Pawloski Case**

274 U.S. 352, 71 L. Ed. 1091, 47 S. Ct. 632

**Pawnee County Case**

12 Kan. 426

**Payme Case**

126 N.J.L. 39, 17 A.2d 167

**Pea Patch Island Case**

F. Cas. No. 18,311

**Peddler Cases**

103 Mo. 941, 15 S.W. 81, 3 I.C. 527; 156 U.S. 296, 39 L. Ed. 430, 15 S. Ct. 367, 5 I.C. 68

68 Tenn. (9 Baxt.) 518; 100 U.S. 676, 25 L. Ed. 754

**Peeping Tom Case**

254 Ala. 482, 48 So. 2d 794

**Peerless Plywood Case**

107 N.L.R.B. 427, No. 106

**Peg O' My Heart Case**

254 F. 737; 258 F. 557; 250 U.S. 638, 63 L. Ed. 1183, 39 S. Ct. 494, 40 S. Ct. 484; 252 U.S. 317, 64 L. Ed. 590, 40 S. Ct. 335

**Pelton Dam Case**

349 U.S. 435, 99 L. Ed. 1215, 75 S. Ct. 832; 211 F.2d 347; 348 U.S. 868, 99 L. Ed. 683, 75 S. Ct. 112

**Pen Register Surveillance Case**

434 U.S. 159, 54 L. Ed. 2d 376, 98 S. Ct. 364

**Penn-Olin Case**

378 U.S. 158, 12 L. Ed. 2d 775, 84 S. Ct. 1710; 375 U.S. 938, 11 L. Ed. 2d 270, 84 S. Ct. 350; 217 F. Supp. 110

**Penniman's Case**

11 R.I. 333; 103 U.S. 714, 26 L. Ed. 602

**Pennington Case**

141 Cal. App. 2d 107, 296 P.2d 351

**Pennington County Bank Cases**

81 Neb. 782, 116 N.W. 669

85 Neb. 226, 122 N.W. 848

87 Neb. 25, 126 N.W. 654

**Pennington Mine Workers Case**

325 F.2d 804; 377 U.S. 929, 12 L. Ed. 2d 294, 84 S. Ct. 1333; 379 U.S. 941, 13 L. Ed. 2d 541, 85 S. Ct. 435

**Pennoyer Case**
F. Cas. No. 10,083; 95 U.S. 714, 24 L. Ed. 565

**Pennsylvania Abortion Cases**
439 U.S. 379, 58 L. Ed. 2d 596, 99 S. Ct. 675, 120 L. Ed. 2d 674, 112 S. Ct. 2791
505 U.S. 833, 120 L. Ed. 2d 674, 112 S. Ct. 2791 (1992)

**Pennsylvania Alien Registration Case**
30 F. Supp. 470; 60 S. Ct. 718; 312 U.S. 52, 85 L. Ed. 581, 60 S. Ct. 399

**Pennsylvania Case (Admiralty Law)**
86 U.S. 125, 22 L. Ed. 148

**Pennsylvania Coal Tax Case**
274 Pa. 448, 118 A. 394; 260 U.S. 245, 67 L. Ed. 237, 43 S. Ct. 83

**Pennsylvania College Cases**
80 U.S. 190, 20 L. Ed. 550
63 Pa. 428

**Pennsylvania Eight Hour Law Case**
43 Pa. Super. 494; 231 Pa. 170, 80 A. 78

**Pennsylvania Insurrection Cases**
2 U.S. 335, 1 L. Ed. 404, F. Cas. No. 15,443
2 U.S. 343, 1 L. Ed. 408
2 U.S. 345, 1 L. Ed. 409
2 U.S. 346, 1 L. Ed. 409
2 U.S. 348, 1 L. Ed. 410
3 U.S. 513, 1 L. Ed. 700, F. Cas. No. 15,442
3 U.S. 515, 1 L. Ed. 701, F. Cas. No. 5,126
F. Cas. No. 5,127

**Pennsylvania Refining Cases**
1 I.C. 717, 1 I.C. 792, 1 I.C. 795, 1 I.C. 811; 2 I.C. 298; 2 I.C. 496; 3 IC 162; 6 I.C.C. 455
2 I.C. 294; 4 I.C. 162; 6 I.C.C. 378; 82 F. 192; 137 F. 343, 70 C.C.A. 23; 208 U.S. 208, 52 L. Ed. 456, 28 S. Ct. 268
2 I.C. 296; 4 I.C. 162; 6 I.C.C. 378; 82 F. 192; 137 F. 343, 70 C.C.A. 23; 208 U.S. 208, 52 L. Ed. 456, 28 S. Ct. 268
2 I.C. 317, 2 I.C. 450, 2 I.C. 451; 4 I.C. 162; 4 I.C. 369, 6 I.C.C. 52; 6 I.C.C. 449; 82 F. 192

**Pension Offset Provision Case**
451 U.S. 504, 68 L. Ed. 2d 402, 101 S. Ct. 1895

**Pentagon Papers Case**
403 U.S. 713, 29 L. Ed. 2d 822, 91 S. Ct. 2140
409 U.S. 1219, 33 L. Ed. 2d 30, 93 S. Ct. 21
446 F.2d 1327
328 F. Supp. 324

**Pentagon Passenger Fares Case**
256 I.C.C. 769; 258 I.C.C. 559; 270 I.C.C. 651; 280 I.C.C. 37; 291 I.C.C. 711

**Peonage Cases**
123 F. 671
136 F. 707
50 F. Supp. 607; 320 U.S. 527, 88 L. Ed. 287, 64 S. Ct. 318

**Pep Boys Case**
247 F. Supp. 221
5 Cal. 2d 784, 55 P.2d 194, 55 P.2d 1186; 5 Cal. 2d 446, 55 P.2d 177; 56 S. Ct. 961; 56 S. Ct. 962; 299 U.S. 198, 81 L. Ed. 122, 57 S. Ct. 147

**Pepco Case**
276 F. 327, 51 App. D.C. 77; 260 U.S. 710, 67 L. Ed. 475, 43 S. Ct. 166; 261 U.S. 428, 67 L. Ed. 731, 43 S. Ct. 445

**Pepto-Bismol Case**
167 F. Supp. 427; 271 F.2d 569, 123 U.S.P.Q. (BNA) 372; 362 U.S. 919, 4 L. Ed. 2d 739, 80 S. Ct. 671

**Peralta Case**
60 U.S. 343, 15 L. Ed. 678

**Percentage Depletion Allowance Case**
451 U.S. 571, 68 L. Ed. 2d 454, 101 S. Ct. 1931

**Performance after Death Case**
31 Cal. 2d 395, 189 P.2d 5

**Periodic Reports Insurance Case**
175 F.2d 540; 175 F.2d 544

**Perjured Testimony Damages Case**
460 U.S. 325, 75 L. Ed. 2d 96, 103 S. Ct. 1108

**Perlman Patent Case**
231 F. 453; 231 F. 734, 146 C.C.A. 18; 247 U.S. 7, 62 L. Ed. 950, 38 S. Ct. 417

**Permanent Disability Proof Case**
201 S.W.2d 234 (Tex.); 146 Tex. 169, 705 S.W.2d 43

**Permian Basin Area Rate Cases**
390 U.S. 747, 20 L. Ed. 2d 312, 88 S. Ct. 1344

**Perpetual Franchise Case**
172 F. 494; 179 F. 455, 102 C.C.A. 601; 230 U.S. 123, 57 L. Ed. 1419, 33 S. Ct. 974; 216 F. 848; 255 F. 801; 250 U.S. 640, 63 L. Ed. 1184, 39 S. Ct. 491

**Personal Products Case**
108 N.L.R.B. 743, No. 109, 227 F.2d 409; 350 U.S. 1004, 100 L. Ed. 867, 76 S. Ct. 650; 352 U.S. 864, 1 L. Ed. 2d 73, 77 S. Ct. 90

**Pest House Cases**
97 Kan. 239, 155 P. 12
103 Ky. 228, 20 Ky. Law Rep. 87, 44 S.W. 667
111 Ky. 361, 23 Ky. Law Rep. 701, 63 S.W. 981

**Pesticide Cases**
428 F.2d 1083
428 F.2d 1093
439 F.2d 584
439 F.2d 598
465 F.2d 528

**Petition Signers' Withdrawal Case**
169 Kan. 653, 219 P.2d 1071

**Petkos Case**
212 F. 275; 214 F. 978, 131 C.C.A. 274

**Peyton Packing Company Case**
49 N.L.R.B. 828,No. 119

**Pfanschmidt Murder Case**
262 Ill. 411, 104 N.E. 804
265 Ill. 180, 106 N.E. 785

**Pfleuger Case**
304 N.Y. 148, 106 N.E.2d 495; 278 A.D. 247, 105 N.Y.S.2d 427; 278 A.D. 1022, 105 N.Y.S.2d 988

**Pharmacy Agreement Case**
440 U.S. 205, 59 L. Ed. 2d 261, 99 S. Ct. 1067

**Phelps Dodge Case**
126 N.L.R.B. 1367, No. 168; 289 F.2d 591

**Philadelphia Cream Cheese Case**
176 A.D. 735, 164 N.Y.S. 71

**Philadelphia National Bank Case**
201 F. Supp. 348; 374 U.S. 321, 10 L. Ed. 2d 915, 83 S. Ct. 1715; 369 U.S. 883, 8 L. Ed. 2d 285, 82 S. Ct. 1156; 370 U.S. 931, 82 S. Ct. 1581

**Philadelphia Parkway Cases**
250 Pa. 257, 95 A. 429
295 Pa. 538, 145 A. 600

**Phileo Case**
257 F.2d 656; 293 F.2d 864, 110 App. D.C. 387; 358 U.S. 876, 79 S. Ct. 120; 358 U.S. 946, 3 L. Ed. 2d 352, 79 S. Ct. 350

**Philippine Island Cases**
183 U.S. 176, 46 L. Ed. 138, 22 S. Ct. 59
195 U.S. 138, 49 L. Ed. 128, 24 S. Ct. 808

**Phillies Case**
1 F. Supp. 283, 14 U.S.P.Q. (BNA) 132

**Phillips Brothers Coal Company Case**
325 F.2d 804; 379 U.S. 941, 13 L. Ed. 2d 541, 85 S. Ct. 435

**Phillips Case**
347 U.S. 672, 98 L. Ed. 1035, 74 S. Ct. 794; 205 F.2d 706; 346 U.S. 934, 98 L. Ed. 424, 74 S. Ct. 374, 348 U.S. 851, 99 L. Ed. 670, 75 S. Ct. 17, 75 S. Ct. 18

**Phoenix Homestead Case**
169 So. 825 (La.)

**Phonograph Price Restriction Case**
225 F. 785; 246 U.S. 8, 62 L. Ed. 551, 38 S. Ct. 257

**Photocopier Parts-and-Service Antitrust Case**
504 U.S. 451, 119 L. Ed. 2d 265, 112 S. Ct. 2072 (1992)
305 F. Supp. 60

**Photograph Authentication Case**
150 Neb. 771, 86 N.W.2d 109

**Photographer Case**
205 N.C. 34, 169 S.E. 825

**Physician-Assisted Suicide Cases**
521 U.S. 702, 138 L. Ed. 2d 772, 117 S. Ct. 2258 (1997)
521 U.S. 793, 138 L. Ed. 2d 834, 117 S. Ct. 2293 (1997)

**Pianola Roll Case**
139 F. 427; 147 F. 226, 77 C.C.A. 368; 209 U.S. 1, 52 L. Ed. 655, 28 S. Ct. 319

**Picketing Cases**
310 U.S. 106, 84 L. Ed. 1104, 60 S. Ct. 746; 310 U.S. 657, 84 L. Ed. 1420, 60 S. Ct. 1072; 60 S. Ct. 582
238 F. 728, 151 C.C.A. 578; 245 U.S. 670, 62 L. Ed. 539, 38 S. Ct. 190; 257 U.S. 184, 66 L. Ed. 189, 42 S. Ct. 72
28 Ala. 527, 189 So. 913; 238 Ala. 162, 189 So. 914; 308 U.S. 547, 84 L. Ed. 460, 60 S. Ct. 296; 310 U.S. 88, 84 L. Ed. 1093, 60 S. Ct. 736
20 Ariz. 7, 176 P. 570; 257 U.S. 312, 66 L. Ed. 254, 42 S. Ct. 124

**Picture Frame Case**
154 Ala. 83, 46 So. 9; 218 U.S. 124, 54 L. Ed. 965, 30 S. Ct. 649

**Piedmont Case**
6 I.C.C. 588; 105 F. 703

**Pierce Case**
245 F. 878; 245 F. 888; 247 U.S. 523, 62 L. Ed. 1247, 38 S. Ct. 428; 252 U.S. 239, 64 L. Ed. 542, 40 S. Ct. 205

**Piggy-Back Case**
350 U.S. 155, 100 L. Ed. 166, 76 S. Ct. 227; 331 Mass. 720, 122 N.E.2d 759; 348 U.S. 969, 99 L. Ed. 755, 75 S. Ct. 533; 350 U.S. 977, 100 L. Ed. 847, 76 S. Ct. 429

**Pike County Case**
268 Mo. 321, 188 S.W. 88

**Pilot Case (Port Fees)**
53 U.S. 299, 13 L. Ed. 996

**Pilot Case (Vessel Forfeiture)**
43 F.2d 491

**Pilot Duel Case**
240 Wis. 161, 1 N.W.2d 887, 2 N.W.2d 871; 243 Wis. 172, 9 N.W.2d 593

**Pilotage Case**
69 Ga. 409; 118 U.S. 90, 30 L. Ed. 115, 6 S. Ct. 988

**Pinch Bottle Case**
118 U.S.P.Q. (BNA) 229

**Pine River Case**
237 Mich. 38, 211 N.W. 115

**Pink Case**
315 U.S. 203, 86 L. Ed. 796, 62 S. Ct. 552; 313 U.S. 553, 85 L. Ed. 1516, 61 S. Ct. 960; 284 N.Y. 555, 32 N.E.2d 552; 259 App Div 871, 20 N.Y.S.2d 665; 259 A.D. 886, 20 N.Y.S.2d 983

**Pioneer Case**
130 F. Supp. 945; 234 F.2d 161, 1956 A.M.C. 1639

**Pipe Case**
230 N.Y. 239, 129 N.E. 889; 230 N.Y. 656, 130 N.E. 932; 187 A.D. 100, 175 N.Y.S. 281

**Pipe Line Cases**
24 I.C.C. 1; 204 F. 798; 234 U.S. 548, 58 L. Ed. 1459, 34 S. Ct. 956
176 Cal. 499, 169 P. 59; 251 U.S. 228, 64 L. Ed. 239, 40 S. Ct. 131

**Piracy Cases**
43 U.S. 210, 11 L. Ed. 239; 25 F. 408
F. Cas. No. 9,080; 24 U.S. 1, 6 L. Ed. 405
F. Cas. No. 14,782, 18 U.S. 153, 5 L. Ed. 57

**Pirate Ship Case**
21 F.2d 231; 32 F.2d 605; 42 F.2d 439

**Pirates Case**
18 U.S. 184, 5 L. Ed. 64

**Pittsburgh Steamship Company Case**
69 N.L.R.B. 1395; 167 F.2d 126; 335 U.S. 857, 93 L. Ed. 404, 69 S. Ct. 130; 337 U.S. 656, 93 L. Ed. 1602, 69 S. Ct. 1283, 1949 A.M.C. 1319; 180 F.2d 731; 339 U.S. 951, 94 L. Ed. 1364, 70 S. Ct. 842; 340 U.S. 498, 95 L. Ed. 479, 71 S. Ct. 453, 1951 A.M.C. 407

**Plain Error Case**
456 U.S. 152, 71 L. Ed. 2d 816, 102 S. Ct. 1584

**Plain View Doctrine Case**
460 U.S. 730, 75 L. Ed. 2d 502, 103 S. Ct. 1535

**Plane View Cases**
476 U.S. 207, 90 L. Ed. 2d 210, 106 S. Ct. 1809; 476 U.S. 227, 90 L. Ed. 2d 226, 106 S. Ct. 1819

**Planer Blade Case**
50 U.S. 109, 13 L. Ed. 66

**Planing Machine Case**
56 U.S. 212, 14 L. Ed. 665

**Plank Road Case**
36 Ala. 410

**Plastic Milk Container Case**
449 U.S. 456, 66 L. Ed. 2d 659, 101 S. Ct. 715

**Platform Gate Case**
132 U.S. 84, 33 L. Ed. 272, 10 S. Ct. 24

**Plauche Electric Company Case**
135 N.L.R.B. 250, No. 41

**Plea Bargain Case**
471 U.S. 453, 85 L. Ed. 2d 462, 105 S. Ct. 2103

**Plessy Case**
163 U.S. 537, 41 L. Ed. 256, 16 S. Ct. 1138; 45 La. Ann. 80, 11 So. 948

**Plochman Case**
140 N.L.R.B. 130, No. 11

**Plumbing Fixture Cases**
295 F. Supp. 33; 298 F. Supp. 483; 298 F. Supp. 484; 302 F. Supp. 795

**Plumbing Materials Case**
187 Md. 610, 51 A.2d 76; 191 Md. 495, 62 A.2d 304, 62 A.2d 582

**Pocahontas Case**
93 F. Supp. 217

**Pocatello Water Company Case**
27 Idaho 603, 150 P. 47

**Pocket Lien Case**
240 U.S. 430, 60 L. Ed. 726, 36 S. Ct. 386

**Pocket Veto Cases**
66 Ct. Cl. 26; 278 U.S. 597, 73 L. Ed. 527, 49 S. Ct. 186; 279 U.S. 655, 73 L. Ed. 894, 49 S. Ct. 463
302 U.S. 583, 82 L. Ed. 439, 58 S. Ct. 395, 84 Ct. Cl. 630; 301 U.S. 681, 81 L. Ed. 1339, 57 S. Ct. 939, 86 Ct. Cl. 765

**Poconoket Case**
61 F. 106; 67 F. 262; 70 F. 640, 17 C.C.A. 309; 168 U.S. 707, 42 L. Ed. 1214, 18 S. Ct. 939

**Poison Bran Case**
133 Neb. 449, 275 N.W. 674; 135 Neb. 232, 280 N.W. 890

**Poisoned Vehicle Cases**
26 M.C.C. 615; 44 M.C.C. 15; 49 M.C.C. 693; 52 M.C.C. 576
47 M.C.C. 597; 52 M.C.C. 511

**Poletown Case**
410 Mich. 616, 304 N.W.2d 455

**Police Board Case**
41 La. Ann. 156, 6 So. 592

**Police Force Citizenship Requirement Case**
55 L. Ed. 2d 287, 98 S. Ct. 1067

**Police Interrogation Case**
417 U.S. 433, 41 L. Ed. 2d 182, 94 S. Ct. 2357

**Police Jurisdiction Statute Case**
439 U.S. 60, 58 L. Ed. 2d 292, 99 S. Ct. 383

**Police Officers Excessive Force Case**
490 U.S. 386, 104 L. Ed. 2d 443, 109 S. Ct. 1865

**Police Pension Case**
131 Md. 315, 101 A. 786

**Policeman's Hair Regulation Case**
425 U.S. 238, 47 L. Ed. 2d 708, 96 S. Ct. 1440

**Political Beliefs Discharge Case**
445 U.S. 507, 63 L. Ed. 2d 574, 100 S. Ct. 1287

**Political Contributions Case**
424 U.S. 1, 46 L. Ed. 2d 659, 96 S. Ct. 612

**Political Patronage Case**
111 L. Ed. 2d 52, 110 S. Ct. 2729

**Political Removal Cases**
F. Cas. No. 3,554; 173 F. 227

**Pollock Case**
157 U.S. 429, 39 L. Ed. 759, 15 S. Ct. 673; 158 U.S. 601, 39 L. Ed. 1108, 15 S. Ct. 912

**Polluted Well Case**
259 S.W.2d 466 (Ky.)

**Pollution—Class Action Case**
414 U.S. 291, 38 L. Ed. 2d 511, 94 S. Ct. 505

**Polo Grounds Case**
26 A.D.2d 372, 274 N.Y.S.2d 805; 20 N.Y.2d 618, 286 N.Y.S.2d 16, 233 N.E.2d 113

**Polymeris Case**
49 F.2d 730; 284 U.S. 601, 76 L. Ed. 516, 52 S. Ct. 13; 284 U.S. 279, 76 L. Ed. 291, 52 S. Ct. 143

**Ponzi Cases**
265 U.S. 1, 68 L. Ed. 873, 44 S. Ct. 424
15 F.2d 113

**Pornography Entrapment Case**
118 L. Ed. 2d 174, 112 S. Ct. 1535

**Port Acres Case**
163 Tex. 417, 357 S.W.2d 364

**Portal to Portal Pay Cases**
321 U.S. 590, 88 L. Ed. 2d 949, 64 S. Ct. 688
169 F.2d 254; 335 U.S. 887, 93 L. Ed. 425, 69 S. Ct. 236
60 F. Supp. 146; 149 F.2d 461; 326 U.S. 706, 90 L. Ed. 416, 66 S. Ct. 91; 328 U.S. 680, 90 L. Ed. 1515, 66 S. Ct. 1187; 329 U.S. 822, 91 L. Ed. 699, 67 S. Ct. 25; 69 F. Supp. 710; 162 F.2d 200; 331 U.S. 784, 91 L. Ed. 1815, 67 S. Ct. 1191
3 F.R.D. 251; 53 F. Supp. 935; 145 F.2d 10; 322 U.S. 756, 88 L. Ed. 1585, 64 S. Ct. 1267; 323 U.S. 707, 89 L. Ed. 570, 65 S. Ct. 434; 325 U.S. 161, 89 L. Ed. 1534, 65 S. Ct. 1063; 325 U.S. 897, 89 L. Ed. 2007, 65 S. Ct. 1550
71 F. Supp. 870; 166 F.2d 317
162 F.2d 774; 166 F.2d 144; 176 F.2d 984

**Portland Fourth Section Case**
22 I.C.C. 366; 24 I.C.C. 34

**Portland Gateway Case**
16 I.C.C. 300; 216 U.S. 538, 54 L. Ed. 608, 30 S. Ct. 417

**Porto Rican Cases**
182 U.S. 1, 45 L. Ed. 1041, 21 S. Ct. 743
182 U.S. 222, 45 L. Ed. 1074, 21 S. Ct. 762

182 U.S. 243, 45 L. Ed. 1086, 21 S. Ct. 827, 36 Ct. Cl. 583
182 U.S. 244, 45 L. Ed. 1088, 21 S. Ct. 770
183 U.S. 151, 46 L. Ed. 128, 22 S. Ct. 62
103 F. 72; 182 U.S. 221, 45 L. Ed. 1065, 21 S. Ct. 742
105 F. 74; 182 U.S. 392, 45 L. Ed. 1146, 21 S. Ct. 827; 109 F. 1058
105 F. 608; 182 U.S. 221, 45 L. Ed. 1065, 21 S. Ct. 742

**Porto Rico Tax Case**
16 F.2d 545; 274 U.S. 732, 71 L. Ed. 1327, 47 S. Ct. 659; 275 U.S. 56, 72 L. Ed. 152, 48 S. Ct. 23

**Possession of Firearm Sentencing Case**
477 U.S. 79, 91 L. Ed. 2d 67, 106 S. Ct. 2411

**Post-Miranda Silence as Evidence of Sanity Case**
474 U.S. 284, 88 L. Ed. 2d 623, 106 S. Ct. 634

**Postmaster Case**
58 Ct. Cl. 199; 45 S. Ct. 350; 272 U.S. 52, 71 L. Ed. 160, 47 S. Ct. 21

**Pot of Gold Case**
146 La. 735, 84 So. 37

**Pot O'Gold Case**
5 T.C. 1333

**Potomac Flats Case**
174 U.S. 196, 43 L. Ed. 946, 19 S. Ct. 649

**Poultry Case**
295 U.S. 495, 79 L. Ed. 1570, 55 S. Ct. 837; 295 U.S. 723, 79 L. Ed. 1676, 55 S. Ct. 651

**Powder Cases**
188 F. 127; 273 F. 869
196 F. 514; 223 F. 881, 139 C.C.A. 319; 248 U.S. 55, 63 L. Ed. 123, 39 S. Ct. 38
183 N.Y. 306, 76 N.E. 153

**Powdered Milk Company Case**
215 F. 922; 222 F. 911, 138 C.C.A. 391; 2 F.2d 107; 7 F.2d 297

**Powell Case**
48 F. Supp. 550; 49 F. Supp. 828

**Prairie State Bank Case**
27 Ct. Cl. 185; 164 U.S. 227, 41 L. Ed. 412, 17 S. Ct. 142

**Pre-Code Food Case**
117 Conn. 128, 167 A. 99
135 Conn. 243, 63 A.2d 158

**Precooling Case**
19 I.C.C. 148; 20 I.C.C. 106; 22 I.C.C. 149; 23 I.C.C. 267; 204 F. 647; 232 U.S. 199, 58 L. Ed. 568, 34 S. Ct. 291

**Pregnancy Benefits Case**
429 U.S. 125, 50 L. Ed. 2d 343, 97 S. Ct. 401

**Pregnancy Disability Case**
479 U.S. 272, 93 L. Ed. 2d 613, 107 S. Ct. 683

**Pregnancy Leave of Absence Case**
434 U.S. 136, 54 L. Ed. 2d 356, 98 S. Ct. 347

**Pregnant Teachers Case**
414 U.S. 632, 39 L. Ed. 2d 52, 94 S. Ct. 791

**Prenatal Injury Cases**
82 Ohio App. 445, 82 N.E.2d 423; 152 Ohio St. 114, 87 N.E.2d 334
184 N.Y.S. 337; 194 A.D. 696, 186 N.Y.S. 278; 232 N.Y. 220, 133 N.E. 567; 195 A.D. 942, 186 N.Y.S. 938

**Preparedness Day Blast Case**
175 Cal. 666, 166 P. 999; 176 Cal. 105, 167 P. 696; 177 Cal. 642, 171 P. 690; 178 Cal. 525, 174 P. 325; 248 U.S. 579, 63 L. Ed. 430, 39 S. Ct. 21

**Prerogative Right of Preference Case**
186 Misc. 438, 54 N.Y.S.2d 330; 269 A.D. 973, 59 N.Y.S.2d 286; 269 A.D. 1024, 59 N.Y.S.2d 623; 295 N.Y. 510, 68 N.E.2d 514; 296 N.Y. 668, 69 N.E.2d 822; 74 N.Y.S.2d 38

**Prescott Case**
44 U.S. 578, 11 L. Ed. 734

**Prescription Drug Advertising Case**
425 U.S. 748, 48 L. Ed. 2d 346, 96 S. Ct. 1817

**President Garfield Assassination Case**
10 F. 161

**President Judges Determination Case**
420 Pa. 243, 216 A.2d 326

**Presidential Campaign Contribution Case**
470 U.S. 480, 84 L. Ed. 2d 455, 105 S. Ct. 1459

**Presidential Civil Liability Case**
520 U.S. 681, 137 L. Ed. 2d 945, 117 S. Ct. 1636 (1997)

**Presidential Immunity Case**
457 U.S. 2d 596, 73 L. Ed. 2d 248, 102 S. Ct. 613

**Presidential Pardoning Power Case**
419 U.S. 256, 42 L. Ed. 2d 430, 95 S. Ct. 379

**Presidential Removal Case**
58 Ct. Cl. 199; 45 S. Ct. 350; 272 U.S. 52, 71 L. Ed. 160, 47 S. Ct. 21

**Presidential Tapes Case**
418 U.S. 683, 41 L. Ed. 2d 1039, 94 S. Ct. 3090
55 L. Ed. 2d 570, 98 S. Ct. 1306

**Press Photographs Case**
386 Pa. 251, 126 A.2d 679; 352 U.S. 1002, 1 L. Ed. 2d 547, 77 S. Ct. 559

**Prest-O-Lite Case**
209 F. 917

**Pretermission Case**
395 Ill. 217, 69 N.E.2d 862

**Pretrial Assistance of Counsel Case**
474 U.S. 159, 88 L. Ed. 2d 481, 106 S. Ct. 477

**Pretrial Detention Case**
481 U.S. 739, 95 L. Ed. 2d 697, 107 S. Ct. 2095

**Pretrial Discovery Dissemination Case**
81 L. Ed. 2d 17, 104 S. Ct. 2199

**Prettyman Case**
93 S.C. 13, 75 S.E. 1012; 97 S.C. 247, 81 S.E. 484

**Pricecutter Termination Antitrust Case**
485 U.S. 717, 99 L. Ed. 2d 808, 108 S. Ct. 1515

**Pride Tobacco Case**
82 N.Y. 519

**Pridgeon Case**
57 F. 200; 153 U.S. 48, 38 L. Ed. 631, 14 S. Ct. 746

**Prima Facie Racial Discrimination Case**
460 U.S. 711, 75 L. Ed. 2d 403, 103 S. Ct. 1478

**Primary Election Cases**
414 U.S. 51, 38 L. Ed. 2d 260, 94 S. Ct. 303
80 Miss. 617, 32 So. 286

**Primary Election Law Cases**
221 Ill. 9, 77 N.E. 321
228 Ill. 522, 81 N.E. 1109
240 Ill. 279, 88 N.E. 821

**Princeton Bank Case**
175 F. 769, 99 C.C.A. 345; 189 F. 432; 193 F. 24, 226 U.S. 110, 57 L. Ed. 145, 33 S. Ct. 78

**Prison Cell Privacy Case**
468 U.S. 517, 82 L. Ed. 2d 393, 104 S. Ct. 3194

**Prison Law Libraries Case**
430 U.S. 817, 52 L. Ed. 2d 72, 97 S. Ct. 1491

**Prison Riot Shooting Case**
475 U.S. 312, 89 L. Ed. 2d 251, 106 S. Ct. 1078

**Prison Visitation Cases**
417 U.S. 817, 41 L. Ed. 2d 495, 94 S. Ct. 2800, 94 S. Ct. 2827
417 U.S. 843, 41 L. Ed. 2d 514, 94 S. Ct. 2811

**Prisoner Disciplinary Proceeding Case**
418 U.S. 539, 41 L. Ed. 2d 935, 94 S. Ct. 2963

**Prisoner Injury Case**
174 F.2d 154

**Prisoners' Rights Case**
425 U.S. 308, 47 L. Ed. 2d 810, 96 S. Ct. 1551

**Private Crossing Case**
319 Mass. 470, 66 N.E.2d 561

**Private Figure Libel Case**
475 U.S. 767, 89 L. Ed. 2d 783, 106 S. Ct. 1558

**Private Individual Libel Case**
418 U.S. 323, 41 L. Ed. 2d 789, 94 S. Ct. 2997

**Private School Race Discrimination Case**
427 U.S. 160, 49 L. Ed. 2d 415, 96 S. Ct. 2586

**Prize Cases**
67 U.S. 635, 17 L. Ed. 459
70 U.S. 514, 18 L. Ed. 200
F. Cas. No. 341; 67 U.S. 635, 17 L. Ed. 459
F. Cas. No. 342; 67 U.S. 635, 17 L. Ed. 459
F. Cas. No. 343; 67 U.S. 635, 17 L. Ed. 459
F. Cas. No. 344
F. Cas. No. 4,937
F. Cas. No. 5,961
F. Cas. No. 6,450; F. Cas. No. 6,451; F. Cas. No. 6,452; 67 U.S. 635, 17 L. Ed. 459
F. Cas. No. 8,637a; F. Cas. No. 8,639
F. Cas. No. 8,638
F. Cas. No. 10,316a; F. Cas. No. 10,317
F. Cas. No. 12,259; F. Cas. No. 12,260; F. Cas. No. 12,261; 70 U.S. 451, 18 L. Ed. 197
F. Cas. No. 13,361
F. Cas. No. 13,362
F. Cas. No. 13,363; F. Cas. No. 13,364; F. Cas. No. 13,685; 70 U.S. 559, 18 L. Ed. 220
F. Cas. No. 17,873
23 N.Y. 192; 67 U.S. 635, 17 L. Ed. 456, 17 L. Ed. 459

**Prize Fight Film Case**
239 U.S. 325, 60 L. Ed. 308, 36 S. Ct. 131

**Processing Tax Cases**
297 U.S. 110, 80 L. Ed. 513, 56 S. Ct. 374
301 U.S. 308, 81 L. Ed. 1122, 57 S. Ct. 764
301 U.S. 337, 81 L. Ed. 1143, 57 S. Ct. 816; 302 U.S. 772, 82 L. Ed. 599, 58 S. Ct. 3
78 F.2d 1; 297 U.S. 1, 80 L. Ed. 477, 56 S. Ct. 312

**Professional Journal Advertising Taxation Case**
475 U.S. 834, 89 L. Ed. 2d 841, 106 S. Ct. 1591

**Profits in Minerals Case**
202 Miss. 602, 30 So. 2d 516

**Prohibition Cases**
255 U.S. 98, 65 L. Ed. 524, 41 S. Ct. 303
264 F. 218; 255 U.S. 81, 65 L. Ed. 516, 41 S. Ct. 298
251 U.S. 311, 64 L. Ed. 280, 40 S. Ct. 154
267 U.S. 132, 69 L. Ed. 543, 45 S. Ct. 280
257 F. 860; 252 U.S. 465, 64 L. Ed. 665, 40 S. Ct. 364
260 F. 486; 251 U.S. 210, 64 L. Ed. 229, 40 S. Ct. 139
264 F. 186; 253 U.S. 350, 64 L. Ed. 946, 40 S. Ct. 486, 40 S. Ct. 588
268 F. 864; 260 U.S. 377, 67 L. Ed. 314, 43 S. Ct. 141
284 F. 596; 251 U.S. 146, 64 L. Ed. 194, 40 S. Ct. 106; 251 U.S. 264, 64 L. Ed. 260, 40 S. Ct. 141
156 Ga. 488, 119 S.E. 302; 267 U.S. 188, 69 L. Ed. 568, 45 S. Ct. 264
24 Kan. 700
100 Ohio St. 385, 126 N.E. 400; 253 U.S. 221, 64 L. Ed. 871, 40 S. Ct. 495
100 Ohio St. 540, 127 N.E. 924; 253 U.S. 231, 64 L. Ed. 877, 40 S. Ct. 498

**Property Tax Equal Protection Case**
488 U.S. 336 102 L. Ed. 2d 688, 109 S. Ct. 633

**Prosecution Injunction Case**
190 Ga. 842, 11 S.E.2d 30

**Prosecutorial Comments Case**
470 U.S. 1, 84 L. Ed. 2d 1, 105 S. Ct. 1038

**Prosecutor's Immunity Case**
424 U.S. 409, 47 L. Ed. 2d 128, 96 S. Ct. 984

**Prostitution Forfeiture Case**
516 U.S. 442, 134 L. Ed. 2d 68, 116 S. Ct. 994 (1996)

**Providence Hospital Case**
175 U.S. 291, 44 L. Ed. 168, 20 S. Ct. 121; 12 App. D.C. 453

**Proxy Solicitation Case**
426 U.S. 438, 48 L. Ed. 2d 757, 96 S. Ct. 2126

**Prudential Insurance Case**
361 U.S. 477, 4 L. Ed. 2d 454, 80 S. Ct. 419; 260 F.2d 736; 358 U.S. 944, 3 L. Ed. 2d 351, 79 S. Ct. 352; 361 U.S. 872, 4 L. Ed. 2d 112, 80 S. Ct. 137

**Prunier Case**
248 F.2d 818, 28 T.C. 19

**Psychotherapist-Patient Privilege Case**
518 U.S. 1, 135 L. Ed. 2d 337, 116 S. Ct. 1923 (1996)

**Public Aid to Nonpublic Schools Case**
421 U.S. 349, 44 L. Ed. 2d 217, 95 S. Ct. 1753

**Public Airport Authority Case**
391 Ill. 237, 62 N.E.2d 809

**Public Condemnee Compensation Case**
469 U.S. 24, 83 L. Ed. 2d 376, 105 S. Ct. 451

**Public Conveyance Exclusion Clause Case**
195 Md. 180, 73 A.2d 1

**Public Free School Attendance Case**
461 U.S. 321, 75 L. Ed. 2d 879, 103 S. Ct. 1838

**Public Property Sign Posting Case**
80 L. Ed. 2d 772, 104 S. Ct. 2118

**Public Recreational Facilities**
417 U.S. 556, 41 L. Ed. 2d 304, 94 S. Ct. 2416

**Public School Search Case**
469 U.S. 325, 83 L. Ed. 2d 720, 105 S. Ct. 733

**Public School Teacher in Parochial School Case**
473 U.S. 402, 87 L. Ed. 2d 290, 105 S. Ct. 3232

**Public Trial Case**
443 U.S. 368, 61 L. Ed. 2d 608, 99 S. Ct. 2898

**Public Utility Anti-Strike Law Cases**
257 Wis. 43, 42 N.W.2d 471; 340 U.S. 874, 95 L. Ed. 636, 71 S. Ct. 124; 340 U.S. 383, 95 L. Ed. 364, 71 S. Ct. 359
258 Wis. 1, 44 N.W.2d 547; 340 U.S. 903, 95 L. Ed. 653, 71 S. Ct. 283; 340 U.S. 383, 95 L. Ed. 364, 71 S. Ct. 359

**Public Utility Condemnation Case**
27 Wash. 2d 694, 179 P.2d 510; 28 Wash. 2d 476, 183 P.2d 802

**Public Utility Regulatory Policies Act Case**
456 U.S. 742, 72 L. Ed. 2d 532, 102 S. Ct. 2126

**Pueblo Case**
F. Cas. No. 12,316

**Pueblo Indian Tax Case**
12 N.M. 139, 76 P. 307

**Puerto Rican Cases**
182 U.S. 1, 45 L. Ed. 1041, 21 S. Ct. 743
182 U.S. 222, 45 L. Ed. 1074, 21 S. Ct. 762
182 U.S. 243, 45 L. Ed. 1086, 21 S. Ct. 827, 36 Ct. Cl. 583
182 U.S. 244, 45 L. Ed. 1088, 21 S. Ct. 770
183 U.S. 151, 46 L. Ed. 128, 22 S. Ct. 62
103 F. 72; 182 U.S. 221, 45 L. Ed. 1065, 21 S. Ct. 742
105 F. 74, 182 U.S. 392, 45 L. Ed. 1146, 21 S. Ct. 827; 109 F. 1058
105 F. 608, 182 U.S. 221, 45 L. Ed. 1065, 21 S. Ct. 742

**Pulaski County Board of Equalization Case**
49 Ark. 518, 6 S.W. 1

**Pullman Cases**
139 U.S. 24, 35 L. Ed. 55, 11 S. Ct. 478; 49 F. 261; 65 F. 158; 72 F. 211; 76 F. 401, 22 C.C.A. 246, 39 U.S. App. D.C. 307; 83 F. 1, 27 C.C.A. 395; 171 U.S. 138, 43 L. Ed. 108, 18 S. Ct. 808

139 U.S. 62, 35 L. Ed. 69, 11 S. Ct. 489

**Pullman Monopoly Case**
50 F. Supp. 123; 53 F. Supp. 908; 55 F. Supp. 985; 64 F. Supp. 108; 67 S. Ct. 71; 330 U.S. 806, 91 L. Ed. 1263, 67 S. Ct. 1078; 331 U.S. 865, 91 L. Ed. 1870, 67 S. Ct. 1195, 67 S. Ct. 1196

**Pullman Porter Case**
157 Ind. 305, 61 N.E. 678

**Pumpkin Papers Case**
185 F.2d 822; 340 U.S. 948, 95 L. Ed. 683, 71 S. Ct. 532; 107 F. Supp. 128; 201 F.2d 372; 345 U.S. 942, 97 L. Ed. 1368, 73 S. Ct. 830; 88 F. Supp. 559; 9 F.R.D. 515

**Punctured Oil Pan Case**
138 W. Va. 369, 76 S.E.2d 244

**Punitive Damages Due Process Case**
509 U.S. 443, 125 L. Ed. 2d 366, 113 S. Ct. 2711 (1993)

113 L. Ed. 2d 1, 111 S. Ct. 1032

**Purchase by Pledge Case**
118 Cal. App. 2d 410, 258 P.2d 497

**Pure Food Case**
220 U.S. 45, 55 L. Ed. 364, 31 S. Ct. 364

**Pure Oil Company Case**
84 N.L.R.B. 315, No. 38

**Pusey and Jones Case**
276 F. 296; 279 F. 488; 286 F. 707; 260 U.S. 712, 67 L. Ed. 476, 43 S. Ct. 13; 261 U.S. 491, 67 L. Ed. 763, 43 S. Ct. 454

**Push Cart Peddler's Case**
167 Misc. 815, 4 N.Y.S.2d 837; 254 A.D. 672, 4 N.Y.S.2d 844; 254 A.D. 720, 4 N.Y.S.2d 997; 278 N.Y. 667, 16 N.E.2d 394

**Pushed Car Case**
196 Tenn. 680, 270 S.W.2d 321

**Pyrites Cinder Case**
15 I.C.C. 9; 18 I.C.C. 624; 188 F. 860; 207 F. 717; 238 U.S. 473, 59 L. Ed. 1414, 35 S. Ct. 888

## Q

**Quadra Case**
3 F.2d 643; 10 F.2d 339; 271 U.S. 652, 70 L. Ed. 1133, 46 S. Ct. 475; 273 U.S. 593, 71 L. Ed. 793, 47 S. Ct. 531

**Qualified Allegiance Cases**
42 F.2d 842; 282 U.S. 832, 75 L. Ed. 740, 51 S. Ct. 90; 283 U.S. 636, 75 L. Ed. 1319, 51 S. Ct. 569
42 F.2d 845; 282 U.S. 832, 75 L. Ed. 740, 51 S. Ct. 90; 283 U.S. 605, 75 L. Ed. 1302, 51 S. Ct. 570

**Qualified Immunity Case**
469 U.S. 464, 83 L. Ed. 2d 878, 105 S. Ct. 873

**Quality Rubber Case**
430 F.2d 519

**Quandt Island Case**
92 F. Supp. 232; 106 F. Supp. 234

**Quarry Nuisance Case**
124 Cal. App. 2d 577, 269 P.2d 81

**Queue Case**
F. Cas. No. 6,546

**Quicksilver Mine Case**
61 U.S. 413, 15 L. Ed. 944; 62 U.S. 445, 16 L. Ed. 185; 69 U.S. 649, 17 L. Ed. 739

**Quitman Field Case**
380 S.W.2d 556 (Tex.)

**Quodrigen Case**
257 F. Supp. 991; 411 F.2d 1390
285 F. Supp. 432; 411 F.2d 48

## R

**Race Covenant Cases**
355 Mo. 814, 198 S.W.2d 679; 331 U.S. 803, 91 L. Ed. 1826, 67 S. Ct. 1751; 334 U.S. 1, 92 L. Ed. 1161, 68 S. Ct. 836; 358 Mo. 364, 214 S.W.2d 525
316 Mich. 614, 25 N.W.2d 638; 331 U.S. 804, 91 L. Ed. 1826, 67 S. Ct. 1754; 68 S. Ct. 162; 68 S. Ct. 204; 68 S. Ct. 215; 68 S. Ct. 348; 334 U.S. 1, 91 L. Ed. 1161, 68 S. Ct. 836
162 F.2d 233, 82 App. D.C. 180; 332 U.S. 789, 92 L. Ed. 371, 68 S. Ct. 100; 68 S. Ct. 162; 68 S. Ct. 205; 68 S. Ct. 206; 68 S. Ct. 217; 68 S. Ct. 349; 68 S. Ct. 457; 334 U.S. 24, 92 L. Ed. 1187, 68 S. Ct. 847
112 Cal. App. 2d 534, 247 P.2d 99; 345 U.S. 902, 97 L. Ed. 1339, 73 S. Ct. 644; 346 U.S. 249, 97 L. Ed. 1586, 73 S. Ct. 1031

**Race-Mare Case**
76 Tenn. (8 Lea) 465

**Race Segregation Case**
165 Ky. 559, 177 S.W. 472; 245 U.S. 60, 62 L. Ed. 149, 38 S. Ct. 16

**Race Track Liability Case**
195 Va. 13, 77 S.E.2d 368

**Racial Bias Voir Dire Case**
476 U.S. 28, 90 L. Ed. 2d 27, 106 S. Ct. 1683

**Racial Disparity Death Penalty Case**
481 U.S. 279, 95 L. Ed. 2d 262, 107 S. Ct. 1756

**Racial or Ethnic Voir Dire Case**
451 U.S. 182, 68 L. Ed. 2d 22, 101 S. Ct. 1629

**Racial Prejudice Voir Dire Case**
424 U.S. 577, 47 L. Ed. 2d 258, 96 S. Ct. 1017

**Racial Steering Case**
455 U.S. 363, 71 L. Ed. 2d 214, 102 S. Ct. 1114

**Racially Mixed Household Custody Case**
461 U.S. 907, 76 L. Ed. 2d 810, 103 S. Ct. 1879

**Racketeering Case**
118 F.2d 684; 314 U.S. 596, 86 L. Ed. 480, 62 S. Ct. 67; 315 U.S. 521, 86 L. Ed. 1004, 62 S. Ct. 642

**Radical Consideration in Redistricting Case**
430 U.S. 144, 51 L. Ed. 2d 229, 97 S. Ct. 996

**Radio Boycott Cases**
180 F.2d 28
10 F.R.D. 487; 92 F. Supp. 794; 71 S. Ct. 743; 342 U.S. 143, 96 L. Ed. 162, 72 S. Ct. 181

**Radio Case**
31 F.2d 630, 58 App. D.C. 386; 280 U.S. 537, 74 L. Ed. 599, 50 S. Ct. 20; 50 S. Ct. 78; 281 U.S. 464, 74 L. Ed. 969, 50 S. Ct. 389

**Radio Officers Case**
347 U.S. 17, 98 L. Ed. 455, 74 S. Ct. 323; 345 U.S. 962, 97 L. Ed. 1382, 73 S. Ct. 947; 196 F.2d 1; 196 F.2d 960; 197 F.2d 719; 212 F.2d 790

**Radio Station State Tax Case**
51 N.M. 332, 184 P.2d 416; 54 N.M. 133, 215 P.2d 819

**Radio Tube Cases**
17 F.2d 90; 28 F.2d 641; 278 U.S. 656, 73 L. Ed. 565, 49 S. Ct. 180
23 F.2d 698; 44 F.2d 931; 282 U.S. 836, 75 L. Ed. 743, 51 S. Ct. 333; 283 U.S. 664, 75 L. Ed. 1339, 51 S. Ct. 563; 284 U.S. 571, 76 L. Ed. 497, 52 S. Ct. 26

**Radioactive Pollutants Case**
426 U.S. 1, 48 L. Ed. 2d 434, 96 S. Ct. 1938

**Radius of Business Case**
33 Wash. 2d 741, 207 P.2d 227

**Raffel Case**
271 U.S. 494, 70 L. Ed. 1054, 46 S. Ct. 566; 15 F.2d 1017

**Ragan Case**
337 U.S. 530, 93 L. Ed. 1520, 69 S. Ct. 1233; 338 U.S. 839, 94 L. Ed. 513, 70 S. Ct. 33; 170 F.2d 987

**Railroad Cases**
35 Wis. 425; 38 Wis. 69

**Railroad Commission Cases**
116 U.S. 307, 29 L. Ed. 636, 6 S. Ct. 334, 6 S. Ct. 388, 6 S. Ct. 1191; 116 U.S. 352, 29 L. Ed. 651, 6 S. Ct. 349,
116 U.S. 366, 29 L. Ed. 652, 6 S. Ct. 391
20 F. 270; 116 U.S. 307, 29 L. Ed. 636, 6 S. Ct. 334
20 F. 468, 116 U.S. 347, 29 L. Ed. 650, 6 S. Ct. 348

**Railroad Connection Case**
137 N.C. 1, 49 S.E. 191

**Railroad Emergency Case**
243 U.S. 332, 61 L. Ed. 755, 37 S. Ct. 298

**Railroad Grant Case**
46 F. 592; 154 U.S. 288, 38 L. Ed. 992, 14 S. Ct. 1030

**Railroad Labor Act Case**
300 U.S. 515, 81 L. Ed. 789, 57 S. Ct. 592

**Railroad Lookout Liability Case**
166 F.2d 278

**Railroad Loss of Baggage Case**
58 So. 2d 185 (Fla.)

**Railroad Reorganization Case**
294 U.S. 648, 79 L. Ed. 1110, 55 S. Ct. 595

**Railroad Retirement Act Cases**
375 U.S. 253, 11 L. Ed. 2d 307, 84 S. Ct. 316, 289 F. Supp. 374

**Railroad Retirement Benefits Case**
439 U.S. 572, 59 L. Ed. 2d 1, 99 S. Ct. 802

**Railroad Retirement Case**
449 U.S. 166, 66 L. Ed. 2d 368, 101 S. Ct. 453

**Railroad Tax Case (Arkansas)**
136 F. 233

**Railroad Tax Case (Illinois)**
92 U.S. 575, 23 L. Ed. 663

**Railroad Tax Cases (California)**
13 F. 722; 116 U.S. 138, 29 L. Ed. 589, 6 S. Ct. 317
18 F. 385; 118 U.S. 394, 30 L. Ed. 118, 6 S. Ct. 1132

**Railroad Tax Cases (Delaware)**
F. Cas. No. 9,645; 85 U.S. 206, 21 L. Ed. 888

**Railroad Tax Cases (Kentucky)**
81 Ky. 492; 115 U.S. 321, 29 L. Ed. 414, 6 S. Ct. 57

**Railroad Telegraphers Case**
362 U.S. 330, 4 L. Ed. 2d 774, 80 S. Ct. 761; 264 F.2d 254; 361 U.S. 809, 4 L. Ed. 2d 58, 80 S. Ct. 56; 362 U.S. 984, 4 L. Ed. 2d 1019, 80 S. Ct. 1056

**Railroad Valuation Cases**
252 U.S. 178, 64 L. Ed. 517, 40 S. Ct. 187
22 F.2d 980; 279 U.S. 461, 73 L. Ed. 798, 49 S. Ct. 384

**Railway Clerks Case**
281 U.S. 548, 74 L. Ed. 1034, 50 S. Ct. 427

**Railway Gross Receipts Case**
82 U.S. 284, 21 L. Ed. 164

**Railway Mail Pay Cases**
65 Ct. Cl. 115; 278 U.S. 588, 73 L. Ed. 522, 49 S. Ct. 18; 279 U.S. 73, 73 L. Ed. 619, 49 S. Ct. 260
65 Ct. Cl. 327; 278 U.S. 588, 73 L. Ed. 522, 49 S. Ct. 18; 279 U.S. 73, 73 L. Ed. 619, 49 S. Ct. 260

**Railway Pension Case**
295 U.S. 330, 79 L. Ed. 1468, 55 S. Ct. 758

**Railway Shopmen's Strike Case**
283 F. 479; 286 F. 228; 290 F. 978

**Railway Tax Cases**
62 Pa. 286; 82 U.S. 232, 21 L. Ed. 146; 82 U.S. 282, 21 L. Ed. 164
66 Pa. 84

**Rancid Oil Case**
135 Cal. App. 2d 245, 286 P.2d 1000

**Rape Death Penalty Case**
433 U.S. 584, 53 L. Ed. 2d 982, 97 S. Ct. 2861

**Rape Seed Case**
105 Wis. 315, 81 N.W. 491

**Rape Shield Case**
114 L. Ed. 2d 205, 111 S. Ct. 1743

**Rape Victims Identification Case**
420 U.S. 469, 43 L. Ed. 2d 328, 95 S. Ct. 1029

**Rat Case**
153 Ohio St. 258, 91 N.E.2d 256, 41 Ohio Op. 274

**Rat Poison Case**
184 Okla. 614, 89 P.2d 340

**Rate Case**
127 N.C. 283, 37 S.E. 266

**Rate Regulation Cases**
196 F. 800; 205 F. 800; 208 F. 35; 210 F. 465
256 F. 929; 255 U.S. 539, 65 L. Ed. 764, 41 S. Ct. 400; 257 U.S. 662, 66 L. Ed. 423, 42 S. Ct. 45
257 F. 467; 255 U.S. 547, 65 L. Ed. 777, 41 S. Ct. 428

**Ray Case**
118 Tex. 331, 15 S.W.2d 541

**Rayl Case**
30 Idaho 41, 166 P. 220

**Raymond Basin Case**
33 Cal. 2d 908, 207 P.2d 17, 339 U.S. 937, 94 L. Ed. 1354, 70 S. Ct. 671

**Rayne Field Case**
381 U.S. 392, 14 L. Ed. 2d 466, 85 S. Ct. 1517
287 F.2d 143

**Re-employment of Veterans Case**
62 F. Supp. 25; 154 F.2d 785; 327 U.S. 775, 90 L. Ed. 1004, 66 S. Ct. 904; 328 U.S. 275, 90 L. Ed. 1230, 66 S. Ct. 1105

**Rea Case**
350 U.S. 214, 100 L. Ed. 233, 76 S. Ct. 292; 218 F.2d 237

**Reader's Digest Murder Case**
303 N.Y. 856, 104 N.E.2d 917; 303 N.Y. 982, 106 N.E.2d 63; 344 U.S. 815, 97 L. Ed. 634, 73 S. Ct. 51; 346 U.S. 156, 97 L. Ed. 1522, 73 S. Ct. 1077; 346 U.S. 842, 98 L. Ed. 362, 74 S. Ct. 13; 306 N.Y. 675, 115 N.E.2d 502, 306 N.Y. 678, 117 N.E.2d 355; 306 N.Y. 867, 118 N.E.2d 918; 307 N.Y. 253, 120 N.E.2d 813; 307 N.Y. 912, 123 N.E.2d 567; 348 U.S. 878, 99 L. Ed. 691, 75 S. Ct. 118; 308 N.Y. 747, 125 N.E.2d 105; 348 U.S. 922, 99 L. Ed. 723, 75 S. Ct. 301; 129 F. Supp. 123; 221 F.2d 626; 308 N.Y. 772, 125 N.E.2d 117; 308 N.Y. 913, 127 N.E.2d 76; 349 U.S. 968, 99 L. Ed. 1289, 75 S. Ct. 906; 308 N.Y. 1021, 127 N.E.2d 862; 75 S. Ct. 908

**Reading Case**
183 F. 427; 226 U.S. 324, 57 L. Ed. 243, 33 S. Ct. 90, 228 U.S. 158, 57 L. Ed. 779, 33 S. Ct. 509; 226 F. 229; 253 U.S. 26, 64 L. Ed. 760, 40 S. Ct. 425; 253 U.S. 478, 64 L. Ed. 1022, 40 S. Ct. 585; 273 F. 848; 259 U.S. 156, 66 L. Ed. 871, 42 S. Ct. 540; 295 F. 551; 300 F. 477

**Real Estate Boards Case**
84 F. Supp. 802; 176 F.2d 631, 85 App. D.C. 165; 70 S. Ct. 189; 339 U.S. 485, 94 L. Ed. 1007, 70 S. Ct. 711

**Real Estate Brokers' Split-Fee Case**
339 Mich. 12, 62 N.W.2d 461

**Reapportionment Cases**
347 U.S. 483, 98 L. Ed. 873, 74 S. Ct. 686
369 U.S. 186, 7 L. Ed. 2d 663, 82 S. Ct. 691; 179 F. Supp. 824; 364 U.S. 898, 5 L. Ed. 2d 193, 81 S. Ct. 230; 175 FS 649; 365 U.S. 838, 81 S. Ct. 799, 365 U.S. 864, 81 S. Ct. 899; 365 U.S. 875, 81 S. Ct. 1025; 366 U.S. 907, 81 S. Ct. 1082; 367 U.S. 804, 82 S. Ct. 28; 206 F. Supp. 341; 222 F. Supp. 684

*Continued*

372 U.S. 368, 9 L. Ed. 2d 821, 83 S. Ct. 801

377 U.S. 533, 12 L. Ed. 2d 506, 84 S. Ct. 1362; 377 U.S. 713, 12 L. Ed. 2d 632, 84 S. Ct. 1459

390 U.S. 474, 20 L. Ed. 2d 45, 88 S. Ct. 1114

397 U.S. 50, 25 L. Ed. 2d 45, 90 S. Ct. 791

**Rear Window Copyright Case**

495 U.S. 207, 109 L. Ed. 2d 184, 110 S. Ct. 1750

**Rearview Mirror Case**

55 N.M. 357, 233 P.2d 1044

**Reasonable Access to Television Case**

453 U.S. 361, 69 L. Ed. 2d 706, 101 S. Ct. 2813

**Reasonableness of Detention Case**

470 U.S. 675, 84 L. Ed. 2d 605, 105 S. Ct. 1568

**Recapture Clause Case**

287 F. 728; 263 U.S. 456, 68 L. Ed. 388, 44 S. Ct. 169

**Reception-Room Theft Case**

30 Wash. 2d 92, 190 P.2d 714

**Reciprocal Wills Case**

189 S.W.2d 889 (Tex.); 144 Tex. 618, 193 S.W.2d 165

**Reconsignment Cases**

11 I.C.C. 90; 149 F. 609; 153 F. 728, 82 C.C.A. 614; 214 U.S. 297, 53 L. Ed. 1004, 29 S. Ct. 678; 18 I.C.C. 607; 19 I.C.C. 533

47 I.C.C. 590

**Rectanus Case**

206 F. 570; 226 F. 545; 242 U.S. 625, 61 L. Ed. 534, 37 S. Ct. 16; 248 U.S. 90, 63 L. Ed. 141, 39 S. Ct. 48

**Red Flag Case**

106 Cal. App. 725, 290 P. 93; 75 L. Ed. 1472, 51 S. Ct. 343; 283 U.S. 359, 75 L. Ed. 1117, 51 S. Ct. 532

**Red Fork Point Case**

122 F. Supp. 115

**Red Kimono Case**

112 Cal. App. 285, 297 P. 91

**Red Light Law Case**

169 Iowa 148, 151 N.W. 81

**Red Oak Cases**

3 F. 117

**Redistricting Cases**

111 Tenn. 234, 80 S.W. 750

**Redmond Cases**

9 F.2d 209

**Reduced Rates Case**

68 I.C.C. 676; 69 I.C.C. 138; 77 I.C.C. 675

**Reelfoot Lake Case**

127 Tenn. 575, 158 S.W. 746

**Refineries Case**

156 U.S. 1, 39 L. Ed. 325, 15 S. Ct. 249; 60 F. 934

**Refrigerator Case**

191 U.S. 1, 48 L. Ed. 65, 24 S. Ct. 1; 128 F. 149

63 Conn. 551, 29 A. 76

**Refrigerator Fixture Case**

115 Colo. 478, 173 P.2d 882

**Refugee Asylum Case**

480 U.S. 421, 94 L. Ed. 2d 434, 107 S. Ct. 1207

**Regents Prayer Case**

18 Misc. 2d 659, 191 N.Y.S.2d 453, 11 A.D.2d 340, 206 N.Y.S.2d 183; 10 N.Y.2d 174, 218 N.Y.S.2d 659, 176 N.E.2d 579; 370 U.S. 421, 8 L. Ed. 2d 601, 82 S. Ct. 1261; 12 N.Y.2d 712, 233 N.Y.S.2d 766, 186 N.E.2d 124; 368 U.S. 924, 7 L. Ed. 2d 189, 82 S. Ct. 367; 368 U.S. 982, 82 S. Ct. 597; 369 U.S. 809, 82 S. Ct. 686

**Regional Rail Reorganization Case**

419 U.S. 102, 42 L. Ed. 2d 320, 95 S. Ct. 335

**Reichmann Case**
145 F. 235

**Reindictment Speedy Trial Case**
172 Kan. 224, 239 P.2d 949; 176 Kan. 203, 270 P.2d 211

**Reinhardt Case**
71 N.J. Eq. 70, 63 A. 1097

**Released Rates Case**
13 I.C.C. 550

**Released Time Cases**
333 U.S. 203, 92 L. Ed. 648, 68 S. Ct. 461

275 A.D. 774, 87 N.Y.S.2d 639; 195 Misc. 531, 90 N.Y.S.2d 750; 198 Misc. 631, 99 N.Y.S.2d 339; 278 A.D. 573, 102 N.Y.S.2d 27; 303 N.Y. 161, 100 N.E.2d 463; 72 S. Ct. 332; 343 U.S. 306, 96 L. Ed. 954, 72 S. Ct. 679

**Relicted Land Case**
252 Mich. 198, 233 N.W. 159

**Religious Freedom Restoration Act Case**
521 U.S. 507, 138 L. Ed. 2d 624, 117 S. Ct. 2157 (1997)

**Religious Guardian Case**
100 Cal. App. 2d 194, 223 P.2d 322; 114 Cal. App. 2d 82, 249 P.2d 578

**Religious Literature Cases**
319 U.S. 103, 87 L. Ed. 1290, 63 S. Ct. 890; 315 U.S. 793, 86 L. Ed. 1196, 62 S. Ct. 903; 316 U.S. 584, 86 L. Ed. 1691, 62 S. Ct. 1231; 318 U.S. 796, 87 L. Ed. 1161, 63 S. Ct. 658; 320 U.S. 719, 88 L. Ed. 423, 64 S. Ct. 423; 135 F.2d 981; 241 Ala. 279, 3 So. 2d 76; 242 Ala. 549, 7 So. 2d 503; 30 Ala. App. 416, 7 So. 2d 503; 202 Ark. 614, 151 S.W.2d 1000; 58 Ariz. 144, 118 P.2d 97

319 U.S. 105, 87 L. Ed. 1292, 63 S. Ct. 870, 63 S. Ct. 891; 319 U.S. 141, 87 L. Ed. 1313, 63 S. Ct. 862; 316 U.S. 584, 86 L. Ed. 1691, 62 S. Ct. 1231; 318 U.S. 748, 87 L. Ed. 1125, 63 S. Ct. 660, 63 S. Ct. 661, 63 S. Ct. 662; 319 U.S. 166, 87 L. Ed. 1330, 63 S. Ct. 882; 149 Pa. Super. 175, 27 A.2d 666

**Religious Organization Reporting Requirements Case**
456 U.S. 228, 72 L. Ed. 2d 33, 102 S. Ct. 1673

**Remarried Divorced Widows Social Security Case**
476 U.S. 340, 90 L. Ed. 2d 316, 106 S. Ct. 1881

**Remington Case**
208 F.2d 567; 343 U.S. 907, 96 L. Ed. 1325, 72 S. Ct. 580; 347 U.S. 913, 98 L. Ed. 1069, 74 S. Ct. 476

**Removal Authority of Prison Administrator Case**
459 U.S. 460, 74 L. Ed. 2d 675, 103 S. Ct. 864

**Removal Cases**
46 Iowa 406; 100 U.S. 457, 25 L. Ed. 593

**Reno Water Rate Case**
300 F. 645

**Rent Regulation Cases**
267 F. 614, 50 App. D.C. 56; 254 U.S. 640, 65 L. Ed. 452, 41 S. Ct. 13; 267 F. 631, 50 App. D.C. 73; 256 U.S. 135, 65 L. Ed. 865, 41 S. Ct. 458

269 F. 306; 256 U.S. 170, 65 L. Ed. 877, 41 S. Ct. 465

51 F. Supp. 597; 320 U.S. 713, 88 L. Ed. 419, 64 S. Ct. 200; 321 U.S. 503, 88 L. Ed. 892, 64 S. Ct. 641

113 Misc. 527, 185 N.Y.S. 632; 194 A.D. 523, 186 N.Y.S. 58; 230 N.Y. 429, 130 N.E. 601; 257 U.S. 665, 66 L. Ed. 424, 42 S. Ct. 47

113 Misc. 536, 185 N.Y.S. 638; 195 A.D. 280, 186 N.Y.S. 63; 230 N.Y. 429, 130 N.E. 601; 257 U.S. 665, 66 L. Ed. 424, 42 S. Ct. 47

**Renton News Case**
136 N.L.R.B. 1297, No. 55

**Reorganization Tax Cases**
4 T.C. 897; 155 F.2d 237; 329 U.S. 701, 91 L. Ed. 611, 67 S. Ct. 62; 331 U.S. 737, 91 L. Ed. 1782, 67 S. Ct. 1489; 332 U.S. 752, 92 L. Ed. 338
4 T.C. 1186; 5 T.C. 351; 155 F.2d 246; 329 U.S. 695, 91 L. Ed. 607, 67 S. Ct. 62, 331 U.S. 737, 91 L. Ed. 1782, 67 S. Ct. 1489; 332 U.S. 752, 92 L. Ed. 338

**Repainted Car Punitive Damages Case**
517 U.S. 559, 134 L. Ed. 2d 809, 116 S. Ct. 1589 (1996)

**Replevin Case**
407 U.S. 67, 32 L. Ed. 2d 556, 92 S. Ct. 1983

**Reporter's Case**
41 Ill. App. 164; 140 Ill. 69, 29 N.E. $88

**Reporters Privilege Cases**
408 U.S. 665, 33 L. Ed. 2d 626, 92 S. Ct. 2646, 92 S. Ct. 2686

**Republic Aviation Case**
51 N.L.R.B. 1186; 142 F.2d 193; 323 U.S. 688, 89 L. Ed. 557, 65 S. Ct. 55; 324 U.S. 793, 89 L. Ed. 1372, 65 S. Ct. 982

**Repurchase Option Case**
72 So. 2d 289 (Fla.)

**Reputation Rights Case**
424 U.S. 693, 47 L. Ed. 2d 405, 96 S. Ct. 1155

**Res Judicata Divorce Case**
160 Fla. 838, 36 So. 2d 774; 59 So. 2d 40; 344 U.S. 878, 97 L. Ed. 680, 73 S. Ct. 165

**Resale Price Maintenance Case**
264 F. 885; 253 U.S. 482, 64 L. Ed. 1024, 40 S. Ct. 584; 257 U.S. 441, 66 L. Ed. 307, 42 S. Ct. 150

**Reserved-Gate Picketing Case**
278 F.2d 282; 364 U.S. 869, 5 L. Ed. 2d 92, 81 S. Ct. 114; 366 U.S. 667, 6 L. Ed. 2d 592, 81 S. Ct. 1285; 123 N.L.R.B. 1547, No. 180; 138 N.L.R.B. 342, No. 38

**Residential Picketing Case**
487 U.S. 474, 101 L. Ed. 2d 420, 108 S. Ct. 2495

**Restricted Rate Case**
20 I.C.C. 426; 225 U.S. 326, 56 L. Ed. 1107, 32 S. Ct. 742

**Restrictions on Commercial Speech Case**
478 U.S. 328, 92 L. Ed. 2d 266, 106 S. Ct. 2968

**Restrictive Covenant Cases**
334 U.S. 1, 92 L. Ed. 1161, 68 S. Ct. 836

**Retail Installment Contracts Statute Case**
227 Ind. 373, 86 N.E.2d 444

**Retained Downpayment Case**
120 Colo. 253, 208 P.2d 1159

**Retaliatory Tax Case**
451 U.S. 648, 68 L. Ed. 2d 514, 101 S. Ct. 2070

**Retired Judges Pay Case**
291 U.S. 339, 78 L. Ed. 836, 54 S. Ct. 379

**Retirement Annuity Deduction Case**
6 T.C. 37; 162 F.2d 379; 176 F.2d 815; 338 U.S. 949, 94 L. Ed. 586, 70 S. Ct. 488; 17 T.C. 1600

**Retroactive Application of Miller Standard Case**
430 U.S. 188, 51 L. Ed. 2d 260, 97 S. Ct. 990

**Reynolds Metal Cases**
236 F.2d 224
125 F. Supp. 481
176 F. Supp. 178
221 Ore 86, 342 P.2d 790

**Rhode Island Case**
48 U.S. 1, 12 L. Ed. 581

**Rice Case**
37 Idaho 73, 217 P. 252

**Rice Millers Case**
297 U.S. 110, 80 L. Ed. 513, 56 S. Ct. 374

**Rich Young Ruler Case**
192 N.C. 251, 134 S.E. 487

**Richardson Valve Case**
113 U.S. 157, 28 L. Ed. 939, 5 S. Ct. 513

**Richmond, Virginia Case**
124 Va. 522, 98 S.E. 643; 256 U.S. 635, 65 L. Ed. 1135, 41 S. Ct. 619

**RICO Antiabortion Protest Case**
510 U.S. 249, 127 L. Ed. 2d 99, 114 S. Ct. 798 (1994)

**RICO Predicate Conviction Case**
473 U.S. 479, 87 L. Ed. 2d 346, 105 S. Ct. 3275

**Riegelman Case**
27 T.C. 833; 253 F.2d 315

**Right of Privacy Case**
155 Fla. 198, 20 So. 2d 243; 159 Fla. 31, 30 So. 2d 635

**Right to Appoint Counsel Case**
440 U.S. 367, 59 L. Ed. 2d 383, 99 S. Ct. 1158

**Right to Be Heard Case**
415 U.S. 452, 39 L. Ed. 2d 505, 94 S. Ct. 1209

**Right to Counsel Cases**
315 U.S. 791, 86 L. Ed. 1194, 62 S. Ct. 639; 316 U.S. 455, 86 L. Ed. 1595, 62 S. Ct. 1252
469 U.S. 91, 83 L. Ed. 2d 488, 105 S. Ct. 490
51 L. Ed. 2d 424, 97 S. Ct. 1232
116 F.2d 690, 313 U.S. 551, 85 L. Ed. 1222, 61 S. Ct. 835; 315 U.S. 60, 86 L. Ed. 680, 62 S. Ct. 457; 315 U.S. 827, 86 L. Ed. 1222, 62 S. Ct. 629, 62 S. Ct. 637

**Right to Die Case**
111 L. Ed. 2d 224, 110 S. Ct. 2841

**Right-to-Reply Case**
418 U.S. 241, 41 L. Ed. 2d 730, 94 S. Ct. 2831

**Rights of Involuntarily Committed Persons Case**
457 U.S. 307, 73 L. Ed. 2d 28, 102 S. Ct. 2452

**Rights of Pretrial Detainees Case**
441 U.S. 520, 60 L. Ed. 2d 447, 99 S. Ct. 1861

**Rigid Steel Conduit Case**
168 F.2d 175; 336 U.S. 902, 93 L. Ed. 1068, 69 S. Ct. 491; 336 U.S. 956, 93 L. Ed. 1110, 69 S. Ct. 888

**River Bed Cases**
20 F.2d 845
20 F.2d 873; 275 U.S. 552, 72 L. Ed. 421, 48 S. Ct. 115; 275 U.S. 555, 72 L. Ed. 423, 48 S. Ct. 116
121 Tex. 515, 50 S.W.2d 1065; 25 S.W.2d 706

**River Rights Cases**
199 A.D. 539, 192 N.Y.S. 211; 235 N.Y. 351, 139 N.E. 474, 236 N.Y. 579, 142 N.E. 291; 271 U.S. 364, 70 L. Ed. 992, 46 S. Ct. 569
199 A.D. 552, 192 N.Y.S. 222; 235 N.Y. 364, 139 N.E. 477; 236 N.Y. 578, 142 N.E. 291; 271 U.S. 403, 70 L. Ed. 1009, 46 S. Ct. 581

**River Road Case**
353 U.S. 30, 1 L. Ed. 2d 622, 77 S. Ct. 635; 353 U.S. 948, 1 L. Ed. 2d 857, 77 S. Ct. 823; 229 F.2d 926

**Riverside Mills Case**
168 F. 987; 168 F. 990; 219 U.S. 186, 55 L. Ed. 167, 31 S. Ct. 164

**Road Cases**
30 Tex. 503
30 Tex. 506

**Roane-Anderson Case**
192 Tenn. 150, 239 S.W.2d 27; 342 U.S. 847, 96 L. Ed. 639, 72 S. Ct. 74; 342 U.S. 232, 96 L. Ed. 257, 72 S. Ct. 257

**Roanoke Rapids Case**
345 U.S. 153, 97 L. Ed. 918, 73 S. Ct. 609; 191 F.2d 796; 343 U.S. 941, 96 L. Ed. 1346, 72 S. Ct. 1034

**Robertson Case**
89 F. 504

**Rochester Telephone Case**
307 U.S. 125, 83 L. Ed. 1147, 59 S. Ct. 754; 23 F. Supp. 634; 59 S. Ct. 252

**Rochin Case**
342 U.S. 165, 96 L. Ed. 183, 72 S. Ct. 205; 101 Cal. App. 2d 140, 225 P.2d 1, 225 P.2d 913

**Rock Island Bridge Cases**
73 U.S. 213, 18 L. Ed. 753
294 U.S. 648, 79 L. Ed. 1110, 55 S. Ct. 595

**Rockaway Rolling Mill Case**
101 N.J. Eq. 192, 137 A. 650; 103 N.J. Eq. 297, 143 A. 334; 8 N.J. Misc. 193, 149 A. 532; 109 N.J. Eq. 608, 158 A. 438

**Rockcastle County Bond Case**
164 Ky. 747, 176 S.W. 185

**Rockne Case**
115 U.S. 600, 29 L. Ed. 477, 6 S. Ct. 201

**Rodin's Hand of God Case**
177 F. Supp. 265, 394 F. Supp. 1390

**Rogers Lumber Company Case**
117 N.L.R.B. 1732, No. 230

**Rogers Silverware Cases**
285 U.S. 247, 76 L. Ed. 740, 52 S. Ct. 387
11 F. 495
70 F. 1017
110 F. 955
17 U.S.P.Q. (BNA) 32
39 Conn. 450
66 N.J. Eq. 119, 57 A. 1037; 66 N.J. Eq. 140, 57 A. 725; 67 N.J. Eq. 646, 60 A. 187, 71 N.J. Eq. 560, 63 A. 977; 72 N.J. Eq. 933, 67 A. 105

**Roller Miller Patent Case**
43 F. 527; 156 U.S. 261, 39 L. Ed. 417, 15 S. Ct. 333

**Roller Rock Bit Case**
215 F.2d 924; 113 F. Supp. 519, 98 U.S.P.Q. (BNA) 131, 113 F. Supp. 527, 98 U.S.P.Q. (BNA) 137, 114 F. Supp. 525, 98 U.S.P.Q. (BNA) 102; 348 U.S. 927, 99 L. Ed. 726, 75 S. Ct. 339; 348 U.S. 965, 99 L. Ed. 753, 75 S. Ct. 521

**Rolling Stock Cases**
143 Ga. 765, 85 S.E. 994; 146 Ga. 489, 91 S.E. 680; 249 U.S. 275, 63 L. Ed. 602, 39 S. Ct. 276
118 Ky. 131, 80 S.W. 490; 81 S.W. 268; 199 U.S. 194, 50 L. Ed. 150, 26 S. Ct. 36
162 Okla. 185, 19 P.2d 168; 290 U.S. 158, 78 L. Ed. 238, 54 S. Ct. 152
107 Pa. 156; 141 U.S. 18, 35 L. Ed. 613, 11 S. Ct. 876
100 Tex. 153, 97 S.W. 71; 210 U.S. 217, 52 L. Ed. 1031, 28 S. Ct. 638
18 Utah 378, 55 P. 639; 177 U.S. 149, 44 L. Ed. 708, 20 S. Ct. 631

**Roman Scandals Case**
23 F. Supp. 519, 37 U.S.P.Q. (BNA) 760; 104 F.2d 661, 42 U.S.P.Q. (BNA) 164; 30 F. Supp. 436, 43 U.S.P.Q. (BNA) 353; 40 F. Supp. 534, 50 U.S.P.Q. (BNA) 372; 150 F.2d 612, 66 U.S.P.Q. (BNA) 9; 66 S. Ct. 471; 327 U.S. 790, 90 L. Ed. 1016, 66 S. Ct. 802, 68 U.S.P.Q. (BNA) 462; 328 U.S. 878, 90 L. Ed. 1646, 66 S. Ct. 1020

**Rome Cable Case**
377 U.S. 271, 12 L. Ed. 2d 314, 84 S. Ct. 1283

**Rome Case**
202 Misc. 893, 114 N.Y.S.2d 27

**Roosevelt Hospital Case**
43 N.Y. 254

**Ropert Case**
15 Haw. 76

**Rose Essay Contest Case**
80 App. D.C. 176; 150 F.2d 585

**Rose Hill Case**
86 Tenn. 1, 5 S.W. 444

**Rosenberg Case**
10 F.R.D. 521; 195 F.2d 583; 344 U.S. 838, 97 L. Ed. 652, 73 S. Ct. 20, 73 S. Ct. 21; 344 U.S. 850, 97 L. Ed. 661, 73 S. Ct. 66; 344 U.S. 889, 97 L. Ed. 687, 73 S. Ct. 134, 73 S. Ct. 180; 108 F. Supp. 798; 200 F.2d 666; 109 F. Supp. 108; 109 F. Supp. 381; 345 U.S. 965, 97 L. Ed. 1381, 73 S. Ct. 949; 345 U.S. 989, 97 L. Ed. 1397, 73 S. Ct. 1151; 345 U.S. 1003, 97 L. Ed. 1408, 73 S. Ct. 1151; 346 U.S. 271, 97 L. Ed. 1607, 73 S. Ct. 1152; 346 U.S. 313, 97 L. Ed. 1629, 73 S. Ct. 1173; 346 U.S. 273, 97 L. Ed. 1607, 73 S. Ct. 1152; 346 U.S. 322, 97 L. Ed. 1633, 73 S. Ct. 1178; 346 U.S. 324, 97 L. Ed. 1634, 73 S. Ct. 1178; 347 U.S. 1021, 98 L. Ed. 1142, 74 S. Ct. 860

**Rosie O'Grady Case**
58 F. Supp. 13, 63 U.S.P.Q. (BNA) 206; 62 F. Supp. 300, 66 U.S.P.Q. (BNA) 6; 67 F. Supp. 736, 70 U.S.P.Q. (BNA) 349; 71 F. Supp. 914, 71 U.S.P.Q. (BNA) 49; 71 F. Supp. 916, 71 U.S.P.Q. (BNA) 143; 7 F.R.D. 190, 72 U.S.P.Q. (BNA) 431; 165 F.2d 784, 76 U.S.P.Q. (BNA) 246

**Rotary Club Sex Discrimination Case**
481 U.S. 537, 95 L. Ed. 2d 474, 107 S. Ct. 1940

**Rothstein Murder Case**
226 A.D. 364, 235 N.Y.S. 112

**Roxalana Druse Case**
41 Hun 640; 103 N.Y. 655, 8 N.E. 733

**Roxy Case**
65 F.2d 324; 290 U.S. 647, 78 L. Ed. 561, 54 S. Ct. 65

**Roy & Sons Case**
118 N.L.R.B. 286, No. 24

**Royal Spy Case**
380 S.W.2d 233 (Ky.)

**Royal Typewriter Case**
228 F.2d 553; 122 F. Supp. 43; 351 U.S. 962, 100 L. Ed. 1483, 76 S. Ct. 1025

**Rozek's Case**
294 Mass. 205, 200 N.E. 903

**Rubber Comb Case**
13 Jones & S. (45 N.Y. Super. Ct.) 258

**Rubber Tip Pencil Case**
F. Cas. No. 12,102; 87 U.S. 498, 22 L. Ed. 410

**Rubber Tire Case**
232 U.S. 413, 58 L. Ed. 663, 34 S. Ct. 403

**Ruberoid Case**
163 F. 977, 90 C.C.A. 195; 220 U.S. 446, 55 L. Ed. 536, 31 S. Ct. 456

**Ruppert Case**
3 N.Y.2d 576, 170 N.Y.S.2d 785, 148 N.E.2d 129; 2 A.D.2d 670, 153 N.Y.S.2d 553; 2 Misc. 2d 744, 152 N.Y.S.2d 327

**Ruptured Tire Case**
267 S.W.2d 83 (Ky.)

**Russell Case**
173 Misc. 943, 18 N.Y.S.2d 821; 260 A.D. 9, 20 N.Y.S.2d 898, 20 N.Y.S.2d 1016

**Russell Motor Car Case**
261 U.S. 514, 67 L. Ed. 778, 43 S. Ct. 428

**Russian Insurance Cases**
214 A.D. 778, 210 N.Y.S. 904; 241 N.Y. 581, 150 N.E. 564; 215 A.D. 796, 213 N.Y.S. 883; 243 N.Y. 524, 154 N.E. 590; 224 A.D. 105, 229 N.Y.S. 554; 225 A.D. 92, 232 N.Y.S. 282; 225 A.D. 801, 232 N.Y.S. 847; 250 N.Y. 449, 166 N.E. 163; 227 A.D. 784, 237 N.Y.S. 867; 228 A.D. 621, 228 A.D. 622, 237 N.Y.S. 868; 136 Misc. 715, 242 N.Y.S. 100; 253 N.Y. 589, 171 N.E. 795; 229 A.D. 673, 243 N.Y.S. 35; 231 A.D. 303, 247 N.Y.S. 160; 255 N.Y. 436, 175 N.E. 121; 256 N.Y. 177, 176 N.E. 133; 256 N.Y. 680, 177 N.E. 191; 284 U.S. 678, 76 L. Ed. 573, 52 S. Ct. 140
219 A.D. 46, 219 N.Y.S. 366; 244 N.Y. 606, 155 N.E. 916; 219 A.D. 825, 220 N.Y.S. 904; 249 N.Y. 538, 164 N.E. 575; 226 A.D. 802, 234 N.Y.S. 747; 229 A.D. 637, 243 N.Y.S. 35; 230 A.D. 834, 244 N.Y.S. 902; 256 N.Y. 528, 177 N.E. 126

*Continued*

223 A.D. 384, 228 N.Y.S. 111; 224 A.D. 726, 229 N.Y.S. 901; 226 A.D. 805, 234 N.Y.S. 865; 227 A.D. 784, 237 N.Y.S. 866; 228 A.D. 618, 237 N.Y.S. 867; 228 A.D. 620, 228 A.D. 621, 237 N.Y.S. 866; 228 A.D. 675, 238 N.Y.S. 905; 253 N.Y. 365, 171 N.E. 572; 229 A.D. 637, 243 N.Y.S. 35; 255 N.Y. 415, 175 N.E. 114; 255 N.Y. 415, 175 N.E. 114, 255 N.Y. 428, 175 N.E. 118; 255 N.Y. 440, 175 N.E. 122; 255 N.Y. 608, 175 N.E. 334; 256 N.Y. 655, 177 N.E. 180; 250 A.D. 711, 294 N.Y.S. 500; 274 N.Y. 545, 10 N.E.2d 543

223 A.D. 378, 228 N.Y.S. 106; 224 A.D. 726, 229 N.Y.S. 901; 226 A.D. 805, 234 N.Y.S. 864; 227 A.D. 702, 236 N.Y.S. 874; 228 A.D. 618, 237 N.Y.S. 867; 229 A.D. 637, 243 N.Y.S. 35, 254 N.Y. 518, 173 N.E. 846; 255 N.Y. 415, 175 N.E. 114; 255 N.Y. 608, 175 N.E. 334

223 A.D. 870, 229 N.Y.S. 285; 225 A.D. 749, 232 N.Y.S. 287; 225 A.D. 750, 232 N.Y.S. 288; 225 A.D. 801, 232 N.Y.S. 847; 229 A.D. 637, 243 N.Y.S. 35; 255 N.Y. 433, 175 N.E. 120; 261 N.Y. 616, 185 N.E. 762; 261 N.Y. 624, 185 N.E. 766; 262 N.Y. 453, 188 N.E. 17

226 A.D. 875, 235 N.Y.S. 858; 252 N.Y. 578, 170 N.E. 150; 229 A.D. 637, 243 N.Y.S. 35; 255 N.Y. 433, 175 N.E. 120; 257 N.Y. 544, 178 N.E. 788

**Ryan Construction Corporation Case**

85 N.L.R.B. 417, No. 76

**Ryan Stevedoring Company Case**

350 U.S. 124, 100 L. Ed. 133, 76 S. Ct. 232; 348 U.S. 948, 75 S. Ct. 435; 349 U.S. 901, 99 L. Ed. 1239, 75 S. Ct. 575; 349 U.S. 926, 99 L. Ed. 1257, 75 S. Ct. 769, 1955 A.M.C. 1422; 211 F.2d 277, 1954 A.M.C. 766; 111 F. Supp. 505, 1953 A.M.C. 755

## S

**Sabbatino Case**
376 U.S. 398, 11 L. Ed. 2d 804, 84 S. Ct. 923

**Sabine Tram Case**
61 Tex. Civ. App. 353, 121 S.W. 256; 128 S.W. xv; 227 U.S. 111, 57 L. Ed. 442, 33 S. Ct. 229

**Sabotage Cases**
348 Pa. 558, 36 A.2d 492

**Saboteur Cases**
47 F. Supp. 431; 317 U.S. 1, 87 L. Ed. 3, 63 S. Ct. 1; 63 S. Ct. 22

**Sacco-Vanzetti Case**
255 Mass. 369, 151 N.E. 839; 259 Mass. 128, 156 N.E. 57; 261 Mass. 12, 158 N.E. 167; 275 U.S. 574, 72 L. Ed. 434, 48 S. Ct. 17

**Sacramento Rate Cases**
231 F. 292; 242 U.S. 178, 61 L. Ed. 233, 37 S. Ct. 24
19 I.C.C. 259

**Sacramento Suburban Fruit Lands Cases**
36 F.2d 907, 36 F.2d 941

**Sacred Heart Case**
350 S.W.2d 814 (Mo.)

**Safe Place to Work Case (Independent Contractor)**
362 Mo. 530, 242 S.W.2d 479

**Safety Appliance Act Case**
164 F. 347; 222 U.S. 20, 56 L. Ed. 72, 32 S. Ct. 2
282 F.2d 569

**Safety Car Heating Case**
155 F.2d 937, 69 U.S.P.Q. (BNA) 401

**Sage Patch Case**
217 Miss. 112, 63 So. 2d 551

**Saginaw Case**
113 Mich. 694, 71 N.W. 1073; 168 U.S. 706, 42 L. Ed. 1214, 18 S. Ct. 947, 115 Mich. 300, 73 N.W. 243; 117 Mich. 246, 75 N.W. 466

**Sainsbury Case**
183 F.2d 548

**Salad Oil Cases**
179 F. 373
192 F. 904

**Salambier Case**
88 F. 990, 31 C.C.A. 596; 170 U.S. 621, 42 L. Ed. 1167, 18 S. Ct. 771

**Sale of Influence Case**
343 U.S. 148, 96 L. Ed. 846, 72 S. Ct. 568; 343 U.S. 954, 96 L. Ed. 1355, 72 S. Ct. 1046; 200 F.2d 639; 345 U.S. 941, 97 L. Ed. 1367, 73 S. Ct. 832; 345 U.S. 971, 97 L. Ed. 1388, 73 S. Ct. 1111

**Salesmen's Unemployment Compensation Case**
72 Ariz. 354, 236 P.2d 44

**Salt Cases**
6 F.2d 315; 293 U.S. 58, 79 L. Ed. 197, 55 S. Ct. 23
92 I.C.C. 388

**Salt Lake City Subscription Solicitors Case**
115 Utah 476, 206 P.2d 153

**Salt Lake County Case**
5 F.2d 34; 269 U.S. 578, 70 L. Ed. 421, 46 S. Ct. 103

**Salton Sea Cases**
172 F. 792, 97 C.C.A. 214; 215 U.S. 603, 54 L. Ed. 345, 30 S. Ct. 405
172 F. 820; 97 C.C.A. 242; 215 U.S. 606, 54 L. Ed. 346, 30 S. Ct. 407

**Salvation Army Case**
63 Mich. 396, 30 N.W. 72

**Sam Langer Case**
82 N.L.R.B. 1028, No. 132; 181 F.2d 34; 341 U.S. 694, 95 L. Ed. 1299, 71 S. Ct. 954

**Sam Spade Case**
216 F.2d 945

**San Antonio Park Case**
446 F.2d 1013; 368 F. Supp. 238

**San Francisco Switching Case**
18 I.C.C. 333; 188 F. 241, 188 F. 929; 234 U.S. 315, 58 L. Ed. 1329, 34 S. Ct. 820

**San Jacinto Tin Company Case**
9 F. 726

**San Mateo Case**
13 F. 722, 116 U.S. 138, 29 L. Ed. 589, 6 S. Ct. 317

**San Pedro Tidelands Cases**
166 Cal. 576, 138 P. 79
166 Cal. 614, 138 P. 94
166 Cal. 627, 138 P. 103
166 Cal. 630, 138 P. 100; 169 Cal. 542, 147 P. 274; 240 U.S. 142, 60 L. Ed. 569, 36 S. Ct. 338
166 Cal. 635, 138 P. 101
167 Cal. 643, 140 P. 587
167 Cal. 651, 140 P. 591
169 Cal. 521, 147 P. 141
169 Cal. 537, 147 P. 274
172 Cal. 692, 158 P. 177
207 Cal. 430, 278 P. 1028
70 Cal. App. 752, 234 P. 426

**San Saba Cases**
190 S.W.2d 126 (Tex.)
190 S.W.2d 130 (Tex.)

**Sanatogen Case**
229 U.S. 1, 57 L. Ed. 1041, 33 S. Ct. 616

**Sand Door Case**
113 N.L.R.B. 1210, No. 123; 241 F.2d 147; 247 F.2d 71; 355 U.S. 808, 2 L. Ed. 2d 27, 78 S. Ct. 13; 357 U.S. 93, 2 L. Ed. 2d 1186, 78 S. Ct. 1011

**Sandoval Case**
198 F. 539; 231 U.S. 28, 58 L. Ed. 107, 34 S. Ct. 1

**Sandpaper Case**
310 F.2d 89, 326 F.2d 517

**Sandy Bayou Mandamus Case**
87 Miss. 125, 40 So. 152

**Sandy Fox Case**
75 F.2d 183

**Sanford Case**
60 U.S. 393, 15 L. Ed. 691

**Sangre de Christo Case**
2 Colo. 411; 93 U.S. 644, 23 L. Ed. 998

**Sani-Flush Case**
81 F. Supp. 935, 81 U.S.P.Q. (BNA) 16; 178 F.2d 461, 84 U.S.P.Q. (BNA) 31; 339 U.S. 948, 94 L. Ed. 1362, 70 S. Ct. 802, 70 S. Ct. 803

**Santa Clara Tax Case**
18 F. 385; 118 U.S. 394, 30 L. Ed. 118, 6 S. Ct. 1132

**Santa Claus Case**
112 Tex. Crim. 612, 18 S.W.2d 625, 20 S.W.2d 196

**Santa's Workshop Case**
282 A.D. 328, 122 N.Y.S.2d 488; 2 A.D.2d 262, 153 N.Y.S.2d 839; 285 A.D. 1210, 140 N.Y.S.2d 524

**Saranac Case**
108 F. 221; 113 F. 884, 51 C.C.A. 514

**Saratoga Springs Cases**
194 N.Y. 326, 87 N.E. 504; 128 A.D. 33, 112 N.Y.S. 374; 137 A.D. 557, 121 N.Y.S. 683; 140 A.D. 943, 125 N.Y.S. 1123; 163 A.D. 768, 149 N.Y.S. 176; 179 A.D. 425, 165 N.Y.S. 1044; 60 Misc. 341, 113 N.Y.S. 458; 83 Misc. 582, 146 N.Y.S. 271
196 N.Y. 421, 90 N.E. 441; 128 A.D. 42, 112 N.Y.S. 381; 133 A.D. 937, 118 N.Y. Supp. 1131; 140 A.D. 802, 125 N.Y.S. 610; 119 N.Y.S. 1151
220 U.S. 61, 55 L. Ed. 369, 31 S. Ct. 337

**Satisfactory Title Case**
265 S.W.2d 386 (Mo.)

**Satisfactory Work Case**
377 Pa. 342, 105 A.2d 126

**Savage Pure Food Case**
225 U.S. 501, 56 L. Ed. 1182, 32 S. Ct. 715

**Save the Baby Case**
37 F.2d 137

**Savings Account Gift Case**
252 Wis. 175, 31 N.W.2d 175

**Savings and Loan Government Liability Case**
518 U.S. 839, 135 L. Ed. 2d 964, 116 S. Ct. 2432 (1996)

**Scaffold Case**
6 N.J. 82, 77 A.2d 245

**Scenic Hudson Case**
354 F.2d 608

**Schechter Case**
295 U.S. 495, 79 L. Ed. 1570, 55 S. Ct. 837; 295 U.S. 723, 79 L. Ed. 1676, 55 S. Ct. 651
76 F.2d 617

**Schenectady Rate Case**
200 A.D. 268, 193 N.Y.S. 186

**Schenectady Six Tickets for a Quarter Case**
2 Dep't Rep. 284

**Schenk Case**
253 F. 212; 249 U.S. 47, 63 L. Ed. 470, 39 S. Ct. 247

**Schiedam Schnapps Cases**
18 How. Pr. 64
15 Abb. Pr. 336

**Schlesinger Cases**
14 F. 682; 120 U.S. 109, 30 L. Ed. 607, 7 S. Ct. 442
14 F. 687; 120 U.S. 264, 30 L. Ed. 656, 7 S. Ct. 546
153 Minn. 88, 189 N.W. 415
153 Minn. 136, 189 N.W. 714

**Schmerber Case**
382 U.S. 971

**Schoharie Valley Railroad Case**
12 Abb. Pr. (n.s.) 394

**School Board Cases**
213 Ala. 106, 104 So. 273
221 Ala. 217, 128 So. 435

**School Bus Case**
132 N.J.L. 98, 39 A.2d 75; 133 N.J.L. 350, 44 A.2d 333; 330 U.S. 1, 91 L. Ed. 711, 67 S. Ct. 504; 330 U.S. 855, 91 L. Ed. 1297, 67 S. Ct. 962

**School Cases**
296 F. 928; 268 U.S. 510, 69 L. Ed. 1070, 45 S. Ct. 571
281 F.2d 452
284 F.2d 377; 163 F. Supp. 637
361 F.2d 250
127 F. Supp. 591
141 F. Supp. 777
142 F. Supp. 916
152 F. Supp. 84
161 F. Supp. 409
161 F. Supp. 610
141 Ct. Cl. 775
142 Ct. Cl. 794; 154 Ct. Cl. 397
145 Ct. Cl. 344
145 Ct. Cl. 723
146 Ct. Cl. 559
162 Ct. Cl. 310
167 Ct. Cl. 106

**School Corporal Punishment Case**
430 U.S. 651, 51 L. Ed. 2d 711, 97 S. Ct. 1401

**School Desegregation Cases**
443 U.S. 449, 61 L. Ed. 2d 666, 99 S. Ct. 2941; 443 U.S. 526, 61 L. Ed. 2d 720, 99 S. Ct. 2971; 99 S. Ct. 2982
112 L. Ed. 2d 715, 111 S. Ct. 630
118 L. Ed. 2d 108, 112 S. Ct. 1430
515 U.S. 70, 132 L. Ed. 2d 63, 115 S. Ct. 2038 (1995)

**School Desegregation Tax Cases**

495 U.S. 1, 109 L. Ed. 2d 1, 110 S. Ct. 1632; 495 U.S. 33, 109 L. Ed. 2d 31, 110 S. Ct. 1651

**School Prayer Cases**

177 F. Supp. 398; 184 F. Supp. 381; 195 F. Supp. 518; 201 F. Supp. 815; 364 U.S. 298, 5 L. Ed. 2d 89, 81 S. Ct. 268; 371 U.S. 807, 9 L. Ed. 2d 52, 83 S. Ct. 25; 371 U.S. 907, 83 S. Ct. 251; 371 U.S. 944, 83 S. Ct. 499; 372 U.S. 901, 83 S. Ct. 715; 374 U.S. 203, 10 L. Ed. 2d 844, 83 S. Ct. 1560; 83 S. Ct. 870

228 Md. 239, 179 A.2d 698; 374 U.S. 203, 10 L. Ed. 2d 844, 83 S. Ct. 1560; 371 U.S. 809, 9 L. Ed. 2d 52, 82 S. Ct. 21; 371 U.S. 907, 83 S. Ct. 251; 371 U.S. 944, 83 S. Ct. 498; 372 U.S. 901, 83 S. Ct. 714; 372 U.S. 901, 83 S. Ct. 715; 83 S. Ct. 869; 232 Md. 368, 193 A.2d 554

18 Misc. 2d 659, 191 N.Y.S.2d 453; 11 A.D.2d 340, 206 N.Y.S.2d 183; 10 N.Y.2d 174, 218 N.Y.S.2d 659, 176 N.E.2d 579; 370 U.S. 421, 8 L. Ed. 2d 601, 82 S. Ct. 1261; 12 N.Y.2d 712, 233 N.Y.S.2d 766, 186 N.E.2d 124; 368 U.S. 982, 82 S. Ct. 597; 369 U.S. 809, 82 S. Ct. 686

**School Segregation Cases**

344 U.S. 873, 97 L. Ed. 676, 73 S. Ct. 173; 345 U.S. 972, 97 L. Ed. 1388, 73 S. Ct. 886; 347 U.S. 497, 98 L. Ed. 884, 74 S. Ct. 693; 348 U.S. 886, 75 S. Ct. 210; 349 U.S. 294, 99 L. Ed. 1083, 75 S. Ct. 753

270 F.2d 209

369 F.2d 55

373 F.2d 75

380 F.2d 955

98 F. Supp. 529; 342 U.S. 350, 96 L. Ed. 342, 72 S. Ct. 327; 345 U.S. 972, 97 L. Ed. 1388, 73 S. Ct. 1118; 347 U.S. 483, 98 L. Ed. 873, 74 S. Ct. 686; 348 U.S. 886, 75 S. Ct. 210; 349 U.S. 294, 99 L. Ed. 1083, 75 S. Ct. 753; 349 U.S. 914, 75 S. Ct. 602

98 F. Supp. 797; 344 U.S. 1, 97 L. Ed. 3, 73 S. Ct. 1; 344 U.S. 141, 97 L. Ed. 152, 73 S. Ct. 124; 345 U.S. 972, 97 L. Ed. 1388, 73 S. Ct. 1118; 347 U.S. 483, 98 L. Ed. 873, 74 S. Ct. 686; 348 U.S. 886, 75 S. Ct. 210; 349 U.S. 294, 99 L. Ed. 1083, 75 S. Ct. 753

103 F. Supp. 337; 344 U.S. 1, 97 L. Ed. 3, 73 S. Ct. 1; 345 U.S. 972, 97 L. Ed. 1388, 73 S. Ct. 1118; 347 U.S. 483, 98 L. Ed. 873, 74 S. Ct. 686; 348 U.S. 886, 75 S. Ct. 210; 349 U.S. 294, 99 L. Ed. 1083, 75 S. Ct. 753

32 Del. Ch. 343, 87 A.2d 862; 33 Del. Ch. 144, 91 A.2d 137; 344 U.S. 891, 97 L. Ed. 689, 73 S. Ct. 213; 345 U.S. 972, 97 L. Ed. 1388, 73 S. Ct. 1118; 347 U.S. 483, 98 L. Ed. 873, 74 S. Ct. 686; 348 U.S. 886, 75 S. Ct. 210; 349 U.S. 294, 99 L. Ed. 1083, 75 S. Ct. 753

**Schowgurow Case**

240 Md. 121, 213 A.2d 475

**Schuyler Fraud Cases**

34 How. Pr. 302; 34 N.Y. 30; 3 Keyes 24; 3 Keyes 363

1 Abb. Pr. 417; 28 How. Pr. 187; 17 N.Y. 592, 7 Abb. Pr. 41; 8 Abb. Pr. 239; 17 How. Pr. 464; 38 Barb. 534; 29 Howpr 89

**Schuylkill Bridge Case**

81 U.S. 442, 20 L. Ed. 867

**Schwegmann Case**

184 F.2d 11; 340 U.S. 928, 95 L. Ed. 669, 71 S. Ct. 491, 341 U.S. 384, 95 L. Ed. 1035, 71 S. Ct. 745; 341 U.S. 956, 95 L. Ed. 1377, 71 S. Ct. 1011

**Schwimmer Case**

27 F.2d 742; 278 U.S. 595, 73 L. Ed. 526, 49 S. Ct. 80; 279 U.S. 644, 73 L. Ed. 889, 49 S. Ct. 448

**Scienter in Rule 10b-5 Case**

446 U.S. 680, 64 L. Ed. 2d 611, 100 S. Ct. 1945

**Scientific Evidence Case**

509 U.S. 579, 125 L. Ed. 2d 469, 113 S. Ct. 2786 (1993)

**Scofield Case**

215 F. 45

**Scopes Case**

152 Tenn. 424, 278 S.W. 57; 154 Tenn. 105, 289 S.W. 363

**Scotch Whiskey Case**

299 F. Supp. 543

**Scott County Sex Abuse Case**

421 N.W.2d 334

**Scottish Clans Case**
151 Mass. 558, 24 N.E. 918

**Scottsboro Cases**
224 Ala. 524, 141 So. 215; 236 Ala. 261, 182 So. 3; 286 U.S. 540, 76 L. Ed. 1278, 52 S. Ct. 648; 287 U.S. 45, 77 L. Ed. 158, 53 S. Ct. 55
224 Ala. 531, 141 So. 195; 286 U.S. 540, 76 L. Ed. 1278, 52 S. Ct. 648; 287 U.S. 45, 77 L. Ed. 158, 53 S. Ct. 55
224 Ala. 540, 141 So. 201; 286 U.S. 540, 76 L. Ed. 1278, 52 S. Ct. 648; 287 U.S. 45, 77 L. Ed. 158, 53 S. Ct. 55
229 Ala. 226, 156 So. 556; 236 Ala. 281, 182 So. 69; 293 U.S. 552, 79 L. Ed. 655, 55 S. Ct. 345, 294 U.S. 587, 79 L. Ed. 1074, 55 S. Ct. 579
229 Ala. 270, 156 So. 567; 234 Ala. 342, 175 So. 371; 293 U.S. 554, 79 L. Ed. 656, 55 S. Ct. 347; 294 U.S. 600, 79 L. Ed. 1082, 55 S. Ct. 575; 302 U.S. 733, 82 L. Ed. 567, 58 S. Ct. 121

**Scrap Metal Theft Case**
187 F.2d 427; 341 U.S. 925, 95 L. Ed. 1356, 71 S. Ct. 796; 342 U.S. 246, 96 L. Ed. 288, 72 S. Ct. 240

**Scrip Book Case**
187 F. 984; 194 F. 444; 203 F. 278

**Scripto Case**
362 U.S. 207, 4 L. Ed. 2d 660, 80 S. Ct. 619; 105 So. 2d 775 (Fla.); 361 U.S. 806, 4 L. Ed. 2d 54, 80 S. Ct. 52

**Sea Dog Case**
371 U.S. 471, 9 L. Ed. 2d 441, 83 S. Ct. 407; 368 U.S. 817, 7 L. Ed. 2d 23, 82 S. Ct. 75; 368 U.S. 973, 82 S. Ct. 477; 370 U.S. 908, 8 L. Ed. 2d 403, 82 S. Ct. 1254; 288 F.2d 366

**Sealing Cases**
24 F.2d 933; 33 F.2d 241

**Seamens Act Cases**
239 F. 583; 248 U.S. 182, 63 L. Ed. 199, 39 S. Ct. 83; 256 F. 631; 250 U.S. 638, 63 L. Ed. 1184, 39 S. Ct. 494; 252 U.S. 348, 64 L. Ed. 607, 40 S. Ct. 350
242 F. 954, 154 C.C.A. 590; 248 F. 670, 160 C.C.A. 570; 248 U.S. 185, 63 L. Ed. 200, 39 S. Ct. 84
244 F. 833; 250 F. 180, 162 C.C.A. 316; 246 U.S. 669, 62 L. Ed. 930, 38 S. Ct. 345; 248 U.S. 205, 63 L. Ed. 208, 39 S. Ct. 89

**Seamen's Sit Down Strike Case**
20 F. Supp. 650

**Seamless Hosiery Case**
7 F.2d 1003

**Search Warrant Cases**
255 U.S. 313, 65 L. Ed. 654, 41 S. Ct. 266
253 F. 239; 253 F. 242; 253 F. 770; 264 F. 839; 255 U.S. 298, 65 L. Ed. 647, 41 S. Ct. 261; 273 F. 506

**Search Warrant 'Totality of Circumstances' Case**
80 L. Ed. 2d 721, 104 S. Ct. 2085

**Searls Case**
49 F.2d 224

**Seat of Government Case**
F. Cas. No. 6,848

**Sebastian Kneipp Case**
82 F. 321, 27 C.C.A. 351

**Second Avenue Bondholders Cases**
188 F. 339; 188 F. 343; 189 F. 661; 190 F. 609; 194 F. 543; 198 F. 721, 117 C.C.A. 503; 204 F. 513
208 F. 168; 208 F. 747; 208 F. 757; 208 F. 777; 216 F. 458

**Second Avenue Case**
165 F. 489; 166 F. 569; 168 F. 937; 170 F. 625; 170 F. 626; 171 F. 1014, 177 F. 925

**Second Boston and Maine Case**
227 A.D. 361, 238 N.Y.S. 27; 254 N.Y. 513, 173 N.E. 844

**Second Clay County Case**
140 So. 2d 576 (Fla.)

**Second Commodities Case**
220 U.S. 257, 55 L. Ed. 458, 31 S. Ct. 387

**Second Coronado Coal Case**
268 U.S. 295, 69 L. Ed. 963, 45 S. Ct. 551

**Second Dooley Case**
183 U.S. 151, 43 L. Ed. 128, 22 S. Ct. 62

**Second Employers' Liability Cases**
173 F. 494; 223 U.S. 1, 56 L. Ed. 327, 32 S. Ct. 169
259 F. 178, 170 C.C.A. 246; 250 U.S. 636, 63 L. Ed. 1183, 39 S. Ct. 490; 253 U.S. 86, 64 L. Ed. 794, 40 S. Ct. 454
50 Cal. App. 161, 195 P. 81; 255 U.S. 567, 65 L. Ed. 789, 41 S. Ct. 377; 259 U.S. 182, 66 L. Ed. 888, 42 S. Ct. 489
82 Conn. 373, 73 A. 762; 223 U.S. 1, 56 L. Ed. 327, 32 S. Ct. 169
168 A.D. 351, 153 N.Y.S. 499; 216 N.Y. 284, 110 N.E. 614; 244 U.S. 147, 61 L. Ed. 1045, 37 S. Ct. 546

**Second Industrial Railways Case**
34 I.C.C. 596; 38 I.C.C. 316

**Second Mutoscope Case**
151 F. 767

**Second New York Milk Case**
6 F. Supp. 297; 293 U.S. 163, 79 L. Ed. 259, 55 S. Ct. 7; 54 S. Ct. 719

**Second Shoe Machinery Case**
264 F. 138, 254 U.S. 666, 65 L. Ed. 465, 41 S. Ct. 217; 41 S. Ct. 9; 258 U.S. 451, 66 L. Ed. 708, 42 S. Ct. 363; 259 U.S. 575, 66 L. Ed. 1071, 42 S. Ct. 585

**Second United Mine Workers' Case**
268 U.S. 295, 69 L. Ed. 963, 45 S. Ct. 551

**Second Whittemore Case**
250 N.Y. 298, 165 N.E. 454

**Secondary Boycott Case**
276 N.Y. 281, 11 N.E.2d 910

**Section 1981 Private Discrimination Case**
491 U.S. 164, 105 L. Ed. 2d 132, 109 S. Ct. 2363

**Section 1993 State-Not-"Person" Case**
491 U.S. 58, 105 L. Ed. 2d 45, 109 S. Ct. 2304

**Securities Act Case**
298 U.S. 1, 80 L. Ed. 1015, 56 S. Ct. 654; 85 F.2d 15

**Securities Fraud Aiding and Abetting Case**
511 U.S. 164, 128 L. Ed. 2d 119, 114 S. Ct. 1439 (1994)

**Securities Transaction Case**
471 U.S. 701, 85 L. Ed. 2d 708, 105 S. Ct. 2308

**Securities Violation Standard of Proof Case**
450 U.S. 91, 67 L. Ed. 2d 69, 101 S. Ct. 999

**Security Trust Company Case**
93 Cal. App. 2d 608, 209 P.2d 657; 339 U.S. 947, 94 L. Ed. 1361, 70 S. Ct. 801, 70 S. Ct. 802; 340 U.S. 47, 95 L. Ed. 53, 71 S. Ct. 111

**Sedalia Case**
299 Mo. 446, 253 S.W. 741

**Sedition Case**
54 F. Supp. 791; 142 F.2d 473, 79 App. D.C. 47; 69 F. Supp. 812

**Seelbach Case**
161 Tex. 250, 339 S.W.2d 521

**Segregation Cases**
See School Segregation Cases

**Segui Case**
35 U.S. 306, 9 L. Ed. 435

**Selden Patent Case**
172 F. 923; 184 F. 893, 107 C.C.A. 215

**Selective Draft Law Cases**
98 U.S. 145, 25 L. Ed. 244
133 U.S. 333, 33 L. Ed. 637, 10 S. Ct. 299
245 U.S. 366, 62 L. Ed. 349, 38 S. Ct. 159
120 F.2d 236
123 F.2d 395

**Selective Service Cases**
470 U.S. 598, 84 L. Ed. 2d 547, 105 S. Ct. 1544
470 U.S. 656, 84 L. Ed. 2d 572, 105 S. Ct. 1524

**Self-Representation Case**
422 U.S. 806, 45 L. Ed. 2d 562, 95 S. Ct. 2525

**Selma March Case**
240 F. Supp. 100

**Selma Station Case**
185 N.C. 435, 117 S.E. 563

**Semicolon Case**
39 Tex. 705

**Seminole Indian Case**
179 F. 13, 103 C.C.A. 1; 224 U.S. 458, 56 L. Ed. 841, 32 S. Ct. 544; 224 U.S. 471, 56 L. Ed. 847, 32 S. Ct. 549

**Seniority Layoff Case**
467 U.S. 561, 81 L. Ed. 2d 483, 104 S. Ct. 2576

**Seniority Systems Cases**
456 U.S. 63, 71 L. Ed. 2d 748, 102 S. Ct. 1534; 456 U.S. 273, 72 L. Ed. 2d 66, 102 S. Ct. 1781

**Sentence Appeal Case**
449 U.S. 117, 66 L. Ed. 2d 328, 101 S. Ct. 426

**Sentencing Guidelines Case**
488 U.S. 361, 102 L. Ed. 2d 714, 109 S. Ct. 647

**Separate Coach Law Case**
186 F. 966, 109 C.C.A. 110; 235 U.S. 151, 59 L. Ed. 169, 35 S. Ct. 69

**Separate Gate Picketing Case**
123 N.L.R.B. 1547, No. 180; 278 F.2d 282; 366 U.S. 667, 6 L. Ed. 2d 592, 81 S. Ct. 1285; 138 N.L.R.B. 342, No. 38

**Separate Roofs Case**
277 A.D. 560, 101 N.Y.S.2d 206

**Separation Agreement Case**
377 Pa. 487, 105 A.2d 608

**Sequestration Cases**
30 Tex. 688
30 Tex. 712
30 Tex. 713
30 Tex. 714

**Servant Apparent Authority Case**
190 Md. 256, 58 A.2d 290

**Service Letter Case**
259 U.S. 530, 66 L. Ed. 1044, 42 S. Ct. 516

**Servicemen's Mortgage Foreclosure Case**
362 Mo. 19, 239 S.W.2d 352

**Services to Relative Case**
131 W. Va. 429, 48 S.E.2d 1

**Set-Back Restrictive Covenant Case**
331 Mich. 323, 49 N.W.2d 314

**Seth Thomas Clock Company Case**
62 Hun 619, 42 N.Y. St. Rep. 60, 16 N.Y.S. 602; 133 N.Y. 323, 31 N.E. 238; 31 N.E. 626

**Seven Cent Fire Cases**
25 F.2d 164; 32 F.2d 1015
26 F.2d 912; 279 U.S. 159, 73 L. Ed. 652, 49 S. Ct. 282; 296 U.S. 667, 73 L. Ed. 1011, 49 S. Ct. 338

**Seven Count Case**
88 N.J.L. 378, 96 A. 587

**Seven Dirty Words Case**
438 U.S. 726, 57 L. Ed. 2d 1073, 98 S. Ct. 3026

**Seven Sons Case**
69 F. 271

**Seven-Up Labor Case**
196 F.2d 424; 344 U.S. 811, 97 L. Ed. 632, 73 S. Ct. 39; 344 U.S. 344, 97 L. Ed. 377, 73 S. Ct. 287

**Seventeen Magazine Cases**
163 F.2d 74, 167 F.2d 969

**Seventeen Townships Case**
81 Pa. 114

**Severance Pay Case**
149 Me. 286, 100 A.2d 726

**Severance Tax Cases**
279 F. 432; 286 F. 365
160 Ark. 17, 254 S.W. 450; 169 Ark. 473, 275 S.W. 741; 273 U.S. 672, 71 L. Ed. 833, 47 S. Ct. 475

**Severin Case**
99 Ct. Cl. 435; 322 U.S. 733, 88 L. Ed. 1567, 64 S. Ct. 1045

**Sewing Machine Cases**
F. Cas. No. 4,884; F. Cas. No. 4,885
F. Cas. No. 12,904
110 Mass. 1; 110 Mass. 70; F. Cas. No. 4,883; 85 U.S. 553, 21 L. Ed. 914

**Sex Stereotype Employment Discrimination Case**
490 U.S. 228, 104 L. Ed. 2d 268, 109 S. Ct. 1775

**Sexual Harassment Cases**
141 L. Ed. 2d 633, 118 S. Ct. 2257 (1998)
141 L. Ed. 2d 662, 118 S. Ct. 2275 (1998)
141 L. Ed. 2d 277, 118 S. Ct. 1989 (1998)
510 U.S. 17, 126 L. Ed. 2d 295, 114 S. Ct. 367 (1993)

**Sexual Psychopath Case**
360 Mo. 1249, 232 S.W.2d 897

**Shadwan Case**
49 F. 379; 55 F. 1002, 5 C.C.A. 381

**Shafer Case**
160 Ohio St. 543, 52 Ohio Op. 443, 117 N.E.2d 438

**Shamrock Dairy Case**
119 N.L.R.B. 998, No. 134

**Shanty Car Cook's Case**
250 U.S. 101, 63 L. Ed. 869, 39 S. Ct. 396

**Shea Chemical Corporation Case**
121 N.L.R.B. 1027, No. 129

**Sheldon Case**
222 F. 685; 243 U.S. 444, 61 L. Ed. 839, 37 S. Ct. 434

**Shelley Cases**
334 U.S. 1, 92 L. Ed. 1161, 68 S. Ct. 836; 316 Mich. 614, 25 N.W.2d 638; 355 Mo. 814, 198 S.W.2d 679; 358 Mo. 364, 214 S.W.2d 525

**Shepang Voting Trust Cases**
60 Conn. 553, 24 A. 32

**Sheppard Case**
65 Pa. 20; 77 Pa. 295

**Sheppard Uxoricide Case**
121 N.E.2d 438; 121 N.E.2d 440; 97 Ohio App. 489, 123 N.E.2d 544; 97 Ohio App. 493, 124 N.E.2d 730; 165 Ohio St. 293, 59 Ohio Op. 398, 135 N.E.2d 340; 352 U.S. 910, 1 L. Ed. 2d 119, 77 S. Ct. 118; 164 Ohio St. 428, 58 Ohio Op. 247, 131 N.E.2d 837; 170 Ohio St. 551, 11 Ohio Op. 2d 406, 167 N.E.2d 94; 100 Ohio App. 345, 60 Ohio Op. 298, 128 N.E.2d 471; 352 U.S. 955, 1 L. Ed. 2d 245, 77 S. Ct. 323; 100 Ohio App. 399, 60 Ohio Op. 332, 128 N.E.2d 504; 384 U.S. 333, 16 L. Ed. 2d 600, 86 S. Ct. 1507

**Sherman Act Jurisdiction Case**
444 U.S. 232, 62 L. Ed. 2d 441, 100 S. Ct. 502

**Sherrer Case**
334 U.S. 343, 92 L. Ed. 1429, 68 S. Ct. 1087, 68 S. Ct. 1097; 320 Mass. 351, 69 N.E.2d 801

**Sherry Wine Case**
F. Cas. No. 14,279

**Ship Chandler Cases**
264 F.2d 400; 28 T.C. 1322
152 F. Supp. 10
260 F.2d 185; 28 T.C. 692

**Ship Recorder Case**
F. Cas. No. 16,129; F. Cas. No. 16,130

**Shipbuilders' Bank Case**
50 Me. 271; 54 Me. 206

**Shipping Pool Case**
216 F. 971; 239 U.S. 466, 60 L. Ed. 387, 36 S. Ct. 212

**Shipwreck-Marking Case**
95 F. Supp. 298, 1951 A.M.C. 230; 193 F.2d 631

**Sho-Me Power Cooperative Case**
356 Mo. 832, 204 S.W.2d 276

**Shoe Buckle Case**
Tres. Dec. 43588; Treas. Dec. 44425, 18 C.C.P.A. 248; Abs. (n.s.) No. 15048

**Shoe Last Case**
F. Cas. No. 8,653

**Shoe Machinery Trust Case**
195 F. 578; 227 U.S. 202, 57 L. Ed. 481, 33 S. Ct. 253

**Shorter Work Day Case**
71 Ore. 259, 139 P. 731; 243 U.S. 426, 61 L. Ed. 830, 37 S. Ct. 435

**Showboat Cases**
17 F.2d 446
47 F.2d 268
13 F. Supp. 123

**Shredded Wheat Cases**
91 F.2d 150, 33 U.S.P.Q. (BNA) 256; 302 U.S. 733, 82 L. Ed. 567, 58 S. Ct. 120; 302 U.S. 777, 82 L. Ed. 601, 58 S. Ct. 139; 302 U.S. 654, 82 L. Ed. 506, 58 S. Ct. 280, 55 U.S.P.Q. (BNA) 214; 96 F.2d 873, 37 U.S.P.Q. (BNA) 475; 304 U.S. 586, 82 L. Ed. 1547, 58 S. Ct. 1052; 58 S. Ct. 1043; 305 U.S. 111, 83 L. Ed. 73, 59 S. Ct. 109; 305 U.S. 674, 83 L. Ed. 437, 59 S. Ct. 246, 59 S. Ct. 247; 39 C.D. 850, 39 U.S.P.Q. (BNA) 296; 22 F. Supp. 801, 37 U.S.P.Q. (BNA) 119; 24 U.S.P.Q. (BNA) 138; 28 U.S.P.Q. (BNA) 179
250 F 960; 244 F. Supp. 508

**Shreveport Rate Case**
23 I.C.C. 31; 205 F. 380; 205 F. 391; 234 U.S. 342, 58 L. Ed. 1341, 34 S. Ct. 833

**Shrimp Peelers Cases**
366 F.2d 117
244 F. Supp. 9, 245 F. Supp. 1019, 260 F. Supp. 193

**Shufflin' Sam Case**
362 U.S. 199, 4 L. Ed. 2d 654, 80 S. Ct. 624; 362 U.S. 985, 4 L. Ed. 2d 1020, 80 S. Ct. 1074

**Shurtleff Case**
189 U.S. 311, 47 L. Ed. 828, 23 S. Ct. 535

**Shut Down Case**
2 F. Supp. 168

**Sibbald Case**
35 U.S. 313, 9 L. Ed. 437

**Sick Chicken Case**
295 U.S. 495, 79 L. Ed. 1570, 55 S. Ct. 837; 295 U.S. 723, 79 L. Ed. 1676, 55 S. Ct. 651

**Sick Engineer Case**
90 A.D. 125, 18 N.Y. Crim. 103, 85 N.Y.S. 1056; 179 N.Y. 518, 71 N.E. 1135

**Side-End Line Case**
98 U.S. 463, 25 L. Ed. 253

**Sidewalk Vault Case**
202 Ind. 233, 171 N.E. 871, 173 N.E. 287

**Sieracki Case**
328 U.S. 85, 90 L. Ed. 1099, 66 S. Ct. 872; 149 F.2d 98, 1945 A.M.C. 407; 57 F. Supp. 724, 1944 A.M.C. 1182; 326 U.S. 700, 90 L. Ed. 413, 66 S. Ct. 58, 1945 A.M.C. 1387; 328 U.S. 878, 90 L. Ed. 1646, 66 S. Ct. 1116

**Signal Switch Case**
246 U.S. 500, 62 L. Ed. 854, 38 S. Ct. 360

**Silberschein Case**
280 F. 917; 285 F. 397; 266 U.S. 221, 69 L. Ed. 256, 45 S. Ct. 69

**Silent Meditation Cases**
471 U.S. 858, 85 L. Ed. 2d 829, 105 S. Ct. 2455; 472 U.S. 38, 86 L. Ed. 2d 29, 105 S. Ct. 2479

**Silicon-Monoxide Case**
36 App. D.C. 181, 11 C.D. 295, 163 Off. Gaz. Pat. Office 729

**Silicosis Case**
352 Mo. 211, 176 S.W.2d 471; 357 Mo. 738, 210 S.W.2d 98; 335 U.S. 809, 93 L. Ed. 365, 69 S. Ct. 41; 337 U.S. 163, 93 L. Ed. 1282, 69 S. Ct. 1018

**Silver Bridge Disaster Case**
311 F. Supp. 1345

**Silver Platter Cases**
232 U.S. 383, 58 L. Ed. 652, 34 S. Ct. 341
338 U.S. 74, 93 L. Ed. 1819, 69 S. Ct. 1372; 331 U.S. 853, 91 L. Ed. 1861, 67 S. Ct. 1737; 333 U.S. 835, 92 L. Ed. 1119, 68 S. Ct. 601; 159 F.2d 798
364 U.S. 206, 4 L. Ed. 2d 1669, 4 L. Ed. 2d 1688, 80 S. Ct. 1437, 80 S. Ct. 1453

**Silverthorne Lumber Company Cases**
251 U.S. 385, 64 L. Ed. 319, 40 S. Ct. 182
265 F. 853; 265 F. 859

**Similitude Clause Case**
Treas. Dec. 38403, 10 Ct. Cust. 165; 257 U.S. 536, 66 L. Ed. 357, 42 S. Ct. 212

**Simultaneous Death Case**
189 Ore. 537, 221 P.2d 892

**Sinclair Contempt Cases**
279 U.S. 263, 73 L. Ed. 692, 49 S. Ct. 268
279 U.S. 749, 73 L. Ed. 938, 49 S. Ct. 471

**Sinclair Refining Case**
187 F. Supp. 225; 290 F.2d 312; 370 U.S. 195, 8 L. Ed. 2d 440, 82 S. Ct. 1328; 370 U.S. 238, 8 L. Ed. 2d 462, 82 S. Ct. 1318

**Singer Case**
41 F. 208; 163 U.S. 169, 41 L. Ed. 118, 16 S. Ct. 1002

**Sinking Fund Cases**
96 U.S. 97, 24 L. Ed. 616
99 U.S. 700, 25 L. Ed. 496, 504
13 Ct. Cl. 401; 99 U.S. 402, 25 L. Ed. 274

**Siphon Case**
205 Cal. 515, 271 P. 1060

**Sister Egan Case**
408 U.S. 41, 33 L. Ed. 2d 179, 92 S. Ct. 2357; 450 F.2d 199

**Sister State Disbarment Case**
64 Nev. 364, 183 P.2d 833

**Sisters of Charity Case**
67 N.Y. 409

**Sit-In Cases**
368 U.S. 157, 7 L. Ed. 2d 207, 82 S. Ct. 248 (1961)
373 U.S. 267, 10 L. Ed. 2d 338, 83 S. Ct. 1122; 373 U.S. 374, 10 L. Ed. 2d 419, 83 S. Ct. 1311; 373 U.S. 375, 10 L. Ed. 2d 420, 83 S. Ct. 1311 (1963)
378 U.S. 130, 12 L. Ed. 2d 754, 84 S. Ct. 1770 (1964)
378 U.S. 146, 12 L. Ed. 2d 766, 84 S. Ct. 1734
378 U.S. 153, 12 L. Ed. 2d 771, 84 S. Ct. 1693
378 U.S. 226, 12 L. Ed. 2d 822, 84 S. Ct. 1814
378 U.S. 347, 12 L. Ed. 2d 894, 84 S. Ct. 1697
379 U.S. 306, 13 L. Ed. 2d 300, 85 S. Ct. 384 (1965)
379 U.S. 684, 13 L. Ed. 2d 603, 85 S. Ct. 635
195 A.2d 379 (Del.)

**Six-Member Jury Case**
413 U.S. 149, 37 L. Ed. 2d 522, 93 S. Ct. 2448
456 F.2d 1379

**Six-Million Suit Cases**
13 Abb. Pr. (n.s.) 25; 58 N.Y. 1; 13 Abb. Pr. (n.s.) 148, 13 Abb. Pr. (n.s.) 419; 14 Abb. Pr. (n.s.) 23
50 How. Pr. 262; 63 N.Y. 194, 63 N.Y. 202; 5 Hun 382; 373 U.S. 244, 10 L. Ed. 2d 323, 83 S. Ct. 1119, 83 S. Ct. 1133; 373 U.S. 262, 10 L. Ed. 2d 335, 83 S. Ct. 1130; 11 Hun 195

**Sixty-Four Count Case**
88 N.J.L. 376, 96 A. 589; 243 U.S. 574, 61 L. Ed. 908, 37 S. Ct. 468

**Sixty Pipes of Brandy Case**
23 U.S. 421, 6 L. Ed. 356

**Skid-Marks Case**
194 Md. 516, 71 A.2d 450

**Skinner's Estate Case**
197 F. Supp. 726; 316 F.2d 517

**Skokie Anti-Parade Case**
432 U.S. 43, 53 L. Ed. 2d 96, 97 S. Ct. 2205 (1985)

**Slaughterhouse Cases**
83 U.S. 36, 21 L. Ed. 394
122 U.S. 636, 30 L. Ed. 1248
9 F. 743; 12 F. 225; 111 U.S. 746, 28 L. Ed. 585, 4 S. Ct. 652
F. Cas. No. 8,408
22 La. Ann. 545; 77 U.S. 273, 19 L. Ed. 915; 83 U.S. 36, 21 L. Ed. 394
33 La. Ann. 930
36 La. Ann. 63; 37 La. Ann. 280
37 La. Ann. 874; 120 U.S. 141, 30 L. Ed. 614, 7 S. Ct. 472
41 La. Ann. 355, 6 So. 508

**Slave Case**
31 F. 327

**Slavers Cases**
69 U.S. 135, 17 L. Ed. 796
69 U.S. 350, 17 L. Ed. 878
69 U.S. 366, 17 L. Ed. 906
69 U.S. 375, 17 L. Ed. 909
F. Cas. No. 16,144; 69 U.S. 383, 17 L. Ed. 911

**Sleepy Lagoon Cases**
66 Cal. 2d 166, 152 P.2d 180
66 Cal. 2d 369, 152 P.2d 450

**Slippery Sidewalk Case**
174 Kan. 686, 257 P.2d 1115

**Slocum Case**
134 F. 592; 159 F. 847, 87 C.C.A. 27

**Slum Clearance Case**
9 F. Supp. 137; 78 F.2d 684; 294 U.S. 735, 79 L. Ed. 1263, 55 S. Ct. 548; 296 U.S. 567, 80 L. Ed. 400, 56 S. Ct. 154; 297 U.S. 726, 80 L. Ed. 1009, 56 S. Ct. 594

**Small Loan Case**
115 Conn. 102, 160 A. 426

**Smallpox Vaccination Case**
See Vaccination Cases

**Smelting Case**
61 N.J. Eq. 458, 48 A. 786
62 N.J. Eq. 729, 48 A. 771
62 N.J. Eq. 729, 48 A. 1116

**Smelting Company Cases**
106 U.S. 447, 27 L. Ed. 226, 1 S. Ct. 389
13 F. 208
F. Cas. No. 12,239a; 104 U.S. 636, 26 L. Ed. 875

**Smith Act Case of 1948**
341 U.S. 494, 95 L. Ed. 1137, 71 S. Ct. 857

**Smith Case**
110 F. 60; 119 F. 114, 55 C.C.A. 216; 194 U.S. 401, 48 L. Ed. 1039, 24 S. Ct. 676

**Smith-Turner Case**
122 Tex. 338, 61 S.W.2d 792

**Smog Cases**
173 Pa. Super. 209, 96 A.2d 163; 379 Pa. 441; 173 Pa. Super. xxix
160 A.2d 465 (Pa.); 388 Pa. 559, 131 A.2d 141
109 A.2d 310 (Pa.)

**Smokador Case**
31 F.2d 255

**Smoke-House Lode Case**
6 Mont. 397, 12 P. 858

**Smoot's Case**
5 Ct. Cl. 490; 131 U.S. Appx. ccvi; 82 U.S. 36, 21 L. Ed. 107

**Smyth Case**
64 F. 165; 100 F. 235; 102 F. 197; 169 U.S. 466, 42 L. Ed. 819, 18 S. Ct. 418; 171 U.S. 361, 43 L. Ed. 197, 18 S. Ct. 888

**Snail Darter Case**
437 U.S. 153, 57 L. Ed. 2d 117, 98 S. Ct. 2279

**Snake Cases**
38 Ala. App. 404, 88 So. 2d 880
291 Ky. 437, 164 S.W.2d 972
229 N.C. 734, 51 S.E.2d 179
188 Tenn. 17, 216 S.W.2d 708
186 Wis. 482, 202 N.W. 295

**Snoozing Case**
392 Pa. 350, 140 A.2d 802

**Snow Bank Cases**
62 Iowa 629, 17 N.W. 901
64 Iowa 652, 21 N.W. 193; 69 Iowa 161, 28 N.W. 487

**Snow Road Case**
95 Ohio Law Abs. 6

**Snuff Case**
78 F. 472, 24 C.C.A. 173

**Snug Harbor Case**
283 F. 1015, 1923 A.M.C. 536; 272 U.S. 675, 71 L. Ed. 472, 47 S. Ct. 289; 29 F.2d 588, 1929 A.M.C. 42; 40 F.2d 27, 1930 A.M.C. 807

**Snyder-Gray Case**
246 N.Y. 491, 159 N.E. 408

**Soap Cases**
102 U.S. 707, 26 L. Ed. 279
50 F.T.C. 494
50 F.T.C. 513
50 F.T.C. 525

**Soap Classification Cases**
2 I.C. 614; 3 I.C. 131; 3 I.C. 374
9 I.C.C. 440; 146 F. 559; 206 U.S. 142, 51 L. Ed. 995, 27 S. Ct. 648

**Sobriety Checkpoint Case**
496 U.S. 444, 110 L. Ed. 2d 412, 110 S. Ct. 2481

**Sobriety Videotape Case**
496 U.S. 582, 110 L. Ed. 2d 528, 110 S. Ct. 2638

**Social Circle Case**
2 I.C. 625; 3 I.C. 682; 4 I.C. 332; 56 F. 925, 9 C.C.A. 689; 162 U.S. 184, 40 L. Ed. 935, 16 S. Ct. 700

**Social Security Cases**
301 U.S. 619, 81 L. Ed. 1307, 57 S. Ct. 904; 301 U.S. 672, 57 S. Ct. 947; 301 U.S. 674, 81 L. Ed. 1336, 57 S. Ct. 792
17 F. Supp. 225; 57 S. Ct. 514; 300 U.S. 644, 81 L. Ed. 858, 57 S. Ct. 668, 57 S. Ct. 674; 301 U.S. 495, 81 L. Ed. 1245, 57 S. Ct. 868
89 F.2d 207; 300 U.S. 652, 81 L. Ed. 863, 57 S. Ct. 673; 57 S. Ct. 755; 301 U.S. 548, 81 L. Ed. 1279, 57 S. Ct. 883

**Social Security Gender Distinction Case**
430 U.S. 199, 51 L. Ed. 2d 270, 97 S. Ct. 1021

**Social Security Spousal Benefits Case**
79 L. Ed. 2d 646, 104 S. Ct. 1387

**Sodomy Laws Case**
478 U.S. 186, 92 L. Ed. 2d 140, 106 S. Ct. 2841

**Soldier Bonus Case**
198 A.D. 928, 188 N.Y.S. 944; 231 N.Y. 465, 132 N.E. 241

**Soldier Compensation Case**
114 Kan. 270, 283, 217 P. 905

**Soldiers Case**
283 F. 845

**Soldiers Civil Relief Case**
222 N.C. 205, 22 S.E.2d 426; 318 U.S. 750, 87 L. Ed. 1126, 63 S. Ct. 770; 319 U.S. 561, 87 L. Ed. 1587, 63 S. Ct. 1223; 320 U.S. 809, 88 L. Ed. 489, 64 S. Ct. 26; 160 F.2d 13; 228 N.C. 199, 45 S.E.2d 261

**Soldiers' Voting Bill Case**
45 N.H. 607

**Solicitation of Contributions Case**
444 U.S. 620, 63 L. Ed. 2d 73, 100 S. Ct. 826

**Solomons Case**
137 U.S. 342, 34 L. Ed. 667, 11 S. Ct. 88; 21 Ct. Cl. 479; 22 Ct. Cl. 335

**Sonoma County Tax Case**
13 F. 789

**Sorrels Case**
57 F.2d 973; 287 U.S. 584, 77 L. Ed. 511, 53 S. Ct. 19; 287 U.S. 435, 77 L. Ed. 413, 53 S. Ct. 210

**South Bend Tax Budget Case**
202 Ind. 214, 172 N.E. 186, 907

**South Carolina Dispensary Case**
199 U.S. 437, 50 L. Ed. 261, 26 S. Ct. 110

**South Dakota Divorce Case**
88 Conn. 689, 92 A. 684

**South Dakota Passenger Rate Case**
210 F. 632

**South Dakota Rate Case**
38 S.D. 227, 161 N.W. 132; 244 U.S. 617, 61 L. Ed. 1352, 37 S. Ct. 656

**Southern Class Rate Investigation Case**
100 I.C.C. 627

**Southern Governors' Cases**
235 I.C.C. 255; 237 I.C.C. 515; 292 I.C.C. 599
301 I.C.C. 100

**Southern Pacific Clerks' Case**
281 U.S. 548, 74 L. Ed. 1034, 50 S. Ct. 427

**Southern Pacific Oil-Land Case**
234 U.S. 669, 58 L. Ed. 1527, 34 S. Ct. 907

**Southern Pacific Tax Case**
238 F. 847; 247 U.S. 330, 62 L. Ed. 1142, 38 S. Ct. 540

**Southwestern Bell Telephone Case**
233 S.W. 425 (Mo.); 262 U.S. 276, 67 L. Ed. 981, 43 S. Ct. 544

**Sovereign Immunity Case**
440 U.S. 410, 59 L. Ed. 2d 416, 99 S. Ct. 1182

**Space Suit Cases**
117 Ohio App. 493, 24 Ohio Op. 2d 290, 192 N.E.2d 99
137 U.S.P.Q. (BNA) 389
137 U.S.P.Q. (BNA) 804

**Spanish Pirates Case**
F. Cas. No. 15,204

**Spark Plug Cases**
299 F. 533
50 F.T.C. 30
50 F.T.C. 54
50 F.T.C. 73

**Special Franchise Tax Cases**
79 A.D. 183, 80 N.Y.S. 85; 174 N.Y. 417, 67 N.E. 69; 199 U.S. 1, 50 L. Ed. 65, 25 S. Ct. 705; 199 U.S. 48, 50 L. Ed. 79, 25 S. Ct. 713; 199 U.S. 53, 50 L. Ed. 85, 25 S. Ct. 715

**Specific Peril Cases**
84 F.2d 10; 23 F. Supp. 424; 96 F.2d 996; 305 U.S. 614, 83 L. Ed. 391, 59 S. Ct. 73
97 F.2d 628

**Speedway Case**
60 A.D. 122, 69 N.Y.S. 994; 168 N.Y. 134, 61 N.E. 158

**Spencer Haywood Case**
325 F. Supp. 1049

**Spendthrift Trust Case**
243 Iowa 312, 51 N.W.2d 412

**Spering's Appeal Case**
71 Pa. St 11

**Spicer Case**
5 Ct. Cl. 34; 82 U.S. 51, 21 L. Ed. 107

**Spielberg Manufacturing Company Case**
112 N.L.R.B. 1080, No. 139

**Spike-Making Machine Case**
F. Cas. No. 14,195; 55 U.S. 193, 14 L. Ed. 383; 56 U.S. 451, 14 L. Ed. 768; F. Cas. No. 14,196; F. Cas. No. 14,197; F. Cas. No. 14,198

**Spike Mike Case**
365 U.S. 505, 5 L. Ed. 2d 734, 81 S. Ct. 679; 275 F.2d 173; 166 F. Supp. 838

**Spiked Shoe Cases**
97 Pa. Super. 275
137 Pa. Super. 41, 8 A.2d 437
197 Pa. Super. 502, 179 A.2d 258
272 Pa. 28, 115 A. 869

**Spiller Cases**
246 F. 1; 249 F. 677; 253 U.S. 117, 64 L. Ed. 810, 40 S. Ct. 466

**Spiritual Advisor Privileged Communication Case**
121 Ind. App. 262, 95 N.E.2d 304

**Split Shingle Case**
46 F.2d 353

**Split Year Teachers' Pay Cases**
62 Cal. App. 2d 706, 145 P.2d 60; 174 Cal. App. 2d 459, 168 P.2d 749

**Spokane Rate Cases**
2 I.C. 452; 4 I.C. 183; 83 F. 249
15 I.C.C. 376

**Spontaneous News Case**
52 F. Supp. 362; 64 S. Ct. 1058; 326 U.S. 1, 89 L. Ed. 2013, 65 S. Ct. 1416; 326 U.S. 802, 90 L. Ed. 489, 66 S. Ct. 6; 326 U.S. 803, 90 L. Ed. 489, 66 S. Ct. 7

**Spot Welder Case**
268 F. 836; 281 F. 680; 260 U.S. 718, 67 L. Ed. 479, 43 S. Ct. 96; 265 U.S. 445, 68 L. Ed. 1098, 44 S. Ct. 533

**Spotted Tobacco Case**
103 F. 868

**Spouse Competency Case**
186 Va. 775, 43 S.E.2d 858

**Spreading Fire Case**
121 Colo. 227, 214 P.2d 793

**Spring Valley Case**
110 U.S. 347, 28 L. Ed. 173, 4 S. Ct. 48
201 Cal. 248, 257 P. 49

**Springfield Mail Robbery Cases**
25 F.2d 90
25 F.2d 92

**Spur Case**
295 U.S. 264, 79 L. Ed. 1429, 55 S. Ct. 689; 229 A.D. 617, 243 N.Y.S. 665; 238 A.D. 832, 262 N.Y.S. 973; 265 N.Y. St. Rep. 170, 192 N.E. 188; 141 Misc. 565, 253 N.Y.S. 743

**Square Yard Cases**
76 U.S. 248, 19 L. Ed. 648
113 U.S. 645, 28 L. Ed. 1130, 5 S. Ct. 624
6 F. 150
F. Cas. No. 5,778; 101 U.S. 278, 25 L. Ed. 845

**St. Agnes Hospital Case**
290 Pa. 388, 139 A. 122

**St. Cloud Case**
8 I.C.C. 346

**St. John Station Case**
80 Utah 455, 15 P.2d 358

**St. Joseph Stockyards Case**
298 U.S. 38, 80 L. Ed. 1033, 56 S. Ct. 720

**St. Louis Bill Board Ordinance Case**
235 Mo. 99, 137 S.W. 929; 231 U.S. 761, 58 L. Ed. 470, 34 S. Ct. 325

**St. Louis Hay and Grain Case**
11 I.C.C. 90; 149 F. 609; 153 F. 728, 82 C.C.A. 614; 214 U.S. 297, 53 L. Ed. 1004, 29 S. Ct. 678; 18 I.C.C. 607; 19 I.C.C. 533

**St. Louis Terminal Cases**
224 U.S. 383, 56 L. Ed. 810, 32 S. Ct. 507; 197 F. 446; 226 U.S. 420, 57 L. Ed. 281, 33 S. Ct. 170
34 I.C.C. 453

**St. Louis Union Trust Cases**
28 B.T.A. 107; 75 F.2d 416; 295 U.S. 727, 79 L. Ed. 1678, 55 S. Ct. 834; 296 U.S. 39, 80 L. Ed. 29, 56 S. Ct. 74
76 F.2d 851; 296 U.S. 564, 80 L. Ed. 398, 56 S. Ct. 122; 296 U.S. 48, 80 L. Ed. 35, 56 S. Ct. 78

**St. Patrick Parade Case**
515 U.S. 557, 132 L. Ed. 2d 487, 115 S. Ct. 2338 (1995)

**Stage Horse Case**
15 Abb. Pr. (n.s.) 51

**Stairway Hole Case**
204 Md. 387, 104 A.2d 628

**Staley Case**
144 F.2d 221; 324 U.S. 746, 89 L. Ed. 1338, 65 S. Ct. 971; 323 U.S. 702, 89 L. Ed. 567, 65 S. Ct. 189; 135 F.2d 453

**Stamp Case**
3 Cal. 2d 689, 46 P.2d 135

**Stan-Jay Case**
179 F. Supp. 481; 182 F. Supp. 949

**Standard Dry Wall Products Case**
91 N.L.R.B. 544, No. 103

**Standard Oil Cases**
148 F. 719; 155 F. 305; 164 F. 376, 90 C.C.A. 364; 212 U.S. 579, 53 L. Ed. 659, 29 S. Ct. 689; 170 F. 988
152 F. 290; 173 F. 177; 221 U.S. 1, 55 L. Ed. 619, 31 S. Ct. 502

**Standard Oil of Indiana Case**
173 F.2d 210; 338 U.S. 865, 94 L. Ed. 530, 70 S. Ct. 140; 339 U.S. 975, 94 L. Ed. 1381, 70 S. Ct. 1018; 340 U.S. 231, 95 L. Ed. 239, 71 S. Ct. 240

**Standard Parts Case**
264 U.S. 52, 68 L. Ed. 560, 44 S. Ct. 239

**Standard Stations Case**
78 F. Supp. 850; 337 U.S. 293, 93 L. Ed. 1371, 69 S. Ct. 1051; 338 U.S. 808, 94 L. Ed. 489, 70 S. Ct. 29

**Standby Counsel Case**
79 L. Ed. 2d 122, 104 S. Ct. 944

**Stanley County Cases**
89 F. 257; 96 F. 284, 37 C.C.A. 484; 113 F. 705, 51 C.C.A. 379; 186 U.S. 484, 46 L. Ed. 1261, 23 S. Ct. 856; 190 U.S. 437, 47 L. Ed. 1126, 23 S. Ct. 811
121 N.C. 394, 28 S.E. 539

**Star Route Case**
40 F. 752

**Starin Case**
115 U.S. 248, 29 L. Ed. 388, 6 S. Ct. 28; 21 F. 593; 22 F. 801

**Starnes Case**
26 F.2d 997

**State Aid to Private Schools Cases**
413 U.S. 455, 37 L. Ed. 2d 723, 93 S. Ct. 2804
340 F. Supp. 1003

**State Bond Taxation Case**
485 U.S. 505, 99 L. Ed. 2d 592, 108 S. Ct. 1355

**State Bonding Cases**
27 N.D. 77, 145 N.W. 425
33 N.D. 76, 156 N.W. 561, 245 U.S. 627, 62 L. Ed. 518, 38 S. Ct. 60

**State Candidate Drug-Testing Case**
520 U.S. 305, 137 L. Ed. 2d 513, 117 S. Ct. 1295 (1997)

**State Fair Automobile Case**
163 A.D. 253, 148 N.Y.S. 479

**State Free Pass Case**
122 N.C. 1052, 30 S.E. 133

**State Freight Tax Cases**
62 Pa. 286; 82 U.S. 232, 21 L. Ed. 146, 82 U.S. 282, 21 L. Ed. 164
66 Pa. 84

**State Gross Receipts Tax Case**
82 U.S. 284, 21 L. Ed. 164

**State Injunction against Picketing Case**
199 Misc. 518, 106 N.Y.S.2d 865; 278 A.D. 936, 105 N.Y.S.2d 857; 303 N.Y. 300, 101 N.E.2d 697; 303 N.Y. 673, 102 N.E.2d 833

**State Legislator's Privilege Case**
445 U.S. 360, 63 L. Ed. 2d 454, 100 S. Ct. 1185

**State Line Case**
235 U.S. 1, 59 L. Ed. 97, 35 S. Ct. 8

**State Normal College Case**
98 Miss. 337, 53 So. 681

**State Officers' Communist Oath Case**
5 N.J. Super. 239, 68 A.2d 761; 3 N.J. 578, 71 A.2d 352

**State Owned Railroad Case**
455 U.S. 678, 71 L. Ed. 2d 547, 102 S. Ct. 1349

**State Railroad Tax Cases**
92 U.S. 575, 23 L. Ed. 663

**State Regulation of Illegal Aliens Case**
424 U.S. 351, 47 L. Ed. 2d 43, 96 S. Ct. 933

**State Regulation of Peaceful Activity Case**
427 U.S. 132, 49 L. Ed. 2d 396, 96 S. Ct. 2548

**State Secrets in Evidence Case**
10 F.R.D. 468; 192 F.2d 987; 343 U.S. 918, 96 L. Ed. 1332, 72 S. Ct. 678; 345 U.S. 1, 97 L. Ed. 727, 73 S. Ct. 528

**State Street Trust Company Case**
263 F.2d 635; 160 F. Supp. 877

**State Tax Law Cases**
54 Mich. 350, 20 N.W. 493
23 N.W. 87; 54 Mich. 417, 23 N.W. 189

**State Tax of Carriers Case**
192 Md. 303, 64 A.2d 284; 339 U.S. 542, 94 L. Ed. 1053, 70 S. Ct. 806

**State Tax on Foreign Held Bonds Cases**
72 U.S. 290, 18 L. Ed. 475
82 U.S. 300, 21 L. Ed. 179

**State Tax on Railway Gross Receipts Cases**
82 U.S. 284, 21 L. Ed. 164, 4 Brewst. 222
104 Pa. 109; 122 U.S. 326, 30 L. Ed. 1200, 7 S. Ct. 1118

**State Tonnage Tax Cases**
43 Ala. 578; 79 U.S. 204, 20 L. Ed. 370
43 Ala. 697; 79 U.S. 204, 20 L. Ed. 370

**State Troopers Affirmative Action Case**
480 U.S. 149, 94 L. Ed. 2d 203, 107 S. Ct. 1053

**State Troopers Presence at Trial Case**
475 U.S. 560, 89 L. Ed. 2d 525, 106 S. Ct. 1340

**State Unemployment Insurance Case**
301 U.S. 495, 81 L. Ed. 1245, 57 S. Ct. 868

**State Use Tax Exemption Case**
198 Md. 398, 84 A.2d 86

**State Welfare Regulation Case**
441 U.S. 600, 60 L. Ed. 2d 508, 99 S. Ct. 1905

**Statham Case**
93 U.S. 24, 23 L. Ed. 789

**Station Facilities Case**
12 I.C.C. 114; 155 F. 512

**Statute of Limitations Cases**
95 U.S. 628, 24 L. Ed. 365; 95 U.S. 637, 24 L. Ed. 534

**Statutory Rape Case**
450 U.S. 464, 67 L. Ed. 2d 437, 101 S. Ct. 1200

**Staunton Mail Robbery Case**
10 F.2d 401; 270 U.S. 663, 70 L. Ed. 788, 46 S. Ct. 471; 271 U.S. 662, 70 L. Ed. 1138, 46 S. Ct. 474

**Steam Shovel Case**
207 N.Y. 81, 100 N.E. 700

**Steam Turbine Case**
204 F. 103; 222 F. 297; 231 F. 162

**Steamboat Monopoly Case**
22 U.S. 1, 6 L. Ed. 23; 14 Johns. 488, 4 Johns. Ch 150; 19 U.S. 448, 5 L. Ed. 302

**Steamship Cases**
58 U.S. 596, 15 L. Ed. 254
78 U.S. 423, 20 L. Ed. 192
83 U.S. 471, 21 L. Ed. 303

**Steel Case**
64 N.J. Eq. 90, 53 A. 601; 64 N.J. Eq. 807, 54 A. 1

**Steel Company Case**
89 F. 721; 96 F. 850, 37 C.C.A. 593; 175 U.S. 727, 44 L. Ed. 339, 20 S. Ct. 1031; 185 U.S. 403, 46 L. Ed. 968, 22 S. Ct. 698

**Steel Seizure Case**
103 F. Supp. 569; 103 F. Supp. 978; 90 App. D.C. 416, 197 F.2d 582; 343 U.S. 937, 96 L. Ed. 1344, 72 S. Ct. 775, 72 S. Ct. 1075; 343 U.S. 952, 72 S. Ct. 1047, 72 S. Ct. 1075; 343 U.S. 579, 96 L. Ed. 1153, 72 S. Ct. 863

**Steel Trader Case**
10 F.2d 248; 13 F.2d 614, 273 U.S. 680, 71 L. Ed. 837, 47 S. Ct. 111; 275 U.S. 388, 72 L. Ed. 326, 48 S. Ct. 162

**Steel Trust Case**
223 F. 55; 240 U.S. 442, 60 L. Ed. 731, 36 S. Ct. 408; 251 U.S. 417, 64 L. Ed. 343, 40 S. Ct. 293

**Steel Window Sash Case**
26 I.C.C. 605; 220 F. 14, 135 C.C.A. 590

**Steelworkers Trilogy Cases**
363 U.S. 564, 4 L. Ed. 2d 1403, 4 L. Ed. 2d 1432, 80 S. Ct. 1343, 80 S. Ct. 1363; 264 F.2d 624
363 U.S. 574, 4 L. Ed. 2d 1409, 80 S. Ct. 1347, 168 F. Supp. 702; 269 F.2d 633
363 U.S. 593, 4 L. Ed. 2d 1424, 80 S. Ct. 1358; 168 F. Supp. 308; 269 F.2d 327

**Stein Case**
346 U.S. 156, 97 L. Ed. 1522, 73 S. Ct. 1077; 303 N.Y. 856, 104 N.E.2d 917; 303 N.Y. 982, 106 N.E.2d 63; 306 N.Y. 675, 116 N.E.2d 502; 306 N.Y. 678, 117 N.E.2d 355; 306 N.Y. 867, 118 N.E.2d 918; 307 N.Y. 253, 120 N.E.2d 813, 307 N.Y. 912, 123 N.E.2d 567, 308 N.Y. 747, 125 N.E.2d 105; 308 N.Y. 772, 125 N.E.2d 117; 308 N.Y. 913, 127 N.E.2d 76; 308 N.Y. 1021, 127 N.E.2d 862; 221 F.2d 626, 129 F. Supp. 123; 344 U.S. 815, 97 L. Ed. 634, 73 S. Ct. 51; 346 U.S. 842, 98 L. Ed. 362, 74 S. Ct. 13; 348 U.S. 878, 99 L. Ed. 691, 75 S. Ct. 118; 348 U.S. 922, 99 L. Ed. 723, 75 S. Ct. 301; 100 L. Ed. 1505, 75 S. Ct. 908

**Steinert Case**
33 T.C. 447

**Stella Dallas Case**
26 F. Supp. 265, 42 U.S.P.Q. (BNA) 7

**Stenographers Case**
100 Me. 271, 61 A. 782

**Stephenson Case**
157 F. 797

**Stepladder Case**
79 Ohio St. 203, 86 N.E. 989

**Sterilization Case**
143 Va. 310, 130 S.E. 516; 274 U.S. 200, 71 L. Ed. 1000, 47 S. Ct. 584

**Sterilization Immunity Case**
55 L. Ed. 2d 331, 98 S. Ct. 1099

**Sterilization of Criminals Cases**
85 N.J.L. 46, 88 A. 963
189 Okla. 235, 115 P.2d 123; 315 U.S. 789, 86 L. Ed. 1193, 62 S. Ct. 488; 316 U.S. 535, 86 L. Ed. 1655, 62 S. Ct. 1110

**Sterling Avenue Subway Case**
334 Mo. 1001, 70 S.W.2d 61

**Sterling-Meaker Case**
140 F. 554; 150 F. 589; 171 F. 111

**Stern Case**
357 U.S. 39, 2 L. Ed. 2d 1126, 78 S. Ct. 1047; 242 F.2d 322; 25 T.C. 1358

**Steubenville Truck Case**
162 Ohio St. 251, 65 Ohio Op. 138, 122 N.E.2d 790

**Stevedore Cases**
234 U.S. 52, 58 L. Ed. 1185, 34 S. Ct. 741
244 U.S. 205, 61 L. Ed. 1086, 37 S. Ct. 524
244 U.S. 255, 61 L. Ed. 1116, 37 S. Ct. 545
253 U.S. 149, 64 L. Ed. 834, 40 S. Ct. 438
259 U.S. 263, 66 L. Ed. 933, 42 S. Ct. 473
264 U.S. 219, 68 L. Ed. 646, 44 S. Ct. 302
272 U.S. 50, 71 L. Ed. 157, 47 S. Ct. 19
276 U.S. 179, 72 L. Ed. 520, 48 S. Ct. 228
278 U.S. 142, 73 L. Ed. 232, 49 S. Ct. 88

**Stevens Cases**
1 Ohio Dec. Reprint 335, 7 W.L.J. 369; 20 Ohio 415
173 F.2d 1015

**Stickney Case**
164 F. 638; 215 U.S. 98, 54 L. Ed. 112, 30 S. Ct. 66

**Sticky Fly Paper Cases**
245 F. 609, 158 C.C.A. 37; 254 F. 219; 246 U.S. 664, 62 L. Ed. 928, 38 S. Ct. 334; 257 F. 394, 168 C.C.A. 434; 8 F.2d 570
114 Mich. 149, 72 N.W. 140

**Stiles Case**
182 Ala. 138, 62 So. 734; 192 Ala. 687, 68 So. 1018; 242 U.S. 111, 61 L. Ed. 176, 37 S. Ct. 58

**Stock Dividends Cases**
242 F. 702; 245 U.S. 418, 62 L. Ed. 372, 38 S. Ct. 158; 252 U.S. 189, 64 L. Ed. 521, 40 S. Ct. 189
274 F. 960

**Stock Exchange Case**
221 A.D. 193, 223 N.Y.S. 64; 248 N.Y. 533, 162 N.E. 514

**Stock-Law Election Case**
7 S.W.2d 105 (Tex.)

**Stock-Option Case**
32 Del. Ch. 219, 83 A.2d 473; 33 Del. Ch. 69, 90 A.2d 652; 33 Del. Ch. 174, 91 A.2d 62; 33 Del. Ch. 395, 94 A.2d 217

**Stockdate Cases**
83 U.S. 156, 21 L. Ed. 350
87 U.S. 323, 22 L. Ed. 348

**Stockham Valves and Fittings Case**
213 Ga. 713, 101 S.E.2d 197; 358 U.S. 450, 3 L. Ed. 2d 421, 79 S. Ct. 357; 214 Ga. 803, 108 S.E.2d 314; 356 U.S. 911, 2 L. Ed. 2d 585, 78 S. Ct. 670

**Stockholders' Patent Rights Case**
362 Mo. 1194, 247 S.W.2d 668

**Stockholders' Right of Action Case**
161 P.2d 817 (Cal.); 28 Cal. 2d 525, 170 P.2d 898

**Stockton Laundry Case**
26 F. 611

**Stockyards Cases**
183 U.S. 79, 46 L. Ed. 92, 22 S. Ct. 30
196 U.S. 375, 49 L. Ed. 518, 25 S. Ct. 276
258 U.S. 495, 66 L. Ed. 735, 42 S. Ct. 397
262 U.S. 1, 67 L. Ed. 839, 48 S. Ct. 470
298 U.S. 38, 80 L. Ed. 1033, 56 S. Ct. 720
3 F. 775
13 F. 3

**Stomach Pump Case**
342 U.S. 165, 96 L. Ed. 183, 72 S. Ct. 205; 101 Cal. App. 2d 140, 225 P.2d 1; 225 P.2d 913; 341 U.S. 939, 95 L. Ed. 1366, 71 S. Ct. 997

**Stop, Look and Listen Case**
10 F.2d 58; 271 U.S. 658, 70 L. Ed. 1136, 46 S. Ct. 632; 275 U.S. 66, 72 L. Ed. 167, 48 S. Ct. 24

**Stoppage of Work Case**
66 Ariz. 162, 185 P.2d 528

**Storer Case**
351 U.S. 192, 100 L. Ed. 1081, 76 St 763

**Storm Drain Cases**
115 Cal. App. 122, 300 P. 993
8 Cal. 2d 741, 68 P.2d 971

**Storm King Case**
354 F.2d 608

**Story Case**
90 N.Y. 122

**Stowers Case**
295 S.W. 257 (Tex.); 15 S.W.2d 544; 39 S.W.2d 956

**Strange Interlude Case**
49 F.2d 603

**Strawberry Case**
122 Md. 215, 89 A. 433; 240 U.S. 34, 60 L. Ed. 511, 36 S. Ct. 230

**Street Car Case**
157 S.C. 1, 153 S.E. 537; 164 S.C. 208, 162 S.E. 74; 166 S.C. 207, 164 S.E. 637; 168 S.C. 409, 167 S.E. 644; 162 S.E. 93; 280 U.S. 551, 74 L. Ed. 609, 50 S. Ct. 162; 281 U.S. 537, 74 L. Ed. 1023, 50 S. Ct. 401; 282 U.S. 187, 75 L. Ed. 287, 51 S. Ct. 94; 282 U.S. 795, 75 L. Ed. 717, 51 S. Ct. 38

**Street Case**
367 U.S. 740, 6 L. Ed. 2d 1141, 81 S. Ct. 1784; 361 U.S. 807, 4 L. Ed. 2d 54, 80 S. Ct. 84; 363 U.S. 825, 4 L. Ed. 2d 1521, 80 S. Ct. 1604; 213 Ga. 279, 99 S.E.2d 101; 215 Ga. 27, 108 S.E.2d 796; 217 Ga. 351, 122 S.E.2d 220

**Street Closing Case**
451 U.S. 100, 67 L. Ed. 2d 769, 101 S. Ct. 1584

**Strikers Case**
67 F. 698

**Strikers Food Stamp Case**
485 U.S. 360, 99 L. Ed. 2d 380, 108 S. Ct. 1184

**Striking Employees Unemployment Compensation Case**
440 U.S. 519, 59 L. Ed. 2d 553, 99 S. Ct. 1328

**Strip Bond Case**
F. Cas. No. 10,455; 102 U.S. 634, 26 L. Ed. 263

**Stuart Case**
97 Fla. 69, 120 So. 335

**Student-Athlete Drug-Testing Case**
515 U.S. 646, 132 L. Ed. 2d 564, 115 S. Ct. 2386 (1995)

**Student Expulsion Case**
420 U.S. 308, 43 L. Ed. 2d 214, 95 S. Ct. 992

**Student Free Speech Case**
478 U.S. 675, 92 L. Ed. 2d 549, 106 S. Ct. 3159

**Student Newspaper Censorship Case**
484 U.S. 260, 98 L. Ed. 2d 592, 108 S. Ct. 562

**Student Suspension Case**
419 U.S. 565, 42 L. Ed. 2d 725, 95 S. Ct. 729
55 L. Ed. 2d 252, 98 S. Ct. 1042

**Student Voting Cases**
164 Wis. 82, 159 N.W. 546
164 Wis. 89, 159 N.W. 549
164 Wis. 91, 159 N.W. 549

**Students Due Process Case**
55 L. Ed. 2d 124, 98 S. Ct. 948

**Students' Religious Publication Case**
515 U.S. 819, 132 L. Ed. 2d 700, 115 S. Ct. 2510 (1995)

**Stuffed Turkey Case**
382 U.S. 111, 15 L. Ed. 2d 194, 86 S. Ct. 258

**Stultz Case**
6 Cal. 2d 688, 59 P.2d 100

**Subiaco Case**
278 U.S. 269, 73 L. Ed. 322, 49 S. Ct. 133

**Submerged Land Cases**
326 U.S. 688, 66 S. Ct. 94; 66 S. Ct. 226, 66 S. Ct. 518; 327 U.S. 764, 90 L. Ed. 995, 66 S. Ct. 524; 66 S. Ct. 954; 66 S. Ct. 1335; 329 U.S. 689, 91 L. Ed. 604, 67 S. Ct. 478; 67 S. Ct. 618; 332 U.S. 19, 91 L. Ed. 1889, 67 S. Ct. 1658; 67 S. Ct. 1747; 332 U.S. 787, 92 L. Ed. 370, 68 S. Ct. 37; 332 U.S. 804, 92 L. Ed. 382, 68 S. Ct. 20; 68 S. Ct. 37; 332 U.S. 806, 92 L. Ed. 383, 68 S. Ct. 103; 332 U.S. 828, 92 L. Ed. 402, 68 S. Ct. 200; 68 S. Ct. 342; 334 U.S. 825, 92 L. Ed. 1754, 68 S. Ct. 1327; 334 U.S. 855, 92 L. Ed. 1776, 68 S. Ct. 1517; 335 U.S. 897, 93 L. Ed. 432, 69 S. Ct. 298; 337 U.S. 952, 93 L. Ed. 753, 69 S. Ct. 1520
335 U.S. 901, 93 L. Ed. 435, 69 S. Ct. 399; 336 U.S. 958, 93 L. Ed. 1111, 69 S. Ct. 887; 337 U.S. 902, 93 L. Ed. 1716, 69 S. Ct. 1040; 337 U.S. 928, 93 L. Ed. 1736, 69 S. Ct. 1490; 338 U.S. 806, 94 L. Ed. 488, 70 S. Ct. 36; 338 U.S. 806, 94 L. Ed. 488, 70 S. Ct. 37; 339 U.S. 669, 94 L. Ed. 1216, 70 S. Ct. 914; 71 S. Ct. 16; 340 U.S. 856, 95 L. Ed. 627, 71 S. Ct. 75; 340 U.S. 899, 95 L. Ed. 651, 71 S. Ct. 275; 340 U.S. 907, 95 L. Ed. 656, 71 S. Ct. 276; 340 U.S. 939, 95 L. Ed. 678, 71 S. Ct. 480
335 U.S. 901, 93 L. Ed. 435, 69 S. Ct. 399; 69 S. Ct. 598; 336 U.S. 958, 93 L. Ed. 1111, 69 S. Ct. 887; 337 U.S. 902, 93 L. Ed. 1716, 69 S. Ct. 1040; 338 U.S. 806, 94 L. Ed. 488, 70 S. Ct. 37; 338 U.S. 807, 94 L. Ed. 488, 70 S. Ct. 37; 70 S. Ct. 236; 339 U.S. 707, 94 L. Ed. 1221, 70 S. Ct. 918

**Subterranean Water Case**
54 So. 2d 673 (Fla.); 73 So. 2d 228

**Suburban Low Income Housing Case**
425 U.S. 284, 47 L. Ed. 2d 792, 96 S. Ct. 1538

**Sugar Bounty Case**
163 U.S. 427, 41 L. Ed. 215, 16 S. Ct. 1120

**Sugar Cane Labor Case**
97 F. Supp. 198; 216 F.2d 466; 348 U.S. 870, 99 L. Ed. 685, 75 S. Ct. 111; 349 U.S. 254, 99 L. Ed. 1040, 75 S. Ct. 719

**Sugar Chest Case**
30 Tenn. 465

**Sugar Lighterage Case**
20 I.C.C. 200; 225 U.S. 306, 56 L. Ed. 1100, 32 S. Ct. 817; 200 F. 779; 231 U.S. 274, 58 L. Ed. 218, 34 S. Ct. 75

**Sugar Monopoly Case**
156 U.S. 1, 39 L. Ed. 325, 15 S. Ct. 249; 60 F. 934

**Sugar Rate Cases**
81 I.C.C. 448

**Sugar Refiners' Case**
54 Hun 355, 22 Abb. N. Cas. 164, 16 Civ. P. Rep. 1, 19 N.Y. St. Rep. 853, 3 N.Y.S. 401; 53 Hun 635, 3 Silv. 26, 23 Abb. N. Cas. 311, 25 N.Y. St. Rep. 569, 6 N.Y.S. 408; 54 Hun 354, 27 N.Y. St. Rep. 282, 7 N.Y.S. 406; 121 N.Y. 582, 25 Abb. N. Cas. 1, 18 Civ. P. Rep. 406, 24 N.E. 834; 121 N.Y. 696, 24 N.E. 1099

**Sugar Trust Cases**
297 U.S. 553, 80 L. Ed. 859, 56 S. Ct. 629
60 F. 934, 9 C.C.A. 297, 17 U.S. App. D.C. 466; 156 U.S. 1, 39 L. Ed. 325, 15 S. Ct. 249
173 F. 823; 218 U.S. 601, 54 L. Ed. 1168, 31 S. Ct. 124
54 Hun 355, 22 Abb. N. Cas. 164, 16 Civ. P. Rep. 1, 19 N.Y. St. Rep. 853, 3 N.Y.Supp. 401, 53 Hun 635, 3 Silv. 26, 23 Abb. N. Cas. 311, 25 N.Y. St. Rep. 569, 6 N.Y.S. 408, 54 Hun 354, 27 N.Y. St. Rep. 282, 7 N.Y.S. 406; 121 N.Y. 582, 25 Abb. N. Cas. 1, 18 Civ. P. Rep. 406, 24 N.E. 834; 121 N.Y. 696, 24 N.E. 1099

23 Abb. N. Cas. 314, 8 N.Y.S. 237; 57 Hun 592, 10 N.Y.S. 632

25 Abb. N. Cas. 438, 12 N.Y.S. 126; 26 Abb. N. Cas. 157, 13 N.Y.S. 873; 59 Hun 619, 37 N.Y. St. Rep. 967, 15 N.Y.S. 157

31 N.Y. St. Rep. 968, 11 N.Y.S. 118; 59 Hun 387, 36 N.Y. St. Rep. 237, 13 N.Y.S. 86

**Suicide Liability Case**

212 S.C. 485, 48 S.E.2d 324

**Sullivan Case**

175 F.2d 657; 10 T.C. 961

**Summerville Hay Case**

6 I.C.C. 257; 71 F. 835; 83 F. 898, 28 C.C.A. 229, 42 U.S. App. D.C. 581; 169 U.S. 644, 42 L. Ed. 889, 18 S. Ct. 502; 175 U.S. 648, 44 L. Ed. 309, 20 S. Ct. 209

**Sun Oil Company Case**

371 U.S. 505, 9 L. Ed. 2d 466, 83 S. Ct. 358; 294 F.2d 465

**Sunday Closing Case**

177 U.S. 164, 44 L. Ed. 716, 20 S. Ct. 666

141 Ill. App. 218; 238 Ill. 593, 87 N.E. 840

**Sunday Closing Law Cases**

175 U.S. 291, 44 L. Ed. 168, 20 S. Ct. 121

268 U.S. 510, 69 L. Ed. 1070, 45 S. Ct. 571

281 U.S. 370, 74 L. Ed. 913, 50 S. Ct. 335

330 U.S. 1, 91 L. Ed. 711, 67 S. Ct. 504

366 U.S. 420, 6 L. Ed. 2d 393, 81 S. Ct. 1101, 81 S. Ct. 1153, 81 S. Ct. 1218; 368 U.S. 869, 7 L. Ed. 2d 69, 7 L. Ed. 2d 70, 82 S. Ct. 21, 82 S. Ct. 22; 220 Md. 117, 151 A.2d 156; 176 F. Supp. 466

366 U.S. 582, 6 L. Ed. 2d 551, 81 S. Ct. 1135; 179 F. Supp. 944, 273 F.2d 954; 266 F.2d 427

366 U.S. 599, 6 L. Ed. 2d 563, 81 S. Ct. 1144; 184 F. Supp. 352

366 U.S. 617, 6 L. Ed. 2d 536, 81 S. Ct. 1122; 176 F. Supp. 466; 178 F. Supp. 336; 362 U.S. 960, 4 L. Ed. 2d 875, 80 S. Ct. 876

**Sunday-Law Cases**

125 A.D. 780, 110 N.Y.S. 210

125 A.D. 784, 110 N.Y.S. 217

125 A.D. 793, 110 N.Y.S. 216

218 S.C. 474, 63 S.E.2d 308

30 Tex. 521

30 Tex. 523

30 Tex. 524

**Sundry Cotton Cases**

10 Ct. Cl. 502; 92 U.S. 651, 23 L. Ed. 756

**Sunflower County Case**

136 Miss. 191, 101 So. 192

**Sunlight Incandescent Gas Lamp Case**

87 F. 221; 102 F. 1007, 41 C.C.A. 683

**Sunshine Biscuit Case**

306 F.2d 48

**Sunstroke Cases**

65 F.2d 232; 290 U.S. 614, 78 L. Ed. 537, 54 S. Ct. 73; 291 U.S. 491, 78 L. Ed. 934, 54 S. Ct. 461

91 Okla. 194, 216 P. 933

**Superman Cases**

111 F.2d 432; 28 F. Supp. 399, 41 U.S.P.Q. (BNA) 182

191 F.2d 594; 93 F. Supp. 349, 87 U.S.P.Q. (BNA) 12; 4 F.R.D. 237, 64 U.S.P.Q. (BNA) 116; 61 U.S.P.Q. (BNA) 435; 67 U.S.P.Q. (BNA) 118

**Supermarket Case**

366 U.S. 617, 6 L. Ed. 2d 536, 81 S. Ct. 1122

78 F. Supp. 388, 77 U.S.P.Q. (BNA) 343; 179 F.2d 636, 84 U.S.P.Q. (BNA) 209; 339 U.S. 947, 94 L. Ed. 1361, 70 S. Ct. 803; 340 U.S. 147, 95 L. Ed. 162, 71 S. Ct. 127; 340 U.S. 918, 95 L. Ed. 663, 71 S. Ct. 349

**Superseding Indictment Case**

474 U.S. 231, 88 L. Ed. 2d 537, 106 S. Ct. 555

**Supp-Hose Case**

191 F. Supp. 652; 299 F.2d 793

**Support Cases**

42 Ky. 2

19 Ky. Law Rep. 686, 41 S.W. 579

**Sureties Contribution Case**

199 Okla. 233, 185 P.2d 205

**Surface Mail Experiment Case**
231 F.2d 483

**Surface Railway Cases**
27 N.Y. 188
50 N.Y. 206

**Surname for Business Case**
44 Wash. 2d 546, 268 P.2d 1006

**Surplus Property Case**
454 U.S. 464, 70 L. Ed. 2d 700, 102 S. Ct. 752

**Susan River Case**
18 Cal. 2d 518, 116 P.2d 442

**Suspect Order Cases**
283 F.2d 817; 365 U.S. 879, 6 L. Ed. 2d 191, 81 S. Ct. 1030; 365 U.S. 881, 6 L. Ed. 2d 192, 81 S. Ct. 1030
287 F.2d 146; 365 U.S. 880, 6 L. Ed. 2d 192, 81 S. Ct. 1031; 365 U.S. 882, 6 L. Ed. 2d 192, 81 S. Ct. 1030
287 F.2d 159
290 F.2d 133; 368 U.S. 823, 7 L. Ed. 2d 27, 82 S. Ct. 41

**Sutter Case**
62 U.S. 170, 16 L. Ed. 119; F. Cas. No. 16,424; 69 U.S. 562, 17 L. Ed. 881

**Suwannee County Case**
122 So. 2d 190 (Fla.); 132 So. 2d 289 (Fla.)

**Swage-Block Case**
68 U.S. 491, 17 L. Ed. 668

**Swaying Vehicle Liability Case**
357 Pa. 369, 54 A.2d 701

**Sweat-Box Case**
80 Miss. 592, 32 So. 9

**Sweat Shop Case**
155 Ill. 98, 40 N.E. 454

**Swedish Conflict of Laws Case**
89 F. Supp. 557, 1950 A.M.C. 868; 185 F.2d 212

**Sweezy Case**
100 N.H. 103, 121 A.2d 783; 354 U.S. 234, 1 L. Ed. 2d 1311, 77 S. Ct. 1203; 352 U.S. 812, 77 S. Ct. 49

**Swift Case**
41 U.S. 1, 10 L. Ed. 865

**Swinging Door Injury Case**
95 Cal. App. 2d 725, 214 P.2d 106

**Swiss Watch Case**
133 F. Supp. 40; 134 F. Supp. 710

**Switching Case**
227 F. 258; 227 F. 273; 242 U.S. 60, 61 L. Ed. 152, 37 S. Ct. 61

**Swope Park Rape Case**
428 S.W.2d 489 (Mo.)
428 S.W.2d 727 (Mo.)

**Syracuse Rate Case (Street Railways)**
25 Dep't Rep. 659

**Systolic Blood Pressure Test Case**
293 F. 1013, 54 App. D.C. 46

## T

**T V A Cases**

21 F. Supp. 57; 97 F.2d 979; 305 U.S. 625, 83 L. Ed. 400, 59 S. Ct. 87

8 F. Supp. 893; 9 F. Supp. 800; 9 F. Supp. 965; 14 F. Supp. 11; 19 F. Supp. 190; 78 F.2d 578; 296 U.S. 562, 80 L. Ed. 396, 56 S. Ct. 145; 297 U.S. 288, 80 L. Ed. 688, 56 S. Ct. 466; 297 U.S. 728, 80 L. Ed. 1011, 56 S. Ct. 588

21 F. Supp. 947; 58 S. Ct. 1042; 305 U.S. 663, 83 L. Ed. 430, 59 S. Ct. 54; 305 U.S. 664, 83 L. Ed. 431, 59 S. Ct. 62; 305 U.S. 665, 83 L. Ed. 431, 59 S. Ct. 154; 306 U.S. 118, 83 L. Ed. 543, 59 S. Ct. 366

**Tacoma 7 Case**

451 F.2d 372

**Taft-Hartley Free Speech Case**

204 F.2d 422

**Taft-Hartley Oath Case**

79 F. Supp. 563; 17 F.2d 247; 335 U.S. 910, 93 L. Ed. 443, 69 S. Ct. 480; 336 U.S. 960, 93 L. Ed. 1112, 69 S. Ct. 887; 339 U.S. 382, 94 L. Ed. 925, 70 S. Ct. 674; 339 U.S. 990, 94 L. Ed. 1391, 70 S. Ct. 1017

**Tailhook Case**

818 F. Supp. 1366 (D. Nev. 1993)

**Take-and-Rail Butter and Egg Rates Case**

29 I.C.C. 45

**Talbot Unemployment Relief Appropriation Case**

308 Pa. 35, 161 A. 697

**Tampa Flogging Case**

123 Fla. 785, 167 So. 687

**Tank Car Case**

34 I.C.C. 179; 227 F. 911; 242 U.S. 208, 61 L. Ed. 251, 37 S. Ct. 95

**Tanker Case**

107 F. Supp. 997, 1952 A.M.C. 2039; 207 F.2d 535, 1953 A.M.C. 1771; 347 U.S. 932, 98 L. Ed. 1083, 74 S. Ct. 631, 1954 A.M.C. 835; 348 U.S. 801, 99 L. Ed. 633, 75 S. Ct. 17, 1955 A.M.C. 1655

**Tap Line Cases**

157 F.2d 112

10 I.C.C. 193

10 I.C.C. 505

14 I.C.C. 364; 17 I.C.C. 338

23 I.C.C. 277; 23 I.C.C. 549; 209 F.2d 244; 209 F. 260; 234 U.S. 1, 58 L. Ed. 1185, 34 S. Ct. 741; 234 U.S. 29, 58 L. Ed. 1196, 34 S. Ct. 748; 31 I.C.C. 490; 34 I.C.C. 116; 240 U.S. 294, 60 L. Ed. 651, 36 S. Ct. 313; 40 I.C.C. 470; 53 I.C.C. 475; 58 I.C.C. 220; 274 F. 372; 257 U.S. 114, 66 L. Ed. 156, 42 S. Ct. 25; 95 I.C.C. 235

**Tapes Case**

418 U.S. 683, 41 L. Ed. 2d 1039, 94 S. Ct. 3090

**Tar Kettle Case**

259 F. 968

**Taranto Case**

132 F. 883

**Tarble's Case**

25 Wis. 390; 80 U.S. 397; 20 L. Ed. 597

**Tavern Code Authority Case**

220 Wis. 25, 264 N.W. 633

**Tax Appeal Cases**

12 G. & J. 117; 44 U.S. 133, 11 L. Ed. 529

**Tax Benefit Rule Case**

460 U.S. 370, 75 L. Ed. 2d 130, 103 S. Ct. 1134

**Tax Commission Cases**

56 Colo. 343, 138 P. 509

68 Mont. 450, 219 P. 817

**Tax Domicile Case**

199 Ind. 262, 157 N.E. 275

**Tax Exemption Contract Case**
224 Ind. 575, 70 N.E.2d 19; 330 U.S. 808, 91 L. Ed. 1265, 67 S. Ct. 1088; 331 U.S. 864, 91 L. Ed. 1869, 67 S. Ct. 1201

**Tax Fraud Penalties Case**
184 F.2d 86

**Tax Immunity Retroactivity Case**
509 U.S. 86, 125 L. Ed. 2d 74, 113 S. Ct. 2510 (1993)

**Tax Matter Practicing Law Case**
188 Misc. 406, 69 N.Y.S.2d 730; 273 A.D. 524, 78 N.Y.S.2d 209; 299 N.Y. 728, 87 N.E.2d 451

**Tax on Imported Goods Case**
459 U.S. 145, 74 L. Ed. 2d 323, 103 S. Ct. 523

**Tax Return Late Filing Case**
469 U.S. 241, 83 L. Ed. 2d 622, 105 S. Ct. 687

**Tax Return Preparation Case**
205 Miss. 865, 39 So. 2d 505

**Tax Title Cases**
105 Tenn. 243, 105 Tenn. 244, 105 Tenn. 245, 58 S.W. 259

**Tax Withholding Case**
419 U.S. 43, 42 L. Ed. 2d 212, 95 S. Ct. 247

**Taxable Gifts Case**
79 L. Ed. 2d 343, 104 S. Ct. 1086

**Taxation of National Bank Shares Case**
164 Minn. 235, 204 N.W. 874, 205 N.W. 375; 269 U.S. 550, 70 L. Ed. 406, 46 S. Ct. 121; 273 U.S. 561, 71 L. Ed. 774, 47 S. Ct. 468

**Taxi Driver's Tip Case**
176 F.2d 221; 10 T.C. 581

**Taxicab Cases**
276 U.S. 518, 72 L. Ed. 681, 48 S. Ct. 404
159 A.D. 907, 144 N.Y.S. 1151; 159 A.D. 899, 144 N.Y.S. 599; 159 A.D. 906, 144 N.Y.S. 1151; 160 A.D. 878, 144 N.Y. Supp.1151; 160 A.D. 935, 145 N.Y.S. 1150 82 Misc. 94, 143 N.Y.S. 279; 159 A.D. 893, 144 N.Y.S. 299; 159 A.D. 888, 144 N.Y.S. 494; 159 A.D. 907, 144 N.Y.S. 1120; 160 A.D. 925, 145 N.Y.S. 1127; 211 N.Y. 597, 105 N.E. 1087; 211 N.Y. 598, 105 N.E. 1086; 212 N.Y. 97, 105 N.E. 803; 212 N.Y. 609, 106 N.E. 1043

**Taxicab Franchise Renewal Case**
475 U.S. 608, 89 L. Ed. 2d 616, 106 S. Ct. 1395

**Taxpayers Damages Suit Case**
454 U.S. 100, 70 L. Ed. 2d 271, 102 S. Ct. 177

**TBA Case**
393 U.S. 223, 21 L. Ed. 2d 394, 89 S. Ct. 429

**Tea Case**
22 U.S. 430, 6 L. Ed. 128

**Tea Rose Cases**
204 F. 211; 208 F. 513; 231 U.S. 756, 58 L. Ed. 468, 34 S. Ct. 324; 58 L. Ed. 1584, 34 S. Ct. 329; 240 U.S. 403, 60 L. Ed. 713, 36 S. Ct. 357

**Teachers' Fifth Amendment Case**
331 Mass. 531, 120 N.E.2d 772

**Teachers' Oath Case**
276 Mich. 662, 268 N.W. 773

**Teachers' Tenure Act Case**
329 Pa. 213, 197 A. 344

**Teapot Dome Cases**
299 F. 620; 273 U.S. 135, 71 L. Ed. 580, 47 S. Ct. 319
5 F.2d 330; 14 F.2d 705; 273 U.S. 686, 71 L. Ed. 840, 47 S. Ct. 332; 275 U.S. 13, 72 L. Ed. 137, 48 S. Ct. 1
6 F.2d 43; 9 F.2d 761; 270 U.S. 640, 70 L. Ed. 775, 46 S. Ct. 356; 273 U.S. 456, 71 L. Ed. 734, 47 S. Ct. 416; 24 F.2d 206; 45 F.2d 821; 55 F.2d 753; 287 U.S. 612, 77 L. Ed. 532, 53 S. Ct. 14
13 F.2d 562; 273 U.S. 733, 71 L. Ed. 864, 47 S. Ct. 242

**Tecumseh Town Site Case**
3 Neb. 267

**Telegraph Franchise Cases**
1 F. 745
3 F. 1; 3 F. 423
3 F. 417
3 F. 430
3 F. 721
F. Cas. No. 10,960; 96 U.S. 1, 24 L. Ed. 708

**Telegraph Patent Case**
56 U.S. 62, 14 L. Ed. 601

**Telephone and Railroad Depreciation Charge Case**
118 I.C.C. 295; 177 I.C.C. 351

**Telephone Cases**
230 U.S. 58, 57 L. Ed. 1389, 33 S. Ct. 988
126 U.S. 1, 31 L. Ed. 863, 8 S. Ct. 778; 15 F. 488, 1983 C.D. 160; 17 F. 604; 22 F. 309, 1984 C.D. 475; 25 F. 725, 1986 C.D. 84; 32 F. 214

**Telephone Directory Case**
91 F.2d 484

**Telephone Patent Cases**
8 F. 509
15 F. 448; 17 F. 604; 126 U.S. 1, 31 L. Ed. 863, 8 S. Ct. 778, 43 Off. Gaz. Pat. Office 377
22 F. 309; 25 F. 725; 126 U.S. 1, 31 L. Ed. 863, 8 S. Ct. 778, 43 Off. Gaz. Pat. Office 377
27 F. 663
29 F. 17
31 F. 729; 145 U.S. 640, 36 L. Ed. 855, 12 S. Ct. 981
32 F. 214; 126 U.S. 1, 31 L. Ed. 863, 8 S. Ct. 778, 43 Off. Gaz. Pat. Office 377
32 F. 591; 128 U.S. 315, 32 L. Ed. 450, 9 S. Ct. 90
65 F. 86; 68 F. 542, 15 C.C.A. 569; 159 U.S. 548, 40 L. Ed. 255, 16 S. Ct. 69; 167 U.S. 224, 42 L. Ed. 144, 17 S. Ct. 809

**Telephone Pole Case**
118 Cal. App. 344, 5 P.2d 58, 6 P.2d 297

**Telephone Rate Cases**
233 S.W. 425 (Mo.); 262 U.S. 276, 67 L. Ed. 981, 43 S. Ct. 544
269 U.S. 531, 70 L. Ed. 397, 46 S. Ct. 22; 39 F.2d 157; 38 F.2d 77; 282 U.S. 133, 75 L. Ed. 255, 51 S. Ct. 65; 283 U.S. 794, 75 L. Ed. 1419, 51 S. Ct. 482; 283 U.S. 808, 75 L. Ed. 1427, 51 S. Ct. 646; 3 F. Supp. 595; 292 U.S. 151, 78 L. Ed. 1182, 54 S. Ct. 658; 98 F.2d 930; 102 F.2d 58, 307 U.S. 648, 83 L. Ed. 1527, 59 S. Ct. 1045

**Temporary Taking Case**
482 U.S. 304, 96 L. Ed. 2d 250, 107 S. Ct. 2378

**Tenancy under Void Lease Case**
191 Md. 289, 60 A.2d 669

**Tenement House Cases**
145 N.Y. 32, 39 N.E. 833
179 N.Y. 325, 72 N.E. 231; 203 U.S. 583, 51 L. Ed. 328, 27 S. Ct. 781

**Tenement House Cigar Case**
33 Hun 374, 2 N.Y. Crim. 346; 98 N.Y. 98, 2 N.Y. Crim. 539

**Tennessee Bank Tax Case**
459 U.S. 392, 74 L. Ed. 2d 562, 103 S. Ct. 692

**Tennessee Bond Cases**
3 F. 673; 114 U.S. 663, 29 L. Ed. 281, 5 S. Ct. 974, 5 S. Ct. 1098
4 F. 97; 114 U.S. 663, 29 L. Ed. 281, 5 S. Ct. 974, 5 S. Ct. 1098

**Tennessee Gasoline Case**
24 F.2d 455; 278 U.S. 235, 73 L. Ed. 287, 49 S. Ct. 115

**Tennessee Valley Authority Case**
21 F. Supp. 57; 97 F.2d 979; 305 U.S. 625, 83 L. Ed. 400, 59 S. Ct. 87

**Tepee Apple Case**
179 F. 985

**Term Limits Case**
514 U.S. 779, 131 L. Ed. 2d 881, 115 S. Ct. 1842 (1995)

**Terminal Case**
224 U.S. 383, 56 L. Ed. 810, 32 S. Ct. 507

**Terminal Cities Case**
231 F. 292; 242 U.S. 178, 61 L. Ed. 233, 37 S. Ct. 24

**Test-Oath Cases**
71 U.S. 277, 18 L. Ed. 356
71 U.S. 333, 18 L. Ed. 366

**Tetracycline Case**
107 F.R.D. 719

**Tex-O-Kan Case**
26 N.L.R.B. 765, No. 83; 122 F.2d 433

**Texas Bond Issue Case**
3 F.2d 160; 269 U.S. 396, 70 L. Ed. 330, 46 S. Ct. 141

**Texas City Disaster Case**
1950 A.M.C. 1084; 197 F.2d 771; 344 U.S. 873, 97 L. Ed. 676, 73 S. Ct. 166; 73 S. Ct. 332; 73 S. Ct. 726; 346 U.S. 15, 97 L. Ed. 1427, 73 S. Ct. 956, 1953 A.M.C. 1175; 346 U.S. 841, 98 L. Ed. 362, 74 S. Ct. 13; 346 U.S. 880, 98 L. Ed. 386, 74 S. Ct. 117; 347 U.S. 924, 98 L. Ed. 1078, 74 S. Ct. 511

**Texas Concrete Pipe Case**
302 F. Supp. 1342

**Texas Corporation Privilege Tax Case**
100 F.2d 515; 306 U.S. 628, 83 L. Ed. 1031, 59 S. Ct. 775; 307 U.S. 611, 83 L. Ed. 1494, 59 S. Ct. 821; 308 U.S. 331, 84 L. Ed. 304, 60 S. Ct. 273; 308 U.S. 640, 84 L. Ed. 531, 60 S. Ct. 385

**Texas Gulf Sulphur Case**
258 F. Supp. 262; 401 F.2d 833

**Texas Highway Load Regulation Cases**
52 F.2d 151; 52 S. Ct. 40; 284 U.S. 598, 76 L. Ed. 513, 52 S. Ct. 207
52 F.2d 730; 56 F.2d 189; 52 S. Ct. 459; 286 U.S. 374, 76 L. Ed. 1167, 52 S. Ct. 581
52 F.2d 737
53 F.2d 509; 53 S. Ct. 88; 287 U.S. 251, 77 L. Ed. 288, 53 S. Ct. 181

**Texas Law School Case**
339 U.S. 629, 94 L. Ed. 1114, 70 S. Ct. 848; 210 S.W.2d 442; 338 U.S. 865, 94 L. Ed. 530, 70 S. Ct. 139; 340 U.S. 846, 95 L. Ed. 620, 71 S. Ct. 13

**Texas Legislative Apportionment Case**
343 F. Supp. 704

**Texas Live Stock Rate Case**
11 I.C.C. 296; 12 I.C.C. 1; 13 I.C.C. 418; 164 F. 645; 30 I.C.C. 721

**Texas Midland Railroad Valuation Case**
75 I.C.C. 1; 84 I.C.C. 150

**Texas Parallelogram Case**
199 S.W. 523 (Tex.)

**Texas Primary Cases**
273 U.S. 536, 71 L. Ed. 2d 759, 47 S. Ct. 446; 286 U.S. 73, 76 L. Ed. 984, 52 S. Ct. 484
321 U.S. 649, 88 L. Ed. 2d 987, 64 S. Ct. 757; 319 U.S. 738, 87 L. Ed. 1697, 63 S. Ct. 1325; 322 U.S. 718; 322 U.S. 769, 88 L. Ed. 1594, 64 S. Ct. 1052; 137 F.2d 593
345 U.S. 461, 97 L. Ed. 1152, 73 S. Ct. 809

**Texas Railroad Commission Cases**
154 U.S. 413, 38 L. Ed. 1028, 14 S. Ct. 1060
154 U.S. 418, 38 L. Ed. 1030, 14 S. Ct. 1062
154 U.S. 420, 38 L. Ed. 1031, 14 S. Ct. 1062
51 F. 529; 154 U.S. 362, 38 L. Ed. 1014, 14 S. Ct. 1047

**Texas Supreme Court Docket Case**
173 S.W. 1186; 184 S.W. 566; 108 Tex. 434, 196 S.W. 502, 196 S.W. 1153

**Texas White Primary Cases**
273 U.S. 536, 71 L. Ed. 759, 47 S. Ct. 446
286 U.S. 73, 76 L. Ed. 984, 52 S. Ct. 484
321 U.S. 649, 88 L. Ed. 987, 64 S. Ct. 757
345 U.S. 461, 97 L. Ed. 1152, 73 S. Ct. 809

**Textile Sample Card Case**
250 F. 863

**Textile Workers Case**
353 U.S. 448, 1 L. Ed. 2d 972, 77 S. Ct. 912, 77 S. Ct. 923; 230 F.2d 81; 233 F.2d 85; 352 U.S. 821, 1 L. Ed. 2d 46, 77 S. Ct. 54; 353 U.S. 547, 1 L. Ed. 2d 1028, 77 S. Ct. 921; 353 U.S. 550, 1 L. Ed. 2d 1031, 77 S. Ct. 920

**Thacher's Distilled Spirits Case**
F. Cas. No. 13,851; F. Cas. No. 15,944; 103 U.S. 679, 26 L. Ed. 535

**Thaw Cases**
209 F. 56; 209 F. 954; 214 F. 423; 235 U.S. 432, 59 L. Ed. 302, 35 S. Ct. 137
138 A.D. 91, 24 N.Y. Crim. 471, 24 N.Y. Crim. 509, 122 N.Y.S. 970
158 A.D. 571, 143 N.Y.S. 854
168 A.D. 553, 153 N.Y.S. 188; 215 N.Y. 339, 109 N.E. 486
59 Misc. 359, 110 N.Y.S. 848
116 N.Y.S. 62, 133 A.D. 159, 117 N.Y.S. 322, 196 N.Y. 525, 89 N.E. 1109
118 N.Y.S. 389
154 N.Y.S. 949; 167 A.D. 104, 33 N.Y. Crim. 128, 152 N.Y.S. 771
154 N.Y.S. 965

**The Flopper Case**
224 A.D. 832, 231 N.Y.S.2d 826; 250 N.Y. 479, 166 N.E. 173

**The Whip Case**
180 Tenn. 471, 176 S.W.2d 804

**Theard Doctrine**
354 U.S. 278, 1 L. Ed. 2d 1342, 77 S. Ct. 1274

**Theatrical Productions Case**
420 U.S. 546, 43 L. Ed. 2d 448, 95 S. Ct. 1239

**Third Avenue-American Surety Company Case**
180 F. 710, 103 C.C.A. 492

**Third Degree Case**
203 Ind. 51, 178 N.E. 570

**Third Party Contract Renegotiation Case**
266 S.W.2d 790 (Ky.)

**Third Phoenix Case**
140 I.C.C. 171; 284 U.S. 370, 76 L. Ed. 348, 52 S. Ct. 183; 49 F.2d 563; 75 F.2d 873

**Thirteen Count Cases**
88 N.J.L. 241, 96 A. 582
88 N.J.L. 367, 96 A. 587; 90 N.J.L. 338, 100 A. 1071

**Thirty-Six Cent Tax Case**
346 Mich. 266, 78 N.W.2d 186

**Thomas Case**
284 U.S. 296, 76 L. Ed. 304, 52 S. Ct. 151; 284 U.S. 599, 76 L. Ed. 515, 52 S. Ct. 7
53 F.2d 192

**Thompson Case**
362 U.S. 199, 4 L. Ed. 2d 654, 80 S. Ct. 624; 362 U.S. 985, 4 L. Ed. 2d 1020, 80 S. Ct. 1074

**Thomson-Ohio Cases**
69 F. 257; 71 F. 886; 71 F. 396, 18 C.C.A. 145; 163 U.S. 685, 41 L. Ed. 315, 16 S. Ct. 1201
80 F. 712, 26 C.C.A. 107

**Thomsonian Medicine Case**
36 Mass. (19 Pick.) 214

**Thornhill Case**
310 U.S. 88, 84 L. Ed. 1093, 60 S. Ct. 736; 28 Ala. App. 527, 189 So. 913; 238 Ala. 162, 189 So. 914; 308 U.S. 547, 84 L. Ed. 460, 60 S. Ct. 296

**Threat to Reindict Case**
54 L. Ed. 2d 604, 98 S. Ct. 663

**Three Brothers Case**
F. Cas. No. 14,009

**Three Circuits Case**
346 U.S. 86, 97 L. Ed. 1470, 73 S. Ct. 998; 201 F.2d 694; 238 F.2d 24

**Three Hundred and Three Case**
47 Barb. 455; 48 N.Y. 374

**Three Mile Limit Cases**
284 F. 890; 262 U.S. 100, 67 L. Ed. 894, 43 S. Ct. 504
285 F. 79; 262 U.S. 100, 67 L. Ed. 894, 43 S. Ct. 504

**Three Schooners Case**
22 U.S. 391, 6 L. Ed. 118

**Three Sisters Bridge Case**
434 F.2d 436; 459 F.2d 1231; 308 F. Supp. 423; 316 F. Supp. 754

**Three Year Limit Case**
287 F. 522; 263 U.S. 694, 68 L. Ed. 510, 44 S. Ct. 36; 264 U.S. 456, 68 L. Ed. 788, 44 S. Ct. 364

**Throckmorton Case**
F. Cas. No. 15,121; 98 U.S. 61, 25 L. Ed. 93

**Thum Case**
111 F. 904, 50 C.C.A. 61

**Thurston Case**
179 F.2d 514

**Ticker Cases**
224 Mass. 365, 113 N.E. 192; 247 U.S. 105, 65 L. Ed. 1006, 38 S. Ct. 438
119 F. 294

**Ticket Brokerage Case**
82 F. 65

**Ticket Register Case**
15 F.2d 257; 273 U.S. 764, 71 L. Ed. 880, 47 S. Ct. 477

**Ticonium Case**
87 U.S.P.Q. (BNA) 20

**Tidelands Oil Cases**
326 U.S. 688, 66 S. Ct. 94; 66 S. Ct. 226; 66 S. Ct. 518; 327 U.S. 764, 90 L. Ed. 995, 66 S. Ct. 524; 66 S. Ct. 954; 66 S. Ct. 1335; 329 U.S. 689, 91 L. Ed. 604, 67 S. Ct. 478; 67 S. Ct. 618; 332 U.S. 19, 91 L. Ed. 1889, 67 S. Ct. 1658; 67 S. Ct. 1747; 332 U.S. 787, 92 L. Ed. 370, 68 S. Ct. 37; 332 U.S. 804, 92 L. Ed. 382, 68 S. Ct. 20; 68 S. Ct. 37; 332 U.S. 806, 92 L. Ed. 383, 68 S. Ct. 103; 332 U.S. 828, 92 L. Ed. 402, 68 S. Ct. 200; 68 S. Ct. 342; 334 U.S. 825, 92 L. Ed. 1754, 68 S. Ct. 1327; 334 U.S. 855, 92 L. Ed. 1776, 68 S. Ct. 1517; 335 U.S. 897, 93 L. Ed. 432, 69 S. Ct. 298; 337 U.S. 952, 93 L. Ed. 753, 69 S. Ct. 1520
335 U.S. 901, 93 L. Ed. 435, 69 S. Ct. 399; 336 U.S. 958, 93 L. Ed. 1111, 69 S. Ct. 887; 337 U.S. 902, 93 L. Ed. 1716, 69 S. Ct. 1040; 337 U.S. 928, 93 L. Ed. 1736, 69 S. Ct. 1490; 338 U.S. 806, 94 L. Ed. 488, 70 S. Ct. 36; 338 U.S. 806, 94 L. Ed. 488, 70 S. Ct. 37; 339 U.S. 669, 94 L. Ed. 1216, 70 S. Ct. 914; 71 S. Ct. 16; 340 U.S. 856, 95 L. Ed. 627, 71 S. Ct. 75; 340 U.S. 899, 95 L. Ed. 651, 71 S. Ct. 275; 340 U.S. 907, 95 L. Ed. 656, 71 S. Ct. 276; 340 U.S. 939, 95 L. Ed. 678, 71 S. Ct. 480
335 U.S. 901, 93 L. Ed. 435, 69 S. Ct. 399; 69 S. Ct. 598; 336 U.S. 958, 93 L. Ed. 1111, 69 S. Ct. 887; 337 U.S. 902, 93 L. Ed. 1716, 69 S. Ct. 1040; 338 U.S. 806, 94 L. Ed. 488, 70 S. Ct. 37; 338 U.S. 807, 94 L. Ed. 488, 70 S. Ct. 37; 70 S. Ct. 236; 339 U.S. 707, 94 L. Ed. 1221, 70 S. Ct. 918
363 U.S. 1, 4 L. Ed. 2d 1025, 80 S. Ct. 961; 364 U.S. 502, 5 L. Ed. 2d 247, 81 S. Ct. 258; 382 U.S. 288, 15 L. Ed. 2d 331, 86 S. Ct. 419

**Tift Lumber Rate Case**
123 F. 789; 138 F. 753; 148 F. 1021, 79 C.C.A. 536; 206 U.S. 428, 51 L. Ed. 1124, 27 S. Ct. 709

**Tiidee Products Case**
426 F.2d 1243

**Tilden Will Case**
18 N.Y. St. Rep. 752, 2 N.Y.S. 584; 54 Hun 231, 7 N.Y.S. 382; 130 N.Y. 29, 28 N.E. 880; 29 N.E. 1033

**Till Case**
3 Neb. 261

**Tillamooks Cases**
329 U.S. 40, 91 L. Ed. 29, 67 S. Ct. 167; 59 F. Supp. 934, 103 Ct. Cl. 494; 87 F. Supp. 938, 115 Ct. Cl. 463; 121 Ct. Cl. 173; 326 U.S. 707, 90 L. Ed. 417, 66 S. Ct. 99
341 U.S. 48, 95 L. Ed. 738, 71 S. Ct. 552; 59 F. Supp. 934; 87 F. Supp. 938, 115 Ct. Cl. 463; 329 U.S. 40, 91 L. Ed. 29, 67 S. Ct. 167; 340 U.S. 873, 95 L. Ed. 635, 71 S. Ct. 121, 117 Ct. Cl. 822; 71 S. Ct. 614

**Timber Cases**
11 F. 81
F. Cas. No. 15673
F. Cas. No. 15864

**Tinsley Case**
222 Ky. 120, 300 S.W. 368

**Tipaldo Women's Wage Case**
156 Misc. 522, 282 N.Y.S. 576; 270 N.Y. 233, 200 N.E. 799; 298 U.S. 587, 80 L. Ed. 1347, 56 S. Ct. 918; 297 U.S. 702, 80 L. Ed. 991, 56 S. Ct. 670; 299 U.S. 619, 81 L. Ed. 456, 57 S. Ct. 4

**Tipper-Tippee Cases**
474 F.2d 514
495 F.2d 228
524 F.2d 275
542 F.2d 307
555 F.2d 1152

**Tisdale Case**
26 Iowa 170; 28 Iowa 12

**Titanic Cases**
233 U.S. 718, 58 L. Ed. 1171, 34 S. Ct. 754
204 F. 259, 124 C.C.A. 347
204 F. 260, 124 C.C.A. 352
204 F. 295
204 F. 298
206 F. 500
209 F. 501; 209 F. 513

**Tobacco Cases**
246 U.S. 79, 62 L. Ed. 587, 38 S. Ct. 233
164 F. 700; 164 F. 1024; 221 U.S. 106, 55 L. Ed. 663, 31 S. Ct. 632
191 F. 371

**Tobacco Inspection Act Case**
19 F. Supp. 211; 95 F.2d 856; 305 U.S. 584, 83 L. Ed. 369, 59 S. Ct. 91; 306 U.S. 1, 83 L. Ed. 441, 59 S. Ct. 379

**Tobacco Pool Cases**
182 Wis. 571, 197 N.W. 936
191 Wis. 586, 211 N.W. 923

**Toilet Case**
276 Mass. 398, 177 N.E. 656; 284 U.S. 684, 76 L. Ed. 578, 52 S. Ct. 201

**Tokyo Rose Case**
180 F.2d 271; 192 F.2d 338

**Toledo Case**
43 F. 533

**Toledo Newspaper Company Case**
247 U.S. 402, 62 L. Ed. 1186, 38 S. Ct. 560; 220 F. 458; 237 F. 986; 62 L. Ed. 1186, 38 S. Ct. 581

**Toll Bridge Barrier Case**
28 Wash. 2d 377, 183 P.2d 473

**Tomahawk Case**
147 F.2d 743; 325 U.S. 880, 89 L. Ed. 1996, 65 S. Ct. 1574; 325 U.S. 880, 89 L. Ed. 1996, 65 S. Ct. 1575

**Tompkins Case**
90 F. 363; 176 U.S. 167, 44 L. Ed. 417, 20 S. Ct. 336

**Ton Mile Tax Case**
207 Iowa 461, 221 N.W. 364; 73 L. Ed. 1016, 49 S. Ct. 482; 280 U.S. 529, 74 L. Ed. 595, 50 S. Ct. 151

**Tonnage Tax Cases**
62 Pa. 286; 82 U.S. 232, 21 L. Ed. 146; 82 U.S. 282, 21 L. Ed. 164
66 Pa. 84

**Too Many Purchasers Case**
77 Ariz. 18, 266 P.2d 739; 77 Ariz. 120, 267 P.2d 895

**Toolson Case**
101 F. Supp. 93; 200 F.2d 198; 345 U.S. 963, 97 L. Ed. 1382, 73 S. Ct. 948; 345 U.S. 963, 97 L. Ed. 1382, 73 S. Ct. 949; 202 F.2d 413; 202 F.2d 428; 346 U.S. 356, 98 L. Ed. 64, 74 S. Ct. 78

**Topeka and Iola Tax Cases**
154 U.S. 617, 22 L. Ed. 463, 14 S. Ct. 1199
F. Cas. No. 2,734; 87 U.S. 655, 22 L. Ed. 455

**Torcaso Case**
223 Md. 49, 162 A.2d 438; 367 U.S. 488, 6 L. Ed. 2d 982, 81 S. Ct. 1680

**Tortfeasor's Contribution Case**
91 A.2d 473 (D.C.)

**Totten Trust Cases**
91 A.D. 609, 86 N.Y.S. 1147
38 Misc. 349, 3 Mills 165, 77 N.Y.S. 928; 89 A.D. 368, 85 N.Y.S. 928; 178 N.Y. 604, 70 N.E. 1110; 179 N.Y. 112, 71 N.E. 748

**Tourist Court Ordinance Case**
254 Ala. 525, 49 So. 2d 108

**Towed Car Case**
37 Wash. 2d 293, 223 P.2d 443

**Tower Case**
3 T.C. 396; 148 F.2d 388; 326 U.S. 703, 90 L. Ed. 415, 66 S. Ct. 55; 327 U.S. 280, 90 L. Ed. 670, 66 S. Ct. 532

**Town and Country Manufacturing Company Case**
136 N.L.R.B. 1022, No. 111; 316 F.2d 846

**Town Cases**
72 Me. 522
75 Me. 141
76 Me. 506

**Townsend Cases**
95 F.2d 362
195 Minn. 107, 261 N.W. 859

**Township and County Bond Cases**
94 U.S. 682, 24 L. Ed. 219
94 U.S. 801, 24 L. Ed. 322
98 U.S. 169, 25 L. Ed. 88
99 U.S. 499, 25 L. Ed. 330
101 U.S. 87, 25 L. Ed. 878
102 U.S. 81, 26 L. Ed. 83
103 U.S. 562, 26 L. Ed. 411
105 U.S. 73, 26 L. Ed. 1024
112 U.S. 325, 28 L. Ed. 744, 5 S. Ct. 157
128 U.S. 102, 32 L. Ed. 359, 9 S. Ct. 18

**Toyo Paper Case**
2 Cust. Ct. 926, Reappr. Dec. 4568

**Track Scales Case**
139 N.C. 126, 51 S.E. 793

**Trade Bank Case**
222 A.D. 799, 226 N.Y.S. 914; 132 Misc. 371, 229 N.Y.S. 93, 222 A.D. 736, 225 N.Y.S. 915, 249 N.Y. 546, 164 N.E. 578

**Trade-Mark Case (Bottle Law)**
77 Ohio St. 438, 83 N.E. 797

**Trade-Mark Cases**
100 U.S. 82, 25 L. Ed. 550

**Trade Secrets Disclosure Case**
240 Mo. App. 1075, 226 S.W.2d 737

**Trading Stamp Cases**
218 U.S. 673, 54 L. Ed. 1205, 31 S. Ct. 223; 219 U.S. 210, 55 L. Ed. 184, 31 S. Ct. 143
128 F. 800; 128 F. 1015; 135 F. 833
137 F. 992
161 F. 219
208 F. 605, 240 U.S. 369, 60 L. Ed. 691, 36 S. Ct. 379
214 F. 827; 240 U.S. 342, 60 L. Ed. 679, 36 S. Ct. 370
219 F. 755
221 F. 512
101 Kan. 789, 168 P. 679
134 Md. 437, 107 A. 189
109 N.Y. 389, 17 N.E. 343
79 Wash. 608, 140 P. 918; 80 Wash. 699, 141 P. 883; 240 U.S. 387, 60 L. Ed. 703, 36 S. Ct. 385
160 Wis. 613, 166 N.W. 54

**Trading Stamp Fair Trade Case**
195 Misc. 151, 89 N.Y.S.2d 215; 277 A.D. 769, 97 N.Y.S.2d 550; 302 N.Y. 61, 96 N.E.2d 177

**Trading Stamps Case**
421 U.S. 723, 44 L. Ed. 2d 539, 95 S. Ct. 1917

**Traffic Cases**
See Trans-Missouri Freight Case
53 F. 440; 58 F. 58, 7 C.C.A. 15, 19 U.S. App. D.C. 36, 4 I.C. 443; 166 U.S. 290, 41 L. Ed. 1007, 17 S. Ct. 540
76 F. 895; 89 F. 1020, 32 C.C.A. 491, 45 U.S. App. D.C. 762; 171 U.S. 505, 43 L. Ed. 259, 19 S. Ct. 25

**Traffic-Stop Drug Seizure Case**
517 U.S. 820, 135 L. Ed. 2d 102, 116 S. Ct. 1777 (1996)

**Train Limit Law Case**
18 F. Supp. 393

**Trans-Alaska Pipeline Case**
436 U.S. 631, 56 L. Ed. 2d 591, 98 S. Ct. 2053

**Trans-Missouri Freight Case**
See Traffic Cases
53 F. 440; 58 F. 58, 7 C.C.A. 15, 19 U.S. App. D.C. 36, 4 I.C. 443; 166 U.S. 290, 41 L. Ed. 1007, 17 S. Ct. 540

**Transamerica Case**
206 F.2d 163; 346 U.S. 901, 98 L. Ed. 401, 74 S. Ct. 225

**Transfer Cases**
199 Ill. 484, 65 N.E. 451
199 Ill. 579, 65 N.E. 470

**Transfer Inheritance Tax Case**
277 Pa. 242, 121 A. 35; 268 U.S. 473, 69 L. Ed. 1058, 45 S. Ct. 603

**Transfer Ticket Case**
210 F. 443; 212 F. 719

**Transferee Estoppel Case**
264 Wis. 220, 58 N.W.2d 641

**Transom Case**
151 U.S. 221, 38 L. Ed. 137, 14 S. Ct. 291

**Travelers Health Association Case**
339 U.S. 643, 94 L. Ed. 1154, 70 S. Ct. 927

**Treasury Note Cases**
59 Mont. 557, 197 P. 988
74 Mont. 1, 238 P. 316

**Tree Fruits Labor Relations Committee Case**
377 U.S. 58, 12 L. Ed. 2d 129, 84 S. Ct. 1063; 374 U.S. 804, 10 L. Ed. 2d 1030, 83 S. Ct. 1693; 308 F.2d 311

**Trem Carr Case**
154 S.W.2d 507 (Tex.); 161 S.W.2d 1022

**Tremolo Patent Case**
F. Cas. No. 6,538; F. Cas. No. 6,539; F. Cas. No. 6,540; 90 U.S. 518, 23 L. Ed. 97

**Trenton Potteries Case**
273 U.S. 392, 71 L. Ed. 700, 47 S. Ct. 377

**Trenton Six Case**
2 N.J. 540, 67 A.2d 298; 88 F. Supp. 774; 10 N.J. 532, 92 A.2d 786

**Trespassing Dog Case**
4 N.J. Super. 475, 67 A.2d 876; 3 N.J. 195, 69 A.2d 576

**Trespassing Light Case**
184 Ore. 336, 198 P.2d 847

**Tri-City Case**
257 U.S. 184, 66 L. Ed. 189, 42 S. Ct. 72

**Tri-State Transit Company Case**
197 Miss. 37, 19 So. 2d 441

**Triangle Conduit and Cable Cases**
168 F.2d 175; 336 U.S. 902, 93 L. Ed. 1068, 69 S. Ct. 491; 336 U.S. 956, 93 L. Ed. 1110, 69 S. Ct. 888

**Triangle Fire Case**
74 Misc. 353, 26 N.Y. Crim. 472, 134 N.Y.S. 409

**Trichinosis Case**
271 N.Y. 131, 2 N.E.2d 513

**Trilogy Cases**
36 U.S. 564, 4 L. Ed. 2d 1403, 4 L. Ed. 2d 1432, 80 S. Ct. 1343, 80 S. Ct. 1363; 264 F.2d 624
363 U.S. 574, 4 L. Ed. 2d 1409, 80 S. Ct. 1347; 168 F. Supp. 702; 269 F.2d 633
363 U.S. 593, 4 L. Ed. 2d 1424, 80 S. Ct. 1358; 168 F. Supp. 308; 269 F.2d 327
372 U.S. 293, 9 L. Ed. 2d 770, 83 S. Ct. 745, 372 U.S. 391, 9 L. Ed. 2d 837, 83 S. Ct. 822; 373 U.S. 1, 10 L. Ed. 2d 148, 83 S. Ct. 1068

**Triner Case**
363 Ill. 559, 2 N.E.2d 929; 299 U.S. 183, 81 L. Ed. 109, 57 S. Ct. 139; 57 S. Ct. 48

**Trinity Church Case**
36 F. 303; 143 U.S. 457, 36 L. Ed. 226, 12 S. Ct. 511

**Trinity Church Corporation Cases**
44 F.2d 716; 283 U.S. 827, 75 L. Ed. 1441, 51 S. Ct. 351; 49 F.2d 908
1 Abb. Pr. 385
179 A.D. 621, 167 N.Y.S. 107
83 N.Y. 348
30 Barb. 537; 22 N.Y. 44
4 Paige 178; 15 Wend. 111; 4 Sandf. Ch. 369; 4 Sandf. Ch. 633
7 Paige 195; 24 Wend. 587

**Triple A Case (AAA)**
297 U.S. 1, 80 L. Ed. 477, 56 S. Ct. 312
297 U.S. 110, 80 L. Ed. 513, 56 S. Ct. 374

**Tronieri Unemployment Compensation Case**
164 Pa. Super. 435, 65 A.2d 426

**Troy Case**
6 I.C.C. 1; 69 F. 227; 74 F. 715, 21 C.C.A. 51, 41 U.S. App. D.C. 453, 5 I.C. 685; 168 U.S. 144, 42 L. Ed. 414, 18 S. Ct. 45

**Troy Press Case**
187 N.Y. 279, 79 N.E. 1006

**Truax-Traer Coal Company Case**
122 W. Va. 530, 11 S.E.2d 111, 123 W. Va. 621, 17 S.E.2d 330

**Truck Length Limitations Case**
450 U.S. 662, 67 L. Ed. 2d 580, 101 S. Ct. 1309

**True Knowledge Case**
214 F.2d 778; 348 U.S. 908, 99 L. Ed. 712, 75 S. Ct. 288

**Truitt Case**
351 U.S. 149, 100 L. Ed. 1027, 76 S. Ct. 753; 224 F.2d 869; 350 U.S. 922, 100 L. Ed. 807, 76 S. Ct. 211

**Trust Beneficiary Party Case**
110 F.2d 539

**Trustee's Retention of Investments Case**
59 N.Y.S.2d 325; 90 N.Y.S.2d 74; 276 A.D. 134, 93 N.Y.S.2d 555; 302 N.Y. 246, 97 N.E.2d 888

**Tub-Kove Case**
213 F.2d 382

**Tuck Creaser Case**
F. Cas. No. 5,151; 94 U.S. 288, 24 L. Ed. 103; 94 U.S. 299, 24 L. Ed. 107

**Tucker Act Case**
282 U.S. 656, 75 L. Ed. 598, 51 S. Ct. 284; 37 F.2d 38; 281 U.S. 714, 74 L. Ed. 1135, 50 S. Ct. 410

**Tucker Bronze Case**
120 U.S. 442, 30 L. Ed. 737, 7 S. Ct. 640

**Tulane Homestead Case**
185 La. 777, 171 So. 28

**Tungsten Lamp Cases**
233 F. 96, 147 C.C.A. 166
244 F. 825; 267 F. 824
261 F. 606; 266 F. 994
277 F. 290; 280 F. 852; 260 U.S. 727, 67 L. Ed. 484, 43 S. Ct. 89
280 F. 846
280 F. 856
286 F. 175; 294 F. 562; 298 F. 579; 266 U.S. 609, 69 L. Ed. 466, 45 S. Ct. 94
286 F. 180
290 F. 967
292 F. 384
294 F. 567
4 F.2d 584
7 F.2d 1020; 10 F.2d 851
27 F.2d 590; 52 F.2d 725
27 F.2d 593
27 F.2d 595; 30 F.2d 99
52 F.2d 603

**Turbine Case**
202 F. 932; 211 F. 124; 232 F. 166; 238 F. 564; 228 U.S. 645; 57 L. Ed. 1003; 33 S. Ct. 722; 234 U.S. 755; 58 L. Ed. 1578; 34 S. Ct. 674; 243 U.S. 637, 61 L. Ed. 941, 37 S. Ct. 402; 246 U.S. 28, 62 L. Ed. 560, 38 S. Ct. 271

**Turner Case**
287 F.2d 821; 178 F. Supp. 239

**Turnpike Cases**
11 Pa. 61
92 Tenn. 369, 22 S.W. 75

**Turntable Cases**
F. Cas. No. 13,503; F. Cas. No. 13,504; 84 U.S. 657, 21 L. Ed. 745
75 Ga. 637; 77 Ga. 102
81 Ill. 76
116 Iowa 410, 90 N.W. 95
22 Kan. 686; 18 Kan. 34
37 Kan. 1, 14 P. 501
21 Minn. 207
65 Mo. 592
75 Mo. 653
67 Hun 604, 22 N.Y.S. 441; 78 Hun 1, 28 N.Y.S. 1097; 145 N.Y. 301, 39 N.E. 1068
57 Tex. 123; 57 Tex. 126

**Turpentine Timber Case**
74 Ga. App. 877, 41 S.E.2d 797; 202 Ga. 820, 44 S.E.2d 783; 76 Ga. App. 135, 45 S.E.2d 266

**Tuskegee Gerrymander Case**
167 F. Supp. 405, 270 F.2d 594; 364 U.S. 339, 5 L. Ed. 2d 110, 81 S. Ct. 125; 364 U.S. 806, 81 S. Ct. 41

**TWA Sex Discrimination Case**
455 U.S. 385, 71 L. Ed. 2d 234, 102 S. Ct. 1127

**Tweed Ring Cases**
58 N.Y. 1; 5 Hun 382; 63 N.Y. 202, 50 How. Pr. 26; 50 How. Pr. 434
6 Thomp. & Cook's 223, 3 Hun 682
5 Hun 353; 63 N.Y. 194, 50 How. Pr. 38
50 How. Pr. 262; 50 How. Pr. 273; 11 Hun 195
50 How. Pr. 280; 50 How. Pr. 286
13 Abb. Pr. (n.s.) 148; 13 Abb. Pr. (n.s.) 25; 13 Abb. Pr. (n.s.) 419

**Tweed's Case**
76 U.S. 425, 19 L. Ed. 678; 83 U.S. 504, 21 L. Ed. 389

**Twelfth Street Rag Case**
115 F. Supp. 754; 221 F.2d 569, 105 U.S.P.Q. (BNA) 178; 223 F.2d 252, 105 U.S.P.Q. (BNA) 460

**Twelve Commitments Case**
19 Abb. Pr. 394

**Twenty-Eight Hour Law Cases**
160 F. 526
218 F. 868

**Twenty-Four Hour Case (Union Elections)**
107 N.L.R.B. 427, No. 106

**Twenty-Ninth Street Case**
1 Hill 189

**Twenty Per Cent Cases (Salaries)**
3 Ct. Cl. 257
3 Ct. Cl. 260
*Continued*

3 Ct. Cl. 263
3 Ct. Cl. 265; 4 Ct. Cl. 554
3 Ct. Cl. 267
4 Ct. Cl. 227
5 Ct. Cl. 523; 80 U.S. 568, 20 L. Ed. 705, 20 L. Ed. 706, 20 L. Ed. 707
9 Ct. Cl. 103
9 Ct. Cl. 152
9 Ct. Cl. 153
9 Ct. Cl. 302; 87 U.S. 179, 22 L. Ed. 339
9 Ct. Cl. 315
9 Ct. Cl. 509

**Twenty Per Cent Cases (Votes)**
144 Wis. 1, 128 N.W. 1041
144 Wis. 58, 128 N.W. 1061

**Twilight Zone Case**
317 U.S. 249, 87 L. Ed. 246, 63 S. Ct. 225; 12 Wash. 2d 349, 121 P.2d 365; 316 U.S. 657, 86 L. Ed. 1736, 62 S. Ct. 1283; 317 U.S. 713, 87 L. Ed. 567, 63 S. Ct. 438

**Two Guys Case**
366 U.S. 582, 6 L. Ed. 2d 551, 81 S. Ct. 1135; 362 U.S. 960, 4 L. Ed. 2d 875, 80 S. Ct. 876; 368 U.S. 869, 7 L. Ed. 2d 69, 82 S. Ct. 21; 266 F.2d 427; 273 F.2d 954; 179 F. Supp. 944

**Two Per Cent Limit Cases**
202 Ind. 28, 169 N.E. 51, 171 N.E. 381
202 Ind. 254, 171 N.E. 378, 173 N.E. 268

**Two States Unemployment Insurance Case**
273 A.D. 391, 77 N YSupp2d 739; 299 N.Y. 232, 86 N.E.2d 577

**Tying Cases**
243 U.S. 502, 61 L. Ed. 871, 37 S. Ct. 416; 235 F. 398; 242 U.S. 637, 61 L. Ed. 540, 37 S. Ct. 21
283 U.S. 25, 75 L. Ed. 816, 51 S. Ct. 340; 43 F.2d 273; 282 U.S. 835, 75 L. Ed. 742, 51 S. Ct. 181
298 U.S. 131, 80 L. Ed. 1085, 56 S. Ct. 701; 13 F. Supp. 11; 56 S. Ct. 593
302 U.S. 458, 82 L. Ed. 371, 58 S. Ct. 288; 89 F.2d 960, 33 U.S.P.Q. (BNA) 261; 302 U.S. 673, 82 L. Ed. 520, 58 S. Ct. 30
306 U.S. 208, 83 L. Ed. 610, 59 S. Ct. 467; 20 F. Supp. 868; 304 U.S. 55, 82 L. Ed. 1146, 58 S. Ct. 768; 58 S. Ct. 523
309 U.S. 436, 84 L. Ed. 852, 60 S. Ct. 618; 27 F. Supp. 959, 41 U.S.P.Q. (BNA) 772; 60 S. Ct. 296
314 U.S. 488, 86 L. Ed. 363, 62 S. Ct. 402; 117 F.2d 968, 48 U.S.P.Q. (BNA) 277; 31 F. Supp. 876, 44 U.S.P.Q. (BNA) 337; 313 U.S. 555, 85 L. Ed. 1517, 61 S. Ct. 1098; 315 U.S. 788, 86 L. Ed. 363, 62 S. Ct. 402; 315 U.S. 826, 86 L. Ed. 1222, 62 S. Ct. 620
314 U.S. 495, 86 L. Ed. 367, 62 S. Ct. 406; 117 F.2d 829, 48 U.S.P.Q. (BNA) 487; 32 F. Supp. 690, 45 U.S.P.Q. (BNA) 418; 313 U.S. 558, 85 L. Ed. 1518, 61 S. Ct. 1117
316 U.S. 265, 86 L. Ed. 1461, 62 S. Ct. 1070; 40 F. Supp. 852; 316 U.S. 713, 86 L. Ed. 1778, 62 S. Ct. 1302; 62 S. Ct. 302
320 U.S. 661, 88 L. Ed. 376, 64 S. Ct. 268; 133 F.2d 803, 56 U.S.P.Q. (BNA) 72; 43 F. Supp. 692, 52 U.S.P.Q. (BNA) 154; 319 U.S. 737, 87 L. Ed. 1696, 63 S. Ct. 1319, 57 U.S.P.Q. (BNA) 568; 321 U.S. 802, 88 L. Ed. 1089, 64 S. Ct. 525; 323 U.S. 672, 89 L. Ed. 546, 65 S. Ct. 77
320 U.S. 680, 88 L. Ed. 396, 64 S. Ct. 278; 133 F.2d 811, 56 U.S.P.Q. (BNA) 80; 142 F.2d 549, 61 U.S.P.Q. (BNA) 464; 43 F. Supp. 878, 52 U.S.P.Q. (BNA) 569; 46 F. Supp. 675; 319 U.S. 739, 87 L. Ed. 1697, 63 S. Ct. 1328, 57 U.S.P.Q. (BNA) 568; 321 U.S. 802, 88 L. Ed. 1089, 64 S. Ct. 526
323 U.S. 386, 89 L. Ed. 322, 65 S. Ct. 373; 46 F. Supp. 541, 55 U.S.P.Q. (BNA) 14; 65 F. Supp. 271, 69 U.S.P.Q. (BNA) 373; 1945 C.D. 654, 65 U.S.P.Q. (BNA) 1; 64 U.S.P.Q. (BNA) 165; 324 U.S. 570, 89 L. Ed. 1198, 65 S. Ct. 815, 1945 C.D. 651, 65 U.S.P.Q. (BNA) 1; 324 U.S. 888
326 U.S. 1, 89 L. Ed. 2013, 65 S. Ct. 1416; 52 F. Supp. 362; 326 U.S. 802, 90 L. Ed. 489, 66 S. Ct. 6; 326 U.S. 803, 90 L. Ed. 489, 66 S. Ct. 7
332 U.S. 392, 92 L. Ed. 20, 68 S. Ct. 12; 6 F.R.D. 302, 71 U.S.P.Q. (BNA) 262; 67 S. Ct. 1199
334 U.S. 100, 92 L. Ed. 1236, 68 S. Ct. 941; 68 F. Supp. 180; 94 F. Supp. 747
334 U.S. 131, 92 L. Ed. 1260, 68 S. Ct. 915; 66 F. Supp. 323, 69 U.S.P.Q. (BNA) 573; 70 F. Supp. 53, 72 U.S.P.Q. (BNA) 46; 75 F. Supp. 1002, 76 U.S.P.Q. (BNA) 296; 85 F. Supp. 881, 82 U.S.P.Q. (BNA) 291; 338 U.S. 802, 94 L. Ed. 486, 70 S. Ct. 61; 339 U.S. 974, 94 L. Ed. 1380, 70 S. Ct. 1031, 70 S. Ct. 1032; 340 U.S. 857, 95 L. Ed. 627, 71 S. Ct. 69, 71 S. Ct. 70; 67 S. Ct. 1752, 73 U.S.P.Q. (BNA) 551; 70 S. Ct. 1032

345 U.S. 594, 97 L. Ed. 1277, 73 S. Ct. 872; 105 F. Supp. 670

**Tyson Case (Jurisdiction of Federal Courts)**
41 U.S. 1, 10 L. Ed. 865

**Tyson Case (Theatre Tickets)**
273 U.S. 418, 71 L. Ed. 718, 47 S. Ct. 426

## U

**U G I Case**
283 F.2d 817

**U-Turn Case**
32 Wash. 2d 427, 202 P.2d 253

**Ulysses Case**
5 F. Supp. 182; 72 F.2d 705

**Unauthorized Use of Photo Case**
119 Ind. App. 643, 86 N.E.2d 306, 88 N.E.2d 55

**Unborn Child Injury Case**
229 Minn. 365, 38 N.W.2d 838

**Uncle Remus Case**
1 F. Supp. 713

**Under Street Parking Case**
324 Mich. 527, 37 N.W.2d 625

**Underassessed Taxes Case**
190 Md. 394, 58 A.2d 672

**Undertaker Insurance Agent Case**
79 F. Supp. 62; 336 U.S. 220, 93 L. Ed. 632, 69 S. Ct. 550

**Underwriter's Monopoly Case**
51 F. Supp. 712; 64 S. Ct. 90; 322 U.S. 533, 88 L. Ed. 1440, 64 S. Ct. 1162; 323 U.S. 811, 89 L. Ed. 646, 65 S. Ct. 26

**Uneeda and Iwanta Biscuit Case**
95 F. 135

**Unemployment Compensation Law Case (Massachusetts)**
296 Mass. 275, 5 N.E.2d 720, 300 U.S. 657, 81 L. Ed. 867, 57 S. Ct. 434

**Unemployment Insurance Case**
301 U.S. 495, 81 L. Ed. 1245, 57 S. Ct. 868

**Unfair Labor Practice Complete Relief Case**
459 U.S. 344, 74 L. Ed. 2d 523, 103 S. Ct. 665

**Unguarded Pit Case**
245 Iowa 270, 60 N.W.2d 240; 246 Iowa 318, 67 N.W.2d 533

**Unharvested Crop Case**
116 Colo. 593, 183 P.2d 889

**Uniform Partnership Act Case**
125 Cal. App. 641, 13 P.2d 999

**Uniform Warehouse Law Case**
221 F. 16, 136 C.C.A. 542; 238 U.S. 624, 59 L. Ed. 1494, 35 S. Ct. 662

**Unilateral Termination of Contract Case**
324 Mich. 433, 37 N.W.2d 162

**Union Bank Case**
37 N.J. Eq. 420; 38 N.J. Eq. 265

**Union Bill of Rights Case**
467 U.S. 526, 81 L. Ed. 2d 457, 104 S. Ct. 2557

**Union Bluestone Company Case**
15 A.D. 602, 44 N.Y.S. 787; 164 N.Y. 401, 58 N.E. 525

**Union Business Agent Discharge Case**
456 U.S. 431, 72 L. Ed. 2d 239, 102 S. Ct. 1867

**Union Cigar Label Case**
39 F. 777

**Union Expulsion Case**
26 Wash. 2d 498, 174 P.2d 523

**Union Liability Case**
459 U.S. 212, 74 L. Ed. 2d 402, 103 S. Ct. 588

**Union News Company Case**
58 F.T.C. 10

**Union Nonmembership Amendment Case (Arizona)**
67 Ariz. 20, 189 P.2d 912; 335 U.S. 538, 93 L. Ed. 222, 69 S. Ct. 258, 69 S. Ct. 260

**Union Officers Discipline Case**
460 U.S. 693, 75 L. Ed. 2d 387, 103 S. Ct. 1467

**Union Organizers Case**
516 U.S. 85, 133 L. Ed. 2d 371, 116 S. Ct. 450 (1995)

**Union Pacific Cases**
76 U.S. 579, 19 L. Ed. 792
169 U.S. 466, 42 L. Ed. 819, 18 S. Ct. 418; 371 U.S. 361, 43 L. Ed. 197, 18 S. Ct. 888; 64 F. 165; 100 F. 235; 102 F. 197
188 F. 102; 226 U.S. 61, 57 L. Ed. 124, 33 S. Ct. 53; 226 U.S. 470, 57 L. Ed. 306, 33 S. Ct. 162
F. Cas. No. 14,378; 85 U.S. 5, 21 L. Ed. 787
F. Cas. No. 14,379
F. Cas. No. 14,380

**Union Stockyard Case**
192 F. 330; 226 U.S. 286, 57 L. Ed. 226, 33 S. Ct. 83

**Unitary Business Tax Case**
77 L. Ed. 2d 545, 103 S. Ct. 2933

**United-Capital Merger Case**
303 F.2d 395

**United Dye Case**
330 F.2d 316

**United Fuel Gas Cases**
13 F.2d 510; 278 U.S. 300, 73 L. Ed. 390, 49 S. Ct. 150
14 F.2d 209; 278 U.S. 322, 73 L. Ed. 402, 49 S. Ct. 157

**United Mine Workers' Cases**
259 U.S. 344, 66 L. Ed. 975, 42 S. Ct. 570; 268 U.S. 295, 69 L. Ed. 963, 45 S. Ct. 551
330 U.S. 258, 91 L. Ed. 884, 67 S. Ct. 677; 70 F. Supp. 42; 329 U.S. 708, 91 L. Ed. 616, 67 S. Ct. 359; 329 U.S. 709, 91 L. Ed. 617, 67 S. Ct. 373; 329 U.S. 710, 91 L. Ed. 618, 67 S. Ct. 485; 91 L. Ed. 1298, 67 S. Ct. 975; 91 L. Ed. 1298, 67 S. Ct. 976; 91 L. Ed. 1298, 67 S. Ct. 977

**United Press Case**
164 N.Y. 406, 58 N.E. 527

**United Shoe Machinery Cases**
195 F. 578; 227 U.S. 202, 57 L. Ed. 481, 33 S. Ct. 253
227 F. 507; 232 F. 1023; 234 F. 127; 264 F. 138; 41 S. Ct. 9; 254 U.S. 666, 65 L. Ed. 465, 41 S. Ct. 217; 258 U.S. 451, 66 L. Ed. 708, 42 S. Ct. 363; 259 U.S. 575, 66 L. Ed. 1071, 42 S. Ct. 585

**United States Bank Case**
17 U.S. 316, 4 L. Ed. 579

**United States Gold Cases**
294 U.S. 240, 79 L. Ed. 885, 55 S. Ct. 407
294 U.S. 317, 79 L. Ed. 907, 55 S. Ct. 428
294 U.S. 330, 79 L. Ed. 912, 55 S. Ct. 432

**United States Hame Company Case**
227 F. 876, 142 C.C.A. 400

**United States Steel Corporation Case**
223 F. 55; 251 U.S. 417, 64 L. Ed. 343, 40 S. Ct. 293

**Universal Camera Case**
179 F.2d 749; 180 F.2d 731; 339 U.S. 951, 94 L. Ed. 1364, 70 S. Ct. 842; 339 U.S. 962, 94 L. Ed. 1372, 70 S. Ct. 998; 340 U.S. 474, 95 L. Ed. 456, 71 S. Ct. 456; 190 F.2d 429

**University Case**
6 F. 443

**University Levy Case**
75 Mont. 429, 244 P. 287

**Unlawful Employment of Child Labor Case**
446 U.S. 238, 64 L. Ed. 2d 182, 100 S. Ct. 1610

**Unrepeated Message Case**
44 I.C.C. 670

**Unreported Accident Limitations Case**
310 Ky. 776, 221 S.W.2d 679

**Unused Tag Case**
21 F. 701

**Uphaus Case**
355 U.S. 16, 2 L. Ed. 2d 22, 78 S. Ct. 57; 100 N.H. 436, 130 A.2d 278; 101 N.H. 139, 136 A.2d 221; 102 N.H. 517, 162 A.2d 611; 356 U.S. 926, 2 L. Ed. 2d 758, 78 S. Ct. 715; 356 U.S. 965, 78 S. Ct. 1005; 360 U.S. 72, 3 L. Ed. 2d 1090, 79 S. Ct. 1040; 5 L. Ed. 2d 29, 81 S. Ct. 22

**Upper Berth Case**
152 Wis. 341, 140 N.W. 70; 238 U.S. 491, 59 L. Ed. 1423, 35 S. Ct. 869

**Upshaw Case**
335 U.S. 410, 93 L. Ed. 100, 69 S. Ct. 170; 168 F.2d 167

**Upton Cases**
91 U.S. 45, 23 L. Ed. 203
91 U.S. 56, 23 L. Ed. 220
91 U.S. 64, 23 L. Ed. 224
91 U.S. 65, 23 L. Ed. 384
95 U.S. 665, 24 L. Ed. 523
96 U.S. 328, 24 L. Ed. 818

**Urban Redevelopment Case**
99 N.H. 161, 106 A.2d 571

**Urban Renewal Cases**
60 So. 2d 663 (Fla.)
115 So. 2d 745 (Fla.)

**Use of Deadly Force Case**
471 U.S. 1, 85 L. Ed. 2d 1, 105 S. Ct. 1694

**Use of Silence for Impeachment Case**
426 U.S. 610, 49 L. Ed. 2d 91, 96 S. Ct. 2240

**Used Car Agent Case**
221 Miss. 293, 72 So. 2d 696

**Utah Election Cases**
114 U.S. 15, 29 L. Ed. 47, 5 S. Ct. 747

**Utica Bridge Cases**
2 Ill. Ct. Cl. 254
2 Ill. Ct. Cl. 272
2 Ill. Ct. Cl. 273
2 Ill. Ct. Cl. 274
2 Ill. Ct. Cl. 276
2 Ill. Ct. Cl. 277
2 Ill. Ct. Cl. 278
2 Ill. Ct. Cl. 279
2 Ill. Ct. Cl. 280
2 Ill. Ct. Cl. 281
2 Ill. Ct. Cl. 282
2 Ill. Ct. Cl. 283
2 Ill. Ct. Cl. 284
2 Ill. Ct. Cl. 285
2 Ill. Ct. Cl. 286
2 Ill. Ct. Cl. 287
2 Ill. Ct. Cl. 288
2 Ill. Ct. Cl. 289
2 Ill. Ct. Cl. 290

**Utica Insurance Cases**
19 Johns. 1; 6 Cow. 606; 8 Cow. 709
8 Cow. 20
3 Wend. 296
3 Wend. 369
4 Wend. 652

## V

**Vacant Building Arson Case**
331 Mich. 490, 50 N.W.2d 137; 343 U.S. 911, 96 L. Ed. 1327, 72 S. Ct. 644

**Vacation Pay Clause Case**
106 Cal. App. 2d 833, 236 P.2d 236

**Vacation Unemployment Compensation Case**
171 Pa. Super. 634, 91 A.2d 315

**Vaccination Cases**
197 U.S. 11, 49 L. Ed. 643, 25 S. Ct. 358
225 S.W. 267 (Tex.); 257 U.S. 650, 66 L. Ed. 416, 42 S. Ct. 53; 260 U.S. 174, 67 L. Ed. 194, 43 S. Ct. 24

**Valuation Case (Rate Making)**
302 U.S. 388, 82 L. Ed. 319, 58 S. Ct. 334; 302 U.S. 771, 82 L. Ed. 598, 58 S. Ct. 3

**Valuation of Common Carrier Properties Case**
295 F. 558; 266 U.S. 438, 69 L. Ed. 369, 45 S. Ct. 153

**Valuation of Corporate Stock Case**
89 A.2d 862 (Del.); 33 Del. Ch. 293, 93 A.2d 107

**Van Camp Case**
207 Cal. 123, 277 P. 324

**Van Rensselaer Cases**
13 N.Y. 299; 9 Barb. 302
19 N.Y. 68, 27 Barb. 104
19 N.Y. 100, 27 Barb. 104
26 N.Y. 558, 24 Barb. 365
26 N.Y. 580, 24 Barb. 365
39 N.Y. 9
110 N.Y. 537, 18 N.E. 357

**Vander Weele Case**
27 T.C. 340; 254 F.2d 895

**Vanderbilt University Case**
129 Tenn. 279, 164 S.W. 1151

**Vansant Cases**
96 Md. 110, 53 A. 711
97 Md. 598, 55 A. 395

**Various Items Case**
40 F.2d 422; 282 U.S. 818, 75 L. Ed. 731, 51 S. Ct. 21; 282 U.S. 577, 75 L. Ed. 558, 51 S. Ct. 282

**Veazie Bank Case**
75 U.S. 533, 19 L. Ed. 482

**Vehicle Identification Search Case**
475 U.S. 106, 89 L. Ed. 2d 81, 106 S. Ct. 960

**Velocipede Case**
150 Ga. 747, 105 S.E. 358

**Veney Raids Cases**
364 F.2d 197
240 F. Supp. 550

**Verbal Abuse Case**
149 Ohio St. 301, 78 N.E.2d 735

**Vermicelli Case**
247 Miss. 575, 156 So. 2d 734

**Vertical Price-Fixing Case**
79 L. Ed. 2d 775, 104 S. Ct. 1464

**Vestris Case**
60 F. 273

**Veterans Benefits Case**
415 U.S. 361, 39 L. Ed. 2d 389, 94 S. Ct. 1160

**Veterans Lifetime Preference Case**
442 U.S. 256, 60 L. Ed. 2d 870, 99 S. Ct. 2282

**Veto Cases**
7 Haw. 229
69 Mont. 325, 222 P. 428

**Victim Impact Evidence Case**
115 L. Ed. 2d 720, 111 S. Ct. 2597

**Victim Impact Statement Case**
482 U.S. 496, 96 L. Ed. 2d 440, 107 S. Ct. 2529

**Victor Talking Machine Cases**
118 F. 50
140 F. 860; 145 F. 189; 145 F. 350, 76 C.C.A. 180; 151 F. 601, 81 C.C.A. 145; 178 F. 577; 183 F. 580, 106 C.C.A. 348
146 F. 534; 148 F. 1022, 79 C.C.A. 536; 213 U.S. 301, 53 L. Ed. 805, 29 S. Ct. 495; 180 F. 778
150 F. 147; 154 F. 58, 83 C.C.A. 170; 213 U.S. 325, 53 L. Ed. 816, 29 S. Ct. 503
158 F. 309; 169 F. 894; 180 F. 777; 183 F. 849; 188 F. 330; 186 F. 625; 188 F. 326
177 F. 248

**Video Tape Recorder Case**
78 L. Ed. 2d 574, 104 S. Ct. 774

**Vigen Case**
213 Minn. 120, 5 N.W.2d 397

**Village Zoning Discrimination Case**
429 U.S. 252, 50 L. Ed. 2d 450, 98 S. Ct. 555

**Vinegar Case**
186 F. 399

**Virgin Island Divorce Case**
214 F.2d 820; 348 U.S. 810, 99 L. Ed. 639, 75 S. Ct. 60; 348 U.S. 885, 99 L. Ed. 696, 75 S. Ct. 205; 349 U.S. 1, 99 L. Ed. 773, 75 S. Ct. 553

**Virginia Coupon Cases**
107 U.S. 769, 27 L. Ed. 468, 2 S. Ct. 91
114 U.S. 269
114 U.S. 270, 29 L. Ed. 185, 5 S. Ct. 903, 5 S. Ct. 962
114 U.S. 307, 29 L. Ed. 199, 5 S. Ct. 923, 5 S. Ct. 962
114 U.S. 309, 29 L. Ed. 198, 5 S. Ct. 924, 5 S. Ct. 962
114 U.S. 317, 29 L. Ed. 202, 5 S. Ct. 928, 5 S. Ct. 962
114 U.S. 323, 29 L. Ed. 204, 5 S. Ct. 931, 5 S. Ct. 962
114 U.S. 325, 29 L. Ed. 205, 5 S. Ct. 932, 5 S. Ct. 962
114 U.S. 338, 29 L. Ed. 240, 5 S. Ct. 1020
17 F. 171; 114 U.S. 311, 29 L. Ed. 200, 5 S. Ct. 925, 5 S. Ct. 962

**Virginia Electric Case**
44 N.L.R.B. 404, No. 75; 20 N.L.R.B. 911, No. 87; 115 F.2d 414; 132 F.2d 390; 312 U.S. 677, 85 L. Ed. 117, 61 S. Ct. 826; 314 U.S. 469, 86 L. Ed. 348, 62 S. Ct. 344; 318 U.S. 752, 87 L. Ed. 1127, 63 S. Ct. 832; 319 U.S. 533, 87 L. Ed. 1568, 63 S. Ct. 1214; 320 U.S. 809, 88 L. Ed. 489, 64 S. Ct. 27

**Virginia Milk Case**
300 U.S. 608, 81 L. Ed. 835, 57 S. Ct. 549

**Virginia Railroad Commission Case**
211 U.S. 210, 53 L. Ed. 150, 29 S. Ct. 67

**Virginia Telegraph Cases**
90 Va. 297, 18 S.E. 280; 41 L. Ed. 1180, 17 S. Ct. 1002
94 Va. 268, 26 S.E. 828
94 Va. 513, 27 S.E. 429

**VMI Sex Discrimination Case**
518 U.S. 515, 135 L. Ed. 2d 735, 116 S. Ct. 2264 (1996)

**Voir Dire Examination Case**
78 L. Ed. 2d 629, 104 S. Ct. 819

**Von Bramer Case**
127 F.2d 149

**Voorhies Memorial Case**
69 Colo. 135, 169 P. 138

**Voting for Corporate Directors Case**
95 Ohio App. 498, 121 N.E.2d 146; 161 Ohio St. 60, 118 N.E.2d 138

**Voting Machine Case**
241 N.Y. 49, 148 N.E. 784

**Voting Rights Act Case**
55 L. Ed. 2d 148, 98 S. Ct. 965
459 U.S. 159, 74 L. Ed. 2d 334, 103 S. Ct. 530

**Voting Rights Act Cases**
512 U.S. 874, 129 L. Ed. 2d 687, 114 S. Ct. 2581 (1994)
512 U.S. 997, 129 L. Ed. 2d 775, 114 S. Ct. 2647 (1994)

**Voting Rights Cases**
364 U.S. 339, 5 L. Ed. 2d 110, 81 S. Ct. 125
369 U.S. 186, 7 L. Ed. 2d 663, 82 S. Ct. 691
377 U.S. 533, 12 L. Ed. 2d 506, 84 S. Ct. 1362

**Voting Trust Cases**
48 N.J. Eq. 208, 21 A. 847
52 N.J. Eq. 178, 28 A. 75
60 N.J. Eq. 17, 46 A. 591
60 N.J. Eq. 179, 47 A. 345
61 N.J. Eq. 658, 47 A. 638

**Vukovich Case**
70 Utah 354, 260 P. 279

**Vulcan Coal Case**
244 U.S. 82, 61 L. Ed. 1007, 37 S. Ct. 584

## W

**Wabash Cases**

22 F. 272; 23 F. 513; 23 F. 863; 25 F. 69; 25 F. 693

46 F. 26

29 F. 618; 30 F. 332; 34 F. 259; 38 F. 63; 145 U.S. 82, 36 L. Ed. 632, 12 S. Ct. 787; 150 U.S. 287, 37 L. Ed. 1085, 14 S. Ct. 86

29 F. 161

**Wade Case**

388 U.S. 218, 18 L. Ed. 2d 1149, 87 S. Ct. 1926

**Wadsworth Case**

81 N.L.R.B. 802, No. 127; 184 F.2d 60; 341 U.S. 947, 95 L. Ed. 1371, 71 S. Ct. 1011; 342 U.S. 843, 96 L. Ed. 637, 72 S. Ct. 20, 72 S. Ct. 21, 72 S. Ct. 22, 72 S. Ct. 23

**Wage Discrimination Case**

452 U.S. 161, 68 L. Ed. 2d 751, 101 S. Ct. 2242

**Wage Stabilization Case**

421 U.S. 542, 44 L. Ed. 2d 363, 95 S. Ct. 1792

**Wagner Act Cases**

301 U.S. 1, 81 L. Ed. 893, 57 S. Ct. 615; 90 F.2d 678

35 N.L.R.B. 621, No. 137; 129 F.2d 410; 317 U.S. 618, 87 L. Ed. 501, 63 S. Ct. 202; 319 U.S. 50, 87 L. Ed. 1250, 63 S. Ct. 905

**Wait-Pierce Case**

191 Wis. 202, 209 N.W. 475, 210 N.W. 822

**Waiver of Counsel Case**

475 U.S. 412, 89 L. Ed. 2d 410, 106 S. Ct. 1135

**Waiver of Right to Counsel Case**

451 U.S. 477, 68 L. Ed. 2d 378, 101 S. Ct. 1880

**Walking Time Case**

60 F. Supp. 146; 149 F.2d 461; 326 U.S. 706, 90 L. Ed. 416, 66 S. Ct. 91; 328 U.S. 680, 90 L. Ed. 1515, 66 S. Ct. 1187; 329 U.S. 822, 91 L. Ed. 699, 67 S. Ct. 25; 331 U.S. 784, 91 L. Ed. 1815, 67 S. Ct. 1191; 69 F. Supp. 710

**Wall-Bed Case**

46 Cal. App. 524, 189 P. 1022

**Wall Case**

164 F.2d 462

**Wall Paper Cases**

148 F. 939, 78 C.C.A. 567; 204 U.S. 673, 51 L. Ed. 673, 27 S. Ct. 787; 212 U.S. 227, 53 L. Ed. 486, 29 S. Ct. 280

287 F. 841

**Walla-Walla Doctrine Case**

60 F. 857; 172 U.S. 1, 43 L. Ed. 341, 19 S. Ct. 77

**Wallamet Bridge Case**

6 F. 326; 6 F. 780; 19 F. 347; 27 F. 673; 125 U.S. 1, 31 L. Ed. 629, 8 S. Ct. 811

**Walnut Street Case**

151 Wis. 520, 139 N.W. 396

**Walters' Case**

278 Pa. 421, 123 A. 408

**Walthall County Case**

97 Miss. 599, 54 So. 257

**Waltham Watch Case**

191 F. 855; 202 F. 225; 209 F. 1007, 126 C.C.A. 668; 232 U.S. 724, 58 L. Ed. 815, 34 S. Ct. 602

**Wanamaker Case**

169 F. 491

**Wanted Flyer Detention Case**

469 U.S. 221, 83 L. Ed. 2d 604, 105 S. Ct. 675

**War Bond Gift Case**
139 N.J. Eq. 316, 51 A.2d 105; 140 N.J. Eq. 474, 55 A.2d 26

**War Brides Case**
338 U.S. 537, 94 L. Ed. 270, 70 S. Ct. 309

**War Materials Reparation Case**
294 I.C.C. 5; 297 I.C.C. 635

**War Minerals Cases**
295 F. 225; 44 S. Ct. 459; 267 U.S. 175, 69 L. Ed. 561, 45 S. Ct. 252
298 F. 839; 267 U.S. 185, 69 L. Ed. 566, 45 S. Ct. 256
47 F.2d 417; 283 U.S. 681, 75 L. Ed. 1466, 51 S. Ct. 654
47 F.2d 421; 283 U.S. 681, 75 L. Ed. 1466, 51 S. Ct. 654
47 F.2d 422; 283 U.S. 817, 75 L. Ed. 1433, 51 S. Ct. 650; 284 U.S. 231, 76 L. Ed. 261, 52 S. Ct. 113
47 F.2d 424; 283 U.S. 817, 75 L. Ed. 1433, 51 S. Ct. 650; 284 U.S. 231, 76 L. Ed. 261, 52 S. Ct. 113; 62 F.2d 863; 289 U.S. 715, 77 L. Ed. 1468, 53 S. Ct. 527; 289 U.S. 510, 77 L. Ed. 1352, 53 S. Ct. 700
59 F.2d 887; 287 U.S. 588, 77 L. Ed. 514, 53 S. Ct. 89; 288 U.S. 97, 77 L. Ed. 638, 53 S. Ct. 293

**War Risk Insurance Cases**
67 F.2d 490; 292 U.S. 616, 78 L. Ed. 1474, 54 S. Ct. 641; 292 U.S. 571, 78 L. Ed. 1434, 54 S. Ct. 840; 80 F.2d 418; 298 U.S. 658, 80 L. Ed. 1384, 56 S. Ct. 683
68 F.2d 442; 292 U.S. 617, 78 L. Ed. 1475, 54 S. Ct. 641; 292 U.S. 571, 78 L. Ed. 1434, 54 S. Ct. 840; 87 F.2d 164; 301 U.S. 683, 81 L. Ed. 1341, 57 S. Ct. 783
165 F.2d 758

**War Time Profits Cases**
23 F. Supp. 676, 1938 A.M.C. 1007; 26 F. Supp. 259; 113 F.2d 301; 311 U.S. 632, 85 L. Ed. 402, 61 S. Ct. 49; 315 U.S. 289, 86 L. Ed. 855, 62 S. Ct. 581

**War Time Prohibition Cases**
260 F. 486; 251 U.S. 210, 64 L. Ed. 229, 40 S. Ct. 139
284 F. 596; 251 U.S. 146, 64 L. Ed. 194, 40 S. Ct. 106; 251 U.S. 264, 64 L. Ed. 260, 40 S. Ct. 141

**Ward Case**
144 F. 524; 136 F. 502; 150 F. 541; 205 U.S. 544, 51 L. Ed. 923, 27 S. Ct. 791

**Warrantless Automobile Search Case**
456 U.S. 798, 72 L. Ed. 2d 572, 102 S. Ct. 2157

**Warrantless Home Arrest Case**
80 L. Ed. 2d 732, 104 S. Ct. 2091

**Warrantless Home Search Pursuant to Arrest Warrant for Another Case**
451 U.S. 204, 68 L. Ed. 2d 38, 101 S. Ct. 1642

**Warren Bridge Case**
6 Pick. (23 Mass) 376; 7 Pick. (24 Mass) 344; 36 U.S. 420, 9 L. Ed. 773

**Warrior Case**
363 U.S. 574; 4 L. Ed. 2d 1409, 80 S. Ct. 1347; 269 F.2d 633; 168 F. Supp. 702; 361 U.S. 912, 4 L. Ed. 2d 183, 80 S. Ct. 255; 363 U.S. 564, 4 L. Ed. 2d 1432, 80 S. Ct. 1363

**Warrior Run Case**
182 Pa. 514, 38 A. 491; 182 Pa. 530, 38 A. 489

**Wash Gray Case**
14 F.2d 196; 19 F.2d 493; 19 F.2d 496; 275 U.S. 518, 72 L. Ed. 403, 48 S. Ct. 118; 277 U.S. 66, 72 L. Ed. 787, 48 S. Ct. 459

**Washburn Insurance Case**
2 F. 633

**Washerwoman's Case**
160 N.C. 450, 76 S.E. 502

**Washington Arbitration Case**
436 Pa. 168, 259 A.2d 437

**Washington Coca Cola Case**
107 N.L.R.B. 299, No. 104; 220 F.2d 380

**Washington Compensation Tax Case**
300 U.S. 577, 81 L. Ed. 814, 57 S. Ct. 524; 300 U.S. 635, 57 S. Ct. 429

**Washington Minimum Wage Case**
185 Wash. 581, 55 P.2d 1083; 300 U.S. 379, 81 L. Ed. 703, 57 S. Ct. 578

**Washington Moral Nuisance Statute Case**
472 U.S. 491, 86 L. Ed. 2d 394, 105 S. Ct. 2794

**Washington Occupation Tax Cases**
188 Wash. 98, 61 P.2d 1269; 57 S. Ct. 671; 301 U.S. 672, 57 S. Ct. 947; 302 U.S. 186, 82 L. Ed. 187, 58 S. Ct. 233
188 Wash. 115, 61 P.2d 1276; 301 U.S. 672, 57 S. Ct. 947; 302 U.S. 186, 82 L. Ed. 187, 58 S. Ct. 233

**Washington Rent Law Case**
256 U.S. 135, 65 L. Ed. 865, 41 S. Ct. 458

**Washingtonian Case**
25 U.S.P.Q. (BNA) 83; 32 U.S.P.Q. (BNA) 113; 98 F.2d 245, 68 App. D.C. 373, 37 U.S.P.Q. (BNA) 429; 305 U.S. 583, 83 L. Ed. 368, 59 S. Ct. 85; 306 U.S. 30, 83 L. Ed. 470, 59 S. Ct. 397; 306 U.S. 668, 83 L. Ed. 1063, 59 S. Ct. 588; 140 F.2d 465, 60 U.S.P.Q. (BNA) 224

**Watchtower Restriction Case**
188 Misc. 978, 69 N.Y.S.2d 385; 272 A.D. 1039, 75 N.Y.S.2d 81; 273 A.D. 759, 75 N.Y.S.2d 660; 273 A.D. 807, 76 N.Y.S.2d 269; 297 N.Y. 805, 78 N.E.2d 349; 297 N.Y. 339, 79 N.E.2d 433; 68 S. Ct. 1342; 335 U.S. 886, 93 L. Ed. 425, 69 S. Ct. 232; 335 U.S. 912, 93 L. Ed. 445, 69 S. Ct. 479

**Water Effluent Limitations Case**
449 U.S. 64, 66 L. Ed. 2d 268, 101 S. Ct. 295

**Water Fluoridation Case**
273 P.2d 859 (Okla.); 348 U.S. 912, 99 L. Ed. 715, 75 S. Ct. 292

**Water Pollution Standards Case**
430 U.S. 112, 51 L. Ed. 2d 204, 97 S. Ct. 965

**Water Power Cases**
148 Wis. 124, 134 N.W. 330
229 U.S. 53, 57 L. Ed. 1063, 33 S. Ct. 667
23 F. Supp. 83; 107 F.2d 769; 309 U.S. 646, 84 L. Ed. 999, 60 S. Ct. 608; 309 U.S. 636, 84 L. Ed. 992, 60 S. Ct. 720; 309 U.S. 638, 84 L. Ed. 994, 60 S. Ct. 806; 311 U.S. 377, 85 L. Ed. 243, 61 S. Ct. 291, 1941 A.M.C. 1; 312 U.S. 712, 85 L. Ed. 1143, 61 S. Ct. 548; 317 U.S. 594, 87 L. Ed. 487, 63 S. Ct. 67

**Waterbury Conspiracy Case**
127 Conn. 543, 18 A.2d 895

**Waterfront Case**
33 F. 721

**Watergate Cases**
407 U.S. 297, 32 L. Ed. 2d 752, 92 S. Ct. 2125
356 F. Supp. 1394
559 F.2d 31
354 F. Supp. 217

**Watergate Tapes Case U.S. v Nixon**
360 F. Supp. 1; 487 F.2d 700; 418 U.S. 683, 41 L. Ed. 2d 1039, 94 S. Ct. 3090

**Waterman Pen Cases**
29 F. 316; 138 U.S. 252, 34 L. Ed. 923, 11 S. Ct. 334
183 F. 118; 193 F. 242; 197 F. 534, 117 C.C.A. 30; 197 F. 536, 117 C.C.A. 32; 235 U.S. 88, 59 L. Ed. 142, 35 S. Ct. 91

**Waters Case**
121 Ky. 611, 85 S.W. 209, 27 Ky. Law Rep. 479; 27 Ky. Law Rep. 586; 85 S.W. 150, 28 Ky. Law Rep. 679

**Waterworks Cases**
84 N.J.L. 611, 87 A. 140
9 N.J. 134, 87 A.2d 325

**Watkins Case**
354 U.S. 178, 1 L. Ed. 2d 1273, 77 S. Ct. 1173; 233 F.2d 681; 352 U.S. 822, 1 L. Ed. 2d 46, 77 S. Ct. 62

**Waukesha Canning Case**
211 F. 927, 128 C.C.A. 305

**Wax Nose Case**
15 F. 747; 119 U.S. 47, 30 L. Ed. 303, 7 S. Ct. 72

**Wayne Township Case**
8 N.J. Super. 468, 73 A.2d 287; 9 N.J. Super. 83, 74 A.2d 609; 13 N.J. Super. 490, 80 A.2d 650; 10 N.J. 165, 89 A.2d 693; 344 U.S. 919, 97 L. Ed. 708, 73 S. Ct. 386

**Weary Erie Case**
304 U.S. 64, 82 L. Ed. 1188, 58 S. Ct. 817; 90 F.2d 603; 98 F.2d 49; 302 U.S. 671, 82 L. Ed. 518, 58 S. Ct. 50; 305 U.S. 637, 83 L. Ed. 410, 59 S. Ct. 108; 305 U.S. 673, 83 L. Ed. 436, 59 S. Ct. 229

**Weaver Case**
27 Idaho 728, 151 P. 1013

**Weber Case**
348 U.S. 468, 99 L. Ed. 546, 75 S. Ct. 480; 364 Mo. 573, 265 S.W.2d 325; 348 U.S. 808, 99 L. Ed. 638, 75 S. Ct. 32

**Webster Case**
59 Mass. (5 Cush.) 295; 59 Mass. (5 Cush.) 386

**Webster Dictionary Cases**
43 F. 450, 53 Off. Gaz. Pat. Office 1409

**Webster-Parkman Case**
59 Mass. (5 Cush.) 295; 59 Mass. (5 Cush.) 386

**Webster Telephone Case**
17 Neb. 126, 22 N.W. 237

**Weeks Case**
232 U.S. 383, 58 L. Ed. 652, 34 S. Ct. 341

**Weirton Case**
7 F. Supp. 255; 10 F. Supp. 55

**Weiser River Case**
33 Idaho 146, 191 P. 206

**Welch Plug Case**
41 F.2d 672

**Well of Loneliness Case**
133 Misc. 611, 233 N.Y.S. 565

**Wentz Case**
108 Neb. 111, 187 N.W. 762; 108 Neb. 124, 187 N.W. 767; 108 Neb. 129, 187 N.W. 769

**Werbe's Estate Case**
273 F.2d 201; 178 F. Supp. 704

**Werfel Case**
231 Ala. 285, 164 So. 383; 230 Ala. 552, 162 So. 103

**West Case**
21 Idaho 410, 121 P. 1039; 235 U.S. 690, 59 L. Ed. 427, 35 S. Ct. 205

**West Coast Communist Case**
354 U.S. 298, 1 L. Ed. 2d 1356, 77 S. Ct. 1064; 225 F2d 146; 350 U.S. 860, 100 L. Ed. 763, 76 S. Ct. 104

**West Coast Hotel Wage Case**
185 Wash. 581, 55 P.2d 1083; 57 S. Ct. 40; 300 U.S. 379, 81 L. Ed. 703, 57 S. Ct. 578

**West of the Rockies Concrete Pipe Case**
303 F. Supp. 507

**West Virginia Passenger Rate Cases**
230 U.S. 513, 57 L. Ed. 1597, 33 S. Ct. 985
236 U.S. 605, 59 L. Ed. 745, 35 S. Ct. 437

**Westbound Meat Case**
210 I.C.C. 13; 263 I.C.C. 9

**Western Grain Case**
164 I.C.C. 619; 173 I.C.C. 511; 205 I.C.C. 301; 215 I.C.C. 83; 223 I.C.C. 235; 223 I.C.C. 556; 225 I.C.C. 401, 231 I.C.C. 793; 237 I.C.C. 145; 243 I.C.C. 83; 258 I.C.C. 337; 259 I.C.C. 629; 293 I.C.C. 479; 298 ICC 261; 301 I.C.C. 29

**Western Grain Company Cases**
247 Ala. 225, 23 So. 2d 577; 247 Ala. 242, 23 So. 2d 592; 247 Ala. 579, 25 So. 2d 384; 252 Ala. 282, 41 So. 2d 641
247 Ala. 363, 24 So. 2d 550; 247 Ala. 579, 25 So. 2d 384; 252 Ala. 282, 41 So. 2d 641
264 Ala. 145, 85 So. 2d 395
265 Ala. 62, 89 So. 2d 534

**Western Hemisphere Trade Case**
28 T.C. 14

**Western Liquid Asphalt Case**
303 F. Supp. 1053

**Western Union Cases**

216 U.S. 146, 54 L. Ed. 423, 30 S. Ct. 280

33 F. 129; 125 U.S. 530, 31 L. Ed. 790, 8 S. Ct. 961; 141 U.S. 40, 35 L. Ed. 628, 11 S. Ct. 889

154 F. 95; 216 U.S. 165, 54 L. Ed. 430, 30 S. Ct. 286

75 Kan. 609, 90 P. 299; 216 U.S. 1, 54 L. Ed. 355, 30 S. Ct. 190

299 N.Y. 177, 86 N.E.2d 162; 274 A.D. 754, 79 N.Y.S.2d 545

**Western Union Income Tax Case**

141 F.2d 774; 322 U.S. 751, 88 L. Ed. 1581, 64 S. Ct. 1262; 322 U.S. 751, 88 L. Ed. 1582, 64 S. Ct. 1268

**Westinghouse Cases**

358 U.S. 184, 3 L. Ed. 2d 210, 79 S. Ct. 180; 249 F.2d 490; 148 F. Supp. 597; 355 U.S. 922, 2 L. Ed. 2d 353, 78 S. Ct. 366

112 F. 417; 117 F. 495, 55 C.C.A. 230

129 F. 604; 173 F. 361, 97 C.C.A. 621; 215 U.S. 608, 54 L. Ed. 347, 30 S. Ct. 409; 225 U.S. 604, 56 L. Ed. 1222, 32 S. Ct. 691

218 F. 646; 233 F. 752; 242 U.S. 640, 61 L. Ed. 541, 37 S. Ct. 112

248 F. 508; 281 F. 453; 260 U.S. 744, 67 L. Ed. 492, 43 S. Ct. 165

210 F. Supp. 483

386 Pa. 306, 125 A.2d 755; 352 U.S. 1024, 1 L. Ed. 2d 596, 77 S. Ct. 589

**Westinghouse Labor Case**

107 F. Supp. 692; 210 F.2d 623; 347 U.S. 1010, 98 L. Ed. 1134, 74 S. Ct. 868; 348 U.S. 437, 99 L. Ed. 510, 75 S. Ct. 489; 349 U.S. 925, 99 L. Ed. 1256, 75 S. Ct. 657

**Whale Oil Case**

Treas. Dec. 45099; Treas. Dec. 45578, 19 C.C.P.A. (Customs) 415; Treas. Dec. 45647; Abs. (n.s.) No. 21863; 287 U.S. 629, 77 L. Ed. 546, 53 S. Ct. 82

**Wharf Case**

141 F. 454; 152 F. 1022, 82 C.C.A. 276; 158 F. 1023, 86 C.C.A. 674; 207 U.S. 588, 52 L. Ed. 353, 28 S. Ct. 255; 214 U.S. 345, 53 L. Ed. 1024, 29 S. Ct. 661

**What-Cheer House Case**

21 Cal. 448

**Wheat Biscuit Case**

244 F. 508; 250 F. 960, 163 C.C.A. 210

**Wheeling Bridge Case**

50 U.S. 647, 13 L. Ed. 294, 52 U.S. 528, 13 L. Ed. 799; 54 U.S. 518, 14 L. Ed. 249; 59 U.S. 421, 15 L. Ed. 435; 59 U.S. 460, 15 L. Ed. 449

**Whip and Collar Case**

299 U.S. 334, 81 L. Ed. 270, 57 S. Ct. 277; 299 U.S. 525, 81 L. Ed. 386, 57 S. Ct. 19

**Whipping Boss Case**

88 Fla. 26, 101 So. 233

**Whiskey Cases**

99 U.S. 594, 25 L. Ed. 399

**Whiskey Rebellion Cases**

2 U.S. 335, 1 L. Ed. 404, F. Cas. No. 15,443

2 U.S. 343, 1 L. Ed. 408

2 U.S. 345, 1 L. Ed. 409

2 U.S. 346, 1 L. Ed. 409

2 U.S. 348, 1 L. Ed. 410

3 U.S. 513, 1 L. Ed. 700, F. Cas. No. 15,442

3 U.S. 515, 1 L. Ed. 701, F. Cas. No. 15,126

F. Cas. No. 15,127

**Whiskey Tax Act Case**

274 F. 420; 255 U.S. 288, 65 L. Ed. 638, 41 S. Ct. 272

**Whisky Trust Cases**

50 F. 469; 51 F. 205

51 F. 213

52 F. 104

**White Bear Brewing Case**

227 F.2d 359; 350 U.S. 1010, 100 L. Ed. 871, 76 S. Ct. 646; 351 U.S. 958, 100 L. Ed. 1480, 100 L. Ed. 1481, 76 S. Ct. 844, 76 S. Ct. 845, 76 S. Ct. 851

**White Cargo Case**

297 F. 625; 12 F.2d 116

**White Cases**

299 F. 855; 270 U.S. 175, 70 L. Ed. 530, 46 S. Ct. 274

322 U.S. 694, 88 L. Ed. 1542, 64 S. Ct. 1248; 320 U.S. 729, 88 L. Ed. 431, 64 S. Ct. 189; 137 F.2d 24; 147 F.2d 603

**White Cross Drug Case**

66 Nev. 166, 207 P.2d 990; 66 Nev. 202, 210 P.2d 454

**White House Tapes Case**

433 U.S. 425, 53 L. Ed. 2d 867, 97 S. Ct. 2777

487 F.2d 700

**White Pine Cases**

56 F.2d 774

64 F.2d 618

**White Primary Cases**

313 U.S. 299, 85 L. Ed. 1368, 61 S. Ct. 1031; 35 F. Supp. 66; 61 S. Ct. 443; 35 F. Supp. 457; 314 U.S. 707, 86 L. Ed. 565, 62 S. Ct. 51

165 F.2d 387, 174 F.2d 391

**White Primary Cases (Texas)**

273 U.S. 536, 71 L. Ed. 759, 47 S. Ct. 446

34 F.2d 464; 49 F.2d 1012; 284 U.S. 601, 76 L. Ed. 516, 52 S. Ct. 24; 76 L. Ed. 1301, 52 S. Ct. 202; 286 U.S. 73, 76 L. Ed. 984, 52 S. Ct. 484

294 U.S. 699, 79 L. Ed. 1236, 55 S. Ct. 351; 295 U.S. 45, 79 L. Ed. 1292, 55 S. Ct. 622

131 F.2d 593; 319 U.S. 738, 87 L. Ed. 1697, 63 S. Ct. 1325; 321 U.S. 649, 88 L. Ed. 987, 64 S. Ct. 757; 322 U.S. 769, 88 L. Ed. 1594, 64 S. Ct. 1052; 322 U.S. 718

345 U.S. 461, 97 L. Ed. 1152, 73 S. Ct. 809; 344 U.S. 883, 97 L. Ed. 684, 73 S. Ct. 180; 345 U.S. 1003, 97 L. Ed. 1408, 73 S. Ct. 1128; 193 F.2d 600; 90 F. Supp. 595

**White Slave Cases**

227 U.S. 326, 57 L. Ed. 528, 33 S. Ct. 285

187 F. 992; 227 U.S. 308, 57 L. Ed. 523, 33 S. Ct. 281; 215 F. 679, 131 C.C.A. 613

114 Vt. 285, 44 A.2d 133

**Whiteside Case**

122 Tex. 369, 61 S.W.2d 804; 124 Tex. 232, 76 S.W.2d 1043; 128 Tex. 324, 98 S.W.2d 993; 81 S.W.2d 1064

**Whitney Case**

8 F.2d 476

**Widow Case**

66 Colo. 407, 181 P. 529

**Widower's Benefits Case**

420 U.S. 636, 43 L. Ed. 2d 514, 95 S. Ct. 1225

**Widow's Election Proration Case**

243 Iowa 1394, 55 N.W.2d 474

**Widow's Property Tax Exemption Case**

416 U.S. 351, 40 L. Ed. 2d 189, 94 S. Ct. 1734

**Wife vs. Husband Negligence Case**

262 S.W.2d 480 (Ky.)

**Wiggins Case**

39 U.S. 334, 10 L. Ed. 481

**Wilcox Cases**

96 Tenn. 148, 33 S.W. 914; 96 Tenn. 328, 34 S.W. 420; 100 Tenn. 538, 46 S.W. 297

96 Tenn. 163, 33 S.W. 917

100 Tenn. 524, 45 S.W. 781

**Wild Goose Case**

258 F. 479; 252 U.S. 416, 64 L. Ed. 641, 40 S. Ct. 382

**Wild Horse Case**

267 F. 665; 269 F. 365; 256 U.S. 690, 65 L. Ed. 1173, 41 S. Ct. 450; 256 U.S. 691, 65 L. Ed. 1173, 41 S. Ct. 450; 256 U.S. 691, 65 L. Ed. 1174, 41 S. Ct. 450

**Wildcat Strike Case**

444 U.S. 212, 62 L. Ed. 2d 394, 100 S. Ct. 410

**Wildenhus Case**

28 F. 924; 120 U.S. 1, 30 L. Ed. 565, 7 S. Ct. 385

**Will Alteration Case**
170 Kan. 407, 227 P.2d 148; 173 Kan. 298, 245 P.2d 979

**Will Option Case**
267 S.W.2d 46 (Mo.)

**Will Renunciation Limitation Case**
189 Md. 116, 54 A.2d 128

**Willamette Valley Lumber Cases**
14 I.C.C. 61, 215 U.S. 226, 54 L. Ed. 169, 30 S. Ct. 89; 177 F. 963; 219 U.S. 433, 55 L. Ed. 283, 31 S. Ct. 288
21 I.C.C. 389; 197 F. 167

**Williams Case (Divorce)**
220 N.C. 445, 17 S.E.2d 769; 315 U.S. 795, 86 L. Ed. 1196, 62 S. Ct. 918; 317 U.S. 287, 87 L. Ed. 279, 63 S. Ct. 207; 222 N.C. 609, 24 S.E.2d 256; 224 N.C. 183, 29 S.E.2d 744; 322 U.S. 725, 88 L. Ed. 1562, 64 S. Ct. 1286; 325 U.S. 226, 89 L. Ed. 1577, 65 S. Ct. 1092; 325 U.S. 895, 89 L. Ed. 2006, 65 S. Ct. 1560

**Williams Case (Veterans)**
23 F.2d 792; 277 U.S. 580, 72 L. Ed. 997, 48 S. Ct. 530; 278 U.S. 255, 73 L. Ed. 314, 49 S. Ct. 97; 73 L. Ed. 1014, 49 S. Ct. 250

**Williamsburg Steel Products Company Case**
289 F.2d 700; 369 U.S. 736, 8 L. Ed. 2d 230, 82 S. Ct. 1107

**Williamson's Case**
26 Pa. 9; 39 Pa. 9

**Willowbrook Case**
393 F. Supp. 715

**Wilson Case**
50 F.2d 1063

**Wiltberger Case**
F. Cas. No. 16,738; 18 U.S. 76, 5 L. Ed. 37

**Winchester Avenue Railway Company Case**
71 F. 192

**Windfall Cases**
16 F. Supp. 801, 90 F.2d 812
17 F. Supp. 120; 89 F.2d 775

**Windfall Profit Tax Case**
76 L. Ed. 2d 427, 103 S. Ct. 2239

**Window Shades Case**
6 I.C.C. 148; 64 F. 723; 6 I.C.C. 548

**Wingfield Bank Case**
55 Nev. 206, 29 P.2d 500

**Wingo Case**
156 F. 152; 216 U.S. 146, 54 L. Ed. 423, 30 S. Ct. 280

**Winnebago Case**
83 U.S. 6, 21 L. Ed. 272

**Winnie Ruth Judd Murder Case**
41 Ariz. 176, 16 P.2d 720; 39 Ariz. 242, 5 P.2d 192

**Winsted Hosiery Case**
258 U.S. 483, 66 L. Ed. 729, 42 S. Ct. 384

**Winston-Salem Case**
19 I.C.C. 303; 195 F. 953

**Wire Cloth Case**
16 Daly 529, 14 N.Y.S. 277; 16 N.Y.S. 384

**Wire Rope Case**
139 F.2d 622; 142 F.2d 909

**Wire Tapping Cases**
302 U.S. 379, 82 L. Ed. 314, 58 S. Ct. 275; 106 F.2d 41; 308 U.S. 338, 84 L. Ed. 307, 60 S. Ct. 266
7 F.2d 756; 7 F.2d 760; 19 F.2d 842; 275 U.S. 557, 72 L. Ed. 424, 48 S. Ct. 117; 276 U.S. 609, 72 L. Ed. 729, 48 S. Ct. 207; 72 L. Ed. 1017, 48 S. Ct. 212; 277 U.S. 438, 72 L. Ed. 944, 48 S. Ct. 564
19 F.2d 850; 275 U.S. 557, 72 L. Ed. 424, 48 S. Ct. 117; 276 U.S. 609, 72 L. Ed. 729, 48 S. Ct. 207; 72 L. Ed. 1017, 48 S. Ct. 212; 277 U.S. 438, 72 L. Ed. 944, 48 S. Ct. 564
118 F.2d 310; 313 U.S. 588, 85 L. Ed. 1543, 61 S. Ct. 1109; 40 F. Supp. 468, 314 U.S. 704, 86 L. Ed. 563, 62 S. Ct. 119; 316 U.S. 129, 86 L. Ed. 1322, 62 S. Ct. 993; 317 U.S. 703, 87 L. Ed. 562, 63 S. Ct. 22

84 F. Supp. 472; 88 F. Supp. 910; 88 F. Supp. 912; 88 F. Supp. 915; 88 F. Supp. 921; 89 F. Supp. 142; 89 F. Supp. 664; 185 F.2d 629; 342 U.S. 920, 96 L. Ed. 688, 72 S. Ct. 362; 91 F. Supp. 867; 191 F.2d 749, 89 App. D.C. 107; 342 U.S. 926, 96 L. Ed. 690, 72 S. Ct. 362

**Wirebounds Patents Case**

37 F.2d 830; 49 F.2d 261; 281 U.S. 711, 74 L. Ed. 1133, 50 S. Ct. 346; 282 U.S. 704, 75 L. Ed. 634, 51 S. Ct. 232; 76 L. Ed. 1300, 52 S. Ct. 125

**Wiretap Notice Case**

429 U.S. 413, 50 L. Ed. 2d 652, 97 S. Ct. 658

**Wiretaps Authorization Cases**

416 U.S. 505, 40 L. Ed. 2d 341, 94 S. Ct. 1820; 416 U.S. 562, 40 L. Ed. 2d 380, 94 S. Ct. 1849, 94 S. Ct. 1858

**Wisconsin Appointment Case**

81 Wis. 440, 51 N.W. 724

**Wisconsin Dividend Tax Cases**

233 Wis. 286, 289 N.W. 677; 310 U.S. 618, 84 L. Ed. 1392, 60 S. Ct. 1076; 311 U.S. 435, 85 L. Ed. 267, 61 S. Ct. 246; 238 Wis. 69, 298 N.W. 186

233 Wis. 305, 298 N.W. 685; 310 U.S. 619, 84 L. Ed. 1393, 60 S. Ct. 1076; 311 U.S. 452, 85 L. Ed. 274, 61 S. Ct. 253; 312 U.S. 712, 85 L. Ed. 1143, 61 S. Ct. 444

**Wisconsin Employment Peace Act Case**

237 Wis. 164, 295 N.W. 791; 315 U.S. 740, 86 L. Ed. 1154, 62 S. Ct. 820

**Wisconsin Minimum Wage Law Case**

300 F. 991

**Wisconsin Motors Case**

145 N.L.R.B. 1097, No. 109

**Wisconsin Passenger Fares Case**

59 I.C.C. 391

**Wisconsin Peaceful Picketing Case**

222 Wis. 383, 268 N.W. 270, 268 N.W. 872; 57 S. Ct. 434; 301 U.S. 468, 81 L. Ed. 1229, 57 S. Ct. 857

**Wisconsin Rate Case**

257 U.S. 563, 66 L. Ed. 371, 42 S. Ct. 232

**Witness Identification Hearing Case**

449 U.S. 341, 66 L. Ed. 2d 549, 101 S. Ct. 654

**Witness Immunity Case**

53 N.M. 513, 212 P.2d 425

**Witness' Volunteered Statement Case**

88 Okla. Crim. 422, 204 P.2d 305

**Wobbly Deportation Case**

254 U.S. 281, 65 L. Ed. 270, 41 S. Ct. 133

**Wolf Case**

338 U.S. 25, 93 L. Ed. 1782, 69 S. Ct. 1359; 117 Colo. 279, 187 P.2d 926; 117 Colo. 321, 187 P.2d 928

**Wolff Packing Company Cases**

262 U.S. 522, 67 L. Ed. 1103, 43 S. Ct. 630; 267 U.S. 552, 69 L. Ed. 785, 45 S. Ct. 441

**Woman Juror Case**

419 U.S. 522, 42 L. Ed. 2d 690, 95 S. Ct. 692

**Women Exclusion Rape Case**

215 Ark. 53, 219 S.W.2d 424

**Women's Minimum Wage Cases**

284 F. 613, 52 App. D.C. 109; 261 U.S. 525, 67 L. Ed. 785, 43 S. Ct. 394

300 F. 991

156 Misc. 522, 282 N.Y.S. 576; 270 N.Y. 233, 200 N.E. 799; 297 U.S. 702, 80 L. Ed. 991, 56 S. Ct. 670; 56 S. Ct. 748; 298 U.S. 587, 80 L. Ed. 1347, 56 S. Ct. 918; 299 U.S. 619, 81 L. Ed. 456, 57 S. Ct. 4

185 Wash. 581, 55 P.2d 1083; 300 U.S. 379, 81 L. Ed. 703, 57 S. Ct. 578

1 Ill. 2d 108, 115 N.E.2d 306; 347 U.S. 949, 98 L. Ed. 1096, 74 S. Ct. 680

**Wood Case**

145 F. 405

**Wood Paper Patent Cases**

F. Cas. No. 320; 90 U.S. 566, 23 L. Ed. 31

F. Cas. No. 322, 75 U.S. 333, 19 L. Ed. 379

**Woodworth Planing Machine Case**
56 U.S. 212, 14 L. Ed. 665

**Wooldridge Case**
295 F. 847; 268 U.S. 234, 69 L. Ed. 932, 45 S. Ct. 489

**Woolworth Cutoff Case**
109 N.L.R.B. 1446, No. 203; 107 N.L.R.B. 732, No. 150; 235 F.2d 319

**Woolworth Labor Discrimination Case**
90 N.L.R.B. 289 No. 41

**Work-Related Expenses Case**
416 U.S. 251, 40 L. Ed. 2d 120, 94 S. Ct. 1746

**Workman's Insufficient Assistance Case**
199 F.2d 91

**Workman's Second Marriage Case**
190 Va. 181, 56 S.E.2d 214

**Workmen's Compensation Cases**
220 F. 378; 243 U.S. 210, 61 L. Ed. 678, 37 S. Ct. 255
169 A.D. 903, 152 N.Y.S. 1149; 216 N.Y. 653; 110 N.E. 1051; 243 U.S. 188, 61 L. Ed. 667, 37 S. Ct. 247
75 Wash. 581, 135 P. 645; 243 U.S. 219, 61 L. Ed. 685, 37 S. Ct. 260
97 Wash. 698, 165 P. 971

**World Publishing Company Case**
35 T.C. 7; 299 F.2d 614

**World War I Excess Profits Case**
3 B.T.A. 622

**World's Fair Case**
93 Ky. 537, 14 Ky. Law Rep. 529, 20 S.W. 901

**Worley Case**
42 F.2d 197; 281 U.S. 339, 74 L. Ed. 887, 50 S. Ct. 291

**Wounded Knee Case**
510 F.2d 808

**Wrapping Paper Case**
235 U.S. 33, 59 L. Ed. 113, 35 S. Ct. 6; 182 F. 150; 191 F. 35

**Wrenn Paper Company Franchise Tax Case**
156 Ohio St. 583, 103 N.E.2d 756; 158 Ohio St. 15, 106 N.E.2d 625

**Written Hearsay Evidence Case**
325 Mich. 127, 37 N.W.2d 779; 329 Mich. 214, 45 N.W.2d 41

**Wrong Lane Driving Case**
266 Wis. 282, 63 N.W.2d 86

**Wrongful Conviction Compensation Case**
247 Wis. 512, 19 N.W.2d 884

**Wycko Case**
361 Mich. 331, 105 N.W.2d 118

## X

**X-ray Evidence Case**
218 S.W.2d 230 (Tex.); 148 Tex. 113, 221 S.W.2d 235

**X-ray Injury Case**
238 N.C. 1, 76 S.E.2d 461

## Y

**Yacht Tax Cases**
190 F. 359; 232 U.S. 261, 58 L. Ed. 596, 34 S. Ct. 421; 232 U.S. 289, 58 L. Ed. 608, 34 S. Ct. 428; 232 U.S. 290, 58 L. Ed. 609, 34 S. Ct. 427; 232 U.S. 292, 58 L. Ed. 610, 34 S. Ct. 427; 232 U.S. 293, 58 L. Ed. 610, 34 S. Ct. 431; 232 U.S. 299, 58 L. Ed. 612, 34 S. Ct. 433, 232 U.S. 308, 58 L. Ed. 616, 34 S. Ct. 437; 232 U.S. 310, 58 L. Ed. 617, 34 S. Ct. 429
190 F. 372, 214 F. 67, 130 C.C.A. 507

**Yale College Case**
67 Conn. 237, 34 A. 1036

**Yankee Blade Case**
F. Cas. No. 16,847; 60 U.S. 82, 15 L. Ed. 554

**Yankton Asylum Case**
6 Dakota 501

**Yarmulke and the Military Case**
475 U.S. 503, 89 L. Ed. 2d 478, 106 S. Ct. 1310

**Yazoo Lands Case**
10 U.S. 87, 3 L. Ed. 162

**Yellow Dog Contract Cases**
208 U.S. 161, 52 L. Ed. 436, 28 S. Ct. 277
236 U.S. 1, 59 L. Ed. 441, 35 S. Ct. 240
305 Pa. 206, 157 A. 588

**Yellow Jackets Case**
93 W. Va. 328, 116 S.E. 687

**Yellow Pine Lumber Cases**
123 F. 789; 138 F. 753; 148 F. 1021, 79 C.C.A. 536; 206 U.S. 428, 51 L. Ed. 1124, 27 S. Ct. 709
10 I.C.C. 505; 206 U.S. 441, 51 L. Ed. 1128, 27 S. Ct. 700

**Yellow Taxi Cases**
156 La. 837, 101 So. 216
120 Misc. 499, 198 N.Y.S. 864
132 Misc. 654, 230 N.Y.S. 343
91 N.J. Eq. 233, 108 A. 763

**Yellowstone County Case**
46 Mont. 439, 128 P. 596

**Yonkers Shorts Case**
274 N.Y. 284, 8 N.E.2d 862

**York Case**
326 U.S. 99, 89 L. Ed. 2079, 65 S. Ct. 1464; 3)3 U.S. 693, 89 L. Ed. 560, 65 S. Ct. 60; 326 U.S. 806, 90 L. Ed. 491, 66 S. Ct. 7; 143 F.2d 503, 164 F.2d 387

**York Switching Case**
295 F. 523; 266 U.S. 191, 69 L. Ed. 243, 45 S. Ct. 43

**Yosemite Valley Case**
41 Cal. 634; 82 U.S. 77, 21 L. Ed. 82

**Young Case**
51 F. 585; 53 F. 895; 59 F. 96, 8 C.C.A. 27

**Youngstown Steel Case**
103 F. Supp. 569, 197 F.2d 582; 343 U.S. 937, 96 L. Ed. 1344, 72 S. Ct. 775, 72 S. Ct. 1075; 343 U.S. 579, 96 L. Ed. 1153, 72 S. Ct. 863

**Youthful Offenders Sentencing Case**
454 U.S. 201, 70 L. Ed. 2d 345, 102 S. Ct. 233

## Z

**Zeiss Case**
277 F.2d 94, 120 U.S.P.Q. (BNA) 100

**Zia Case**
108 N.L.R.B. 1134, No. 140; 109 N.L.R.B. 312, No. 50, 109 N.L.R.B. 862, No. 130

**Zipp Case**
28 T.C. 314; 259 F.2d 119

**Zoning Ordinance Cases (St. Louis)**
301 Mo. 1, 256 S.W. 474
301 Mo. 130, 256 S.W. 495
301 Mo. 231, 256 S.W. 489

**Zoning Regulation Condemnation Case**
167 P.2d 515 (Cal.); 30 Cal. 2d 763, 185 P.2d 585

**Zoo Case**
318 Mo. 910, 1 S.W.2d 1021

**Zorach Case**
343 U.S. 306, 96 L. Ed. 945, 72 S. Ct. 679; 303 N.Y. 161, 100 N.E.2d 463; 278 A.D. 573, 102 N.Y.S.2d 27; 198 Misc. 631, 99 N.Y.S.2d 339

## 1

**1983 Exhaustion of Remedies Case**
475 U.S. 496, 73 L. Ed. 2d 172, 102 S. Ct. 2557